Mastering
Exchange Server 2013

Mastering
Exchange Server 2013

David Elfassy

SYBEX®
A Wiley Brand

Acquisitions Editor: Mariann Barsolo

Development Editor: Candace Cunningham

Technical Editor: J. Peter Bruzzese

Production Editor: Dassi Zeidel

Copy Editor: Linda Recktenwald

Editorial Manager: Pete Gaughan

Vice President and Executive Group Publisher: Richard Swadley

Associate Publisher: Chris Webb

Book Designers: Maureen Forys, Happenstance Type-O-Rama; Judy Fung

Proofreader: Sarah Kaikini, Word One New York

Indexer: Ted Laux

Project Coordinator, Cover: Katherine Crocker

Cover Designer: Wiley

Cover Image: @Getty Images, Inc./Thomas Northcutt

Dear Reader,

Thank you for choosing *Mastering Exchange Server 2013*. This book is part of a family of premium-quality Sybex books, all of which are written by outstanding authors who combine practical experience with a gift for teaching.

Sybex was founded in 1976. More than 30 years later, we're still committed to producing consistently exceptional books. With each of our titles, we're working hard to set a new standard for the industry. From the paper we print on to the authors we work with, our goal is to bring you the best books available.

I hope you see all that reflected in these pages. I'd be very interested to hear your comments and get your feedback on how we're doing. Feel free to let me know what you think about this or any other Sybex book by sending me an email at contactus@sybex.com. If you think you've found a technical error in this book, please visit http://sybex.custhelp.com. Customer feedback is critical to our efforts at Sybex.

Best regards,

Chris Webb
Associate Publisher
Sybex, an Imprint of Wiley

This book is dedicated to my loving, gorgeous wife, Gillian, and to my three daily inspirations, Zachary, Zoe, and Savannah. Thank you for enduring all my late nights and continuously encouraging me through this journey. I love you all.

— D

Acknowledgments

Thank you once again, Microsoft, for a great release of Exchange Server. This is now the seventh major release of the well-known premiere messaging system. In this release, we can see the effort and the ingenuity come together in solving customer problems to create a truly superior product. Congratulations!

As the team that is working on this book completes the final steps required to send it to the printer, I continue to bring some real-world expertise into the content. I have deployed several Exchange Server 2013 infrastructures to date, but this product is so vast and so broad that I continue to find design options, best practices, and architecture recommendations on a daily basis. I'm pretty sure that I will be updating the content up to the last minute!

When I was approached to take on this book, several months before Exchange Server 2013 was about to release to manufacturing, my reaction was, "What about Jim?" Jim McBee, having authored three previous editions of this book, has been the pillar of the *Mastering Exchange Server* series and an inspiring role model in my own Exchange Server consulting career. I consider it to be a true honor to take over for Jim McBee as the lead author for this book, and I hope that this edition has adequately followed through on his tradition.

Throughout the book, I have tried to keep the tone and language similar to what was used in the previous editions of this book, so if you are familiar with Jim's writing style, you should find comfort in these pages. In addition, I have removed some of the introductory technical information from previous editions, to reflect the depth of initial experience of the readers.

Taking on the responsibility of a 900+ -page manual is no simple task and not one that can be undertaken by only one person. Along the way, I have invited several contributors to this effort. Their knowledge and expertise have added incredible value to this book. Having written anywhere from several paragraphs to complete chapters, Chris Crandall, Devin Ganger, Mahmoud Magdy, Adam Micelli, Bob Reinsch, Jeffrey Rosen, and Michael Smith are Exchange Server gurus who have provided key content for this book. Some of this has been outside my areas of expertise and a great contribution to this effort. Thank you!

There is also a man who has kept us all honest and has been the gatekeeper for technical accuracy in this book, and he has helped revise a couple of chapters more substantially. J. Peter Bruzzese agreed to take on the responsibility of technical reviewer for this book and has done a formidable job. When I received a chapter back from Peter with only very few red marks, I considered it an achievement! Peter, thank you!

The great folks at Wiley have been patient beyond belief when it comes to deadlines, content, and outline changes as well as our ever-changing list of contributors. They include acquisitions editor Mariann Barsolo, developmental editor Candace Cunningham, and production editor Dassi Zeidel.

Along the way, several Exchange Server experts have answered my questions, calmed my nerves, and listened to my rants about configuration frustrations. I would like to acknowledge them, even if some of them answered my questions without knowing it. They include Paul Adare, David Espinosa, Stan Reimer, Paul Robichaux, Scott Schnoll, Ross Smith, Greg Taylor, and Brian Tirch. And a big thank-you goes to Corey Hynes and Kim Frank for providing me with some very useful virtual server environments.

I would also like to acknowledge those who have helped me in my own Exchange Server path, from Sandra Ford, who hired me to teach my first Exchange Server 5.0 course, to Ken Rosen, who inspired me to write my first course on Exchange Server 2003, to Jennifer Morrison, who pushed to hire me on my first large Microsoft project. Thank you!

I would also like to thank my business partner and friend, Jonathan Long, for doing the work I was supposed to be doing when I was writing this book and for supporting me through this latest writing effort.

And a special acknowledgement to those in my daily life, my father, Elie Elfassy; my uncle, Leon Elfassy; my sister, Celine Elfassy; and my father-in-law, Sam Katz: thank you for always being supportive of all my endeavors.

About the Author

David Elfassy, MCSE, MCT, and MVP: Exchange Server, is an international presenter and trainer, having presented on messaging technologies to thousands of Microsoft clients since the late 1990s. David collaborates with Microsoft on certification, courseware, and key development projects. As a senior technical advisor for two Microsoft Gold Certified Partners, including Netlogon Technologies, where he specializes in large enterprise consulting and technical writing, and Kalleo, where he specializes in small business network management (overseeing a team of consultants and network technicians), David is a project lead on many migrations and implementations of Microsoft infrastructure technologies for government and corporate organizations. Helping organizations migrate to the latest versions of Microsoft Exchange Server has always been a key focus of David's consulting commitments. David is a regular presenter at international conferences such as TechEd North America and TechEd Europe. David was also the coauthor of the previous edition of this book, *Mastering Exchange Server 2010* (Sybex, 2010) with Jim McBee.

When David is not troubleshooting SMTP connections or working on Microsoft projects, he's usually snowboarding or skateboarding, depending on the season. He also spends a fair bit of time running after his three young children, Zachary, Zoe, and Savannah, and hanging out with his supporting, lovely wife, Gillian.

Contents at a Glance

Contents

Introduction

Thank you for purchasing (or considering the purchase of) *Mastering Exchange Server 2013*; this is the latest in a series of Mastering Exchange Server books that have helped thousands of readers to better understand Microsoft's excellent messaging system. Along the way, we hope that this series of books has made you a better administrator and allowed you to support your organizations to the best of your abilities.

When we started planning the outline of this book more than a year before its release, Exchange Server 2013 appeared to be simply a minor series of improvements over Exchange Server 2010. Of course, the further we explored the product, the more we found that was not the case. Many of the improvements in Exchange Server 2013 were major improvements (such as DAG management) and sometimes even complete rewrites (such as in the case of the Client Access server role) of how the product worked previously.

Another challenge then presented itself. The market penetration of Exchange Server 2010 was fairly dominant, but we found that many organizations still run Exchange Server 2007. Though increasingly smaller, a percentage of Exchange Server customers are still using Exchange Server 2003. Thus, we needed to explain the differences for not only Exchange Server 2010 administrators but also for the Exchange Server 2007 and even Exchange Server 2003 administrators.

We took a step back and looked at the previous editions of the book to figure out how much of the previous material was still relevant. Some of the material from the Exchange Server 2010 book is still relevant but needed updating. Some required completely new chapters to cover new technologies introduced in Exchange Server 2013 or technologies that have since taken on more importance in deployments and management. We faced the challenge of explaining two management interfaces, Exchange Management Shell and Exchange Admin Center, as well as describing the new roles and features.

We started working with the Exchange Server 2013 code more than a year before we expected to release the book. Much of the book was written using the RTM code that was first made available in October 2012, but as we continued writing the book, we made updates to changes introduced in Cumulative Update 1 and Cumulative Update 2. So, you can safely assume when reading this book that it is based on the latest bits of Exchange Server 2013 that released in late summer 2013. In writing this book, we had a few goals for the book and the knowledge we wanted to impart to the reader:

- We wanted to provide an appropriate context for the role of messaging services in an organization, outlining the primary skills required by an Exchange Server administrator.

- We wanted the reader to feel comfortable when approaching an Exchange Server environment of any size. The content in this book can assist administrators of small companies with only one server, as well as administrators who handle large Exchange Server farms.

- We wanted the skills and tasks covered in this book to be applicable to 80 percent of all organizations running Exchange Server.

- We wanted the book to educate not only "new to product" administrators but also those "new to version" administrators who are upgrading from a previous version.

◆ We wanted the book to familiarize administrators with Office 365 environments and the implementation of hybrid coexistence with on-premises Exchange Server deployments.

◆ We wanted to provide familiar references for administrators of previous versions, ensuring that Exchange Server 2003, 2007, and 2010 administrators can easily find equivalent solutions in Exchange Server 2013.

Microsoft listened to the advice of many of its customers, its internal consultants at Microsoft Consulting Services (MCS), Microsoft Certified Systems Engineers (MCSEs), Most Valuable Professionals (MVPs), Microsoft Certified Solutions Masters (MCSMs), and Microsoft Certified Trainers (MCTs) to find out what was missing from earlier versions of the product and what organizations' needs were. Much of this work started even before Exchange Server 2013 was released.

Major Changes in Exchange Server 2013

This book covers the many changes in Exchange Server 2013 in detail, but we thought we would give you a little sample of what is to come in the chapters. As you can imagine, the changes are once again significant, considering the tremendous effort that Microsoft sinks into the Exchange Server line of products. Exchange Server is a significant generator of revenue for Microsoft and is also a foundational service for Office 365. Microsoft has every reason to continue improving this most impressive market leader of email and collaboration services.

The primary changes in Exchange Server 2013 since the latest release (Exchange Server 2010) have come in the following areas:

◆ Replacement of the Exchange Management Console by the web-based console Exchange Admin Center

◆ Integration of Transport services into the Client Access and Mailbox server roles and subsequent removal of the Hub Transport server role

◆ Integration of Unified Messaging services into the Client Access and Mailbox server roles and subsequent removal of the Unified Messaging server role

◆ Reconfiguration of public folders to be stored in mailbox databases within a *public folder mailbox*

◆ Improved integration with SharePoint Server 2013 and Lync Server 2013, including options for archiving Lync conversations in Exchange Server

◆ Completely rewritten Information Store processes, now named the *Managed Store*

◆ Significant improvement in database maintenance, database availability group management, and overall site resiliency functionalities

◆ Significant improvement in Transport rules, mainly through the implementation of the new Data Loss Prevention (DLP) policies

Of course, many more changes have been introduced in Exchange Server 2013, but the preceding list stands out to us as the most noteworthy improvements. Chapter 2, "Introducing the Changes in Exchange Server 2013," contains an exhaustive list of all significant changes, as well as changes since specific versions of Exchange Server (for example, Exchange Server 2003 versus Exchange Server 2013).

How This Book Is Organized

This book consists of 25 chapters, divided into five broad parts. As you proceed through the book, you'll move from general concepts to increasingly detailed descriptions of hands-on implementation.

This book won't work well for practitioners of the time-worn ritual of chapter hopping. Although some readers may benefit from reading one or two chapters, we recommend that you read most of the book in order. Even if you have experience as an Exchange Server administrator, we recommend that you do not skip any chapter, because they all provide new information since the previous iterations of Exchange Server. Only if you already have considerable experience with these products should you jump to the chapter that discusses in detail the information you are looking for.

If you are like most administrators, though, you like to get your hands on the software and actually see things working. Having a working system also helps many people as they read a book or learn about a new piece of software because this lets them test new skills as they learn them. If this sounds like you, then start with Chapter 7, "Exchange Server 2013 Quick Start Guide." This chapter will take you briefly through some of the things you need to know to get Exchange Server running, but not in a lot of detail. As long as you're not planning to put your quickie server into production immediately, there should be no harm done. Before you put it into production, though, we strongly suggest that you explore other parts of this book. Here's a guide to what's in each chapter.

Part 1: Exchange Fundamentals

This part of the book focuses on concepts and features of Microsoft's Windows Server 2012, Exchange Server 2013, and some of the fundamentals of operating a modern client/server email system.

Chapter 1, "Putting Exchange Server 2013 in Context," is for those administrators who have been handed an Exchange Server organization but who have never managed a previous version of Exchange Server or even another mail system. This will give you some of the basic information and background to help you get started managing Exchange Server and, hopefully, a little history and perspective.

Chapter 2, "Introducing the Changes in Exchange Server 2013," introduces the new features of Exchange Server 2013 as contrasted with previous versions.

Chapter 3, "Understanding Availability, Recovery, and Compliance," helps even experienced administrators navigate some of the new hurdles that Exchange Server administrators must overcome, including providing better system availability, site resiliency, backup and restoration plans, and legal compliance. This chapter does *not* cover database availability groups in detail; instead, that information is covered in Chapter 20, "Creating and Managing Database Availability Groups."

Chapter 4, "Virtualizing Exchange Server 2013," helps you decide whether you should virtualize some percentage of your servers, as many organizations are doing.

Chapter 5, "Introduction to PowerShell and the Exchange Management Shell," focuses on and uses examples of features that are enabled in PowerShell through the Exchange Server

2013 management extensions for PowerShell. All administrators should have at least a basic familiarity with the Exchange Management Shell extensions for PowerShell even if you rarely use them.

Chapter 6, "Understanding the Exchange Autodiscover Process," helps you to come up to speed on the inner workings of the magic voodoo that is Autodiscover, a feature that greatly simplifies the configuration of both internal and external clients.

Part 2: Getting Exchange Server Running

This section of the book is devoted to topics related to meeting the prerequisites for Exchange Server and getting Exchange Server installed correctly the first time. While installing Exchange Server correctly is not rocket science, getting everything right the first time will greatly simplify your deployment.

Chapter 7, "Exchange Server 2013 Quick Start Guide," is where everyone likes to jump right in and install the software. This chapter will help you quickly get a single server up and running for your test and lab environment. While you should not deploy an entire enterprise based on the content of this one chapter, it will help you get started quickly.

Chapter 8, "Understanding Server Roles and Configurations," covers the primary services that run on the two Exchange Server roles: Mailbox server and Client Access server. It also covers the architecture of communications between the roles.

Chapter 9, "Exchange Server 2013 Requirements," guides you through the requirements (pertaining to Windows Server, Active Directory, and previous versions of Exchange Server) that you must meet in order to successfully deploy Exchange Server 2013.

Chapter 10, "Installing Exchange Server 2013," takes you through both the graphical user interface and the command-line setup for installing Exchange Server 2013.

Chapter 11, "Upgrades and Migrations to Exchange Server 2013 or Office 365," helps you decide on the right migration or transition approach for your organization. It recommends steps to take to upgrade your organization from Exchange Server 2007 or 2010 to Exchange Server 2013 or to Office 365. Also included in this chapter are recommendations for migration phases and hybrid coexistence with Office 365.

Part 3: Recipient Administration

Recipient administration generally ends up being the most time-consuming portion of Exchange Server administration. Recipient administration includes creating and managing mailboxes, managing mail groups, creating and managing contacts, and administering public folders.

Chapter 12, "Management Permissions and Role-based Access Control," introduces one of the most powerful features of Exchange Server 2013, Role-based Access Control, which enables extremely detailed delegation of permissions for all Exchange Server administrative tasks. This feature will be of great value to large organizations.

Chapter 13, "Basics of Recipient Management," introduces you to some concepts you should consider before you start creating users, including how email addresses are generated and how recipients should be configured.

Chapter 14, "Managing Mailboxes and Mailbox Content," is at the core of most Exchange Server administrators' jobs since the mailboxes represent our direct customer (the end user). This chapter introduces the concepts of managing mailboxes, mailbox data (such as personal archives), and mailbox data retention.

Chapter 15, "Managing Mail-enabled Groups, Mail-enabled Users, and Mail-enabled Contacts," covers management of these objects, including creating them, assigning email addresses, securing groups, and allowing for self-service management of groups, and it offers guidelines for creating contacts.

Chapter 16, "Managing Resource Mailboxes," discusses a key task for most messaging administrators. A resource can be either a room (such as a conference room) or a piece of equipment (such as an overhead projector). Exchange Server 2013 makes it easy to allow users to view the availability of resources and request the use of these resources from within Outlook or Outlook Web App.

Chapter 17, "Managing Modern Public Folders," introduces you to the new public folder storage and management features in Exchange Server 2013. Although public folders are being deemphasized in many organizations, other organizations still have massive quantities of data stored in them. Microsoft has reinvented public folders in this latest release of Exchange Server.

Chapter 18, "Managing Archiving and Compliance," covers not only the overall concepts of archiving and how the rest of the industry handles archiving but also the exciting archival and retention features.

Part 4: Server Administration

Although recipient administration is important, administrators must not forget their responsibilities to properly set up the Exchange server and maintain it. This section helps introduce you to the configuration tasks and maintenance necessary for some of the Exchange Server 2013 roles as well as safely connecting your organization to the Internet.

Chapter 19, "Creating and Managing Mailbox Databases," helps familiarize you with the changes in Exchange Server 2013 with respect to mailbox database, storage, and basic sizing requirements. Many exciting changes have been made to support large databases and to allow Exchange Server to scale to support more simultaneous users.

Chapter 20, "Creating and Managing Database Availability Groups," is a key chapter in this book that will affect all administrators from small to large organizations. Exchange Server 2013 relies heavily on Windows Failover Clustering for its site resilience and high availability functionalities. This chapter covers the implementation and management of high availability solutions.

Chapter 21, "Understanding the Client Access Server," introduces you to the critical Client Access server role and the components running on the Client Access server.

Chapter 22, "Managing Connectivity with Transport Services," brings you up to speed on the Transport services that run on the Mailbox and Client Access server roles. This chapter discusses mail flow and the transport pipeline in detail.

Chapter 23, "Managing Transport, Data Loss Prevention, and Journaling Rules," shows you how to implement a feature set that was first introduced in Exchange Server 2007 but has since been greatly improved: the transport rule feature. This chapter also discusses message journaling and the new Data Loss Prevention policies.

Part 5: Troubleshooting and Operating

Troubleshooting and keeping a proper eye on your Exchange servers' health are often neglected tasks. You may not look at your Exchange servers until there is an actual problem. In this part we discuss some tips and tools that will help you proactively manage your Exchange Server environment, ensuring that you can track down problems as well as restore any potential lost data.

Chapter 24, "Troubleshooting Exchange Server 2013," introduces you not only to troubleshooting the various components of Exchange Server 2013 but also to good troubleshooting techniques. This chapter also includes a discussion of some of the Exchange Server 2013 built-in tools, such as the Exchange Management Shell test cmdlets and the Remote Connectivity Analyzer.

Chapter 25, "Backing Up and Restoring Exchange Server," includes discussions on developing a backup plan for your Exchange Server 2013 servers as well as how to implement appropriate backup solutions for Exchange Server configuration, databases, logs, and any other relevant information.

Conventions Used in This Book

We use the code-continuation character on PowerShell commands to indicate that the line of text is part of a previous command line.

Many of the screen captures in this book have been taken from lab and test environments. However, sometimes you will see screen-captures that came from an actual working environment. We have obscured any information that would identify those environments.

Any examples that include IP addresses have had the IP addresses changed to private IP addresses even if we are referring to Internet addresses.

Remember, Exchange Server is designed to help your organization do what it does better, more efficiently, and with greater productivity. Have fun, be productive, and prosper!

The Mastering Series

The *Mastering* series from Sybex provides outstanding instruction for readers with intermediate and advanced skills, in the form of top-notch training and development for those already working in their field and clear, serious education for those aspiring to become pros. Every *Mastering* book includes the following:

- ◆ Real-World Scenarios, ranging from case studies to interviews, that show how the tool, technique, or knowledge presented is applied in actual practice

- ◆ Skill-based instruction, with chapters organized around real tasks rather than abstract concepts or subjects

- ◆ Self-review test questions, so you can be certain you're equipped to do the job right

Part 1

Exchange Fundamentals

- ◆ Chapter 1: Putting Exchange Server 2013 into Context
- ◆ Chapter 2: Introducing the Changes in Exchange Server 2013
- ◆ Chapter 3: Understanding Availability, Recovery, and Compliance
- ◆ Chapter 4: Virtualizing Exchange Server 2013
- ◆ Chapter 5: Introduction to PowerShell and the Exchange Management Shell
- ◆ Chapter 6: Understanding the Exchange Autodiscover Process

Chapter 1

Putting Exchange Server 2013 in Context

Email is one of the most visible services that IT professionals provide; most organizations have become dependent on "soft" information to run their business. As a result, users have developed an attachment to email that goes beyond the hard value of the information it contains. If there's a problem with email, it affects users' confidence in their ability to do their jobs—and their confidence in IT.

Microsoft's Exchange Server products play a key role in electronic messaging, including email. This chapter is a high-level primer on Exchange Server–based email administration and good administration practices, and it prepares you to put Exchange Server 2013 into the proper context. An experienced email administrator may want to proceed to more-technical chapters. However, if you are new to the job or need a refresher, or maybe you just want to put email services back into perspective, this chapter is for you!

In this chapter, you will learn to:

◆ Understand email fundamentals

◆ Identify email-administration duties

Email's Importance

If you're responsible for electronic messaging in your organization, no one has to tell you about its steadily expanding use—you see evidence every time you check the storage space on your disk drives or need an additional tape to complete the backup of your mail server. This section discusses some aspects of electronic mail and the ever-changing nature of email. Even experienced Exchange Server administrators may want to review this section to better understand how their users and requirements are evolving.

Billions of emails are sent every day (more than 500 billion worldwide, according to Research firm The Radicati Group). That's a lot of email messages, on a lot of servers—many of them Exchange servers.

Sure, sending simple text email and file attachments is the most basic function, but email systems (the client and/or the server) may also perform the following important functions:

♦ Act as a personal information manager, providing storage for and access to personal calendars, personal contacts, to-do and task lists, personal journals, and chat histories.

♦ Provide the user with a single "point of entry" for multiple types of information, such as voicemail, faxes, and electronic forms.

♦ Provide shared calendars, departmental contacts, and other shared information.

♦ Provide notifications of workflow processes, such as finance/accounting activities, IT events (server status information), and more.

♦ Archive important attachments, text messages, and many other types of information.

♦ Allow users to access their "email data" through a variety of means, including clients running on Windows computers, Apple computers, Unix systems, web browsers, mobile phones, and even a regular telephone.

♦ Perform records management and enable long-term storage of important information or information that must be archived.

♦ Enable near-time communication of sales and support information with vendors and customers.

These are just a few of the types of things that an email system may provide to the end user either via the client interface or as a result of some function running on the server.

How Messaging Servers Work

At the core of any messaging system, you will find a common set of basic functions. These functions may be implemented in different ways depending on the vendor or even the version of the product. Exchange Server has evolved dramatically over the past 18 years, and its current architecture is almost nothing like Exchange Server 4.0 from 1996. Common components of most messaging systems include the following:

♦ A message transport system that moves messages from one place to another. Examples include the Simple Mail Transport Protocol (SMTP).

♦ A message storage system that stores messages until a user can read or retrieve them. Messages may be stored in a client/server database, a shared file database, or even in individual files.

♦ A directory service that allows a user to look up information about the mail system's users, such as a user's email address.

♦ A client access interface on the server that allows the clients to get to their stored messages. This might include a web interface, a client/server interface, or the Post Office Protocol (POP).

♦ The client program that allows users to read their mail, send mail, and access the directory. This may include Outlook, Outlook Web App, and a mobile device such as a Windows Phone, an iPhone, or an Android device.

Working in tandem with real-time interactive technologies, electronic messaging systems have already produced a set of imaginative business, entertainment, and educational applications with high payoff potential. All of this action, of course, accelerates the demand for electronic messaging capabilities and services.

Most organizations that deploy an email system usually deploy additional components from their email software vendor or third parties that extend the capabilities of the email system or provide required services. These include the following:

- Integration with existing phone systems or enterprise voice deployments to pull voice messages into the mailbox

- Message-hygiene systems that help reduce the likelihood of a malicious or inappropriate message being delivered to a user

- Backup and recovery, disaster recovery, and business continuity solutions

- Message archival software to allow for the long-term retention and indexing of email data

- Electronic forms routing software that may integrate with accounting, order entry, or other line-of-business applications

- Mail gateways to allow differing mobile devices, such as BlackBerry devices, to access the mail server, along with native access through Exchange ActiveSync

- Email security systems that improve the security of email data either while being transferred or while sitting in the user's mailbox

- A link load balancer to balance the load between multiple Internet-facing servers or internal servers

What Is Exchange Server?

In its simplest form, Exchange Server provides the underlying infrastructure necessary to run a messaging system. Exchange Server provides the database to store email data, the transport infrastructure to move the email data from one place to another, and the access points to access email data via a number of different clients.

However, Exchange Server, when used with other clients such as Outlook or Outlook Web App, turns the "mailbox" into a point of storage for personal information management such as your calendar, contacts, task lists, and any file type. Users can share some or all of this information in their own mailbox with other users on the message system and start to collaborate.

The Outlook and Outlook Web App clients also provide access to public folders. Public folders look like regular mail folders in your mailbox, except that they are in an area where they can be shared by all users within the organization. A folder can have specialized forms associated with it to allow the sharing of contacts, calendar entries, or even other specialized forms. Further, each public folder can be secured so that only certain users can view or modify data in that folder.

The Unified Messaging features in Exchange Server 2013 further extend the functions of Exchange Server in your organization by allowing your Exchange Server infrastructure to also act as your voicemail system and direct voicemails and missed-call notifications automatically to the user's mailbox.

While integrated voicemail solutions are nothing new for Exchange Server customers, Microsoft is now providing these capabilities out of the box rather than relying on third-party products.

Exchange Server 2013 tightens the integration of collaborative tools in its integration with Lync Server 2013, the Lync client, and the Lync Mobile client. Lync provides a core set of SIP-based enterprise voice capabilities that allows it to act as a PBX in many cases. With Exchange Server, Lync, Outlook, and the Lync client, users enjoyed full Unified Messaging with software-based telephony from their computer, including the new voicemail and missed-call notification provided by Exchange Server and Outlook. Furthermore, Lync could log chat and instant-message conversation logs to a folder in the user's mailbox. Exchange Server 2013 further pushes this integration, embedding basic IM and presence capabilities into the Outlook Web App premium experience.

The capabilities of the client can be extended with third-party tools and forms-routing software so that electronic forms can be routed through email to users' desktops.

About Messaging Services

Electronic messaging is now far more than email. Together, Exchange Server 2013 and its clients perform a variety of messaging-based functions. These functions include email, unified messaging, message routing, scheduling, and support for several types of custom applications. Together these features are called messaging services.

Many Modes of Access

For years, the only way to access your email system was to use a Windows, Macintosh, or Unix-based client and access the email system directly. In the case of Outlook and Exchange Server, this access was originally in the form of a MAPI client directly against the Exchange server. As Exchange Server has evolved, it has included support for the POP3 and IMAP4 protocols, then web-based email access, and finally mobile device access. Exchange Server 2013 doesn't offer any radically new modes of mailbox access as Exchange Server 2007 did, but it does provide ongoing support and refinement of existing Exchange Server 2007 technologies, such as Exchange Web Services, that can provide additional mechanisms for accessing data in mailboxes and a move away from RPC in client connectivity in favor of RPC over HTTPs, also known as Outlook Anywhere.

Outlook Web App (OWA) has evolved quickly and, in Exchange Server 2013, bears almost no resemblance to the original version found in Exchange Server 5.0 in terms of features, functions, and the look of the interface. Exchange Server 2013 OWA is even a radical step beyond Exchange Server 2010. It also expands the previous option configuration experience of the Exchange Control Panel (ECP), which gives users a much greater degree of control over their mailbox, contacts, and group memberships. ECP is now built into the Outlook Web App interface. Using ECP, end users can create and join distribution groups (where permissions have been assigned), track their own messages throughout the organization, and perform other functions that previously required help-desk or IT professional intervention. Another significant feature of Outlook Web App is the ability to use the web-based interface when working offline and completely disconnected from the network.

With Exchange Server 2013, Exchange ActiveSync (EAS) continues to offer significant partnerships with and control over mobile devices. Many vendors have licensed EAS to provide their mobile devices with a high-performance, full-featured push mobile synchronization experience now extending beyond mobile phones and into tablet devices.

With all of these mechanisms for retrieving and sending email, it is not unusual for users to access their mailbox using more than one device. In some cases, we have seen a single user accessing her mailbox from her desktop computer, her tablet device using Outlook Anywhere, and her Windows Phone device.

In medium and large organizations, the fact that users are now accessing their mailbox from more than one device or mechanism will affect not only hardware sizing but also, potentially, your licensing costs.

WHAT'S GONE?

When Exchange Server 2007 was released, Microsoft introduced new core APIs (including Web Services, the new management API based on the .NET Framework) intended to replace existing Exchange Server APIs. Several of those legacy APIs were completely removed, whereas others were *deprecated*—while they still worked, developers were encouraged to port their applications over to the new APIs. The deprecated APIs were not guaranteed to be continued in future versions of Exchange Server.

With Exchange Server 2010, those deprecated APIs were eliminated. One of the biggest was WebDAV, which was the previous HTTP-based access protocol prior to Exchange Web Services. WebDAV calls are somewhat simpler to develop but are more fundamentally limited in what they can do.

HOW MESSAGING SERVICES ARE USED

Certainly, email is a key feature of any messaging system, and the Outlook Calendar is far better than previous versions of Microsoft's appointment and meeting-scheduling software. Outlook 2013 together with Exchange Server 2013 introduces even more synergy. Figure 1.1 and Figure 1.2 show the Outlook 2013 client Calendar and Inbox in action.

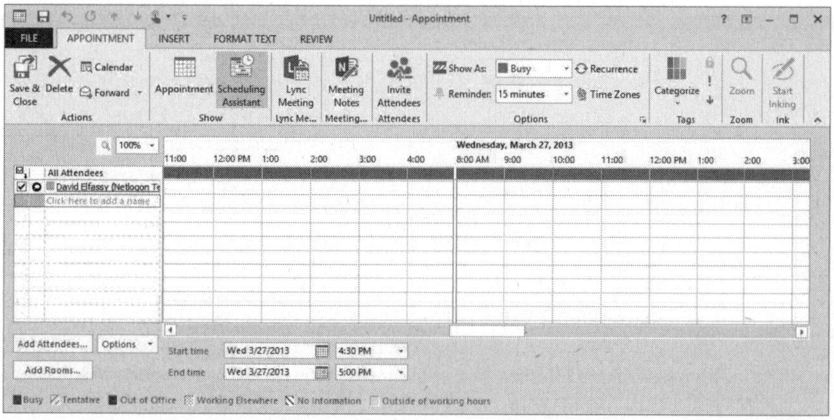

FIGURE 1.1
Outlook 2013 Appointment scheduling on an Exchange Server 2013 mailbox

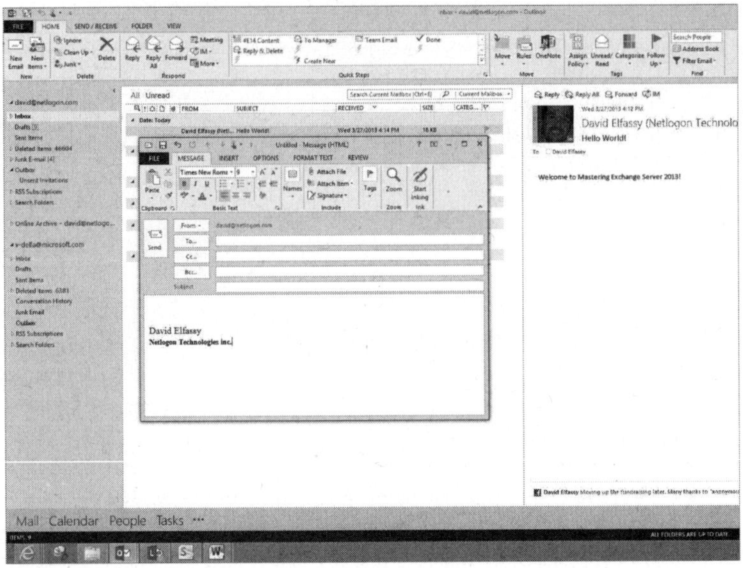

FIGURE 1.2
The Outlook 2013 client Inbox on an Exchange Server 2013 mailbox

Figure 1.3 shows the new Outlook Web App 2013 web browser client. For the first time, Outlook Web App 2013 provides the full premium user experience for browsers other than Internet Explorer; it also supports Mac OS X Safari, Firefox, and Chrome. Those coming from previous versions will immediately notice a cleaner, less-cluttered interface in OWA 2013 and amazing new functionalities such as Offline Usage.

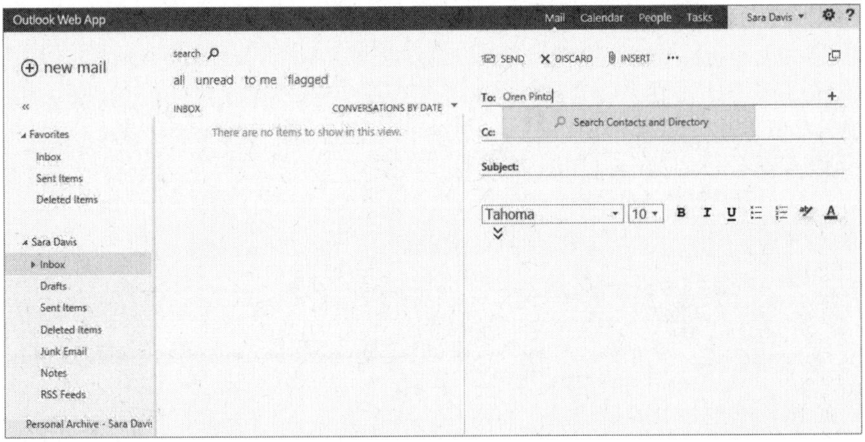

FIGURE 1.3
Outlook Web App on an Exchange Server 2013 mailbox

Email clients are exciting and sexy, but to get the most out of Exchange Server 2013 you need to throw away any preconceptions you have that messaging systems are only for email and scheduling. The really exciting applications are not those that use simple email or scheduling but those that are based on the routing capabilities of messaging systems. These applications bring people and computers together for improved collaboration.

The Universal Inbox

Email systems are converging with their voicemail and enterprise voice-solution cousins. The concept of unified messaging is nothing new to email users. For the past 20 years, third-party vendors have included email integration tools for voicemail, network faxing solutions, and third-party integration. However, for most organizations, integrated voicemail remains the exception rather than the rule. Exchange Server 2007 introduced integrated voice, which Exchange Server 2013 continues to improve on.

Organizations with IP-based telephone systems or telephone systems with an IP gateway can easily integrate a user's voicemail with the Exchange Server user's mailbox. The Exchange Server 2013 Unified Messaging features handle the interaction between an organization's telephone system and Exchange Server mailboxes. Inbound voicemail is transferred into the user's mailbox as a cross-platform-friendly MP3 file attachment; this message includes an Outlook or OWA form that allows the user to play the message. As well, the voicemail text can be transcribed into the body of the email message for quick reading by the user during meetings or rapid glancing at the Inbox. Because the default format is MP3 in Exchange Server 2013 (it was a Windows Media file in Exchange Server 2007, using a custom codec), this file can be easily played on mobile devices from any manufacturer, allowing easy on-the-go access to voicemail. A short voicemail message may be anywhere from 40 KB to 75 KB in size, whereas longer voicemail messages may be range from 200 KB to 500 KB in size. One estimate that is frequently used for the size of a voicemail message is around 5 KB per second of message.

Inbound voicemail increases the demands on your Exchange server from the perspective of required disk space and possible additional server hardware. As an administrator, you need to consider this.

JUST THE FAX, MA'AM

In Exchange Server 2007, the Unified Messaging features included the out-of-the-box capability to capture incoming facsimile (fax) messages. There were some limitations, but it provided good basic functionality. For outbound fax capability, organizations had to deploy some other solution, typically a third-party fax package.

For Exchange Server 2010 and Exchange Server 2013, Microsoft made the decision to cut this feature. When talking with the product group, it's not hard to figure out why; the inbound-only fax functionality wasn't enough for the customers who needed fax integration. Exchange Server 2013 needed to either add outgoing fax capability and beef up its feature set (and lose other desired functionality) or drop the existing functionality since the majority of Exchange Server 2007 customers needed a third-party product anyway. While it's always disappointing to lose a feature, most of the organizations we've talked to didn't use it to begin with. We think that Microsoft definitely made the right call, if you'll pardon the pun.

Architecture Overview

Understanding a bit about how Exchange Server works from an architectural perspective will help make you a better administrator. You don't have to be able to reproduce or write your own client/server messaging system, but it helps to know the basics.

THE EXTENSIBLE STORAGE ENGINE

The Exchange Server database uses a highly specialized database engine called the Extensible Storage Engine (ESE). Generically, you could say it is almost like SQL Server, but this is technically not true. It is a client/server database and is somewhat relational in nature, but it is designed to be a single-user database (the Exchange server itself is the only component that directly accesses the data). Further, the database has been highly tuned to store hierarchical data, such as mailboxes, folders, messages, and attachments.

Without going into a lot of techno-babble on the database architecture, it is important that you understand the basics of what the database is doing. Figure 1.4 shows conceptually what is happening with the ESE database as data is sent to the database. In step 1, an Outlook client sends data to the Exchange server (the information store service); the information store service places this data in memory and then immediately writes the data out to the transaction log files associated with that database.

FIGURE 1.4
Exchange data and transaction logs

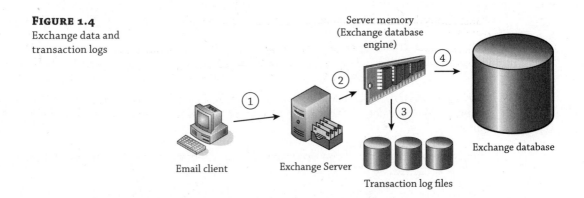

Server memory (Exchange database engine)

Email client

Exchange Server

Transaction log files

Exchange database

The transaction log that is always written to is the current transaction log for that particular database (e00.log, for example). Each transaction log file is exactly 1 MB in size, so when the transaction log is filled up, it is renamed to the next sequential number. For example, an old transaction log file might be named like this: e000004032.log. I often get questions about the logic of the transaction logs, and how they reserve space on the disk, whether they are empty or full. An easy way to look at it is to compare a log file to a carton of milk. When you have a carton of milk, it always takes up the same space in your fridge, empty or full. The same is true of the log files. Empty log files (current log file and *reserved* log files) are empty, or partially full; the renamed, *old*, log files are full. However, they take up the same amount of space on the disk.

The data, such as new email messages that enter my organization, is retained in RAM for some period of time (maybe as little as 5 seconds or maybe even 60 seconds or more) before it is flushed to the database file. The actual period that data is retained in memory will depend on how much cache memory is available, what types of operations are happening in the data, and how busy the server is. The important operation, though, is to make sure that as soon as the data is sent to the Exchange server, it is immediately flushed to the transaction log files. If the server crashes before the data is written to the database file, the database engine (the store process) will automatically read the transaction log files once the server is brought back up and compare them with the data that's stored in the corresponding mailbox databases. Any inconsistency is resolved by replaying the missing data operations from the transaction logs back into the database, assuming that the entire transaction is present; if it's not, the operations are not written (and you can be confident that the operation wasn't completed at the time the crash happened). This helps ensure that the integrity of the mailbox database is preserved and that half-completed data operations aren't written back into the database and allowed to corrupt good data.

The transaction log files are important for a number of reasons. They are used by Microsoft replication technologies (as you'll learn in Chapter 19, "Creating and Managing Mailbox Databases"), but they can also be used in disaster recovery. The transaction logs are not purged off the log disk until a full backup is run; therefore, every transaction that occurred to a database (new data, modifications, moves, deletes) is stored in the logs. If you restore the last good backup to the server, Exchange Server can replay and rebuild all the missing transactions back into the database—provided you have all the transactions since the last full backup.

In previous versions of Exchange Server, you had two separate mail store objects: the *storage group*, which was a logical container that held an associated set of transaction logs, and the *mailbox database*, a set of files that held the actual permanent copies of user mailboxes. You often had multiple mailbox databases per storage group, meaning that one set of transaction logs contained interwoven transaction data for multiple databases (which could have detrimental effects on performance, space, and backups). In Exchange Server 2007, the recommendation changed; while you could still assign mailbox databases to a storage group in a many-to-one ratio, Microsoft encouraged you to assign them 1:1. In fact, to use the continuous-replication features in Exchange Server 2007, you had to do so.

In Exchange Server 2013, you still have mailbox databases. However, storage groups were removed in Exchange Server 2010; each mailbox database now has its own integral set of transaction log files. In fact, mailbox databases—which were once tightly coupled with specific servers—can have copies on multiple servers in the organization, even spread across multiple sites. This functionality was introduced by moving the mailbox databases from the Server hierarchy to the Organization hierarchy, essentially rendering them a *shared* object that can become active on any server in the organization. The *database availability group* container is now available to contain servers that participate in the replication of mailbox databases with each other.

EXCHANGE AND ACTIVE DIRECTORY

We could easily write two or three chapters on how Exchange Server interacts with the Active Directory, but the basics will have to do for now. Exchange Server relies on the Active Directory for information about its own configuration, user authentication, and email-specific properties for mail-enabled objects such as users, contacts, groups, and public folders. Look at Figure 1.5 to see some of the different types of interactions that occur between Exchange Server and the Active Directory.

FIGURE 1.5

Active Directory and Exchange
Server

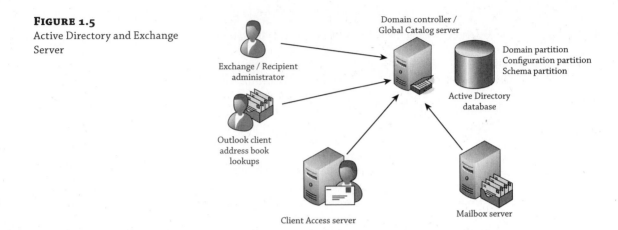

Because most of the Exchange Server configuration data for an Exchange server is stored in the Active Directory, all Exchange Server roles must contact a domain controller to request its configuration data; this information is stored in a special partition of the Active Directory database called the configuration partition. The configuration partition is replicated to all domain controllers in the entire Active Directory forest.

Each of the individual Exchange Server roles uses the Active Directory for different things. Here is a list of some of those functions:

Mailbox Servers   Exchange Server Mailbox servers must query the Active Directory to authenticate users, enumerate permissions on mailboxes, look up individual mailbox limits, and determine which mailboxes are on a particular server. They also require access to global catalog servers to look up email addressing information, distribution list membership information, and other data related to message routing.

Client Access Servers   Exchange Server Client Access servers require access to the Active Directory to look up information about users, Exchange ActiveSync, and Outlook Web App user restrictions.

Controlling Mailbox Growth

As users have become more savvy and competent at using Outlook and the features of Exchange Server, and email messages themselves have become more complex, the need for email storage has grown. Back in the days of Exchange Server 4.0, an organization that gave its users a 25 MB mailbox was considered generous. With Exchange Server 2003, a typical user's mailbox may have a storage limit of 300 to 500 MB, with power users and VIPs requiring even more. At TechEd 2006, Exchange Server gurus were tossing about the idea that in the future a default mailbox limit would be closer to 2 GB as users start incorporating Unified Messaging features. Current discussions now look forward to and assume 20 GB mailboxes within the next few years.

We all see users with mailbox sizes in the gigabyte range, but is your organization prepared for a typical user with a 20 GB mailbox size limit? What sort of concerns will you face when your average user has 5 GB, 10 GB, 15 GB, or even 20 GB of content (not just email!) in their mailbox?

Certainly the need for more disk storage will be the first factor that organizations need to consider. However, disk storage is reasonably cheap, and many larger organizations that are supporting thousands of mailbox users on a single Mailbox server already have more disk space than they can practically use. This is due to the fact that they require more disk spindles to accommodate the number of simultaneous I/Os per second (IOPS) that are required by a large number of users. While early versions of Exchange Server were primarily *performance-bound* /meaning that they would require more drive performance before they required more disk capacity/versions since Exchange Server 2007 have solidly pushed that to being *capacity-bound*. With the performance characteristics and capacities of modern drives, it becomes feasible to economically provision Exchange Server storage in support of large mailboxes.

For more administrators with large amounts of mail storage, the primary concern they face is the ability to quickly and efficiently restore data in the event of a failure. These administrators are often faced with service-level agreements that bind them to maximum restoration times. In even the most optimal circumstances, a 300 GB mailbox database will take some time to restore from backup media. However, these issues have largely been mitigated by the use of database availability groups (DAGs), which ensure constant *copies* of mailbox databases that reside on other servers, essentially providing a constant *live* backup of mailbox databases on other servers, and in other datacenters.

Microsoft recommends that you do not allow an Exchange Server mailbox database to grow larger than 200 GB unless you are implementing continuous-replication technologies in Exchange Server 2013. If you use database availability groups to replicate databases to multiple servers, the maximum database size recommendation goes up (way up) to 2 TB. However, the maximum supported database size is actually 64 TB. If you require more than the maximum recommend database storage, Exchange Server 2013 Standard Edition allows you to have up to 5 mailbox databases and Exchange Server 2013 (CU2 and later) Enterprise Edition allows you to have up to 100.

The solution in the past was to restrain the user community by preventing them from keeping all of the mail data that they might require on the mail server. This was done by imposing low mailbox limits, implementing message-archival requirements, keeping deleted items for only a few days, and keeping deleted mailboxes for only a few days.

However, as Unified Messaging data arrives in a user's mailbox and users have additional mechanisms for accessing the data stored in their mailbox, keeping mail data around longer is a demand and a requirement for your user community. The Exchange Server 2013 archive mailbox feature also drives the need for more storage, as message archival moves away from the PST files and back into Exchange Server in the form of archive mailboxes. Those archive mailboxes can be *segregated* to a dedicated mailbox database and be set to a different backup schedule and their own set of management practices.

Personal Folders or PST Files

And while we're on the subject of PST files, let's discuss this pesky feature of client management. The Outlook Personal Folder, or PST files, can be the very bane of your existence. Outlook allows users to create a local database, named Personal Folder, in which users can create folders and archive email. Although this seems like a good feature on the surface, there are a few downsides:

◆ Once data is in a user's PST file, you, as the server administrator, have lost control of it. If you ever had to find all copies of a certain message, perhaps for a lawsuit, you would be out of luck. PSTs can become a management and security nightmare as data is suddenly distributed all over your network.

◆ The data in PST files take up more space than the corresponding data on the server.

◆ The default location for a PST is the local portion of the user's profile; this means it is stored on the local hard disk of their computer and is not backed up.

◆ PST files can get corrupted, become misplaced, or even be lost entirely. PSTs are not designed for access over a network connection; they're meant to be on the local hard drive, which wastes space, as well as complicates the backup and management scenarios.

◆ Starting with Exchange Server 2010, Personal Archives stored on the server can be populated from PST files, therefore offering a true alternative to those pesky local files.

Email Archiving

Sometimes, managing a mail server seems like a constant race between IT and users to keep users from letting their mailbox run out of space. Users are pack rats and generally want to keep everything. If there is a business reason for them to do so, you should look at ways to expand your available storage to accommodate them.

However, as databases become larger and larger, the Exchange server will be more difficult to manage. You might start requiring hundreds and hundreds of gigabytes (or even terabytes) of storage for email databases. Worse still, backups and data recovery take longer.

As discussed in the previous section, Exchange Server 2013 does provide some archiving features, such as the Personal Archive. Also, large mailboxes could be moved to an Office 365 subscription, in a hybrid coexistence model.

For those organizations that are *not* opting to head out to the cloud or do *not* choose Office 365 as their email solution, this is where email archiving becomes useful. The last time we counted, there were several dozen companies in the business of supplying email archiving tools and services. Archiving products all have a lot of functions in common, including the ability to keep data long term in email archival, to allow the users to search for their own data, and to allow authorized users to search the entire archive.

If you look at how email is archived, archive systems generally come in one of three flavors:

◆ Systems that depend on journaling to automatically forward every email sent or received by specified users on to the archive system.

◆ Systems that perform a scheduled "crawl" of specified mailboxes, looking for messages that are eligible to be moved or copied to the archive.

◆ Systems that move data to the archive by copying the log files from the production Mailbox servers and then replaying the logs in to the archive. This is called log shipping.

Each of these methods has its advantages and disadvantages with respect to using storage, providing a complete archive, and dealing with performance overhead.

In the previous section, I discussed briefly the archive mailbox as an alternative to the management of PST files. However, its ability goes beyond the manual move of email messages to a dedicated location on the server. For any user who requires email archival, a Personal Archive, can be created for that user. As email ages past a certain point, the mail is moved from the active mailbox to the archive mailbox by using Retention Policies. The user can still access and search the archive mailbox from Outlook Web App or Outlook, though. The email data remains on the Exchange server and thus does not require an additional email archival infrastructure.

We often get asked if this information can be made available offline; keep in mind that it cannot. Personal Archives cannot be included in Offline Stores (OST) files. This is by design, and we're kind of glad that it works this way, since we are continuously trying to reduce the email footprint on the client computers. OST files get very large, very fast, and can cause plenty of headaches as well.

IF I USE A THIRD-PARTY SOLUTION, DOES IT MATTER HOW I ARCHIVE?

Every third-party archival vendor is going to tell you how their product is best and give you long technical reasons why their approach is so much better than the competition's. The dirty little secret is that all three approaches have their pros and cons:

Journaling is based on SMTP. If content doesn't run across SMTP, it won't get journaled and thus won't get archived. Journaling is great for capturing messaging and calendaring traffic that involve multiple parties or external entities, but it won't capture what happens to messages and other mailbox data once they're in the mailbox. Journaling can also place an additional load on the Hub Transport servers, depending on the amount and type of messaging traffic your users generate.

Crawling can capture changes only at certain intervals; it can't capture every single change, even though it overcomes many of the limitations of journaling. For example, if one user sends a message to another in violation of policy and both hard-delete their copy of the message before the next crawl interval, that message won't be detected and archived. The more often you schedule the crawl, the more of a performance impact your Mailbox servers will suffer.

Log shipping is the best of all options; it captures every transaction and change, allowing you to capture the entire history of each object while offloading the performance hit from your Exchange servers. However, the Exchange Server product team does not like the concept of log shipping and tries to discourage its use—mainly because there are vendors who try to inject data back into Exchange Server by modifying logs. This, needless to say, results in mailbox data that won't be supported by Microsoft.

Public Folders

The end-user experience for public folders has not changed in Exchange Server 2013, though the architecture has changed a lot—mainly the storage of the public folders which is now in a mailbox database, instead of the public folder database. Public folders are for common access to messages and files. Files can be dragged from file-access interfaces, such as Windows Explorer, and dropped into public folders. The whole concept of public folders has many organizations in a quandary as they try to figure out the best place for these collaborative applications. Increasingly, applications that were once "best suited" for a public folder are now better suited for web pages or portals, such as SharePoint workspaces. Although the whole concept of public folders is perceived as being deemphasized since Exchange Server 2007, Microsoft continues to support public folders, and many organizations will continue to find useful applications for public folders for the foreseeable future.

A key change in public-folder storage occurs in Exchange Server 2013, one that finally breaks the paradigm of dedicated public folder databases and public folder replication. Although we discuss this change in Chapter 2, "Introducing the Changes in Exchange Server 2013," we just briefly note here that public folders are now stored in mailbox databases and can be replicated as mailbox database copies in a database availability group.

You can set up sorting rules for a public folder so that items in the folder are organized by a range of attributes, such as the name of the sender or creator of the item or the date that the item was placed in the folder. Items in a public folder can be sorted by conversation threads. Public folders can also contain applications built on existing products such as Word or Excel or built with Exchange Server or Outlook Forms Designer, client or server scripting, or the Exchange Server API set. You can use public folders to replace many of the maddening paper-based processes that abound in every organization.

For easy access to items in a public folder, you can use a *folder link*. You can send a link to a folder in a message. When someone navigates to the folder and double-clicks a file, the file opens. Everyone who receives the message works with the same linked attachment, so everyone reads and can modify the same file. As with document routing, applications such as Microsoft Word can keep track of each person's changes to and comments on file contents. Of course, your users will have to learn to live with the fact that only one person can edit an application file at a time. Most modern end-user applications warn the user when someone else is using the file and if so allow the user to open a read-only copy of the file, which of course can't be edited.

Things Every Email Administrator Should Know

The information in this section is something that we often find even our own email administrators and help-desk personnel are not aware of. Sometimes the most important skill any technology administrator has is not a specific knowledge of something but generic knowledge that they can use to quickly find the right answer.

A Day in the Life of the Email Administrator

We know and work with a lot of email administrators, and we can honestly say that no two people have the same set of tasks required of them. Your CEO, director of information technology, or even your supervisor is going to ask you to pull rabbits out of your hat, so don't expect each day to be the same as the last one. (And invest in some rabbits.) Keep up with your technology and supporting products so that you can be ready with answers or at the very least intelligent responses to questions.

DAILY ADMINISTRATIVE TASKS

So, what are some typical tasks that you may perform as part of your duties as an email administrator? These tasks will depend on the size of your organization, the number of administrators you have running your Exchange Server organization, and how administrative tasks are divided up.

Recipient Management Tasks   These are certainly the biggest day-to-day tasks that most Exchange Server administrators in medium and large organizations will experience. Recipient management tasks may include:

- ◆ Assigning a mailbox to a user account

- ◆ Creating mail-enabled contacts

- ◆ Creating and managing mail groups

- ◆ Managing mail-enabled object properties such as users' phone numbers, assigning more email addresses to a user, or adding/removing group members

Basic Monitoring Tasks   These ensure that your Exchange servers are healthy and functioning properly:

- ◆ Checking queues for stalled messages

- ◆ Verifying that there is sufficient disk space for the databases and logs

- ◆ Making sure that the message-hygiene system is functioning and up to date

- ◆ Running and verifying daily backups

- ◆ Reviewing the event logs for unusual activity, errors, or warnings

Daily Troubleshooting Tasks   These include the following:

- ◆ Reviewing non-delivery report messages and figuring out why some mail your users are sending might not have been delivered

- ◆ Looking up errors and warnings that show up in the event logs to determine if they are serious and warrant corrective action

- ◆ Looking at mail flow in the organization to identify why delivery is taking a long time to some recipients

Security-Related Tasks   Some of these are performed daily, while others are performed only weekly or monthly:

- ◆ Looking at server and service uptimes to ensure that servers are not rebooting unexpectedly

- ◆ Reviewing the event logs for warnings that may indicate users are inappropriately accessing other users' data

- ◆ Saving the IIS and SMTP and connectivity logs or even reviewing their content

Email Client Administration Tasks   These include the following:

- ◆ Troubleshooting Autodiscover connectivity and client connectivity issues

- ◆ Diagnosing problems with mobile or tablet devices that use Exchange ActiveSync connectivity

Application Integration Tasks These are performed on an as-needed basis and may include the following:

◆ Establishing and diagnosing SMTP connectivity with email-enabled third-party applications such as web servers

◆ Configuring, testing, and troubleshooting Unified Messaging interoperability with voice and SIP systems

◆ Configuring, testing, and troubleshooting connectivity with SharePoint Server 2013 site mailboxes.

COMMUNICATING WITH YOUR USERS

Communicating with your users is probably one of the most important things you do. Keeping your users informed and delivering good customer service are almost as important as delivering the IT service itself. Keeping users informed of full or partial service outages such as mobile or iPhone support or web connectivity may not score any immediate points, but users appreciate honest, forthright information. Remember how you felt the last time you were waiting for an airplane to arrive that kept on being delayed and delayed, and all the airline could do was be evasive?

Also remember to have multiple avenues of communication available to your users. For example, you may need to get out to your users the message that you will be having downtime on the weekend. Postings on your company intranet or even the bulletin board in the cafeteria or on the wall of the elevator are good ways to keep your users informed.

PREPARING REPORTS

Maybe we have just worked in a large IT environment for too long now, but it seems to us that information technology is more and more about reports and metrics. We are frequently asked to provide reports, statistics, and information on usage—not necessarily information on performance (how well the system performed for the users) but other types of metrics. Depending on your management, you may be asked to provide the following:

◆ Total number of mailboxes and mailbox sizes

◆ Top system users and top source/destination domains

◆ Antispam and message-hygiene statistics

◆ Disk space usage and growth

◆ System availability reports indicating how much unscheduled downtime may have been experienced during a certain reporting period

Exchange does not provide you with a way to easily access most of this data. The mailbox statistics can be generated using the Exchange Management Shell, but many of these will actually require an additional reporting product, such as System Center 2012 R2.

Something that you can do to prepare for a reporting requirement is to ensure that you are keeping two to four weeks' worth of message-tracking and protocol logs.

Scheduled Downtime, Patches, and Service Packs

As the discussion over moving to "the cloud" becomes more prevalent in most industries, the common argument that keeps on coming back in favor for moving Exchange Server services to some version of Exchange Online or Office 365 is server availability. No one likes downtime, whether it is scheduled or not. Management may actually be holding you to a specific service-level agreement (SLA) that requires you to provide so many hours of uptime per month or to provide email services during certain hours. Unscheduled downtime is anything that happens during your stated hours of operation that keeps users from accessing their email.

Even a small organization can provide very good availability for its mail services, and without large investments in hardware. Good availability begins with the following:

◆ Server hardware should always be from a reputable vendor and listed in the Microsoft Server Catalog.

◆ Server hardware should be installed using the vendor recommended procedures and updated regularly. Problems with servers are frequently caused by outdated firmware and device drivers.

◆ Once the server is in production, it should not be used as a test bed for other software. Keep an identically configured server that uses the same hardware for testing updates.

Don't underestimate the importance of training and documentation. In general, the industry formula for providing better availability for any system is to spend more money to purchase redundant servers and build failover clusters. But often better training for IT personnel and a simple investment in system documentation, as well as system policies and procedures can improve availability, and for less money.

⊕ Real World Scenario

INTERNAL STAFF TRAINING IS JUST AS IMPORTANT AS YOUR INFRASTRUCTURE

Company LMNOP invested hundreds of thousands of dollars in their infrastructure to improve server uptime. Three months into the operation of the new system, an untrained operator accidentally brought down a 15,000-mailbox database availability group (DAG) simply because he had been asked to do a task he had never done before and the organization did not have documentation on how to proceed. So keep in mind that documentation, training, and procedures are very important in improving uptime.

Even the biggest mailbox servers in large database availability groups need some scheduled downtime. Even if it is scheduled in the wee hours of the morning, undoubtedly someone, somewhere, somehow will need access when you are working on the system. Thankfully, the DAG solution for high availability ensures that users may never notice the scheduled server downtime, since mailbox services can be switched over to another member server in the DAG. That being said, when you are driving your car with no spare tire in the trunk, you are more vulnerable to a flat tire. The same is true of the DAG, because when a member server is offline for maintenance, the DAG loses a potential mailbox server that is capable of taking over in the event of server failure.

When your scheduled downtime will affect components that can impact server availability for your users, that downtime should be well communicated. Also, You should document your scheduled downtime as part of your operational plans and let your user community know about these plans. The specific time window for maintenance should always be the same; for some organizations, this might be 6:30 p.m.–10:30 p.m. on Thursday once per month, whereas other organizations might schedule downtime from 11:00 p.m. Saturday until 4:00 a.m. every Sunday.

The number-one reason for downtime is to apply updates and fixes to the operating system or to the applications running on the server. Microsoft releases monthly security updates for the operating system and applications if vulnerabilities are discovered. Every few months, Microsoft releases updates for Exchange Server 2013 that fix bugs or that may even add slight functionality.

Microsoft's updates are usually downloaded to your servers shortly after they are released. The server can download them directly from Microsoft, or they can be downloaded from Windows Software Update Service (WSUS), Microsoft Systems Center 2012 R2, or another third-party server inside your network. Whichever you choose, it is important that you make sure that the machine is a server and not a workstation. For example, make sure the automatic updates component of Windows Server is configured correctly. Figure 1.6 shows the Change Settings options for Windows Update.

FIGURE 1.6
Configuring automatic updates

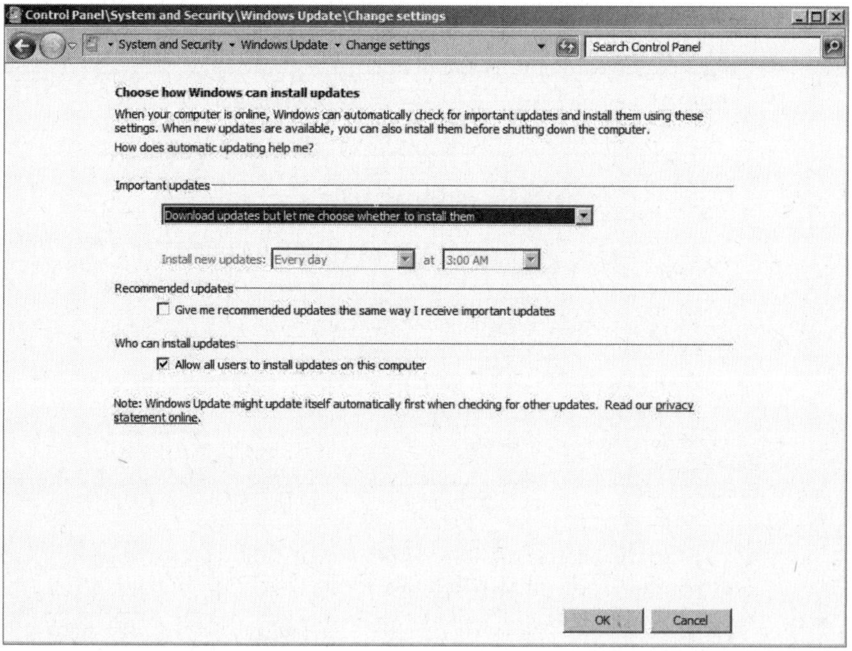

For production Exchange servers, you should configure the server with the option Download Updates But Let Me Choose Whether To Install Them. This is an important setting because if you choose the Install Updates Automatically (Recommended) option, the server will automatically apply any update within a day or so of downloading it. This is not a desirable action for a production mail server. Instead, you want the server to download the updates and notify you via the updates icon in the system tray. You can then investigate the updates and schedule appropriate downtime to apply them manually.

Finding Answers

This topic deserves special attention. One of our jobs is working in Tier 3 support for a large organization. The thing we respect the most about the administrators who actually run the system and handle the trouble tickets is that they have done their homework prior to coming to us with a problem.

Too often techies make up an answer when they are not sure about something. Don't do that! When you are asked a question that you don't know the answer to, it is okay to say you don't know the answer. But follow that up by indicating that you will find the answer. Knowing the right resources (where to get answers) is therefore just as important as the technical knowledge it takes to implement the answer. Key players in your organization will respect you much more when they know that you are willing to accept the limitations of your knowledge and have the appropriate resources to find the resolution to a problem or the answer to a question.

HELPFUL RESOURCES

Exchange Server has to be one of the most documented and discussed products (short of maybe Windows) that Microsoft produces. This means that most of the questions that we have about Exchange Server we can usually answer via the right search or by looking in the right place. The most obvious place to start when you have a problem or a question is to perform an Internet search, but many other resources are available:

Exchange Server Documentation There is a world of free information on the Internet, but let's start right on the local hard disk of your Exchange Server or any place you have installed the admin tools. Microsoft has done an excellent job of providing better and better documentation for Exchange Server over the past few years. The Exchange Server 2013 documentation is comprehensive and so readable you will wonder if it is really from Microsoft. Figure 1.7 shows an example of the Exchange Server 2013 documentation. Look for the following file,

```
C:\Program Files\Microsoft\Exchange Server\v15\Bin\ExchHelp.chm
```

or run it from the Microsoft Exchange Server 2013 folder on the Start menu.

FIGURE 1.7
Viewing the
Exchange 2013
documentation

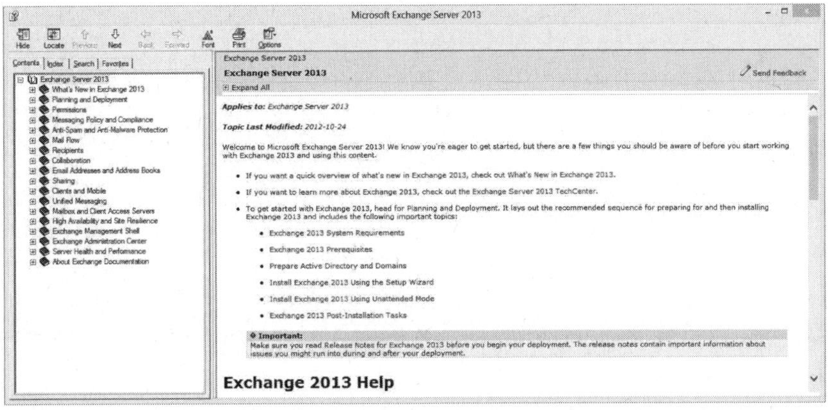

You can also download updated versions of `ExchHelp.chm` from the following URL:

`http://technet.microsoft.com/en-us/exchange/fp179701`

Exchange Server Release Notes   Another good resource for "I wish I had known that" types of things is the release notes. You should be able to find a link to the release notes here:

`C:\Program Files\Microsoft\Exchange Server\v15\`

Exchange Server Forums   If you have a question on which you have done your due diligence in searching and researching the problem but you don't have an answer, it is time to ask the world. A good place to start is the Microsoft forums, also known as social.technet.microsoft .com. You can find the Exchange Server section here:

`http://social.technet.microsoft.com/forums/en-US/category/exchangeserver/`

When you post your question, please take a moment to think about what information the other readers are going to need to answer your question. While you can post a question like "Exchange is giving me an error," doing so is only going to result in (at best) delays while other forum participants have to request specific information from you. Instead, post the exact error message and any error codes you are seeing. Also indicate, at minimum, what version of the software you are using (including service pack), the role of the server, and what operating system you are using.

You Had Me at EHLO   This is the Microsoft Exchange Team's blog. This is the best site on the Internet for getting the inside scoop on how Exchange Server works, best practices, and the future of Exchange Server. You can read articles written by Exchange Server developers and Customer Support Services engineers. When changes to the product are announced, or customers are requesting changes in the product, you will hear *first* from the product group engineers about the way they have chosen to deal with the issue.

`http://blogs.technet.com/b/exchange/`

MSExchange.Org Website   One of the best sites on the Internet for free, easy-to-access content about Exchange Server is `www.msexchange.org`. The articles are written by Exchange Server gurus from all over the world and are usually in the form of easy-to-read and easy-to-follow tutorials. There is also a forums section where you can post questions or read other people's questions.

CALLING FOR SUPPORT

If your system is down or your operations are seriously hindered and you don't have a clue what to do next, it is time to call in the big guns. Sure, you should do some Internet searches to try to resolve your problem, but Internet newsgroups and forums are not the place to get support for business-critical issues.

Microsoft Product Support Services (PSS) is Microsoft's technical support organization. Its home page is `http://support.microsoft.com`. Professional support options (ranging from peer-to-peer support to telephone support) can be found at the following URL, where a web browser–based wizard guides you through your support options:

`https://gettechsupport.microsoft.com/default.aspx?locale=en-us&supportregion=en-us&pesid=14886`

If you do not have a Microsoft Premier agreement, Microsoft telephone support may seem to be a bit expensive, but believe me, when an Exchange server is down and the users are burning you in effigy in the company parking lot, a few hundred dollars for business hours support is cheap.

When you call and get a support technician on the phone, don't be surprised or offended if they start at the beginning and ask you a lot of elementary questions. They have to double-check everything you have done before they can look into more advanced problems. Frequently, one of these basic questions will help you locate a problem that you were convinced was more complicated than it really was. Though the beginning of the call may be underwhelming, the technician will stay with you on the phone until the problem is resolved or some kind of an acceptable resolution is put in place.

I always encourage people to call PSS if they truly need assistance. But PSS engineers are not mind readers, nor do they know every bit of Exchange Server code. You will do both yourself and the PSS engineer a big favor if you have all of your ducks in a row before you call. Do the following before you call:

- Attempt a graceful shutdown and restart of the server in question, if applicable.

- Perform a complete backup if possible.

- Have a complete, documented history of everything you have done to solve the problem. At the first sign of trouble, you should start keeping a chronological log of the things you did to fix the problem.

- Find out if you are allowed to initiate support sessions with remote support personnel through a tool like Lync 2013 or WebEx.

- Be at a telephone that is physically at the server's console, or be in a place where you can access the server remotely via the Remote Desktop client. Your support call will be very brief if you cannot immediately begin checking things for the PSS engineer.

- Have the usernames and passwords that will provide you with the right level of administrative access. If you don't have those, have someone nearby who can log you in.

- Save copies of the event logs. Be prepared to send these to PSS if requested.

- Know the location of your most recent backup and how to access it when needed.

- Keep copies of all error messages. Don't paraphrase the message. Screen captures work great in this case. Pressing Alt+Print Scrn and pasting into a WordPad document works great, too. We usually create a document with screen captures along with notes of what we were doing when we saw each message.

Be patient; telephone support is a terribly difficult job. A little kindness, patience, and understanding on your part will most certainly be returned by the PSS engineer.

Tools You Should Know

Out of the box, Exchange Server is an excellent product, but sometimes the base software that you install can use some assistance. Some of these tools are actually installed with Exchange Server, whereas you may need to download other tools.

PowerShell and the Exchange Management Shell   Even here in the very first chapters, we are extolling the virtues of the new Windows management shell (or command-line and scripting interface) called PowerShell. PowerShell enables some basic Windows management functions, such as managing event logs and services, to be performed via a command-line interface. This interface is simple to use and easy to learn, even for a GUI guy like this author. The Exchange Server team pioneered the adoption of PowerShell when they built the entire Exchange Server 2007 management interface, known as the Exchange Management Shell (EMS), as an extension to PowerShell. Exchange Server 2010 and Exchange Server 2013 continues to follow this pattern.

Although almost every chapter in this book will include at least some information about using EMS to perform Exchange Server management tasks, we have dedicated all of Chapter 5, "Introduction to PowerShell and the Exchange Management Shell," to helping you learn your way around EMS.

Exchange Management Shell Test Cmdlets   The Exchange Management Shell has a series of command-line tools that are very good for testing and diagnosing problems. These include tools for testing Outlook Web App connectivity, Unified Messaging connectivity, Outlook connectivity, and even mail flow. They are installed when you install the Exchange Server 2013 Management Tools. For more information, at the EMS prompt type `Get-Excommand test*`.

Microsoft Remote Connectivity Analyzer (Previously Exchange Remote Connectivity Analyzer)   Available at www.testexchangeconnectivity.com, the Remote Connectivity Analyzer is likely going to be the most useful tool in your troubleshooting arsenal. Initially started as a side project by two Microsoft employees, this website acts as the ultimate connectivity troubleshooting catch-all. The basic troubleshooting scenarios for Exchange Server 2013 (on-premises) are shown in Figure 1.8.

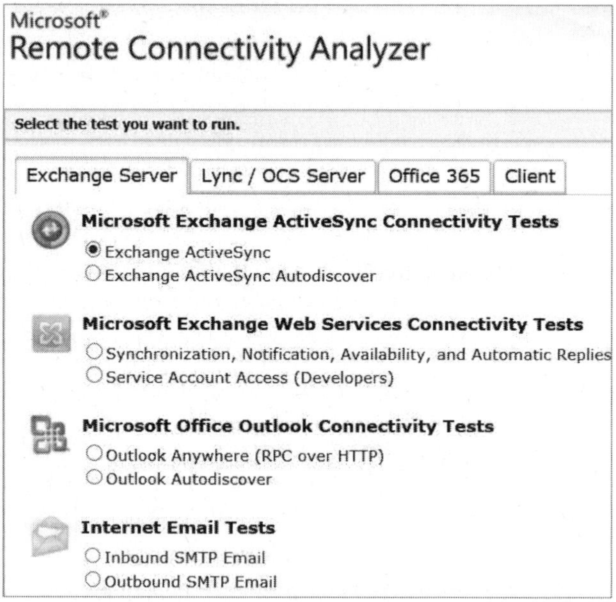

FIGURE 1.8
Viewing the Microsoft Remote Connectivity Analyzer

Those of you who have used "analyzers" from Microsoft in the past may remember the Exchange Best Practices Analyzer (ExBPA), the Remote Connectivity Analyzer should not be confused with the ExBPA. In fact, a new version of the ExBPA has not been released for Exchange Server 2013, as of the writing of this book, and will likely not be released.

ADModify.NET   If you need to make bulk changes to Active Directory objects such as users, groups, contacts, or even public folders, then you need ADModify.NET (shown in Figure 1.9). This powerful and free tool allows you to find and select objects from the Active Directory and then use a simple interface to modify one or more attributes of the selected objects. You can even use other attributes of that object to build a new attribute.

FIGURE 1.9

The main search screen of ADModify.NET

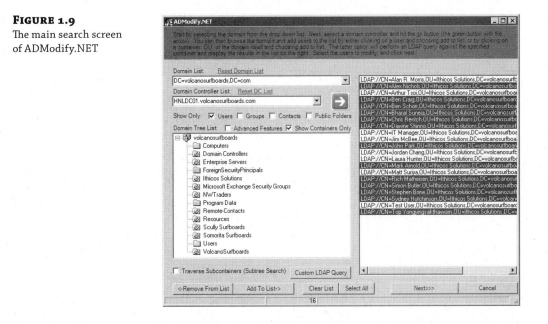

There are a few important things to note about ADModify. You must run it from your local hard disk, and the Microsoft .NET Framework v2.0 is required. Another important item to note is that it has an "undo" feature; you can back out a bulk change that you made if it turns out to be wrong. You can download ADModify from `www.codeplex.com/admodify`.

Quest ActiveRoles Management Shell for Active Directory   Quest Software is giving away one of the most useful add-on tools for Microsoft PowerShell that we have ever used. Its Management Shell for Active Directory allows you to manage users and groups using PowerShell even if you don't yet have Exchange Server 2013. We use this tool almost daily in organizations that have not yet migrated to Exchange Server 2013. You can download this free tool from Quest at: `www.quest.com/powershell/activeroles-server.aspx`.

PowerGUI   If you like the Quest ActiveRoles Management Shell, you will also like PowerGUI. PowerGUI is a graphical interface that "wraps itself" around PowerShell and allows you to see the results of PowerShell cmdlets. It will help you in writing scripts utilizing PowerShell and extensions to PowerShell.

You can download PowerGUI from `http://powergui.org`.

The Bottom Line

Understand email fundamentals.   To gain the best advantage from Exchange Server 2013, you should have a good grounding in general email applications and principles.

Master It   What two application models have email programs traditionally used? Which one does Exchange Server use? Can you name an example of the other model?

Identify email-administration duties.   Installing an Exchange Server system is just the first part of the job. Once it's in place, it needs to be maintained. Be familiar with the various duties and concerns that will be involved with the care and feeding of Exchange Server.

Master It   What are the various types of duties that a typical Exchange Server administrator will expect to perform?

Chapter 2

Introducing the Changes in Exchange Server 2013

Email clients used to be fairly simple and text based. Email servers had few connectivity options, no high-availability features, and no integrated directory. Then, beginning in the mid-1990s, we saw a big push toward providing email service to most of our user communities. We also saw email go from an occasionally used convenience to a business-critical tool. Business management and users demanded more features, better availability, and more connectivity options as the email client and server evolved.

Microsoft released Exchange Server 4.0 (the first version of Exchange Server) in 1996, and the product has been evolving ever since. Exchange Server 2013 is the seventh major release of the Exchange Server family and represents continued evolution of the product. The features and functions of this new release include not only feature requests from many thousands of Microsoft's customers but also requirements shared internally at Microsoft by Microsoft Consulting Services and their own IT department, which supports more than 100,000 mailboxes.

We'll explore how some product features have evolved to this latest release, providing context for functionalities that were added, removed, modified, renamed, or reinvented. And because as of this writing most Exchange Server customers are still using Exchange Server 2010 rather than Exchange Server 2013, we'll discuss the changes that have been made to Exchange Server since Exchange Server 2010.

In this chapter, you will learn to:

◆ Understand the changes in the Exchange Server roles

◆ Understand the changes in Exchange server architecture

Getting to Know Exchange Server 2013

It seems that we approach any new release of Exchange Server with a sense of both excitement and trepidation. We look forward to the new features and capabilities that are introduced with a newer version of the product. Certainly the new site-resiliency features, compliance functionalities, resource management, management features, and security features will allow us to deliver better, more reliable messaging services to our end users.

On the other side of the coin is the feeling that we have to learn a whole new series of features inside and out so that we can better use them. Sure, we know Exchange Server 2010 pretty well, but there will be new details to learn with Exchange Server 2013. Sometimes we have to learn these implementation or management details the hard way.

However, this milestone in the evolution of Exchange Server is a good one. We can't help but be excited about learning about this new version and sharing what we have learned. We hope that you will feel the same sense of excitement. We have picked a top-ten list of new features that we like and hope that you will investigate further as you start to learn Exchange Server 2013. Some of these are summarized in this chapter and many of these you will find in more detail in later chapters.

1. ◆ Powerful message transport rules applied through Data Loss Prevention (DLP) policies

2. ◆ Smarter database availability group (DAG) features that provide simpler restore scenarios

3. ◆ Outlook Web App available when working offline

4. ◆ A move away from role-based installations and a simplified installation process

5. ◆ Improved search and e-discovery features that includes the ability to search across mailboxes and archives

6. ◆ Integration with SharePoint Server 2013 and Lync Server 2013 through Lync archives and site mailboxes

7. ◆ Message routing now based on multiple boundaries, including the database availability group and the Active Directory site

8. ◆ Introduction of the Exchange Administration Center to replace the (always too slow) Exchange Management Console and the (always with too sparsely featured) Exchange Control Panel

9. ◆ A much easier migration path to Exchange Server 2013 than to previous versions

10. ◆ Public folders hosted as mailboxes

LEARN THE EXCHANGE MANAGEMENT SHELL (AND WEAR SUNSCREEN!)

To those of you who have been around the Internet long enough to remember the "Wear Sunscreen" email, that was supposedly the 1997 commencement address to MIT given by Kurt Vonnegut but was in reality a column written by the *Chicago Sun Tribune*'s Mary Schmich, I give you "Learn the Management Shell":

◆ If we could offer you one important tip when learning Exchange Server 2013, it would be that you should get to know the Exchange Management Shell (EMS). Sure, it looks intimidating and nearly everything you will ever need to do is in the Exchange Administration Center. Many Exchange Server gurus will back us up on the value and usefulness of the new EMS, whereas they might not agree with us on things such as using real-time block lists, making full backups daily, and keeping lots of free disk space available.

◆ Make regular Exchange Server data backups.

◆ Document.

◆ Don't believe everything you read from vendors; their job is to sell you things.

◆ Don't put off maintenance that might affect your uptime.

◆ If you get in trouble, call for help sooner rather than later. A few hundred dollars for a phone call to your vendor or Microsoft Product Support Services is better than a few days of downtime.

◆ Share your knowledge and configuration information with coworkers.

◆ Accept certain inalienable truths: disks will fail, servers will crash, users will complain, viruses will spread, and important messages will sometimes get caught in the spam filter.

◆ Get to know your users and communicate with them.

◆ Implement site resiliency and high availability for mailboxes but also for public folder mailboxes.

◆ Make regular backups of your Active Directory.

◆ If a consultant is telling you something that you know in your gut is wrong, double-check their work or run their recommendation by another colleague. Second opinions and another set of eyes are almost always helpful.

◆ Think twice. Click once.

But trust me on the EMS.

In this chapter, we will cover the features of Exchange Server 2013 not only to give experienced Exchange Server administrators the proper perspective on Exchange Server 2013 but also to educate newly minted Exchange Server administrators on just how powerful Exchange Server has become. Some features we'll discuss in this chapter aren't brand new, but they are so key to the product and have been so greatly improved in this release that we are compelled to mention them at the onset.

Exchange Server Architecture

Over the last several releases, a number of significant changes have been made to the architecture of Exchange Server. These changes positively improve the performance and scalability of Exchange Server, but they also make some pretty significant changes in the platform on which you support Exchange Server.

x64 Processor Requirement

Exchange Server 2013 uses only 64-bit extensions. This change was made in Exchange Server 2010 and was one of the most controversial at the time. It meant your production servers would have to have x64 architecture–based Intel Xeon and Pentium processors or AMD64 architecture–based AMD Opteron and Athlon processors. This change also prompted the Windows Server teams to make similar radical changes. When Windows Server 2008 R2 was introduced, it also supported only 64-bit extensions. The same is true of Windows Server 2012.

Although many people are thrilled with this change in the architecture, there are, no doubt, folks screaming, "What? I have to buy new hardware just to upgrade?" A good response to this concern is that in most messaging-system upgrades, the hardware is replaced anyway. Certainly this is true for hardware that has been in production for three or four years. Add to this the fact that there is no "in-place" upgrade from Exchange Server 2000, 2003, 2007, or 2010 to Exchange Server 2013, and there is really no question that new hardware will be necessary to deploy Exchange Server 2013.

Windows Server 2008 R2 and Windows Server 2012

Because of some of the underlying requirements of Exchange Server 2013, you must run Windows Server 2008 R2 Service Pack 1 or Windows Server 2012. The following editions of Windows Server will support Exchange Server 2013:

◆ Windows Server 2008 Standard Edition R2 SP1 (only for non-DAG members)

◆ Windows Server 2008 Enterprise Edition R2 SP1

◆ Windows Server 2008 Datacenter Edition R2 SP1

◆ Windows Server 2012 Standard Edition

◆ Windows Server 2012 Datacenter Edition

Many administrators will immediately notice that a leap of architecture exists also for the Windows Server layer on which Exchange Server depends. We recommend that administrators with only Windows Server 2003 experience take the time to familiarize themselves with the Windows Server 2012 platform. The user interface of Windows Server 2012 presents a brave new world for those coming from previous platforms.

As of the writing of this chapter, Windows Server 2012 R2 was just released as a Preview edition. I have recently tested an Exchange Server 2013 Cumulative Update 1 (CU1) installation on a Windows Server 2012 R2 server and could not find any problems with my Exchange server installation. It's definitely early on in the game, and no official support stance has been announced by Microsoft, but it would seem that Exchange Server 2013 will purr like a kitten on Windows Server 2012 R2.

Installer, Service Pack, and Patching Improvements

The setup process in Exchange Server 2000/2003 had some serious annoyances; actually, the whole process of getting a server up and running was pretty annoying. If a server did not meet the prerequisites, you had to close the Setup program, fix the problem, and then restart Setup. Once you got the release to manufacturing (RTM) or "gold" version installed, you had to install the most recent version of the Exchange Server service pack. Finally, you had to research all the post-service pack–critical fixes and apply them (sometimes in a specific order).

Microsoft has improved the setup process for Exchange Server 2013 as well as simplified patching. These improvements have been made in five key areas:

◆ A simplified wizard with a much cleaner user experience and instructions. You no longer need to research the implications of your answers during the setup process and wonder if you've made a critical mistake that cannot be reverted.

◆ The Exchange Server 2013 Setup program downloads and installs all missing prerequisites, letting you fix the missing prerequisites and then continue without starting over (unless a reboot is required after installing a prerequisite).

◆ The entire setup process can be scripted by using PowerShell cmdlets.

◆ Service packs are released as a complete installation pack; all updates are built into the service pack and you can install a complete Exchange Server directly from the latest service pack. That means no more installing the RTM version and then applying the latest service pack.

◆ The Setup program downloads and applies all updates and patches to Exchange Server 2013. So, you are always sure that you are running the latest and greatest version of Exchange Server immediately after the installation.

If you plan to perform some unattended server installations, all you have to do is download the latest cumulative update. Once those files are available locally, you can use the `/UpdatesDir` parameter as part of your setup command to allow the Exchange Server Setup program to update itself and provide an up-to-date installation that uses already downloaded update files.

ABOUT APPLYING UPDATES

For Exchange Server 2013, Microsoft has replaced the traditional model of applying hotfixes with a predictable and reliable cumulative update process. Microsoft has committed to implementing a quarterly cadence to released cumulative updates to the Exchange Server product. The cumulative updates will be released as full build packages and deployed as build-to-build upgrades. This solution provides many benefits to administrators, such as the ability to plan adequately for these updates, and removes a lot of the guessing-game we played in previous versions of Exchange Server.

Server Roles

In Exchange Server 2013, what's old is new again. Nowhere is this more true than the major change in server roles. Exchange Server 2007 was the first release to officially introduce the concept of server roles. At the time, the challenge was to separate Exchange Server functionalities to separate physical servers that would each run an individual role. The result was that each server would only provide a specific set of features for the infrastructure and could scale nicely for large organizations. Limitations in hardware were the main technical drivers behind role-based installation and the need to segregate feature sets to different servers.

For most Exchange Server 2007 and 2010 organizations, this meant three primary roles. Client Access server, Mailbox server, and Hub Transport server roles were required in each site where Exchange Server features were supported and were your primary installation choices. There were two other roles as well, the Unified Messaging server and the Edge Transport server, which served very specific purposes and were installed only when those feature sets were required.

Exchange Server 2013 contains only two server roles the Client Access server role and the Mailbox server role. We will provide much more detail on these roles later, but this section highlights how the roles have changed. During the installation of Exchange Server 2013, the administrator will be presented with the choices shown in Figure 2.1.

So let's take a peek at those two Exchange Server 2013 roles and highlight some of the key departures from Exchange Server 2010.

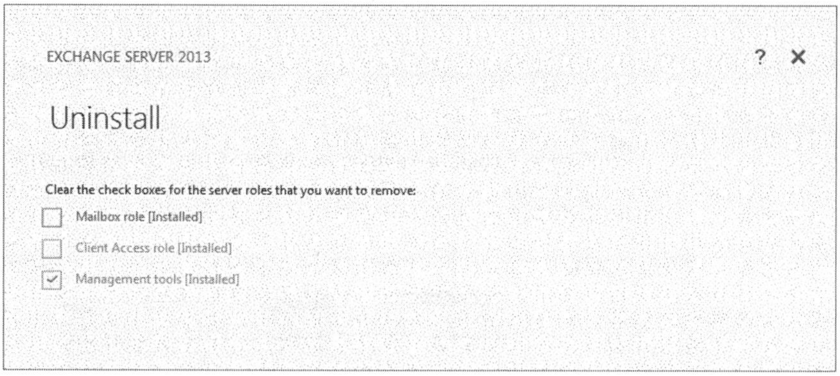

FIGURE 2.1
Specifying
server roles

> **HIGH-AVAILABILITY DECISIONS**
>
> High-availability decisions do not need to be made at installation time. Unlike in Exchange Server 2007 and previous versions, high availability for Exchange Server 2013 databases is added incrementally *after* the initial deployment of the Mailbox server. There is no clustered Mailbox server installation option; however, administrators create database availability groups to implement high availability. High availability is discussed in detail in Chapter 20, "Creating and Managing Database Availability Groups." Mailbox databases can be added to database availability groups at any point in the game. The databases can be removed from database availability groups as well, as needed. Essentially, the high-availability decisions can be done incrementally after a deployment has occurred, and reversed if they no longer serve the needs of the organization.

1)   The Mailbox server role handles all mailboxes, public folder mailboxes, and database replication, as it has in previous versions. However, it now also handles Transport service and Unified Messaging features.

2)   The Client Access server role acts as a thin server that essentially proxies most client requests to Mailbox servers. The major change for this role is that it also handles Transport services (more on that little surprise later in this chapter) and no longer performs the heavy lifting for client connections, such as rendering Outlook Web Access pages and acting as a client endpoint.

This brings us back to the idea that what's old is new again. Well, the model of having a thin front-end server and a thick backend (aka Mailbox) server is very reminiscent of Exchange Server 2003, where we had two roles: the Front End and the Back End server roles.

THE MAILBOX SERVER ROLE

The Mailbox server role is responsible for so much, yet changes in the architecture have ensured that it requires very few resources to perform all its necessary tasks. We will discuss, in later chapters, the database improvements in database schema and memory utilization in Exchange Server 2013; these improvements are really designed to enhance the ability of a Mailbox server to do so much more with so much less.

The primary departure for Mailbox servers is the inclusion of Transport services. Transport had been segregated to its own role, the Hub Transport server role, but Transport is now mostly integrated into the Mailbox server roles. The Processes tab of the Task Manager shows familiar services that used to be associated with Hub Transport servers now running on a Mailbox server (Figure 2.2). Since this figure shows a server that runs both the Mailbox server and Client Access server roles, a keen eye will also identify the Front End Transport service that is associated with the Client Access server role.

FIGURE 2.2

Transport services

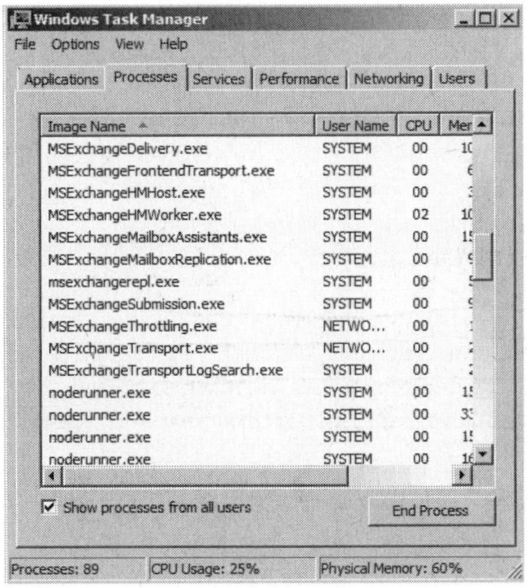

Another very significant change in the Mailbox server role is the number of Client Access features that are now handled on this role. In fact, most of the features handled by Client Access servers in Exchange Server 2010 are now handled by Mailbox servers. In Exchange Server 2013, a Mailbox server handles the data rendering for client requests, runs all of the client access protocols, and still maintains all mailboxes.

THE CLIENT ACCESS SERVER ROLE

In the prerelease days of Exchange Server 2013, the acronym for this newly modified role was CAFÉ—Client Access on the Front End. Its goal was to be a leaner, less-rigid, less-depended-on affinity Client Access server role that could be decoupled from the Mailbox server, that could provide cross-site access to mailbox, and, most importantly, that would be *stateless*. Well, those are some pretty hefty requirements, but in this latest release Microsoft was able to reinvent the Client Access server role (and make it look a lot like the Front End role in Exchange 2003).

Client Access servers provide client authentication and some limited client redirection but mostly proxy all client requests to the Mailbox servers. One very notable point regarding the Client Access server role (and one that did not exist in the Exchange Server 2003 Front End role) is the ability to run Transport services. Client Access servers are the SMTP inbound endpoints for your organization and therefore accept connections over TCP port 25.

Be aware, though, that Client Access servers do not store any email messages; they do not queue any email either; they simply proxy and redirect connection. So, you might be able to guess by now that since the Client Access servers do not store any email, they cannot be used to act upon email messages either. Transport rule agents, content-filtering agents, and other agents that require access to the content or headers of email messages to perform tasks on email messages all run on the Mailbox server.

Edge Transport Services

Edge Transport services are not available yet in Exchange Server 2013. However, an administrator can deploy an Exchange Server 2010 or Exchange Server 2007 Edge Transport server on the network, and it will coexist quite nicely with the Exchange Server 2013 servers. This section describes the behavior of Exchange Server 2010 Edge Transport servers on your network.

The amount of spam and viruses that some organizations receive is staggering. Even small organizations are receiving tens of thousands of pieces of spam, dozens of viruses, and hundreds of thousands of dictionary spamming attacks each week. Some organizations estimate that more than 90 percent of all inbound email is spam or other unwanted content. Keeping this unwanted content away from your Exchange servers is important. A common practice for messaging administrators is to employ additional layers of message hygiene and security. The first layer is usually some type of appliance or third-party SMTP software package that is installed in the organization's perimeter network. The problem with these third-party utilities is that the administrator has to become an expert on an additional technology.

IS THE EDGE TRANSPORT SERVER ROLE REQUIRED?

A common misconception is that the Edge Transport role is required for an Exchange Server organization. This is not the case. Inbound email can be sent directly to the Client Access server role, or you can continue to use your existing third-party antispam/message-hygiene system to act as an inbound message relay for Exchange Server.

Microsoft's solution to this dilemma is the Edge Transport server. The Edge Transport server is a stand-alone message transport server that is managed using the EMS and the same basic management console that is used to manage Exchange Server 2013. A server functioning in an Edge Transport role should not be a member of the organization's internal Active Directory, although it can be part of a separate management forest used in a perimeter network.

Functions such as transport rules are identical to those that run on an Exchange Server 2013 Mailbox server. Content filtering and Microsoft Forefront Security for Exchange are implemented on the Edge Transport server through content filtering and other antispam features all run on the mailbox server as well as for for organizations that do not have Edge Transport servers.

An example of how an organization might deploy an Edge Transport server is shown in Figure 2.3. Inbound email is first delivered to the Edge Transport servers that are located in the organization's perimeter network, where the message is inspected by the content filter, Forefront Security for Exchange, and any message transport rules. The inbound message is then sent on to the internal servers. Additionally, the Exchange Server Mailbox servers are configured to deliver mail leaving the organization to the Edge Transport servers rather than configuring the internal servers to deliver mail directly to the Internet.

FIGURE 2.3
Deploying an
Edge Transport
server

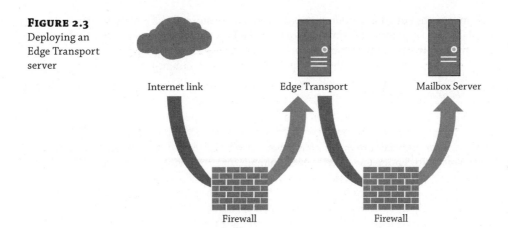

The Edge Transport server is a fully functional SMTP message-hygiene system with many of the same features that are found in expensive message-hygiene software packages and appliances. The following features are included:

◆ Per-user safe-sender, safe-recipient, and blocked-sender lists are automatically replicated from the user's mailbox to the Edge Transport server. Recipient filtering is enabled when valid recipients are synchronized to the Edge Transport server's local Active Directory Application Mode (ADAM) or Active Directory Lightweight Directory Services (AD LDS) database.

◆ Sender and recipient filtering can be configured via administrator-controlled lists.

◆ Integrated Microsoft content filter is included for spam detection. Spam can be rejected, deleted, quarantined, or delivered to the user's Junk email.

◆ Multiple message-quarantines allow messages that are highly likely to be spam to be quarantined and sent to a quarantine mailbox on your Exchange server. A separate quarantine exists in the form of the user's Junk email folder for messages that are still tagged as spam but with a lower Spam Confidence Level.

◆ Microsoft Forefront Security for Exchange Server is available for the Edge Transport server when Enterprise client access licenses are used. However, this will be a short-lived solution, since Microsoft has announced that the entire suite of Forefront products is being decommissioned. Instead, Exchange administrators could use a third-party solution or a cloud-based solution.

◆ Daily content filter and virus signature updates are available for organizations using Microsoft Forefront Security for Exchange Server.

◆ Real-time block lists and the IP Reputation Service allow an IP address to be checked to see if it is a known source of spam. Reputation filters can be updated on a daily basis.

◆ Sender ID filters allow for the verification of the mail server that sent a message and whether it is allowed to send mail for the message sender.

◆ Sender reputation filters allow a sender to be temporarily placed on a block list based on characteristics of mail coming from that sender, such as message content, sender ID verification, and sender behavior.

Unified Messaging

Another concept that has been integrated into the Mailbox server role, but is still very present in Exchange Server 2013, is Unified Messaging. The concept of Unified Messaging means that information from multiple sources is accessed in a single location. This concept is by no means a new one; third-party vendors have had fax and voicemail gateways for most major email systems. This can make users more efficient by providing a single location for inbound information; voicemails can be read via Outlook Web App, Outlook, or Windows Phone devices. In addition, missed-call information (someone who calls but does not leave a voicemail message) is sent to the user's mailbox. Also in Exchange Server 2013, Unified Messaging integration with Lync Server 2013 is greatly improved. Organizations that have Lync Server 2013 deployed with Enterprise Voice functionalities can take advantage of enhanced Unified Messaging for all Lync users.

Figure 2.4 shows an example of a voicemail that has been delivered to a user. The form you see in the figure is in Outlook Web App and includes a player control for playing the message via the PC speakers.

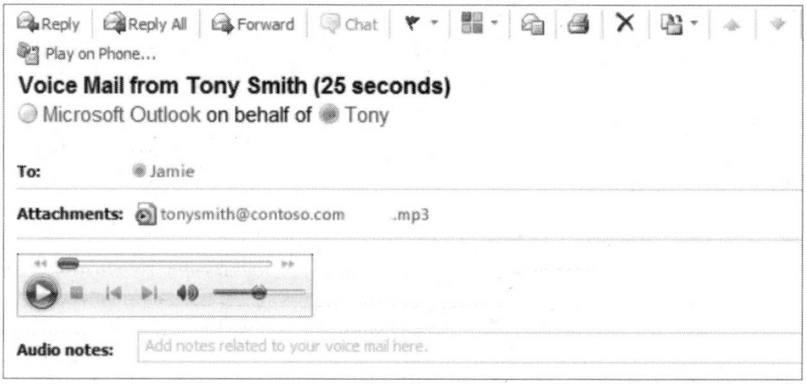

FIGURE 2.4

Viewing a voicemail message sent via Unified Messaging

The message also includes the ability to play the voice message on your desk phone. The Play On Phone option allows you to instruct the Unified Messaging server, also known as a Mailbox server, to call you at a specified extension (or optionally an external phone if the Unified Messaging dial-plan allows).

Further, the user can call the Unified Messaging server via the telephone and listen to their voicemail, have their email read to them, listen to their calendar, rearrange appointments, or look up someone in the global address book. Unified Messaging also allows the administrator to build a customized auto-attendant for call routing. In our experience, a typical voicemail (using the default MP3 codec) takes between 2 KB and 3 KB per second of message time, but this amount can be changed. However, with higher-quality recordings come larger message sizes.

The Unified Messaging server role functions as just another Exchange server in your organization, but this role includes components that allow IP-based phone systems and IP/PBX (public branch exchange) gateways to interface directly with Exchange Server over the network. This can take place provided the IP phone system or IP/PBX can communicate using Session Initiation Protocol (SIP) over TCP or Real-time Transport Protocol (RTP) for voice communication.

Not all voice systems are going to support this feature "right out of the box." More and more vendors (such as Cisco and Mitel) are tweaking their Voice over Internet Protocol (VoIP) systems to talk directly to Exchange Server 2010 Unified Messaging, but you may still require a VoIP gateway of some type. Many traditional "hard-wired" PBXs will require a PBX-to-VoIP gateway, but even some VoIP systems will require a VoIP-to-VoIP gateway.

If you are like us, you are more of a specialized network administrator. We have never managed a phone system in the past and are only slightly familiar with some of the phone terminology. We just assumed that VoIP was VoIP and that was that. Working with the folks who manage your telephone system will be a new and exciting experience. We were quite surprised to learn that there are more than 100 implementations of SIP on the market.

As of 2013, Unified Messaging solutions have only about a 15 percent market penetration—that is, of course, depending on whose survey you read and how you define Unified Messaging. However, the outlook is bright for Unified Messaging because of the popularity of Lync Server 2013. Lync Server 2013 is enjoying a surge in popularity since its release in the third quarter of 2012. Most Lync Server administrators see the benefits of integrating their environment with Exchange Unified Messaging and are already familiar with the configuration requirements to manage Unified Messaging. If we had a crystal ball, we would surely see many Lync Server 2013 administrators working in tandem with Exchange Server administrators to deploy and manage end-to-end solutions for Enterprise Voice and Unified Messaging.

UNIFIED MESSAGING MESSAGE SIZES

A typical voicemail uses the default MP3 codec between 2 KB and 3 KB per second of message time, but this size can be changed. Exchange Server 2013 unified messaging features that run on the Mailbox servers support the MP3, WMA, G.711 PCM, and GSM codecs for encoding and storing voicemail messages. However, with higher-quality recordings come larger message sizes.

Client Connectivity

Previously, in all versions of Outlook and Exchange Server, the Outlook client (using MAPI over RPC, not RPC over HTTP) had to be configured to connect to a specific Exchange server.

In Exchange Server 2007, an absolute game changer for all Exchange administrators was introduced—the Autodiscover service, a feature that allows the client application, in most cases Outlook, to automatically configure itself with the necessary information required for a successful connection. (For a full discussion of the topic, see Chapter 6, "Understanding the Exchange Autodiscover Process.")

Autodiscover is not new for Exchange Server 2013; however, *what Autodiscover configures* is new. In previous versions of Exchange Server, the famous client connection endpoint was the fully qualified domain name (FQDN) of the server that hosted a user's mailbox. In some cases, that FQDN was masked by a unified namespace, also known as Client Access Array (available only in Exchange Server 2010).

In Exchange Server 2013, Autodiscover configures a new connection point for Outlook clients that contains the globally unique identifier of the user's mailbox and the SMTP suffix of the user's primary email address. By removing the FQDN of a server or a Client Access Array as a connection point, moving a mailbox is now seamless to the user and will not prompt the user to restart Outlook.

In the gamut of changes in Exchange Server 2013, the one that surprised me the most was the move away from RPC. RPC is no longer supported as a remote access protocol in this latest release. What does this mean for Outlook clients? RPC over HTTP, later renamed to Outlook Anywhere, is now the only way to connect to an Exchange Server 2013 server. The major caveat here is the supported version of Outlook. Officially, Microsoft will support only Outlook 2007 or later with Exchange Server 2013. There is, however, anecdotal evidence that Outlook 2003 works fine as well. I have had mixed results in my tests with Outlook 2003, so I would definitely recommend using a newer version.

One Outlook client connectivity component that remains identical in the eyes of the user is public folder server connectivity. Public folders, as they were in previous versions, no longer exist in Exchange Server 2013. Outlook continues to display the public folders, though the client does not establish an RPC connection to the Mailbox server to display that information. The connection is still established to the Mailbox server but only to retrieve the public folder mailbox, the new public folder storage, that contains all public folder content. This change in architecture is hidden from the end users but means that administrators now have a greater set of high-availability options when managing public folders. Of course, an even greater benefit is the departure from the problem-ridden public folder replication.

The Managed Store

As far back as we can remember, the Information Store service has been referred to as the primary service or feature that manages the databases that contain the user mailboxes. In Exchange Server 2013, the Information store, also known as the *Managed Store*, has been completely rewritten in managed code and replaces the infamous Store.exe process. The Managed Store is now tied to the Microsoft.Exchange.Store.Service.exe and Microsoft.Exchange.Store.Worker.exe processes. The database engine, however, remains unchanged, continuing to prefer Extensible Storage Engine (ESE) over other database technologies. To learn more about the Exchange Server 2013 store, review the contents of Chapter 19, "Creating and Managing Mailbox Databases."

IS EXCHANGE SERVER USING SQL SERVER TO STORE ITS DATABASE?

Over the years, the rumors of the Exchange Server team moving to SQL Server as its database storage engine have flourished. A lot of those rumors were based on truth. The Exchange Server team actually tested SQL Server with Exchange Server. They went as far as deploying test servers with mailbox databases stored on SQL Server. However, in 2010 Microsoft announced their continued commitment to use ESE databases with Exchange Server and cooled off all the rumors.

What drove that final decision to leave SQL Server in the dust? We believe that the Exchange Server team wanted to maintain their independence in driving innovation forward. The great number of performance improvements in Exchange Server 2013 make us feel like it was the right decision.

A key difference in the Managed Store that you will quickly notice is that each database runs under its own process. The result of this is a complete isolation of each database in the event of memory, store, or other server issues.

Microsoft also boasts some pretty impressive numbers when discussing the resource requirements of Exchange Server 2013. Many of those numbers are tied to the changes in the database schema over previous versions of Exchange Server and are discussed in detail in Chapter 19.

High-Availability Features

One of the biggest enemies of high availability is slow restoration times. As mailbox databases get larger and larger, restore times get longer and longer. Often this is used as a rationale for limiting users' mailbox sizes to less than what they need to do their jobs effectively.

When Microsoft released Exchange Server 2007 Service Pack 1, they introduced a new technology called continuous replication. This technology allowed Microsoft to introduce three new features to improve high availability: local continuous replication (LCR), cluster continuous replication (CCR), and standby continuous replication (SCR). These features allowed a database to be initially seeded with another copy and then the log files to be replicated in near real time and replayed to the copy of the database. The database copy could then be restored quickly (in the case of LCR) or brought online in the event of a server failure.

Exchange Server 2007 CCR leveraged Windows failover clustering so that in the event of a server failure the server could automatically be recovered. SCR was used so that even a single database failure could be recovered by being brought online (manually) on a remote Exchange server. CCR was designed as a high-availability solution, whereas SCR was designed to provide resiliency.

Exchange Server 2010 and Exchange Server 2013 take the continuous replication and clustering technologies even further so that the lines between high availability and resiliency have been blurred. Failover Clustering is now used much differently than it was in the past, and the complexities of clustering are better hidden from the Exchange Server administrator. The Exchange Server 2013 high-availability technology is easy to incorporate with existing Mailbox servers. Individual databases can now be replicated to multiple servers and, failover can automatically occur, not at the server level but at the database level.

There have been very few changes in high-availability features between Exchange Server 2010 and 2013; the few changes are mostly tied to the changes in database architecture discussed in the previous section. The architectural changes enable faster database failover and better physical disk failure handling.

Exchange Server 2010 and Exchange Server 2013 make building a failover cluster so much simpler than with past versions that the technology is easy to implement even for small organizations with no clustering expertise.

Continuous Replication Basics

The continuous replication technology is compelling. It supports the ability to replicate a database to one or more additional Exchange Server Mailbox servers within your organization. If you are familiar with Exchange Server 2010, you will be able to manage this technology easily in Exchange Server 2013.

Unlike many tools from third-party vendors, which replicate data either at the disk block level or by taking snapshots of the disk and replicating changes, Exchange Server continuous replication is more similar to the SQL Server *log shipping* technology. This is considered similar to a *pull* model, but the active copy of the database does the work. The replication service managing the passive copy of the database communicates with the active copy and indicates which logs the passive copy needs to keep the database in sync. The active source Exchange Server database, logs, and database engine do not even realize they are being copied. The Microsoft Exchange Mailbox Replication Service handles copying the logs and managing the passive databases.

Initially (as when continuous replication is set up or reconfigured) the current copy of the database is copied to the passive location; this is called *seeding*. As an Exchange Server transaction log is filled up and renamed (that is, when the E00.LOG file is filled and then renamed to E000000001.LOG), the renamed and closed log file is copied to the passive location. The Information Store service then verifies the log file and commits it to the passive copy of the database. So the actual database file is not replicated at all, but it is kept in sync by copying the log files and replaying them. Figure 2.5 shows an example of how this process works.

FIGURE 2.5
How continuous replication works

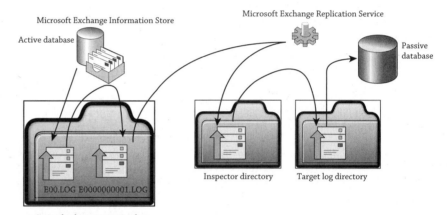

If continuous replication is enabled, the Microsoft Exchange Mailbox Replication Service copies the E0000000001.LOG file to the Inspector directory. This folder exists on any server within the database availability group that has a copy of the database.

The service performs an intensive verification of the log files in the Inspector directory to ensure they are not corrupted. Once the log files are verified as not being corrupted, they are checked to ensure that they are in the correct sequence. Once this is verified, the Replication service copies the log file (E0000000001.LOG) to the target log file directory. The Information Store service then replays the transactions found in the E0000000001.LOG file and the transactions are committed to the passive copy of the database.

At any given time, the most out-of-sync a passive copy of the database will be is approximately 15 minutes. The 15-minute lag time would be in a worst-case scenario, such as in the dead of night when there is absolutely no activity on the mailbox database. During a normal workday in which users are actively using the database, the passive copy of the database will be no more than a few minutes behind.

If a database is dismounted or the Information Store service is stopped, all the data is committed to the active database and the log files are pulled over to the servers that hold a passive copy of the database. If the administrator has to manually switch over to the passive copy of the database, the passive copy should be completely synchronized with the active copy of the database.

Mailbox Database Mobility

Exchange Server 2010 introduced the concept of *database mobility*. Continued in Exchange Server 2013, database mobility is a set of technologies and features that allow a mailbox database to be replicated to more than one Exchange server in an organization and that database to be brought online if the active copy of the database is no longer available. High availability is no longer tied to a specific server but rather to individual databases.

A mailbox database can be replicated to any Exchange Server 2013 Mailbox server within the same DAG. The DAG is a collection of 1 to 16 Exchange Server 2013 Mailbox servers that can be configured to host a set of databases. The DAG is the boundary of database replication and can span multiple Active Directory sites and geographic locations.

Figure 2.6 shows a simplified example of a DAG. This group has three Exchange Server Mailbox servers as members, and each of the servers has a single "active" mailbox. The server in Tokyo has an active mailbox database called Executives, but a copy of this database is replicated to the Denver and Honolulu servers. The database can be replicated to one or more servers in the DAG.

FIGURE 2.6
Simple database availability group

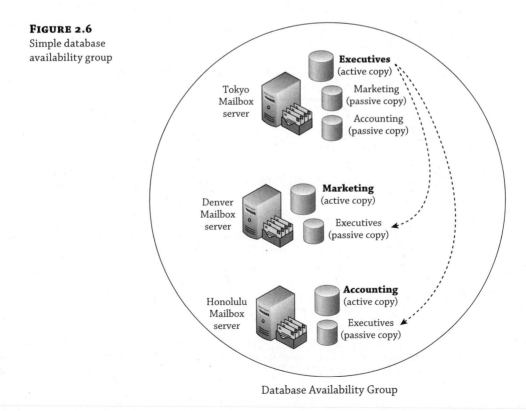

Database Availability Group

In the event of a failure on the Tokyo Mailbox server or a problem with the Executives database on the Tokyo Mailbox server, the database on either the Denver or the Honolulu server will be made active and users will be redirected to the new "active" location.

Database mobility replaces the SCR, CCR, LCR, and single copy cluster features that were available in previous versions of Exchange.

🌐 Real World Scenario

HIGH AVAILABILITY AND RESILIENCY FOR A COMPANY WITH TWO OFFICES

ImportantAmericanDocs Corporation has a main headquarters office in South Florida and another one in Colorado. Each office has a data center. In recent years, the South Florida office has had several instances when they had to close the office and shut down their data center because of hurricanes. This means the South Florida office loses not only Exchange Server services but also all users in the eastern United States that connect remotely to the Florida office.

ImportantAmericanDocs requires a high-availability solution that provides email access in the event of an Exchange server failure in the local office and also provides a contingency in case their office headquarters has to be shut down. Email should automatically be accessible from all users to the Colorado office in the event that the Florida office has to be closed. The solution must be smooth and simple, and it should not degrade the level of service for users during regular operations.

The company decided to implement two Exchange Server 2013 database availability groups. The Eastern US DAG has two Mailbox servers: one in South Florida and one in Colorado. The Western US DAG has two Mailbox servers: one in Colorado and one in South Florida. All mailbox databases in each office are replicated to the other office. Each DAG contains a file share witness in its respective office. The benefit of this design is to ensure that users always connect to a mailbox in their local office, unless their Mailbox server is unavailable. As well as, because each DAG contains a file share witness in its respective office, the design will not force a failover of the DAG resources if a network failure between the offices were to occur. This is my preferred design for high-availability solutions, and it also works if the company has more than two offices but may only have two primary data centers. The design is simple, is well tested, and provides as much failover as any other DAG design.

Content Storage

As we mentioned earlier, email systems have evolved not only in their own complexity but also in the complexity (and size!) of the messages and mailbox content being sent and stored. Users' demands for improved searching and indexing of their mailboxes have stretched the limits of most server hardware.

MAILBOX DATABASES

Even in a small or medium-size organization, mailbox size constraints are often based solely on the ability to restore a certain amount of data given a specified maximum amount of time. To scale to larger mailboxes, the administrator must create more mailbox stores. Whereas in Exchange Server 2003 Enterprise Edition administrators could create 20 mailbox databases spread across four storage groups, later versions of Exchange Server changed this paradigm not only by removing storage groups but also by increasing the number of databases available. The Exchange Server 2000/2003 term *mailbox store* has been replaced simply with the term *mailbox database*. For so many years, the term *store* has been associated with the database and the server that it resides on. In Exchange Server 2013, the mailbox database has completed its disassociation from the store by no longer being a server-based configuration. Mailbox databases are configured under the Organization object and belong to the organization as a whole. The primary benefit of this additional paradigm change is the flexibility to have a mailbox database be active on *any* server in the organization.

To allow a server to scale to support larger mailbox sizes or more mailboxes, Exchange Server 2013 RTM and CU1 Enterprise Edition allowed up to 50 mounted mailbox databases. This limit was increased to 100 mounted mailbox databases in Exchange Server 2012 CU2 Enterprise Edition. Exchange Server 2013 Standard Edition supports a maximum of 5 databases. The databases have a practical limit of 16 TB, but Microsoft does not provide database size limits for either edition of Exchange Server 2013.

MAXIMUM NUMBER OF DATABASES ON DATABASE AVAILABILITY GROUPS

When you hear of a maximum of 100 mailbox databases on a server, we are always talking of *mounted* databases, of course. However, keep in mind that a *passive* or *unmounted* database can at any point become *active*. The maximum number of mailbox databases should include both the mounted and the unmounted copies. You must take this calculation into consideration when planning database availability groups.

Exchange Server Management

Server management with Exchange Server 2013 becomes increasingly complex as administrators try to make Exchange Server work within their organizations, particularly in larger organizations. Exchange Server 2000/2003 management of mail recipients was performed through the Active Directory Users and Computers console, while management of Exchange Server–related tasks and global recipient tasks was performed through the Exchange Server System Manager console. In Exchange Server 2010 and 2013, all recipient administration tasks are performed through the Exchange Administration Center or the Exchange Management Shell (EMS).

Although making bulk changes or manipulating Exchange servers might seem like a simple task (after all, Windows, Active Directory, and Exchange Server are all from the same company), the truth of the matter is that these tasks were not that simple to perform via script. That all changed with the introduction of Windows PowerShell. Bulk recipient tasks, such as creating multiple mailboxes, changing many email addresses, and configuring bulk properties, can be performed through an application programming interface (API) or scripting interface such as, Active Directory Services Interface (ADSI). However, the EMS provides a vastly simpler way to manage all Exchange Server and email recipient properties.

Manipulation of Exchange Server operations—such as, mounting and dismounting of databases, queue management, diagnostics logging, switching over databases, and tracking log management—should be handled through the EMS interface. In fact, some actions can only be performed from the EMS and are not available in the Exchange Administration Center.

With Exchange Server 2010, the management interface was rewritten from the ground up. All management operations related to Exchange Server management—whether they are performed against an Exchange server, Active Directory, the registry, or the Internet Information Server (IIS) metabase—were broken up into unique tasks. All Exchange Server tasks could be performed from the EMS. This infrastructure, called Role-based Access Control (RBAC), has remained mostly identical in Exchange Server 2013.

The Exchange Administration Center (shown in Figure 2.7) is a completely redesigned management interface to make it easier to use, to better organize Exchange Server management tasks, to reduce the complexity, and to make administrative tasks more discoverable.

FIGURE 2.7
The new
Exchange
Administration
Center

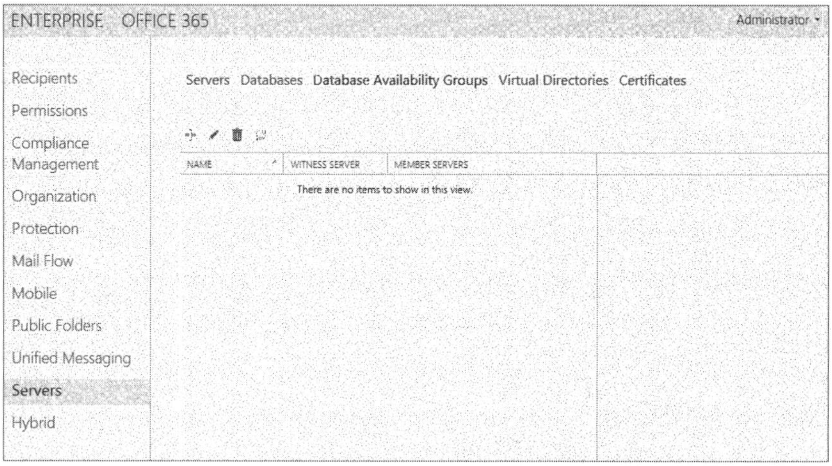

The new Exchange Administration Center is built on top of PowerShell and a set of Exchange Server-specific extensions called the Exchange Management Shell cmdlets (pronounced "command-lets").

Improved Message and Content Control

All messaging-system administrators can relate to challenges, such as adequately managing the content that is stored on their mail servers, keeping business-essential information available when it is required, removing content that is no longer necessary, controlling the flow of messaging information, and preventing disclosure of information. If one or more of these challenges has been a problem for you, then Exchange Server 2013 has solutions.

Built-in Archiving

The market for third-party tools to support Exchange Server has grown rapidly since the release of Exchange Server 2003. At one point, there were more than 60 third parties providing email archive solutions for Exchange Server. The sheer volume of email that users receive and the users' demand that they be able to keep their historical email have made these tools very attractive.

Exchange Server 2010 introduced, and Exchange Server 2013 continues, a premium feature that allows for the integration of email archiving. The email archiving feature is actually a series of features that interact directly with the user's mailbox:

Archive Mailbox   Defined on a user-by-user basis since all users might not need an archive mailbox. The content in the archive mailbox can be accessed by users using the Outlook 2010 or later client or Outlook Web App 2013.

Retention Policies   Define the types of mail and how long the mail can be retained within the user's primary mailbox. Retention policies can be defined to control when items are permanently deleted or when they are moved into the archive mailbox. With Outlook 2010 or later, end users can participate in the retention process by applying retention tags to messages or an entire folder.

eDiscovery (aka Multi-mailbox and Federated Search)   Allows an authorized user to search for content across multiple data sources (both the user's "active" mailbox as well as their "personal archive mailbox") within an organization. You're able to search for information across Exchange, SharePoint, and Lync archives, as well as use the eDiscovery Center in SharePoint 2013 to search for content in Exchange Server. Discovery managers can also export mailbox content to a .pst file from the SharePoint 2013 eDiscovery console.

In-place Hold   Allows the administrator to place a "hold" on a user's mailbox so that deleted and edited items are held during the hold period. This would be necessary in the event of legal action or an investigation regarding the conduct of one or more of your users.

Ultimately, the new Exchange Server 2013 archiving and retention policies are intended to replace the messaging records-management features that were introduced in Exchange Server 2007.

Message Transport Rules

Message transport rules are quite similar to Outlook rules and are even created using a wizard similar to one used to create Outlook rules. However, these rules are quite a bit more powerful and are executed on Mailbox servers. Since all messages are processed by a Mailbox server whether they are inbound, outbound, or for local delivery, you can build powerful policies to control the messages and data that flow within your organization. Transport rules can also be defined at your organization's perimeter by using an Exchange Server 2010 Edge Transport server.

The following is a taste of what you can do with transport rules:

◆ Append disclaimers to outgoing messages

◆ Implement message-journaling based on recipients, distribution lists, message classification, or message importance

◆ Prevent users or departments from sending emails to each other by creating an ethical wall (aka a Chinese wall, named after the size of the Great Wall of China)

◆ Intercept messages based on content or text patterns using regular expressions (regex) found in the message subject or message body

- Apply message classifications to messages based on sender or message content

- Take action on a message with a certain attachment, attachment type, or an attachment size that exceeds a specified limit

- Examine and set message headers or remove data from the message header

- Redirect, drop, or bounce messages based on certain criteria

- Apply Microsoft Rights Management Service (RMS) encryption-based transport rule conditions

In Exchange Server 2013, transport rules have been updated with several new predicates and actions. Also, the coolest new feature to hit transport rules is Data Loss Prevention (DLP) policies. DLP policies are designed to prevent users from sharing sensitive information with unauthorized users.

Every transport rule has three components: conditions, actions, and exceptions. The conditions specify under what circumstances the rule applies, whereas the exceptions specify under what conditions it will not apply. The actions are the interesting part of the transport rule. Figure 2.8 shows the conditions on the New Rule window of the Transport Rule Wizard; this screen has three parts. The first part is checking on which object to take action, the second is simply checking the actions to take, and the third part specifies more details about the action.

FIGURE 2.8
Examining a
transport rule

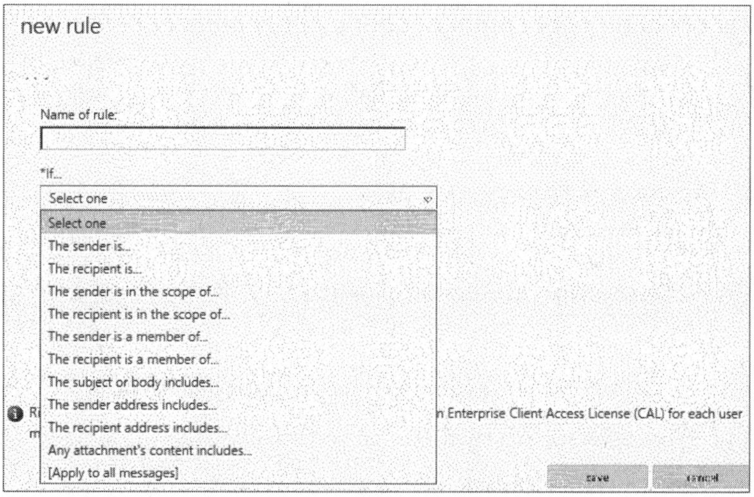

Message Classifications

Organizations that send confidential, proprietary, or classified information via email often implement message-classification templates. However, these client-side templates display the message classification only for the sender and the recipients; in earlier versions of Exchange Server, such as Exchange Server 2003, there was nothing within the message transport that could evaluate or take action on a classified message.

Exchange Server 2013 allows a message to enforce rules based on the classification of a message, such as Do Not Forward, Partner Mail, Attachment Removed, Company Confidential, Company Internal, Attorney/Client Privilege, and customized classification levels. The sender can assign the classification using Outlook 2007, Outlook 2010, Outlook 2013, or Outlook Web App; message transport rules can assign a classification based on sender, recipient, message content, importance, and so on.

Rights Management Service Message Protection

If you are concerned about message content protection, one of the cool features of Exchange Server 2013 is its integration with the Microsoft Active Directory Rights Management Services (RMS). While RMS has been integrated with the Outlook client for quite a few years now, Exchange Server 2013 introduces significantly better integration. Features include the following:

◆ Transport rules can apply rights management protection to messages and attachments based on rule conditions.

◆ The Transport service can be configured to allow decryption of Information Rights Management (IRM)–protected messages in transit in order to apply message policies to the message.

◆ IRM provides protection for Unified Messaging voicemail messages.

◆ IRM protection is available from Outlook Web App and Outlook.

Programming Interfaces

Much of what is now the underlying infrastructure of Exchange Server 2013 was completely rewritten when Exchange Server 2010 was released. As a result, many of the APIs used to access Exchange Server data and to manage Exchange Server components were replaced with new APIs.

EXCHANGE MANAGEMENT

Management of Exchange Server–related components and recipient objects is performed with the new management API that was released in Exchange Server 2010. All operations that can be performed have been defined as tasks. The management API provides access to all management functions via the EMS tasks, also known as cmdlets. The EMS is a set of extensions for the Windows PowerShell. Exchange Server management functionality can be extended and accessed via managed code, and custom scripts can integrate with and use .NET objects.

TRANSPORT AGENTS

All messages and message content traveling through the message transport system (on a Mailbox server or Edge Transport server) can be manipulated using transport agents. Transport agents are written using managed code. They replace Exchange Server 2000/2003 transport event sinks.

EXCHANGE SERVER–MANAGED APIs

Exchange Server–managed APIs extend the Microsoft .NET Framework by providing classes and data structures that allow custom programs to access and manipulate different parts of email message content. Functions include accessing MIME content; filtering email body content; converting message content between plain-text, HTML, and RTF formats; and reading or writing calendar items.

WEB SERVICES

One of the most exciting APIs is the Web Services API. It lets developers write applications that can remotely access mailboxes, folders, and message content. Many of the Client Access server Exchange Server services—such as the Autodiscover service and the Availability service—use the Web Services API. Services can be developed to send notifications to client applications and provide synchronization of mailbox folders and items. The Web Services API provides these features:

◆ Ability to manage folders in a user mailbox, including creating, deleting, copying, changing, searching, viewing, and moving folders

◆ Ability to manage messages in a user mailbox, including creating, deleting, copying, changing, searching, viewing, moving, and sending messages as well as accessing message content

◆ Ability to enumerate distribution group memberships

New and Improved Outlook Web App

Those of us who gushed when we saw the Outlook Web Access interface in Exchange 2003 thought a web interface could not get much better. For Outlook Web App in Exchange 2013, the Exchange team started over from scratch to build a much more functional interface than ever before. Here are some of the features in Outlook Web App 2013:

◆ Offline access to user mailboxes

◆ Ability to view multiple calendars

◆ Ability to use Outlook Web apps, such as Bing Maps

◆ Ability to browse the global address list (GAL)

◆ Ability to manage and remotely wipe Windows Phone devices

◆ Improved meeting-booking features

◆ Ability to perform full-text searches on mailbox content

◆ Selectable message format (HTML or plain text) when composing a message

◆ Ability to set out-of-office messages, define them as internal or external, and schedule when they start

◆ Ability to manage voicemail features such as their greeting, reset their voicemail PIN, and turn on missed-call notifications

◆ Conversation view, which provides threaded views of email conversations

An important thing to note about the functionality of Outlook Web App is that S/MIME controls are no longer available. Users can still use S/MIME from Outlook 2007 or higher.

Mobile Clients and Improved Security

With the proliferation of mobile device, tablets, and many other personal devices that are appearing in offices across the world, there is a renewed focus on controlling these devices in an efficient manner. The bring your own device (BYOD) phenomenon is a major thorn in network administrators' sides. What connections to the network can these devices make? Should they be able to use the camera feature? Can we protect the data on these devices if they're lost? All of those questions, and many more, must be answered by network administrators before allowing BYOD on their network. A piece of that puzzle is Exchange ActiveSync (EAS) and specifically EAS policies.

Windows Phone and EAS device support are certainly not new features to Exchange Server 2013. Exchange Server 2003 had good support for mobile devices, and you could even support mobile devices using Microsoft Mobile Information Server and Exchange Server 2000. However, support for EAS has been extended to many other mobile device types, such as the recently released Microsoft Surface, which now has a built-in mail client that connects to Exchange Server by using EAS.

If you have supported mobile devices, you realize how important centralized policies and security can be for your organization and your users. EAS has improved greatly over the years. The newest features can be assigned to users based on a mobile device mailbox policy that is assigned to the user. Figure 2.9 shows two of the advanced properties pages.

FIGURE 2.9

Examples of mobile device mailbox policies

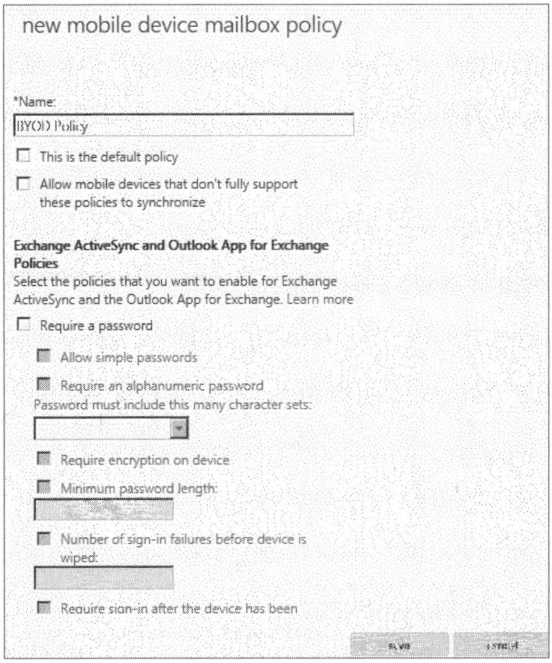

Now, Where Did That Go?

As new and better functions and APIs have been introduced, naturally some functions are no longer emphasized or supported. We've already mentioned a few features that have been removed, but there are many more. There has been a lot of confusion surrounding what will continue to be supported in Exchange Server 2013 and what will no longer work. The phrase "no longer supported" itself tends to generate a lot of confusion because an unsupported function may continue to work because it has not truly been removed. Your mileage may vary when it comes to features that are no longer supported.

What's been removed from Exchange Server really depends on your perspective. Are you an Exchange Server 2007 expert? Is Exchange Server 2010 your comfort zone? I've broken down the next section of removed features based on your perspective.

Features No Longer Included

As Exchange Server has evolved into its current form, the code has experienced significant changes. Some features and APIs have been completely removed. Although most of these features will not affect the majority of Exchange Server deployments, you should keep them in mind and thoroughly evaluate your existing messaging environment to make sure you are not dependent on a feature that has no equivalent in Exchange Server 2013. If you require any of the features or APIs that were not carried over from Exchange Server 2007 or 2010, you may need to keep an older version of Exchange Server in operation.

> **EXCHANGE SERVER 2013 ESCHEWS EXCHANGE SERVER 2003**
>
> Only Exchange Server 2007 and Exchange Server 2010 can coexist with Exchange Server 2013 in the same organization. If you still require features provided by the Exchange Server 2003 platform, you are not even going to be able to transition to Exchange Server 2013 until you can replace that particular feature requirement with newer software.

EXCHANGE SERVER 2007 FEATURES REMOVED FROM EXCHANGE SERVER 2013

Although Exchange Server 2007 did not enjoy wide deployment, some organizations will be transitioning from Exchange Server 2007 to Exchange Server 2013. A number of features have been removed from Exchange Server since Exchange Server 2007; this list is in addition to the features that were removed since Exchange Server 2003. The following Exchange Server 2007 features are no longer available:

- Local continuous replication
- Single copy clustering
- Cluster continuous replication
- Standby continuous replication

- Unified Messaging inbound faxing functions

- Streaming backups

- Storage groups

- SharePoint document library and network share access via Outlook Web Access

- 32-bit management tools

EXCHANGE SERVER 2010 FEATURES REMOVED FROM EXCHANGE SERVER 2013

Unlike Exchange Server 2007, Exchange Server 2010 enjoyed great popularity and deployment in thousands of organizations. Likely the most popular version of Exchange Server to date, Exchange Server 2010 is strongly tied to Exchange Server 2013 in features. I have already reviewed most of the key differences between those two versions, such as client connectivity and performance improvements; now I will discuss some more granular changes. The following features have been removed from Exchange Server 2013:

- Spell check in Outlook Web App. (Though it should be noted that spell-checking can be performed by the web browser, providing the browser has that ability.)

- Many PowerShell cmdlets have been added and others have been removed. A notable cmdlet that has been replaced is the `Set-TransportServer` cmdlet, which has been replaced by the `Set-TransportService` cmdlet.

- Management of the antispam agents from the GUI-based console (must be managed from the Exchange Management Shell).

- Managed folders. (This one is a bit confusing, since the cmdlets for MRM are all still available in Exchange Server 2013; however, they are not processed.)

- Exchange Best Practice Analyzer, the mail flow troubleshooter, Performance Monitor, and Performance Troubleshooter (though the latest rumor in the halls of Redmond is that it will make a well-deserved return to the fold very soon).

- Public folder databases. (Although public folders are still available in Exchange Server 2013, they are available only through the creation of public folder mailboxes.)

Clearing Up Some Confusion

We mentioned earlier that Exchange has certainly been hyped a lot during the design and beta-testing process. This has generated a lot of buzz in the information technology industry, but this buzz has also generated a lot of confusion and some misinformation. Here we'll clear up the confusion by answering a few of the common questions about Exchange 2013.

Do I have to have two servers to run each of the server roles?   In the days of Exchange Server 2010, Microsoft recommended deploying different roles to different servers in large organizations. They reserved the consolidated server approach for small environments. However, the performance capabilities of Exchange Server 2013 surpass the previous versions to such an extent that they now recommend that all Exchange servers run both the Mailbox and Client Access server roles. Separation of roles, unless for unique requirements, is no longer necessary.

Is there a 32-bit version of Exchange Server?   No 32-bit version of Exchange Server 2013 is available.

Is the Edge Transport server required?   No, Edge Transport servers are not required. You can use any third-party message-hygiene system in your perimeter network, or you can direct inbound and outbound mail through your internal servers, or both. Also, the Edge Transport server role is not available in Exchange Server 2013 as of the RTM release.

Is EMS knowledge required? Do I have to learn scripting?   Most common administrative tasks can be performed through the Exchange Administration Center graphical user interface. Command-line management and scripting for Exchange Server 2013 have been greatly improved through the use of the EMS. Many tasks are simplified or more powerful through the EMS, but it is not necessary to learn scripting in order to start working with Exchange Server 2013. We strongly encourage you to get to know many of the powerful features of the EMS as you get comfortable with Exchange Server 2013. A number of advanced administration tasks do not have a graphical user interface option.

What is happening with public folders?   The use of public folders with Exchange Server 2013 is still available and supported, but their use is being deemphasized as newer collaborative technologies such as websites and portals have become commonplace. We urge you to examine your public folder applications with an eye toward migrating them to systems such as Microsoft SharePoint Server 2013. Also, remember that the traditional public folder databases are no longer available in Exchange Server 2013 and that you must now store all public folders in a public folder mailbox.

Do I need to use every Exchange Server 2013 server role to have a functional Exchange Server 2013 system?   To build a completely functional Exchange Server 2013 system, you need both the Mailbox and Client Access server roles in each Active Directory site where either server role is deployed.

The Bottom Line

Understand the changes in the Exchange Server roles.   Significant changes were made to the Exchange Server 2013 architecture to improve the scalability, security, and stability. Requiring an x64-based operating system and hardware dramatically provides scalability and performance of Exchange Server 2013. The database schema changes in this latest release have greatly reduced the performance toll that database writes and reads put on the server. This greatly improves the Exchange Server 2013 disk I/O profile over previous versions. The x64 architecture also means that Exchange Server 2013 can now access more than 3 GB of physical memory. Microsoft has tested server configurations with several hundreds of GB of physical memory. The additional physical memory means that data can be cached and written to disk more efficiently.

> **Master It**   You are planning your Exchange Server 2013 infrastructure to provide basic messaging functionality (email, shared calendars, and Windows phones). Which Exchange Server roles will you need to deploy?

Understand the changes in Exchange Server architecture.   Microsoft introduced not only role consolidation in Exchange Server 2013, but also a new mechanism from client connectivity. RPC connectivity has not only been replaced by an "all-in" move to Outlook Anywhere, but Client Access is also now your entry point for email messages coming from the Internet. In Exchange Server 2010, Outlook Anywhere was the *recommended* mechanism for connectivity from Outlook clients. In Exchange Server 2013, Outlook Anywhere is the *only* mechanism for connectivity from Outlook clients. In Exchange Server 2010, the Hub Transport and Edge Transport roles were the *only* server roles that handled SMTP connectivity. In Exchange Server 2013, *neither* of those two roles exist, and all SMTP connectivity is handled by *both* the Client Access and Mailbox server roles.

Master It   You are planning a training session for your junior administrators to prepare them in their SMTP connectivity troubleshooting tasks. Which server role should you recommend they inspect when attempting to troubleshoot email delivery problems?

Chapter 3

Understanding Availability, Recovery, and Compliance

The modern business world is getting more complex, not less; email in turn evolves to keep up. As an Exchange Server administrator or implementer, you need to know more about a wider variety of topics without losing your core competency in Exchange Server.

In this chapter, you will learn to:

◆ Distinguish between availability, backup and recovery, and disaster recovery

◆ Determine the best option for disaster recovery

◆ Distinguish between the different types of availability meant by the term *high availability*

◆ Implement the four pillars of compliance and governance activities

Changing from a Technology to a Business Viewpoint

You've probably heard the old proverb that "every cloud has a silver lining." It can be a comfort to know that good can usually be found during even the worst of occasions. When a mailbox database server's RAID controller goes bad and corrupts the drive array containing the executive mailboxes, you have the opportunity to validate your backup strategy and demonstrate that it works perfectly under pressure.

However, the unacknowledged corollary is Murphy's Law: "Anything that can go wrong will go wrong." Every feature and functionality and component that is added to a messaging infrastructure increases complexity and the number of potential failures. If you think for a moment about the spread of email and how it has changed from a luxury to a utility, you can see that electronic messaging administrators have become victims of their own success.

Gone are the days where you simply had to worry about editing and publishing the correct DNS records for your domains, provisioning and configuring your T1 routers, and wrestling with server hardware. Today's challenges involve meeting more goals, supporting more complex environments, meeting business requirements, and analyzing risks. These are common scenarios:

◆ Ensuring that mailbox servers have the proper storage back-end design to allow backups to happen within a defined window

◆ Ensuring that your users continue to have access to their mailboxes even when a server fails, a flaky router takes a site offline, or power fails for an entire rack of servers

♦ Ensuring that a plan exists for enabling dial-tone mailbox functionality for your users after a major storm takes out the region for several days

♦ Ensuring that the messages users send to external clients are in compliance with all business policies and regulations

♦ Determining the risks associated with failing to provide disaster recovery plans and the risks associated with a failure to meet service-level agreements

♦ Balancing business costs versus risks associated with providing recovery, ensuring compliance, and providing a specified level of service

What's in a Name?

Backup and recovery, *high availability*, *disaster recovery*, and *compliance and governance*—you have likely heard of these many times. Each plays a role in the overall protection strategy for your organization's data.

Each of these topics must be evaluated by every modern Exchange Server administrator and professional, along with appropriate business stakeholders, even if they are not actively addressed in every deployment of Exchange Server 2013. When you do need to address them in your planning, Exchange Server 2013 provides a variety of options to ensure that the deployment meets the particular needs of your business. One size and one set of capabilities do not fit all organizations. To make the best use of the tools that Exchange Server gives you, you must clearly understand the problems that each capability is designed to solve. It doesn't do to use a screwdriver as a hammer—and you can't solve a disaster-recovery problem by using an eDiscovery search.

In this section, a common vocabulary will be presented for discussing these topics. This will enable you to get the most from our discussions of the new features and functionality in Exchange Server 2013 that are covered in later chapters. You should clearly understand how Microsoft intended Exchange Server 2013's features to be deployed and used, so that you have confidence that they will meet your business goals.

Backup and Recovery

Let us begin with a topic that is one of the core tasks for any IT administrator, not just Exchange Server administrators: backup and recovery.

Backup is the process of preserving one or more point-in-time copies of a set of data, regardless of the number of copies, frequency and schedule, or media type used to store them. With Exchange Server, there are four main types of backups:

Full Backups (Normal)   Full backups capture an entire set of target data; in legacy versions of Exchange Server, this is a storage group with the transaction log files and all the associated mailbox databases and files. Beginning with Exchange Server 2010 and continuing in Exchange Server 2013, each mailbox database is a separate backup target, since there is now an enforced 1:1 relationship between mailbox databases and transaction logs (it was "strongly recommended" in earlier versions). Full backups take the most time to perform and use the most space. If circular logging is disabled for a mailbox database, full backups must be executed on a regular basis. A successful full backup informs Exchange Server that the databases and transaction logs have been preserved and that saved transaction logs can be purged. Circular logging will be discussed more later.

Copy Backups   Copy backups are exactly like full backups, except that saved transaction logs are not purged.

Incremental Backups   Incremental backups capture only a partial set of the target data—specifically, the data that has changed since either the last full backup or the last incremental backup. For Exchange Server, this means any new transaction logs. Incremental backups are designed to *minimize how often* full backups are performed, as well as *minimize the space used* by any particular backup set. As a result, a backup set that includes incremental backups can be more time-consuming and fragile to restore; successful recovery includes first recovering the latest full backup and then each successive incremental backup. Incremental backups also instruct Exchange Server to purge the saved transaction logs after the backup is complete. Incremental backups are not available when circular logging is enabled.

Differential Backups   Differential backups also capture only a partial set of the target data—specifically, the data that has changed since the last full backup. All other backups (incremental and differential) are not considered. For Exchange Server, this means any transaction logs generated since the last full backup. Differential backups are designed to *minimize how many* recovery operations you have to perform in order to fully restore a set of data. In turn, differential backups use more space than incremental backups, but they can be recovered more quickly and with fewer opportunities for data corruption; successful recovery includes first recovering the latest full backup and then the latest differential backup. A differential backup does not purge saved transaction logs. Differential backups are not available when circular logging is enabled.

Recovery   Also known as restoration, recovery is the process of taking one or more sets of the data preserved through backups and making it once again accessible to administrators, applications, and/or end users. Most recovery jobs require the restoration of multiple sets of backup data, especially when incremental and differential backups are in use. Two metrics are used to determine if the recovery time and the amount of data recovered are acceptable:

Recovery Time Objective   Recovery Time Objective (RTO) is a metric commonly used to help define successful backup and restore processes. The RTO defines the time window in which you must restore Exchange Server services and messaging data after an adverse event. You may have multiple tiers of data and service, in which case it could be appropriate to have a separate RTO for each tier. Often, the RTO is a component of (ideally, an input into, but that's not always the case) your service-level agreements. As a result, the RTO is a critical factor in the design of Exchange Server mailbox database storage systems; it's a bad idea to design or provision mailbox databases that are larger than you can restore within your RTO.

Recovery Point Objective   Recovery Point Objective (RPO) is a metric that goes hand in hand with the RTO. While the RTO measures a time frame, the RPO sets a benchmark for the maximum amount of data (typically measured in hours) you can afford to lose. Again, multiple tiers of service and data often have separate RPOs. The RPO helps drive the backup frequency and schedule. It's worth noting that this metric makes an explicit assumption that all data within a given category is equally valuable; that's obviously not true, which is why it is important to properly establish your categories. Remember, though, if you have too many classes or categories, you'll just have confusion.

One thing to note about Exchange Server 2013 is that it supports only online backups and restores created through the Windows Volume Shadow Copy Service (VSS). VSS provides several advantages compared to other backup methods, including the ability to integrate with third-party storage systems to speed up the backup and recovery processes. The most important benefit VSS gives, though, is that it ensures that the Exchange Server information store flushes all pending writes consistently, ensuring that a backup dataset can be cleanly recovered.

We will use the phrase "backup set" several times. A *backup set* is a copy of all of the various backups that are required to perform a particular recovery. This will almost always include at least the last full backup and may include one or more incremental or differential backups

HOW MUCH DATA GETS COPIED?

One thing that Volume Shadow Copy Service does not natively provide is the ability to reduce the amount of data that must be copied during a backup operation. VSS simply creates either a permanent or temporary replica (depending on how the invoking-application requested the replica be created) of the disk volume; it's then up to the application to sort out the appropriate files and folders that make up the dataset. Usually, this is the entire disk volume, but depending on the selected *VSS writers* it may only be a portion of a disk volume or specific files on a disk volume. Many Exchange Server–aware backup applications simply copy the various transaction log files and mailbox database files to the backup server.

Some applications, however, are a bit more intelligent; they keep track of which blocks have changed in the target files since the last backup interval. These applications can copy just those changed blocks to the backup dataset—typically some percentage of the blocks in the mailbox database file as well as all the new transaction log files—thus reducing the amount of data that needs to travel over the network and be stored. Block-level backups help strike a good balance between storage, speed, and reliability. As you go forward with VSS-aware Exchange Server–compatible backup solutions, be sure to investigate whether they offer this feature. Microsoft's System Center Data Protection Manager does offer this feature.

Disaster Recovery

Regular backups are important; the ability to successfully restore them is even more important. This capability is a key part of your extended arsenal for problem situations. Restoring the occasional backup is fairly straightforward but assumes that you have a functional Exchange server and the dependent network infrastructures. What do you do if an entire site or datacenter goes down and your recovery operations extend beyond a single Exchange Server mailbox database? The answer to this question is a broad topic that can fill many books, blog postings, and websites of its own.

Disaster recovery (DR) is the practice of ensuring that critical services can be restored when some disaster or event causes large-scale or long-term outage. A successful DR plan requires the identification of critical services and data, creation of documentation that lists the necessary tasks to re-create and restore them, and modification of the relevant policies and processes within your organization to support the DR plan.

It's not enough to consider how to rebuild Exchange servers and restore Exchange Server mailbox databases. Exchange Server is a complex application with many dependencies, so your plans need to accommodate the following issues:

Network Dependencies   These include subnets, IP address assignments, DHCP services, switch configurations, network/Internet access, and router configurations. Are you rebuilding your services to have the same IP addresses or new ones? Whatever you decide, you'll need to make sure that required services and clients can reach the Exchange servers.

Active Directory Services   These include associated DNS zones and records. Exchange Server cannot function without reliable access to global catalog servers and other domain controllers. Which forests and domains hold objects Exchange Server will need to reference? Does your existing replication configuration meet those needs during a DR scenario?

Third-Party Applications   These include monitoring, backup, archival, or other programs and services that require messaging services or interact with those services. Don't just blindly catalog everything in production; be sure these systems are also being addressed as part of the disaster-recovery plan.

There's a blurry line between disaster recovery and the associated concept of *business continuity* (also called *business continuance*). Business continuity (BC) is the ability of your organization to continue providing some minimum set of operations and services necessary to stay in business during a large-scale outage, such as during a regional event or natural disaster (for example, a hurricane or earthquake). In a business continuity plan, your organization will identify and prioritize the most critical services and capabilities that need to provide at least some level of operational capacity as soon as possible, even without full access to data or applications.

It's important to note that the business continuity plan is designed and implemented alongside your disaster-recovery efforts. In many organizations, they will be maintained by two separate groups of professionals. It is imperative that these groups should have good lines of communication in place.

⊕ Real World Scenario

DRAWING THE LINE BETWEEN DISASTER RECOVERY AND BUSINESS CONTINUITY

There's a lot of confusion over exactly how disaster recovery and business continuity relate to each other. We have good news and bad news: the good news is that it's a simple relationship. The bad news is, "It depends."

Both types of plans are ultimately aimed at the goal of repairing the damage caused by extended outages. The biggest difference is the scope; many business-continuity plans focus very little on technology and look instead at overall business processes. In contrast, disaster-recovery plans of necessity have to be concerned with the finer details of IT administration. The reality is that both levels of focus are often needed—and must be handled in parallel, with coordination, and in support of any additional ongoing crisis management.

We'll try to clarify the difference by providing an example. Acme Inc. is a national manufacturer and supplier of various goods, mainly to wholesale distributors but with a small and thriving mail-order retail department for the occasional customer who needs quality Acme products but has no convenient retail outlet in their locale. Acme's main call center has a small number of permanent staff but a large number of contract call center operators.

Unfortunately, Acme's main order fulfillment center—for both bulk wholesale orders, as well as the relatively small amount of mail-order traffic—gets hit by a large fragment in a meteor shower, causing a fire that rapidly transforms the entire site into smoking rubble even as all personnel are safely evacuated. The call center and supporting datacenter are completely destroyed and, conservatively, will take several months to fully rebuild. Obviously, Acme is going to suffer some sort of setback, but with proper planning they can minimize the effects. What types of actions would Acme's BC and DR plans each be taking?

Acme's BC plan is concerned with getting the minimum level of operational function back online as quickly as possible. In this case, it's going to take a while before they can resume call center operations. Their immediate needs are to establish at least some level of messaging support for the temporary call center workers the BC plan brings in. Their BC plan does not assume that they will have in-house capability, so it makes provisions—if required—to use hosted Exchange Server services as a short-term stopgap so that communications with customers and wholesalers will proceed until Acme's IT staff can bring up sufficient Exchange servers to switch back to on-premises services.

Acme's DR plan is concerned with rebuilding critical structures. In addition to restoring critical network infrastructure services, Acme's Exchange Server administrators are tasked with first rebuilding sufficient Exchange servers in their DR location to recover the mailbox databases for the call center's permanent staff. They also need to then create sufficient Exchange servers to allow the recovery of operator mailbox databases to extract message data pertaining to currently open cases that need investigation. Once the datacenter is rebuilt, they can build the rest of the Exchange servers and restore operations from the DR site.

Location, Location, Location

One factor tends to consistently blur the line between regular backups, disaster recovery, business continuity, and even high availability: where your solution is located. We have talked to many administrators who have the false assumption that once a recovery activity moves off-site, that automatically makes it disaster recovery (or business continuity, or high availability). This is an understandable misconception—but it's still not true.

In reality, the question of "where" is immaterial. If you're taking steps to protect your data, it's backup and recovery. If you're taking steps to rebuild services, it's disaster recovery. If you're taking steps to ensure you can still do business, it's business continuity. This is obviously an oversimplification, but it'll do for now unless we start looking at all the ways the lines can blur. We do want to touch on one of those complications now, however: where you deploy your recovery operations. There are three overall approaches: on-premises, off-premises, or a combination of the two.

On-Premises Solutions

Most of what we do as Exchange Server administrators, especially in backup and restore work, is *on-premises*. In an on-premises solution, you have one or more sites where your Exchange servers are deployed, and those same sites host the backup and disaster recovery operations. Note that this definition of "on-premises" differs somewhat from traditional disaster recovery terminology, which talks about *dedicated disaster recovery sites*. These sites are still part of your premises and so are still "on-premises" for our purpose.

Many organizations can handle all their operations in this fashion through the use of Exchange Server, storage and networking devices, and third-party applications. Some, however, can use additional help. When you need on-premises help in the Exchange Server world, there are two broad categories:

Appliances   Appliances are self-contained boxes or servers, usually a sealed combination of hardware and software, placed into the network. They are designed to interface with or become part of the Exchange Server organization and provide additional abilities. Appliances are useful for smaller organizations that want sophisticated options for disaster recovery but don't have the budget or skill level to provide their own. Appliances can be used to provide services such as cross-site data replication, site monitoring, or even additional services aimed at other types of functionality.

On the upside, appliances are typically easy to install. On the downside, they can quickly become a single point of failure. The temptation to place an appliance and treat it as a "fire-and-forget" solution is high. In reality, most appliances need to be tested, monitored, and upgraded on a regular basis.

Remote Managed Services   Remote managed services (or remote management) are service offerings. Instead of buying a sealed black box, the customer purchases a period of service from a vendor. The service provider provides design, deployment, and ongoing maintenance services as part of the offering for the customer—sometimes as a package, sometimes as a set of a la carte offerings. Like appliances, these offerings can extend beyond traditional disaster-recovery offerings.

These types of service providers are able to provide trained Exchange Server expertise on a scale that is typically available only to very large organizations. They can do this through economies of scale; by using these highly trained personnel to monitor, maintain, and troubleshoot many disparate customer organizations of all sizes and types, they can both afford this type of staff and offer them the kind of challenges necessary to retain them.

Some solutions exist that combine these two approaches; customers purchase both an appliance, as well as a managed service offering.

OFF-PREMISES SOLUTIONS

Some problems are easier to solve—or more efficient to solve—if you let someone else deal with them. In the Exchange Server world, this translates to *hosted services*—services or offerings provided by a third party. Hosted services may provide a large variety of functionality to an Exchange Server organization, ranging from backup, disaster recovery, and business continuity to such services as message hygiene, archival, and compliance and governance.

There's a close similarity between hosted services and remote managed services. Both are provided by an external service model. They can both offer a combination of features, performance, and convenience that makes them attractive to small- and medium-sized organizations. The difference is that with hosted services, messaging traffic is targeted— whether externally or internally—to the hosting provider, which then performs specific actions.

Depending on the specific service, traffic may then be rerouted back to the organization or it may continue to reside at the hosting provider.

Most hosted services charge on a per-user or per-mailbox basis. Because of this, they were often originally favored by smaller organizations or for specific portions of a larger enterprise. However, today's costs for hosted services are so low that even very large organizations have deployed hosted services. Hosted services can also require a large amount of bandwidth, depending on the overall amount of traffic between your organization and the service. This can drive the costs higher than just the up-front per-user price.

One of the main differences between hosted services and remote managed services is that a hosted service provider usually (but not always) has an internal Exchange Server deployment that is designed to host multiple tenants. For many years, the retail version of Exchange Server was designed around the assumption that each deployment would be used for a single organization or corporate entity.

Beginning with Exchange Server 2000, Microsoft began adding enhancements to Exchange Server to provide better support for multi-tenant deployments. However, it was not until after the release of Exchange Server 2007 and Microsoft's own initial multi-tenant offering (BPOS – Business Productivity Online Suite) that Microsoft began to invest significant resources into improving the Exchange Server story around multi-tenant support. These improvements continued with Exchange Server 2010 and have further continued with Exchange Server 2013.

With Office 365 Wave 15, Microsoft is hosting millions of mailboxes based on Exchange Server 2013. Exchange Server 2013 can be run on-premises, in the cloud, or in a hybrid configuration of the two. In each case, the available functionality is almost identical irrespective of where the mailboxes are located (on-premises or in the cloud).

Management Frameworks

There's a lot of great guidance out there (including fine books such as this one) on the technical aspects of designing, installing, configuring, and operating Exchange servers and organizations. There's a lot less material that provides a coherent look at the issues of the entire life cycle of IT management in general, let alone Windows or Exchange Server deployments in particular. There may be, however, more than you think: every organization of every size struggles with common nontechnical issues and needs a good defined framework for managing IT resources. Having this type of framework in place makes it easier to properly plan for disaster recovery and business continuity concerns, as well as other common management tasks.

There are several frameworks you may wish to examine, or with which you are already familiar in some fashion:

◆ The *Information Technology Infrastructure Library (ITIL)* is the 900-pound gorilla of the IT management framework world. ITIL provides a generic set of tools for IT professionals to use as template concepts and policies when developing their own management processes of their IT infrastructure and operations.

◆ Microsoft has developed the *Microsoft Operations Framework (MOF)*, a detailed framework based on the concepts and principles of ITIL. MOF takes the generic framework offered by ITIL and provides greater detail optimized for Windows and other Microsoft technologies.

◆ Like Microsoft, IBM offers its own ITIL-centric framework: the *IBM Tivoli Unified Process (ITUP)*. ITUP provides guidance on taking generic ITIL concepts and processes and linking them into real-world processes and tasks that map to real IT objectives.

◆ The *Control Objectives for Information and Related Technologies (COBIT)* best practices framework was initially created as a way to help organizations develop IT governance processes and models. While COBIT is typically thought of as optimized for IT audits, it offers supplemental practices suitable for IT management.

So how necessary are management frameworks in real deployments? Why are we wasting valuable space talking about ITIL and MOF when we could be cramming in a couple more nuggets of yummy Exchange Server 2013 technical goodness? The answer is simple: we can't include everything. No matter how thorough (and long) the book, there will always be more technical details that we can't include. Instead, we wanted to include at least an introduction to some of the nontechnical areas that can give you an advantage.

While a deep dive into any of these alternatives is out of scope for this book, we do want to take a short peek at two of them: first ITIL and then MOF. Although you don't have to know anything about these subjects to be a low-level Exchange Server administrator (but you should!), Microsoft has begun introducing exposure to these concepts into the training for their high-level Exchange Server certifications.

ITIL

The best way to learn about ITIL is to go through one of the training and certification events. Outside such classes, ITIL is in essence a collection of best practices in the discipline of IT service management. IT service management is just what it sounds like: effective and consistent management of IT services. IT management is in many respects nonintuitive and offers several specific challenges that are not common to many other management disciplines; most people need specific training to learn how to manage IT in the most effective way. ITIL represents the most accepted IT management approach in the world.

ITIL was developed by the UK Central Computer and Telecommunications Agency in an attempt to develop a centralized management standard for IT throughout the various British government agencies. This effort was not successful—in part due to the change from mainframe-based computing to personal computers and networks and the resulting lowering of barriers to server acquisition and deployment. However, it did allow the formation of existing best practices and thoughts on IT service management into a single collection of best practices and procedures, supported by tasks and checklists IT professionals can use as a starting point for developing their own IT governance structures. ITIL is supported and offered by a wide variety of entities, including many large enterprises and consulting firms, with training and certification available for IT professionals.

ITIL has been through several iterations. The most current version, ITIL 2011, became available in July 2011 and consists of five core texts:

Service Strategy   Demonstrates how to use the service management discipline and develop it as both a new set of capabilities, as well as a large-scale business asset

Service Design   Demonstrates how to take your objectives and develop them into services and assets through the creation of appropriate processes

Service Transition   Demonstrates how to take the services and assets previously created and transition them into production in your organization

Service Operation   Demonstrates the processes and techniques required to manage the various services and assets previously created and deployed

Continual Service Improvement   Demonstrates the ongoing process of improving on the services and assets

For more information on ITIL, see its official website at www.itil-officialsite.com/. And for a great improvement over the official ITIL texts, see *ITIL Foundation Exam Study Guide* (Sybex, 2012).

MOF

Microsoft has worked with ITIL for more than 10 years, beginning in 1999. As ITIL has developed and grown in popularity, Microsoft has seen that its customers needed more specific guidance for using the principles and concepts of ITIL in the context of Microsoft technologies and applications. As a result, they created the Microsoft Operations Framework, which they describe in the following manner:

> *The Microsoft strategy for IT service management is to provide guidance and software solutions that enable organizations to achieve mission-critical system reliability, availability, supportability, and manageability of the Microsoft platform. The strategy includes a model for organizations and IT pros to assess their current IT infrastructure maturity, prioritize processes of greatest concern, and apply proven principles and best practices to optimize performance on the Microsoft platform.*

MOF is not a replacement for ITIL; it is one specific implementation of ITIL, optimized for environments that use Microsoft products. It's specifically designed to help IT professionals align business goals with IT goals and develop cohesive, unified processes that allow the creation and management of IT services throughout all portions of the IT life cycle. It is currently on version 4.0, which aligns with ITIL v3.

MOF defines four stages of the IT service management life cycle:

Plan   Plan is the first stage of the cycle: new IT services are identified and created, or necessary changes are identified in existing IT services that are already in place.

Deliver   Deliver is the second stage: the new service is implemented for use in production.

Operate   Operate is the final stage of the cycle: the service is deployed and monitored. It feeds back into the Plan stage in order to affect incremental changes as necessary.

Manage   Manage is not a separate stage; instead, it is an ongoing set of processes that take place at all times throughout the cycle to measure and monitor the effectiveness of your efforts. This is illustrated in Figure 3.1.

FIGURE 3.1
The four stages of the Microsoft IT service management life cycle

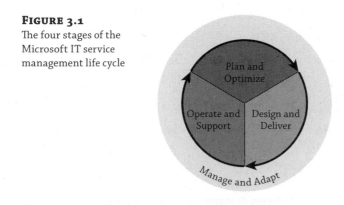

For more information on MOF, see the following web page:

`http://technet.microsoft.com/en-us/library/cc506049.aspx`

WHAT ARE YOU MEASURING?

Let's demonstrate the practical value of some of this "management framework" mumbo-jumbo by tackling a hot topic: availability and uptime. We've heard a lot of executives talk about "five nines of availability"—but what, exactly, does that mean? You can't have a meaningful discussion about availability without knowing exactly what kind of availability you're talking about (which we'll get to later in this chapter), and without knowing that, you can't measure it, let alone to the ludicrous degree of detail that five nines represents.

Now let's discuss uptime. Uptime has a pretty well-defined meaning; you just need to know what scope it applies to. Are you talking server uptime, mailbox uptime, or service uptime? Once you have that defined, you can take measurements and apply numbers for quantitative comparisons.

ITIL and MOF give you not only the conceptual framework for agreeing on what you're measuring but also guidance on how to put the process of measurement into place. That kind of discipline can give you a lot of long-term advantages and help keep your Exchange Server deployment better managed than you could do on your own. The thing to remember is that these frameworks are starting points; they're not cast in stone, and they're not laws you must rigidly obey. If you find some aspect that doesn't work for your organization, you should first make sure you understand what the purpose of that feature is and how it's intended to work. Once you're sure that it doesn't apply as is, feel free to make documented changes to bring it into alignment with your needs.

A Closer Look at Availability

We've already talked about disaster recovery and how it can be confused with general data protection (backup and recovery) and business continuity. Perhaps an even more common confusion, though, is the distinction between high availability and disaster recovery. This is a common enough error that we felt it was worth devoting a separate section of this chapter.

High availability (HA) is a design strategy. The strategy is simple: try to ensure that users keep access to services, such as their Exchange Server mailboxes or Unified Messaging servers, during periods of outage or downtime. These outages could be the result of any sort of event:

- Hardware failure, such as the loss of a power supply, a memory module, or the server motherboard

- Storage failure, such as the loss of a disk, disk controller, or data-level corruption

- Network failure, such as the cutting of a network cable or a router or a switch losing configuration

- Some other service failure, such as the loss of an Active Directory domain controller or a DNS server

HA technologies and strategies are designed to allow a given service to continue to be available to users (or other services) in the event of these kind of failures. No matter which technology is involved, there are two main approaches, one or both of which is used by each HA technology and strategy:

Fault Tolerance and Redundancy   This involves placing resources into a pool so that one can take up the load when another member of the pool fails. This strategy removes the presence of a single point of failure. Fault tolerance needs to be accompanied by some mechanism for selecting which of the redundant resources is to be used. These mechanisms are either *round-robin* or *load balancing*. In the former, each resource in the pool is used in turn, regardless of the current state or load. In the latter, additional mechanisms are used to direct users to the least loaded member of the resource pool. Many higher-end hardware systems use redundant parts to make the overall server system more redundant to many common types of hardware failures. Exchange Server 2013 can use CAS arrays to provide fault tolerance and redundancy to client access servers. If a CAS fails, any other CAS in the same Active Directory site can immediately take over.

Replication   This process involves making copies of critical data between multiple members of a resource pool. If replication happens quickly enough and with a small enough time interval, when one member of the resource pool becomes unavailable, another member can take over the load. Most replication strategies, including Exchange Server's database replication features, are based on a *single master* strategy, where all updates happen to the master (or active) copy and are replicated to the additional copies. Some technologies such as Active Directory are designed to allow *multimaster replication*, where updates can be directed to the closest member. Exchange Server 2013 can use database availability groups (DAGs) to replicate copies of data from one Mailbox server to another and to provide failover in the event the database where the mailbox resides fails.

To achieve complete availability with Exchange Server, you'll use both strategies. However, you also need to think of the different levels of availability that you'll need to ensure.

MEASURING AVAILABILITY

It is not uncommon to find that availability of a system is measured differently depending on the organization. Typically, to report the percentage of availability, you take the amount of time during a measurement period and then subtract the total downtime during that period. Finally, you divide that number by the total elapsed time.

So, let's say that during a 30-day period of time, there was no *scheduled* downtime, but there was a 4-hour period of time when patches were applied to the system. So, 30 days − .17 days = 29.8 days of total uptime, and 29.8/30 = 99.3 percent availability.

This is just a sample calculation, of course. In the real world, you may have a maintenance window during your operations that would not count against your availability numbers. You want to do your very best to minimize the amount of unplanned downtime, but you also have to take in to consideration scheduled maintenance and planned downtime.

In some organizations, no downtime, planned or unplanned, is acceptable. You must design your systems accordingly.

SERVICE AVAILABILITY

When we have discussions with people about high availability in Exchange Server organizations, we find that the level of high availability that most of them are actually thinking about is *service availability*. That is, they think of the Exchange Server deployment as an overall service and think of how to ensure that users can get access to everything (either that, or they think solely of hardware clusters, storage replication, and the other low-end technologies). It is important to note that when discussing service availability, this term may mean different things to different people.

Service availability is an important consideration for the overall availability strategy. It doesn't make a lot of sense to plan for redundant server hardware if you forget to deploy sufficient numbers of those servers with the right Exchange Server roles in the appropriate locations. (We'll discuss the proper ratios and recommendations for role and server placement in Chapter 8, "Understanding Server Roles and Configurations.") To ensure true service availability, you need to consider all the other levels of availability.

The other aspect of service availability is to think about what other services Exchange Server is dependent on:

◆ The obvious dependency is Active Directory. Each Exchange server requires access to a domain controller, as well as global catalog servers. The more Exchange servers in the site, the more of each Active Directory role that the site requires. If your domain controllers are also DNS servers, you need enough DNS servers to survive the loss of one or two. If you lose all DNS servers or all domain controllers in an Active Directory site, Exchange Server will fail.

◆ What type of network services do you need? Do you assign static IP addresses and default gateways or do you use DHCP and dynamic routing? Do you have extra router or switching capacity? What about your firewall configurations—do you have only a single firewall between different network zones or are those redundant as well?

◆ What other applications do you deploy as part of your Exchange Server deployment? Do you rely on a monitoring system such as Microsoft System Center Operations Manager? What will occur if something happens to your monitoring server; is there a redundant or backup system that takes over, or will additional faults and failures go unnoticed and be allowed to impact the Exchange Server system? Do you have enough backup agents and servers to protect your Mailbox servers?

Service availability typically requires a combination of redundancy and replication strategies. For example, you deploy multiple Active Directory domain controllers in a site for redundancy, but they replicate the directory data between each other.

NETWORK AVAILABILITY

The next area we want to talk about is network availability. By this, we don't mean the types of network services we mentioned in the previous section. Instead, what we mean is the ability to ensure that you can receive new connection requests from clients and other servers, regardless of whether your organization uses Exchange servers, PBX systems and telephony gateways, or external mail servers. Network availability is a key part of Exchange Server infrastructure and must be considered as a part of your overall service availability.

The typical strategy for network availability is load balancing. This is network-level redundancy. Simple network load balancers use a round-robin mechanism to alternately and evenly (on the basis of numbers) distribute incoming connections to the members of the resource pool. Other solutions use more sophisticated mechanisms, such as monitoring each member of the pool for overall load and assigning incoming connections to the least-loaded member.

For larger organizations and complex Exchange Server deployments, it's common to use hardware load balancers. Hardware systems are typically more expensive and represent yet more systems to manage and maintain, so they add a degree of complexity that is often undesirable to smaller organizations. Smaller organizations often prefer to use software-based load-balancing solutions, such as Windows Network Load Balancing (WNLB).

Unfortunately, WNLB isn't generally suitable for Exchange Server 2013 deployments. This is the official recommendation of both the Exchange Server product group and the Windows product group, the folks who develop the WNLB component. WNLB has a few characteristics that render it unsuitable for use with Exchange Server in any but the smallest of deployments or test environments:

♦ WNLB simply performs round-robin balancing of incoming connections. It doesn't detect whether members of the load-balance cluster are down, so it will keep sending connections to the downed member. This could result in intermittent and confusing behavior for clients and loss or delay of messages from external systems. If you must deploy WNLB, also consider deploying scripts that can monitor application health and updated WNLB accordingly, as demonstrated here:

```
http://msdn.microsoft.com/en-us/library/windows/desktop/cc307934.aspx
```

♦ WNLB is incompatible with the Windows Failover Clustering. This means that small shops can't deploy a pair of servers with the Mailbox and Client Access roles and then use WNLB to balance the Client Access role or use continuous replication to replicate the mailbox databases. They'd have to deploy four servers at a minimum.

Even when using hardware network load balancing, there are several things to remember and best practices to follow. (For more information on load balancing, DNS, and WNLB, see Chapter 21, "Understanding the Client Access Server.")

DATA AVAILABILITY

We've seen many Exchange Server organization designs and deployment plans. Most of them spend a lot of time ensuring that the mailbox data will be available.

In all versions of Exchange Server prior to Exchange Server 2007, having high availability for mailbox databases meant using Windows Failover Clustering (WFC), which was a feature of Windows Enterprise Edition. One of the features provided by WFC is the ability to create groups of servers (clusters) that share storage resources. Within this cluster of servers, one or more instances of Exchange Server would be running and controlling the mailbox databases. If one hardware node were to fail, the active server instance would fail over to another hardware node, and the shared storage resources would move with it.

Failover clustering is a common HA strategy, and WFC is a proven technology. This turned out to be a good strategy for many Exchange Server organizations. However, failover clustering has some cons. For clusters that rely on a shared quorum, the biggest is the reliance on shared storage—typically a storage area network. Shared storage increases the cost and complexity of the clustering solution, but it doesn't guard against the most common cause of Exchange Server outage: disk failure or corruption.

Exchange Server 2007 introduced a new data-availability solution called *continuous replication* to help overcome some of the weaknesses associated with failover clustering and to allow more organizations to take advantage of highly available deployments. Continuous replication, also known as log shipping, copies the transaction logs corresponding to a mailbox database from one Mailbox server to another. The target then replays the logs into its own separate copy of the database, re-creating the latest changes.

Exchange Server 2010 added more features to continuous replication, including data encryption and compression. With both Exchange Server 2010 and Exchange Server 2013, a Mailbox server can have up to 15 replication partners. You now join servers into a *database availability group*; members of that group can replicate one or more of their mailbox databases with the other servers in the group. Each database can be replicated separately from others and have one or more replicas. A DAG can cross Active Directory site boundaries, thus providing site resiliency. And activation of a passive copy can be automatic.

We'll go into more detail about DAGs and continuous replication in Exchange Server 2013 in Chapter 20, "Creating and Managing Database Availability Groups."

HA vs. DR: Not the Same

We'll provide a quick comparison between the typical Exchange Server HA deployment and DR deployment. If you think that by having disaster recovery you have availability, or vice versa, think again.

In an HA Exchange Server environment, the focus is usually on keeping mailboxes up and running for users, transferring mail with external systems, and keeping Exchange Server services up. In a DR environment, the focus is usually on restoring *a bare minimum* of services, often for a smaller portion of the overall user population. In short, the difference is that of *abundance* versus *triage*.

For Exchange Server, an HA design can provide several advantages beyond the obvious availability goals. A highly available Exchange Server environment often enables server consolidation; the same technologies that permit mailbox data to be replicated between servers or to keep multiple instances of key Exchange Server services also permit greater user mailbox density or force the upgrading of key infrastructure (like network bandwidth) so that a greater number of users can be handled. This increased density can make proper DR planning more difficult by increasing the requirements for a DR solution and making it harder to identify and target the appropriate user populations.

That's not to say that HA and DR are incompatible. Far from it; you can and should design your Exchange Server 2013 deployment for both. To do that effectively, though, you need to have a clear understanding of what each technology and feature actually provide you, so you can avoid design errors. For example, if you have separate groups of users who will need their mailboxes replicated to a DR site, set them aside in separate mailbox databases, rather than mingling them in with users whose mailboxes won't be replicated.

Storage Availability

Many administrators and IT professionals immediately think of storage designs when they hear the word *availability*. Although storage is a critical part of ensuring the overall service availability of an Exchange Server organization, the impact of storage design is far more than just availability; it directly affects performance, reliability, and scalability.

An Overview of Exchange Storage

In medium-sized and large organizations, the Exchange Server administrator is usually not also responsible for storage. Many medium-sized and large organizations use specialized storage area networks that require additional training to master. Storage is a massive topic, but we feel it is important that you at least be able to speak the language of storage.

From the very beginning, messaging systems have had a give-and-take relationship with the underlying storage system. Even on systems that aren't designed to offer long-term storage for email (such as ISP systems that offer only POP3 access), email creates demands on storage:

◆ The transport components must have space to queue messages that cannot be immediately transmitted to the remote system.

◆ The delivery component must be able to store incoming messages that have been delivered to a mailbox until users can retrieve them.

◆ The message store, in systems like Exchange Server, permits users to keep a copy of their mailbox data on central servers.

◆ As the server accepts, transmits, and processes email, it keeps logs with varying levels of detail so administrators can troubleshoot and audit activities.

Although you'll have to wait for subsequent chapters to delve into the details of planning storage for Exchange Server, the following sections go over the two broad categories of storage solutions that are used in modern Exchange Server systems: direct attached storage (DAS) and storage area networks (SANs). The third type of storage, network-attached storage (NAS), is generally not supported with Exchange Server 2010 or Exchange Server 2013.

Direct attached storage is the most common type of storage in general. DAS disks are usually internal disks or directly attached via cable. Just about every server, except for some high-end varieties, such as blade systems using boot-over-SAN, uses DAS at some level; typically, at least the boot and operating system volumes are on some DAS configuration. However, in versions of Exchange Server prior to Exchange Server 2010, DAS has drawbacks: it doesn't necessarily scale as well for either capacity or performance. Further, organizations that have invested significant amounts of money in their SANs may still require that Exchange Server use the SAN instead of DAS.

To solve these problems, people looked at NAS devices as one of the potential solutions. These machines—giant file servers—sit on the network and share their disk storage. They range in price and configuration from small plug-in devices with fixed capacity to large installations with more configuration options than most luxury cars (and a price tag to match). Companies that bought these were using them to replace file servers, web server storage, SQL Server storage—why not Exchange Server?

However, the only version of Exchange Server that supported NAS was Exchange Server 2003. Instead of continuing to support NAS, the Exchange Server development team switched to reducing the overall I/O requirements so that DAS configurations become practical for small to midsized organizations. Exchange Server 2007 moved to a 64-bit architecture to remove memory-management bottlenecks in the 32-bit Windows kernel, allowing the Exchange Information Store to use more memory for intelligent mailbox data caching and reduce disk I/O. Exchange Server 2010 in turn made aggressive changes to the on-disk mailbox database structures, such as moving to a new database schema that allows pages to be sequentially written to the end of the database file rather than randomly throughout the file. The schema updates improve indexing and client performance, allowing common tasks, such as updating folder views to happen more quickly while requiring fewer disk reads and writes. These changes help improve efficiency and continue to drive mailbox I/O down.

Exchange Server 2013 continued making significant changes to the I/O profile presented by Exchange Server. Between Exchange Server 2010 and Exchange Server 2013, Microsoft reduced I/O requirements between 33 percent and 50 percent. From Exchange Server 2003 to Exchange Server 2013, I/O requirements have been reduced by over 90 percent, granted, at a cost in memory! However, these reductions in I/O requirements now make it practical to reexamine DAS as solution for Exchange Server storage (and, in fact, DAS is recommended by Microsoft for Exchange Server 2013).

The premise behind SAN is to move disks to dedicated storage units that can handle all the advanced features you need—high-end RAID configurations, hot-swap replacement, on the fly reconfiguration, rapid disk snapshots, tight integration with backup and restore solutions, and more. This helps consolidate the overhead of managing storage, often spread out on dozens of servers and applications (and their associated staff), into a single set of personnel. Then, dedicated network links connect these storage silos with the appropriate application servers. Yet this consolidation of storage can also be a serious pitfall since Exchange Server is usually not the only application placed on the SAN. Applications, such as SharePoint, SQL, archiving, and file services may all be sharing the same aggregated set of spindles and cause disk contention, which leads to poor performance.

Direct Attached Storage

As used for legacy Exchange Server storage, DAS historically displays two main problems: performance and capacity. As mailbox databases got larger and traffic levels rose, pretty soon people wanted to look for alternatives; DAS storage under Exchange Server 2000 and Exchange Server 2003 required many disks to meet I/O requirements, because Exchange Server's I/O profile was optimized for the 32-bit memory architecture that Windows provided at the time.

To get more scalability on logical disks that support Exchange Server databases, you can always try adding more disks to the server. This gives you a configuration known as Just a Bunch of Disks (JBOD).

Although JBOD can usually give you the raw disk storage capacity you need, it has three flaws that render it unsuitable for all but the smallest of legacy Exchange Server deployments:

JBOD Forces You to Partition Your Data Because each disk has a finite capacity, you can't store data on that disk if it is larger than the capacity. For example, if you have four 250 GB drives, even though you have approximately 1 TB of storage in total, you have to break that up into separate 250 GB partitions. Historically, this has caused some interesting design decisions in messaging systems that rely on filesystem-based storage.

JBOD Offers No Performance Benefits Each disk is responsible for only one chunk of storage, so if that disk is already in use, subsequent I/O requests will have to wait for it to free up before they can go through. A single disk can thus become a bottleneck for the system, which can slow down mail for all your users (not just those whose mailboxes are stored on the affected disk).

JBOD Offers No Redundancy If one of your disks dies, you're out of luck unless you can restore that data from backup. True, you haven't lost all your data, but the one-quarter of your users who have just lost their email are not likely to be comforted by that observation.

Several of the Exchange Server 2010 design goals focused on building in the necessary features to work around these issues and make a DAS JBOD deployment a realistic option for more organizations. Exchange Server 2013 design goals included continuing to reduce the total I/O requirement necessary for Exchange Server, making DAS even more realistic for many organizations. In fact, Office 365 runs off DAS!

However, legacy versions of Exchange Server contain no mechanisms to work around these issues. Luckily, some bright people came up with a great generic answer to JBOD that also works well for legacy Exchange Server: the Redundant Array of Inexpensive Disks (RAID).

The basic premise behind RAID is to group the JBOD disks together in various configurations with a dedicated disk controller to handle the specific disk operations, allowing the computer (and applications) to see the entire collection of drives and controller as one very large disk device. These collections of disks are known as arrays; the arrays are presented to the operating system, partitioned, and formatted as if they were just regular disks. The common types of RAID configurations are shown in Table 3.1.

TABLE 3.1: RAID configurations

RAID LEVEL	NAME	DESCRIPTION
None	Concatenated drives	Two or more disks are joined together in a contiguous data space. As one disk in the array is filled up, the data is carried over to the next disk. Though this solves the capacity problem and is easy to implement, it offers no performance or redundancy whatsoever and makes it more likely that you're going to lose all your data, not less, through a single disk failure. These arrays are not suitable for use with legacy Exchange servers.
RAID 0	Striped drives	Two or more disks have data split among them evenly. If you write a 1 MB file to a two-disk RAID 0 array, half the data will be on one disk, half on the other. Each disk in the array can be written to (or read from) simultaneously, giving you a noticeable performance boost. However, if you lose one disk in the array, you lose all your data. These arrays are typically used for fast, large, temporary files, such as those in video editing. These arrays are not suitable for use with Exchange Server; while they give excellent performance, the risk of data loss is typically unacceptable.

TABLE 3.1: RAID configurations *(CONTINUED)*

RAID LEVEL	NAME	DESCRIPTION
RAID 1	Mirrored drives	Typically done with two disks (although some vendors allow more), each disk receives a copy of all the data in the array. If you lose one disk, you still have a copy of your data on the remaining disk; you can either move the data or plug in a replacement disk and rebuild the mirror. RAID 1 also gives a performance benefit; reads can be performed by either disk, because only writes need to be mirrored. However, RAID 1 can be one of the more costly configurations; to store 500 GB of data, you'd need to buy two 500 GB drives. These arrays are suitable for use with legacy Exchange Server volumes, depending on the type of data and the performance of the array.
RAID 5	Parity drive	Three or more disks have data split among them. However, one disk's worth of capacity is reserved for parity checksum data; this is a special calculated value that allows the RAID system to rebuild the missing data if one drive in the array fails. The parity data is spread across all the disks in the array. If you had a four-disk 250 GB RAID 5 array, you'd have only 750 GB of usable space. RAID 5 arrays offer better performance than JBOD but worse performance than other RAID configurations, especially on the write requests; the checksum must be calculated and the data + parity written to all the disks in the array. Also, if you lose one disk, the array goes into degraded mode, which means that even read operations will need to be recalculated and will be slower than normal. These arrays are suitable for use with legacy Exchange Server mailbox database volumes on smaller servers, depending on the type of data and the performance of the array. Due to their write performance characteristics, they are usually not well matched for transaction log volumes.
RAID 6	Double parity drive	This RAID variant has become common only recently and is designed to provide RAID 5 arrays with the ability to survive the loss of two disks. Other than offering two-disk resiliency, base RAID 6 implementations offer mostly the same benefits and drawbacks as RAID 5. Some vendors have built custom implementations that attempt to solve the performance issues. These arrays are suitable for use with Exchange Server, depending on the type of data and the performance of the array.

TABLE 3.1:   RAID configurations   *(CONTINUED)*

RAID LEVEL	NAME	DESCRIPTION
RAID 10 RAID 0+1 RAID 1+0	Mirroring plus striping	A RAID 10 array is the most costly variant to implement because it uses mirroring. However, it also uses striping to aggregate spindles and deliver blistering performance, which makes it a great choice for high-end arrays that have to sustain a high level of I/O. As a side bonus, it also increases your chances of surviving the loss of multiple disks in the array. There are two basic variants. RAID 0+1 takes two big stripe arrays and mirrors them together; RAID 1+0 takes multiple mirror pairs and stripes them together. Both variants have essentially the same performance numbers, but 1+0 is preferred because it can be rebuilt more quickly (you only have to regenerate a single disk) and has far higher chances of surviving the loss of multiple disks (you can lose one disk in each mirror pair). These arrays have traditionally been used for high-end highly loaded legacy Exchange Server mailbox database volumes.

Note that several of these types of RAID arrays may be suitable for your Exchange server. Which one, if any, should you use? The answer to that question depends entirely on how many mailboxes your servers are holding, how they're used, and other types of business needs. Beware of anyone who tries to give hard-and-fast answers like, "Always use RAID 5 for Exchange Server database volumes." To determine the true answer, you need to go through a proper storage-sizing process, find out what your I/O and capacity requirements are really going to be, think about your data recovery needs and service-level agreements (SLAs), and then decide what storage configuration will meet those needs for you in a fashion you can afford. There are no magic bullets.

In every case, the RAID controller you use—the piece of hardware, plus drivers, that aggregates the individual disk volumes for you into a single pseudo-device that is presented to Windows—plays a key role. You can't just take a collection of disks, toss them into slots in your server, and go to town with RAID. You need to install extra drivers and management software, you need to take extra steps to configure your arrays before you can even use them in Windows, and you may even need to update your disaster-recovery procedures to ensure that you can always recover data from drives in a RAID array. Generally, you'll need to test whether you can move drives in one array between two controllers, even those from the same manufacturer; not all controllers support all options. *After* your server has melted down and your SLA is fast approaching is not a good time to find out that you needed to have a spare controller on hand.

If you choose the DAS route (whether JBOD or RAID), you'll need to think about how you're going to house the physical disks. Modern server cases don't leave a lot of extra room for disks; this is especially true of rack-mounted systems. Usually, this means you'll need some sort of external enclosure that hooks back into a physical bus on your server, such as SAS or eSATA disks. Make sure to give these enclosures suitable power and cooling; hard drives pull a lot of power and return it all eventually as heat.

Also make sure that your drive backplanes (the physical connection points) and enclosures support hot-swap capability, where you can easily pull the drive and replace it without powering the system down. Keep a couple of spare drives and drive sleds on hand, too. You don't want to have to schedule an outage of your Exchange server in order to replace a failed drive in a RAID 5 array, letting all your users enjoy the performance hit of a thrashing RAID volume because the array is in degraded mode until the replacement drives arrive.

RAID CONTROLLERS ARE NOT ALL CREATED EQUAL

Beware! Not all kinds of RAID are created equal. Before you spend a lot of time trying to figure out which configuration to choose, first think about your RAID controller. There are three kinds of them, and unlike RAID configurations, it's pretty easy to determine which kind you need for Exchange Server:

Software RAID   Software RAID avoids the whole problem of having a RAID controller by performing all the magic in the operating system software. If you convert your disk to dynamic volumes, you can do RAID 0, RAID 1, and RAID 5 natively in Windows 2008 without any extra hardware. However, Microsoft strongly recommends that you not do this with Exchange Server, and the Exchange Server community echoes that recommendation. It takes extra memory and processing power, and it inevitably slows your disks down from what you could get with a simple investment in good hardware. You will also not be able to support higher levels of I/O load with this configuration, in our experience.

BIOS RAID   BIOS RAID attempts to provide "cheap" RAID by putting some code for RAID in the RAID chipset, which is then placed either directly on the motherboard (common in workstation-grade and low-end server configurations) or on an inexpensive add-in card. The dirty little secret is that the RAID chipset isn't really doing the RAID operations in hardware; again it's all happening in software, this time in the associated Windows driver (which is written by the vendor) rather than an official Windows subsystem. If you're about to purchase a RAID controller card for a price that seems too good to be true, it's probably one of these cards. These RAID controllers tend to have fewer ports, which limits their overall utility. Although you can get Exchange Server to work with them, you can do so only with a very low number of users. Otherwise, you'll quickly hit the limits these cards have and stress your storage system. Just avoid them; the time you save will more than make up for the up-front price savings.

Hardware RAID   This is the only kind of RAID you should even be thinking about for your Exchange servers. This means good-quality, high-end cards that come from reputable manufacturers that have taken the time to get the product on the Windows Hardware Compatibility List (HCL). These cards do a lot of the work for your system, removing the CPU overhead of parity calculations from the main processors, and they are worth every penny you pay for them. Better yet, they'll be able to handle the load your Exchange servers and users throw at them.

If you can't tell whether a given controller you're eyeing is BIOS or true hardware RAID, get help. Lots of forums and websites on the Internet will help you sort out which hardware to get and which to avoid. And while you're at it, spring a few extra bucks for good, reliable disks. We cannot stress enough the importance of not cutting corners on your Exchange Server storage system; while Exchange Server 2013 gives you a lot more room for designing storage and brings back options you may not have had before, you still need to buy the best components that you can to make up the designed storage system. The time and long-term costs you save will be your own.

Storage Area Networks

Initial SAN solutions used fiber-optic connections to provide the necessary bandwidth for storage operations. As a result, these systems were incredibly expensive and were used only by organizations with deep pockets. The advent of Gigabit Ethernet over copper and new storage bus technologies, such as SATA and SAS, has moved the cost of SANs down into the realm where midsized companies can now afford both the sticker price and the resource training to become competent with these new technologies.

Over time, many vendors have begun to offer SAN solutions that are affordable even for small companies. The main reason they've been able to do so is the iSCSI protocol: block-based file access routed over TCP/IP connections. Add iSCSI with ubiquitous Gigabit Ethernet hardware, and SAN deployments have become a lot more common.

Clustering and high-availability concerns are the other factors in the growth of Exchange Server/SAN deployments. Exchange Server 2003 supported clustered configurations but required the cluster nodes to have a shared storage solution. As a result, any organization that wanted to deploy an Exchange Server cluster needed some sort of SAN solution (apart from the handful of people who stuck with shared SCSI configurations). A SAN has a certain elegance to it; you simply create a virtual slice of drive space for Exchange Server (called a LUN, or logical unit number), use Fibre Channel or iSCSI (and corresponding drivers) to present it to the Exchange server, and away you go. Even with Exchange Server 2007—which was reengineered with an eye toward making DAS a supportable choice for Exchange Server storage in specific CCR and SCR configurations—many organizations still found that using a SAN for Exchange Server storage was the best answer for their various business requirements. By this time, management had seen the benefits of centralized storage management and wanted to ensure that Exchange Server deployments were part of the big plan.

However, SAN solutions don't fix all problems, even with (usually because of) their price tag. Often, SANs make your environment even more complex and difficult to support. Because SANs cost so much, there is often a strong drive to use the SAN for all storage and make full use of every last free block of space. The cost per GB of storage for a SAN can be between 3 and 10 times as expensive as DAS disks. Unfortunately, Exchange Server's I/O characteristics are very different than those of just about any other application, and few dedicated SAN administrators really know how to properly allocate disk space for Exchange Server:

◆ SAN administrators do not usually understand that total disk space is only one component of Exchange Server performance. For day-to-day operations, it is far more important to ensure enough I/O capacity. Traditionally, this is delivered by using lots of physical disks (commonly referred to as "spindles") to increase the amount of simultaneous read/write operations supported. It is important to make sure the SAN solution provides enough I/O capacity, not just free disk space, or Exchange Server will crawl.

◆ Even if you can convince them to configure LUNs spread across enough disks, SAN administrators immediately want to reclaim that wasted space. As a result, you end up sharing the same spindles between Exchange Server and some other application with its own performance curve, and then suddenly you have extremely noticeable but hard-to-diagnose performance issues with your Exchange servers. Shared spindles will crater Exchange Server performance.

◆ Although some SAN vendors have put a lot of time and effort into understanding Exchange Server and its I/O needs so that their salespeople and certified consultants can help you deploy Exchange Server on their products properly, not everyone does the same. Many vendors will shrug off performance concerns by telling you about their extensive write caching and how good write caching will smooth out any performance issues. Their argument is true—up to a point. A cache can help isolate Exchange Server from the effects of transient I/O events, but it won't help you come Monday morning when all your users are logging in and the SQL Server databases that share your spindles are churning through extra operations.

The moral of the story is simple: don't believe that you need to have a SAN. This is especially true with Exchange Server 2013; there have been a lot of under-the-hood changes to the mailbox database storage to ensure that more companies can deploy a 7200 RPM SATA JBOD configuration and be able to get good performance and reliability from that system, especially when you are using database availability groups and multiple copies of your data.

If you do find that a SAN provides the best value for your organization, get the best one you can afford. Make sure that your vendors know Exchange Server storage inside and out; if possible, get them to put you in contact with their on-staff Exchange Server specialists. Have them work with your SAN administrators to come up with a storage configuration that meets your real Exchange Server needs.

Needless to say, the hints we've scattered here should have given you clues that storage and the Mailbox role have undergone some radical changes in Exchange Server 2013. We'll go into more details about Exchange Server storage in Chapter 19, "Creating and Managing Mailbox Databases."

Compliance and Governance

Quite simply, today's legal system considers email to be an official form of business communication just like written memos. This means that any type of legal requirement or legal action against your organization (regarding business records) will undoubtedly include email. Unless you work in a specific vertical market, such as healthcare or finance, the emergence of compliance and governance as topics of import to the messaging administrator is a relatively recent event. The difference between compliance and governance can be summarized simply:

> *Governance is the process of defining and enforcing policies, while compliance is the process of ensuring that you meet external requirements.*

However, both of these goals share a lot of common ground:

◆ They require thorough planning to implement, based on a detailed understanding of what behaviors are allowed, required, or forbidden.

◆ Though they require technical controls to ensure implementation, they are at heart about people and processes.

◆ They require effective monitoring in order to audit the effectiveness of the compliance and governance measures.

In short, they require all the same things you need in order to effectively manage your messaging data. As a result, there's a useful framework you can use to evaluate your compliance and governance needs: Discovery, Compliance, Archival, and Retention, also known as the DCAR framework.

DCAR recognizes four key pillars of activity, each historically viewed as a separate task for messaging administrators. However, all four pillars involve the same mechanisms, people, and policies; all four in fact are overlapping facets of messaging data management. These four pillars are described in the following list:

Discovery Finding messages in the system quickly and accurately, whether for litigation, auditing, or other needs. There are generally two silos of discovery: *personal discovery*, allowing users to find and monitor the messages they send and receive, and *organizational discovery*, which encompasses the traditional litigation or auditing activities most messaging administrators think about. It requires the following:

◆ Good storage design to handle the additional overhead of discovery actions

◆ The accurate and thorough indexing of all messaging data that enters the Exchange Server organization through any means

◆ Control over the ability of users to move data into and out of the messaging system through mechanisms such as personal folders (PSTs)

◆ Control of the user's ability to delete data that may be required by litigation

Compliance Meeting all legal, regulatory, and governance requirements, whether derived from external or internal drivers. Although many of the technologies used for compliance also look similar to those used by individual users for *mailbox management*, compliance happens more at the organization level (even if not all populations within the organization are subject to the same regimes). It requires the following:

◆ Clear guidance on which behaviors are allowed, required, or prohibited, as well as a clear description of which will be enforced through technical means

◆ The means to enforce required behavior, prevent disallowed behavior, and audit for the success or failure of these means

◆ The ability to control and view all messaging data that enters the Exchange Server organization through any means

Archival The ability to preserve the messaging data that will be required for future operations, including governance tasks. Like discovery, archival happens on two broad levels: the *user archive* is a personal solution that allows individual users to retain and reuse historical personal messaging data relevant to their job function, while the *business archive* is aimed at providing immutable organization-wide benefits such as storage reduction, eDiscovery, and knowledge retention. It requires the following:

◆ Clear guidance on which data must be preserved and a clear description of procedural and technical measures that will be used to enforce archival

◆ The accurate and thorough indexing of all messaging data that enters the Exchange Server organization through any means

◆ Control over the ability of users to move data into and out of the messaging system through mechanisms such as personal folders

Retention The ability to identify data that can be safely removed without adverse impact (whether immediate or delayed) on the business. Although many retention mechanisms are defined and maintained centrally in the organization, it is not uncommon for many implementations to either depend on voluntary user activity for compliance or allow users to easily define stricter or looser retention policies for their own data. It requires the following:

◆ Clear guidance on which data is safe to remove and a clear description of the time frames and technical measures that will be used to enforce removal

◆ The accurate identification of all messaging data that enters the Exchange Server organization through any means

◆ Control over the ability of users to move data into and out of the messaging system through mechanisms, such as personal folders

If many of these requirements look the same, good; that emphasizes that these activities are all merely different parts of the same overall goal. You should be realizing that these activities are not things you do with your messaging system so much as they are activities that you perform while managing your messaging system. The distinction is subtle but important; knowing your requirements helps make the difference between designing and deploying a system that can be easily adapted to meet your needs and one that you will constantly have to fight. Some of these activities will require the addition of third-party solutions, even for Exchange Server 2013, which includes more DCAR functionality out of the box than any other previous version of Exchange Server.

What makes this space interesting is that many of these functions are being filled by a variety of solutions, include both on-premise and hosted solutions, often at a competitive price. Also interesting is the tension between Microsoft's view of how to manage messaging data in the Exchange Server organization versus the defined needs of many organizations to control information across multiple applications. More than ever, no solution will be one-size-fits-all; before accepting any vendor's assurance that their product will meet your needs, first make sure that you understand the precise problems you're trying to solve (instead of just the set of technology buzzwords that you may have been told will be your magic bullet) and know how their functionality will address the real needs.

WHERE JOURNALING FITS INTO DCAR

In our discussion of DCAR, we deliberately left out a common keyword that you inevitably hear about. *Journaling* is a common technology that gets mentioned whenever compliance, archival, and discovery are discussed. However, it often gets over-discussed. Journaling is not the end goal; it's simply a mechanism for getting data out of Exchange Server into some other system that provides the specific function that you really want or need.

Very simply, journaling allows Exchange Server administrators to designate a subset of messaging data that will automatically be duplicated into a *journal report* and sent to a third party—another mailbox in the Exchange Server organization, a stand-alone system in the organization, or even an external recipient, such as a hosted archival service. The journal report includes not only the exact, unaltered text of the original message but also additional details that the senders and recipients may not know, such as any BCC recipients, the specific SMTP envelope information used, or the full membership list and recipient distribution lists (as they existed at the time of message receipt). These reports are commonly used for one of two purposes: to capture data into some other system for archival or to provide a historical record for compliance purposes.

We don't know a single Exchange Server administrator who has ever come up to us and said, "I want to journal my data." Instead, they say, "I need to archive my data and I have to use journaling to get it to my archival solution." Journaling isn't the end goal; it's the means to the end. If journaling is a potential concern for you, you should stop and ask yourself why:

◆ What information am I trying to journal?

◆ What do I want the journaled information for?

◆ Perhaps most important, what am I going to do with the journaled information?

Understanding why you need journaling will give you the background you need to effectively design your Exchange Server organization, journaling requirements, and appropriate add-on applications and hosted solutions. It will also help you identify when journaling may not be the answer you need to solve the particular business problems you're facing.

You should also understand the impact that journaling will have on your system, as well as know what limitations journaling has. There are certain types of data that never get journaled, and if you need that data, you'll have to at a minimum supplement your solution with something that captures that data.

We will discuss Exchange Server 2013's journaling and archiving features in greater detail in Chapter 23, "Managing Transport, Data Loss Prevention, and Journaling Rules." For now, just be aware that they are merely tools that help you solve some other problem.

The Bottom Line

Distinguish between availability, backup and recovery, and disaster recovery. When it comes to keeping your Exchange Server 2013 deployment healthy, you have a lot of options provided out of the box. Knowing which problems they solve is critical to deploying them correctly.

Master It You have been asked to select a backup type that will back up all data once per week but on a daily basis will ensure that the server does not run out of transaction log disk space.

Determine the best option for disaster recovery. When creating your disaster-recovery plans for Exchange Server 2013, you have a variety of options to choose from. Exchange Server 2013 includes an improved ability to integrate with external systems that will widen your recovery possibilities.

Master It What are the different types of disaster recovery?

Distinguish between the different types of availability meant by the term *high availability*. The term *high availability* means different things to different people. When you design and deploy your Exchange Server 2013 solution, you need to be confident that everyone is designing for the same goals.

Master It What four types of availability are there?

Implement the four pillars of compliance and governance activities.   Ensuring that your Exchange Server 2013 organization meets your regular operational needs means thinking about the topics of compliance and governance within your organization.

Master It   What are the four pillars of compliance and governance as applied to a messaging system?

Chapter 4

Virtualizing Exchange Server 2013

Virtualization started as a technique for making better use of mainframe computer resources, but in the last decade it has made the jump to servers in the datacenter. While some organizations dabbled with virtualizing Exchange Server 2003 and 2007, Exchange Server virtualization matured with Exchange Server 2010. In this chapter, we will discuss virtualizing Microsoft Exchange Server 2013.

In this chapter, you will learn to:

◆ Evaluate the possible virtualization impacts

◆ Evaluate the existing Exchange environment

◆ Determine which roles to virtualize

Virtualization Overview

It is important to be clear what kind of virtualization is under discussion. The modern datacenter offers a number of virtualization strategies and technologies: platform virtualization, storage virtualization, network virtualization, and desktop virtualization. Although all of these can affect an Exchange deployment, Exchange virtualization usually refers to *platform virtualization*, also known as *hardware or host virtualization*. Platform virtualization gives you the ability to create multiple independent instances of operating systems on a single physical server. These virtual instances are treated as separate servers by the operating system but are assigned physical resources from the host system. The administrator configures the required amount of physical resources to each virtual machine. Here are some of the resources you can manage and present to your virtual machines:

◆ CPU sockets and cores

◆ RAM

◆ Storage interfaces

◆ Number and type of hard drives

◆ Network interface cards

Platform virtualization is one of the key technologies in the current datacenter trends to reduce power and cooling and deploy private cloud implementations. There are several types of platform virtualization, but the type used for Exchange is *hardware-assisted virtualization*, which uses a hypervisor to manage the physical host resources while minimizing the overhead of the virtualization solution. Depending on the solution used, the hypervisor can either be a full server operating system or a stripped-down minimalist kernel. Hypervisors do not provide emulation; the guest virtual machines provide the same processor architecture as the host server does. Modern hypervisors rely on specific instruction sets in the hardware processors designed to increase performance for virtual guests while decreasing hypervisor overhead.

There are compelling reasons to consider virtualization for your infrastructure, although not all situations or applications lend themselves equally to a positive virtualization experience. Some of these reasons will be covered a bit later in the chapter. You may even encounter both positive and negative experiences.

Technology continues to evolve, and we have seen great strides taken in the virtualization world over the past few years. Although there are multiple vendors in the virtualization game, VMware and Microsoft are at the top of the pile for virtualizing Exchange. These solutions provide the most rigorous and detailed guidance for successfully deploying Exchange on their virtualization solutions. Figure 4.1 gives a virtualization overview.

Terminology

Table 4.1 contains terms you need to be familiar with as you move through this chapter and the virtualization world.

FIGURE 4.1
A look at virtualization

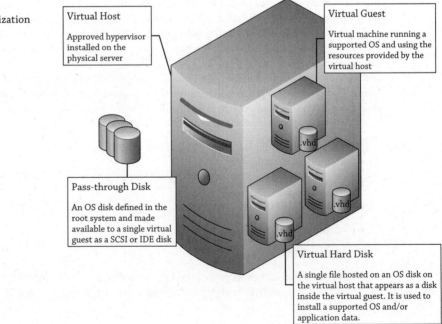

Virtual Host
Approved hypervisor installed on the physical server

Virtual Guest
Virtual machine running a supported OS and using the resources provided by the virtual host

Pass-through Disk
An OS disk defined in the root system and made available to a single virtual guest as a SCSI or IDE disk

Virtual Hard Disk
A single file hosted on an OS disk on the virtual host that appears as a disk inside the virtual guest. It is used to install a supported OS and/or application data.

TABLE 4.1: Virtualization terms

TERM	DEFINITION
Virtual host, Host, Root, Parent	The physical server that is running the virtualization product. This is the computer that is sharing its physical resources to the virtual guests.
Virtual guest, Guest	Virtual machine running a supported OS and using the resources provided by the virtual host.
Database availability group (DAG)	A group of Mailbox servers that host a set of databases and provide automatic database-level recovery from failures.
Pass-through disk, Raw disk mapping (RDM)	Virtual hard disks that are directly linked to unformatted volumes on the host server, whether on local disks or some sort of storage array. These disks hold the operating system, applications, and other data for the virtual guest.
Virtual hard disk (VHD)	Virtual hard disks that are stored as files on a formatted volume on the host server, whether on local disks or some sort of storage array. These disks hold the operating system, applications, and other data for the virtual guest.
Fixed VHD	A VHD whose underlying file on the host storage occupies its maximum size. For example, a 100GB fixed disk with only 25GB used in the guest will still use 100 GB on the host storage.
Dynamic VHD	A VHD whose underlying file on host storage occupies only the amount of space used in the guest. For example, a 100 GB dynamic VHD that is only 25 percent used in the guest will use only 25 GB on the host storage. There is a performance hit as the disk grows, and dynamic VHDs can be extremely fragmented in the file even when the logical structure inside the disk seems to be defragmented.
Differencing VHD	A multiple-part VHD, with a read-only fixed or dynamic VHD as the baseline, and a second VHD for all writes. New or updated disk blocks are written to the differencing VHD, not to the baseline VHD. Any changes can be rolled back to a previous state, and a baseline VHD can be used with many different differencing VHDs. These disks have significant performance penalties, for the increased level of I/O abstraction and CPU, as well as for the fragmentation in the differencing VHD file.

Understanding Virtualized Exchange

Exchange Server 2003 was the first version of Exchange that Microsoft officially supported under virtualization, although that support came late in the product's lifetime. Although customers had been virtualizing Exchange under VMware products for years, Microsoft's official support permitted Exchange Server 2003 to be run only under Microsoft's own Virtual Server product.

In 2008, Microsoft announced their new Server Virtualization Validation Program (SVVP). This program provides a central mechanism for on-premises and hosted virtualization providers to get their solutions validated in specific configurations. The SVVP allows Windows customers to get official Microsoft support for virtualized Windows servers and applications that are running on SVVP-certified virtualization configurations. Later the same year, Microsoft released their virtualization support statement for Exchange Server 2007 SP1 and later versions, building off of the baseline provided by the SVVP. This moved Exchange into the mainstream for applications that could take advantage of the benefits of virtualization.

Microsoft's support guidelines for virtualizing Exchange Server 2007 and Exchange Server 2010 have undergone many changes. Under the terms of the SVVP, Windows Server 2008 SP2 and Windows Server 2008 R2 were the only operating systems supported for virtual Exchange Server 2007 and 2010 deployments. Initially, the Unified Messaging role was not supported under virtualization, but an updated media component was introduced in Exchange Server 2010 SP1. At the same time, Microsoft relaxed some of their restrictions on the use of hypervisor availability features with Exchange. Now, with Exchange Server 2013, a lot of the guidance for previous versions no longer applies because of the changes in service architecture.

The support for Exchange is a constantly evolving story, especially after Cumulative Update packs are released. When in doubt, visit http://technet.microsoft.com/en-us/library/jj619301.aspx to view the latest version of Microsoft's guidelines and recommendations for virtualizing Exchange Server 2013. The virtualized instances of Exchange must still meet the basic Exchange requirements.

MICROSOFT RECOMMENDATIONS

Make sure you have read and are familiar with the "Exchange Server 2013 Virtualization" article at:

http://technet.microsoft.com/en-us/library/jj619301.aspx

The following hypervisor technologies are unsupported for use in your production Exchange Server 2013 servers:

◆ The use of hypervisors or hosting platforms that are not on the SVVP

◆ The use of file-level protocols (Network File System or Server Message Block—NFS or SMB) for storage pools used for Exchange VHDs or partitions

◆ Deploying on Windows Azure virtual machines

◆ Hypervisor snapshots of the Exchange virtual machines

◆ Differencing VHDs

◆ Host-based clustering and migration technologies that rely on saving Exchange virtual machine memory state to disk files

- Virtual-to-logical processor ratios greater than 2:1

- Any applications other than management software running on the hypervisor host

There is one exciting new change in these requirements involving the SMB 3.0 protocol, which is new in Windows Server 2012 and other modern storage solutions that license this protocol. Under SMB 3.0 (and SMB 3.0 *only*), you can configure your hypervisor environment to mount SMB 3.0 file shares and store fixed-length virtual hard drive files on those mounts; these virtual hard drives can then be used to store Exchange data. In this configuration, the new features of SMB 3.0 help ensure that the specific type and order of Exchange data writes are preserved all the way to the physical disks, removing the typical risk of data loss or corruption that is present when using other file-based protocols.

This change helps simplify storage requirements for virtual Exchange Server deployments, but only if all of the following conditions are met:

- Both the client (the hypervisor) and the storage solution (SAN, Windows Server 2012 server, or other device) support the SMB 3.0 protocol and are configured to use it.

- Both the client and storage solution are not configured to fall back to an earlier version of SMB.

- The SMB 3.0 file share is mounted by the hypervisor systems and not directly by the Exchange server.

- The Exchange data is stored on fixed-length (full-size) virtual hard drive files on the SMB 3.0 mount.

Understanding Your Exchange Environment

Before virtualizing your Exchange environment, you must define your current environment. The better you understand your environment, the more prepared you will be to define the virtualized environment. Here is some of the information you need to gather:

- Number of users

- User profiles

- Number of messages sent/received per day, per user

- Server CPU utilization

- Server memory utilization

- Server network utilization

- Database sizes

- Storage patterns

- Storage type

- Current high-availability model

- Concurrently connected users

◆ Number and types of clients accessing the system

◆ Exchange connectors

◆ Administration model

As you gather this information, you will be painting a picture of your Exchange environment. This information will be placed into various calculations throughout the process to ensure that you have done a complete evaluation before moving forward with virtualization. This information will have a significant impact on the Exchange system moving forward.

Each bit of the information you gather will add another piece to the puzzle. As you put the puzzle together, you will have a good idea whether virtualization will meet your needs. You also will be able to validate whether you will get the performance from the virtualized environment that your users require.

Effects of Virtualization

The popularity of virtualization in the datacenter is due to the many benefits it brings, both tangible and intangible. However, not all applications are created equal. While virtualizing Exchange Server is technically possible, there are a number of additional impacts and issues that you should consider.

Environmental Impact

For most organizations, the environmental impact is one of the major driving factors behind virtualization initiatives. The concept is simple: reduce the number of servers and reduce the amount of power. Active servers consume electricity and convert it to heat, indirectly consuming more electricity in the form of cooling systems. Consolidating underutilized servers and replacing older servers with less-efficient hardware can result in a significant amount of saved power. This number is a completely fluid number and is dependent on the environment that you want to virtualize. An organization with 100 servers will see a much different impact than a company with only 15 servers. However, an organization with 100 lightly loaded servers will likewise see a much different impact than a company with 100 heavily loaded servers.

Space Impact

Environmental impact is important, but server consolidation has an impact that may not be as immediately obvious: reduced rack space in the server room or datacenter. Not all organizations will feel this impact, depending on their choice of host hardware.

Organizations that pay for server hosting in a separate facility may find that paying attention to this area of impact can result in additional cost savings. These savings may include the following basic costs associated with hosting:

◆ Rack mounting space for the physical servers

◆ Power

◆ Network connectivity

◆ Cooling

There may also be optional costs associated with your servers, such as the following:

◆   Monitoring of the hardware

◆   Additional firewall capabilities

◆   Out-of-band access to the servers

By deploying powerful physical hardware running a hypervisor environment, you can increase your physical hosting costs in a predictable, building-block fashion, build virtual application servers without having to visit the datacenter, and still provide cost efficiency. Depending on the workload of the servers before you virtualized them, you may need to deploy larger servers, which may increase the per-server cost for the space. Be sure to do the math before deciding that this approach will save you money.

Complexity Impact

Many savings estimates overlook the additional complexity that a virtualized environment can bring to the table. Depending on the level of availability required, the additional host servers and networking gear required to provide clustering and spare capacity—as well as the higher class of hardware to provide redundant components within the host servers—can whittle away the initial estimated savings.

Once the virtual servers are deployed, complexity almost always strikes in the operational processes and technical operational skills of your staff. Having the additional hypervisor layers in the networking, storage, and server stack can drive up the time involved in keeping virtual Exchange Server 2013 servers operating. The additional layers of dependency can also bring down the expected SLAs for the Exchange services in the event of an outage and lengthen the time it takes to troubleshoot problems.

Virtual Exchange deployments can also get bit by the complexity bug when the designs do not adequately consider failure domains. Consider the impact of a failure of a host server and the corresponding virtual machines. Consider also the specific hypervisor features that cannot be used with Exchange, such as differencing disks, hypervisor snapshots, or file-level storage; determine the impact on the organization if those features are used with Exchange virtual machines and there is a problem. What features of Exchange, such as native data protection, are you going to be unable or less likely to use in a virtual deployment without offsetting the projected cost savings? Are these risks high enough to offset the value of virtualizing Exchange?

Additional Considerations

One of the ways companies are saving money is by virtualizing underused servers. By doing this, they reduce the power and cooling footprints that we have talked about. An underused server is thought to use less than 20 percent of its physical hardware. If your current Exchange environment has been sized properly, Exchange servers should not fall into the underused category.

This does not mean that you will not benefit from virtualizing Exchange; you need to do your research. For a good background on the impact virtualization can have, check out the white paper, "Comparing the Power Utilization of Native and Virtual Exchange Environments," available at http://technet.microsoft.com/en-us/library/dd901773.aspx. It was written for Exchange Server 2007, but the information is still applicable. The study shows a reduction of 50 percent in power utilization for the servers used in the study. The total power reduction for the servers and storage was between 34 and 37 percent depending on the storage solution.

🌐 **Real World Scenario**

ARE MY EXCHANGE SERVERS UNDERUTILIZED?

With stand-alone Exchange Server 2013 servers, the process to determine utilization is relatively simple: first, establish a baseline performance set by running the Windows Performance Monitor (PerfMon) for at least a week using a combination of common counters for processor, memory, disk, and network resources. Once this baseline is established, you can use it to compare current performance levels when experiencing issues to identify notable areas of change.

At the time of this writing no specific performance guidance has been published for Exchange Server 2013, but at some point Microsoft will likely provide specific counter and threshold guidance. Until then, use a combination of the counters for an Exchange Server 2010 multirole server combined with some common sense and healthy skepticism to establish your current server baseline. If any specific counter (other than RAM) averages above 60 percent utilization or has frequent spikes above that threshold, the server may be undersized or misconfigured.

One point to keep in mind is that DAG member Mailbox servers or Client Access servers in a load-balancing pool can't be directly measured. To ensure you accurately measure the load on these servers, take your measurements while they are running at the designed and expected maximum load. If your DAG is designed to lose two servers, then simulate the loss of two servers to perform your baseline measurement.

Hypervisor and storage vendors usually give specific guidance for virtualizing Exchange. Make sure you obtain, read, and understand this guidance to ensure that your virtual Exchange deployment will be successful throughout its life.

Virtualization Requirements

Just as with any software you deploy, there are hardware and software requirements that you need to meet when you virtualize.

Hardware Requirements

For the modern virtualization technologies, make sure that your hardware supports the proper level of virtualization. Most of the current market-leading servers do have the proper BIOS, motherboard, and CPU support, but older models may not support the specific CPU extensions or technologies required by the hypervisors you will need to run Exchange Server 2013 on Windows Server 2008 R2 or Windows Server 2012. If you are building a server from scratch, review the hardware requirements for the hypervisor you will be using to make sure the server you are building will perform the way you intend it to perform. Also make sure that you follow the reference processor and memory recommendations and server ratios that are posted on TechNet. These guidelines should always be your first stop for planning.

Know what servers will be virtualized. You will find that there are different pitfalls for the virtual host than you normally see with physical servers. Since you will be sharing the virtual host's physical resources, make sure that you have an idea what servers will be virtualized on the host, as well as what spare capacity the host will be expected to have and what virtual machines will be added to the workload during maintenance or outage. This will allow you to verify that you have enough RAM, processors, and network connections. Gather the physical requirements of each confirmed and provisional guest. Knowing what your guest virtual machines will need before you enter the planning stages for virtualization will put you in a better position for success.

Plan based on system resources.   No matter what workloads or how many servers you will be virtualizing, you need to plan. The virtual host will require resources before the virtual guests are even started. Once you have started the virtual machines, your resources can deplete very quickly. Make sure that you have enough system resources to go around and that you have some breathing room.

Plan for your virtual hosts to consume a CPU overhead of 5–10 percent. This will differ from installation to installation, but it is a good number to use when sizing your equipment and laying out your virtual guests. Try to validate your configuration in a lab (or by configuring your production hardware as a lab) before moving into production.

Plan based on storage requirements.   Knowing which workloads will be virtualized will also enable you to plan the proper storage for the virtual guests. Storage is a major design point for virtualizing Exchange. Exchange Server 2013 continues the trend of I/O improvements that favor disk capacity over disk performance. Virtual Exchange servers may have a significant amount of I/O overhead, depending on the specific storage options you have chosen; pass-through disks on local or iSCSI storage will have much lower overhead than VHDs. Begin your storage design with the Exchange storage calculator and size your storage appropriately; then use that as input for the calculators for your virtualization and storage solutions to ensure that you're meeting all expectations.

Make sure that you have properly partitioned your storage. You don't want to have spindle contention between your virtual host OS and the storage for your virtual guest OS or application data. For the majority of virtual workloads, you should have the underlying storage in a RAID configuration. The level of RAID that you choose is up to you and depends on the project requirements. However, if you are taking the option of using direct-attached storage on your virtual host to provide storage for Exchange mailbox databases in a DAG and you plan to take advantage of Exchange-native data protection, you may not need RAID.

When you are creating your virtual guest OS VHDs, or logical unit numbers (LUNs), include enough space for operation of the virtual machine, including space for updates, additional applications, and the page file. Use the following calculation to determine the minimum VHD size that will be needed for the virtual guest:

OS requirement + Virtual guest RAM = Minimum OS VHD size

For normal virtual workloads, the disk requirements should include space for the memory state file (such as the .VSV and .BIN files used in Hyper-V during Quick Migration and VM pause operations). However, Microsoft's support guidelines are very emphatic: *the use of disk-based memory states is not supported with virtual Exchange servers.*

Plan based on networking configuration.   In addition to the storage-capacity requirements, make sure you have the appropriate bandwidth for all your virtual guests to access your storage subsystem. Exchange Server 2013 storage should be fixed VHDs, pass-through, or iSCSI

LUNs. Microsoft recommends that you use pass-through disks or iSCSI LUNs to host the databases, transaction logs, and mail queues.

WHY CAN'T I USE NFS OR SMB?

One of the most commonly violated support guidelines for virtual Exchange deployments is the prohibition on file-level protocols in the storage stack. For some hypervisor deployments, such as VMware, it is very common to use network-attached storage or storage access networks (NAS or SAN storage) using NFS to provide the data stores used to hold virtual machine drives files. Often, the storage solution is entirely dedicated to the NFS partitions, and the entire virtual environment provisioning process is automated around building out the virtual machine disks (VMDKs). It's efficient, it's relatively inexpensive, and most importantly it's already working. Having to reclaim storage space only to carve it out as iSCSI LUNs or raw device mappings (RDMs) is a lot of work and will require a complete overhaul of the associated backup routines. You're already using VMDKs over NFS for all your other workloads. Why is it necessary to throw this big wrench in the works?

The answer is simple: you're putting your data at risk by lying to Exchange.

In order to maximize performance and keep your data safe, the Exchange storage engine has a very specific sequence of events for how it handles writes to disk. All writes to the database first must be written out to a transaction log file, and the updates to the various files and blocks have to happen in a very specific sequence or database corruption and data loss results. To make sure this happens, Exchange has to assume it's talking to the raw disk blocks; only by doing so can it ensure that all the data and metadata gets written to the disk in the correct order within the correct timeframe. Block-level protocols (iSCSI, FC, SATA/SAS, etc.) and pass-through disks can all make this guarantee. Even when write caching is in the mix (and it should be, using a proper battery backing), the caching controller is taking on the responsibility of ensuring the writes get committed to disk.

With file-level protocols, such as NFS and SMB (before SMB 3.0 when mounted by the hypervisor host), you don't have those same commitments. That's not to say that these protocols won't try to keep your data safe, because they do, but the ways they do it—and the features they provide, such as file locking and caching and disconnect time-outs—are very different than a block-level protocol would. As a result, Exchange is relying on one set of behaviors because it thinks it's talking to a physical disk, but by slipping NFS or SMB into the stack, you've silently changed those behaviors. The translations between the two work most of the time, but when they don't, the results can be amazingly destructive.

If you're going to deploy your Exchange VMs on file-level virtual hard disks, be smart. You can use these solutions for the base operating-system partition, but don't install Exchange on those drives. Instead, provision additional pass-through drives, RDMs, or block-level LUNs for your Exchange databases, logs, and binaries. Keep your Exchange data on volumes where it has a straight block-based path all the way back to the spindles. The data (and job) you save will be your own.

Make sure you have planned your network bandwidth. You are going to be sharing a limited number of physical network ports on your virtual host with your virtual guests. Depending on your virtual guest layout and requirements, you will exhaust your physical network ports in short order.

You may end up needing to install multiple quad-port network interface cards (NICs) to get the port density required to support your Exchange design. Keep in mind that you may need several NICs per virtual guest. Depending on the role of the server, there may be replication traffic as well as client traffic. For virtual hosts that will be hosting Exchange mailbox servers in a DAG, the replication NICs in the guests should not be bound to either of the following physical NIC types in the host:

◆ Any host NIC that connects to storage (such as iSCSI SANs)

◆ The host NICs bound to the primary guest client NICs

If you use NIC teaming on the host to increase bandwidth or provide availability, ensure that the teaming vendor supports the use of teamed NICs for virtualization in general and guest virtual networks that will be used with Exchange Server in particular.

Consider your physical server type.   You are not locked into one type of physical server for the virtual host. You can use a standard server, or you may choose to use blade servers. Blade servers require a bit more planning than standard servers. Since you are sharing resources before you start your virtualization, be sure you have carved out your disks, network traffic, and storage traffic adequately.

Software Requirements

Your software requirements for the host OS will differ depending on which hypervisor you have decided to use. Check with your hypervisor provider to ensure that you have all the required software before you begin. There are differences in the base OSs that may preclude you from loading any hypervisor without a complete reload of the server. Although this is not a huge deal, it is time consuming, and if you purchased the incorrect version, it is also expensive. Make sure that you know how many servers will be virtualized on the host servers as well. This may have an impact on what version of the OS you need to install to minimize the number of guest Windows licenses you need to purchase. Make certain that you have completed the virtual guest configuration before you start to load Exchange.

For the virtual guest, the software requirements and installation are straightforward. Once you have made the initial configurations for the virtual guest, load the appropriate Windows operating system for the designed Exchange roles. There are no requirements from a virtualization perspective as to which version of Windows you need to load as long as the version of hypervisor and Windows guest (virtual machine) are validated on the SVVP list. The guest OS will be driven by the business and technical requirements for the application and configuration you will be deploying. This is where your requirements-gathering will guide you to the correct OS and application versions. For example, if you are going to be using DAGs in your virtual guests, you must install the Standard version of Windows Server 2012 to ensure that the clustering components are available.

In addition to the normal requirements for Exchange servers, ensure that the latest hypervisor integration drivers are loaded. For Microsoft Hyper-V guests, the Hyper-V integration components are part of the base Windows OS and service packs, although if the version of Windows the Hyper-V hosts are running is newer than the version in the guests, you may need to install the additional Hyper-V integration components. The other hypervisor vendors all have their own integration components or guest toolkits to load.

Regardless of which hypervisor you are using, it is critically important to keep your guests up to date on the latest integration drivers. As your hosts are updated to newer versions and patch levels, ensure that all of the guests on the host (or cluster) are running the latest drivers before hosts are upgraded to the new version, especially if not all of the virtualization hosts in the cluster will be upgraded at the same time. Exchange can be extremely sensitive to mismatches between the integration drivers and the host version, with catastrophic impacts to performance.

Operations

Operations include many factors, such as the patching and monitoring of the OS and application, daily maintenance, and troubleshooting. A popular misconception is that your operating costs will magically decrease when you start to virtualize, while your uptime and service availability will frolic with unicorns and rainbows. The reality is that without careful planning and the creation of mature processes, the chances are good that your costs will actually increase, as will your downtime. The reason for this mismatch between expectations and reality is that adding virtualization brings more to the table than just the technology. To have a successful virtual Exchange deployment, you need not only technology but also processes and personnel.

Virtualization technology is mature, but most virtualization guidance makes the assumption that all applications are the same in terms of ignorance about the underlying hardware. Over the years, Microsoft has gone to a lot of trouble to make Exchange as reliable as it can and to ensure that if there is unavoidable data loss, it is as small as possible. The friction between Exchange's assumptions about the hardware stack and the widespread scalability best practices for virtual environments can create a combination where Exchange is less reliable.

Balancing the virtual guests' needs against the host's resources and the users' requirements can be a daunting task. Doing so for Exchange guests typically increases the complexity by creating Exchange-specific technology challenges. These challenges can all be solved at the technology level, but doing so requires additional cross-training for your staff and specific exceptions in your virtualization processes and policies.

The size of your IT organization and the number and location of servers will affect the cost of operations. If you have enough staff to learn the virtualization technology, there may not be a huge impact to the bottom line. If you don't have adequate staff, you will most likely be looking for additional personnel to support your virtualization efforts. When you virtualize your Exchange servers, you still have to take care of the guest Windows installation and the Exchange application as well as the hypervisor hosts and environment.

Virtual Exchange servers have 100 percent of the daily operational requirements that physical Exchange servers do. You still have to test and patch your systems. You still have systems that will experience issues, and you need to spend time troubleshooting. On top of that, you now have added the hypervisor layer. This layer may or may not be familiar to your support and engineering staff. You can't just reboot a virtual host because you feel that it is the best solution for a situation. You now have to expand your thought process to include the Exchange servers that are virtualized on that host and take these factors into consideration:

◆ What Exchange services will be affected by shutting down this host?

◆ Exchange virtual guests are on the virtual host, but how will the users be affected when they are shut down?

◆ Do the affected services have a redundant nature?

◆ Are the redundant services located on the same virtual host or on a different host? (If they are on the same virtual host, are they really redundant?)

Deciding What to Virtualize

No matter how many Exchange servers you plan to virtualize, you must do your research as you are planning the architecture for your environment. Plan your virtual guests just as though they are physical servers. Then include the additional overhead for the virtual host. Make sure that you are thinking about the end product that you will deliver to your users. Consider the possible differences between the physical and virtualized environment. Will your user base be as happy with a virtualized environment if it means a decrease in performance? If you set the expectations, size the environment appropriately, and test appropriately, there should not be a noticeable difference for your end users.

As with any architecture, things that you do can make positive or negative impacts. With Exchange Server 2007, Microsoft changed the Extensible Storage Engine (ESE) to allow Exchange Server 2007 to utilize as much RAM as needed to cache as much mailbox information as possible to drive down read I/O operations. In Exchange Server 2007 and Exchange Server 2010, the Exchange ESE—a monolithic Information Store process that handles all the databases on the server—uses all available physical memory in the system for this cache. If your server that has 16 GB of memory, you can expect that ESE will consume roughly 14 GB of it until other processes need the resources. At that point Exchange will not let go of that memory but will instead allow the operating system to place memory pages in the disk-based page file. With Exchange Server 2013, the ESE has been rewritten to spawn a separate process for each mailbox database on the server, completely changing how memory management works.

Understanding how these changes affect the behavior of the Exchange server allows you to properly plan and deploy virtual Exchange servers. You should know, for example, that using new or popular techniques like memory overallocation or dynamic memory allocation would be a bad match for Exchange servers—and in fact, neither is supported by Microsoft for Exchange. However, overallocation of CPU resources is supported up to a ratio of two virtual CPUs to every one physical CPU core. When looking at resource allocations, don't forget to plan for outages and ensure that having to move Exchange virtual machines in an emergency won't bump these allocations over the recommended numbers.

With Exchange Server 2013, you can support mixing native Exchange and hypervisor high-availability technologies, as long as you stay within the Microsoft support boundaries. You can deploy Exchange DAGs on virtual clusters and move active DAG members around using hypervisor migration technologies, as long as you avoid using technologies that write the current memory state of the Exchange guest to a disk-based file. These technologies are commonly used to enhance availability and even disaster recovery at the hypervisor level without requiring the virtual machine operating system or application to explicitly support them. These technologies include the following:

◆ Hyper-V's Live Migration and VMware's vMotion both transfer memory pages of an active virtual machine from the source host to the target using a direct network connection. These methods, and others like them on other SVVP-validated hypervisors, are supported for use with virtual Exchange machines because they ensure that the memory of the transitioned machines won't grow overly stale compared with the other DAG members or cause the store caches to get out of sync with the on-disk data.

◆ Hyper-V's Quick Migration, and other technologies like it, is not supported. Quick Migration writes the memory state to a disk-based file. This slows down the transition and puts the virtual machine at risk of having a mismatch between the machine memory and the state of the other DAG members or the database cache and data on disk.

◆ Virtual snapshots create a file-based dump of memory. If the machine is ever rolled back to this snapshot, the on-disk database data will be severely out of date. Permanent data loss could result. Using virtual snapshots and rolling back virtually, guarantees that you'll screw up your databases—and because Microsoft doesn't support virtual snapshots and rollbacks, you'll be on your own to clean up the mess.

◆ Technologies that bring up a failed virtual machine on another host, such as VMware's high availability, are supported as long as they bring up that new instance from a cold boot. But think carefully about whether you really want a failed Exchange server to come back up automatically without having a chance to analyze what's going on with it. In the worst-case scenario, you could have an Exchange server bouncing through the hosts in your virtual cluster, wreaking havoc on them.

◆ Technologies, such as VMware's Distributed Resources Scheduler and Hyper-V's integration with the System Center suite, have the capability to dynamically move virtual machines from one host to another to ensure resource utilization is balanced or stays within thresholds. This is a good capability in principle, but again, for Exchange servers this feature can create more problems than it solves. You should never allow multiple DAG members to be active on the same host; without careful management, these features can put your data at greater risk.

The introduction of DAGs makes it easier to plan for, configure, and maintain both high availability and site resilience in the Exchange application. Since DAGs are application-aware, your servers are always in control of any Exchange data. When in a DAG, the Exchange servers are in constant communication about the status of a database in the DAG; there should be minimal impact if a server or database goes down for any reason.

Exchange Roles

Previous versions (and service packs) of Exchange Server limited the roles you could virtualize. These limitations are gone with Exchange Server 2013; you can virtualize both the Mailbox and Client Access roles or even combine them into a single multirole virtualized server. With the latest generation of hypervisors permitting high-performance large-scale virtual machines, combined with the licensing and edition changes in Windows Server 2012, you should seriously consider deploying a smaller number of multirole Exchange Server 2013 servers. Doing so saves you overhead, licensing fees, and complexity, but you should balance this with the required level of redundancy.

However you deploy your roles, make sure to follow common-sense best-practice guidelines:

◆ Don't place two of the same role on the same virtual host, especially Mailbox servers in a DAG.

◆ In a virtual cluster, leave a host or two free of Exchange guests so you have the freedom to move Exchange virtual machines to respond to outages or emergencies.

◆ When planning capacity, don't forget to account for the impact of losing an Exchange guest. A Mailbox server that provides sufficient free headroom when the entire DAG is up and running may tip the host over to processor or memory overutilization when you take a DAG member down for patching.

Testing

As with any engineering effort, you need to make sure that you have a testing plan for the virtualized guests and host. Your plan needs to include testing all your virtual guests at the same time. One of the worst things you can do is to test only a single server at a time. Instead, test as close to real-world operating conditions as possible. Test the entire solution and not pieces of the solution. The solution should include any third-party applications that are in the environment, as well. Anything that you leave out of the testing cycle could come back to haunt you when you move to production.

Use the Microsoft Exchange–specific validation tools to test your configuration and ensure that you have all the settings properly dialed in. Jetstress, newly released for Exchange Server 2013 and downloadable from Microsoft Downloads, is one of the key tools used to test the performance of the disk subsystem before Exchange is installed in the virtual machines. The information that Jetstress gives you should line up with the performance requirements you gathered early in the project. Load Generator for Exchange Server 2010, also available for free from Microsoft Downloads, will simulate the different client connections that will be in your environment. You will be able to define how many simulated clients will use each connection protocol and how much email traffic they will send and receive. When using the testing tools, try to emulate the user base that is currently in the environment. If none of your users use Outlook Web App (OWA), then don't put OWA in the test cases. If your organization includes heavy users of Exchange ActiveSync, make sure that you have included the correct information to heavily test for Exchange ActiveSync. At the time of this writing, Load Generator has not yet been updated for Exchange Server 2013.

Remember: in the virtualized environment, you should do everything you would normally do in a physical environment. Don't fall into the trap of thinking that because it is a virtualized environment, it is a different solution. You are the only one who should know that these servers are virtualized. The end users and the first line of the help desk should never be able to tell the difference.

Possible Virtualization Scenarios

In this section we will look at several scenarios that could lead to a positive virtualization experience. These scenarios are not guarantees of success but examples of what *may* work. (Once you start testing your environment, you may find situations in which physical servers are the best solution.) We will discuss possible hardware for both the virtual host and the virtual guest, but this is just an estimation of hardware that may be needed; we will not be looking at the physical specifications. These scenarios have not been tested in a lab for performance. They are merely examples of what could be virtualized.

Small Office/Remote or Branch Office

In this scenario, our office has a relatively small number of users, and we need to provide email services to them. We have determined that users would be better off using local Exchange servers than pulling email across the WAN. Because the users are in a remote office, we will be supplying directory services as well. We want to provide redundancy and high availability where possible. By using a small number of physical hosts as a virtual cluster, we can deploy the necessary servers, keep costs down, and meet our availability requirements.

We have determined through research, interviews with staff members, and data collection that we have light email users. The Client Access server (CAS) and Mailbox roles will be combined, and we will be providing high availability via DAG. We also have a requirement for site resilience, so we will extend the DAG to the main datacenter.

As we start to build this solution, we must determine which virtual servers will be placed on which virtual hosts. We see a need for the following:

◆ Two multirole Exchange servers

◆ Two domain controllers

◆ A file server (which we can use as the file-share witness)

◆ A backup server

We can put this solution together with a minimum of two physical servers and storage, although for full redundancy—for patching, outages, and the like—we would want three. The exact specifications on the servers and storage are not being discussed. When we create the DAG, we will specify the correct location for the file-share witness. We must not create an issue where the file-share witness ends up being on the same virtual host as a Mailbox server in the DAG. If this were to happen and we created the file-share witness on Virtual Host 1 or 3, then we'd have two voting members of the DAG on the same physical hardware. This is not a recommended solution.

Virtual Host 1 will have the following virtual guests:

◆ Domain Controller 1

◆ Exchange 1

Virtual Host 2 will have the following virtual guests:

◆ Domain Controller 2

◆ File server

Virtual Host 3 will have the following virtual guests:

◆ Exchange 2

◆ Backup

With proper specifications, our physical servers will not be overutilized by the planned workloads; there will be enough spare capacity to ensure that virtual machines can be moved for short periods of time. Instead of having six servers in use, we will have three servers—a 50 percent reduction in servers for this location.

Site Resilience

In this scenario, we'll set up a second location for site resilience. We assume that the primary datacenter is fully functional with Exchange Server 2013 physical servers. We have been handed a new requirement to provide site resilience for all users in our organization. We will also need to provide the same level of performance and reliability as the primary datacenter. Our primary datacenter has four Mailbox servers in a DAG and four CAS roles.

To meet the requirements, we will be deploying 12 virtual guests: four domain controllers, four Mailbox servers, and four CAS roles. We are using four domain controllers to keep down the number of virtual processors and RAM on each domain controller.

We will need five physical servers for the solution. For ease of ordering, we will order all servers with the same hardware specifications. Since we have to provide the same level of performance as the primary datacenter, we will leave the CAS and Mailbox roles separated. If we didn't have to meet performance requirements for the primary datacenter, we could have combined the CAS and Mailbox roles and possibly met the performance needs on four physical servers.

Virtual Host 1 will have the following virtual guests:

- ◆ Domain Controller 1
- ◆ Mailbox Server 1

Virtual Host 2 will have the following virtual guests:

- ◆ Domain Controller 2
- ◆ Mailbox Server 2
- ◆ CAS role 1

Virtual Host 3 will have the following virtual guests:

- ◆ Domain Controller 3
- ◆ CAS role 2

Virtual Host 4 will have the following virtual guests:

- ◆ Domain Controller 4
- ◆ Mailbox Server 3
- ◆ CAS role 3

Virtual Host 5 will have the following virtual guests:

- ◆ Mailbox Server 4
- ◆ CAS role 4

In this scenario, we would manually place the file-share witness on CAS 2. You may recall that the file-share witness is used when there is an even number of servers in the DAG. We have that here, but there are enough servers to separate the witness without putting the DAG in jeopardy.

By separating the virtual guests across five virtual hosts, we have accomplished the task at hand. If we had chosen to mirror the production environment and use physical servers, we would have needed 12 servers. At a minimum, we cut our servers by 50 percent with the inclusion of the domain controllers. The flip side of this is that we probably increased the number of processors and amount of RAM in the virtual hosts. By doing this, we also increased the cost of the virtual hosts. The cost increase may be minimal, but you should calculate it before implementing this solution.

Mobile Access

For the mobile solution, we have a customer that must react quickly to an emergency. They need to have their entire infrastructure physically with them. They do not need to tie back into a corporate environment, but they will be connecting to the Internet and must be able to send and receive email and surf the Internet. They also require a database server, file/print capabilities, and collaboration. There will be an external appliance to provide firewall protection. This is also considered a short-term solution. Once the disaster is over or a permanent datacenter has been established, the mobile solution will be decommissioned. This solution brings in several different technologies in addition to Exchange.

The customer has only 50 users, but they will be sending and receiving a large amount of email. With this number of users, there will not be a huge draw on any of the servers. Knowing this, we are able minimize the server requirements. We can keep the file-share witness separated from the Mailbox servers. We will place a node of the database cluster on the same virtual host as one of the Mailbox servers. This is not a recommended solution for environments with higher requirements, but since we have a small number of users and low demand, we should be fine with the layout.

Virtual Host 1 will have the following virtual guests:

◆ Domain Controller 1

◆ Exchange Server 1

◆ Database Server Node 1

Virtual Host 2 will have the following virtual guests:

◆ Domain Controller 2

◆ Exchange Server 2

◆ Collaboration Server 2

Virtual Host 3 will have the following virtual guests:

◆ File and Print Node

◆ Database Server Node 2

◆ Collaboration Server 2

We are able to meet the requirements for the customer with only three physical servers. If during testing we decide that we need additional capacity, we can add another server or increase the specs on the existing servers. Looking at the numbers, you can see that we have decreased the number of servers from nine to three, which is a 66 percent reduction.

> ### 🌐 Real World Scenario
>
> #### VIRTUALIZE THE LAB
>
> You will plenty of opportunities to virtualize Exchange. One of those opportunities is in the lab. When you virtualize your lab, you can either do an equal virtualization to what is going to be in production, or you can have a different layout. There are benefits to both.
>
> If you are able to duplicate the lab and production, you can include performance testing. Duplicating the lab to production means not only matching the number of servers and role designations but also determining whether they will be physical servers. If you are going to virtualize in production, this test will give you accurate results and a baseline for the production environment. You will also increase the hardware requirement for the virtual hosts and the storage that you will be using.
>
> If you are not able to duplicate the lab, you must prepare yourself and management that the lab is for functional testing only. If you were to do any performance testing, the results would not be accurate. By using this method, you will save on hardware for the virtual hosts and storage.
>
> Both scenarios will give you a good base for testing your virtualized Exchange environment. One gives you the ability to test performance and functionality with an added hardware cost, while the other gives you the ability to do a functional test with minimal hardware costs.

The Bottom Line

Evaluate the possible virtualization impacts.   Knowing the impacts that virtualization can have will help you make the virtualization a success. Conversely, failure to realize how virtualization will impact your environment can end up making virtualization a poor choice.

   Master It   What kind of impact would virtualizing Exchange have in your environment?

Evaluate the existing Exchange environment.   Before you can determine the feasibility of a virtualized Exchange environment, you must know how your current systems are performing.

   Master It   Are your Exchange servers good candidates for virtualization?

Determine which roles to virtualize.   There will be times when virtualization of one or more roles is successful and times when it is not.

   Master It   Which roles will you virtualize?

Chapter 5

Introduction to PowerShell and the Exchange Management Shell

Microsoft PowerShell is an extensible, object-oriented command-line interface for the Windows operating system. The Exchange Management Shell (EMS) is a set of Exchange Server-specific extensions to Microsoft's PowerShell. The EMS was introduced with Exchange Server 2007 and has been further enhanced with Exchange Server 2013, including the ability to connect to remote sessions on other Exchange Server 2013 servers without the Exchange Management tools.

In this chapter, we introduce you to both PowerShell and the EMS. We hope to give you a basic idea of some of the capabilities and encourage you to learn more.

Is knowledge of the EMS required? Some administrators will manage their Exchange servers for years and rarely use the EMS, whereas others use it daily. However, we think it is safe to say that at least limited knowledge of the EMS will be required by all administrators because some specialized configuration options can be set only from the EMS.

We hope that this chapter will provide you with enough of an introduction to PowerShell that you won't dread getting to know it.

In this chapter, you will learn to:

- ◆ Use PowerShell command syntax

- ◆ Understand object-oriented use of PowerShell

- ◆ Employ tips and tricks to get more out of PowerShell

- ◆ Get help with using PowerShell

Why Use PowerShell?

Based on discussions in Internet newsgroups, web forums, and classrooms about the decision to put the management architecture of Exchange Server 2007 on top of PowerShell, you would think that this was one of the most controversial decisions that Microsoft has ever made. Indeed, there has been enthusiastic debate (and name-calling) on both sides of the fence. Some experienced Exchange Server administrators will tell you that the Exchange Management Shell is the best improvement Microsoft has made since Exchange Server 2003.

We have to admit to becoming big supporters of the EMS. All it took was spending a bit of time with it and getting to know some of the basic functionality. The biggest fear that many administrators have is that they will have to learn not only some of the shell's commands (called cmdlets) but also a scripting language just to manage Exchange Server 2013. That is not the case.

The intent of the EMS is to provide a consistent interface for performing management tasks for Exchange Server 2013 servers, whether performing automation tasks, writing scripts, or extending the management capabilities. Tasks or operations that once required multiple programming APIs and hundreds of lines of scripting can now be accomplished in a single command. Single commands can be joined together—the output of one command can be piped to another command as input—to perform extremely powerful functions.

The base PowerShell that ships with Windows Server 2012 provides more than 2,300 built-in cmdlets, and there are more than 700 additional Exchange Server–related cmdlets that you can use in the EMS; the goal is to cover all Exchange Server–related administrative tasks. You will find cmdlets that manipulate other data in Active Directory (such as, cmdlets for managing user accounts) and control Exchange Server–related data in the registry or Internet Information Services, but the cmdlets will only manipulate or manage data related to Exchange Server. The Exchange team is expecting other internal Microsoft teams, such as the Active Directory or Internet Information Server team, to provide their own extensions to the management shell.

There are a lot of very good reasons for Microsoft to create this management layer across all its products. It provides a consistent management and scripting interface for all server products, develops a secure method for remote scripting, improves batching, and provides you with an easy way to automate and repeat anything you can do in the GUI. In fact, PowerShell, first integrated in Exchange Server 2007 is now the de facto management interface for all Microsoft enterprise products, such as System Center 2012, SQL Server 2012, and Lync Server 2013.

Understanding the Command Syntax

The problem with a lot of scripting languages and command shells is that as they get more complex and powerful, the command syntax gets more and more cryptic. PowerShell and the EMS seek to make using the command-line interface and scripting more intuitive. To this end, most PowerShell and EMS cmdlets consist of two components: a verb and a noun.

JUST IN CASE

PowerShell cmdlets and the EMS extensions for PowerShell are case insensitive. That means that you can type everything in uppercase, type everything in lowercase, or mix and match the case of the letters in your commands.

For readability and per suggestions from folks on the Exchange Server team at Microsoft, we are using Pascal-casing in this book. When you use Pascal casing, the first character of each word is in uppercase; if the cmdlet has more than one word, the first letter in each word is in uppercase. All other letters in the cmdlet are lowercase. So the cmdlet that is used to retrieve mailbox statistics is written as `Get-MailboxStatistics`.

Verbs and Nouns

The verb identifies the action that is being taken, and the noun indicates the object on which the action is being taken. The verb always comes first, and the verb and noun are separated by a hyphen (such as, `Get-Mailbox`). The following list shows some of the common verbs you'll use in the EMS; some of these are specific to the EMS, but most are generic to Windows PowerShell.

Get   Get is probably the most common verb that you will use. Get retrieves information about the specified object and outputs information about the object.

Set   Set is probably the second most common verb that you will use. Set allows you to update properties of the object specified in the noun.

New   New creates new instances of the object specified in the noun.

Enable   Enable activates or enables a configuration on the object specified, such as enabling an existing user account.

Add   Add can be used to add items to an object or to add properties of an object.

Remove   Remove deletes an instance of the object specified in the noun.

Disable   Disable disables or deactivates the object specified in the noun. An example of this is removing a mailbox from an existing user (but not deleting the user account).

Mount   Mount is used to mount an Exchange Server 2013 mailbox or public folder database.

Dismount   Dismount is used to dismount an Exchange Server 2013 mailbox or public folder database.

Move   Move can be used to activate a database copy on a mailbox server.

Test   Test performs diagnostic tests against the object specified by the noun and the identity option.

Update   Update is used to update specified objects.

The actual nouns that are used in conjunction with these verbs are too numerous to mention in even a few pages of text. The following is a list of common nouns; later in this chapter you'll learn how to use the online help to find more cmdlets that you need. The nouns in this list can be used in conjunction with verbs, such as the ones in the preceding list, to manipulate the properties of Exchange Server–related objects. However, not all verbs work with all nouns, and unfortunately it sometimes requires some trial and error to determine what works and what doesn't.

ActiveSyncMailboxPolicy   Properties of ActiveSync policies that can be assigned to a mailbox

CASMailbox   Properties of a mailbox relating to client features such as OWA and Exchange ActiveSync

ClientAccessServer   Properties specific to an Exchange Server Client Access server role

DistributionGroup   Properties relating to mail-enabled distribution groups

DynamicDistributionGroup   Properties relating to a dynamic distribution group

EmailAddressPolicy   Properties relating to the policies that are used to define email addresses

ExchangeServer   Properties related to Exchange servers

Mailbox   Properties related to user mailboxes

MailboxDatabase   Properties related to mailbox databases

MailboxServer   Properties specific to an Exchange Server Mailbox server role

MailContact   Properties relating to mail-enabled contact objects

MailUser   Properties relating to a user that has an email address but not a mailbox

MoveRequest   Properties and actions related to move mailbox requests

ReceiveConnector   Properties relating to Receive connectors

SendConnector   Properties relating to Send connectors

TransportConfig   Properties specific to Exchange Server Transport services

UMMailbox   Properties relating to Unified Messaging

User   Properties relating to user objects

CMDLETS WORK ONLY WITH REMOTE POWERSHELL IN EXCHANGE SERVER 2013

One important thing to keep in mind with cmdlets is that they are not individual executables but rather .NET classes that are only accessible from within PowerShell and only if the Exchange Server extensions to PowerShell are loaded.

With Exchange Server 2013, though, you can connect to a remote session on a remote Exchange Server 2013 computer to perform commands on that remote computer. This is often referred to as *remote PowerShell*, or the ability to connect remotely to a PowerShell session. *Whether you use the shell to administer a local server or administer a server across the country, remote PowerShell is used to perform the operation in Exchange Server 2013.*

Unlike in Microsoft Exchange Server 2007, which uses a local Windows PowerShell, Windows PowerShell connects to the closest Exchange Server 2013 server using Windows Remote Management 3.0. The PowerShell module then performs authentication checks and then creates a remote session. When the remote session is created, the user sees and has access only to the cmdlets and the parameters associated with the management role groups and management roles assigned to the user.

Help

There is a more detailed section near the end of this chapter titled, "Getting Help"; however, as you start your journey into learning PowerShell and the EMS, you should know how to get quick and basic help. At any time you can use the `Get-Help` cmdlet to show what parameters any cmdlet takes. This is much like the `man` command on Linux systems:

```
Get-Help Get-Mailbox
```

The -Identity Parameter

For cmdlets that require input, usually the first parameter provided is the `-Identity` parameter. For example, if you want to retrieve information about a mailbox called Lawrence Cohen in the Corporate organizational unit (OU), you would type this:

```
Get-Mailbox -Identity 'Netlogon.com/Corporate/Lawrence Cohen'
```

However, you will quickly find that the `-Identity` parameter is not required. And, if your aliases or account names are unique, even the domain and organizational unit information is not required. For example, this command would yield the same result:

```
Get-Mailbox 'netlogon.com/Corporate/Lawrence Cohen'
```

As long as there is only one Lawrence Cohen in Active Directory, you can even drop the domain and the OU name and this cmdlet will yield the same result:

```
Get-Mailbox 'Lawrence Cohen'
```

YOU CAN QUOTE ME ON THAT

Anytime the identity you are using has a space in it, you must use quotes. Either single or double quotes will work as long as you are consistent.

The -Identity parameter is optional by design. As you will find shortly, the input for one cmdlet can even be piped in from the output of another cmdlet.

If you are not sure what input can be specified for the -Identity parameter, you can easily look up this information either in the Exchange Server online help or by using the EMS command-line help (more on this later in this chapter). For now, let's look at one small piece of the Get-Mailbox help screen that shows the different values that can be used to identify a mailbox:

```
-Identity <MailboxIdParameter>
    The Identity parameter identifies the mailbox. You can use one of the
following values:
      * GUID
      * Distinguished name (DN)
      * Domain\Account
      * User principal name (UPN)
      * LegacyExchangeDN
      * SmtpAddress
      * Alias
```

You can see that the -Identity parameter will take the mailbox GUID, the user's distinguished name, the domain name and account, the UPN name, the legacy Exchange Server distinguished name, the SMTP address, or the Exchange Server alias.

CMDLET VS. COMMAND

You will notice that sometimes we use "command" and sometimes we use "cmdlet" when talking about PowerShell. There is a subtle difference:

- ◆ A cmdlet is the verb-noun combination that performs a specific task; it is the base PowerShell object that takes input, does something to it, and produces some output.

- ◆ A complete command is the cmdlet along with any necessary options that the task might require. The command necessary to retrieve information about a specific mailbox looks like this:

```
Get-Mailbox "Gillian Katz"
```

Cmdlet Parameters

PowerShell and EMS cmdlets support a number of command-line parameters that are useful. Parameters can be categorized as mandatory or not and as positional or not. When a parameter is *mandatory*, PowerShell requires you to add the parameter with a given cmdlet and specify a value for it. If the use of a parameter is not mandatory, you are allowed to include it, but you don't have to. The cmdlet New-Mailbox illustrates this behavior nicely. When creating a new mailbox-enabled user, you have to include the parameter UserPrincipalName, but you are free to include the parameter OrganizationalUnit. The EMS will prompt you for the value of any mandatory parameter you forget to specify. Next to being mandatory or not, it is not always necessary to include the parameter name. When a parameter is *positional*, you can just add the value and leave out the parameter name. The cmdlet Get-Mailbox has no mandatory parameters but does have a positional parameter, namely -Identity. If we run the following EMS line, the shell will return the properties of a mailbox-enabled user whose Exchange alias is Oliver.Cohen:

```
Get-Mailbox Michael.Brown
```

Name	Alias	ServerName	ProhibitSendQuota
Oliver.Cohen	Oliver.Cohen	Ex1	unlimited

This is the same as running this:

```
Get-Mailbox -Identity Oliver.Cohen
```

Name	Alias	ServerName	ProhibitSendQuota
Oliver.Cohen	Oliver.Cohen	EX1	unlimited

However, if we run the following command, the shell will complain that it doesn't know any mailbox-enabled user by the name of Ex1, because the parameter Server is not positional:

```
Get-Mailbox Ex1
The operation couldn't be performed because object 'Ex1' couldn't be
found on 'dc01.netlogon.com'.
    + CategoryInfo    : NotSpecified: (:) [Get-Mailbox],
ManagementObjectNotFoundException
    + FullyQualifiedErrorId : 3FEDEA30,Microsoft.Exchange.Management.
RecipientTasks.GetMailbox
```

However, if you apply the proper -Server parameter in your command, the server name becomes apparent to the Exchange server.

```
Get-Mailbox -Server Ex1
```

Name	Alias	ServerName	ProhibitSendQuota
Administrator	Administrator	EX1	unlimited
DiscoverySearchMailbox...	DiscoverySearchMa...	EX1	unlimited
Clayton Kamiya	Clayton.Kamiya	EX1	unlimited

```
Jordan Chang          JordanChang        EX1        unlimited
Tyler M. Swartz       Tyler M. Swartz    EX1        unlimited
Anita Velez           AnitaVelez         EX1        unlimited
John Rodriguez        JohnRodriguez      EX1        unlimited
Jonathan Long         JonathanLong       EX1        unlimited
Kevin Wile            KevinWile          EX1        unlimited
John Park             JohnPark           EX1        unlimited
Julie R. Samante      JulieR.Samante     EX1        unlimited
Jim McBee             JimMcBee           EX1        unlimited
Chuck Swanson         ChuckSwanson       EX1        unlimited
Kelly Siu             KellySiu           EX1        unlimited
Gerald Nakata         GeraldNakata       EX1        unlimited
```

The following are some of the parameters that cmdlets accept. Not all cmdlets will accept all of these parameters; these are usually optional, and, of course, some of them will not be relevant.

-Identity   -Identity specifies a unique object on which the cmdlet is going to act. The -Identity parameter is a positional parameter, which means that it does not necessarily have to be on the command line; PowerShell will prompt you for the identity if it is not specified. As noted previously, in most cases you do not need to specify the -Identity parameter but just the unique object name.

-WhatIf   -WhatIf tells the cmdlet to simulate the action that the cmdlet would actually perform but not actually make the change.

-Confirm   -Confirm asks the cmdlet to prompt for confirmation prior to starting the action. This option type is Boolean, so you need to include either $True or $False. Some cmdlets (such as, New-MoveRequest-) ask for confirmation by default, so you could specify -Confirm:$False if you did not want the confirmation request to occur.

-Validate   -Validate will check the prerequisites of the cmdlet to verify that it will run correctly and let you know if the cmdlet will run successfully.

-Credential   -Credential allows you to specify alternate credentials when running a PowerShell command.

-DomainController   -DomainController allows you to specify the FQDN of a specific domain controller that you want to perform a PowerShell task against.

-ResultSize   The -ResultSize option allows you to specify a maximum number of results when working with Get- cmdlets.

-SortBy   The -SortBy option allows you to specify a sorting criteria when outputting data that is usually the result of a Get- cmdlet.

-Verbose   -Verbose instructs Get- cmdlets to return more information about the execution of the cmdlet.

-Debug   -Debug instructs the cmdlet to output more information and to proceed step-by-step through the process of performing a task. -Debug returns more information than a typical administrator needs to perform daily tasks.

If you are piping output of one cmdlet into another, the parameters must be within the cmdlet that you want the parameter to affect.

Tab Completion

In order to be descriptive and helpful, some of the cmdlets are pretty long. Consider if you had to type **Get-DistributionGroupMember** several times! However, PowerShell includes a feature called tab completion. If we type part of a command and then press the Tab key, PowerShell will complete the cmdlet with the first matching cmdlet it can find. For example, if we type **Get-Distri** and press Tab, PowerShell will automatically fill out Get-DistributionGroup. If we press Tab again, PowerShell will move on to the next matching cmdlet, or in this case Get-DistributionGroupMember.

The tab completion feature also works for cmdlet parameters. If you type a cmdlet followed by a space and a hyphen, such as **Get-Mailbox -**, and then press Tab, you will cycle through all the parameters for that particular cmdlet. When you include parameters with your cmdlet, it is not necessary to specify their full names. It is sufficient to enter enough letters to make sure the EMS can figure out which parameter you meant to define. For example, if you enter **Get-Mailbox -Se server1** you will be given a list of all mailboxes housed on server1. But tab completion can be useful to help you keep an overview of your EMS lines.

Alias

PowerShell and the EMS also include aliases that allow you to invoke cmdlets using a familiar synonym. A typical example here is entering **Dir** to get a list of all files in the directory that you are in and all subdirectories after that directory, which is in fact an alias for the cmdlet Get-ChildItem. Table 5.1 shows some common aliases that are built into PowerShell.

TABLE 5.1: PowerShell common aliases

ALIAS	DEFINITION
Dir	Get-ChildItem
Ls	Get-ChildItem
Type	Get-Content
Cat	Get-Content
Write	Write-Output
Echo	Write-Output
cd	Set-Location
sl	Set-Location
cls	Clear-Host

But it is important to remember that entering an alias in the end is like entering a cmdlet, thus imposing some constraints that do not apply when entering the aliases from Table 5.1 in a command prompt. If you would like to get a list of all files, and files located in subdirectories, you would be inclined to enter **dir /s**, but when doing so you will be faced with the following error message:

```
dir /s
Get-ChildItem : Cannot find path 'C:\s' because it does not exist.
At line:1 char:4
+ dir  <<<< /s
```

Using PowerShell, you know you need to include any parameter by adding a hyphen followed by the parameter name,

```
dir -Recurse:$True
```

or:

```
dir -r
```

Object-oriented Use of PowerShell

One of the reasons PowerShell is so flexible is that the output of commands is not text based but rather object based. PowerShell uses an object model that is based on the Microsoft .NET Framework. PowerShell cmdlets accept and return structured data. Don't let the terms "object model" or "object-oriented" scare you, though. This is really quite simple. For example, Figure 5.1 shows the output of the Get-Mailbox cmdlet.

FIGURE 5.1
Output of the Get-Mailbox cmdlet

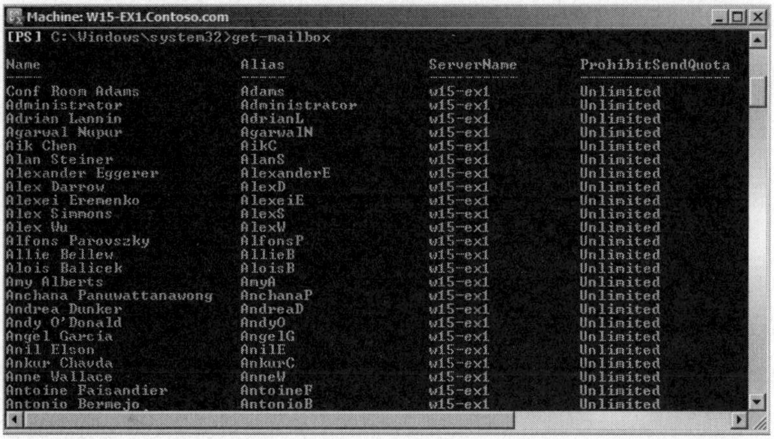

What you see on the screen is text to the user interface, but to PowerShell it is really a list of objects. You can manipulate the output to see the properties you want, filter the output, or pipe the output (the objects) to another cmdlet.

Filtering Output

In Figure 5.1, you can see that the cmdlet we used (Get-Mailbox) outputs every mailbox in the entire organization. There are a number of ways that you can filter or narrow the scope of the output that you are looking for from a specific cmdlet. In the case of Get-Mailbox and other cmdlets, you can specify just the identity of the mailbox that you are looking for.

PowerShell includes two options that can be used specifically for filtering the output. These are the Where-Object (or Where alias) and the Filter-Object (or Filter) objects. The Where clause can be used on most cmdlets and the filter is applied at the client. The Filter clause is available only on a subset of the commands because this filter is applied by the server.

In the following command, the output of the Get-Mailbox cmdlet is piped to the Where clause, which filters the output:

```
Get-Mailbox | Where-Object {$_.MaxSendSize -gt 25000000}
```

In this case, the output is any mailbox whose -MaxSendSize parameter is greater than 25,000,000 bytes. Did you notice the portion of the Where statement $_.MaxSendSize? The $_ portion represents the current object that is being piped to the Where-Object cmdlet, and .MaxSend Size represents the MaxSendSize property of that object.

For nonprogrammers, this might seem a little difficult at first, but we promise it gets much easier as you go along. The operators are also simple to remember. Table 5.2 shows common operators that can be used in clauses such as Where-Object or just the Where alias. The Operator column defines how the value defined as an object property is treated.

TABLE 5.2:   Shell values and operators

SHELL VALUE	OPERATOR	FUNCTION
-eq	Equals	The object.property value must match exactly the specified value.
-ne	Not equals	The object.property value must not match the specified value.
-gt	Greater than	-gt works when the object.property value is an integer.
-ge	Greater than or equal to	-ge works when the object.property value is an integer.
-lt	Less than	-lt works when the object.property value is an integer.
-le	Less than or equal to	-le works when the object.property value is an integer.
-like	Contains	-like is used when the object.property value is a text string. The matching string can either match exactly or contain wildcards (*) at the beginning or end of the string.
-notlike	Does not contain	-notlike is used when the object.property value is a text string and you want to see if the values do not match the string. The matching string can contain wildcards (*) at the beginning or end of the string.

Sometimes, finding all of the properties that can be used with a particular cmdlet can be difficult. There are a couple of tips that we would like to share that will help illustrate or discover these properties. Let's take the Set-Mailbox cmdlet as an example. First, you can simply use the available online help such as this:

```
set-mailbox -?


NAME
    Set-Mailbox

SYNOPSIS
    Use the Set-Mailbox cmdlet to modify the settings of an existing mailbox. You
can use this cmdlet for one mailbox
    at a time. To perform bulk management, you can pipeline the output of various
Get- cmdlets (for example, the
    Get-Mailbox or Get-User cmdlets) and configure several mailboxes in a single-
line command. You can also use the
    Set-Mailbox cmdlet in scripts.


SYNTAX
    Set-Mailbox -Identity <MailboxIdParameter> [-AcceptMessagesOnlyFrom
<MultiValuedProperty>]
    [-AcceptMessagesOnlyFromDLMembers <MultiValuedProperty>]
[-AcceptMessagesOnlyFromSendersOrMembers
    <MultiValuedProperty>] [-AddressBookPolicy
<AddressBookMailboxPolicyIdParameter>] [-Alias <String>]
    [-AntispamBypassEnabled <$true | $false>] [-ApplyMandatoryProperties
<SwitchParameter>] [-Arbitration
    <SwitchParameter>] [-ArbitrationMailbox <MailboxIdParameter>]
[-ArchiveDatabase <DatabaseIdParameter>]
    [-ArchiveDomain <SmtpDomain>] [-ArchiveName <MultiValuedProperty>]
[-ArchiveQuota <Unlimited>] [-ArchiveStatus
    <None | Active>] [-ArchiveWarningQuota <Unlimited>] [-AuditAdmin
<MultiValuedProperty>] [-AuditDelegate
    <MultiValuedProperty>] [-AuditEnabled <$true | $false>] [-AuditLogAgeLimit
<EnhancedTimeSpan>] [-AuditOwner
    <MultiValuedProperty>] [-BypassLiveId <SwitchParameter>]
[-BypassModerationFromSendersOrMembers
    <MultiValuedProperty>] [-CalendarLoggingQuota <Unlimited>]
[-CalendarRepairDisabled <$true | $false>]
    [-CalendarVersionStoreDisabled <$true | $false>] [-ClientExtensions <$true |
$false>] [-Confirm
    [<SwitchParameter>]] [-CreateDTMFMap <$true | $false>] [-CustomAttribute1
<String>] [-CustomAttribute10 <String>]
    [-CustomAttribute11 <String>] [-CustomAttribute12 <String>]
[-CustomAttribute13 <String>] [-CustomAttribute14
```

```
    <String>] [-CustomAttribute15 <String>] [-CustomAttribute2 <String>]
[-CustomAttribute3 <String>]
    [-CustomAttribute4 <String>] [-CustomAttribute5 <String>] [-CustomAttribute6
<String>] [-CustomAttribute7
    <String>] [-CustomAttribute8 <String>] [-CustomAttribute9 <String>]
[-Database <DatabaseIdParameter>]
    [-DefaultPublicFolderMailbox <MailboxIdParameter>]
[-DeliverToMailboxAndForward <$true | $false>] [-DisplayName
    <String>] [-DomainController <Fqdn>] [-DowngradeHighPriorityMessagesEnabled
<$true | $false>] [-EmailAddresses
    <ProxyAddressCollection>] [-EmailAddressPolicyEnabled <$true | $false>]
[-EndDateForRetentionHold <DateTime>]
    [-EvjctLiveId <SwitchParameter>] [-ExtensionCustomAttribute1
<MultiValuedProperty>] [-ExtensionCustomAttribute2
    <MultiValuedProperty>] [-ExtensionCustomAttribute3 <MultiValuedProperty>]
[-ExtensionCustomAttribute4
    <MultiValuedProperty>] [-ExtensionCustomAttribute5 <MultiValuedProperty>]
[-ExternalOofOptions <InternalOnly |
    External>] [-FederatedIdentity <String>] [-Force <SwitchParameter>]
[-ForwardingAddress <RecipientIdParameter>]
    [-ForwardingSmtpAddress <ProxyAddress>] [-GMGen <$true | $false>]
[-GrantSendOnBehalfTo <MultiValuedProperty>]
    [-HiddenFromAddressListsEnabled <$true | $false>] [-IgnoreDefaultScope
<SwitchParameter>] [-ImmutableId <String>]
    [-IssueWarningQuota <Unlimited>] [-Languages <MultiValuedProperty>]
[-LinkedCredential <PSCredential>]
    [-LinkedDomainController <String>] [-LinkedMasterAccount <UserIdParameter>]
[-LitigationHoldDate <DateTime>]
    [-LitigationHoldDuration <Unlimited>] [-LitigationHoldEnabled <$true |
$false>] [-LitigationHoldOwner <String>]
    [-MailboxPlan <MailboxPlanIdParameter>] [-MailRouting <$true | $false>]
[-MailTip <String>] [-MailTipTranslations
    <MultiValuedProperty>] [-ManagedFolderMailboxPolicy
<MailboxPolicyIdParameter>]
    [-ManagedFolderMailboxPolicyAllowed <SwitchParameter>] [-Management <$true |
$false>] [-MaxBlockedSenders <Int32>]
    [-MaxReceiveSize <Unlimited>] [-MaxSafeSenders <Int32>] [-MaxSendSize
<Unlimited>]
    [-MessageTrackingReadStatusEnabled <$true | $false>]
[-MicrosoftOnlineServicesID <SmtpAddress>] [-ModeratedBy
    <MultiValuedProperty>] [-ModerationEnabled <$true | $false>] [-Name <String>]
[-NetID <NetID>] [-OABGen <$true |
    $false>] [-Office <String>] [-OfflineAddressBook
<OfflineAddressBookIdParameter>] [-OldPassword <SecureString>]
    [-Password <SecureString>] [-PrimarySmtpAddress <SmtpAddress>]
[-ProhibitSendQuota <Unlimited>]
    [-ProhibitSendReceiveQuota <Unlimited>] [-PublicFolder <SwitchParameter>]
[-QueryBaseDN
```

```
    <OrganizationalUnitIdParameter>] [-QueryBaseDNRestrictionEnabled <$true |
$false>] [-RecipientLimits <Unlimited>]
    [-RecoverableItemsQuota <Unlimited>] [-RecoverableItemsWarningQuota
<Unlimited>] [-RejectMessagesFrom
    <MultiValuedProperty>] [-RejectMessagesFromDLMembers <MultiValuedProperty>]
[-RejectMessagesFromSendersOrMembers
    <MultiValuedProperty>] [-RemoteAccountPolicy
<RemoteAccountPolicyIdParameter>] [-RemoteRecipientType <None |
    ProvisionMailbox | ProvisionArchive | Migrated | DeprovisionMailbox |
DeprovisionArchive | RoomMailbox |
    EquipmentMailbox | SharedMailbox | TeamMailbox>]
[-RemoveManagedFolderAndPolicy <SwitchParameter>] [-RemovePicture
    <SwitchParameter>] [-RemoveSpokenName <SwitchParameter>] [-RequireSecretQA
<$true | $false>]
    [-RequireSenderAuthenticationEnabled <$true | $false>]
[-ResetPasswordOnNextLogon <$true | $false>]
    [-ResourceCapacity <Int32>] [-ResourceCustom <MultiValuedProperty>]
[-RetainDeletedItemsFor <EnhancedTimeSpan>]
    [-RetainDeletedItemsUntilBackup <$true | $false>] [-RetentionComment
<String>] [-RetentionHoldEnabled <$true |
    $false>] [-RetentionPolicy <MailboxPolicyIdParameter>] [-RetentionUrl
<String>] [-RoleAssignmentPolicy
    <MailboxPolicyIdParameter>] [-RulesQuota <ByteQuantifiedSize>]
[-SamAccountName <String>] [-SCLDeleteEnabled
    <$true | $false>] [-SCLDeleteThreshold <Int32>] [-SCLJunkEnabled <$true |
$false>] [-SCLJunkThreshold <Int32>]
    [-SCLQuarantineEnabled <$true | $false>] [-SCLQuarantineThreshold <Int32>]
[-SCLRejectEnabled <$true | $false>]
    [-SCLRejectThreshold <Int32>] [-SecondaryAddress <String>]
[-SecondaryDialPlan <UMDialPlanIdParameter>]
    [-SendModerationNotifications <Never | Internal | Always>] [-SharingPolicy
<SharingPolicyIdParameter>]
    [-SimpleDisplayName <String>] [-SingleItemRecoveryEnabled <$true | $false>]
[-SKUAssigned <$true | $false>]
    [-SKUCapability <None | BPOS_S_Deskless | BPOS_S_Standard | BPOS_S_Enterprise
| BPOS_S_Archive | BPOS_L_Standard |
    BPOS_B_Standard | BPOS_B_CustomDomain | TOU_Signed | FederatedUser | Partner_
Managed | MasteredOnPremise |
    ResourceMailbox | ExcludedFromBackSync | UMFeatureRestricted |
RichCoexistence | OrganizationCapabilityUMGrammar |
    OrganizationCapabilityUMDataStorage | OrganizationCapabilityOABGen |
OrganizationCapabilityGMGen |
    OrganizationCapabilityClientExtensions | BEVDirLockdown |
OrganizationCapabilityUMGrammarReady |
    OrganizationCapabilityMailRouting | OrganizationCapabilityManagement |
OrganizationCapabilityTenantUpgrade>]
    [-StartDateForRetentionHold <DateTime>] [-TenantUpgrade <$true | $false>]
[-ThrottlingPolicy
```

```
        <ThrottlingPolicyIdParameter>] [-Type <Regular | Room | Equipment | Shared>]
[-UMDataStorage <$true | $false>]
        [-UMDtmfMap <MultiValuedProperty>] [-UMGrammar <$true | $false>]
[-UsageLocation <CountryInfo>]
        [-UseDatabaseQuotaDefaults <$true | $false>] [-UseDatabaseRetentionDefaults
<$true | $false>] [-UserCertificate
        <MultiValuedProperty>] [-UserPrincipalName <String>] [-UserSMimeCertificate
<MultiValuedProperty>] [-WhatIf
        [<SwitchParameter>]] [-WindowsEmailAddress <SmtpAddress>] [-WindowsLiveID
<SmtpAddress>] [<CommonParameters>]
```

```
DESCRIPTION
    You need to be assigned permissions before you can run this cmdlet. Although
all parameters for this cmdlet are
    listed in this topic, you may not have access to some parameters if they're
not included in the permissions
    assigned to you. To see what permissions you need, see the "Recipient
Provisioning Permissions" section in the
    Recipients permissions topic.
```

```
RELATED LINKS
    Online Version http://technet.microsoft.com/EN-US/library/a0d413b9-d949-4df6-
ba96-ac0906dedae2(EXCHG.150).aspx
```

```
REMARKS
    To see the examples, type: "get-help Set-Mailbox -examples".
    For more information, type: "get-help Set-Mailbox -detailed".
    For technical information, type: "get-help Set-Mailbox -full".
    For online help, type: "get-help Set-Mailbox -online"
```

The Set-Mailbox -? command generates a lot of output to the screen, and it is compressed into a hard-to-read format. Since the Set-Mailbox cmdlet is manipulating the same object as the Get-Mailbox cmdlet, you could also use the following command to view all the properties that have been set on a particular mailbox (Oliver.Cohen in this example):

```
Get-Mailbox Oliver.Cohen | Format-List
```

```
RunspaceId                        : 0e354b66-d0e3-431b-8a54-2d1d1cf21a8b
Database                          : MDB01
UseDatabaseRetentionDefaults      : True
RetainDeletedItemsUntilBackup     : False
DeliverToMailboxAndForward        : False
LitigationHoldEnabled             : False
SingleItemRecoveryEnabled         : False
```

```
RetentionHoldEnabled                  : False
EndDateForRetentionHold               :
StartDateForRetentionHold             :
RetentionComment                      :
RetentionUrl                          :
LitigationHoldDate                    :
LitigationHoldOwner                   :
ManagedFolderMailboxPolicy            :
RetentionPolicy                       :
AddressBookPolicy                     :
CalendarRepairDisabled                : False
ExchangeGuid                          : f90babd1-abc9-4795-80f2-91495908b37e
ExchangeSecurityDescriptor            : System.Security.AccessControl.Raw
                                        SecurityDescriptor
ExchangeUserAccountControl            : None
AdminDisplayVersion                   : Version 15.0 (Build 466.6)
MessageTrackingReadStatusEnabled      : True
ExternalOofOptions                    : External
ForwardingAddress                     :
ForwardingSmtpAddress                 :
RetainDeletedItemsFor                 : 14.00:00:00
IsMailboxEnabled                      : True
Languages                             : {}
OfflineAddressBook                    :
ProhibitSendQuota                     : Unlimited
ProhibitSendReceiveQuota              : Unlimited
RecoverableItemsQuota                 : Unlimited
RecoverableItemsWarningQuota          : Unlimited
CalendarLoggingQuota                  : Unlimited
DowngradeHighPriorityMessagesEnabled  : False
ProtocolSettings                      : {}
RecipientLimits                       : Unlimited
IsResource                            : False
IsLinked                              : False
IsShared                              : False
IsRootPublicFolderMailbox             : False
LinkedMasterAccount                   :
ResetPasswordOnNextLogon              : False
ResourceCapacity                      :
ResourceCustom                        : {}
ResourceType                          :
SamAccountName                        : OliverC
SCLDeleteThreshold                    :
SCLDeleteEnabled                      :
SCLRejectThreshold                    :
SCLRejectEnabled                      :
SCLQuarantineThreshold                :
```

```
SCLQuarantineEnabled                 :
SCLJunkThreshold                     :
SCLJunkEnabled                       :
AntispamBypassEnabled                : False
ServerLegacyDN                       : /o=First Organization/ou=Exchange
Administrative Group
(FYDIBOHF23SPDLT)/cn=Configuration/cn=Servers/cn=EX1
ServerName                           : EX1
UseDatabaseQuotaDefaults             : True
IssueWarningQuota                    : Unlimited
RulesQuota                           : 64 KB (65,536 bytes)
Office                               : 16/112
UserPrincipalName                    : OliverC@netlogon.com
UMEnabled                            : True
MaxSafeSenders                       :
MaxBlockedSenders                    :
ReconciliationId                     :
WindowsLiveID                        :
MicrosoftOnlineServicesID            :
ThrottlingPolicy                     :
RoleAssignmentPolicy                 : Default Role Assignment Policy
DefaultPublicFolderMailbox           :
SharingPolicy                        : Default Sharing Policy
RemoteAccountPolicy                  :
MailboxPlan                          :
ArchiveDatabase                      :
ArchiveGuid                          : 00000000-0000-0000-0000-000000000000
ArchiveName                          : {}
ArchiveQuota                         : Unlimited
ArchiveWarningQuota                  : Unlimited
ArchiveDomain                        :
ArchiveStatus                        : None
ArchiveState                         : None
RemoteRecipientType                  : None
DisabledArchiveDatabase              :
DisabledArchiveGuid                  : 00000000-0000-0000-0000-000000000000
QueryBaseDN                          :
QueryBaseDNRestrictionEnabled        : False
MailboxMoveTargetMDB                 :
MailboxMoveSourceMDB                 :
MailboxMoveFlags                     : None
MailboxMoveRemoteHostName            :
MailboxMoveBatchName                 :
MailboxMoveStatus                    : None
MailboxRelease                       :
ArchiveRelease                       :
```

```
IsPersonToPersonTextMessagingEnabled   : False
IsMachineToPersonTextMessagingEnabled  : True
UserSMimeCertificate                   : {}
UserCertificate                        : {}
CalendarVersionStoreDisabled           : False
ImmutableId                            :
PersistedCapabilities                  : {}
SKUAssigned                            :
AuditEnabled                           : False
AuditLogAgeLimit                       : 90.00:00:00
AuditAdmin                             : {Update, Move, MoveToDeletedItems,
SoftDelete, HardDelete, FolderBind,
                                         SendAs, SendOnBehalf, Create}
AuditDelegate                          : {Update, SoftDelete, HardDelete, SendAs,
Create}
AuditOwner                             : {}
WhenMailboxCreated                     : 6/28/2012 6:29:43 AM
Usage                          :
IsSoftDeletedByRemove                  : False
IsSoftDeletedByDisable                 : False
IncludeInGarbageCollection             : False
WhenSoftDeleted                        :
InPlaceHolds                           : {}
Extensions                             : {52238, OliverC@netlogon.com}
HasPicture                             : True
HasSpokenName                          : False
AcceptMessagesOnlyFrom                 : {}
AcceptMessagesOnlyFromDLMembers        : {}
AcceptMessagesOnlyFromSendersOrMembers : {}
AddressListMembership                  : {\Mailboxes(VLV), \All Mailboxes(VLV), \
All Recipients(VLV), \Default Global
                                         Address List, \All Users}
Alias                                  : OliverC
ArbitrationMailbox                     :
BypassModerationFromSendersOrMembers   : {}
OrganizationalUnit                     : netlogon.com/Domain Users
CustomAttribute1                       :
CustomAttribute10                      :
CustomAttribute11                      :
CustomAttribute12                      :
CustomAttribute13                      :
CustomAttribute14                      :
CustomAttribute15                      :
CustomAttribute2                       :
CustomAttribute3                       :
CustomAttribute4                       :
CustomAttribute5                       :
```

```
CustomAttribute6                        :
CustomAttribute7                        :
CustomAttribute8                        :
CustomAttribute9                        :
ExtensionCustomAttribute1               : {}
ExtensionCustomAttribute2               : {}
ExtensionCustomAttribute3               : {}
ExtensionCustomAttribute4               : {}
ExtensionCustomAttribute5               : {}
DisplayName                             : Oliver Cohen
EmailAddresses                          : {eum:52238;phone-context=myExDP.
netlogon.com,

                                          EUM:oliverc@netlogon.com;phone-
context=myExDP.netlogon.com,

                                          SMTP:oliverc@netlogon.com}
GrantSendOnBehalfTo                     : {}
ExternalDirectoryObjectId               :
HiddenFromAddressListsEnabled           : False
LastExchangeChangedTime                 :
LegacyExchangeDN                        : /o=First Organization/ou=Exchange
Administrative Group
(FYDIBOHF23SPDLT)/cn=Recipients/cn=f1e9a9f8cb614b6ea3d6d902e2ffff7c-oliver
MaxSendSize                             : Unlimited
MaxReceiveSize                          : Unlimited
ModeratedBy                             : {}
ModerationEnabled                       : False
PoliciesIncluded                        : {8a8da36c-4784-4ffb-8112-97ae37386e06,
{26491cfc-9e50-4857-861b-0cb8df22b5d7}}
PoliciesExcluded                        : {}
EmailAddressPolicyEnabled               : True
PrimarySmtpAddress                      : oliverc@netlogon.com
RecipientType                           : UserMailbox
RecipientTypeDetails                    : UserMailbox
RejectMessagesFrom                      : {}
RejectMessagesFromDLMembers             : {}
RejectMessagesFromSendersOrMembers      : {}
RequireSenderAuthenticationEnabled      : False
SimpleDisplayName                       :
SendModerationNotifications             : Always
UMDtmfMap                               : {reversedPhone:21105550841+,
emailAddress:936395,

                                          lastNameFirstName:524693639,
firstNameLastName:936395246}
WindowsEmailAddress                     : oliverc@netlogon.com
MailTip                                 :
MailTipTranslations                     : {}
```

```
PartnerObjectId                : 00000000-0000-0000-0000-000000000000
Identity                       : Contoso.com/Domain Users/Oliver Cohen
IsValid                        : True
ExchangeVersion                : 0.20 (15.0.0.0)
Name                           : Oliver Cohen
DistinguishedName              : CN=OliverCohen,OU=Domain
Users,DC=netlogon,DC=com
Guid                           : f6e99cf0-9a6a-4232-b857-af26269da3ae
ObjectCategory                 : netlogon.com/Configuration/Schema/Person
ObjectClass                    : {top, person, organizationalPerson, user}
WhenChanged                    : 6/28/2012 6:37:53 AM
WhenCreated                    : 2/13/2012 5:16:20 PM
WhenChangedUTC                 : 6/28/2012 1:37:53 PM
WhenCreatedUTC                 : 2/14/2012 1:16:20 AM
OrganizationId                 :
OriginatingServer              : EX1.netlogon.com
ObjectState                    : Unchanged
```

Note that some of the properties you see as a result of a Get- cmdlet cannot be set since they are system-controlled properties or they are manipulated using other cmdlets, such as ExchangeGuid or Database.

The third way to view all of the properties associated with an object is to simply use the Get-Member cmdlet. Here is an example where the Get-Mailbox cmdlet pipes its output to the Get-Member cmdlet and filters only the members that are properties. The output is a partial listing only, since a full listing would include a few pages of information you can easily look up yourself and will provide little value to this discussion:

```
Get-Mailbox | Get-Member -MemberType Property


    TypeName: Microsoft.Exchange.Data.Directory.Management.Mailbox


Name                        MemberType Definition
----                        ---------- ----------
AcceptMessagesOnlyFrom          Property
Microsoft.Exchange.Data.MultiValuedProperty'1[[Microsoft.Exchange....
AcceptMessagesOnlyFromDLMembers Property
Microsoft.Exchange.Data.MultiValuedProperty'1[[Microsoft.Exchange....
AddressListMembership           Property
Microsoft.Exchange.Data.MultiValuedProperty'1[[Microsoft.Exchange....
Alias                           Property    System.String Alias
{get;set;}
{get;set;}
ArbitrationMailbox              Property    Microsoft.Exchange.Data.Directory
ArbitrationMailbox {g...
ArchiveGuid                     Property    System.Guid ArchiveGuid {get;}
ArchiveName                     Property
Microsoft.Exchange.Data.MultiValuedProperty'1[[System.String, msco...
```

```
ArchiveQuota                    Property
Microsoft.Exchange.Data.Unlimited'1[[Microsoft.Exchange.Data.ByteQ...
ArchiveWarningQuota             Property
Microsoft.Exchange.Data.Unlimited'1[[Microsoft.Exchange.Data.ByteQ...
BypassModerationFromSendersOrMembersProperty
Microsoft.Exchange.Data.MultiValuedProperty'1[[Microsoft.Exchange....
CalendarRepairDisabled          Property   System.Boolean
CalendarRepairDisabled {get;set;}
CalendarVersionStoreDisabled    Property   System.Boolean
CalendarVersionStoreDisabled {get;set;}
CustomAttribute1                Property   System.String CustomAttribute1
{get;set;}
CustomAttribute10               Property   System.String CustomAttribute10
{get;set;}
CustomAttribute11               Property   System.String CustomAttribute11
{get;set;}
CustomAttribute12               Property   System.String CustomAttribute12
{get;set;}
CustomAttribute13               Property   System.String CustomAttribute13
{get;set;}
CustomAttribute14               Property   System.String CustomAttribute14
{get;set;}
```

Formatting Output

If you look at the output of the Get-Mailbox cmdlet shown in Figure 5.1, you might be tempted to think that the output capabilities of PowerShell are limited, but this is far from the truth. The output shown in Figure 5.1 was the default output for the Get-Mailbox cmdlet. The programmer decided that the output should be in a formatted table with the Name, Alias, ServerName, and ProhibitSendQuota properties as columns. However, you can select the properties you want by merely piping the output of the Get-Mailbox cmdlet to either the Format-Table (FT for short) or Select cmdlet:

```
Get-Mailbox | FT Name,ProhibitSendQuota,ProhibitSendReceiveQuota
```

Figure 5.2 shows the output of the preceding command.

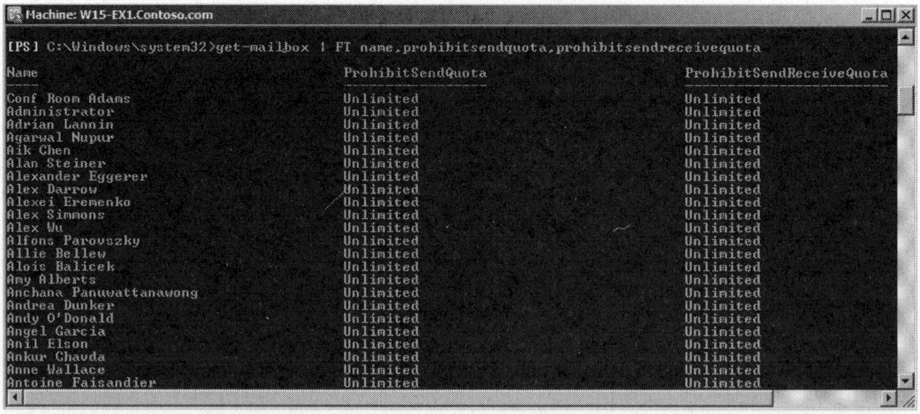

FIGURE 5.2
Formatting output into a formatted table

The output of the Get-Mailbox cmdlet was directed to the Format-Table or FT cmdlet; the result was columns for the Name, ProhibitSendQuota, and ProhibitSendReceiveQuota limits.

You may be wondering how you can learn all the properties of an object. The default output of the Get-Mailbox cmdlet, for example, is probably not the most useful for your organization. We discuss getting help in PowerShell and the Exchange Management Shell later in this chapter, but here is a simple trick to see all the properties of an object: just direct the output of a Get-cmdlet to the Format-List (FL for short) cmdlet instead of the default Format-Table cmdlet.

When you direct the output of a cmdlet, such as Get-Mailbox to the Format-List cmdlet, you will see *all* the properties for that object. Figure 5.3 shows an example where we have directed the output of a Get-Mailbox cmdlet to the FL (Format-List) cmdlet. You will notice in Figure 5.3 that the properties filled up more than one screen. However, you will find that outputting all the properties of an object using the Format-List cmdlet is very useful if you need to know specific property names.

FIGURE 5.3
Formatting output to a formatted list

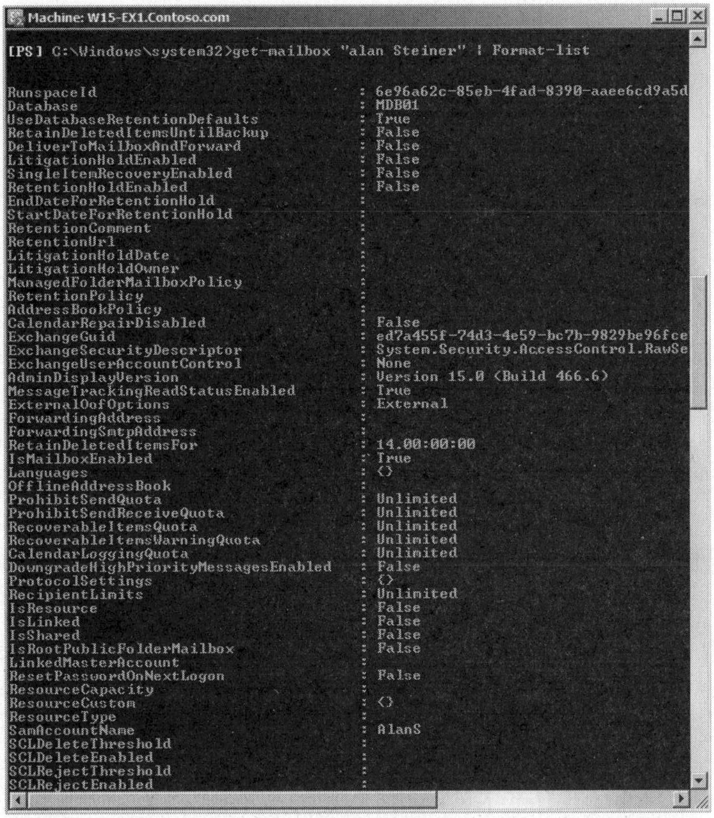

The command we used is as follows:

```
Get-Mailbox "Alan Steiner" | Format-List
```

Directing Output to Other Cmdlets

You have already seen a couple of examples where we used the pipe symbol (|) to direct the output of one command to be used as input for the next command, such as `Get-Mailbox | Format-Table`. You can do this because PowerShell commands act on objects, not just text. Unlike with other shells or scripting languages, you don't have to use string commands or variables to pass data from one command to another. The result is that you can use a single line to perform a query and complex task—something that might have required hundreds of lines of programming in the past.

One of our favorite examples is making specific changes to a group of people's mailboxes. Let's say you need to ensure that all executives in your organization can send and receive a message that is up to 50 MB in size rather than the default 10 MB to which the system limits the user. Earlier we showed you how you could get the properties of the mailbox that you were interested in, such as the `MaxSendSize` and `MaxReceiveSize` properties.

First, let's use the `Get-DistributionGroupMember` cmdlet to retrieve the members of the Executives distribution group:

```
Get-DistributionGroupMember "Executives"
Name                                     RecipientType
----                                     -------------
Gillian Katz                             MailboxUser
Jim McBee                                MailboxUser
Brian Tirch                              MailboxUser
Paul Robichaux                           MailboxUser
Devin Ganger                             MailboxUser
Stephen Rose                             MailboxUser
Cynthia Wang                             MailboxUser
```

Remember that although you see the text listing of the group members, what is actually output are objects representing each of the members.

It is important to note that while piping the output of one cmdlet as input for another cmdlet works frequently, it does not work all the time. Piping input to a cmdlet will always work when the noun used by the two cmdlets is the same, such as this:

```
Get-Mailbox -Server Ex1 | Set-Mailbox -CustomAttribute1 "I am on a ↵
great server! "
```

For cmdlets that do not support piping between them, you can usually use a trick, such as using the `foreach` cmdlet to process the data.

So, now let's pipe the output of that cmdlet to the `Set-Mailbox` cmdlet and do some real work! To change the maximum incoming and outgoing message size for the members of the #Executives group, you would type the following command:

```
Get-DistributionGroupMember "#Executives" | Set-Mailbox ↵
 -MaxSendSize:50MB -MaxReceiveSize:50MB ↵
 -UseDatabaseRetentionDefaults:$False
```

Notice that the `Set-Mailbox` cmdlet did not require any input because it will take as input the objects that are output from `Get-DistributionGroupMember`. When you run these two commands, there will be no output unless you have specified other options. But you can easily check the results by requesting the membership of the #Executives group, piping that to the `Get-Mailbox` cmdlet, and then piping that output to the `Format-Table` cmdlet, as shown here:

```
Get-DistributionGroupMember "#Executives" | Get-Mailbox | Format-Table ↵
Name,MaxSendSize,MaxReceiveSize
Name                  MaxSendSize              MaxReceiveSize
----                  -----------              --------------
Gillian Katz          50 MB (52,428,800 bytes) 50 MB (52,428,800 bytes)
Jonathan Long         50 MB (52,428,800 bytes) 50 MB (52,428,800 bytes)
Jim McBee             50 MB (52,428,800 bytes) 50 MB (52,428,800 bytes)
Brian Tirch           50 MB (52,428,800 bytes) 50 MB (52,428,800 bytes)
Paul Robichaux        50 MB (52,428,800 bytes) 50 MB (52,428,800 bytes)
Stephen Rose          50 MB (52,428,800 bytes) 50 MB (52,428,800 bytes)
```

Pretty cool, eh? After just a few minutes working with PowerShell and the EMS extensions, we hope that you will be as pleased with the ease-of-use as we are.

PowerShell v3

Exchange Server 2013 uses PowerShell v3, whereas Exchange Server 2010 used PowerShell v2 and Exchange Server 2007 used the power of PowerShell v1 (or v2 with Exchange Server 2007 SP2). PowerShell v3 includes some amazing features, like remoting and eventing, which enable it to manage any IT environment even better than before.

Remote PowerShell

Exchange Server 2013 doesn't use local PowerShell anymore but relies on remote PowerShell to manage its roles.

You won't see any difference between using remote or local shell to manage Exchange Server. When you click the Shell shortcut, Windows PowerShell connects to the closest Exchange Server 2013 Client Access server using Windows Remote Management 2.0, performs an authentication check, and then creates a remote session for you to use. It's thanks to Remote PowerShell that Role-based Access Control (RBAC) can be fully implemented. (For more information about RBAC, refer to Chapter 12, "Management Permissions and Role-based Access Control").

Another advantage of introducing Remote PowerShell is the ability to launch the shell and manage your Exchange servers by connecting to an Exchange Server 2013 server, without requiring you to install the management tools locally on that machine; this was a requirement in Exchange Server 2007.

Tips and Tricks

In this section we discuss handling data output, sending output to a file, sending email from the PowerShell, and debugging.

Managing Output

Let's start by exploring how to massage or manipulate the output of PowerShell and EMS cmdlets. In this section, we are going to focus on the Get-MailboxStatistics cmdlet; we are using this cmdlet in our example because in our opinion its default output format is the least desirable of *all* the EMS cmdlets. Whoever set the defaults for this cmdlet's output clearly expected the user to be proficient at manipulating the output.

If you are coming from an Exchange Server 2007 environment, you may be used to running the Get-MailboxStatistics cmdlet with no parameters. Exchange Server 2013 expects you to specify either a mailbox name, server name (-Server), or mailbox database (-Database) in the command line. Here is an example of the Get-MailboxStatistics cmdlet's output specifying a mailbox server:

```
Get-MailboxStatistics -Server Ex1

DisplayName               ItemCount StorageLimitStatus    LastLogonTime
-----------               --------- ------------------    -------------
John Park                 7         BelowLimit
SystemMailbox{21db5e47... 1         BelowLimit
Chuck Swanson             6         BelowLimit
Online Archive - Tyler... 0         NoChecking
Microsoft Exchange        1         BelowLimit
Microsoft Exchange App... 1         BelowLimit
Gillian Katz              7         BelowLimit
Administrator             2         BelowLimit            8/9/2013 1:24:44 AM
Jim McBee                 6         BelowLimit
Discovery Search Mailbox  1         BelowLimit
Clayton K. Kamiya         27        NoChecking            7/24/2013 12:17:44 AM
Microsoft Exchange App... 1         BelowLimit
Tyler M. Swartz           6         BelowLimit
Julie R. Samante          6         BelowLimit
Michael G. Brown          9         BelowLimit
Jonathan Long             6         BelowLimit
SystemMailbox{94c22976... 1         BelowLimit
Kevin Wile                8         BelowLimit
John Rodriguez            6         BelowLimit
Anita Velez               6         BelowLimit
```

Obviously this output is not very useful for most of us.

OUTPUT TO LISTS OR TABLES

Keep in mind that internally, when PowerShell is retrieving data, everything is treated as an object. However, when you are displaying something to the screen, you see just the textual information. Most cmdlets output data to a formatted table, but you can also output the data to a formatted list using the Format-List cmdlet or FL alias. Here is an example of piping a single mailbox's statistics to the Format-List cmdlet:

```
[PS] C:\>Get-MailboxStatistics "Clayton K. Kamiya" | Format-List


RunspaceId            : 3a8e6797-44a5-4c71-8a21-3022b379cb57
AssociatedItemCount   : 16
DeletedItemCount      : 0
```

```
DisconnectDate          :
DisplayName             : Clayton K. Kamiya
ItemCount               : 27
LastLoggedOnUserAccount : netlogon\Clayton.Kamiya
LastLogoffTime          : 7/24/2013 9:54:13 AM
LastLogonTime           : 7/24/2013 12:17:44 AM
LegacyDN                : /O=Netlogon/
OU=EXCHANGE ADMINISTRATIVE GROUP (FYDIBOHF23SPDLT)/
CN=RECIPIENTS/CN=CLAYTON K. KAMIYA
MailboxGuid             : a9e676e9-f67b-4206-817e-ad07eca52659
ObjectClass             : Mailbox
StorageLimitStatus      : NoChecking
TotalDeletedItemSize    : 0 B (0 bytes)
TotalItemSize           : 949.5 KB (972,245 bytes)
Database                : MBX1
ServerName              : Ex1
DatabaseName            : MBX1
MoveHistory             :
IsQuarantined           : False
IsArchiveMailbox        : False
Identity                : a9e676e9-f67b-4206-817e-ad07eca52659
MapiIdentity            : a9e676e9-f67b-4206-817e-ad07eca52659
OriginatingServer       : Ex1.netlogon.com
IsValid                 : True
```

This example shows you all the properties that can be displayed via the
Get-MailboxStatistics cmdlet.

The following are the default results of filtering the command through the Format-Table or
FT alias:

```
Get-MailboxStatistics "Clayton K. Kamiya" | FT

DisplayName      ItemCount  StorageLimitStatus  LastLogonTime
-----------      ---------  ------------------  -------------
Clayton Kamiya   1063       BelowLimit          8/9/2013 1:33:31 PM
```

However, the Format-Table and Format-List cmdlets allow you to specify which properties
you want to see in the output list. Let's say that you want to see the user's name, item count, and
total item size. Here's the command you would use:

```
Get-MailboxStatistics "Clayton Kamiya" | FT DisplayName, ↵
ItemCount,TotalItemSize

DisplayName          ItemCount TotalItemSize
-----------          --------- -------------
Clayton K. Kamiya         1063 4.00 MB (4,190,207 bytes)
```

There we go—that is a bit more useful. It's not perfect, mind you, but the output format is
getting better.

SORTING AND GROUPING OUTPUT

Any output can also be sorted based on any of the properties that you are going to display. If you are using the Format-Table command, you can also group the output by properties. First, let's go back and look at the original example where we are outputting all the mailbox statistics for the local mailbox server. Let's say we are interested in sorting by the maximum mailbox size. To do so, we can pipe the output of Get-MailboxStatistics to the Sort-Object cmdlet. Here is an example:

```
Get-Mailbox | Get-MailboxStatistics -Server Ex1 | Sort-Object ↵
TotalItemSize -Descending | Format-Table DisplayName, ↵
ItemCountTotalItemsize

DisplayName          ItemCount      TotalItemSize
-----------          ---------      -------------
Mike Brown                 306      22.92 MB (24,030,192 bytes)
Clayton Kamiya            1063      21.34 MB (22,376,612 bytes
Lawrence Cohen               2      221.3 KB(226,596 bytes)
Oliver Cohen                 2      71.75 KB (73,469 bytes)
Brian Tirch                  2      50.00 KB(51,200 bytes)
Oren Pinto                   6      50.00 KB(51,200 bytes)
```

This example used the command Sort-Object TotalItemSize -Descending, but we could also have used the -Ascending option. There are several far more sophisticated examples in PowerShell help.

We can take this a step further when using the Format-Table cmdlet by adding a -GroupBy option. Here is an example where we are exporting this data and grouping it using the StorageLimitStatus property:

```
Get-Mailbox | Get-MailboxStatistics | Sort-Object TotalItemSize ↵
-Descending | Format-Table DisplayName, ItemCount, TotalItemSize ↵
-GroupBy StorageLimitStatus

   StorageLimitStatus: MailboxDisabled

DisplayName          ItemCount      Total Item Size
-----------          ---------      ---------------
Mike Brown                 314      21.25 MB (21,763 bytes)

   StorageLimitStatus: ProhibitSend

DisplayName          ItemCount      Total Item Size
-----------          ---------      ---------------
Clayton Kamiya            1066      5.02 MB (5,145 bytes)

   StorageLimitStatus: BelowLimit
```

```
DisplayName          ItemCount      Total Item Size
-----------          ---------      ---------------
Lawrence Cohen               8      1.09 MB (1,119 bytes)
Oliver Cohen                 6      286 B (286 bytes)
Oren Pinto                   6      286 B (286 bytes)
```

OUTPUT TO FILE

Outputting data to the screen is great, but it does not help you with reports. You can also output data to CSV and XML files. Two cmdlets make this easy to do:

◆ Export-Csv exports the data to a CSV file.

◆ Export-Clixml exports the data to an XML file.

Simply direct the output you want sent to a file, and these cmdlets will take care of converting the data to the proper format. Let's take our earlier example where we want a report of all mailboxes and their ProhibitSend and ProhibitSendAndReceive limits. We can't use the Format-Table cmdlet in this instance; we have to use the Select-Object or Select cmdlet to specify the output because we will be directing this output to another cmdlet. Here is an example of the Get-Mailbox cmdlet when using the Select command:

```
Get-Mailbox | Select Name, ProhibitSendQuota, ProhibitSendReceiveQuota
```

The output of this cmdlet is shown here:

```
Name                 ProhibitSendQuota         ProhibitSendReceiveQuota
----                 -----------------         ------------------------
Oren Pinto               unlimited                     unlimited
Zachary Elfassy          unlimited                     unlimited
Zoe Elfassy              unlimited                     unlimited
Savannah Elfassy         unlimited                     unlimited
Mike Brown               unlimited                     unlimited
Dan Holme                unlimited                     unlimited
Russ Zimmer              unlimited                     unlimited
Tyler Swartz             unlimited                     unlimited
Chris Pfennig            unlimited                     unlimited
```

To direct this output to the C:\report.csv file, we simply pipe it to the Export-Csv cmdlet as shown here:

```
Get-Mailbox | Select Name, ProhibitSendQuota, ProhibitSendReceiveQuota | ↵
Export-Csv c:\report.csv
```

If you want to export the report to an XML file, simply use the Export-Clixml cmdlet instead of Export-Csv.

Finally, just as when working with the DOS prompt, you can redirect output of a command to a text file. To send the output of the `Get-Mailbox` to the file `c:\mailboxes.txt`, you would type this:

```
Get-Mailbox > c:\mailboxes.txt
```

PUTTING IT ALL TOGETHER

Let's consider one more example of `Get-MailboxStatistics` piping. Hopefully this will be an example that you can use in the future. We will create a report of the mailbox statistics using the `Get-MailboxStatistics` cmdlet. Then we will export the mailbox statistics for a specific server. We will limit the output by using the `Where-Object` command, choose the properties to output using the `Select` command, and finally pipe that output to the `Export-Csv` cmdlet:

```
Get-MailboxStatistics -Server Ex1 | Sort-Object TotalItemSize ⏎
-Descending | Select-Object DisplayName,ItemCount,TotalItemSize ⏎
| Export-CSV c:\StorStats.csv
```

If you are thinking that this looks a bit sticky to implement, you are probably right. Getting this syntax together took the better part of an afternoon, and arguably, you should be able to perform common tasks like exporting mailbox storage statistics from the GUI. However, on the bright side, now we have the command we need to run each time we want to generate this report; further, the knowledge to do this particular type of report within PowerShell carries over into many other tasks.

Running Scripts

PowerShell scripts are easy to build and to run, but there are a few things you need to know to write your own scripts and/or to read others' scripts. Though this is certainly not a comprehensive briefing on PowerShell scripting or variables, we hope it will give you a quick introduction to a few things that we found interesting and helpful when we got started.

◆   The file extension for a PowerShell script is `.PS1`.

◆   You can't run the script from the source directory. You actually have to preface the script name with the path.

Say we have a script called `c:\scripts\Report.ps1`. We can't just change it to the `c:\reports` directory and run `report.ps1`, so we would have to type **`.\report.ps1`**.

◆   PowerShell (and scripts) use variables preceded with a $ symbol. You can set a variable within a script or just by typing it at the command line. The PowerShell variable is an object, so you can associate an object or an entire list of objects with a single variable.

For example, the following command associates the variable $Zach with the entire object for the user Zachary Elfassy:

```
$Zach = Get-User "Zachary Elfassy"
```

We could then use just specific properties of that object. For example, if we want to just output Zachary's display name, we could type this:

```
$Zach.DisplayName
```

Even better, we could then set Zachary's display name to a variable called $ZachDisplayName by doing this:

```
$ZachDisplayName = $Zach.DisplayName
```

We can set a single variable to a lot of objects and then manipulate them all at once via a script. Here is an example where we set the $AllUsers variable to all the users in the domain:

```
$AllUsers = Get-Users
```

Now here are some interesting things we can do with that variable. We can obtain a count of how many objects it contains:

```
$AllUsers.Count
944
```

Further, each of the 944 objects contained in the $AllUsers variable is treated as an item in an array, so we can retrieve individual ones, such as object number 939:

```
AllUsers[939] | FL SamAccountName,DisplayName,WindowsEmailAddress,Phone,↵
Office


SamAccountName       : Andrew.Roberts
DisplayName          : Andrew Roberts (Operations)
WindowsEmailAddress  : andrew.roberts@Netlogon.com
Phone                : 011-77-8484-4844
Office               : Tokyo
```

SENDING EMAIL FROM THE EXCHANGE MANAGEMENT SHELL

Sometimes the smallest new features are among the best features. In this particular case, we are talking about a PowerShell cmdlet called Send-MailMessage that allows you to easily send an email from within PowerShell. While you could accomplish this in Exchange Server 2007 and PowerShell v1.0, doing so was a bit cumbersome.

For example, if you want to send an email message from the alias SystemMessages@Netlogon.com to HelpDesk@Netlogon.com, it would look something like this:

```
Send-MailMessage -To HelpDesk@netlogon.com -Subject "This is a test ↵
message" -From SystemMessages@netlogon.com -BodyAsHtml -Body "This ↵
is the body of the message" -SmtpServer Ex1
```

Note that you must specify an SMTP server that will either accept this connection or relay the message for you by using the -SmtpServer parameter, as shown in the preceding example.

Running Scheduled PowerShell Scripts

Frequently PowerShell advocates will extol the virtues of creating simple PowerShell scripts (PS1 files) that you can schedule to perform routine tasks. There are quite a few articles and newsgroup postings about how easy this is to do. However, running the PS1 script using a scheduled task is a bit trickier. You can't just run a PS1 script from the DOS command prompt or the Task Scheduler. Before a PS1 script can be run, PowerShell has to be run, the Exchange Management Extensions have to be loaded, and then the script or command can be called.

The PowerShell executable (powershell.exe) is found in the C:\Windows\System32\WindowsPowerShell\v3.0\ folder. PowerShell needs to be told from which Exchange server it will need to import the Exchange Server session (using the Import-PSSession cmdlet).

Finally, we need the name and the location of the script we are going to run, so let's say we are going to execute this command:

```
Get-Mailbox | Select Name, ProhibitSendQuota, ProhibitSendReceiveQuota ↩
| Export-Csv c:\report2.csv
```

Rather than pasting all this into the job scheduler, we can create a simple batch file that looks like this:

```
@echo off
cls
C:\Windows\System32\WindowsPowerShell\v1.0\PowerShell.exe ↩
-command "& { c:\scripts\Report1.ps1 }"
```

Now we need to create the Report1.ps1 script that will run once PowerShell is opened:

```
$Session = New-PSSession -ConfigurationName Microsoft.Exchange ↩
-ConnectionUri http://hnlmbx01/PowerShell/
Import-PSSession $session
Get-Mailbox | Select Name, ProhibitSendQuota, ProhibitSendReceiveQuota ↩
| Export-Csv c:\report2.csv
```

Debugging and Troubleshooting from PowerShell

PowerShell has a lot of features that will help you test your scripts and one-line commands.

Set-PSDebug   The cmdlet Set-PSDebug is designed to allow you to debug PowerShell scripts. To use this, add this command to your script: Set-PSDebug -Trace 1. This will allow you to examine each step of the script. You can enable more detailed trace logging by setting the trace level to 2: Set-PSDebug -Trace 2. If you add the -Step option to the command line, you will be prompted for each step. To turn off trace logging, use this command: Set-PSDebug -Off.

-WhatIf   Most cmdlets support the -WhatIf option. If you add the -WhatIf option to the command line, the cmdlet will run and tell you what will happen without actually performing the task. This is useful for checking to make sure the command you are about to run will really do what you want.

-Confirm   Most cmdlets support the -Confirm option and many cmdlets that perform more destructive types of options, such as those that begin with Remove-, Move-, Dismount-, Disable-, and Clear-, have the -Confirm option turned on by default. If this is turned on, the cmdlet will not proceed until you have confirmed it is OK to proceed. For cmdlets that confirm by default, you can include the -Confirm:$False option if you do not want to be prompted.

-ValidateOnly   The -ValidateOnly option is a bit more powerful than -WhatIf. The -ValidateOnly option will perform all the steps the cmdlet is specifying without actually making any changes and then will summarize what would have been done and if this would have caused any problems.

Getting Help

We have shown you a few simple yet powerful examples of how to use PowerShell and the EMS. Once you dig in and start using the EMS, you will need some references to help you figure out all the syntax and properties of each of the cmdlets.

Exchange Server 2013 Help File

A great starting place for just reading about the cmdlets is in the Microsoft Exchange Server 2013 help file. The help file documents explain how to do most common operations through the graphical user interface, as well as through the EMS.

We strongly recommend you take advantage of the help file that is included with Exchange Server. In fact, you might want to even copy the file and save it to your workstation. The filename is ExchHelp.chm.

Help Files and Other Documentation Updated Regularly

Microsoft tends to update the help file more frequently than it updates the service packs. Visit the Exchange Server downloads site to make sure you have the latest help file:

    http://technet.microsoft.com/en-us/library/bb124558.aspx

The online documentation is updated even more frequently than the help file; the following page has the latest documentation on the Exchange Admin Center and the Exchange Management Shell, such as the help, shown in Figure 5.4:

    http://technet.microsoft.com/en-us/library/bb123778(v=exchg.150).aspx

---

Help from the Command Line

Information is also available on the cmdlets from within PowerShell. For a good starting point, you can just type the help command and this will give you a good overview of using PowerShell and how to get more help. The following list summarizes common methods of getting help on PowerShell and Exchange Management Shell cmdlets:

help   Provides generic PowerShell help information.

help *Keyword*   Lists all cmdlets that contain the keyword. For example, if you want to find all PowerShell v2 cmdlets that work with the Windows event log, you would type **help *EventLog***. To find all Exchange Server cmdlets that work with mailboxes, type **Get-ExCommand *mailbox***. You cannot use the help alias to locate all available Exchange Server cmdlets.

Get-Command ***Keyword***   Lists all PowerShell cmdlets and files (such as help files) that contain the keyword.

Get-Command   Lists all cmdlets (including all PowerShell extensions currently loaded, such as the EMS cmdlets).

Get-ExCommand   Lists all Exchange Server cmdlets.

Get-PSCommand   Lists all PowerShell cmdlets.

Help *Cmdlet* or Get-Help *Cmdlet*   Lists online help for the specified cmdlet and pauses between each screen. Provides multiple views of the online help (such as detailed, full, examples, and default).

Cmdlet -?   Lists online help for the specified cmdlet.

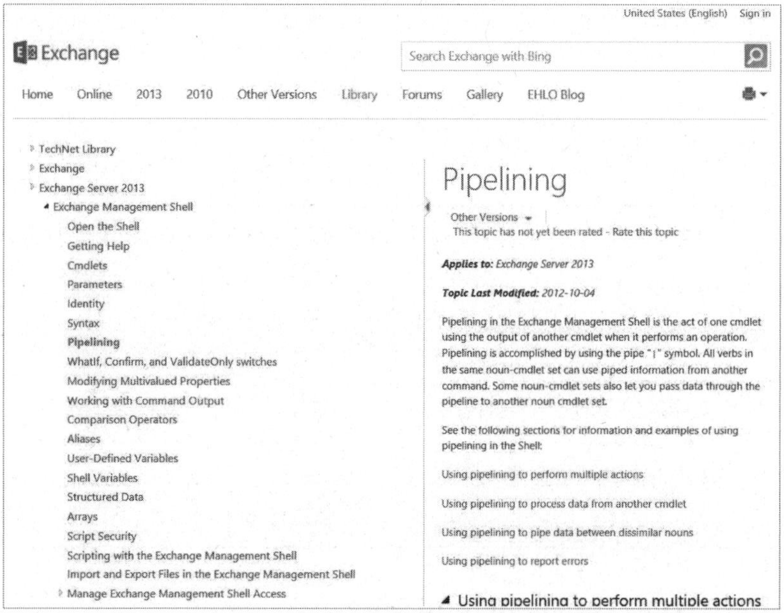

FIGURE 5.4
Online help for
pipelining using
the Exchange
Management Shell

When working with help within PowerShell, help topics are displayed based on the view of help that you request. In other words, you can't just type Get-Help and see everything about that cmdlet. The Get-Help cmdlet includes four possible views of help for each cmdlet. The following list explains the four primary views along with the parameters view:

Default View   Lists the minimal information to describe the function of the cmdlet and shows the syntax of the cmdlet

Example View   Includes a synopsis of the cmdlet and some examples of its usage

Detailed View   Shows more details on a cmdlet, including parameters and parameter descriptions

Full View   Shows all the details available on a cmdlet, including a synopsis of the cmdlet, a detailed description of the cmdlet, parameter descriptions, parameter metadata, and examples

Parameters View   Allows you to specify a parameter and get help on the usage of just that particular parameter

The Full option for Get-Help includes in its output each parameter's metadata. The metadata is shown in the following list:

Required?   Is the parameter required? This value is either true or false.

Position?   Specifies the position of the parameter. If the position is named, the parameter name has to be included in the parameter list. Most parameters are named. However, the -Identity parameter is 1, which means that it is always the first parameter and the -Identity tag is not required.

Default value   Specifies what a value will be for a parameter if nothing else is specified. For most parameters this is blank.

Accept pipeline input?   Specifies if the parameter will accept input that is piped in from another cmdlet. The value is either true or false.

Accept wildcard characters?   Specifies if the parameter accepts wildcard characters, such as the asterisk or question mark character. This value is either true or false.

Still not clear about what each view gives you? Perhaps Table 5.3 can shed some more light on the issue. This table shows you the various sections that are output when using each view option.

TABLE 5.3:   Information output for each Get-Help view

	DEFAULT VIEW	EXAMPLE VIEW	DETAILED VIEW	FULL VIEW
Synopsis	✓	✓	✓	✓
Detailed description	✓		✓	✓
Syntax	✓		✓	✓
Parameters			✓	✓
Parameter metadata				✓
Input type				✓
Return type				✓
Errors				✓
Notes				✓
Example		✓	✓	✓

To use these parameters, you would use the `Get-Help` cmdlet and the view option. For example, to see the example view for the `Get-Mailbox`, you would type the following:

```
Get-Help Get-Mailbox -Example
```

We feel it is important for administrators to understand the available online help options, so let's look at a couple more detailed examples for the `Get-MailboxStatistics` cmdlet. We are picking a cmdlet (`Get-MailboxStatistics`) that we feel is pretty representative of the EMS cmdlets but that also does not have a huge amount of help information. First, let's look at the default view:

```
Get-Help Get-MailboxStatistics

NAME
    Get-MailboxStatistics

SYNOPSIS
    Use the Get-MailboxStatistics cmdlet to obtain information about a mailbox,
such as the size of the mailbox, the number of messages it contains, and the
last time it was accessed. In addition, you can get the move history or a move
report of a completed move request.
SYNTAX
    Get-MailboxStatistics -Identity <GeneralMailboxIdParameter> [-Archive
<SwitchParameter>] [-DomainController <Fqdn>] [-IncludeMoveHistory
<SwitchParameter>] [-IncludeMoveReport <SwitchParameter>] [<CommonParameters>]

    Get-MailboxStatistics -Database <DatabaseIdParameter> [-DomainController
<Fqdn>] [<CommonParameters>]

    Get-MailboxStatistics -Server <ServerIdParameter> [-DomainController <Fqdn>]
[<CommonParameters>]

DESCRIPTION
    On Mailbox servers only, you can use the Get-MailboxStatistics cmdlet
without parameters. In this case, the cmdlet returns the statistics for all
 mailboxes on all databases on the local server.
    The Get-MailboxStatistics cmdlet requires at least one of the following
 parameters to complete successfully: Server, Database, or Identity.
    You can use the Get-MailboxStatistics cmdlet to return detailed move history
and a move report for completed move requests to troubleshoot a move request.
To view the move history, you must pass this cmdlet as an object. Move histories
are retained in the mailbox database and are numbered incrementally, and the last
executed move request is always numbered 0. For more information, see "EXAMPLE
6,"
"EXAMPLE 7," and "EXAMPLE 8" later in this topic.
    You can only see move reports and move history for completed move requests.
    You need to be assigned permissions before you can run this cmdlet. Although
all parameters for this cmdlet are listed in this topic, you may not have access
to some parameters if they're not included in the permissions assigned to you.
```

To see what permissions you need, see the "Recipient Provisioning Permissions"
section in the Mailbox Permissions topic.

```
RELATED LINKS
    Online Version http://technet.microsoft.com/EN-US/library/cec76f70-941f-
4bc9-b949-35dcc7671146(EXCHG.140).aspx

REMARKS
    To see the examples, type: "get-help Get-MailboxStatistics -examples".
    For more information, type: "get-help Get-MailboxStatistics -detailed".
    For technical information, type: "get-help Get-MailboxStatistics -full".
```

The default view (as you could have predicted from Table 5.3) includes the synopsis, syntax,
and detailed description sections. Let's change our approach and look at the example view:

```
[PS] C:\>Get-Help Get-MailboxStatistics -Examples

NAME
    Get-MailboxStatistics

SYNOPSIS
Use the Get-MailboxStatistics cmdlet to obtain information about a mailbox,
such as the size of the mailbox, the number of messages it contains, and
the last time it was accessed. In addition, you can get the move history or
a move report of a completed move request.


    ------------------------ EXAMPLE 1 --------------------------

This example retrieves the mailbox statistics for all mailboxes on the
local server. You can use the Get-MailboxStatistics cmdlet without
parameters only on a Mailbox server, and it defaults to the local mailbox
database.

    Get-MailboxStatistics

    ------------------------ EXAMPLE 2 --------------------------

This example retrieves the mailbox statistics for all mailboxes on
the server MailboxServer01.

Get-MailboxStatistics -Server MailboxServer01

    ------------------------ EXAMPLE 3 --------------------------

This example retrieves the mailbox statistics for the specified
mailbox.
```

```
Get-MailboxStatistics -Identity contoso\chris
```

```
-------------------------- EXAMPLE 4 --------------------------
```

This example retrieves the mailbox statistics for all mailboxes in the specified mailbox database.

```
Get-MailboxStatistics -Database "Mailbox Database"
```

```
-------------------------- EXAMPLE 5 --------------------------
```

This example retrieves the mailbox statistics for all disconnected mailboxes. This example uses a WHERE clause. The $_ variable is used to specify the object passed on the pipeline. The -ne operator means not equal.

```
Get-MailboxStatistics | Where {$_.DisconnectDate -ne $null}
```

```
-------------------------- EXAMPLE 6 --------------------------
```

This example returns the summary move history for the completed move request for Ayla Kol's mailbox. If you dont pipeline the output to the Format-List cmdlet, the move history doesn't display.

```
Get-MailboxStatistics -Identity AylaKol -IncludeMoveHistory | Format-List
```

```
-------------------------- EXAMPLE 7 --------------------------
```

This example returns the detailed move history for the completed move request for Ayla Kol's mailbox. This example uses a temporary variable to store the mailbox statistics object. If the mailbox has been moved multiple times, there will be multiple move reports. The last move report is always MoveReport[0].

```
$temp=Get-MailboxStatistics -Identity AylaKol -IncludeMoveHistory
$temp.MoveHistory[0]
```

```
-------------------------- EXAMPLE 8 --------------------------
```

This example returns the detailed move history and a verbose detailed move report for Ayla Kol's mailbox. This example uses a temporary variable to store the move request statistics object and outputs the move report to a CSV file.

```
$temp=Get-MailboxStatistics -Identity AylaKol -IncludeMoveReport
$temp.MoveHistory[0] | Export-CSV C:\MoveReport_AylaKol.csv
```

The example view does not have as much data, but a lot of techies learn by looking at examples, so we find this view particularly useful. Next, let's look at the detailed view; because this view includes the parameters, it will have quite a bit more information:

```
[PS] C:\>Get-Help Get-MailboxStatistics -Detailed

NAME
    Get-MailboxStatistics

SYNOPSIS
    Use the Get-MailboxStatistics cmdlet to obtain information about
    a mailbox, such as the size of the mailbox, the number of messages it
    contains, and the last time it was accessed. In addition, you can get
    the move history or a move report of a completed move request.

SYNTAX
    Get-MailboxStatistics -Identity <GeneralMailboxIdParameter>
    [-Archive <SwitchParameter>] [-DomainController <Fqdn>]
    [-IncludeMoveHistory <SwitchParameter>] [-IncludeMoveReport
    <SwitchParameter>] [<CommonParameters>]

    Get-MailboxStatistics -Database <DatabaseIdParameter>
    [-DomainController <Fqdn>] [<CommonParameters>]

    Get-MailboxStatistics -Server <ServerIdParameter>
    [-DomainController <Fqdn>] [<CommonParameters>]

DESCRIPTION
    On Mailbox servers only, you can use the Get-MailboxStatistics
    cmdlet without parameters. In this case, the cmdlet returns the
    statistics for all mailboxes on all databases on the local server.
    The Get-MailboxStatistics cmdlet requires at least one of the
    following parameters to complete successfully: Server, Database,
    or Identity.
    You can use the Get-MailboxStatistics cmdlet to return detailed
    move history and a move report for completed move requests to
    troubleshoot a move request. To view the move history, you must pass
    this cmdlet as an object.
    Move histories are retained in the mailbox database and are numbered
    incrementally, and the last executed move request is always numbered 0.
    For more information, see "EXAMPLE 6," "EXAMPLE 7," and "EXAMPLE 8"
    later in this topic.
    You can only see move reports and move history for completed move
    requests. You need to be assigned permissions before you can run this
    cmdlet. Although all parameters for this cmdlet are listed in this
    topic, you may not have access to some parameters if they're not
```

included in the permissions assigned to you. To see what permissions
you need, see the "Recipient Provisioning Permissions" section in
the Mailbox Permissions topic.

```
PARAMETERS
    -Database <DatabaseIdParameter>
        The Database parameter specifies the name of the mailbox
database. When you specify a value for the Database parameter,
the Exchange Management Shell returns statistics for all the mailboxes
on the database specified.
            You can use the following values:
            * GUID
            * Server\Database
            * Database
            This parameter accepts pipeline input from the Get-MailboxDatabase
cmdlet.

    -Identity <GeneralMailboxIdParameter>
        The Identity parameter specifies a mailbox. When you specify
a value for the Identity parameter, the command looks up the mailbox
specified in the Identity parameter, connects to the server where the
mailbox resides, and returns the statistics for the mailbox. You can
use one of the following values:
            * GUID
            * Distinguished name (DN)
            * Domain\Account
            * User principal name (UPN)
            * Legacy Exchange DN
            * SMTP address
            * Alias

    -Server <ServerIdParameter>
        The Server parameter specifies the server from which you
want to obtain mailbox statistics. You can use one of the following values:
            * Fully qualified domain name (FQDN)
            * NetBIOS name
            When you specify a value for the Server parameter, the command
returns statistics for all the mailboxes on all the databases, including
recovery databases, on the specified server. If you don't specify this
parameter, the command returns logon statistics for the local server.

    -Archive <SwitchParameter>
        The Archive switch parameter specifies whether to return
mailbox statistics for the archive mailbox associated with the
specified mailbox. You don't have to specify a value with this parameter.

    -DomainController <Fqdn>
        The DomainController parameter specifies the fully qualified
```

domain name (FQDN) of the domain controller that retrieves data from
Active Directory.

    -IncludeMoveHistory <SwitchParameter>
        The IncludeMoveHistory switch specifies whether to return
additional information about the mailbox that includes the history of
a completed move request, such as status, flags, target database, bad
items, start times, end times, duration that the move request was in
various stages, and failure codes.

    -IncludeMoveReport <SwitchParameter>
        The IncludeMoveReport switch specifies whether to return a
verbose detailed move report for a completed move request, such as
server connections and move stages.
        Because the output of this command is verbose, you should
send the output to a .CSV file for easier analysis.

    <CommonParameters>
        This cmdlet supports the common parameters: Verbose, Debug,
        ErrorAction, ErrorVariable, WarningAction, WarningVariable,
        OutBuffer and OutVariable. For more information, type,
        "get-help about_commonparameters".

    ------------------------- EXAMPLE 1 -------------------------

    This example retrieves the mailbox statistics for all mailboxes on the
local server. You can use the Get-MailboxStatistics cmdlet without
parameters only on a Mailbox server, and it defaults to the local mailbox
database.

    Get-MailboxStatistics

Notice in the preceding output that we left out most of the examples because we had already
shown them to you earlier. We did this with the full view as well since it contains even more
information than the detailed view. The full view includes the metadata for each parameter, as
well as examples:

    Get-Help Get-MailboxStatistics -Full

NAME
    Get-MailboxStatistics

SYNOPSIS
    Use the Get-MailboxStatistics cmdlet to obtain information
about a mailbox, such as the size of the mailbox, the number of
messages it contains, and the last time it was accessed. In
addition, you can get the move history or a move report of a
completed move request.

SYNTAX
```
    Get-MailboxStatistics -Identity <GeneralMailboxIdParameter>
[-Archive <SwitchParameter>] [-DomainController <Fqdn>]
[-IncludeMoveHistory <SwitchParameter>] [-IncludeMoveReport
<SwitchParameter>] [<CommonParameters>]

    Get-MailboxStatistics -Database <DatabaseIdParameter>
[-DomainController <Fqdn>] [<CommonParameters>]

    Get-MailboxStatistics -Server <ServerIdParameter>
[-DomainController <Fqdn>] [<CommonParameters>]
```

DESCRIPTION
    On Mailbox servers only, you can use the Get-MailboxStatistics cmdlet
without parameters. In this case, the cmdlet returns the statistics for all
mailboxes on all databases on the local server.
    The Get-MailboxStatistics cmdlet requires at least one of the following
parameters to complete successfully: Server, Database, or Identity.
    You can use the Get-MailboxStatistics cmdlet to return detailed move
history and a move report for completed move requests to troubleshoot a move
request. To view the move history, you must pass this cmdlet as an object.
Move histories are retained in the mailbox database and are numbered
incrementally, and the last executed move request is always numbered 0.
For more information, see "EXAMPLE 6," "EXAMPLE 7," and "EXAMPLE 8" later
in this topic.
    You can only see move reports and move history for completed move
requests. You need to be assigned permissions before you can run this
cmdlet. Although all parameters for this cmdlet are listed in this topic,
you may not have access to some parameters if they're not included in the
permissions assigned to you.
To see what permissions you need, see the "Recipient Provisioning
Permissions" section in the Mailbox Permissions topic.

PARAMETERS
    -Database <DatabaseIdParameter>
        The Database parameter specifies the name of the mailbox
database. When you specify a value for the Database parameter, the
Exchange Management Shell returns statistics for all the mailboxes
on the database specified.
        You can use the following values:
        * GUID
        * Server\Database
        * Database
        This parameter accepts pipeline input from the Get-MailboxDatabase
cmdlet.

```
     Required?                  true
     Position?                  Named
     Default value
     Accept pipeline input?     True
     Accept wildcard characters?  false


 -Identity <GeneralMailboxIdParameter>
     The Identity parameter specifies a mailbox. When you specify
 a value for the Identity parameter, the command looks up the mailbox
 specified in the Identity parameter, connects to the server where the
 mailbox resides, and returns the statistics for the mailbox. You can
 use one of the following values:
     * GUID
     * Distinguished name (DN)
     * Domain\Account
     * User principal name (UPN)
     * Legacy Exchange DN
     * SMTP address
     * Alias

     Required?                  true
     Position?                  1
     Default value
     Accept pipeline input?     True
     Accept wildcard characters?  false


 -Server <ServerIdParameter>
     The Server parameter specifies the server from which you
 want to obtain mailbox statistics. You can use one of the following
 values:
     * Fully qualified domain name (FQDN)
     * NetBIOS name
     When you specify a value for the Server parameter, the
 command returns statistics for all the mailboxes on all the databases,
 including recovery databases, on the specified server. If you don't
 specify this parameter, the command returns logon statistics for
 the local server.

     Required?                  true
     Position?                  Named
     Default value
     Accept pipeline input?     True
     Accept wildcard characters?  false


 -Archive <SwitchParameter>
     The Archive switch parameter specifies whether to return
 mailbox statistics for the archive mailbox associated with the
```

specified mailbox. You don't have to specify a value with this parameter.

```
Required?                    false
Position?                    Named
Default value
Accept pipeline input?       False
Accept wildcard characters?  false
```

-DomainController <Fqdn>
    The DomainController parameter specifies the fully
qualified domain name (FQDN) of the domain controller that
retrieves data from Active Directory.

```
Required?                    false
Position?                    Named
Default value
Accept pipeline input?       False
Accept wildcard characters?  false
```

-IncludeMoveHistory <SwitchParameter>
    The IncludeMoveHistory switch specifies whether to
return additional information about the mailbox that includes
the history of a completed move request, such as status, flags,
target database, bad items, start times, end times, duration that
the move request was in various stages, and failure codes.

```
Required?                    false
Position?                    Named
Default value
Accept pipeline input?       False
Accept wildcard characters?  false
```

-IncludeMoveReport <SwitchParameter>
    The IncludeMoveReport switch specifies whether to return
a verbose detailed move report for a completed move request, such
as server connections and move stages. Because the output of this
command is verbose, you should send the output to a .CSV file for
easier analysis.

```
Required?                    false
Position?                    Named
Default value
Accept pipeline input?       False
Accept wildcard characters?  false
```

<CommonParameters>
    This cmdlet supports the common parameters: Verbose,

```
Debug, ErrorAction, ErrorVariable, WarningAction, WarningVariable,
OutBuffer and OutVariable. For more information, type,
"get-help about_commonparameters".

INPUTS

OUTPUTS

TERMINATING ERRORS
    (Category: )

    Type:
    Target Object Type:
    Suggested Action:

NON-TERMINATING ERRORS
    (Category: )

    Type:
    Target Object Type:
    Suggested Action:

    ------------------------- EXAMPLE 1 -------------------------

    This example retrieves the mailbox statistics for all
mailboxes on the local server. You can use the Get-MailboxStatistics
cmdlet without parameters only on a Mailbox server, and it defaults
to the local mailbox database.

    Get-MailboxStatistics
```

Yes, that's a lot of text for examples of one cmdlet, but we hope that these examples will make it easier for you to quickly learn the capabilities of all cmdlets and how you can use them.

The EMS help system also gives you some options with respect to getting help on parameters. For example, here is an example if you want help on just the -Database parameter of the Get-MailboxStatistics cmdlet:

```
Get-Help Get-MailboxStatistics -Parameter Database

-Database <DatabaseIdParameter>
    The Database parameter specifies the name of the mailbox database.
When you specify a value for the Database parameter, the Exchange
Management Shell returns statistics for all the mailboxes on the
database specified.
    You can use the following values:
    * GUID
    * Server\Database
    * Database
    This parameter accepts pipeline input from the
```

```
Get-MailboxDatabase cmdlet.

    Required?                   true
    Position?                   Named
    Default value
    Accept pipeline input?      True
    Accept wildcard characters? false
```

The -Parameter option also accepts the asterisk (*) wildcard. Here is an example if you want to see help on all the parameters that contain SCLQuarantine for the Set-Mailbox cmdlet:

```
[PS] C:\>Get-Help Set-Mailbox -Parameter *SCLQuarantine*

-SCLQuarantineEnabled <Nullable>
    The SCLQuarantineEnabled parameter specifies whether messages
that meet the SCL threshold specified by the SCLQuarantineThreshold
parameter are quarantined. If a message is quarantined, it's sent
to the quarantine mailbox where the messaging administrator can
review it. You can use the following values:
    * $true
    * $false
    * $null

    Required?                   false
    Position?                   Named
    Default value
    Accept pipeline input?      False
    Accept wildcard characters? false


-SCLQuarantineThreshold <Nullable>
    The SCLQuarantineThreshold parameter specifies the SCL
at which a message is quarantined, if the SCLQuarantineEnabled
parameter is set to $true. You must specify an integer from 0 through 9
inclusive.

    Required?                   false
    Position?                   Named
    Default value
    Accept pipeline input?      False
    Accept wildcard characters? false
```

Getting Tips

You may have noticed a useful tip each time you launched the Exchange Management Shell (EMS). Figure 5.5 shows the Tip of the Day text that you see each time you launch the EMS. There are more than 100 of these tips.

FIGURE 5.5

Viewing the
Tip of the Day

```
Machine: W15-EX1.Contoso.com                                                    _ □ ×
[PS] C:\Windows\system32>get-tip
Tip of the day #60:

To retrieve the current status of an Exchange server or database, use the Status parameter. For example:

Get-ExchangeServer -Status | Format-List
Get-MailboxDatabase -Server <Server Name> -Status | Format-List
```

If you want to view additional tips, just type **Get-Tip** at the Exchange Management Shell prompt.

You can even add your own tips if you don't mind editing an XML file; the tips for English are found in C:\program files\Microsoft\Exchange Server\v15\bin\extips.xml.

The Bottom Line

Use PowerShell command syntax.   The PowerShell is an easy-to-use, command-line interface that allows you to manipulate many aspects of the Windows operating system, registry, and filesystem. The Exchange Management Shell extensions allow you to manage all aspects of an Exchange Server organization and many Active Directory objects.

PowerShell cmdlets consist of a verb (such as Get, Set, New, or Mount) that indicates what is being done and a noun (such as Mailbox, Group, ExchangeServer) that indicates on which object the cmdlet is acting. Cmdlet options such as -Debug, -Whatif, and -ValidateOnly are common to most cmdlets and can be used to test or debug problems with a cmdlet.

> **Master It**   You need to use the Exchange Management Shell cmdlet Set-User to change the telephone number (the phone property) to (808) 555-1234 for user Matt.Cook, but you want to first confirm that that the command will do what you want to do without actually making the change. What command should you use?

Understand object-oriented use of PowerShell.   Output of a cmdlet is not simple text but rather objects. These objects have properties that can be examined and manipulated.

> **Master It**   You are using the Set-User cmdlet to set properties of a user's Active Directory account. You need to determine the properties that are available to use with the Set-User cmdlet. What can you do to view the available properties?

Employ tips and tricks to get more out of PowerShell.   PowerShell (as well as extensions for PowerShell, such as the Exchange Management Shell) is a rich, powerful environment. Many daily administrative tasks, as well as tasks that previously may have been difficult to automate, can be performed via PowerShell.

One of the most powerful features of PowerShell is the ability to pipe the output of one cmdlet to another cmdlet to use as input. While this is not universally true, cmdlets within the same family can usually be used, such as cmdlets that manipulate or output mailbox information.

> **Master It**   You need to set the custom attribute 2 to have the text "Marketing" for all members of the marketing department. There is a distribution group called Marketing that contains all of these users. How could you accomplish this using a single command (a one-liner)?

Get help with using PowerShell. Many options are available when you are trying to figure out how to use a PowerShell cmdlet, including online help and the Exchange Server documentation. PowerShell and the EMS make it easy to "discover" the cmdlets that you need to do your job.

Master It How would you locate all the cmdlets available to manipulate a mailbox? You are trying to figure out how to use the Set-User cmdlet and would like to see an example. How can you view examples for this cmdlet?

Chapter 6

Understanding the Exchange Autodiscover Process

Being an Exchange Server administrator is rewarding and, at times, frustrating. One of the most common sources of frustration we've encountered is managing the interactions between our Exchange servers and the Outlook desktop client. In large organizations, two separate groups maintain these pieces of the common puzzle. In smaller organizations, though, the same people can handle both the server and the clients. It's in organizations like these that you learn the truth of the fact that Exchange Server and Outlook were developed by two separate product groups.

Historically, many Outlook client issues were the result of mismatches between the Outlook profile settings and the actual server configurations. In Exchange Server 2007, Microsoft introduced the Autodiscover service, a component of the Client Access role, which was intended to allow both clients (such as Outlook, Windows Mobile, and Entourage) and other Exchange servers to automatically discover how your Exchange Server organization is configured and determine the appropriate settings without direct administrator involvement.

Many Exchange Server 2007 organizations ran into two main problems getting Autodiscover properly configured and deployed: understanding the concepts and getting the certificates properly deployed. By deploying Exchange Server 2010, administrators increased their knowledge of the Autodiscover processes. In this latest release of Exchange Server, the update is a much simpler, much more evolved, and a more *administrator-friendly* feature.

In this chapter, you will learn to:

◆ Work with Autodiscover

◆ Troubleshoot Autodiscover

◆ Manage Exchange Server certificates

Autodiscover Concepts

Let's share an unpleasant truth that a lot of administrators have not yet learned: the Autodiscover service is *not an optional component* of an Exchange Server organization. It may seem as if it's optional, especially if you haven't yet deployed a version of Outlook, Windows Phone, or Entourage that takes advantage of it. More than that, you can't get rid of it—Autodiscover is on from the moment that you install the first server in the organization. You can't shut it off, you can't disable it, and you can't keep clients and Exchange servers from trying to contact it (although you can cause problems by not properly configuring Autodiscover, breaking features, and forcing fallback to older, more error-prone methods of configuration).

We know several Exchange Server 2007 organizations that limped along seemingly just fine with Autodiscover improperly configured or just plain ignored. However, when Autodiscover has been neglected this inevitably signals an Exchange Server organization with other problems—and this is even truer in Exchange Server 2013 than in previous versions. Autodiscover is more than just a way to ease administration of Outlook client profiles. Other Exchange Server components, servers, and services also use Autodiscover to find the servers and settings they need to communicate with. In order for the Outlook (2007 or later) client to leverage many of the advanced features of Exchange Server 2013, including the high-availability features, the client depends on a functional Autodiscover service. And if you want to use the external calendar sharing or Lync integration, you'd better get Autodiscover squared away.

In order to properly plan and deploy Autodiscover, you have to work through some of the most potentially confusing aspects of an Exchange Server 2013 deployment. The good news, though, is that once you have these issues solved, you will have headed off some confusing and annoying errors that might otherwise cause problems down the road. These issues include namespace planning and certificate management. Trust me that getting these issues sorted will make your client access deployment and your overall management tasks a lot easier.

What Autodiscover Provides

Autodiscover is necessary for far more reasons than that it makes configuring your Outlook clients easier. In Exchange Server 2007, the clients did benefit a great deal, which is part of the reason why many people did not see the point of learning about the service. Either that, or it worked subtly behind the scenes, and some administrators lived in ignorant bliss, once some configuration was done. In Exchange Server 2013, both the client and the server benefits get better. The information provided by Autodiscover includes the following:

◆ Outlook client connection configuration

◆ Configuration URLs for the offline address book (OAB)

◆ Configuration URLs for free and busy information

◆ Outlook profile configuration information

Client Benefits

Exactly what benefits you get from Autodiscover depends on which client you're using:

◆ Outlook 2007 (SP3 recommended), Outlook 2010, and Outlook 2013 fully support Autodiscover. Outlook versions prior to 2007 do not use Autodiscover, but they are not supported as clients of Exchange Server 2013 either—so why are you still using them?

◆ Windows Mobile 6.1, Windows Phone 7.x/8.x and later support Autodiscover, and many mobile users today rely on Autodiscover for easy configuration of a new device.

◆ The Windows Mail app that is built into the Windows 8 Pro and Windows RT devices also uses Autodiscover to configure client settings (incidentally, those clients are then configured as Exchange Server ActiveSync clients).

◆ Entourage 2008 for Mac, Web Services Edition, which fully supports Exchange Web Services, also takes full advantage of Autodiscover. If you're a Mac user, you may prefer using Outlook for Mac 2011. This new version of Outlook works in a similar way to the PC version, except it does not support service connection point (SCP) lookup. (SCP lookup is a method used for locating services, or more specifically the servers that run the services, and is explained later on in this chapter.)

Even though you get all these great benefits from Autodiscover, likely the only time you will see Autodiscover working is when configuring a client, such as Outlook, for the first time. When running through an initial configuration wizard, a user is prompted to configure Outlook to connect to an email server. Their computer will then look up the correct details using Autodiscover and configure the Outlook profile automatically as seen in Figure 6.1.

FIGURE 6.1
Completing Outlook initial configuration using Autodiscover

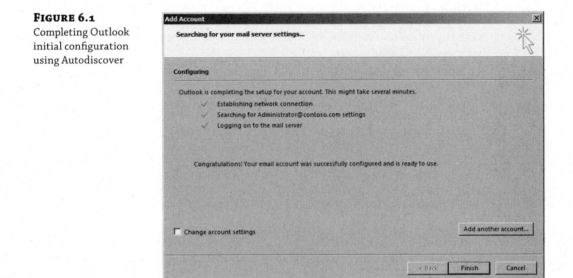

Although these are the main Autodiscover-aware clients, they're not the only ones. For example, the Microsoft Lync client and devices use Autodiscover and Exchange Web Services. The behavior of Autodiscover has been clearly documented by Microsoft, so other third-party clients and mobile devices also make use of it. Features that Outlook and Windows Phone will leverage include the following:

Support for DNS A Records   By default, external clients attempt to find the Autodiscover service through DNS lookups against well-known hostname (A) records.

Support for DNS SRV Records   Due to popular demand, starting in Exchange Server 2010, the Exchange Server and Outlook teams provided support for the use of Service Locator (SRV) records for organizations that couldn't use A records and didn't want to use CNAMEs.

Support for Active Directory Service Connection Point Objects   Domain-joined clients that can contact Active Directory—effectively any Windows client running Outlook 2007 or later—can make use of an Active Directory feature called service connection points. SCPs provide a number of benefits that aren't available with plain DNS lookups. SCPs allow clients to locate resources via SCP objects within the Active Directory. The SCP object contains the list of Autodiscover URLs for the Active Directory forest. You can use the `Set-ClientAccessServer` cmdlet to modify the SCP object. (And of course you can use `Get-ClientAccessServer` to view the object.)

Internal Organization Settings   Services on Exchange Server 2013 Client Access servers have both internal URLs for clients within the firewall (such as Outlook and Lync on domain-joined Windows machines) and external URLs for pretty much everything else. Internal settings use the appropriate Exchange Server FQDNs by default, unless you modify them (such as when using load balancers).

External Organization Settings   External settings allow services to be reached through Internet-available FQDNs. For some reason, many organizations don't like publishing the internal FQDNs of their Exchange servers. Using external settings may also ensure that connections are load balanced or sent through firewalls, such as Forefront Threat Management Gateway 2010 (TMG).

Location of the User's Mailbox Server   In previous versions of Exchange Server, the user's Mailbox server was located in Active Directory, stamped on the user object. However, with the architectural changes to Exchange Server 2013, Outlook can connect to one of several Client Access servers in a site. The connection is stateless; in other words, there is no session affinity, so from one hour to the next a different Client Access server may be handling the connection. This makes Autodiscover all the more important. Now using the users' mailbox GUID plus the domain name from the SMTP address of the user, Outlook finds a connection point to a Client Access server. Previously, Outlook had a direct affinity to the Mailbox server or a Client Access server with the Client Access array feature introduced in Exchange Server 2010. Client Access arrays, the virtual RPC endpoint available in Exchange Server 2010, no longer exists in Exchange Server 2013; but then again it's no longer necessary either.

Location of the Availability Service   Calendar items are stored in each user's mailbox. However, their free/busy information has historically been placed in a system public folder, which could suffer from latency due to replication lag. The Exchange Availability Service allows current information to be quickly looked up by clients (both in the organization and in federated organizations) as they need it, rather than having them dependent on stale data in public folders as was the case in previous versions.

Location of the Offline Address Book Service   OABs in Exchange Server 2013 are generated by an arbitration mailbox, known as an Organization mailbox. This creates the files that a Client Access server will deliver to Outlook clients via HTTPS. In previous versions, clients could retrieve this from a public folder. Locating the OAB URL is essential, because Outlook runs in cached mode by default and relies on the OAB for address book lookups. Autodiscover directs Outlook to the OAB URL that can fetch the changes a client requires. If this or any other Exchange Web Services URL might change on the Exchange server, the client periodically checks the Autodiscover service to receive those updates and changes. Autodiscover is contacted not only during the startup process of Outlook but other times as well.

Outlook Anywhere Settings   With Exchange Server 2013, all Outlook connections use RPC over HTTPS, aka Outlook Anywhere. This is now the connection method for internal, as well as external connections, and this latest version of Exchange Server no longer accepts MAPI over RPC connections from Outlook clients. Now, having the external URL information is a good start for clients outside your corporate firewall, but more settings, such as the certificate validation name, are necessary for a successful Outlook Anywhere session to be established.

Later in this chapter, we'll walk through a typical Outlook 2013 Autodiscover session and show how all this information is used. For now, just be aware that the value of many of these options can be user dependent (such as the mailbox location) or site dependent. As a result, the Autodiscover service is a vital part of spreading load throughout the entire organization, minimizing traffic over WAN links between sites and branches, and ensuring that your users are connecting to the best servers they can reach at the time.

SERVER BENEFITS

Autodiscover isn't just useful for clients connecting to the Exchange Server infrastructure; it's also useful for other servers, both within the organization and without:

◆ Servers within the same organization and Active Directory forest use Autodiscover to locate various services on a user's behalf. For example, when a user performs a logon to Outlook Web App, the Client Access server role handling the OWA session needs several of the pieces of information provided by Autodiscover. Using Autodiscover reduces the load on Active Directory domain controllers and global catalog servers and removes reliance on cached information. This is true whether you're in a mixed Exchange Server 2013/2010/2007 organization or are deploying Exchange Server 2013 fresh.

◆ Servers within the same organization but in a different Active Directory forest depend on cross-forest service connection points and internal Autodiscover to cross the forest boundaries and discover the appropriate servers to use. In this situation, one Client Access server in the source forest will often act as a proxy for the appropriate services in the target forest, or it may simply redirect the client. In multiple-forest deployments, the use of Autodiscover is pretty much mandatory to ensure that Exchange servers in separate forests can interoperate properly.

◆ Servers within separate federated organizations require the use of the external Autodiscover information to reach federated availability services. This, plus the relevant authentication information, allows users to securely share calendar and free/busy information with their counterparts in federated Exchange Server organizations. With other Exchange Server organizations, federation greatly simplifies the configuration and management of these types of operations.

So, let's take a look at the nitty-gritty of how Autodiscover works.

How Autodiscover Works

Don't be fooled by the seeming complexity you're about to see. Autodiscover is pretty simple to understand. The biggest complications come from certificates and namespace planning, which we'll get to in a bit and which have gotten significantly simpler in Exchange Server 2013 with fewer namespaces required.

THE SERVICE CONNECTION POINT OBJECT

The first piece of the Autodiscover puzzle lies with the service connection point (SCP) object. As each Client Access role instance is installed into your organization, it creates an SCP object in the Configuration-naming partition of the Active Directory domain to which it is joined, at the following location:

CN=<*CAS Server NetBIOS Name*>, CN=Autodiscover, CN=Protocols, CN=<*CAS Server NetBIOS Name*>, CN=Servers, CN= Exchange Administrative Group (FYDIBOHF23SPDLT), CN=Administrative Groups, CN=<*Organization Name*>, CN=Microsoft Exchange,CN=Services,CN=Configuration,DC=<*domain name*>,DC=<*domain suffix*>

Here's what a typical SCP object looks like when dumped from the LDP (LDP.EXE) tool:

```
Expanding base
'CN=EX1,CN=Autodiscover,CN=Protocols,CN=EX1,CN=Servers,CN=Exchange
Administrative Group (FYDIBOHF23SPDLT),CN=Administrative Groups,CN=First
Organization,CN=Microsoft Exchange,CN=Services,CN=Configuration,DC=Netlogon,
DC=com'...
Getting 1 entries:
Dn: CN=EX1,CN=Autodiscover,CN=Protocols,CN=EX1,CN=Servers,CN=Exchange
Administrative Group (FYDIBOHF23SPDLT),CN=Administrative Groups,CN=First
Organization,CN=Microsoft Exchange,CN=Services,CN=Configuration,DC=Netlogon,
DC=com
cn: EX1;
distinguishedName:
CN=EX1,CN=Autodiscover,CN=Protocols,CN=EX1,CN=Servers,CN=Exchange
Administrative Group (FYDIBOHF23SPDLT),CN=Administrative Groups,CN=First
Organization,CN=Microsoft Exchange,CN=Services,CN=Configuration,DC=Netlogon,
DC=com;
dSCorePropagationData: 0x0 = (  );
instanceType: 0x4 = ( WRITE );
keywords (2): Site=Default-First-Site-Name; 77378F46-2C66-4aa9-A6A6-3E7A48B19596;
name: EX1;
objectCategory: CN=Service-Connection- Point,CN=Schema,CN=Configuration,DC=Netlog
on,DC=com;
objectClass (4): top; leaf; connectionPoint; serviceConnectionPoint;
objectGUID: 44f44e8c-164a-446a-9eb8-f21a59b11b65;
serviceBindingInformation:
https://ex1.netlogon.com/Autodiscover/Autodiscover.xml;
serviceClassName: ms-Exchange-AutoDiscover-Service;
serviceDNSName: EX1;
showInAdvancedViewOnly: TRUE;
systemFlags: 0x40000000 = ( CONFIG_ALLOW_RENAME );
uSNChanged: 184521;
uSNCreated: 184521;
whenChanged: 8/1/2012 6:05:05 PM Pacific Daylight Time;
whenCreated: 8/1/2012 6:05:05 PM Pacific Daylight Time;
```

There are a few key properties of these entries you should take note of:

◆ The objectClass property includes the serviceConnectionPoint type. This identifies the entry as an SCP, allowing it to be easily searched using LDAP.

◆ The serviceClassName property identifies this particular SCP as an ms-Exchange-AutoDiscover-Service entry. The computers searching for Autodiscover records can thus determine that this is an entry pertaining to Autodiscover and that they should pay attention to it. The client searches the configuration-naming context for any objects that have a `serviceClassName= ms-Exchange-Autodiscover-Service`. Using the combination of `objectClass` and `serviceClassName` allows computers to efficiently find all relevant SCP entries (through an indexed search from a domain controller) without knowing any computer names ahead of time.

◆ The `serviceBindingInformation` points to the actual Autodiscover XML file that the client should access in order to retrieve the current Autodiscover information. More on this later.

◆ The `keywords` property holds additional information that the clients use. Specifically, take note of the `Site=` value. This value helps you control site affinity, ensuring that clients use nearby servers that aren't in far-off sites to provide their Exchange Server services (unless that is desirable).

The rest of the properties on an SCP object are fairly standard for Active Directory objects, so we won't discuss them further.

Now that you know what a service connection point is and where they're located, you're mostly set. The distinguished name of each SCP object uniquely identifies the host associated without that object. If the client search returns multiple SCP objects that the client will use, it will select among them according to alphabetic order. This is can be useful to know.

Note also that a Client Access server instance publishes its corresponding SCP object to Active Directory only when it is installed (which is done automatically for you). If you change something about the Client Access server —such as which site it's located in—it will not update its SCP object. You have to do that manually. The best way is to use Exchange Management Shell. Here is a sample command that configures a server named CAS1 to have an internal URL for the XML file location and also sets it to be authoritative for two sites:

```
Set-ClientAccessServer -Identity CAS1 -AutodiscoverServiceInternalURI "https://
mail.netlogon.com/autodiscover/autodiscover.xml" -AutoDiscoverSiteScope "Site1",
"Site2"
```

THE DNS OPTION

The SCP is used when the client or server is joined to an Active Directory domain and can perform the search against the domain controllers. When the discovering computer is external or not domain joined, another mechanism is used: DNS lookups.

The following list describes the DNS lookups that are performed for the Autodiscover service in a given domain. For this example, let's use the user `UserA@netlogon.com`. The client (or server) takes the domain portion (`netlogon.com`) of this address and performs the following lookups in order until it finds a match:

1. A DNS A record (or CNAME record) for `netlogon.com` that points to a web server that responds to the HTTPS URL `https://netlogon.com/Autodiscover/Autodiscover.xml`

2. A DNS A record (or CNAME record) for `autodiscover.netlogon.com` that points to a web server that responds to the HTTPS URL `https://autodiscover.netlogon.com/Autodiscover/Autodiscover.xml`

3. A DNS A record (or CNAME record) for `netlogon.com` that points to a web server that responds to the HTTP URL `http://autodiscover.netlogon.com/Autodiscover/Autodiscover.xml` (Note that this URL should be configured to redirect to the actual HTTPS location of the Autodiscover service.)

4. A DNS SRV record for `autodiscover._tcp.netlogon.com` (this record should contain the port number 443 and a hostname, such as `mail.netlogon.com`, allowing the client to try the HTTPS URL `https://mail.netlogon.com/Autodiscover/Autodiscover.xml`)

If the requested hostname is returned through either a CNAME record or an SRV record, then be aware that your clients (Outlook in particular) may display a warning dialog with the following text:

```
Allow this website to configure UserA@netlogon.com server settings?
https://mail.netlogon.com/autodiscover/autodiscover.xml
Your account was redirected to this website for settings.
You should only allow settings from sources you know and trust.
```

This warning will appear every time the client performs Autodiscover unless you check the Don't Ask Me About This Website Again check box. You can also prepopulate the registry key to prevent this warning. See the Knowledge Base article at `http://support.microsoft.com/kb/2480582`.

Note that Autodiscover expects the use of SSL. Don't publish it over insecure HTTP and expect clients to be happy about it. You have a lot of sensitive information going through Autodiscover, including user credentials. As a result, SSL certificate considerations will play a large part in your Autodiscover configuration.

🌐 Real World Scenario

WHICH OPTION SHOULD I CHOOSE?

There are several methods that you can use to publish Autodiscover services through DNS. In the end, the option you choose is up to you and your business needs. However, you should consider these points to see how they align with your business objectives. Again, let's consider the case of `netlogon.com`.

◆ Publishing Autodiscover under `https://netlogon.com` doesn't require you to have an extra DNS name. If you have HTTPS published on this hostname already, you don't need to use an extra certificate or hostname as long as you can ensure that the Autodiscover virtual directory can be published under the existing website. Most organizations will probably already have this namespace published in their DNS, but it could result in name-resolution collisions if the URL that it points to does not have the Autodiscover information.

◆ Publishing Autodiscover under `https://autodiscover.netlogon.com` requires you to have an extra DNS name, but it's a hostname that isn't likely to be used by any other servers. However, you'll need to have a Subject Alternative Name (SAN) certificate or a wildcard certificate (not recommended—see the section "Planning Certificate Names") or use multiple certificates and a second virtual website. Publishing a second website is quite a bit more complicated than simply using the defaults, so keep that in mind.

◆ Publishing Autodiscover under the HTTP redirect not only requires you to have an extra DNS name but also invokes the security warning for each user. You'll need to configure the appropriate redirect, and you'll need to have a SAN certificate or a wildcard certificate or use multiple certificates and a second virtual website. This option may make sense for organizations that are hosting multiple servers or SMTP namespaces within a single Exchange Server organization.

◆ Publishing Autodiscover under an SRV redirect requires you to have external DNS servers that handle the SRV type. Most modern DNS servers can handle this, but some DNS hosting services do not. Additionally, this redirect invokes the security warning for each user. Finally, you'll need to have a SAN certificate or a wildcard certificate or use multiple certificates and a second virtual website.

In my experience, the second option (`https://autodiscover.netlogon.com`) is the best combination of simplicity and control. It's the one that most organizations we've worked with have used. When Exchange Server 2007 was first introduced, certificate authorities that could provide SAN certificates were rare and the certificates themselves were expensive, making the alternative more palatable. Now, however, that is no longer the case. If you hesitate to deploy SAN certificates, there is a lot of good guidance out there to help you—including the section, "Deploying Exchange Certificates," later in this chapter—and Exchange Server 2013 gives you better tools to manage them.

TWO STEP-BY-STEP EXAMPLES

Enough theory. Let's dive into our example with a company that has the `contoso.com` domain and show you a walk through of a common scenario: a domain-joined Outlook 2013 client performing Autodiscover behind the organization firewall. To illustrate this scenario, we'll use a tool every Exchange Server administrator should know well: the Outlook Test E-mail AutoConfiguration tool, shown in Figure 6.2. As shown in this example, when using this tool be sure to uncheck the Use Guessmart and Secure Guessmart Authentication options in order to get only the results of an Autodiscover query. The great thing about this tool is that it exposes all the URLs that are returned to the Outlook client. This allows the administrator to quickly identify misconfigured URLs and rule out several potential problems when troubleshooting connectivity.

You can access this tool from Outlook by holding down the Ctrl key while right-clicking the Outlook icon in the notification area on the taskbar. This opens the menu shown in Figure 6.3. From this menu, select the Test E-mail AutoConfiguration option.

When a domain-joined machine performs Autodiscover, it steps through the following process:

1. It performs an LDAP search for all SCP objects in the forest. Outlook enumerates the returned results based on the client's Active Directory site by sorting the returned SCP records using the keywords attribute; if there are no SCP records that contain a matching site value, all nonmatching SCP records are returned. If there are multiple matching SCP objects, Outlook simply chooses the oldest SCP record since the list is not sorted in any particular order.

2. Outlook attempts to connect to the configured URL specified in the SCP record's ServiceBindingInformation attribute: `https:// mail.contoso.com/Autodiscover/ Autodiscover.xml`.

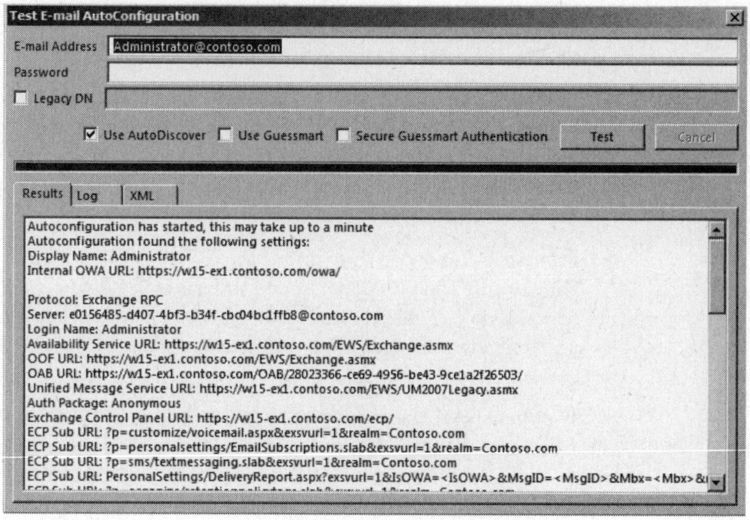

FIGURE 6.2
Using the Test Email
AutoConfiguration tool

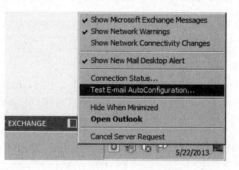

FIGURE 6.3
Accessing the Test Email
AutoConfiguration tool

3. When Outlook attempts to connect to the URL, the XML file is generated from the client request, and then the client successfully receives the XML file shown in Listing 6.1. (This output can be seen on the XML tab in the Test-Email AutoConfiguration screen.)

LISTING 6.1: An Autodiscover XML response

```
<?xml version="1.0" encoding="utf-8"?>?
<Autodiscover xmlns="http://schemas.microsoft.com/exchange/autodiscover/
responseschema/2006">
  <Response xmlns="http://schemas.microsoft.com/exchange/autodiscover/outlook/
responseschema/2006a">
    <User>
      <DisplayName>Administrator</DisplayName>
```

```
    <LegacyDN>/o=First Organization/ou=Exchange Administrative Group
(FYDIBOHF23SPDLT)/cn=Recipients/cn=215e037c2b5645999bc82d0efd528cbe-Admin</
LegacyDN>        <AutoDiscoverSMTPAddress>Administrator@netlogon.com</
AutoDiscoverSMTPAddress>
    <DeploymentId>5ac1eb86-fca8-45e6-8c4e-b48bc3d9c8bd</DeploymentId>
  </User>
  <Account>
    <AccountType>email</AccountType>
    <Action>settings</Action>
    <MicrosoftOnline>False</MicrosoftOnline>
    <Protocol>
      <Type>EXCH</Type>
      <Server>e0156485-d407-4bf3-b34f-cbc04bc1ffb8@netlogon.com</Server>
      <ServerDN>/o=First Organization/ou=Exchange Administrative Group
(FYDIBOHF23SPDLT)/cn=Configuration/cn=Servers/cn=e0156485-d407-4bf3-b34f-
cbc04bc1ffb8@netlogon.com</ServerDN>
      <ServerVersion>73C081D2</ServerVersion>
      <MdbDN>/o=First Organization/ou=Exchange Administrative Group
(FYDIBOHF23SPDLT)/cn=Configuration/cn=Servers/cn=e0156485-d407-4bf3-b34f-
cbc04bc1ffb8@netlogon.com/cn=Microsoft Private MDB</MdbDN>
      <PublicFolderServer>EX1.Netlogon.com</PublicFolderServer>
      <AD>w15-dc.Netlogon.com</AD>
      <AuthPackage>Anonymous</AuthPackage>
      <ASUrl>https://ex1.netlogon.com/EWS/Exchange.asmx</ASUrl>
      <EwsUrl>https://ex1.netlogon.com/EWS/Exchange.asmx</EwsUrl>
      <EmwsUrl>https://ex1.netlogon.com/EWS/Exchange.asmx</EmwsUrl>
      <EcpUrl>https://ex1.netlogon.com/ecp/</EcpUrl>
      <EcpUrl-um>?p=customize/voicemail.aspx&amp;exsvurl=1&amp;realm=Netlogon
.com</EcpUrl-um>
      <EcpUrl-aggr>?p=personalsettings/EmailSubscriptions.slab&amp;exsvurl=1&amp
;realm=Netlogon.com</EcpUrl-aggr>
      <EcpUrl-mt>PersonalSettings/DeliveryReport.aspx?exsvurl=1&amp;IsOWA=&lt
;IsOWA&gt;&amp;MsgID=&lt;MsgID&gt;&amp;Mbx=&lt;Mbx&gt;&amp;realm=Netlogon.com</
EcpUrl-mt>
      <EcpUrl-ret>?p=organize/retentionpolicytags.slab&amp;exsvurl=1&amp;realm=N
etlogon.com</EcpUrl-ret>
      <EcpUrl-sms>?p=sms/textmessaging.slab&amp;exsvurl=1&amp;realm=Netlogon
.com</EcpUrl-sms>
      <EcpUrl-publish>customize/calendarpublishing.slab?exsvurl=1&amp;FldID=&lt;
FldID&gt;&amp;realm=Netlogon.com</EcpUrl-publish>
      <EcpUrl-photo>PersonalSettings/EditAccount.aspx?chgPhoto=1&amp;realm=Netlo
gon.com</EcpUrl-photo>
      <EcpUrl-tm>?ftr=TeamMailbox&amp;exsvurl=1&amp;realm=Netlogon.com</EcpUrl-
tm>
      <EcpUrl-tmCreating>?ftr=TeamMailboxCreating&amp;SPUrl=&lt;SPUrl&gt;&amp;Ti
tle=&lt;Title&gt;&amp;SPTMAppUrl=&lt;SPTMAppUrl&gt;&amp;exsvurl=1&amp;ExchClientVe
r=15&amp;realm=Netlogon.com</EcpUrl-tmCreating>
      <EcpUrl-tmEditing>?ftr=TeamMailboxEditing&amp;Id=&lt;Id&gt;&amp;exsvurl=1&
amp;realm=Netlogon.com</EcpUrl-tmEditing>
```

```
        <EcpUrl-extinstall>Extension/InstalledExtensions.slab?exsvurl=1&amp;realm=
Netlogon.com</EcpUrl-extinstall>
        <OOFUrl>https://ex1.netlogon.com/EWS/Exchange.asmx</OOFUrl>
        <UMUrl>https://ex1.netlogon.com/EWS/UM2007Legacy.asmx</UMUrl>
        <OABUrl>https://ex1.netlogon.com/OAB/28023366-ce69-4956-be43-
9ce1a2f26503/</OABUrl>
        <ServerExclusiveConnect>off</ServerExclusiveConnect>
      </Protocol>
      <Protocol>
       <Type>EXPR</Type>
       <Server>ex1.netlogon.com</Server>
       <SSL>Off</SSL>
       <AuthPackage>Ntlm</AuthPackage>
       <ASUrl>https://mail.netlogon.com/EWS/Exchange.asmx</ASUrl>
       <EwsUrl>https://mail.netlogon.com/EWS/Exchange.asmx</EwsUrl>
       <EmwsUrl>https://mail.netlogon.com/EWS/Exchange.asmx</EmwsUrl>
       <OOFUrl>https://mail.netlogon.com/EWS/Exchange.asmx</OOFUrl>
       <UMUrl>https://mail.netlogon.com/EWS/UM2007Legacy.asmx</UMUrl>
       <ServerExclusiveConnect>on</ServerExclusiveConnect>
<EwsPartnerUrl>https://mail.netlogon.com/EWS/Exchange.asmx</EwsPartnerUrl>
      </Protocol>
      <Protocol>
       <Type>WEB</Type>
       <Internal>
         <OWAUrl AuthenticationMethod="Basic, Fba">https://ex1.netlogon.com/
owa/</OWAUrl>
          <Protocol>
            <Type>EXCH</Type>
            <ASUrl>https://ex1.netlogon.com/EWS/Exchange.asmx</ASUrl>
          </Protocol>
       </Internal>
      </Protocol>
      <Protocol>
       <Type>EXHTTP</Type>
       <Server>ex1.netlogon.com</Server>
       <SSL>Off</SSL>
       <AuthPackage>Ntlm</AuthPackage>
       <ASUrl>https://ex1.netlogon.com/EWS/Exchange.asmx</ASUrl>
       <EwsUrl>https://ex1.netlogon.com/EWS/Exchange.asmx</EwsUrl>
       <EmwsUrl>https://ex1.netlogon.com/EWS/Exchange.asmx</EmwsUrl>
       <EcpUrl>https://ex1.netlogon.com/ecp/</EcpUrl>
       <EcpUrl-um>?p=customize/voicemail.aspx&amp;exsvurl=1&amp;realm=Netlogon
.com</EcpUrl-um>
        <EcpUrl-aggr>?p=personalsettings/EmailSubscriptions.slab&amp;exsvurl=1&amp
;realm=Netlogon.com</EcpUrl-aggr>
        <EcpUrl-mt>PersonalSettings/DeliveryReport.aspx?exsvurl=1&amp;IsOWA=&lt
;IsOWA&gt;&amp;MsgID=&lt;MsgID&gt;&amp;Mbx=&lt;Mbx&gt;&amp;realm=Netlogon.com</
EcpUrl-mt>
```

```
        <EcpUrl-ret>?p=organize/retentionpolicytags.slab&amp;exsvurl=1&amp;realm=N
etlogon.com</EcpUrl-ret>
        <EcpUrl-sms>?p=sms/textmessaging.slab&amp;exsvurl=1&amp;realm=Netlogon
.com</EcpUrl-sms>
        <EcpUrl-publish>customize/calendarpublishing.slab?exsvurl=1&amp;FldID=&lt;
FldID&gt;&amp;realm=Netlogon.com</EcpUrl-publish>
        <EcpUrl-photo>PersonalSettings/EditAccount.aspx?chgPhoto=1&amp;realm=Netlo
gon.com</EcpUrl-photo>
        <EcpUrl-tm>?ftr=TeamMailbox&amp;exsvurl=1&amp;realm=Netlogon.com</EcpUrl-
tm>
        <EcpUrl-tmCreating>?ftr=TeamMailboxCreating&amp;SPUrl=&lt;SPUrl&gt;&amp;Ti
tle=&lt;Title&gt;&amp;SPTMAppUrl=&lt;SPTMAppUrl&gt;&amp;exsvurl=1&amp;ExchClientVe
r=15&amp;realm=Netlogon.com</EcpUrl-tmCreating>
        <EcpUrl-tmEditing>?ftr=TeamMailboxEditing&amp;Id=&lt;Id&gt;&amp;exsvurl=1&
amp;realm=Netlogon.com</EcpUrl-tmEditing>
        <EcpUrl-extinstall>Extension/InstalledExtensions.slab?exsvurl=1&amp;realm=
Netlogon.com</EcpUrl-extinstall>
        <OOFUrl>https://ex1.netlogon.com/EWS/Exchange.asmx</OOFUrl>
        <UMUrl>https://ex1.netlogon.com/EWS/UM2007Legacy.asmx</UMUrl>
        <OABUrl>https://ex1.netlogon.com/OAB/28023366-ce69-4956-be43-
9ce1a2f26503/</OABUrl>
        <ServerExclusiveConnect>On</ServerExclusiveConnect>
      </Protocol>
    </Account>
  </Response>
</Autodiscover>
```

There are six key sections to note in Listing 6.1:

◆ The User and Account sections list the user information for the authenticated user.

◆ The EXCH protocol section (identified by the EXCH tag) is for connections inside the firewall. Remember, all Outlook connections are now over HTTPS. The URLs provided in this section are based on the InternalURL values.

◆ The EXPR protocol section (identified by the EXPR tag) is Outlook Anywhere—RPC over HTTPS. The URLs provided in this section are based on the ExternalURL values.

◆ The WEB protocol section (identified by the WEB tag) is used for OWA and other types of clients. The URLs provided in this section are for clients and are based on the best URL for the users to use.

◆ You will notice what looks like a new provider, ExHTTP, in the list of returned providers to the Outlook client. However, ExHTTP isn't a provider; it just looks like one in the Autodiscover log. It is a calculated set of values from the EXCH and EXPR settings that are processed only by Outlook 2013 clients.

If the client had been outside the firewall, it would have followed a similar process, but instead it steps through the hostnames and URLs as described in the previous section on DNS names. An external client (for the domain `netlogon.com`) using Autodiscover goes through these steps:

1. The client tries to connect to the Active Directory SCP but is unable to do so.

2. The client performs a DNS query for either `netlogon.com` or `autodiscover.netlogon.com` and tries to connect to the Autodiscover URL.

3. The client retrieves `autodiscover.xml` from the Autodiscover HTTPS host.

4. The client parses through the `WEB` sections of the `autodiscover.xml` file in order to determine the correct URL to which it should connect.

5. The client initiates a connection to the appropriate external URL.

To help step through and troubleshoot external connectivity, you should be aware of the Microsoft Remote Connectivity Analyzer tool, available online from `http://testexchangeconnectivity.com/`. This web-based tool from Microsoft provides a secure, reliable suite of tests to help diagnose problems with not only Autodiscover but all of the web-based Exchange Server remote client access protocols and also server-to-server tests like SMTP connectivity and connectivity from other clients such as Lync 2013.

I can't say enough about this great troubleshooting weapon, initially developed as a pet project by a couple of Microsoft engineers. Especially in the early days of Exchange Server 2010, this tool saved me in many situations. Today, I used it more as a validation tool than a troubleshooting tool, but regardless of your level of expertise with Autodiscover, you'll find happiness somewhere in the Remote Connectivity Analyzer.

Site Affinity (aka Site Scope)

You've gotten through the basics of Autodiscover, so you're ready for some advanced concepts, such as how site affinity works.

To understand the point of site affinity, consider an organization that has multiple locations—we'll say in Seattle, Washington (code SEA); Toledo, Ohio (code TOL); and New Orleans, Louisiana (code MSY). There are Exchange servers and users in each of these locations. The links between these locations run over WAN links from Seattle to Toledo and Toledo to New Orleans; it is neither optimal nor desired to allow users in Seattle to use Client Access servers in New Orleans (or vice versa). Using site affinity, we can use the following commands to help ensure this does not happen:

```
Set-ClientAccessServer -Identity "sea-cas01" ↵
-AutodiscoverServiceInternalURI "https://sea-cas01.netlogon.com/↵
autodiscover/autodiscover.xml" -AutodiscoverServiceSiteScope ↵
"Site-SEA","Site-TOL"

Set-ClientAccessServer -Identity "sea-cas02" ↵
-AutodiscoverServiceInternalURI "https://sea-cas02.netlogon.com/↵
autodiscover/autodiscover.xml" -AutodiscoverServiceSiteScope ↵
"Site-SEA","Site-TOL"

Set-ClientAccessServer -Identity "tol-cas01" ↵
```

```
-AutodiscoverServiceInternalURI "https://tol-cas01.netlogon.com/↵
autodiscover/autodiscover.xml" -AutodiscoverServiceSiteScope ↵
"Site-SEA","Site-TOL","Site-MSY"

Set-ClientAccessServer -Identity "tol-cas02" ↵
-AutodiscoverServiceInternalURI "https://tol-cas02.netlogon.com/↵
autodiscover/autodiscover.xml" -AutodiscoverServiceSiteScope ↵
"Site-SEA","Site-TOL","Site-MSY"

Set-ClientAccessServer -Identity "msy-cas01" ↵
-AutodiscoverServiceInternalURI "https://msy-cas01.netlogon.com/↵
autodiscover/autodiscover.xml" -AutodiscoverServiceSiteScope ↵
"Site-TOL","Site-MSY"

Set-ClientAccessServer -Identity "msy-cas02" ↵
-AutodiscoverServiceInternalURI "https://msy-cas02.netlogon.com/↵
autodiscover/autodiscover.xml" -AutodiscoverServiceSiteScope ↵
"Site-TOL","Site-MSY"
```

When clients perform Autodiscover, they will match only the records for those Client Access servers that match the site they are currently in.

Clients in Seattle will match only the SEA-CAS01, SEA-CAS02, TOL-CAS01, and TOL-CAS02 SCP objects. Because there are multiple objects, they will perform their initial discovery to TOL-CAS01 (this was the last server configured), which will then return URLs for the servers in the Seattle site.

Likewise, clients in New Orleans will match only the MSY-CAS01, MSY-CAS02, TOL-CAS01, and TOL-CAS02 SCP objects. Because there are multiple objects, they will perform their initial discovery to MSY-CAS01, which will then return URLs for the servers in the New Orleans site.

Clients in Toledo will match all six SCP objects. Because there are multiple objects, they will perform their initial discovery to MSY-CAS01, which will then return URLs for the servers in the Toledo site.

If these are not the required behaviors, you should take a close look at the Exchange Server 2007 Autodiscover white paper at http://technet.microsoft.com/en-us/library/bb332063 .aspx. Although this paper is for Exchange Server 2007, the concepts transfer to Exchange Server 2013 without much damage.

Planning Certificates for Autodiscover

The other hard part for Autodiscover is managing the required SSL certificates. After working with a number of Exchange Server 2007 deployments, we began to realize that the biggest difficulty with Autodiscover certificates was inevitably the need to use a SAN certificate. While other scenarios are possible (such as creating a separate Autodiscover website on a separate IP address and using a second single-name certificate) as outlined in the Exchange Server 2007 Autodiscover white paper, these options ended up being far more complicated to run.

So what's so difficult about SAN certificates? We think that most people don't understand what certificates really are or how they work. Certificates and Public Key Infrastructures (PKI) are black magic—stark-naked voodoo—mainly because they've traditionally been complicated to deploy and play with. Getting even an internal PKI like the Windows Server 2012 Active Directory Certificates Services in place and running can be hard to manage unless you already know what to do and what the results should look like. Add to that the difficulty of managing certificates with the built-in Windows tools, and most Exchange Server administrators we know want to stay far away from Transport Layer Security (TLS) and Secure Socket Layer (SSL).

Although Exchange Server 2013 follows the lead of Exchange Server 2010 and 2007 and installs self-signed certificates on each new server, these certificates are not meant to take you into production for all scenarios. It's technically possible to leave the self-signed certificate on Mailbox servers, but Client Access servers are the ones that absolutely require the self-signed certificate to be replaced before entering into a production environment. Internal Outlook clients *can* use the self-signed certificates, but Outlook does not ignore improperly matched names or expired certificates. Internal Outlook clients will just ignore the fact that the certificate is from an untrusted certificate authority.

External or web-based clients won't accept a self-signed certificate without you manually importing the root certificate—which is a huge administrative burden for mobile clients. For externally facing deployments, you either need to have a well-managed PKI deployment or use a third-party commercial certificate authority. Make sure that you use one whose root and intermediate CA certificates are well supported by the operating systems and devices that will be connecting to your network.

The X.509 Certificate Standard

The digital certificates that Exchange Server and other SSL/TLS-aware systems use are defined by the X.509 v3 certificate standard. This standard is documented in RFC 2459 (and other related RFCs). The X.509 certificates were developed as part of the X.500 family of standards from the Open Source Initiative but proved to be useful enough that they were adopted by other standards organizations.

The X.509 certificates are based on the concept of *private key cryptography*. In this system, you have an algorithm that generates a pair of cryptographic keys for each entity that will be exchanging encrypted message traffic: a *private key* that only that entity knows and a corresponding *public key* that can be freely transmitted. As long as the private keys are kept safe, the system can be used not only to securely encrypt messages but also to prove that messages were sent from the claimed sender. The exclusivity of the private key provides authentication as well as security.

For example, If UserA and UserB want to exchange encrypted messages using a private key system (S/MIME), here's how it works:

1. Both UserA and UserB ensure that they have secure private keys. They have exchanged their corresponding public keys—maybe through email, by sending a digitally signed email, by publishing them on their websites, or by locating them in Active Directory.

2. UserA, when sending a message to UserB, will use UserA's public key and UserB's public key to encrypt and sign the message. This ensures that only UserB will be able to decrypt the message and provides authenticity of sender via the signature.

3. UserB receives the encrypted messages and uses his private key and UserA's public key to decrypt the message. This ensures that the message actually came from UserA.

When UserB receives the message, he uses his own private key to decrypt the message. If UserB wants to send a message to UserA in return, he simply reverses the process: he uses his public key and UserA's public key to encrypt, and UserA uses his private key. If UserB later needs to open the message in his Sent Items folder, he would use his private key to decrypt it.

Digital certificates help streamline this process and expand it for more uses than just message encryption by providing a convenient wrapper format for the public keys plus some associated metadata. For our purposes, though, we're concerned about using certificates for server authentication and establishing the symmetric shared session key for the TLS session.

In Windows, you can view digital certificates, examine their properties, and validate the certificate chain through the MMC. Although Windows doesn't include a preconfigured Certificate console, it does include the Certificates snap-in. Open an instance of `MMC.exe` and add the Certificates snap-in, configured for the local machine, as shown in Figure 6.4. You can now view and manage the server certificates that will be used by Exchange Server.

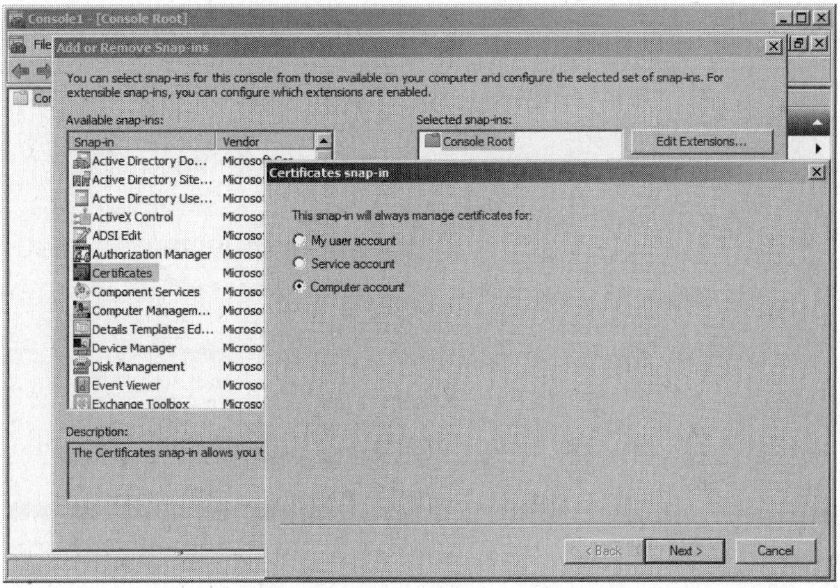

FIGURE 6.4
The Certificates
MMC snap-in

While you can view the properties of a certificate using the Certificate console, all certificates that are used by Exchange Server (for HTTPS, SMTP, UM Call Router, IMAP, or POP) should be managed using either the Exchange Admin Center or the Exchange Management Shell.

Let's take a look at the typical properties of an X.509v3 digital certificate as provisioned for Exchange Server (some of which are shown in Figure 6.5):

Subject Name   This property provides the identity of the entity the certificate applies to. This can be in X.500 format, which looks like LDAP, or in DNS format if intended for a server.

Subject Alternate Name   This is an optional property that lists one or more additional identities that will match the certificate. If the hostname in the URL that the client attempts to connect to doesn't match the subject name or subject alternate name properties, the certificate will not validate. Without this property, a certificate can only match a single hostname.

Common Name Also known as the friendly name, this property provides a useful text tag for handling and managing the certificate once you have a collection of them.

Issuer This property lists the identity of the issuing certificate authority (CA). This can be a root CA or an intermediate CA. Combined with the digital signature from the CA's own digital signature, this property allows establishment of the certificate chain of trust back to the root CA. What distinguishes a root CA? The fact that this property (plus signature) is self-signed.

Serial Number This property allows the certificate to be easily published on a certificate revocation list (CRL) by the certificate authority if the certificate has been revoked. The location(s) of the CRL is usually included on the issuer's certificate. This is typically a URL. Many applications, including Outlook, attempt to check the CRL to verify that the certificate has been revoked.

Thumbprint This property (and the corresponding thumbprint algorithm) is a cryptographic hash of the certificate information. This thumbprint is commonly used by Exchange Server as an easy identifier for certificates.

Valid From and Valid To These properties define the effective duration of the certificate. They are evaluated as part of the certificate validation.

Public Key This property contains the entity's associated cryptographic public key. The corresponding private key is never viewed with the certificate.

FIGURE 6.5
Viewing the properties of an Exchange Server digital certificate

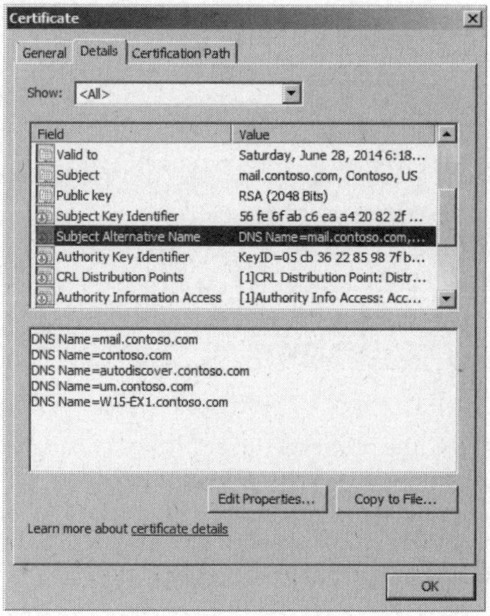

In Figure 6.6, we can see the certificate trust chain and verify that we have the proper CA certificates installed. When installing a third-party or an internally generated certificate, it is essential that the Exchange server trusts all certificates in the certificate chain, similarly to the certificate validation that occurs on a client computer. The trust chain uses a simple transitive logic for trusting certificates. Certificates are issued by certification authorities that are already trusted by the Exchange servers. Or, as it was described to me in college, if you trust your father, and your father trusts his father, then you automatically trust your grandfather.

FIGURE 6.6
Viewing a certificate trust chain

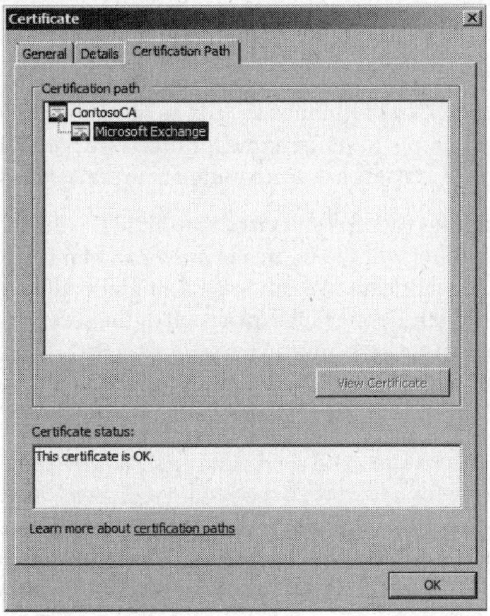

Deploying Exchange Certificates

Now that we've talked about certificates in general, let's dive into the issues of getting them deployed on your Exchange Server 2013 servers.

PLANNING CERTIFICATE NAMES

The first part of creating digital certificates for your Exchange Server 2013 servers is deciding on which names you need. For the Client Access servers, it's highly recommended that you accept the need for a SAN certificate. Although SAN certificates are more expensive than single-name certificates, you can often configure them so that you can reuse them on multiple servers. Otherwise, you need to use a lot of single-name certificates—potentially with multiple websites and virtual directories on your Client Access server instances. This can become an overwhelming amount of operational overhead.

Sure, you can use wildcard certificates for some scenarios, such as Outlook and Windows Phones. The wildcard certificate is issued for an entire domain, such as `*.netlogon.com`. This certificate could then be used by multiple servers and sites. Naturally, wildcard certificates are usually more expensive than certificates issued for a single host. Be aware, also, that not all clients (such as earlier Windows Mobile phones) will recognize wildcard certificates. The Exchange Server product group does not recommend wildcard certificates, and neither do we. They present a bigger risk than SAN certificates, which point to specific named resources. That being said, for small organizations that do not have significant security concerns, a wildcard certificate can sometimes be a simpler overall deployment option.

Let's take the three-site `contoso.com` example from earlier in this chapter and some of the factors to consider when requesting certificates:

◆ For Internet connectivity, a single site will act as the gateway for all inbound Internet connectivity. That site will host the initial Autodiscover service and therefore the domain name `autodiscover.contoso.com`

◆ We'll use the FQDN `mail.contoso.com` as our generic external access name. We don't need to use a separate domain name for this—we could easily use `autodiscover.contoso.com`, but users are accustomed to an easier-to-understand name.

◆ Having two names could mean either multiple IP addresses and websites or a SAN certificate. We don't want to incur the overhead of multiple certificates and websites, so we will use a SAN certificate. We can issue a single certificate for all the Client Access servers each site. We'll include the FQDNs of each of the servers in the SAN. Most commercial CAs have a price increase after five names on a SAN certificate, so you need to keep that in consideration. But always consider all the places you may want to use a certificate, such as on multiple Client Access servers for load balancing.

So, if we have multiple sites, the certificate will require the distinctive names of the locations (such as `Canada.contoso.com` and `Europe.contoso.com`), as well as `mail.contoso.com` and `autodiscover.contoso.com`. We don't need to include the NetBIOS names of our servers— Exchange Server and its clients don't use them unless we choose to configure them otherwise.

It is important to note as you start requesting certificates that poor namespace planning or separate internal namespaces (such as `contoso.com` for external clients but `contoso.local` for internal clients) will result in more complex certificate requirements. Ensure that you have carefully thought out the internal and external URL requirements as you are planning your Exchange Server 2013 deployment. Something to watch for is that you set the common name to be the preferred name that users will access the most and the one that is seen on the first properties page, so in our example we would most probably select `mail.contoso.com` as the common name in the certificate.

ISSUING AND ENABLING CERTIFICATES WITH EXCHANGE ADMIN CENTER

In Exchange Server 2007, you had to do all your certificate requests and imports either through the Certificate MMC snap-in (which was a pain) or through the EMS. In Exchange Server 2013 if you click the Server node in the EAC, you can view, manage, and even request new certificates for your Exchange Server 2013 servers.

On the Domains page of the wizard, you need to specify the domain(s) for which each access type is available. For example, you may select OWA and ActiveSync for contoso.com.

On the next page of the wizard, you will see the different types of names that you can include in your certificate request. For example, we could add mail.contoso.com and ex1.contoso.com to populate the SAN names.

Note in Figure 6.7 that this server's internal OWA name is ex1.contoso.com and the external name is mail.contoso.com. For some of these fields, the New Exchange Certificate Wizard is making a "best guess" at the correct names, but you will need to fill in some of the others manually, depending on your naming preferences and what you have configured in DNS.

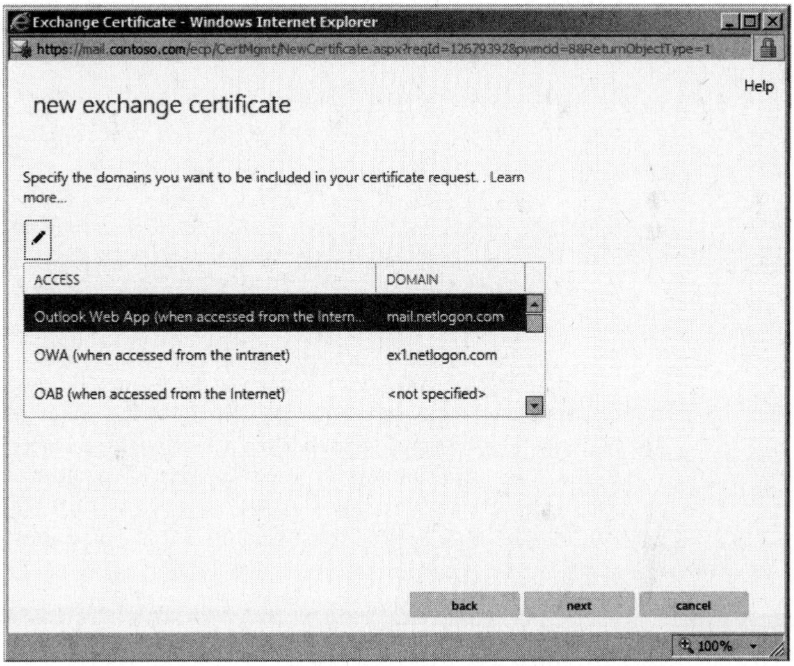

FIGURE 6.7

Viewing the domains to be included in the certificate request

In Figure 6.8, you can see the Certificate Domains page; this page allows you to specify additional fully qualified domain names that will show up in the certificate request. The wizard is making another "best guess" for this certificate request by adding all of the accepted domains as well. You may want to check that the hostname Autodiscover is present for each of these domain names.

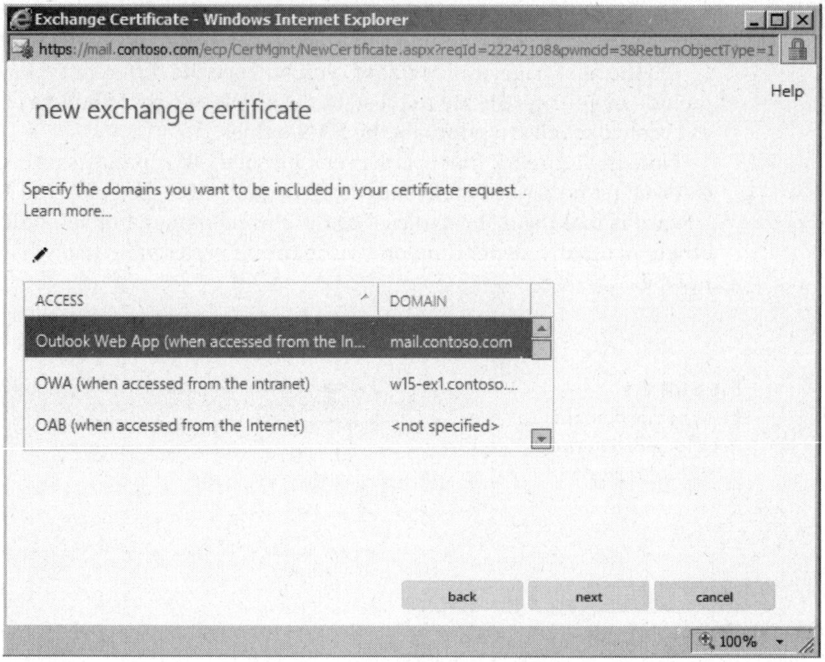

FIGURE 6.8
The Certificate
Domains wizard
page

The Organization and Location page of the wizard requests information that most administrators who have already configured a certificate request will recognize. This includes the organization information, department, city, state, and country.

On the last page in the wizard you must provide a name and path where the certificate request file will be created. The completion of this wizard will execute the relevant cmdlet for you. In this case, the cmdlet New-ExchangeCertificate is being run, such as is shown here:

```
New-ExchangeCertificate
    {PrivateKeyExportable=True, FriendlyName=mail, SubjectName=System.Security
.Cryptography.X509Certificates.X500DistinguishedName, DomainName={ex1
.netlogon.com, mail.netlogon.com, EX1}, RequestFile=\\ex1\c$\cert.req,
GenerateRequest=True, Server=EX1, KeySize=2048}
```

(This cmdlet comes, of course, with Get- and Set- partners as well, to view and configure the certificate.)

You can now submit to a certificate authority the contents of the file that was created. Once you have received back a signed certificate, you use the Complete Pending Request Wizard to complete the process. Start this by clicking Complete next to the certificate showing a pending state. This wizard will load the signed certificate into the certificate store on the appropriate server.

The final process after the certificate is fully loaded is to assign the certificate to be used by the appropriate services (such as SMTP or IIS). Select the certificate in the work pane and then click the Edit button on the toolbar, and select the services node on the left. On the Services node of the wizard (shown in Figure 6.9) select the appropriate services. When you select Internet Information Services (IIS), that includes OWA, the Exchange Admin Center (EAC), the Exchange Control Panel (ECP), Exchange Web Services (EWS), and ActiveSync. Note that a service can be assigned to only one certificate at a time.

FIGURE 6.9
Selecting services that will use the certificate

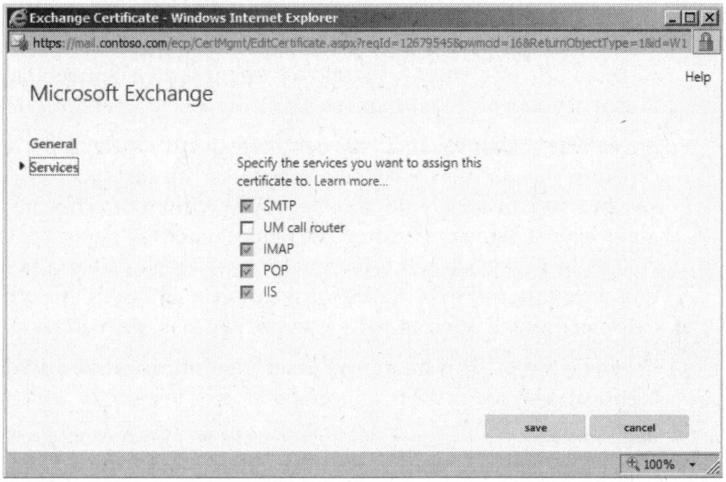

A WORD OF WARNING

Whichever tool you use to request certificates should be the tool you use to import them. Although you should be able to mix and match them in theory, we've seen odd results. Also, don't use the certificate wizard in IIS to request Exchange Server certificates, especially if you need SAN certificates. Stick to the Exchange Server tools for certificate management and also for renewals; the non-Exchange Server tools will not install certificates or manage certificates in the appropriate locations or in the appropriate manner.

ISSUING AND ENABLING CERTIFICATES WITH EMS

Although Exchange Server 2013 provides an Exchange Admin Center interface for managing certificates, you can still manage certificates through the EMS. If you have done this in the past with Exchange Server 2007, you will have to learn a few new tricks in order to work with certificates from the EMS. Because of the way PowerShell works via Remoting now, you can no longer specify a path for a certificate request file. Instead, the certificate request is output to the shell, so you must capture that to a variable. Here's the command you would issue to generate a certificate request for the URL mail.netlogon.com and capture it to the $Data variable:

```
$Data = New-ExchangeCertificate -GenerateRequest -SubjectName "c=US, ↵
o=Netlogon, cn=mail.netlogon.com" -DomainName netlogon.com ↵
–PrivateKeyExportable $true
```

Next, we need to take output the value stored in the $Data variable to the file c:\CertRequest.req using this command:

```
Set-Content -path "C:\Docs\MyCertRequest.req" -Value $Data
```

Here are the details of the New-ExchangeCertificate cmdlet (discussed earlier, in the section "Issuing and Enabling Certificates with Exchange Admin Center"):

GenerateRequest   This parameter tells Exchange Server to generate a certificate request. Had we left it off, the command would have generated a new self-signed certificate. That's usually not what you want. This request is suitable for either an internal PKI or a commercial CA.

PrivateKeyExportable   This parameter is extremely important and is the cause of most certificate headaches we've seen. When a certificate request is generated, it includes the public key, but the private key stays in the secure Windows certificate store. If the CA is configured to allow export of the private key, the request must explicitly ask for the private key to be exportable in the first place. If this parameter wasn't included or was set to $false, we wouldn't be able to export the certificate's private key to import to the other CAS instance or on to the external firewall, such as a TMG server, which is often done.

FriendlyName   This parameter is set for administrative convenience. If we have multiple certificates issued to the machine, it allows us to identify which certificate we're dealing with.

DomainName   This parameter allows us to set one or more domain names. If we specify more than one, Exchange Server will automatically create and populate the SAN property with all the requested hostnames and set the subject name of the certificate to the first hostname in the list. Although the cmdlet provides additional parameters to explicitly set the subject and alternate names, *you don't need them*.

A successful run of the cmdlet will generate the request output and a thumbprint of the request. Submit the request to your CA, download the corresponding certificate, and then import the certificate back on the same machine, like in the following example:

```
Import-ExchangeCertificate -FileData $(Get-Content ↵
-Path c:\CertImport.pfx -Encoding byte) ↵
-Password:(Get-Credential).password
```

This cmdlet will import the saved certificate if it matches a pending request and print out the thumbprint of the newly imported certificate. Ensure that you look after the PFX file that is used here. We've seen administrators leaving this on the desktop or the C: drive of Exchange servers. Best practice is *not* to store a copy of this on the server itself. By all means keep a copy in a safe place if it will not be possible or convenient to download a copy in the future.

You can now view the certificate in the Certificates snap-in in MMC or from the certificate management functionality in the Exchange Admin Center. From here you can view the details about the certificate, such as the thumbprint, SAN names, and which services the certificate is assigned to, as shown in Figure 6.10.

FIGURE 6.10
Viewing certificate properties

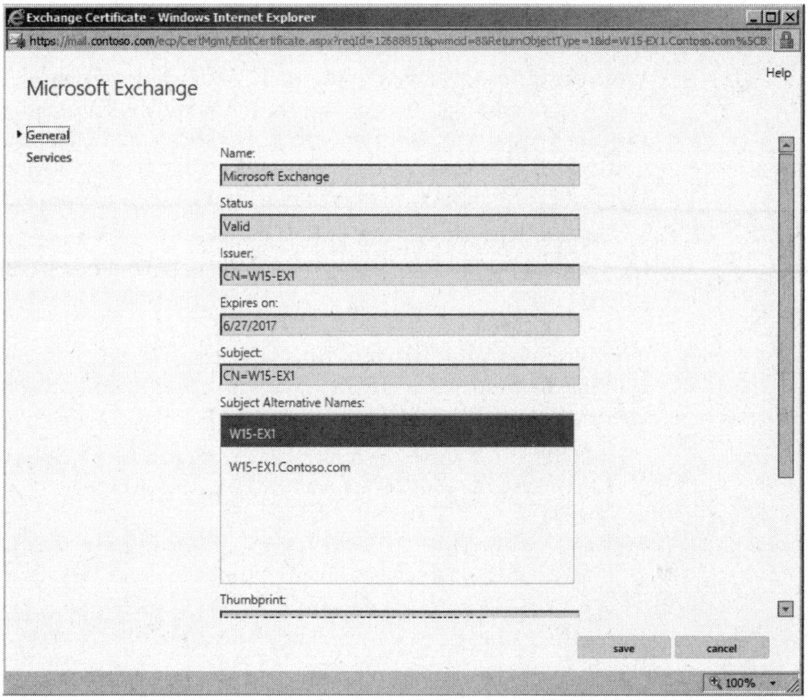

The final step is to enable Exchange Server services against the certificate:

```
Enable-ExchangeCertificate -Thumbprint <certificate thumbprint>
-Services <services>
```

<services> is a comma-separated list of one or more of the following values, depending on the protocols you have enabled and the roles you have installed:

SMTP   For use with SMTP + TLS for front-end/backend transport services

UM Call Router   For use with the Unified Messaging services' call router and connecting to the Client Access server

UM   For use with general Unified Messaging services

Federation   For use when configuring federated services with the Microsoft Federation Gateway (You cannot assign this service with this cmdlet; it is configured when configuring a federated trust.)

IIS   For use with Client Access servers, including Autodiscover

IMAP   For use with Client Access servers that are serving the IMAP client protocol

POP   For use with Client Access servers that are serving the POP3 client protocol

The Bottom Line

Work with Autodiscover.   Autodiscover is a key service in Exchange Server 2013, both for ensuring hassle-free client configuration as well as keeping the Exchange servers in your organization working together smoothly. Autodiscover can be used by Outlook 2007, Outlook 2010, Outlook 2013, Entourage, Outlook for Mac 2011, Windows Mobile/Windows Phone 6.1 and later, and other mobile devices like Android, iOS, and even Windows RT devices.

Master It   You are configuring Outlook 2013 to connect to Exchange Server and you want to diagnose a problem that you are having when connecting. What tool can you use?

Troubleshoot Autodiscover.   In a large organization with multiple Active Directory sites or multiple namespaces, it is essential to track the Autodiscover traffic and understand where client queries will be directed.

Master It   If you have multiple Active Directory sites, what should you do to control the client flow of requests for Autodiscover information?

Manage Exchange Server certificates.   Exchange Server 2013 servers rely on functional X.509v3 digital certificates to ensure proper SSL and TLS security.

Master It   Which tools will you need to create and manage Exchange Server certificates?

Part 2

Getting Exchange Server Running

Chapter 7

Exchange Server 2013 Quick Start Guide

Reading through a Mastering book just to figure out how to get a quick installation of Exchange Server 2013 up and running may seem like a daunting task—especially if all you want to do is get a look at Exchange and play around. With that in mind, here we'll present the steps for getting a lab or test server up and running quickly.

The purpose of building a test server is to learn and optimize the installation and configuration experience. Exchange is a feature-rich application and, as such, has many different ways to configure settings for optimization, performance, and stability. Using a test server to try various scenarios provides for a better production deployment—and a better-prepared administrator.

We won't cover every little detail on every setting or extensive design and best practices in this chapter. That's what the rest of this book is for. But we will discuss the requirements for getting a typical Exchange Server 2013 server up and running. A typical Exchange server is one that holds both roles required in an Exchange Server 2013 organization: the Mailbox role, where user mailboxes reside and which handles all data-rendering for those users' connections; and the Client Access role, which provides transparent connection authentication and routing. In Exchange Server 2013, the functionality, provided by the legacy Hub Transport and Unified Messaging roles, is now provided by the Mailbox and Client Access roles. Exchange Server 2013 doesn't include the Edge Transport role; if you intend to use it, you'll need to use the Exchange Server 2010 SP3 Edge Transport role. Unified Messaging and Edge Transport are optional roles and outside what we'll cover in this chapter.

In this chapter, you will learn to:

◆ Quickly size a typical server

◆ Install the necessary Windows Server 2012 or Windows Server 2008 R2 prerequisites

◆ Install a multifunction Exchange Server 2013 server

◆ Configure Exchange to send and receive email

◆ Configure recipients, contacts, and distribution groups

Server Sizing Quick Reference

Although properly sizing a server for production is extremely important, sizing for a lab or test server is somewhat less involved if you're only interested in pushing some buttons and "kicking the tires" of Exchange Server 2013. For instance, a lab server might have enough storage for a few users, but a production server might be configured for many hundreds or thousands.

However, in order to have a responsive lab or evaluation environment, there are still basics that you should pay attention to when building a test server.

Hardware

In this section, we'll look at the hardware required to quickly set up a lab server. We'll focus on memory, processors, storage, operating system, and virtualization considerations.

Memory

Exchange Server 2013 is the third generation to use 64-bit architecture. Although this gives overall better memory management, including the ability to handle higher amounts of physical memory, it also means that the baseline memory requirements have increased when compared to all previous versions of Exchange. The Exchange Server 2013 architecture, while reducing the number of roles required, necessarily increases the number of processes running on the typical server.

The baseline requirement for the Client Access role is 4 GB of RAM, whereas the baseline for the Mailbox role (or a combined Mailbox/Client Access server role) is 8 GB of RAM. Although these minimums aren't enforced by the setup program, Exchange will run very sluggishly without enough RAM. The ESE database component, in particular, requires more RAM even on a lightly loaded server; it has been completely rewritten in managed code and spawns a separate service for each mailbox database. This overhead adds up on low-end servers like test servers but scales for better caching and efficiency in servers with many users.

The final piece for memory utilization is to properly configure your Windows page file. By default, Windows will manage the page file on its own, but you need to change this to keep even lightly loaded lab Exchange servers from excessive paging. As shown in Figure 7.1, set the page file to a static fixed size: physical RAM plus 10 MB.

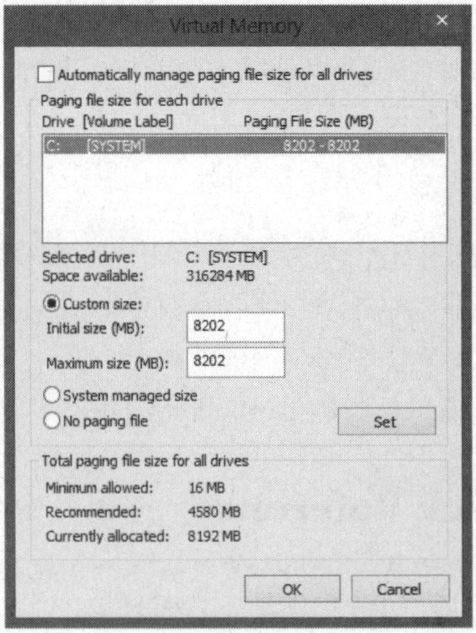

FIGURE 7.1
Setting a static page file for 8 GB of RAM

PROCESSORS

Server hardware that will host Exchange Server 2013 requires 64-bit processors. This includes either x64 Intel or AMD64 CPUs. Itanium IA64 processors are not supported for Exchange Server 2013. The minimum recommended number of processor cores for a lightweight test Exchange server is two. Even in a lab, two processor cores may not provide enough performance, so consider using four to eight processor cores. With a single core, expect to take an inordinately long time installing and for many odd transient errors to occur during normal operations.

DISK SPACE

Basic Exchange Server 2013 storage requirements include space for the Exchange binary files, message-tracking logs, mailbox databases and transaction logs, and transport-queue databases and transaction logs.

A typical installation requires at least the following:

◆ 30 GB available on the installation drive for binaries. Don't forget to keep free space available for utilities and upgrades.

◆ 200 MB available on the system drive (typically C:), aside from the space used by the page file and any spare space you keep for system updates and normal operations (such as IIS logs).

◆ 500 MB available for the transport queue, by default on the installation drive.

◆ Space for mailbox databases and transaction logs.

When installing on Windows Server 2012, the system drive must, of course, be formatted with NTFS, as must all volumes used for Exchange Server 2013. While the new Resilient File System (ReFS) feature in Windows Server 2012 has many attractive features for file servers and servers using low-end storage, it is not supported by Exchange: not for the binary installation data and not for database volumes.

NETWORK

Exchange Server 2013 servers should have at least one 1 GB Ethernet network interface card. Additional cards can be used but aren't required, although they are recommended if you're going to use DAGs. If you are using multiple network interfaces, put them on separate subnets.

Network teaming is supported with Exchange Server 2013, but you should determine whether it's really necessary, especially for your quick-start environment. There's no point in teaming interfaces that are used for replication networks; if you have multiple ports, create multiple replication networks, each with its own IP subnet. Ensure that you have the latest teaming and network drivers for your hardware to prevent bugs from causing irritating issues.

If you're deploying a DAG on multirole servers, you still can't use Windows network load balancing on the Mailbox roles. However, with the new Client Access architecture, simple DNS round-robin records may be sufficient to test load balancing in a lab environment.

Finally, whether you're using IPv6 or not, there's no real advantage to disabling it. Windows (and Exchange) are tested with IPv6 enabled. If you do disable it, follow the Windows IPv6 FAQ guidelines on completely disabling IPv6, including keeping IPv4 enabled. Don't simply unbind it from your network adapters. This practice does not ensure that IPv6 components are no longer active in the network stack and has been the source of past Exchange network and stability issues.

⚡ SERVER VIRTUALIZATION

Both Exchange Server 2013 roles are supported in virtual environments when all the following conditions are true:

- The hardware virtualization software is running one of the following:

  - Windows Server 2008 R2 with Hyper-V technology

  - Microsoft Hyper-V Server 2008 R2

  - Windows Server 2012

  - Microsoft Hyper-V Server 2012

  - Any third-party hypervisor that has been validated under the Windows Server Virtualization Validation Program

  Although you can't run production Exchange Server 2013 virtual machines under the Windows Azure virtualization service, you can run lab or test machines.

- The Exchange Server guest virtual machine meets all of the following requirements:

  - Running Microsoft Exchange Server 2013.

  - Deployed on Windows Server 2008 R2 SP1 or later.

  - Not backed up and restored using virtual machine snapshots; only Exchange-supported backup mechanisms are supported.

  - Not protected by virtualization HA mechanisms that use disk-based state save files such as Hyper-V's Quick Migration.

- The virtual machine configurations meet the following conditions:

  - No memory oversubscription or dynamic memory allocation is used.

  - Processor oversubscription is at a ratio of no more than 2:1.

- The virtual storage meets the following conditions:

  - If virtual hard drives are used, they should be a fixed size for performance and data stability, not dynamically expanding.

  - It doesn't use differencing drives.

  - It doesn't use any file-based storage, such as SMB or NFS at any layer in the stack, with the exception of SMB 3.0 when used to host fixed-size virtual drives; under no circumstances can you use file-based storage to direct-mount and host Exchange data files (see the "Microsoft Recommendations" sidebar in Chapter 4, "Virtualizing Exchange Server 2013," for more information).

  - The operating system drive should be at least 15 GB plus the size of the virtual memory, although realistically in many lab scenarios you will want this drive to be large enough for the boot partition, the operating system, the page file, the Exchange binaries, and patches and the default Exchange databases.

Operating Systems

Exchange Server 2013 supports the following operating systems:

- ◆ Windows Server 2008 R2 (Standard, Enterprise, or Datacenter Edition)
- ◆ Windows Server 2012 (Standard or Datacenter Edition)

Trial versions of each of these operating systems are available for download from Microsoft's website. They will provide months of use and can be installed over and over for testing. You cannot use the Server Core installation of either version of Windows for Exchange Server 2013 machines, however.

Windows Server 2012 is the latest version of the Windows operating system and it includes many stability-, performance-, and security-related updates from its predecessors. Additionally, Windows Server 2012 provides the necessary clustering components required by DAGs in the Standard Edition; with Windows Server 2008 R2, you need Enterprise or Datacenter Edition to get these components. When looking at a new mail platform, it makes sense to use the latest operating system because of all the enhancements available. Building a test server is a perfect time to get some experience with the new operating system. Additionally, it makes sense to deploy an operating system that will still be in mainstream support during the typical life cycle of a newly deployed server. Although Exchange Server 2013 is supported on Windows Server 2008 R2, Windows Server 2012 includes many of the prerequisites required for Exchange, making deployment quicker and easier than with Windows Server 2008 R2.

Since we are focusing on getting an Exchange server up and running quickly in this chapter, we assume the following:

- ◆ The server is joined to an Active Directory domain, and the Active Directory domain is isolated from any production domains.

- ◆ The Active Directory forest and domain are at a minimum functionality level of Windows Server 2003.

- ◆ The server has a static IP address assigned.

- ◆ Test Active Directory user accounts have been created.

- ◆ You have an administrative account that is a member of the Schema Admins, Domain Admins, and Enterprise Admins security groups.

- ◆ The server is not a domain controller.

- ◆ There are no other Exchange servers in the domain.

- ◆ There is a domain controller in the same Active Directory site that the Exchange server will reside in.

- ◆ If you have multiple domains in the forest, the first site you will install an Exchange server in contains a writeable global catalog server from each domain.

Based on these assumptions, you should be able to go through this chapter and build a functioning Exchange Server 2013 server quickly.

🌐 Real World Scenario

CONSIDER SETTING UP A LAB ENVIRONMENT

In many environments, space is at a premium, and administrators may see no need for a lab environment—or feel that they don't have the time, energy, or budget to get one approved by management. If you enjoy managing your Exchange organization in a reactive fashion—always fixing problems after the fact, always finding out the hard way about software incompatibilities, always realizing two hours after your maintenance window was supposed to end that you're actually not sure how a particular feature works—then you absolutely don't need a lab—or this chapter. Everyone else, read on.

Labs are one of the big factors that make the difference between on-time, on-budget Exchange deployments and cost/time overruns. If ever management feels the need for a lab, give them the following list:

◆ Labs allow you to test new patches and updates before risking production systems. Although it's not the norm, occasionally Windows and Exchange updates have problems that take down Exchange services. You have a better chance of finding these problems before they take you down by updating your lab first.

◆ Labs allow you to be better trained and work out bugs and omissions in your procedures. If you've never applied updates to a DAG cluster before (or it's been a while since the last time), a lab is invaluable for clearing out the cobwebs. If you have a special work sequence that has to be performed, you can fine-tune that process in the safety of your lab. Want to make sure your disaster recovery (DR) staff knows how to perform a site-level failover? Do it in your lab.

◆ Labs can end up saving you time and money on support incidents. By replicating a problem in the lab before calling support, you can often narrow down the precise factors that are contributing to the problem. Whether you have a concise set of repro steps or end up finding the answer, you're likely to waste less time playing phone or email tag with support providers.

To meet these goals, however, your lab needs to meet a few essential criteria:

IT HAS TO BE A SEPARATE FOREST.

Remember, you can have only a single Exchange organization in an Active Directory forest. Keep that forest roughly in sync, though. If you have mixed levels of domain controllers in production, have one of each in the lab. Consider a forest trust and cross-forest group memberships so that your Exchange administrators can use their regular administrative credentials in the lab rather than juggle yet another username and password. Keep the DNS and AD namespaces as close to the production namespaces as possible. Consider a regular Active Directory dump of users from production to the lab.

SIMPLICITY IS KEY.

Introduce only as much complexity as you need—only your key third-party apps, client types, and systems need to be in the lab. You don't have to have a lab copy of each Exchange server in production, and you don't have to replicate all the sites. If you have multiple DAGs, note that your lab needs only one—and it needs only two or three members, not the full number in production. Your lab DR site doesn't typically need a fully redundant number of DAG members.

You don't need a full load balancer when a Windows box with Internet Information Server (IIS) and the Application Request Routing extension may give you the functionality you actually need in the lab. However, if you need your operators to be comfortable using these additional components as part of their normal processes, they should be in the lab.

DON'T FORGET CLIENTS.

Labs are fantastic for troubleshooting client issues if you include clients in the lab. Keep them up to date with the production clients. Don't waste time synching up plug-ins and additional add-ons unless you are troubleshooting a problem that includes those components.

KNOW WHEN TO BREAK THE RULES.

Labs are a perfect place to use virtualization technologies and to ruthlessly exploit the benefits of virtualization, such as VM snapshots. While these features aren't supported in production environments, they're time-savers for a lab. However, when you're taking snapshots, capture *all* of the virtual machines (domain controllers, Exchange servers, clients, and everything else) at the same time so rollbacks all come back to a consistent known spot.

MAKE LAB MAINTENANCE A REGULAR ACTIVITY.

Keep time on the schedule to patch and update your lab. Spread the load for various maintenance tasks among your staff so that no one person gets stuck maintaining the entire lab while everyone else trashes it. Ensure that everyone knows the appropriate policies and procedures for resetting the lab and that there's an override in place for situations (such as support calls) when changes to the lab should not take place.

Having a badly implemented lab can require a lot of work. However, done smartly, a lab can increase your productivity and help you become more proactive about managing your Exchange organization.

Configuring Windows

In this section, we'll look at prerequisites. This includes those for Active Directory as well as the server and its operating system. We'll start with Active Directory.

Active Directory Requirements

It's important to keep your test environment isolated from your production environment. Exchange Server 2013 requires many changes to Active Directory through schema updates, and it introduces new objects and adds many parameters to existing objects. Exchange Server 2013 has the following Active Directory requirements:

◆ Domain controllers and global catalogs in the same site are Windows Server 2003 Service Pack 2 (SP2) or higher.

◆ Read-only domain controllers and read-only global catalogs in the same Active Directory site are ignored by Exchange Server 2013. Because of this, a conventional writeable domain controller and global catalog must exist in the AD site.

Active Directory forest and domain functionality modes must be at least Windows Server 2003 to install Exchange Server 2013. To verify that they are, follow these steps:

1. Log onto a domain controller as a domain administrator.

2. Click Start ➣ All Programs ➣ Administrative Tools ➣ Active Directory Domains And Trusts.

3. Right-click the domain in the left pane and choose Properties.

4. On the General tab of the properties dialog box, look for Domain functional level and Forest functional level; both appear in the lower half of the screen, as shown in Figure 7.2.

FIGURE 7.2
Checking the domain and forest functional levels

If the forest or domain is not Windows Server 2003 or higher, it must be raised before Exchange can be installed.

Although installing Exchange Server 2013 on a domain controller is a supported scenario, Microsoft strongly recommends not doing so for a number of reasons. Performance and security are enhanced when Exchange Server 2013 is installed on a member server. Once Exchange is installed, that server cannot be promoted to a domain controller or demoted to a member server. When Exchange is installed on a domain controller, that server must be configured as a global catalog because Exchange will not use any other domain controller. However, in this configuration, Name Service Provider Interface (NSPI) services are provided by the global catalog functionality and not by the Exchange Server NSPI component, which causes loss of functionality for features, such as address-book policies. Finally, this combined server cannot be a member of a supported DAG configuration.

Operating-system Prerequisites

The prerequisites vary depending on which version of Windows Server you choose. This quick-start guide assumes you will be preparing Active Directory for Exchange Server 2013 from the first server you install Exchange Server 2013 on.

WINDOWS SERVER 2012 PREREQUISITES

To install the Exchange Server 2013 prerequisites for Windows Server 2012, follow these steps:

1. Open an administrative instance of PowerShell by right-clicking its icon and selecting Run As Administrator.

2. Whether you are installing one role or both, run the following command:

```
Install-WindowsFeature AS-HTTP-Activation, Desktop-Experience,
NET-Framework-45-Features, RPC-over-HTTP-proxy, RSAT-Clustering,
RSAT-Clustering-CmdInterface, RSAT-Clustering-Mgmt,
RSAT-Clustering-PowerShell, Web-Mgmt-Console, WAS-Process-Model,
Web-Asp-Net45, Web-Basic-Auth, Web-Client-Auth, Web-Digest-Auth,
Web-Dir-Browsing, Web-Dyn-Compression, Web-Http-Errors,
Web-Http-Logging, Web-Http-Redirect, Web-Http-Tracing, Web-ISAPI-Ext,
Web-ISAPI-Filter, Web-Lgcy-Mgmt-Console, Web-Metabase, Web-Mgmt-Console,
Web-Mgmt-Service, Web-Net-Ext45, Web-Request-Monitor, Web-Server,
Web-Stat-Compression, Web-Static-Content, Web-Windows-Auth, Web-WMI,
Windows-Identity-Foundation
Install-WindowsFeature RSAT-ADDS
```

Once you press Enter, the server will install the required roles and features and then automatically restart. Note that it is normal to see yellow warning text scroll by while this code is running, showing that a reboot is required.

3. Locate the following add-in components from the Microsoft Downloads website and install them in the following order:

   a. Microsoft Unified Communications Managed API 4.0, Core Runtime 64-bit

   b. Microsoft Office 2010 Filter Pack 64-bit (required only on the Mailbox role)

   c. Microsoft Office 2010 Filter Pack SP1 64-bit (required only on the Mailbox role)

WINDOWS SERVER 2008 R2 PREREQUISITES

To install the Exchange Server 2013 prerequisites for Windows Server 2008 R2, follow these steps:

1. Open an administrative instance of PowerShell by right-clicking its icon and selecting Run As Administrator.

2. Whether you are installing one role or both, run the following commands:

```
Import-Module ServerManager
Add-WindowsFeature Desktop-Experience, NET-Framework, NET-HTTP-Activation,
RPC-over-HTTP-proxy, RSAT-Clustering, RSAT-Web-Server, WAS-Process-Model,
Web-Asp-Net, Web-Basic-Auth, Web-Client-Auth, Web-Digest-Auth,
Web-Dir-Browsing, Web-Dyn-Compression, Web-Http-Errors, Web-Http-Logging,
Web-Http-Redirect, Web-Http-Tracing, Web-ISAPI-Ext, Web-ISAPI-Filter,
Web-Lgcy-Mgmt-Console, Web-Metabase, Web-Mgmt-Console, Web-Mgmt-Service,
Web-Net-Ext, Web-Request-Monitor, Web-Server, Web-Stat-Compression,
Web-Static-Content, Web-Windows-Auth, Web-WMI
Add-WindowsFeature RSAT-ADDS
```

Once you press Enter, the server will install the required roles and features and then automatically restart. Note that it is normal to see yellow warning text scroll by while this code is running, showing that a reboot is required.

Next, locate the following add-in components from the Microsoft Downloads website and install them in the following order:

1. Microsoft .NET Framework 4.5.

2. Windows Management Framework 3.0.

3. Microsoft Unified Communications Managed API 4.0, Core Runtime 64-bit.

4. Microsoft Office 2010 Filter Pack 64-bit (required only on the Mailbox role).

5. Microsoft Office 2010 Filter Pack SP1 64-bit (required only on the Mailbox role).

6. Hotfix KB974405: Windows Identity Foundation.

7. Hotfix KB2619234: Enable the association cookie/GUID that is used by RPC over HTTP to also be used at the RPC layer in Windows 7 and in Windows Server 2008 R2.

8. Hotfix KB2533623: Insecure library loading could allow remote code execution.

DO I NEED THE OFFICE FILTER PACKS?

Exchange Server 2013 now uses the new Search Foundation to provide the search services for Exchange databases, replacing the indexing technology used in Exchange Server 2007 and Exchange Server 2010. In these versions, you needed to register specific iFilters with the search engine so that it could look at attached and embedded documents of particular formats, such as the Office application formats and third-party formats, such as PDF. Without the correct iFilter installed, the indexing process would skip over the unfamiliar documents, leaving them out of the search results. In Exchange Server 2013, the Search Foundation no longer uses the iFilter format and includes native support for common application formats. Given this change, do you need the Office Filter Packs?

Yes—if you want transport to be able to search through content in message attachments. In general, as new service packs for the Office Filter Pack (or new versions) are put out, put them on your servers and update them. The transport services do not use the Search Foundation for any transport actions that look inside document attachments and still rely on iFilters. Although Exchange Server 2013 does include the iFilters for some document formats, not all are included (and bugs in the included ones may be fixed by future Office Filter Pack updates). If you rely on transport rules (such as for data loss prevention), be sure to include the latest Filter Pack.

You no longer, however, need to manually register the filters after installing Exchange. The Exchange installation process takes care of this for you, as it has since Exchange Server 2010 SP1.

Installing Exchange Server 2013

The installation of Exchange Server 2013 requires an account with specific permissions. Installation must be performed with an account that has membership in the following groups:

◆ Domain Admins

◆ Schema Administrators (first server)

◆ Enterprise Administrators (first server)

During the installation, the Active Directory schema will be extended with attributes necessary for Exchange Server 2013, which is why the Schema Administrators group membership is required. A more detailed explanation of the Exchange Server 2013 installation, including the command-line procedure, is presented in Chapter 10, "Installing Exchange Server 2013."

At this point, you're ready to install Exchange Server 2013. You can use the GUI to install Exchange, or you can use the command line. Each approach has its advantages. First, let's look at the GUI-based installation.

GUI-based Installation

Download or mount the Exchange Server 2013 installation media (yet another reason to run on Windows Server 2012; you can right-click an .iso file and select Mount to have Windows treat it as a virtual CD or DVD), navigate to the root of the folder, and run setup.exe, as shown in Figure 7.3.

FIGURE 7.3
Launch the Exchange Server 2013 installer.

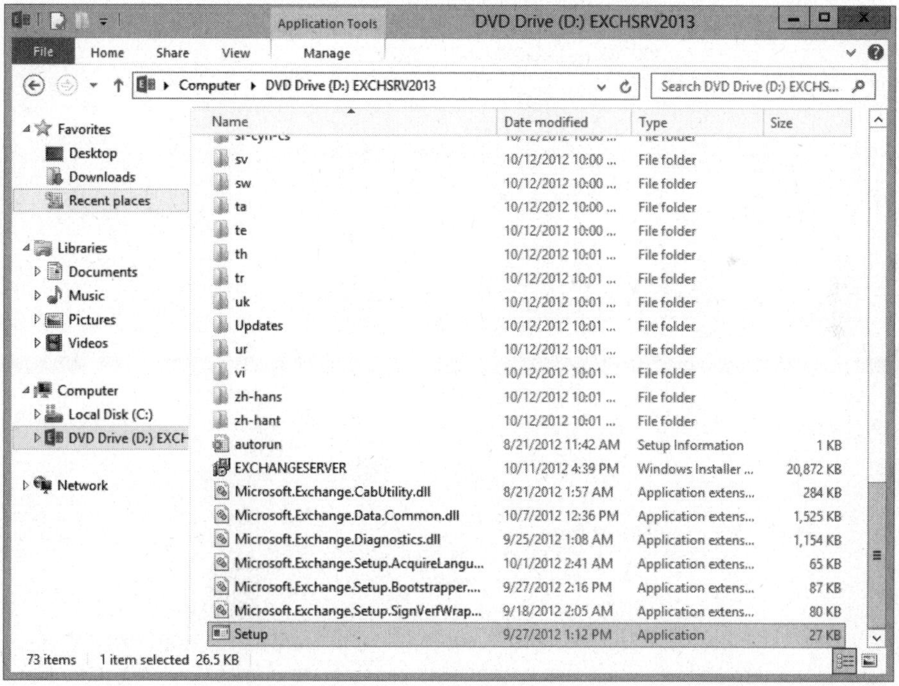

Once the Exchange Setup process starts, the first thing that you will see is the option to go online and check for updates for the installer. Once updates are downloaded (if any are found), Setup will copy files and prepare other tasks necessary for the installation. Once these are done, you'll see the introduction screen. This screen contains links to the TechNet documentation, supported languages, and the Exchange Server 2013 Deployment Assistant. Click Next to move on to the license agreement. Accept it and click Next to move on.

On the next screen, choose whether to send usage feedback to Microsoft and (more importantly) check for additional data online when errors occur. Choose an option and click Next to move on to the meat of the installation: the Server Role Selection screen, shown in Figure 7.4. Because this is the first Exchange Server 2013 server in the organization, you don't have the option to select only the management tools; you must select one of the two main server roles.

FIGURE 7.4
Select the server role.

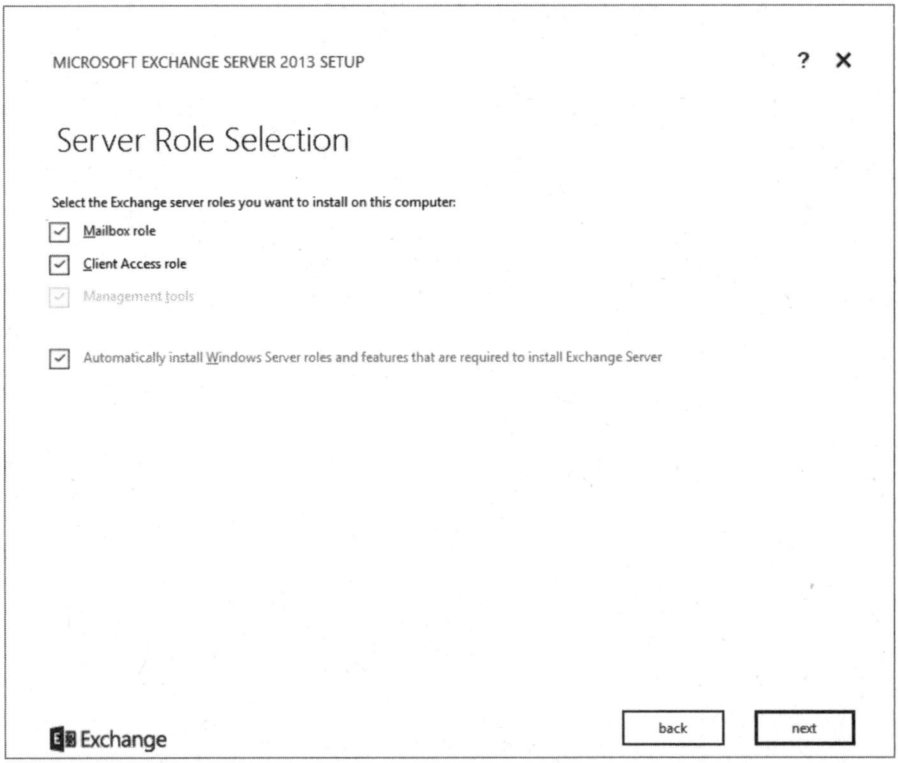

If you have not already installed the prerequisites manually, you can check the option to install them. This also serves as a confirmation that you've gotten the prerequisites installed properly. Even though you can do them here, it's recommended to install them ahead of time to make sure you can run Windows Update to fix any bugs or problems. Click Next to move on.

Your next chore, should you choose to accept it, is to accept the default installation location or select a new location. For a test environment, this may not matter much. This screen also allows you to confirm that you have sufficient free space in your chosen folder. Once you make a selection, click Next to move on, as shown in Figure 7.5. If you want to change the path for the installation, click Browse, specify the appropriate folder, and then click OK. Click Next.

FIGURE 7.5
Choosing the installation location

> MICROSOFT EXCHANGE SERVER 2013 SETUP   ?   ✕
>
> # Installation Space and Location
>
> Disk space required: 7869.3 MB
>
> Disk space available: 110500.7 MB
>
> Specify the path for the Exchange Server installation:
>
> [C:\Program Files\Microsoft\Exchange Server\V15]   [browse]
>
> ⊞ Exchange   [back] [next]

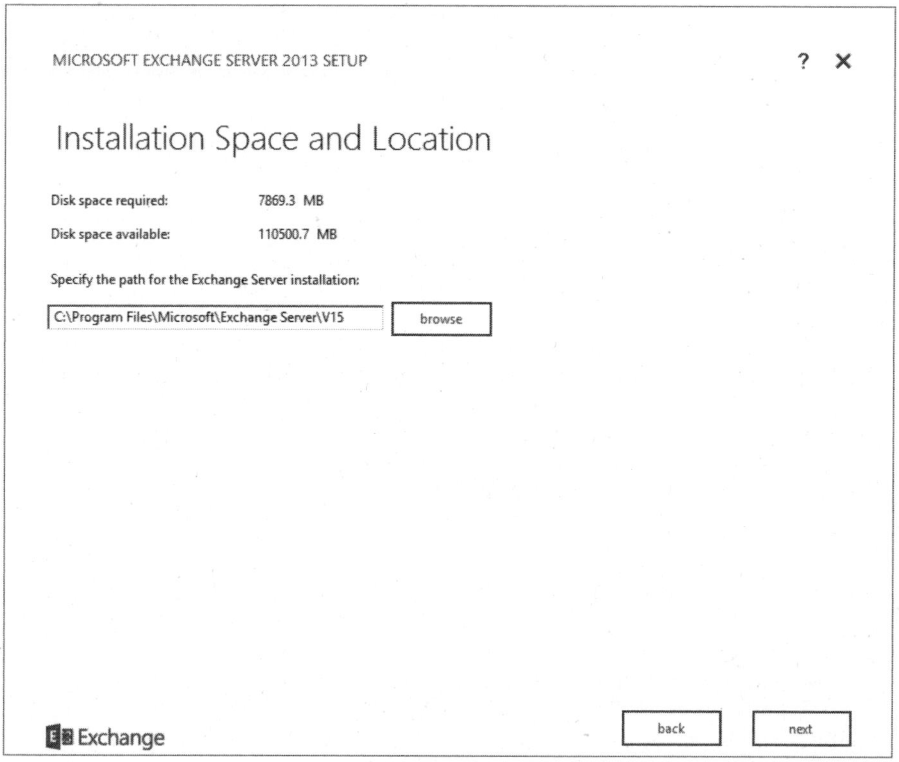

Since this is the first Exchange Server 2013 server in your organization, you are presented with the Exchange Organization screen (Figure 7.6). Type a name for your Exchange organization. This can be any name, such as your company name. The Exchange organization name can contain only the following characters:

◆ Letters *A* through *Z*, uppercase or lowercase

◆ Numbers 0 through 9

◆ Space (not leading or trailing)

◆ Hyphen or dash

The organization name can't be more than 64 characters long and can't be blank. When you've finished typing the name, click Next.

FIGURE 7.6
Organization
name

MICROSOFT EXCHANGE SERVER 2013 SETUP   ? ✕

Exchange Organization

Specify the name for this Exchange organization:

QuickGuide

☐ Apply Active Directory split permissions security model to the Exchange organization

The Active Directory split permissions security model is typically used by large organizations that completely separate the responsibility for the management of Exchange and Active Directory among different groups of people. Applying this security model removes the ability for Exchange servers and administrators to create Active Directory objects such as users, groups, and contacts. The ability to manage non-Exchange attributes on those objects is also removed.

You shouldn't apply this security model if the same person or group manages both Exchange and Active Directory. Click '?' for more information.

E:B Exchange   back   next

Exchange Server 2013 includes built-in malware screening that is by default enabled. If for some reason you feel the need to turn this off, choose that option on the next screen. Click Next to move on.

On the Readiness Checks screen, the setup routine will take some time to inspect the system to verify that Exchange can be successfully installed. This is based on the settings you've chosen, the rights of the user account, and the operating-system prerequisites.

If Exchange finds everything in order, this is your last chance to stop before making modifications to your Active Directory forest. Exchange even warns you that this is the point of no return:

> Setup is going to prepare the organization for Exchange Server 2013 by using 'Setup / PrepareAD'. No Exchange Server 2010 server roles have been detected in this topology. After this operation, you will not be able to install any Exchange Server 2010 server roles.

This is expected; it's simply a notice that legacy versions of Exchange can't be installed after Exchange Server 2010 is installed into an organization.

View the status of the remaining items to determine whether the organization and server role prerequisite checks completed successfully. If they have not completed successfully, you must resolve any reported errors before you can install Exchange Server 2013. After resolving an error, click Retry to rerun the prerequisite checks. However, some conditions may require you to quit Setup and run it again at a later time.

If all the other readiness checks have completed successfully, click Install to install Exchange Server 2013. The Setup program will display the Progress screen, which will show you each step of the process, as well as the outcome. Once the installation process is finished, the Setup Completed screen will display.

At this point, you can click the link shown in Figure 7.7 to pull up the current list of post-installation tasks (shown in Figure 7.8), select the check box to launch Exchange Administration Center, or do neither. Whatever you choose, click Finish to exit the installer.

FIGURE 7.7
Setup complete screen

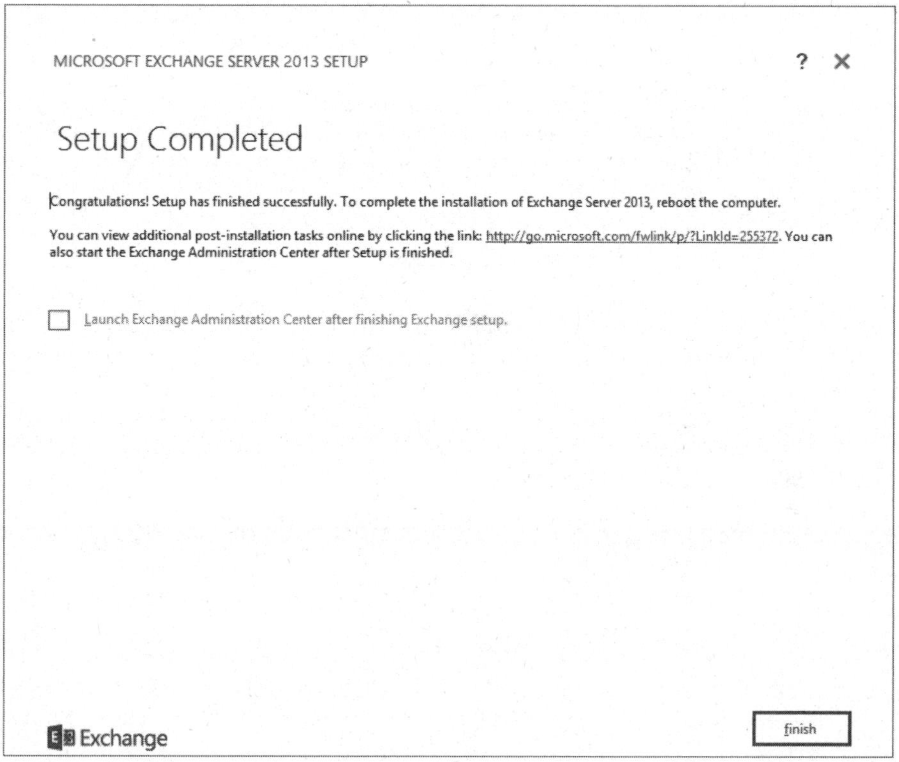

MICROSOFT EXCHANGE SERVER 2013 SETUP   ? ✕

Setup Completed

Congratulations! Setup has finished successfully. To complete the installation of Exchange Server 2013, reboot the computer.

You can view additional post-installation tasks online by clicking the link: http://go.microsoft.com/fwlink/p/?LinkId=255372. You can also start the Exchange Administration Center after Setup is finished.

☐ Launch Exchange Administration Center after finishing Exchange setup.

Exchange   finish

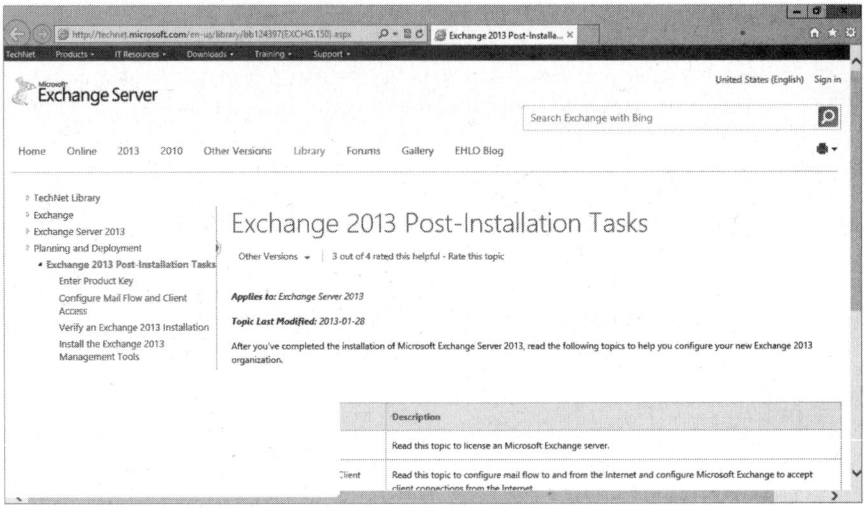

FIGURE 7.8
Exchange Server 2013
post-installation
checklist

At some point, be sure to run Windows Update to install any critical updates that may now be required. Even if you are not prompted, reboot the server to complete installation of Exchange Server 2013.

Command-line Installation

As mentioned earlier, you can also install Exchange Server 2013 from the command line. The setup routine allows you to specify all necessary parameters in one line, and thus avoid having to click on things through a GUI. You do, however, need to manually prepare the Active Directory forest and domain in a separate step.

To install your first multirole Exchange Server 2013 server from the command line, open a command prompt with administrative privileges and navigate to the DVD drive. From there, use the following commands:

```
Setup.exe /PAD /IAcceptExchangeServerLicenseTerms
Setup.exe /m:install /r:mb,ca /on:"<organization name>"
```

To find out more of the options available, run the following command:

```
Setup.exe /h:install
```

When the setup routine finishes, reboot the server as prompted. Once these steps are completed, continue with the rest of the configuration, as explained in the next section.

Post-installation Configuration Steps

Once the server has rebooted, take a few minutes and verify that things are working the way they should. If you didn't look at the setup log at the end of the installation, review it now. It's located at `<system drive>\ExchangeSetupLogs\ExchangeSetup.log`. Look for errors and warnings.

Next, open the Exchange Management Shell and use the `Get-ExchangeServer` cmdlet to get the information about installed roles. Here is an example:

```
Get-ExchangeServer | FT Name,ServerRole -auto
```

The output of this command will list installed roles for the Exchange server. You should see `Mailbox` and `ClientAccess` listed under `ServerRole`.

Next, let's take a look using Event Viewer for any signs of problems. Click Start ➢ All Programs ➢ Administrative Tools ➢ Event Viewer. Navigate to Windows Logs ➢ Application. Look for errors and warnings that may indicate a problem. It's common to see warnings about various processes that haven't yet had a chance to complete.

When you're sure that the installation has been successful, you can move on to post-installation configuration. We'll start with the Exchange Administration Center. To open that, open Internet Explorer and enter the following URL:

```
https://servername/ecp
```

Accept any certificate warnings from the default self-signed certificate (you shouldn't see any if you're running IE from the same server you are connecting to), enter your credentials, and wait for the EAC to come up.

Final Configuration

Now that you're logged into the EAC, finish the steps necessary for the final basic configuration.

SETTING THE OFFLINE ADDRESS BOOK

First, set an offline address book (OAB) on the default mailbox database. The OAB, which Outlook uses when running in cached mode, contains a copy of the global address list. Use the following steps to associate the default OAB with the mailbox databases:

1. In the left pane, click Servers.

2. In the middle pane, click Databases.

3. Select the default mailbox database.

4. Click the pencil icon to edit the database properties.

5. On the left side of the property window, click Client Settings.

6. Click Browse next to Offline Address Book.

7. Click OK, and then click Save.

You can do the same in the Exchange Management Shell using both the `Get-MailboxDatabase` and `Set-MailboxDatabase` cmdlets together:

```
Get-MailboxDatabase | Set-MailboxDatabase -OfflineAddressBook ↵
"\Default Offline Address Book"
```

SETTING SMTP DOMAINS

By default, Exchange Server 2013 configures a default accepted domain and email-address policy using the fully qualified domain name of the domain you installed into. If you need to add a new SMTP domain and create a matching email-address policy, you can do so from the EAC:

1. In the left pane, click Servers.

2. In the middle pane, click Accepted Domains.

3. Click the plus icon to create a new accepted domain.

4. Give the accepted domain a display name and SMTP domain name for which Exchange will receive email.

5. Click Authoritative Domain to indicate that Exchange is responsible for delivering email for that domain in the Exchange organization.

6. Click Save.

7. Select the newly created accepted domain.

8. Click the pencil icon to edit the properties of the accepted domain.

9. Select the Set As Default check box.

10. Click Save.

You can accomplish the same thing in the Exchange Management Shell using the New-AcceptedDomain cmdlet and the Set-AcceptedDomain cmdlet together:

```
New-AcceptedDomain -Name your.domain ↵
-DomainName *.your.domain ↵
-DomainType authoritative | ↵
Set-AcceptedDomain -MakeDefault $true
```

Email-address policies define how email addresses are assigned to recipients within the organization. Configure one for your new domain using these steps in the EAC:

1. In the left pane, click Servers.

2. In the middle pane, click Email Address Policies.

3. Click the plus icon to create a new email address policy.

4. Give the policy a name and SMTP domain name for which Exchange will receive email.

5. Enter a name for the policy.

6. Under Email Address Format, click the plus icon to create the email format.

7. Choose the new accepted domain from the pull-down list.

8. Select your chosen email-address format.

9. Click Save to close the email-address format window.

10. Click Save to close the email-address policy window. Accept the warning.

11. Select the new address policy.

12. In the right pane, click Apply.

13. At the warning, click Yes.

14. Click Close once the policy is applied.

As with all the previous configuration settings, you can use the Exchange Management Shell to make these changes using the `New-EmailAddressPolicy` and `Update-EmailAddressPolicy` cmdlets together:

```
New-EmailAddressPolicy -Name ehloworld.com ↵
-EnabledPrimarySMTPAddressTemplate "SMTP:%g.%s@your.domain" ↵
-IncludedRecipients AllRecipients -Priority 1 | ↵
Update-EmailAddressPolicy
```

ENABLING EXTERNAL MAIL FLOW

In order for mail to flow in and out of the new Exchange organization, you need to modify the default connectors. The Send connector is an object that holds configuration information on how Exchange servers can send email out of the organization. There are no Send connectors by default.

Create a new Send connector to handle all outbound traffic from the EAC:

1. In the left pane, click Servers.

2. In the middle pane, click Send Connectors.

3. Click the plus icon to create a new Send connector.

4. Give the connector a name, such as Default Internet.

5. Under Type, select Internet.

6. Click Next.

7. Accept the default network settings to allow your Exchange server to perform its own DNS lookups, and click Next.

8. Under Address Space, click the plus icon to create the default address space.

9. Under Fully Qualified Domain Name, enter *. Click Save.

10. Click Next.

11. Under Source Server, click the plus icon. Ensure the new Exchange server is selected, click Add, and then click OK.

12. Click Finish.

To accomplish this in the Exchange Management Shell, use the New-SendConnector cmdlet:

```
New-SendConnector -name "Default Internet" ↵
-AddressSpaces "*" -DNSRoutingEnabled $true ↵
-SourceTransportServers "YOURSERVER" -Usage Internet
```

In a lab environment, it is common to pass all outgoing messages to a designated smart host rather than rely on looking up MX records for the target domains through DNS resolution. If this is the case in your lab, change the Send connector settings to use a smart host instead of DNS resolution.

A Receive connector is just the opposite of a Send connector. Receive connectors hold configuration for how Exchange will receive mail. This can include mail from client machines as well as from the Internet and other Exchange servers.

When Exchange Server 2013 is installed, multiple Receive connectors are created. Those associated with the Client Access role are proxy connectors. The Default Frontend Receive connector on each Exchange server with a CAS role is configured to receive email from the Internet from anonymous senders. Again, you must either configure external servers to send messages to your test Exchange domains to your Exchange mail servers or establish the appropriate MX records in DNS for your lab domains.

TESTING THE CONFIGURATION

You now have a significant portion of the configuration finished in Exchange. You can test Exchange using some built-in PowerShell cmdlets. To begin, start the Exchange Management Shell and type **Test-mailflow.** Check the results in the **TestMailflowResult** column. It should say Success.

Next, test MAPI client connectivity using Test-MAPIConnectivity. You should see Success under Result for each database.

You can verify that all necessary Exchange-related services are running by using Test-ServiceHealth. The output of this cmdlet breaks down the services needed for each of the installed server roles. If everything is running correctly, you should see True for each of the RequiredServicesRunning results.

CREATING AN SSL CERTIFICATE

In a production environment, using a third-party trusted secure sockets layer (SSL) certificate to secure client and server communications is highly recommended. When Exchange Server 2013 is installed, Exchange installs a self-signed certificate valid for five years. This is perfectly fine for testing in a lab environment. When testing Exchange using Outlook Web App (OWA), for example, you will be presented with a screen indicating that the security certificate was not issued by a trusted certificate authority if you connect from another machine. You can ignore these warnings during testing.

Creating a certificate request and installing a new certificate are outside the scope of this chapter. See Chapter 21, "Understanding the Client Access Server," for more details.

ENTERING THE PRODUCT KEY

You don't have to enter a product key in order to test Exchange Server 2013. However, if you do have a product key and would like to enter it into the server, it's very simple to do using these steps:

1. In the left pane, click Servers.

2. In the middle pane, click Servers.

3. In the right pane, click Enter Product Key.

4. Enter the digits for the product key.

5. When finished, click Save.

As with any other configuration, you can set the product key using the Exchange Management Shell with the `Set-ExchangeServer` cmdlet and the `-ProductKey` parameter:

```
Set-ExchangeServer –identity '<server>' -ProductKey <product key>
```

TESTING OUTLOOK WEB APP

You can now also test OWA, the web-based email client for Exchange Server 2013:

1. Open a web browser and type `https://<servername>/owa`.

2. If you receive a server warning, click Continue To This Website (Not Recommended) at the certificate prompt.

3. Enter the domain and username for a user that was mailbox-enabled previously, and enter a password. Click OK.

4. Set your language and time zone, and click OK.

You will now be logged into Outlook Web App, and you can test mailbox and ECP functionality. As mentioned earlier, since you're using an internal certificate, features that require a certificate will yield a certificate prompt first if you are using a machine other than the server. In all cases, you can click Continue To This Website (Not Recommended) to continue testing.

Configuring Recipients

There are various types of recipients in Exchange Server 2013, including mailboxes, distribution groups, and contacts. Mailboxes can be further broken down, and that is explained elsewhere in this book. We'll focus on creating mailbox-enabled users and mail contacts.

Mailbox-enabled users are Active Directory accounts that have a mailbox located in Exchange. Take these steps to create a mailbox-enabled user from the EAC:

1. In the left pane, click Recipients.

2. In the middle pane, click Mailboxes.

3. Click the plus icon to create a new mailbox.

4. Give the new mailbox an alias.

5. Select New User and fill in the account name details.

6. Provide the User Logon Name (typically the same as the alias) and select the appropriate UPN suffix (typically the same as the primary SMTP domain).

7. Type in the password and password confirmation.

8. Click Save.

Creating mailbox-enabled users in the Exchange Management Shell is quite simple; you'll use the Enable-Mailbox cmdlet to enable an existing user account:

```
Enable-Mailbox -Identity TestUser
```

Mail-enabled contacts are objects in the global address list that represent external recipients, such as vendors or clients. Take these steps to create a new mail-enabled contact:

1. In the left pane, click Recipients.

2. In the middle pane, click Contacts.

3. Click the plus icon to create a new contact.

4. Fill in the contact-name details.

5. Give the new contact an alias.

6. Provide the external email address associated with the contact.

7. Click Save.

Creating a mail contact in the Exchange Management Shell is quite simple using the New-MailContact cmdlet:

```
New-MailContact -Name "Test Contact" -ExternalEmailAddress "user@domain.local"
```

To create a distribution group in the EAC, follow these steps:

1. In the left pane, click Recipients.

2. In the middle pane, click Groups.

3. Click the plus icon to create a new distribution group.

4. Fill in the group display name and alias.

5. Under Members, click the plus sign, select mail-enabled recipients to be members of the new group, click Add, and click Save.

6. Click Save.

You can accomplish both creating a distribution group and adding members in one line of code in the Exchange Management Shell using something like this:

```
New-DistributionGroup -name "Group Name" |
Add-DistributionGroupMember -member "User"
```

CONFIGURING A POSTMASTER ADDRESS

A postmaster address is needed for the sending of non-delivery reports (NDRs) and other related messages to recipients outside the Exchange organization and is required by RFC 2821. Configuring your environment takes two steps. First, either create a new mailbox for the postmaster or assign the address to an existing mailbox, such as Administrator. Second, use the Exchange Management Shell to set the external postmaster address in Exchange. To do so, open the Exchange Management Shell and use the `Set-TransportConfig` cmdlet and the `-ExternalPostmasterAddress` parameter, using the following format:

```
Set-TransportConfig -ExternalPostmasterAddress 
<ExternalPostmasterSMTPAddress>
```

Here's an example:

```
Set-TransportConfig -ExternalPostmasterAddress 
postmaster@quickstart.local
```

The Bottom Line

Quickly size a typical server.   Having a properly equipped server for testing can yield a much more positive experience. Taking the time to get the right hardware will avoid problems later.

Master It   What parameters must be kept in mind when sizing a lab/test server?

Install the necessary Windows Server 2012 or Windows Server 2008 R2 prerequisites. Certain configuration settings must be performed before installing Exchange Server 2013.

Master It   What is involved in installing and configuring the prerequisites?

Install a multifunction Exchange Server 2013 server.   You should provide a basic, bare-bones server for testing and evaluation.

Master It   What installation methods are available for installing Exchange Server 2013?

Configure Exchange to send and receive email.   Your new Exchange server should be interacting with other email systems.

Master It   What are the configuration requirements for sending and receiving email?

Configure recipients, contacts, and distribution groups.   Add mailbox-enabled users, mail-enabled contacts, and distribution groups to Exchange.

Master It   How are recipients created, and what's the difference between them?

Chapter 8

Understanding Server Roles and Configurations

Exchange Server 2013, similarly to Exchange Server 2010, provides a role-based installation procedure. This procedure provides only two server role choices: the Client Access server role and the Mailbox server role. As discussed in previous chapters, the former Hub Transport and Unified Messaging server role functionalities have been rolled into the other existing roles, providing a simplified installation process and deployment architecture. In some cases, installing both the Mailbox and Client Access server roles on the same server is the best implementation choice, and in other cases installing those roles on separate servers is the preferred option. This chapter will discuss the server roles, their preferred deployment options, and the components installed with each role.

In this chapter, you will learn to:

- ◆ Understand the importance of server roles
- ◆ Understand the Exchange Server 2013 server roles
- ◆ Explore possible server role configurations

The *Roles* of Server Roles

Although the concept of roles is not new, the number of roles available in Exchange Server 2013 has changed from previous versions. In Exchange Server 2007 and Exchange Server 2010, you had five roles to select from during installation: Mailbox, Hub Transport, Client Access, Unified Messaging, and Edge Transport. In Exchange Server 2013, up to CU2, the number of roles has been reduced to two: Mailbox and Client Access. Many of the components of the Hub Transport role and Unified Messaging role have been stripped down and placed into the Mailbox and Client Access roles.

EDGE TRANSPORT IN THE FUTURE?

Although the Edge Transport role is currently unavailable in Exchange Server 2013, Microsoft is rumored to be adding it back into the product for later releases. Based on the short time frame to release Exchange Server 2013, it would seem that the Exchange team ran out of time for this role. I'm speculating here, since no one really knows what will happen with the Edge Transport role or whether it will ever return to the Exchange family of products. I also cannot ignore the push to the cloud and the availability of a cloud-based solution to replace the Edge Transport role: Exchange Online. For administrators who require the features available in the Edge Transport role on-premises, the current recommendation is to implement an Exchange Server 2010 server on the network.

A key benefit of having role-based installation has always been the ability to segregate or separate Exchange Server functionalities onto separate servers. Maximizing the usage of server resources has traditionally been a driver for architects designing Exchange Server messaging solutions, and role-based installation has been used as a solution to achieve a more optimal design. Virtualization solutions have provided an alternate solution to use these hardware resources appropriately. At the time of this writing, the need to segregate Exchange Server roles is becoming less relevant and beneficial. Sure, there are still advantages to separating roles, such as simplified troubleshooting, administrative delegation, and others, but they are sometimes overshadowed by the administrative overhead required to administer multiple servers.

Depending on what your company's business priorities may be—more control or simplified deployment—you might find yourself on either side of that deployment option: only one role on each server or both roles on each server. The choice is yours.

THE SEEDS OF SERVER ROLES

The concept of an Exchange Server role is not new. Microsoft officially introduced the concept in Exchange Server 2007, and it's been carried over to Exchange Server 2013, but in Exchange Server 2003 you did have server roles, such as a Mailbox server, a front-end server, or a bridgehead server.

What was different is that for an Exchange Server 2003 Front End server, you installed the entire Exchange Server 2003 package, including the database engine, the message transport (SMTP), and other Exchange Server functions.

Once all the Exchange Server 2003 software was installed, you then had to make configuration changes and disable services to make the server provide only the services you required of that specific "role."

Whatever that choice may be, during installation, you are prompted to choose which server roles a particular Exchange server will be providing. Figure 8.1 shows the screen that you will see if you choose a custom setup of Exchange Server 2013 CU1. You are prompted for which server roles you need to install.

FIGURE 8.1
Selecting the
Exchange
Server 2013
roles

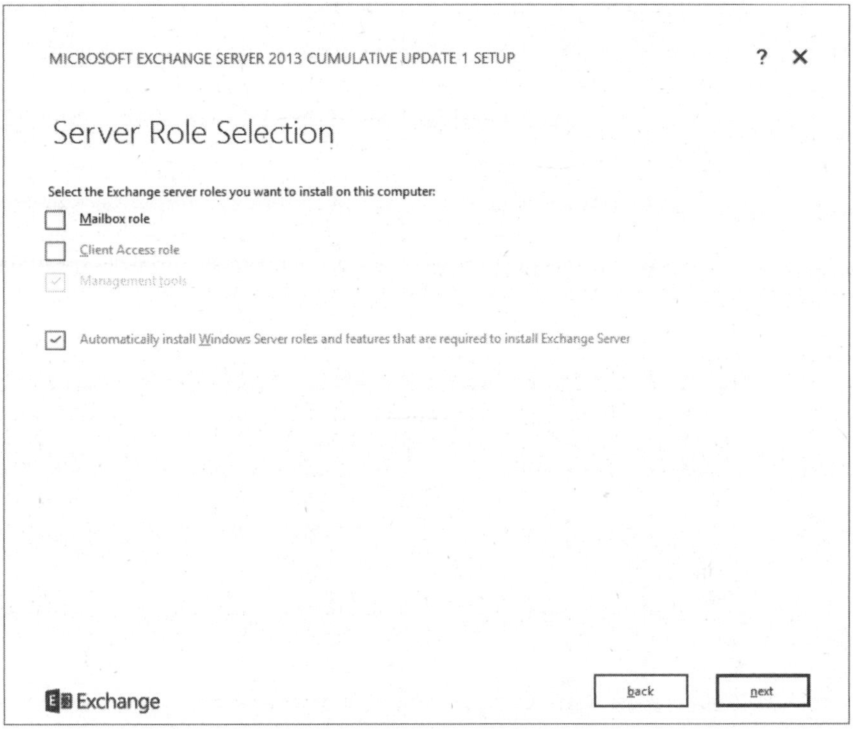

There are some clear and important advantages to this approach, such as the following:

◆ Server configuration complexity is reduced.

◆ Unnecessary components are no longer installed. Additional steps to disable services or lock down a component are not necessary.

◆ Server security is improved because now unnecessary components are not even installed, thus reducing a server's potential attack surface.

Exchange Server 2013 Server Roles

Now let's take a look at the specific Exchange Server 2013 roles that you may find in your organization. Enjoy those roles now, because I predict that in the next revision of Exchange Server, role-based installations will be nothing but a relic of the past.

Mailbox Server

The Mailbox server role is at the center of the Exchange Server 2013 universe. In Exchange Server 2013 the Mailbox role is much more than a placeholder of the mailbox database. The functionality of the deprecated Hub Transport and Unified Messaging roles has been moved to the Mailbox and Client Access roles. Some of the responsibilities owned by the Client Access role in Exchange Server 2010 have been moved to the Mailbox role in Exchange Server 2013. One of the major changes was moving the OWA rendering from the Client Access server back to the Mailbox server. This section will cover the common Mailbox role functionality that is similar to legacy versions of Exchange, as well as the substantial changes that have been introduced in Exchange Server 2013 to the Mailbox role.

> ### WHERE ARE ACTIVE AND PASSIVE CLUSTERED MAILBOXES?
>
> If you have worked with Exchange Server 2007, you may be wondering where the Active Clustered Mailbox and Passive Clustered Mailbox server roles are. They are no longer necessary: clustering can be achieved after installation because the concept of a clustered mailbox server no longer exists as it did in previous versions. This concept is achieved through the implementation of Database Availability Groups (DAGs) and relies on the Failover Clustering feature built into Windows Server 2012.

MAILBOX AND PUBLIC FOLDER DATABASES

Just like in previous versions of Exchange Server, the Mailbox server role hosts mailbox databases. The mailbox database can be replicated to other Mailbox servers when the Mailbox server is a member of a DAG, just like in Exchange Server 2010.

Unlike in previous versions, you can no longer create public folder databases in Exchange Server 2013. Public folders are stored within a public folder mailbox. End users now connect to a public folder mailbox to retrieve public folder content. This means that public folder high availability is based on mailbox database replication and not on the all-too-troublesome public folder replication.

TRANSPORT SERVICES

Mail delivery (even mail going from one mailbox on a local database to another mailbox on the same database) is routed through Transport services on the Mailbox server and sometimes through the Client Access server. This is a major change from legacy versions of Exchange Server, which used the services on the Hub Transport server to deliver email messages. Three Transport services are created when the Mailbox role is installed: Microsoft Exchange Mailbox Transport Submission, Microsoft Exchange Mailbox Transport Delivery, and Microsoft Exchange Transport. There is also a Transport service on the Client Access server, the Front End Transport service, which will be discussed later in this chapter.

Let's quickly see how these services handle email messages. When an email message is sent to a recipient on a different Mailbox server in a different delivery group, the message is picked up by the Mailbox Transport Submission service and passed to the Transport service that is located on the least-cost route. Then, the Transport service submits the message to the Mailbox Transport Delivery service, and then finally, the email message is written to the mailbox database.

UNIFIED MESSAGING

Another major change in the Mailbox role is that it is now responsible for all of the Unified Messaging features. In fact, the services that were installed on the Unified Messaging role for an Exchange Server 2007 or 2010 server are now installed on the Mailbox role for Exchange Server 2013. It should be noted that the Client Access server is the first server in the communication path for all inbound calls or Session Initiation Protocol (SIP) requests for Unified Messaging. However, once the traffic passes through the Client Access server, the Mailbox server receives unified communication and establishes the RTP and SRTP channels with the IP PBX or VOIP gateway.

MEMORY ALLOCATION

Memory allocation for database cache has been tweaked in Exchange Server 2013. When looking at memory consumption in Exchange Server 2007 and Exchange Server 2010, the information store would consume, by far, the largest portion of the available memory. Memory consumption in Exchange Server 2013 servers running the Mailbox role is very different. The Mailbox server reserves 25 percent of the total RAM for database caches. Memory allocation in Exchange Server 2013 is based on the following:

◆ Total amount of memory

◆ Total number of active databases

◆ Total number of passive databases

◆ The max number of active databases

Essentially, the Exchange server looks at its memory requirements and then ensures that the most important process running on the server has enough resources available to function effectively.

When the Information Store service is started, a worker process and database cache is allocated per database. Based on the state of a database being active or passive, the amount of RAM allocated to the database cache will vary. An active copy of a mailbox database will use all of the allotted database cache. A passive database copy will only use 20 percent of the allocated database cache. Let's use this example:

◆ The Mailbox server has 100 GB of RAM.

◆ Ten mailbox database copies exist on this server.

◆ Five mailbox database copies are active and five mailbox database copies are passive.

Since 25 percent of the available memory is allocated to the database cache, the total amount of memory allocated for the database cache is 25 GB. This means that each database is allocated 2.5 GB of the database cache. Each passive copy uses only 20 percent of the allocated database cache; thus the passive databases have a database cache of 512 MB.

If at any point a passive copy becomes activated, the database cache for that database copy will change from 512 MB to 2.5 GB. Figure 8.2 illustrates the memory allocation from this example, whereas, DB1 through DB5 are active databases, and DB6 through DB10 are passive databases.

FIGURE 8.2
Memory allocation

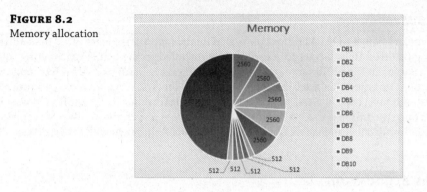

Since the database cache is determined when the Information Store service is started, when a new database is added to an Exchange server, you must restart the Information Store service. (The requirement for a service restart after the creation of a new database is new to Exchange Server 2013 and is a direct result of the new database cache allocation scheme.) This includes the creation of a new database or the addition of a passive copy of a mailbox database. You'll see the warning message shown in Figure 8.3 when adding a new database to a Mailbox server.

FIGURE 8.3
The warning message when adding a new database to a Mailbox server

> **warning**
>
> Please restart the Microsoft Exchange Information Store service on server ALL-1 after adding new mailbox databases.
>
> [ok]

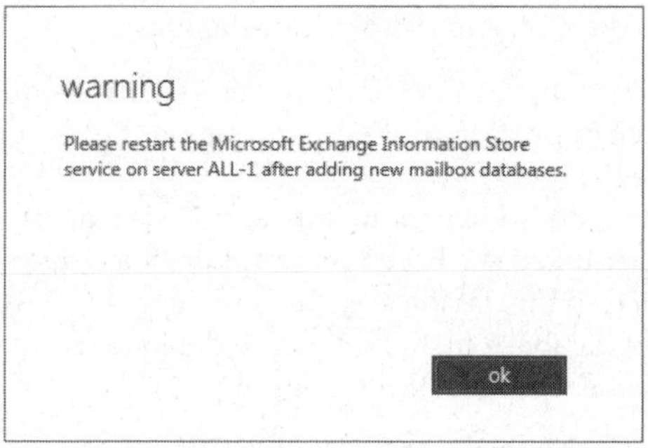

Note that this is only a warning message and does not indicate an immediate problem. Performance issues may arise in the future if the Information Store service is not restarted and a new mailbox database becomes populated with a large number of mailboxes.

The formula used to determine memory sizing is as follows:

$$\text{Active database cache allocated} = (\text{total server memory}) \times 25\% \div$$
$$(\text{number of max allowed active databases} + [(\text{total number of databases on a server}) -$$
$$(\text{number of max allowed active databases})] \times 20\%)$$

If max allowed active databases is not set, then max allowed active databases = total number of databases on a server.

SERVICES

On an Exchange Server 2013 server that is dedicated to providing only Mailbox server functionality, you will still find quite a few Exchange services running. The Exchange Server 2013 Mailbox server services are as follows:

Microsoft Exchange Active Directory Topology/MSExchangeADTopology/ADTopology-Service.exe Locates Active Directory domain controllers and global catalog servers, and provides Active Directory topology information to Exchange Server services. Most Exchange Server services depend on this service; if it does not start, the Exchange server will probably not function.

Microsoft Exchange Anti-spam Update/MSExchangeAntispamUpdate/Microsoft .Exchange.AntispamUpdateSvc.exe This service is responsible for updating anti-spam signatures.

Microsoft Exchange Diagnostics/MSExchangeDiagnostics/Microsoft.Exchange .Diagnostics.Service.exe Uses an agent to monitor the health of the Exchange server.

Microsoft Exchange EdgeSync\MSExchangeEdgeSync\Microsoft.Exchange.EdgeSyncSvc .exe Keeps recipient and configuration data up to date when an Edge server is subscribed to the same AD site the Mailbox server is a member of.

Microsoft Exchange Health Manager/MSExchangeHM/MSExchangeHMHost.exe Monitors the health and performance of key services on the Exchange server.

Microsoft Exchange IMAP4 Backend/MSExchangeIMAP4BE/Microsoft.Exchange .Imap4Service.exe Provides IMAP4 clients with access to Exchange Server mailboxes. This service retries IMAP4 requests from the Client Access server. This service is set to manual by default.

Microsoft Exchange Information Store/MSExchangeIS/store.exe The information store is the actual Exchange database engine (also known as ESE). This service manages the mailbox databases. If the store.exe service does not start, databases will not be mounted.

Microsoft Exchange Mailbox Assistants/MSExchangeMailboxAssistants/MSExchange-MailboxAssistants.exe Handles background processing functions for Exchange Server mailboxes.

Microsoft Exchange Mailbox Replication\MSExchangeMailboxReplication\MSEx-changeMailboxReplication.exe This service is responsible for mailbox moves.

Microsoft Exchange Mailbox Transport Delivery\MSExchangeDelivery\MSExchange-Delivery.exe Accepts email messages from the Transport service and delivers the email messages to the mailbox.

Microsoft Exchange Mailbox Transport Submission\MSExchangeSubmission\MSEx-changeSubmission.exe Pulls the email messages from a mailbox and finds the best Transport service to send the message to.

Microsoft Exchange POP3 Backend\MSExchangePOP3BE\Microsoft.Exchange.Pop3Ser-vice.exe Receives POP3 requests from the Client Access server. Once the request is processed, the Mailbox server provides access to the mailbox over POP3. The service startup type is manual by default.

`Microsoft Exchange Replication/MSExchangeRepl/msexchangerepl.exe` Provides the continuous replication service to copy log files from an active database to a server that hosts a passive copy of the database.

`Microsoft Exchange RPC Client Access/MSExchangeRPC/Microsoft.Exchange.RpcClientAccess.Service.exe` Handles the RPC connections for the Exchange server.

`Microsoft Exchange Search/MSExchangeFastSearch/Microsoft.Exchange.Search.Service.exe` Handles content indexing and queuing of Exchange Server data.

`Microsoft Exchange Search Host Controller\HostControllerService\hostcontrollerservice.exe` Provides service management and deployment for applications on the local host.

`Microsoft Exchange Server Extension for Windows Server Backup/wsbexchange/wsbexchange.exe` Allows the Windows Server Backup utility to back up and restore Exchange Server data.

`Microsoft Exchange Service Host/MSExchangeServiceHost/Microsoft.Exchange.ServiceHost.exe` Provides a service host for Exchange Server components that do not have their own service. These include components such as configuring registry and virtual directory information.

`Microsoft Exchange Throttling/MSExchangeThrottling/MSExchangeThrottling.exe` Handles the limits on the rate of user operations to prevent any single user from consuming too many server resources.

`Microsoft Exchange Transport\MSExchangeTransport\MSExchangeTransport.exe` Handles SMTP connections from Edge, Client Access server, Submission and Delivery services, and other SMTP connection points.

`Microsoft Exchange Transport Log Search/MSExchangeTransportLogSearch/MSExchangeTransportLogSearch.exe` Handles the remote search capabilities for the Exchange Server transport log files.

`Microsoft Exchange Unified Messaging\MSExchangeUM\umservice.exe` Handles UM requests from Client Access servers. This service is responsible for unified communication to the Exchange server.

Client Access Server

Since Exchange Server 2007, the responsibilities of the Client Access role have changed dramatically from version to version. The common thread between the Exchange Server 2010 Client Access role and the Exchange Server 2013 Client Access role is that it provides most of the interface for accessing email data. This means that when a user connects to their mailbox, the connection from the client is established on a server running the Client Access role. The server running the Client Access role will authenticate the request, locate the mailbox, and proxy or redirect the client request to the appropriate Mailbox server. On top of all the client access services, the Client Access role is also responsible for parts of mail routing and Unified Messaging. I'll give you a second for that to sink in; the Client Access server is no longer just responsible for handling client requests. Microsoft made this change to simplify the deployment and management of Exchange Server 2013. Instead of having multiple servers acting as an entry point for a variety of services, the Client Access server can handle client requests, mail flow, and phone calls.

As you can see in Figure 8.4, the Client Access server, rather than the Mailbox server, sits at the center of the client's universe.

FIGURE 8.4
Placement of the Client Access server

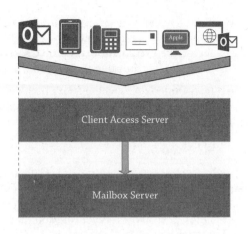

The Client Access server coordinates all communication between clients. The functions of the Client Access server include the following:

◆ Supporting connections from Outlook Anywhere (RPC over HTTP).

◆ Supporting connections from mobile devices using Microsoft ActiveSync technology.

◆ Supporting connections from POP3 and IMAP4 clients.

◆ Proxying SMTP message for inbound and outbound email messages to/from the Internet.

◆ Supporting connections from other Exchange Web Services (EWS) applications.

◆ Proxying connections from various email clients to the relevant Exchange Server Mailbox server.

◆ Serving as an initial communication point for inbound calls and faxes.

◆ Proxying or redirecting connections from external Outlook Anywhere, Offline Address Book, Exchange Web Services, Outlook Web App, or Exchange ActiveSync clients to Client Access servers in other Active Directory sites. The actual mechanics of the connection depend on the client that is being used and the location of the mailbox:

   ◆ If an OWA user's mailbox is on an Exchange Server 2007 server, then the Exchange Server 2013 CAS redirects the user to the Exchange Server 2007 CAS based on the external URL set on the OWA virtual directory.

   ◆ If an OWA user's mailbox is on an Exchange Server 2010 server and the external URL on that server matches the external URL on the Exchange Server 2013 server, the Exchange Server 2013 CAS proxies the request to an Exchange Server 2010 server running the CAS role in the same AD site the mailbox is in.

◆ If an OWA user's mailbox is on an Exchange Server 2010 server and the external URL on that server *does not* match the external URL on the Exchange Server 2013 server, the Exchange Server 2013 CAS redirects the request to the external URL set on the Exchange Server 2010 server.

◆ If an ActiveSync user's mailbox is on an Exchange Server 2010 or 2007 server and the external URL on that server matches the external URL on the Exchange Server 2013 server, the Exchange Server 2013 CAS proxies the request to an Exchange Server 2010 or 2007 server running the CAS role in the same AD site the mailbox is in.

◆ If an Outlook Anywhere user's mailbox is on an Exchange Server 2010 or 2007 server and the external URL on that server matches the external URL on the Exchange Server 2013 server, the Exchange Server 2013 CAS proxies the request to an Exchange Server 2010 or 2007 server running the CAS role in the same AD site the mailbox is in.

When the hardware is properly sized, a Client Access server can accept thousands and thousands of simultaneous connections from different types of clients and connect on behalf of those clients to the Mailbox server. This section covers the new responsibilities that have been assigned to the Client Access server role and that are distinctively different from previous versions of Exchange Server.

MAIL ROUTING

Mail routing is now a responsibility of servers running the Client Access role. The Client Access server provides a proxy service for inbound and outbound email messages. During the installation of the Client Access role, three default receive connectors are created that are associated to the Microsoft Exchange Front End Transport service. One of the receive connectors that is created during install listens over port 25 and is configured with proper permissions to accept email messages from the Internet.

When the Client Access role and the Mailbox role are installed on the same server, the Microsoft Exchange Front End Transport service still listens on port 25 and the Microsoft Exchange Transport service listens on port 2525. Figure 8.5 shows an export of netstat from a multirole Exchange Server 2013, with the Front End Transport service listening on port 25 and the Edge Transport service listening on port 2525.

FIGURE 8.5
Netstat export showing the ports Exchange Server 2013 services are listening on

```
Active Connections

  Proto  Local Address            Foreign Address         State
  TCP    0.0.0.0:25               0.0.0.0:0               LISTENING
  [MSExchangeFrontendTransport.exe]
  TCP    0.0.0.0:2525             0.0.0.0:0               LISTENING
  [edgetransport.exe]
```

UNIFIED MESSAGING

Much like the Mailbox role, the Client Access role now plays an integral part of Unified Messaging. The Microsoft Exchange Unified Messaging Call Router service now runs on the Client Access servers and is responsible for redirecting SIP traffic from an incoming call to a Mailbox server.

CLIENT ACCESS SERVERS IN THE PERIMETER NETWORK

If your organization is going to allow external clients (Outlook Web App, mobile phones, Outlook Anywhere) to connect to your Exchange servers from the Internet, a common question is whether the Client Access server should be in the perimeter or DMZ (demilitarized zone) network. We can tell you that the answer to this question is an unequivocal, no.

Microsoft has dedicated blogs on this topic and their official statement on putting a Client Access server in the DMZ is as follows:

> *Starting with Exchange Server 2007 and current as of Exchange Server 2013, having network devices blocking ports/protocols between Exchange servers within a single organization or between Exchange servers and domain controllers in an organization is not supported. A network device may sit in the communication path between the servers, but a rule allowing "ANY/ANY" port and protocol communication must be in place allowing free communication between Exchange servers as well as between Exchange servers and domain controllers.*

While it can sometimes be temping to place Client Access servers in the DMZ, especially since Microsoft has discontinued the Forefront Threat Management Gateway, there are better approaches to this problem. One solution that is picking up steam is to not place pre-authentication or reverse proxy to accept inbound connections from the Internet. Although a firewall appliance would still be placed in front of the Exchange servers, once the traffic goes through the firewall appliance, the packets would be sent directly to the Exchange servers. Before your chin hits the table, Microsoft has been diligent over the years in securing Exchange Server services out of the box. This might not be the right approach for all organizations, but it is worth considering.

HOW MANY CLIENT ACCESS SERVERS DO I NEED?

Each Active Directory site that contains an Exchange Server 2013 Mailbox server must have at least one Client Access server. Microsoft recommends a ratio of one Client Access processor core for every four Mailbox server processor cores. This is, of course, a generic recommendation and your mileage may vary depending on the number of simultaneous clients and the types of users (light, medium, heavy). You should keep up with Microsoft's current recommendations for sizing because they change over time.

SERVICES

When you look in the service console on an Exchange Server 2013 Client Access server, you will see a number of services that may or may not be familiar to you. The Client Access server is dependent on many of the Internet Information Server web services, so they are also required. The services found on an Exchange Server 2013 Client Access server are as follows:

Microsoft Exchange Active Directory Topology/MSExchangeADTopology/ADTopology-Service.exe   Locates Active Directory domain controllers and global catalog servers, and provides Active Directory topology information to Exchange Server services. Most Exchange Server services depend on this service; if it does not start, the Exchange server will probably not function.

Microsoft Exchange Diagnostics/MSExchangeDiagnostics/Microsoft.Exchange .Diagnostics.Service.exe   Uses an agent to monitor the health of the Exchange server.

Microsoft Exchange Frontend Transport/MSExchangeFrontEndTransport/ MSExchangeFrontendTransport.exe   Provides SMTP proxy for inbound and outbound email messages from/to the Internet.

Microsoft Exchange Health Manager/MSExchangeHM/MSExchangeHMHost.exe   Monitors the health and performance of key services on the Exchange server.

Microsoft Exchange IMAP4/MSExchangeImap4/Microsoft.Exchange.Imap4Service .exe   Authenticates the connection and passes the request to the appropriate Mailbox server. This service is set to manual by default.

Microsoft Exchange Unified Messaging Call Router/MSExchangeUMCR/Microsoft .Exchange.UM.CallRouter.exe   Provides call-routing features.

Microsoft Exchange POP3/MSExchangePop3/Microsoft.Exchange.Pop3Service .exe   Authenticates the client connection and passes the request to the appropriate Mailbox server. This service is set to manual by default.

Microsoft Exchange Service Host/MSExchangeServiceHost/Microsoft.Exchange .ServiceHost.exe   Provides a service host for Exchange Server components that do not have their own service. These include components such as configuring registry and virtual directory information.

WHAT ABOUT THE EDGE TRANSPORT SERVER?

The Edge Transport server, which has provided a slimmed-down version of the Exchange server message transport functionality that requires neither Active Directory nor components such as the information store, is not available in Exchange Server 2013 RTM, CU1, or CU2. With that said, legacy versions of Edge Transport will still function correctly with Exchange Server 2013 servers with the Mailbox role installed.

It's important to note that an Edge Transport server is *not* required in any Exchange Server organization. It's only *an option*. Administrators may choose to deploy third-party SMTP relay or message hygiene solutions, instead of using a legacy Edge Transport server.

Possible Role Configurations

There are many possible configurations for Exchange Server 2013; unfortunately, there is no magic formula that will help you determine the exact number of servers you need and the roles those servers should host—well, at least not a simple formula. Knowing exactly when to scale Exchange Server 2013 from a single combined-function server to multiple dedicated server roles depends on a lot of factors:

◆ Server roles that your organization requires. Note that all Exchange Server organizations require at least one Mailbox and Client Access server.

◆ The number of simultaneous users who will be using the system and their usage profile (light, average, heavy).

◆ The number of messages sent and received per hour and the average size of those messages.

◆ An organization's high-availability requirements.

◆ The distribution of your users (across various offices) as well as the WAN link speeds and latency between the offices.

◆ The number of transport rules, journaling rules, daily messaging records management events, daily archiving, and other Exchange Server features that are required.

◆ Any third-party products that place additional transport, mailbox, or I/O load on the server, such as discovery, compliance, antivirus, antispam, archiving, or mobile devices.

You might need to segment server roles in a situation where you need to simplify server configuration by ensuring that only specific server roles reside on a single Windows server.

Combined-function Server

For many companies, a single Windows Server 2012 running Exchange Server 2013 with the Mailbox and Client Access server roles will be just fine depending on their usage patterns and number of simultaneous users. A company with only a few hundred users will fit perfectly well on a single server.

When properly configured with sufficient memory, disk capacity, and CPU resources, the combined-function server or multirole server can easily support your user base. The combined-function server is an economical solution provided you don't overload the server and you have good disaster-recovery documentation. The disaster-recovery documentation is important since all server roles are on a single server, so if it ever has to be rebuilt, all server roles have to be recovered at the same time.

Picking the right server hardware configuration is especially important when running a multirole server. When you're looking at megacycles for a Client Access server, determine the total megacycles and divide by 25 percent. For example, if you have 10,000 users and the number of megacycles for each user is 10, your formula would look like this:

Total CAS required megacycles = 10,000 users × 10 megacycles × 0.25 = 25,000 megacycles

Whatever you do, do not skimp on the RAM or CPU.

⊕ **Real World Scenario**

EXCHANGE SERVER 2013 AND DOMAIN CONTROLLERS COEXISTING

In almost no circumstances do we recommend installing Exchange Server 2013 on the same machine as a domain controller. Too many problems have arisen in every previous version of Exchange Server. Troubleshooting one or the other becomes more difficult when both Exchange Server and Active Directory are hosted on the same Windows server. We certainly see the logic that can be applied when buying server hardware, though.

For a company that is supporting only 50 mailboxes (and does not want to use a legacy Small Business server), it seems foolish to purchase two separate physical machines that will both be very lightly loaded. (Keep in mind that in those scenarios, Microsoft recommends a deployment of Office 365 to meet the needs of the company.)

A company that one of the authors worked with has 50 users; at any given time only about 30 of those users were using the email server. With the help of their consultant, they decided to use a host Windows Server 2012 x64 operating system and run a domain controller on one Hyper-V virtual machine and the Exchange Server 2013 server on a different Hyper-V virtual machine. This kept the applications separated on different operating systems but did not require the purchase of two physical servers. A third Hyper-V machine was configured to run SharePoint and an additional web application and to act as their file/print server.

The actual physical machine running these three guest operating systems had a dual quad-core processor and 128 GB of physical memory.

Scaling Exchange Server 2013 Roles

If you have determined that you are unable to host both your Exchange Server roles on a single physical machine, you will need to start splitting the roles off to multiple Windows servers. This is usually because you need to scale to support a larger user load than a single server can provide, or you're using a virtualization solution that can't meet sizing requirements with both roles on the same virtual server.

One of the biggest design decisions organizations will face with Exchange Server 2013 deployments is the placement of roles. Each organization is different, but the process to determine the best approach for Exchange Server 2013 deployments is simple. Planning for Exchange Server 2013 is covered is earlier chapters, but proper planning based on the user types, technical requirement, and business requirements will drive the how Exchange Server 2013 is deployed within your organization. In most organizations, you must evaluate the impact on a server's resources, as well as the overall impact of where servers are deployed and whether roles must coexist.

For example, take an organization that needs to support 4,000 mailboxes and requires high availability for the Mailbox and Client Access roles. In this example the organization has purchased four servers. Each server has been sized to support up to 2,000 active mailboxes while running the Client Access services. By installing the Client Access role and Mailbox role on the same physical server, the organization can place 1,000 mailboxes on each server and add all the Mailbox servers to the same DAG. This approach allows the organization to sustain two servers failing before reaching the 2,000-mailbox limit per server.

The preceding is a straightforward example of role placement. In more complex environments the options aren't always as cut and dried. As organizations look to streamline server deployments by using the same hardware or require all servers to be virtualized, many Exchange Server administrators find themselves between a rock and a hard place when it comes to role placement. Should you scale out and segregate the servers? Should you tell the customer not to virtualize and buy physical servers that can support the Mailbox and Client Access roles? Many times the company's IT strategy doesn't align with the best deployment option. In these situations you should provide the customer with two project plans. Each project plan should contain the pros, cons, and overall cost of each design.

The Bottom Line

Understand the importance of server roles.   For medium-size and large organizations, server roles allow more flexibility and scalability by providing you with the ability to isolate specific Exchange Server 2013 functions on different Windows servers. By installing only the necessary Exchange Server roles on a Windows server, there is less likelihood that one set of functions will consume all the server's resources and interfere with the operation of the other functions. The flip side of segregating roles onto different host Windows servers is that this normally increases the number of servers that are deployed within the organization. Increasing the number of servers in the organization will result in higher cost of support, management, and licensing.

Consolidation and segregation of roles per host should be considered during the planning phase of an Exchange Server 2013 project. The path that you choose will directly impact the implementation of Exchange Server 2013 within your organization.

Master It   You are the administrator for an Exchange Server organization with 1,700 mailboxes. Your design calls for a dedicated Mailbox server based on hardware limitations. Your boss has asked you to explain some of the reasons why you need to segment the Mailbox role to a dedicated server.

Understand the Exchange Server 2013 server roles.   Exchange Server 2013 supports two unique server roles. The features of the roles in Exchange Server 2007 and Exchange Server 2010 have been moved to the Client Access and Mailbox server roles in Exchange Server 2013. Also, some of the services that were performed by the Client Access role in Exchange Server 2010 have been moved to the Mailbox role in Exchange Server 2013.

The Mailbox server handles much more in Exchange Server 2013 than just the Exchange Server database engine. The Mailbox role now handles Unified Messaging, Client Access, and Transport services.

The Client Access server in many cases is a stateless server. A server running just the Client Access role can be quickly added or removed from an Exchange Server organization with little to no impact within the environment. With that said, a server running the Client Access role holds a lot of key responsibilities. It is still the end point for most of the protocols in the organization, such as SMTP, HTTP, and RTP. The main functions of the Client Access server are to authenticate an incoming request, locate the next hop for the request, and proxy or redirect the request to the next hop.

Master It   Which Exchange Server role provides access to the mailbox database for Outlook Web App and Outlook clients?

Explore possible server role configurations.   Server roles can be mixed and matched to meet most configuration requirements and organizational requirements.

For small organizations, a combined-function server that hosts the Mailbox and Client Access roles will suffice provided it has sufficient hardware even if it needs to support 500 or more mailboxes.

We do not recommend installing Exchange Server 2013 on a domain controller.

All server roles can be virtualized. Depending on the client load, Mailbox servers may also be virtualized as long as you remain within Microsoft's support boundaries. It is important to size out your Exchange Server 2013 deployment before committing to a virtual or physical server deployment.

Master It   Your company has approximately 400 mailboxes. Your users require only basic email services (email, shared calendars, Outlook, and Outlook Web App). You already have two servers that function as domain controllers/global catalog servers. What would you recommend to support the 400 mailboxes?

## Chapter 9

Exchange Server 2013 Requirements

When you get ready to start installing Exchange Server 2013, one thing that may slow you down is meeting all the necessary prerequisites. Depending on your expertise with Exchange Server, Active Directory, and supported versions of Windows Server, it may take hours or even days before you are ready to install Exchange Server 2013.

Things that can slow you down include, operating system and Active Directory prerequisites (software versions, patches, updates) as well as having the required permissions. If you are upgrading from a previous version of Exchange Server, you must make sure you are at the right version and service pack for all your existing servers.

In this chapter, we will make sure you are aware of all these prerequisites so that when you are ready to install Exchange Server 2013 you will breeze through the installation quickly and without interruption.

In this chapter, you will learn to:

- Use the right hardware for your organization

- Configure Windows Server 2008 R2 and Windows Server 2012 to support Exchange Server 2013

- Confirm that Active Directory is ready

- Verify that previous versions of Exchange Server can interoperate with Exchange Server 2013

Getting the Right Server Hardware

One of the things you can depend on when looking at any manufacturer's hardware specifications is that the specs will provide the minimum recommendations necessary to run the product. However, Microsoft has learned that recommending a minimum configuration often yields unhappy customers, which is why when Microsoft suggests hardware configurations, you will typically see two minimum and recommended.

The minimum hardware configuration works just fine if you are building a test lab or a classroom environment. But for production environments you want to make sure that your hardware can support a typical everyday workload plus a bit more. In this section, we will make some recommendations that are partially based on our own experiences and partially based on Microsoft's best practices.

Note that hardware configuration can vary quite a bit depending on the server's role and its workload. You may be supporting a single server with 100 mailboxes or a multiserver site with 100,000 mailboxes. You should plan to comfortably support your maximum expected load and allow some room for growth.

🌐 Real World Scenario

HARDWARE FOUNDATIONS: STABILITY, CONFIGURATION, AND MANAGEMENT

There are three key factors to ensuring that your Exchange servers function reliably and efficiently: stable hardware, correctly configured software, and proper management. If you fail to get any one of these right, the result will be poor performance, downtime, data loss, and unhappy users.

Windows hardware stability and compatibility are probably the most important factors in your choice for a server platform. These include not only the server model itself but also the components you will be using, such as network adapters and any third-party software. Selecting a stable hardware platform and vendor can be critical to a successful implementation.

Many vendors may be available to you. Local support, service-level agreements, quality, and performance should all be considerations when you select a vendor.

Choose a server model that will provide you with the card slots and available disk drives. When evaluating server models, ensure that the server model is near the beginning of its model life rather than near the end. It is not uncommon to purchase a server through a discount outlet that is near or at the end of its model life.

As you build your Windows servers, ensure that you are running reasonably recent versions of all supporting software, such as device drivers, and that the operating system is patched. Plan accordingly for physical deployments or virtual deployments (discussed in Chapter 4, "Virtualizing Exchange Server 2013").

You will also want to implement a comprehensive management strategy. You can do some monitoring of your Exchange Server deployment by using some of the built-in tools, such as Performance Monitor, Resource Monitor, and Event Viewer. You will notice after you have deployed Exchange Server in your environment that a number of different Exchange Server–specific objects and counters are now available in Performance Monitor. These counters can provide you an abundance of data that you can use to tune your deployment.

Other tools from Microsoft that you may have access to include: System Center Operations Manager and System Center Configuration Manager. It is worth noting that Exchange Server and the System Center tools are designed to work together, and one dovetails into the other as part of a comprehensive management solution.

You may also have researched and chosen to implement one of the many third-party network and application-monitoring tools. Some of these tools may be coming from your systems vendor, while others are stand-alone applications. Prior to purchase, you will want to research those applications, including talking with your peers in Exchange Server user groups and various web forums.

Regardless of the management tools you choose to implement, a solution is only as good as the information you can draw from the data. Bad or incomplete data can lead to poor decisions being made about your configuration and that leads to dissatisfied users. Monitor over time, and tune your systems for optimum performance.

The Typical User

If you have worked with more than one organization, you have probably reached the same conclusion that we have: no two Exchange Server organizations are exactly alike. Even businesses within the same industry can have dramatically different usage patterns based on slightly different business practices.

Where does this put the poor hapless person in charge of figuring out how much hardware to buy and how much capacity that hardware should have? If you are currently running an earlier version of Exchange Server, at least you have a leg up over other people.

You can use tools, such as Performance Monitor, to measure the number of messages sent and received per day and disk I/O capacity. If you are currently using Exchange Server 2010, you can generate a report on mailbox sizes by running the `exchange2010MailboxReportV1.ps1` PowerShell script from Microsoft; see:

```
http://gallery.technet.microsoft.com/office/Exchange-2010-Mailbox-Size-c3746baf
```

For Exchange Server 2007, you can use the `Get-MailboxStatistics` Exchange Management Shell cmdlet to acquire information regarding your mailboxes. You can enable message tracking and use tools, such as the Exchange Server Profile Analyzer (64-bit for Exchange Server 2007 or Exchange Server 2010) at `www.microsoft.com/en-us/download/details.aspx?id=10559` or Promodag Reports (`www.promodag.com`), to report how much mail each user sends and receives per day (and more).

Microsoft has done a lot of research in this area and has published some statistics on what they consider to be light, average, heavy, very heavy, and extra heavy Outlook users. They have also calculated that the average email message is 50 KB in size. Table 9.1 shows how Microsoft has defined each type of user.

TABLE 9.1:   Microsoft Outlook user types

USER TYPE	MESSAGES SENT PER DAY	MESSAGES RECEIVED PER DAY
Light	5	20
Average	10	40
Heavy	20	80
Very heavy	30	120
Extra heavy	40	160

Just relying on emails sent and received may not give you the best estimate of the hardware capacity required. We will talk about other factors throughout the book, but here we'll just list some factors that can adversely affect performance:

◆ Email archiving

◆ Mobile device user (the Blackberry can place a load four times higher on a server than that of a typical Outlook user)

◆ Antivirus scanning

◆ Messaging records management

◆ Transport rules

◆ Database replication

CPU Recommendations

Exchange Server 2013 runs only on Windows Server 2008 R2 and Windows Server 2012 and therefore only on hardware (physical or virtualized hardware) that is capable of supporting the x64 processor extensions. The primary benefit of 64-bit processing is the ability to take advantage of larger amounts of both virtual and physical memory. The processor should be at least 1.6 GHz, though you will certainly benefit from processors faster than 2 GHz as well as multicore processors. The processor must be one of the following:

◆ Intel Xeon or Intel Pentium x64 that supports the Intel 64 architecture (formerly known as EM64T)

◆ AMD Opteron 64-bit processor that supports the AMD64 platform

The Intel Itanium IA64 processor family is not supported.

Table 9.2 shows the processor recommendations from Microsoft for different Exchange Server 2013 roles.

TABLE 9.2:   Processor recommendations based on server role

EXCHANGE SERVER 2013 SERVER ROLE	MINIMUM	RECOMMENDED	RECOMMENDED MAXIMUM
Client Access	2 processor cores	8 processor cores	12 processor cores
Mailbox	2 processor cores	8 processor cores	24 processor cores
Combined function (combinations of Client Access and Mailbox server roles)	2 processor cores	8 processor cores	24 processor cores

This may seem like a lot of processor power, and in some ways it is. But remember that an Exchange Server 2013 server is doing a lot more than previous versions of Exchange Server. For example, on a combined-function server that is running the Mailbox and Client Access server roles, not only are the database engine, web components, and message transport running, but components, such as transport rules, messaging records management, mailbox archival, and client access functions are also running.

If you have worked with Exchange Server in the past, you may also note that the CPU recommendations for the Exchange Server 2013 Client Access server are higher than in Exchange Server 2007 or Exchange Server 2010. One of Microsoft's recommendations for the Client Access server role is a modification to the CAS-to-Mailbox server ratio. In Exchange Server 2010, that ratio was three CAS servers to every four Mailbox servers, but today, due to changes in the way the CAS handles clients, Microsoft recommends one CAS server to every four Mailbox servers. That said, for availability and load-balancing purposes, Microsoft recommends a minimum of two CAS servers.

If you are planning to use existing server hardware, consult your manufacturer's documentation for specific information on the processors and cores.

If you are not sure whether your existing hardware supports the x64 extensions, you can check this in a number of ways, including confirming it with the hardware vendor. If the computer is already running Windows, you can get a handy little program called CPU-Z from www.cpuid.com that will check your processor. Figure 9.1 shows the CPU-Z program.

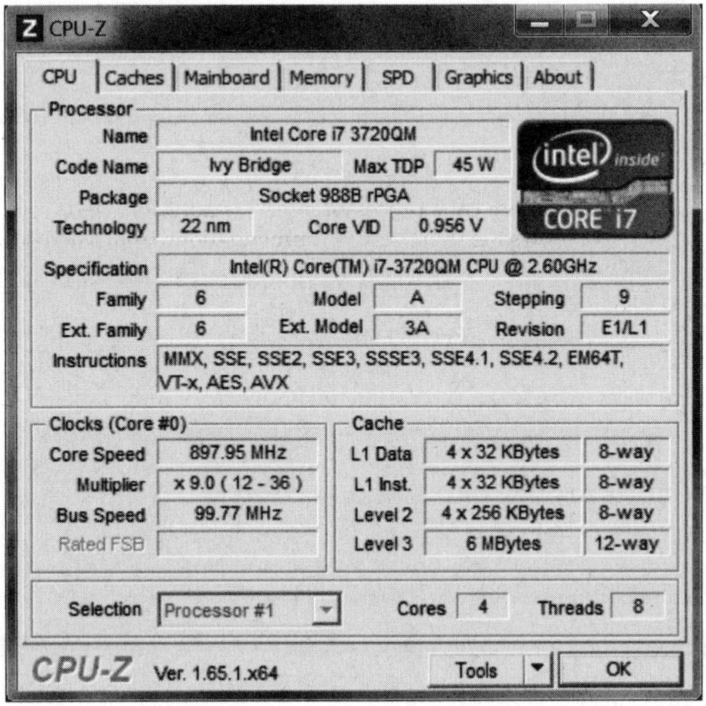

FIGURE 9.1
Using CPU-Z to identify the CPU type

Notice in the Instructions line of CPU-Z that this particular chip supports a variety of instruction sets, most important being EM64T, Intel's 64-bit extension to the Intel 32-bit instruction set.

The point of using a tool like CPU-Z is to assess the complete capabilities of the processor. Granted, you could simply look at the Computer/Properties page of a system running a Windows operating system, and that would help you determine the model and speed of the processor but may not provide you with a complete description of the processor and its capabilities.

CLIENT ACCESS SERVER CPU CONSIDERATIONS

All access to mailbox content is now handled through the Client Access server (see the sidebar "The Disappearance of the Hub Transport Role"). Mobile devices, web clients, Outlook clients, POP3, and IMAP4 clients now go through the Client Access server. One significant change to the client environment is that in Exchange Server 2007 and 2010, the Outlook client connected to Exchange Server using MAPI, while Outlook Anywhere connected to the Client Access server role via RPC over HTTPS. In Exchange Server 2013, both internal and external Outlook users will use MAPI commands issued to the server via remote procedure calls (RPC) over HTTPS (TCP port 443).

THE DISAPPEARANCE OF THE HUB TRANSPORT ROLE

One of the significant changes to Exchange Server 2013 is the removal of the Hub Transport role as a separate role. The functionality of the Hub Transport role has been retained, but it's now split between the Client Access server role and the Mailbox server role.

Although this is a good thing for the Mailbox server, it means that the Client Access server has more work to do. A Client Access server in an environment with a few hundred mailboxes can probably use a two-CPU core processor, but as the number of simultaneous users climbs, the processor power required will also climb. These additional factors may affect CPU requirements:

- Implementing SSL (secure sockets layer) access on the Client Access server

- Supporting larger numbers of POP3, IMAP4, Outlook Web Access, or Windows Mobile clients (since these clients require messages to be converted)

MAILBOX SERVER CPU CONSIDERATIONS

The number of processors required on a Mailbox server mostly depends on the total number of simultaneous users. According to Microsoft, a dedicated Mailbox server with sufficient memory and a four-processor-core server should be able to support 2,000+ mailboxes. Microsoft estimates a factor for calculating CPU requirements is one CPU core for each 1,000 mailboxes; this guideline is based on some assumptions about the usage profiles of those 1,000 users. In this case, Microsoft assumes that 750 of those are active and heavy-usage mailboxes. Sizing your mailbox servers for 10 to 20 percent more capacity than you think you are going to need is a good practice.

A number of factors affect CPU requirements, including the usage profile of the typical user and the concurrency rate (the percentage of your users who are accessing the server at any given time). If you are planning to support 2,000 very heavy users who use Outlook 90 percent of the day, you may need more CPU capacity. Factors that affect mailbox server CPU requirements include the following:

- Number of simultaneous users and usage profile

- Email archiving processes

- Mobile device usage

SCALING TO DEDICATED SERVERS ROLES

Many Exchange Server administrators never have to worry about more than a single server because their entire user community can fit nicely onto a single, combined function server. At some point, though, you may be required to add dedicated Exchange Server 2013 server roles to your organization. Here are some scenarios that may require dedicated server roles:

- The Active Directory site has more than one Mailbox server role.

- The Client Access functions place too much overhead on a single server.

- The requirements for high availability and/or load balancing demand more than one point of failure.

Exactly how many Client Access servers do you require? As with almost everything related to an Exchange Server configuration, this depends largely on your user community and the load they place on the server. Microsoft has a guideline based on the number of processor cores that the Mailbox server has versus the number of supporting Client Access server processor cores.

The ratio for Client Access servers has changed primarily because of the change in load placed on the Client Access server by the improved IOP efficiency in Exchange Server 2013. A typical environment should have one Client Access CPU core for every four Mailbox server cores, a change from the 3:4 ratio in Exchange Server 2010.

If you have a dedicated Mailbox server with eight CPU cores, an array of dedicated Client Access servers should have at least four CPU cores. This configuration provides redundancy and takes into consideration some additional factors that might increase processing load, such as enabling SSL or some transport rules.

Memory Recommendations

As mentioned previously, the advantage Exchange Server gets out of the x64 architecture is the ability to access more physical memory. Additional physical memory improves caching, reduces the disk I/O profile, and allows for the addition of more features.

Microsoft recommends a minimum of 4 GB of RAM in each Exchange Server 2013 server. This amount depends on the roles that the server is supporting. Table 9.3 shows the minimum, recommended, and maximum memory for each of the server roles.

TABLE 9.3: Minimum, recommended, and maximum RAM for Exchange Server 2013 roles

SERVER ROLE	MINIMUM	RECOMMENDATION	MAXIMUM
Mailbox	8 GB	8 GB of base memory plus mail volume calculation (generally 3 MB per every 50 messages sent/received daily per mailbox; see Table 9.4)	64 GB
Client Access	8 GB	2 GB per CPU core	16 GB
Multiple roles	8 GB	8 GB for Client Access plus the per-mailbox calculation* (see Table 9.4)	64 GB

*For more information, see: http://technet.microsoft.com/en-us/library/dd346700.

Although Microsoft's minimum RAM recommendation for any server hosting the Mailbox role is 8 GB, we strongly recommend a minimum of 12 GB based on calculated requirements (12 GB should be adequate based on an 8-GB base, a message volume of 100 messages per day for 600 users, and rounded up). Once you have calculated the minimum amount of RAM that you require for the server, if you are configuring a Mailbox server, you will need to add some additional RAM for each mailbox. This amount will depend on either your user community's estimated message profile or the mailbox size. In other words, you should calculate the memory requirement based on not only the usage profile of your users but also the mailbox size; then use the larger of these two calculations. Let's start with the amount of memory required based on usage profiles. Table 9.4 shows the additional memory required based on the number of mailboxes supported. The user profiles were defined previously in Table 9.1. The general rule from Microsoft is 3 MB of RAM for every 50 messages sent or received daily.

TABLE 9.4:   Additional memory factor for Mailbox servers

USER PROFILE	PER-MAILBOX MEMORY RECOMMENDATION
Light	Add 1.5 MB per mailbox
Average	Add 3 MB per mailbox
Heavy	Add 6 MB per mailbox
Very heavy	Add 9 MB per mailbox
Extra heavy	Add 12 MB per mailbox

Next, let's look at the recommendations based on the mailbox size. Table 9.5 shows Microsoft's per-mailbox memory recommendations for mailboxes of different sizes.

TABLE 9.5:   Memory required based on mailbox size

MAILBOX SIZE	PER-MAILBOX MEMORY RECOMMENDATION
Small (0 to 1 GB)	Add 2 MB per mailbox
Medium (1 to 3 GB)	Add 4 MB per mailbox
Large (3 to 5 GB)	Add 6 MB per mailbox
Very large (5 to 10 GB)	Add 8 MB per mailbox
Extra large (10 GB+)	Add 10 MB per mailbox

So, for example, a server handling a Mailbox server role should have 4 GB of memory plus the additional RAM per mailbox shown in Table 9.4 or the memory shown in Table 9.5 (whichever is larger). Let's do the calculations for a simple organization. If the Mailbox server is supporting 1,000 mailboxes and it is estimated that 500 of the users are average (1.75 GB of RAM if assuming 4 MB per mailbox) and 500 are heavy users (2.5 GB of RAM if assuming 6 MB per mailbox), the server should have about 9 GB of RAM. For good measure, we would recommend going with 10 or 12 GB of RAM so that there is additional RAM just in case it is required.

However we perform the additional calculation based on mailbox size, we may arrive at a different amount of RAM. Of the 1,000 mailboxes that this server supports, 400 of these users have an average mailbox size that is in excess of 10 GB, whereas the remainder of the mailboxes average around 6 GB. That would require 4 GB of RAM (400 times 10 MB per mailbox) for the extra-large mailboxes and about 5 GB of RAM (600 times 8 MB per mailbox) for the very large mailboxes. That is a total of about 9 GB of RAM.

So in this case, going with at least 10 GB to 12 GB of RAM for mailbox caching will definitely be a good design decision. Remember that these RAM estimates are just that: estimates. Additional factors (message hygiene software, continuous replication, email archiving, and so on) may require more or less RAM (usually more) than the calculations and recommendations here. For example, antivirus and antispam software on Mailbox servers can place a significant burden on RAM. Microsoft has released the Exchanger Server 2013 Server Role Requirements Calculator, which can be useful when estimating RAM requirements; see this article on the Exchange Team Blog for more information:

```
http://blogs.technet.com/b/exchange/archive/2013/05/14/released-exchange-2013-
server-role-requirements-calculator.aspx
```

Network Requirements

With previous versions of Exchange Server, recommending network connectivity speeds was often a gray area because of the variety of networking hardware that most organizations were using. Essentially, not everyone had a Gigabit Ethernet backbone for their servers. Today, however, Gigabit Ethernet is present in most datacenters at least for the datacenter backbone.

So, the recommendation is pretty simple. All Exchange Server 2013 servers should be on a Gigabit Ethernet backbone. Will Exchange Server 2013 work on a 100-MB or even a 10-MB network? Sure, it will, but you will get the best results in even a medium-sized network if you are using Gigabit Ethernet.

In organizations that have put their Exchange Server roles onto different Windows servers (physical or virtual), a lot of communication is taking place between the Client Access servers and the Mailbox servers. All Exchange Server roles should be Gigabit Ethernet.

All of the "client-to-server" communication traffic now takes place between the client (usually Outlook) and the Client Access server. The MAPI traffic that took place between Outlook clients and Mailbox servers hosting public folders in previous versions of Exchange Server no longer exists, because all client communication for public folders occurs over RPC over HTTPS. This is because the public folders in Exchange Server 2013 are actually specialized private mailboxes with a very similar structure. (For in-depth information on public folders, see Chapter 17, "Managing Modern Public Folders.")

If you are planning to implement database availability groups (DAGs) between two or more Exchange Server 2013 Mailbox servers, each server will need a second network adapter installed. The first network adapter will be used for production LAN communications, while the second adapter will be used for replication of the information stores. The replication network will be on its own IP subnet and should also have Gigabit Ethernet connectivity to the physical network. In large environments with multiple servers and dozens of databases in a DAG, consider adding additional network adapters that act as replication or MAPI network connections.

If you are planning to put DAG members on a separate physical network to facilitate site resiliency, the maximum network latency between members should not exceed 500 milliseconds (ms), and there must be sufficient bandwidth to keep up with the volume of replication traffic.

Disk Requirements

When calculating disk requirements for some applications, it is easy to decide that a single 500 GB hard disk will solve your storage needs. You might be tempted to think the same thing about Exchange Server.

With earlier versions of Exchange Server, getting the disk requirements sized correctly could be a bit tricky. That is not to say that doing so cannot still be tricky with Exchange Server 2013. This is because sizing a disk is not just a matter of figuring out how much storage you need. Physical storage requirements are a big part of the sizing, of course, because if you don't get large enough disks to support your users, you will be going back to the boss for more money to buy more disks.

But asking the boss to buy more physical disk drives because the users' mailboxes are full is at least something tangible you can ask for. The other side of the sizing requirement is ensuring that the disk I/O capacity will keep up with the database engine. The more users using Exchange Server, the greater the disk I/O capacity required by the disk subsystem. Try explaining to your boss that the disks have plenty of storage available but can't keep up with the database load.

The disk subsystem that you choose has to be able to support not only the *amount* of storage required but also the I/O *load* that the users will place on the disk subsystem. Therefore, understanding the I/O profile as well as the amount of storage required is important. Helpfully, Microsoft has improved the I/O profile with every iteration of Exchange Server, and Exchange Server 2013 is no exception, most notably improving the Input/Output Operations Per Second (IOPS) performance when replicating information store data between DAG nodes.

A full discussion of all the factors you may need to take into consideration when calculating disk storage is beyond the scope of a single chapter in this book. Something that you may find of benefit relative to Exchange Server 2013 is the following web page, which addresses a number of factors associated with various storage architectures, physical disk types, and best practices:

`http://technet.microsoft.com/en-us/library/ee832792%28v=exchg.150%29.aspx`

IMPROVED CACHING AND REDUCED I/O PROFILES

By and large, Client Access servers require far less disk I/O capacity than Mailbox servers, but the I/O profiles have changed significantly because of the incorporation of all message-routing functionality into the Client Access and Mailbox server roles. The information in this section applies to servers that are hosting the Mailbox server role.

Hundreds of pages of material have been written on the concept of optimizing Exchange Server for maximizing performance by improving I/O performance with Exchange Server—and we certainly can't do the concept justice in just a few paragraphs—but understanding the basic IOPS requirements of users is helpful. Microsoft and hardware vendors have done much research on I/O requirements based on the mailbox size and the average load that each user places on the server. One of the things that you may find helpful is gaining an understanding of the differences between Exchange Server 2010 I/O versus Exchange Server 2013 I/O. A good starting point for Exchange Server 2010 is this information from TechNet:

```
http://technet.microsoft.com/en-us/library/dd351197(EXCHG.140).aspx
```

You can then follow that up with this article on Exchange Server 2013 IOPS performance that was put together by Microsoft's Exchange Team. This breaks down a number of factors regarding sizing and capacity planning:

```
http://blogs.technet.com/b/exchange/archive/2013/05/13/3570595.aspx
```

One area Microsoft has continuously improved is IOPS. Since Exchange Server 2003, we've witnessed a number of changes to the structure of Exchange Server and its databases to improve performance. The most obvious improvement moving from Exchange Server 2003 to Exchange Server 2007 was the removal of the .STM database, a database for streamed Internet content. The .EDB database was modified to support that same content. Microsoft wasn't finished there.

The Exchange Server database team worked at further improving the I/O performance of Exchange Server 2010 Mailbox Server Role. One of the key factors that the database team focused on with Exchange Server 2010 was to further improve the I/O performance so that most types of affordable disk drive could be used (such as SATA, SAS, or SCSI). They did this by further optimizing the use of cache memory, increasing database page sizes, changing the database schema, and optimizing how the database arranges data to be written to the disk.

The resulting improvements to the Exchange Server 2010 database engine further reduced the I/O requirements for the standard usage profiles. I/O requirements, of course, are just estimates, but they generally provide a pretty good guideline for the IOPS requirements for the disks that will host Exchange Server databases. The disks that will host the Exchange Server transaction logs will require approximately 10 to 20 percent of the IOPS requirements for their corresponding database.

There have been significant changes to the way Exchange Server 2013 interacts with information stores, but some numbers from Microsoft, as shown in Table 9.6, reflect the continuous improvement in I/O performance.

TABLE 9.6: User type, database volume IOPS, and messages sent and received per day for Exchange Server 2013

USER TYPE	DATABASE VOLUME IOPS	MESSAGES SENT/RECEIVED PER DAY*
Light	0.017	5 sent/20 received
Average	0.034	10 sent/40 received
Heavy	0.067	20 sent/80 received
Large	0.101	30 sent/120 received

Assumes average message size is approximately 50 KB.

It is reasonable to assume that there has been some variation in the testing methodology used to generate the data over the years. A lot of things have changed since Exchange Server 2003, but the fact is that Microsoft has worked to improve the overall performance of I/O operations as they relate to Mailbox servers. For an in-depth breakdown on performance improvements to Exchange Server 2013, check out this blog entry from the Microsoft Exchange Team:

```
http://blogs.technet.com/b/exchange/archive/2013/05/13/3570595.aspx
```

Mailbox Storage

Exchange servers holding the Mailbox server role consume the most disk space. Exchange Server system designers often fall short in their designs by not allowing sufficient disk space for mail storage, transaction logs, and extra disk space. Often the disk space is not partitioned correctly, either. Here are some important points to keep in mind when planning your disk space requirements:

◆ Transaction log files should be on a separate set of physical disks (spindles) from their corresponding Exchange Server database files if you are deploying only a single data-base copy. RAID 1 or RAID 0+1 arrays provide better performance for transaction logs. However, if you are implementing a DAG, it is unnecessary to separate the database copy and the transaction log files, because recovery takes place via a replicated copy hosted on another machine rather than a backup.

◆ Allow for 7 to 10 days' worth of transaction logs to be stored for each database. The esti-mated amount of transaction logs will vary dramatically from one organization to another, but a good starting point is about 4 GB of transaction logs per day per 1,000 mailboxes. This is just one estimate of a specific usage profile, though, and your actual mileage may vary. Tools like the Exchange Storage Calculator can be used to assist in disk space requirements.

◆ Allow for whitespace estimates in the maximum size of each of your database files. (The whitespace is the empty space that is found in the database at any given time.) The size of the whitespace in the database can be approximated by the amount of mail sent and received by the users with mailboxes in that database. For example, if you have one hun-dred 2 GB mailboxes (a total of 200 GB) in a database where users send and receive an aver-age of 10 MB of mail per day, the whitespace is approximately 1 GB (100 mailboxes × 10 MB per mailbox). Factor in 5 to 10 percent additional disk space for the content index databases. You will have one content index database for each production database.

◆ Allocate enough free space on the disk so that you can always make a backup copy of your largest database and still have some free disk space. A good way to calculate this is to take 110 percent of the largest database you will support because that also allows you to defrag-ment the database using Eseutil if necessary.

◆ Consider additional disk space for message tracking, message transport, and RPC client access, as well as HTTP, POP3, and IMAP4 log files if you have combined-function servers.

◆ Always have recovery in mind, and make sure you have enough disk space to be able to restore a database to a recovery database.

Microsoft has a number of excellent guidelines for estimating disk space requirements and database sizing, including the Storage Calculator. Here is another article that is worth reading:

```
http://technet.microsoft.com/en-us/library/bb738147.aspx
```

Let's move on to an example of a server that will support 1,000 mailboxes. We are estimating that we will provide the typical user with a Prohibit Send size warning of 500 MB and a Prohibit Send And Receive limit of 600 MB. In any organization of 1,000 users, you have to take into account that 10 percent will qualify as VIPs who will be allowed more mail storage than a typical user; in this case, let's allow 100 VIP users to have a Prohibit Send And Receive limit of 2 GB.

These calculations result in 540 GB of mail storage requirements (600 MB × 900 mailboxes) for the first 900 users plus another 200 GB (2 GB × 100 mailboxes) for the VIP users. This results in a maximum amount of mail storage of 740 GB. However, this estimate does not include estimates for deleted items in a user's mailbox and deleted mailboxes, so we want to add an additional overhead factor of about 15 percent, or about 111 MB, plus an additional overhead factor of another 15 percent (another 111 MB) for database whitespace.

So at any given time, for these 1,000 mailboxes we can expect mail database storage (valid email content, deleted data, and empty database space) to consume approximately 962 GB, but because we like round numbers, we'll round that up to 1,000 GB, or 1 TB.

In this example, let's say that we have decided the maximum database size we want to be able to back up or restore is 100 GB. This means that we need to split the users' mailboxes across 10 mailbox databases.

For the transaction logs, we estimate that we will generate approximately 5 GB of transaction logs per day. We should plan for enough disk space on the transaction log disk for at least 50 GB of available disk space.

Next, because full-text indexing is enabled by default, we should allow enough disk space for the full-text index files. In this case, we will estimate that the full-text index files will consume a maximum of about 10 percent of the total size of the mail data, or approximately 100 GB. If we combine the full-text index files on the same disk drive as the database files, we will need about 1.3 TB of disk space.

Anytime you are not sure how much disk space you should include, it is a good idea to plan for more rather than less. Although disk space is reasonably inexpensive, unless you have sophisticated storage systems, adding additional disk space can be time consuming and costly from the perspective of effort and downtime.

PLANNING FOR MAIL GROWTH

Growth? You may be saying to yourself, "I just gave the typical user a maximum mailbox size of 600 MB and the VIPs a maximum size of 2 GB! How can my users possibly need more mailbox space?" Predicting the amount of growth you may need in the future is a difficult task. You may not be able to foresee new organizational requirements, or you might be influenced by future laws that require specific data-retention periods.

In our experience, though, mailbox limits, regardless of how rigid we plan to be, are managed by exception and by need. In the preceding example, we calculated that we would need 1.3 TB of disk space for our 1,000 mailboxes. Would we partition or create a disk of exactly that size? Possibly. One of the facts that Microsoft has taken into consideration is the increasing size factor as hard drives as large as 8 TB are becoming available on the market at an increasingly attractive price point.

Instead of carving out exactly the amount of disk space you anticipate needing, add a "fluff factor" to your calculations. As a baseline, we recommend adding approximately 20 to 25 percent additional capacity to the anticipated amount of storage you think you will require. In this example, we might anticipate using 1.3 TB of disk space if we added 25 percent to our expected requirements. Here are some factors that you may want to consider when deciding how much growth you should expect for your mailbox servers:

◆ Average annual growth in the number of employees

◆ Acquisitions, mergers, or consolidations that are planned for the foreseeable future

◆ Addition of new mail-enabled applications, such as Unified Messaging features or electronic forms routing

◆ Government regulations that require some types of corporate records (including email) to be retained for a number of years

Conversely, potential events in your future could reduce the amount of mailbox storage you require. Many organizations are now including message archival and long-term retention systems in their messaging systems. These systems archive older content from a user's mailbox and move it to some type of external storage such as disk, storage area network, network-attached storage, optical, or tape storage.

Email Archiving and Mail Storage

Email has emerged as the predominant form of business communications. Sales, marketing, ordering, human resources, legal, financial, and all other types of information are now disseminated via email.

Myriad companies provide archiving solutions for email systems. Some of these companies provide in-house solutions, whereas some are hosted solutions. There are just about as many reasons to implement an email archive system as there are archive vendors. The following are some of the reasons to implement email archiving:

◆ Reduces the size of mailbox databases and mailboxes (smaller databases and smaller mailboxes improve disaster-recovery response times and improve performance)

◆ Provides long-term retention of email data

◆ Provides users with a searchable index of their historical email data

◆ Allows for eDiscovery of email (message content, attachments, as well as email metadata) that often must be indexed for legal proceedings

◆ Eliminates the use of Outlook personal folder (PST) files

Third-party archive systems are great for organizations that must retain much of the information in their mailboxes but want to move it to external storage. However, depending on the system, you don't want to archive everything older than five days, for example, because that may prevent the user from accessing it via Outlook Web App or mobile devices. Further, once the content is archived and no longer residing in the user's mailbox, it will no longer be accessible from a user's desktop search engine, such as the Google Desktop or the Windows Desktop search engine. So keeping a certain amount of content in the user's mailbox always makes sense.

Exchange Server 2013 has retained the email archive system created in Exchange Server 2010. Microsoft's approach is to establish an extra archive mailbox for each user who requires archiving. The email archive mailbox can reside on the same mailbox database as the user's mailbox or a different mailbox database hosted on a different server. This approach does serve the goal of reducing the size of the user's primary mailbox, but it does not reduce the size of the aggregate database volume. Furthermore, it allows users who may have been using PST files as an archival storage mechanism to return that email back into an Exchange Server archive mailbox for the purposes of eDiscovery and long-term archival.

If you are planning to use the Exchange Server 2013 mailbox archive feature, you will need to take this into account and plan for additional storage as needed.

Software Requirements

After you have the right hardware chosen to support Exchange Server 2013, you need to make sure that the software is ready. This includes getting the right version and edition of the operating system, software updates, and any prerequisite Windows roles or functions.

Operating System Requirements

The operating system requirements for Exchange Server 2013 are pretty cut and dried. Windows Server 2008 R2 and Windows Server 2012 are the only operating systems supported in the following configurations:

- Windows Server 2012 Standard Edition
- Windows Server 2012 Datacenter Edition
- Windows Server 2008 R2 Standard Edition with SP1
- Windows Server 2008 R2 Enterprise Edition with SP1
- Windows Server 2008 R2 Datacenter Edition RTM or later

If you want to implement database availability groups, avoid Windows Server 2008 R2 Standard Edition, because it does not come with the Failover Clustering feature that is required to support DAGs.

Additionally, you may be a fan of the Server Core installation, but Exchange Server 2013 does not run on Server Core.

If you are unsure as to whether you have the correct Service Pack installed on your system, you can acquire this information by opening `Control Panel\Programs\Programs and Features\Installed Updates`. There you will see a comprehensive list of all Service Packs, Cumulative Rollups, and Hot Fixes that have been applied to your system.

Real World Scenario

NAME THE SERVER QUICKLY!

Once you have installed Windows Server 2008 R2 or Windows Server 2012, make sure that the server is assigned the correct name before you proceed. During installation, the Windows Server setup assigns a random name to the server. More than likely, this name will not be the one you want to use. Once Exchange Server 2013 is installed, you cannot change this name.

WINDOWS SERVER 2008 R2 ROLES AND FEATURES

You must add a number of roles and features to the default installation of Windows Server 2008 R2 to support the functionality of Exchange Server 2013. The roles and features are required for all versions of the host operating system, whether Standard, Enterprise, or Datacenter. If you are unsure as to whether the necessary roles and features have already been installed, you can check Server Manager or open a PowerShell session and use the `Get-Module` cmdlet.

Mailbox Server Role or Combined Mailbox Server/Client Access Server

The preferred method for installing all of the prerequisite roles and features on a Windows Server 2008 R2 host to support Exchange Server 2013 is by using PowerShell. Follow these steps:

1. Open a PowerShell session as an administrator with adequate rights to modify the server. You can verify which modules have been loaded by running the following cmdlet:

   ```
   Get-Module -ListAvailable
   ```

2. Load the Server Manager module by running the following cmdlet:

   ```
   Import-Module ServerManager
   ```

3. Install the required components by using the `Add-WindowsFeature` cmdlet:

   ```
   Add-WindowsFeature Desktop-Experience, NET-Framework, NET-HTTP-Activation,
   RPC-over-HTTP-proxy, RSAT-Clustering, RSAT-Web-Server, WAS-Process-Model, Web-
   Asp-Net, Web-Basic-Auth, Web-Client-Auth, Web-Digest-Auth, Web-Dir-Browsing,
   Web-Dyn-Compression, Web-Http-Errors, Web-Http-Logging, Web-Http-Redirect,
   Web-Http-Tracing, Web-ISAPI-Ext, Web-ISAPI-Filter, Web-Lgcy-Mgmt-Console,
   Web-Metabase, Web-Mgmt-Console, Web-Mgmt-Service, Web-Net-Ext, Web-Request-
   Monitor, Web-Server, Web-Stat-Compression, Web-Static-Content, Web-Windows-
   Auth, Web-WMI
   ```

This completes the required features that are native to the Windows Server 2008 R2 SP1 operating system, but there are some additional items that need to be installed and in the order displayed:

1. Microsoft .NET Framework 4.5

   ```
   http://msdn.microsoft.com/en-us/library/5a4x27ek%28VS.110%29.aspx
   ```

2. Windows Management Framework 3.0

   ```
   http://www.microsoft.com/en-us/download/details.aspx?id=34595
   ```

3. Microsoft Unified Communications Managed API 4.0, Core Runtime 64-bit

   ```
   http://www.microsoft.com/en-us/download/details.aspx?id=34992
   ```

4. Microsoft Office 2010 Filter Pack 64-bit

   ```
   http://www.microsoft.com/en-us/download/details.aspx?id=17062
   ```

5. Microsoft Office 2010 Filter Pack SP1 64-bit

   `http://www.microsoft.com/en-us/download/details.aspx?id=26604`

6. Windows Identity Foundation Extension (Microsoft Knowledge Base article KB974405)

   `http://support.microsoft.com/?kbid=974405`

7. Association Cookie/GUID Hotfix (Microsoft Knowledge Base article KB2619234)

   `http://support.microsoft.com/?kbid=2619234`

8. Microsoft Security Advisory Package (Microsoft Knowledge Base article KB2533623)

   `http://support.microsoft.com/?kbid=2533623`

If you have installed the operating system with all available updates, you may not need to install all of these additional components, because they may have been included with installed updates.

Client Access Server Role Only

This procedure is very similar to the installation of the Mailbox/CAS role from the previous section but with fewer software requirements:

1. Open a PowerShell session as an administrator with adequate rights to modify the server.

2. Load the Server Manager module by running the following cmdlet:

   ```
   Import-Module ServerManager
   ```

3. Install the required components by using the `Add-WindowsFeature` cmdlet:

   ```
   Add-WindowsFeature Desktop-Experience, NET-Framework, NET-HTTP-Activation,
   RPC-over-HTTP-proxy, RSAT-Clustering, RSAT-Web-Server, WAS-Process-Model, Web-
   Asp-Net, Web-Basic-Auth, Web-Client-Auth, Web-Digest-Auth, Web-Dir-Browsing,
   Web-Dyn-Compression, Web-Http-Errors, Web-Http-Logging, Web-Http-Redirect,
   Web-Http-Tracing, Web-ISAPI-Ext, Web-ISAPI-Filter, Web-Lgcy-Mgmt-Console,
   Web-Metabase, Web-Mgmt-Console, Web-Mgmt-Service, Web-Net-Ext, Web-Request-
   Monitor, Web-Server, Web-Stat-Compression, Web-Static-Content, Web-Windows-
   Auth, Web-WMI
   ```

Once again, you must install additional components prior to installing Exchange Server 2013 as a Client Access server. The components and order are identical to those detailed in the preceding "Mailbox Server Role or Combined Mailbox Server/Client Access Server" section.

WINDOWS SERVER 2012 ROLES AND FEATURES

You must add a number of roles and features to the default installation of Windows Server 2012 to support the functionality of Exchange Server 2013. The roles and features are required for all versions of the host operating system.

Mailbox Server Role or Combined Mailbox Server/Client Access Server

You will want to use PowerShell once again to install the prerequisite features on Windows Server 2012. There are some minor differences between the combination role of Mailbox/Client Access server and a Client Access server supporting existing Mailbox servers.

1. Open a PowerShell session with the appropriate administrative rights to modify the installation.

2. Run the Install-WindowsFeature cmdlet:

```
Install-WindowsFeature AS-HTTP-Activation, Desktop-Experience, NET-Framework-
45-Features, RPC-over-HTTP-proxy, RSAT-Clustering, RSAT-Clustering-
CmdInterface, RSAT-Clustering-Mgmt, RSAT-Clustering-PowerShell, Web-Mgmt-
Console, WAS-Process-Model, Web-Asp-Net45, Web-Basic-Auth, Web-Client-Auth,
Web-Digest-Auth, Web-Dir-Browsing, Web-Dyn-Compression, Web-Http-Errors,
Web-Http-Logging, Web-Http-Redirect, Web-Http-Tracing, Web-ISAPI-Ext, Web-
ISAPI-Filter, Web-Lgcy-Mgmt-Console, Web-Metabase, Web-Mgmt-Console, Web-Mgmt-
Service, Web-Net-Ext45, Web-Request-Monitor, Web-Server, Web-Stat-Compression,
Web-Static-Content, Web-Windows-Auth, Web-WMI, Windows-Identity-Foundation
```

After that command is complete, you will need to install the following supplemental components in the order listed:

1. Microsoft Unified Communications Managed API 4.0, Core Runtime 64-bit

   http://www.microsoft.com/en-us/download/details.aspx?id=34992

2. Microsoft Office 2010 Filter Pack 64-bit

   http://www.microsoft.com/en-us/download/details.aspx?id=17062

3. Microsoft Office 2010 Filter Pack SP1 64-bit

   http://www.microsoft.com/en-us/download/details.aspx?id=26604

Client Access Server Role Only

Unlike a Windows Server 2008 R2 deployment of Exchange Server 2013, there is a difference in the required components and packages when installing the Client Access server role by itself compared to a Mailbox server role system. To install the prerequisite features to support a Client Access server, take the following steps:

1. Open a PowerShell session with the appropriate administrative rights to modify the installation.

2. Run the Install-WindowsFeature cmdlet:

```
Install-WindowsFeature AS-HTTP-Activation, Desktop-Experience, NET-Framework-
45-Features, RPC-over-HTTP-proxy, RSAT-Clustering, RSAT-Clustering-
CmdInterface, RSAT-Clustering-Mgmt, RSAT-Clustering-PowerShell, Web-Mgmt-
Console, WAS-Process-Model, Web-Asp-Net45, Web-Basic-Auth, Web-Client-Auth,
Web-Digest-Auth, Web-Dir-Browsing, Web-Dyn-Compression, Web-Http-Errors,
```

```
Web-Http-Logging, Web-Http-Redirect, Web-Http-Tracing, Web-ISAPI-Ext, Web-
ISAPI-Filter, Web-Lgcy-Mgmt-Console, Web-Metabase, Web-Mgmt-Console, Web-Mgmt-
Service, Web-Net-Ext45, Web-Request-Monitor, Web-Server, Web-Stat-Compression,
Web-Static-Content, Web-Windows-Auth, Web-WMI, Windows-Identity-Foundation
```

After you have completed the installation of those features, you have one additional package to install:

◆ Microsoft Unified Communications Managed API 4.0, Core Runtime 64-bit

```
http://www.microsoft.com/en-us/download/details.aspx?id=34992
```

Windows 7 and Windows 8 Management Consoles

You can create a management console for your Exchange Server 2013 deployment on a domain-joined Windows 8 (64-bit) system with no additional configuration. The default installation is supported.

You can also configure a domain-joined Windows 7 (64-bit only) to function as a management console for your Exchange Server 2013 deployment, but there are prerequisites that must be met before you can do that:

1. Open Control Panel.

2. Select Programs.

3. Select the option Turn Windows Features On or Off.

4. Select Internet Information Services.

5. Select Web Management Tools.

6. Select IIS 6 Management Compatibility.

7. Turn on the IIS 6 Management Console.

8. Click OK (see Figure 9.2).

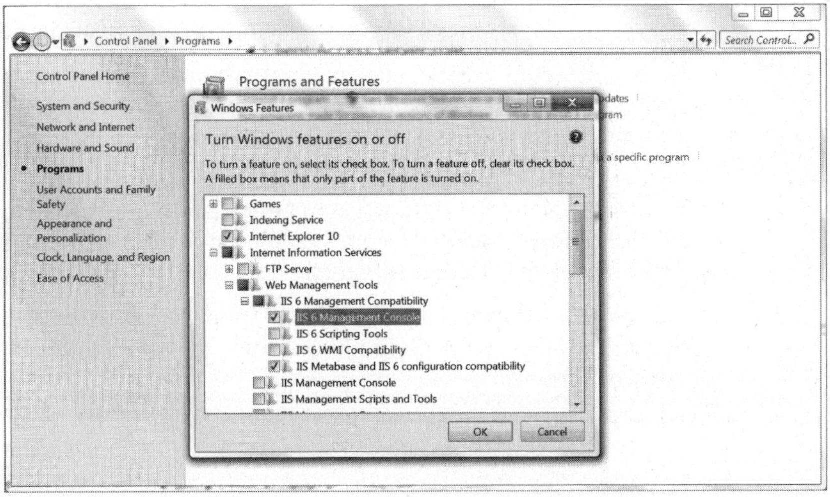

FIGURE 9.2
Installing the IIS 6
Management Console
on Windows 7

After you have done that, you must install three additional components, in the order listed here:

1. Microsoft .NET Framework 4.5

   `http://msdn.microsoft.com/en-us/library/5a4x27ek%28VS.110%29.aspx`

2. Windows Management Framework 3.0

   `http://www.microsoft.com/en-us/download/details.aspx?id=34595`

3. Windows Identity Foundation Extension (Microsoft Knowledge Base article KB974405)

   `http://support.microsoft.com/?kbid=974405`

Additional Requirements

In addition to making sure that the hardware and server software can support Exchange Server 2013, you need to consider a few infrastructure requirements. These include making sure that your Active Directory infrastructure can support Exchange Server 2013 and that you have the necessary permissions to prepare the forest and domain.

Active Directory Requirements

The Active Directory domain controller requirements to install Exchange Server 2013 into your forest can be a bit confusing. We've created a summary of the required settings for you. Here are some AD settings that you must conform to when ensuring that your Active Directory infrastructure will properly support Exchange Server 2013:

◆ All domain controllers in each Active Directory site where you plan on deploying Exchange Server 2013 must be running Windows Server 2003 SP2 at a minimum.

◆ The Active Directory forest must be in Windows Server 2003 forest functional level. Each Active Directory site in which you will install Exchange Server 2013 servers should contain at least two global catalog servers to ensure local global catalog access and fault tolerance.

◆ For organizations using domain controllers running x86 Windows, each Active Directory site that contains Exchange servers should have one domain controller processor core for each four Exchange Server Mailbox server processor cores.

◆ For organizations using domain controllers running x64 Windows and having enough RAM installed for the entire `NTDS.DIT` to be loaded into memory, each Active Directory site that contains Exchange servers should have one domain controller processor core for each of the eight Exchange Server Mailbox server processor cores.

◆ Always take into account that domain controllers may not be dedicated to just Exchange Server. They may be handling authentication for users logging into the domain and for other applications.

◆ Exchange Server 2013 doesn't use read-only domain controllers and global catalog servers; so do not include their presence in your domain controller planning.

Installation and Preparation Permissions

It might seem that the easiest possible way to get Exchange Server 2013 installed is to log on to a Windows Server 2008 R2 SP1 or Windows Server 2012 computer as a member of Domain Admins, Schema Admins, and Enterprise Admins. Indeed, using a user account that is a member of all three of those groups will give you all the rights you need.

In some larger organizations, though, getting a user account that is a member of all three of these groups is impossible. In some cases, the Exchange Server administrator may have to make a request from the Active Directory forest owner to perform some of the preparation tasks on behalf of the Exchange Server team. For this reason, it is important to know the permissions that are required to perform the different setup tasks, as shown in Table 9.7.

TABLE 9.7:   Task permissions

TASK	GROUP MEMBERSHIP
Setup /PrepareSchema or setup /ps	Schema Admins and Enterprise Admins
Setup /PrepareAD or setup /p	Enterprise Admins
Setup /PrepareDomain or setup /pd	Domain Admins
Install Exchange Server 2013	Administrators group on the Windows server and Exchange Organization Management

Coexisting with Previous Versions of Exchange Server

Exchange Server is fairly widely deployed in most organizations, so it is likely that you will be transitioning or migrating your existing Exchange Server organization over to Exchange Server 2013. For some period of time (hopefully short), your Exchange Server 2013 servers will be inter-operating with either Exchange Server 2010 or Exchange Server 2007 servers. For this reason, you must know the factors necessary to ensure successful coexistence.

The recommended order for installing Exchange Server 2013 servers and transitioning messaging services over to those new servers is as follows:

1. Install Client Access servers and decide how you will handle legacy OWA clients (via proxying, redirection, or direct connections). Depending on the clients you need to support, you will want to enable Outlook Web App, Windows Mobile, Outlook Anywhere, POP3, and IMAP4 clients on the new Client Access servers.

2. Install Mailbox servers and begin to transition mailboxes and public folders from the legacy servers to the new servers.

COEXISTENCE WITH EXCHANGE SERVER 2007

If you are currently using Exchange Server 2007, prior to installing the first Exchange Server 2013 server ensure that you meet the following prerequisites:

- ◆ All Exchange Server 2007 servers within the Active Directory where you are planning to introduce Exchange Server 2013 must be running a minimum of Exchange Server 2007 Service Pack 3 with Update Rollup 10.

- ◆ The Active Directory forest must be at the Windows Server 2003 forest functional level.

- ◆ Each Active Directory site must have at least one global catalog server running Windows Server 2003 SP2 or later.

- ◆ Exchange 2013 servers must have Cumulative Update 2 (CU 2) installed.

COEXISTENCE WITH EXCHANGE SERVER 2010

If you are currently using Exchange Server 2010, prior to installing the first Exchange Server 2013 server, ensure that you meet the following prerequisites:

- ◆ All Exchange Server 2010 servers, including the Edge Transport server, must be at Exchange Server 2010 Service Pack 3.

- ◆ All Exchange Servers 2013 servers must have CU 2 (or later) installed.

The Bottom Line

Use the right hardware for your organization. There are several tools provided online to help you properly size the amount of RAM, as well as the hard disk configuration for your deployment. One other resource that you should not overlook is your hardware vendor. Very often vendors have created custom tools to aid in the proper sizing of your environment relative to your organizational needs.

If you want to get a fair idea as to what you should plan, use the tables in this chapter, based on both mailbox size and message volume. Remember, you should try both sizing methods and select the option that projects the most RAM and the largest storage volume. You can never have enough RAM or storage space.

Ensure that the processor core ratio for Client Access servers to Mailbox servers is adequate to keep up with the load clients will place on these servers. For Client Access servers, use a ratio of one processor core for every four Mailbox server processor cores.

Explore the possibilities with the Exchange Server 2013 Server Role Requirements Calculator, and try different combinations of options. It can serve as a solid guideline for deployments, from small-to medium-size companies, as well as large multinational organizations.

If you are missing a component, you will receive feedback from Exchange Server 2013 when you attempt to install the application. The components are going to differ from server operating system to server operating system and from role combination to role combination.

If you find it necessary to integrate Exchange Server 2013 with either Exchange Server 2007 or Exchange Server 2010, you will want to ensure that you have installed the latest Service Packs and updates for the host operating systems and the server applications.

Master It   What is the primary tool you can use to ascertain the appropriate configuration of an Exchange Server 2013 deployment based on the number of users and message volume?

Configure Windows Server 2008 R2 and Windows Server 2012 to support Exchange Server 2013.   Make sure you have all of the prerequisite features and modules. Using PowerShell is the most efficient method for quickly and completely installing all of the necessary components.

Master It   You need to verify that all of prerequisites are met. How can you accomplish this from PowerShell?

Confirm that Active Directory is ready.   Make sure that you have set your Active Directory domain and forest functional levels to Windows Server 2003 at a minimum. You should not encounter any problems if you set your domain and forest functional levels to Windows Server 2008, 2008 R2, or Windows Server 2012.

Avoid frustration during installation or potential problems in the future that may result from domain controllers or global catalog servers running older versions of the software.

Master It   You must verify that your Active Directory meets the minimum requirements to support Exchange Server 2013. What should you check?

Verify that previous versions of Exchange Server can interoperate with Exchange Server 2013.   Exchange Server 2013 will interoperate only with specific previous versions of Exchange Server.

Master It   You must verify that the existing legacy Exchange servers in your organization are running the minimum versions of Exchange Server required to interoperate with Exchange Server 2013. What should you check?

Chapter 10

Installing Exchange Server 2013

People who install Exchange Server 2013 fall into two camps. The first camp—and probably most fall into this one—contains people who simply run the Setup program with no command-line options and choose the default roles. The second camp consists of those who want to install specific Exchange Server roles on different servers or make custom configurations to the default settings at the time of installation and who may need the command-line options to successfully install those servers.

Regardless of which camp you fall into, getting the prerequisites out of the way first will ensure a smooth installation. Further, knowing your setup options will help to make sure you get everything right the first time.

In this chapter, you will learn to:

- ◆ Implement important steps before installing Exchange Server 2013

- ◆ Prepare the Active Directory forest for Exchange Server 2013 without actually installing Exchange Server

- ◆ Employ the graphical user interface to install Exchange Server 2013

- ◆ Determine the command-line options available when installing Exchange

Before You Begin

When you run the Exchange Server 2013 Setup program, it checks a number of things to ensure that not only Windows Server but also Active Directory and your specific permissions all meet the necessary prerequisites. Some missing prerequisites are easy to resolve, whereas others may take hours or even days.

You don't want these missing pieces and prerequisites to slow you down. If you have not already read Chapter 9, "Exchange Server 2013 Requirements," you should do so. Here we'll review only the prerequisites and best practices:

- ◆ If you have existing Exchange Servers in your environment, run the Exchange Best Practices Analyzer (ExBPA). Make sure you correct any serious problems that the ExBPA finds. Although ExBPA has been retired in Exchange Server 2013, it will still provide valuable information about problems in your current environment that could interrupt a smooth transition.

- ◆ The Active Directory forest should be at least Windows 2003 Forest Functional mode.

- The Active Directory Schema Master role must be on a Windows 2003 Standard or Enterprise SP2 domain controller or later.

- Every Exchange 2010 server in the organization, including Edge Transport servers, must be running at least Exchange Server 2010 SP3 in order for you to install the first Exchange 2013 server into the organization.

- All existing Exchange 2007 servers, including Edge Transport servers, must be running at least Update Rollup 10 (UR10) for Exchange 2007 SP3.

- All Active Directory sites in which you plan to install Exchange 2013 servers should have at least one global catalog server running at least Windows 2003 Standard or Enterprise SP2.

- Client Access servers must have at least 4 GB of RAM and 30 GB of hard disk space free. For Mailbox servers, ensure that you have performed the proper disk space and memory requirement calculations and that you are providing the right amount of disk space and physical memory. A minimum of 8 GB of RAM is required.

- Windows Server 2008 R2 or Windows Server 2012 must be the operating system used on any server that will run Exchange Server 2013.

- If you have *storage area networks* (SANs), get your device drivers configured and your storage and *logical units* (LUNs) connected ahead of time. Don't mix Exchange trouble-shooting with SAN troubleshooting.

- Install the required Windows Server roles and features.

- Confirm that you have the Exchange installation files (including any additional language packs above and beyond English) that you require. We recommend that you copy them onto a network share so that they are easily accessible.

Preparing for Exchange 2013

In some large organizations, you may find it necessary to prepare your Active Directory prior to installing Exchange Server 2013. You may need to do this for a number of reasons. Remember that the various steps to prepare the forest require membership in the Schema Admins and Enterprise Admins groups as well as Domain Admins membership in each of the forests' domains.

In a small- or medium-size business, you may be where the proverbial buck stops. You may have a user account that has all of these permissions, and you can run everything easily by yourself. In that case, simply log on as a user with the necessary permissions and run Setup.

However, large organizations are a bit different. Here are a few points you should consider:

- Large organizations may have configuration control and change management in place. Those are best practices. You may need to document the steps that you will take, request permissions to proceed, and schedule the forest preparation.

- Large Active Directories may have many Active Directory sites and domain controllers.

- Organizations that are distributed across large geographic areas may have replication delays on their domain controllers of anywhere from 15 minutes to seven days. Replication of schema and domain changes may need to be completed prior to proceeding with Exchange Server installations.

◆ Permissions to update the schema, configuration partition, and child domains are sometimes spread across a number of different individuals or departments. You may need to have another administrator log in for you to run various preparation steps.

If you have to prepare the Active Directory forest, you'll need to take a few steps. The number of steps will vary depending on the following factors:

◆ Whether you have a previous version of Exchange Server running

◆ The number of domains in your forest

◆ The permissions within the forest root domain and the child domains

---

IMPORTANT STEPS PRIOR TO PREPARING ANY DOMAIN

Before running any of the Active Directory preparation steps, make sure that the machine from which you are running the setup.exe program is in the same Active Directory site as the Schema Master and has good connectivity to the Schema Master as well as a domain controller from each domain within the forest. If you're using Windows 2008 R2, Microsoft .NET Framework 4.5 and Windows Management Framework 3.0 must be installed. These are included by default with Windows Server 2012. Further, ensure that you have installed the Active Directory management tools by running Add-WindowsFeature RSAT-ADDS on your Windows 2008 R2 server or Install-WindowsFeature RSAT-ADDS on your Windows 2012 server.

Existing Exchange Organizations

Exchange 2013 supports coexistence with only Exchange 2007 or later. If you have Exchange 2003 in your organization, you must upgrade to Exchange 2007 or 2010 before introducing Exchange 2013 or else install Exchange 2013 into a new forest.

If you have Exchange 2007 or 2010 servers in your organization, you must prepare each server so that Exchange Server 2013 can properly communicate with it. To do this, install Exchange 2010 SP3 on every Exchange 2010 server in the forest, and install Exchange 2007 SP3 RU10 on every Exchange 2007 server in the forest, including Edge Transport servers. (This is a slight deviation from the upgrade guidance for previous versions, where only legacy Exchange servers in the same site where the new version was being introduced needed to be patched. Now Microsoft requires that all legacy servers in the organization be patched.)

If you have more than one site, the preferred sequence is to upgrade any Internet-facing sites first and then upgrade the internal sites. The first Internet-facing site that you should upgrade, if there are multiple, is the one where Autodiscover requests from the Internet are received. More information on upgrading from previous versions of Exchange can be found in Chapter 11, "Upgrades and Migrations to Exchange Server 2013 or Office 365."

Preparing the Schema

Next is the step that usually scares Active Directory administrators the most: extending the Active Directory schema. Essentially, the schema is the set of rules that define the structure (the objects and the attributes of those objects) for Active Directory. This operation requires the user account running this operation to have both Enterprise Admins and Schema Admins group memberships.

This scares Active Directory administrators for a couple of reasons. First, schema changes cannot be undone. Ever. Second, once the schema changes are made, they replicate to every domain controller in the entire forest.

Naturally, schema changes are not made to an Active Directory forest very often. When schema changes are performed, often the Active Directory administrators want to know exactly what is being changed. This is a bit difficult to document for Exchange because of the sheer number of changes. An Active Directory that has never been prepped for Exchange will have more than 3,000 changes made to the schema, including new classes (object types), new attributes, new attributes being flagged for the global catalog replication, and existing attributes being flagged to replicate to the global catalog. If you want to point your Active Directory administrators to a specific list of changes, this URL is helpful:

```
http://technet.microsoft.com/en-us/library/bb738144.aspx
```

If you, or your Active Directory administrators, are curious about what is being changed, take a look at the LDF files in the \Setup\Data folder within the Exchange 2013 setup files. For the most part, you probably don't have to worry about this unless you have done something nonstandard with your Active Directory, such as defining your own classes or attributes without giving them unique names and unique object identifiers.

To extend the schema affectively, the server from which you are running the schema preparation must be in the same Active Directory site as the schema master domain controller. You can locate that domain controller using the Schema Management console; the console is not available by default, so you first must register it. At the command prompt, type regsvr32 .exe schmmgmt.dll; you will see a message indicating the schmmgmt.dll registration succeeded.

Then you can run the Microsoft Management Console program (mmc.exe) and add the Active Directory Schema snap-in. This snap-in will not appear unless the schmmgmt.dll registered properly. Once you have the Active Directory Schema console open, right-click Active Directory Schema and choose Operations Master. The Change Schema Master dialog (Figure 10.1) will show you which server currently holds the Schema Master role.

FIGURE 10.1
Determining which domain controller holds the Schema Master role

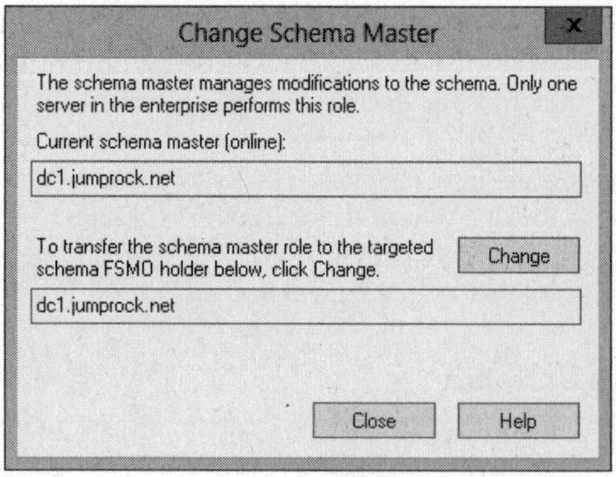

To extend the schema, run the following command from within the Exchange 2013 Setup folder:

```
Setup.exe /PrepareSchema /IAcceptExchangeServerLicenseTerms
```

Note that this can take between 15 and 30 minutes depending on the speed of the computer on which you are running Setup, the speed of the Schema Master domain controller, and the network connection between the computers.

Preparing the Active Directory Forest

The next step is to prepare the Active Directory forest to support an Exchange organization. Although this process does not make as many changes to the forest, it does make quite a few more noticeable changes, such as creating the various Exchange configuration containers and creating Exchange security groups. Figure 10.2 shows an example of the configuration containers that are created.

Here are some of the tasks the Active Directory preparation process includes:

♦ Defining the Exchange organization name if it does not exist already in the Microsoft Exchange container under the Services container of the Active Directory configuration partition

♦ Creating configuration objects and containers under the Exchange organization container (see Figure 10.2)

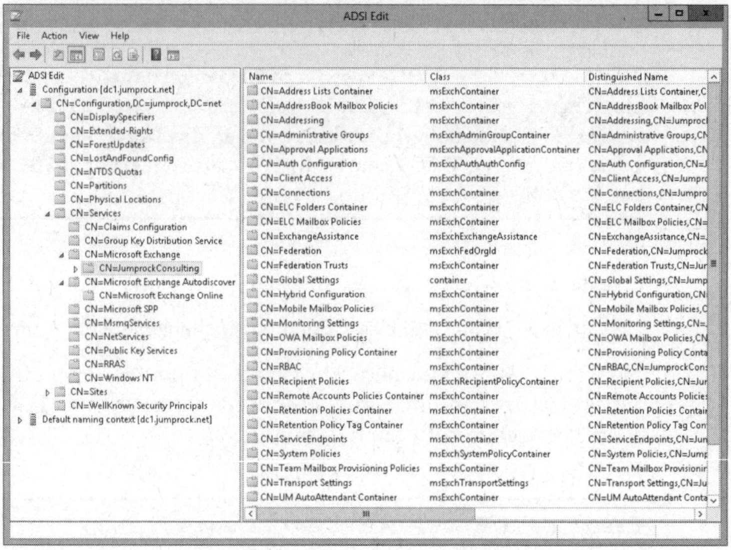

FIGURE 10.2
Exchange configuration containers that are found in the Active Directory configuration partition

◆ Creating the Microsoft Exchange Security Groups organizational unit in the forest root domain and then creating the Exchange universal security groups:

  ◆ Compliance Management

  ◆ Delegated Setup

  ◆ Discovery Management

  ◆ Exchange Servers

  ◆ Exchange Trusted Subsystem

  ◆ Exchange Windows Permissions

  ◆ ExchangeLegacyInterop

  ◆ Help Desk

  ◆ Hygiene Management

  ◆ Organization Management

  ◆ Public Folder Management

  ◆ Recipient Management

  ◆ Records Management

  ◆ Server Management

  ◆ UM Management

  ◆ View-only Organization Management

- Importing new Exchange-specific extended Active Directory rights and assigning the necessary permissions in Active Directory

- Creating the Microsoft Exchange System Objects container in the forest root domain

- Preparing the forest root domain for Exchange Server 2013

To run the forest preparation, you must be logged on as a member of the Enterprise Admins group. Further, you should run the forest-preparation process from a server that is in the same Active Directory site and domain that holds the Schema Master FSMO role.

You must use the Setup /PrepareAD option to prepare the Active Directory. You have two options when running /PrepareAD; the option you choose will depend on whether you have an existing Exchange organization. For example, to prepare a forest that has never supported any version of Exchange Server and to use the organization name JumprockConsulting, you would run the following command from the Exchange 2013 setup folder:

```
Setup /PrepareAD /OrganizationName:JumprockConsulting /
IAcceptExchangeServerLicenseTerms
```

CHOOSING AN EXCHANGE ORGANIZATION NAME

In previous versions of Exchange Server, choosing the right organization name was often a source of great anxiety. With Exchange 5.5 and earlier, when you built an Exchange site, if you did not pick the right organization name, you could not replicate that site's global address list to the rest of the organization.

Even with Exchange 2000/2003, the organization name was visible at the top of the global address list and within the Exchange System Manager administrative console. Once the organization name is set, it cannot be changed. Fears of acquisitions, mergers, and company name changes still drive people to be concerned about this name.

Although we still recommend naming your organization something descriptive, the actual name is not as important because it is not going to be seen by the end users and is rarely (if ever) seen by the administrators. You can always set the organization name to something generic like ExchangeOrganization if you want something that would not be affected by a reorganization.

When you pick an organization name, use a name that is 64 characters or less and uses only valid Active Directory characters for a container name. We recommend you stick to the basics:

- A–Z

- a–z

- 0–9

- Spaces and hyphens

However, if the forest already supports a previous version of Exchange Server, the /OrganizationName option is not necessary. You can simply run this command:

```
Setup /PrepareAD /IAcceptExchangeServerLicenseTerms
```

When the /PrepareAD process runs, it will check to see if the /PrepareSchema step needs to be run. If so, Setup will check to see if you have the necessary permissions and then run it if so. However, if running /PrepareSchema is necessary and you do not have the required permissions, you will see an error and Setup will fail.

Preparing Additional Domains

If you have only a single domain in your Active Directory forest, the Setup option /PrepareAD will prepare that domain and you will be ready to proceed with your first Exchange Server installation.

However, if you have additional domains in your Active Directory forest and they contain mail-enabled recipients or Exchange servers, you may have to prepare these additional domains. To do so, use the /PrepareDomain or /PrepareAllDomains Setup option. This process includes the following:

◆ Assigning to the domain container various permissions to the Authenticated Users and Exchange universal security groups that are necessary for viewing recipient information and performing recipient-management tasks.

◆ Creating a Microsoft Exchange System Objects container in the root of the domain; this container holds mail-enabled recipient information for organization objects such as Exchange databases.

To prepare a single domain, you must be logged on as a member of that domain's Domain Admins group, and there should be a domain controller for that domain in the same site as the server from which you are running Setup. The domain controller should be running a minimum of Windows Server 2003 SP2. To prepare a domain called eu.jumprock.local, type this command:

```
Setup /PrepareDomain:eu.jumprock.local /IAcceptExchangeServerLicenseTerms
```

If you have a user account that is a member of the Enterprise Admins group, you can run this command and prepare all domains in the entire forest:

```
Setup /PrepareAllDomains /IAcceptExchangeServerLicenseTerms
```

Graphical User Interface Setup

The simplest way to install Exchange Server 2013 is to use *the graphical user interface* (GUI). The GUI will be sufficient for most Exchange Server installations. We recommend first copying the Exchange Server 2013 installation files to the local hard disk or using a locally attached CD/DVD from which to run the Exchange installation. Copying the Exchange binaries to the local hard disk will speed up the installation time.

From the Exchange Server installation folder, run Setup.exe to see the initial setup screen, which will ask you if you want to check for updates. If you say yes, Setup will check the Microsoft website to see if there is a more recent Service Pack or Cumulative Update available.

After the Check for Updates page, Setup will copy files, prepare resources, and then display the Microsoft Exchange Server 2013 Setup Wizard's introduction page. Click Next to proceed. On the next page, you will see the License Agreement screen. Select the I Accept The Terms In The License Agreement radio button and then click Next.

The fourth page of the setup wizard is titled Recommended Settings. Here you can specify whether you want to enable error reporting and participate in the Customer Experience Improvement Program (CEIP).

Enabling *error reporting* will prompt Exchange to check online for solutions to errors and send reports of problems automatically to Microsoft. The server will send information back to Microsoft via HTTPS; this information may prove valuable for Microsoft in identifying errors in their software. Passing along this information also provides you (the customer) with good value because it means that Microsoft can more quickly identify bugs and software issues. The report sent back to Microsoft usually does not contain any information specific to your organization or to your server, but some organizations' Information Security departments will want you to block this anyway. If you are concerned about this, select Don't Use Recommended Settings. You can read more about the Microsoft Online Crash Analysis program, as well as Microsoft's privacy statement and what information might be collected, at `http://oca .microsoft.com/en/dcp20.asp`.

If you participate in the *Microsoft Exchange Customer Experience Program*, the server will periodically upload usage and configuration data that helps Microsoft when designing future versions of Exchange Server. The program is completely anonymous and will not be used to gather information about your organization. We recommend participating in the program, but this is a decision that each person installing Exchange must make. For more information on the CEIP, visit:

`www.microsoft.com/products/ceip/en-us/default.mspx`

Selecting Use Recommended Settings will enable both error reporting and participation in the CEIP. Selecting Don't Use Recommended Settings will disable both error reporting and participation in the CEIP. These settings can be changed later and managed individually after the installation has completed. When you have made your choice, click Next.

The next page on the wizard is the Server Role Selection screen (Figure 10.3). Here, you specify whether you want to install the Mailbox role, the Client Access role, or both. If you select neither option, only the Management tools will be installed. Be aware that after you've run Setup and installed any Exchange 2013 server role, you will not be able to use the GUI version of Setup to install any additional roles. The only options for installing additional roles, after Exchange 2013 is installed, are to use Add or Remove Programs from the Windows Control Panel or use `Setup.exe` from the command line.

On this page, there is also an option to allow Windows to automatically install Windows Server roles and features that are required to install Exchange. Keep in mind, this will not guarantee that all software prerequisites are installed—just the ones that are a part of the native operating system. If you do choose to use this option, it is possible that you will need to reboot the server to complete the installation of some of the Windows features before Setup can proceed with the installation of Exchange.

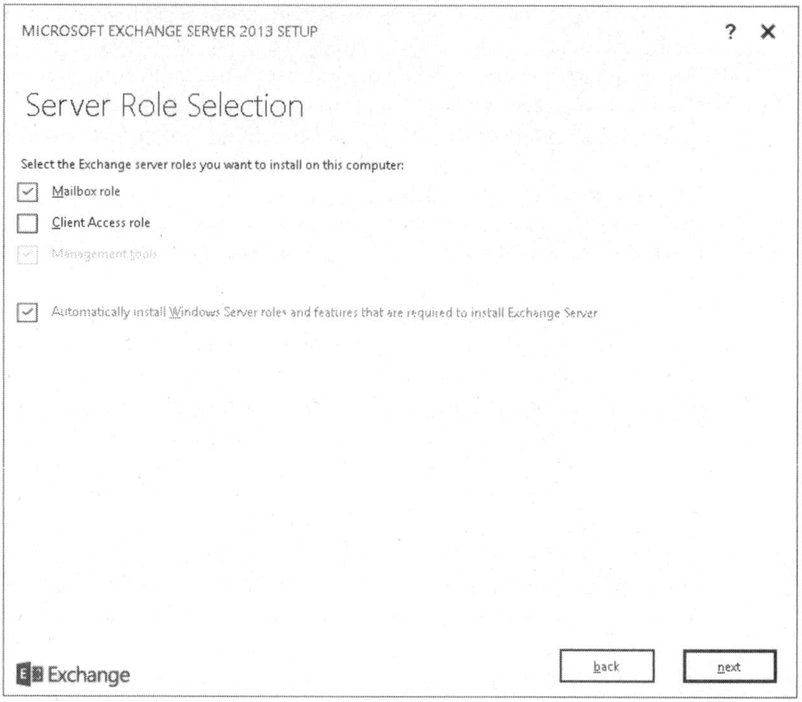

FIGURE 10.3
Server Role
Selection screen

Real World Scenario

ENSURE SUCCESS BY INSTALLING COMPONENTS MANUALLY

The option Automatically Install Windows Server Roles And Features That Are Required To Install Exchange Server has been known to not work as expected. In order to save yourself some time and ensure a successful installation on the first try, a better option might be to install the required components manually beforehand using PowerShell. Microsoft has made things easy by publishing the PowerShell syntax to install the required components on the following URL:

    http://technet.microsoft.com/en-us/library/bb691354(v=exchg.150).aspx

For example, to install the operating system prerequisites for a Windows Server 2012 computer that will have the Client Access and Mailbox roles installed, you would run the following command:

```
Install-WindowsFeature AS-HTTP-Activation, Desktop-Experience, NET-Framework-45-
Features, RPC-over-HTTP-proxy, RSAT-Clustering, RSAT-Clustering-CmdInterface,
RSAT-Clustering-Mgmt, RSAT-Clustering-PowerShell, Web-Mgmt-Console, WAS-
Process-Model, Web-Asp-Net45, Web-Basic-Auth, Web-Client-Auth, Web-Digest-
Auth, Web-Dir-Browsing, Web-Dyn-Compression, Web-Http-Errors, Web-Http-Logging,
Web-Http-Redirect, Web-Http-Tracing, Web-ISAPI-Ext, Web-ISAPI-Filter, Web-Lgcy-
Mgmt-Console, Web-Metabase, Web-Mgmt-Console, Web-Mgmt-Service, Web-Net-Ext45,
Web-Request-Monitor, Web-Server, Web-Stat-Compression, Web-Static-Content, Web-
Windows-Auth, Web-WMI, Windows-Identity-Foundation
```

ROLE-INSTALLATION ORDER

If you are installing the first Exchange 2013 server into your environment and plan to install roles separately, *be sure to install the Mailbox role first*. This guidance is contrary to recommendations from past versions. The reason for this change is that in Exchange 2013, the Client Access server is stateless, used only for authentication, proxy, and redirection. All of the actual rendering and processing occurs on the Mailbox role.

So, if you were to install the Client Access server first, you would not be able to manage it using tools such as Exchange Management Shell or Exchange Admin Center until a Mailbox server was installed as well.

The next page in the Setup wizard is the Installation Space And Location screen, where you can choose the installation path for the Exchange program files. Once you select an installation path for the Exchange program files, Setup will provide a comparison of the amount of disk space required to the amount that is currently available. The amount required will depend on which roles you chose to install on the previous screen.

When specifying a path for the Exchange program files, remember that by default this is where all Exchange databases and log files will be stored. Most of these you can (and should) move after the installation, but you want to make sure that the volume on which the Exchange program files are stored has at least 30 GB of free space.

Next, the Malware Protection Settings screen provides the administrator with the ability to disable malware scanning on the Mailbox server role. You might want to do this if you are using a third-party product to handle message hygiene on the server. This setting can also be changed later, after Exchange is installed.

The last screen analyzes all of the selections you have made and uses that information to determine if the server has all of the software prerequisites necessary to proceed with the Exchange installation. If required Windows roles or features are missing and you opted to have Setup install them, it will do so now. If you did not opt to have Setup install them, it will notify you so that you can take the necessary action. If you find anything about the configuration that should be changed, you must resolve those matters before continuing.

One of the nice things about the Microsoft Exchange Server 2013 Setup Wizard is that if it detects a missing component or something that must be done prior to starting the Exchange setup, you can fix the issue and then click the Retry button. The Setup program will recheck the prerequisites and pick up where it left off.

Once the prerequisites have all been met and the readiness check is complete, you must click the Install button to initiate the installation. What you observe on the screen after clicking the Install button will depend on which server roles you opted to install and whether you took previous steps to prepare Active Directory manually or are allowing Setup to do it for you. If this is the first time you are installing Exchange Server 2013 in your environment, you are installing both server roles, and you are allowing Setup to handle the Active Directory preparations, then you will see a total of 15 steps in a successful installation.

Don't be alarmed if the Setup process appears to be hung during installation. This can be normal, particularly during Step 8 (Mailbox Role: Transport service). As long as Setup does not return errors or explicitly state that it has failed, be patient. You can also check

ExchangeSetup.log located in c:\ExchangeSetupLogs for more details about what Setup is doing at any given time.

Command-Line Setup

The Exchange Server 2013 Setup program includes a powerful set of command-line options that can help you automate an Exchange server setup or perform custom setup options that you could not do through the GUI. The command-line setup options are broken into six categories:

- Installing Exchange server roles

- Removing Exchange server roles

- Recovering an existing Exchange server

- Preparing Active Directory to support Exchange

- Creating delegated or pre-provisioned servers

- Adding or removing Unified Messaging language packs

For all of these options, you run the same setup.exe program that you use for launching the GUI.

Real World Scenario

THE USEFULNESS OF COMMAND-LINE INSTALLATIONS

A lot of Exchange administrators wonder why the command-line setup options even exist since the graphical user interface is so easy to use and has most of the same options. Consider the case of an organization that is installing 30 Mailbox servers and 18 Client Access servers.

Due to the organization's requirements for certifying a production IT system, all server builds have to be thoroughly documented prior to being deployed. By generating the installation scripts ahead of time, their Exchange team can ensure that each server is built exactly to the design specifications and with the necessary options. This speeds up the overall installation and ensures that nothing is overlooked.

Command-Line Installation Options

By and large, the server role installation options are probably the most useful for a typical person installing or configuring Exchange. They are certainly the most numerous. Some of these setup.exe options have required parameters. For example, if you use the /mode:install option, you will have to specify which server role or roles you are installing. Table 10.1 lists the command-line installation options in alphabetical order.

TABLE 10.1:   Exchange Server 2013 command-line installation options

Option	Optional (O) or Required (R)	Explanation
/ActiveDirectorySplit Permissions	O	Specifies whether to enable or disable the Active Directory split-permissions mode when preparing the Exchange organization. Disabled by default.
/AnswerFile	O	Allows you to specify a text file that contains answers to some of the advanced setup parameters.
/CustomerFeedback Enabled	O	Configures Exchange Server to report usage information to Microsoft automatically. All server roles can use this information.
/DbFilePath	O	Specifies the path and name to the default database file. This is used in conjunction with the /Mdbname and the /LogFolderPath switches.
/DisableAMFiltering	O	Allows you to turn off malware scanning on the Mailbox role. Enabled by default.
/DomainController	O	Allows you to specify the NetBIOS name or the FQDN of a domain controller.
/DoNotStartTransport	O	Tells Setup not to allow the Transport service on a Hub Transport or Edge Transport server.
/EnableErrorReporting		Configures Exchange Server to report errors automatically to Microsoft. All server roles can use this option. The default is not to enable this feature.
/IAcceptExchangeServer LicenseTerms	R	Specifies that you understand and accept the terms of the Exchange Server license.
/InstallWindowsComponents	O	Allows you to have Setup automatically install any required Windows roles or features.
/LogFolderPath	O	Specifies the path for the log files for the default database when installing a Mailbox server role.
/Mdbname	O	Specifies the name of the default mailbox database when installing a Mailbox server.

TABLE 10.1:   Exchange Server 2013 command-line installation options   *(CONTINUED)*

OPTION	OPTIONAL (O) OR REQUIRED (R)	EXPLANATION
/mode or /m	R	Specifies whether the Setup program is installing a new role or removing it. Valid options are as follows: /mode:install /mode:uninstall /mode:upgrade
/OrganizationName	O	Allows you to specify an organization name; this is necessary only if this is the first server being installed in the Active Directory forest and the /PrepareAD step has not previously been done.
/roles or /r	R	Specifies which roles are being installed. These are the valid role types: Client Access, CA, C Mailbox, MB, M ManagementTools, MT, T
/SourceDir	O	Specifies the location for the Exchange installation files.
/TargetDir	O	Allows you to specify an optional path for the Exchange program files rather than the default location on the C:\ drive.
/TenantOrganizationConfig	O	Specifies the path to the file that contains configuration data about your Office 365 tenant. This file is created by running the Export-OrganizationConfig cmdlet in your Office 365 tenant.
/UpdatesDir	O	Specifies a path to a directory that contains updates that should be applied as a part of the installation process.

> ### ABBREVIATIONS AND SHORTCUTS
>
> Most of the command-line switches and options have a long and short option. For example, the following three commands accomplish exactly the same thing (installing the Mailbox role):
>
> ◆ `setup /m:install /r:m`
>
> ◆ `setup /m:install /r:mb`
>
> ◆ `setup /m:install /r:Mailbox`
>
> In this chapter, we have chosen to spell out the options completely to more clearly illustrate the commands and in the hope that you will remember them more easily. However, once you learn the long version of the options, you will probably find it easier to use the shorter versions. They are just a bit cryptic when you are learning.

Command-Line Server-Recovery Options

There may come a time when you have to recover an Exchange Server from a backup. This process will involve rebuilding the Windows server and then reinstalling Exchange Server using the Recover Server mode. This option will read most of the configuration of the server from the Active Directory rather than installing the server from scratch. Several options are available when recovering a server, as shown in Table 10.2.

TABLE 10.2:   Exchange Server 2013 server-recovery setup options

Option	Optional (O) or Required (R)	Explanation
/DomainController	O	Allows you to specify the NetBIOS name or the FQDN of a domain controller.
/DoNotStartTransport	O	Tells Setup to not allow the Transport service on a Hub Transport or Edge Transport server to start. This is useful during a recovery if you do not want messages to start flowing until you are sure the server is fully recovered.
/EnableErrorReporting	O	Configures Exchange Server to report errors automatically to Microsoft. All server roles can use this option. The default is set to not enable this feature.
/IAcceptExchangeServer LicenseTerms	R	Specifies that you understand and accept the terms of the Exchange Server license.
/mode:RecoverServer	R	Specifies that the installation mode is to be the Recover Server option.

TABLE 10.2:   Exchange Server 2013 server-recovery setup options   *(CONTINUED)*

OPTION	OPTIONAL (O) OR REQUIRED (R)	EXPLANATION
/TargetDir	O	Allows you to specify an optional path for the Exchange program files rather than the default location on the C:\ drive.
/UpdatesDir	O	Specifies a path to look for updates after the installation is completed.

Command-Line Delegated Server Installation

In some large organizations, the person who is installing the Exchange servers may not have an account with sufficient Active Directory permissions to create the server objects in the Active Directory. For this reason, someone else may have to create the necessary server objects, and the installer can then set up the servers.

This is where the delegated server installation is handy. The person with the necessary rights to set up the servers can "prestage" the servers in the Active Directory. Table 10.3 shows a list of the options available for delegated server setup.

TABLE 10.3:   Exchange Server 2013 delegated setup options

OPTION	OPTIONAL (O) OR REQUIRED (R)	EXPLANATION
/IAcceptExchangeServer LicenseTerms	R	Specifies that you understand and accept the terms of the Exchange Server license.
/NewProvisionedServer	O	Creates a new provisioned server with the name specified on the command line, such as this: `Setup.exe /NewProvisionedServer:HNLMBX`
/RemoveProvisionedServer	O	Removes a server that was previously configured with the /NewProvisionedServer option.

Installing Language Packs

If you are supporting an Exchange 2013 server for only English-speaking users and administrators, you do not need to worry about installing additional language packs. Exchange Server 2013 automatically includes native support for the U.S. English (en-US) messaging language pack (and it can't be removed), as well as many other languages. For a full list of languages supported by default from both the server and client, please refer to this URL:

```
http://technet.microsoft.com/en-us/library/dd298152.aspx
```

Depending on the cultural diversity of your environment and users, you should know how to install additional Unified Messaging language packs.

Table 10.4 shows the valid options for installing Unified Messaging language packs. Note that the Unified Messaging language pack options are available only on servers that already have the Mailbox role installed.

TABLE 10.4: Exchange Server 2013 language pack options

OPTION	OPTIONAL (O) OR REQUIRED (R)	EXPLANATION
/AddUmLanguagePack	O	Adds the specified Unified Messaging language pack. You must specify the language pack name that you want to install; for French, you would use this command: Setup /AddUmLanguagePack:fr-fr
/IAcceptExchangeServer LicenseTerms	R	Specifies that you understand and accept the terms of the Exchange Server license.
/RemoveUmLanguagePack	O	Removes the specified Unified Messaging language pack.
/SourceDir	O	Specifies the source folder for the Unified Messaging language pack.
/UpdatesDir	O	Specifies the path for updates for the Unified Messaging language pack.

The Bottom Line

Implement important steps before installing Exchange Server 2013.   One of the things that slows down an Exchange Server installation is finding out you are missing some specific Windows component, feature, or role. Reviewing the necessary software and configuration components will keep your installation moving along smoothly.

Server hardware should match the minimum requirements, including at least 30 GB of free space and 4 GB of RAM for the Client Access role or 8 GB of RAM for the Mailbox server role. Ensure that you are using Windows Server 2008 R2 or Windows Server 2012 with the most recent updates. Install the Windows Server roles and features necessary for the Exchange Server's role requirements.

Master It   You are working with your Active Directory team to ensure that the Active Directory is ready to support Exchange Server 2013. What are the minimum prerequisites that your Active Directory must meet in order to support Exchange Server 2013?

Prepare the Active Directory forest for Exchange Server 2013 without actually installing Exchange Server.   In some organizations, the Exchange administrator or installer may not have the necessary Active Directory rights to prepare the Active Directory schema, the forest, or a child domain. Here is a breakdown of the steps involved and the associated group membership requirements to complete each:

◆ Running the Exchange Server 2013 setup.exe program from the command line with the /PrepareSchema option allows the schema to be prepared without installing Exchange. A user account that is a member of the Schema Admins group is necessary to extend the Active Directory schema.

◆ Running the Exchange Server 2013 setup.exe program from the command line with the /PrepareAD option allows the forest root domain and the Active Directory configuration partition to be prepared without installing Exchange. A user account that is a member of the Enterprise Admins group is necessary to make all the changes and updates necessary in the forest root. When preparing a child domain, a member of the Enterprise Admins group or the child domain's Domain Admins group may be used.

Master It   You have provided the Exchange 2013 installation binaries to your Active Directory team so that the forest administrator can extend the Active Directory schema. She wants to know what she must do in order to extend only the schema to support Exchange Server 2013. What must she do?

Employ the graphical user interface to install Exchange Server 2013.   The graphical user interface can be used for most Exchange Server installations that do not require specialized pre-staging or nonstandard options. The GUI will provide all the necessary configuration steps, including Active Directory preparation.

The GUI allows you to install the Mailbox and Client Access roles on a server.

Master It   You are using the GUI for the Exchange Server 2013 installation program to install the Mailbox and Client Access roles onto the same Windows Server 2012 system. You must install both of these roles. Which setup option must you choose?

Determine the command-line options available when installing Exchange.   The Exchange 2013 command-line installation program has a robust set of features that allow all installation options to be chosen from the command line exactly as if you were installing Exchange Server 2013 using the graphical user interface.

Master It   You are attempting to use the command line to install an Exchange Server 2013 Mailbox server role. What is the proper command-line syntax to install this role?

Chapter 11

Upgrades and Migrations to Exchange Server 2013 or Office 365

According to Microsoft 2013 public financials, the Office product lines (Exchange Server, SharePoint, Lync, Office 365, and the Office client applications) accounted for over $22 billion of Microsoft sales. Exchange Server itself became a billion-dollar business in 2004 and has enjoyed double-digit growth almost every year since. (See: http://redmondmag.com/articles/2005/01/20/exchange-joins-microsofts-billiondollar-club.aspx and http://exchangepedia.com/blog/2005/01/exchange-joins-microsofts-billion.html.) The Radicati Group, Inc. states that in 2012, Exchange Server was the email system used by 53 percent of businesses and will be used by 68 percent of businesses by 2016.

Today, very few of those businesses are using Exchange Server 2013 on-premises. Large numbers of mailboxes (in the millions) are running Exchange Server 2013 as a part of Office 365 Wave 15, although, as of this writing that migration is not complete.

You need to know how to move from an older version of Exchange Server to Exchange Server 2013 or Office 365. Depending on the software you have used in the past, you may be used to in-place upgrades, where you have an existing version of the software on a computer, run the installer, and end up with the new version of the software. However, there is no in-place upgrade path for organizations running either Exchange Server 2007 or Exchange Server 2010.

This seems to complicate life, but it actually simplifies the migration path from a legacy version of Exchange Server. Using new Exchange servers means that they are more stable, and it will ease interoperability during the migration.

In this chapter, you will learn to:

- Choose between an upgrade and a migration

- Choose between on-premises deployment and Office 365

- Determine the factors you need to consider before upgrading

- Understand coexistence with legacy Exchange servers

- Perform an interorganization migration

Upgrades, Migrations, Transitions, and Deployments

Let's take a moment to clear up matters of terminology. Through the release of Exchange Server 2003, it was possible to *upgrade* from one major Exchange Server version to the next—on the same server. Since that time, every major version of Exchange Server has required deployment to new servers and migration of the data from the old servers to the new servers. Some Microsoft documentation (and lots of other documentation as well) makes a strong distinction between *upgrade* and *migration* because of this. That distinction no longer makes any difference. Every Exchange Server upgrade is a migration.

However, when your upgrade involves movement between an existing Exchange Server organization and a new Exchange Server organization, you'll see upgrades referred to as *interorganizational migrations* or *transitions*. The terms are interchangeable.

There are two variations you need to know: *deployment* (in which Exchange Server does not connect to Office 365) and *hybrid deployment* (which occurs when you configure your Exchange Server organization to reside both on-premises and in Office 365).

Finally, when we refer to moving data between organizations, we will explicitly say *migration strategy*. This helps us be clear and stay consistent with the documentation provided for Exchange Server 2013.

Factors to Consider Before Upgrading

Are you ready to upgrade? Not so fast! Before you pull the trigger and double-click setup.exe from the Exchange Server 2013 installation media, you must take into account a number of factors. Let's take some time to go over them in more detail so that your upgrade is successful.

Prerequisites

Before you can begin upgrading your Exchange Server organization, you have to ensure that the organization meets the prerequisites. We've gone over some of these in previous chapters from the context of a fresh installation of Exchange Server 2013, but let's look at them again, this time keeping in mind how your existing Exchange Server organization may affect your ability to meet those prerequisites.

HARDWARE AND OPERATING SYSTEM

Exchange Server 2013 is available only in a 64-bit version. This means it must run on a 64-bit operating system that is running on 64-bit hardware. The 64-bit hardware must conform to x64 specifications (note that this excludes Intel Itanium).

Since the operating systems supported by Exchange Server 2013 are available only in 64-bit versions, that does simplify the choices. Do be aware that Exchange Server 2013 does not support the use of Server Core mode in Windows Server. You must use the full GUI mode operating system.

Nowadays, multicore processors are increasingly common—both Intel and AMD. Although Windows recognizes multiple cores as separate processors when managing processes and threads, Microsoft licensing does not make a distinction between single-core and multicore processors. This fact is to your benefit because Exchange Server will obtain significant benefits from additional cores.

You can run Exchange Server 2013 on any edition of Windows Server 2012 or any edition of Windows Server 2008 R2 with Service Pack 1 (SP1). This means that to reuse existing server hardware, you must have at least one spare server and be prepared to reinstall Windows Server and Exchange Server on your servers as you go. We discuss this topic in more detail in the section, "An Overview of the Upgrade Process," later in this chapter.

ACTIVE DIRECTORY

Because Exchange Server 2013 depends on Active Directory, you should take a good look at the domain controllers and global catalog servers in your Active Directory forest before starting the upgrade process.

Exchange Server 2013 requires all domain controllers that may be accessed by Exchange Server 2013 have a minimum operating system version of Windows Server 2003 with SP2. This includes the schema master domain controller (usually the first domain controller installed in your Active Directory forest) and all global catalog servers that will be used by Exchange Server 2013. If your domain controllers are not running at least Windows Server 2003 with SP2, Exchange Server will ignore them. If Exchange Server 2013 cannot find domain controllers at the required versions, then installation will fail.

Our recommendation is to upgrade all your domain controllers to at least Windows Server 2003 R2 with SP2. Windows Server 2003 (pre-R2) is end-of-life and even Windows Server 2003 R2 with SP2 will go end-of-life on July 14, 2015. At this writing, Windows Server 2012 is available, and July 14, 2015, is less than two years away. Best practice would be for you to find a way to upgrade your infrastructure all the way to Windows Server 2012.

CHECK THE HEALTH OF YOUR ACTIVE DIRECTORY SITE BEFORE UPGRADING

It is extremely important that Active Directory be healthy before you upgrade to Exchange Server 2013. Among other things, Exchange Server 2013 relies directly on your Active Directory site structure for message-routing information. Most configuration information for Exchange Server 2013 is stored in Active Directory.

Whether you upgrade all your domain controllers or just the minimum number, you need to prepare a list of all the Active Directory domains in which you will either install Exchange Server 2013 or create Exchange Server 2013 recipient objects, such as users, contacts, and distribution groups. For each of these domains, ensure that the domain functional level is set to Windows Server 2003 or higher. The Active Directory forest functional level must also be Windows Server 2003 or higher.

Exchange Server 2013 supports domain functional levels and forest functional levels from Windows Server 2003 all the way to Windows Server 2012. While Exchange Server 2013 does not mandate that you move to higher domain and forest functional levels, there are Active Directory benefits and features that are available if you do so. A major one is the Active Directory Recycle Bin introduced in Windows Server 2008 R2.

Exchange Server performance is directly impacted by Active Directory performance. Therefore, it is important for your domain controllers to perform well. While your domain controllers can be either 32-bit or 64-bit, performance is enhanced when your domain controllers are running a 64-bit operating system and have enough memory to load the entirety of your Active Directory database (NTDS.DIT) into memory.

It is technically supported to install Exchange Server onto a domain controller (although it must be a global catalog server). However, it is not recommended. Exchange Server and its ancillary services will consume most of the memory available on any server where Exchange Server is installed. This can have a significant negative impact on Active Directory performance. Also, restoring such a combination server, in the event of a catastrophic failure of the server, is much more difficult than restoring a server with just Active Directory or just Exchange Server.

EXCHANGE SERVER 2013 AND DCPROMO

DCPROMO is a part of Active Directory Domain Services used to either promote a computer to be a domain controller or to demote a computer from being a domain controller to a normal member computer. After Exchange Server is installed, it is *not* supported to change the domain controller status of the computer. That is, you may not promote the computer to a domain controller or demote the computer from being a domain controller. It will break Exchange Server. Don't do it.

LEGACY EXCHANGE

In order to upgrade to Exchange Server 2013 in your current Exchange Server organization, your existing Exchange Server environment must meet certain minimum requirements.

If you have Exchange Server 2007 servers in your organization, they must be upgraded to a minimum of Exchange Server 2007 Service Pack 3 with Update Rollup 10 (Exchange Server 2007 SP3 UR10). This includes Edge Transport servers. If you have Exchange Server 2010 servers in your organization, they must be upgraded to a minimum of Exchange Server 2010 Service Pack 3 (Exchange Server 2010 SP3). This also includes Edge Transport servers. If you have both Exchange Server 2007 and Exchange Server 2010 servers in your organization, the same minimums apply.

In all cases, the minimum destination version of Exchange Server 2013 is Exchange Server 2013 RTM with Cumulative Update 2 (Exchange Server 2013 RTM CU2). We'll talk more about coexistence with legacy Exchange Servers later in this chapter.

HYBRID DEPLOYMENTS

In a hybrid scenario, some part of your Exchange Server organization is on-premises and another part is in Office 365. Exchange Server 2013 supports hybrid deployments with new Office 365 tenants and with Office 365 tenants that have been migrated to Wave 15 (the migration to Wave 15 is scheduled to be complete by January 1, 2014).

For a hybrid deployment, your on-premises Exchange servers must be updated to the same minimum versions as described in the section, "Legacy Exchange." However, you must also install at least one Exchange Server 2013 RTM CU2 (or later) server on-premises in order to configure a hybrid deployment. Depending on the size of your current environment, you may need more than one.

Only E* plans (Office 365 for Enterprises) and A* plans (Office 365 for Education) support hybrid deployments.

OTHER POSSIBLE HYBRID DEPLOYMENTS

While the URL quoted indicates that only Enterprise (Office 365 for Enterprises) and Academic (Office 365 for Education) licenses support hybrid deployments, it is also true that government licensing and non-profit/charity licensing provide hybrid deployment capabilities and support. Those will be made available based on a specific license agreement with Microsoft.

OFFICE 365 FOR EDUCATION

Microsoft provides Office 365—for academic environments—for free. This is a so-called basic experience. It includes Exchange Online, Lync Online, SharePoint Online, and Office Web Apps, and is currently known as plan A2. There is also a plan for Alumni, which is also free, that includes only Exchange Online.

Plans with more feature content are available for nominal fees, including Office Pro Plus, home use rights for five PCs, Exchange voicemail, Exchange archiving, Access, Excel, Infopath, and others; this increment is available for only USD $2.50 per user per month. Taking that plan and adding full voice capabilities is only an additional USD $0.50 per user per month.

These plans are discussed at `http://www.microsoft.com/liveatedu/learn-about-office-365.aspx`. Or if the URL disappears, you can search for "Office 365 for education" at `www.microsoft.com`.

After configuring a hybrid deployment, you can no longer configure EdgeSync. Another way of saying that is if you want to deploy Edge servers, you should do so before configuring your hybrid deployment.

A somewhat hidden but important prerequisite is to ensure that a user's userPrincipalName (UPN) matches their primary email address. While this is not strictly a requirement, it simplifies hybrid deployments significantly. It will also enable you to deploy single sign-on (SSO) between your local Active Directory and Office 365.

Finally, you need to be prepared to install and configure the Windows Azure Active Directory Synchronization (WAADS, commonly known as DirSync) tool or Active Directory Federation Services. These tools will synchronize your users, groups, and contacts with Office 365. A large number of attributes for each of these objects are also synchronized (but not all of them). The tools also provide for synchronization of the global address list (GAL) between your on-premises and Office 365 environments.

Choosing Your Strategy

Now that you are aware of the various preparations that must be completed to upgrade Exchange Server, it is time to figure out how to do it. As we discussed earlier, there are three options in front of us: *upgrade*, *transition*, and *hybrid deployment*.

Hybrid deployment is a special case because it involves first performing either an upgrade or a migration and then integrating with Office 365. Because of that, we will discuss upgrades and transitions first and then return to discuss integration with Office 365.

If you're like many readers, you probably have at least some preference for your upgrade strategy already in mind. Before you set that choice in stone, though, read through this section and see whether there are any surprises (good or bad) that might allow you to address some aspect of the upgrade that you hadn't previously considered. If, on the other hand, you're not sure which strategy would be best for you, this section should give you enough information to begin making a well-informed decision.

Let's start with an overview of how the two strategies stack up. Table 11.1 lists several points of comparison between the transition and upgrade strategies.

TABLE 11.1: Comparison of Exchange Server 2013 upgrade strategies

POINT OF COMPARISON	TRANSITION STRATEGY	UPGRADE STRATEGY
Tools	You will need a combination of free Microsoft tools to manage the multiple sets of data that need to be migrated (Active Directory user information and third-party tools to manage/migrate the Exchange Server mailbox data at a minimum). These tools usually result in at least some minor information loss, such as delegates and folder permissions.	You can use the built-in tools in Exchange Server 2013 and Windows Server to control all aspects of the transition, including building the new servers, reconfiguring Active Directory, or moving mailbox data.
Hardware	You will usually require a significant amount of new hardware. You may not need to have a complete spare set of replacement hardware, but you'll need enough to have the basic infrastructure of your new Exchange Server 2013 organization in place.	You can accomplish this strategy, but you must ensure that you have sufficient hardware in place to handle loads, such as the additional load placed on the Exchange Server 2013 servers. Exchange Server 2013 requires significantly more memory than earlier versions of Exchange Server and needs more cores for the best experience. Using older hardware is unlikely to be feasible.
Active Directory and DNS	You must create a new Active Directory forest. Typically, this means that you cannot reuse the same Active Directory domain names (although you will be able to share the same SMTP domain names).	You can make use of your existing Active Directory and DNS deployment; however, you may need to upgrade your existing domain controllers and global catalogs to meet the prerequisites.
User accounts	You must move your user accounts to the new AD forest or re-create them.	Your users will be able to use their existing accounts without any changes.

TABLE 11.1:   Comparison of Exchange Server 2013 upgrade strategies   *(CONTINUED)*

POINT OF COMPARISON	TRANSITION STRATEGY	UPGRADE STRATEGY
Message routing	Your SMTP domains must be split between your legacy organization and your new organization; one of them must be configured to be nonauthoritative and to route to the other. This configuration may need to change during the course of the migration. Additionally, you must set up explicit external SMTP connectors between the two organizations or play tricks with name resolution.	Your organization continues to be a single entity, with full knowledge of all authoritative domains shared among all Exchange servers. Message flow between organizations can be controlled by normal Send and Receive connectors along with AD site links.
Outlook profiles	You will need to either create new Outlook profiles (manually or using the tools found in the matching version of the Microsoft Office Resource Kit) or use third-party tools to migrate them over to the new organization. This may cause loss of information, such as any personalizations made to Outlook.	As long as you keep the legacy mailbox servers up and running during an appropriate transition phase, Outlook will transparently update your users' profiles to their new Mailbox server the first time they open it after their mailbox is moved to Exchange Server 2013.

For the most part, Table 11.1 speaks for itself; if any point requires more in-depth discussion, we address it properly in the detailed sections that follow.

Transitioning Your Exchange Organization

From the overview given in Table 11.1, it may seem as if we have a grudge against upgrading to Exchange Server 2013 by using the transition strategy. Although we have to admit it's not our favorite strategy, we'll hasten to say that transition offers many advantages that a normal upgrade doesn't offer:

◆ It is the only realistic way to consolidate two or more separate Exchange Server organizations into a single organization. This kind of consolidation can happen as the result of a major reorganization inside one company or a merger or acquisition.

◆ It allows you to set up a *greenfield* (a term used to denote the ideal state of implementation) deployment of Exchange Server 2013. No matter how conscientious you are as an admin, any real network is the product of a number of design compromises. After a while, the weight of those compromises and workarounds adds up; the design and structure of your network can reflect imperatives and inputs that no longer exist, or are no longer relevant, in your organization. It's nice to be able to wipe the slate clean, especially if that ends up being less work than trying to start with your current mess and clean it up.

◆ It permits you to move your Exchange servers out of your existing Active Directory forest and establish them in their own forest. If you're in an environment that separates administrative control between Active Directory and the Exchange Server organization, having a separate forest for Exchange Server can make it a lot easier to accomplish many of the day-to-day management tasks on your servers. (We don't know about you, but we'd much prefer to have control of the OU structure and Group Policy objects that affect our Exchange servers.) If the benefits of a multiforest deployment outweigh the drawbacks, this configuration may improve the efficiency of the split between directory/account administration and Exchange Server administration.

◆ It gives you the chance to easily define new policies and procedures that apply equally to everyone, from account provisioning to server-naming conventions. With the importance of regulatory compliance and strong internal IT controls and auditing rising on a daily basis, this can be a strong motivator.

◆ It allows you to perform additional configuration and testing of your new organization before you move the bulk of your live data and users to it. Being able to perform additional validation, perhaps with a pilot group of users, gives you additional confidence in the strength of your design and affords you extra opportunities to spot problems and correct them while you can.

Now that we've said that, we should point out that a transition strategy usually involves more work, more money, or both. Sometimes, though, it's what you have to do.

Here's what a transition might look like:

1. Deploy a new Active Directory forest and root domain, as well as any additional domains. These will probably be named something different from the domains in use in your current network so that you can operate in both environments (and your users can as well). You could be using this forest as an Exchange Server resource forest, or you could be moving all your servers and desktops as well. Because transitions don't happen overnight, you'll need some sort of forest trust between your forests so that accounts and permissions will work properly while the transition is in progress. This step is outside the scope of this book; for more information see: *Mastering Microsoft Windows Server 2012 R2* by Mark Minasi, et al (Sybex, 2013).

2. Move a suitable set of user accounts to the new forest. Perhaps you're concentrating on one site at one time to minimize confusion; if so, you need to move each user account in the site to the corresponding site in the new Active Directory forest. Again, this step is outside the scope of this book.

3. Install Windows Server 2012 and Exchange Server 2013 on a suitable number of 64-bit servers to form the core of your new Exchange Server organization. You don't need to have new servers for everything, but you usually should have at least a site's worth of equipment on hand. You'll need to configure SMTP connectors between the two organizations, and you must have some sort of directory synchronization going on between the two forests. That way, as users get moved into the new forest, each GAL is properly updated to ensure that internal mail is delivered to the right Exchange Server organization.

4. Move the mailbox data for the site from the legacy Exchange Server Mailbox servers to the new Exchange Server 2013 Mailbox servers. Update your users' Outlook profiles so that they can get to their mailboxes, and ensure that the GAL information is updated so that mail follows these users to their new mailbox servers. Once everything is working, you can remove the legacy Exchange servers from this site.

5. Don't forget that you may have to join your users' desktops, as well as any other Windows member servers (such as file/print, database, and web servers) to the new forest if it isn't being used exclusively as an Exchange Server resource forest. This step is outside the scope of this book.

6. Continue this process one site at a time until you've moved all your user accounts and mailbox data into the Exchange Server 2013 organization and have decommissioned the remaining legacy Exchange servers.

Now you can see why we consider the transition strategy to be the labor-intensive route. You don't have the luxury of accepting your existing Active Directory structure and accounts. Although you can move message data over to a new organization, more effort is involved in making sure users' profiles are properly updated. Alternatively, you can rebuild your users' profiles and accept some data loss. If you're upgrading the desktop clients to Outlook 2010 or Outlook 2013, you have the additional worry of whether you need to move the desktop machines into a new forest.

On the other hand, if you have an Active Directory deployment with serious structural problems (whether through years of accumulation or the results of previous mistakes), if you need to extract your Exchange servers into a separate Active Directory forest, or if there is some other reason why upgrading your existing organization isn't going to work for you, a transition has a lot to offer.

Transitions require you to keep track of a lot of details and separate types of information. Although you can move all the important information—mailboxes, public folders, GAL data—using the freely available Microsoft tools, you'll have a harder time migrating some of the smaller details that aren't mission critical but nonetheless can add up to a negative user experience if omitted. If users' first experience on the new messaging system is having to reconfigure Outlook with all their preferences, they're going to be less than happy about the experience. The cost of third-party tools may well prove to be a good investment that saves you time, reduces complexity, and gains you the goodwill of your users.

Upgrading Your Exchange Organization

The process of upgrading your Exchange Server organization to Exchange Server 2013 resembles the process required to upgrade from Exchange Server 2003 to Exchange Server 2007 or Exchange Server 2010. If you have experience in those particular upgrades, relax; transitioning to Exchange Server 2013 is much easier. All you're doing is moving mailboxes and public folder information, so it's easy—well, as easy as these types of projects get.

Let's take a closer look at the average upgrade to Exchange Server 2013.

AN OVERVIEW OF THE UPGRADE PROCESS

Imagine that you have an Exchange Server 2010 organization that has eight Mailbox servers, two Client Access servers, and two Hub Transport servers that handle all SMTP traffic with the Internet. For the sake of illustration, say that all your existing Exchange servers are already on 64-bit hardware; you have spares that you plan on using during the upgrade to keep your new hardware costs to a minimum.

In this organization, the upgrade process would look something like this:

1. Ensure that your organization meets all the prerequisites we discussed earlier. Run the PrepareSchema step of setup to upgrade the Active Directory forest schema with the Exchange Server 2013 extensions and to create the proper objects in the forest and the root domain.

2. If you have additional Active Directory domains in your forest, prepare each of them by running the PrepareDomain step of setup.

3. Install the first Exchange Server 2013 Client Access server into your organization. Once it is configured, you can bring it into production use and decommission the first Exchange Server 2010 CAS provided you have an additional Exchange Server 2010 CAS to handle proxy communications. You can then reuse this hardware to install the second Exchange Server 2013 CAS and decommission the second Exchange Server 2010 front-end server.

4. Install Windows Server 2012 on your spare 64-bit Mailbox server hardware. Install Exchange Server 2013 on it as the first Exchange Server 2013 Mailbox server in the organization.

5. Reconfigure Exchange Server 2013 to handle the offline address book generation and distribution. If you still have Outlook 2003 clients, they will not be able to access the OAB generated by Exchange Server 2013. You may need to leave an Exchange Server 2010 CAS around to handle that until you get Outlook clients upgraded.

6. Reconfigure Exchange Server 2013 to handle outgoing SMTP traffic.

7. Move the mailboxes from the first Exchange Server 2010 Mailbox server onto the first Exchange Server 2013 Mailbox server. Remove the first Exchange Server 2010 Mailbox server from the organization.

8. Perform a clean installation of Windows Server 2012 on this server and then install the Exchange Server 2013 Mailbox role. Move the mailboxes from the second Exchange Server 2010 server onto this new Mailbox server.

9. Continue the process in step 8 one server at a time until you have moved all mailboxes onto Exchange Server 2013 Mailbox servers and you have no remaining Exchange Server 2010 Mailbox servers left in the organization. At this point, you will have the same number of spare servers you started with.

10. Once all Exchange Server 2010 mailboxes have been moved to Exchange Server 2013, you can then retire the Exchange Server 2010 CAS, Hub Transport, and Mailbox servers.

It sounds like a lot of work, but many people have favored this kind of approach even in previous upgrades to Exchange Server. It gives you the advantage of having a clean installation of

Windows to work with and allows you to configure the operating system exactly the way you want it.

Order of Installation for Exchange Server 2013 Roles

Unlike with prior versions of Exchange, Microsoft makes no specific recommendations on the order in which you should install the various Exchange Server 2013 roles. Of course, since there are now only two roles, the process is quite a bit simpler than it was previously. However, installing roles in a certain order may simplify your upgrade to Exchange Server 2013.

CLIENT ACCESS SERVERS

We recommend that the Client Access role be the first Exchange Server 2013 instance you install into a legacy Exchange Server organization. The reasons for this are simple: First, once you actually have mailboxes on Exchange Server 2013 servers and your users attempt to access them in any way, you will need to have an Exchange Server 2013 Client Access server to provide that protocol access. Second, the Exchange Server 2013 CAS will act as a stateless proxy for client protocols to all legacy servers. This potentially allows you to switch client and web protocol access to Exchange Server 2013 quite early on in the upgrade process. For more information, see Chapter 21, "Understanding the Client Access Server."

In smaller organizations, it is common to deploy all roles on the same physical server. In fact, this is the standard Exchange Server 2013 installation option when you use the GUI setup.

> **CLIENT ACCESS ROLE REQUIREMENTS AND BEST PRACTICES**
>
> Upgrading the Client Access servers first has long been an Exchange Server best practice; even when applying Service Packs, you always want the CAS running the most recent version of Exchange Server. Although this is not a requirement in Exchange Server 2013, this rule of thumb still applies.

When you are determining the number of Client Access servers you need, remember that you should have at least one CAS in each Active Directory site where you will have an Exchange Server 2013 Mailbox server. Although any CAS can answer an incoming request, it is more efficient for the client to use a CAS in the same AD site as the Mailbox server.

The CAS role is mandatory in an Exchange Server 2013 organization even if you do not plan to support Outlook Web App, ActiveSync, POP, or IMAP clients. Outlook clients must use the Microsoft Exchange RPC Client Access service to access mailbox data; Outlook 2007 and later use the CAS for Autodiscover as well as accessing free/busy information and downloading the offline address book.

MAILBOX SERVERS

After you have suitable CAS servers in a given site, you can begin deploying the Mailbox role. Until you have mailboxes hosted on Exchange Server 2013, the advanced features of Exchange Server 2013 cannot be used.

In Exchange Server 2013, most of the Hub Transport role functionality was merged into the Mailbox role. This is also true of Unified Messaging role functionality. As you may surmise, the client protocol handling was moved onto the CAS. With this role consolidation, the Mailbox role now requires more memory and processor resources than it did in the past. However, the total number of servers required in an Exchange Server organization may decrease. You will have to evaluate this for your own organization.

Now, intraorganizational message flow happens between Mailbox servers. Incoming messages from the Internet enter a CAS, which connects to the destination Mailbox server and proxies the message to the proper mailbox. Outgoing messages to the Internet originate from a Mailbox server, are routed to a CAS in the same AD site if available (to another site if not), and proxied to the Internet. But administration is mainly unchanged.

When moving mailboxes to Exchange Server 2013 Mailbox servers, you should use only the Exchange Server 2013 Exchange Admin Center New Migration Batch Wizard or the Exchange Management Shell New-MoveRequest or New-MigrationBatch cmdlets. In particular, do not use the wizard or cmdlets in legacy versions of Exchange Server or you could break the mailboxes.

The Mailbox role is mandatory in an Exchange Server 2013 organization.

Real World Scenario

HANDLING OF EDGE TRANSPORT AND UNIFIED MESSAGING

Exchange Server 2013 does not have an Edge Transport role. According to some sources, one may be coming with Exchange Server 2013 SP1. From a realistic perspective, this means that if you want to use Edge Transport servers, you need to deploy them before you remove Exchange Server 2007 or Exchange Server 2010 from your organization. Exchange Server 2013 Mailbox servers can operate with Exchange Server 2007 and Exchange Server 2010 Hub Transport servers for sending and receiving mail.

Although configuring and using Unified Messaging capabilities are not within the scope of this book, we can make a few general observations about deploying it. This is probably the last role to configure in your organization; it requires working CAS and Mailbox servers in the organization. For your users to make use of the Unified Messaging functionality, you must have sufficient Enterprise Client Access Licenses for those users.

On-premises Coexistence

As you proceed with your Exchange Server 2013 upgrade, you will almost certainly have a period of time during which your Exchange Server 2013 servers will be required to coexist with legacy Exchange servers. During this time, there are several points you should consider:

♦ Outlook Web App (OWA) with single sign-on between Exchange Server 2013 and Exchange Server 2010 requires a minimum of Exchange Server 2013 RTM CU1. It will also be necessary to enable either Basic Authentication or Integrated Windows Authentication on the Exchange Server 2010 CAS. SSO is not possible if only Forms-based Authentication is enabled.

♦ OWA with SSO between Exchange Server 2013 and Exchange Server 2007 requires a minimum of Exchange Server 2013 RTM CU2. It will also be necessary to enable either Basic Authentication or Integrated Windows Authentication on the Exchange Server 2007 CAS.

◆ By default, a Send connector is not present for Internet messages. You must create one before you can send Internet email.

◆ The Unified Messaging role cannot offer services for recipients whose mailboxes are on legacy servers. You must retain the legacy UM servers and update the dial plan(s) to include the new Exchange Server 2013 servers (or create new dial plans that include the legacy servers).

Office 365

We are certainly not here to make a pitch for you to move to Office 365. That being said, for many organizations, a cloud-based communication platform makes sense, and that's primarily what Office 365 is about. Exchange Online provides for cloud-based email and scheduling, Lync Online provides for cloud-based instant messaging and videoconferencing, and SharePoint Online provides for cloud-based file sharing and rich websites.

The price point, if you exclude licensing of the Office client software, is quite low. In fact, we have to wonder if Microsoft actually makes a profit at it! If you have not yet considered it, it is a fair bet that your management will expect you to soon.

However, for many other companies, cloud-based solutions don't make sense. Moving your operations to the cloud represents a significant loss of control and, potentially, concerns about security of your data.

The process of moving onto Office 365 from on-premises systems (or other cloud providers) is known as *onboarding*. Similarly, the process of moving off Office 365 to another provider is known as *offboarding*. We suggest that you not onboard your Exchange Server organization without some plan in place to offboard. Many companies have moved and then retired from Office 365 quickly after finding that they cannot accept the restrictions of the services.

Very detailed descriptions of the services are available and a very interesting read. The descriptions include detailed explanations of exactly what is, and is not, available as part of the online services when compared to the on-premises solutions:

```
http://technet.microsoft.com/en-us/library/office-365-service-descriptions.aspx
```

Should that URL disappear, search for "Office 365 service descriptions" on `http://technet .microsoft.com` or your favorite search engine.

Surprisingly, perhaps, preparing for either a hybrid deployment of Exchange Server 2013 with Office 365 or a full transition to Office 365 requires the same steps as for an on-premises deployment of Exchange Server 2013.

Microsoft has invested heavily in making the onboarding process easy—at least as easy as an on-premises upgrade.

Office 365 Options

When moving to Office 365, there are four basic mechanisms to do so:

Hybrid Deployment In this case, you will maintain a local Exchange Server environment, as well as an Exchange Server environment in Office 365. You may also have to use a hybrid deployment when you expect that onboarding to Office 365 will take an extended period of time or when you cannot use any of the following mechanisms.

Cutover Exchange Migration With a Cutover Exchange Migration (CEM), your local Exchange Server organization has fewer than 1,000 mailboxes. All of the mailboxes are moved in a single batch. To be obvious, while mailboxes are moved in a single batch, the length of time the mailbox move requires is dependent on your Internet connectivity, the size of the mailboxes, and on throttling on the Office 365 servers. Mailboxes and users are automatically created in Office 365 when performing a CEM.

Staged Exchange Migration In the case of a Staged Exchange Migration (SEM), you can move multiple groups of users, across a period of time, to onboard them onto Office 365. The source servers may be only Exchange Server 2003 or Exchange Server 2007. Prior to executing an SEM to onboard your users, you must use some type of directory synchronization (such as WAADS discussed in the "Hybrid Deployments" section earlier in this chapter) in order to create your users in Office 365. You must take some care with SEM in order to ensure that mailflow works properly.

IMAP Migration This approach also allows you to move multiple groups of users, across a period of time, to onboard them onto Office 365. The source servers may be any IMAP server (including Exchange Server). Prior to executing an IMAP Migration to onboard your users, you must use some tool to create users and mailboxes in Office 365. (See the section "Exchange Server Deployment Assistant" later in this chapter.) You must take some care in order to ensure that mailflow works properly.

In every case, users are onboarded to Office 365 by moving their mailboxes using one of two PowerShell cmdlets (or the equivalent in the Exchange Admin Center). That process is discussed in the upcoming section, "Moving Mailboxes."

Office 365 Coexistence

When we begin to discuss different mechanisms for coexisting with an on-premises Exchange Server organization and Office 365, the water begins to get murky. There are many options. However, there are certain key factors:

◆ Some type of directory synchronization is required. Microsoft provides a prepackaged solution in WAADS and in AD FS. If you have the resources and Identity Management experts, you can use Forefront Identity Manager, the Shibboleth Identity Provider (SIP), or the older Identity Lifecycle Manager. You may also, if you have specific needs, implement your own solution. Regardless, users, groups, contacts, and a significant set of attributes must be copied from the on-premises environment to Office 365. AD FS or SIP is required for a true single sign-on experience (or an equivalent federation partner).

◆ You must have updated your on-premises organization as described previously.

◆ You must have an on-premises Internet-accessible Exchange Server 2013 CAS with autodiscover DNS records pointing to it.

◆ You must configure the on-premises Exchange Admin Center to connect to both your on-premises Exchange Server organization and your Office 365 tenant.

◆ CAS servers that will be referenced when using the Hybrid Configuration Wizard (HCW) must have a valid third-party SSL certificate installed on them, and the autodiscover and Exchange Web Services (EWS) configured names must be valid subject alternate names on the certificates.

You should verify that AD FS or WAADS is working properly (verifying that users and their attributes are present within Office 365). Next, verify that your configuration is correct by using the Microsoft Remote Connectivity Analyzer at http://www.testexchangeconnectivity.com.

Once both of those tests are successful, you are ready to execute the Hybrid Configuration Wizard. To start the HCW, log in to the EAC on one of your on-premises CAS servers. Select the Hybrid node and click Enable. This will start the HCW, and then you simply select the appropriate options for your organization. They are self-explanatory.

When the HCW successfully completes, your hybrid deployment is live. At this time, you can move mailboxes back and forth between the cloud and on-premises. For more information on that topic, see, "Moving Mailboxes" later in this chapter.

Performing an On-premises Interorganization Migration

This part of this chapter focuses on moving from an Exchange Server 2010 organization into a new or separate Exchange Server 2013 organization. This type of migration is somewhat more difficult than an intraorganization upgrade, may be more disruptive for your users, and often leaves you with fewer options than a normal upgrade. However, you may be faced with an organizational configuration that leaves you no choice.

INTRAORGANIZATION VS. INTERORGANIZATION UPGRADE

An intraorganization upgrade occurs within your current Exchange Server organization. An interorganization upgrade (or migration) occurs between your current Exchange Server organization and another Exchange Server organization.

Is Interorganization Migration the Right Approach?

An interorganization migration is quite a bit more complex for both the person handling the migration and the users. The "upgrade" migration is by far the simplest type of Exchange Server 2013 migration. Before you choose an interorganization migration over an upgrade, you want to make sure you are choosing the right (and simplest) upgrade path.

Most organizations that are moving to Exchange Server 2013 will not need to perform an interorganization migration. If the following checklist sounds like your organization, you should perform an "upgrade" instead:

- You have a single Active Directory forest and no resource forests.

- You are running Exchange Server 2007 or Exchange Server 2010.

- Your Exchange Server organization is part of your existing Active Directory.

Does this sound like you? If so, go back and read the first part of this chapter because performing a normal upgrade is what you need to do. Because you already have Exchange Server in your Active Directory, there is no need for the extra effort of an interorganization migration.

So, who needs to perform an interorganization migration? You might need to perform an interorganization migration for a number of reasons:

- ◆ You are consolidating one or more separate Exchange Server organizations.

- ◆ You are moving Exchange Server resources from a resource forest into your accounts forest.

- ◆ You are moving from Exchange Server 2003 or earlier to Exchange Server 2013.

- ◆ You are moving from a different messaging system to Exchange Server 2013.

If you have multiple organizations that you need to consolidate or some other item in the preceding list, you have no choice but to proceed down the interorganization migration path. Proceeding down this path means different things to different organizations, but most of these interorganization migrations face a number of challenges:

- ◆ Finding the tools necessary to perform the migration based on your needs

- ◆ Moving mail data between two systems

- ◆ Moving directory data between two systems

- ◆ Maintaining directory synchronization and messaging between two systems during some period of interoperability

- ◆ Ensuring that email flows correctly between the email systems during the transition

- ◆ Figuring out how and when to transition services, such as public folders, MX records, mobile phones, and web mail

Choosing the Right Tools

When you're planning an interorganization migration, it is important to pick the right tools to help you create accounts, move data, synchronize directories, create forwarders, and perform other migration tasks. Naturally, the most powerful and flexible of these tools are all provided by third parties rather than by Microsoft. However, Microsoft does provide some basic tools that you can use to perform Exchange Server 2007/2010 to Exchange Server 2013 interorganization migrations.

Active Directory Migration Tool   If the user accounts have not yet been created or migrated into your target Active Directory, consider migrating the accounts from their original Active Directory rather than creating new user accounts. The Active Directory Migration Tool (ADMT) is a free tool from Microsoft that will help you migrate users, groups, and computers from one Windows domain or Active Directory to another. The big advantages of this tool are that it preserves the source domain's security identifier (SID) in the target account's SID history attribute and that it preserves group membership.

You can download the Active Directory Migration Tool v3.2 and its associated documentation from the download center of Microsoft's website at `http://microsoft.com/downloads`.

New-MoveRequest and New-MigrationBatch Cmdlets   The Exchange Server 2013 `New-MoveRequest` cmdlet and the `New-MigrationBatch` cmdlet have options that allow you to migrate mailbox data from separate Exchange Server 2007 or 2010 organizations, and there are automated options for them to create an account for you if one does not exist. We cover these tools in more detail later in this chapter in the section, "Moving Mailboxes."

`Export-Mailbox` and `New-MailboxImportRequest` Cmdlets   If you have a small number of users (fewer than 50), you might opt to export all their mail from their old mail server using a tool like `Export-Mailbox` (or even ExMerge or Outlook, yikes!) and then use the Exchange Server 2013 `New-MailboxImportRequest` cmdlet to import mail data from these PST files into the users' new mailboxes. This is a basic solution, but it saves you from having to learn the `New-MoveRequest` cmdlet, and you still get to move your users' mail data. Keep in mind, though, that if you use this method, you will lose things like folder rules and delegates that users have assigned to their folders.

Third-party Tools   If you have more than a few hundred users, a lot of public folder data, or very large mailboxes, or if you will need to maintain some level of interoperability between your old Exchange Server 2007 or 2010 system and your new Exchange Server 2013 system for a long period of time (longer than a few weeks), you should consider a third-party tool. These are often a tough sell after an organization has invested a lot of money in a new mail system, but they can make your migration much easier and allow for better long-term interoperability.

Maintaining Interoperability

During either a true migration or a transition migration from one messaging system to another, the period of interoperability is always one of the biggest headaches. One of the first factors we always want to take into consideration when faced with an interorganization migration is developing a plan that will minimize the time during which the old system and the new system must coexist.

The transition type of migration is the simplest type if you are going to need two systems to coexist for some period of time. However, this approach is not always an option. In that case, you need to figure out if you can perform an "instant" or light-switch migration or if you must have some period of interoperability.

LIGHT-SWITCH MIGRATIONS

For a relatively small number of users (fewer than 1,000 mailboxes, for example), we try to find a way to perform a light-switch migration. On Friday afternoon when a user leaves work, she is using the old system. On Monday morning when she returns to work, she is using the new system. This is a light-switch migration; from the user's perspective the transition occurs very quickly.

We like the light-switch migration strategy because it usually does not require us to perform any sort of destructive migration on the source system, and everything is migrated all at once. We have performed successful light-switch migrations for 20-user organizations all the way up to 1,500-user organizations. A number of factors will determine if a light-switch migration is possible in your organization. Here are some of the factors to consider:

◆   Can all of the data be moved in a short period of time?

◆   Can users' Outlook clients and ActiveSync devices be directed or reconfigured to use the new servers effectively and accurately?

◆   Are there sufficient help desk and information technology resources to support the user community on "the morning after"?

◆   If new accounts have to be created for users, can the old passwords be synchronized or can new passwords be distributed to the users?

If you can properly support the light-switch migration, it is best for minimizing interoperability between two systems. The first goal has to be minimizing disruption for the user community, but a long transition between two mail systems can often be more disruptive if the interoperability issues are not properly addressed.

A lot of factors are involved in planning any interorganization migration strategy, but here is a list of major factors in roughly the order in which they should be done:

- Deploy the new messaging system and test all components, including inbound/outbound mail routing and web components.

- Develop a plan for migrating Outlook profiles such as using Outlook 2007/2010/2013 Autodiscover or a script that creates a new profile.

- Create mailboxes and establish email addresses that match the existing mailboxes on the source system.

- Move older data (mailboxes and public folders) if possible.

- Restrict user access to the older mail system and start the migration.

- Switch inbound email to the new mail system.

- Switch Outlook profiles to the new servers.

- Switch over inbound HTTP/HTTPS access to mailboxes.

- Replicate public folder data.

- Move mailbox data; if using a third-party migration tool, try to replicate older mailbox data prior to migration day.

- Keep the old mail system up and running for a month or two just in case you need to retrieve something.

INTEROPERABILITY FACTORS

In migrations, we try to avoid keeping two mail systems operating in parallel for very long. Without the right tools, interoperability is a royal pain in the neck. That being said, you are probably wondering what some of the issues of interoperability are. Here is a partial list of things you need to be concerned about or that your migration utilities should address:

- Email forwarding between domains should work seamlessly; email should be delivered to the right location regardless of whether someone has been migrated.

- Directory/address book synchronization should work seamlessly; users should be able to continue to use the GAL and it should accurately reflect the correct address of the user.

- Mail distribution groups should continue to work properly regardless of where the member is located.

- Users should still be able to reply to email messages that were migrated to the new system.

- Public folder data and free/busy data should be synchronized between the two systems.

- ◆ You should have a plan that includes how to transition from one web-based mail system and mobile device system to another.

- ◆ Your plan should include migrating users in groups or by department if possible.

- ◆ Your plan or migration utilities should also include a mechanism to migrate (or help the user to reproduce) rules, folder permissions, and mailbox delegate access.

Preparing for Migration

You can do some things to get ready for your interorganization migration; these tasks will make things go more quickly for you. This preparation includes gathering information about what you have to migrate as well as preparing for the actual steps of migration. Here is a partial list:

- ◆ Because you are migrating your users from an existing Exchange Server organization to a new Exchange Server 2013 organization, have all the target systems' Exchange Server 2013 servers installed, tested, and ready to use before starting the migration.

- ◆ Document everything relevant about your source organization, including connectors, email flow, storage/message size limits, mail-enabled groups, and web access configuration (OWA, ActiveSync, IMAP4, POP3).

- ◆ Ensure that DNS name resolution between the two Active Directories is working correctly. You may need to configure conditional forwarders or zone transfers to achieve this.

- ◆ Ensure that WINS name resolution between all resources in both domains works properly. This step may not be necessary, but it never hurts.

- ◆ Make sure there are no firewalls between the two systems; if there are, ensure that the necessary ports are open between the systems.

- ◆ Configure trust relationships between the two systems.

- ◆ Ensure that you have Domain Administrator and Exchange Administrator permissions in both the source and target systems.

- ◆ If you are planning to use the Active Directory Migration Tool (ADMT) to migrate user accounts, you must establish name resolution, a trust relationship, and admin accounts in both domains.

Moving Mailboxes

Exchange Server 2013 includes the `New-MoveRequest` cmdlet, which can be used to move either mailboxes within an organization (intraorganization) or between two different Exchange Server organizations (interorganization). For interorganization migrations, `New-MoveRequest` can be used whether the source server is running Exchange Server 2003 or Exchange Server 2007/2010/2013; the target server must always be running Exchange Server 2013. For online mailbox moves, the source server must be Exchange Server 2010 or Exchange Server 2013.

The `New-MoveRequest` cmdlet is a powerful tool with many parameters and options. In this section, we focus just on its use when moving mail data between one Exchange Server organization and another. Keep in mind that one requirement for using the `New-MoveRequest` cmdlet is that the global catalog servers in both the source and target forests must be running Windows Server 2003 with Service Pack 2 or later.

Exchange Server 2013 introduces the concept of *batches* and of *migration endpoints*. A batch of mailboxes seems fairly self-explanatory—it is simply a group of mailboxes. A batch always connects to a local server and to a migration endpoint. Batch moves are used for cross-forest migrations of every type. The types are discussed in the section, "Office 365 Options," earlier in this chapter. A batch move must always be executed in the target Exchange Server environment (this means that all migrations are "pulled" across from the source environment).

A migration endpoint, which is used only for cross-forest moves, is used to identify the configuration settings and connection mechanism for the source mailboxes that will be used by the batch move request. Therefore, if you are executing a batch move to onboard to Office 365, you will create a migration endpoint and execute a batch move either from the Office 365 Exchange Admin Center or when connected to the Office 365 environment via remote PowerShell.

The cmdlet that is used to create a migration endpoint is `New-MigrationEndpoint`. The cmdlet that is used to create a new migration batch is `New-MigrationBatch`. There are also many other batch-related cmdlets. The cmdlets provide ways to control the movement of mailboxes via batch, including ways to stop a batch from executing, suspend it, get the status and statistics associated with a currently executing batch, and so on. You can find information on all the batch cmdlets at `http://technet.microsoft.com/en-us/library/jj218644(v=exchg.150).aspx` or by searching for "Exchange 2013 move and migration cmdlets" using your favorite search engine.

Migration batches are preferred over the use of `New-MoveRequest` in Exchange Server 2013, but both mechanisms are supported. Migration batches can be fully controlled and monitored from within the EAC, and that is the recommended method for doing so. The batch cmdlets have many options and many different usage scenarios depending on whether you are onboarding or offboarding to Office 365, performing cross-forest moves, doing staged Exchange Server migrations or cutover Exchange Server migrations, or even just performing local (same forest) mailbox moves.

As a person who was very resistant to the EAC in the beginning, I will say that it provides a great interface for executing and monitoring batch moves.

Migrating User Accounts

Using either of the cross-forest move mechanisms (individual move requests or migration batches) requires that a mail-enabled user account be created in the destination forest before the mailbox move is initiated. As noted in our prior section "Office 365 Coexistence," this can be accomplished in a number of different ways. Microsoft documents the attributes that *must* be copied and that *may* be copied at this URL:

`http://technet.microsoft.com/en-us/library/ee633491`

If that URL should disappear, then on `http://technet.microsoft.com` (or your favorite Internet search engine) search for "prepare mailboxes for cross-forest move requests."

Another resource for creating users and copying attributes that we have not previously discussed can be very handy. As part of Exchange Server 2013, the Exchange Server team shipped a script named `Prepare-MoveRequest.ps1`. This script is located in the `$ExScripts` directory, normally at `C:\ Program Files\Microsoft\Exchange Server\V15\Scripts`. It is extremely useful if you are planning some type of custom migration where none of the earlier tools are useful, for whatever reason. Using this script is discussed at:

```
http://technet.microsoft.com/en-us/library/ee861103
```

Or you can find the most current link by searching for "prepare mailboxes for cross-forest moves using the `Prepare-MoveRequest.ps1` script in the shell."

Permissions Required

When you are moving mailboxes between forests, you need to have accounts in both the source and destination forests that will give you the necessary permissions to move mailbox data between the two organizations. Usually, the accounts you use for the source and target organizations will *not* be the same account. Permissions required are pretty simple: you need to be a recipient administrator for all the accounts you will be moving. In the case of Office 365, you need to be a tenant administrator.

Importing Data from PSTs

Exchange Server 2013 adds the native (that is, does not depend on Outlook) capability to import personal folder (PST) files into a mailbox. Similar to mailbox batches discussed in the prior section, there is an entire suite of cmdlets controlling this capability. Unlike with mailbox batches, there is a not a nice, pretty interface in the Exchange Admin Center, which is unfortunate.

Regardless, the new cmdlets are as follows:

- `Get-MailboxImportRequest`

- `Get-MailboxImportRequestStatistics`

- `New-MailboxImportRequest`

- `Remove-MailboxImportRequest`

- `Resume-MailboxImportRequest`

- `Set-MailboxImportRequest`

- `Suspend-MailboxImportRequest`

Before you begin trying to import PST data into an existing mailbox, make sure that you have the necessary permissions. By default, just because you are an Exchange Server administrator does not mean you can import data. Use the EMS `New-ManagementRoleAssignment` cmdlet to give your account the necessary permissions. Here is an example where we give user Rena .Dauria permission to import or export user data from mailboxes:

```
New-ManagementRoleAssignment -Role "Mailbox Import Export" ↵
-User "Rena.Dauria"
```

Once you have the necessary permissions to the mailbox and have opened an instance of the Exchange Management Shell, you can proceed. Here is an example of importing a PST file called `ARoberts.PST` into the mailbox `Andrew.Roberts`:

```
New-MailboxImportRequest Andrew.Roberts -FilePath \\Server\PSTshare\ARoberts.PST
```

Unlike in earlier versions of this cmdlet, the dumpster is included by default. You can also specify that you want the data imported into the user's archive versus the main mailbox, the specific folders you want to include and exclude, and many other options. Unfortunately, unlike the `Import-Mailbox` cmdlet that was present in Exchange Server 2010, there is no way to specify a date range.

For more details about the `New-MailboxImportRequest` cmdlet, see,

`http://technet.microsoft.com/en-us/library/ff607310.aspx`

or search for, "Exchange 2013 New-MailboxImportRequest."

Tasks Required Prior to Removing Legacy Exchange Servers

If you are performing an upgrade or are migrating completely to Office 365, the time will come when all of the upgrade and/or migration tasks are complete (at least, we hope so!).

Now you are ready to start removing the old servers. No, you can't just cut them off and be done with it. Exchange Server has hooks deep into your Active Directory, and if you have new servers (or are going to continue with directory synchronization to the cloud), you *must* clean up the remnants of the old servers. If you don't, they are guaranteed to come back and haunt you.

To actually remove an installation of Exchange Server from a server, you need Organization Admin privileges, plus local Administrator privileges on that server.

Before you begin the process of removing Exchange Server, there are some items that you should verify for completeness:

- ◆ If you will be using public folders, you need to ensure that replication has completed and that the migration is completed on the target environment.

- ◆ If you will not be using public folders, you need to ensure that all replicas of both system and normal public folders have been removed from all public folder databases and that the public folder databases have been deleted.

- ◆ All CAS configuration is pointing to Exchange Server 2013 CAS (including EWS, EAS, Outlook Anywhere, Autodiscover, and the like).

- ◆ All Send and Receive connectors are pointing to Exchange Server 2013 servers.

- ◆ All user mailboxes have been moved to Exchange Server 2013.

- ◆ All system mailboxes have been moved to Exchange Server 2013 (including arbitration and discovery search mailboxes).

- ◆ All mailbox databases on the legacy servers have been removed.

- ◆ All Exchange Server 2010 client access arrays have been removed.

- ◆ All applications that may be using Exchange Server services (SMTP relay, for example) have been reconfigured to use Exchange Server 2013 servers.

Once all of these tasks are complete and verified, you are now ready to begin removing legacy Exchange servers.

Removing Exchange Server from a server is as simple as choosing Add/Remove Programs (for Windows Server 2003) or Programs and Features (for Windows Server 2008 and later) ➢ Exchange Server ➢ Uninstall. Simply follow the uninstallation wizard. If you have forgotten to perform any of the steps listed previously, the wizard will let you know. At that point, you should correct the problem and rerun the wizard.

Exchange Server Deployment Assistant

Beginning with Exchange Server 2010, Microsoft made available an online tool to assist in the planning and deployment process for Exchange Server. The web-based tool, known as the Microsoft Exchange Server Deployment Assistant (EDA), allows a user to specify their starting configuration and desired end result. Then the tool produces the broad outline of a plan to reach the desired end result.

EDA, especially with common deployment scenarios, can be a great time-saver. While EDA does not cover every scenario or diagram of everything that must be done, especially when third-party messaging systems or extensions come into play, it does provide extensive links to the relevant TechNet literature. Relevancy is the key. TechNet is a huge repository of data, and determining what is relevant to a particular deployment can be challenging. That is where EDA comes in.

Here's what EDA covers:

◆ On-premises upgrades and transitions from Exchange Server 2007 and Exchange Server 2010 to Exchange Server 2013

◆ Hybrid deployments using the following versions of Exchange Server: Exchange Server 2007, Exchange Server 2010, and Exchange Server 2013

◆ Transitions to cloud-only solutions (that is, moving your entire messaging infrastructure to Office 365)

As of this writing, you can find EDA at `http://technet.microsoft.com/en-us/exchange/jj657516.aspx`. Should that link disappear, you can search for "Microsoft Exchange Server Deployment Assistant" on TechNet, using your favorite Internet search engine.

The Bottom Line

Choose between an upgrade and a migration.   The migration path that you take will depend on a number of factors, including the amount of disruption that you can put your users through and the current version of your messaging system.

> **Master It**   Your company is currently running Exchange Server 2010 and is supporting 3,000 users. You have a single Active Directory forest. You have purchased new hardware to support Exchange Server 2013. Management has asked that the migration path you choose have minimal disruption on your user community. Which type of migration should you use? What high-level events should occur?

Choose between on-premises deployment and Office 365.   A common choice today is deciding whether to move your mailbox data into the cloud. Office 365 is Microsoft's cloud solution, of which Exchange Online is a part.

Master It You work at a university using Exchange Server 2007 on-premises for 10,000 students. You want to offer the functionality present in Exchange Server 2013 to your students, but you have budgetary constraints and cannot replace all of the required servers. What is your best course of action?

Determine the factors you need to consider before upgrading. Organizations frequently are delayed in their expected deployments due to things that they overlook when preparing for their upgrade.

Master It You are planning your Exchange Server 2013 upgrade from an earlier version. What are some key factors that you must consider when planning the upgrade?

Understand coexistence with legacy Exchange servers. Coexistence with earlier versions of Exchange Server is a necessary evil unless you are able to move all your Exchange Server data and functionality at one time. Coexistence means that you must keep your old Exchange servers running for one of a number of functions, including message transfer, email storage, public folder storage, or mailbox access. One of the primary goals of any upgrade should be to move your messaging services (and mailboxes) over to new servers as soon as possible.

Master It You are performing a normal upgrade from Exchange Server 2010 to Exchange Server 2013. Your desktop clients are a mix of Outlook 2003 and Outlook 2007. You quickly moved all your mailbox data to Exchange Server 2013. Why should you leave your Exchange Server 2010 mailbox servers online for a few weeks after the mailbox moves have completed?

Perform an interorganization migration. Interorganization migrations are by far the most difficult and disruptive migrations. These migrations move mailboxes as well as other messaging functions between two separate mail systems. User accounts and mailboxes usually have to be created for the new organization; user attributes, such as email addresses, phone numbers, and so forth must be transferred to the new organization. Metadata such as "reply-ability" of existing messages as well as folder rules and mailbox permissions must also be transferred.

Although simple tools are provided to move mailboxes from one Exchange Server organization to another, large or complex migrations may require third-party migration tools.

Master It You have a business subsidiary that has an Exchange Server 2007 organization with approximately 2,000 mailboxes; this Exchange Server organization is not part of the corporate Active Directory forest. The users all use Outlook 2010. You must move these mailboxes to Exchange Server 2013 in the corporate Active Directory forest. What four options are available to you to move email to the new organization?

Part 3

Recipient Administration

Chapter 12

Management Permissions and Role-based Access Control

In Exchange Server 2013, methodology for managing access permissions to user and administrative functionality is the same as it was in Exchange Server 2010. This technology, called Role-based Access Control (RBAC), provides more-powerful and -granular control over what people can do than what was available in earlier versions of Exchange.

To use it effectively, we need to take an in-depth look at how RBAC works and how it differs from the permission model in previous versions of Exchange. Then we'll examine the tools and processes for configuring and managing RBAC. After that, we can dig deeper into the topic of roles and how to assign them to users and administrators.

In this chapter, you will learn to:

◆ Determine what built-in roles and role groups provide you with the permissions you need

◆ Assign permissions to administrators using roles and role groups

◆ Grant permissions to end users for updating their address list information

◆ Create custom administration roles and assign them to administrators

◆ Audit RBAC changes using the Exchange Management Shell and built-in reports in the Exchange Administration Center

RBAC Basics

The goal in this section is to give you a broad and high-level understanding of what RBAC is and how it works. As we discuss these various topics throughout this chapter, we will build on this knowledge and you will gain deeper insights into RBAC. This will help you learn what RBAC can do for you and how you can use it.

Differences from Previous Exchange Versions

In the most basic sense, RBAC is the permissions model for Exchange Server 2013. Anyone who has had to customize permissions in Exchange versions prior to Exchange 2010 can understand the inconvenience of making permission changes in Active Directory and keeping track of what permission modifications were made. Permission configuration prior to RBAC's introduction used access control lists (ACLs) on various Active Directory objects. Each object to which you wanted to delegate permissions had its own ACL. Each ACL was further composed of multiple access control entries (ACEs) that defined what permissions each user or group had on that object. To make this process a bit more manageable, Exchange used property sets. A *property set* is a group of attributes that can share a common ACE. For example, instead of setting an ACE on 15 different attributes, those attributes could be added to a property set so that applying the ACE to the property set would update the ACLs on each of the attributes.

RBAC is a significantly different approach to solving this problem. Since the management of Exchange Server 2013 is brokered through PowerShell cmdlets, it makes more sense to apply the permissions at the administrative level instead of on the Active Directory object. RBAC does this by using roles to define which Exchange cmdlets can be run and what parameters can be used with those cmdlets. By moving these permissions to the cmdlet level, you ensure that access control is enforced by PowerShell. This allows Exchange to do some really powerful things, such as presenting administrators with only the cmdlets that they have permissions to run.

AVAILABLE COMMANDS BASED ON ROLE GROUP ASSIGNMENT

If an administrator doesn't have access to run the `Set-Mailbox` cmdlet, the cmdlet will not even be available to that administrator when the Exchange Management Shell (EMS) is used. Not only will the cmdlet not be found if the administrator tries to run it, but it won't even be a part of tab completion in the EMS.

How RBAC Works

To illustrate how RBAC works, let's look at an example. Suppose that in your Exchange infrastructure, you have a group of people who provide support for your end users. This group is primarily responsible for creating new accounts, mail-enabling users, configuring mailbox properties, and similar tasks. To enable this group of people to do their job, you could assign the Mail Recipients role to their accounts. When these users are assigned this role, they gain the permissions to run the Exchange cmdlets that this role allows. In this example, the users will have access to cmdlets, such as `Enable-Mailbox`, `Set-Mailbox`, and `Get-MailboxStatistics`.

The previous example illustrates only one aspect of RBAC: the ability to assign roles to various levels of Exchange administrators. But there is another aspect of RBAC that allows you to assign roles to end users. The types of roles that end users would have are different than the roles that an Exchange administrator would have. Whereas the Exchange administrator's roles are geared toward managing Exchange, the end user's roles are geared toward managing the end-user's contact information, mailbox settings, marketplace apps, team mailboxes, and distribution groups. For example, if you want your users to be able to update their own phone numbers in the global address list (GAL), you can assign them the MyContactInformation or MyPersonalInformation role.

To understand how RBAC defines and distributes roles, you will need to become familiar with a few new terms:

Management Role   A management role, also referred to simply as a *role*, represents a grouping of Exchange cmdlets that can be run by people who are assigned the role. These cmdlets are also referred to as management role entries.

Management Role Entry   A management role entry, also known simply as a *role entry*, is the term used to refer to each Exchange cmdlet and parameter that are defined on a role. There is also a special type of role that allows your role entries to be PowerShell scripts or non-Exchange cmdlets.

Scope   The scope defines the boundary of objects that a role can be applied to. By default, the scope of impact on roles is not very restrictive. However, you can create custom scopes that make the scope of impact for a role more restrictive, such as restricting a role to only an organizational unit (OU) of recipients.

Role Group   A role group is a security group in Active Directory that defines who gets which roles applied to them. Along with the specific roles, a role group can also define the scope to which those roles are applied. An administrator can create a role group that contains a collection of common roles that are grouped together in a related job function. For example, there is a built-in role group in Exchange called Help Desk. This role group contains the roles that help desk personnel would need to perform their job function. Rather than assigning management roles directly to Active Directory accounts, we recommend that you add the account to the appropriate role group.

Role Assignment Policy   A role assignment policy is similar to a role group, because it is a representation of a collection of management roles. However, the role assignment policy is used for distributing roles to end users, whereas the role group is used for assigning roles to Exchange administrators.

Management Role Assignment   Management role assignments, also known as *role assignments*, are what pull everything together. RBAC defines who (the role group or user account) has what permissions (the roles) and where (the scope) those permissions are in effect. The role assignment pulls this together by assigning a management role to a role group, a user account, or a role assignment policy. Each time a role is assigned to a unique role group, user account, or role assignment policy, a different role assignment is created. Each role assignment assigns only one role to one role group, user account, or role assignment policy.

Two different processes define how the RBAC components interact with one another. The process for assigning permissions to Exchange administrators is different than the process for assigning permissions to end users, though there is some overlap. In both instances, management roles are used to define what the assignee can do. Management roles contain management role entries. The difference, however, is in how management roles are assigned.

RBAC for Administrators

When assigning roles to administrators, management role groups are the basic method used for defining which roles administrators have. These groups are universal security groups in Active Directory. When you want to give an administrator a group of roles, you add the administrator's Active Directory account to the appropriate management role group. Each of these groups is assigned one or more management roles.

Management role assignments allow you to assign one or more management roles to management role groups. For example, the Organization Management role group has several roles associated with it. Each of these roles is associated with the role group by using a unique management role assignment. Within this management role assignment, you can also define the scope of the role. Suppose you want to create a group of administrators who can manage only the mailboxes belonging to the users in the Baltimore OU. You can create a role group called Baltimore Mailbox Administrators and use a management role assignment to assign the Mail Recipients role to that group for only users in the Baltimore OU.

To better illustrate how these components come together, see Figure 12.1. Management role entries are defined on management roles. Management role assignments tie a management role to a management role group. Administrator accounts are added as members of the role group. Once in the group, those administrators have access to the functionality defined by the roles that are assigned to the group.

FIGURE 12.1

The interaction among the RBAC components for granting permissions to administrators

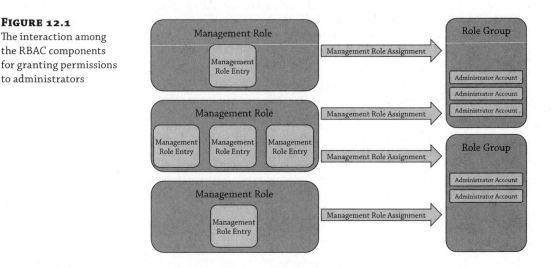

RBAC FOR END USERS

The process for assigning roles to end users is different than the process for assigning roles to administrators. End users still use management roles and management role entries. However, the roles are assigned to user accounts using a role assignment policy. The role assignment policy has management roles assigned, just as role groups do. The difference is that role assignment policies aren't groups to which users can be added. Therefore, a user cannot have multiple role assignment policies. Like other types of policies in Exchange, a user account can have only one role assignment policy assigned to it. The roles that users have in Exchange are defined by that policy.

Figure 12.2 describes how this process takes place for user accounts. Contrasting this with Figure 12.1, you can see that each end-user account gains its roles by specifying the policy that takes effect on it, but each administrator account gains its roles by being a part of the role group.

Managing RBAC

As you are managing RBAC, multiple areas need your attention. When you deploy Exchange, you have to manage the various RBAC components. This work consists of assigning the roles, modifying role groups, setting role assignments, and much more. You will also have to manage the role distribution, which consists of managing the role groups and the role assignment policies. And before anyone can manage those things, you must delegate the RBAC management permissions to the appropriate people.

FIGURE 12.2
How RBAC is used to grant permissions to end users

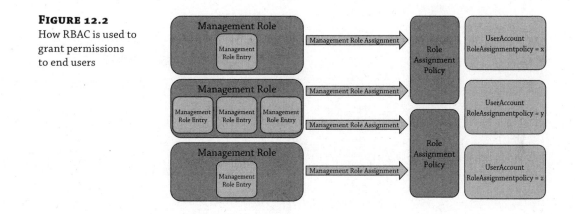

There are primarily two built-in tools you can use to manage these various aspects of RBAC. There is also a downloadable tool from www.codeplex.com named RBAC Manager. In this section, we'll look at these tools and discuss what they enable you to do at a high level. Throughout the remainder of this chapter, we will be using these tools and examining them in more detail.

Exchange Administration Center

The first tool that we will look at is the Exchange Administration Center (EAC). The EAC is a web-based management console used to manage Exchange Server 2013 features and services.

When you log into the EAC, you will navigate to the Permissions task in the Feature pane. Notice the two tabs, Admin Roles and User Roles, shown in Figure 12.3. If you don't have these tabs available, you likely don't have the appropriate permissions to manage the roles.

FIGURE 12.3
Managing administrator roles and user roles in the EAC

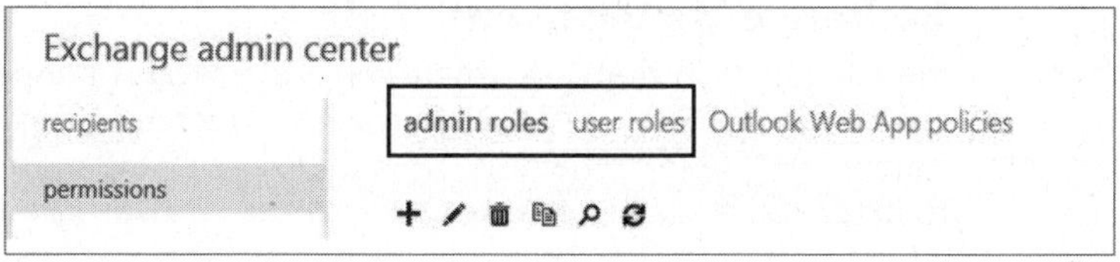

When you click the Admin Roles tab, the role groups are listed alphabetically. This list includes both the built-in role groups and any custom role groups that you may have created. If you select a role group, the Details pane on the right will display the description of the role group, the roles that the group is assigned, and the members of the group. This is shown in Figure 12.4.

FIGURE 12.4
Viewing role group details in the EAC

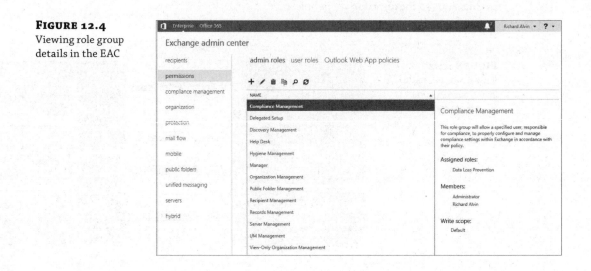

You can also create a new role group, delete a role group, copy a role group, and edit the role group. The steps for doing this are described in the "Distributing Roles" section, later in this chapter.

When you click the User Roles tab in the EAC, you are presented with a list of role assignment policies that exist in your organization. In a manner similar to the Admin Roles tab, you can select the role assignment policy from the list and view the details of the policy in the Details pane on the right. You can also edit the user roles that are assigned to this policy, create a new assignment policy, and delete an assignment policy that is not associated with a mailbox. This is covered later in the section, "Distributing Roles." Figure 12.5 shows the information available on the User Roles tab of the EAC.

This is the extent to which you can manage RBAC inside the EAC. Therefore, most of the tasks required to set up RBAC and configure it will require you to use the EMS or RBAC Manager.

Exchange Management Shell

The EMS is the built-in tool where you will probably be spending most of your time when you are managing RBAC. Table 12.1 lists which cmdlets are available for managing each RBAC component. These cmdlets are further discussed and used throughout the remainder of this chapter.

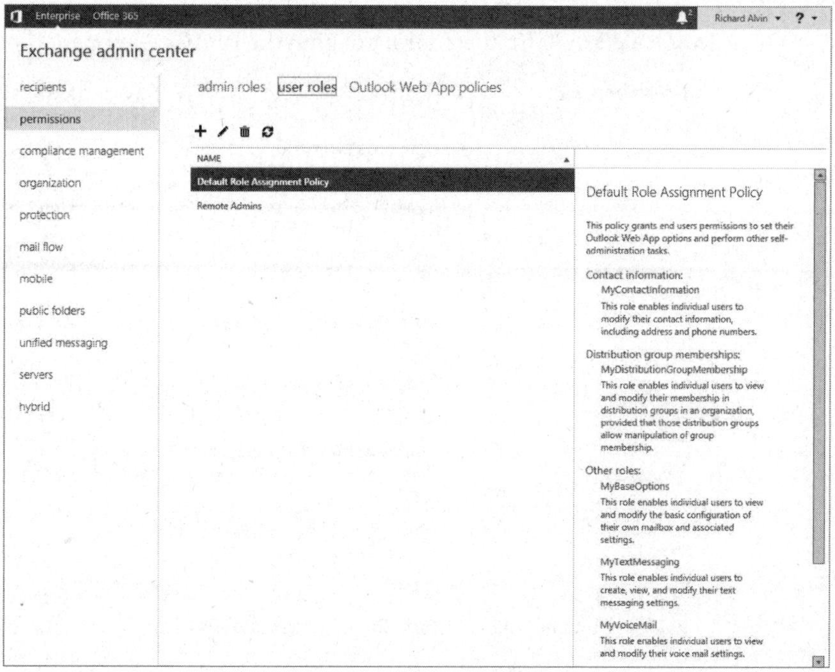

FIGURE 12.5
Viewing the user role information in the EAC

Exchange admin center

recipients

permissions

compliance management

organization

protection

mail flow

mobile

public folders

unified messaging

servers

hybrid

admin roles   **user roles**   Outlook Web App policies

NAME

Default Role Assignment Policy

Remote Admins

Default Role Assignment Policy

This policy grants end users permissions to set their Outlook Web App options and perform other self-administration tasks.

Contact information:
MyContactInformation
This role enables individual users to modify their contact information, including address and phone numbers.

Distribution group memberships:
MyDistributionGroupMembership
This role enables individual users to view and modify their membership in distribution groups in an organization, provided that those distribution groups allow manipulation of group membership.

Other roles:
MyBaseOptions
This role enables individual users to view and modify the basic configuration of their own mailbox and associated settings.

MyTextMessaging
This role enables individual users to create, view, and modify their text messaging settings.

MyVoiceMail
This role enables individual users to view and modify their voice mail settings.

TABLE 12.1:   Cmdlets for managing the RBAC components

COMPONENT	CMDLET	DESCRIPTION
Management role	New-ManagementRole	Creates a new role
	Get-ManagementRole	Gets the list of roles or the properties of a specific role
	Remove-ManagementRole	Deletes a role
Management role entry	Add-ManagementRoleEntry	Adds a role entry to an existing role
	Get-ManagementRoleEntry	Retrieves the list of role entries on a role
	Remove-ManagementRoleEntry	Removes a role entry from a role
	Set-ManagementRoleEntry	Sets the parameters on an already defined role entry
Role group	Get-RoleGroup	Gets the list of role groups or the properties of a specific role group

TABLE 12.1: Cmdlets for managing the RBAC components *(CONTINUED)*

COMPONENT	CMDLET	DESCRIPTION
	New-RoleGroup	Creates a new role group
	Remove-RoleGroup	Deletes a role group
	Set-RoleGroup	Changes the properties of the role group
	Add-RoleGroupMember	Adds an administrator to a role group
	Get-RoleGroupMember	Lists the members of a role group
	Remove-RoleGroupMember	Removes an administrator from a role group
	Update-RoleGroupMember	Modifies the role group membership in bulk
Role assignment policy	Get-RoleAssignmentPolicy	Retrieves the list of role assignment policies or retrieves the details of a specific role assignment policy
	New-RoleAssignmentPolicy	Creates a new role assignment policy
	Remove-RoleAssignmentPolicy	Deletes a role assignment policy
	Set-RoleAssignmentPolicy	Configures the properties of a role assignment policy, including whether the policy is the default policy for the domain
Management role assignment	Get-ManagementRoleAssignment	Retrieves the list of role assignments or the details of a specified role assignment
	New-ManagementRoleAssignment	Creates a new role assignment
	Remove-ManagementRoleAssignment	Deletes a role assignment
	Set-ManagementRoleAssignment	Configures the properties of the role assignment, including the scope that the assignment uses
Management scope	Get-ManagementScope	Retrieves management scopes, orphaned scopes, and exclusive or regular scopes

TABLE 12.1:   Cmdlets for managing the RBAC components   *(CONTINUED)*

COMPONENT	CMDLET	DESCRIPTION
	New-ManagementScope	Creates a regular or exclusive management scope for recipients or Exchange objects
	Remove-ManagementScope	Removes management scopes that are orphaned
	Set-ManagementScope	Updates the existing configuration of a management scope

RBAC Manager

RBAC Manager provides a GUI interface to manage the implementation of RBAC within your organization. You can perform common RBAC management tasks through the EAC; however, some tasks cannot be performed through the EAC.

RBAC Manager connects to a specific Exchange Server 2013 server and domain controller, and you can specify a user account to connect with. RBAC Manager, by default, also maintains a log file on the computer that RBAC Manager was accessed from.

In the RBAC Manager window there are four tabs that can be used to manage your RBAC configuration:

- Show Management Roles
- Show Assignment Policies
- Show Role Groups
- Show Management Scopes

Figure 12.6 shows the tabs available in RBAC Manager—from left to right, they are Show Management Roles, Show Role Assignment Policies, Show Role Groups, and Show Management Scopes.

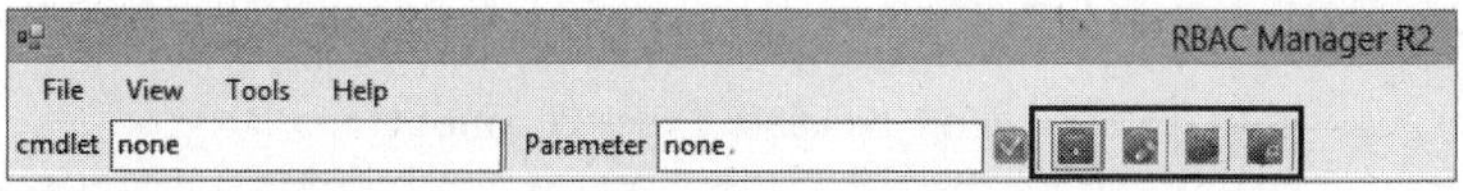

FIGURE 12.6
Tabs to manage roles, role assignment policies, role groups, and scopes

The Show Management Roles tab (brown briefcase image) displays all the built-in management roles that are created during the installation of Exchange Server 2013. Any custom management roles are stored underneath the parent management role. Built-in management roles are listed in green and custom management roles are listed in blue.

The Show Role Assignment Policies tab displays all the mailbox role assignment policies in the right pane. Much like the Show Management Roles tab, the default role assignment policy that is created during install is listed in green and any new role assignment policy is listed in blue.

To see all the administrators and security groups that have been assigned a role, you can use the Show Role Groups tab. All security groups that have been assigned a role are displayed as green and roles that have been assigned directly to a user are displayed in blue.

The last tab, Show Management Scopes, provides a list of all the custom management scopes that you have created in your organization.

Defining Roles

The management role is the key component of RBAC. This section will go into a little more detail about roles and show you how to choose an existing role to assign and how to create a custom role if it's necessary.

What's in a Role?

At the most basic level, a management role is a grouping of Exchange cmdlets and parameters. Anyone who is assigned the management role has permissions to execute those cmdlets with those parameters. To illustrate this more clearly, let's examine a management role. The Mailbox Import Export role is a built-in role in Exchange, meaning that Exchange created this role by default during setup. There are many built-in roles, but we'll look at Mailbox Import Export in particular for this example.

The Mailbox Import Export role allows assignees to run the following cmdlets:

- `Set-MailboxExportRequest`
- `New-MailboxImportRequest`
- `New-MailboxExportRequest`
- `Get-Notification`
- `Set-MailboxImportRequest`
- `Get-MailboxImportRequest`
- `Set-Notification`
- `Get-MailboxExportRequest`
- `Get-Mailbox`
- `Write-AdminAuditLog`
- `Suspend-MailboxImportRequest`
- `Suspend-MailboxExportRequest`
- `Set-ADServerSettings`
- `Search-Mailbox`
- `Resume-MailboxImportRequest`
- `Resume-MailboxExportRequest`

- Remove-MailboxImportRequest

- Remove-MailboxExportRequest

- Get-MailboxImportRequestStatistics

- Get-MailboxExportRequestStatistics

To get the list of the management role entries for a management role, run this command:

```
Get-ManagementRoleEntry "Mailbox Import Export\*" | fl name
```

Having the Get-Mailbox cmdlet as a part of this role is especially important. If you don't have any Get-* cmdlets defined in your roles, the assignee cannot retrieve the data they are modifying. With each one of these cmdlets, the role defines which parameters the assignee can use. If the parameter isn't in this list, it can't be used. For example, the Mailbox Import Export role doesn't specify that the assignees can use the Database parameter with the Get-Mailbox cmdlet. Because of this, the assignee can't list all the mailboxes on a database unless they are assigned another role that has those permissions.

To get the list of the parameters that are available for a specific role entry, run this command:

```
(Get-ManagementRoleEntry "Mailbox Import Export\get-mailbox").parameters
```

Since PowerShell is the underlying command-execution engine in Exchange, you can see how this level of granularity is very powerful. In RBAC terms, these cmdlets are referred to as management role entries. There is another type of management role that allows you to use PowerShell scripts and non-Exchange cmdlets as management role entries, but we'll look at that a little later, in the section, "Unscoped Top-Level Roles: The Exception." Figure 12.7 shows the relationship between management roles and management role entries.

FIGURE 12.7
The relationship between a management role and its management role entries

As discussed earlier in this chapter, the RBAC data is stored in Active Directory. Each management role has an associated object of the object type msExchRole in Active Directory. The role objects are stored in the Configuration Naming Context inside the following container: Services\Microsoft Exchange\Org Name\RBAC\Roles. If you were to examine this in ADSI Edit, you would see something similar to Figure 12.8.

FIGURE 12.8

The role objects in Active Directory

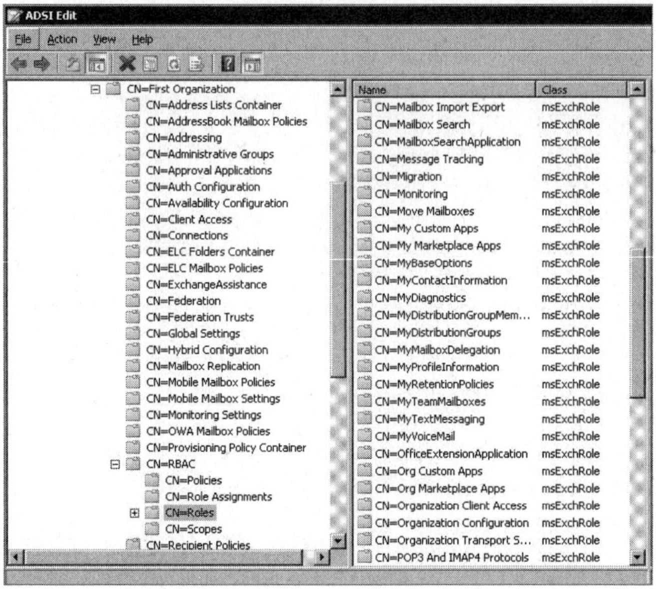

If you were to open up the Mailbox Import Export role object (CN=Mailbox Import Export), you would see the properties dialog shown in Figure 12.9.

FIGURE 12.9

The properties for the Mailbox Import Export role object

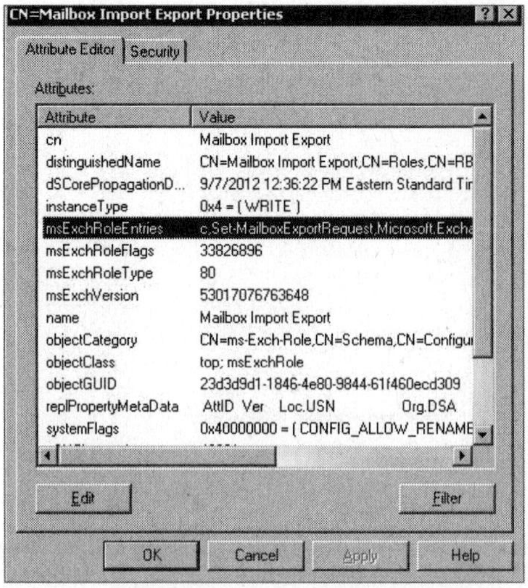

You will notice that one of the attributes on this object is the msExchRoleEntries attribute. This is a multivalued string attribute that lists each management role entry and the parameters that role assignees can run. Figure 12.10 shows the values that the Mailbox Import Export object has for its msExchRoleEntries attributes, as viewed in ADSI Edit.

FIGURE 12.10

The management role entries for the Mailbox Import Export role as seen in ADSI Edit

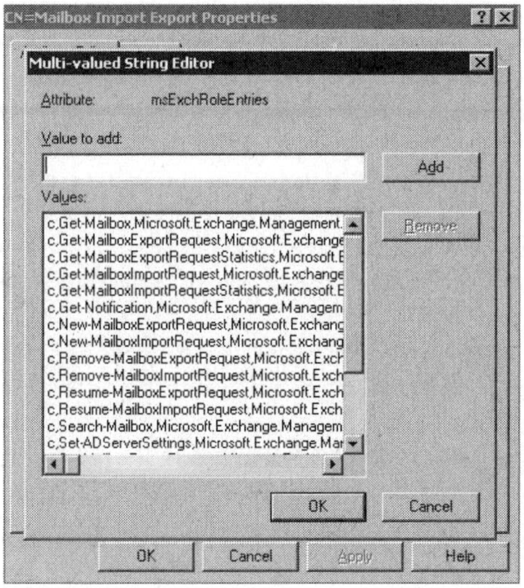

So as you can see, management role entries are added to management roles as an attribute of the management role. The management role itself is its own object. Each of these management role entries defines an Exchange cmdlet that an assignee can run.

Choosing a Role

Exchange already has several management roles defined out of the box. These defined roles give you a great degree of flexibility without having to create and customize your own management roles. For the sake of simplicity and manageability, these built-in roles should be used whenever possible.

But how do you know which built-in role to use? Let's pretend that you didn't know the Mailbox Import Export role existed. However, you have an ongoing legal investigation and you need to give your lawyer, Richard, the ability to import mail stored on the personal folder store to a specific mailbox. To determine which role you need to assign to Richard, you can use the Get-ManagementRoleEntry cmdlet. With it, you can specify wildcards to determine the following:

◆ Which management role contains a particular management role entry

◆ Which management role entries are allowed for a particular management role

To determine which role allows Richard to run the New-MailboxImportRequest cmdlet, you can run the following EMS command:

```
Get-ManagementRoleEntry "*\New-MailboxImportRequest"
```

Name	Role	Parameters
New-MailboxImportRequest	Mailbox Import Export	{AcceptLargeDataLoss…

As you can see from the command's output, the `New-MailboxImportRequest` cmdlet is added only to the Mailbox Import Export role. There are no other options by default in Exchange. If you want to use the built-in roles, you must assign the Mailbox Import Export role to Richard.

You will also notice that in the command we specified `*\New-MailboxImportRequest` as the management role entry that we were looking for. When working with management role entries, the identity of each entry is in the following format: *management role\management role entry*. By specifying a wildcard character (*) in place of the *management role* portion, we told the cmdlet to retrieve every management role that has the `New-MailboxImportRequest` cmdlet defined on it. You can use wildcards in different places and retrieve different results.

For example, let's pretend that you stumbled across the Mailbox Import Export role and you want to find out what management role entries this management role allows. Again, you can use the `Get-ManagementRoleEntry` cmdlet to find this information. However, this time you will place the wildcard at the end of the role entry's identity instead of the beginning. The following command retrieves the management role entries that the Mailbox Import Export management role allows:

```
Get-ManagementRoleEntry "Mailbox Import Export\*"
```

Name	Role	Parameters
Set-MailboxExportRequest	Mailbox Import Export	{AcceptLargeDataLoss…
New-MailboxImportRequest	Mailbox Import Export	{AcceptLargeDataLoss…
New-MailboxExportRequest	Mailbox Import Export	{AcceptLargeDataLoss…
Get-Notification	Mailbox Import Export	{Debug…
Set-MailboxImportRequest	Mailbox Import Export	{AcceptLargeDataLoss…
Get-MailboxImportRequest	Mailbox Import Export	{BatchName…
Set-Notification	Mailbox Import Export	{Confirm…
Get-MailboxExportRequest	Mailbox Import Export	{BatchName…
Get-Mailbox	Mailbox Import Export	{Anr…
Write-AdminAuditLog	Mailbox Import Export	{Comment…
Suspend-MailboxImportRequest	Mailbox Import Export	{Confirm…
Suspend-MailboxExportRequest	Mailbox Import Export	{Confirm…
Set-ADServerSettings	Mailbox Import Export	{…
Search-Mailbox	Mailbox Import Export	{Confirm…
Resume-MailboxImportRequest	Mailbox Import Export	{Confirm…
Resume-MailboxExportRequest	Mailbox Import Export	{Confirm…
Remove-MailboxImportRequest	Mailbox Import Export	{Confirm…
Remove-MailboxExportRequest	Mailbox Import Export	{Confirm…
Get-MailboxImportRequestSta...	Mailbox Import Export	{Debug…
Get-MailboxExportRequestSta...	Mailbox Import Export	{Debug …

By using `Mailbox Import Export\*` in the command, we told the cmdlet to retrieve every management role entry that is defined on the Mailbox Import Export management role. When deciding which roles you need to assign to administrators, it's very important to look at not only what role allows the administrator to do their job but also what other permissions the administrator will gain when using one of the built-in roles.

Customizing Roles

You should always turn to the built-in management roles first and determine if you can use what's already there before attempting to customize your own roles. However, there may be times when the built-in roles offer you too much access. To illustrate this, let's continue with the scenario of your legal struggles. In the previous section, we determined that to give Richard, your lawyer, the ability to import mail stored in PST files, you could assign him the Mailbox Import Export role. This role allows him to run these cmdlets:

- `Set-MailboxExportRequest`
- `New-MailboxImportRequest`
- `New-MailboxExportRequest`
- `Get-Notification`
- `Set-MailboxImportRequest`
- `Get-MailboxImportRequest`
- `Set-Notification`
- `Get-MailboxExportRequest`
- `Get-Mailbox`
- `Write-AdminAuditLog`
- `Suspend-MailboxImportRequest`
- `Suspend-MailboxExportRequest`
- `Set-ADServerSettings`
- `Search-Mailbox`
- `Resume-MailboxImportRequest`
- `Resume-MailboxExportRequest`
- `Remove-MailboxImportRequest`
- `Remove-MailboxExportRequest`
- `Get-MailboxImportRequestStatistics`
- `Get-MailboxExportRequestStatistics`

Now let's suppose that you run a very tight ship. When you examined the Mailbox Import Export role, you noticed that not only does the role give Richard the ability to import mail, but it also gives him the ability to export it. Knowing this, you've decided that you don't want your lawyer to be able to export mail from people's mailboxes. In this case, you can create a custom management role.

HOW A CUSTOM ROLE WORKS

To create a new custom management role, you must start with an existing management role. You cannot create a custom management role from scratch (however, there is one exception that we will discuss shortly, in the section, "Unscoped Top-Level Roles: The Exception"). Each custom role that you create must inherit properties from an existing management role that is already in place. This forms a parent/child relationship between an existing role (the parent) and the custom role (the child). Let's take a closer look at the Mailbox Import Export role to understand this more clearly.

To fulfill the scenario that we just discussed of allowing Richard to only import mail, you would have to create a custom role that is similar to the Mailbox Import Export role but that doesn't have the ability to export mail. Since every custom role must have a parent management role that already exists, we can make the Mailbox Import Export role the parent to our new custom role. We'll call this new role Mailbox Import Only.

When we create the custom role, it will be able to use only the same management role entries that the parent role uses. This will give the Mailbox Import Only role access to the same management role entries defined on its parent role, Mailbox Import Export. We cannot add any role entries to our new custom role that aren't already included in the Mailbox Import Export role. This restriction applies not only to the cmdlets but also to the parameters on the cmdlets. Because of this, the role entries that the child role can have are limited to the role entries defined on the parent. Even though we don't have the ability to add role entries to the Mailbox Import Only role, we do have the ability to remove them. In this case, you would remove access to all the `MailboxExportRequest` cmdlets.

This leaves the Mailbox Import Only role without any of the `MailboxExportRequest` cmdlets. Figure 12.11 illustrates the relationship between the parent and child roles.

FIGURE 12.11
The relationship between a parent role and a child role

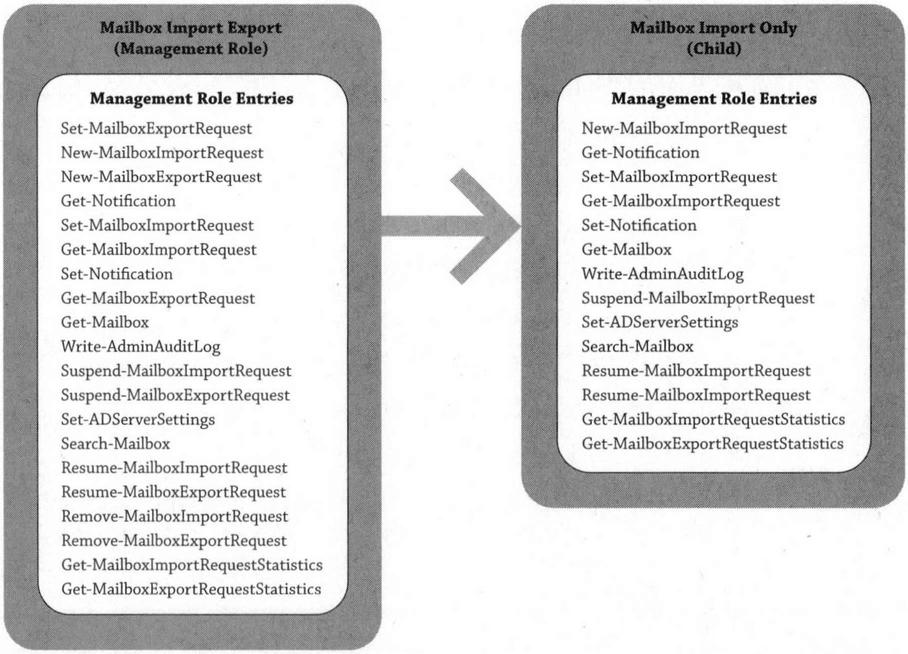

Mailbox Import Export (Management Role)	Mailbox Import Only (Child)
Management Role Entries	**Management Role Entries**
Set-MailboxExportRequest	New-MailboxImportRequest
New-MailboxImportRequest	Get-Notification
New-MailboxExportRequest	Set-MailboxImportRequest
Get-Notification	Get-MailboxImportRequest
Set-MailboxImportRequest	Set-Notification
Get-MailboxImportRequest	Get-Mailbox
Set-Notification	Write-AdminAuditLog
Get-MailboxExportRequest	Suspend-MailboxImportRequest
Get-Mailbox	Set-ADServerSettings
Write-AdminAuditLog	Search-Mailbox
Suspend-MailboxImportRequest	Resume-MailboxImportRequest
Suspend-MailboxExportRequest	Resume-MailboxImportRequest
Set-ADServerSettings	Get-MailboxImportRequestStatistics
Search-Mailbox	Get-MailboxExportRequestStatistics
Resume-MailboxImportRequest	
Resume-MailboxExportRequest	
Remove-MailboxImportRequest	
Remove-MailboxExportRequest	
Get-MailboxImportRequestStatistics	
Get-MailboxExportRequestStatistics	

DEFINING CUSTOM ROLES

To create custom roles, you must use the EMS or RBAC Manager. The EAC does not give you the ability to manage custom roles. When defining these roles, you will use the following cmdlets:

New-ManagementRole   Creates a new custom role

Remove-ManagementRole   Deletes a custom role that you previously created

Add-ManagementRoleEntry   Adds a role entry onto an existing role

Remove-ManagementRoleEntry   Removes a role entry that you previously added

Set-ManagementRoleEntry   Adjusts the parameters that can be used on a role entry that has already been added to a role

To continue with the legal scenario, let's create the Mailbox Import Only role using the New-ManagementRole cmdlet. When using the cmdlet, you specify the name of the new role and the parent from which the role is inheriting its management role entries. The following example creates the Mailbox Import Only role that we've been discussing:

```
New-ManagementRole "Mailbox Import Only" -Parent "Mailbox Import Export"


Name                           RoleType
----                           --------
Mailbox Import Only            MailboxImportExport
```

You can run the Get-ManagementRoleEntry cmdlet on this newly created role to see that, by default, the custom role defines all the same role entries that the parent role has:

```
Get-ManagementRoleEntry "Mailbox Import Only\*"
Name                        Role                    Parameters
----                        ----                    ----------
Set-MailboxExportRequest    Mailbox Import Only     {AcceptLargeDataLoss…
New-MailboxImportRequest    Mailbox Import Only     {AcceptLargeDataLoss…
New-MailboxExportRequest    Mailbox Import Only     {AcceptLargeDataLoss…
Get-Notification            Mailbox Import Only     {Debug…
Set-MailboxImportRequest    Mailbox Import Only     {AcceptLargeDataLoss…
Get-MailboxImportRequest    Mailbox Import Only     {BatchName…
Set-Notification            Mailbox Import Only     {Confirm…
Get-MailboxExportRequest    Mailbox Import Only     {BatchName…
Get-Mailbox                 Mailbox Import Only     {Anr…
Write-AdminAuditLog         Mailbox Import Only     {Comment…
Suspend-MailboxImportRequest Mailbox Import Only    {Confirm…
Suspend-MailboxExportRequest Mailbox Import Only    {Confirm…
Set-ADServerSettings        Mailbox Import Only     {…
Search-Mailbox              Mailbox Import Only     {Confirm…
Resume-MailboxImportRequest Mailbox Import Only     {Confirm…
Resume-MailboxExportRequest Mailbox Import Only     {Confirm…
Remove-MailboxImportRequest Mailbox Import Only     {Confirm…
Remove-MailboxExportRequest Mailbox Import Only     {Confirm…
Get-MailboxImportRequestSta... Mailbox Import Only  {Debug…
Get-MailboxExportRequestSta... Mailbox Import Only  {Debug …
```

Now that the role is created, you can remove the `MailboxExportRequest` cmdlets from the list of role entries. To do so, you run the `Remove-ManagementRoleEntry` cmdlet and specify the role entry that you want to remove. Since there are multiple cmdlets with `MailboxExportRequest`, you will first run `Get-ManagementRoleEntry` and pipe the results to `Remove-ManagementRoleEntry`. When you run this command, you will be prompted with a confirmation message that asks you if you are sure that you want to remove the role entry. You can bypass this message by adding the `-Confirm:$False` parameter to the command. The following example demonstrates the command that you would use to remove the `MailboxExportRequest` cmdlets from the Mailbox Import Only role, bypassing the confirmation message:

```
Get-ManagementRoleEntry "Mailbox Import Only\*-MailboxExportRequest" | Remove-
ManagementRoleEntry -confirm:$false
```

To verify that the role entry was removed, you can run the `Get-ManagementRoleEntry` cmdlet again to retrieve the management role entries on the management role. You will notice that all the management role entries for `MailboxExportRequest` have been removed:

```
Get-ManagementRoleEntry "Mailbox Import Only\*"
Name                           Role                    Parameters
----                           ----                    ----------
Get-MailboxExportRequestSta... Mailbox Import Only     {Debug, DomainControl
Get-MailboxImportRequestSta... Mailbox Import Only     {Debug, DomainControl
Remove-MailboxImportRequest    Mailbox Import Only     {Confirm, Debug, Doma
Resume-MailboxImportRequest    Mailbox Import Only     {Confirm, Debug, Doma
Search-Mailbox                 Mailbox Import Only     {Confirm, Debug, Dele
Set-ADServerSettings           Mailbox Import Only     {ConfigurationDomainC
Suspend-MailboxImportRequest   Mailbox Import Only     {Confirm, Debug, Doma
Write-AdminAuditLog            Mailbox Import Only     {Comment, Confirm, De
Get-Mailbox                    Mailbox Import Only     {Anr, Credential, Deb
Set-Notification               Mailbox Import Only     {Confirm, Debug, Doma
Get-MailboxImportRequest       Mailbox Import Only     {BatchName, Database,
Set-MailboxImportRequest       Mailbox Import Only     {AcceptLargeDataLoss,
Get-Notification               Mailbox Import Only     {Debug, DomainControl
```

UNSCOPED TOP-LEVEL ROLES: THE EXCEPTION

Earlier in this section, we stated that there was an exception to the fact that custom management roles require an existing management role to be the parent. That exception is a special type of management role called the *unscoped top-level role*. This type of role does not have a parent. The unscoped top-level role allows you to define both PowerShell scripts and non-Exchange cmdlets as its role entries. This type of role is highly customized, so it can't affectively have a parent role because there is no starting point for it. You would typically want to use an unscoped top-level role when you want to strictly limit what an administrator can do, such as only giving them access to predefined scripts.

By default, no one has permissions to create unscoped top-level roles. If you want to grant these permissions to an administrator, you will need to assign the role called Unscoped Role Management to the administrator who needs to create unscoped top-level roles.

To create the unscoped top-level role, use the New-ManagementRole cmdlet with the UnscopedTopLevel parameter. If the UnscopedTopLevel parameter isn't available, that means you have not been assigned the Unscoped Role Management role. The following example creates an unscoped top-level role called Run Custom Scripts:

```
New-ManagementRole "Run Custom Scripts" -UnScopedTopLevel
```

```
Name                                          RoleType
----                                          --------
Run Custom Scripts                            UnScoped
```

After the role is created, you can use the Add-ManagementRoleEntry cmdlet to add custom scripts or non-Exchange cmdlets as role entries on the role. When you run this cmdlet, specify the script with the syntax of *Management Role\Script*. Also specify the type of role entry that you are adding (script or cmdlet), and use the UnScopedTopLevel parameter. You can also use the Parameters parameter to specify what parameters can be used with the script. For example, to add the custom script called CheckServerHealth.ps1 to the Run Custom Scripts role, you would use the following command:

```
Add-ManagementRoleEntry "Run Custom Scripts\CheckServerHealth.ps1" ↵
-UnScopedTopLevel -Type Script -Parameters CheckServices, CheckLogs
```

Lastly, you need to assign the unscoped role to a security group or a user.

Distributing Roles

After you have defined the roles you want to use in your RBAC implementation, you must distribute those roles to administrators and end users. This section will discuss the important aspects of role distribution and show you how to distribute roles to both administrators and end users.

Determining Where Roles Will Be Applied

When distributing roles, one important detail that should not be overlooked is where those roles apply. In RBAC, this is referred to as the role's *scope*. The scope defines what objects (such as recipients or servers) the role can impact. As you'll see throughout this section, scopes are extremely flexible. They allow roles to be applied throughout the organization or even restricted to just a particular OU of recipients in Active Directory.

INHERITED SCOPES

Every role has a scope. When a role is created, it has a default scope, also known as an *implicit* scope. There are two types of implicit scopes: a recipient scope and a configuration scope. The recipient scope defines which recipients the role can impact. The configuration scope defines which configuration components the role can impact. To illustrate how this applies to a role, let's look at our example of the Mailbox Import Export role. We can use the Get-ManagementRole cmdlet to view the implicit scope defined on this role:

```
Get-ManagementRole "Mailbox Import Export" | fl *scope*
```

```
ImplicitRecipientReadScope  : Organization
```

```
ImplicitRecipientWriteScope : Organization
ImplicitConfigReadScope     : OrganizationConfig
ImplicitConfigWriteScope    : OrganizationConfig
```

The first thing you will notice is that there are four scope attributes on the role. Each type of scope (recipient and configuration) has both a read scope and a write scope associated with it. In most cases, the read and write scope are the same. However, there are a few roles where they are different. If you run the following command, you can see the roles that have different read and write scopes defined. As you can tell from the output of the command, the cases where the read and write scope differ make sense. For example, the View-only Configuration role can read the configuration of Exchange but not write to it.

```
Get-ManagementRole | where { ↵
$_.ImplicitRecipientReadScope -ne $_.ImplicitRecipientWriteScope -or ↵
$_.ImplicitConfigReadScope -ne $_.ImplicitConfigWriteScope} | ↵
fl Name, *scope*

Name                        : Legal Hold
ImplicitRecipientReadScope  : Organization
ImplicitRecipientWriteScope : Organization
ImplicitConfigReadScope     : OrganizationConfig
ImplicitConfigWriteScope    : None

Name                        : View-Only Configurat
ImplicitRecipientReadScope  : Organization
ImplicitRecipientWriteScope : None
ImplicitConfigReadScope     : OrganizationConfig
ImplicitConfigWriteScope    : None

Name                        : View-Only Recipients
ImplicitRecipientReadScope  : Organization
ImplicitRecipientWriteScope : None
ImplicitConfigReadScope     : OrganizationConfig
ImplicitConfigWriteScope    : None

Name                        : MyDistributionGroups
ImplicitRecipientReadScope  : MyGAL
ImplicitRecipientWriteScope : MyDistributionGroups
ImplicitConfigReadScope     : OrganizationConfig
ImplicitConfigWriteScope    : None

Name                        : MyMailboxDelegation
ImplicitRecipientReadScope  : MyGAL
ImplicitRecipientWriteScope : MailboxICanDelegate
ImplicitConfigReadScope     : OrganizationConfig
ImplicitConfigWriteScope    : None

Name                        : View-Only Audit Logs
ImplicitRecipientReadScope  : Organization
```

```
ImplicitRecipientWriteScope : None
ImplicitConfigReadScope     : OrganizationConfig
ImplicitConfigWriteScope    : None
```

Table 12.2 shows the various types of the scope parameters and what each of these values means.

TABLE 12.2:   Implicit scope values

SCOPE	APPLIES TO RECIPIENT SCOPE	APPLIES TO CONFIGURATION SCOPE	DESCRIPTION
MyDistributionGroups	Yes	No	If in the read scope, allows read access to distribution groups owned by the user. If in the write scope, allows users to create or modify distribution lists that they own.
MyGAL	Yes	No	View the properties of recipients in the GAL. Valid only with the read scope.
None	Yes	Yes	Disallows access to the scope that it's applied to.
Organization	Yes	No	If in the read scope, gives users read access to all recipients in the organization. If in the write scope, gives users the ability to create or modify recipients in the organization.
OrganizationConfig	No	Yes	If in the read scope, allows the user to view the configuration of any server in the organization. If in the write scope, the user can modify configuration settings on any server.
Self	Yes	No	If in the read scope, users can only view their own properties. If in the write scope, users can modify their properties.

The implicit scope that is defined on a role cannot be changed. When you define a custom role, the same implicit scopes on the parent role also apply to the custom role, and they cannot be changed. However, the implicit scopes defined on the roles can be overwritten. To overwrite the implicit scopes, you can set an explicit scope on the role assignment, instead of configuring it on the role. *Explicit* scopes are scopes that you apply, as opposed to the implicit scopes that Exchange has already applied. Explicit scopes come in two forms: predefined scopes and custom scopes.

> **OVERWRITING THE WRITES**
>
> Explicit scopes only overwrite the write scopes associated with the role. The read scopes will always apply, regardless of any explicit scope defined in the role assignment. Because of this, you can't specify an explicit write scope that isn't within the read scope of the management role. For example, if the read scope on a role is Self, you can't specify a write scope of Organization.

USING PREDEFINED SCOPES

Predefined scopes are explicit scopes that Exchange makes available to you by default. These predefined scopes apply only to the recipient scope type. Exchange creates the following predefined scopes:

MyDistributionGroups   Allows users to create distribution groups and modify the properties of distribution groups where they are defined as the owner.

Organization   Allows users that hold the role to modify recipients in the entire organization. For example, if the role allows users to change the recipient display name, this scope would allow the role holders to change it for any recipient in the organization.

Self   Allows users to modify only their own properties. For example, if the role allows users to change the recipient display name, this scope would allow the role holder to change only their own display name.

CREATING CUSTOM SCOPES

Aside from using an existing predefined scope, you can create a custom scope that offers more flexibility. Custom scopes are extremely useful because they allow you to narrow down the scope of a role to a very granular level. For example, you can narrow down the scope of recipients to a specific OU or only recipients with a specific attribute set on their accounts. For servers, you can narrow down the configuration scope to a specific site or even name the servers themselves. For databases, you can select a static set of databases or use a filter to manage databases that have a common configuration.

Along with configuring which objects a custom scope is applied to, you can configure if the scope is exclusive or regular. By default, all new scopes are created as regular; however, you can specify that a custom scope be an exclusive scope. An exclusive scope and a regular scope act almost the same. The major difference between them is that an exclusive scope prevents any administrator that is not associated with an exclusive scope from making changes to objects even if the object falls within the boundaries of a regular scope. Once you set a scope as an exclusive scope, the deny action takes effect immediately. For example, if you have a role group named Baltimore IT, with the custom write scope of the Baltimore OU, members of the Baltimore IT group would be able to manage users in the Baltimore OU based on the roles applied to the Baltimore IT group. If you created a new exclusive scope with a filter to include anyone with "Manager" in the Department field, administrators of the Baltimore IT group would not be able to edit users in the Baltimore OU that have "Manager" in the Department field unless they have been associated with the new exclusive scope or an equivalent exclusive scope. Figure 12.12 illustrates the implementation of an exclusive scope (note that the -eq command stands for equal).

FIGURE 12.12
Implementation
of an exclusive scope

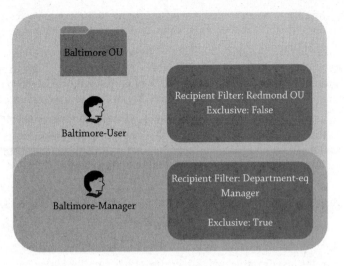

Like predefined scopes, custom scopes are applied to the role assignments and not the roles themselves. However, unlike with predefined scopes, you can specify a configuration scope as well as a recipient scope. You can create a custom scope using the New-ManagementScope cmdlet. When you create the scope, you have several options that give you the ability to narrow the scope as granularly as you want. You have the following options when creating the scope:

DatabaseList   Allows you to specify a list of databases that this scope applies to.

DatabaseRestrictionFilter   Allows you to define a filter based on databases' attributes to which that the scope applies. For example, you can filter out databases that match a certain string.

RecipientRestrictionFilter   Gives you the ability to define a filter based on attributes on the recipient. For example, you can define a scope whose recipients include only the people on the fourth floor of a specific building.

RecipientRoot   Allows you to restrict the scope to an OU in Active Directory.

To illustrate how this works, let's create a couple of custom scopes:

ServerList   Allows you to specify a list of servers that this scope applies to.

ServerRestrictionFilter   Allows you to define a filter based on server attributes to which that the scope applies. For example, you can filter out the servers based on the Active Directory site that they are in.

For our first example, we'll say that you want to create a scope that allows you to confine certain roles to only servers in Baltimore. To accomplish this, we'll use the New-ManagementScope cmdlet with the ServerRestrictionFilter parameter. In this parameter, we'll create a filter that specifies only servers in the Baltimore Active Directory site. The following command would be used:

```
New-ManagementScope -Name "Baltimore Site" -ServerRestrictionFilter { ↵
ServerSite -eq "CN=Baltimore,CN=Sites,CN=Configuration,DC=contoso,DC=com"}
```

For the next example, we'll build a custom recipient scope that applies only to users in the Accounting OU in Active Directory. Referring to the preceding list, you can see that you will need to use the RecipientRoot parameter. You are also required to specify a RecipientRestrictionFilter, but you can set this to be all accounts that are user mailboxes. This command creates a scope that includes all user mailboxes in the Accounting OU:

```
New-ManagementScope -Name "Accounting Only" -RecipientRoot ↵
"OU=Accounting,DC=contoso,DC=com" -RecipientRestrictionFilter ↵
{RecipientType -eq "UserMailbox"}
```

You can also create a custom recipient scope based only on a filter. The following command creates a scope that includes only mailboxes that are considered Discovery Mailboxes:

```
New-ManagementScope -Name "Discovery Mailboxes" -RecipientRestrictionFilter ↵
{RecipientTypeDetails -eq "DiscoveryMailbox"}
```

In the last example, you can create a filter for all mailbox databases that start with "Baltimore" in the string and ensure that only administrators assigned this role can manage the Baltimore mailbox databases by using the Exclusive parameter:

```
New-ManagementScope -Name "Baltimore Databases" -DatabaseRestrictionFilter ↵
{Name -Like "Baltimore*"} -Exclusive -Force
```

After the scope is created, you can apply the role assignment. This is discussed in more detail in the next section.

🌐 Real World Scenario

GEOGRAPHIC ROLES VS. TIERED ROLES

RBAC gives you great flexibility in designing the access model for your Exchange implementation. There are many models that you can use when defining your roles. The rule of thumb is that the RBAC model you adopt should mirror how you manage your Exchange organization. There are two models in particular that we've frequently encountered in various Exchange organizations.

The geographic management model divides the management of Exchange into different physical regions. Suppose you're working with an organization that wanted to have central control of the Exchange organization maintained from one region but also allow other regions to manage their own Exchange servers and recipients. This organization could use RBAC to define server scopes based on sites and recipient scopes based on regional OUs.

Another organization might use a tiered management model. In this model, the lower tier (Tier 1 in this case) handles basic recipient management tasks. Higher tiers (Tier 2 and Tier 3) handle more advanced tasks. As you get to higher tiers of support, the permissions get less and less restrictive. Eventually you would reach the top tier of support, providing an administrator or a group of administrators the rights to manage all tasks within the Exchange organization. This organization could also use RBAC to their benefit by creating different role groups for each tier of support and assigning the necessary roles to the appropriate tiers. In this case, the scope of management is the entire organization, so there would be no need to specify an explicit scope.

Assigning Roles to Administrators

The process for assigning roles to administrators is different than the process for assigning roles to end users. The roles that administrators are assigned are inherently different from the roles that users are assigned. Administrators need to have the permissions to manage and configure Exchange. Before we go further and show you how to assign roles to administrators, you should first understand how role assignments work for administrators.

How Roles Are Assigned to Administrators

When assigning roles to administrators, you have two options. The first option is to assign the role to a management role group and then add the administrator to the role group. This is the easiest and preferred method of assigning roles to administrators. The second option is to assign the role directly to the administrator's account using a direct role assignment.

Regardless of which method you use, management roles are assigned to either the management role group or the administrator's account using a management role assignment. In Active Directory, an msExchRoleAssignment object is created that represents the role assignment between the account and the role. These role assignment objects are stored in the Configuration Naming Context under the container Services\Microsoft Exchange\<Org Name>\RBAC\Role Assignments.

When these role assignments are created, the default name of the assignment object is the name of the role, followed by a hyphen, followed by the name of the object that it's being assigned to. Figure 12.13 shows an example of a role assignment. Here, the Mail Recipients role is assigned to the Organization Management role group.

FIGURE 12.13

A role assignment object is created in Active Directory when assigning roles.

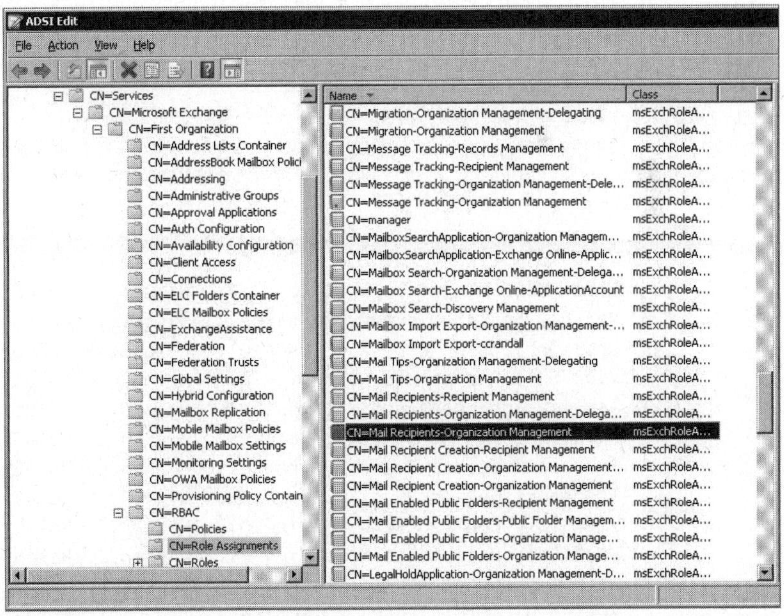

If you were to take a closer look at the role assignment object, you would see that the msExchRoleLink attribute corresponds to the Mail Recipients role's AD object and the msExchUserLink attribute corresponds to the distinguished name of the Organization Management security group (Figure 12.14). This is how a role is united with the assignee.

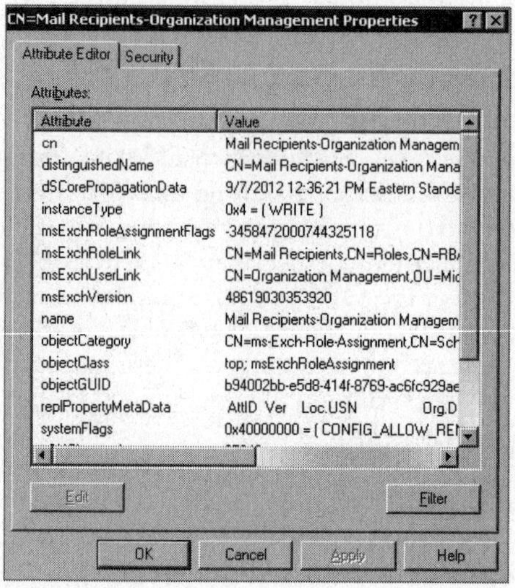

FIGURE 12.14
A deeper look at the role assignment object in Active Directory

You can retrieve a list of the role assignments in the EMS by running the Get-ManagementRoleAssignment cmdlet with no parameters. Several role assignments are created by default. The following example is only a partial listing:

```
Get-ManagementRoleAssignment
```

Name	Role	RoleAssig neeName	RoleAssig neeType	Assignmen tMethod	Effectiv eUserNam e
View-Only Configuratio...	View-O...	Delega...	RoleGroup	Direct	All G...
Legal Hold-Discovery M...	Legal ...	Discov...	RoleGroup	Direct	All G...
Mailbox Search-Discove...	Mailbo...	Discov...	RoleGroup	Direct	All G...
User Options-Help Desk	User O...	Help Desk	RoleGroup	Direct	All G...
View-Only Recipients-H...	View-O...	Help Desk	RoleGroup	Direct	All G...
ApplicationImpersonati...	Applic...	Hygien...	RoleGroup	Direct	All G...
Receive Connectors-Hyg...	Receiv...	Hygien...	RoleGroup	Direct	All G...
Transport Agents-Hygie...	Transp...	Hygien...	RoleGroup	Direct	All G...
Transport Hygiene-Hygi...	Transp...	Hygien...	RoleGroup	Direct	All G...
View-Only Configuratio...	View-O...	Hygien...	RoleGroup	Direct	All G...
View-Only Recipients-H...	View-O...	Hygien...	RoleGroup	Direct	All G...
Active Directory Permi...	Active...	Organi...	RoleGroup	Direct	All G...
Active Directory Permi...	Active...	Organi...	RoleGroup	Direct	All G...
...					

Figure 12.15 illustrates the relationship between management role assignments, scopes, management roles, and management role groups. This figure shows that a management role assignment object is used to assign a role to a role group.

FIGURE 12.15
The relationship between management role assignments, scopes, management roles, and management role groups

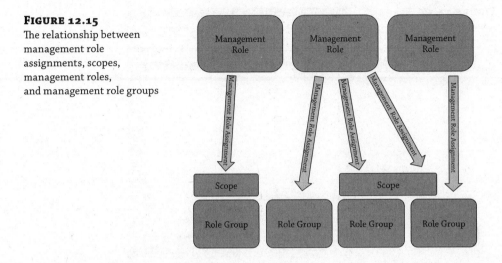

ADDING ADMINISTRATORS TO A MANAGEMENT ROLE GROUP

You can add an administrator's account to a management role group using the EMS, EAC, RBAC Manager, or by adding the account directly to the group in Active Directory using a tool, such as Active Directory Users and Computers. When you add an administrator's account to a management role group, the account gains every role that is specified on the role group. Roles are added cumulatively, so if an administrator's account is a member of another role group, the account will retain those permissions in addition to the permissions assigned by the roles of the new role group.

To add an administrator to a management role group, use the `Add-RoleGroupMember` cmdlet. To use the cmdlet, specify the name of the management role group and the administrator's account in the command. The following example shows the command for adding lawyer Jennifer Fox's account to the Lawyers role group, which has permissions only to export mail from a mailbox:

```
Add-RoleGroupMember "Lawyers" -Member "Jennifer Fox"
```

After you execute this command, you can verify that the administrator was added to the group by enumerating the group membership using the `Get-RoleGroupMember` command and specifying the name of the management role group:

```
Get-RoleGroupMember "Lawyers"

Name                                              RecipientType
----                                              -------------
Jennifer Fox                                      UserMailbox
Richard Alvin                                     UserMailbox
```

If you look in the Active Directory security group that represents the Lawyers group, you will also notice that Jennifer Fox's account has been added as a member (Figure 12.16).

FIGURE 12.16
Administrator accounts are added to the AD group that represents management role groups.

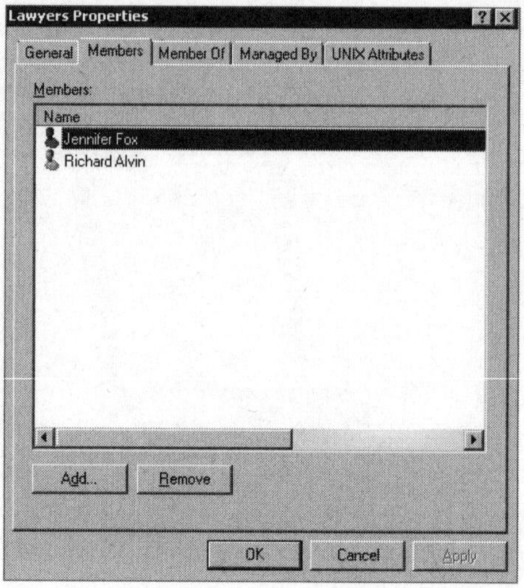

You can also add the administrator's account to the role group through the EAC. This provides a convenient method for modifying permissions without having to open a remote PowerShell connection. You can use the following steps to add an administrator account to a management role group in the EAC:

1. On your client computer, open a web browser and browse to the ECP URL. This URL should be the name of your client access server with /ECP appended to the end. If you don't know the URL for EAC, you can use the Outlook Web App URL and specify **/ECP** instead of **/owa** at the end of the URL. For example, for Contoso, the EAC URL might be https://mail.contoso.com/ECP.

2. When prompted with the authentication page, type in your name and password and log in.

3. In the Feature pane, in the left column of the EAC, select Permissions.

4. In the toolbar across the top of the EAC, select the Admin Roles tab. The role groups are populated in the list in the center of the EAC, as shown in Figure 12.17.

5. Double-click the role group to which you want to add the administrator's account.

   The management role group's details will be displayed in a separate web browser dialog.

6. In the role group's dialog, click the Add button (+ sign) under the Members list, as shown in Figure 12.18.

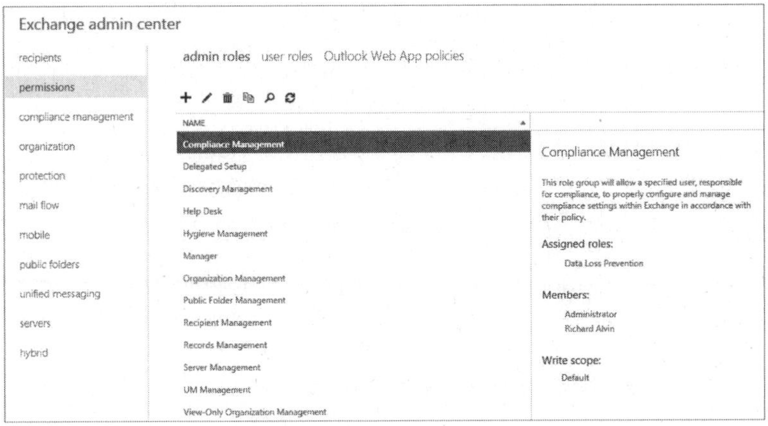

FIGURE 12.17
The list of management
role groups is populated
into the EAC.

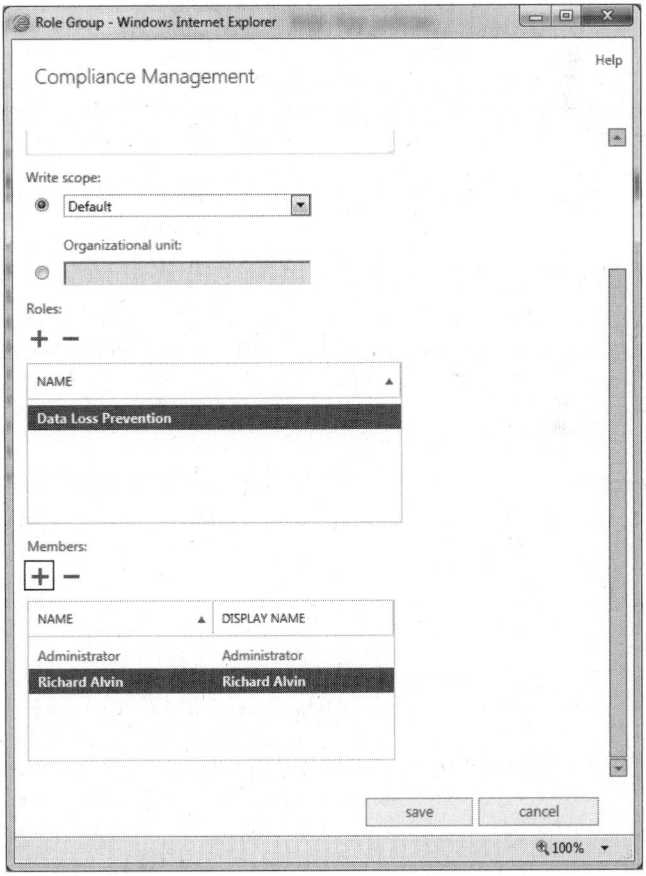

FIGURE 12.18
Click the Add button
to add a member of a role
group in the EAC.

7. The Select Members dialog will be displayed, listing the accounts that can be added to the role group. Select the accounts that you want to add one at a time, or highlight a group of accounts and click the Add button to add them to the list. After you have added all the accounts in the Select Members dialog, click OK.

8. When you are returned to the details dialog for the role group, the accounts that you added are displayed in the Members list. Click the Save button to close this dialog and return to the EAC.

Whether you decide to use the EAC to add administrator accounts to management role groups or you use the EMS cmdlets or RBAC Manager, the result is the same: the administrators gain the permissions they need to do their job.

MODIFYING ROLE GROUPS

You may find that a role you want to assign is not available on any of the existing role groups. You can modify the existing role groups or even create your own custom role groups to assign the management roles that you want to use. To add a role to an existing role group, you have to create a role assignment for the group.

For example, let's suppose your legal team is a member of the Discovery Management role group. The Discovery Management role group is assigned the roles Legal Hold and Mailbox Search. The legal team needs to be able to search all mail content for users in the Accounting OU over the last six years. The legal team discovers that some of the mail content has been moved to PST files. You need to give the legal team the ability to import messages from the PST files to mailboxes in the Accounting OU. To do this, you can modify the Discovery Management role group and add the Mailbox Import Only role to the group.

To modify an existing role group, use the `New-ManagementRoleAssignment` cmdlet to create the role assignment between the Mailbox Import Only role and the Discovery Management role group. When running the command, specify the `SecurityGroup` parameter to indicate that the role is being assigned to a group and to identify the group that the role is being assigned to. The following command demonstrates adding the Mailbox Import Only role to the Discovery Management role group:

```
New-ManagementRoleAssignment -Role "Mailbox Import Only" -SecurityGroup ↵
"Discovery Management"

Name                      Role       RoleAssig RoleAssig Assignmen Effectiv
                                     neeName   neeType   tMethod   eUserNam
                                                                   e

----                      ----       --------- --------- --------- --------
Mailbox Import Only-Di... Mailbo...  Discov... RoleGroup Direct
```

When assigning a role to a role group, you have the ability to specify the scope that the role impacts. Earlier in this chapter, we showed you how to use explicit scopes and how to create your own custom scopes. If you want to apply a custom scope that you created, specify the `CustomConfigWriteScope` and `CustomRecipientWriteScope` parameters. For example, if you want to apply the Mailbox Import Only role to the users in the Accounting OU, you can use the custom scope called Accounting Only that we created earlier in this chapter. The following command would apply this:

```
New-ManagementRoleAssignment -Role "Mailbox Import Only" -SecurityGroup ⏎
"Discovery Management" -CustomRecipientWriteScope "Accounting Only"
```

In most cases, the preferred method is to create a new role group and then use the previous command to create the role assignment to assign the necessary roles to it. To create a role group, use the New-RoleGroup cmdlet. Specify the name of the role group that you are creating and at least one role that will be assigned to the role group. In the following example, we're creating the role group called Lawyers and assigning the Mailbox Import Only role to it:

```
New-RoleGroup "Lawyers" -Roles "Mailbox Import Only"
```

Name	DisplayName	AssignedRoles	RoleAssignments	ManagedBy
Lawyers		{Mailbox Exp...	{Mailbox Exp...	{contoso.com...

After the role group is created, you can manage it just like any existing role group. For the steps to add administrator accounts to this role group, see the previous section.

DIRECTLY ASSIGNING ROLES TO ADMINISTRATORS

Instead of adding administrator accounts to management role groups, you can assign management roles directly to the administrator's account. Although this method is available, it's not necessarily preferred. When you use this method of assigning permissions, it's harder to track the roles that you delegate to administrators and it's more difficult to manage the access.

Assigning Roles to End Users

When you are assigning roles to end users, the process is a little different than when assigning roles to administrators. User roles serve a different purpose than do administrator roles. Whereas administrators will need permissions assigned to manage Exchange, users only need to be assigned permissions to modify contact information, mailbox settings, marketplace apps, team mailboxes, and distribution groups. Not only is the scope different between the administrators and users, but users will be managing their own mailboxes instead of other people's mailboxes.

HOW ROLES ARE ASSIGNED TO END USERS

As discussed in the previous section, administrators are assigned to roles by either adding the administrator's account to a management role group that contains the necessary roles or by assigning the management role directly to the administrator's account. This process is quite different for end users.

Roles are assigned to end users using a role assignment policy. Each mailbox can have only one role assignment policy attached to it. Management roles are tied to the role assignment policy with management role assignments. Exchange creates a management role assignment object in Active Directory that links the management role with the management role assignment policy. If you are browsing the management role assignment objects in Active Directory, you will notice that among the assignments that link roles to role groups, you will also find assignments that link roles to assignment policies. Most roles that are assigned to users start with "My"—for example, MyBaseOptions or MyTeamMailboxes. Figure 12.19 shows the MyBaseOptions role assigned to the Default role assignment policy using a role assignment object.

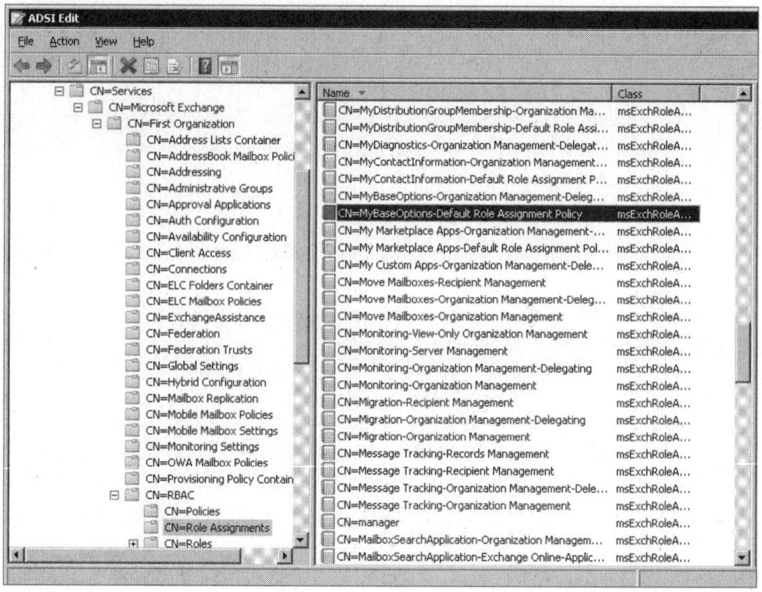

FIGURE 12.19
Role assignment objects are also used for assigning roles to role assignment policies.

DEFAULT USER ROLES

Every mailbox gets a role assignment policy by default when the mailbox is created. The role assignment policy called Default is created when Exchange is installed and is set to be the default policy for new mailboxes. On this default policy, seven roles are assigned by default, as follows:

MyBaseOptions   Allows users to modify basic mailbox settings for their own mailbox. This includes settings for managing their ActiveSync device, inbox rules, and so on.

MyContactInformation   Gives users the ability to update their contact information in Active Directory.

MyDistributionGroupMembership   Gives users the ability to change their own distribution group memberships. They can use this role to add or remove themselves from distribution groups.

MyMarketPlaceApps   Allows users to manage their marketplace apps.

MyTeamMailboxes   Allows users to create a site mailbox and connect it to SharePoint sites.

MyTextMessaging   Allows users to manage their text messaging settings.

MyVoiceMail   Allows users to change their voicemail settings, which includes the ability to do things like changing their PIN.

The Default role assignment policy doesn't have to remain as the default policy. You can designate a different role assignment policy that you created to be the default policy. When you do this, new mailboxes will use the new policy that you defined instead of the one that

Exchange created. The existing mailboxes that were using the Default role assignment policy will remain with that policy.

To change the Default role assignment policy, use the `Set-RoleAssignmentPolicy` cmdlet with the `IsDefault` parameter. The following EMS command changes the Default role assignment policy to a different policy:

```
Set-RoleAssignmentPolicy "Contact Update Only Policy" -IsDefault
```

WORKING WITH ROLE ASSIGNMENT POLICIES

Role assignment policies can be managed using the EAC, RBAC Manager, or the EMS. In the EAC, you can add and remove certain user-specific roles to and from the role assignment policy. You can do this by performing the following steps:

1. On your client computer, open a web browser and browse to the EAC URL. This URL should be the name of your Client Access server with /ECP appended to the end. If you don't know the URL for EAC, you can use the Outlook Web App URL and specify **/ECP** instead of **/owa** at the end of the URL. For example, for Contoso, the EAC URL might be `https://mail.contoso.com/ECP`.

2. When prompted with the authentication page, type in your name and password and log in.

3. On the Feature pane of the EAC, select Permissions.

4. In the toolbar across the top of the EAC, select the User Roles tab. The role assignment policies are populated in the list in the center of the EAC.

5. Select the role assignment policy on which you want to assign or unassign roles.

   When you select the role assignment policy, the Details pane to the right of the list will display some information about the policy. The roles assigned to the assignment policy are segregated into these categorizes:

   ◆ Contact information

   ◆ Profile information

   ◆ Distribution groups

   ◆ Distribution group memberships

   ◆ Other roles

6. After you have selected the role assignment policy that you want to modify, click the Edit button or double-click the role assignment policy.

7. A new window will open displaying the role assignment policy you selected to edit. You can assign or unassign roles by checking or unchecking the roles. The list of roles for the Default role assignment policy will look like Figure 12.20.

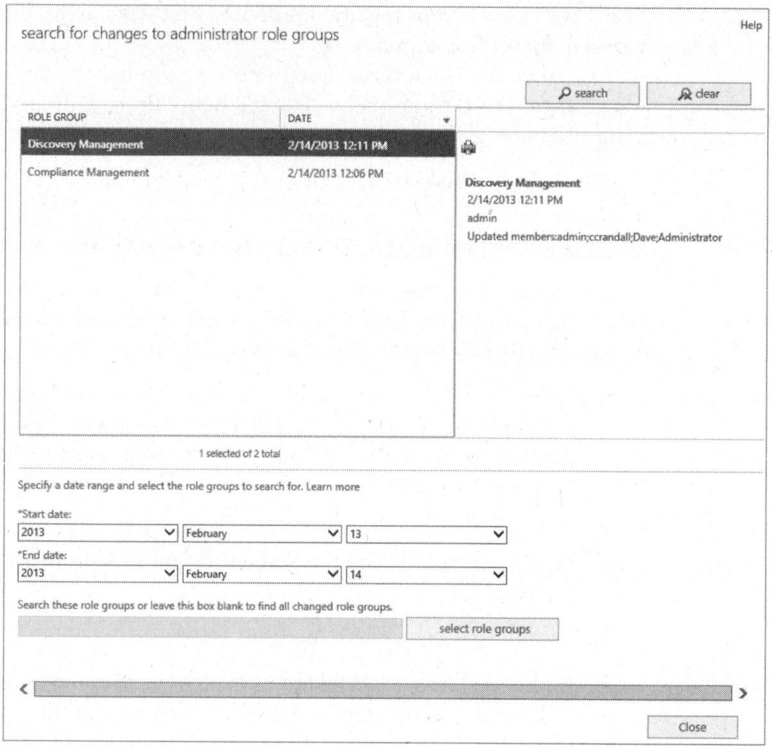

FIGURE 12.20
Check and uncheck
the roles that you
want to add to or
remove from the
role assignment policy.

8. After you have chosen the roles that you want to be assigned to the policy, click the Save button at the bottom of the dialog.

   If you are prompted with a Warning dialog indicating that this policy change will affect many users, click Yes to tell it that you want to continue.

Although you can assign roles to role assignment policies, this option does not give you a lot of flexibility because you can't create or configure role assignment policies. To do this, you must use the EMS or RBAC Manager to manage the role assignment policies.

To start off, you can view a list of the role assignment policies that are currently in existence by running the Get-RoleAssignmentPolicy cmdlet. No parameters are needed to run this command. With a fresh Exchange organization, you should see only the Default role assignment policy. The following example demonstrates the use of this command and the output:

```
Get-RoleAssignmentPolicy | fl Name, IsDefault, Description, RoleAssignments, ↵
AssignedRoles

Name           : Default Role Assignment Policy
IsDefault      : True
Description    : This policy grants end users permissions to set their...
```

```
RoleAssignments    : {MyDistributionGroupMembership-Default Role Assignment...
AssignedRoles      : {MyDistributionGroupMembership, MyBaseOptions...
```

You can view the roles that are tied to the policy by using the Get-ManagementRoleAssignment cmdlet with the RoleAssignee parameter. Just specify the name of the policy and the roles will be enumerated for you. The following command demonstrates this by listing all the roles in the Default role assignment policy:

```
Get-ManagementRoleAssignment -RoleAssignee "Default Role Assignment ↵
Policy" | ft Name, Role
```

```
Name                                                   Role
----                                                   ----
MyDistributionGroupMembership-Default Role Assignment... MyDistributionGrou...
MyBaseOptions-Default Role Assignment Policy           MyBaseOptions
MyContactInformation-Default Role Assignment Policy    MyContactInformati...
MyTextMessaging-Default Role Assignment Policy         MyTextMessaging
MyVoiceMail-Default Role Assignment Policy             MyVoiceMail
MyTeamMailboxes-Default Role Assignment Policy         MyTeamMailboxes
My Marketplace Apps-Default Role Assignment Policy     My Marketplace Apps
```

If you can't use an existing role assignment policy, you can create a custom policy and add your own set of roles to it. To create the policy itself, use the New-RoleAssignmentPolicy cmdlet. The following example creates a new role assignment policy that is similar to the default policy but removes some of the functionality in the MyBaseOptions role:

```
New-RoleAssignmentPolicy "Limited Assignment Policy"
```

You can add a role to an existing policy by creating a new management role assignment. This is serviced by the New-ManagementRoleAssignment cmdlet in the EMS. Specify the role that you are adding to the role assignment policy along with the name of the role assignment policy itself. Let's say that you don't want users to have access to the message-tracking features that come with the MyBaseOptions role. Therefore, you've created a custom role based on MyBaseOptions, called MyLimitedBaseOptions, and removed the message-tracking role entries from the role. The following command adds the MyLimitedBaseOptions role to the policy that we just created:

```
New-ManagementRoleAssignment -Role "MyLimitedBaseOptions" -Policy ↵
"Limited Assignment Policy"
```

After the role assignment policy is created and configured with the management roles that you want to use, you can start applying that policy to end users. To apply a role assignment policy to end users, use the Set-Mailbox cmdlet in the EMS. When you do, specify the name of the mailbox to which you are applying the policy as well as the name of the policy that you are applying. The following example sets the role assignment policy on Lincoln's account to the Limited Assignment Policy that we created previously:

```
Set-Mailbox "Lincoln Alexander" -RoleAssignmentPolicy "Limited Assignment Policy"
```

Auditing RBAC

As the previous sections have illustrated, there are a lot of moving parts in implementing and managing an RBAC deployment. When RBAC is not working as expected, it can be difficult to gather usable information to pinpoint where the problem lies and search the changes made to your RBAC configuration. This section will cover how to reveal what changes were made to your RBAC configuration and find out which roles have been assigned to your users.

Seeing What Changes Were Made

Since RBAC provides administrators with control over an Exchange Server 2013 organization, it is critical that you closely monitor any changes made to the roles assigned to your users. With any administrative change made in your Exchange Server 2013 organization, the change is recorded in the administrator audit log. Using the administrator audit log, you will be able to reveal any modifications made to the RBAC implementation. There are a couple ways to do this.

EXCHANGE ADMINISTRATION CENTER

You can generate an administrator role group report through the EAC. This provides a convenient method of retrieving changes made to roles groups without having to filter through the administrator audit logs. You can use the following steps to run a role group report in the EAC:

1. On your client computer, open a web browser and browse to the EAC URL. This URL should be the name of your Client Access server with /ECP appended to the end. If you don't know the URL for EAC, you can use the Outlook Web App URL and specify **/ECP** instead of **/owa** at the end of the URL. For example, for Contoso, the EAC URL might be https://mail.contoso.com/ECP.

2. When prompted with the authentication page, type in your name and password and log in.

3. On the Feature pane of the EAC, select Compliance Management.

4. In the toolbar across the top of the EAC, select the Auditing tab. The built-in reports are populated in the center of the EAC.

5. Select Run An Administrator Role Group Report.

6. A new window will open displaying all changes made to your roles groups in the last two weeks. The new window is broken down into four sections:

   - The name and date of the role group(s) modified

   - Lists of changes made against the role group and the user who made the change

   - Date range to search for changes made against role groups

   - The Select Role Groups button, which allows you to search for a specific role group

In Figure 12.21 you see that an administrator named Chris changed the group membership of the Compliance Management role group.

FIGURE 12.21
Auditing RBAC
changes using the EAC

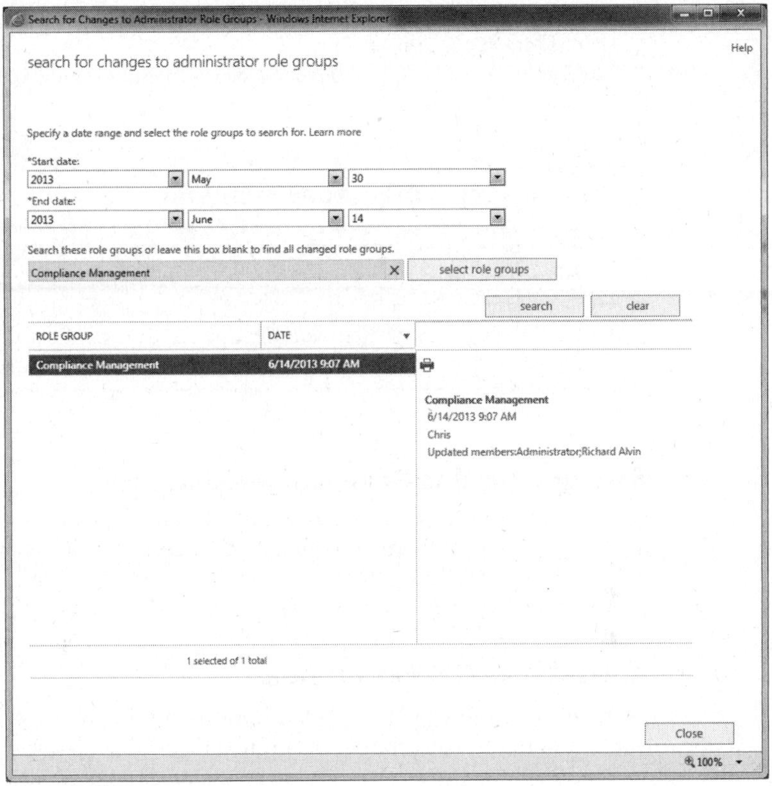

EXCHANGE MANAGEMENT SHELL

The administrator role group report does not provide all the RBAC changes made in your Exchange Server 2013 organization. Using the Search-AdminAuditLog cmdlet, you can search the administrator audit log for a specific cmdlet and parameter. For example, let's use the previous example when we changed the role assignment policy of Lincoln's mailbox to Limited Assignment Policy. To change Lincoln's role assignment policy to Limited Assignment Policy, we used the Set-Mailbox cmdlet with the RoleAssignmentPolicy parameter. To search the administrator audit log for role assignment policy changes, you can run the following command to search the administrator audit log:

```
Search-AdminAuditLog -Cmdlets Set-Mailbox -Parameters ↵
RoleAssignmentPolicy -StartDate 01/24/2013 -EndDate 02/14/2013


...
ObjectModified     : contoso.com/Users/Lincoln Alexander
SearchObject       : lincoln
CmdletName         : Set-Mailbox
```

```
CmdletParameters   : {RoleAssignmentPolicy, Identity}
ModifiedProperties : {}
Caller             : contoso.com/Baltimore/Accounts/Admin
...
```

ENABLE ACTIVE DIRECTORY AUDITING

Role groups in RBAC are any security groups that have been assigned a role. When members are added to or removed from a role group using the Exchange Server 2013 tools, the change is recorded in the administrator audit log. However, if a member is added to a role group using Active Directory tools, Exchange Server 2013 does not log the change in the administrator audit logs. To ensure that any members added to a role group are recorded, you must enable Active Directory auditing.

Seeing Who Has Been Assigned Rights

Generating audit logs is a great way in determining what changes have been made, but in many cases you will need to find out what Exchange Server 2013 permissions have already been allocated to users. Using the EMS you will be able to discover the roles, role groups, and how the permissions have been allocated to your users.

ADMINISTRATOR PERMISSIONS

Using the `Get-ManagementRoleAssignment` cmdlet with the `GetEffectiveUsers` parameter, you can output how each role is assigned to an administrator. In most cases, roles are assigned to administrators through group membership, but an administrator could have a direct assignment or a policy application. In the following example, Richard Alvin has access to the roles Legal Hold and Mailbox Search because he is a member of the Discovery Management role group and the role Mailbox Import Only has been directly assigned to Richard Alvin:

```
Get-ManagementRoleAssignment -GetEffectiveUsers | ↵ ?{$_.EffectiveUserName -eq
"Richard Alvin"} | ft Name, Role, RoleAssigneeName
```

```
Name                                    Role          RoleAssigneeName
----                                    ----          ----------------
Legal Hold-Discovery Management         Legal Hol...  Discovery Management
Mailbox Search-Discovery Management      Mailbox S...  Discovery Management
Mailbox Import Only-Dave                Mailbox m...  Richard Alvin
```

You can also use the `Get-ManagementRoleAssignment` cmdlet with the `GetEffectiveUsers` parameter and search which users have access to a specific role. Using the `Unique` parameter will ensure that each administrator is shown only once, even if they have access to the role through different role assignments. In the following example, all the administrators listed under `EffectiveUserName` have access to the Mailbox Search role group:

```
Get-ManagementRoleAssignment -Role 'Mailbox Search' ↵
    -GetEffectiveUsers  | select EffectiveUserName -Unique
```

```
EffectiveUserName
```

```
-----------------
All Group Members
Admin
Richard Alvin
```

End-user Permission

When multiple role assignment policies have been created and applied to mailboxes, the `Where-Object` cmdlet can be used to search all mailboxes that have a specific role assignment policy applied. Using the Limited Assignment Policy we created earlier in this chapter, you can search all mailboxes for a specific role assignment policy. By running the following command, any mailbox with the role assignment policy of Limited Assignment Policy will be displayed:

```
Get-Mailbox -ResultSize Unlimited | Where-Object ⏎
{$_.RoleAssignmentPolicy -eq "Limited Assignment Policy"} | FT

Name
----
Lincoln Alexander
```

The Bottom Line

Determine what built-in roles and role groups provide you with the permissions you need. Exchange Server 2013 includes a vast number of built-in management roles out of the box. Many of these roles are already assigned to role groups that are ready for you to use. To use these built-in roles, figure out which roles contain the permissions that you need. Ideally, determine which role groups you can use to gain access to these roles.

Master It As part of your recent email compliance and retention initiative, your company hired a consultant to advise you on what you can do to make your Exchange implementation more compliant. The consultant claims that he needs escalated privileges to your existing journal rules so he can examine them. Since you tightly control who can make changes to your Exchange organization, you don't want to give the consultant the ability to modify your journal rules, though you don't mind if he is able to view the configuration details of Exchange. What EMS command can you run to find out what role the consultant can be assigned to view your journal rules but not have permissions to modify them or create new ones? What role do you want to assign to the consultant?

Assign permissions to administrators using roles and role groups. When assigning permissions to administrators, the preferred method is to assign management roles to role groups and then add the administrators account to the appropriate role group. However, Exchange allows you to assign management roles directly to the administrator's account if you want.

Master It Earlier in the day, you determined that you need to assign a certain role to your email compliance consultant. You've created a role group called Email Compliance Evaluation and you need to add your consultant to this role group. What command would you use in the EMS to add your consultant, Sam, to this role group?

Grant permissions to end users for updating their address list information. RBAC doesn't apply only to Exchange administrators. You can also use RBAC to assign roles to end-user accounts so users can have permissions to update their personal information, Exchange settings, and their distribution groups.

Master It You've decided that you want to give your users the ability to modify their contact information in the global address list. You want to make this change as quickly as possible and have it apply to all existing users and new users coming into your Exchange organization immediately. You determine that using the EAC would be the easiest way to make this change. What would you modify in the EAC to make this change?

Create custom administration roles and assign them to administrators. If you can't find an existing role that meets your needs, don't worry! You can create a custom role in Exchange Server 2013 and assign the permissions you need to the custom role.

Master It Your company has asked you to allow administrators in the Baltimore office to manage mailbox settings for all users in the Baltimore OU. Your company does not want the administrators in the Baltimore office to be able to change the mailbox storage limits for individual mailboxes. What would you implement to ensure administrators in the Baltimore office can only manage mailboxes in the Baltimore OU and are not able to change the mailbox storage limits?

Audit RBAC changes using the Exchange Management Shell and built-in reports in the Exchange Administration Center. Assigning RBAC permissions is the easy part, determining who has been assigned what permissions can be a bit tricky. Luckily EMS can be used to determine the roles assigned to users.

Master It Your company has purchased a partner company, which has an administrator named Dave. You have been tasked with providing Dave with the same level of RBAC permissions in your Exchange Server 2013 organization that he has in his Exchange Server 2013 organization. What command would you run in your partner's organization to determine the roles assigned to Dave?

Chapter 13

Basics of Recipient Management

The term *Exchange recipient* defines any mail or mailbox-enabled object in Active Directory used to send or receive email within an Exchange organization.

Depending on the size of your organization, recipient management (handling the user accounts, groups, contacts, public folders, and other resources that can receive email) may consume the vast majority of Exchange administration time. In a small organization, you may be responsible for every aspect of your Exchange server, including creating and managing recipients. In a larger organization with lots of changes, new users, and users leaving the organization, recipient administration will probably be handled by a person or team that is separate from the person or team that manages the Exchange Server infrastructure (message routing, backups, server maintenance, and so on).

This chapter discusses the basics of recipient management. It examines the environment configurations that must exist to support recipient management and the tools you use to manage recipients. It also examines Exchange address lists and how email addresses are defined.

In this chapter, you will learn to:

◆ Identify the various types of recipients

◆ Use the Exchange Admin Center to manage recipients

◆ Configure accepted domains and define email address policies

Understanding Exchange Recipients

There are different types of users in your organization, as well as different types of needs for messaging delivery. To account for those differences, Exchange provides various recipient types. Each one fills a specific need within your messaging environment.

Mailbox-enabled Users

A mailbox-enabled user has an account in Active Directory and a mailbox on an Exchange server. A mailbox-enabled user can send and receive email messages within the Exchange organization and through the Internet, plus has access to a personal calendar, contact list, and other services provided by the Exchange servers. In most organizations, all corporate users have mailboxes and therefore store all emails on the Exchange servers.

Users who have a mailbox can use various client applications to access mailbox content or send emails. For example, they can use Office Outlook, Outlook Web App, or Exchange ActiveSync to access all mailbox content.

When you create a mailbox-enabled user, you can create multiple types of mailboxes. For example, you can create a standard mailbox that is associated with a user and then used by a company employee to send and receive emails, or you can create a resource mailbox that can be used to represent a company's resources, such as a conference room. Additionally, the concept of the shared mailbox in Exchange Server 2013 provides a more fluid solution for mailbox sharing within the Exchange organization. More detailed information about mailbox-enabled users is available in Chapter 14, "Managing Mailboxes and Mailbox Content."

Mail-enabled Users and Contacts

A mail-enabled user is quite different from a mailbox-enabled one—the distinction is more than just a few letters. A mail-enabled user has a user account in Active Directory and an *external* email address associated with the account. The mail-enabled user has *no* mailbox on an Exchange Server inside your organization.

All mail-enabled users who appear in the corporate global address list can be used as delivery recipients by any user inside your organization (assuming that there are no restrictions in place to prevent delivery) and can be used to manage certain aspects of those recipients.

So why would a company *not* create a mailbox for a user? Why would they only associate an external email address with their user accounts? The answer is that mail-enabled users fill a specific need: the need to make an external *contact* appear in the internal address list. Yes, but there is already an object that fills that need, the *mail-enabled contact* (more on that recipient type later in this section). The caveat here is that the external *contact* needs access to internal network resources by using an Active Directory user account. An example of this would be an onsite contract employee who requires access to the network but needs to continue receiving email through their existing email address. As a result, the mail-enabled user appears in the global address list and other users can easily locate and send email to the address, even though the user does not have a mailbox in the Exchange organization. Note also that a mail-enabled user *cannot* send or receive email by using the internal Exchange servers. Mail-enabled contacts are exactly that: *contacts* for individuals who are external to your organization. A mail-enabled contact is an individual who has neither a security principal in Active Directory nor a mailbox on an internal Exchange server. Mail-enabled contacts are visible in the global address list, but they receive all email on an external messaging system. Any internal user can send an email message to a contact simply by selecting the contact from an address list.

So what is the real-world purpose of a mail-enabled contact? Imagine a company that has a large number of suppliers or customers, with whom many internal users regularly communicate. You may want to make it very easy for your internal users to locate and identify these external contacts; by adding these contacts to Active Directory, you are making them available from a central location and accessible to all internal users. This also provides you with a way to include the suppliers in distribution groups that are used for mass mailings.

Contacts can be created in Active Directory without an Exchange infrastructure in place, but in that case, they are essentially useless. After working with Active Directory since 1999, I am still looking for a compelling reason to create non-mail-enabled contacts. More information about mail-enabled users and mail-enabled contacts is available in Chapter 15, "Managing Mail-enabled Groups, Mail-enabled Contacts, and Mail-enabled Users."

Table 13.1 shows the core differences between mailbox-enabled users, mail-enabled users, and mail-enabled contacts.

TABLE 13.1:   Mailbox-enabled users, mail-enabled users, and mail-enabled contacts

RECIPIENT	NEEDS ACCESS TO INTERNAL RESOURCES?	NEEDS A MAILBOX IN EXCHANGE?
Mailbox-enabled user	Yes	Yes
Mail-enabled user	Yes	No
Mail-enabled contact	No	No

Real World Scenario

CONTACTS: USED IN A SYNCHRONIZATION SCENARIO

We certainly don't want to oversimplify or minimize the purpose of mail-enabled contact objects. These seemingly minimal objects, which have no access rights, are key elements of some of the most complex Exchange environments. If your organization has long-lasting business relationships with other organizations, you may want to maintain a *somewhat* unified address list where all users from the partner companies appear.

To achieve this goal, your company will create contact objects for all users in the other companies, and vice versa. Though this doesn't actually result in a *single* global address list, it is a way to make the address lists look identical.

Additionally, some organizations that implement rich coexistence scenarios with Office 365 may want to create mail-enabled contact objects as part of their coexistence scenario and unified global address list solution.

In scenarios where coexistence between multiple directories is in place, generally a synchronization solution must be put in place. Microsoft Forefront Identity Manager 2010 can be used to achieve such coexistence scenarios.

In scenarios of coexistence between on-premises Active Directory infrastructures and an Office 365 tenant, the Microsoft Online Services Directory Synchronization tool is used to synchronize address lists.

Mail-enabled Groups

A mail-enabled group is an Active Directory group that has been tagged with all the appropriate Exchange mail attributes, including an email address. Once a group has been mail-enabled, any internal or external user can send mail to the group (assuming that there are no restrictions preventing message delivery to the group). The group membership can then be modified to configure who receives emails that are sent to the group.

An Active Directory forest that does not include any Exchange organization already uses groups to manage access to resources and permissions. With the integration of an Exchange organization into Active Directory, the same groups (security groups) can be mail-enabled or new groups (distribution groups) that will only be used as a *distribution list* can be created and then mail-enabled.

Active Directory contains two types of groups: distribution and security. Some organizations may decide to mail-enable only distribution groups to prevent the likelihood of mistakenly adding users to a group and assigning them access to secured resources. This decision should be made early in an Exchange deployment to ensure consistent use of groups.

A mail-enabled group can contain any type of Exchange recipients, including other mail-enabled groups. In Exchange Server 2013, you can mail-enable only groups that are set to the universal group scope. The groups can be either security groups or distribution groups. Dynamic distribution groups, groups that have an automatically updated membership, can be mail-enabled as well.

More information about mail-enabled groups is available in Chapter 15.

Mail-enabled Public Folders

A public folder is an electronic version of a bulletin board. Public folders can be used to store messages, contacts, or calendars that must be accessed by multiple users in your organization. Users can create public folders by using Microsoft Outlook, and administrators can create public folders by using the Exchange Administration Center. In Exchange Server 2013, public folders are often referred to as *modern* public folders.

A mail-enabled public folder is one that has been tagged with all the appropriate Exchange mail attributes. Mail-enabled public folders have an email address and can receive email from any internal or external user from your organization (assuming that the appropriate permissions have been configured for the folder).

Mail-enabled public folders are particularly useful if you need to have a "virtual" mailbox shared between multiple users. For example, you may want to have multiple individuals in the HR department review the job applications that are sent to your company. You can create a mail-enabled public folder and provide an email address of hr@yourcompany.com. You would then provide the necessary permissions to individuals in the HR department to review the contents of the folder, without having a large number of emails polluting their inboxes. The shared mailbox recipient type—new to Exchange Server 2013—provides the same functionality. Other than an enhanced mechanism for accessing the shared mailbox from Outlook, the type of information stored in a shared mailbox is identical to that stored in a public folder. For those reading the writing on the wall, we see feature duplication between those two products that will soon result in a product ending up on the cutting room floor. The shared mailbox feels to us like another attempt to create a departure from public folders.

Although in the front of the house not much has been changed in terms of user access and client functionality for public folders in Exchange Server 2013, the key changes are present in the back end. The main difference is related to public folder storage and public folder replication. Public folders are stored in public folder mailboxes, which reside on mailbox databases. Public folder mailboxes must be created by an administrator from the Exchange Administration Center or the Exchange Management Shell.

More information about shared mailboxes and mail-enabled public folders is available in Chapter 15, and Chapter 17, " Modern Public Folders."

Defining Email Addresses

Before we discuss how to create mail-enabled users, groups, or contacts, we'll first discuss how these objects get their email addresses. Those of you who are familiar with Exchange 2003 probably remember that email addresses were defined by a recipient policy. Once the recipient policy was defined, the Microsoft Exchange System Attendant's Recipient Update Service (RUS) would establish email addresses for any mail-enabled recipient at some point in the future (hopefully just a minute or two).

This process is just a bit different in Exchange 2013. Email addresses are generated for the object at the time the mail-enabled recipient is created, and they are generated by an Exchange Management Shell (EMS) task or the Exchange Administration Center—still with a background EMS task, though. Recipient policies from Exchange Server 2003 have been broken up into two separate concepts:

◆ Email domains for which your organization will accept mail, also known as *accepted domains*

◆ Policies that define the syntax of email addresses, also known as *email address policies*

For addresses that will be assigned to mailboxes on your Exchange Server 2013 servers, you define both an accepted domain and an email address policy.

Accepted Domains

An accepted domain is an SMTP domain name (aka SMTP namespace) for which your Exchange Server 2013 servers will accept mail. The servers will either deliver the mail to an Exchange mailbox or relay it to internal or external SMTP mail servers. If you migrate from a previous version of Exchange Server, the list of accepted domains in Exchange Server 2013 will include all accepted domains from the previous environment. Accepted domains must be defined for all email addresses that will be routed into your organization. Most small- and medium-size organizations will have only a single accepted domain.

ABOUT DOMAIN TYPES

One tricky thing about defining an accepted domain is that you must define how Exchange is to treat a message for it. You can choose from three types of domains when creating an accepted domain:

Authoritative Domains   These are SMTP domains for which you accept the inbound message and deliver it to an internal mailbox within your Exchange organization.

Internal Relay Domains   These are SMTP domains for which your Exchange Server will accept inbound SMTP mail. The Exchange Server must have mail-enabled contacts or mail-enabled users who specify forwarding addresses for users in those domains. The Exchange Server then relays the message on to another internal mail system. Internal relay domains are used when two Exchange organizations are doing global address list synchronization.

External Relay Domains   These are SMTP domains for which your Exchange organization will accept inbound SMTP mail and then relay that mail on to an external SMTP mail server, usually one that is outside of the organization's boundaries. If Edge Transport servers are used, they handle external relay domains.

SETTING UP AN ACCEPTED DOMAIN USING THE EXCHANGE ADMINISTRATION CENTER

Accepted domains are found within the Mail Flow window. When you choose the Accepted Domains link in the top banner, you will see a list of the accepted domains that have been defined for your organization, such as those shown in Figure 13.1.

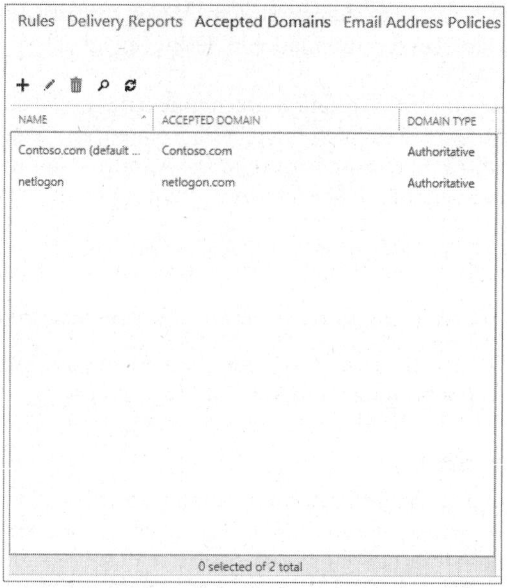

FIGURE 13.1
List of accepted
domains

When you create an Exchange organization, a single accepted domain is automatically created and given a name. This is the name of the Active Directory forest root domain; for many organizations this will not be correct because the naming conventions for Active Directory domain names and SMTP domain names may be different. For example, your Active Directory name may be Netlogon.local whereas your public domain name for email is Netlogon.com.

Accepted domains are simple to create and require little input. To create a new accepted domain, open the New Accepted Domain window by clicking the + sign in the Actions list. You need to provide only a descriptive name for the accepted domain, the SMTP domain name, and an indication of how messages for this domain should be treated when messages are accepted by Exchange Server 2013 (see Figure 13.2).

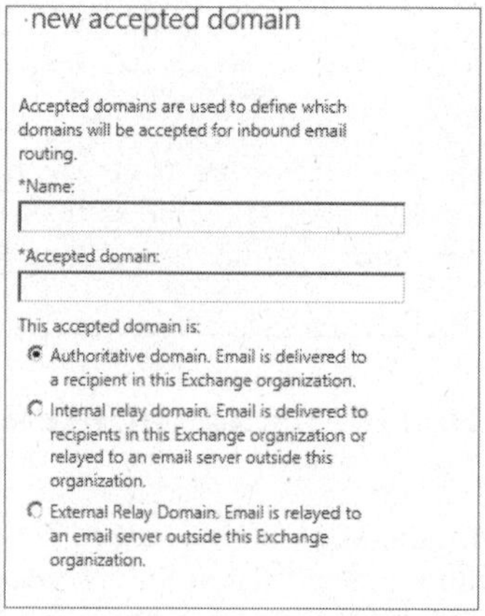

FIGURE 13.2
Creating a new
accepted domain

Keep in mind that you cannot change the domain name of an accepted domain once it is created. (You can change the domain type, however.)

SETTING UP AN ACCEPTED DOMAIN USING THE EMS

You can also manage accepted domains using the following EMS cmdlets:

- `New-AcceptedDomain`
- `Set-AcceptedDomain`
- `Get-AcceptedDomain`
- `Remove-AcceptedDomain`

For example, to create a new accepted domain for a Canadian division of KonoPizza Incorporated, use the following EMS command:

```
New-AcceptedDomain -Name "KonoPizza Canada" -DomainName "KonoPizza.ca"
 -DomainType "Authoritative"
```

Email Address Policies

Exchange email address policies are the configuration objects used by Exchange when new mail objects are created. Each policy's conditions are examined to see if they apply to the object that is being created; if they do, the new mail-enabled object's email address policies are generated based on the email-address-generation rules.

Using the Exchange Administration Center, you can find email address policies in the Mail Flow window. Select the Email Address Policies tab to see a list of the email address policies in the organization. In Figure 13.3, we have only the default policy assigned by the Exchange Server 2013 installation.

FIGURE 13.3
Email address policies for an Exchange Server 2013 organization

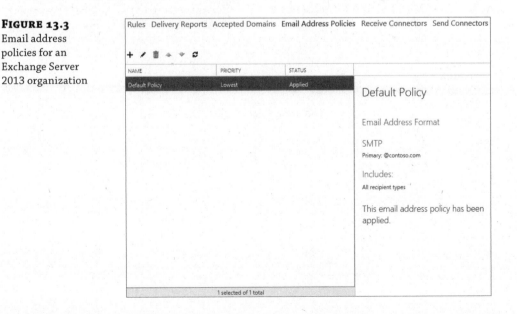

The default policy is the lowest priority policy and applies if no others above it do. This is just like having multiple recipient policies in Exchange Server 2003.

CHANGING AN EXISTING POLICY

The default email-address-generation rule uses the object's Exchange alias and the domain name of the Active Directory forest root. Suppose you want to make two changes to the email address policy:

♦ You want to change the SMTP domain name that is on the default policy to something else.

  For example, this is relevant when the default domain name for the Active Directory forest root is different from the public domain name used for SMTP, and you need to fix this.

♦ You want all email addresses to be generated using the first name, followed by a period, then the last name, and then the domain name.

To perform those tasks, follow these steps:

1. Define an accepted domain. If the default accepted domain is not correct for your organization, you need to create a new accepted domain because Exchange 2013 does not allow you to change an accepted domain. Let's say that your Active Directory forest root is called fourthcoffee.com but your public SMTP domain is Contoso.com. First, under the Accepted Domains tab, create a new authoritative accepted domain for Contoso.com.

2. Change the default email address policy so that it uses the new domain name and generates an address using the *firstname.lastname* format, such as josh.maher@Contoso.com. Locate the default policy by clicking the Email Address Policies tab, highlight the default policy, and double-click to edit the policy. On the Email Addresses Format page, you see the list of all domain names used to generate email addresses. Click the domain name you want to modify, in this case @contoso.com, and then click the Edit button to see the SMTP Email Address dialog box. The default setting in the email address policy is to use the user's alias to generate the email. This can be modified to multiple combinations, as Figure 13.4 shows.

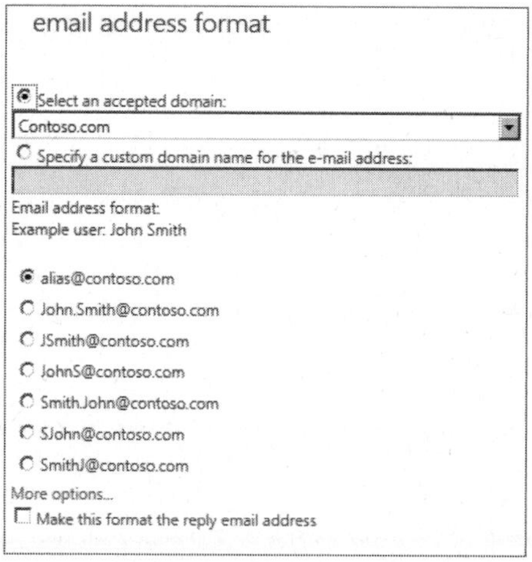

FIGURE 13.4
Changing how the SMTP address is generated

3. Click the Apply To link on the next tab to select the scope of the policy. The setting allows you to choose which recipients will be affected by the email address policy.

Once the email address policy is modified, it will run automatically at its preset interval. In order to force the application of the policy to recipients, an administrator must run the `Update-EmailAddressPolicy` cmdlet.

Of course, you can also create email address policies using the EMS; Table 13.2 shows the EMS cmdlets for creating, deleting, modifying, and updating email address policies.

TABLE 13.2: EMS cmdlets used to manipulate email address policies

EMS CMDLET	DESCRIPTION
New-EmailAddressPolicy	Creates a new email address policy
Set-EmailAddressPolicy	Changes properties of the email address policy specified
Update-EmailAddressPolicy	Updates mail-enabled objects in the Active Directory if the conditions of the policy specified apply to those objects
Get-EmailAddressPolicy	Retrieves a list of email address policies and their properties
Remove-EmailAddressPolicy	Deletes the specified email address policy

The following is an example of an EMS command that would create an email address policy for the domain `Kalleo.ca`:

```
New-EmailAddressPolicy -Name 'Kalleo Solutions' -IncludedRecipients
'MailboxUsers' -ConditionalCustomAttribute1 'test' -Priority '1'
-EnabledEmailAddressTemplates 'SMTP:%g.%s@Kalleo.ca'
```

Finally, if you want to see the email addresses that have been applied to a mail-enabled object, you can also use an EMS cmdlet to retrieve that information. (You could use EAC for this task, but it would require hours of work.) You would use `Get-Mailbox`, `Get-MailContact`, or `Get-DistributionGroup`. To retrieve the email addresses for a mailbox whose alias is `Julie.Samante`, for instance, you could type the command,

```
Get-Mailbox "julie.samante" | Format-List DisplayName,EmailAddresses
```

and see output similar to this:

```
DisplayName    : Julie Samante
EmailAddresses : {smtp:Julie.Samante@kalleo.ca,
SMTP:Julie.Samante@contoso.com}
```

CREATING A NEW EMAIL ADDRESS POLICY

If you have a small- or medium-size organization, you probably support only a single SMTP domain for your users. However, even companies with a handful of mailboxes can sometimes require two or three SMTP domain names. Let's take as an example an organization that has two divisions, each of which requires its own unique SMTP addresses.

Previously you changed the default policy for an organization so that all users would get an SMTP address of @kalleo.ca. Let's extend that a bit further. Let's say that this organization has another division called Volcano Surfboards and its SMTP domain is @volcanosurfboards.com. Anyone whose company attribute in the Active Directory contains *Volcano Surfboards* should have an SMTP address of *firstname.lastname*@volcanosurfboards.com, and that address should be set as the mailbox default reply address.

🌐 Real World Scenario

CREATE A NEW ADDRESS POLICY OR MODIFY THE DEFAULT ADDRESS?

This is one of the questions we hear the most often: Should I create a new address list when I need to add a new SMTP domain, or should I simply modify the default address list?

Let's look at an example to illustrate when you need to use one or the other. Also, keep in mind that only one email address policy can be applied to a new user that is created in your organization. When you create a new user, Exchange checks to see which policy matches the new recipient, based on conditions and filters. If multiple policies apply to the user, it will apply only the policy with the highest priority and then ignore all others. If no custom policies apply to the user, then the default policy is applied. (A policy must always be applied when you create a mailbox-enabled user, which is why you cannot remove or delete the default email address policy.)

Now on to our scenario. One of this book's authors was called in because "the Internet was broken and not sending emails." (We love those descriptions!) We quickly noticed that the organization had five different email address policies. Each address policy had a different SMTP domain and was configured to apply to *all users*. So, you now know that when a new user was created in their company, the user received only the highest priority email address policy and was therefore assigned only a single SMTP address that matched that policy. There is an easy fix to this: simply remove all the custom email address policies, and then add the SMTP domains to the default email address policy. Then reapply the policy and all users are assigned correct addresses.

So now to answer the initial question: Create a custom email address policy when you need to assign a separate SMTP domain to a *subset* of your users. Modify the default email address policy when you want to add domains to *all users* in your organization.

The first thing you need to do is define volcanosurfboards.com as an authoritative accepted domain. If you don't define the accepted domain, you will receive an error message when you try to create a policy based on that domain. The accepted domain must always exist first.

Next, you want to create the email address policy. To create a new email address policy, click the Email Address Policy tab in the Mail Flow window in the Actions pane. On the first page of the New Email Address Policy window, you will be prompted for the name of the policy, the accepted domain associated with the policy, and what type of objects this policy applies to.

In this example, the policy is being created for the Kalleo company users and you want the policy to apply only to mailboxes, so you will provide that information on the screen shown in Figure 13.5. When you have provided this information, click Save to create the email address policy.

FIGURE 13.5
Naming the email
address policy
and defining the
accepted domain

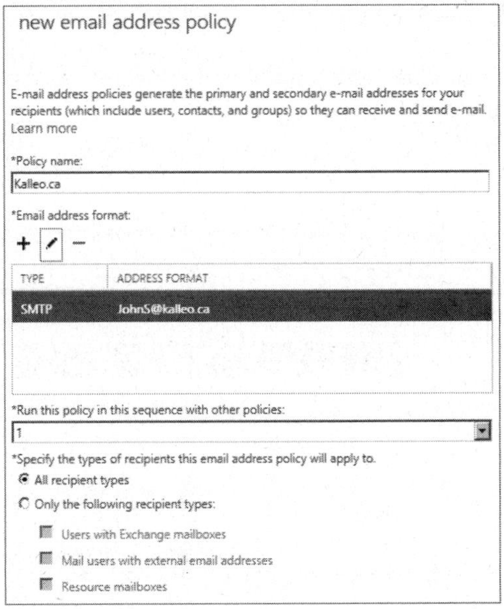

On the next page, click the Rules button, and you can define the conditions that can be used to apply the policy. This is built as an additional filter, essentially if you want to more granularly define the target of the policy. Figure 13.6 shows the conditions available for the rule. You can select such criteria as the state or province, department, or company name of the object.

FIGURE 13.6
Conditions
available in the
email address
policy rules

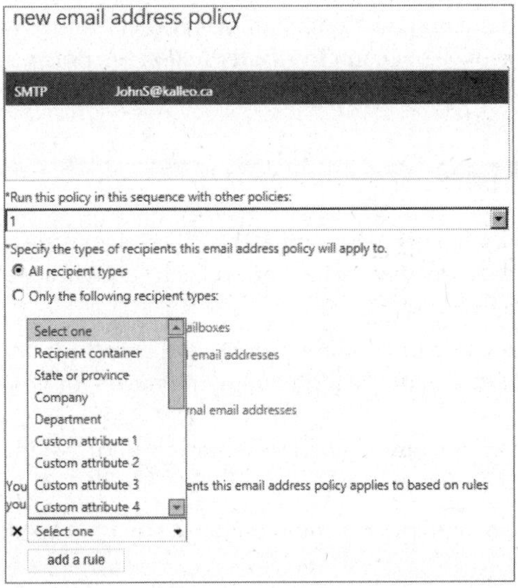

In this example, you want the policy to apply to anyone whose company name attribute contains *Kalleo*.

Once you select the Company condition, the Specify Words Or Phrases window opens; there you enter the company name (see Figure 13.7).

FIGURE 13.7
Specifying words for a rule in an email address policy

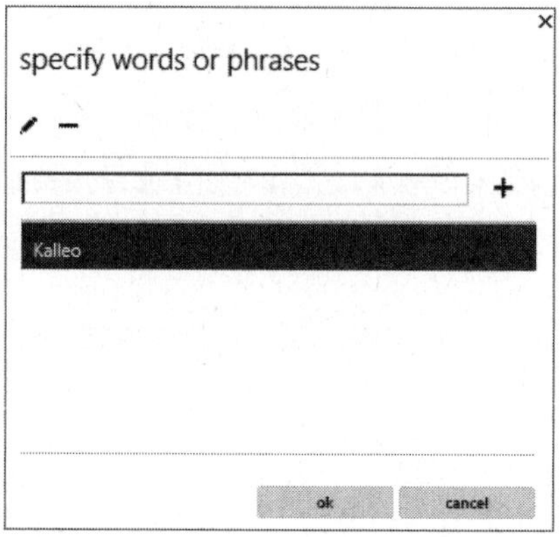

specify words or phrases

✎ —

[   ] +

Kalleo

ok   cancel

When you have entered the necessary company information (in this case, just a single company called Kalleo), click OK to close the window. You can verify that the conditions are defined correctly by clicking the Preview Recipients The Policy Applies To link on the Conditions page. That displays the Email Address Policy Preview dialog box; you should see users that have a mailbox and whose company name is Kalleo.

The Preview Recipients The Policy Applies To link is also helpful in confirming that attributes are being entered correctly in Active Directory. Administrators may not recognize if everyone in a 10,000-user company exists in the Email Address Policy Preview dialog box, but hopefully it will give them an idea that the information is being entered correctly. In this case, if a user's company name does not contain exactly *Kalleo*, the policy conditions will not be met and the user's mailbox will have the email addresses from the default policy.

The Bottom Line

Identify the various types of recipients. Most recipient types in Exchange Server 2013 have been around since the early days of Exchange. Each serves a specific purpose and has objects that reside in Active Directory.

Master It Your company has multiple Active Directory domains that exist in a single forest. You must make sure that the following needs for your company are met:

◆ Group managers cannot, by mistake, assign permissions to a user by adding someone to a group.

◆ Temporary consultants for your company must not be able to access any internal resource.

Use the Exchange Administration Center to manage recipients. Historically, Exchange administrators mainly used a combination of Active Directory tools and Exchange-native tools to manage Exchange servers and objects. That has all changed with Exchange Server 2013, mainly with the advent of the remote PowerShell implementation of the Exchange Management Shell, but also with the browser-based version of the Exchange Administration Center.

Master It You are responsible for managing multiple Exchange organizations and you need to apply identical configurations to servers in all organizations. If you are just starting out with Exchange Server 2013 and you are not yet familiar with Remote PowerShell and Exchange Management Shell, you need some guidance regarding the commands that must be used. What should you do?

Configure accepted domains and define email address policies. Accepted domains and email address policies, once a single concept, have been broken up since Exchange Server 2007, and that it is still the case in Exchange Server 2013. It gives you more flexibility in managing email address suffixes and SMTP domains that will be accepted by your Exchange servers.

Master It You plan to accept mail for multiple companies inside your organization. Once accepted, the mail will be rerouted to the SMTP servers responsible for each of those companies. What do you need to create in your organization?

Chapter 14

Managing Mailboxes and Mailbox Content

In a small- or medium-sized business, you may be the sole person responsible for all Exchange Server tasks, such as backing up the server, checking the queues, reviewing event logs, and managing mailboxes. In other organizations, you might have a specific task, such as running backups or managing mobile devices.

In most Exchange Server organizations, the single biggest day-to-day administration task is the management of end-user mailboxes. The majority of mailbox-management tasks involve creating mailboxes, moving them to the correct database, setting mailbox properties or policies, and managing email addresses. Mailbox management also may entail management of the actual content, such as purging the Deleted Items folder, moving content to other folders, or removing content from a user's mailbox.

In this chapter, you will learn to:

- ◆ Create and delete user mailboxes
- ◆ Manage mailbox permissions
- ◆ Move mailboxes to another database
- ◆ Perform bulk manipulation of mailbox properties
- ◆ Use Messaging Records Management to manage mailbox content

Managing Mailboxes

This first section on mailbox management tackles the most common tasks: creating, managing, and deleting mailboxes associated with a real user account. If you are upgrading from Exchange Server 2007/2010 to Exchange Server 2013, you will immediately notice the absence of the Exchange Management Console and the Exchange Control Panel. All GUI-based management operations are performed via the Exchange Admin Center (EAC).

Using the EAC to Assign a Mailbox

Let's start with a common task: assigning a mailbox to an existing user. You may hear this process referred to as "mailbox-enabling" a user or simply creating a mailbox. Let's say we have a user who requires a mailbox. Her unique location and distinguished name are as follows:

```
tsxen.com/Corporate/Amany Bakr
CN=Amany Bakr,OU=Corporate,DC=tsxen,DC=com
```

To assign this user a mailbox, you must use either the Exchange Management Shell (EMS) or the EAC.

A WIZARD BY ANY OTHER NAME

You had several options available, such as the Exchange Management Console, the Exchange Control Panel, and the venerable Exchange System Manager in earlier versions of Exchange Server. In Exchange Server 2013, you can use the Exchange Management Shell, or you have a unified GUI experience in the EAC to perform an action, enabling you to do your tasks more efficiently and consistently.

Launch the Exchange Admin Center and navigate to the Mailboxes section of the Recipients option on the feature pane (Figure 14.1). Above the list of recipients you'll notice the plus sign in the Actions bar. This launches the New User Mailbox Wizard, which will allow you to create a user mailbox and associate it with an existing user account, create a new user account with a mailbox, or link a mailbox.

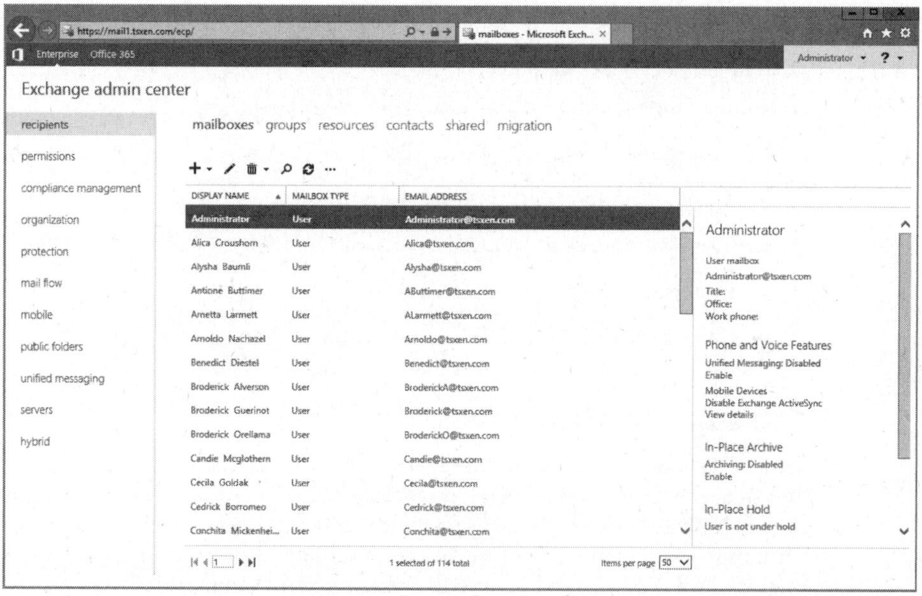

FIGURE 14.1
The Mailboxes section of the EAC's Recipient Configuration work center

User Mailbox   This wizard creates a mailbox for an existing user in the same Active Directory domain. The user could be a new user (without a user account) or an existing user without a mailbox account.

Linked Mailbox   This wizard also creates a disabled user account, assigns it a mailbox, and prompts the administrator to provide a user account in a separate, trusted forest. The account in the other forest is considered the owner of this mailbox and has the Associated External

Account permissions to the mailbox. This is used in organizations that install Exchange Server in a resource forest. If you are creating linked mailboxes, the user account in your forest must remain disabled.

In this example, you are associating a mailbox with a user account that has no mailbox associated to it, thus creating a mailbox-enabled user. To proceed, you would click the Browse button to locate the user account that you want to associate with the new mailbox. After you have selected the user account, you can specify the user's Exchange Server alias, define the mailbox database on which the mailbox will be hosted (or allow Exchange Server to select one for you automatically), create an archive, and assign an Address Book policy to the user if needed. Figure 14.2 shows the wizard.

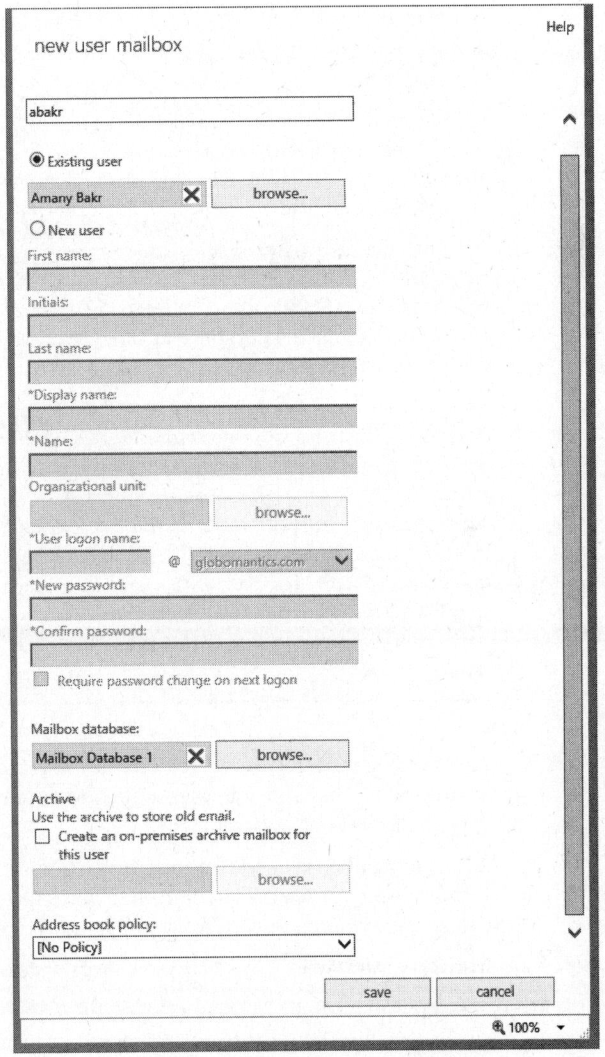

FIGURE 14.2
In the mailbox wizard, you can select a mailbox database for a user, as well as enable an archive mailbox and an address book policy.

Help

new user mailbox

abakr

● Existing user

Amany Bakr ☒ browse...

○ New user

First name:

Initials:

Last name:

*Display name:

*Name:

Organizational unit:

browse...

*User logon name:

@ globomantics.com ▼

*New password:

*Confirm password:

☐ Require password change on next logon

Mailbox database:

Mailbox Database 1 ☒ browse...

Archive
Use the archive to store old email.
☐ Create an on-premises archive mailbox for this user

browse...

Address book policy:

[No Policy] ▼

save   cancel

🔍 100% ▼

AUTOMATICALLY ASSIGNING A MAILBOX TO A DATABASE

Exchange Server 2010's management tools introduced a great feature that automatically assigned a user to a mailbox database, and Exchange Server 2013's EAC inherited this feature. Historically, some mailbox administrators would select the first mailbox database in the list. This feature is a benefit to organizations that have trouble balancing mailboxes on mailbox databases.

Exchange Server 2013 has some load-balancing provisioning logic built into moving mailboxes and creating new mailboxes (as did Exchange Server 2010). You don't need to specify a database name when doing a mailbox creation or mailbox move. The logic is as follows:

1. Gather all databases in the organization.

2. Exclude any databases that are marked to be excluded for mailbox load.

3. Exclude any that are not in the same Active Directory site as the provisioning server.

4. Pick a database at random; check if it's "up" according to Active Manager. If yes, use it. If no, repeat step 4.

If you want to use the load-balancing logic, specifying a mailbox type or profile type won't benefit you, because mailboxes will be randomized across all databases. Microsoft has always recommended that you balance the distribution of the mailbox population and not scope stores with specific classes of users.

Given that, there are scenarios where you may have defined specific databases on which you do not want automatic distribution of mailboxes (such as when you're defining journaling based on the database). You can exclude these databases from the provisioning logic by changing the properties on the database via the Set-MailboxDatabase cmdlet. You have two options: IsExcludedFromProvisioning and IsSuspendedFromProvisioning.

The two options have the same net effect (causing the database to be excluded from the load-balancer algorithm), but one is intended to be short term and the other long term. The scenario for off (IsExcludedFromProvisioning) is used when you have a mailbox database that you want to permanently exclude from provisioning. Let's say it's full or it's a special VIP database. The scenario for temporarily off (IsSuspendedFromProvisioning) is used when you are temporarily taking a server out of rotation for new mailboxes. The reason why this distinction is interesting is that you might wish to identify databases that are permanently off from those that are temporarily off if you are trying to manage the load balancing via automation. If you're turning on and off load balancing to particular databases, you want to make sure you're doing this only for the subset of databases that you would not want to keep permanently excluded.

After you have determined which mailbox database you wish to assign the new mailbox to, there are some other settings you will need to address. From the Mailbox Settings page, you specify the following information:

Alias The alias is used to generate the default SMTP addresses as well as other internal Exchange Server functions. The alias defaults to be the same as the user account name, but you can change it if you need it to conform to other standards.

Mailbox Database This browse list consists of mailbox databases found in the organization.

Create On-premises Archive   The archive mailbox enables the user to archive the emails to an on-premises mailbox, saving the inconvenience of local Personal Storage Table (PST) and lost emails. This can be configured manually or based on retention policies.

Address Book Policy   The Address Book policy enables you to assign a custom address book for that user, hiding some aspects of the GAL from the user.

When you are convinced that the parameters for the mailbox you are creating are correct, click the Save button on the New User Mailbox screen. The EAC then launches an EMS cmdlet that enables the mailbox in the Active Directory.

ASSIGNING A MAILBOX TO MORE THAN ONE USER?

The EAC does not offer the ability to create or assign multiple mailboxes at the same time. In order to do that, you must use the Exchange Management Shell (the PowerShell command-line tool for Exchange Server) to create and assign mailboxes in one shot. In the next section, "Assigning a Mailbox to a User from the EMS," we will explore how to do that in detail.

Assigning a Mailbox to a User from the EMS

In a larger organization, you will probably want to streamline or script the creation of new mailboxes and/or user accounts. The EMS allows you to do this easily. For now, though, let's look at the example you just completed from the EAC graphical user interface. You enabled a mailbox for an existing user, assigned that user a mailbox in a mailbox database. The cmdlet executed is as follows:

```
Enable-Mailbox -Identity ABakr -Alias Abakr -Database MBX-002 –ArchiveName Abakr
-AddressBookPolicy "Engineering AB Policy"
```

This works because there is only a single mailbox database in the entire organization called MBX-002. If you have not established a naming standard for databases, you should do so. Unique database names are required for Exchange Server 2010/2013, because Exchange Server mailbox databases are associated with the organization rather than the individual server as they were in Exchange Server 2007 and earlier versions. When considering database names, we recommend against including the server name since the active copy of a database may move from one server to another if you are using database availability groups.

ASSIGNING PERMISSIONS TO A MAILBOX USING THE EMS

On some occasions, you may need to assign a user the permission necessary to access another user's mailbox. With Exchange Server 2010, you could accomplish this by using the Manage Full Access Permission task in the Actions pane. In Exchange Server 2013, however, you need to open the user's mailbox and navigate to the Mailbox Delegation tab. The permissions available for a selected mailbox are shown in Figure 14.3; these are the Send As, Send On Behalf Of, and Full Access permissions.

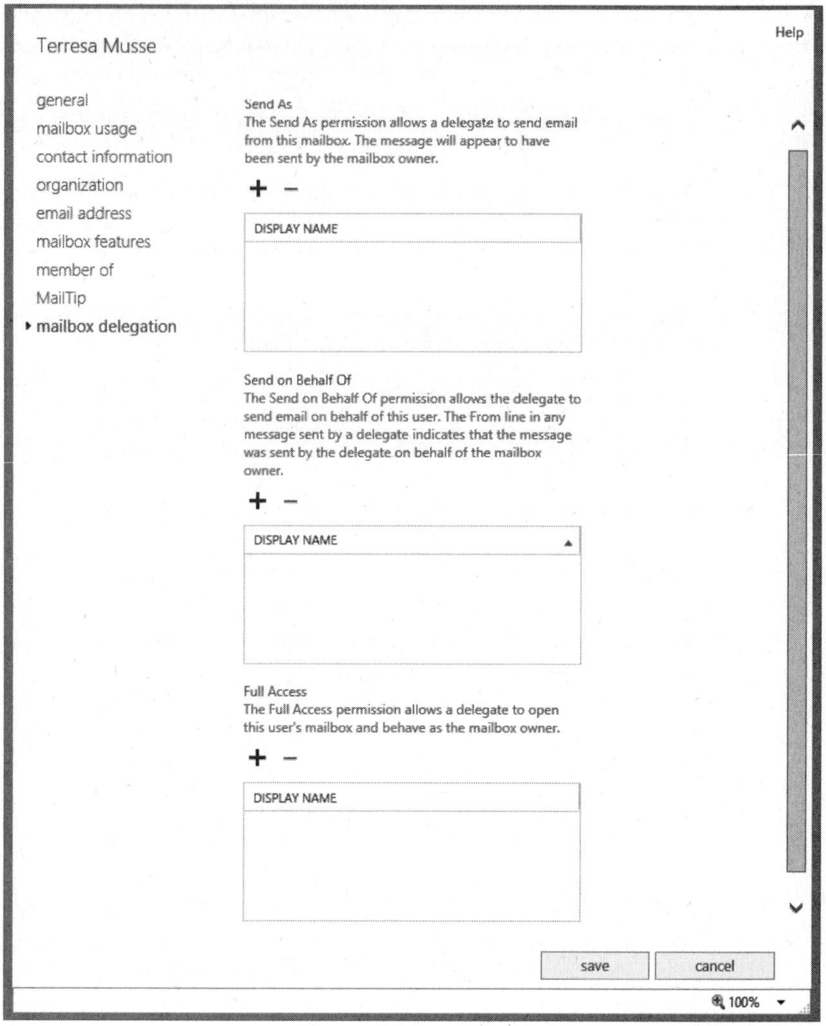

FIGURE 14.3
Permissions
available

Terresa Musse

general
mailbox usage
contact information
organization
email address
mailbox features
member of
MailTip
▸ mailbox delegation

Help

Send As
The Send As permission allows a delegate to send email from this mailbox. The message will appear to have been sent by the mailbox owner.

➕ ➖

DISPLAY NAME

Send on Behalf Of
The Send on Behalf Of permission allows the delegate to send email on behalf of this user. The From line in any message sent by a delegate indicates that the message was sent by the delegate on behalf of the mailbox owner.

➕ ➖

DISPLAY NAME

Full Access
The Full Access permission allows a delegate to open this user's mailbox and behave as the mailbox owner.

➕ ➖

DISPLAY NAME

save   cancel

🔍 100% ▾

- The Full Access permission lets another user open the mailbox and view any message or folder within it.

- The Send As permission lets another user send a message that appears to be coming from the user whose mailbox it is.

- The Send On Behalf Of permission lets another user send a message that appears as (on behalf of) the original user.

  For example, Terresa Musse grants John Rodriguez the Send On Behalf permission, the result being that when John Rodriguez sends a message on behalf of Terresa while logged on to his Outlook or OWA client, the recipient will notice that it is from John Rodriguez on behalf of Terresa Musse. This implies that John Rodriguez is authorized by the owner of the mailbox to send out messages on the owner's behalf, much as one might expect from an executive assistant. This is a bit different than the Send As permission, which does not indicate that the message was sent on behalf of a user and, in fact, grants a degree of impersonation upon the user granted that permission.

FULL ACCESS VS. SEND AS VS. RECEIVE AS PERMISSIONS

Giving a user Full Access permission to another user's mailbox will allow the user to open the other user's mailbox and view any folder or message within the user's mailbox. This is performed via the `Add-MailboxPermission` cmdlet. However, if the user needs to be able to send a message as another user, Full mailbox permission is not sufficient. Send As permissions are intended to be used on shared mailboxes on behalf of a team or department.

Third-party products, such as Research in Motion's BlackBerry Enterprise Server (BES), may require Receive As permissions for the mailboxes that the service account manages. And the BES service account must have Send As permissions on the Active Directory object. You can add Receive As mailbox permissions by using the `Add-MailboxPermission` cmdlet by specifying the `-ExtendedRights Receive-As` parameter. You can add Send As permissions through the EAC or using the `Add-ADPermission` cmdlet. Full Access permissions must be assigned through the `Add-MailboxPermission` cmdlet as well.

If you have been managing Exchange Server organizations for some time, you may remember a time when giving users full mailbox rights would allow them to see all the messages and folders as well as send messages that would originate from that mailbox's address. However, that changed with an Exchange Server 2003 post–Service Pack 2 hotfix. Now Send As permissions must be assigned separately.

ASSIGNING FULL ACCESS PERMISSION

To assign Full Access permissions, simply select the mailbox to which you want to add more permissions, and double-click it to open up the mailbox properties. From the Mailbox Properties interface (the assigned user appears at the top left), select the Mailbox Delegation option on the feaure list, and then you can scroll down and you'll notice the Full Access section. You can click the plus sign to add the selected user to the list of users with full access to this mailbox.

You could also do this using the EMS cmdlet `Add-MailboxPermission`. In this example, we are assigning user abakr permissions to access Haya Mahmoud's mailbox:

```
Add-MailboxPermission -Identity hmahmoud -User abakr -AccessRights FullAccess
```

If you want to assign an administrator permissions to access all mailboxes (such as to import or export mailbox content), you can use the Role-based Access Control (RBAC) management role called Mailbox Import Export. For example, if we want to assign user abakr the role that would allow him to open all mailboxes, we could use this command:

```
New-ManagementRoleAssignment -Role "Mailbox Import Export" -User abakr
```

ASSIGNING SEND AS PERMISSION

To assign Send As permissions, use the same page as for assigning Full Access permission, but in the Send As section, click the plus sign, and add the user who will be assigned the Send As permissions.

You can perform the same task using the EMS; here is an example of giving user abakr Send As permissions to Haya Mahmoud's user account:

```
Add-ADPermission -Identity hmahmoud -User abakr
-AccessRights ExtendedRight -ExtendedRights "Send As"
```

You can remove the permissions you have assigned via the EMS with the following command:

```
Remove-ADPermission -Identity hmahmoud  -User abakr
-ExtendedRights Send-As
```

ASSIGNING SEND ON BEHALF OF PERMISSION

To assign Send On Behalf Of permissions, use the same page as for assigning Full Access and Send As permissions, but in the Send On Behalf Of section, click the plus sign and add the user who will be assigned the Send On Behalf Of permissions.

To achieve the same goal using the Exchange Management Shell, use this cmdlet:

```
Set-Mailbox -Identity hmahmoud -GrantSendOnBehalfTo abakr
```

To remove permissions from the shared mailbox Tsxen Help Desk, you could use this cmdlet:

```
Set-Mailbox "Tsxen Help Desk" -GrantSendOnBehalfTo @{remove="abakr@tsxen.com"}
```

Creating a New User and Assigning a Mailbox Using the EAC

Previously, you saw how to assign a mailbox to an existing user via the EAC; now we will explore how to create a new user and assign the new user a mailbox at the same time (as shown in Figure 14.4).

On the New User Mailbox screen, you provide some basic account information, such as the first name, middle initials, last name, user principal name, pre–Windows 2000 account name, and a new password. You must also specify the organizational unit (OU) in which the user account will be created. You must have the Active Directory permissions necessary to create user accounts in that OU.

The rest of the wizard is exactly the same as if you were enabling a mailbox for an existing user, though there are some small differences in the parameters of the cmdlet. To create a user named Maya.Mahmoud in the Corporate OU, assign her mailbox to the MBX-003 mailbox database and assign her an archive mailbox. Here is the command that the EAC performs:

```
$password = Read-Host "Enter password" -AsSecureString
New-Mailbox -UserPrincipalName mahmoud@tsxen.com -Alias maya -Database "MBX-003"
-Name MayaMahmoud
-OrganizationalUnit Corporate -Password $password
-FirstName Maya -LastName Mahmoud -DisplayName "Maya Mahmoud"
-ResetPasswordOnNextLogon $true
```

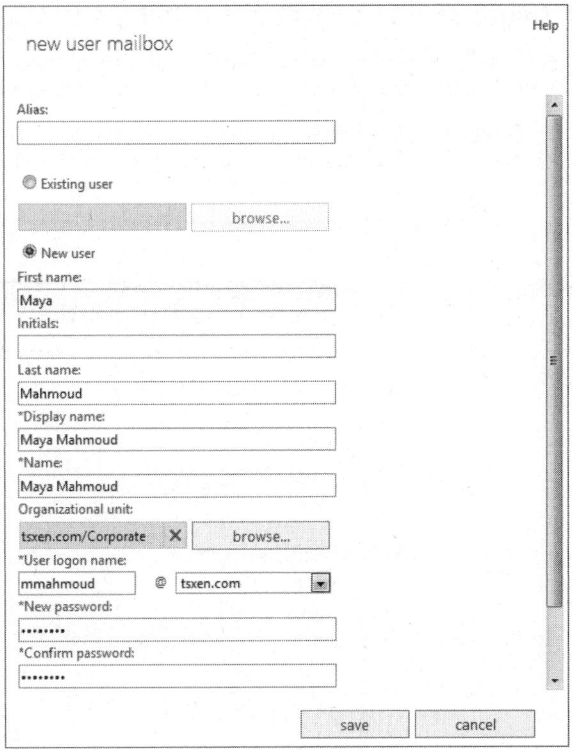

FIGURE 14.4

Creating a user account from the Exchange Administration Center

Because the MBX-003 mailbox database is unique for the Exchange Server organization, no additional identifying information is necessary.

When you include the `$password = Read-Host "Enter password" -AsSecureString` option, you are prompted to enter the password for the user; this helps prevent the password from being compromised. Notice that the cmdlet is not `Enable-Mailbox` as it was in the earlier section, "Assigning a Mailbox to a User from the EMS." That cmdlet is used to assign a mailbox to an *existing* user account. The cmdlet used here is `New-Mailbox`; this cmdlet creates the user account as well as enables the mailbox. Notice that there is an `-OrganizationalUnit` parameter that allows you to specify the domain and the OU name in the canonical name format, such as `tsxen.com/Corporate`.

The `New-Mailbox` cmdlet also has parameters for setting the password, pre–Windows 2000 account name and UPN.

Managing User and Mailbox Properties

Many of the user account properties managed through the Active Directory Users and Computers console can now be managed through the EAC or the EMS. Naturally, using the EAC is a little easier than using the command line, but the EMS is more flexible and efficient in the long term. The tips feature of the Exchange Management Shell allows you to see the EMS cmdlet and syntax necessary to update an object, so your learning curve will be minimized.

USING THE EAC TO MANAGE USER AND MAILBOX PROPERTIES

Let's start with managing user and mailbox properties using the EAC. We'll take a look at a few of the things that you can do and some of the user property pages.

General The General page (Figure 14.5) has some interesting information on it, including the user ID of the last person to access the mailbox, the mailbox size, and the mailbox database name.

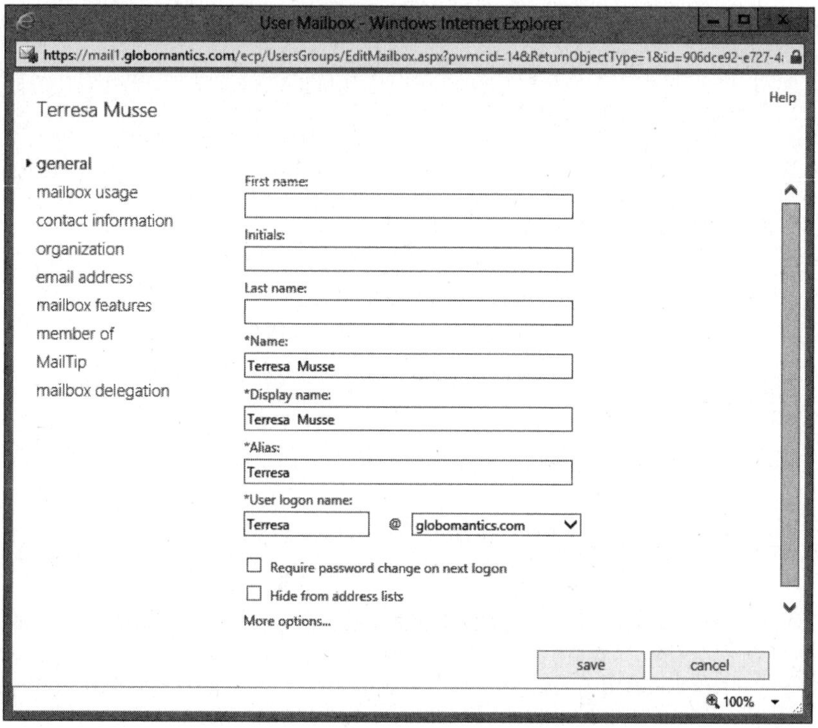

FIGURE 14.5
General properties page for a mailbox

On the General page, you'll notice the Hide From Exchange Address Lists check box. This setting prevents the mailbox from appearing in the global address list (GAL) and other custom address lists. The General page also includes a Custom Attributes section that allows you to access all 15 custom attributes (extension attributes).

Mailbox Usage A new feature of Exchange Server 2013 is Last Logon, which displays when that user logged onto their mailbox. This is useful in determining the frequency of user access. Another option is storage quotas to override mailbox database storage quotas for individual users. This allows the administrator to modify storage quotas up and down depending on the needs of the user.

On the bottom of the Storage Quotas dialog is the individual deleted item retention period. By default, each Exchange Server mailbox database will keep a user's data that has been emptied from the Deleted Items folder, or hard-deleted, for 14 days. Although this does somewhat increase the size of the mailbox database, it also greatly helps reduce the necessity of restoring single items or folders that a user may have accidentally deleted. If you have a user who frequently comes back to you after deleting something more than two weeks past and has to have it restored right away, you could increase their individual deleted item retention time.

Contact Information and Organization   These pages expose most of the attributes available through AD, like Street, City, Country, Company, and Manager.

Email Address   This page is where you can manage the SMTP addresses (and other address types) that are assigned to the mailbox, as Figure 14.6 shows.

FIGURE 14.6
Email Address properties of a mailbox

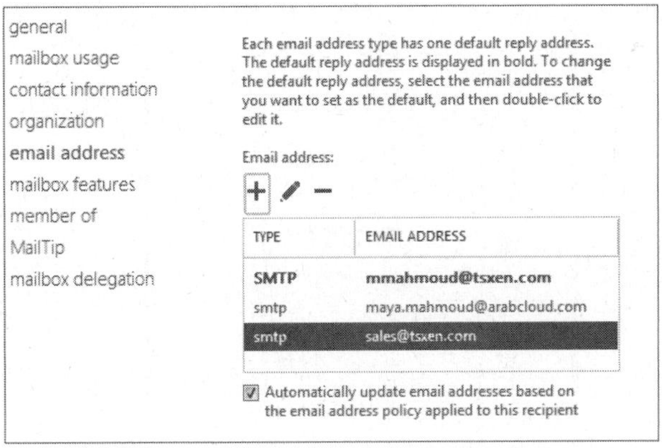

Regardless of how many email addresses are assigned to this mailbox, when an Exchange Server user clicks the Reply button to reply to a message sent to any of these addresses, the Set As Reply address is the one that is always used as the Reply To address. In Figure 14.6, this is the address shown in bold. You can change this by selecting another address, double-clicking the address or selecting the edit button, and clicking the Set As Reply button. If you clear the Automatically Update Email Addresses Based On The Email Address Policy Applied To This Recipient check box, any changes to the email address policy that affect the mailbox will not be made. Clearing this check box also permits you to reassign the Set As Reply email address. This option is not available if the check box is checked.

Email address policies affect the email addresses assigned to an account. As additional email address policies are created, more email addresses will be associated with that user's or resource's mailbox. If a policy that affects the default SMTP address is changed, the email address policy can change a user's primary email address.

Notice in Figure 14.6 that user Maya Mahmoud has addresses from two different domains: mmahmoud@tsxen.com and maya.mahmoud@arabcloud.com. All inbound email for both email addresses will be directed to her mailbox. This is a useful feature for organizations that have more than one domain. Any email to which she replies will have mmahmoud@tsxen.com as the source address. Exchange Server does not allow a user to select which address will be used in the From field of a message.

Mailbox Features   On the Mailbox Features property page (Figure 14.7), there are a number of configuration items, some of which are newly exposed in the GUI in Exchange Server 2013. Depending on your environment, you might want to customize some of these settings.

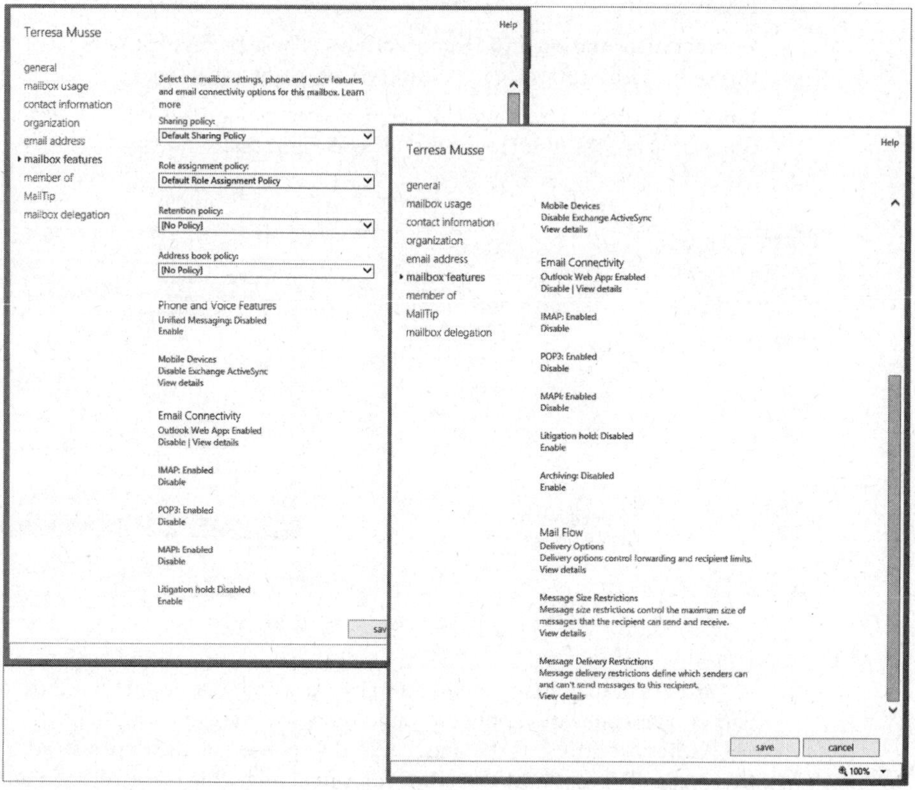

FIGURE 14.7
Mailbox Features
properties

The first of these settings is Sharing Policy, which offers the Federated Sharing Policy option. This is useful only if you have configured the federated sharing features of Exchange Server 2010/2013 to share calendars and contacts across multiple Exchange Server 2010/2013 organizations.

The second setting shows the Role Assignment policies that have been assigned to the owner of the mailbox. Role-based Access Control (RBAC) is discussed in Chapter 12, "Management Permissions and Role-based Access Control," but this where you can change the policy that grants the user a specific RBAC role.

The third section allows an admin to assign the Retention Policy for messages. The Retention Policy defines when messages are moved to an archive mailbox, if the user has one, as well as deletion rules after a retention period has expired.

The fourth section is where Address Book policies can be assigned to the user. A user can only have one Address Book policy assigned to a mailbox at a time.

Below the policy settings are the Phone And Voice Features section, the Email Connectivity section, and the Mail Flow section.

Phone And Voice Features options include:

♦ Enable/Disable Unified Messaging and assign a Unified Messaging mailbox policy

♦ Enable/Disable Exchange ActiveSync, assign a mobile device mailbox policy, and manage mobile devices

Email Connectivity options include:

♦ Enable/Disable Outlook Web App and assign an Outlook Web App mailbox policy

♦ Enable/Disable the IMAP, POP3, and MAPI client protocols

♦ Enable/Disable Litigation Hold

♦ Enable/Disable Archiving

Mail Flow options include:

♦ Delivery Options, such as message forwarding, to mailboxes or recipient groups and placing a limit on the number of recipients

♦ Message Size Restrictions for messages sent and received

♦ Message Delivery Restrictions, with allow lists and rejection lists and requirements for authentication for inbound mail

The Delivery Options page provides the option to deliver messages to an alternate recipient (known as the forwarding address). The recipient that you specify must be a mailbox in your organization or a mail-enabled contact that you find within your GAL.

If you select a mail-enabled contact that you have created in your global address list, this would let you forward all of this user's mail to an external mail system. That can be useful if someone has left the organization and wants to keep getting their mail. It could also be a disaster if that person has left your organization and gone to work for a competitor, so use this feature with caution.

If the Deliver Message To Both Forwarding Address And Mailbox check box is enabled, the message is delivered to both places. This is useful when a manager wants her assistant to receive all her mail but she wants to see the mail as well.

Finally, the bottom part of the Delivery Options page allows you to specify the maximum number of recipients to which this person can send a message. The global default is 5,000, but some organizations want to reduce this figure and allow only the VIPs or authorized users, such as Human Resources personnel, to send messages to large numbers of users.

The Message Size Restrictions allow you to specify the maximum size of messages the user can send or receive. If limits are not specified, the user is limited by the global defaults or the connector defaults.

The last set of configuration options under the Mail Flow Settings section is Message Delivery Restrictions (Figure 14.8). With these options, you can restrict who is allowed to send mail to this particular mailbox. For example, if this is a VIP, you might want to restrict who can send to this mailbox to only a subset of users within the organization. Conversely, you could configure a mailbox to reject mail from a specific set of users.

By default, all mail received from the Internet is received anonymously. Selecting the Require That All Senders Are Authenticated check box will prevent anonymous Internet email from being received as well as cut down on spam.

> You need an Exchange Server enterprise client access license (eCAL) for every user using personal archive mailboxes, retention policies, transport journaling, advanced features of ActiveSync, and Unified Messaging features.

USING THE EMS TO MANAGE USER AND MAILBOX PROPERTIES

You can also manage mailbox and user properties from the Exchange Management Shell. For doing any type of mailbox administration in bulk, you will want to learn how to use the EMS. There are three cmdlet pairs that you should know about in order to manage most of the properties: Get-User and Set-User, Get-Mailbox and Set-Mailbox, and Get-CasMailbox and Set-CasMailbox.

Get-User and Set-User   These cmdlets manage user account properties that are unrelated to Exchange Server. Say that we want to update user Stan.Reimer's mobile phone number. We would type this:

```
Set-User Stan.Reimer -MobilePhone "(808) 555-1234"
```

The Set-User cmdlet has quite a few useful parameters (see the following list). You can retrieve them from within the EMS by typing **Set-User -?** or **Help Set-User**.

City   Sets the city or locality name.

Company   Sets the company name.

Department   Sets the department name.

DisplayName   Updates the user's display name, which appears in the GAL.

Fax   Specifies the fax number.

FirstName   Specifies the given or first name.

HomePhone   Sets the home phone number.

LastName   Specifies the surname or last name.

Manager   Sets the name of the user's manager; the input value must be a distinguished name in canonical name format, such as fourthcoffee.com/Corporate/BenCraig.

MobilePhone   Sets the mobile/cell phone number.

Phone   Sets the business phone number.

PostalCode   Sets the zip or postal code.

StateOrProvince   Sets the state or province.

StreetAddress   Sets the street address.

Title   Sets the title or job function.

You can retrieve the list of properties for Set-User by using the Get-User cmdlet, specifying a username, and then piping the output to the Format-List cmdlet. Piping the output of a Get- cmdlet to Format-List is a great way to enumerate the properties of an object and also to learn the property names. Here is an example of some of the properties that are returned; we removed some properties to save space.

```
Get-User Matthew.Cook | FL

IsSecurityPrincipal       : True
SamAccountName            : Matthew.Cook
SidHistory                : {}
UserPrincipalName         : Matthew.Cook@tsxen.com
ResetPasswordOnNextLogon  : False
CertificateSubject        : {}
RemotePowerShellEnabled   : True
NetID                     :
OrganizationalUnit        : tsxen.com/Corporate
AssistantName             :
City                      : Honolulu
Company                   : Somorita Surfboards
```

```
CountryOrRegion           :
Department                : Surfboard Design
DirectReports             : {}
DisplayName               : Matthew Cook
Fax                       : (808) 555-6657
FirstName                 : Matthew
HomePhone                 :
Initials                  :
LastName                  : Cook
Manager                   :
MobilePhone               : (808) 555-7777
Notes                     :
Office                    : Honolulu Surfboard Design
OtherFax                  : {}
OtherHomePhone            : {}
OtherTelephone            : {}
Pager                     : (808) 555-5545
Phone                     : (808) 555-1234
PhoneticDisplayName       :
PostalCode                : 96816
PostOfficeBox             : {}
RecipientType             : UserMailbox
RecipientTypeDetails      : UserMailbox
SimpleDisplayName         : Matt Cook (Honolulu)
StateOrProvince           : Hawaii
StreetAddress             : 550 Kalakaua Avenue, Suite 201
Title                     : Senior Systems Engineer
UMDialPlan                :
UMDtmfMap                 : {emailAddress:62884392665,
lastNameFirstName:26656288439, firstNameLastName:62884392665}
AllowUMCallsFromNonUsers  : SearchEnabled
WebPage                   :
TelephoneAssistant        :
WindowsEmailAddress       : MatthewCook@tsxen.com
UMCallingLineIds          : {}
IsValid                   : True
ExchangeVersion           : 0.10 (14.0.100.0)
Name                      : Matthew Cook
DistinguishedName         : CN=Matthew Cook,OU=Corporate,
DC=tsxen,DC=com
OriginatingServer         : HNLMBX01.tsxen.com
```

Not only does the Get-User cmdlet allow you to view this information about a user account, but it also allows you to see all the property names. For example, if you did not know what the property name was for the state, you could look in the output listing and see that it is -StateOrProvince. You could then change the user's state by typing the following EMS command:

```
Set-User vlad.mazek -StateOrProvince "Florida"
```

You can pipe the output of one cmdlet together with another one in order to perform bulk administration. Let's say that we want to set the office name of all users who are in Honolulu. We can use a combination of Get-User and Set-User to accomplish this:

```
Get-User | Where-Object {$_.city -eq "Honolulu"} | ↵
Set-User -Office "Main Office"
```

In this example, we piped the output of the Get-User cmdlet to a local filter (using the Where-Object cmdlet). This provided us with a subset of only the users whose city property is equal to Honolulu; the output of that was then piped to the Set-User cmdlet and the office property was updated. That's not too difficult once you see it, is it?

Get-Mailbox and Set-Mailbox   The Set-User and the Get-User cmdlets help you with non–Exchange Server–specific properties of a user account, but the Get-Mailbox and the Set-Mailbox cmdlets will help you view and set the properties of a mailbox-enabled user account. In fact, you have already seen these cmdlets earlier in this book when we talked about setting mailbox storage limits. Let's take a quick look at some ways you can use these cmdlets. For example, if you want to change the user Cheyne.Manalo's rules quota, you would type this:

```
Set-Mailbox cheyne.manalo -RulesQuota 128KB
```

You can set a lot of properties through the EMS and the Set-Mailbox cmdlet. A few of the most useful ones are listed here:

AntispamBypass Enabled   If set to True, this specifies that this mailbox should not have its mail filtered by the Exchange Server 2007 content-filtering component on the Edge Transport or Hub Transport server. The default is False.

CustomAttribute1   Specifies the value for Custom Attribute 1 (Extension Attribute 1). Fifteen custom attributes can be set through the EMS; referred to as CustomAttribute1 through CustomAttribute15.

EmailAddressPolicy Enabled   Specifies whether this mailbox should have its email addresses updated by email address policies.

ForwardingAddress   Specifies an address to which mail sent to this mailbox will be forwarded. The value must be in canonical name format, such as volcanosurfboards.com/Corporate/MikeBrown.

HiddenFromAddress ListsEnabled   If set to True, this mailbox will not appear in any of the Exchange Server address lists. The default is False.

IssueWarningQuota   Specifies the mailbox size above which users will receive a warning message indicating they are over their mailbox quota.

MaxReceiveSize   Specifies the maximum size for messages that can be received into this mailbox.

MaxSendSize   Specifies the maximum size for messages that can be sent by this mailbox.

ProhibitSendQuota   Specifies the mailbox size above which the user will not be able to send any new messages.

ProhibitSend ReceiveQuota Specifies the mailbox size above which the mailbox will reject new mail and the user will not be able to send any messages.

RecipientLimits Specifies the maximum number of recipients per message that a user can send to.

RulesQuota Specifies the maximum amount of rules a user can have in a folder. Note that having more than 32 KB of rules per folder requires the Outlook 2007 client.

SCLDeleteEnabled Specifies if messages above the value of the SCLDeleteThreshold property should be deleted. There are additional SCL threshold options that are not listed in this table.

SCLDeleteThreshold Specifies the SCL (spam confidence level) value at and above which messages flagged as spam should be deleted.

UseDatabaseQuota Defaults If set to False, the mailbox uses the storage quotas set on the mailbox. If set to True (the default), the mailbox uses the mailbox storage quotas that are defined for the mailbox database on which the mailbox is located.

If you want to look up these parameters, from the EMS type **Set-Mailbox -?** or **Help Set-Mailbox.** As we showed you previously with Get-User, you can pipe the output for a mailbox to the Format-List (or FL) cmdlet and see all the properties for that mailbox. The following code shows examples of some of the properties; we did trim out a few of the properties to save space. You may notice that there are some properties that you will find by issuing the Get-User cmdlet as well. That is expected; remember, many of these properties for both Get-User and Get-Mailbox are stored as properties on the same Active Directory user object.

```
Get-Mailbox matthew.cook | Format-List

Database                           : MBX-003
DeletedItemFlags                   : DatabaseDefault
UseDatabaseRetentionDefaults       : True
RetainDeletedItemsUntilBackup      : False
DeliverToMailboxAndForward         : False
LitigationHoldEnabled              : False
SingleItemRecoveryEnabled          : False
RetentionHoldEnabled               : False
EndDateForRetentionHold            :
StartDateForRetentionHold          :
RetentionComment                   :
RetentionUrl                       :
ManagedFolderMailboxPolicy         :
RetentionPolicy                    :
CalendarRepairDisabled             : False
ExchangeUserAccountControl         : None
MessageTrackingReadStatusEnabled   : True
ExternalOofOptions                 : External
```

```
ForwardingAddress                       :
RetainDeletedItemsFor                   : 14.00:00:00
IsMailboxEnabled                        : True
OfflineAddressBook                      :
ProhibitSendQuota                       : unlimited
ProhibitSendReceiveQuota                : unlimited
RecoverableItemsQuota                   : unlimited
RecoverableItemsWarningQuota            : unlimited
DowngradeHighPriorityMessagesEnabled    : False
ProtocolSettings                        : {}
RecipientLimits                         : unlimited
IsResource                              : False
IsLinked                                : False
IsShared                                : False
ResourceCapacity                        :
ResourceCustom                          : {}
ResourceType                            :
SamAccountName                          : Matthew.Cook
SCLDeleteThreshold                      :
SCLDeleteEnabled                        :
SCLRejectThreshold                      :
SCLRejectEnabled                        :
SCLQuarantineThreshold                  :
SCLQuarantineEnabled                    :
SCLJunkThreshold                        :
SCLJunkEnabled                          :
AntispamBypassEnabled                   : False
ServerName                              : hnlmbx01
UseDatabaseQuotaDefaults                : True
IssueWarningQuota                       : unlimited
RulesQuota                              : 64 KB (65,536 bytes)
Office                                  :
UserPrincipalName                       : Matthew.Cook@tsxen.com
UMEnabled                               : False
MaxSafeSenders                          :
MaxBlockedSenders                       :
RssAggregationEnabled                   : True
Pop3AggregationEnabled                  : True
WindowsLiveID                           :
ThrottlingPolicy                        :
RoleAssignmentPolicy                    : Default Role Assignment Policy
SharingPolicy                           : Default Sharing Policy
RemoteAccountPolicy                     :
MailboxPlan                             :
ArchiveGuid                             : 00000000-0000-0000-0000-
000000000000
ArchiveName                             : {}
ArchiveQuota                            : unlimited
ArchiveWarningQuota                     : unlimited
```

```
QueryBaseDNRestrictionEnabled          : False
MailboxMoveTargetMDB                    :
MailboxMoveSourceMDB                    :
MailboxMoveFlags                        : None
MailboxMoveRemoteHostName               :
MailboxMoveBatchName                    :
MailboxMoveStatus                       : None
IsPersonToPersonTextMessagingEnabled    : False
IsMachineToPersonTextMessagingEnabled   : False
UserSMimeCertificate                    : {}
UserCertificate                         : {}
CalendarVersionStoreDisabled            : False
Extensions                              : {}
HasPicture                              : False
HasSpokenName                           : False
AcceptMessagesOnlyFrom                  : {}
AcceptMessagesOnlyFromDLMembers         : {}
AcceptMessagesOnlyFromSendersOrMembers  : {}
AddressListMembership                   : {\Mailboxes(VLV),
\All Mailboxes(VLV),\All Recipients(VLV), \Default Global
Address List, \All Users}
Alias                                   : MatthewCook
ArbitrationMailbox                      :
BypassModerationFromSendersOrMembers    : {}
OrganizationalUnit                      : tsxen.com/Corporate
CustomAttribute1                        :
CustomAttribute2                        :
DisplayName                             : Matthew Cook
EmailAddresses                          : {SMTP:MatthewCook@tsxen.com}
GrantSendOnBehalfTo                     : {}
HiddenFromAddressListsEnabled           : False
LegacyExchangeDN                        : /o=tsxen Solutions LLC
/ou=Exchange Administrative Group (FYDIBOHF23SPDLT)/cn=Recipients
/cn=Matthew Cook
MaxSendSize                             : unlimited
MaxReceiveSize                          : unlimited
ModeratedBy                             : {}
ModerationEnabled                       : False
PoliciesExcluded                        : {}
EmailAddressPolicyEnabled               : True
PrimarySmtpAddress                      : MatthewCook@tsxen.com
RecipientType                           : UserMailbox
RecipientTypeDetails                    : UserMailbox
RejectMessagesFrom                      : {}
RejectMessagesFromDLMembers             : {}
RejectMessagesFromSendersOrMembers      : {}
RequireSenderAuthenticationEnabled      : False
SimpleDisplayName                       :
SendModerationNotifications             : Always
```

```
UMDtmfMap                             : {emailAddress:62884392665,
  lastNameFirstName:26656288439, firstNameLastName:62884392665}
WindowsEmailAddress                   : MatthewCook@tsxen.com
MailTip                               :
MailTipTranslations                   : {}
ExchangeVersion                       : 0.10 (14.0.100.0)
Name                                  : Matthew Cook
DistinguishedName                     : CN=Matthew Cook,OU=Corporate,DC=tsxen,
  DC=com
```

MODIFYING MAILBOX PARAMETERS

Keep in mind that not all properties can be modified, even using the EMS. Many of the properties listed here are system properties and are either created or managed by the system.

Get-CasMailbox and **Set-CasMailbox** Properties specific to the mailbox using a Client Access server are viewed and set using the Get-CasMailbox and Set-CasMailbox cmdlets. These include properties related to ActiveSync, Outlook Web App, POP, IMAP, and MAPI. Here are some of the attributes that can be set using the Set-CasMailbox cmdlet:

```
Get-CASMailbox Matthew.Cook | Format-List

EmailAddresses                   : {SMTP:MatthewCook@tsxen.com}
LegacyExchangeDN                 : /o=tsxen Solutions LLC/ou=Exchange
Administrative Group (FYDIBOHF23SPDLT)/cn=Recipients/cn=Matthew Cook
LinkedMasterAccount              :
PrimarySmtpAddress               : MatthewCook@tsxen.com
SamAccountName                   : Matthew.Cook
ServerLegacyDN                   : /o=tsxen Solutions LLC/ou=Exchange
Administrative Group (FYDIBOHF23SPDLT)/cn=Configuration/cn=Servers
/cn=HNLMBX01
ServerName                       : hnlmbx01
DisplayName                      : Matthew Cook
ActiveSyncAllowedDeviceIDs       : {}
ActiveSyncBlockedDeviceIDs       : {}
ActiveSyncMailboxPolicy          : Default
ActiveSyncMailboxPolicyIsDefaulted : True
ActiveSyncDebugLogging           : False
ActiveSyncEnabled                : True
HasActiveSyncDevicePartnership   : False
OwaMailboxPolicy                 :
OWAEnabled                       : True
ECPEnabled                       : True
EmwsEnabled                      : False
PopEnabled                       : True
PopUseProtocolDefaults           : True
PopMessagesRetrievalMimeFormat   : BestBodyFormat
```

```
PopEnableExactRFC822Size          : False
PopProtocolLoggingEnabled         : False
ImapEnabled                       : True
ImapUseProtocolDefaults           : True
ImapMessagesRetrievalMimeFormat   : BestBodyFormat
ImapEnableExactRFC822Size         : False
ImapProtocolLoggingEnabled        : False
MAPIEnabled                       : True
MAPIBlockOutlookNonCachedMode     : False
MAPIBlockOutlookVersions          :
MAPIBlockOutlookRpcHttp           : False
IsValid                           : True
ExchangeVersion                   : 0.10 (14.0.100.0)
Name                              : Matthew Cook
DistinguishedName                 : CN=Matthew Cook,OU=Corporate,
DC=tsxen,DC=com
```

Moving Mailboxes

Moving mailboxes from one mailbox database to another is a pretty common task for most Exchange Server administrators. Often mailbox databases need to be balanced out because too many large mailboxes have been created on a single mailbox database. You may also need to decommission a server or database and thus move all the mailboxes to a new mailbox database.

If you are an experienced Exchange Server administrator and you are transitioning to Exchange Server 2013 from Exchange Server 2010, you don't need to learn new tricks; mailbox moves in Exchange Server 2013 are largely the same as in 2010. If you are transitioning from older versions, there is a lot to learn.

You must always use the 2013 EAC or the New-MoveRequest cmdlet to move mailboxes to, or between, Exchange Server 2013 mailboxes. Do not use the old Exchange Server 2007 Move-Mailbox cmdlet to do this. The process for moving mailboxes to Exchange Server 2010/2013 databases is significantly different than it was in earlier releases.

Mailboxes are now moved in the background by the Microsoft Exchange Server Mailbox Replication service (MRS) running on a Client Access server. The process is as follows:

1. The administrator submits a new move mailbox request.

2. The New-MoveRequest or new-migrationbatch request updates the Active Directory and adds the mailbox to be moved to a queue by adding a message to the system mailbox on the target mailbox database. The status of the request at this point is Queued.

3. An instance of the MRS (now running on the Mailbox server role, not the CAS as it did in Exchange Server 2010) in the Active Directory site that contains the target mailbox will see the move request. The MRS services on each mailbox periodically query the system mailbox on each database within the local site.

4. The MRS begins to move the mailbox data from the source database to the target database and updates the queue status to InProgress.

5. Near the end of the move, the mailbox is locked, a final synchronization occurs, and the status is changed to CompletionInProgress.

6. When the move is completed, the Active Directory attributes are updated, the old mailbox on the source database is deleted, and the new mailbox is activated. The status is changed to Completed. Client accesses to this mailbox will now be directed to the new mailbox database.

7. The administrator can clear the move request via the `Remove-MoveRequest` or `new-migrationbatch` cmdlet or via the Exchange Administration Center.

There are a number of advantages to this change, including that the mailbox is always available during the move and the actual move is handled server-to-server rather than through a computer running the admin tools. Further, items in the dumpster are also retained. Administrators may find it handy to have statistics readily available about mailbox moves. They can retrieve this information using the `Get-MailboxStatistics` cmdlet.

Mailbox move operations can be quite lengthy depending on a number of factors, including bandwidth between servers, server speed, available RAM, and disk I/O. For typical servers on LAN-speed network segments, we estimate that you can move from 3 GB to 5 GB per hour. For better or worse, your results may vary. Depending on your Active Directory infrastructure and replication times, Outlook Web App users might not be able to reconnect to their mailboxes for up to 15 minutes because the home mailbox database attribute must replicate to all domain controllers.

As with all Exchange Server management tasks, you can perform move mailbox operations using the 2013 Exchange Administration Center or the Exchange Management Shell using `New-MoveRequest` or `New-MigrationBatch`.

Moving Mailboxes Using the EAC

Mailboxes can be moved via the GUI using the Exchange Administration Center. Open the Recipients work center of the EAC, select one or more mailboxes, and then select the Move Mailbox To Another Database task in the Details pane. This launches the New Local Mailbox Move Wizard.

New Local Mailbox Move Wizard

The most important information is found on the Move Configuration page of the New Local Mailbox Move Wizard (see Figure 14.9). You can define the new migration batch name, the target database for the mailbox, the target database for the archive mailbox (if it exists), the maximum bad item limit, and the large item limit.

Occasionally the properties of a message get corrupted. This often happened with previous versions of Exchange Server if a pointer between one table and another table got corrupted. Corrupted messages are much less likely in Exchange Server 2010/2013 since the single-instance storage (SIS) feature has been removed from this version. If a mailbox has more than the maximum number of corrupted messages specified under Bad Item Limit, that particular mailbox will not be moved to the destination database.

When you click Next, you will be presented with the migration batch settings, including the option to select multiple users, specify a CSV file that contains all the users that you want to move, specify a recipient of the message that will be sent when the batch is complete, define if the batch will start automatically or manually, and determine if the move operations will be completed automatically or wait for administrative intervention (see Figure 14.10).

new local mailbox move
Move configuration

Help

These configuration settings will be applied to the new batch. Learn more

*New migration batch name:

Move Amany Bakr

Archive:

◉ Move the primary mailbox and the archive mailbox if one exists

○ Move primary mailbox only, without moving archive mailbox
This option is only valid for mailboxes on Exchange 2010 or Exchange 2013.

○ Move archive mailbox only, without moving primary mailbox
This option is only valid for mailboxes on Exchange 2010 and Exchange 2013.

Target database:
Enter the database name you'd like to move this mailbox to:

Gold DB   ✕   browse...

Target archive database:
Enter the database name you'd like to move the archive mailbox to:

                                                      browse...

Bad item limit:

50

next   cancel

new local mailbox move
Start the batch

Help

A new migration batch will be created after you click new. Learn more

*After the batch is complete, a report will be sent to the following recipients. You must select at least
one recipient to receive this report.

Administrator   ✕   browse...

You can start the batch automatically or start it later by selecting it in the migration dashboard and
then clicking Start.
◉ Automatically start the batch
○ Manually start the batch later

If you don't choose the option below, you will have to manually complete the migration batch by
clicking the "Complete this migration batch" link on the right pane, after the link becomes active.
☑ Automatically complete the migration batch

back   new   cancel

MIGRATION DASHBOARD

As you look at the Recipients tab of the EAC, you'll notice a tab named Migration to the right. This allows you to launch the migration dashboard, another new Exchange Server 2013 feature. The migration dashboard displays very useful information about currently running migration batches and their progress.

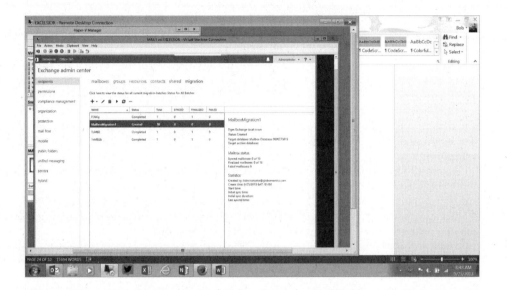

Figure 14.11 shows the mailbox synced and waiting for completion; you can complete the migration batch by clicking the Complete This Migration Batch link. This link is available only if you do not select the Automatically Complete The Migration Batch check box, shown previously in Figure 14.10.

FIGURE 14.11
Migration progress in the migration dashboard

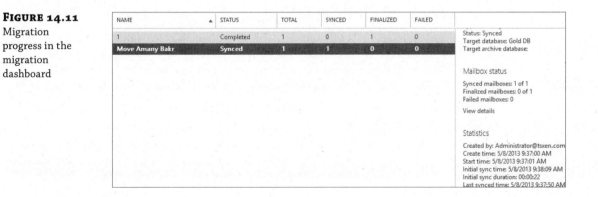

There are multiple handy operations that you can do from the control panel of the migration dashboard. When you click the plus sign, you can create a migration batch, either to a new database or from another forest to your current forest.

Once you are finished, you can edit the batch properties and upload the CSV file to move the users list into the CSV. The CSV file format is very simple, specifying in each line the user's email address.

In the Actions bar that appears during the migration, you can select to stop the migration batch for any reason and resume it later.

NEW MIGRATION ENDPOINT WIZARD

Exchange Server 2013 offers the new concept of migration endpoints. Migration endpoints can be in either your AD forest or a Microsoft Office 365 hosted location in the cloud. In a hybrid deployment, mailboxes can be stored in a locally hosted environment or hosted on the Internet by the Microsoft Office 365 cloud. Endpoints can be either a source or a destination, and to facilitate movement back and forth between your location and the cloud location, they are kept persistent and used later by migration batches to move mailboxes back and forth between endpoints.

To create a migration endpoint, expand the Actions bar by clicking More and select Migration Endpoints. This will open the Migration Endpoint list, displaying the configured endpoints. To add a new one, click the plus sign; this will open the New Migration Endpoint Wizard.

Creating a new migration endpoint is very straightforward; you need to enter the source mailbox, the source administrator account, and the password.

Once you click Next, the wizard will try to verify the settings via autodiscover. If it's not successful, it will ask you to enter the FQDN of the Mailbox Replication Service (MRS) server URL.

Moving Mailboxes Using the EMS

In the previous section, one of the example mailboxes moved belonged to a user named Glenn Chang. We decided that his mailbox should be moved to a mailbox database called MBX-001. To make this move, we opened the Exchange Management Shell and ran the `New-MoveRequest` cmdlet:

```
New-MoveRequest –Identity Glenn.Chang -TargetDatabase 'MBX-001' -BadItemLimit 2
```

This command would also have moved the mailbox:

```
New-MoveRequest –Identity "Glenn Chang" -TargetDatabase 'MBX-001' -BadItemLimit 2
```

If you want to include the bad item count, you could include the parameter `-BadItemLimit:2` in the command. Notice that this cmdlet asks you to confirm that you want the mailbox to be moved. To avoid the confirmation prompt, you can include in the command line `-Confirm:$False` and the cmdlet will not prompt you. That command line would look like this:

```
New-MoveRequest –Identity Glenn.Chang -TargetDatabase 'MBX-001'
-Confirm:$False -BadItemLimit:2
```

A couple other tricks may prove useful for you when you are using the `New-MoveRequest` cmdlet. Let's look at two quick examples. In this first example, you want to move everyone who is a member of the Executives group to the mailbox database called MBX-001. You would use the

Get-DistributionGroupMember cmdlet to enumerate the membership of the Executives group and pipe that output to the New-MoveRequest cmdlet:

```
Get-DistributionGroupMember "#Executives" | New-MoveRequest
-TargetDatabase "MBX-001" -Confirm:$False
```

Additionally, you can move the mailboxes via a migration batch. In the following example, you start with the New-MigrationBatch cmdlet to define the batch job by giving it a name (MoveToGold) and specifying its arguments. You can see that it's a local move (not going to the Internet), the name of the migration batch procedure, followed by the list of mailboxes to migrate from the CSV file. The cmdlet then reads the file from the defined path to a destination database.

```
New-MigrationBatch -Local -Name MoveToGold -CSVData ([System.
IO.File]::ReadAllBytes("C:\Users\Administrator\Desktop\Goldusers.csv"))
-TargetDatabases mbdb-laxmb01-15
```

Then you can start the migration batch:

```
Start-MigrationBatch -Identity MoveToGold
```

Another useful set of cmdlets enumerates everyone whose mailbox is located on one mailbox database and then moves them to another database. You need to use the Get-Mailbox cmdlet and narrow the scope of the search using the -Database parameter so that you output only the objects for mailboxes located on a specific database. Here is an example that includes the output of the New-MoveRequest cmdlet:

```
Get-Mailbox -Database mbx-001 | New-MoveRequest -TargetDatabase MBX-003
```

DisplayName	Status	TotalMailboxSize	TotalArchiveSize	PercentComplete
Michael Brown	Queued	59.54 KB (60,966 bytes)		0
Grace Tanaka	Queued	59.19 KB (60,610 bytes)		0
Cheryl Tung	Queued	80.89 KB (82,831 bytes)		0
Jonathan Core	Queued	59.4 KB (60,822 bytes)		0
Glenn Chang	Queued	59.13 KB (60,547 bytes)		0

With a little creativity, you can probably figure out a number of other ways to accomplish this task or tasks similar to it.

Once you have submitted move requests, you have different ways to check on the status of the moves to see if they are completed. The simplest way is to use the Get-MoveRequest cmdlet to see a list of all the move requests that have been submitted:

```
Get-MoveRequest
```

DisplayName	Status	TargetDatabase
Tyler M. Swartz	Queued	MBX-001
Grace Tanaka	Queued	MBX-001
Cheryl Tung	Queued	MBX-001
Julie R. Samante	Queued	MBX-001

```
Suriya Supatanasakul         Queued              MBX-001
Clayton K. Kamiya            InProgress          MBX-001
Michael G. Brown             InProgress          MBX-001
Jordan Chang                 InProgress          MBX-001
```

If you want to see details of the move and how far along a move request is, you can use the Get-MoveRequestStatistics cmdlet to view a specific move request. Here is an example of Ivan Baker's mailbox performing an intraorganization move. We have piped this to the Format-List cmdlet so that you can see all the properties:

```
Get-MoveRequestStatistics ivan.baker | Format-List

UserIdentity                      : tsxen.com/Corporate/Ivan Baker
DistinguishedName                 : CN=Ivan Baker,OU=Corporate,
DC=tsxen,DC=com
DisplayName                       : Ivan Baker
Alias                             : IvanBaker
ArchiveGuid                       :
Status                            : InProgress
StatusDetail                      : CreatingInitialSyncCheckpoint
SyncStage                         : CreatingInitialSyncCheckpoint
Flags                             : IntraOrg, Pull
MoveType                          : IntraOrg
Direction                         : Pull
IsOffline                         : False
Protect                           : False
Suspend                           : False
SuspendWhenReadyToComplete        : False
IgnoreRuleLimitErrors             : False
SourceVersion                     : Version 14.0 (Build 639.0)
SourceDatabase                    : MBX-001
TargetVersion                     : Version 14.0 (Build 639.0)
TargetDatabase                    : MBX-003
RemoteHostName                    :
RemoteGlobalCatalog               :
BatchName                         :
RemoteCredentialUsername          :
RemoteDatabaseName                :
RemoteDatabaseGuid                :
TargetDeliveryDomain              :
BadItemLimit                      : 0
BadItemsEncountered               : 0
QueuedTimestamp                   : 11/27/2009 10:45:38 AM
StartTimestamp                    : 11/27/2009 10:46:55 AM
LastUpdateTimestamp               : 11/27/2009 10:47:16 AM
InitialSeedingCompletedTimestamp  :
FinalSyncTimestamp                :
CompletionTimestamp               :
```

```
SuspendedTimestamp              :
MoveDuration                    : 00:01:42
TotalFinalizationDuration       :
TotalSuspendedDuration          :
TotalFailedDuration             :
TotalQueuedDuration             : 00:01:13
TotalInProgressDuration         : 00:00:29
TotalStalledDueToCIDuration     :
TotalStalledDueToHADuration     :
TotalTransientFailureDuration   :
MoveServerName                  : HNLMBX01.tsxen.com
TotalMailboxSize                : 4.355 MB (4,566,443 bytes)
TotalMailboxItEACount           : 44
TotalArchiveSize                :
TotalArchiveItEACount           :
BytesTransferred                : 22.55 KB (23,089 bytes)
BytesTransferredPerMinute       : 56.31 KB (57,657 bytes)
ItemsTransferred                : 0
PercentComplete                 : 15
PositionInQueue                 :
FailureCode                     :
Message                         :
FailureTimestamp                :
IsValid                         : True
ValidationMessage               :
```

You can also pipe the output of all move requests currently queued, in progress, or completed using this command:

```
Get-MoveRequest | Get-MoveRequestStatistics
```

DisplayName	Status	TotalMailbox Size	TotalArchive Size	PercentComplete
Grace Tanaka	Queued	115.4 KB ...		0
Clarence A. ...	Queued	59.74 KB ...		0
Clayton K. K...	InProgress	3.895 MB ...		29
Michael G. B...	Completed	116.1 KB ...		100
Jordan Chang	CompletionInProg...	401.6 KB ...		95
Tyler M. Swartz	InProgress	272.5 KB ...	3.427 KB (3	89
Anita Velez	Completed	59.24 KB ...		100

You can use the Get-MoveRequest cmdlet to retrieve information about a specific user's remove request. Here is one example:

```
Get-MoveRequest "Ivan Baker" | FL
```

```
RunspaceId                      : 49ca8abe-886f-4203-82f5-c3cf750f5d1b
ExchangeGuid                    : e8c489ba-3513-4133-a046-aeab6139a325
```

```
SourceDatabase                : MBX-003
TargetDatabase                : MBX-001
Flags                         : IntraOrg, Pull
RemoteHostName                :
BatchName                     :
Status                        : Completed
MoveType                      : IntraOrg
Direction                     : Pull
IsOffline                     : False
Protect                       : False
Suspend                       : False
SuspendWhenReadyToComplete    : False
Alias                         : IvanBaker
DisplayName                   : Ivan Baker
RecipientType                 : UserMailbox
RecipientTypeDetails          : UserMailbox
IsValid                       : True
ExchangeVersion               : 0.10 (14.0.100.0)
Name                          : Ivan Baker
DistinguishedName             : CN=Ivan Baker,OU=Corporate,DC=tsxen,DC=com
Identity                      : tsxen.com/Corporate/Ivan Baker
Guid                          : e48f79c2-af8d-4ef1-9641-2e23b70e23d3
OrganizationId                :
OriginatingServer             : HNLMBX01.tsxen.com
```

You can also use Get-MigrationStatistics to display the migration batch statistics:

```
RunspaceId                    : 8077d2a0-1dd9-43cf-82ab-2aef5c008225
Identity                      :
TotalCount                    : 2
ActiveCount                   : 0
StoppedCount                  : 0
SyncedCount                   : 0
FinalizedCount                : 2
FailedCount                   : 0
PendingCount                  : 0
ProvisionedCount              : 0
MigrationType                 : ExchangeLocalMove
DiagnosticInfo                :
IsValid                       : True
ObjectState                   : Unchanged
```

If you'd like, you can use PowerShell to stop the migration batch:

```
Get-MigrationBatch | Stop-MigrationBatch
```

Alternatively, you can remove the migration batch:

```
Get-MigrationBatch | Remove-MigrationBatch
```

The mailbox object has some specific information about the mailbox's move request as well. Here is an example of how to retrieve that information using the Get-Mailbox cmdlet:

```
Get-Mailbox Ivan.Baker | FL Displayname,*move*

DisplayName                 : Ivan Baker
MailboxMoveTargetMDB        : MBX-001
MailboxMoveSourceMDB        : MBX-003
MailboxMoveFlags            : IntraOrg, Pull
MailboxMoveRemoteHostName :
MailboxMoveBatchName        :
MailboxMoveStatus           : Completed
```

The Get-MailboxStatistics cmdlet also includes some fascinating information with respect to the move history, but you have to include the -IncludeMoveHistory option in the command line. Look at the MoveHistory property in this example:

```
Get-MailboxStatistics ivan.baker -IncludeMoveHistory | Format-List

AssociatedItEACount     : 12
DeletedItEACount        : 0
DisconnectDate          :
DisplayName             : Ivan Baker
ItEACount               : 32
LastLoggedOnUserAccount : ITHICOS\Ivan.Baker
LastLogoffTime          :
LastLogonTime           : 11/27/2009 1:34:31 PM
ObjectClass             : Mailbox
StorageLimitStatus      : BelowLimit
TotalDeletedItemSize    : 0 B (0 bytes)
TotalItemSize           : 4.356 MB (4,568,055 bytes)
Database                : MBX-003
ServerName              : HNLMBX01
DatabaseName            : MBX-003
MoveHistory             : {(11/21/2009 10:48:01 AM: TargetMDB=MBX-003,
Size=4.355 MB (4,566,443 bytes), Duration=00:02:18), (11/26/2009
11:31:02 PM: TargetMDB=MBX-001, Size=4.301 MB (4,510,383 bytes),
Duration=00:02:03)}
IsQuarantined           : False
IsArchiveMailbox        : False
```

Once you are sure that you no longer need the information about a move request, you can remove the completed or queued move requests using the Remove-MoveRequest cmdlet. This removes the move status information from Active Directory but does not remove the move history from the mailbox statistics. To remove user Ivan.Baker's move request information, use this command:

```
Remove-MoveRequest Ivan.Baker -Confirm:$False
```

You can also remove all move requests that completed successfully using this command:

```
Get-MoveRequest | Where {$_.Status -eq "Completed"} | Remove-MoveRequest
```

> ### 🌐 Real World Scenario
>
> #### MANAGE THE MIGRATION BATCH
>
> A lot of architects and consultants spend a great deal of time staring at mailboxes as they move; this is extremely frustrating. To avoid this, don't move the mailboxes in specific move windows after the environment is entirely built. Rather, create a move batch that does not complete immediately and allows you to suspend the batch, providing you with more flexibility regarding when the batch file will complete. That way, you can complete your infrastructure, doing the necessary consulting work while the mailboxes are being moved.
>
> Once you are ready to complete the move batch, the move batch will resync the emails and find what has changed, resync the changes, and complete the move; this will complete the migration. Creating the migration batch takes a little time, but launching it takes a few seconds, and the migration takes place over hours instead of days.

Retrieving Mailbox Statistics

Frequently, Exchange Server mailbox administrators need to run a report and list the amount of storage that each mailbox is consuming. With previous versions of Exchange Server, this information was available via the GUI, but now it is available via the EMS cmdlet `Get-MailboxStatistics`. The `Get-MailboxStatistics` cmdlet requires one of three parameters:

- **-Identity** Retrieves the mailbox statistics for a specific mailbox
- **-Database** Retrieves statistics for all mailboxes on a specific mailbox database
- **-Server** Retrieves statistics for all mailboxes on a specific server

Here is an example using this cmdlet with a single mailbox on the database MBX-003:

```
Get-MailboxStatistics Clayton.Kamiya
```

```
DisplayName          ItEACount   StorageLimitStatus        LastLogonTime
-----------          ---------   ------------------        -------------
Clayton K. Kamiya    35                      NoChecking 11/27/2009 1:34:31 PM
```

And here is an example for all of that database's mailboxes:

```
Get-MailboxStatistics -Database MBX-003
```

```
DisplayName               ItEACount StorageLimitStatus        LastLogonTime
-----------               --------- ------------------        -------------
Suriya Supatanasakul      4                     BelowLimit 11/25/2009 9:55:28 AM
Online Archive - Chuck... 0                     NoChecking 12/15/2009 7:47:41 AM
Michael G. Brown          4                     BelowLimit 11/26/2009 9:01:12 AM
Chuck Swanson             9
Jason Crawford            5                     BelowLimit 11/27/2009 3:53:09 PM
Jordan Chang              11                    BelowLimit
Luke Husky                4                     BelowLimit 12/21/2009 5:23:48 PM
Clayton K. Kamiya         35                    NoChecking 12/23/2009 6:48:12 AM
Ivan Baker                32                    BelowLimit 12/13/2009 7:13:38 PM
```

Not a real attractive report, is it? However, keep in mind that what is being output to the PowerShell are objects (and those objects' properties), so that provides you with the building blocks to produce a report that contains the information you require.

There are a few useful properties that are part of the objects that output when you use the `Get-MailboxStatistics` cmdlet. You can use these properties to constrain the output that is sent to the screen, as well as the output if you redirect this information to a file. The following are some of the properties of the objects that are output when you use the `Get-MailboxStatistics` cmdlet:

DisplayName   Name of the mailbox.

ItEACount   Total number of items stored in the entire mailbox.

TotalItemSize   Total size of all of the items in the mailbox except for items in the deleted item cache.

TotalDeletedItemsSize   Total size of items that are in the deleted item cache.

StorageLimitStatus   Status of the mailbox storage limits; the limits you may see are as follows:

- `-BelowLimit`—Mailbox is below all limits.

- `-IssueWarning`—Mailbox storage is above the issue warning limit.

- `-ProhibitSend`—Mailbox is above the prohibit send limit.

- `-MailboxDisabled`—Mailbox is over the prohibit send and receive limit.

Database   Name of the database, such as MBX-002, on which the mailbox is located.

ServerName   Name of the mailbox server on which the database is active.

LastLogoffTime   Date and time of the last time someone logged off the mailbox.

LastLogonTime   Date and time of the last time someone logged on to the mailbox.

LastLoggedOnUserAccount   Domain name and username of the last person to access the mailbox.

DisconnectDate   Date and time when the mailbox was deleted or disconnected.

IsArchive   Indicates if this is an archive mailbox (`True`) or not (`False`).

IsQuarantined   Indicates if this mailbox has been flagged as having problems and has been quarantined (`True`).

MoveHistory   Includes the history (date/time/mailbox database) of mailbox moves if the `-IncludeMoveHistory` parameter is used.

So, perhaps you want to look at a mailbox report that includes only the display name, the total size of the mailbox, the total number of items, and the storage limit status. Further, you can include the where clause and filter out any mailbox whose name contains the word *system*. The following example shows what this would look like:

```
Get-MailboxStatistics -Database MBX-003 | where {$_.displayname -notlike ↵
"*System*"} | FT displayname, @{expression={$_.totalitemsize.value.ToKB()}; ↵
width=20;label="Mailbox Size(kb) "},ItEACount,StorageLimitStatus
```

DisplayName	Mailbox Size(kb)	ItEACount	StorageLimitStatus
Julie R. Samante	114	4	BelowLimit
Suriya Supatanas...	117	4	BelowLimit
Ken Vickers	114	4	BelowLimit
John Park	402	11	BelowLimit
Online Archive -...	1	0	NoChecking
Michael G. Brown	117	4	BelowLimit
Chuck Swanson	184	9	
Online Archive -...	3	0	NoChecking
Clarence A. Birtcil	115	4	BelowLimit
Jonathan Core	117	4	BelowLimit
Matthew Badeau	115	4	BelowLimit
Kevin Wile	116	4	BelowLimit
Jason Crawford	145	5	BelowLimit

One way to modify the output is by using the Expression feature of the PowerShell language and converting the mailbox size to kilobytes. Depending on the size of your typical mailbox, you might want to convert the mailbox size report to megabytes or gigabytes. Here is an example of the expression necessary to convert to megabytes:

```
expression=($_TotalItemSize.Value.ToMB()
```

You can redirect the output to a text file using the > character and a filename:

```
Get-MailboxStatistics -Database MBX-003 | where {$_.displayname -notlike
"*System*"} | FT displayname, @{expression={$_.totalitemsize.value.ToKB()};
width=20;label="Mailbox Size(kb) "},ItEACount,StorageLimitStatus
> c:\Mailbox.txt
```

You could also pipe the output to the Export-Csv, Export-Clixml, or ConvertTo-Html cmdlet and send the data to a CSV, XML, or HTML file. Take a look at Chapter 5, "Introduction to PowerShell and the Exchange Management Shell," for more detailed examples of how to tune the output of Get-MailboxStatistics.

Here are a few more useful examples of things that you can do with the Get-Mailbox Statistics cmdlet. This command lets you report on mailboxes that have not been accessed in the last 30 days; it uses the PowerShell cmdlet Get-Date but subtracts 30 days from the current date:

```
Get-MailboxStatistics -Database MBX-003 | where {$_.LastLogonTime -lt
(Get-Date).AddDays(-30)} -And $_DisplayName -notlike "*System*"} |
Format-Table displayName,lastlogontime,lastloggedonuseraccount,servername
```

Here is a command that lets you see a list of all the mailboxes that have been disconnected over the last seven days on server HNLMBX01:

```
Get-MailboxStatistics -Server HNLMBX01 | Where-Object {$_.DisconnectDate
-gt (Get-Date).AddDays(-7)} | Format-Table displayName,ServerName,
DatabaseName,TotalItemSize -Autosize
```

Deleting Mailboxes

Deleting mailboxes might not seem like such a complicated task until you look at the Actions bar once you have selected a mailbox in the Recipients Configuration work center. There are few options with respect to deleting a mailbox, including simply disconnecting the mailbox from a user account, deleting both the account and the mailbox, and purging a previously deleted mailbox. We'll also look at how to reconnect a deleted mailbox.

USE CAUTION WHEN DELETING!

In Exchange Server 2013, the Actions bar provides you with the default Delete action, which will delete the mailbox and the user account. If you want to delete only the mailbox, make sure to click More and select Disable.

Deleting the Mailbox but Not the User

If you choose the Disable option, the mailbox is disconnected from the user account, but the user account remains in the Active Directory. This is the equivalent of using the EMS cmdlet `Disable-Mailbox`. For example, to remove a mailbox from an existing user, you could type this:

```
Disable-Mailbox Damion.Jones -Confirm:$False
```

All this command does is disconnect the mailbox from the user account; the user account remains in the Active Directory. After the deleted mailbox recovery time expires, the mailbox will be permanently removed from the mailbox database.

Deleting Both the User and the Mailbox

If you choose the Remove option, the mailbox is disconnected from the user account, *and* the user account is deleted from the Active Directory. You can accomplish the same thing from the EMS using the `Remove-Mailbox` cmdlet. Here is an example:

```
Remove-Mailbox Cheyne.Manalo
```

This command will prompt you to verify that you want to remove the mailbox; you can avoid the confirmation prompt by including the `-Confirm:$False` parameter. If you want to delete the mailbox and the account and prevent the mailbox from being recovered, you can include the `-Permanent:$True` parameter. Here is an example that automatically confirms the deletion and permanently removes the mailbox:

```
Remove-Mailbox Jonathan.Long -Permanent:$True -Confirm:$False
```

Permanently Purging a Mailbox

By default, after the deleted mailbox recovery time has expired, the mailbox will be permanently purged from the mailbox database. If you have already deleted the mailbox and want to permanently purge the mailbox from the mailbox database, you can also do that, but it requires two lines. The first line sets a variable ($Temp) that retrieves the mailbox object for a mailbox whose display name is Martha Lanoza. The second line uses that variable along with the `MailboxGuid` property of that mailbox to remove that mailbox from the VIP Mailboxes database. Here are the two commands that would need to be executed:

```
$Temp = Get-User "Martha Lanoza" | Get-MailboxStatistics
Remove-Mailbox -Database "VIP Mailboxes" -StoreMailboxIdentity
$Temp.MailboxGuid
```

This example assumes there would be only a single mailbox whose display name is Martha Lanoza and that there is only a single mailbox database named VIP Mailboxes. With a little creativity, you can permanently purge mailboxes in other ways, but this is a basic EMS method for doing so.

Reconnecting a Deleted Mailbox

Exchange Server allows you to undelete a mailbox that you may have accidentally disconnected from a user account. The simplest way to do this is to use the EAC, but you can also do it using the EMS.

RECONNECTING A MAILBOX USING THE EAC

One the right side of the Actions menu of the Mailbox tab, you will see an ellipsis (…). Hovering your mouse over the ellipsis shows that this is the More button. Selecting that gives you a drop-down menu with options to add/remove columns, export to a PST file, export data to a CSV file, connect to a mailbox, or perform an advanced search. Once you select the Connect action from the More button, you will be prompted with the Connect A Mailbox Wizard. You can open the drop-down menu to select a specific mailbox server (see Figure 14.12).

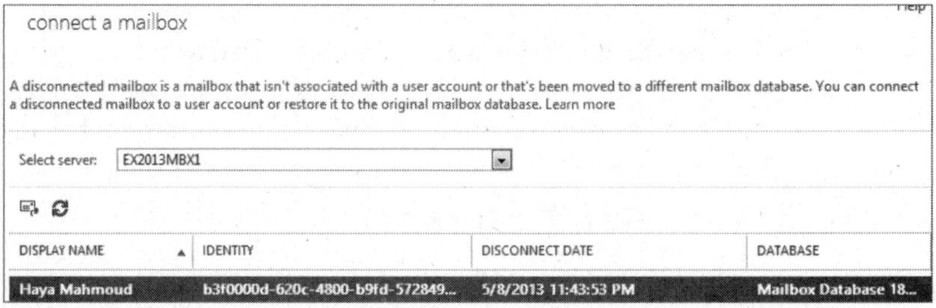

FIGURE 14.12
Reconnecting a mailbox that has been deleted

From the list of disconnected mailboxes in this example, we will select the disconnected mailbox for Haya Mahmoud and reconnect it to her account. When you click Connect, you will be asked if you want to connect the mailbox to the original account (which might be the case if you deleted that mailbox by mistake) or a different account.

If you select to connect to a different user account, you will be prompted with another screen asking you to select from existing user accounts in Active Directory. These accounts must be valid and not have associated mailboxes; this is a useful scenario if a user left the company and you want to associate that user's mailbox with the person hired to replace that employee, for example.

Select the type of mailbox that you are connecting—User mailbox, Room Resource mailbox, Equipment Resource mailbox, or Linked mailbox—and click the Next button. You will be prompted with the list of options; select the appropriate user account and click Finish.

You could generate the same list using the Get-MailboxStatistics command and filter based on viewing only objects whose DisconnectDate property contains data:

```
Get-MailboxStatistics -Server HNLMBX01 | Where {$_.DisconnectDate ⏎
-ne $null} | Format-Table DisplayName,DisconnectDate
```

```
DisplayName          DisconnectDate
-----------          --------------
Micah Hoffmann       12/10/2009 3:13:37 AM
David Elfassy        12/02/2000 3:13:23 AM
Paul Agamata         11/25/2009 3:13:55 AM
Brian Tirch          11/20/2009 3:13:47 AM
Clayton Kamiya       11/16/2009 3:13:01 AM
```

NO MORE WORRIES ABOUT DISCONNECT MAILBOXES

In previous versions of Exchange Server, if you deleted a mailbox you would needed to run `clean-mailboxdatabase` to clean up the database so disconnected mailboxes would appear in the Disconnected Mailboxes section.

In Exchange Server 2013, the `Disable-Mailbox` cmdlet runs a cleanup process immediately after you disconnect a user's mailbox, updating the database to reflect the disconnected status.

RECONNECTING A MAILBOX USING THE EMS

To reconnect a deleted mailbox using the EMS, you use the `Connect-Mailbox` cmdlet. This cmdlet takes an identifier for the mailbox you are trying to connect to using either the unique mailbox GUID, the display name, or the legacy Exchange Server distinguished name. The display name of the mailbox is the easiest to use. You also must provide the name of the database in which the mailbox is located and the user account you wish to connect to the mailbox.

Before you do this, let's take a quick look at another iteration of the `Get-MailboxStatistics` cmdlet and how to enumerate the information you need to reconnect a mailbox. This output displays the database name and the display name:

```
Get-MailboxStatistics -Server HNLMBX01 | Where {$_.DisconnectDate ⏎
-ne $null} | Format-Table DisplayName,Database
```

```
DisplayName                   Database
-----------                   --------
Aran Hoffmann                 MBX-001
Paul Agamata                  MBX-002
Donny Shimamoto               MBX-003
Clayton Kamiya                MBX-003
```

Let's say you have accidentally deleted user Clayton Kamiya's mailbox from the Executives mailbox database; this user also had a managed folder policy and an ActiveSync policy. To reconnect this user's mailbox to user account volcanosurf\Clayton.Kamiya, here is the command you would execute:

```
Connect-Mailbox "Clayton Kamiya" -Database:"MBX-003" -Alias:"Clayton.Kamiya"
-User:"volcanosurf\Clayton.Kamiya" -ManagedFolderMailboxPolicy:"All Employees"-
MobileMailboxPolicy:"Standard User ActiveSync Policy"
```

Bulk Manipulation of Mailboxes Using the EMS

Arguably the most useful feature of the PowerShell and the EMS is the ability to perform bulk manipulation of objects.

Managing Mailbox Properties with the EMS

Let's say you want to do something like turn off OWA for all users. This is set using the `Set-CASMailbox` cmdlet (not `Set-Mailbox`). You could do this with a one-liner, though, by retrieving a list of all mailboxes in the organization and then piping each mailbox to the `Set-CASMailbox` cmdlet:

```
Get-Mailbox | Set-CASMailbox -OWAEnabled:$False
```

Does this look powerful? Does this look dangerous? We say yes on both counts. You can easily do something you did not intend to do, so take care when using the EMS if you are performing any type of bulk administration.

You are probably not interested in making mass changes to every mailbox or user account in your organization, at least not usually. That is why group membership comes in so handy. A few cmdlets are useful when it comes to using the membership of a group. The `Get-DistributionGroup` cmdlet will list all of the distribution groups in the organization, but it does not provide you with a membership list:

```
Get-DistributionGroup

Name                 DisplayName         GroupType           PrimarySmtpAddress
----                 -----------         ---------           ------------------
$Operations Group$Operations Group    Global, Security… OperationsGroup@…
$Executives and …$Executives and …   Global, Security… ExecutivesandVIP…
DirectoryUpdateS…!Directory Updat…    Universal           DirectoryUpdateS…
Executives           Executives          Universal           Executives@somor…
VIPs                 VIPs                Universal, Secur… VIPs@somorita.com
Executives           Somorita Executives Universal, Secur… SomoritaExecutiv…
Somorita Sales a…   Somorita Sales a…   Universal, Secur… SomoritaSalesand…
```

To retrieve a list of objects that are members of a distribution group, you need the `Get-DistributionGroupMember` cmdlet. Here is the output (remember that this is not text within the PowerShell environment; these are unique objects that can be piped as input to another cmdlet):

```
Get-DistributionGroupMember "Executives"

Name                               RecipientType
----                               -------------
Goga Kukrika                       UserMailbox
Pavel Nagaev                       UserMailbox
Ryan Tung                          UserMailbox
George Cue                         UserMailbox
Chris Eanes                        UserMailbox
Bthaworn Thaweeaphiradeemaitree    UserMailbox
Jason Sherry                       UserMailbox
```

Do you remember the cmdlet we used to override the mailbox quotas for one mailbox? Let's expand on that and set that quota for all members of the Executives group. Here is an example:

```
Get-DistributionGroupMember "Executives" | Set-Mailbox -ProhibitSendQuota:250MB
-IssueWarningQuota:200MB -UseDatabaseQuotaDefaults:$False
-ProhibitSendReceiveQuota:300MB
```

This cmdlet retrieves the membership list for the Executives distribution group and then passes those objects as input to the `Set-Mailbox` cmdlet.

How about another common task? Let's say you need to move all of the mailboxes in the Executives group to a mailbox database called Executives. Here is the command to do that:

```
Get-DistributionGroupMember "Executives" | New-MoveRequest -BadItemLimit:2 ↩
```

You could extend that and move all mailboxes on a specific server by using the `-Server` option of the `Get-Mailbox` cmdlet to help you narrow your listing of mailboxes:

```
Get-Mailbox -Server:HNLEX04 | New-MoveRequest -TargetDatabase:MBX-003
```

What if you want to move only the mailboxes on a specific database? Here is another example:

```
Get-Mailbox -Database MBX-004 | New-MoveRequest -TargetDatabase "MBX-003"
-Confirm:$False
```

With a little creativity, you can probably figure out a number of other ways to accomplish this or similar tasks.

Scripting Account Creation

In some organizations, many accounts are created at one time. The EMS and PowerShell give you the ability to automate this process by reading the data in from a text or CSV file. Although you could probably automate the process if you created a massive one-liner, it is much easier to create a simple PowerShell script. First, let's look at a CSV input file of new user accounts:

```
Name,Database,OrganizationalUnit,UserPrincipalName
Saul Tigh,MB-DB1,colonialfleet.int/Military,Saul.Tigh@fleet.int
Helena Cain, MB-DB1,colonialfleet.int/Military,Helena.Cain@fleet.int
Felix Gaeta, MB-DB1,colonialfleet.int/Military,Felix.Gaeta@fleet.int
Tory Foster, MB-DB1,colonialfleet.int/Civilians,Tory.Foster@fleet.int
Tom Zarek,MB-DB1,colonialfleet.int/Civilians,Tom.Zarek@fleet.int
Samuel Anders,MB-DB1,colonialfleet.int/Civilians,Samuel.Anders@fleet.int
Hera Agathon,MB-DB1,colonialfleet.int/Civilians,Hera.Agathon@fleet.int
```

This CSV file has four columns; they represent the absolute minimum necessary to create an account and assign it a mailbox. Naturally, in real life you would have more columns (first name, last name, SAM account name, Exchange Server alias, and so on). Also, the OUs in the Active Directory must exist for these users.

Here is the script for creating these mailboxes:

```
# Read the c:\demo\newaccounts.csv file. The first line is the header.
# Each additional line represents a user object.
# Read all of these in to the $Users variable.
$Users = Import-Csv C:\Demo\newaccounts.csv
```

```
# Output the contents of the $Users variable.
# This command is not necessary as it only outputs the list to the screen.
$Users

# Prompt the person running the script for a password.
# This password will be assigned to each user created.
$Password = Read-Host "Please enter a password" -AsSecureString

# A simple Foreach loop to create the new users
# For each line in the $Users variable, run the New-Mailbox cmdlet.
# $User.Database represents the value of the Database field for user.
Foreach ($User in $Users) {
  New-Mailbox -Name $User.Name -Database $User.Database -OrganizationalUnit ⏎
$User.OrganizationalUnit -UserPrincipalName $User.UserPrincipalName ⏎
-Password $Password
}
```

Managing Mailbox Content

The need to control mailbox content and size is often due to limited disk space for mailbox databases, but it may also be due to company security policies, archiving, electronic discovery (eDiscovery) requirements, or regulatory compliance. But you may just want to help your users clean the junk out of their mailboxes. Over the years, many solutions for managing mailbox and folder content have come and gone.

Many organizations are now employing archival solutions that will remove content from users' mailboxes and store it in long-term storage, such as tape, optical, network-attached storage (NAS), or storage area networks (SANs). In some cases, archival solutions are put in place merely to reduce the size of the Exchange Server databases but still allow users long-term access to their old mail data. In other cases, an organization is required to keep certain types of message content, such as financial data, official company communications, and healthcare-related data.

Mailbox archiving has raised new issues and challenges not only for the Exchange Server administrator but for management and users as well. Some types of messages may need to be retained for long periods of time, but not necessarily one copy of each message in each mailbox. There has to be some method of determining which messages should be retained or archived, and sometimes that task may fall on the user.

Organizations that are concerned about meeting regulatory requirements with respect to message archiving and long-term retention of certain types of messages may also be interested in keeping a journaled copy of messages.

Exchange Server 2007 introduced the basics of mailbox contents management; Exchange Server 2010 leaped forward with retention policies and retention tags. Exchange Server 2013 continues with the policies and tags from previous editions with some modifications. In this section, we will explore retention policies and tags in detail.

Understanding the Basics of Messaging Records Management

Before diving into how you would set up and implement Messaging Records Management (MRM), let's discuss some basics. We'll explore possible usage scenarios, what the user would see, and the basics of getting started.

First, let's get some terminology out of the way. Messaging Records Management encompasses management of email content "at rest." This means that you are managing the content while it is sitting in a folder in someone's mailbox. Don't get this concept confused with transport rules, which are discussed in more detail in Chapter 23, "Managing Transport, Data Loss Prevention, and Journaling Rules."

MESSAGING RECORDS MANAGEMENT AND LICENSING

Exchange Server 2013 licensing for MRM is simple; you can use the default type of retention policies. Default policies are applied to the entire mailbox.

If you wish to use personal or custom policies, you will need to purchase an enterprise CAL. The following web page contains more information:

```
http://office.microsoft.com/en-us/exchange/microsoft-exchange-server-licensing-
licensing-overview-FX103746915.aspx
```

USER PARTICIPATION

Keep in mind that MRM does not include "important message pixie dust." A popular misconception is that content that should be retained will automatically be moved to the appropriate managed folder. Messages do *not* get organized automatically. Users must participate in MRM by moving their relevant content into the appropriate managed folders.

There are two different perspectives on what you can implement with MRM—without user participation and with user participation. You can do certain tasks without user involvement, such as purging mail in existing folders or moving mail to a message archive. However, the real mission of MRM is to get the user to participate in the process. You can use the MRM process to create custom retention tags in the user's mailbox, but it is up to the user to determine where and when to apply this tag. Figure 14.13 shows a set of custom tags.

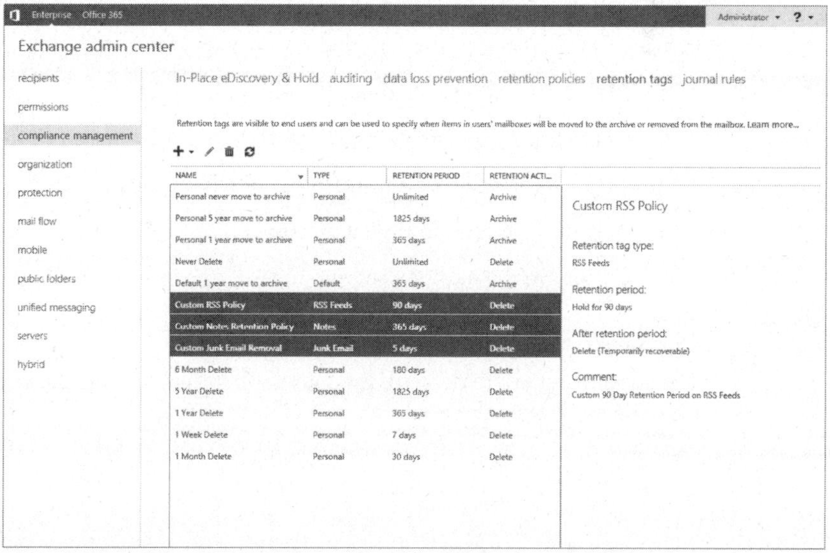

FIGURE 14.13
Custom retention tags defined

The administrator defines the policy name, the retention action, and the period in days before the retention action should be applied, and it is up to the user to apply those retention tags. Users are trained to categorize their mailbox content and apply personal retention tags to them. This will allow the Exchange server to take actions based on the policies applied and delete/move items based on the retention tags' settings. The most crucial thing to realize is that *the user must participate in the process.*

POSSIBLE SCENARIOS

Even if your organization does not perform mailbox archiving or does not have to deal with regulatory compliance, you will probably find many useful scenarios for MRM, such as these:

◆ Creating custom retention tags that are used by users to categorize or organize information that must be retained

◆ Deleting items in the Sync Issues folder

◆ Archiving emails in a shared mailbox on a daily basis and emptying it

◆ Enforce deletion of Inbox messages after the defined retention period

◆ Automate the movement of messages from one folder to another

◆ Archive, delete, or move voicemail messages after a period of time

These are just a few of the possible uses for MRM.

Getting Started with Messaging Records Management

Retention policies and tags can be defined in the EAC or the EMS. For most of the actions we will be describing, we will show you the EAC interface and follow up with EMS commands as necessary.

The retention policies and tags are located in the Compliance Management section in the EAC. You cannot set up MRM using a single dialog or wizard. A few steps are involved in getting started. We'll go into more detail later in the chapter on how to do each of these steps, but let's start with a basic outline of how you would get started with a policy:

1. Create a retention tag (default, personal, or custom).

2. Define retention tag settings and actions.

3. Create a retention policy, through which tags are applied.

4. Assign the retention policy to users.

5. Configure the mailbox servers to run the Managed Folder Assistant on a schedule.

Managing Default Folders

A mailbox's default folders are the folders that the Outlook client automatically creates the first time the mailbox is accessed.

The Managed Default Folder list (found in the Folders section when you create a new policy that is applied to a folder) is static; you cannot create additional default folders through either the EAC or the EMS. The following is a list of default folders:

◆ Calendar

◆ Conversations History

◆ Deleted Items

◆ Drafts

◆ Inbox

◆ Journal

◆ Junk E-mail

◆ Notes

◆ Outbox

◆ RSS Feeds

◆ Sent Items

◆ Sync Issues

Creating Retention Tags

When creating a retention policy, you must select which type of tag you will create. Three types of tags are available:

Applied Automatically To Entire Mailbox   This retention tag is applied via policy to the entire mailbox and its folder; you can't customize it on a folder level or item level.

Applied Automatically To A Folder   This retention tag is applied via policy to a folder and its subfolders; you can't apply it to a mailbox level or item level.

Applied By Users To Items And Folders   This is applied manually by users to items and folders; this cannot be automatically assigned and it requires an enterprise CAL.

The retention period is specified in days; when the item reaches this age, the policy is applied to that item (see Figure 14.14).

You apply different actions when an item reaches a specific retention period:

Delete And Allow Recovery   This deletes the item from the mailbox and moves it to the Deleted Items folder. Users can recover that item from there. You can apply this to the entire mailbox, to a folder, and to personal tags.

Permanently Delete   This purges the item entirely from the mailbox. You can apply this to the entire mailbox, to a folder, and to personal tags.

Move To Archive   This moves the item to the archive mailbox. You can apply this action to the entire mailbox and personal tags only.

FIGURE 14.14
New retention tag

FIGURE 14.14
New retention tag

```
                                                                    Help
  new tag applied by users to items and folders (personal)

  *Name:
  [Delete sales notifications after 30 days              ]

  Retention action:
    ● Delete and Allow Recovery
    ○ Permanently Delete
    ○ Move to Archive

  Retention period:
    ○ Never
    ● When the item reaches the following age (in days):
      [30        ]

  Comment:
  [This will delete the sales notifications generate by the system]
  [after 30 days                                                  ]
  [                                                               ]
  [                                                               ]

  ⓘ Personal tags are a premium feature. Mailboxes with
    policies containing these tags require an Enterprise Client
    Access License (CAL) or Exchange Online Archiving
    License. Learn more

                                        [  save  ]   [ cancel ]
```

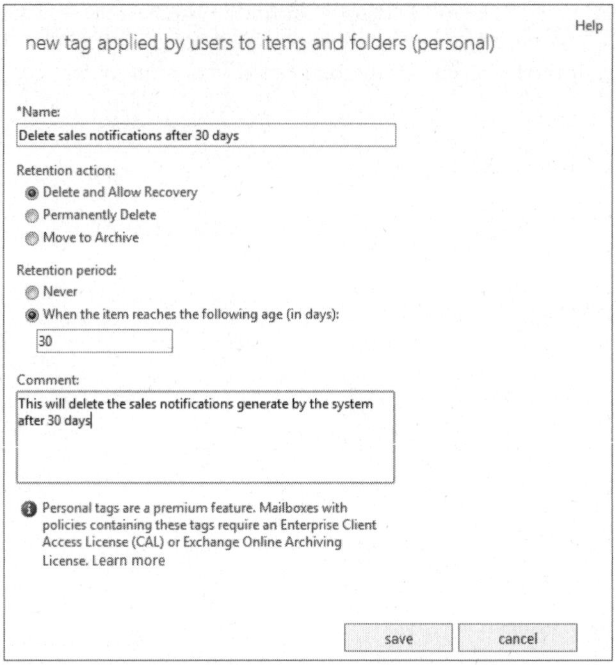

The final field in this dialog is for a comment. This comment is extremely useful in displaying a small tip pertaining to the tag for end users.

🌐 Real World Scenario

KEEPING THE DELETED ITEMS FOLDER CLEAN WITH RETENTION TAGS

One pet peeve of many Exchange Server administrators is that users will delete messages from their Inbox or Sent Items folder but never empty the Deleted Items folder. It is not uncommon to find hundreds of megabytes of message content in a user's Deleted Items folder. In the following example, you set up conditions on the Deleted Items folder so that nothing older than seven days is kept in the Deleted Items folder, but users can recover the deleted message from the deleted item cache after you empty their Deleted Items folder.

Let's create a new retention tag to purge items older than seven days from the Deleted Items folder. To do this through the EAC, choose Compliance Management ➤ Retention Tags and create a new tag that is automatically applied to a default folder. Select the Deleted Items folder and specify the retention action to permanently delete after seven days.

```
new tag applied automatically to a default folder                         Help


*Name:
Remove Items from the deleted items after 7 days

Apply this tag to the following default folder:
Deleted Items                                    ▾

Retention action:
○ Delete and Allow Recovery
◉ Permanently Delete

Retention period:                       ┌─────────────────────────┐
○ Never                                 │ Users can move items to │
◉ When the item reaches the following   │ the archive or delete   │
  age (in days):                        │ them before their       │
  ┌──────────────┐                      │ retention period. You   │
  │ 7            │                      │ can place users on      │
  └──────────────┘                      │ In-Place Hold to        │
                                        │ preserve items either   │
Comment:                                │ for a specific duration │
┌──────────────────────────────┐        │ or indefinitely to meet │
│                              │        │ retention or eDiscovery │
│                              │        │ requirements.           │
│                              │        └─────────────────────────┘
│                              │
└──────────────────────────────┘



                                           ┌────────┐  ┌────────┐
                                           │  save  │  │ cancel │
                                           └────────┘  └────────┘
```

Here is the EMS command to define this managed-content setting:

```
New-RetentionPolicyTag -Name "Remove Items from the deleted items ↵
after 7 days" -Type "DeletedItems" -RetentionAction PermanentlyDelete ↵
-RetentionEnabled $True -AgeLimitForRetention 7.00:00:00
```

Note that although you have defined the retention tag settings for this particular folder, it will not yet apply to anyone's mailbox, nor will any server enforce it. Managing retention policies and scheduling the Managed Folder Assistant are covered later in this chapter.

Managing Retention Policies

Creating retention tags is just part of the equation when implementing MRM. Now you have to assign those retention tags to mailboxes with a retention policy. Once you have created a retention policy, you can assign the policy to one or more mailboxes.

ONE RETENTION POLICY PER MAILBOX

Each mailbox can have only one retention policy assigned to it.

CREATING RETENTION POLICIES

Retention policies are found in the Retention Policies section of the Compliance Management work center. By default, there is one policy; it contains all the default tags created in Exchange Server 2013 during the installation.

A retention policy has few properties. When you launch the New Retention Policy Wizard, you are asked to provide a name for the policy, and you must provide the retention tags that will be assigned through this policy. Figure 14.15 shows the New Mailbox Policy page of this wizard.

FIGURE 14.15
Creating a
retention policy

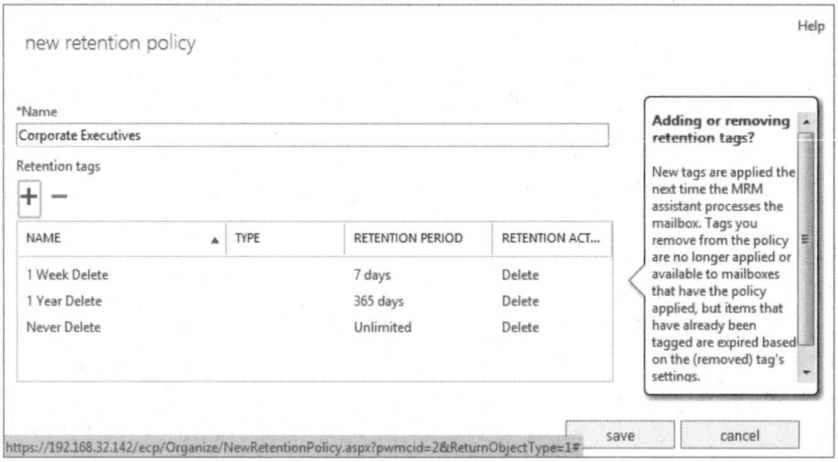

When creating retention policies, you must remember that each user can be assigned to one retention policy only, so you must design your policies carefully.

The resulting EMS command that is executed to create this policy is as follows:

```
New-RetentionPolicy –Name "Corporate Executives" –RetentionPolicyTagLinks "1 Week
Delete", "1 Year Delete", "Never Delete"
```

ASSIGNING RETENTION POLICIES TO USERS

After you define a retention policy, the next step is to assign it to a user. You can do this in one of two ways. The first way is to assign the policy to a user in the EAC after the mailbox is created. Figure 14.16 shows the Mailbox Features page of the mailbox's properties. You can open the drop-down list and select the policy you want to assign for that use.

The second way to assign a policy to a user is by using the Exchange Management Shell. Exchange Server 2013 introduces a change in the options in the Enable-Mailbox, Set-Mailbox, or New-Mailbox command line. You now use -RetentionPolicy instead of -ManagedFolderMailboxPolicy to set the RetentionPolicy property on the mailbox. Here is an example of an EMS command that would enable a mailbox and set the managed folder mailbox policy:

```
Enable-Mailbox 'volcanosurfboards.com/VolcanoSurfboards/Nikki Char' -Alias 'Nikki
Char' -Database 'MBX-001' -RetentionPolicy 'Corporate Executives'
```

FIGURE 14.16
Assigning a
retention policy
to a user's
mailbox

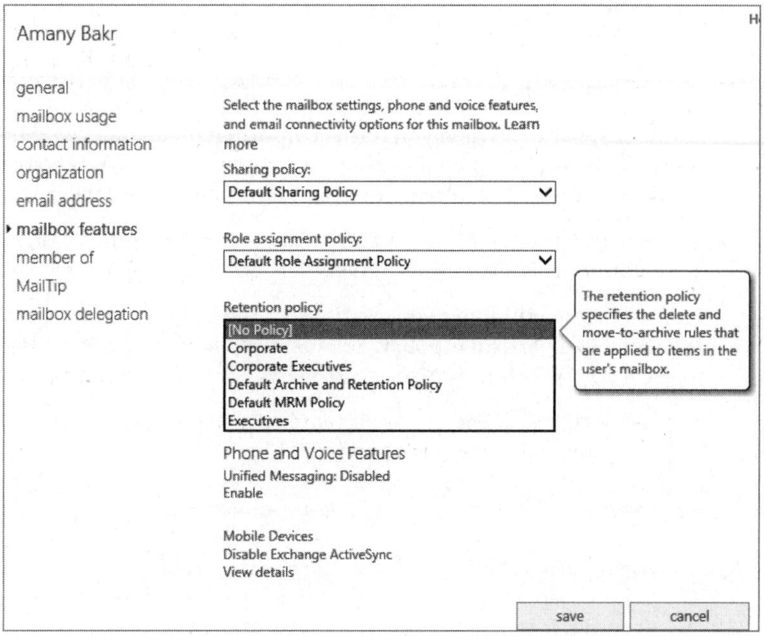

If the mailbox already exists, you can assign the policy using the EMS. For example, if you want to assign user Supatana to the Executives Managed Folder Mailbox policy, you would type the following EMS cmdlet:

```
Set-Mailbox "Supatana" -RetentionPolicy "Executives Managed Folder Mailbox
Policy"
```

If you know that you have to assign a group of mailboxes to a specific policy, it is much easier to do using the EMS. For example, if you want to assign everyone in the Executives group to a managed folder mailbox policy, you can use a single EMS command to accomplish this. Before we show you the command, we'll break it into pieces.

First, you want to enumerate the objects that are members of the Executives distribution group. You would use the Get-DistributionGroupMember cmdlet:

```
Get-DistributionGroupMember "Executives"
Name                               RecipientType
----                               -------------
Saso Erdeljanov                    UserMailbox
Jordan Chang                       UserMailbox
Don Nguyen                         UserMailbox
Goga Kukrika                       UserMailbox
```

```
Pavel Nagaev                          UserMailbox
George Cue                            UserMailbox
Julie Samante                         UserMailbox
Chris Eanes                           UserMailbox
Bthaworn Thaweeaphiradeemaitree       UserMailbox
Cheyne Manalo                         UserMailbox
Jason Sherry                          UserMailbox
Konrad Sagala                         UserMailbox
```

Remember that when you retrieve information using PowerShell, what is actually output is the objects; you can pipe those objects to other cmdlets. You want to pipe this command to the Set-Mailbox cmdlet in order to assign the ManagedFolderMailboxPolicy property:

```
Get-DistributionGroupMember "Executives" | Set-Mailbox ↵
-RetentionPolicy "Executives Managed Folder Mailbox Policy"
```

Another useful thing you can do from the EMS is to list the mailboxes that are already assigned to a particular policy. You just need to implement the Where cmdlet and filter only the objects whose RetentionPolicy property contains the word Executive. Here is an example:

```
Get-Mailbox | Where {$_.RetentionPolicy -like "*Executive*"} ↵
| Format-Table Name,RetentionPolicy
```

```
Name                      RetentionPolicy
----                      ---------------------------
Nathan Nakanishi          Corporate Executive
Lily Ebrahimi             Corporate Executive
Aran Hoffmann             Corporate Executive
Ryan Tung                 Corporate Executive
```

ENABLING MESSAGING RECORDS MANAGEMENT ON THE MAILBOX SERVER

The final piece of enabling MRM is to configure the mailbox servers to schedule and run the Managed Folder Assistant. Managed custom folders do not get created, nor do the content settings get enforced, unless the Managed Folder Assistant is run. The Managed Folder Assistant also processes retention policies for personal mailbox archives. Previously, you could define the Managed Folder Assistant agent via the GUI. In Exchange Server 2013 you cannot do that; *you must manage it from the EMS.*

First, we'll show how you can view the default Managed Folder Assistant settings. To do that, use the following cmdlet:

```
Get-MailboxServer | fl name,*managedFolder*
```

The output of this cmdlet is as follows:

```
Name                                  : EX2013MBX1
ManagedFolderWorkCycle                : 1.00:00:00
ManagedFolderWorkCycleCheckpoint      : 1.00:00:00
ManagedFolderAssistantSchedule        :
LogPathForManagedFolders              : C:\Program Files\Microsoft\Exchange
  Server\V15\Logging\Managed Folder Assistant
LogFileAgeLimitForManagedFolders      : 00:00:00
```

```
LogDirectorySizeLimitForManagedFolders      : Unlimited
LogFileSizeLimitForManagedFolders           : 10 MB (10,485,760 bytes)
RetentionLogForManagedFoldersEnabled        : False
JournalingLogForManagedFoldersEnabled       : False
FolderLogForManagedFoldersEnabled           : False
SubjectLogForManagedFoldersEnabled          : False
```

By default, the Managed Folder Assistant is configured to scan all emails within one day. You can set that through individual user settings; you can also run it manually. If you run `Start-ManagedFolderAssistant` from the EMS on a Mailbox server, no parameters are necessary. However, if you want to run it on a remote Mailbox server, you would type this (substituting the name of your server):

```
Start-ManagedFolderAssistant hnlex03
```

You can also run the Managed Folder Assistant against a specific mailbox, as in this example:

```
Start-ManagedFolderAssistant -Mailbox Suriya.Supatanasakul
```

The Bottom Line

Create and delete user mailboxes.   Exchange Server 2013 supports the same types of mail-enabled users as previous versions of Exchange Server. These are mailbox-enabled users who have a mailbox on your Exchange server and the mail-enabled user account. The mail-enabled user account is a security principal within your organization (and would appear in your global address list), but its email is delivered to an external email system.

There are four different types of mailbox-enabled user accounts: a User mailbox, a Room Resource mailbox, an Equipment Resource mailbox, and a Linked mailbox. You can perform mailbox management tasks via either the Exchange Administration Center or the Exchange Management Shell.

Master It   Your Active Directory forest has a trust relationship to another Active Directory forest that is part of your corporate IT infrastructure. The administrator in the other forest wants you to host their email. What type of mailboxes should you create for the users in this other forest?

Master It   You must modify user Nikki.Char's office name to say Honolulu. You want to do this using the Exchange Management Shell. What command would perform this task?

Master It   You need to change the maximum number of safe senders allowed for user Jeff.Bloom's mailbox to 4,096. You want to make this change using the Exchange Management Shell. What command would you use?

Manage mailbox permissions   A newly created mailbox allows only the owner of the mailbox to access the folders within that mailbox. An end user can assign someone else permissions to access individual folders within their mailbox or to send mail on their behalf using the Outlook client. The administrator can assign permissions to the entire mailbox for other users. Further, the administrator can assign a user the Send As permission to a mailbox.

Master It   All executives within your organization share a single administrative assistant whose username is Chris.Rentch; all of the executives belong to a mail distribution group called #Executives. All of the executives want user Chris.Rentch to be able to access all of the folders within their mailboxes. Name two ways you can accomplish this.

Move mailboxes to another database.   Exchange Server 2013 implements an entirely new way to move mailbox content from one mailbox database to another. The administrative tools (the Exchange Administration Center and the New-MoveRequest cmdlet) are no longer responsible for moving mailbox data. The Microsoft Exchange Server Mailbox Replication service that runs on each Client Access server role handles mailbox moves.

Master It   You want to use the Exchange Management Shell to move mailbox Brian .Desmond from mailbox database MBX-001 to MBX-002. The move should ignore up to three bad messages before it fails. What command should you use?

Master It   You have submitted a move request for user Brian.Desmond. You want to check the status and statistics of the move request to see if it has completed; you want to use the Exchange Management Shell to do this. What command would you type?

Perform bulk manipulation of mailbox properties.   By taking advantage of piping and the EMS, you can perform bulk manipulation of users and mailboxes in a single command that previously might have taken hundreds of lines of scripting code.

Master It   You want to move all of your executives to a single mailbox database called MBX-004. All of your executives belong to a mail distribution group called #Executives. How could you accomplish this task with a single command?

Use Messaging Records Management to manage mailbox content.   Messaging Records Management provides you with control over the content of a user's mailbox. Basic MRM features allow you to automatically purge old content, such as deleted items or junk email. You can create new managed folders within the user's mailbox as well as move content to these folders.

Master It   You are managing an Exchange Server organization that was transitioned from Exchange Server 2010. You have found that many of your users are not emptying the contents of their Deleted Items and Junk E-mail folders. You want to automatically purge any content in these folders after 14 days. What are the steps you should take to do this?

Chapter 15

Managing Mail-enabled Groups, Mail-enabled Users, and Mail-enabled Contacts

We're now well into the discussion on Exchange recipients, and you are aware of the different recipient types that are available to messaging administrators in Exchange Server 2013. (If you need a refresher, look back to Chapter 13, "Basics of Recipient Management.")

Mail-enabled groups are one type of recipient that makes things a bit more interesting—and by *interesting* I mean complex. Most administrators are familiar with the concept of groups but not necessarily with mail-enabled groups. This essentially provides the group with all the necessary attributes to be listed in the Exchange-specific directories and to be identified as a recipient object.

All the benefits of groups, as Active Directory objects, still apply to mail-enabled groups. They are objects that allow us to apply permissions in *bulk*, or allow us to send email messages in *bulk*—essentially making our lives as administrators and email users a little easier.

Mail-enabled users and mail-enabled contacts serve more specific purposes that don't apply to all organizations. They are used to segregate your user permissions from Exchange attributes, and they may not be used in organizations that require only standard usage of permissions and Exchange recipients.

In this chapter, you will learn to:

◆ Create and mail-enable contact objects

◆ Manage mail-enabled contacts and mail-enabled users in a messaging environment

◆ Choose the appropriate type and scope of mail-enabled groups

◆ Create and manage mail-enabled groups

◆ Explore the moderation features of Exchange Server 2013

Understanding Mail-enabled Groups

If your organization is like most organizations today, you make significant use of mail groups. You may refer to these as mail-enabled groups, distribution groups, or distribution lists. The official term for a mail group, though, is *mail-enabled group*—essentially, a group that *lives* in Active Directory but is managed as a mail-enabled object from the Exchange Server administrative tools. Within Active Directory are two basic types of groups:

Security Groups   These are groups that can be assigned permissions to resources or rights to perform certain tasks. Security groups can be mail-enabled and can be used for addressing mail by Exchange Server recipients.

Distribution Groups   These are groups that are not security principals; they have no security identifier and thus cannot be assigned any rights or permissions. Distribution groups are intended for use with a mail system that integrates with Active Directory, such as Exchange Server.

> **Dynamic Distribution Groups**   There is a subset of distribution groups called a dynamic distribution group (DDG). (You may also see these referred to as query-based distribution groups.) A DDG's membership list is dynamic, based on some criteria the administrator defines. DDGs are managed only by using the Exchange Administration Center or the Exchange Management Shell.

When you create a new group using the Active Directory Users and Computers interface, you must provide a scope for the group in addition to defining the group type (see Figure 15.1).

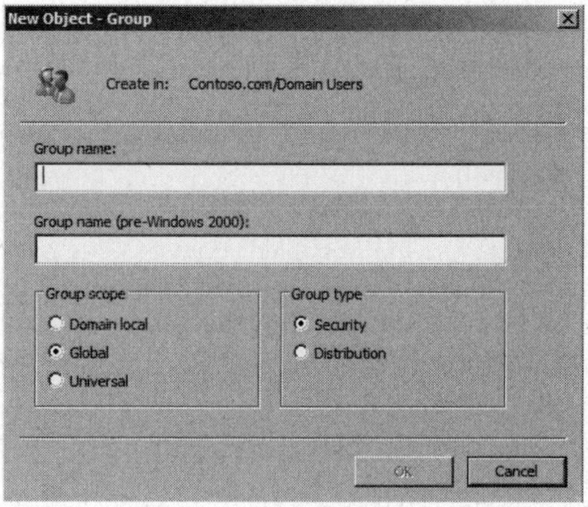

FIGURE 15.1
Creating a new group in
Active Directory

All groups utilized by Exchange Server 2013 must be set to the Universal scope. This tells the Active Directory that the membership list attribute for that group should be replicated to all global catalog servers in the organization.

In earlier versions of Exchange Server, such as Exchange Server 2007, you could mail-enable groups that have the global or the domain local group scope. However, this could cause mail-delivery problems in organizations that have multiple Active Directory domains, since the membership of a global group, for example, is not replicated to a global catalog server. In previous versions of Exchange Server this possibly resulted in lost emails.

Naming Mail-enabled Groups

Decisions about group naming are often made before groups are created. An important consideration when creating group names is to create a standard for mail-enabled group display names. This allows them to all be grouped together in the global address list. For example, you may include special characters in front of the group names, mostly to illustrate how they will sort together in the global address list. Remember that special characters will be sorted before letters or numbers in the global address list.

When selecting a name for the groups, pick a standard that will work for your organization and that your users will clearly understand. The key is to identify a naming convention that represents static units (based on geography or company-wide) and that is, therefore, less likely to have to be modified. Departmental groups are common.

Creating Mail-enabled Groups

The simplest way to create and manage mail-enabled groups is to use the Exchange Admin Center graphical interface. Just using Active Directory Users and Computers will not define any mail (Exchange Server) attributes.

To create a mail-enabled group, open Exchange Admin Center, navigate to the Recipients area work center, and click the + icon on the top-left corner. Select one of the three group types from the list of available group types: distribution groups, security groups, or dynamic distribution groups, as shown in Figure 15.2.

FIGURE 15.2
Viewing the group choices in the Exchange Admin Center

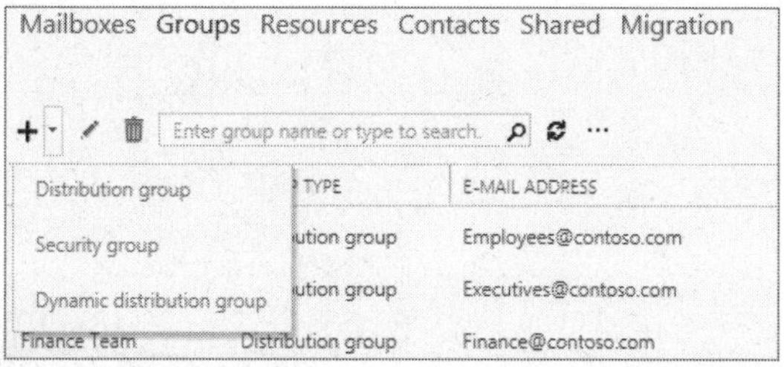

Selecting a group type launches the New Group creation window. From here you can open the New Distribution Group window, as shown in Figure 15.3, from which you can populate the following options:

Display Name   Enter the name of the group. The name will be visible from the Exchange Admin Center and the global address list.

Alias   The alias will be used to generate the group's email address.

Description   The description can be used to provide context for the group when viewing from the global address list.

Organizational Unit   The location where the group will be created in the Active Directory infrastructure.

Owners   Owners of the group are users who can change the membership of the group by using Microsoft Outlook or the Outlook Web App. Additionally, any user that has the appropriate Recipient Management Role assigned can modify the membership of a group from Outlook Web App or Outlook.

Members   At the time of creation of the group or later, you can add members to the group. Members can be any recipient type, including other mail-enabled groups. Additionally, this section contains options that control the membership of the group. Group membership join can be set to Open, Closed, or Owner Approval. Only distribution groups can be set to Open or Closed. Because of the risk of inadvertently assigning unnecessary permissions to users, security groups can only be set to Owner Approval.

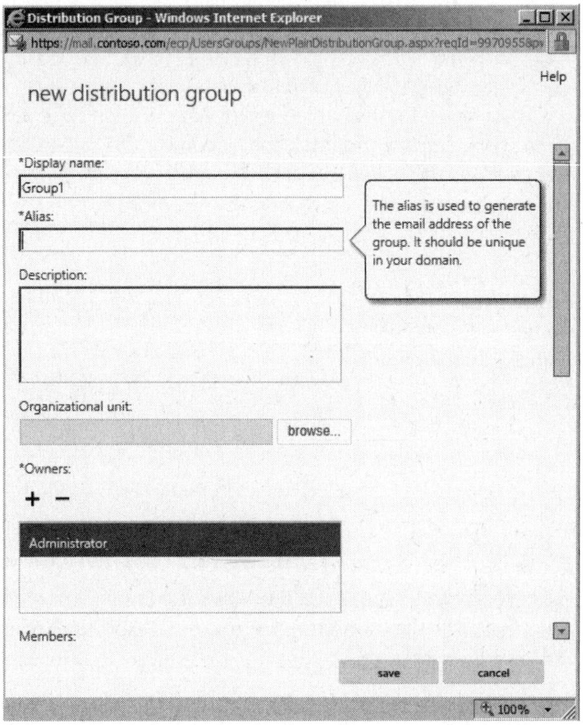

FIGURE 15.3
Opening the New Distribution Group window

In the event that you want to mail-enable an existing distribution or security group, this action cannot be performed from the Exchange Admin Center. You must use the Exchange Management Shell. The following sample command can be used to enable a group named Group1 that has been previously created in Active Directory:

```
Enable-DistributionGroup -Identity:'Contoso.com/Groups/ ↵
IT Operations' -DisplayName: Group1 ↵
-Alias: Group1
```

Real World Scenario

MAIL-ENABLED GROUPS: WHAT NOT TO DO

There are many examples of companies misusing or overusing technology. Unfortunately, inappropriate management of group permissions, as well as the lack of a standard naming convention, can cause havoc for administrators and end users.

The most blatant representation of this problem became painfully obvious during a recent visit to a new customer. Their Active Directory infrastructure had lost all default and standard security provisions for minimizing administrative rights. This was one of those networks where everyone was a domain administrator. So beyond the obvious security implications, this issue had snowballed into a messaging issue where the global address list included more than 50,000 objects for a company of fewer than 200 users.

A large group of support users was in charge of creating mail-enabled groups for anyone who requested them. Requests came from everyone, with little more reason than, "I need a group for Project X. Please add me to that group. We need to send emails to each other as well." The company did not have a standard group-naming convention, so it was difficult to identify the purpose of each group. The groups were never purged from Active Directory, most of them had been stale for many years, and all were mail-enabled.

This was a sad illustration of improper planning in implementing both Active Directory and Exchange Server. A large offline address book, a security risk (when mail-enabled security groups are mistaken for distribution groups), and an inefficient Active Directory structure are only some of the possible impacts of inadequate group management.

CREATING DYNAMIC DISTRIBUTION GROUPS

Do you have a problem keeping your distribution groups up to date? Dynamic distribution groups (DDGs) may be the solution you have been looking for. Mail is sent to users in a DDG based on one or more criteria, such as organizational unit, city, or department. As a user's Active Directory properties are changed or updated, the DDG membership changes automatically.

DDGs are created a little differently than regular mail-enabled groups because you have to define the filter settings and the conditions of the group. From the Exchange Admin Center, you can launch the New Dynamic Distribution Group window by clicking the + sign in the top-left corner. The General page shows some typical information required for creating a new group object. This page requires that you specify the organizational unit in which you want the object created, the display name, and the Exchange alias of the group.

Once you have specified the information necessary on the General page, the filter settings (Figure 15.4) allow you to specify which recipient container (or the entire domain) you want to apply to the filter and which types of recipients you want to display.

FIGURE 15.4
Filter settings for a dynamic distribution group

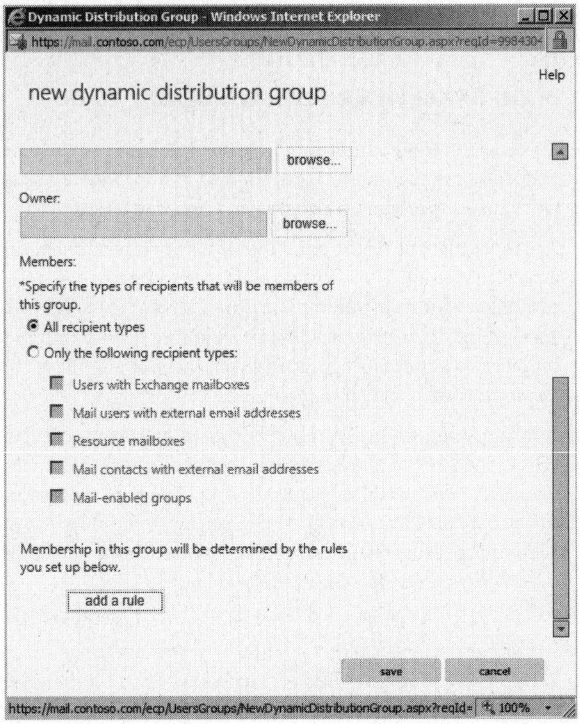

The following recipient types can be included in the filter settings:

◆ All recipients types

◆ Users with Exchange mailboxes (mailbox-enabled user accounts)

◆ Users with external email addresses (mail-enabled user accounts)

◆ Resource mailboxes (room and equipment)

◆ Contacts with external email addresses

◆ Mail-enabled groups

After selecting the recipient type and OU scope for the DDG, you can further refine the scope of the group membership by clicking the Add A Rule button and then filtering based on the keywords set for a specific attribute. For example, if you have a custom attribute that is populated for all recipients, you may want to filter the dynamic distribution group by using this attribute. The following attributes can be used to filter DDG membership with the rules in the new dynamic distribution group:

◆ Recipient container

◆ State or province

◆ Department

- Company

- Custom attribute 1 through 15

After you've created the DDG, the Preview button on the group's General page is helpful in confirming that your scope and rules are defined properly. By clicking this button, you will see the Dynamic Distribution Group Preview dialog box. Here, you should verify that the membership appears to be what you expected.

Of course, as with all actions in the Exchange Admin Center, you can also create DDGs by using the EMS. An example EMS command that you can use is the following:

```
New-DynamicDistributionGroup -Name '#Everyone in Quebec ⏎
-IncludedRecipients 'MailboxUsers, MailUsers' ⏎
-ConditionalStateOrProvince 'Quebec' ⏎
-OrganizationalUnit 'Contoso.com/Users' ⏎
-Alias '_EveryoneINquebec' ⏎
-RecipientContainer 'Contoso.com/Recipients'
```

Managing Mail-enabled Groups

Once groups have been mail-enabled, you can configure their properties to achieve advanced messaging results. Though the core function of a group is to facilitate the delivery of mail messages to multiple users, and its subsequent management, there are many specific group features that you can set.

HAVE YOU HEARD OF THE SHARED MAILBOX YET?

A new mailbox type—the shared mailbox—was introduced in Exchange Server 2010 and is still available in Exchange Server 2013 to provide some functionality previously provided by mail-enabled groups. Some organizations use mail-enabled groups to create a single entry point for emails for a team of special users, a functionality that can now be served quite well with a shared mailbox, as long as the team's users do not require their own mailboxes. More information about the shared mailbox is available in Chapter 14, "Managing Mailboxes and Mailbox Content."

Let's start with Delivery Management (Figure 15.5). This page, accessed from the group's properties, includes two components you can configure: whether the group can receive email messages only from users in the organization or whether they can receive email messages from any user. As well, you can configure the group to receive email messages only from a subset of senders. Note that in order to select a sender, the sender must already exist in the global address list. For example, if you want to include a specific external sender, you must create that sender as a mail-enabled contact in the organization. We often recommend that you restrict who is allowed to send email to large groups or groups that contain VIPs. This prevents accidents and keeps unwanted mail content from your VIPs.

Once you browse through the group options, you will quickly realize that some settings are not available from the Exchange Admin Center. Some settings, such as the Message Size restrictions, must be set from the Exchange Management Shell. Message Size restrictions can help prevent misuse of distribution groups or the accidental distribution of large files. By using the `Set-DistributionGroup` cmdlet, you can use either the `-MaxRecieveSize` parameter to prevent large messages from landing in the mailbox of each recipient in the group or the `-MaxSendSize` parameter to prevent the group from being used as the sender of large messages.

The Email Options properties page shows the email addresses that can be used to address a message to the group. You can edit the existing addresses or add new ones by using the Exchange Management Shell.

If a distribution list is used entirely within your organization, the Reply To address will not be particularly important. However, if you use lists both internally and externally, keep in mind that the Reply To address is the one that will be seen by people outside the organization. For example, if someone sends a message to your `HelpDesk@company.com` address and internal users reply to that message and copy (Cc) the distribution group, the original sender will see the Reply To address of the distribution group. You must also keep in mind that all addresses set on the Email Options properties page must have an associated accepted domain. Again, the sharing functionalities of a mailbox between several users can now be provided by the Shared Mailbox feature.

There are other settings that you can configure from the properties of a distribution group that you should be aware of, such as the Hide This Group From Address Lists setting.

This check box (unchecked by default) allows you to prevent a mail-enabled group from being displayed in the address lists. This might be useful for specialized groups that are used just for mail distribution by an automated system or for users who know the SMTP address.

You should be aware that several group configuration properties are not available from the Exchange Admin Center and must be modified from the Exchange Management Shell.

The most relevant example is the Expansion Server setting that must be set by using the Set-DistributionGroup cmdlet.

Message expansion is the process of enumerating the members of a mail-enabled group and figuring out where each member is, either within your organization or externally. Expansion of large mail-enabled groups can be a pretty intensive process for an Exchange Server as well as the Active Directory global catalog server that it is using.

The Expansion Server list provides you with a list of all the servers in your organization. By default, Expansion Server is set to any server in the organization. This means that the first Exchange Server Mailbox server receiving the message is responsible for expanding the mail-enabled group. In some environments, you may want to manually specify which server handles expansion, especially environments where multiple versions of Exchange Server will be responsible for mail delivery. Special considerations should be taken in an environment where Exchange Server 2007 Hub Transport servers will coexist with Exchange Server 2013 mailbox servers. Keep in mind that Exchange Server 2007 servers that are used for expansion are unaware of features introduced in Exchange Server 2010 or Exchange Server 2013, therefore completely bypassing features such as group moderation. An expansion server should be chosen by using the following criteria:

1. Is running the latest version of Exchange Server

2. Has a reliable and rapid connection to domain controllers

3. Has enough resources available to manage the additional demand coming from group expansion

The above criteria are not requirements, but simply recommendations in selecting an expansion server. Many organizations choose to identify a dedicated expansion server for all distribution groups to facilitate the troubleshooting process and provide clear process flow should mail delivery problems arise.

MANAGING MODERATION FOR DISTRIBUTION GROUPS

We're always gratified when an often-requested feature appears in a release of the product. Such is the case of moderated groups. This feature first appeared in Exchange Server 2010, and it is still available in Exchange Server 2013.

Now any group can be enabled for moderation. Once moderation is enabled, you can define one or more moderators, as well as exceptions to the moderation process. Although moderation is handled on the back end, you configure the moderation options in the properties of the moderated groups. Figure 15.6 shows the moderated group configuration options on the Message Approval page. Note that you can also configure moderated groups from the Exchange Control Panel. A group owner, or an administrator who has been assigned the necessary RBAC role, can enable groups for moderation and add multiple moderators.

All groups have moderation disabled by default (moderation has been enabled in Figure 15.6). The first feature you will immediately need to configure is the moderator(s) for the group. A moderator will be notified each time a message is sent to the group. The moderator will receive a copy of the message and will then be able to perform an action against the message. The moderator can accept or reject messages sent to the group. Messages are not delivered to the group until a moderator of the group has approved the message. You can define multiple moderators, but you can assign only users (not groups) as moderators.

FIGURE 15.6
Configuration options for moderated groups

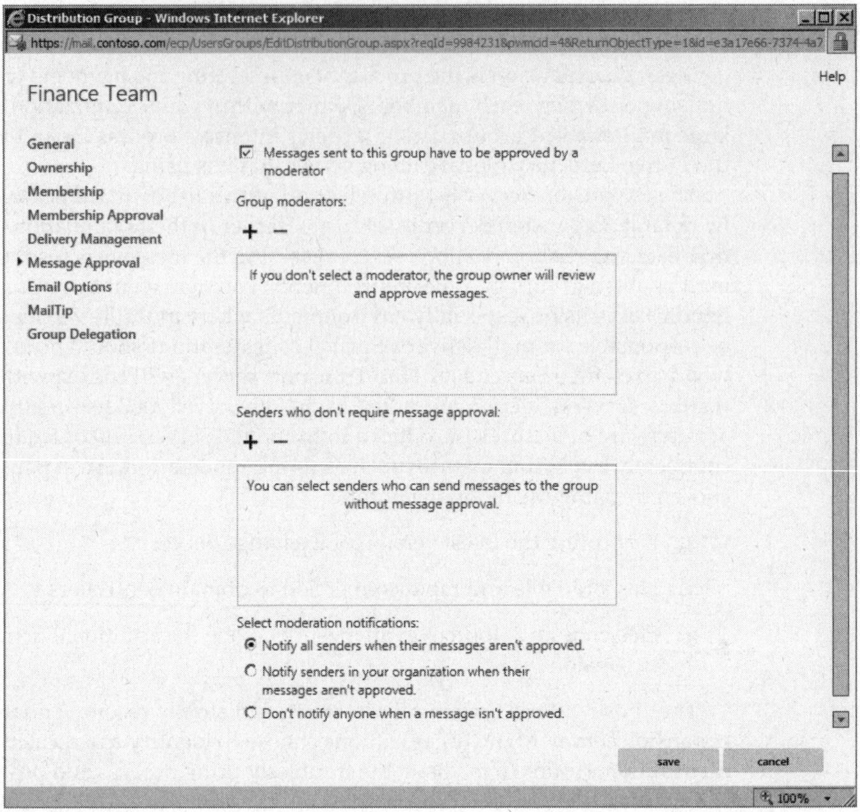

An administrator can also exempt a specific user from being moderated. Users listed in the Senders Who Don't Require Message Approval list are able to send email messages to the group without being moderated.

The Select Moderation Notifications settings, available from the group properties, provide the ability to notify or silently drop messages sent to the list. If you choose to notify senders of rejected messages, you can select to notify only internal senders or all senders.

Note that moderation is not limited to groups; an administrator can also moderate email sent to mailboxes or mail contacts in the same way as mail sent to distribution groups. Email sent from a specific mailbox can be moderated by using a transport rule, which contains moderation as an action.

CONVERTING GLOBAL OR LOCAL DISTRIBUTION GROUPS TO UNIVERSAL GROUPS

In multidomain environments in previous versions of Exchange server, creating groups of type global and domain local could cause problems with distribution list expansion. If the Exchange Server that performed the group expansion pointed to a domain controller from a domain that did not contain the membership list for a domain local or global group, the group would not be expanded and the message would not be delivered. Worse, the message sender might not get a notification that there was a problem.

For this reason, Microsoft is enforcing that all groups created for Exchange Server mail distribution be universal groups. If you create a domain local or global group using Active Directory Users and Computers and then try to mail-enable it using the Exchange Management Shell, you will not even see the group in the list of available groups.

In an organization that was upgraded or transitioned from a previous version of Exchange Server to Exchange Server 2013, you may have some mail-enabled groups that are not universal groups. You can still manage those groups from either the Exchange Admin Center or the Exchange Management Shell.

For groups that you want to change to universal groups, you can modify the group type using Active Directory Users and Computers, of course. On the General properties page for the group (shown in Figure 15.7), simply select the Universal radio button and click OK to convert the group.

FIGURE 15.7

Converting a group to a universal group using Active Directory Users and Computers

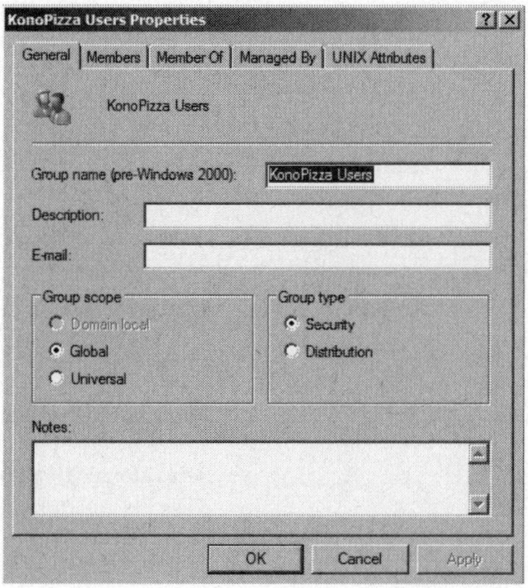

You can also convert a group to a universal group from the EMS.
You can convert groups one at time with the `Set-Group` cmdlet like this:

```
Set-Group "Operations Group" -Universal
```

However, one at a time is probably not the best use of your time. We recommend you convert all groups used for mail distribution but not necessarily your non-mail groups. You can generate a list of just these groups with the `Get-DistributionGroup` cmdlet and a `Where-Object` filter; here is an example:

```
Get-DistributionGroup | Where {$_.RecipientType ⏎
-eq "MailNonUniversalGroup"}
```

```
Name                  DisplayName         GroupType         PrimarySmtpAddress
----                  -----------         ---------         ------------------
$Operations Group     $Operations Group   Global, Security… OperationsGroup@…
```

```
$Executives and …  $Executives and …  Global, Security… ExecutivesandVIP…
Field Research G…  Field Research G…  Global, Security… FieldResearchGro…
Failure Analysis…  Failure Analysis…  Global            FailureAnalysisT…
```

This outputs a list of all groups that are mail-enabled and that are not universal groups. Converting them all at once is just a matter of piping this as input to the Set-Group cmdlet. Here is the command necessary to convert all of these groups to universal groups:

```
Get-DistributionGroup | Where {$_.RecipientType ↵
-eq "MailNonUniversalGroup"} | Set-Group -Universal
```

Note that this command does not change whether the group is a security group or a distribution group.

USING THE EXCHANGE MANAGEMENT SHELL TO MANAGE GROUPS

If you are just getting started with Exchange Server 2013 and the EMS, managing groups is going to be a little tougher using the EMS than it will be if you use the Exchange Admin Center. However, we want to review the cmdlets that are available for managing and manipulating mail-enabled groups so that as you learn more about the EMS, you will have these cmdlets in your management arsenal. Table 15.1 lists the EMS cmdlets you can use to manage groups and mail-enabled groups.

TABLE 15.1:   EMS and PowerShell cmdlets for group management

CMDLET	FUNCTION
Get-Group	Retrieves information about all Active Directory groups.
Set-Group	Sets information about an Active Directory group; this will work for any Active Directory group, not just mail-enabled ones.
Get-DistributionGroup	Retrieves information related to mail-enabled groups.
Set-DistributionGroup	Sets properties of mail-enabled groups.
New-DistributionGroup	Creates a new group in Active Directory and mail-enables that group.
Enable-DistributionGroup	Mail-enables an existing group that was previously created in Active Directory.
Disable-DistributionGroup	Removes mail attributes from a mail-enabled group but does not remove the group from Active Directory.
Remove-DistributionGroup	Deletes the mail attributes of a mail-enabled group and removes the group from Active Directory.

TABLE 15.1:   EMS and PowerShell cmdlets for group management   *(CONTINUED)*

CMDLET	FUNCTION
Get-DistributionGroupMember	Retrieves membership list information from a mail-enabled group.
Add-DistributionGroupMember	Adds members to a mail-enabled group.
Remove-DistributionGroupMember	Removes members from a mail-enabled group.
Get-DynamicDistributionGroup	Retrieves information about a dynamic distribution group.
Set-DynamicDistributionGroup	Sets properties for dynamic distribution groups.
New-DynamicDistributionGroup	Creates a new dynamic distribution group.
Remove-DynamicDistributionGroup	Removes mail properties from a dynamic distribution group and deletes the group from Active Directory.

For our purposes in this chapter, we'll focus on only a few of the cmdlets listed in Table 15.1 and some common properties that can be used with them. The best way to illustrate them is to use some examples.

In the first example, let's say you have a universal group in the Corporate OU in the Active Directory. The group is called Finance. You want to set up this group as a distribution group.

Because the group already exists in the Active Directory, you'll use the Enable-Distribution Group cmdlet. You need to assign the group an Exchange Server alias (the -Alias property) and a display name (-DisplayName). The following command would accomplish these tasks:

```
Enable-DistributionGroup Finance -DisplayName:Finance ⏎
-Alias:Finance
```

If the group does not yet exist in Active Directory and you wanted to create it in addition to mail-enabling it, you would use the New-DistributionGroup cmdlet. The following example creates the Finance group in the Corporate OU; the -OrganizationalUnit property is required. The -SamAccountName property is also required if the group will be a security group:

```
New-DistributionGroup -Name:Finance -Type:'Distribution' ⏎
-OrganizationalUnit:'contoso.com/Corporate' ⏎
-SamAccountName:Finance -DisplayName:Finance ⏎
-Alias:Finance
```

To add members to a group, you use the Add-DistributionGroupMember cmdlet. Conversely, you can use the Remove-DistributionGroupMember cmdlet to remove members. For example, if you want to add user Jonathan Long to the Finance group, you would type the following command:

```
Add-DistributionGroupMember Finance -Member "Jonathan.Long"
```

To enumerate the members of a group, you use the Get-DistributionGroupMember cmdlet. Here is an example and the resulting output:

```
Get-DistributionGroupMember Finance

Name             RecipientType
----             -------------
Jonathan Long    UserMailbox
```

You can modify the properties of a distribution group by using the Set-DistributionGroup cmdlet. Specifically, you can modify the moderation properties with this cmdlet. The following example enables moderation for a group and then configures the moderators, along with the exceptions and the notification settings:

```
Set-DistributionGroup Finance -ModerationEnabled $true ⏎
-ModeratedBy "David@contoso.com","gillian@contoso.com" ⏎
-ByPassModerationFromSendersOrMembers "Administrators" ⏎
-SendModerationNotifications Internal
```

Table 15.2 lists some of the common properties that you can define for a mail-enabled group.

TABLE 15.2:   Common mail-enabled group properties

PROPERTY	FUNCTION
Alias	Sets the Exchange Server alias for the group. By default, the alias is used when SMTP addresses are generated.
CustomAttribute1 through CustomAttribute15	Sets 1 of the 15 custom attributes (aka extension attributes).
DisplayName	Sets the display name of the mail-enabled group; the display name is what is visible in address lists.
HiddenFromAddressLists Enabled	Sets whether the group will be displayed in address lists. The default is that the objects are visible. You can set this to $True and it will hide the lists.
MaxReceiveSize	Sets the maximum size message that can be sent to the group.
ModerationEnabled	Enables or disables moderation for a group.

You can view the group's properties using the EMS cmdlet Get-DistributionGroup. You can modify any of these using the Set-DistributionGroup cmdlet.

Finally, if you no longer need a group, you can use Remove-DistributionGroup to get rid of it completely (including the group object in the Active Directory) or Disable-DistributionGroup to simply remove the mail attributes from it.

Let's now look at an example where you create and manage a dynamic distribution group using the EMS. Let's say that you need to create a group called All Research that consists only of mailbox-enabled users. You want to create the Active Directory object in the contoso.com domain and in the Research organizational unit. Further, let's say that the maximum receive size should be only 750 KB.

To create this DDG, you would use the following cmdlet:

```
New-DynamicDistributionGroup -Name "All Research" ↵
-IncludedRecipients 'MailboxUsers' ↵
-ConditionalDepartment 'Research' ↵
-OrganizationalUnit 'contoso.com/Research' ↵
-Alias 'AllResearch' ↵
-RecipientContainer 'contoso.com/Corporate'
```

After you create the group, you use the Set-DynamicDistributionGroup cmdlet to update the maximum receive size:

```
Set-DynamicDistributionGroup -Name "All Research" ↵
-MaxReceiveSize 750KB
```

ALLOWING END USERS TO MANAGE GROUP MEMBERSHIP

A handy feature of Outlook is that when you locate a distribution group in the global address list and select its properties, if you have the right permissions you can add and remove users, contacts, or groups from the group's membership. Figure 15.8 shows the Outlook interface that allows you to manage the membership of a mail-enabled group.

FIGURE 15.8
Managing group membership
from within Outlook

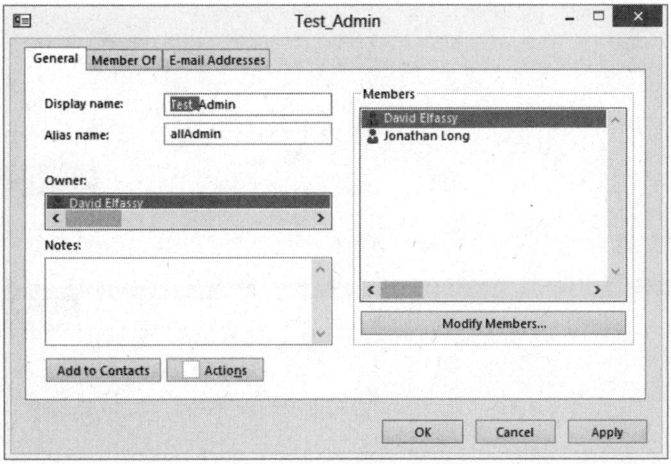

Note that only mail-enabled groups can have their membership managed by an Outlook client. This feature is not available for dynamic distribution groups.

Each distribution group's configuration page includes a Managed By field that allows you to set the "manager" or "owner" of the group. Disappointingly, this Managed By option alone does not allow the manager to manage the membership list; the ability to manage a distribution group membership is delegated through the management roles. In addition to being designated as an owner, a user must be assigned a management role assignment policy that contains the My Distribution Groups and My Distribution Group Membership roles to manage the membership of the group. By default, all users are assigned those roles in the role assignment policy. You need to add these roles to the policy only if you previously removed them. (Management roles and role-based access control are covered in detail in Chapter 12, "Management Permissions and Role-based Access Control.") That takes an extra step (or two). In Active Directory Users and Computers, locate the group and then display its properties. On the Managed By properties page, you should see the option to define the manager and a Manager Can Update Membership List check box.

From Outlook Web App, administrators and users with permissions can modify the properties of groups by using a web-based administrative console, as well. The Exchange Server Control Panel, available from Outlook Web App, can be used, once permissions have been properly delegated, to create or manage groups and group memberships. Figure 15.9 shows how an administrator can modify the membership of an existing distribution group.

FIGURE 15.9
Modify the membership of a mail-enabled distribution group from the Exchange Control Panel.

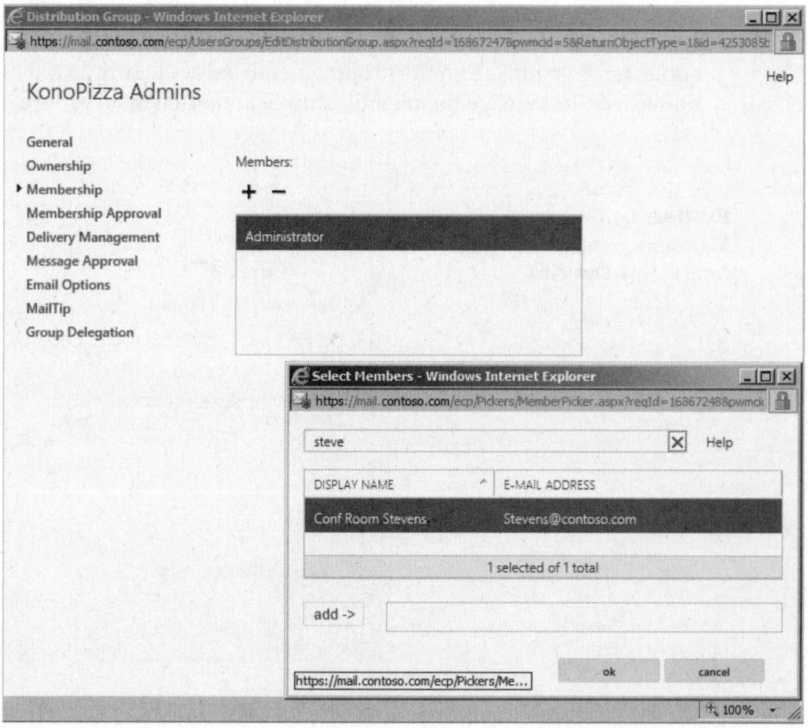

An administrator (or a user with elevated privileges) can also use the Exchange Admin Center or the Exchange Management Shell to add a member to a distribution group. From the Exchange Admin Center, simply locate the group in the group list and then modify the properties of the Member tab. From the Exchange Management Shell, you can use the `Add-DistributionGroupMember` cmdlet. For example, we used the following command to add four users to the distribution group named Vegetarians:

```
Add-DistributionGroupMember -identity Vegetarians ↵
  -Member "Gillian@contoso.com, Zachary@contoso.com, ↵
Zoe@contoso.com, Savannah@contoso.com"
```

Creating and Managing Mail-enabled Contacts and Users

So what is the use of a mail-enabled contact? Many organizations like to have their users' frequently used contacts in the organization's address lists so they are accessible to all, rather than having users add the addresses to their individual contacts folders or address books. Mail-enabled contacts appear in your organization's address lists, but they direct email to an external mail system. The email addresses of these external contacts are almost always SMTP, so we are going to limit our discussion to that type of contact.

In Exchange Server 2013, a contact object can be created in Active Directory, but it will not be mail-enabled and thus will not appear in the Exchange Server address lists. This is different from Exchange Server 2003, where you could mail-enable a contact using the Active Directory Users and Computers snap-in. The process of mail-enabling the contact will have to occur as a second step, described later, in the section "Managing Mail-enabled Contacts and Users via the EMS."

Creating a contact object in Active Directory requires minimal information; you can simply create a new contact and specify the contact's name information. Figure 15.10 illustrates the context options for creating contact objects from the Active Directory Users and Computers console.

FIGURE 15.10
Creating a new contact object in Active Directory

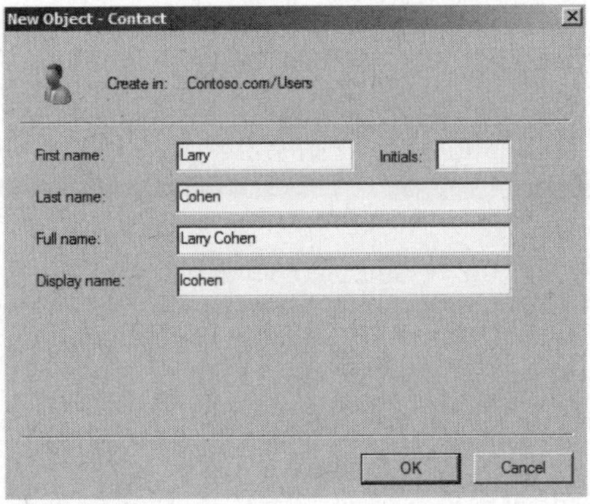

However, you may notice that there is no way to provide email address information when you create a contact object from Active Directory Users and Computers. If you look at the contact's information (shown in Figure 15.11), you will see an E-mail property, but Exchange

Server will not include the contact information in the address lists with just this information populated. The complete mail attributes must be set on the contact.

FIGURE 15.11
Contact information in Active Directory

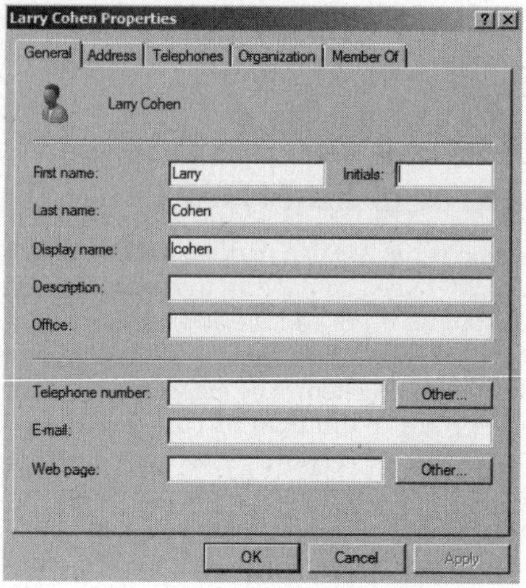

To properly mail-enable a contact for use with Exchange Server, you must use the Exchange Admin Center or the Exchange Management Shell.

🌐 Real World Scenario

MAKING THINGS EASY FOR YOUR USERS

I worked with a company that had a large number external suppliers—contacts—that were often used in communications by internal users. Users often shared this contact information with one another, by forwarding emails and using old-fashioned pen and paper. That solution was inefficient and error prone.

Using the company's billing system, we were able to locate the list of suppliers in an existing electronic format, within a SQL Server database. The next step was to export the database using SQL tools. We decided to use a SQL Server database export command to export to a comma-separated value (CSV) file.

With the CSV file, we were able to use the trusted Active Directory export/import tool, CSVDE.exe, to import all suppliers and thus create all the contacts.

The last step was mail-enabling the contacts. Once we completed this task, the contact information for all suppliers became visible from the global address list to all internal users.

Keep in mind that when a user copies a contact to a personal address book, the contact then becomes a *local* object and any updates that may occur in Active Directory will not be pulled down to the local object.

Managing Mail-enabled Contacts and Users via the EAC

Let's start by examining how you would create and manage a mail-enabled contact using the Exchange Admin Center. In the Recipients area of the Exchange Admin Center, click the Contacts option. You will see a window that lists all mail-enabled users and mail-enabled contacts in the organization. That's right; although the window is called Contacts, it is actually the area from which you view and manage all mail-enabled contacts and mail-enabled users.

And now for the all-important definition of these two object types: The *mail-enabled contact* is an object that appears in the Active Directory and Exchange Server address lists, but it is not a security principal. You cannot put the mail-enabled contact into any security groups and assign it any permissions because it does not have a security identifier. This type of contact is useful when you need to make an external email address appear in your address lists. However, the external user associated with the email address does not need any sort of permissions in your organization.

The *mail-enabled user* is a user account in your organization but not one for which you host a mailbox. For example, you might need to create a user account for an accounting auditor who will be working at one of your workstations for a few months. You want that person to appear in your Exchange Server address lists, but their mailbox is hosted somewhere else. This is also called a mail user. The easiest way to understand the difference between a mail-enabled user and a mailbox-enabled user is that you are *not* responsible for a mail-enabled user's email storage, but you are responsible for a mailbox-enabled user's email storage. The mailbox-enabled user was covered in Chapter 13.

This short list describes the three principal recipients in Exchange Server 2013 and the ways in which they are different:

◆ Mailbox-enabled user (see Chapter 13)

  ◆ User exists *inside* your organization.

  ◆ Mailbox exists *inside* your organization.

  ◆ Recipient appears in your address lists by default or can be hidden.

◆ Mail-enabled user

  ◆ User exists *inside* your organization.

  ◆ Mailbox exists *outside* your organization.

  ◆ Recipient appears in your address lists by default or can be hidden.

◆ Mail-enabled contact

  ◆ User exists *outside* your organization.

  ◆ Mailbox exists *outside* your organization.

  ◆ Recipient appears in your address lists by default or can be hidden.

Let's look at creating a mail-enabled contact. Simply click + icon on the top-left corner of the Contacts area of the Recipients window. The New Mail Contact window asks you some pretty basic information about the contact you are about to create, as shown in Figure 15.12.

FIGURE 15.12

Creating a mail-enabled contact

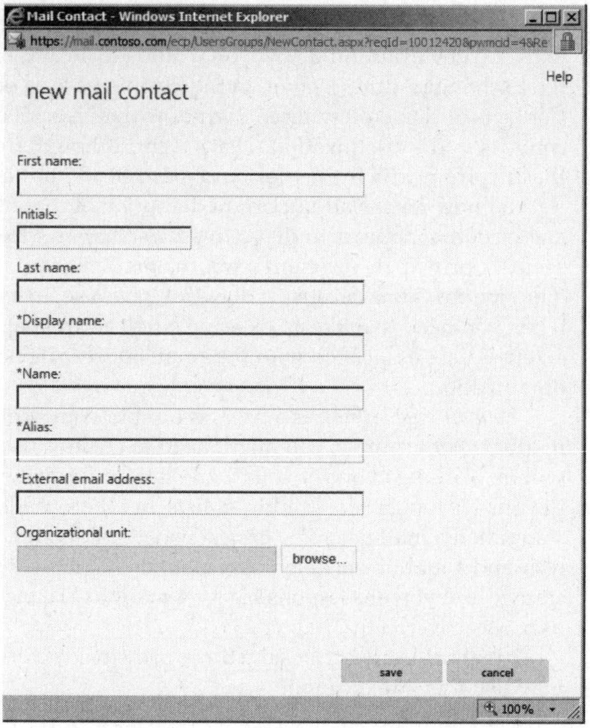

If you are so inclined, and you prefer to use the Exchange Management Shell to manage your contacts, you can use the following EMS command to mail-enable a contact for an external user named Jonathan Long:

```
Enable-MailContact -Identity 'contoso.com/Users/Jonathan Long' ↵
-ExternalEmailAddress 'SMTP:jlong@netlogon.com' -Alias 'Jlong'
```

Before we look at the mail-related properties of a contact, let's look at the creation of a mail-enabled user. You can simply select the + sign from the Contacts area of the Recipients window but select the New User option. In the New User window, select similar options to those available in the New Mail Contact window. Alternatively, run the following command from the Exchange Management Shell:

```
New-MailUser -Name 'Gillian Katz' -Alias 'gkatz' -OrganizationalUnit ↵
'contoso.com/Users' ↵
-UserPrincipalName 'GKatz@contoso.com' ↵
-SamAccountName 'GKatz' -FirstName 'Gillian' -Initials '' -LastName 'Katz' ↵
-Password 'System.Security.SecureString' -ResetPasswordOnNextLogon $false ↵
-ExternalEmailAddress 'SMTP:gkatz@netlogon.com'
```

Most properties of a mail-enabled contact or a mail-enabled user are similar to those you have seen in previous chapters for mail-enabled mailboxes, so we won't bore you with a lot of repetition. We want to remind you, though, that a mail-enabled user can be a member of a distribution group, have a telephone number attribute, and have an SMTP email address.

Managing Mail-enabled Contacts and Users via the EMS

Once you become proficient at Exchange Admin Center, as with many other tasks, you may want to try your hand at creating mail-enabled contacts or mail-enabled users from the EMS instead of the GUI. Table 15.3 shows the cmdlets that can be used to manipulate mail-enabled contacts and users.

TABLE 15.3:   Exchange Management Shell cmdlets for mail-enabled contacts and users

CMDLET	DESCRIPTION
New-MailContact	Creates a new contact in Active Directory and mail-enables that contact
Enable-MailContact	Mail-enables a previously existing contact
Set-MailContact	Sets mail properties for a mail-enabled contact
Get-MailContact	Retrieves properties of a mail-enabled contact
Remove-MailContact	Removes the mail properties from a contact and deletes that contact from Active Directory
Disable-MailContact	Removes the mail properties from a contact
New-MailUser	Creates a new user in Active Directory and mail-enables that user
Enable-MailUser	Mail-enables a previously existing user
Set-MailUser	Sets mail properties for a mail-enabled user
Get-MailUser	Retrieves properties of a mail-enabled user
Remove-MailUser	Removes the mail properties from a user and deletes that user from Active Directory
Disable-MailUser	Removes the mail properties from a user

The best way to learn how to use the EMS to create mail-enabled contacts and users is to look at some examples.

Let's say a user named Oliver Cohen is a contractor who works for your company occasionally. He requires a desk and a company logon, so you have already created his Oliver .Cohen user account in the Active Directory domain; the account is in an OU called Corporate. You want Oliver to appear in the address lists, but he should receive his email at an external address: Oliver.Cohen@IAmAHumongousSupplier.com. Here is the command you would use to mail-enable Oliver's user account. In this example, you are using his Common Name attribute instead of his username:

```
Enable-MailUser "Oliver Cohen" -Alias 'Oliver.Cohen' ⏎
-ExternalEmailAddress 'SMTP:Oliver.Cohen@IAmAHumongousSupplier.com'
```

Let's extend this example now to a mail-enabled contact. You have a contact that you want to appear in your address lists, but this contact does *not* need to access any resources on your network. The contact does not yet exist, so you will create a mail-enabled contact in the Corporate OU for contact named Oren Pinto, whose external address will be Oren.Pinto@Netlogon.com:

```
New-MailContact ⏎
-ExternalEmailAddress 'SMTP:Oren.Pinto@Netlogon.com' ⏎
-Name 'OrenPinto' -Alias 'OrenPinto' ⏎
-OrganizationalUnit 'Netlogon.com/Corporate' ⏎
-FirstName 'Oren' -LastName 'Pinto'
```

When setting properties for the mail-enabled contact and mail-enabled user objects, you should keep in mind some useful properties. Table 15.4 shows some of the common properties that these two object types share.

TABLE 15.4:   Useful properties of mail contact and mail user objects

PROPERTY	DESCRIPTION
Alias	Sets the object's Exchange Server alias.
CustomAttribute1 through CustomAttribute10	Sets custom attributes 1 through 10; these are also known as the extension attributes.
DisplayName	Sets the display name of the object.
ExternalEmailAddress	Sets the address that is to be used to deliver mail externally to the user or contact.
HiddenFromAddressLists Enabled	Specifies whether the object is hidden from address lists. The default is $False, but it can be set to $True.
MaxSendSize	Sets the maximum size of a message that can be sent to this recipient.

The Bottom Line

Create and mail-enable contact objects.   In some cases, you should *not* create mail-enabled users and instead choose the less-well-known mail-enabled contacts. Mail-enabled contacts can be used to provide easy access to external email contacts by using your internal address lists. Mail-enabled users can be used to provide convenient access to internal resources for workers who require an externally hosted email account.

a) **Master It**   You periodically update the email addresses for your Active Directory contacts. However, some users report that they are not seeing the updated contact address and that they receive non-delivery reports (NDR) when sending mail to some contacts. What should you do?

Manage mail-enabled contacts and mail-enabled users in a messaging environment.   All Exchange Server–related attributes for mail-enabled users and contacts are not available from Active Directory Users and Computers. To manage all Exchange Server–related attributes, you must use the Exchange Admin Center or EMS tools.

b) **Master It**   Whether you want to manage users in bulk, need to create multiple users in your domain or multiple mail-enabled contacts in your organization, or simply want to change the delivery restrictions for 5,000 recipients, what tool should you use?

Choose the appropriate type and scope of mail-enabled groups.   Although you can modify your group scope or group type at any time after the group has been created, it's always a best practice to create all groups as universal groups in an environment that contains Exchange servers.

c) **Master It**   Your company needs to ensure that if an administrator adds a user to a distribution list, that user will not get any unnecessary access to resources on the network. How should you ensure that this type of administrative mistake does not impact the security of your networking environment?

Create and manage mail-enabled groups.   Creating and managing distribution groups can mostly be done from the Exchange Admin Center, with only limited options that require the Exchange Management Shell.

D) **Master It**   You want to simplify the management of groups in your organization. You recently reviewed the functionalities of dynamic distribution groups and decided that this technology can provide the desired results. You need to identify the tools that should be used to manage dynamic distribution groups. What tools should you identify?

Explore the moderation features of Exchange Server 2013.   Moderation and moderated groups are one of the features of Exchange Server 2013 that were only recently introduced. As part of the self-service focus of Exchange Server 2013, moderation allows a user to review messages sent to an email address on your server.

e) **Master It**   If you want to use moderated groups in a mixed organization that contains both Exchange Server 2013 servers and Exchange Server 2007 Hub Transport servers, what group feature should you configure?

p. 397

Chapter 16

Managing Resource Mailboxes

Resource mailboxes play an important role in the scheduling of various tools and facilities—conference rooms, projectors, laptop computers, smart boards, company vehicles, and any other sort of location or tool that is in demand but may have limited availability. To that end, it becomes increasingly important to maintain a calendar and mailbox for these resources, as well as define who can schedule access. Exchange Server 2013, Outlook Web App, and Outlook give you the ability to schedule these resources and view their availability quite easily.

In some respects, managing resource mailboxes is the same as managing user mailboxes. But there are some unique features and settings that can enhance the use of resource mailboxes.

In this chapter, you will learn to:

- ◆ Understand how resource mailboxes differ from regular mailboxes

- ◆ Create resource mailboxes

- ◆ Configure resource mailbox booking and scheduling policies

- ◆ Migrate resource mailboxes

The Unique Nature of Resource Mailboxes

As mentioned in Chapter 14, "Managing Mailboxes and Mailbox Content," there are four possible choices for mailbox types: the user mailbox, a room mailbox, an equipment mailbox, and a linked mailbox. We covered user and linked mailboxes in Chapter 14; in this chapter, we'll focus on the other two, room mailbox and equipment mailbox:

Room Mailbox   A room mailbox is simply a resource mailbox assigned to a meeting location, such as conference and training rooms and auditoriums. A room mailbox can be included in a meeting request as a resource.

Equipment Mailbox   An equipment mailbox is a resource mailbox assigned to a resource that is not generally location specific, such as a projector, specialty AV equipment, or even a company car. Like room mailboxes, equipment mailboxes can be included in meetings requests as resources.

Both room and equipment mailboxes are created as disabled mailbox-enabled accounts in Active Directory. They are not intended to be logged into like a normal user mailbox. The icons associated with resource mailboxes in the global address list are different than the icons associated with user and group accounts. Additionally, certain configurable attributes on the mailboxes allow them to be utilized as resources. They are otherwise the same as standard user accounts.

Exchange 2013 Resource Mailbox Features

Resource mailboxes are handy when it comes to booking resources, such as conference rooms or equipment, such as projectors. In Exchange Server 2013, resource mailboxes for rooms allow you to accept or decline meeting requests, and the room mailbox properties can include information about the seating capacity as well as information about permanent items in the room, such as whiteboards and teleconferencing tools. Resource mailboxes for other pieces of equipment can provide you with descriptions about that device, such as the make and model information for a laptop computer or a company car. Various clients, including Outlook, Outlook Web App, and mobile clients, can utilize resource mailboxes to streamline the process of reserving resources quickly and easily through the same Calendar and Availability services you would use to invite meeting attendees.

Myriad features are available for resource mailboxes: from customization features to booking policy features that determine whether a meeting request is accepted or rejected. By utilizing resource mailboxes, overbooking problems can be eliminated while also enforcing some rules, such as how long a resource can be reserved, who can reserve it, and what to do with certain information within requests.

Delegation of resource room mailboxes provides for manual approval or rejection of meeting requests while also allowing some people to reserve resources outside the defined policies.

Creating Resource Mailboxes

Creating resource mailboxes isn't much different than creating standard mailboxes. You can use the Exchange Administration Center (EAC) or the Exchange Management Shell (EMS). Both just require an added parameter to define the mailbox as a resource mailbox.

Creating and Defining Resource Mailbox Properties

We'll begin with a resource mailbox for a conference room called Conference Room South. You'll create it in the EAC just like you create standard user accounts. To do so, select Recipients from the Feature pane, and then navigate to the Resources tab, click the Add button on the toolbar, and select Room Mailbox; fill in the information in the New Room Mailbox Wizard (shown in Figure 16.1).

If an organizational unit (OU) is not defined, the resource mailbox will be placed in the Users OU. If you would like it placed elsewhere in your Active Directory structure, click the Browse button immediately to the right of the Organizational Unit field and select the appropriate OU.

The rest of the mailbox settings are the same as when you're creating a standard user mailbox. As the wizard completes, a disabled account is created for the resource mailbox.

To create a room resource account using the EMS, you'll use the New-Mailbox cmdlet and specify the -Room parameter. Here's an example:

```
New-Mailbox -Name 'Conference Room East' -Alias 'cr_east' -OrganizationalUnit
'ehloworld.local/ehloworld/Resource Mailboxes' -UserPrincipalName 'cr_east@
ehloworld.local' -SamAccountName 'creast' -FirstName 'Conference Room' -LastName
'East' -Database 'MB01SG01MS01' -Room
```

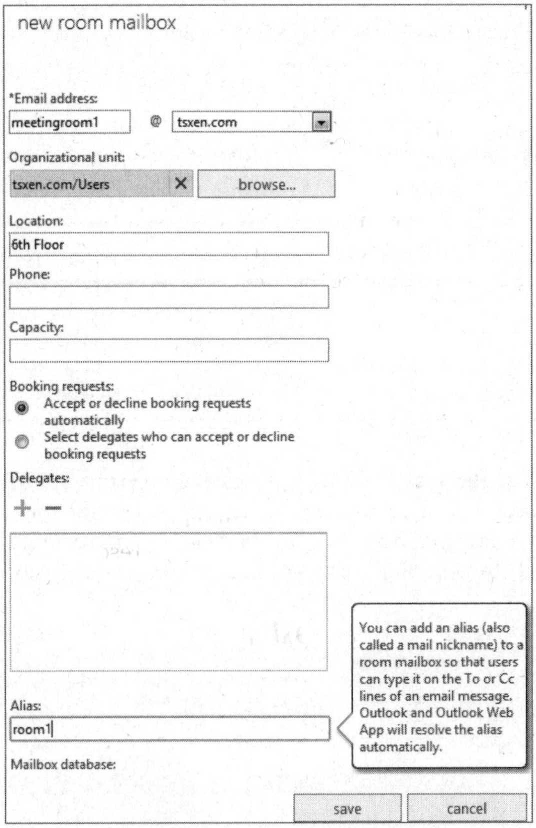

FIGURE 16.1
Defining user
information for a
conference-room
mailbox

In Exchange Server 2013, additional attributes are added to resource accounts. These include different values for RecipientTypeDetails, as well as use of the attributes ResourceType, ResouceCapacity, and ResourceCustom. You can see examples of these using the Get-Mailbox cmdlet. An example is shown here, along with sample output:

```
Get-Mailbox "Conference Room South" | Format-List Name, *recipient*, *resource*

Name                  : Conference Room South
RecipientLimits       : unlimited
RecipientType         : UserMailbox
RecipientTypeDetails  : RoomMailbox
IsResource            : True
ResourceCapacity      :
ResourceCustom        : {}
ResourceType          : Room
```

Table 16.1 shows the details of these attributes when using resource mailboxes.

TABLE 16.1:   Recipient-related attributes for mailboxes

ATTRIBUTE	VALUE/PURPOSE
RecipientType	Set to UserMailbox, regardless of whether the mailbox is a standard user mailbox or resource mailbox
RecipientTypeDetails	Set to either RoomMailbox or EquipmentMailbox
ResourceType	Set to either Room or Equipment
ResourceCapacity	For defining room capacity to assist in determining the correct room for the number of participants
ResourceCustom	For defining additional properties for a resource mailbox

Having these additional attribute settings allows Exchange Server to enable specific handling of meeting requests for these accounts, as well as to provide for easier recognition of resource mailboxes versus user mailboxes. An example is shown in Figure 16.2, where a user can choose the All Rooms address book to see just a list of room resource accounts.

FIGURE 16.2
Viewing room resources in the Address Book using Outlook

As you can see, this simplifies locating and viewing rooms without the clutter of the entire global address list.

Defining Advanced Resource Mailbox Features

At this point, you've created a resource mailbox. With Exchange Server 2013, you can now specify additional parameters for the mailbox to help make it more convenient for end users when they are scheduling meetings that may involve this resource: the ResourceCapacity and ResourceCustom attributes of a mailbox. ResourceCapacity allows you to define the capacity of a room, which can certainly help in finding the correctly sized room for an event.

To define the number of attendees a room can host, set the Capacity property of a room mailbox. Open the mailbox in the EAC by either double-clicking the resource or clicking the Edit button on the toolbar, and click the General tab. Enter the room capacity in the appropriate field, as shown in Figure 16.3.

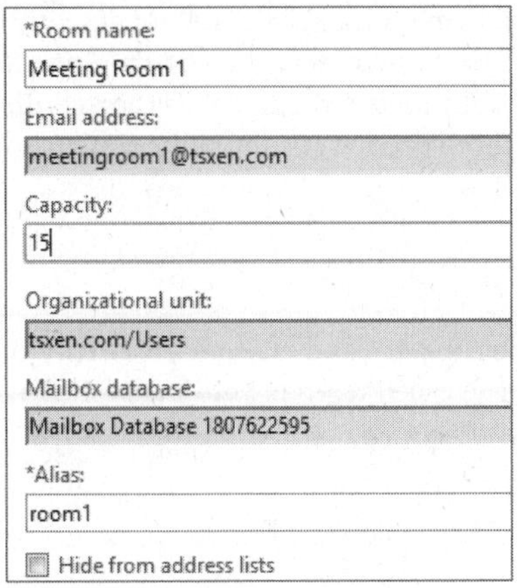

FIGURE 16.3
Entering room
capacity for a
resource mailbox

```
*Room name:
Meeting Room 1

Email address:
meetingroom1@tsxen.com

Capacity:
15

Organizational unit:
tsxen.com/Users

Mailbox database:
Mailbox Database 1807622595

*Alias:
room1

☐ Hide from address lists
```

Resource capacity can be defined from the EMS as well, using the Set-Mailbox cmdlet. Let's say you want to define the room capacity of Conference Room North as 15 people. To do so, use this:

```
Set-Mailbox "Conference Room North" -ResourceCapacity 15
```

What good is finding a conference room with the correct capacity if you can't find one with all the equipment or resources you need? Some organizations have certain conference rooms equipped with TVs, projectors, and so forth. This is where the ResourceCustom attribute comes into play.

To configure ResourceCustom for any resource mailbox, you need to configure the Resource property by modifying the resource object attributes in the Active Directory schema. You do this using the Set-ResourceConfig cmdlet. With Set-ResourceConfig, the attribute needed is ResourcePropertySchema. You can also use Get-ResourceConfig to see the current settings. An example of the default configuration is shown here:

```
Get-ResourceConfig | FL Name,ResourcePropertySchema

Name                  : Resource Schema
ResourcePropertySchema : {}
```

Let's say you want to define an additional type of resource property for TV, Projector, and Speakerphone. Note that Set-ResourceConfig replaces the existing value with the new value, so make sure you include the existing properties when using Set-ResourceConfig. All entries must begin with either Room/ or Equipment/. To set those properties, use the following example:

```
Set-ResourceConfig -ResourcePropertySchema("Room/TV","Room/Projector", "Room/
Speakerphone")
```

Once the resource property schema includes TV, Projector, and Speakerphone, you can verify that they've been added to the schema by using the Get-ResourceConfig cmdlet.

To set these attributes via the EMS, use the Set-Mailbox cmdlet with the –ResourceCustom attribute. You can specify the room capacity at the same time using the –ResourceCapacity attribute, as shown here:

```
Set-Mailbox "Conference Room North" -ResourceCustom ("TV","Speakerphone",
"Projector") -ResourceCapacity 15
```

This will configure both the capacity and custom properties of the room mailbox. You can then verify the settings using the Get-Mailbox cmdlet, as shown here with sample output:

```
Get-Mailbox "Conference Room North" | FL Name, *resource*

Name              : Conference Room North
IsResource        : True
ResourceCapacity  : 15
ResourceCustom    : {TV, Speakerphone, Projector}
ResourceType      : Room
```

Defining Resource Scheduling Policies

In Exchange Server 2013 (as in 2010), the processing of meeting requests is much more streamlined and far more feature rich than in older releases. Among the options are who can book automatically or via a delegate, how to handle conflicting requests, and when and for how long meetings can be scheduled.

Exchange Server 2013 provides two different interfaces for configuring these settings: Exchange Administration Center and Exchange Management Shell. We'll look at both here.

DEFINING RESOURCE SCHEDULING POLICIES USING THE EAC

When you open a resource mailbox in the EAC, you can see that two of the five tabs on the resource property page (Figure 16.4) are related to resource configuration: Delegates and Booking Options.

Delegates   Defines whether scheduling requests will be automatically rejected or accepted based on the booking policy or whether delegates will be responsible for accepting or rejecting requests manually.

Booking Options   Defines whether recurring meetings are allowed, when meetings can be scheduled during the work week, advanced scheduling options, and message replies to meeting organizers.

Click the Booking Options tab to view the settings available. An example of some default settings is shown in Figure 16.5.

The list of options here includes settings to define what is acceptable for a meeting request to be approved. These include recurring meeting requests, how long meetings can be, and how far in the future they can be booked. We've broken down the individual settings in Table 16.2, including how they are referenced in the EAC and the EMS.

FIGURE 16.4
General tab for a resource mailbox

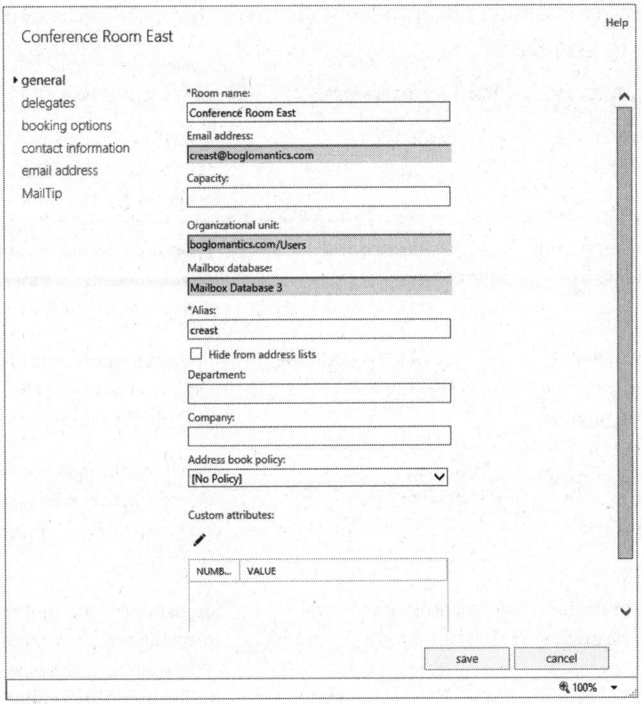

FIGURE 16.5
Booking Options settings for a room mailbox

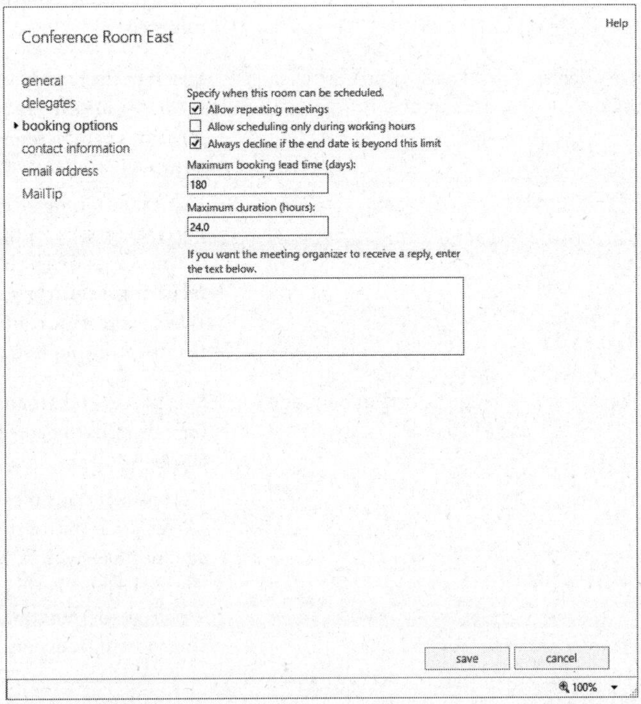

TABLE 16.2:   Booking Options tab features and EMS equivalents

EAC PARAMETER	EMS PARAMETER	DESCRIPTION
(Not available in EAC)	-AllowConflicts	Specifies whether to allow conflicting meeting requests. If enabled, this will allow multiple meetings to be accepted for the same date and time.
Allow repeating meetings	-AllowRecurring Meetings	Specifies whether to allow recurring meetings. When enabled, recurring meeting requests, such as those for every Monday at 9 a.m., are accepted.
Allow scheduling only during working hours	-ScheduleOnlyDuring WorkHours	Specifies whether to allow meetings to be scheduled outside work hours. If checked, meeting requests for times outside the mailbox's working hours will be rejected.
Maximum booking lead time (days)	-Booking WindowInDays	Specifies the maximum number of days in advance that the resource can be reserved. Maximum is 1080. When set to 0, the resource can be reserved at any date in the future.
Maximum duration (Hours)	-MaximumDuration InMinutes	Specifies the maximum duration allowed for incoming meeting requests. Valid input is 0 through 2147483647. When set to 0, the maximum duration of a meeting is unlimited. This applies to individual meetings in the case of recurring meeting requests. The EAC specifies hours in the booking options, but the shell specifies minutes.
(Not available in EAC)	-MaximumConflict Instances	Specifies the maximum number of conflicts for new recurring meeting requests when the Allow Repeating Meetings parameter is checked. Valid input ranges from 0 through 2147483647.
		If a new recurring meeting request conflicts with existing reservations for the resource more than the number of times specified by Maximum Conflict Instances, the recurring meeting request is automatically declined. When set to 0, no conflicts are permitted for new recurring meeting requests.
	-ConflictPercentage Allowed	Specifies the maximum percentage of meeting conflicts for new recurring meeting requests. Valid input is 0 through 100.
		If a new recurring meeting request conflicts with existing reservations for the resource more than the percentage specified by the Conflict Percentage Allowed value, the recurring meeting request is automatically declined. When set to 0, no conflicts are permitted for new recurring meeting requests.

TABLE 16.2: Booking Options tab features and EMS equivalents *(CONTINUED)*

EAC PARAMETER	EMS PARAMETER	DESCRIPTION
	-ResourceDelegates	Specifies a list of users who are resource mailbox delegates. Resource mailbox delegates can approve or reject requests sent to this resource mailbox.
	-ForwardRequestsTo Delegates	Specifies whether to forward incoming meeting requests to the delegate(s) defined for the mailbox.
	-EnforceScheduling Horizon	Enforces an end date for recurring meetings based on the BookingWindowInDays setting.

There are settings that will help you standardize how meeting requests appear in the resource mailbox calendar. Those settings are listed in Table 16.3, along with their EMS equivalents where available.

TABLE 16.3: Resource information settings and their EMS equivalents

EMS PARAMETER	DESCRIPTION
-DeleteAttachments	Specifies whether to remove attachments from all incoming messages.
-DeleteComments	Removes any text in the message body of incoming meeting requests.
-DeleteSubject	Removes the subject of incoming meeting requests.
-DeleteNonCalendar Items	Removes all non-calendar items received by the mailbox.
-AddOrganizerTo Subject	Specifies whether the meeting organizer's name is used as the subject of the meeting request.
-RemovePrivate Property	Clears the private flag for incoming meeting requests.
-OrganizerInfo	Resource mailboxes send organizer information when a meeting request is declined because of conflicts.
-Additional Response	Specifies the additional information to be included in responses to meeting requests.
-AllowNewRequests Tentatively	Specifies whether to mark pending requests as tentative on the calendar. If set to $false, pending requests are marked as free.
-RemoveForwarded MeetingNotifications	Specifies whether meeting forwarding notifications are moved to Deleted Items after processing.
-RemoveOldMeeting Messages	Specifies whether old and redundant updates and responses are removed.

Through the Booking Policy parameters in the Set-CalendarProcessing cmdlet, you can define which users are automatically approved to schedule access to a resource, as well as those that are subject to delegate approval. This can be just a specific group of people or everyone. Those settings, and their EMS version where available, are listed in Table 16.4.

TABLE 16.4: Resource in-policy request features and their EMS equivalents

EMS PARAMETER	DESCRIPTION
-BookInPolicy	Specifies a list of users who are allowed to submit in-policy meeting requests. These are automatically approved.
-RequestInPolicy	Specifies a list of users who are allowed to submit in-policy meeting requests. These require approval from a resource mailbox delegate.
-AllBookInPolicy	Specifies whether to automatically approve in-policy requests from all users.
-AllRequestInPolicy	Specifies whether to allow all users to submit in-policy requests. These would require approval from a resource mailbox delegate.

Requests by users defined as being "out of policy" are sent to resource mailbox delegates. These policy definitions can only be assigned via the EMS and can include requests for meetings outside of working hours, longer duration, and so forth, and are listed in Table 16.5.

TABLE 16.5: Resource out-of-policy request settings and their EMS Equivalents

EMS PARAMETER	DESCRIPTION
-RequestOutOfPolicy	Specifies a list of users who are allowed to submit out-of-policy requests. These require approval from a resource mailbox delegate.
-AllRequestOutofPolicy	Specifies whether to allow all users to submit out-of-policy requests. These require manual approval from a resource mailbox delegate.

DEFINING RESOURCE SCHEDULING POLICIES USING THE EXCHANGE MANAGEMENT SHELL

You can also use the EMS to configure the settings. To view resource scheduling policies in the EMS, you use the Get-CalendarProcessing cmdlet, shown here along with its output:

```
Get-CalendarProcessing "Conference Room South" | Format-List

RunspaceId                     : 53135a92-3a51-4db4-
a0aa-7a45c231fb91
AutomateProcessing             : AutoAccept
AllowConflicts                 : False
```

```
BookingWindowInDays                     : 180
MaximumDurationInMinutes                : 1440
AllowRecurringMeetings                  : True
EnforceSchedulingHorizon                : True
ScheduleOnlyDuringWorkHours             : False
ConflictPercentageAllowed               : 0
MaximumConflictInstances                : 0
ForwardRequestsToDelegates              : True
DeleteAttachments                       : True
DeleteComments                          : True
RemovePrivateProperty                   : True
DeleteSubject                           : True
AddOrganizerToSubject                   : True
DeleteNonCalendarItems                  : True
TentativePendingApproval                : True
EnableResponseDetails                   : True
OrganizerInfo                           : True
ResourceDelegates                       : {}
RequestOutOfPolicy                      :
AllRequestOutOfPolicy                   : False
BookInPolicy                            :
AllBookInPolicy                         : True
RequestInPolicy                         :
AllRequestInPolicy                      : False
AddAdditionalResponse                   : False
AdditionalResponse                      :
RemoveOldMeetingMessages                : True
AddNewRequestsTentatively               : True
ProcessExternalMeetingMessages          : False
RemoveForwardedMeetingNotifications     : False
Identity                                : ehloworld.local
/ehloworld/Resource Mailboxes/Conference Room South
```

Setting an attribute in EMS is straightforward using the `Set-CalendarProcessing` cmdlet. For example, let's say you want to add a resource delegate to Conference Room South. You can accomplish that in one line:

```
Set-CalendarProcessing "Conference Room South" -ResourceDelegates ↵
"Alex Bossio"
```

As with other EMS commands, you can supply multiple attributes in one command. If you want to, say, add a delegate and also add the meeting organizer's name to the subject, you could use this:

```
Set-CalendarProcessing "Conference Room South" -ResourceDelegates ↵
"Alex Bossio" –AddOrganizerToSubject $true
```

A complete description of each of the attributes is listed in Table 16.2 through Table 16.4 earlier in this chapter.

SETTINGS THAT CAN BE CONFIGURED ONLY IN THE EMS

Some settings can be configured only by using the Exchange Management Shell. They include working hours and days, time zone, and default reminder settings. You can see an example of these by using the Get-MailboxCalendarConfiguration cmdlet:

```
Get-MailboxCalendarConfiguration "Conference Room South" | ↵
Format-List

RunspaceId            : 53135a92-3a51-4db4-a0aa-
7a45c231fb91
WorkDays              : Weekdays
WorkingHoursStartTime : 08:00:00
WorkingHoursEndTime   : 17:00:00
WorkingHoursTimeZone  : Pacific Standard Time
WeekStartDay          : Sunday
ShowWeekNumbers       : False
TimeIncrement         : ThirtyMinutes
RemindersEnabled      : True
ReminderSoundEnabled  : True
DefaultReminderTime   : 00:15:00
Identity              :
IsValid               : True
```

Setting options here is possible via the Set-MailboxCalendarConfiguration cmdlet. For example, if you need to change the WorkingHoursTimeZone, you can use this:

```
Set-MailboxCalendarConfiguration "Conference Room South" ↵
-WorkingHoursTimeZone "Eastern Standard Time"
```

A complete breakdown of the attributes is shown in Table 16.6.

TABLE 16.6:   Set-MailboxCalendarConfiguration attributes

PARAMETER	DESCRIPTION
WorkDays	Specifies which days are defined as workdays in the OWA calendar
WorkingHoursStartTime	Specifies the start of the workday in hours, minutes, and seconds
WorkingHoursEndTime	Specifies the end of the workday in hours, minutes, and seconds
WorkingHoursTimeZone	Specifies the time zone used to determine start and end times
WeekStartDay	Specifies which day of the week is the start of the workweek
ShowWeekNumbers	Specifies whether the OWA date picker shows the week number
TimeIncrement	Specifies in which increments the OWA calendar shows time frames
RemindersEnabled	Specifies whether OWA events trigger a reminder
DefaultReminderTime	Specifies the default time frame before a scheduled event that OWA displays the reminder

Automatic Processing: AutoUpdate vs. AutoAccept

Automatic processing of meeting requests is enabled by an attribute on resource mailboxes called `AutomateProcessing`. By default, when a resource mailbox is created or an existing mailbox is converted to a resource mailbox, the `AutomateProcessing` attribute is set to `AutoUpdate`. `AutoUpdate` processes requests automatically but doesn't validate the request against any booking policy settings. This is generally not ideal for an organization.

The alternative value available for `AutomateProcessing` is `AutoAccept`. When a resource mailbox is configured for `AutoAccept`, the attendant validates the meeting request against the configured policy settings before determining whether the meeting request is accepted or rejected. For the settings in the resource policy to be effective, the `AutomateProcessing` attribute on a resource mailbox needs to be changed to `AutoAccept`. Changing this attribute on a resource mailbox is simple, regardless of whether you use the EMS or OWA.

In OWA, choose Options ➤ Settings ➤ Resource, and check the box that reads Automatically Process Meeting Requests And Cancellations. Then click Save. This will change `AutomateProcessing` to `AutoAccept`, and future meeting requests will be validated against the policy settings for that mailbox.

In the EMS, you set the `AutomateProcessing` attribute using the `Set-CalendarProcessing` cmdlet, like this:

```
Set-CalendarProcessing "Conference Room South" ↵
-AutomateProcessing AutoAccept
```

You can also use the EMS to make the change across all resource mailboxes:

```
Get-Mailbox -filter {IsResource -eq $true} | ↵
Set-CalendarProcessing -AutomateProcessing AutoAccept
```

Using any of these methods will change the resource mailbox to `AutoAccept`.

Migrating Resource Mailboxes

Moving resource mailboxes from a pre–Exchange Server 2007 version to Exchange Server 2013 involves a few steps. Exchange Server is not intelligent enough to know that a mailbox called Conference Room South is a resource, and thus to make it a resource mailbox you must tell Exchange Server that this is the case. Follow these steps:

1. Document all resource mailboxes that need to be moved, as well as any settings configured via third-party solutions or scripts.

2. Disable any automatic processing configured via script or third-party solutions.

3. Move the mailboxes to Exchange Server 2013 using either the EAC or the EMS. This process is detailed in Chapter 17, "Managing Modern Public Folders."

4. Use the EMS to convert the mailboxes from user mailboxes to room mailboxes.

5. Configure the appropriate policy settings for the resource mailboxes.

Converting a standard user mailbox to a resource mailbox is quick and simple in the EMS using the `Set-Mailbox` cmdlet, usineg the –Type argument, and specifying the Room or Equipment attribute, as in this example:

```
Set-Mailbox "Conference Room South" -Type Room
```

You should then set the room resource mailbox to automatically process appointments using a command like this:

```
Get-Mailbox "Conference Room South" | Set-CalendarProcessing -AutomateProcessing
AutoAccept
```

Once this occurs, Exchange Server considers the mailbox a room mailbox, and the ability to configure it via the EAC, EMS, or OWA is enabled.

Real World Scenario

ELIMINATING CONFERENCE ROOM HIJACKING

Organization KLMN is a large community church; it is not like most churches. With more than 400 staff, volunteers, and interns, there are constant meetings, conferences, and gatherings in the building's five conference rooms. And to complicate matters, the scheduling process for the conference rooms was antiquated and inconvenient. In the building's lobby were three-ring binders for each conference room. Each contained pages for each calendar day. Those wishing to reserve a conference room had to go to the lobby, look through the binder for the desired conference room, and try to decipher sometimes-cryptic entries. Additionally, when meetings were cancelled, meeting organizers didn't always remove the entry in the binder to allow the conference room to be rescheduled. Since some of KLMN's staff worked outside the main building, the process was even more cumbersome when trying to find a conference room that was available. The process was so inconvenient that many would just hijack a conference room without scheduling it. This sometimes led to "musical conference rooms" and a lot of user frustration.

When KLMN moved to resource mailboxes in Exchange Server, users could immediately reserve conference rooms by merely adding the conference room to the meeting request. Additionally, since the resource room mailboxes were configured with capacity and special features defined, finding a conference room that best fit the needs of the users was much easier. Remote users had the same experience as local users, and the number of conference room "hijackings" dropped to nearly zero.

This process has improved the adoption of using Outlook Meeting Requests, the Outlook Calendar in general, and the correct process for booking conference rooms. Users no longer have to walk to the other end of the building or go down three floors just to find when a conference room might be reserved. They can simply open Outlook or OWA or use a mobile device to schedule their meeting, including all attendees, the conference room, and any necessary equipment.

The Bottom Line

Understand how resource mailboxes differ from regular mailboxes. Resource mailboxes serve a different purpose in Exchange Server 2013 than standard user mailboxes and thus have different features and capabilities. Understanding how resource mailboxes are different, including what added features are provided, can help improve the end-user experience and increase adoption rate.

a) **Master It**   You are planning to create resource mailboxes to support conference room and other resource scheduling. Identify how the resource mailboxes are different from regular user mailboxes.

Create resource mailboxes.   Creating resource mailboxes is easy using various tools in Exchange Server. Users need resource mailboxes for conference rooms and equipment to allow for easier, more informative scheduling.

b) **Master It**   What tools are available to create resource mailboxes and to define additional schema properties for resource mailboxes?

Configure resource mailbox booking and scheduling policies.   Properly configured resource mailboxes help users find the correct resource and determine whether it is available when needed. When the resource mailbox is properly configured, users can quickly and easily find conference rooms that have the proper capacity and features needed to hold a meeting.

c) **Master It**   You need to configure a resource mailbox to handle automatic scheduling. What tools can you use?

Migrate resource mailboxes.   Moving resource mailboxes from legacy versions of Exchange Server requires proper planning and execution to ensure that Exchange Server 2013 features and capabilities for resource mailboxes are available. Resource mailboxes in Exchange Server versions prior to 2007 were standard user accounts, and they need to be migrated and converted to resource mailboxes in Exchange Server 2013.

d) **Master It**   You have moved a resource mailbox from an Exchange Server 2003 Mailbox server to an Exchange Server 2013 Mailbox server. You need to convert this resource to an Exchange Server 2013 resource mailbox. What steps should you take?

Chapter 17

Managing Modern Public Folders

Public folders are a major part of many Exchange Server deployments. Public folders are a powerful way to share knowledge and data with users throughout an organization, they've been a staple of Exchange Server since 1996.

Back in Exchange Server 2007, there were rumors that public folders might not exist in subsequent editions because they used a separate management and replication architecture that was difficult to scale. In Exchange Server 2013, Microsoft has dramatically changed the public folder architecture to make it more scalable, which makes it possible to support public folders for many years to come.

In this chapter, you will learn to:

◆ Understand the architectural changes made to public folders

◆ Manage public folders

Understanding Architectural Changes for Modern Public Folders

Despite the rumors of their demise, public folders are alive and well, and, in some ways, they're better in Exchange Server 2013 than they ever have been.

In Exchange Server 2013, Microsoft changed the public folder architecture, branding them as "modern public folders." This change enables Microsoft and those implementing Exchange Server 2013 to easily support and scale the infrastructure, overcoming the challenges and limits from previous editions.

Modern Public Folders and Exchange Server 2013

In the previous editions of Exchange Server, the public folder database stored public folders. In addition, public folders used a separate replication architecture known as PF replication.

To scale and simplify the public folder architecture, Microsoft decided to move away from the legacy public folder database and public folder replication. In Exchange 2013, public folders are now stored in a special type of mailbox called a public folder mailbox, but in essence those public folder mailboxes are normal mailboxes and Exchange Server treats them as it does users' mailboxes.

Because mailboxes now store public folders, there is no longer public folder replication based on a multi-master model. The database availability group (DAG) replicates public folder mailboxes and their contents as it does any other mailboxes in the organization. Thus, there is no need to manage and troubleshoot public folders separately, and there is no black magic to use in troubleshooting public folder replication.

In Exchange Server 2013, as we explained, mailboxes store public folders and mailboxes are hosted on a mailbox database. End users do not see any difference; they use public folders as they were using them in the previous versions of Exchange Server. What has changed is how public folders are stored and replicated.

To create a public folder, first you need to create a public folder mailbox that will host the public folder's hierarchy and contents. There can be only one primary hierarchy in an organization. The primary hierarchy is writable and the secondary hierarchy copies are read-only. The primary hierarchy mailbox is the first public folder mailbox created in the Exchange Server organization, although the hierarchy can be replicated to every public folder mailbox.

The primary hierarchy holds the public folder tree hierarchy and folder structure, which helps identify permissions on the folders and the parents and children of that folder.

When users connect, they connect to their home hierarchy, which contains a copy of the primary hierarchy (in read-only format if they are not connecting to the primary hierarchy), and they access public folder contents located on a mailbox hosting the contents in their site via their local Client Access server (CAS). If they are accessing content that resides in a different public folder mailbox, the CAS will connect the user to that public folder mailbox directly, even if the content is remote or on a different site, since there is no local copy of this content.

Modern Public Folders and Replication

Modern public folders do not use public folder replication as previous Exchange Server versions did; since public folders are stored in mailboxes, the DAG must replicate the mailboxes. However, there is a mentality shift here; there is only one writable copy of the contents at any time. Contents in every public folder mailbox are not writable as they were previously.

From a high-availability point of view, public folder mailboxes are treated as normal mailboxes; they are replicated via the DAG. Public folder failover occurs in the same fashion as normal mailbox database failover. In case of failure, the passive copy of the mailbox database that holds the public folder mailbox in the DAG will take ownership and serve the users. We will explore in detail the high-availability considerations for modern public folders later in this chapter.

If there are no changes to the hierarchy, the hierarchy will be replicated to every public folder mailbox every 24 hours. If there is a change to the hierarchy, the replication is triggered immediately via the incremental change synchronization process, which helps in monitoring the mailbox contents. When users are connected to content mailboxes, the synchronization occurs every 15 minutes. If the node hosting the hierarchy is part of a DAG, it will failover to the database passive copy within the DAG should the mailbox database with the public folder primary hierarchy fail.

Modern Public Folder Limitations and Considerations

If you have been using public folders for years, you are probably already aware of their limitations. However, there are new considerations for modern public folders:

◆ The maximum recommended mailbox size is 100 GB and the maximum recommended mailbox database size is 2 TB. You may need to consider splitting your public folder into multiple public folder mailboxes. End users will see the same folder structure regardless of how the public folders are stored.

◆ There is no more public folder replication; thus public folder replication does not replicate contents independently. DAG replicates public folder mailboxes. There is only one writable copy of the content, and users must connect to this copy to update the content.

◆ You must use Outlook 2007 or later to access modern public folders.

◆ Users cannot delete public folders from Outlook Web Access, but they can perform any other operation.

◆ You cannot apply retention policies to public folder mailboxes.

Moving Public Folders to Exchange Server 2013

If you are migrating from Exchange Server 2007/2010 to Exchange Server 2013 and you are planning to continue to use public folders, you will need to extract the public folder statistics via Export-PublicFolderStatistics.ps1, create a mapping between public folders and public folder mailboxes, and create a migration request to move the public folders, as detailed in these steps:

1. To document the current public folder hierarchy, run the following command from your Exchange Server 2007/2010 server to export the public folder structure to CSV:

   ```
   Get-PublicFolder -Recurse | ConvertTo-CSV C:\PFmigration\
   E12PFfoldersdocumentation.csv
   ```

2. To document the current folders' sizes, items, and owners, run the following command from your Exchange Server 2007/2010 server:

   ```
   Get-PublicFolder -Recurse | Get-PublicFolderStatistics | ConvertTo-CSV C:\
   PFmigration \E12PFfoldersitemsdocumentation.csv
   ```

3. Download the migration scripts from http://www.microsoft.com/en-us/download/ details.aspx?id=38407 to your Exchange Server 2007/2010 server, and then export the folders and sizes via the C:\Program Files\Microsoft\Exchange Server\V15\ Scripts> command from the following path:

   ```
   .\Export-PublicFolderStatistics.ps1 ts-ex2010.tsxen.com C:\PFmigration\
   e12PFstatistics.csv
   ```

   In this case, we have four public folders (Engineering, Marketing, Sales, and R&D), each in a different size. Figure 17.1 shows the command output.

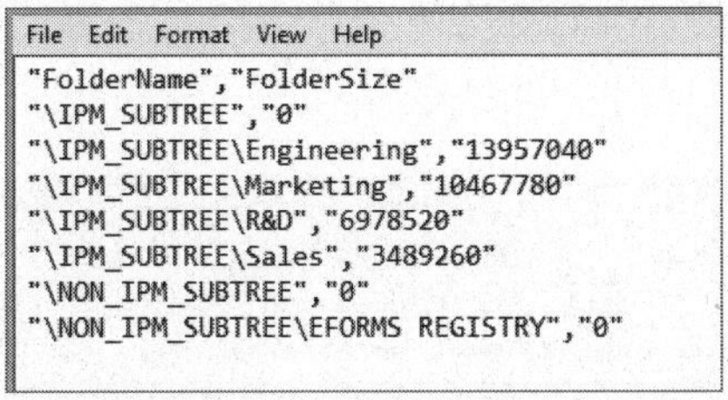

FIGURE 17.1
Public folder statistics

```
 File  Edit  Format  View  Help
"FolderName","FolderSize"
"\IPM_SUBTREE","0"
"\IPM_SUBTREE\Engineering","13957040"
"\IPM_SUBTREE\Marketing","10467780"
"\IPM_SUBTREE\R&D","6978520"
"\IPM_SUBTREE\Sales","3489260"
"\NON_IPM_SUBTREE","0"
"\NON_IPM_SUBTREE\EFORMS REGISTRY","0"
```

4. Create a folder-to-mailbox mapping using the following command, which imports the file and configures the maximum size of the public folder mailbox to 100 GB. You can always open the map file and edit the folder-to-mailbox mapping:

```
.\PublicFolderToMailboxMapGenerator.ps1 100000000000 C:\PFmigration\
e12PFstatistics.csv C:\PFmigration\e12PFmap.csv
```

5. Create the first public folder mailbox. Because it will hold the primary hierarchy, you must create it with the –HoldForMigration switch. On your Exchange Server 2013 server, issue the following command:

```
New-Mailbox -PublicFolder mailbox1 –HoldForMigration
```

This will set the new public folder mailbox to the migration status.

6. On the Exchange Server 2013 server, insert the path to the map CSV file that was created in step 4 (C:\PFmigration\e12PFmap.csv). Now you are ready to kick off the migration:

```
New-PublicFolderMigrationRequest -SourceDatabase (Get-PublicFolderDatabase
-Server ts-ex2010.tsxen.com) -CSVData (Get-Content C:\PFmigration\e12PFmap.csv
-Encoding Byte)
```

Once the migration starts, you can use `Get-PublicFolderMigrationRequest` to see how the migration is progressing.

You will know the migration is working when it reaches `InProgress` status. Once it reaches `AutoSuspended`, proceed to the next step. Figure 17.2 shows the migration progress from `Queued` to `InProgress`, and Figure 17.3 shows that the migration has reached the `AutoSuspended` stage.

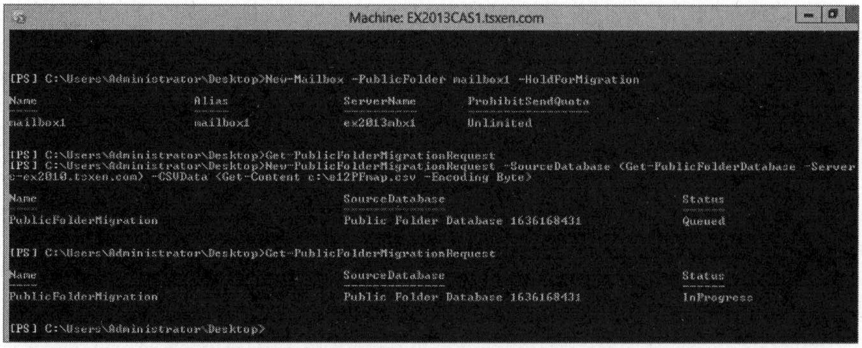

FIGURE 17.2
Public folder migration progress

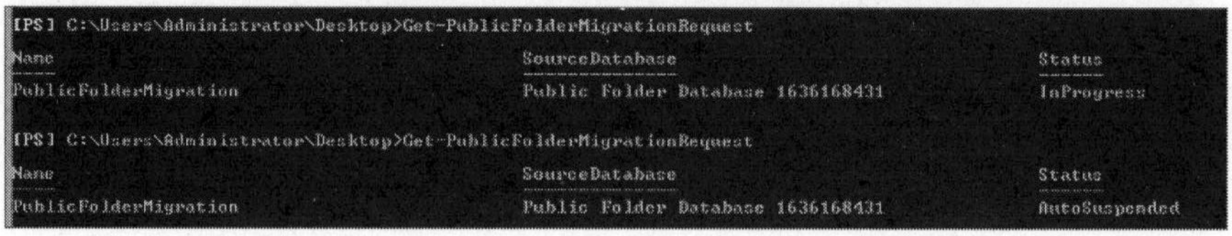

FIGURE 17.3
Public folder migration autosuspended

7. To prevent users from accessing the old public folder, issue the following command to lock it down:

```
Set-OrganizationConfig -PublicFoldersLockedForMigration:$true
```

8. At this point, you need to remove the `PreventCompletion` flag and resume the migration request. Issue the following commands, which will allow the migration to complete:

```
Set-PublicFolderMigrationRequest -Identity \PublicFolderMigration
-PreventCompletion:$false
```

9. Then issue the following command:

```
Resume-PublicFolderMigrationRequest -Identity \PublicFolderMigration
```

10. You can view the migration progress via this command:

```
Get-PublicFolderMigrationRequest | Get-PublicFolderMigrationRequestStatistics
-IncludeReport | fl
```

Congratulations—you have completed your public folder migration! The final steps depend on how many changes have occurred since your migration reached `AutoSuspended` status (in step 6), because it will incrementally sync the data. Thus, it is highly recommended to move the data as quickly as possible.

Now that your public folders are on Exchange Server 2013, we'll show how you can manage them.

Managing Public Folder Mailboxes

We have gone through creating public folder mailboxes in the previous section, but here we discuss how to create them from the Exchange Administration Center (EAC) and control their properties.

You can create a dedicated public folder mailbox for every folder or group of folders as you wish. As with other public folder changes, this will not affect end users' experience; they will still see the public folders in the hierarchy you specified.

You can use the EAC or PowerShell to create public folders. To create a public folder mailbox from the EAC, open the EAC, browse to Public Folder Mailboxes, and click the plus sign to open the Public Folder Mailbox Wizard (see Figure 17.4).

If this is your first public folder mailbox, it will contain the primary hierarchy, as shown in Figure 17.5. Keep in mind that you cannot create a primary hierarchy mailbox when you are migrating from previous versions of Exchange Server (2007/2010) because it must be created in the `HoldForMigration` status.

To edit the public folder, click the Edit button, which opens the public folder mailbox's properties. On the General page, shown in Figure 17.6, you can rename the mailbox and view its organizational unit and the mailbox database that hosts that mailbox.

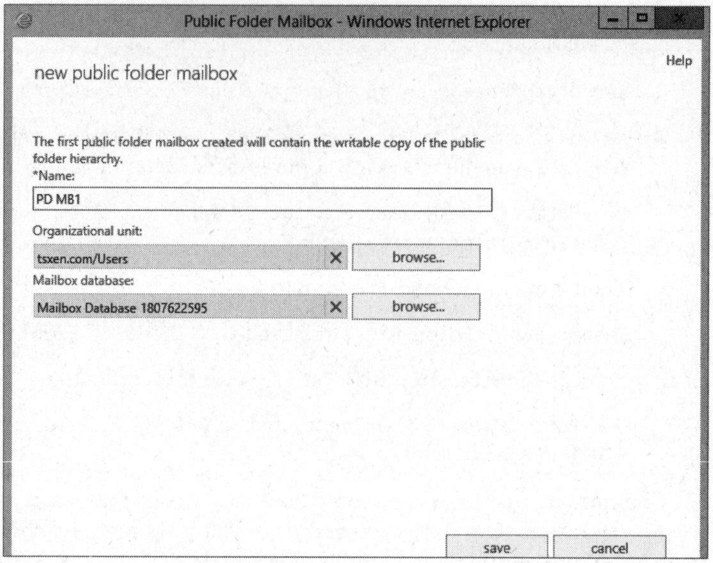

FIGURE 17.4
New Public
Folder Mailbox
screen

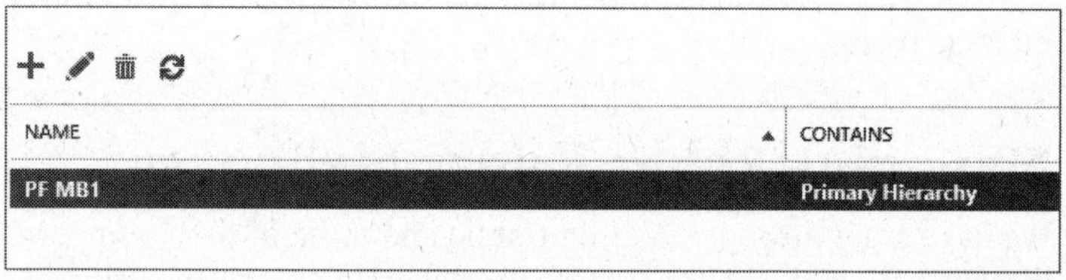

FIGURE 17.5
The public folder
mailbox contain-
ing the primary
hierarchy

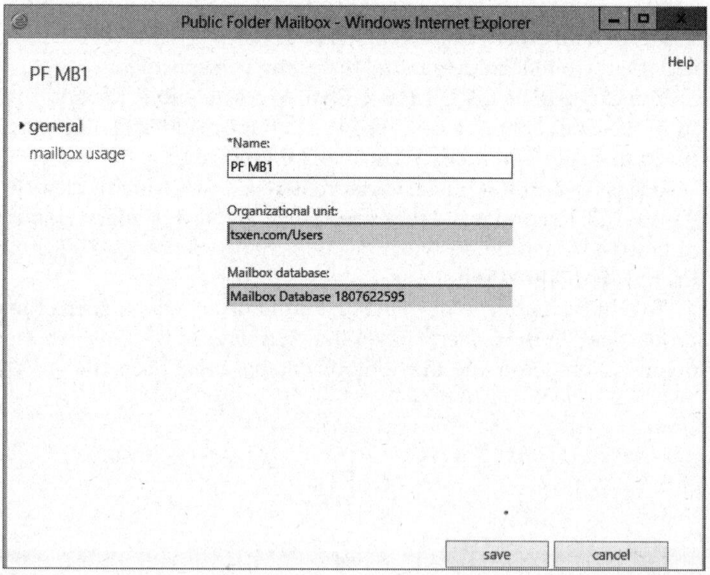

FIGURE 17.6
Primary hierarchy
mailbox properties

The Mailbox Usage page displays the mailbox size limit and how much it consumes, and it defines the mailbox limits, including the following:

◆ Issue Warning at (MB): Defines when the public folder users will receive a warning when it reaches a certain size

◆ Prohibit Post at (MB): Defines a size at which users will not be able to post to the public folder

◆ Maximum Item Size (MB): Defines the maximum size of items that can be sent to that public folder

You can set this configuration via PowerShell. The following cmdlets are used to create and manage a public folder mailbox:

`New-Mailbox -PublicFolder` Creates a new public folder mailbox

`Set-Mailbox -PublicFolder` Sets the properties of a public folder mailbox

`Get-Mailbox -PublicFolder` Retrieves a list of public folder mailboxes and their properties

`Remove-Mailbox -PublicFolder` Deletes a public folder mailbox

VOILÀ—NO MORE "DATABASE WILL NOT MOUNT" ERROR MESSAGES

In previous versions of Exchange Server, after creating public folders, it was common that the public folder database would not mount. That was because of Active Directory replication, and sometimes the Exchange server was speaking to a different domain controller. Now that public folders are hosted in mailboxes and on the mailbox database, there are no more public folder mount errors!

Managing Public Folders

Now that you have a public folder mailbox created, let's look at creating the public folders within the public folder mailbox using the EAC.

To add a folder to the public folder mailbox, navigate to the public folders and click the plus sign to add a public folder to the root. The New Public Folder screen will open, as shown in see Figure 17.7. You use the New Public Folder screen to fill in two attributes of the public folder— the name of the public folder, and the path of the public folder should it be nested in a public folder hierarchy.

To mail-enable the public folder, which will allow users to post to that public folder via email, click the Enable link under the Mail Settings section on the right hand side of the EAC. This will launch a wizard, which will ask if you are sure you want to enable the public folder. Click Yes to enable the public folder for emails. The email address will be taken from the name of the Public Folder and the default email address policy for the organization. If you have created a Public Folder and given it a name that includes a space, the space will be removed during the creation of the folder's email address. Given that we started with a Public Folder named sales, and our default email address domain is tsxen.com, we can now send email to this folder from outside the organization by addressing mail to `sales@tsxen.com` after the email address has been enabled.

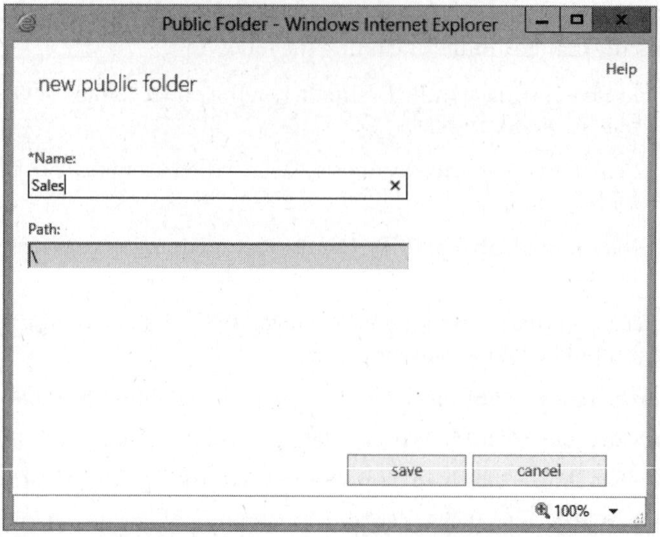

FIGURE 17.7
Adding a new
public folder

PUBLIC FOLDER PROPERTIES

The default permissions on a folder deny anonymous users to contribute to a folder. The permissions can be viewed by selecting the Manage button beneath the Folder Permissions section of the Details pane in the EAC, or by using the EMS to run the `Get-PublicFolderClientPermission` cmdlet. To look at the client permissions on a folder called Sales, you would run the following cmdlet:

```
Get-PublicFolderClientPermission "\Sales"
```

In this example, the path is listed as `"\Sales"`, indicating that the folder was created at the root of the public folder mailbox. If there were a parent folder named, "Departments" in which the "Sales" folder was nested, the path would be "\Departments\Sales."

To view the public folder's properties, click the Edit icon to open the public folder's properties page, which is divided into several subpages:

General   Displays the public folder's general information like name, item count, and the database hosting the public folder mailbox that hosts the public folder, as shown in Figure 17.8.

Statistics   Displays the item counts, deleted items, total items sizes, and the like. Figure 17.9 shows the Statistics properties page.

Limits   Sets the public folder limits, including the following (see Figure 17.10):

◆ Issue Warning At (MB): Defines when the public folder users will receive a warning about the folder reaching a certain size.

◆ Prohibit Post At (MB): Defines a size at which users will not be able to post to the public folder.

FIGURE 17.8
Public folder General
properties page

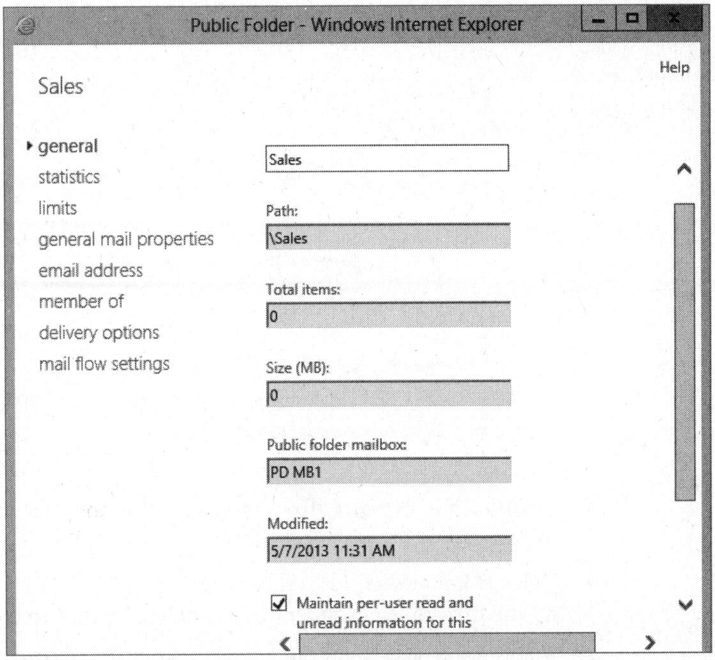

FIGURE 17.9
Public folder Statistics properties
page

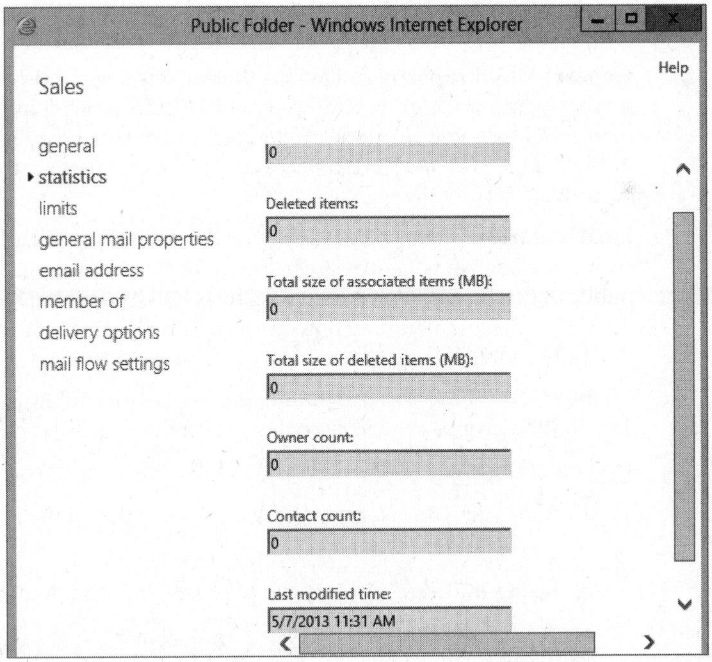

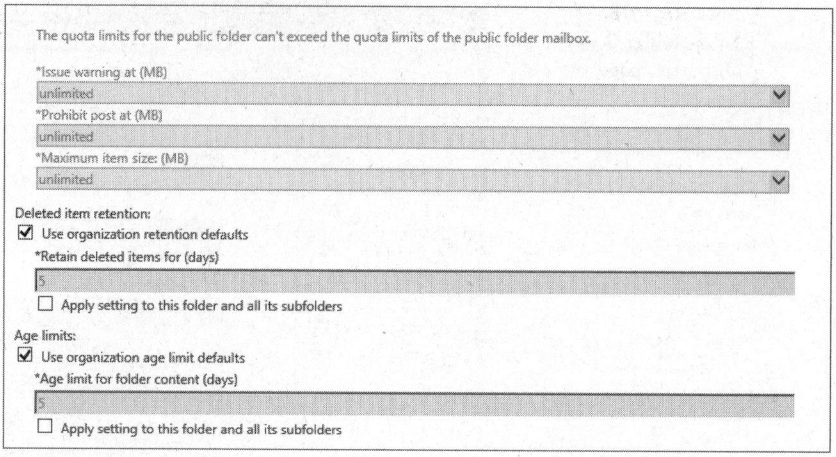

FIGURE 17.10
Public folder
properties,
Limits page

The quota limits for the public folder can't exceed the quota limits of the public folder mailbox.

*Issue warning at (MB)
unlimited

*Prohibit post at (MB)
unlimited

*Maximum item size: (MB)
unlimited

Deleted item retention:
☑ Use organization retention defaults
   *Retain deleted items for (days)
   5
   ☐ Apply setting to this folder and all its subfolders

Age limits:
☑ Use organization age limit defaults
   *Age limit for folder content (days)
   5
   ☐ Apply setting to this folder and all its subfolders

- ◆ Maximum Item Size (MB): Defines the maximum size for items sent to that public folder.

- ◆ Deleted Item Retention: Allows you to use the global organization's settings or specify the maximum number of days deleted items are kept; by default it is 5 days.

- ◆ Age Limits: Allows you to use the global organization settings and to instruct the database to delete any item in any folder on this database that exceeds the specified age limit. This is useful if you want to delete or age out older content, but it is probably better to apply this property on a folder-by-folder basis.

General Mail Properties Defines the various general properties including alias and display name in the global address list (GAL). You can change these to meet your requirements and how you want the public folder to be displayed in the GAL. You can also hide the public folder from the GAL if necessary or define custom attributes that will be used in your organization.

Email Address Lets you change the public folder's email address or add additional email addresses. Each email address can be used by users (internally or externally) to post to the public folder. By default, the email address will be updated based on the email address policy defined in the organization; however, you can disable that to define the email address(es) for that public folder.

Member Of Shows the distribution lists (DLs) this public folder is a member of. Public folder distribution groups are a very cool way of archiving DL conversations.

Delivery Options Allows you to grant the following permissions:

- ◆ Send As: Allows you to grant a user or a group the permissions to send email as that public folder.

- ◆ Send On Behalf: Allows you to grant send-on-behalf permissions to a user or group.

- ◆ Forward To: Lets you forward all the emails sent or received via this public folder to another DL, mailbox, or public folder.

Additionally, you can define the maximum sending and receiving message sizes in MB, and you can define whether this public folder will receive emails from all senders or from specific senders or groups. You can also specify specific senders who will be rejected (see Figure 17.11).

FIGURE 17.11
Message delivery restrictions

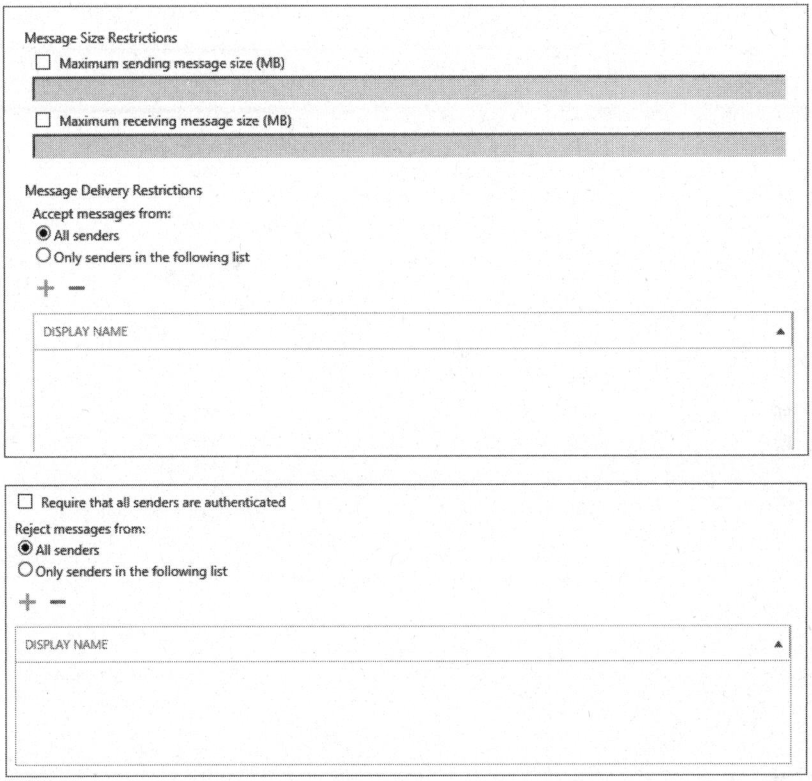

Message Flow Settings   Allows you to manage the following settings:

- Message Size Restrictions for Maximum Sending Message Size and Maximum Receive Message Size.

- Message Delivery Restrictions (Accept), defining whether to accept messages from All Senders, or only senders listed in the list gathered from the Global Address List.

- Message Delivery Restrictions (Reject), defining whether to reject message from All Senders, or only senders listed in the list gathered from the Global Address List.

The Message Delivery Restrictions (Accept) option allows you to require that users must be authenticated before their messages will be accepted by the Public Folder, see Figure 17.12.

Departments

general
statistics
limits
general mail properties
email address
member of
delivery options
▸ mail flow settings

Help

Message Size Restrictions
☐ Maximum sending message size (MB)

☐ Maximum receiving message size (in MB)

Message Delivery Restrictions
Accept messages from:
◉ All senders
○ Only senders in the following list

➕ ➖

DISPLAY NAME ▲

☐ Require that all senders are authenticated
Reject messages from:
◉ All senders
○ Only senders in the following list

➕ ➖

DISPLAY NAME ▲

save   cancel

🔍 100% ▼

All of the properties of public folder can be managed from the Exchange Management Shell.

WHEN PUBLIC FOLDERS PROVIDE EASY BUSINESS SOLUTIONS

Public folders have been around for a while. Organizations of various sizes have been using public folders to provide easy solutions to sometimes-complex problems. Sometimes, it seems that using a public folder is truly the easiest solution to a business requirement. Maybe that is the secret to the longevity of this simple technology.

The simplest aspect of public folders, and one that some companies forget to implement, is the ability to send and receive mail on a public folder. You can mail-enable a public folder and then configure it to receive emails. This solution is typically used for public folders that must receive information from external senders or users who do not use a client application that supports public folder access.

For example, we encountered a company that needed a solution for collecting resumes for job postings. The company needed to be able to accept resumes from external individuals applying for positions. The specific need was for external individuals to be able send an email by using the external email address. The solution was easy. All we did was mail-enable a public folder, hence converting the folder into an email recipient. Whenever an email came into the public folder, internal HR employees responsible for selecting applicants could review the attached resume.

A user must have permissions to post to the folder to successfully send a message to the folder's email address. If you are setting up a mail-enabled public folder that will receive email from outside your organization, make sure that anonymous users have Contributor permissions to the public folder. The Contributor role contains two rights: the right to post to a folder and the right to see the folder in a folder list.

Suppose we select a folder called Sales in the List view pane and then click the Manage Folder Permissions task from the Details pane. This will open the Public Folder Permissions screen and will allow us to add/remove user permissions based on different levels of permissions, as shown in Figure 17.13.

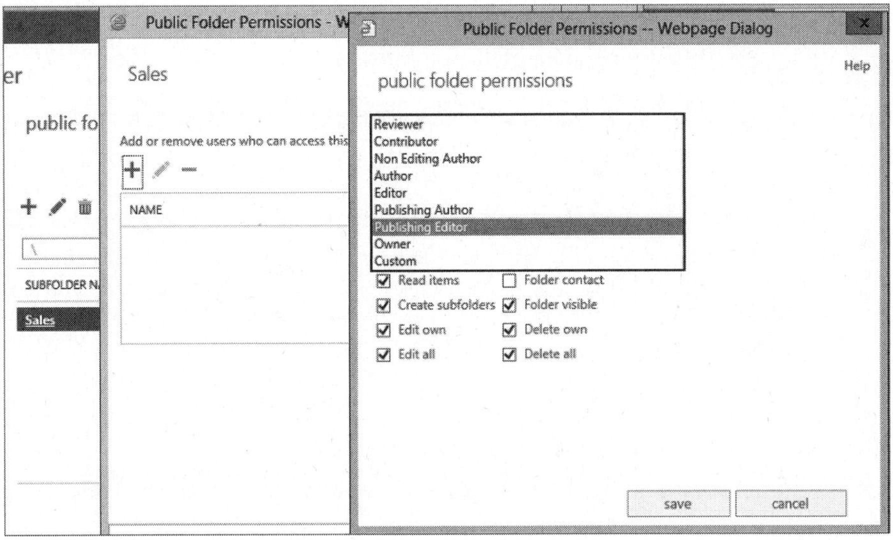

FIGURE 17.13
Opening the folder permissions

The client permissions in Exchange Server 2013 are the same as in the previous versions (Owner, Contributor, Editor, and so on). In our example we will assign a user the Owner permissions on the Sales folder.

> **DEFINING THE DEFAULT PUBLIC FOLDER SERVER**
>
> In previous version of Exchange Server, you were required to specify the default public folder database for users; this was done by setting the default public folder on the user's mailbox database. In Exchange Server 2013, this is no longer required because Exchange Server calculates the public folder mailbox to be accessed based on the site this user belongs to and the hierarchy information.

Defining Public Folder Administrators

In a small- or medium-sized organization, one or two administrators are responsible for all Exchange Server administrative tasks, including managing the public folders. However, in very large organizations, you may need to delegate the public folder administration tasks to a different person or group. Exchange Server 2013 automatically creates a group in the Microsoft Exchange Security Groups OU called Public Folder Management. Members of this group can manage the Exchange Server public folder attributes and perform public folder operations, including these tasks:

- Creating public folders
- Creating top-level public folders
- Modifying public folder permissions
- Modifying public folder administrative permissions
- Modifying public folder properties, such as content expiration times, storage limits, and deleted item retention time
- Modifying public folder replica lists
- Mounting and dismounting public folder databases
- Mail-enabling/disabling public folders

Using the Exchange Management Shell to Manage Public Folders

Exchange Server 2013 includes the Exchange Management Shell and the ability to manage public folders from the command line. As there have been many changes to the way public folders could be implemented in Exchange 2013, the EMS has been updated as well to reflect those changes.

ABOUT TYPING LONG LINES IN THE EXCHANGE MANAGEMENT SHELL

In some of the following examples, you'll see lines terminated by a ◄ character. This character tells you that what follows is a continuation of the same, single command line. You can also use the back-tick (`) character if you want to continue typing on the next line. PowerShell uses the back-tick character for line termination; it tells the shell that the logical line of input will be continued on the next physical line. This allows you to break up long lines for display and still ensure that they work correctly when you enter them.

PERFORMING GENERAL PUBLIC FOLDER TASKS

These cmdlets apply to the entire public folder hierarchy at once and provide broad control of your public folder infrastructure:

Get-PublicFolderStatistics This cmdlet provides a detailed set of statistics about the public folder hierarchy on a given server:

```
Get-PublicFolderStatistics -Server "MBX01"
```

If the -Server parameter is not specified, the cmdlet will default to displaying the statistics on the local server.

Suspend-PublicFolderMigrationRequest This cmdlet suspends all public folder content migration. You may want to suspend public folder migration if, for example, huge network traffic occurred or you want to pause it during working hours.

Resume-PublicFolderMigrationRequest This cmdlet re-enables all public folder content migration from previous versions if it was suspended.

New-PublicFolderMoveRequest This cmdlet creates a new public folder move request, and moves public folders from one public folder mailbox to another. You must specify the public folders you wish to move my path, as well as the public folder mailbox that is the destination, as in this example:

```
New-PublicFolderMoveRequest -Folders \Departments\Sales -TargetMailbox
ManagedPublicFolders -Name \PublicFolderMove
```

Suspend-PublicFolderMoveRequest This cmdlet suspends the public folder move from one mailbox to another. As move requests can be given names, you can reference the name in the cmdlet. If you have not given the original move request a name, it is referred to as \PublicFolderMove, as referenced in the example:

```
Suspend-PublicFolderMoveRequest -Identity \PublicFolderMove
```

Resume-PublicFolderMoveRequest This cmdlet resumes the public folder move from one mailbox to another mailbox. Here's an example:

```
Resume-PublicFolderMoveRequest -Identity \PFMoveRequest1
```

You may want to move a specific public folder to another mailbox to reduce the size of the original mailbox or move it to another mailbox database.

MANIPULATING INDIVIDUAL PUBLIC FOLDERS

These cmdlets are designed to work with a specific public folder:

Get-PublicFolder This cmdlet retrieves the properties for the specified public folder:

```
Get-PublicFolder -Identity "\Jobs\Posted" -Server "MBX01"
```

If you don't name a public folder by specifying a value for the -Identity property, it will default to the root public folder.

By default, the Get-PublicFolder cmdlet returns the values for only a single folder. The -Recurse switch changes the behavior to report on all subfolders as well:

```
Get-PublicFolder -Identity "\Jobs\Posted" -Server "MBX01" -Recurse
```

If you want to see system folders, you'll need to set the -Identity property to a value beginning with the string \NON_IPM_SUBTREE:

```
Get-PublicFolder -Identity \NON_IPM_SUBTREE -Recurse
```

New-PublicFolder This cmdlet creates a new public folder. The -Path property is required and provides the name and location of the new public folder:

```
New-PublicFolder -Name New -Path "\Jobs" -Server "MBX01"
```

Remove-PublicFolder This cmdlet deletes a public folder. The -Path property is required and provides the name and location of the public folder to be deleted:

```
Remove-PublicFolder -Path "\Jobs\Old" -Server "MBX01"
```

By default, the Remove-PublicFolder cmdlet removes only the named public folder. The -Recurse switch will delete all subfolders as well, which is handy for removing an entire group of folders at once.

Set-PublicFolder This cmdlet allows you to set most of the properties for the named public folder, such as limits, replicas, replication schedules, and more:

```
Set-PublicFolder -Identity "\Jobs\Posted" -Server "MBX01"
```

You cannot use the Set-PublicFolder cmdlet to mail-enable a public folder or to change its mail-related attributes. See the next section, "Manipulating Public Folder Mail Attributes," for the cmdlets to use for these tasks.

Update-PublicFolderMailbox This cmdlet starts the hierarchy-synchronization process for the named public folder mailbox. The -Identity property is required:

```
Update-PublicFolderMailbox -Identity "PF Mailbox2"
```

MANIPULATING PUBLIC FOLDER MAIL ATTRIBUTES

These cmdlets are designed to work with a specific public folder, mail-enable it, and modify the attributes it receives when it is mail-enabled:

Enable-MailPublicFolder This cmdlet renders an existing public folder mail-enabled. The optional -HiddenFromAddressListsEnabled switch allows you to hide the folder from your address lists:

```
Enable-MailPublicFolder -Identity "\Jobs\New"
-HiddenFromAddressListsEnabled $true -Server "MBX01"
```

Disable-MailPublicFolder This cmdlet renders an existing mail-enabled public folder mail-disabled:

```
Disable-MailPublicFolder -Identity "\Jobs\New"
```

You set the mail-related attributes separately using the Set-MailPublicFolder cmdlet.

Get-MailPublicFolder This cmdlet retrieves the mail-related properties for the specified public folder:

```
Get-MailPublicFolder -Identity "\Jobs\Old" -Server "MBX01"
```

If you don't name a public folder by specifying a value for the -Identity property, it will default to the root public folder.

Set-MailPublicFolder This cmdlet allows you to set the mail-related properties for the named public folder, such as an alias, email addresses, send and receive sizes, permitted and prohibited senders, and so on:

```
Set-MailPublicFolder -Identity "\Jobs\Posted"  -Alias PostedJobs ↲
-PrimarySmtpAddress "Jobs@Ithicos.com"
```

Keep in mind that to be able to modify the mail-related attributes for a public folder, you must first mail-enable it using the Enable-MailPublicFolder cmdlet.

MANAGING PUBLIC FOLDER DATABASES

These cmdlets allow you to manage the public folder mailbox:

Get-mailbox -PublicFolder This cmdlet provides the functionality used by the EAC and allows you to view the properties of existing public folder databases:

```
Get-Mailbox –Publicfolder -Server "MBX01"
```

This cmdlet takes one of two parameters: -Identity or -Server. The parameters are not compatible with each other. Use only one of them to narrow your selection.

New-mailbox -PublicFolder This cmdlet allows you to create a new public folder mailbox.

```
New-Mailbox –Publicfolder –Name "PF MB1"
```

Remove-Mailbox -publicfolder This cmdlet deletes an existing public folder mailbox from the active configuration of the server:

```
Remove-Mailbox -PublicFolder -Identity "PF Mailbox2"
```

If this mailbox is a hierarchy mailbox and there are other mailboxes below it in the hierarchy, you will have to delete the other mailboxes first and then delete the primary hierarchy mailbox.

MANAGING PUBLIC FOLDER PERMISSIONS

These cmdlets allow you to modify and monitor the permissions on your public folders. You can control the client permissions as well as the administrative permissions through EMS. The Exchange Server 2013 documentation contains the list of specific permissions that you can apply.

Add-PublicFolderClientPermission   This cmdlet lets you add a client permission entry to a given public folder. You can specify a single access right or list multiple rights at once using the syntax shown here:

```
Add-PublicFolderClientPermission -User Cohen.Oliver -Identity "\Jobs\Posted"
-AccessRights CreateItems, DeleteItems
```

Get-PublicFolderClientPermission   This cmdlet lets you view the client permission entries on a given public folder:

```
Get-PublicFolderClientPermission  -Identity "\Jobs\Posted"
```

Remove-PublicFolderClientPermission   This cmdlet lets you remove a client permission entry from a given public folder:

```
Remove-PublicFolderClientPermission -User Bouganim.Mike -Identity "\Jobs\
Posted" -AccessRights CreateItems
```

USING ADDITIONAL SCRIPTS FOR COMPLICATED TASKS

Although the cmdlets described in the preceding sections are certainly great for single-folder operations, performing common operations on entire groups of folders starts getting sticky. Because most of us aren't scripting gurus, Exchange Server 2013 provides some example EMS scripts that allow you to perform more complicated server and management tasks that affect groups of folders:

◆ AddUsersToPFRecursive.ps1 allows you to grant user permissions to a folder and all folders beneath it.

◆ Export-MailPublicFoldersForMigration.ps1 exports all mail-enabled public folders to an XML file.

◆ Export-PublicFolderStatistics.ps1 generates a CSV file with public folder sizes.

◆ Import-MailPublicFoldersForMigration.ps1 imports a list of mail-enabled public folders from the XML file.

◆ merge-publicfoldermailbox.ps1 merges the content of a given public folder with the destination public folder mailbox.

◆ move-publicfolderbranch.ps1 moves a branch public folder and all its subfolders to another mailbox.

◆ PublicFolderToMailboxMapGenerator.ps1 creates a mapping between branch public folders and mailboxes; we used this script in the migration steps earlier in the "Moving Public Folders to Exchange Server 2013" section.

- `RemoveUserFromPFRecursive.ps1` removes the given user's access permissions from the given public folder and all its subfolders.

- `ReplaceUserPermissionOnPFRecursive.ps1` replaces existing user permissions with a new set of permissions for the folder provided as well as all folders beneath that folder when you run the script.

- `ReplaceUserWithUserOnPFRecursive.ps1` copies one user's access permissions on a given public folder and all its subfolders to a second user while retaining permissions for the first user.

You can find these scripts in the Scripts subfolder of the Exchange Server 2013 installation folder. Note that with the default Windows PowerShell configuration, you just can't click these scripts and run them; you must invoke them from within the EMS, usually by navigating to the folder and calling them explicitly.

Using Outlook to Create a Public Folder

Mailbox-enabled users can also create Exchange Server public folders in their email clients. Here are the steps for doing so in Outlook:

1. Open Outlook and make sure the folder list is displayed.

2. Double-click Public Folders in the folder list, or click the plus sign just in front of Public Folders. Notice that the plus sign becomes a minus sign when a folder is expanded to show the folders within it.

   You've now expanded the top-level folder for public folders, which contains two subfolders: Favorites and All Public Folders.

3. Expand the All Public Folders folder. If your organization uses public folders, you probably have many subfolders listed here.

4. Right-click All Public Folders, select a child folder, and select New Folder from the menu that pops up. This brings up the Create New Folder dialog box (see Figure 17.14).

FIGURE 17.14
Creating a new folder

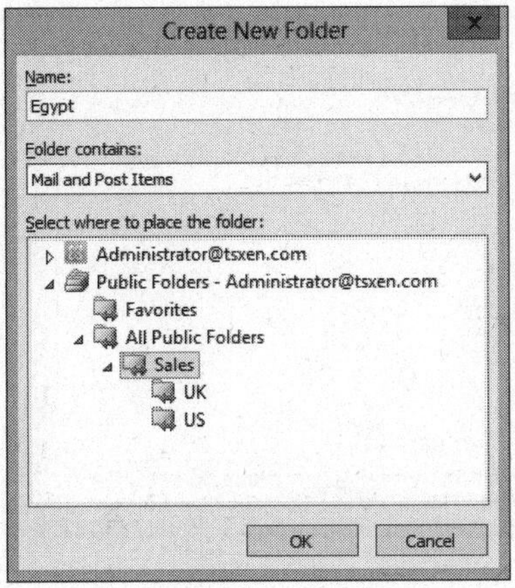

5. Enter a name for the folder. We've given ours the name Egypt since it will be a new Sales branch and will require a dedicated public folder.

   Note that the folder will hold two different kinds of items:

   ◆ Email items that are messages.

   ◆ Posted items that contain a subject and text. You can post an item in a folder designed to hold posts without having to deal with messaging attributes, such as to whom the item is sent. To post an item, click the down arrow near the New icon on the main Outlook window, and select Post In This Folder from the drop-down menu.

6. When you've finished creating your folder, click OK.

   If you're told that you don't have sufficient permissions to create the folder, you need to have those permissions assigned using one of the other Exchange Server public folder management tools. If you have Exchange Server administrative permissions, you can make this change yourself.

   The new public folder now shows up under the All Public Folders hierarchy. If you can't see the full name of your new folder, make the Folder List pane a little wider.

7. To set additional properties for your folder, right-click your new folder and select Properties from the context menu.

   The properties dialog box for the Egypt folder is shown in Figure 17.15.

FIGURE 17.15
The Outlook client's properties dialog box for a public folder

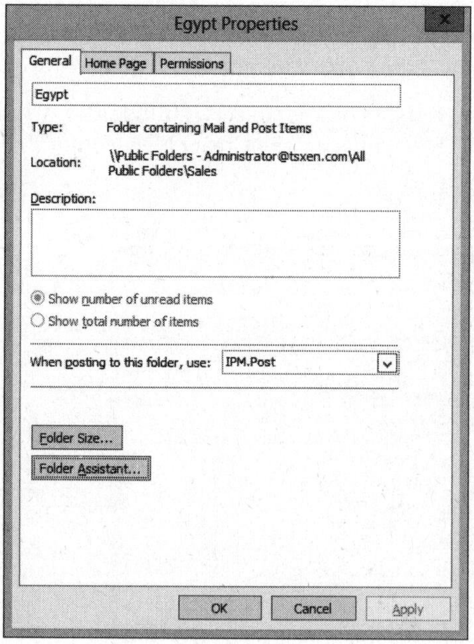

Among other things, mailbox owners use a public folder's properties dialog box to do the following:

◆ Add a description for other mailbox owners who access the folder

◆ Make the folder available on the Internet

◆ Set up a default view of the folder, including grouping by such things as the subject or sender

◆ Set up administrative rules on folder characteristics, access, and such

◆ Set permissions for using the folder

If your Exchange Server organization has a large number of public folders, you can drag the ones that you use a lot to your Favorites subfolder. This makes them easier to find. Folders in the Favorites folder are also the only ones that are available when you work offline without a connection to your Exchange server. Only public folders that are in a user's Favorites folder, and that have been selected by the user, will be downloaded when working in local cache mode.

Understanding the Public Folder Hierarchy

A public folder hierarchy, or public folder tree, is a list of public folders and their subfolders that are stored in the default public folder database on the Exchange servers in an Exchange Server organization. The hierarchy also includes the name of the server on which a copy of each folder resides. The hierarchy does not contain any of the actual items in your various public folders. There is one organization-wide public folder hierarchy object.

THE THREE PIECES OF THE PUBLIC FOLDER PUZZLE

The public folder hierarchy can be confusing, so here's an overview of the objects and components that make up public folders.

Public Folder Hierarchy   As outlined earlier, the hierarchy is essentially the list of public folder names available in your organization. This list is viewed from the Exchange Server 2013 EAC or from the Outlook client when viewing all public folders. When you are delegating administrative permissions over Exchange Server public folders, the hierarchy is the target of the permissions.

Public Folder Content   These are the items that are contained in the folder. These items could be files, emails, posts, or any other content type that Outlook supports. When you are delegating client permissions to public folders, the content is the target of the permissions.

Public Folder Recipient Object   When a public folder is mail-enabled, a recipient object is created for the folder. Since the recipient must be added to the Exchange Server address lists, this object is created in Active Directory. When you delegate recipient management permissions over Exchange Server objects, the permissions will apply to a public folder recipient object.

Exploring Public Folder High Availability

As we stated earlier, there is no specific public folder replication architecture in 2013. Public folder high availability shifted from public folder replication to database replication via DAG, as you have seen. Public folders are hosted in mailboxes, which are hosted in mailbox databases. Thus, they are treated as any other mailbox and replicated via DAG architecture, with no special configuration or separate administration needed.

This could be challenging when migrating from the existing public folder implementations with multiple geographical locations to Exchange Server 2013. Previously, people were redirected to their local replica, where they could perform different operations (read, write, and delete), and changes got synchronized later according to the synchronization schedule. Since there is only one writable replica in modern public folders, user traffic might traverse the WAN in an undesired manner to access the writable contents. Thus, you need to pay close attention when moving public folders from Exchange Server 2007/2010 to Exchange Server 2013 and reconsider your public folder structure.

Here some factors to consider when planning Exchange Server 2013 public folder high availability:

◆ The size of your public folder has implications on the total size of the database and whether it will be hosted on a shared database with other mailboxes or on a separate database replicated to designated mailbox servers and whether you will use the same DAG for mailboxes or a different DAG.

◆ Based on the new architecture, there is only a single writable instance of the public folder. Mailboxes are replicated via DAG, and if a mailbox or a mailbox database fails, one of the passive copies become active on another member of the DAG.

◆ Since there is only a single writable instance of the public folder, the write operations are performed on a single mailbox hosted on a designated server; the write operation is single-master (not multimaster as it was previously). If you were distributing your mailbox contents geographically before, this will not work anymore. Users might have to cross the WAN to access their contents, so you might need to reconsider your public folder architecture and how users will access the public folders.

◆ You need to carefully plan for DAG failover. Failing over a mailbox database will have a great effect on users' access to public folders.

◆ You no longer add public folder replicas; you add a replica of the mailbox database that hosts the public folder mailbox. You need to plan this as part of your DAG deployment strategy and allocate space accordingly.

Real World Scenario

HIGH AVAILABILITY—A PRACTICAL EXAMPLE

Hayacorp is a multinational company with three branches in the United States, the United Kingdom, and Egypt. The company currently has three datacenters distributed among the branches running Exchange Server 2010 SP3.

The sales team at Hayacorp heavily uses the public folders across the three branches; they use it to share weekly and monthly reports, as well as other information. The administrators configured one top-level Sales public folder and three subfolders—one for each branch underneath it. They also configured a single Exchange Server public folder database that holds a replica of the three folders in each site; thus, users from each site access the local replica and can see the three folders. They can post as they wish in collaboration with the other teams. Data in the public folders is replicated via public folder replication after working hours.

When designing the migration to Exchange Server 2013, Hayacorp's team decided to create three public folder mailboxes, each hosting a single public folder mailbox and each public folder mailbox holding a public folder. After reviewing that design, they realized that there will be some impact on the network because there is a single writable copy of a public folder; users will see the data, but they must cross the WAN when they access the other countries' sales folders.

For example, when the U.S. team is working with the Egyptian team on a new lead, the U.S. team can post to the Egypt public folder in their replica, and vice versa. In the new system, there is no local replica, so the U.S. team will have to cross the WAN to post to the Egypt Sales public folder.

For the DAG design, they decided to create two mailbox database copies, one local and one in the closest datacenter. Thus, the US public folder mailbox database will have two copies—one locally and one in the UK, and vice versa. The Egypt public folder mailbox database will have two copies—one locally and one in the UK.

Managing Public Folder Permissions

You can manage folder permissions in one of two ways. The simplest is just to use Outlook. Navigate to the public folder, right-click to display its properties, and select the Permissions tab (shown in Figure 17.16).

Of course, when you are using Outlook, your user account must be one of the owners of the folder. Otherwise, the Permissions properties page will not be displayed. The Permissions properties page shows the permissions that the groups (mail-enabled groups) or users have to the folder.

You can use the Permissions properties page to assign specific folder access rights to Exchange Server users and distribution groups, who can then work with a public folder using their Outlook client. For emphasis, we'll restate what we just said in a somewhat different form: *You grant public folder access permissions to Exchange Server recipients, not to Active Directory users and groups.* Once access to a public folder is granted, Exchange Server recipients access the folder in their Outlook client while connected to their mailbox.

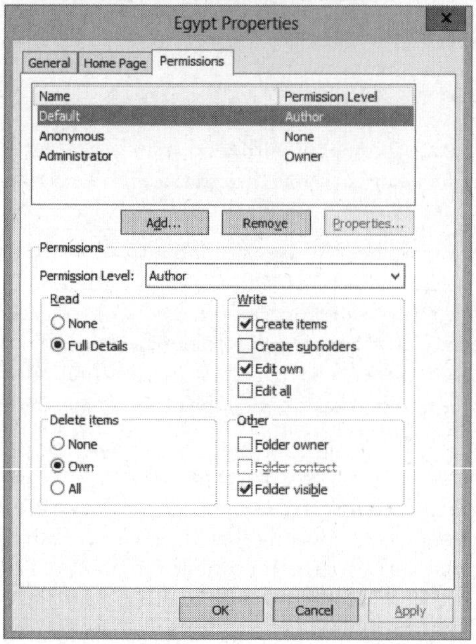

FIGURE 17.16
Managing public
folder permissions
via Outlook

For a graphic reinforcement of this point, click Add, on the Public Folder Permissions page, to start adding a new user or group who will have access to this public folder. This action opens a dialog box that looks very much like the Outlook address book that you use to select recipients to send a message to.

If a user has the correct permissions on a public folder, that user can change access permissions on the folder for other users. Permissions on a public folder can only be modified from within the Outlook client using the Permissions properties page for a public folder.

There is a group named Default that includes all Exchange Server recipients not separately added to the Name list box. When the folder is created, this group is automatically given the default role of Author. Authors can edit and delete only their own folder items, but they do not own the folder and cannot create subfolders.

To make assigning permissions easier, Microsoft has created predefined roles. Each role has a specific combination of permissions to the folder. The roles are Owner, Publishing Editor, Editor, Publishing Author, Author, Nonediting Author, Reviewer, Contributor, and Custom—each with a different combination of client permissions.

Comparing Public Folders, Site Mailboxes, and Shared Mailboxes

Exchange Server 2013 introduces a revamped public folder architecture that makes it scalable for most uses. It also introduces another new collaboration feature known as site mailboxes, which rely on SharePoint 2013 to display documents and email in Outlook.

When you design a collaboration solution, you must understand the capabilities and limitations of each option to provide the best solution for your organization. When you wish to implement a mailbox that needs to be accessible to a number of users located in the same site, it is hard to decide whether public folders, site mailboxes, or shared mailboxes should be used, but the following points will help you decide:

- Public folders provide a great way to share knowledge and archive that knowledge within the organization. For example, they fit well for HR in receiving resumes via email and they can be used to document conversation between distribution list members or to host a small forum.

- Site mailboxes provide a group of users working on a shared pool of resources (documents and emails) with a shared area where related documents and emails are stored in a single location and viewed via Outlook. This setup is perfect for a group of users working on the same project or task. You need to be aware that site mailboxes require SharePoint 2013, which has its own infrastructure and servers to manage and operate.

- Shared mailboxes fit virtual entities like sales or support, which need to receive shared emails and respond on behalf of the entity.

The Bottom Line

Understand the architectural changes made to public folders.   If you're coming new to Exchange Server 2013 or don't have a lot of investment in public folders in your current Exchange Server organization, you probably haven't been too worried about the rumors of the demise of public folders. These rumors are fortunately not true; public folders are still supported in Exchange Server 2013.

A)   **Master It**   You are the administrator of a distributed messaging environment that runs Exchange Server 2013. You plan to deploy a collaboration solution, and you are currently evaluating public folders as well as site mailboxes and shared mailboxes. You need to identify the limitations of each solution and present recommendations to your company's executives. What information should you present?

Manage public folders.   You are managing a large distributed Exchange Server infrastructure, and you want to create a hierarchy of public folders to reflect the organizational structure of your enterprise environment. How you can do it in Exchange Server 2013?

B)   **Master It**   Start with the Public Folder Mailbox, then define the various Departments within your folder structure. You can add various nested folders underneath the Departments parent folder, and manage the folder structure underneath, and make modifications to the permission structure to reflect the needs of the organization.

Chapter 18

Managing Archiving and Compliance

Since the rise of archiving systems in business more than a decade ago in response to storage concerns on Exchange servers, the technology has gone through some very impressive growth and technology improvements. The need for archiving systems is also growing with ever-increasing stringent regulations and litigation procedures.

Messaging systems such as Microsoft Exchange Server 2013—Microsoft's latest version of Exchange Server—have also seen their share of changes and improvements in archiving and compliance.

In this chapter, you will learn to:

- ◆ Understand the basic principles of email archiving

- ◆ Ensure your company complies with regulations

- ◆ Enable Exchange Server 2013 in-place archiving

- ◆ Use Exchange Server 2013 retention policies

- ◆ Use Exchange Server 2013 In-Place eDiscovery and Hold

Introduction to Archiving

Over time, archiving products have evolved significantly. They have gone from simple storage-size-reduction software to sophisticated enterprise content-management systems that not only offer the storage management of Exchange servers but have moved beyond email to managing filesystems, SharePoint, Lotus Notes, GroupWise, and even databases. Don't be intimidated by archiving products; they can resolve many pain points in your organization, and in some ways they can even be seen as an insurance policy.

One of the main things to understand is that the way business communications are handled has drastically changed over the last 15 years or so. In the past, most of the communications and even business contracts were done by either fax or paper records. Nowadays, more than 90 percent of business communications take place by electronic means—email and instant messaging (IM), for instance—and this number is increasing on an annual basis.

A couple of famous corporate failures in 2002 sparked massive lawsuits. One of the world's largest accounting firms, Arthur Andersen, collapsed due to evidence that was brought up through email in the Enron scandal.

Citibank nearly suffered a similar fate and was forced to pay some $400 million in penalties after the attorney general of New York State demanded emails that originated from stock analyst Jack Grubman and Citigroup chairman Sanford I. Weill. In 2004, the stock price of insurance broker Marsh & McLennan had dropped a devastating 50 percent after evidence surfaced from emails about investments they publicly praised but internally described as disasters. And the list of these cases goes on, with Merrill Lynch and PricewaterhouseCoopers having gone through public court cases over information in emails. Because of lawsuits/litigations, external compliance investigations, and even internal human resources (HR) investigations, ediscovery (that is, the discovery of electronic information) has become entrenched in current business. In the United States, all these cases have resulted in the courts deciding that organizations have to retain and be able to recover emails within a "reasonable" time frame and also to prove, when these records are provided, that the emails have not been tampered with and are complete.

To clarify this process, amendments were made to the Federal Rules of Civil Procedure (FRCP). These amended rules went into effect on December 1, 2006, and require that companies create, document, and enforce policies to retain emails or dispose of them as part of operating procedures. One of the most important parts of the new FRCP rules is that, as mentioned already, organizations must now discover and disclose relevant information and emails within a reasonable time frame, so stalling tactics no longer work.

Archiving systems are used throughout the world in many different scenarios, largely depending on industry and country. Some of the scenarios are as follows:

◆ Storage management of Exchange Server

◆ Simple compliance data capture by using journaling

◆ Complete data capture using journaling and archiving

◆ Ediscovery and litigation support

◆ Enterprise content management (beyond just Exchange Server)

Benefits of Archiving

Archiving generally refers to the process of removing data from one storage location and moving it to another, cheaper storage location. Archiving systems can be tailored or tweaked for use with specific case scenarios.

Retention

These days it is an accepted fact that business email is considered a record or controlled record and that these records need to be archived under either your corporate policy or government regulatory requirements. A defined email-retention policy informs employees as to what email must be archived and for how long. For an email-retention policy to be effective, you have to distribute this policy in written format to all employees. A written retention policy should include several of these details:

Effective Date   This leaves no doubt as to whether the policy is currently in effect or is an old one that should be discarded.

Last Change Date and Changes Made   This information confirms the policy's authenticity and appropriateness because regulations change over time.

Person or Department Responsible for the Policy   This gives employees or their managers someone to contact with questions regarding the policy.

Scope/Coverage   This includes the geographic limits of the policy (if any), affected departments and offices, and a definition of what company information is covered.

Purpose of the Policy/Policy Statement   This can include a company philosophy statement about the business, legal, or regulatory reasons for records retention.

Definitions   This area defines what constitutes business records and applicable exceptions.

Responsibilities   This area covers the following:

- Business units, subsidiaries, and special departments (such as the legal department).
- General employees.
- Records-retention coordinators.
- Procedures for retention and deletion of email and attachments (if no automated email-archiving system is employed).
- How the emails should be stored (usually in a personal storage table [PST] file).
- Where those PSTs should be stored, like a network storage target or shared drive; however, many would argue that PSTs are not a good form for archiving/compliance.
- How often those files should be cleaned out.
- How duplicate and convenience copies are treated.

Consequences   This describes what happens if the policy isn't adhered to.

Appendix A   This appendix should include litigation-hold and stop-destruction policies, including a backup procedure.

Appendix B   Appendix B should include a current list of department records-retention coordinators and contact information.

A manually managed email-retention policy relies on employees understanding and following the policy. The obvious fact is that each employee will interpret the policy a little differently, so in practice organizations will have many different email-retention policies. This fact is the main reason you need to adopt an automated email-archiving solution.

The benefits of automating your email-retention policy are multifold:

Regulatory Compliance   Email retention for regulatory compliance isn't a choice but a requirement. The only choice is how you meet the requirements: manually or with email-archiving automation. Automating your email-retention policy lowers your overall risk of non-compliance and ensures that you are keeping your email for the required time period.

Legal-risk Management   When you can show the court that you keep your email-retention policy current and enforce it, you can demonstrate retention intent and that you might not have purposely destroyed information in case of litigation.

Document Retention for Corporate Governance   Businesses rely on the generation, use, and reference of data to make ongoing business decisions. The data the business generates has a value to the business if that data can be used efficiently. An effective retention policy ensures that valuable information is available for some period of time, and an automated email-archiving system allows for quick search and reference.

Discovery

One of the primary reasons United States–based organizations use archiving software is to aid in electronic discovery, also known as ediscovery. This refers to the process of finding electronically stored information for litigation reasons and generally isn't restricted to searching for email. While it is very common for emails, including attachments, to be requested as a part of an ediscovery case, it is almost just as likely for general office productivity documents not specifically involved in email transmissions to also be requested (which means Word and Excel files on your file server and desktops are part of the litigation). Metadata does play an important role in this process and is referred to as *chain of custody*—a verifiable record of who had access to the data and whether the data could have been altered or changed during the ediscovery process.

Eliminating PST Files

It is our opinion that there are no good reasons to have PST files in a corporate environment other than handing them over to a lawyer for review. Starting to see the trend here? Archiving systems can be your friend, but you will start working closely with your HR and legal people. PST files have become popular because of mailbox quotas, which were implemented to help curb the growth of Exchange Server databases. These easy-to-implement policies were for the longest time the only option an Exchange Server administrator had to gain some sort of control over this growth. Now the problem is that the quotas have a nasty side effect: end users who are unable to find the Delete key on their keyboards are forced to groom their inboxes for old email messages to delete when they hit their mailbox limit.

They then naturally create PST files. In the past, this approach was encouraged by Exchange Server administrators. These files were created either locally on the desktop or laptop or on the file server, where they would take up valuable storage space. PST files use up more storage than if the data were kept in Exchange Server in the first place. We could probably write an entire book on eliminating PST files, but here's the gist: Large mailboxes together with an archiving product can be your best allies here, helping you find the PST files and bring them back under control, which ultimately reduces the storage footprint of PST files in your environment.

Reducing Storage Size

Reducing the storage size of production Exchange Server databases was the first reason archiving systems became popular. In the late 1990s, Standard editions of Exchange Server still had a 16 GB mailbox store limit, and having a 5 or 10 MB mailbox limit was extremely common. People were looking for other ways to offload content from their mailbox stores, not only to keep the databases in line for storage limits but also to reduce the backup times. A reduced backup size also means a reduced recovery size, which is something you start to appreciate once you have gone through a full-blown Exchange Server disaster recovery. Archiving systems can offload email to the archiving storage system, while either leaving a shortcut behind to open up the archived email or simply removing the entire message. Doing this can substantially reduce the size of your Exchange Server databases—sometimes up to 90 percent.

Disaster Recovery

You are probably wondering what disaster recovery has to do with archiving. The whole idea is related to storage management. Probably 90 percent of the data stored in Exchange Server databases is never accessed again by end users; however, this data is backed up daily to either tape or disk, and in case of a disaster this data will also have to be restored. Archiving can help you remove this data from Exchange Server and therefore reduce not only the backup time but also the amount of time it would take to recover a database.

Compliance

Compliance makes most people cringe, but you need to understand it. The odds are that your company is subject to some regulation that enforces you to retain records. Some industries—especially healthcare and finance—face stricter and more-complex rules than others. Regulatory compliance is either already part of your daily Exchange Server life or soon will be. Let's briefly go over some of the current laws that might be applicable to your organization:

Federal Rules of Civil Procedure   The Federal Rules of Civil Procedure (FRCP) implemented in 2006 impact how companies retain, store, and produce electronic data, including email for litigation. The rules that most often affect organizations are as follows:

Rules 16 and 26   These rules call for organizations to "give early attention to issues relating to electronic discovery, including the frequently recurring problems of the preservation of the evidence…." This means being ready to discuss a strategy for dealing with electronically stored evidence at the very first meeting with other parties in litigation.

Rule 34(b)   This rule requires organizations to produce electronically stored information in its native format with its metadata intact and to prove chain of custody. While the duty to preserve evidence is narrowed only to relevant data, the potential repercussions are great. For example, if a defensible process is not demonstrated, opponents may be granted access to an organization's network.

Rule 37(f)   This rule provides a "safe harbor" for data destruction. *Safe harbor* means that organizations face no penalties for deleting electronically stored information in keeping with routine operation of IT systems if the party took "reasonable" steps to preserve it. However, any destruction must be the result of routine operation and done in good faith, a systematic framework must be in place, and this systematic framework must have integrated litigation hold procedures.

Sarbanes-Oxley Act   The Sarbanes-Oxley Act (SOX) was passed mostly in response to the front-page news headlines of corporate corruption and financial scandals (namely Enron and WorldCom) in the early part of the last decade. SOX provides severe criminal penalties, including jail sentences, for corporate executives who knowingly destroy business documents and other information that is used in the daily operations of their organization. It also describes specific records that need to be retained and requires a records retention period of seven years.

Financial Industry Regulatory Authority   The Financial Industry Regulatory Authority (FINRA) rules (formerly known as SEC Rules 17a-3 and a-4) focus on brokers and traders and require these people to retain and store specific records, such as customer communications and customer account trading activities, for a specific period of time on nonrewritable electronic media and to make them ready for easy review by the SEC within a reasonable time frame, typically 24 hours.

Health Insurance Portability and Accountability Act   One part of the Health Insurance Portability and Accountability Act (HIPAA) requires that an organization's patient records and related data (including related email) be archived and retained in a secure manner that ensures privacy and content integrity for at least two years after the death of the patient.

ISO 15489 (Worldwide)   This standard offers guidelines on the classification, conversion, destruction, disposition, migration, preservation, tracking, and transfer of records.

Title 17 Code of Federal Regulations Part 1   This regulation allows record keepers for futures-trading companies to store information either on electronic media or on micrographic media. This regulation also requires that "record keepers store required records for the full five-year maintenance period" while continuing to provide commission auditors and investigators with timely access to a reliable system of records.

Federal Energy Regulatory Commission Part 125   This rule sets specific retention periods for the public utilities industry and states that the records must have a life expectancy equal to or greater than the specified retention periods.

National Archives and Records Administration Part 1234   The National Archives and Records Administration (NARA) regulations specify which government agency records are kept, for how long, and in what form and how they are to be accessed.

Freedom of Information Act   The Freedom of Information Act (FOIA)—which applies to federal agencies—allows for the full or partial disclosure of previously unreleased information and documents controlled by the U.S. government. The act, which relies on the NARA regulations, defines federal agency records subject to disclosure and outlines mandatory disclosure procedures and, under certain circumstances, time frames for response.

The USA PATRIOT Act   The USA PATRIOT Act (fully named Uniting and Strengthening America by Providing Appropriate Tools Required to Intercept and Obstruct Terrorism) requires the Secretary of the Treasury to prescribe regulations "setting forth the minimum standards for financial institutions and their customers regarding the identity of the customer that shall apply in connection with the opening of an account at a financial institution." Broker-dealers must have a fully implemented customer identification program that includes procedures for making and maintaining a record of all information obtained.

Federal Employment–Related Regulations   Largely unknown to many Exchange Server administrators, federal employment regulations exist that require some sort of records retention, and they apply to all companies with employees. Some of the best-known are as follows:

- Title VII of the Civil Rights Act of 1964

- Age Discrimination in Employment Act

- Americans with Disabilities Act

- Family and Medical Leave Act

- Equal Pay Act of 1963

- Vocational Rehabilitation Act

- Employee Retirement Income Security Act of 1974

- National Labor Relations Act

- Fair Labor Standards Act

Each of these regulatory acts introduces its own set of requirements for data retention and stewardship, which the employer is responsible for. So, any company that employs people should be familiar with these and consider email archiving as a way to meet these regulations.

The regulatory requirements listed are the relatively well-known U.S. federal government drivers for record retention and cover quite a bit, including email data. However, this is not a complete list. There are more than 10,000 records-retention regulations effective in the United States, and many of these are state-mandated, so reviewing the regulations in the states your company operates in is a great idea.

🌐 Real World Scenario

IMPLEMENTING ARCHIVING

A city in the Midwest was using Microsoft Exchange Server for its email-communication infrastructure. However, due to ever-increasing messaging volume, the network was slowly starting to become unmanageable. One of the reasons was that employees were retaining all of their email dating back to the early 1990s outside their mailboxes in PST files. This resulted in backups and storage capacity being strained to the limit. Because many state and local governments do business electronically, and with the paperless initiatives taking off, the problem was only getting worse. Any efforts to bring the PST sprawl under control manually by asking employees to clean up were futile, and because end users continued to save all their email in local PST files, the problems reached a boiling point when the PST files started to experience corruption and monopolized costly storage space on file shares, desktops, and laptops.

To ensure that data was preserved, retained, and protected properly, the city government decided to move ahead and implement archiving. A project was initiated to locate all the PST files in the environment and bring them under centralized control. This strategy ensured that legal, general counsel, and city officials could perform retention management and search all the email content easily for discovery when the city got a request for public records. This allowed the city to comply with the U.S. Department of State Freedom of Information Act requirements.

Industry Best Practices

Organizations that are planning to deploy an archiving system in their environment soon realize that the deployment can be a daunting task. Email archiving is a critical application for driving down the cost of managing email for corporate governance, litigation support, and regulatory compliance. Doing something wrong can result in some serious trouble (the worst is jail time). So in this chapter we want to give you some insight into the industry's best practices (that is, guidelines for doing things right the first time).

Storage Management

One of the main reasons that many organizations want to use archiving is storage management. Think of offloading of old email messages as filing away your IRS tax records. You don't keep your IRS records on the table forever; you file them away where you have easy access to them. In the years that we've been working with and deploying archiving solutions, one thing has stood out when it comes to storage management: nearly all emails older than six months are never accessed again, and then you start to wonder why you keep them on your Exchange server.

Most administrators mistakenly think that the performance of the Exchange Server database is related to the size of the database or the size of the mailbox. Microsoft Knowledge Base article 905803 (http://support.microsoft.com/kb/905803) describes how Microsoft Office Outlook users experience poor performance when they work with a folder that contains many items on a server that is running any version of Exchange Server from Exchange Server 2000 all the way up to Exchange Server 2010. The issue is caused because Outlook must perform several operations against the Exchange server to retrieve the contents of a folder, and the more items there are in a folder, the more time it takes to respond to the requests. The reason for this is restricted views; see: http://technet.microsoft.com/en-us/library/cc535025.aspx to learn more about this topic. While the article doesn't specifically mention Exchange Server 2013, it does apply to this release as well. You can now have about 10,000 items per folder before performance degradation starts to take place, so these issues will arise a lot less. You can help avoid the performance degradation in Outlook by managing the number of items in heavily used folders, including inbox, sent items, and calendars.

Archiving solutions reduce the storage footprint, but traditionally administrators will only perform archiving because they want to allow end users to have transparent access to data. When that happens, you will run into the item-limit counts, because even though the stubbed archived messages are only a few kilobytes in size, they count toward the item limits.

A few storage-management options are available; here we'll go over two that we've seen work at organizations:

Time Based   With this option you archive data pretty much from day one, but you don't create stubs in the mailbox; instead, you delete all data from the mailbox that's older than a specific age. The philosophy behind this approach is that you don't want to possibly confuse the end user with stubbed or archived messages. The time frame in which you want to delete the older data depends on how users use email in your organization, but deleting anything older than six months or a year is generally safe. You have to realize that even though you delete it from the mailbox, the data is in the archiving system, so end users can get access to the data if they need to do so. In some situations, however, organizations deploy an organizational archive and do not allow end users to access the data.

Stub and Time Based   This option combines the first one—deleting data older than six months or a year—with stubbing or archiving messages. This means that you can squeeze out a bit more storage savings by replacing the large emails that are younger than six months or so.

We can't tell you exactly what will work in your environment; however, don't create a stubbing policy that acts on data that is younger than a few days. Not only would that create frustration for your end users, but it would also result in data ping-pong, because end users would constantly want to restore archived data to their mailboxes.

Archiving PSTs

PSTs are notoriously bad for your environment. We often compare them to those pesky blackberries in your garden that take over the entire yard if you don't keep them in line. Most administrators know what PST files are because we've been using them daily since we started to use Exchange Server and Outlook. Archiving these days has almost become a standard practice as part of a process to get the messaging data under centralized management.

Two versions of PST files are available. Originally, PSTs created by Outlook 2002 or earlier used the American National Standards Institute (ANSI) format, which has an overall size limit of 2 gigabytes (GB). Today, the most common and current version, known as Unicode, has a theoretical 32 TB file size limit. In the real world, however, the Unicode PST file could cause performance degradation beyond 5 GB in file size if you do not have adequately performing hardware. Beyond 10 GB, according to Microsoft, you will encounter short pauses on almost all hardware (see http://support.microsoft.com/kb/2695805 for more details).

For more than a decade, users controlled the creation and location of PST files. The lack of centralized management tools played a major role in the sprawl of PST files. A company we worked with reported that it had close to 300 TB of data in PST files that were spread across desktops, laptops, servers, and backup tapes. Some users' PST file storage far exceeded what would be considered feasible to make available via an Exchange Server primary mailbox, resulting in major headaches. The company needed to consider segregating the data into an archive mailbox in order to bring the data under centralized management.

An archiving system can make your life easier. To comply with laws and regulations, you can't simply ignore and delete PST files. It fascinates us that organizations often spend a small fortune on protecting their messaging infrastructure with data-leak-prevention software to block sensitive data from leaving the organization unchecked. By forgetting about PST files, they have neglected to close a major security leak. One of the most common ways for end users to take their mailbox data with them is to simply export all the contents of their mailbox to a PST file and store it on a thumb drive or even MP3 player. They then can walk out the door with your company's sensitive information, contracts, and intellectual property, all unchecked.

Even if you have managed to retain the information in your infrastructure, the cost of storing data in PST files is enormous. The file format itself is so bloated that it uses more storage than if the data were kept in the Exchange Server database.

So how do you affectively eradicate PST files from your environment? We recommend implementing a multistep process:

1. Write a project plan.   A project plan will come in handy, particularly for large companies. A project plan allows you to prepare and think about exceptions that you didn't consider. For instance, what are you going to do with data from employees who have left your organizations? How are you going to handle password-protected PST files? A good plan will save you time.

2. Prevent further growth of the problem.   Some good Microsoft system management (Group Policy object) policies are available, which allow you to restrict users from creating PST files. You can download them from http://go.microsoft.com/fwlink/?LinkId=78161. Use them. We love, for instance, the option Prevent Users From Adding New Content To PST Files. This option allows end users to open their PST files but prevents them from adding any new content.

3. Discover all existing PST files.   This task probably will take up the most time, because you will have to find *all* the files on your network. If you run scripts to do this, ensure that you don't do an all-out search, because it will saturate your network with network traffic. It takes such a long time because you'll find PST files on servers, tapes, laptops, and workstations. Think about how you are going to deal with people who work remotely. (See the sidebar, "The Microsoft Exchange Server PST Capture Tool.")

4. Archive PST data. Archiving PST data allows you to bring the data back under your control. One of the reasons you shouldn't bring it into Exchange Server directly is because there is a good chance that you might not have the required storage available. A big advantage is that if the data is in an archive, it allows you to set retention and gives you additional benefits when it comes to ediscovery, risk management, and early case assessment.

THE MICROSOFT EXCHANGE SERVER PST CAPTURE TOOL

This tool can assist with both searching for PST files across your network and importing them into Exchange Server. The tool consists of a central service, a console, and agents (the latter of which can be pushed out to all the computers in your organization). The agents can be scheduled to search for PST files and send them back to the server, where the central service is running, for import into Exchange Server. General information on the PST Capture tool can be found at `http://technet .microsoft.com/en-us/library/hh781036(EXCHG.141).aspx`. Additionally, version 2.0 of the tool with support for Exchange Server 2013 has been released and is available at `http://www .microsoft.com/en-us/download/details.aspx?id=36789`.

---

5. Give end users access to their archived PSTs. Taking away PST files from end users and not giving them access to their own data is the quickest way to start a revolt. Give end users access to the archived data—they need access to the data for productivity reasons.

AVOID EXCESSIVE USE OF STUBS

Stub files are shortcuts in the mailbox pointing to the archived item that now resides in the archive—it's no longer on Exchange Server. Excessive use of stubs can create problems on Exchange Server with whitespace, fragmentation, and major I/O overhead.

---

6. Disable PST file creation. This final step is important because, after all, what good would it do if you bring everything under control and then you do not prevent your users from creating PST files again? Use the policies that we referred to in step 2.

Retention Policies

Deciding on your retention categories or how long you want to retain information within the archive will probably take up the most planning time. This process will involve most of the departments in your organization, from the storage team to the Exchange Server team, management, legal counsel, and even HR.

Retention controls the creation, filing, storage, and disposal of records in a way that is not only legally correct but also administratively possible. Retention has to serve multiple purposes, fulfill the operational needs, and provide a way to preserve an adequate historical record of the information. It is very important to implement and practice proper retention management, because it allows your organization to accomplish the following:

- Reduce compliance and litigation risks by proactively managing the retention and disposition of all potentially discoverable information

- Reduce storage costs by storing only important and relevant information in the archive

- Have only the relevant information in the archive, which will also make it easier and faster to find relevant information

- Increase the reliability of information by managing the appropriate versions of information assets and ensuring that they have high value as evidence if they are needed in a court of law

There are significant benefits to developing your retention policies before automating and implementing an archiving solution:

More-effective Regulatory Compliance   You don't have a choice when it comes to email retention for regulatory compliance; it is an absolute requirement. The only choice your company has is in how you meet the requirements: manually or with an email-archiving automation system. Creating and automating your email-retention policy lowers your overall risk of noncompliance and ensures that all required email is kept for the required time period.

Better Legal Risk Management   The ability to show a court an updated and regularly enforced email-retention policy can demonstrate retention policy intent and counter the claims of "spoliation," or purposeful destruction of evidence, by the plaintiff's attorney.

More-consistent Corporate Governance   Organizations these days rely on the active generation, use, and leverage/reference of data for business processes and decisions. The data that a business generates has a value to the business if that data can be used efficiently. An effective retention policy will ensure that this information will remain available for some period of time, and an email-archiving system allows for quick search and reference.

More information about retention policies, and how they are used specifically within Exchange Server 2013, will be discussed later in this chapter.

Archiving with Exchange Server 2013

Microsoft has made several key improvements to the archiving, retention, search, and hold capabilities in Exchange Server 2013. These new features allow for more-granular control over how information is preserved and accessed, while also allowing end users to manage their mailboxes according to their own filing habits.

The following messaging and compliance features are new to Exchange Server 2013:

- Preservation of mailbox data based on specific criteria, known as *query-based hold*

- Preservation of mailbox data based on a date range, known as *time-based hold*

- Ability to conduct searches across SharePoint 2013, Lync 2013, and Exchange Server 2013 from one interface

- New all-in-one GUI for conducting In-Place eDiscovery and Hold operations

- Support for Calendar and Tasks folders when creating retention tags

Exchange In-Place Archive vs. Third-Party Enterprise Archives

Although significant strides continue to be made to improve the native functionality available within Exchange Server, it will be up to each organization to determine if it meets all of their needs. Exchange Server 2013 should not be confused or compared with an "enterprise" scaled solution like a Symantec Enterprise Vault or Mimosa NearPoint. Microsoft refers to these solutions as "enterprise archives," whereas Exchange Server 2013 is more of a "personal archive." We need to set the record straight on this—when it comes down to compliance archiving or enterprise records retention, you can't afford to make mistakes.

So when should you use the In-Place Archive (previously known as "personal archive") feature that is available in Exchange Server 2013, and when should you use an enterprise archive solution available through third parties? In essence, the decision has to be made based on the requirements and functionality offered by these solutions. Microsoft positions Exchange Server 2013 as a personal archive and not as an enterprise archive solution. Microsoft's basic archiving solution enables organizations to get rid of PST files, implement large mailboxes, and provide advanced search. It does not provide records management or preservation of electronic information beyond Exchange Server or support for write-once, read-many (WORM) storage. Organizations that have strict requirements to retain information beyond email or have the need to store information on WORM storage should look at an enterprise archive solution. Organizational archiving goes beyond the scope of the In-Place Archive and delivers full mailbox capture for all users, full single-instance storage across all data, and advanced search and case-management tools for ediscovery.

By way of comparison, a typical third-party email-archival solution can be expected to deliver all or a portion of the following key functions in addition to the In-Place Archive functionality in Exchange Server 2013:

◆ Logs, WORM, read-only

◆ Single instancing/compression

◆ Configuration auditing

◆ Mailbox auditing

◆ Regulatory accreditation

◆ Federated discovery, retention, and reporting across multiple content sources

◆ Data mining and visualization

◆ Case management and advanced ediscovery

◆ Content monitoring and supervisory tools

◆ Archiving for Bloomberg data and other non-Microsoft instant messaging data

◆ Archiving for both files and SharePoint

Microsoft is positioning the archiving functionality in Exchange Server 2013 for basic storage management, PST archiving, and discovery while leaving the door open for third-party vendors to offer additional value that is necessary for organizational archiving. Small organizations will find the basic features of Exchange Server 2013 satisfactory to reduce the strain on storage growth and eliminate PST files. However, for organizations that require full email retention and advanced ediscovery, a third-party email-archiving solution is the answer for the next few years.

Retention Policies and Tags

The technology used in Exchange Server 2013 to maintain records management is called Message Records Management (MRM) and helps organizations reduce legal risks associated with email and other communications. It is much easier to make an organization comply with company policies and regulatory needs with MRM, and within Exchange Server 2013 this is accomplished with retention policies. Each mailbox can have one retention policy assigned to it, and each retention policy can have multiple retention tags. Exchange Server 2013 has multiple types of retention tags available for maintaining and moving data between the primary and archive mailboxes:

Default Policy Tag   Default policy tags (DPTs) are used to apply retention policies to untagged mailbox items. Untagged items are mailbox items that either didn't receive a retention tag from the folder that they are located in or didn't get a policy applied explicitly by the user. DPTs are created by specifying the type All.

A retention policy should not contain more than one DPT with the MoveToArchive action and one DPT with the DeleteAndAllowRecovery or PermanentlyDelete action. Also, if both a deletion tag and an archive tag exist on a retention policy, the archive tag should always have the shorter retention period.

Personal Tags   Personal tags are available to users in their mailbox as part of their retention policy, and they can apply these tags to folders they create themselves or to individual items. This allows end users to tag information they consider critical and therefore apply a longer retention period to it.

Retention Policy Tag   A retention policy tag (RPT) applies retention settings to the default folders (Inbox, Deleted Items, and Sent Items) in a mailbox, and all items that are in these default folders inherit the folders' policy tag. Users are not able to change the tag that is applied to a default folder, but they can apply a different tag to individual items in one of the default folders. You can create RPTs for the following default folders:

- Calendar
- Conversation History
- Deleted Items
- Drafts
- Inbox
- Journal
- Junk Email
- Notes
- Outbox
- Recoverable Items

- ◆ RSS Subscriptions
- ◆ Sent Items
- ◆ Sync Issues
- ◆ Tasks

New in Exchange Server 2013, RPTs support the Calendar, Journal, Notes, and Tasks folders. However, you still cannot use the MoveToArchive retention action with RPTs. The MoveToArchive action is reserved for use with default policy tags and personal tags only, both of which we will discuss next.

You can define retention tags with the following actions:

Move To Archive   Automatically moves messages from the primary mailbox to the personal archive. The DPT created by Exchange Server setup has a retention action of MoveToArchive and a retention period of 730 days (two years), but any number of days or Never can be configured. This policy can help keep the mailbox under quota. The policy works like the Outlook Auto-Archive functionality without creating the PST file and will create a folder name that matches the primary mailbox folder name from which the item was moved. This action can only be applied to default policy tags or personal tags; it cannot be applied to retention policy tags. Any policy tag that uses this action is referred to as an *archive tag*.

Delete And Allow Recovery   Emulates the behavior when the Deleted Items folder is emptied or the user deletes a message using Shift+Delete. Messages move to the Recoverable Items folder when deleted item retention is configured for either the mailbox database or the user. Recoverable Items, also known as the *dumpster*, gives the user another chance to recover deleted messages. Any policy tag that uses this action or the Permanently Delete action is known as a *deletion tag*.

Permanently Delete   Permanently deletes a message. A message is purged from the mailbox when this policy is applied; this is similar to a deleted message being removed from Recoverable Items. Once this happens, the user can no longer recover the message (although when single-item recovery or legal hold is enabled, the item is placed in the Purges folder of Recoverable Items and thus can be recovered by administrators).

Mark As Past Retention Limit   Marks a message as expired after it has reached its retention age. In Outlook 2010 or later and Outlook Web App, expired items are displayed with a notification stating "This item has expired" and "This item will expire in 0 days." Expired items in Outlook 2007 are displayed using strikethrough text. This action is not available when configuring retention tags using the EAC, only via PowerShell.

The priority in which policies take effect is pretty simple. Explicit policies have a higher priority over default policies, and longer-term policies apply over shorter-term policies. Remember that you can't apply a managed folder policy to a mailbox that has an archive mailbox enabled. The managed folder settings created can't use the MoveToArchive action. Managed folder policies are a remnant from MRM 1.0 first introduced in Exchange Server 2007. While they are still supported for backward-compatibility purposes in Exchange Server 2013, they are fundamentally different from the MRM 2.0 framework used in Exchange Server 2013, and therefore both cannot coexist on the same mailbox.

During setup, Exchange Server creates a default retention policy, called Default MRM Policy, which includes several archive tags, as shown in Table 18.1.

TABLE 18.1: Default archive tags

RETENTION TAG NAME	TAG TYPE	DESCRIPTION
Default 2-Year Move To Archive	Default	Applies to items in the entire mailbox that do not have a retention tag applied explicitly or inherited from the folder. Messages are automatically moved to the archive mailbox after two years.
Personal 1-Year Move To Archive	Personal	Messages are automatically moved to the archive mailbox after 365 days.
Personal 5-Year Move To Archive	Personal	Messages are automatically moved to the archive mailbox after five years.
Personal Never Move To Archive	Personal	Messages are never moved to the archive mailbox.

The default retention policy is automatically assigned to each mailbox that has archiving enabled. The tags will be made available to the mailbox user after the Managed Folder Assistant has processed the mailbox. The user can then use these tags and apply them to folders or messages.

MOVING ITEMS BETWEEN FOLDERS

When an item is moved from one folder to another, it inherits the retention tag from the new folder location. If there is no retention-policy tag active on that particular folder, the item automatically gets the default policy tag. However, when the item has a specific personal tag assigned to it, this tag will travel with the item and always take priority over any folder-level tags or the default tag.

SETTING A RETENTION TAG

You can assign retention policies directly to a mailbox or to all mailboxes that are members of a distribution group. When assigning a retention policy to a distribution group, keep in mind that any new members added to a distribution group after the fact will not automatically receive that given retention policy, and you should run the distribution group policy cmdlet at regular intervals. The following example applies the Finance retention policy to John Doe's mailbox:

```
Set-Mailbox "John Doe" -RetentionPolicy "Finance"
```

The next example applies the Finance retention policy to members of the distribution group Seattle-Finance:

```
Get-DistributionGroupMember -Identity "Seattle-Finance" | Set-Mailbox - ↩
RetentionPolicy "Finance"
```

It is also possible to use the EAC to assign a retention policy to one or more mailboxes simultaneously. To assign a retention policy to a single mailbox, follow these steps:

1. Log on to EAC and navigate to the Recipients ➢ Mailboxes pane.

2. In the list view, select the mailbox you want to assign a retention policy to, and click the Edit button.

3. In the properties of the mailbox, click Mailbox Features.

4. From the Retention Policy drop-down menu, select the policy you want to assign, and then click Save (see Figure 18.1).

FIGURE 18.1
Assigning a retention policy to a single mailbox

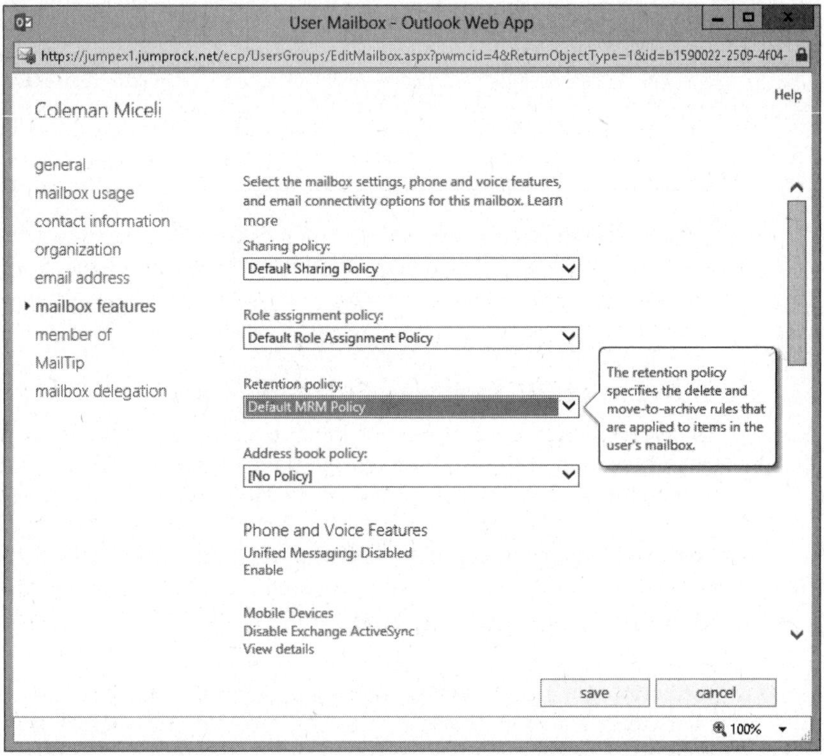

To assign a retention policy to multiple mailboxes simultaneously, use these steps:

1. Log on to EAC and navigate to the Recipients ➢ Mailboxes pane.

2. In the list view, use the Shift or Ctrl keys to select the mailboxes you want to assign the policy to.

3. In the details pane, click More options.

4. Under Retention Policy, click Update.

5. In the Bulk Assign Retention Policy dialog box, select the retention policy that you want to assign from the drop-down menu, and then click Save.

CHANGING A RETENTION POLICY

You can also change the policy that is applied to mailboxes in a new policy. The following two-step example applies the new retention policy "New-Retention-Policy" to all mailboxes that have the old policy "Old-Retention-Policy":

```
$OldPolicy=(Get-RetentionPolicy "Old-Retention-Policy"}.distinguishedName

Get-Mailbox -Filter {RetentionPolicy -eq $OldPolicy} -Resultsize Unlimited | ↵
Set-Mailbox -RetentionPolicy "New-Retention-Policy"
```

DELETING AND REMOVING A RETENTION TAG

When you remove a retention tag from the retention policy that is applied to the mailbox, it is no longer available to the user and therefore can no longer be applied to items in the mailbox. Items that have been specifically stamped with this tag, however, will continue to be processed by the Mailbox Assistant with these settings.

Deleting a tag using the Remove-RetentionPolicyTag cmdlet will not only remove the retention tag from being available to the user but also remove the tag from Active Directory. The next time the Mailbox Assistant runs, it will restamp all the items that had the removed policy applied and apply the default policy tag. If you remove the tag from a large number of mailboxes and items, this could result in a significant increase in resource consumption on your mailbox servers.

RETENTION HOLD

Retention might take actions on new email messages before end users get to them when they are away or unable to access email due to vacation or other reasons. Depending on the policies that may be active and applied to the user, this could mean that messages may have been moved from the primary mailbox to the archive or even deleted. For these users, you have the option to temporarily suspend the retention policies from processing the mailbox for a set amount of time by placing the mailbox on a retention hold. You can specify a retention comment that will notify and inform the user (or another user who might have access to the mailbox) about this hold and explain when it begins and ends. These retention holds are visible only in supported Outlook clients, however, and can be localized in the language of the user's preferred language setting.

Applying a retention hold will not modify or change mailbox quota limits if they are applied, and it might be advisable if you have end users leaving for an extended period of time to increase or remove the mailbox quotas. Also, it might take the user a while to catch up on email after he returns, so give the user some time after he returns to work to go through the messages before removing the retention hold status. Retention hold works in a similar fashion to litigation hold but with some distinct differences, such as the fact that users on retention hold can proactively purge data from the mailbox permanently. Litigation hold will be discussed in more detail later in this chapter.

PLACING A MAILBOX ON RETENTION HOLD

In Exchange Server 2013, when you place a mailbox on retention hold, the Managed Folder Assistant stops processing the retention tags on the retention policy that exists on that particular mailbox. End users can still log on to their mailbox as they normally would during a legal hold and send, delete, or change emails. However, when the user searches her mailbox, she will not be able to find items that were older than the retention time period because they are stored in the Purges folders of Recoverable Items. You can configure Exchange Server to leave a comment when you place a mailbox on retention hold. This comment will be displayed in supported versions of Outlook.

You can only use PowerShell to place a mailbox on retention hold. The following example places John Doe's mailbox on retention hold from June 2, 2013, until June 12, 2013:

```
Set-Mailbox "John Doe" -RetentionHoldEnabled $true -StartDateForRetentionHold
  "6/2/2013" -EndDateForRetentionHold "6/12/2013"
```

This example removes the retention hold from John Doe's mailbox:

```
Set-Mailbox "John Doe" -RetentionHoldEnabled $false
```

Enabling Archiving

You have two ways to archive-enable a mailbox:

◆ Through the Exchange Admin Center (EAC)

◆ Through PowerShell

To enable an existing mailbox for archiving within the EAC, follow these steps:

1. Click Recipients in the Feature pane on the left, then the Mailboxes tab, and select the mailbox that you would like to enable.

2. Select the Edit button from the toolbar.

3. Click Mailbox Features and scroll down until you see the Archiving option.

4. Click Enable.

5. In the dialog box, you can optionally specify the database where you would like the archive mailbox to reside.

6. Click Save.

To enable new users that are created through the EAC with the wizard, you simply select the check box Create An On-Premises Archive Mailbox For This User (see Figure 18.2).

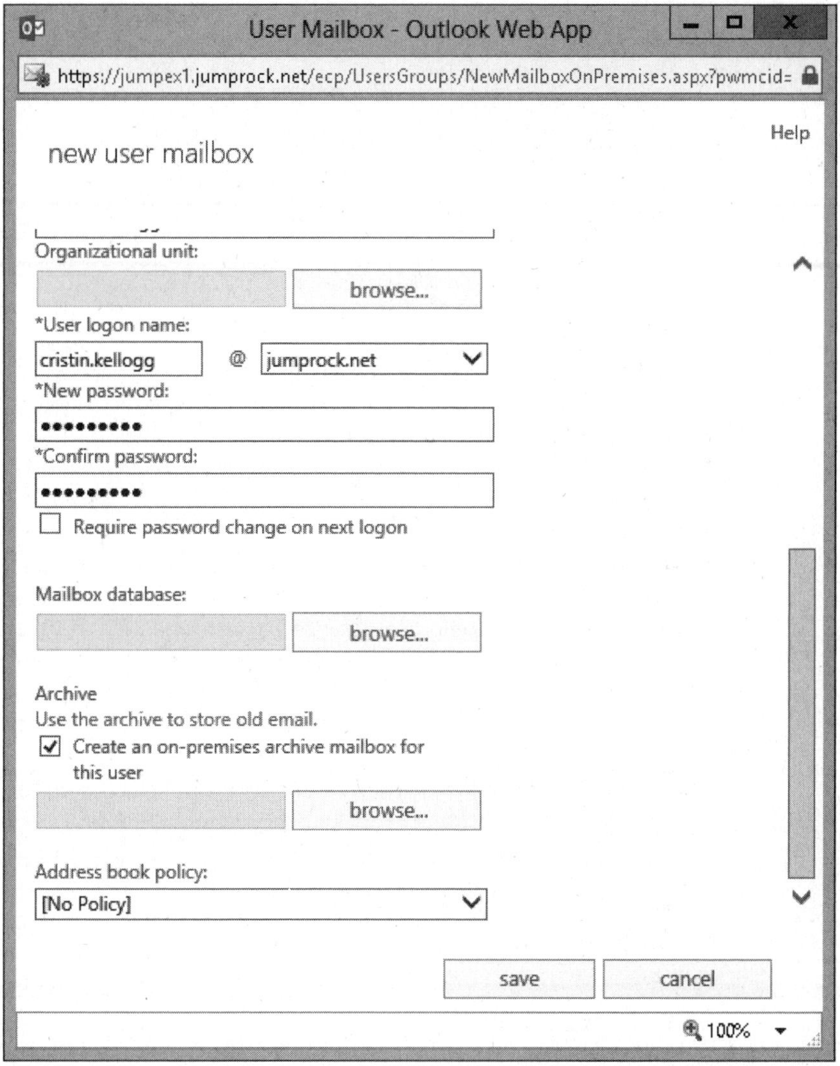

FIGURE 18.2
Select the
Create An
On-Premises
Archive
Mailbox For
This User
option.

You can use PowerShell to enable it as well, and your cmdlet would look like this:

```
Enable-Mailbox "John Doe" –archive
```

Disabling a mailbox from being archive-enabled can be done in the same way: by navigating to the properties of the mailbox in the EAC and selecting Disable Archiving, or by selecting the Disable Archiving option in the Details pane on the right side of the EAC when you highlight the mailbox. If you want to do it with a cmdlet, the command will look like this:

```
Disable-Mailbox "John Doe" –archive
```

Disabling ensures that the data remains but that no new data can be added. This is basically the same as disconnecting a primary mailbox from an account.

The Remove command will delete the archive mailbox from Exchange Server, and the command looks like this:

```
Remove-Mailbox "John Doe" -archive
```

Using the Exchange Server 2013 In-Place Archive

For an end user to get access to his archived data with Exchange Server 2013, he will either have to use Outlook Web App or have Outlook 2010 or later installed. Outlook 2007 with the Office 2007 Cumulative Update for February 2011 can also support an In-Place Archive, but with some reduced functionality. An end user can drag and drop email from his PST files directly into the personal archive, but mail in the primary mailbox can also be moved automatically using retention and archive policies that can be set on the mailbox, folder, or item level.

You can set a quota on the archive mailbox separately from the primary mailbox, as we'll discuss next.

Archive Quotas

Many organizations enforce quotas on users' mailboxes, and archive mailboxes are designed to allow users to store historical data outside their primary mailboxes. Mailbox quotas are one of the primary reasons end users have started using PST files. To attempt to remove end users' desire and need for using PST files, you must ensure that the archive mailbox has enough storage available for the end users to store all of their data. However, organizations may want to cap the growth of archive mailboxes for cost reasons or storage-expansion planning. You can configure an end user's archive mailbox with two options:

ArchiveWarningQuota When an end user's archive mailbox exceeds this limit, an event is logged in the Application event log. The default is 45 GB.

ArchiveQuota When an end user's archive mailbox exceeds this limit, moving data to the archive mailbox is prohibited. The default is 50 GB.

Like most of the archiving functionality in Exchange 2013, you have two ways to configure quotas:

- Through the EAC
- Through PowerShell

To set personal archive quotas within the EAC, select Recipients from the Feature pane on the left, click the Mailboxes tab, and select the mailbox that you would like to configure. In the Details panes, under In-Place Archive, click View Details. Fill in the storage values in gigabytes, or choose an option from the drop-down menu.

You can configure both the ArchiveQuota and ArchiveWarningQuota settings with PowerShell. To set an ArchiveQuota of 20 GB and an ArchiveWarningQuota of 18 GB for an end user, use this command:

```
Set-Mailbox -Identity "John Doe" -ArchiveQuota 20GB -ArchiveWarningQuota ↵
18GB
```

Offline Access

Most users have Outlook configured to synchronize their mailbox with Exchange Server using an Offline Storage Tables (OST) file. This gives users an offline cache so that they can still read their email when they are not connected to the network. The archive mailbox is not integrated with the OST file, which means that when data has been moved from a user's mailbox to their archive, the data will not be in the offline cache. If the user requires access to this data, she has two options: get access through OWA or move the data back to her live mailbox.

Understanding Litigation and In-Place Hold

Organizations use litigation hold to preserve all forms of relevant information when litigation is reasonably anticipated. It prevents deletions and preserves record changes to mailbox items in both the user's primary mailbox and archive mailboxes. Within Exchange Server 2013, Microsoft uses the term "In-Place Hold" to refer to litigation hold. While retention hold simply disables MRM policies, litigation hold keeps the policies enabled but simply does not purge data and is either enabled or disabled (that is, there are no time frames for litigation hold). What is nice is that you can send alerts to the end users that their mailbox data is on hold, which eliminates manually notifying users and telling them that they can't delete data. Once mailboxes are put on In-Place Hold, compliance officers can conduct searches against them using eDiscovery. There is very tight integration within the EAC between placing a mailbox on In-Place Hold and eDiscovery. Both are handled using the same wizard, which you will see.

Placing a Mailbox on In-Place Hold

A lot of improvements have been made to the legal-hold functionality in Exchange Server 2013. With Exchange Server 2010, it was only possible to place *everything* in the mailbox on hold for an indefinite period of time, until the hold was removed. This could result in a lot of unnecessary data retention and misused storage. Now administrators and compliance officers can search one or more mailboxes for data based on a very specific set of criteria and place only those items on hold. Those criteria can include keywords, date ranges, sender, recipient, and message type. Additionally, you can define how long the items should be kept on hold, in terms of days since they were received or created in the mailbox. When you place a mailbox on In-Place Hold, policies are still acted on and applied, but the relevant data is never purged from the mailbox. End users can log on to their mailbox as they normally would during a legal hold and send, delete, or change emails. However, when the user searches her mailbox, she will not be able to find items that are older than the retention time period. And any messages that are modified by the user will have a copy of the original saved to a hidden folder within the mailbox that is inaccessible to the mailbox owner but remains subject to searches. This is known as copy-on-write (COW).

Although litigation hold can still be enabled on a mailbox through PowerShell using the `Set-Mailbox` cmdlet with the `-LitigationHoldEnabled` parameter, this is discouraged in Exchange Server 2013. Instead, a new tool called the In-Place eDiscovery & Hold Wizard is available in the EAC, and it can be used for performing both single- and multi-mailbox searches, as well as for implementing In-Place Holds. We will walk through the wizard later in this chapter, in "Using the In-Place eDiscovery & Hold Wizard."

Implementing eDiscovery

The ability to search for relevant content within mailboxes is provided in Exchange Server 2013 through the eDiscovery feature. These searches are common practice within organizations that are dealing with litigations and lawsuits or that want to ensure they are in compliance with organizational rules, rules that are enforced by their business bylaws, or rules that are enforced on their business by legislation.

The eDiscovery functionality uses the existing content indexes created by Exchange Search, which has been revamped in Exchange Server 2013 to use Microsoft Search Foundation rather than Windows Search. Microsoft Search Foundation offers significant improvements in the areas of indexing and query performance. Instead of the PowerShell queries used in Exchange Server 2007 to do cross-mailbox and -server search, there is now an easy search interface, but behind the scenes it is still a PowerShell cmdlet (search-mailbox). One of the reasons for this change is that it is fairly rare to find a lawyer or HR person who is fluent in PowerShell, and the GUI is much more suited for them. Since cross-mailbox and -server search is a "powerful" right to have (that is, you technically could look in everyone's mailbox), it is a restricted permission. Use Role-based Access Control (RBAC) to add the Mailbox Search role to give nontechnical people access to this search functionality without disclosing administrative permissions.

WHEN DO YOU USE EDISCOVERY?

There are a few scenarios for which you would use the eDiscovery option. The main usage scenarios are as follows:

Legal eDiscovery   More and more organizations are forced to provide information to support litigation or lawsuits. Traditionally, you had to manually search multiple servers, and if you were lucky you could use some of the PowerShell cmdlets. No matter what you used, it was a time-consuming and costly exercise. Exchange Server 2013 eDiscovery fills a niche; you can search across your entire organization without using cmdlets (which is important for HR or legal people).

HR   Corporate human resources departments commonly must respond to requests to research and monitor email content or complaints. For instance, in a case where an employee feels that the email content he has received from peers is offensive in content and in violation with HR policies, HR should investigate this matter.

SAFEGUARDING AGAINST UNWARRANTED MAILBOX ACCESS

Within the EAC, there is an easy search interface, but behind the scenes it is still a PowerShell cmdlet (New-MailboxSearch). (It is fairly rare to find a lawyer or HR person who is fluent in PowerShell, so the GUI is helpful for them.) Since cross-mailbox and -server search is a powerful right to have (that is, you technically could look in everyone's mailbox), it is a restricted permission. Add nontechnical personnel to the Discovery Management security group to grant them the Role-based Access Control permissions necessary to perform ediscovery searches without disclosing administrative permissions.

Organizational Investigations   Many organizations are involved in legal matters that involve an external party. In this case the internal legal department will respond to a formal request for information as part of a legal matter and will have a limited amount of time to respond to this request.

USING THE IN-PLACE EDISCOVERY & HOLD WIZARD

To use the Exchange Server 2013 In-Place eDiscovery & Hold Wizard, a user should be added to the Discovery Management role group. By default, this group does not have any members. Administrators who have the Organizational Management role are restricted from doing any In-Place eDiscovery searches without being added to the Discovery Management role group. In-Place eDiscovery is a powerful feature that allows anyone with the appropriate permissions to have potential access to all the email records stored in your entire organization. Therefore, it is critical to control and monitor who gets access to the Discovery Management role and keep a close eye on the In-Place eDiscovery actions.

You can use PowerShell to add a user to the Discovery Management role group. To add, for instance, user John Doe, the cmdlet looks like this:

```
Add-RoleGroupMember "Discovery Management" -User Jdoe
```

After you have gotten permission, you can open the Discovery Manager console by going to https://servername.local.com/ecp and logging in with your credentials (see Figure 18.3).

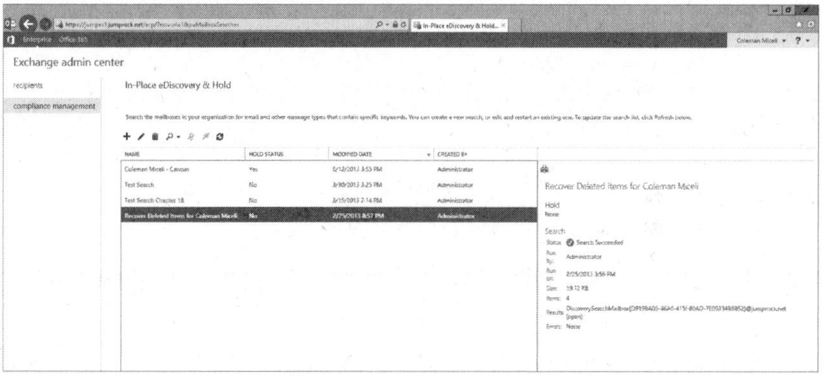

FIGURE 18.3
Exchange Server 2013 In-Place eDiscovery & Hold Console

Once logged in, you can create a new In-Place eDiscovery search or In-Place Hold by clicking Compliance Management in the Feature pane and then selecting the In-Place eDiscovery & Hold tab. Give the search a name that is descriptive, so that it will make sense to you and others later, since you will be sharing this view of the console with others in the Discovery Management group. Select what you want to search. You have the option to search all mailboxes, specific mailboxes, or mailboxes that belong to a distribution group. In Figure 18.4, we are searching specific mailboxes, as well as mailboxes for all members of the Sales group.

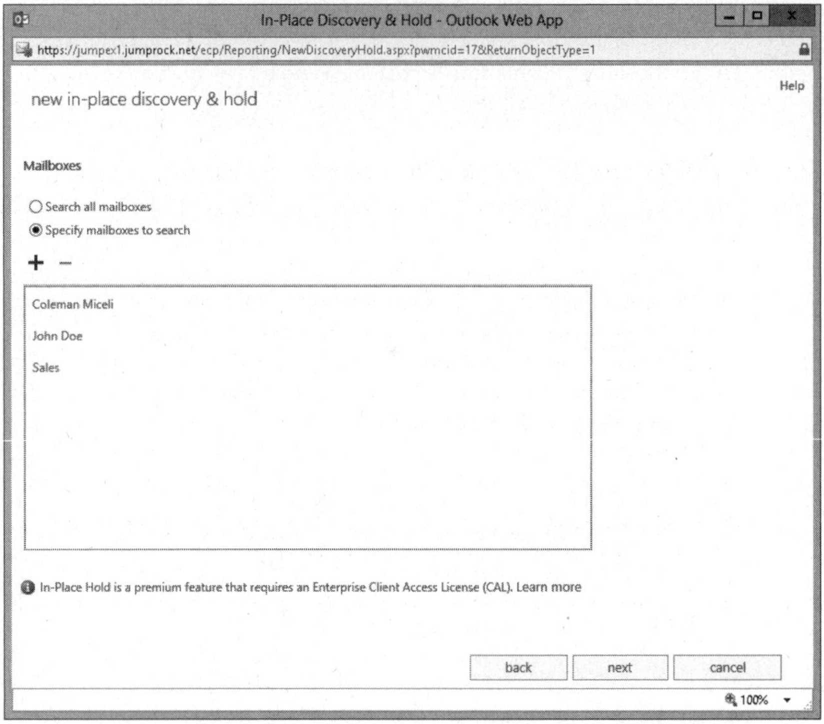

FIGURE 18.4
Selecting
mailboxes in
the In-Place
eDiscovery &
Hold Wizard

FIGURE 18.4
Selecting mailboxes in the In-Place eDiscovery & Hold Wizard

On the Search Query page, define the content that you want to search for. You can search the entire mailbox, or you can narrow your search by selecting keywords, message types, to and from addresses, a date range, and specific senders or recipients. To filter based on keywords, as in Figure 18.5, you can simply type basic words, or to be more specific, you can build complex queries based on Keyword Query Language.

If you want to preserve the results of your search, check the box to place the matching content on hold (see Figure 18.6). You have the option to put the contents on hold indefinitely or for a specific number of days. After you click Finish, Exchange Server will queue the search.

VIEWING THE SEARCH RESULTS

Once the search is completed, you will be able to see a summary of the results in the Details pane of the EAC, including the total number of items, aggregate size, and keyword statistics. Next, you can preview the results within the browser or export them to a Discovery Search mailbox. Be conscious of the amount of data you are exporting, the mailbox you are exporting to, and the database and volume where that mailbox resides. You don't want to cause an outage because you filled up the drive with exported data. You can select the default Discovery Search mailbox, or you can create additional ones and use them. There are also export options for whether to include unsearchable items and to enable deduplication and thread compression.

During the export, In-Place eDiscovery will create a new folder in the target mailbox that has the same name you gave to the search, and a subfolder will be created below that for each mailbox that had information that matches the search query.

FIGURE 18.5
Defining a
search query

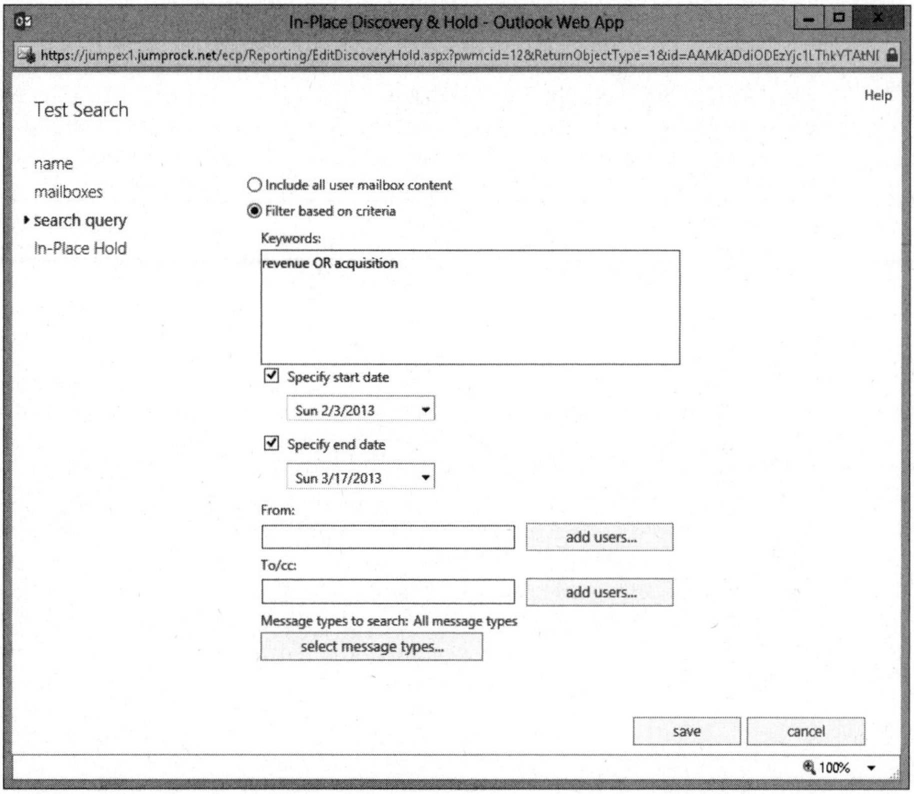

FIGURE 18.6
Placing search
results on
In-Place Hold

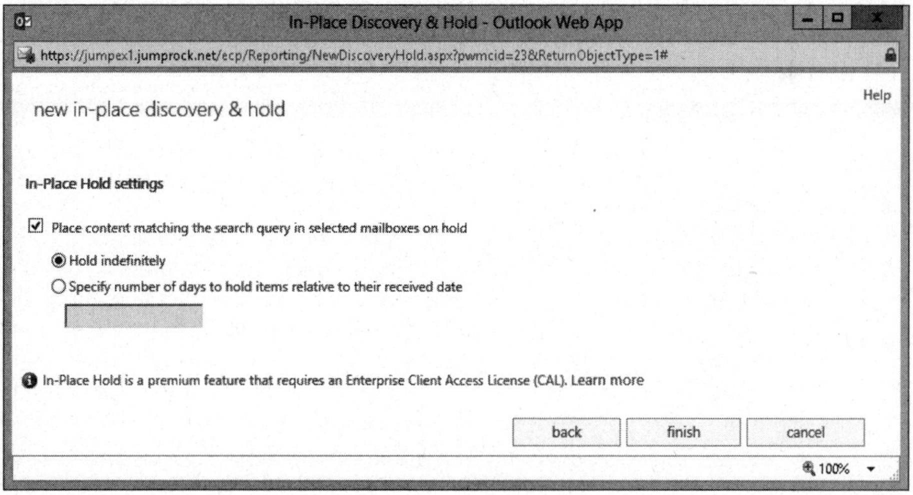

Requirements and Considerations

There are many important factors to consider before implementing Exchange Server 2013 to address archiving, compliance, and data management within your organization. As we've discussed throughout this chapter, while the native functionality available within Exchange Server has matured greatly over the past several releases of the product and may suit many companies, it still might not have all of the features necessary to meet your needs. Be sure to understand what laws and regulations impact your organization's business and what your obligations are in terms of data retention and stewardship. Here are some other factors to consider before moving forward with any strategy.

Licensing

The archiving functionality in Exchange Server 2013 is marketed as a way that organizations can get archiving for free, without purchasing an expensive third-party business archive solution. But as with lots of marketing, you have to lift up the curtains a bit to get the correct answer.

As a starter, the archiving functionality requires an enterprise client access license, also known as an eCAL, which adds some cost on top of the regular license cost of Exchange Server. Also, you need at least Outlook 2010 to take advantage of the full archiving and compliance capabilities. Of course, you can use Outlook Web Access for lots of the functionality, but it's smart to deploy Exchange Server 2013 in combination with Outlook 2010 or later since the full archiving functionality in Exchange Server 2013 is available only with Outlook 2010 or later. This isn't in line with the "free" marketing theme, but it is embedded within the product.

Server Storage

When it comes to archiving software, proper storage planning is important. With Exchange Server 2013 there are a few additional "curveballs" you have to work with. Depending on the version of Exchange Server you are transitioning from, you may need to consider some architectural changes present within the Exchange Server database structure in Exchange Server 2013. Single-instance storage (SIS) has been removed in favor of better performance and reduced input/output per second (IOPS) requirements. SIS refers to storing a single copy of a message or item once, even though it is stored in multiple locations. On average, the SIS savings were about 20 percent. But for an Exchange Server database that has had its mailboxes moved from Exchange Server 2007 to Exchange Server 2013, this increase has largely been mitigated by the page-compression features that were added in the Extensible Storage Engine (ESE) functionality.

Additionally, when you bring in PST files with Exchange Server 2013, you need to ensure that the additional capacity is available. The problem gets more interesting when you start deploying database availability groups and replicate data. You will replicate not only the primary mailbox but also the archived data in the personal archive. This could mean that your storage requirements grow exponentially. There is a reason why Microsoft provides the option to put the archive mailbox on the same database as the primary mailbox it belongs to: Microsoft spent a lot of time making Serial Advanced Technology Attachment (SATA) storage a viable option for Exchange Server 2013 for both performance and capacity. If you decide to go with SATA, there is no reason to split the personal archive and primary mailbox onto separate databases because you are already on the cheapest disks out there. In addition, keep in mind that disk capacity is continuing to increase while performance isn't; this means that if you continue to split the data onto different drives, you are not maximizing the efficiency of the drives (either capacity or performance).

If your organization is going to use the in-place archiving functionality extensively, be prepared for the additional storage requirements as well. This is, of course, because of the removal of SIS; however, the added page compression does provide some mitigation against this. A rapid increase in storage needs could occur when someone creates a large search result set that is copied to the Discovery Search Mailbox. When you quickly export those results and provide them to the legal team, this might be only a short-term problem.

Client Requirements

As mentioned earlier, only Outlook 2010 or later and Outlook Web App provide full MRM capabilities. While Outlook 2007 with the Office 2007 Cumulative Update for February 2011 will give the end user access to the archive, it has some limitations. First, searches across both primary and archive mailboxes are not supported. Selecting All Mailbox Items when conducting a search will return results only from the mailbox you are searching, primary or archive. Second, users are not able to apply personal tags to items in their primary mailbox. However, administrators are still able to move data to the archive through default and retention tags, and users can manage personal tags via Outlook Web App as an alternative.

The Bottom Line

Understand the basic principles of email archiving.   An archiving solution not only provides a way to ease the pain of storage problems on Exchange Server whether they are with the databases or with PST files but also assists in helping organizations become compliant and make discovery of email easier.

>   **Master It**   How can government organizations actively comply with regulations on open records laws to taxpayers?

Ensure your company complies with regulations.   It is extremely important that your messaging system be configured in such a way that email data is managed according to laws and regulations.

>   **Master It**   Which laws and regulations are in effect in your business, and what does it mean for your organization?

Enable Exchange Server 2013 in-place archiving.   Exchange Server 2013 allows for more efficient management of the user's primary mailbox by enabling the mailbox for archiving and using policies to move the content between the mailbox and the archive.

>   **Master It**   How does archiving allow for moving older email content automatically from the primary mailbox to the In-Place Archive?

Use Exchange Server 2013 retention policies.   Retention policies define how long data must be retained before it is automatically removed when the time setting has been met.

Master It   You can create as many policies as you need; however, in many organizations retention policies will be created per department (for instance, finance).

Use Exchange Server 2013 In-Place eDiscovery and Hold.   In certain situations you may need to prevent deletion of email for a period of time while an end user is away and unable to attend to their mailbox.

Master It   Without retention hold, and depending on the policies that may be active and applied to the user, messages may have been moved from the primary mailbox to the archive or even deleted. What is the cmdlet to put a mailbox on retention hold?

Part 4

Server Administration

Chapter 19

Creating and Managing Mailbox Databases

An Exchange server at its core is a database-management server. When we remember the days of Exchange Server 5.0, Exchange Server handled its databases, Internet connectivity, directory service, and SMTP connectivity. In Exchange Server 2000/2003, SMTP became a function of Internet Information Services (IIS). After this brief trip, SMTP is now back under Exchange Server's umbrella. Many other responsibilities have been passed on to other Windows components, except for the management of the message information stores. Database and storage management is what Exchange Server does best, and in Exchange Server 2010 and Exchange Server 2013 we find some of the most impressive improvements.

In this chapter, you will learn to:

- ◆ Identify the core components of Exchange Server database storage

- ◆ Plan for disk storage requirements for Exchange Server databases

- ◆ Configure Exchange Server Mailbox servers with the appropriate storage solution

Getting to Know Exchange Server Database Storage

To end users Exchange Server is all about reading their email. For the administrator, it's about making sure users' email is available and up to date. Of course, there's a lot more to it than that, but the basic job of Exchange Server is to store and process messages for users. To this end, it is important to understand how the database technology works "under the hood."

Exchange Server 2007 (Third Generation)

The rumors of Exchange Server moving to a SQL-based storage technology proved untrue. In fact, Microsoft pushed forward with Extensible Storage Engine (ESE) and increased its investment, introducing database-replication technologies and essentially providing greater availability options to administrators, now stressed out about their ever-growing databases. ESE had proved to be a successful database technology over the preceding years for Exchange Server since version 4.0, through to the present time.

Exchange Server 2007 introduced two major changes in database management. First, the maximum number of available mountable databases, still organized in storage groups, was increased to 50. Second, finally recognizing the need for large mailboxes, Microsoft removed all database hard file-size limits. There were many other changes, but a notable one was the graceful removal of the STM file from Exchange Server, ensuring that the EDB was once again riding solo, storing all content in a single database file.

Exchange Server 2010 (Fourth Generation)

Exchange Server 2010 introduced a version of ESE that was reengineered to denote years of customer feedback, experience, and the reality of larger user mailbox requirements. The changes in Exchange Server 2010 were mostly the kind of changes that most administrators would not notice when working with middle-of-the-range servers or hardware. However, for administrators who manage Mailbox servers with 500 or more mailboxes, the importance of the changes became very real, very fast.

Online defragmentation running at runtime, new database tables, a larger page size, and an aggressive compression solution, to name just a few, were some of the architectural changes in storage for Exchange Server 2010. Exchange Server 2010 vastly reduced random IOPS (input/output operations per second) requirements by up to 90 percent (when compared to Exchange Server 2003). Many administrators had to rethink their strategy for disk storage, because it brought about the possibility of using cheaper, lower-performance JBOD (just a bunch of disks) in many scenarios.

Exchange Server 2013 (Current Generation)

Several years of lessons learned from experience accrued in Exchange Server 2010 environments have led Microsoft to further improve how mailbox databases are handled in Exchange Server 2013. Database schema changes have been introduced, and resource utilization for disk access has been decreased further, improving overall performance. We've seen some numbers floating around that decreased utilization by over 97 percent from the days of Exchange Server 2003. Though those numbers are really impressive, they are only marginally more than what Exchange Server 2010 was already able to achieve. It is important to note that many of the improvements are unseen by the administrator but are notable in disk and server sizing. Many changes in database management also provide enhanced failover experiences and replication mechanisms within database availability groups. Refer to Chapter 20, "Creating and Managing Database Availability Groups," to review many of those changes.

Basics of Storage Terminology

In this section, we'll visit the basics of storage terminology and explain why these terms should be relevant to you in a discussion on storage.

MAILBOX DATABASE

In Exchange Server 2013, the mailbox database (called a mailbox store in Exchange Server 2003) is the configuration object that provides management for all database settings. From the mailbox database properties, an administrator can configure the location of the database file, the transaction log file settings, and some settings that apply to mailboxes stored in the mailbox database.

Each Exchange Server 2013 server that has the Mailbox server role installed has a mailbox database named Mailbox Database <GUID> (the GUID suffix is there to ensure that the database name is unique; more on that later in this chapter).

This database is created during the installation process and has an EDB (Exchange database) file named `Mailbox Database <GUID>.edb`, stored in the default Mailbox folder in the Exchange Installation directory. (The EDB file may also be stored in an alternate location if you specified one during the Exchange Server installation by using the `/DBFilePath` parameter.) On an Exchange Server 2013 Standard Edition Mailbox server, an administrator can create up to 5 mailbox databases; Enterprise Edition allows creation of up to 50 mailbox databases (though most administrators will likely *not* want to create so many). Exchange Server 2013 Cumulative Update 1 is the latest version released, as of the writing of this book, though Microsoft has already announced that Cumulative Update 2 will provide administrators the ability to concurrently mount 100 mailbox databases.

Administrators often ask me why they should ever need to create more than one Exchange database, especially since the maximum mailbox database size is *unlimited.* Later in this chapter we will discuss the organizational and business reasons why having multiple mailbox databases may be the right solution for your Exchange Server environment.

TRANSACTION LOGS

Transaction logging is obscure to most administrators. It is easy to forget about transaction logging, since it all occurs automatically (or *automagically*). For every transaction that enters your messaging server (new email, deleted email, a change to an email message, a modified attachment, and so on), the information is written to a transaction log file. When transaction log files are filled up with data, new transaction log files are created in a perpetual fashion that bears resemblance to a factory production line.

Transaction log files always have the same size, 1024 KB. We compare them to milk containers (whether empty or full, they are always one-gallon containers, or one-liter containers for those using the metric system). Transaction log files are created at the 1,024 KB size and then filled to capacity. These files will be persistent on the hardware. Later in this chapter, we will discuss the recommended methods for administrators to purge or remove older transaction log files.

🌐 Real World Scenario

WHO OWNS THE STORAGE?

The databases are more than physical files on the hard drive. The databases store information, and the properties of these databases have to be configured and managed according to the purpose they serve. One way to better understand how Exchange Server manages them is to compare them to a rental property. The organization is the top-level entity in Exchange Server. It is the name that describes the configuration boundary for Exchange Server, much like a forest describes the boundary for Active Directory.

Databases are created and managed at the organization level. They are affectively "owned" by the landlord, the organization, much like a building would be. Databases can have one or more copies on individual mailbox servers. These servers are in effect leasing the database from the landlord, because the organization is still the point of management. More on database management shortly.

Storage in Exchange Server 2013

There are many notable characteristics of database storage and architecture in Exchange Server 2013. These are important to point out since they have a far-reaching impact on Exchange Server deployments and the overall strategy that an organization takes with its messaging infrastructure. Let's look at some of those characteristics, or at least the ones most relevant to Exchange Server administrators:

◆ Most write transactions to the Exchange Server databases are performed as sequential writes rather than traditional *random* writes. Why should you care? Well, it means that the hard disk arm does not move; the disk is spinning, but the arm is not moving. This characteristic, which may seem like a detail at first, is significant in reducing the number of required disks or IOPS for Mailbox servers and improving overall database access performance. (Note that some write transactions are still performed as random writes to handle database space compactness or for other specific architectural reasons.)

◆ The database itself received a brand-new schema in Exchange Server 2010, and it was updated again in this latest release of Exchange Server 2013. (By the way, this new database schema is the main reason why you cannot perform an in-place upgrade from previous versions of Exchange Server.)

◆ Well, it can't all be good. Single instance storage (SIS) was removed as a database feature as of Exchange Server 2010. (Keep in mind that SIS was affectively gone in Exchange Server 2007 when it no longer applied to email attachments.) SIS had become decreasingly important, to the point that it would be detrimental to performance to attempt to implement this solution at the database level.

◆ The database page (each transaction resulting in new data creates at least one database page) size is 32 KB. In essence, this means that a 5 KB message will require a 32 KB block of space in the database. However, a 16 KB message is now stored in a single page, rather than two pages as in versions of Exchange Server previous to Exchange Server 2010.

◆ Database pages are compressed to mitigate the risk of an increased database size potentially caused by the new larger page size and other new database architectural changes.

🌐 Real World Scenario

How Should I Think About Storage?

Wouldn't it be great if you could walk into your boss's office and ask for the budget to give every user a 100 GB mailbox so they would never (well, not for a while at least) have to delete anything? Then you could create as many databases on your Exchange server as you could before your fingers go numb and let the users go to town.

Unfortunately, we all have constraints we have to live within; that goes for system administrators, end users, and our VIP users. So, thinking about adding more storage and allowing larger mailboxes or databases, what are some of the constraints that we face? Some of these are technological in nature and some are budgetary or political. We're hoping that you already know most of these and can skim right through them:

◆ Exchange Server 2013 Standard Edition supports a maximum of 5 mailbox databases.

◆ Exchange Server 2013 Enterprise Edition supports a maximum of 50 mailbox databases. In Exchange Server 2010, this number was 100 and it will be that number again in Exchange Server 2013 Cumulative Update 2.

◆ For earlier editions of Exchange Server, the disk I/O limitations affected storage design. In Exchange Server 2013, this limitation now has a lessened impact on storage design.

◆ The bigger a mailbox is, the longer it takes to back up and restore. For typical backups of Exchange Server databases, the restore time will be twice as long as the backup time. There are many solutions today that limit the need of implementing regular backups—personal archives, retention policies, journaling, and others.

◆ Microsoft recommends a maximum Exchange Server database of 2 TB when you have two or more copies of your databases.

◆ You need to plan for 7 to 10 days' worth of transaction logs; a good starting point for estimating how much space transaction logs will consume is about 9 GB of transaction logs for each 1,000 average users. However, we will discuss later, in "Managing Mailbox Databases," how some organizations will want to enable circular logging and therefore not require additional disk space to store transaction logs.

◆ If you implement database replication with a database availability group and multiple replication partners, remember that log files will only purge after a successful replication (even when circular logging is enabled). Therefore, you must account for network outages where replication will fail and transaction log files can queue on your physical disks. Depending on the time necessary to troubleshoot or repair the problem that is preventing successful replication, enough disk space must be available before databases will begin to shut down.

◆ You should assume that each database needs to contain 10 to 15 percent additional space for deleted items (known as the recoverable item space or the database dumpster) and for database whitespace. Also, note that whitespace can continue to grow if the online maintenance process does not complete during its scheduled interval. Make sure that your online maintenance interval is large enough to allow a completed process. You can check this in Event Viewer.

An Additional Factor: the Personal Archive (aka the Archive Mailbox)

A personal archive is what we call the "Siamese" mailbox to a user's primary mailbox. It's a secondary mailbox that is "joined at the hip" to a user's primary mailbox and provides a second location for storing older, rarely accessed emails. We'll briefly discuss the personal archive in this chapter, since it does have an effect on the overall storage solution. Let's look at some of the features unique to the personal archive:

◆ A personal archive is created by using the `Enable-Mailbox <mailbox> -Archive` command, or you can use `Enable-Mailbox <mailbox> -RemoteArchive` if you plan to create an archive mailbox in Office 365 for a user who has a mailbox in an on-premises deployment of Exchange Server 2013.

◆ A personal archive and a primary mailbox for a user do not have to be stored in the same mailbox database.

◆ The personal archive cannot be cached locally on an Outlook client through an offline store (OST).

◆ A personal archive can only be accessed by Outlook 2010 or newer or with Outlook Web App.

◆ Personal archives allow administrators to provide larger storage solutions for users, while still providing access to all email.

◆ Do not confuse a personal archive with a personal folder. Personal folders, or PSTs, are containers for email messages and other Outlook content. PSTs are always stored on client computers, are portable, and can be used as a means of back up by individual users.

We want to address a couple of questions that often arise around personal archives. First, as there is typically a trend toward ever-larger primary mailboxes, why not just give users a bigger primary mailbox? Actually, some organizations do just that. However, in my opinion, the biggest benefit of using personal archives is the reduction in OST file size. Since the personal archive is not available offline, it will reduce OST file bloat while still providing remote access through Outlook Web App, therefore minimizing disk space issues on client computers.

The other question is, "Why bother?" Now that it's possible to separate the primary mailbox and the personal archive into different databases, the administrator has more options. For example, an organization may take the view that archive items by definition are not being accessed as frequently, so they can exist in databases that rest on cheaper storage, thus saving the organization money. It can also decrease the time taken to recover the primary mailbox in the event of a disaster. So for archive mailboxes, it's well worth a look to see if it makes more sense to move mail out from the primary mailbox and to import mail from PSTs!

Disk Size vs. I/O Capacity

Historically, Exchange Server has been limited by the performance of its disks rather than by the space available on those disks. In Exchange Server 2010, there was somewhat of a role reversal between those two characteristics, and Exchange Server 2013 has improved this situation. The improvements and reductions in I/O requirements permit administrators to use lower-cost SATA disks (or equivalent) to handle storage.

For many Exchange Server administrators (the authors of this book included), the knowledge and understanding of disk I/O capacity constraints came slowly. For some reason, we kept thinking that the disk technology far outperformed the database capacity. But as Exchange servers got more heavily loaded with more simultaneous users and larger databases, the demands on the disk grew.

Let's take a look at a quick example. Say you have an 18 GB SCSI disk from the olden days; that disk may be able to support 100 reads and/or writes to the disk each second. That's not a big deal if you have 50 users, but what if you have 500 users? Can the disk subsystem service the I/O requests that those 500 users will put on it? If the disk system is not properly sized—both for capacity and for the required I/O load—then users will see performance problems.

This load is normally measured (and planned) in terms of the IOPS profile of the users who will use the system. The Exchange Server team at Microsoft has done much research into the type of load that users place on an Exchange server; they have broken that down based on different types of users, from a *light user* who may send 5 messages per day and receive 20, to an *extra heavy* user who may send 40 messages per day and receive 160.

Note that the reductions in IOPS between recent Exchange Server versions are significant, to the point that an Exchange Server 2013 deployment requires only small fraction (a few percentage points) of the IOPS required by a server that ran Exchange Server 2003. IOPS has truly become one of the least significant disk and hardware elements used in calculating server size for Exchange Server 2013.

What's Keeping Me Up at Night?

We spend quite a bit of time wondering if we have our storage configuration optimized. Ask yourself these questions about your own environment:

♦ Am I giving my users enough mailbox space to store enough historical information to do their jobs? Or (*shudder*) too much?

♦ Are users wasting mail storage on personal or non-work-related content, such as MPG files of cats playing the piano (http://www.youtube.com/watch?v=npqx8CsBEyk)?

♦ Should I employ an email archival solution to move older content off the mailbox database and onto alternative storage? Should I use the built-in personal archive solution or a third-party solution? If I use either solution, how much "recent" content should be left on the Exchange server versus moved out to the archive?

♦ Do I need to be keeping copies of certain types of messages (such as for regulatory, legal, or business reasons)?

♦ Are my databases growing so fast that I may run out of disk space before I notice?

♦ Do I have the right balance of databases, size of disk, frequency of backups, and deployment of redundancy?

Planning Mailbox Storage

When estimating mailbox database size for a given configuration, as a worst-case scenario we once estimated that a single database could grow to 1.3 TB in size. Although Exchange Server can technically support a database that large, it would take forever to back up, and worse, it would take forever to restore. (Okay, maybe not forever but longer than what would make operational sense.) Even if you are using snapshot technologies, if the snapshot backup software performs database verification, the verification would take far too long. So a database size of 1.3 TB is just not practical in organizations that have not yet implemented a DAG with log replication.

Maximum Database Sizes

Microsoft recommends that you keep each mailbox database under about 200 GB if you are not using any type of replication technology. If you are using a DAG and maintaining at least two copies of each database, you can consider allowing a maximum database size of 2 TB. In practical terms, there are very good reasons to keep it far smaller, such as the time necessary to back up and restore the files and the time necessary to repair the files, but this number is only a general idea of what you should attempt to stay under.

These numbers are based on some simple principles. Consider that if you *don't* use replication for your mailbox databases, you have to account for the time necessary to restore a database and the impact of a restore operation. A smaller database, in the case of loss or hardware failure, can be restored quickly, ensuring minimal impact on users. When database replication is put in place, the replica of the database in essence acts as a backup and, depending on the number of mailbox database copies, may never be used in a restore operation. In that case, a large database is more efficient, because it simplifies administration by reducing the number of databases in the organization.

We urge you to consider your existing environment when you think about these maximum sizes. Ultimately, you need to consider how much time it will take to restore one of these databases from a backup; if the absolute longest time you can take to restore a database from your backup media is two hours, and your system restores at a rate of 30 GB per hour, then the largest database size you should consider supporting is 60 GB. Your company's recovery time objective/recovery point objective (RTO/RPO) will most likely dictate recovery time and therefore will help you in calculating what your maximum database sizes should be.

Replication technologies in Exchange Server 2013 provide options for quicker access to a mailbox database, in the event of a server or disk failure. Naturally, this requires a proper implementation and configuration of a DAG.

Determining the Number of Databases

A common way to improve the scalability of Mailbox servers is to add mailbox databases. Though this might not improve overall server performance or a user's perceived response time, it allows you to break up the amount of data you are storing and spread it across multiple smaller mailbox databases. In turn, this enables you to support larger mailboxes. Keep in mind that as you increase the number of mailboxes that each Mailbox server supports, increasing the amount of RAM will help improve performance and reduce the disk I/O profile.

Some administrators may want to create multiple mailbox databases to gain underlying performance benefits. Each mailbox database is configured with a 20 MB checkpoint depth. This means that 20 MB of outstanding transactions can be written to the logs but not immediately committed to the database. If you have one mailbox database, then that database's default checkpoint depth is 20 MB; for databases that are replicated, the default checkpoint depth is 100 MB. Note that in Exchange Server 2007 and earlier, the recommendation was to create multiple storage groups that each had a single mailbox store, rather than a single storage group with multiple mailbox stores. This recommendation was in place to ensure that the checkpoint depth, which was unique to the log stream of the storage group, would not have to be shared by the multiple mailbox stores in the storage group. Instead, you were urged to have only a single mailbox store per storage group. In Exchange Server 2013, this issue no longer has relevance, since all mailbox databases maintain their own checkpoint depth and log stream.

When creating additional mailbox databases that do not use database replication with a DAG, you should plan to place each database's transaction logs on separate disk spindles from the database files. This can help improve performance (due to the nature of the I/O differences), though it mainly improves recoverability. If you are using a DAG and have two copies or more, you can safely place the transaction logs and the database files on the same spindles or disks.

Planning for Mailbox Databases

A company named ABC is planning to migrate their existing messaging infrastructure to Exchange Server 2013. ABC has 1,200 users who connect to a server farm in the company's main office. During their planning process, administrators are attempting to determine the number of databases required to support their requirements.

They have identified the following requirements:

◆ Minimize the time necessary to perform a restore in the event of a single disk failure.

◆ Minimize the time necessary to perform an offline operation on the database files.

◆ Provide all users with at least 1 GB of storage but support even much larger mailboxes. (Today, it's becoming the norm for users to expect mailboxes that have unlimited storage; the new generation of users is increasingly familiar with cloud storage and cheap disk storage.)

When looking at each requirement, ABC has determined that they should design the following storage solution:

Create Multiple Mailbox Databases   By having multiple mailbox databases, ABC feels that they will be able to split up the 1,200 users and therefore keep the database files to a manageable size. With smaller database files, database restore and offline database operation times are minimized.

Configure Mailbox Size Limits   To ensure that a user or a group of users does not overrun the amount of disk space used, ABC has decided to implement mailbox size limits on the mailbox databases. Hard disk drives have been purchased to support up to 5 GB of storage for each user. For now, administrators plan to configure users to receive a warning message when their storage reaches 4 GB.

Though a single Mailbox server can support the company's users, ABC has also determined that they should plan for mailbox resiliency by using a DAG and database replication across multiple Mailbox servers.

Note that this scenario does not take into consideration the performance requirement of the mailbox databases. ABC must also analyze the backup/restore needs, service-level agreements, and user profiles and then provide a storage configuration that will meet the I/O and performance requirements.

Allocating Disk Drives

The traditional logic for Exchange Server design was to place databases on a set of physical disk drives separate from the transaction log files. As Exchange Server 2000/2003 servers scaled upward to support thousands of mailboxes, administrators placed the transaction log files for each storage group on separate spindles (or physical disks) and placed the database files for each group on a different set of spindles.

Although placing different files on separate disks is pretty good advice, today many of us use Fibre Channel or iSCSI SANs to store our Exchange Server data. The SAN is usually some aggregation of a large number of disks in a RAID 5, RAID 1+0, or another redundant configuration. The person who manages the SAN (hereafter known as one of the SAN people) carves up the amount of storage you request from that large aggregation of disk space and assigns it to you as a logical unit number (LUN) of disk space. You then configure your Windows server to connect to those LUNs across the iSCSI or Fibre Channel network (or fabric).

We were skeptical at first of putting Exchange databases on a *networked storage* device, but we have come to see the advantages for many medium and large organizations. The ability to combine large numbers of disks into a very large volume and then allocate pieces of that large volume to the applications (such as Exchange Server) that need disk space can help reduce your storage costs and allow you to take advantage of technologies, such as snapshot backups and improved recoverability features. Further, because some of the storage is not physically connected to the server, a disaster that befalls the server hardware may not affect the storage system.

If you are a SAN user, you should ask your SAN people for two LUNs for each mailbox database. One LUN should be sized to hold a mailbox database's transaction log files and the other should be sized to hold that database file—that is, of course, for a Mailbox server role and does not account for the backup requirements. By putting one database and one transaction log on each LUN, you ensure that the granularity of snapshot solutions is per database. Dedicating LUNs to specific tasks helps you isolate I/O for those tasks; you should avoid placing the data for other applications on those LUNs that would affect I/O. This also allows you to configure the LUN characteristics to suit that data type. For example, RAID 1 would be more suited to transaction logs, whereas RAID 5 would be more suited to database files.

A lot has been done in Exchange Server 2013 to optimize storage for lower-cost disk solutions. A storage configuration that has no built-in redundancy (RAID-less) and mid-range SATA disks is a reality. Microsoft talks about JBOD (just a bunch of disks, a pretty self-explanatory terminology) configurations, providing a solution where storage capacity can dramatically increase while keeping storage costs very low. (A caveat in this design is that it depends entirely on a high-availability solution that uses a DAG for database replication. You should not consider using JBOD without it being part of a DAG solution.)

Those of you who think about disks and disk performance may be wondering about all of those LUNs being carved out of the same logical disk. If your SAN is improperly sized and does not have enough spindles, performance can be a problem. A properly engineered SAN solution should provide enough total I/O capacity for all the LUNs and the applications that will use those LUNs to function correctly.

One new feature in Exchange Server 2013 is the concept of multiple databases per disk. This feature means that Exchange servers that are members of a DAG do not require a dedicated LUN for the storage of each database. So now, several databases can be stored on the same LUN.

Managing Mailbox Databases

Although Exchange Server 2013 Cumulative Update 1 allows up to 50 mailbox databases, the examples here will be limited to a single mailbox database. As discussed earlier, some Exchange deployments may only require a single mailbox database, since the recommended maximum size is now 2 TB for mailbox databases that have multiple copies.

Viewing Mailbox Databases

You can view the current mailbox database for each server using the EAC, or you can use the Get-MailboxDatabase cmdlet to list all the mailbox databases stored on an Exchange Server, as shown here:

```
Get-MailboxDatabase -server MTLEXC01
```

Name	Server	Recovery	ReplicationType
Mailbox Database 1	MTLEXC01	False	None
Mailbox Database 2	MTLEXC01	False	None

A new parameter for the Get-MailboxDatabase cmdlet is -includePreExchange2013. This parameter instructs the cmdlet to return information for all mailbox databases in the organization, including those on servers that run previous versions of Exchange Server. For example, the following command will return all mailbox databases in a mixed organization:

```
Get-MailboxDatabase -IncludePreExchange2013
```

Of course, you can narrow the scope of this output to just a specific server or a specific storage group using the Where-Object cmdlet (well, just the Where alias). Here are some examples:

```
Get-MailboxDatabase -IncludePreExchange2013 | Where {$_.Server -eq "MTLEX03"}
Get-MailboxDatabase -IncludePreExchange2013| Where {$_.StorageGroupName -eq ↵
"Executives SG"}
```

Creating Mailbox Databases

To create a new mailbox database in EAC, on the left pane, select Servers. In the middle pane at the top, click Databases. Then click the plus sign to create a new database. This launches the New Database screen, shown in Figure 19.1. To create a new database, provide a name for the database and then enter the name of the server that will store the database; the path will automatically be completed and the database's EDB file will be put in the same path as the transaction logs. The paths can always be changed later to ensure that the database files are in a safe location.

FIGURE 19.1
Creating a new database using the Exchange Admin Center

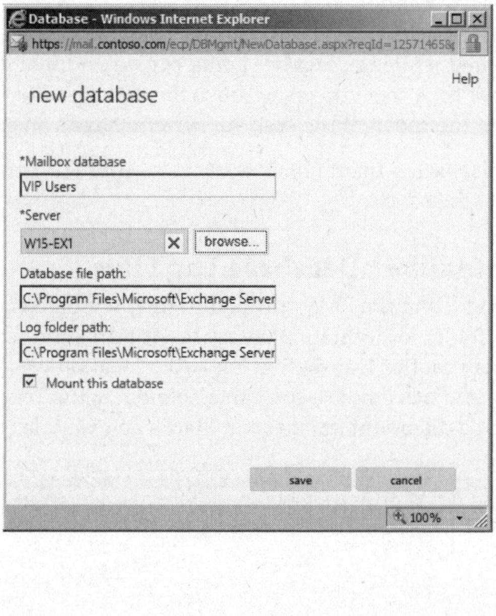

When creating a new database, name it something that is standardized and descriptive but unique in the entire organization. Note that a mailbox database can be activated and then mounted on any Mailbox server in your organization, given that it's part of the same DAG. This functionality introduced in Exchange Server 2010 created the requirement for unique mailbox database names within an organization. Also, making sure the filename matches the display name of the database will ensure that it's easier to manage. For example, a database name of MBX-Sales-Montreal-01 can adequately describe the mailboxes stored in the database, as well as include a numerical trailer to allow for growth in the Sales department.

Normally, you would modify the database file and transaction log paths and select a correct location for the mailbox database now, but we will show you how to move the mailbox database in the next section.

The EAC creates the configuration for the database and then mounts the database. This will initialize a new empty database file. The New-MailboxDatabase cmdlet is used in the command to create the database and the Mount-Database cmdlet is used in the command to mount the database. The resulting commands are as follows:

```
New-MailboxDatabase -Name 'Executives' -EdbFilePath
'F:\executiveslogs\Executives.edb'-Server MTLEX1.Contoso.com

Mount-Database -Identity Executives
```

Notice that when the database was created, the distinguished name of the database was not used. This is because we know that the database name is unique, therefore the location does not need to be specified. All databases are always created in the same location under the Exchange Server organization.

Moving the Mailbox Database EDB File

We created the database in the default path (see Figure 19.1) so we could illustrate the process of moving it. Using Exchange Management Shell, you can move the database by using the Move-DatabasePath cmdlet.

When you specify that you want to move the database files, you are warned that the database will be dismounted while the files are being copied and that it will be inaccessible.

The amount of time that it takes to move the database file will depend both on the size of the database file and the speed of the disk subsystem. Here's an example:

```
Move-DatabasePath -Identity Executives -EdbFilePath 'F:\ExecutivesDB\
Executives.edb'
```

Moving the Mailbox Database Log Files

The same method using the EMS outlined in the previous section can be used to move the Transaction log folder location for a database. Administrators of previous versions of Exchange Server remember that the Transaction log folder location was tied to a storage group. By using the Move-DatabasePath cmdlet, you can also modify the Transaction log folder path. You are also warned that a dismount must occur. Here's an example:

```
Move-DatabasePath -Identity Executives -LogFolderPath F:\Databases\Logs
```

As you have seen for the last two commands, the database must be taken offline to perform these actions. It is therefore better to plan ahead and implement the desired paths at the time of database creation to avoid downtime in the future or to plan to modify the database path before you move mailboxes to your database. The more mature a database is, the longer it is likely to be offline during a move, due to its size.

Properties of a Mailbox Database

Now let's look at some of the properties of a mailbox database. Figure 19.2 shows the General section of the mailbox database's properties dialog box. At the top is the display name of the mailbox database. From here, you can rename the database if you need to conform to a new database-naming standard. The path to the database is shown, but you cannot change the path here; you must use the Move-DatabasePath cmdlet.

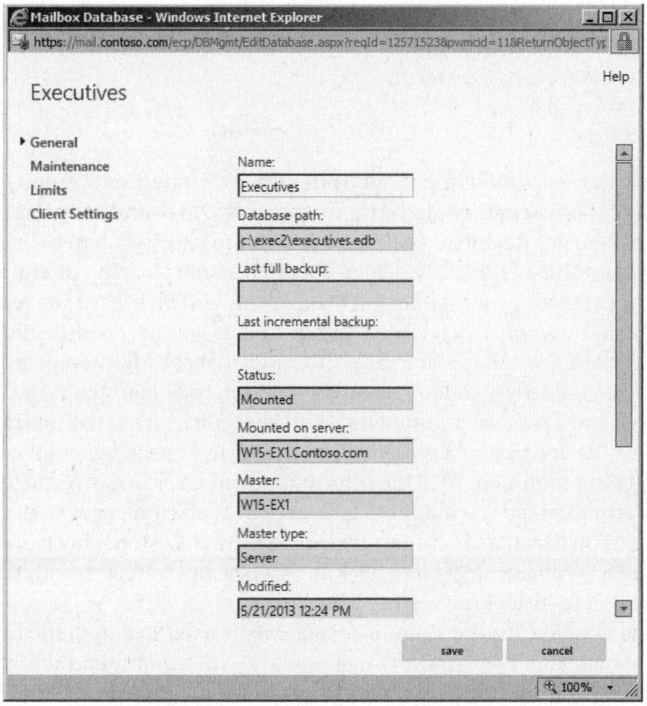

FIGURE 19.2
General section of the mailbox database's properties dialog box

A lot of dynamic state information resides on the General tab as well, including the following:

Last Full Backup   Indicates the last time a full or normal Exchange Server–aware VSS backup was performed. Transaction logs would have also been purged at that time.

Last Incremental Backup   Indicates the last time an incremental backup was run. This backup type will back up the database's transaction logs and then purge them.

Status   Indicates if the database is mounted or dismounted.

Master Indicates if the copy of the database is the master copy in a DAG deployment.

Master Type Indicates the type of master copy of the database that exists on the server.

Modified Shows the date and time the database properties in Active Directory were last changed.

This information (including the dynamic information) can be retrieved using the -Status option of the Get-MailboxDatabase cmdlet:

```
Get-MailboxDatabase MTL-EX1 -Status | FL Name,*last*,Mounted
```

```
Name                             : Executives
SnapshotLastFullBackup           : False
SnapshotLastIncrementalBackup    :
SnapshotLastDifferentialBackup   :
SnapshotLastCopyBackup           :
LastFullBackup                   : 6/22/2013 1:45:47 AM
LastIncrementalBackup            :
LastDifferentialBackup           :
LastCopyBackup                   :
Mounted                          : True
```

The next section in the mailbox database's properties screen is Maintenance. Here you find a potpourri of various configurations that relate to overall database file and content management.

The Journal Recipient option allows you to specify a journaling recipient for all mailboxes located on this mailbox database. If this is enabled, a copy of any message or delivery receipt sent or received by a mailbox on this system will be sent to the journal mailbox.

The Maintenance Schedule settings allows you to schedule online maintenance for this particular database. The Enable Background Database Maintenance (24 × 7 ESE Scanning) option, which is enabled by default, ensures that database maintenance occurs at runtime. If you disable this option, database maintenance will run only during the maintenance schedule.

The Do Not Mount This Database At Startup check box allows you to prevent the database from being mounted after the information store service is restarted. This might be useful when you want to make the mailbox databases available one or two at a time rather than all at once.

The This Database Can Be Overwritten By A Restore check box is used when you must restore a database file from a backup. An attempt to restore a database without this checked will result in a failure of the restore procedure.

The Enable Circular Logging check box is used to automatically purge transaction log files on the disk. In a DAG deployment scenario, we recommend that you enable this option if you are using mailbox database replication as a backup solution. For organizations that use VSS-aware backup solutions, circular logging should remain at its default setting of Disabled. In any case, for a stand-alone Mailbox server scenario, circular logging should not be enabled, since it will allow you to recover your mailbox database to the exact point of a total failure when combining with an older backup. When circular logging is not enabled, transaction log files will only be purged following a successful Full or Incremental backup or when the transaction logs have been successfully copied to another server in a DAG.

The next section on the properties screen is Limits. The Storage Limits section allows you to specify the amount of storage that the mailbox is allowed to have. Administrators used to previous versions of Exchange Server will be surprised to learn that newly created mailbox databases have defaults. *Everyone* will be surprised to see the actual default values:

◆ Issue Warning At (GB) is set to 1.9 GB. When a mailbox reaches this limit, users will receive an email message informing them that they have reached a limit on their mailbox and they should clean up some data in it.

◆ Prohibit Send At (GB) is set to 2 GB. Once the mailbox hits this limit, the user will be unable to send new messages or reply to existing messages. Both Outlook and Outlook Web App will inform users if they try to send a message while they are over this limit.

◆ Prohibit Send And Receive At (GB) is set to 2.3 GB. When a mailbox exceeds this limit, the mailbox is closed or disabled. Even though the user can access the mailbox, the server will not allow the user to send new messages or reply to existing messages. In addition, the mailbox will not receive any incoming mail from other Exchange Server users or from outside the organization.

Outlook has a neat new feature that will inform users of how close they are to their limit or if they are over their limit. Simply right-click the bottom bar in Outlook, and select Quota Information On. You can then see in the bottom-left corner the quota utilization, as shown in Figure 19.3.

An administrator can also determine mailbox utilization using the EAC by selecting a user from Recipients in the left pane and then clicking Mailbox Usage on the properties for that user, as shown in Figure 19.4.

The Warning Message Interval drop-down list determines the interval at which Exchange Server generates a warning message informing users that they are over their Issue Warning limit. By default, this is sent once daily at 1:00 a.m. local time. You can customize this to another time, but be careful. The Limits dialog box (shown in Figure 19.5) has a detail view option of either 1 hour or 15 minutes.

FIGURE 19.3
Quota limit in
Outlook

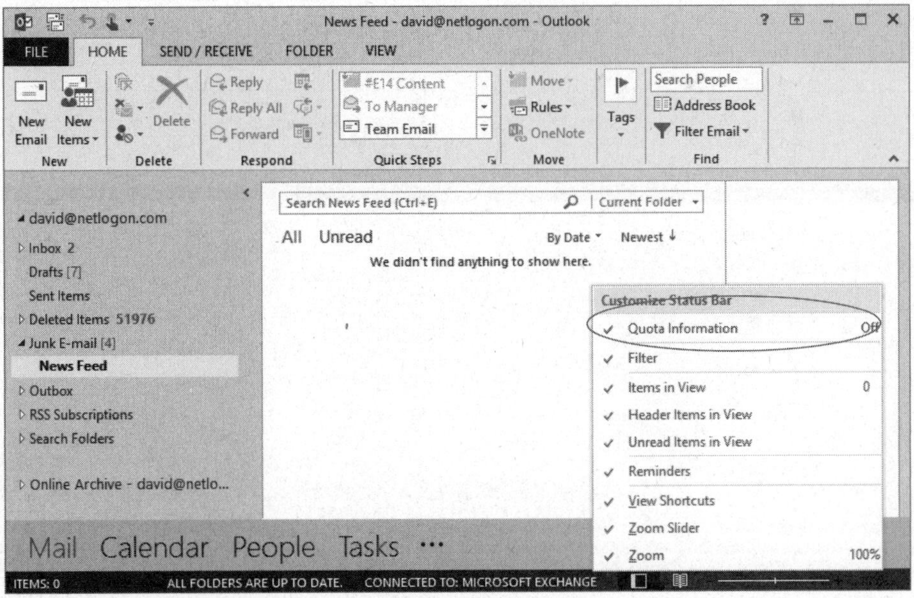

FIGURE 19.4
Quota limit in
EAC

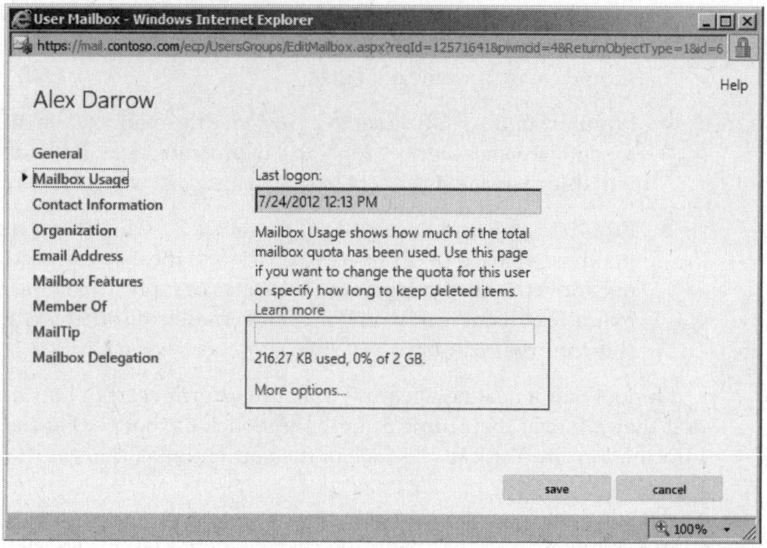

FIGURE 19.5
Using the Limits
dialog box

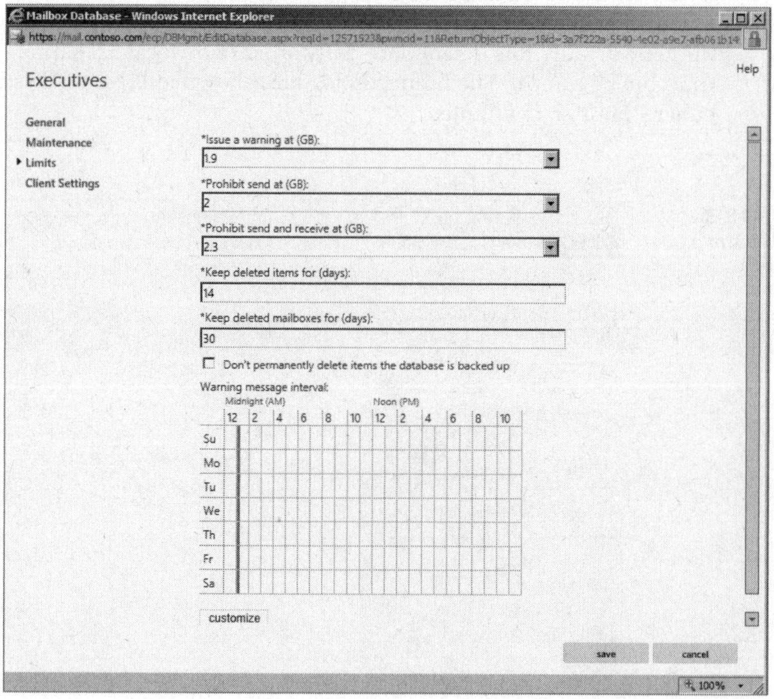

> **USE CAUTION WITH SCHEDULE BOXES**
>
> When using any schedule box that has both a 1-hour view and a 15-minute view, switch to the 15-minute view to set a schedule. If you select an entire hour, whatever process you are scheduling will run four times per hour. In this case, if you select an entire hour, a warning message will be sent to all mailboxes over their warning limit four times per hour. The users will *not* be amused.

The deletion settings of the Limits section allows you to configure how long the server will retain deleted items for this mailbox and how long the server will retain a mailbox once it is deleted. The Keep Deleted Items For (Days) option specifies how many days the Exchange server will keep items that have been deleted either from the Deleted Items folder or via a hard delete (Shift+Delete) from another folder. Once a message has been in the deleted items cache for longer than this period (14 days by default for Exchange Server 2013), the user will no longer be able to retrieve the message using the Recover Deleted Items feature.

The Keep Deleted Mailboxes For (Days) option specifies how long the mailbox database will keep a deleted mailbox before it is permanently purged. The default is 30 days, which is reasonable for most organizations. A mailbox that has been deleted but not purged can be recovered using EAC's Connect a Mailbox feature or via the Exchange Management Shell's `Connect-Mailbox` cmdlet.

The Don't Permanently Delete Items The Database Is Backed Up check box tells the server that it should not permanently purge an item or a mailbox until the mailbox database has been backed up. This ensures that a copy of the deleted item or deleted mailbox could be recovered from backup media if necessary.

The Client Settings section (shown in Figure 19.6) allows you to specify which offline address book (OAB) an Outlook client should download; this affects clients that work in offline mode or local cache mode. The default OAB contains the default global address list and is sufficient for most small- and medium-size businesses.

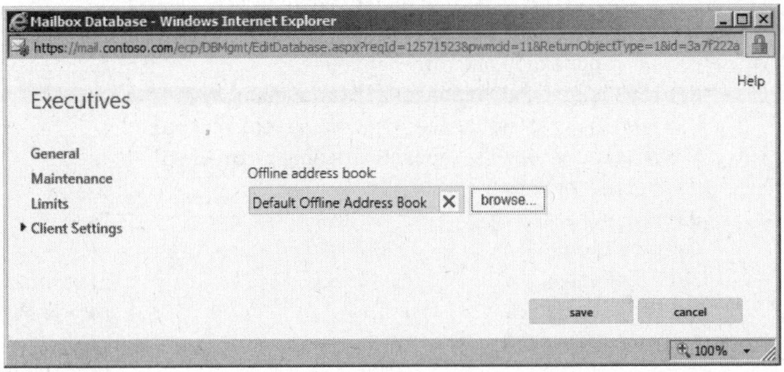

FIGURE 19.6
Client Settings properties of a mailbox database

The properties you have just examined using the graphical user interface can also be examined using the Get-MailboxDatabase cmdlet. The following example retrieves mailbox database properties and sends them to a formatted list:

```
Get-MailboxDatabase 'Executives' | FL

RunspaceId                                  : b47e6666-6396-4fb7-8ef8-
1811a0deaae7
JournalRecipient                            :
MailboxRetention                            : 30.00:00:00
OfflineAddressBook                          :
OriginalDatabase                            :
PublicFolderDatabase                        :
ProhibitSendReceiveQuota                    : 2.3 GB (2,469,396,480 bytes)
ProhibitSendQuota                           : 2 GB (2,147,483,648 bytes)
RecoverableItemsQuota                       : 30 GB (32,212,254,720 bytes)
RecoverableItemsWarningQuota                : 20 GB (21,474,836,480 bytes)
CalendarLoggingQuota                        : 6 GB (6,442,450,944 bytes)
IndexEnabled                                : True
IsExcludedFromProvisioning                  : False
IsExcludedFromInitialProvisioning           : False
IsSuspendedFromProvisioning                 : False
IsExcludedFromProvisioningBySpaceMonitoring : False
DumpsterStatistics                          :
DumpsterServersNotAvailable                 :
ReplicationType                             : None
AdminDisplayVersion                         : Version 15.0 (Build 466.6)
AdministrativeGroup                         : Exchange Administrative Group
(FYDIBOHF23SPDLT)
AllowFileRestore                            : False
BackgroundDatabaseMaintenance               : True
ReplayBackgroundDatabaseMaintenance         :
BackgroundDatabaseMaintenanceSerialization  :
BackgroundDatabaseMaintenanceDelay          :
ReplayBackgroundDatabaseMaintenanceDelay    :
MimimumBackgroundDatabaseMaintenanceInterval :
MaximumBackgroundDatabaseMaintenanceInterval :
BackupInProgress                            :
DatabaseCreated                             : True
Description                                 :
EdbFilePath                                 : c:\exec2\executives.edb
ExchangeLegacyDN                            : /o=First Organization/ou=Exchange
Administrative Group
                                              (FYDIBOHF23SPDLT)/
    cn=Configuration/cn=Servers/cn=W15-EX1/cn=Microsoft
                                              Private MDB
DatabaseCopies                              : {Executives\W15-EX1}
InvalidDatabaseCopies                       : {}
```

```
AllDatabaseCopies                    : {Executives\W15-EX1}
Servers                              : {W15-EX1}
ActivationPreference                 : {[W15-EX1, 1]}
ReplayLagTimes                       : {[W15-EX1, 00:00:00]}
TruncationLagTimes                   : {[W15-EX1, 00:00:00]}
RpcClientAccessServer                : W15-EX1.Contoso.com
MountedOnServer                      :
DeletedItemRetention                 : 14.00:00:00
SnapshotLastFullBackup               :
SnapshotLastIncrementalBackup        :
SnapshotLastDifferentialBackup       :
SnapshotLastCopyBackup               :
LastFullBackup                       :
LastIncrementalBackup                :
LastDifferentialBackup               :
LastCopyBackup                       :
DatabaseSize                         :
AvailableNewMailboxSpace             :
MaintenanceSchedule                  : {Sun.1:00 AM-Sun.5:00 AM, Mon.1:00
AM-Mon.5:00 AM, Tue.1:00 AM-Tue.5:00

                                       AM, Wed.1:00 AM-Wed.5:00 AM,

Thu.1:00 AM-Thu.5:00 AM, Fri.1:00
                                       AM-Fri.5:00 AM, Sat.1:00 AM-

Sat.5:00 AM}
MountAtStartup                       : True
Mounted                              :
Organization                         : First Organization
QuotaNotificationSchedule            : {Sun.1:00 AM-Sun.1:15 AM, Mon.1:00
AM-Mon.1:15 AM, Tue.1:00 AM-Tue.1:15

                                       AM, Wed.1:00 AM-Wed.1:15 AM,

Thu.1:00 AM-Thu.1:15 AM, Fri.1:00
                                       AM-Fri.1:15 AM, Sat.1:00 AM-

Sat.1:15 AM}
Recovery                             : False
RetainDeletedItemsUntilBackup        : False
Server                               : W15-EX1
MasterServerOrAvailabilityGroup      : W15-EX1
WorkerProcessId                      :
AutoDagExcludeFromMonitoring         : False
AutoDatabaseMountDial                : GoodAvailability
MasterType                           : Server
ServerName                           : W15-EX1
IssueWarningQuota                    : 1.899 GB (2,039,480,320 bytes)
EventHistoryRetentionPeriod          : 7.00:00:00
Name                                 : Executives
LogFolderPath                        : c:\exec2
TemporaryDataFolderPath              :
```

```
CircularLoggingEnabled                  : False
LogFilePrefix                           : E04
LogFileSize                             : 1024
LogBuffers                              :
MaximumOpenTables                       :
MaximumTemporaryTables                  :
MaximumCursors                          :
MaximumSessions                         :
MaximumVersionStorePages                :
PreferredVersionStorePages              :
DatabaseExtensionSize                   :
LogCheckpointDepth                      :
ReplayCheckpointDepth                   :
CachedClosedTables                      :
CachePriority                           :
ReplayCachePriority                     :
MaximumPreReadPages                     :
MaximumReplayPreReadPages               :
DataMoveReplicationConstraint           : None
IsMailboxDatabase                       : True
IsPublicFolderDatabase                  : False
AdminDisplayName                        : Executives
ExchangeVersion                         : 0.10 (14.0.100.0)
DistinguishedName                       : CN=Executives,CN=Databases,CN=Exch
  ange Administrative Group

                                          (FYDIBOHF23SPDLT),CN=Administrati

  ve Groups,CN=First

                                          Organization,CN=Microsoft
                                          Exchange,CN=Services,CN=Configurat
  ion,DC=Contoso,DC=com
Identity                                : Executives
Guid                                    : 3a7f222a-5540-4e02-a9e7-
afb061b149a6
ObjectCategory                          : Contoso.com/Configuration/Schema/
  ms-Exch-Private-MDB
ObjectClass                             : {top, msExchMDB, msExchPrivateMDB}
WhenChanged                             : 5/21/2013 12:24:11 PM
WhenCreated                             : 5/21/2013 12:15:29 PM
WhenChangedUTC                          : 5/21/2013 7:24:11 PM
WhenCreatedUTC                          : 5/21/2013 7:15:29 PM
OrganizationId                          :
OriginatingServer                       : w15-dc.Contoso.com
IsValid                                 : True
ObjectState                             : Changed
```

Some of these properties can be changed through the EMS using the Set-MailboxDatabase cmdlet. For example, to change the Prohibit Send At (KB) quota to 100 MB, you would type this:

```
Set-MailboxDatabase 'Executives' -ProhibitSendQuota:100MB
```

Not all of the properties that you see in the output of the Get-MailboxDatabase cmdlet can be changed. Some of them are system properties. The mailbox database location must be changed using the Move-MailboxDatabase cmdlet.

The Bottom Line

Identify the core components of Exchange Server database storage.   The ability to identify the components of your Exchange servers that provide storage functionality will allow you to properly plan and troubleshoot storage.

> **Master It**   You plan to have redundancy for Mailbox servers. You need to establish how redundancy for databases has changed since Exchange Server 2003. What major change should you identify?

Plan for disk storage requirements for Exchange Server databases.   A major paradigm shift has occurred in the Exchange Server messaging world. Up to now, administrators have been focused on their IOPS and the capacity of their disks to handle the client requests. Today, administrators have to rethink the way they plan for server storage, though they still need to think about IOPS and capacity, new storage capabilities, and limits. Calculate your IOPS requirements based on the number and profiles of your users. By using Microsoft's user profile guidelines, you can reliably predict your IOPS requirements.

> **Master It**   When planning for storage requirements for Exchange, you must take many factors into consideration. Many of them have to do with storage type, capacity, load, and redundancy. However, many administrators don't always plan for the number of databases that need be created and opt for a reactionary approach to mailbox database creation.

Configure Exchange Server Mailbox servers with the appropriate storage solution.   Storage groups no longer exist in Exchange Server 2013 and Exchange Server 2010. All storage group configuration options have been moved to the mailbox database objects.

> **Master It**   You need to prepare your junior administrator to manage the properties of your mailbox databases. Though most administrators have experience managing Exchange Server, most of their experience was attained in previous versions of Exchange Server. What are some of the issues you want to be aware of when managing mailbox databases?

Chapter 20

Creating and Managing Database Availability Groups

Messaging services for most organizations are deemed business-critical and need to be online with minimal to no data loss during a variety of failure scenarios. Organizations are also looking for more flexibility in managing a Mailbox server during business hours while minimizing the impact on end users. To assist organizations with these requirements, Exchange Server 2007 and later include new solutions for high availability. Through a process called continuous replication, a mailbox database can be copied to one or more Mailbox servers and the database is kept up to date through transaction log shipping and replay into the passive copy (or copies) of the database. In Exchange Server 2010 this continuous-replication process matured as database availability groups (DAGs).

You add Mailbox servers into the DAG as members, and then you can determine which databases will be replicated to which member servers. The value here is simple. If the Mailbox server hosting the active database were to fail or if maintenance is going to be performed on a Mailbox server, a copy of that mailbox database can be activated on a different Mailbox server with minimal to no interruption of mailbox services to the end users.

Long before the DAG is created and Mailbox servers are added, a design is created laying out the configuration of the DAG. The configuration should be built around business and technical requirements while taking into consideration the limitations of the existing environment. For many organizations, the business and technical requirements drive the configuration of the DAG to be stretched across multiple datacenters, which requires additional implementation and management considerations.

A single misstep in the configuration of a component can have catastrophic effects, ranging from prolonged outages to loss of email data. This chapter covers the essential components of a DAG and how they operate together.

In this chapter you will learn to:

◆ Understand database replication

◆ Manage a database availability group

◆ Understand Active Manager

◆ Understand site resiliency for Exchange Server 2013

Understanding Database Replication in Exchange Server 2013

In Exchange Server 2007, Microsoft introduced continuous replication. The concept of continuous replication was enhanced in Exchange Server 2010 with the introduction of a database availability group. Exchange Server 2013 uses the DAG as the boundary to replicate database content between Mailbox servers. By default, Mailbox servers that are members of a DAG and have copies of the same mailbox database use continuous replication, which is performed by the Microsoft Exchange Replication Service, to seed or reseed a mailbox database copy and to replicate transaction logs between the active mailbox copy and the passive mailbox copies.

When an active mailbox database is added to a Mailbox server that is a member of a database availability group, continuous replication kicks in. The Mailbox server that was added as a passive database copy opens a TCP connection to the Mailbox server hosting the active database copy, and the mailbox database is seeded from the source server to the target server. Once the mailbox database has been seeded, continuous replication uses the same procedure to replicate transaction log information between the source and the target Mailbox servers.

The TCP port used to connect the target and source replication services can be changed. If Windows Firewall is enabled on the Mailbox server, you must add the updated replication port in the Windows Firewall settings. The default port used is TCP 64327; the replication port can be changed by running this command:

```
Set-DatabaseAvailabilityGroup -Identity (name of DAG) -ReplicationPort (new
replication port)
```

As part of the replication process in Exchange Server 2013, Mailbox servers that are members of the same DAG replicate content indexing. Each mailbox database maintains a separate content index and the content index is replicated across all the Mailbox servers that hold a copy of the same mailbox database. The health of the content index, much like the health of a mailbox database itself, is critical to monitor. For example, if the health of the content index were to reach a failed state on the Mailbox server holding the active database copy, the Mailbox server may move the mailbox database to another server that has a healthy copy of the content index database.

The main purpose of the content index is to maintain a catalog of key components of email items so end-user searches or eDiscovery searches can be performed quickly. A major change in Exchange Server 2013 is that Microsoft has integrated the FAST search engine for better indexing and search performance.

File Mode vs. Block Mode

Before we dig into file mode and block mode, you need to understand how transactions are stored on a Mailbox server. As you know by now, Exchange Server stores transaction log files and the corresponding mailbox database on disk. The contents in the transaction log files are played into the mailbox database. We will not cover this process in great detail. What is important to understand for this chapter is how content is written to a transaction log. Every database, no matter if it is the active copy or the passive copy, stores transactions in memory, which is called the log buffer. When the log buffer is flushed from memory, it is written to a transaction log.

Now that you know where transactions are stored on a Mailbox server, let's take a look at the two types of continuous replication. *File mode* is used to replicate closed transaction logs to all

Mailbox servers that hold a passive mailbox database copy. Since transaction log files are only 1 MB in Exchange Server 2013, if replication falls behind by a couple logs and a failure occurs, the impact of the data loss will be minimal. In Exchange Server 2007 and the RTM version of Exchange Server 2010, the only way to replicate database changes between Mailbox servers that held a database replica was using file mode.

Microsoft wanted to improve how content was replicated between mailbox copies and introduced *block mode* in Exchange Server 2010 SP1. This feature has been carried over to Exchange Server 2013. As mentioned earlier, file mode must be up to date before block mode is used. As updates are written to the log buffer of the active copy, the log buffer content is sent to the log buffer of all passive copies. When the log buffer is full, each database copy commits the log buffer content from memory to disk in the form of a transaction log file. By replicating changes in the log buffer, the passive copies have the latest changes performed against a mailbox database. To limit the amount of data loss during an unexpected failure of the active database copy, you can use block mode replication when file mode replication is up to date.

To determine whether a passive copy is using block mode or file mode, you can use the Get-Counter cmdlet. The value 1 indicates the Mailbox server holding a passive copy is using block mode and the value 0 indicates the Mailbox server holding a passive copy is using file mode.

```
Get-Counter -ComputerName all-3 -Counter ↵
 "\MSExchange Replication(*)\Continuous replication - block mode Active"


Timestamp                 CounterSamples
---------                 --------------
3/11/2013 4:11:07 PM      \\all-3\\msexchange replication(db2)\continuous
replication - block mode active : 1



Get-Counter -ComputerName all-2 -Counter ↵
 "\MSExchange Replication(*)\Continuous replication - block mode Active"


Timestamp                 CounterSamples
---------                 --------------
3/11/2013 4:22:21 PM      \\all-2\\msexchange replication(db3)\continuous
replication - block mode active : 0
```

The Anatomy of a Database Availability Group

A DAG is a grouping of up 16 Mailbox servers that uses components of Windows Failover Clustering and continuous replication to provide a high-availability solution for mailbox databases. Once a DAG is formed and Mailbox servers are added as members, those member Mailbox servers can be assigned passive copies of mailbox databases to provide fault tolerance during a datacenter outage, network interruption, storage subsystem failure, Mailbox server failure, database failure, or a component failure of the Mailbox server, hence allowing for higher levels of availability.

You can create a DAG using the EAC or EMS. Creating a DAG in the EAC or EMS is a straightforward process and can be performed with minimal effort. Before creating a DAG, however, let's discuss the Microsoft requirements and recommendations that a DAG configuration should adhere to:

◆ Mailbox servers that are members of the same DAG must be in the same domain.

◆ Microsoft doesn't support adding a Mailbox server to a DAG that is installed on domain controllers. (Note that Exchange Server roles should not be installed on domain controllers.)

◆ The DAG name must be 15 characters or fewer.

◆ You can add a mix of Mailbox servers running Exchange Server 2013 Standard and Exchange Server 2013 Enterprise to the same DAG.

◆ At least one network adapter on each Mailbox server must be able to communicate to all other DAG members.

◆ All DAG members should have the same number of network adapters.

◆ If more than one adapter is used on a Mailbox server, each network adapter must be on a different network subnet.

◆ The round-trip latency between DAG members should be no more than 500 milliseconds.

◆ A Mailbox server that is a member of a DAG should not be used as the file share witness.

Additionally, because Windows Failover Clustering components will be used for Mailbox servers that are a member of a DAG, a Mailbox server must be installed on one of these operating systems:

◆ Windows Server 2008 Enterprise

◆ Windows Server 2008 Datacenter

◆ Windows 2012 Standard

◆ Windows 2012 Datacenter

Before adding Mailbox servers to a DAG, ensure that all Mailbox servers are running the same version of Windows. A Mailbox server running Windows 2008 R2 cannot be added to a DAG that already has a Mailbox server running Windows 2012. If the DAG members are running Windows Server 2012, the Cluster Name Object (CNO) must be pre-staged before adding members to the DAG. To pre-stage a CNO use the "Pre-Stage the Cluster Name Object for a Database Availability Group" topic in the help file.

Now that you've met all the prerequisites and created a DAG, let's review the steps performed when a Mailbox server is added to the DAG and it is the first Mailbox server added to the DAG. The following changes occur:

◆ Windows Failover Clustering is installed on the Mailbox server.

◆ The CNO object is created in Active Directory (if the CNO object wasn't already pre-staged).

◆ An A record is created in DNS with the IP address and the name of the DAG.

◆ The DAG AD object is updated with the Mailbox server that was added to the DAG.

- Any mailbox databases mounted on the Mailbox server added to the DAG are updated in the cluster database.

- A failover cluster is created using the DAG name.

Once a DAG has been populated with a Mailbox server, any additional Mailbox servers that are added to the DAG run through the following changes:

- Windows Failover Clustering services are installed on the Mailbox server.

- The DAG Active Directory object is updated with the Mailbox server that was added to the DAG.

- Any mailbox databases mounted on the Mailbox server added to the DAG are updated in the cluster database.

- The Mailbox server is added as a node in the cluster.

- The quorum model of the DAG automatically changes (discussed further in a moment).

After creating the DAG and adding Mailbox servers to it, the availability of the DAG is based on maintaining quorum. Quorum is maintained when a majority of the Mailbox servers are online. A simple formula of N/2+1 can be used to determine how many voting servers are needed to maintain quorum. For example, if you have a seven-node DAG, four voters are needed to maintain quorum (7 / 2 = 3.5; always round down, thus 3 + 1 = 4). Using this example, a DAG that contained seven Mailbox servers (remember all Mailbox servers that are members of a DAG are also members of the same cluster) could sustain a loss of three Mailbox servers. If another Mailbox server were to go offline, quorum would be lost and the cluster would be marked as offline, and all the databases would be dismounted mailbox databases.

As Mailbox servers are added and removed as members of a DAG, the cluster's quorum model changes. When an even number of mailbox servers are members of a DAG, the quorum model is set to A Node and File Share Majority. When an odd number of Mailbox servers are members of a DAG, the quorum model is set to A Node Majority. The main difference between the two models is that the A Node and File Share Majority model uses a witness server as a tiebreaker when quorum is in question.

Dynamic Quorum with Windows Server 2012

Dynamic quorum is a new feature, enabled by default, with Windows Server 2012. Dynamic quorum enables the cluster to dynamically manage the number of votes needed to maintain cluster services. This is done by adjusting the number of votes needed to maintain quorum after a node fails. This has the potential to make Exchange Server more resilient to multiple node failures, even maintaining the cluster with one final "last-man-standing" node.

Let's return to our earlier example. If three of the seven Mailbox servers were to fail, the cluster would adjust the number of votes needed to maintain quorum to three. If anther server were to fail, the cluster would adjust the number of votes needed to maintain quorum.

It's important to keep in mind that this is a newer feature and does have some limitations. For example, it's required that servers fail sequentially, not all at once. Sequential failures allow the cluster to readjust as opposed to simultaneous failures of a majority of voting members.

To view the settings of dynamic quorum run the following command:

```
cluster node All-1 /prop

Listing properties for 'All-1':

T  Node                 Name                              Value
-- -------------------- --------------------------------- --------------------
DR All-1                DynamicWeight                     1 (0x1)
```

HEARTBEATS

After the server has been added to a DAG, the cluster monitors the availability of the Mailbox server by issuing a heartbeat request. A cluster heartbeat is a network communication sent between the nodes within a cluster to validate that the cluster service is online and responding. It's like a ball being bounced back and forth. If you throw the ball and it doesn't come back, you assume there is a problem. In a similar line of reasoning, if the heartbeat request goes unanswered after five requests, the node representing the Mailbox server in the cluster is marked as offline. To view the heartbeat threshold, run this command from a DAG member:

```
Cluster /prop
Listing properties for 'DAG-2':

T   Cluster             Name                              Value
--  --------            ------                            ------
...
D   DAG-2               CrossSubnetDelay                  1000 (0x3e8)
D   DAG-2               CrossSubnetThreshold              5 (0x5)
...
D   DAG-2               SameSubnetDelay                   1000 (0x3e8)
D   DAG-2               SameSubnetThreshold               5 (0x5)
```

File Share Witness

A witness server is a domain-joined computer that is not part of a DAG and can be used to maintain quorum when a DAG contains an even number of Mailbox servers. As discussed earlier in this chapter, a DAG with an even number of Mailbox servers uses the A Node and File Share Majority quorum model. This model uses the witness server as a tiebreaker when half the Mailbox servers are either offline or can no longer communicate to each other. The witness server per se doesn't get a vote for the cluster quorum; what happens is that a Mailbox server that has placed a lock on the witness.log file has a weighted vote. In scenarios where a DAG is stretched across two datacenters and an even number of Mailbox servers are located at each datacenter, the location of the witness server will determine which datacenter will hold quorum if communication between the two datacenters were to fail. For example, a DAG is stretched across two datacenters and each datacenter houses four Mailbox servers (for a total of eight members of the DAG). The quorum formula would require five voters to maintain quorum (8 / 2 + 1 = 5). The datacenter that can lock the witness.log file will get an "extra" vote and be able to grab the cluster services.

Even though the witness server is not used to maintain quorum when a DAG contains an odd number of Mailbox servers, the witness server is still configured within the DAG. DAG members can fluctuate due to an administrator adding or removing Mailbox servers from the DAG. Once the number of DAG members changes from even to odd or odd to even, the DAG cluster automatically switches the quorum model. The Windows Failover Cluster MMC can be used to monitor the status of the file share witness, as shown in Figure 20.1.

FIGURE 20.1

Witness server status from the Windows Failover Cluster MMC

▲ Cluster Core Resources		
Name		Status
Default		
📄 File Share Witness (\\cas-1.jennchris.com\DAG-2.jennchris.com) (\\cas-1.jennchris.com\DAG-2.jennchris.com)	◉	Online

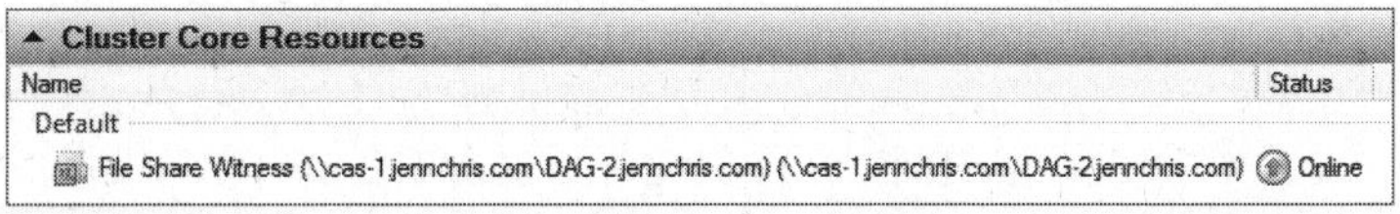

Creating a Database Availability Group Using the EAC

Prior to the establishment of your DAG and the inclusion of member servers, you want to have a few design and deployment concepts and configurations in mind. You obviously want to know how many Mailbox servers you will be adding to your DAG and what kind of design for resiliency you are planning. For the servers you plan on making members of the DAG, it would be in your best interest to ensure they have more than one network adapter (although having just one *is* supported). You want to configure the adapters properly to ensure both replication and MAPI traffic stay organized. To learn more about this see the section, "Managing a DAG Network."

In the Exchange Admin Center (EAC) you can create, edit, or remove a DAG, add a new DAG network, or manage DAG membership. You need to perform several steps on a Mailbox server before adding a server as a DAG member. One of the most important tasks is configuring the network cards on each Mailbox server. For more information on managing network cards please see the "Managing a DAG Network" section. To create a DAG from the EAC, use the following steps:

1. On your client computer, open Internet Explorer and browse to the Exchange Admin Center URL. This URL should be the name of your Client Access server with /ECP appended to the end. If you don't know the URL for the EAC, you can use the Outlook Web App URL and specify /ECP instead of /owa at the end of the URL. For example, for Contoso, the EAC URL might be `https://mail.contoso.com/ECP`.

ECP vs. EAC

ECP, used in the URL in step 1 here, stands for Exchange Control Panel and is a throwback to the terminology used for the web-based administrative options in Exchange Server 2010, which have been renamed Exchange Admin Center, or EAC.

---

2. When prompted with the authentication page, type in your name and password and log in.

3. In the Feature pane, on the left column of the EAC, select Servers.

4. In the toolbar across the top of the EAC, select the Database Availability Groups tab. Any existing DAGs will be listed below.

5. Click the Add (+) button to create a new DAG. Remember, if the DAG will host servers running Windows Server 2012, you must pre-stage the DAG computer.

6. In the new database availability group windows, enter the name of the DAG in the Database Availability Group Name text box. This should match the CNO you pre-staged earlier.

7. You can leave the Witness Server and Witness Directory fields blank if there is a server running just the CAS role in the same AD site as the first Mailbox server that is added to the DAG. If you want to specify a server, enter the server name in the Witness Server text box and the file path in the Witness Directory text box, as displayed in Figure 20.2.

8. In the Database Availability Group IP Addresses text box, enter the IP address or addresses that will be associated with the DAG. If the text box is left blank, the DAG will use DHCP.

9. Click Save when you've added all required details.

FIGURE 20.2
Creating a new
DAG in the EAC

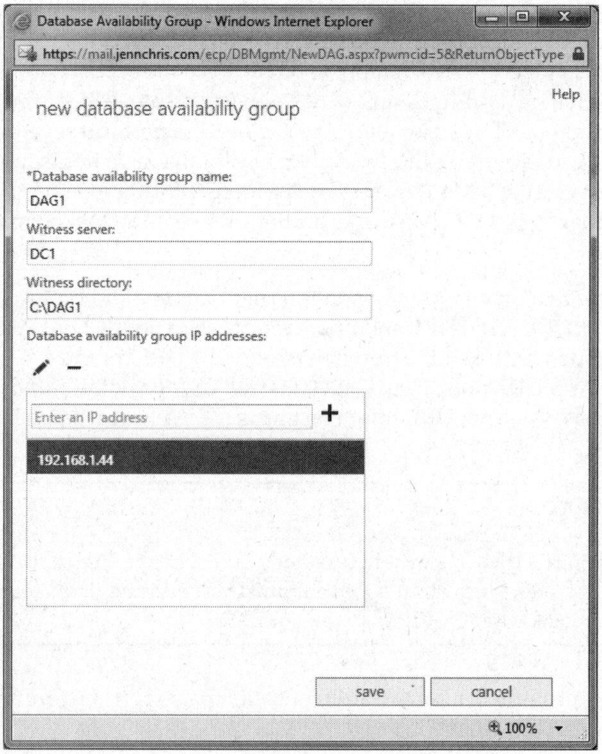

10. After the DAG has been created, you can add the first Mailbox server to the DAG by highlighting the DAG and selecting the Manage DAG Membership icon (the one with the small gear in front of the rectangle).

11. In the Manage Database Availability Group Membership window, click the Add button.

12. Highlight the Mailbox server that will be added to the DAG and click the Add (+) button. You will see servers available to add to the DAG. You can select multiple servers; however, it's better to add them one at a time to ensure a smoother process.

13. Once you add a Mailbox server, click the Save button.

Creating a Database Availability Group Using EMS

The `New-DatabaseAvailabilityGroup` cmdlet is used to create a new DAG in EMS. The same options that are available in the EAC are available when creating a new DAG in the EMS. The following command creates a new DAG using DC1 as the witness server:

```
New-DatabaseAvailabilityGroup -Name DAG1 -WitnessServer DC1 ↵
 -WitnessDirectory C:\DAG1 -DatabaseAvailabilityGroupIpAddresses 192.168.1.44
```

Once the DAG has been created, Mailbox servers can be added to the DAG using the `Add-DatabaseAvailabilityGroupServer` cmdlet:

```
Add-DatabaseAvailabilityGroupServer -Identity DAG1 -MailboxServer MBX-1
```

Managing a Database Availability Group

Once you've created a DAG and added Mailbox servers to it, you can modify multiple settings within the DAG and those Mailbox servers to meet the business and technical requirements of your organization. Covering all the settings that can be modified within a DAG falls outside the scope of this book. Instead, we'll concentrate on some of the common changes made after a DAG has been formed and some of the new DAG features introduced in Exchange Server 2013.

Managing a DAG in EMS

Using the Exchange Management Shell, you can create, edit, or remove a DAG, modify DAG-specific changes on a Mailbox server or mailbox database, and modify the state a of DAG member. For a full list of the parameters for each of the following cmdlets, please reference the Exchange Server 2013 Help file.

Set-DatabaseAvailabilityGroup   Modifies the settings of an existing DAG. In the example here, DC2 has been added as the alternate file share witness for DAG-2:

```
Set-DatabaseAvailabilityGroup -Identity DAG-2 -AlternateWitnessDirectory C:\
DAGFileShareWitnesses\DC2.jennchris.com -AlternateWitnessServer DC2
```

Remove-DatabaseAvailabilityGroup   Removes the DAG after all Mailbox servers have been removed from a DAG. The following example removes DAG-2 from the organization:

```
Remove-DatabaseAvailabilityGroup DAG-2
```

Set-MailboxServer   Helps manage the configuration of Mailbox servers in a DAG. The following example sets the maximum number of active mailbox databases on All-1 to 50:

```
Set-MailboxServer All-1 -MaximumActiveDatabases 50
```

Set-MailboxDatabase   Changes the mailbox database settings for databases that are part of a DAG. In the following example, a single database copy alert is turned off for DB4:

```
Set-MailboxDatabase DB4 -AutoDagExcludeFromMonitoring $False
```

Add-DatabaseAvailabilityGroupServer   Adds Mailbox servers to a DAG. The following command adds All-2 to DAG-2 and bypasses the validation of the DAG quorum model and the health check for the witness server:

```
Add-DatabaseAvailabilityGroupServer -Identity DAG-2
 -MailboxServer All-2 -SkipDagValidation
```

Remove-DatabaseAvailabilityGroupServer   To remove a Mailbox server from a DAG use this cmdlet. All-2 will be removed from DAG-2 when this command completes:

```
Remove-DatabaseAvailabilityGroupServer DAG-2 -MailboxServer All-2
```

Stop-DatabaseAvailabilityGroup   Marks a Mailbox server, that is a member of a DAG, as failed so no Exchange Server resources can be activated on this server. Mailbox server All-2 is offline. Using the ConfigurationOnly switch, All-2 can be marked as failed even though the server is offline:

```
Stop-DatabaseAvailabilityGroup DAG-2 -MailboxServer All-2
        -ConfigurationOnly
```

Restore-DatabaseAvailabilityGroup   Performs a datacenter switchover process when quorum is lost. The following command starts the restore of DAG services in the Charlotte AD site:

```
Restore-DatabaseAvailabilityGroup DAG-2
 -ActiveDirectorySite Charlotte
```

Start-DatabaseAvailabilityGroup   Reinstates a DAG member to the DAG. Here Mailbox server All-2 is reinstated in DAG-2:

```
Start-DatabaseAvailabilityGroup DAG-2 -MailboxServer All-2
```

Multiple Databases per Volume

Managing and planning for a DAG goes beyond configuring parameters in EAC and EMS. Part of managing and planning a DAG is determining the placement of databases on physical spindles. Exchange Server 2010 did not support having multiple databases on the same physical disk. This limitation was a big drawback for organizations that were planning a Just a Bunch Of Disks (JBOD) storage solution (see Figure 20.3).

There are two problems that jump out in Figure 20.3. The first is the size of the mailbox; 200 GB is less than half of the disk size, 500 GB, resulting in an organization wasting available storage. In this example, 300 GB are left over. Second, each Mailbox server has a dedicated disk for a passive copy. The IOPS load is unevenly dispersed between the physical disks, again wasting the resources of the physical disk. A JBOD storage solution for a DAG in Exchange Server 2010 left a lot to be desired.

Fast-forward to Exchange Server 2013: Microsoft has nipped this problem by now supporting multiple database copies on the same physical disk (passive and active). Now a JBOD deployment is a more appealing storage solution because an organization can squeeze the resources out of each physical disk. Before running to your storage team demanding they purchase a JBOD storage solution, you must take into account considerations for the number of database copies and database placement of those copies. A good rule of thumb to follow is the number of copies of each database should be equal to the number of database copies per physical disk. This type of design is referred to as symmetric design. Take the example in Figure 20.4. All three Mailbox servers host three database copies on drive E:\ and each database has three copies.

FIGURE 20.3
Exchange Server
2010 JBOD
configuration

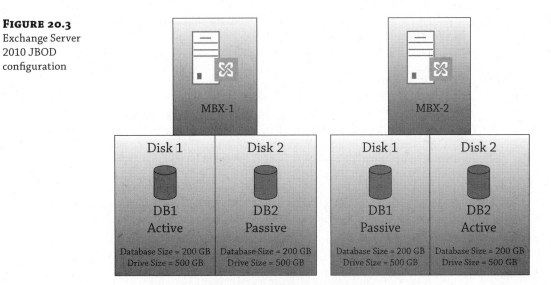

FIGURE 20.4
Mailbox databases
symmetrically
placed between
the Mailbox
servers

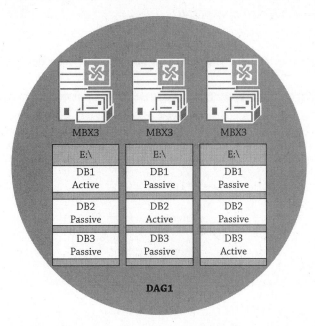

Microsoft has made the following recommendations for deploying multiple databases on the same physical disk:

◆ There should be a single logical disk partition per physical disk.

◆ The number of copies of each database should be equal to the number of database copies per physical disk.

◆ The activation preference of each database copy should be balanced between the Mailbox servers in the DAG.

Managing a DAG Network

Creating a DAG and adding the first Mailbox server to it establishes a DAG network. A DAG network consists of one or more subnets that are used for continuous replication and client connectivity (MAPI network). If a Mailbox server with a single network adapter is added to the DAG, the subnet of that network adapter is used for both client connectivity and continuous replication. The Microsoft preferred deployment is to add Mailbox servers to a DAG that have multiple network adapters. Once a Mailbox server with multiple network adapters is added to the DAG, one or more network adapters can be used for continuous replication and only one network adapter can be used for client connectivity.

Before adding a Mailbox server to a DAG, it is important to set up the network interface cards (NIC) on a Mailbox server. As stated previously, only one NIC can be used for client communication. This NIC is often referred as the MAPI NIC. Any other NIC can be used for replication. These NICs are often referred to as the replication NICs. The MAPI NIC should have the following configuration:

◆ Use the default gateway.

◆ Enable File and Printer Sharing for Microsoft Networks.

◆ Enable Client for Microsoft Networks.

◆ Register in DNS.

◆ Use the first adapter listed in the network binding order (see Figure 20.5).

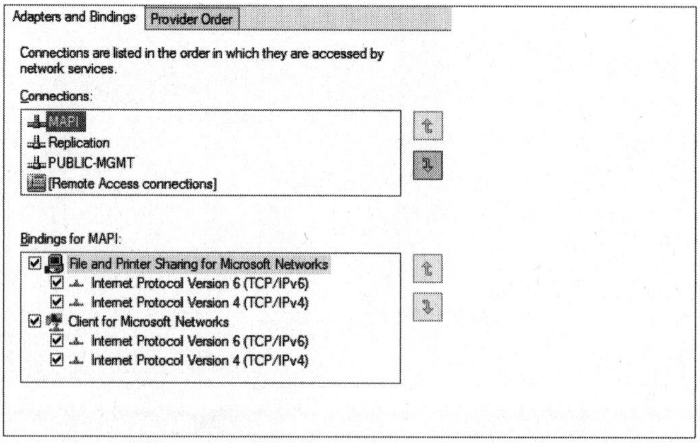

FIGURE 20.5
The network binding order that should be in place before adding a Mailbox server to a DAG

The network binding order is found under Advanced Settings for your network adapter on the Adapters and Bindings tab, and this helps determine the order accessed by network services.

The replication NICs should have the following configuration:

◆ Use a subnet separate from the MAPI network.

◆ Do not use the default gateway.

◆ Disabled File and Print Sharing for Microsoft Networks.

◆ Disabled Client for Microsoft Networks.

◆ Do not register in DNS.

AUTOMATIC DAG NETWORK MANAGEMENT

A new feature in Exchange Server 2013 is automatic management of DAG networks by the system; this feature is enabled by default. When the system manages DAG networks, the network adapters of the Mailbox servers that are added to the DAG are checked, and based on the configuration of each network adapter, the system determines if the network adapter can be used for client connectivity, replication, or both.

There are two types of DAG networks: a single subnet and a multi-subnet. When all members of the DAG are in the same subnet, this normally means the DAG is not stretched across multiple datacenters, and the DAG is considered a single subnet. When members of the DAG are in different subnets, this normally means the DAG is stretched across two or more datacenters, and the DAG is considered a multi-subnet.

When a multi-subnet DAG is configured and the automatic management of DAG networks is enabled, the system pairs the proper network subnets for client connectivity and continuous replication based on the configuration of the network adapters.

One of the downsides of having automatic DAG network configuration enabled is that the DAG network settings—including managing the DAG network settings through the EAC—are disabled. Figure 20.6 shows the information available when automatic DAG network configuration is enabled versus when it's disabled (giving you more manual options).

FIGURE 20.6
DAG network settings in the EAC when automatic DAG network configuration is enabled (left) and disabled (right)

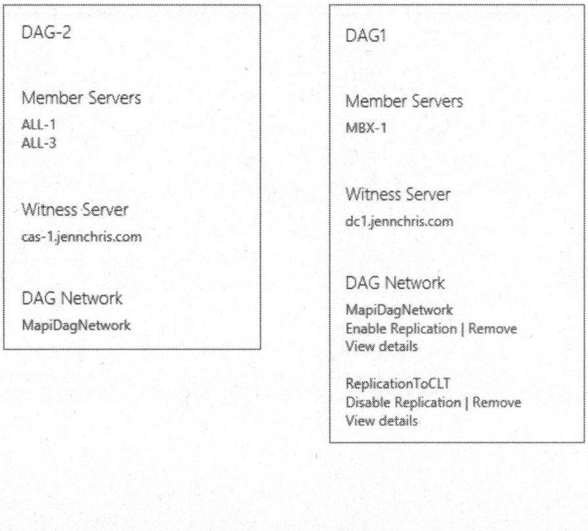

DAG-2

Member Servers
ALL-1
ALL-3

Witness Server
cas-1.jennchris.com

DAG Network
MapiDagNetwork

DAG1

Member Servers
MBX-1

Witness Server
dc1.jennchris.com

DAG Network
MapiDagNetwork
Enable Replication | Remove
View details

ReplicationToCLT
Disable Replication | Remove
View details

Managing a DAG Network from EMS

You can use EMS to manage, add, and remove DAG networks and manage DAG network settings in the DAG via the following cmdlets:

Set-DatabaseAvailabilityGroup Changes DAG settings. To disable the automatic management of the DAG networks by the system, run the following command:

```
Set-DatabaseAvailabilityGroup DAG-2 -ManualDagNetworkConfiguration $true
```

New-DatabaseAvailabilityGroupNetwork Creates a new DAG network. Automatic network configuration must be turned off to run this cmdlet. To create a DAG network that will be used for replication, run this command:

```
New-DatabaseAvailabilityGroupNetwork -DatabaseAvailabilityGroup DAG-2↵
 -Name ReplicationToCLT -Subnets 10.1.0.0/16 -ReplicationEnabled:$true
```

Set-DatabaseAvailabilityGroupNetwork Helps manage the DAG networks. Automatic network configuration must be turned off to run this cmdlet. Replication for the MAPI network will be disabled in this example:

```
Set-DatabaseAvailabilityGroupNetwork DAG-2\MapiDagNetwork ↵
    -ReplicationEnabled:$false
```

Remove-DatabaseAvailabilityGroupNetwork Deletes a DAG network. In this example the DAG network ReplicationToCLT will be removed from DAG-2:

```
Remove-DatabaseAvailabilityGroupNetwork -Identity DAG-2\ReplicationToClT
```

Get-DatabaseAvailabilityGroupNetwork Retrieves the DAG networks. To see all the DAG networks, run this command:

```
Get-DatabaseAvailabilityGroupNetwork
Identity                 ReplicationEnabled       Subnets
--------                 ------------------       -------
DAG-2\MapiDagNetwork     True                     {{192.168.0.0/16,Up}}
DAG1\MapiDagNetwork      False                    {{192.168.0.0/16,Up}}
DAG1\ReplicationToCLT    True                     {{10.1.0.0/16,Up}}
```

---

iSCSI and DAG Networks

Any network adapter on a Mailbox server is discovered and exposed as a DAG network. This can be a problem when iSCSI storage is configured on a Mailbox server. Microsoft recommends that any network adapter used for iSCSI must be excluded from the DAG network. To disable the use of iSCSI adapters, run the following command against all iSCSI networks:

```
Set-DatabaseAvailabilityGroupNetwork DAG-2\iSCSI ↵
 -ReplicationEnabled:$false -IgnoreNetwork:$true
```

Adding a Mailbox Database to a DAG

Developing a database layout is part of the process of adding mailbox databases in a DAG. It consists of spreading the database copies across Mailbox servers and determining the activation preference of each database copy. For example, in Figure 20.7 there are four Mailbox servers and each mailbox database is replicated to each Mailbox server.

The preference of a database is used during the Best Copy and Server Selection process, which is covered later in this chapter. However, it's important to note that database preference is used as a tiebreaker *only* when Active Manager chooses which database to activate. For example, if *all things were equal* for the mailbox database copy of DB1 on MBX1 and MBX2, Active Manager would activate DB1 on MBX1 because MBX1 has the low mailbox database preference. So, while you want to establish the activation preference that makes sense to you with regard to the order in which you would like Mailbox servers to host the active database copy, your preference is not considered of primary importance during the failover process.

FIGURE 20.7
Mailbox database layout

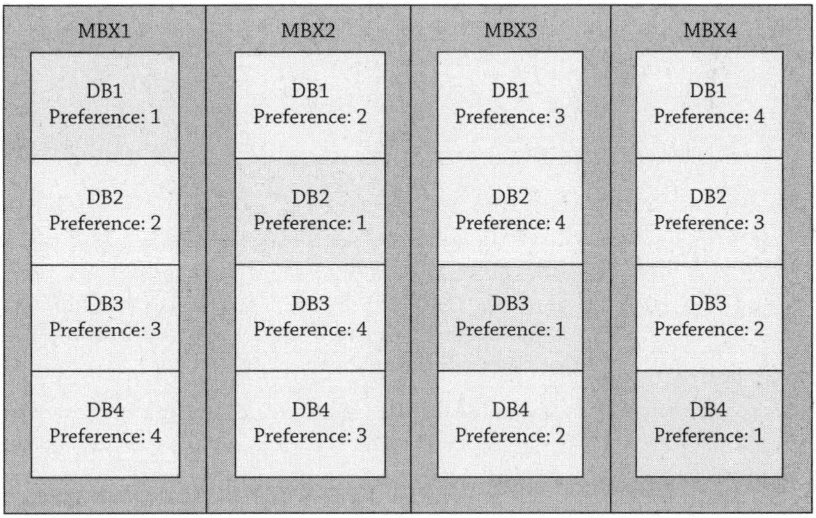

MBX1	MBX2	MBX3	MBX4
DB1 Preference: 1	DB1 Preference: 2	DB1 Preference: 3	DB1 Preference: 4
DB2 Preference: 2	DB2 Preference: 1	DB2 Preference: 4	DB2 Preference: 3
DB3 Preference: 3	DB3 Preference: 4	DB3 Preference: 1	DB3 Preference: 2
DB4 Preference: 4	DB4 Preference: 3	DB4 Preference: 2	DB4 Preference: 1

If MBX1 and MBX2 were to fail, Active Manager would initiate a failover request, find the best database copy to mount (more information on the best database copy to mount can be found in the "Understanding Active Manager" section), and mount the mailbox database. In Figure 20.8 Active Manager selected the next preferred mailbox database copy to mount. (Active Manager will be covered in greater detail later in this chapter.)

FIGURE 20.8
Mailbox database
activation after
a failure on MBX1
and MBX2

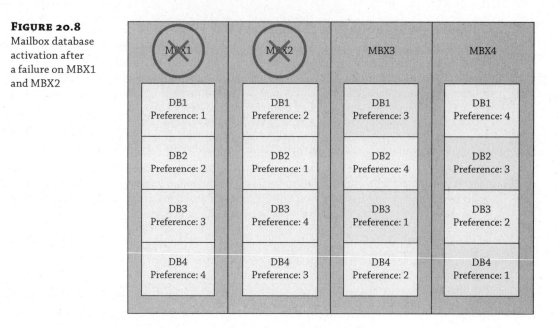

MANAGING MAILBOX DATABASE COPIES IN THE EAC

To create a mailbox database and add passive copies from the EAC, use the following steps:

1. On your client computer, open Internet Explorer and browse to the ECP URL. This URL should be the name of your Client Access server with /ECP appended to the end. If you don't know the URL for the EAC, you can use the Outlook Web App URL and specify / ECP instead of /owa at the end of the URL. For example, for Contoso, the EAC URL might be https://mail.contoso.com/ECP.

2. When prompted with the authentication page, type in your name and password and log in.

3. In the Feature pane, on the left column of the EAC, select Servers.

4. In the toolbar across the top of the EAC, select the Databases tab. Mailbox databases will be listed below. This includes legacy databases.

5. Click the Add (+) button to create a new database.

6. In the Mailbox Database Name text box, provide the name of the database.

7. Under Server click the Browse button and select a Mailbox server that is a member of the DAG.

8. Once the Mailbox server has been selected, the Database File Path and Log Folder Path text boxes will be autopopulated. To change the location where the database and transaction log will be stored, clear the content in each text box and enter a different storage location.

9. The Mount This Database check box is checked by default. The database will be mounted on the Mailbox server specified, as shown in Figure 20.9

FIGURE 20.9
Creating a new
database from
the EAC

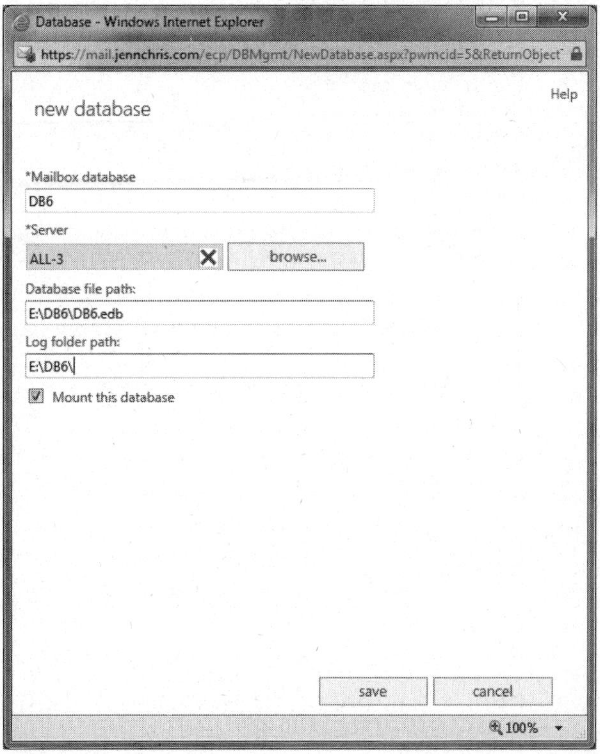

10. To add a passive copy of the newly created database (Figure 20.10), highlight the mailbox database, click the More button (a row of three dots), and select Add Database Copy. (After creating the database, it might take a minute or two for this option to become available.)

11. Under Specify Mailbox Server, click the Browse button and choose the Mailbox server that you want to add a replica to.

12. In the drop-down box under Activation Preference Number, select a number. The lower the number, the higher the preference.

13. To see additional (optional) settings, click More Options.

◆ Use the Replay Lag Time (Days) text box if you want to make this database a lagged database copy.

◆ Checking the Seeding Postponed check box will delay the copying of the mailbox database to the Mailbox server being added as a replica.

FIGURE 20.10
Adding a mailbox
database to a
Mailbox server

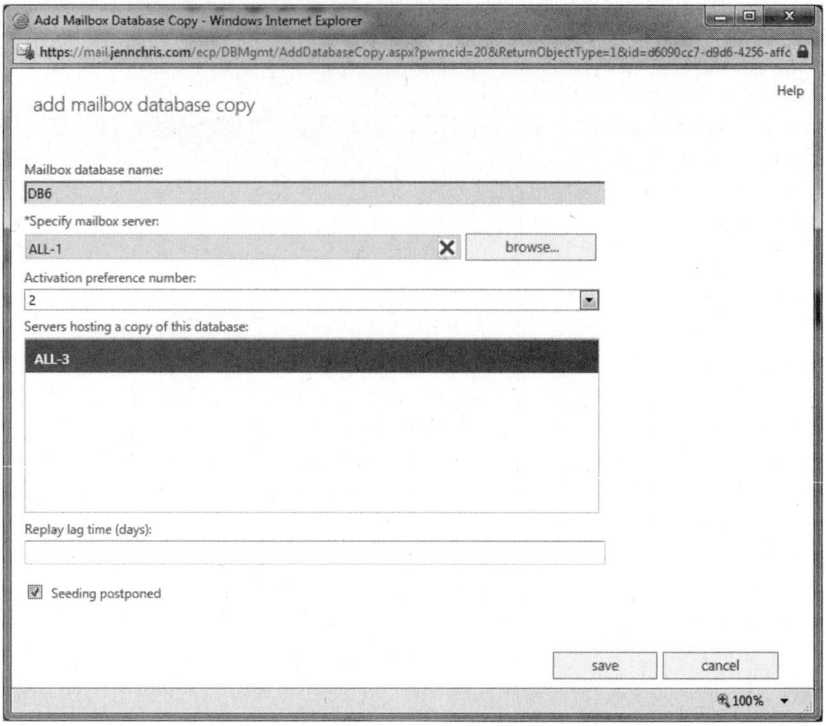

Once you select Save, a copy of the mailbox database will be added to the Mailbox server and information within the DAG and Active Directory will be updated to reflect this change.

After the mailbox database has been added to the Mailbox server, you can prevent this copy of the mailbox database from automatically being activated by Active Manager during a mailbox database or Mailbox server failover, by enabling activation block:

1. Highlight the mailbox database you just added a replica to.

2. In the Details pane select Suspend (see Figure 20.11) on the mailbox database copy you want to enable the activation block on.

3. In the Suspend Database Copy window check the box next to "This copy can only be activated by manual intervention" and click Save.

   When Active Manager builds the list of available databases after a failover, the mailbox copy with activation block enabled will be excluded from the list.

MANAGING A MAILBOX DATABASE IN THE EMS

Using the Exchange Management Shell, you can specify unique settings to each database copy, validate the health of each database copy, pause and resume replication, reseed a database copy, or remove a database copy. For a full list of the parameters for each of the following cmdlets, please reference the Exchange Server 2013 Help file.

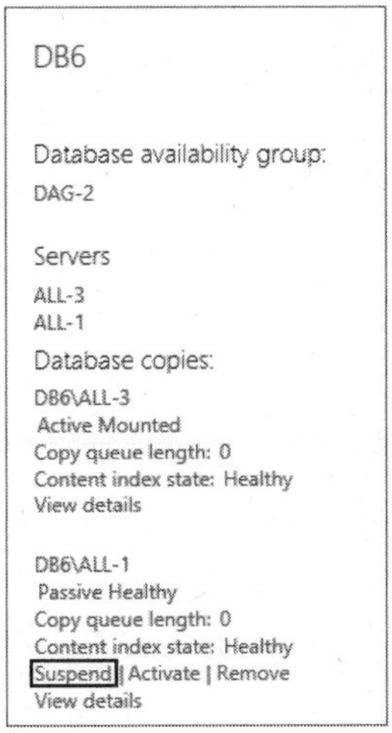

FIGURE 20.11
Database options
from the Details
pane in EAC

```
DB6

Database availability group:
DAG-2

Servers

ALL-3
ALL-1
Database copies:
DB6\ALL-3
 Active Mounted
Copy queue length: 0
Content index state: Healthy
View details

DB6\ALL-1
 Passive Healthy
Copy queue length: 0
Content index state: Healthy
Suspend | Activate | Remove
View details
```

Add-MailboxDatabaseCopy   Adds a replica to an existing mailbox database. The Mailbox server All-1 will be added as a passive copy of DB6 and will postpone the seeding of the mailbox database:

```
Add-MailboxDatabaseCopy DB6 -MailboxServer All-1 ↵
-ActivationPreference 2 -SeedingPostponed
```

Suspend-MailboxDatabaseCopy   Enables activation block and stops the copying and replay of transaction logs from the active database copy. To suspend replication of DB6 on Mailbox server All-1, run this command:

```
Suspend-MailboxDatabaseCopy DB6\All-1 -SuspendComment ↵
  "Taking storage offline"
```

Resume-MailboxDatabaseCopy   Removes activation block or resumes the copying and replay of transaction logs from the active database copy. Replication will resume for DB6 on the Mailbox server All-1:

```
Resume-MailboxDatabaseCopy DB6\All-1
```

Remove-MailboxDatabaseCopy   Removes a mailbox database copy from a Mailbox server. The Mailbox server All-1 will be removed as a replica of mailbox database DB6:

```
Remove-MailboxDatabaseCopy DB6\All-1
```

Update-MailboxDatabaseCopy   Seeds or reseeds a mailbox database. This cmdlet can be used to update both the database and content index or just the database or content index. DB6 on All-1 will seed the mailbox only from All-3 and remove any existing database files:

```
Update-MailboxDatabaseCopy -Identity DB6\All-1 -SourceServer ↵
     All-3 -DeleteExistingFiles -DatabaseOnly -Network MapiDagNetwork
```

Set-MailboxDatabaseCopy Changes a mailbox database copy to a lagged copy or changes the activation preference. To change the activation preference to 1 for DB6 on Mailbox server All-1, run this command:

```
Set-MailboxDatabaseCopy DB6\All-1 -ActivationPreference 1
```

Move-ActiveMailboxDatabase Moves the active mailbox database to a different server. In the following example, DB6 is being activated on Mailbox server All-1:

```
Move-ActiveMailboxDatabase DB6 -ActivateOnServer All-1
```

Get-MailboxDatabaseCopyStatus Shows the replication status of all the mailbox databases homed on the Mailbox server the cmdlet was run from:

```
Get-MailboxDatabaseCopyStatus -ConnectionStatus
```

The Get-MailboxDatabaseCopyStatus cmdlet is very useful in determining the replication state of each mailbox database on a specific Mailbox server. (For more information on mailbox database replication, please see the "Understanding the Best Copy and Server Selection" section, later in this chapter.) To see a list of the replication states for all the Mailbox servers, you can add Get-MailboxServer in front of Get-MailboxDatabaseCopyStatus:

```
Get-mailboxserver | Get-MailboxDatabaseCopyStatus -CoonectionStatus
```

Name	Status	CopyQueueLength	ReplayQueueLength
DB6\ALL-1	Mounted	0	0
DB6\All-3	Healthy	0	0

Set-MailboxServer Applies global settings to all databases homed on a specific Mailbox server. The following example prevents any database from automatically being activated on All-1:

```
Set-MailboxServer All-1 -DatabaseCopyAutoActivationPolicy Blocked
```

IMPLEMENTING LAGGED MAILBOX DATABASE COPIES

A lagged mailbox database copy is not a new concept in Exchange Server 2013, but significant changes have been made in Exchange Server 2013 that have a direct impact on lagged databases. A *lagged mailbox database copy* is a replication partner of an active database and for the most part operates in the same manner as other passive database copies. As a replication partner, it replicates transactions to the server hosting the lagged database copy, and the integrity of the transaction logs is inspected before committing the changes into the database. The difference between a standard passive copy and the lagged passive copy is that the transaction log files are not committed to the mailbox after inspection.

A *lagged copy* is defined by the replay lag time setting of a mailbox database copy. The replay lag time specifies how long after the inspection of the transaction log the Mailbox server will wait to commit the changes in the transaction log into the copy of the mailbox database. Having the database hold off on committing changes immediately gives you the ability to restore the mailbox database copy to a specific point and time.

Another parameter that you can manipulate on a lagged database is the *truncation lag time*. The truncation lag time defines when the transaction log file will be deleted from disk. The truncation lag time does not kick in until after the replay lag time. If the replay lag time is set to

5 days and the truncation lag time is set to 5 days, the transaction log file will not be removed from disk until 10 days after the transaction log file was replicated and inspected. The main advantage of setting the truncation lag time is having a copy of the transaction log in case a catastrophic failure were to occur on the active database copy, and you needed to replay missing logs into the database to restore older email content.

You can set the truncation and replay lag times on a lagged database by using the `Add-MailboxDatabaseCopy` and `Set-MailboxDatabaseCopy` cmdlets. The following examples set the replay lag time and truncation lag time to 1 day.

The following sets the replay and truncation lag times using the `Add-MailboxDatabaseCopy` cmdlet:

```
Add-MailboxDatabaseCopy -Identity DB1 -MailboxServer All-2 ↵
            -ReplayLagTime 1.00:00:00 -TruncationLagTime 1.00:00:00 ↵
                -ActivationPreference 4
```

The following sets the replay and truncation lag times by using the `Set-MailboxDatabaseCopy` cmdlet:

```
Set-MailboxDatabaseCopy -Identity DB4\all-2 -ReplayLagTime 1.00:00:00 ↵
    -TruncationLagTime 1.00:00:00
```

The introduction of Safety Net, which is covered in Chapter 22, "Managing Connectivity with Transport Services," has replaced the functionality of the transport dumpster that was used in Exchange Server 2007 and 2010. When an email message has been delivered to the active copy of the mailbox database, a copy of the message is stored in the queue. Each active mailbox database retains its own queue. By default the messages stored in the Safety Net queue are retained for 2 days.

The use of lagged databases in an organization will directly impact the configuration of the Safety Net. The duration of time set in the `ReplayLagTimes` parameter on a lagged database copy, should match the duration of time Safety Net stores email messages. For example, if you set a lagged database to play transaction logs after 5 days, messages should be removed from the Safety Net queue after 5 days. If you have multiple lagged database copies throughout your organization, set the Safety Net threshold to the highest `ReplayLagTimes` value. It is important to note that the longer you set the Safety Net queue, the more storage you will need for it.

Keeping on the theme of new features in Exchange Server 2013, lagged databases can now bypass the replay lag time setting, in certain scenarios, by automatically replaying log files into the mailbox database. This process is referred to in the Microsoft documentation as, *play down* of log files. The following scenarios invoke play down of log files:

- When there are fewer than three healthy databases copies (active or passive) for more than 24 hours

- When page patching is needed to fix physical corruption of the mailbox database

- When the free disk space falls below the defined free disk space percentage threshold

By default, lagged copy play down is disabled on a DAG. Using the `Set-DatabaseAvailabilityGroup` cmdlet with the `ReplayLagManagerEnabled` parameter, you can enable lagged copy play down:

```
Set-DatabaseAvailabilityGroup DAG1 -ReplayLagManagerEnabled $true
```

Once the `ReplayLagManagerEnabled` parameter has been set to true on a given DAG, you can modify the registry on the Mailbox server hosting a lagged copy to change the number of available database copies and free disk space threshold before play down occurs.

The following sets the number of available database copies:

```
HKLM\Software\Microsoft\ExchangeServer\v15\Replay\Parameters\
ReplayLagManagerNumAvailableCopies
```

And this sets the free disk space percentage:

```
HKLM\Software\Microsoft\ExchangeServer\v15\Replay\Parameters\
ReplayLagPlayDownPercentDiskFreeSpace
```

Automatic Reseed (aka AutoReseed)

During the lifetime of a DAG, it is almost inevitable that a database copy will enter into a failed state. In Exchange Server 2010, if resuming continuous replication didn't fix the problem, reseeding the mailbox was required to bring the replica back to a healthy state. Reseeding the mailbox database from a healthy copy was a manual process in Exchange Server 2010. In Exchange Server 2013, new parameters have been added to the DAG to allow for automatic reseed. This feature empowers Exchange Server to automatically restore the state of the database copy on the local server. The configuration of Automatic Reseed involves pre-mapping volumes and using mount points. To start out with, let's review the Automatic Reseed process flow:

◆ The Exchange Replication Service checks for mailbox database copies that have a status of FailedAndSuspended.

◆ When the Exchange Replication Service finds a database copy with a status of FailedAndSuspended, prerequisite checks are performed to determine if there is single-copy situation, if a spare disk is available, and if the system can perform an Automatic Reseed.

◆ If the all checks pass, the Exchange Replication Service starts the Automatic Reseed process by allocating and remapping a spare drive.

◆ Seeding is performed on the failed mailbox database.

◆ Once seeding has finished, the Exchange Replication Service checks to see if the seeded database is in a healthy state.

The configuration and implementation of Automatic Reseed can be a bit tricky the first time through. To ease the pain, Figure 20.12 illustrates an Automatic Reseed configuration for a single database. Starting from the top, two folders are created on the root of the `C:\` drive, ExVols and ExDBs. ExVols contains two folders, Volume1 and Volume2. These folders are used as mount points for Physical Disk 1 and Physical Disk 2. DB1 is located under the ExDBs folder. The DB1 folder will be used as a mount point that maps to `C:\ExVols\Volume1`. The DB1 folder stores the DB1.DB and DB1.Logs folders.

Now that the mount points are in place, what's next? Parameters within the DAG must be updated to reflect the Automatic Reseed design in Figure 20.12. The following parameters will be changed:

FIGURE 20.12
Automatic Reseed
configuration

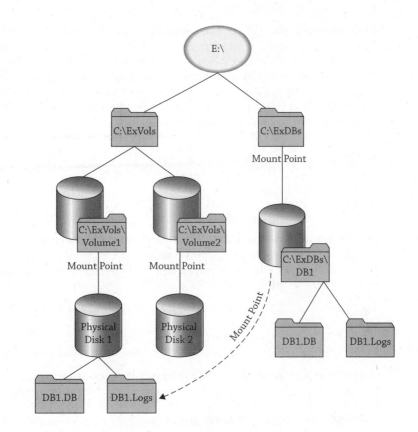

AutoDagVolumesRootFolderPath   The mount point that contains all of the available volumes (C:\ExVols)

AutoDagDatabasesRootFolderPath   The mount point that contains all of the databases (C:\ExDBs)

AutoDagDatabaseCopiesPerVolume   The number of database copies per volume (one database copy on Disk 1 and one database copy on Disk 2)

Next, a new mailbox database is created, the database path is set to C:\ExDBs\DB1\DB1.DB\ DB1.edb and the transaction log path is set to C:\ExDBs\DB1\DB1.Log. The database and log files will be stored on Disk 1 through the mount point C:\ExDBs\DB1.

And that's it, Automatic Reseed is ready. Database copies can be added to the newly created database and if the replication status of this database copy changes to FailedAndSuspended, AutoReseed would kick in and reseed the database to C:\ExVols\Volume2 (Disk 2).

Understanding Active Manager

Active Manager runs on all Mailbox servers inside the Microsoft Exchange Replication Service and is responsible for many aspects of mailbox availability. Each Mailbox server is designated with an Active Manager role. When the Mailbox server is a member of a DAG, there are two

Active Manager roles, Primary and Standby. Only one server in the DAG can hold the Primary Active Manager (PAM) role at a time; all the other Mailbox servers in the DAG hold the Standby Active Manager (SAM) role. When a Mailbox server is not a member of a DAG, the Active Manager role is set to stand-alone. If a stand-alone server is added to the DAG, the Mailbox server will update its role to SAM. The Mailbox server in the DAG that is designated as the PAM always has ownership of the cluster quorum resources. If the PAM server were to fail, another Mailbox server in the DAG would pick up the PAM role. To determine the Mailbox server that holds the PAM role, run either one of these commands:

```
Get-DatabaseAvailabilityGroup -Identity DAG-1 -Status | ↵
            fl name, PrimaryActiveManager


Name                : DAG-1
PrimaryActiveManager : ALL-1
```

(Note that the server names ALL-1, ALL-2, ALL-3, ... used here are just examples. In each environment the naming will vary. This is but one admin's naming convention.)

Or from one of the DAG members you run the command `cluster group`:

```
Cluster DAG-1 GROUP
Group                 Node             Status
-------------------   --------------   ------
Available Storage     ALL-1            Offline
Cluster Group         ALL-1            Online
```

The PAM role can be moved to another Mailbox server by using the `Cluster` cmdlet. The Mailbox server that is taking on the PAM role will record the process, shown in Figure 20.13, in the Operational log found underneath `Event Viewer\Applications and Service Logs\ Microsoft\Exchange\HighAvailability\`.

To move the PAM role to a different Mailbox server, run this command:

```
Cluster DAG-1 group "Cluster group" /moveto: All-3

Moving resource group 'Cluster group'...

Group                 Node             Status
-------------------   --------------   ------
Cluster group         ALL-3            Online
```

Mailbox servers that hold the SAM role provide information to the PAM. The SAM notifies the PAM of databases that are active on the local server. If a database or a component were to fail, the SAM would communicate to the PAM to start a failover to a passive database copy. If a Mailbox server were to fail, the Mailbox server holding the PAM role would mark the server as down in cluster resources and start the process of activating the mailbox databases on a different Mailbox server. The server that owns the PAM role has several responsibilities, including the following:

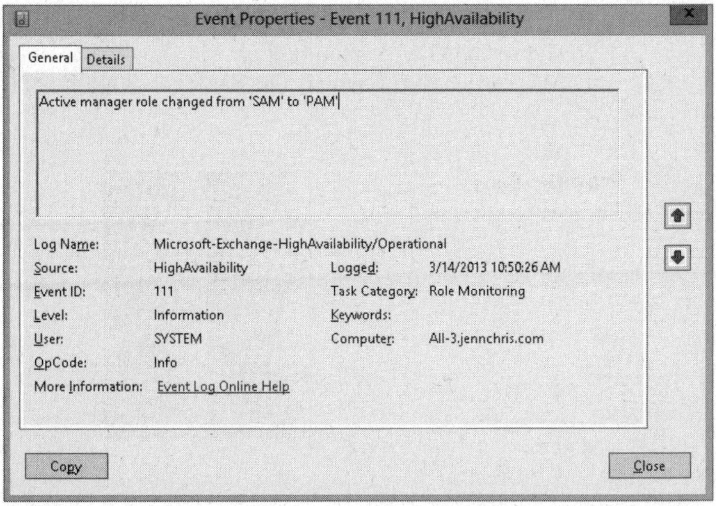

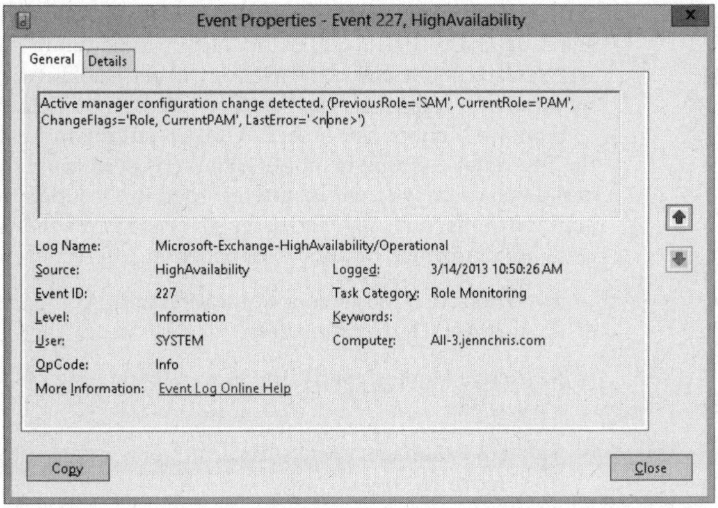

FIGURE 20.13
Event 111 records the Active Manager role changing from SAM to PAM, and Event 227 notes the change of the Active Manager role to the PAM role.

- ◆ Determining which Mailbox server has the active copy of each mailbox database
- ◆ Monitoring and acting on failures
- ◆ Notifying DAG members of topology changes
- ◆ Maintaining database and server state information

Active Manager makes a resubmission request of email messages that are stored in the queue database. This process is covered in Chapter 22.

ACTIVE MANAGER AT WORK

In Figure 20.14 DB7 is mounted on ALL-3, which is the server currently running as a SAM. The PAM is server ALL-1, which also has a passive copy of the database DB7.

FIGURE 20.14

DB7 is activated on ALL-3

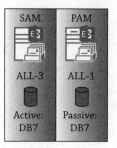

A lot of the information that Active Manager uses to determine the best database copy to activate is stored in the registry. When a Mailbox server is a member of a DAG, Active Manager stores database, server, and Safety Net information in the registry. This information is used when selecting the best database copy to activate during a failover scenario. See the next section for more information on the Best Copy and Server Selection process.

Suppose Mailbox server ALL-3 fails, resulting in Active Manager on ALL-1 determining the best database copy to mount. The steps performed by Active Manager on ALL-1 to find the best database copy to mount are recorded in the Operational logs found under `Event Viewer\ Applications and Service Logs\Microsoft\Exchange\HighAvailability\`. The following steps are performed by Active Manager on ALL-1:

1. When ALL-1 loses communication with ALL-3, ALL-3 is marked as down in Windows Failover Cluster Manager.

2. Active Manager starts the process of moving DB7 from ALL-3 to a different Mailbox server.

3. Active Manager checks the health of key components on Mailbox server ALL-1 (Figure 20.15).

4. DB7 on ALL-1 is deemed the best copy and Active Manager automatically mounts DB7 on ALL-1. (The next section of this chapter provides more insight on the process for best copy and server selection.)

5. As part of the failover process, Active Manager tries to copy any missing transaction logs from the Mailbox server that last held the active copy to the Mailbox server the database is moving to. In this example, since ALL-3 was the last server to hold the active copy of DB7, this process fails to copy transaction logs to ALL-1, since ALL-3 is offline (Figure 20.16).

6. After DB7 is mounted, Active Manager requests Safety Net to resubmit messages that it doesn't have because of the failover.

FIGURE 20.15
The health status of
components on ALL-1

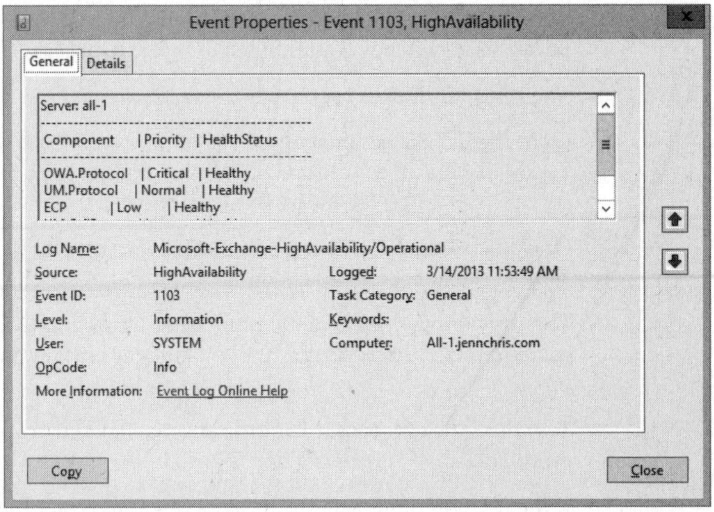

Event Properties - Event 1103, HighAvailability

General | Details

```
Server: all-1
---------------------------------------------------
Component    | Priority | HealthStatus
---------------------------------------------------
OWA.Protocol | Critical | Healthy
UM.Protocol  | Normal   | Healthy
ECP          | Low      | Healthy
```

Log Name: Microsoft-Exchange-HighAvailability/Operational
Source: HighAvailability   Logged: 3/14/2013 11:53:49 AM
Event ID: 1103   Task Category: General
Level: Information   Keywords:
User: SYSTEM   Computer: All-1.jennchris.com
OpCode: Info
More Information: Event Log Online Help

Copy   Close

FIGURE 20.16
An attempt to copy
remaining transaction
log files

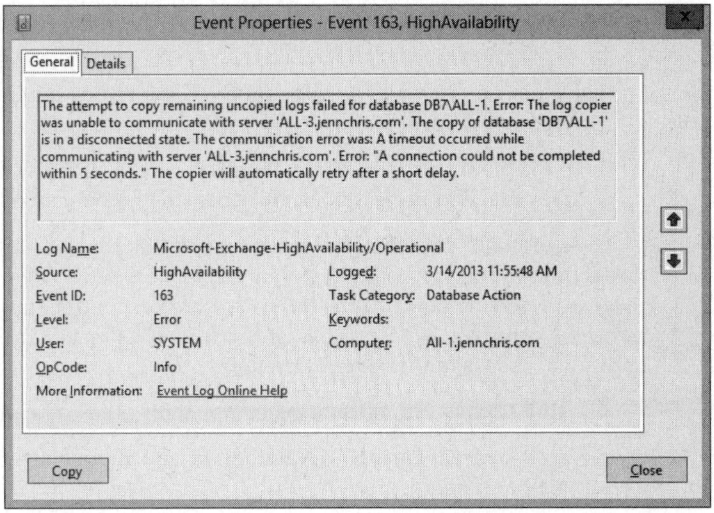

Event Properties - Event 163, HighAvailability

General | Details

The attempt to copy remaining uncopied logs failed for database DB7\ALL-1. Error: The log copier was unable to communicate with server 'ALL-3.jennchris.com'. The copy of database 'DB7\ALL-1' is in a disconnected state. The communication error was: A timeout occurred while communicating with server 'ALL-3.jennchris.com'. Error: "A connection could not be completed within 5 seconds." The copier will automatically retry after a short delay.

Log Name: Microsoft-Exchange-HighAvailability/Operational
Source: HighAvailability   Logged: 3/14/2013 11:55:48 AM
Event ID: 163   Task Category: Database Action
Level: Error   Keywords:
User: SYSTEM   Computer: All-1.jennchris.com
OpCode: Info
More Information: Event Log Online Help

Copy   Close

Understanding the Best Copy and Server Selection Process

The Best Copy and Server Selection (BCSS) process is new and improved in Exchange Server 2013. The core concept of BCSS is the same as in Exchange Server 2010 (when it was called Best Copy Selection, or BCS). If a failure is detected or an administrator performs a switchover without specifying a target server, the Mailbox server holding the PAM role will evaluate the best passive database to mount. The process to mount a passive database is as follows:

1. A failure is detected by Managed Availability or Active Manager, or an administrator performs a switchover without specifying a target server.

2. The PAM Mailbox server starts the BCSS algorithm.

3. Once the BCSS has determined the mailbox database to activate, the Attempt Copy Last Log (ACLL) process is kicked off. ACLL tries to copy any missing logs from the Mailbox server that hosted the active mailbox database.

4. Once the ACLL process has completed, the value of the copy queue length is compared against the `AutoDatabaseMountDial` parameter of the mailbox database.

   The copy queue length is the number of transaction logs that were not successfully replicated to the Mailbox server Active Manager is attempting to mount the mailbox database on.

   To mount the database, the `AutoDatabaseMountDial` parameter defines the acceptable number of missing transaction logs.

5. If the number of missing transaction logs is greater than the value of `AutoDatabaseMountDial`, Active Manager will try to mount the next-best database copy. If there are no other acceptable database copies, the database will be in offline state.

6. If the number of missing transaction logs is less than or equal to the value of `AutoDatabaseMountDial`, move on to the next step.

7. A mount request is issued from the PAM to the Mailbox server that is hosting the passive copy over RPC.

8. If the mount request works, the passive copy of the mailbox database becomes the active copy and end users are able to access their mail content again.

The process of determining which passive database to activate looks almost identical to how it was in Exchange Server 2010. Looks can be deceiving, however. Microsoft changed the BCSS process by adding new health checks that are part of the Managed Availability monitoring component. During the BCSS process (step 2 from the preceding list), Active Manager performs four additional checks in the order listed here:

1. All Healthy—All monitoring components are in a healthy state.

2. Up to Normal Healthy—All monitoring components with a normal priority are in a healthy state.

3. All Better Than Source—All monitoring components are in a better health state on a Mailbox server that the database is being moved to than on the Mailbox server the database is being moved from.

4. Same As Source—All monitoring components are in the same health state on a Mailbox server that the database is being moved to and the Mailbox server the database is being moved from.

After the health checks are performed, Active Manager begins the best copy selection by building a list of available database copies. Any database that is unreachable or its activation block is enabled is not added to the database list. If `AutoDatabaseMountDial` is set to Lossless, all transaction logs must be present before the database is mounted on a different Mailbox server and Active Manager sorts the list of available database copies in ascending order by activation preference. When `AutoDatabaseMountDial` is set to anything other than Lossless, Active Manager sorts the available database copies by copy queue length. If multiple database copies have the same copy queue length, the list is sorted a second time using activation preference as a tiebreaker.

Active Manager also looks at the state of the replay queue length, which defines the number of logs that have been copied to a passive Mailbox server but haven't been written to the mailbox database.

Next, Active Manager processes each database copy against 10 sets of criteria to determine which database copy is the best database to mount. Active Manager attempts to find database copies with a replication status of Healthy, DisconnectedAndHealthy, DisconnectedAndResynchronizing, or SeedingSource and evaluates the databases against 10 sets of criteria. Each passive mailbox copy goes through the evaluation process to determine the best suited database to mount. If multiple databases fall within the same criteria, then the Active Manager tries to activate the first mailbox database in the database list. Each database is evaluated against the 10 sets of criteria in Table 20.1.

> **WHAT HAPPENS WHEN A FAILOVER IS ISSUED**
>
> It is worth noting that if a failover is issued by a health service, some of the 10 steps in Table 20.1 are not performed. For example, if the failover is issued because the index status is in a failed state, Active Manager will not activate a database copy on a Mailbox server that also has a failed database index.

TABLE 20.1:   Active Manager evaluation of each database copy

CRITERIA SET	DESCRIPTION
1	Content index is in a Healthy state.
	Copy queue length is less than 10.
	Replay queue length is less than 50.
2	Content index is in a Crawling state.
	Copy queue length is less than 10.
	Replay queue length is less than 50.
3	Content index is in a Healthy state.
	Replay queue length is less than 50.

TABLE 20.1: Active Manager evaluation of each database copy *(CONTINUED)*

CRITERIA SET	DESCRIPTION
4	Content index is in a Crawling state.
	Replay queue length is less than 50.
5	Replay queue length is less than 50.
6	Content index is in a Healthy state.
	Copy queue length is less than 10.
7	Content index is in a Crawling state.
	Copy queue length is less than 10.
8	Content index is in a Healthy state.
9	Content index is in a Crawling state.
10	The database copy status is Healthy, DisconnectedAndHealthy, DisconnectedAndResynchronizing, or SeedingSource.

If none of the databases meet the 10 criteria sets, the mailbox database will not be automaticity mounted on a passive Mailbox server. If a passive copy of the database is found that matches one of the 10 criteria sets and the replay queue length is less than the amount of acceptable logs loss, specified by the `AutoDatbaseMountDial` parameter, the chosen passive mailbox database is mounted.

EXAMPLES OF BEST COPY AND SERVER SELECTION

The BCSS process is confusing, so to ease the pain let's use some real-world examples to understand how the BCSS process works. As we go through the examples, it is important to note that the order listed in Table 20.1 is the order Active Manager uses to determine which Mailbox server should be used to mount the mailbox database.

Our fictional company has deployed four Mailbox servers ranging from MBX1 to MBX4. The Mailbox server MBX1 has three active mailbox databases, DB1 through DB3, and each database is replicated to the other three Mailbox servers. In this example, let's say that MBX1 has a hardware failure. Active Manager must now evaluate each Mailbox server and its corresponding passive database copy to determine which database will be activated. To simplify the BCSS process, none of the databases are set to Lossless and all protocols are in a healthy state. Tables

20.2 through 20.4 provide the status of the passive copies before MBX1 failed. After each table a description is provided of which database would be activated and why.

TABLE 20.2:   DB1 replication status

DATABASE COPY	ACTIVATION PREFERENCE	COPY QUEUE LENGTH	REPLAY QUEUE LENGTH	CONTENT INDEX STATE	DATABASE STATE
MBX2\DB1	2	9	37	Healthy	Healthy
MBX3\DB1	3	5	0	Crawling	Healthy
MBX4\DB1	4	2	15	Healthy	DisconnectedAndHealthy

Sorting databases on copy queue length

MBX4\DB1

MBX3\DB1

MBX2\DB1

Databases in order of the criteria state they are related to based on Table 20.1

MBX4\DB1 - Criteria Set 1

MBX3\DB1 - Criteria Set 2

MBX2\DB1 - Criteria Set 1

Result

Active Manager would try to activate the database copy MBX4\DB1 since it is missing the fewest transaction logs (copy queue length) and meets the first set of criteria.

TABLE 20.3:   DB2 replication status

DATABASE COPY	ACTIVATION PREFERENCE	COPY QUEUE LENGTH	REPLAY QUEUE LENGTH	CONTENT INDEX STATE	DATABASE STATE
MBX2\DB1	4	4	39	Healthy	Healthy
MBX3\DB1	2	5	0	Healthy	Healthy
MBX4\DB1	3	4	15	Healthy	Healthy

Sorting databases on copy queue length *and* activation preference

(Here activation preference is used as the tiebreaker since two of the databases have the same copy queue length.)

MBX4\DB1

MBX2\DB1

MBX3\DB1

Database results of the criteria sets

MBX4\DB1 - Criteria Set 1

MBX2\DB1 - Criteria Set 1

MBX3\DB1 - Criteria Set 1

Result

Active Manager would try to activate the database copy MBX4\DB1 since it is missing the fewest transaction logs (copy queue length), is the preferred activation preference, and meets the first set of criteria.

TABLE 20.4: DB3 Replication Status

Database Copy	Activation Preference	Copy Queue Length	Replay Queue Length	Content Index State	Database State
MBX2\DB1	3	41	67	Failed	Healthy
MBX3\DB1	4	13	107	Crawling	Healthy
MBX4\DB1	2	27	51	Healthy	DisconnectedAndHealthy

Sorting databases on copy queue length

MBX3\DB1

MBX4\DB1

MBX2\DB1

Database results of the criteria sets

MBX3\DB1 - Criteria Set 9

MBX4\DB1 - Criteria Set 8

MBX2\DB1 - Criteria Set 10

Result

Even though MBX3\DB1 has the lowest copy queue length, Active Manager would try to activate the database copy MBX4\DB1 first, since it matches the requirements in criteria set 8 and MBX3\DB1 matches the requirements in criteria set 9.

Understanding Site Resiliency for Exchange Server 2013

In Exchange Server 2013, Microsoft set out to simplify the deployment and management of having a DAG stretched across multiple datacenters. One of the many changes Microsoft has introduced in Exchange Server 2013 is the removal of clients connecting to specific namespaces and the use of clients connecting to mailbox resources over RPC. These changes have a massive impact on site resiliency. In Exchange Server 2010, clients connected using a specific namespace listed in the RpcClientAccessServer parameter of a mailbox database. Many organizations changed the RpcClientAccessServer parameter to point to a shared namespace that resolved to a Virtual IP (VIP). If the server or appliance in the primary site that was responsible for the VIP went offline, end users would no longer be able to access their email content and, depending on the severity of the issue, a datacenter switchover had to be performed to restore email services. In Exchange Server 2010, mailbox availability was dependent not only on the availability of the mailbox database but also the availability of the Exchange servers that held the CAS role.

Microsoft has severed the dependency of the Mailbox role from the Client Access role for site resiliency. Continuing with the scenario from the previous paragraph, if the server or appliance responsible for the VIP fails, a datacenter switchover is not required. A client can communicate to an Exchange server with the CAS role in a secondary datacenter without administrator intervention. The Exchange servers with the CAS role in the secondary datacenter can then proxy the client's request back to a Mailbox server in the primary datacenter.

OK, this sounds too good to be true, but Microsoft has stressed making site resiliency…well, more *resilient*. When performing a datacenter switchover, a namespace doesn't need to move with the DAG and a DAG doesn't need to move with a namespace. Since a majority of clients will connect using HTTP, Microsoft has harnessed the built-in resiliency of HTTP. A namespace can resolve to multiple IP addresses and/or be load-balanced by a hardware appliance. For example, let's use the namespace mail.jennchris.com. In DNS you can create multiple A records for the namespace mail.jennchris.com that resolve to different IPs. If a client using HTTP is unable to connect to the first IP address returned by DNS, the client will move on to the next IP address in DNS for mail.jennchris.com. This configuration also works well for intermittent interruptions of service. If a client is connected to mail.jennchris.com and loses connectivity, the client will query DNS for a different IP address to connect to.

So bringing this full circle, Mailbox server site resiliency does not have to depend on client access site resiliency. The following sections on this topic cover the Mailbox server options for site resiliency in Exchange Server 2013.

Page Patching

When replicating mailbox databases between datacenters, there is always the possibility that the database copies in the secondary datacenter are not up to date with the latest transactions. In scenarios where the secondary datacenter is behind in the transaction log stream and a failure occurs in the primary datacenter resulting in a datacenter switchover, database or transaction log divergence will be present between the mailbox copy in the secondary datacenter and the mailbox copy in the primary datacenter.

When a database has divergence at either the database or page level, Exchange Server 2013 will implement page patching. This means that the email data on one of the passive servers is different from the email data in the active database/log files. The Replication Service tries to determine the divergence point by reading the logs from both the active source and the passive target. Once the divergence is found, the Replication Service updates the log stream to match the database/log information found on the active database.

Page patching and divergence are important to understand. Take, for example, this scenario: if a failover were to occur and the replication between the active and passive mailbox databases was behind by 10 log files, once the passive copy is forcibly made the active copy, the passive copy will create the 10 logs as part of own its log stream. The result of this is that the 10 log files in each datacenter would have different email content. If you were to resynchronize the databases once the Mailbox server in the primary datacenter comes back online, the 10 log files would be overwritten and the data in the 10 log files that were never replicated to the passive copy would be lost.

During a datacenter failover, you should note the last log replicated before bringing the passive mailbox database online. Once the primary datacenter is active, determine if any of the log files are missing between the primary and secondary datacenter before the failover. If they are, copy the log files and the mailbox database to a different location. Once the copy is complete, replay the logs files into the mailbox database to bring the database to a clean state and mount the mailbox database as a recovery mailbox database. You can then export the missing content into a PST file.

Datacenter Activation Coordination

Microsoft recommends that any DAG that has three or more members that have been deployed in a multi-datacenter configuration should have Datacenter Activation Coordination (DAC) mode enabled, since it is disabled by default. In most deployments a majority of the quorum voters will be placed in the primary datacenter. If a single DAG is used to service active users in two datacenters, the file share witness is typically located where the majority of your users' mailboxes reside, although it can be placed in a third datacenter. In a scenario where a majority of voters are offline, the DAG will be marked as offline and all mailbox databases will be dismounted. When a DAG is offline there are two options: wait for the majority of voters to be brought back online or manually restore the DAG service.

When choosing to manually restore the DAG service, DAC mode is used to prevent split brain syndrome. Split brain syndrome occurs when the nodes in each datacenter own a version cluster quorum. Without DAC mode, Active Manager does not communicate with all the other active Mailbox servers before mounting a database copy. Without communicating to the other Mailbox servers, split brain syndrome could occur, allowing the same mailbox databases to be mounted in multiple datacenters.

Consider an organization that has deployed a DAG between two datacenters and didn't enable DAC mode. In this example, assume that a majority of the nodes are in the primary datacenter. During a catastrophic event, the WAN connection failed and all the Exchange servers in the primary datacenter lost power for an extended period of time, forcing this organization to restore DAG services in the secondary datacenter. All mailbox databases are now mounted on Mailbox servers in the secondary datacenter. Once power has been restored in the primary datacenter, all the Mailbox servers in the primary site are brought online. Since a majority of the cluster nodes are homed in the primary datacenter, the cluster in the primary site has quorum and Active Manager starts mounting databases on those Mailbox servers. Each database is mounted twice; one instance is mounted in the primary datacenter and the other instance is mounted in the secondary datacenter. Because multiple instances of a database are mounted, divergence has been introduced into the organization.

DAC mode uses the Datacenter Activation Coordination Protocol (DACP) to find the state of the DAG and determine if Active Manager can mount a mailbox database on the Mailbox server. When Active Manager starts on a Mailbox server, DACP is set in memory as a bit with the value of 0. The value of 0 informs Active Manager not to mount any mailbox databases on the local Mailbox server. Active Manager does not update the bit value in memory from 0, Don't Mount Mailbox Databases, to 1, Mount Mailbox Databases, until another Active Manager in the DAG can be located with the value of 1.

Continuing with our example, suppose that this time the organization enabled DAC mode before the catastrophic event occurred. Once power is restored in the primary datacenter and the Mailbox servers are brought online, Active Manager on the Mailbox servers in the primary datacenter would not mount any mailbox database even though the cluster is online in the primary datacenter. This is because all the Mailbox servers in the primary datacenter would have a DACP value of 0. Not until the WAN connection between the datacenters has been restored and PowerShell cmdlets have been run would Active Manager then allow mailbox databases to be mounted on the local server.

The other major benefit of enabling DAC mode is only EMS cmdlets are needed to perform a datacenter switchover. DAC mode can be enabled on a DAG by running the following command:

```
Set-DatabaseAvailabilityGroup DAG-2 -DatacenterActivationMode DAGonly
```

🌐 Real World Scenario

BYE-BYE, BACKUPS

Ever wonder what it would be like to never have to worry about backups again? Well, that is a possibility in Exchange Server 2013 by using lagged database copies, page patching, litigation hold, and single-item recovery.

When evaluating native Exchange Server features to maintain email content, you must review all the possible failure scenarios and the process to recover email content in each scenario. It is also critical to review all single points of failure in the Exchange Server 2013 design. A single point a failure could be the use of shared storage or a shared enclosure. You never want one catastrophic failure to result in vaporizing a mailbox database.

Along the lines of reviewing the single points of failure, choosing the number of database copies and where to place each database copy is important in maintaining email content during failure events. One of the authors of this book assisted a customer in moving away from traditional backups and toward native Exchange Server 2013 features to maintain email content. The author's design included three copies of every database and the three copies did not include the lagged database copy that was added to each mailbox database.

Lastly the design included other native Exchange Server features, such as single-item recovery, changing the deleted item retention window, enabling continuous replication circular logging, using In-Place Archive, In-Place Hold, and so on. These features were used to meet the customers' requirements for long-term data storage and recovery after accidental deletion.

One of the major drawbacks of not using traditional backups is that logical database corruption cannot be accounted for. On the rare occasion when logical corruption of a database occurs, using built-in features of Exchange Server 2013 may not be sufficient. Since logical corruptions can be masked for a long time, determining when the logical corruption occurred is almost impossible. Native backups can be used to restore a mailbox database that has experienced logical corruption. The only caveat is that you must have a repository of database backups and test each restore to determine if the restored copy contains the logical corruption.

Implementing Site-resiliency Scenarios

Based on business and technical requirements for a given organization, the design of a site-resilient DAG will differ dramatically. This section covers three common site-resilient DAG configurations, along with their pros and cons.

SINGLE DAG BETWEEN TWO AD SITES

When stretching a single DAG between two datacenters, as shown in Figure 20.17, the primary datacenter should always contain the majority of the Mailbox servers. When an even number of Mailbox servers are placed in each datacenter, the witness server should be a located in the primary datacenter. When connectivity between the primary and secondary datacenters is lost, the DAG members in the primary datacenter would have the majority of voters and therefore quorum would be maintained in the primary datacenter.

FIGURE 20.17
Single DAG between two AD sites

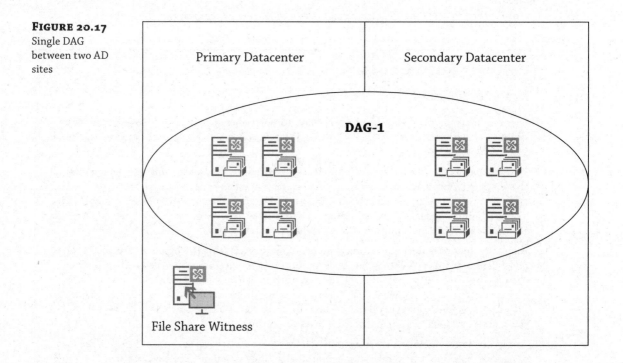

This configuration is appealing to customers who have a secondary datacenter designated for disaster recovery only or to organizations with only two viable datacenters.

There are a couple drawbacks with this site-resiliency deployment. First and foremost, if end users are located in each datacenter and the WAN connection between the datacenters were to fail, end users in the secondary datacenter would lose email services.

The other concern with this deployment is if all the Mailbox servers in the primary datacenter were to fail, an administrator would have to manually restore mailbox services in the secondary datacenter.

SINGLE DAG BETWEEN THREE AD SITES

Microsoft is touting the three AD sites' DAG configurations as the most site-resilient solution. This is because if a catastrophic failure occurs in one of the three datacenters, quorum is kept and mailbox databases are still online.

As displayed in Figure 20.18, two of the three datacenters have the same number of Mailbox servers and the third datacenter holds the file share witness.

FIGURE 20.18
Single DAG between
three AD sites

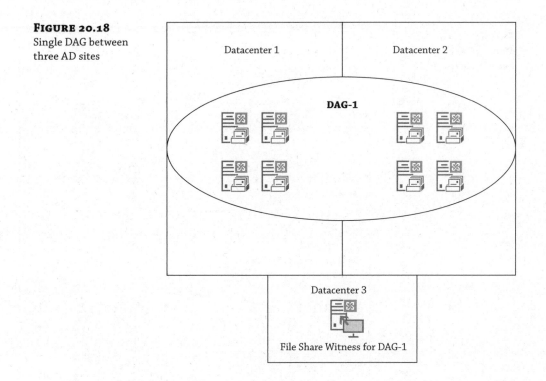

The only limitations with this deployment are first, your organization must have three data-centers with WAN connections between them, and second, if a datacenter that contains active users loses WAN connectivity, the end users could lose access to their mailboxes until WAN connectivity is restored.

MULTIPLE DAGS BETWEEN TWO AD SITES

Consider the following: Your organization has two offices and each office is used as a datacenter. After doing your research you've determined that the WAN connection between the offices is slow and unreliable. In this case, you would not create a single DAG that stretched across the two offices, but you would create a DAG at each office to ensure your design meets the company's requirements. The other option in this scenario is to work with your company and upgrade your WAN connection.

Creating multiple DAGs is an optimal deployment when the WAN connection between the datacenters does not have the throughput to support continuous replication or an organization requires mailbox databases to be replicated between the datacenters and requires mailbox services to be online in both datacenters when a WAN connection fails.

The implementation of two DAGs stretched across multiple datacenters is essentially the same configuration as stretching a single DAG between two datacenters, as shown in Figure 20.19.

FIGURE 20.19
Multiple DAGs between two AD sites

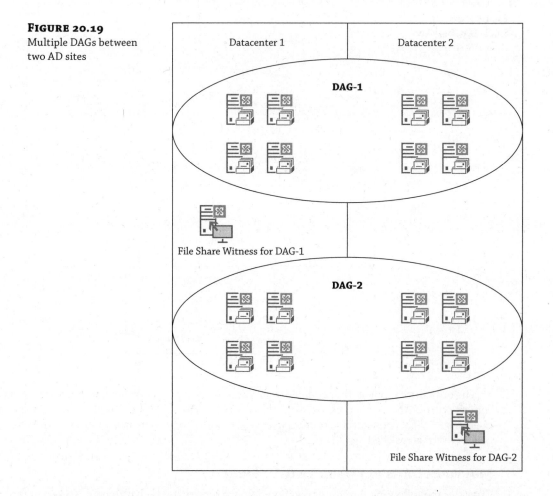

When deploying multiple DAGs, normally more hardware (servers, storage, and so on) is required and the support staff has to manage both DAGs and additional servers (patching, monitoring, and the like).

The steps to perform a site recovery are covered in the Microsoft Exchange Server 2013 Help file that can be downloaded from Microsoft's TechNet website. Depending on the configuration of a DAG, the steps to initiate a datacenter switchover will vary. Microsoft has published through TechNet a slew of information on how to fail over and switch over from one datacenter to another. Failovers occur automatically, whereas switchovers require manual intervention.

The Bottom Line

Understand database replication.   Mailbox databases can be replicated between Mailbox servers in different AD sites. Replicating databases between AD sites ensures mailbox services could be online and available if the Mailbox server in the primary site were to fail.

a) **Master It**   Your company has a DAG that is stretched across two datacenters. All databases should be mounted in the primary datacenter where the end users are located. Last week, a server had a hardware failure, causing all the databases on that Mailbox server to fail over. After the failover you noticed that some of the databases were mounted on Mailbox servers in the secondary datacenter. What solution should be put in place to prevent mailbox databases from being activated in the secondary datacenter?

Manage a database availability group.   Lagged database copies maintain an older database state by suppressing when transaction logs are written to the mailbox database. A lagged database can be used to restore mailbox content that has been removed or manipulated.

b) **Master It**   A user has reported that email messages are missing from her Inbox. After checking the client and the dumpster, the messages are still missing. The user's mailbox is on a mailbox database that has a passive lagged copy. What steps should you perform to restore the lagged database copy?

p.525

Understand Active Manager.   Behind the scenes you have a primary active manager (PAM) that is responsible for ensuring best copy and server selection in the event of a failure that causes a failover of the active database.

c) **Master It**   You have a four-member DAG split evenly across two sites. You have configured your activation preferences for failover of active databases for your database; however, when you test the process by manually bringing down the server handling the active database, the failover never goes toward your preferred server. Why are your selections being ignored?

Understand site resiliency for Exchange Server 2013.   When designing a DAG, Service Level Agreement (SLA), Recovery Time Objective (RTO), Recovery Point Objective (RPO), business requirements, and technical requirements should be used to model how the DAG is implemented.

d) **Master It**   Your company has three datacenters spread across the continental United States. Each datacenter has a low-latency, high-throughput WAN connection to the other datacenters. Users are located in two of the three datacenters. Management requires that mailbox services must be online if the power fails in one of the datacenters. Due to budget restrictions, the solution must use the minimum number of servers. How would you design a DAG solution to meet management's requirements?

Chapter 21

Understanding the Client Access Server

There is an old saying, "What's old is new again." People who have been working with Exchange Server for a long time will see striking similarity between the Exchange Server 2013 architecture and Exchange Server 2003. Once again, the Client Access role is a "simple" proxy to the mailbox backend, where the heavy lifting is performed. However, this similarity is only on the surface, and this chapter will illustrate how while the architecture looks familiar, there are some fundamental improvements to the design.

Similar to previous versions, the Client Access server role brokers all client communications, including Outlook Web App, IMAP4/POP3, Exchange ActiveSync, and Outlook Anywhere. In a change from previous versions, public folder access and unified messaging are now also client endpoints on the Client Access server role. Additionally, Exchange Server 2013 brings an end to direct remote procedure call (RPC), or MAPI, connectivity. All Outlook client connections take place using RPC over HTTP (also called Outlook Anywhere).

Perhaps one of the most exciting changes to the Client Access server role is the addition of SMTP transport services acting as a proxy to the Mailbox server role. This model is the next step in Microsoft's plan to abstract all transport and data-access functions out of the information store and away from the Mailbox server role.

Because of this dramatic change in mailbox access, there are some new capabilities that you will want to explore and some additional knowledge to be gained in understanding the Client Access server role.

Many things have not changed, however, including the Web Services model implemented in Exchange Server 2007 and 2010. For many of the services performed by the Client Access server, everything still works similarly to how it did. The Web Services model in Client Access servers forms the basis of many features used.

This chapter introduces the new features of the Client Access server role and shows you the steps required to get the most out of them.

In this chapter, you will learn to:

- ◆ Understand architecture changes in the CAS role

- ◆ Design a CAS proxy and redirection solution

- ◆ Consider Client Access servers and coexistence with previous versions of Exchange Server

- ◆ Generate valid Subject Alternative Name certificates

- ◆ Understand Front End Transport architecture changes

- ◆ Understand Unified Messaging CAS architecture changes

Learning the Client Access Server Role Architecture

Exchange Server 2000 and 2003 had the concept of a front end server that clients could connect to, and it would proxy connections to the back end server, where all of the processing and rendering would occur. Then, in Exchange Server 2007 there was a shift to move client access to a dedicated role that could do more than just proxy. If a user's mailbox server failed over, clients might not be impacted because the Client Access server (CAS) they were connected to would maintain session information, essentially decoupling the user experience from backend processing. Exchange Server 2010 continued with this design, and while it achieved its goals of providing a good user experience, it came at the cost of complexity. I always told administrators designing Exchange Server 2007/2010 that it's a misconception that the most difficult part of planning was mailbox or storage. Client access was significantly more complex and took careful planning and a good knowledge of load balancing and networking. In Exchange Server 2007 and 2010, the Client Access server was responsible for the application programming interface (API) as well as the business logic for processing client connections. In Exchange Server 2013, this functionality has been moved to the Mailbox server role, leaving the Client Access role to continue handling authentication, proxy, and redirection functionality.

Exchange Server 2013 enhances the legacy design by moving all client access to the CAS. MAPI connections from Outlook no longer exist—all Outlook connectivity now leverages RPC over HTTP (aka Outlook Anywhere). Figure 21.1 illustrates the new client connectivity model. Notice the addition of the Front End Transport service and Unified Messaging Call Router service and how Outlook, OWA, PowerShell, and EAS all use HTTP for mailbox access.

FIGURE 21.1
CAS 2013 unifies all client access.

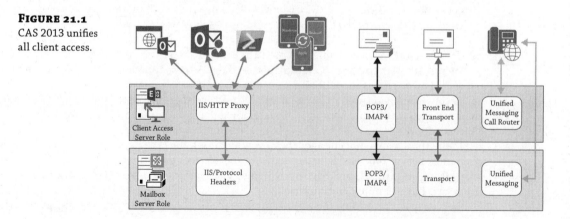

Requirements for the Client Access Server Role

When the Client Access server (CAS) was first introduced in Exchange Server 2007, the hardware requirements were more demanding than in its predecessor, the front end server in Exchange Server 2000/2003. The CAS was given a lot of responsibility because it was doing things that Mailbox servers used to do. In Exchange Server 2010, the CAS was given even more responsibility, and as a result, the system requirements were again increased. In Exchange Server 2013, because CAS is a stateless proxy, it is less demanding on resources than in these previous versions.

CAS Operating System Requirements

One of the first decisions when designing the Client Access server role is determining what version of the Windows Server operating system to run. The following is a list of the supported OS versions:

◆ Windows Server 2012 Standard or Datacenter

◆ Windows Server 2008 R2 Standard with Service Pack 1

◆ Windows Server 2008 R2 Enterprise with Service Pack 1

◆ Windows Server R2 Datacenter RTM or later

There are significant changes between Windows Server 2008 R2 and Windows Server 2012 with respect to licensing and functionality. Windows Server 2012 greatly simplifies things by including most of the functionality in the Standard edition that previously was only included in the 2008 R2 Enterprise edition. Ultimately, there are very few reasons to run Exchange Server 2013 on the Datacenter editions, though it is supported.

EXCHANGE SERVER 2013 REQUIRES A GUI VERSION OF THE OS

Exchange Server 2013 must be installed with the graphical version of the OS. For installations running Windows Server 2008 R2, this means the core installation is not supported, and you must reinstall the OS as a full installation. Windows Server 2012 can be converted from core mode by running the following PowerShell command:

```
Install-WindowsFeature Server-Gui-Mgmt-Infra, Server-Gui-Shell-Restart
```

CAS Hardware Recommendations

The next consideration when planning the installation of the Client Access server role is what hardware to use. As mentioned in the introduction, much of the workload has been moved off to the Mailbox server role, so the Client Access role has lowered the hardware requirements. Because of the reduced footprint, a multirole server is a great way to consolidate servers. A multirole server combines both Exchange Server 2013 roles on the same hardware. Later on in this chapter, we will look at the concept of multirole servers in more detail. The Client Access server role now has transport components, namely the Front End Transport service, as well. Like the Client Access services, the Front End Transport service is also stateless and does not queue or write any information to disk storage. The Front End Transport service is discussed in detail later in this chapter.

So what does this mean in terms of hardware? This means that the CAS is lighter with the use of the processor, memory, storage, and network resources. The recommendations and requirements are as follows:

Processor

◆ As with all versions of Exchange Server, x64 architecture–based processors are required. Two-socket systems are preferred over four-socket systems.

Memory

◆ The minimum RAM recommendation is 4 GB for a stand-alone CAS and 8 GB for a multi-role server. When purchasing memory, you want to pack as much memory on a single chip as possible. Large chips are generally more expensive, but they give you the option to scale up later if the load turns out to be heavier than you expected.

Storage

◆ There must be at least 30 GB of space on the drive on which you install Exchange Server for the Exchange Server binaries.

◆ Plan for at least 200 MB of available space on the system drive.

◆ The page file size minimum and maximum must be set to physical RAM plus 10 MB. This file must reside on the boot volume of the server.

Network Resources

◆ The Client Access server role puts the most of its resources toward networking, and eliminating network bottlenecks is especially important if you're servicing clients from multiple sites. This is particularly important in Exchange Server 2013, since Client Access servers now handle all client traffic and need good connectivity to Mailbox servers. Therefore, it is recommended to use Gigabit Ethernet where possible.

CALCULATING NETWORK BANDWIDTH

The Exchange Client Network Bandwidth Calculator is a useful tool when trying to model and estimate network traffic. Detailed usage of the calculator is beyond the scope of this book, but more information can be found here:

```
http://gallery.technet.microsoft.com/office/Exchange-Client-Network-8af1bf00
```

Services the Client Access Server Provides

Before we start digging deeper into the Client Access server role, we want to explain the services that the CAS provides. The Client Access server is the first point of contact for all access to mailbox data. It is also responsible for additional services, such as helping clients get their configuration. The CAS helps Exchange Server 2013 solutions scale efficiently and increase availability by creating load-balanced arrays.

Remote PowerShell

Exchange Server 2013 allows administrators to remotely connect to the Exchange Management Shell (EMS) and issue commands from another computer. This is made possible by the PowerShell virtual directory. In fact, when you open the EMS locally on an Exchange server, it connects to the PowerShell virtual directory that is running on the server itself. The PowerShell virtual directory shows up in the Internet Information Services (IIS) Manager as a web service, just like the other Exchange Server virtual directories. You can view the properties of the

PowerShell virtual directory using IIS Manager, though Microsoft recommends using the EMS cmdlets to view and make changes to the PowerShell virtual directory when possible. It is also possible to configure the PowerShell virtual directory with the Exchange Admin Center. This can be found on the Servers node, in the Virtual Directories tab.

Like other virtual directories in Exchange Server, the EMS provides a set of cmdlets that can be used for configuring the web service. Exchange Server includes the following cmdlets for PowerShell:

- `Get-PowerShellVirtualDirectory`

- `Set-PowerShellVirtualDirectory`

- `New-PowerShellVirtualDirectory`

- `Remove-PowerShellVirtualDirectory`

- `Test-PowerShellConnectivity`

Of particular note is the `Test-PowerShellConnectivity` cmdlet, which you can use to test the connection to the PowerShell virtual directory. You can specify various options with this cmdlet to test things such as the authentication method, the certificate, and the URL of the web service. This following example command will test the PowerShell connection using Basic authentication and ignoring certificate problems:

```
Test-PowerShellConnectivity -TrustAnySSLCertificate
-ConnectionUri https://mail.pacific.contoso.com -Authentication Basic
CasServer  LocalSite    Scenario      Result    Latency(MS) Error
---------  ---------    --------      ------    ----------- -----
           Honolulu     Logon User    Success      890.45
```

As you can see from the output, the test provides some useful information, such as the success of the connection and even the latency encountered.

WHAT IF I GET AN ERROR?

If you have not configured the test user account, when you run the `Test-PowerShellConnectivity` cmdlet, you will get an error. You may need to run the `new-TestCasConnectivityUser.ps1` PowerShell script first. The script is located by default in the `/Scripts` directory in the location where the Exchange Server 2013 binaries are located.

Outlook Web App

Outlook Web App (OWA) underwent several changes in Exchange Server 2013 to match the user experience in the Office 2013 suite. Some of the most interesting changes are listed here:

Modern GUI Interface   The new UI matches the new Office suite and provides a clean, minimalist view that lets you focus on data and not the interface.

Touch Experience   To support the ever-growing use of tablets and mobile devices, OWA features a touch mode interface. This changes the icons and screen layout to make it easier to work with touch-enabled devices. It is also possible to force this mode by adding ?layout=twide to the end of the OWA URL, for example, https://mail.rosenexchange .com/owa/?layout=twide.

"Three-Screen" Rendering   For full PCs, OWA will render in a three-column view. For tablets, OWA renders in a smaller two-column view, and for smartphones, the interface adapts to show in a single column. Users do not need to know different OWA URLs to get this functionality. The adaptive rendering is accomplished by Exchange when the device accesses the OWA URL. This is a great benefit to users because OWA provides a familiar user experience independent of the device being used.

Support for OWA Applications   OWA applications are the new extensibility model for Outlook and OWA. These are web applications that a third party can host and safely run inline inside the application. OWA ships with a number of built-in apps, such as Bing Maps, Suggested Meetings, and Unsubscribe.

Office Web Apps Server Integration   Previous versions of Exchange Server shipped with web-ready document viewing, which allowed users to view Office documents from a web browser. Office Web Apps are browser-based versions of Office (Word, PowerPoint, Excel, and OneNote) that allow substantially more functionality than web-ready viewing, including editing.

Access to Modern Public Folders (with CU1)   Modern public folders replace the legacy public folders in Exchange Server 2013. Modern public folders provide a similar user experience but are designed to take advantage of the high-availability and site-resilience architecture. At Exchange Server 2013's product release, OWA lacked the ability to access these folders. Cumulative Update 1 included the ability to add public folders by selecting specific folders to be added to the user's Favorites folder.

Exchange Admin Center Replaces the Exchange Control Panel   OWA leverages the new EAC. This will be covered in a little more detail in the next section.

Display Options (with CU1)   The initial release of OWA 2013 did not allow users to customize the location of the reading pane or hide it. With CU1 this functionality is back along with a few other display options.

Another major new benefit is offline email access. This requires a relatively new browser, such as Internet Explorer 10, Chrome 24 or later, or Safari 6 or later; it is dependent on the OS as well.

The new OWA relies on HTML5 technologies such as the Application Cache (AppCache)—a new feature of HTML5 that lets web developers create offline web applications. Essentially, the browser is able to take a URL offline and cache all of the scripts needed to run OWA offline. What data is available offline?

◆   150 emails or the last three days of content (whichever is larger)

◆   Inbox, drafts, recently used items (used within the previous seven days)

◆   All contacts

◆   One month prior and one year in the future of calendar information (primary calendar only)

There is some functionality that is not available offline, such as the following:

◆ Attachments

◆ Archive and team folders, tasks, and favorites

◆ Searching and sorting items

This is configured within OWA by clicking the settings gear icon ➢ Offline Settings, as shown in Figure 21.2.

FIGURE 21.2
Configuring OWA for offline use

Finally, there are some features that didn't make the cut and may eventually make their way back into the product:

S/MIME   OWA does not have the ability to create or read emails encrypted with S/MIME. Hopefully, this is on the roadmap to bring back into the product. This was the case with OWA 2010, where S/MIME functionality was added in a Service Pack. If S/MIME is required, you can use the full Outlook client.

Spell Checker   Spell-checking is now provided by the web browser, such as in Internet Explorer 10.

Customizable Filters   OWA lost the ability to have customizable filtered views and to save those views to Favorites. These features have been replaced with a number of standard, fixed filters such as View All Messages, Unread Messages, Messages Sent To User, or Flagged Messages.

Document Access   OWA cannot access SharePoint document libraries and Windows file shares. The document-access capability has been completely removed. A new Exchange Server 2013 feature, Site Mailboxes, which requires integration with SharePoint 2013, could be a good replacement but is not yet available in OWA.

Exchange Admin Center

In earlier versions of Exchange Server, users would manage their configurations with the Exchange Control Panel (ECP), and administrators would use the Exchange Management Console (EMC) to manage servers and organization configuration. Exchange Server 2013 combines the functionality of these technologies into a single web-based application named the Exchange Admin Center (EAC).

Figure 21.3 shows the results of an administrator (left side) accessing EAC compared to a user (right side) accessing it.

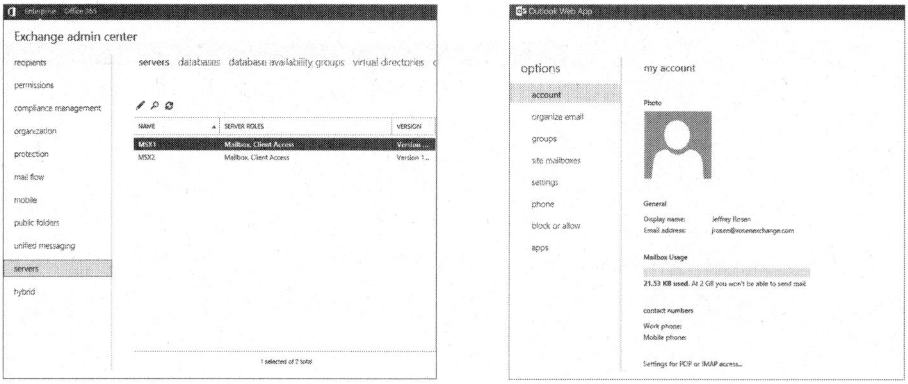

FIGURE 21.3
Side-by-side comparison of EAC for users and for administrators

The virtual directory for the EAC still references ECP. The default directory is `https://servername.domain.com/ecp`, where `servername` is the CAS server.

CONSISTENCY OF THE OWA AND ECP EXPERIENCE

Because ECP and OWA go hand in hand, you should keep the virtual directory settings similar. For example, don't require SSL on OWA but not ECP. Since the two are integrated, you want the user's experience to flow from OWA to ECP without any additional authentication prompts or other annoyances.

EAC for End Users

EAC for end users is very similar to the legacy ECP options found in Outlook Web App. Some functionality has been introduced to support new features, such as managing site mailboxes, managing your account information, and uploading a high-resolution photo.

Users can upload a photo as large as 20 MB or 648×648 pixel, and the photo is stored in a hidden folder in the mailbox. Exchange will automatically resize the photo for use by Active Directory (48×48 pixel) or by other Office applications, such as Outlook and OWA (96×96 pixel). This feature is accessible by clicking the gear icon and selecting Account. At the bottom of the My Account page, click Edit Information, which pops up a new window where a user can upload a photo or change other contact information.

Other options will be familiar to users coming from legacy versions of Exchange Server. Carried over from the ECP is the ability to manage Inbox rules and email signatures and wipe EAS mobile devices.

In addition, users can manage their own group membership, and also manage groups that they are owners on. This group-management component is a powerful new feature for users. Not only can they create distribution groups, edit their properties, and manage their memberships, but they can also determine how group membership is approved and whether the messages sent to the group are moderated. For example, the user who owns the group can determine that they want the group to require owner approval, meaning that users can only join if the owner approves. This powerful group-management component is a significant advancement in browser-based email access.

EAC for Administrators

A frequent complaint about the EMC is that it must be installed on a 64-bit workstation or lacked support for the latest operating systems. Because EAC runs entirely as a web application, all administrators need is a supported browser. To see the list of supported browsers, check the latest online help at:

```
http://technet.microsoft.com/en-us/library/jj150562%28v=exchg.150%29.aspx#SB
```

Browsers are categorized as Premium, Supported, or Unsupported.

Premium   Supports all functionality and is fully tested.

Supported   Has the same functional feature support as Premium, but features are missing from the browser or operating system (e.g., offline OWA).

Unsupported   The browser and operating system are unsupported or have not been tested and therefore may not work correctly.

Since the administration can be done with a web-based tool, this may raise security concerns. EAC provides flexibility by allowing the web application to be disabled for Internet access. This option can only be configured with PowerShell; see the following cmdlet example. Note that IISReset is used to force the change to take place immediately.

```
Set-ECPVirtualDirectory -Identity "CAS01\ecp (default web site)" -AdminEnabled
$false
IISReset /noforce
```

Note that this disables EAC access for the virtual directory, regardless of whether the `internalURL` or `externalURL` is used to access the website. Therefore, it is recommended to configure a second virtual directory for internal access to allow EAC for administrators to access internally.

Autodiscover

The Autodiscover service was introduced in Exchange Server 2007 and remains largely the same in Exchange Server 2013. This valuable service, which runs on Client Access servers, provides automatic configuration of Outlook profiles for Outlook 2007 and newer versions. This provides a way to get users up and running in an easy manner on a new machine without using scripts, running Custom Installation Wizard installations, or relying on users to set up their own account (which is always dangerous!). When setting up an Outlook profile while connected to the domain, users only have to click the Next button a few times because Outlook picks up all the relevant information from the account the user logged in with. If they're not connected to the domain, users are simply asked to enter their email address and password. (Note that users must specify their primary address; otherwise, Autodiscover may not work.)

Aside from the profile configuration, Autodiscover also provides Outlook with the information needed for downloading the offline address book, connecting to Outlook Anywhere, and even for connecting to Exchange Web Services, which, among other things, provides calendar availability information.

WINDOWS MOBILE SUPPORT FOR AUTODISCOVER

Windows Mobile 6.1 introduced the use of Autodiscover for configuring devices for Exchange ActiveSync. It's interesting to note that Windows Mobile devices use Autodiscover differently than Outlook does. While Outlook clients continuously use Autodiscover to ensure that the client is up to date, Windows Mobile uses it only on the initial configuration of the profile.

Autodiscover works in two ways, depending on whether the client is on the internal LAN and a member of the forest where the mailbox is held or is external to the LAN.

INTERNAL AUTODISCOVER

When a computer is connected to the Active Directory domain, the Autodiscover process is different than when the computer is not currently connected to the domain. The method used when Autodiscover is used on a client within the LAN is described here and shown in Figure 21.4.

1. When Outlook is launched, it checks to see if an Outlook profile exists. If there is none, it automatically fills in the user's email address and password from Active Directory.

2. Outlook then searches for a Service Connection Point (SCP) object in Active Directory for Autodiscover. An SCP is a special object that gives computers a mechanism for advertising an application or service that it is hosting. Figure 21.5 shows location of the SCP for Autodiscover.

SCP objects in Active Directory aren't only used for Exchange Server. Other applications can use SCPs as well to publish information about that service. For Exchange Server, the information published in the Autodiscover SCP gives Outlook the service-binding information of the servers hosting the Autodiscover service (the Client Access servers).

3. Outlook queries the CAS using the URL that it got from the SCP.

4. The CAS locates a Mailbox server, and the Mailbox server prepares an XML file specifically for the user.

5. The Autodiscover XML file is downloaded by the Outlook client, which applies the settings and connects the user to their mailbox.

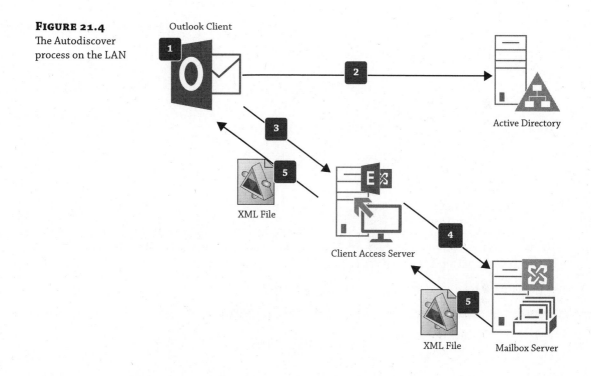

FIGURE 21.4
The Autodiscover process on the LAN

EXTERNAL AUTODISCOVER

If the user is outside the Active Directory forest (for example, on a machine that is not domain joined) or on a machine that is outside the LAN, the internal Autodiscover process is not used. If the client cannot contact the Active Directory domain, then it can't read the SCP. So the Outlook client needs another way to find out where the Autodiscover service is running. This is accomplished using the following process, which is demonstrated in Figure 21.6.

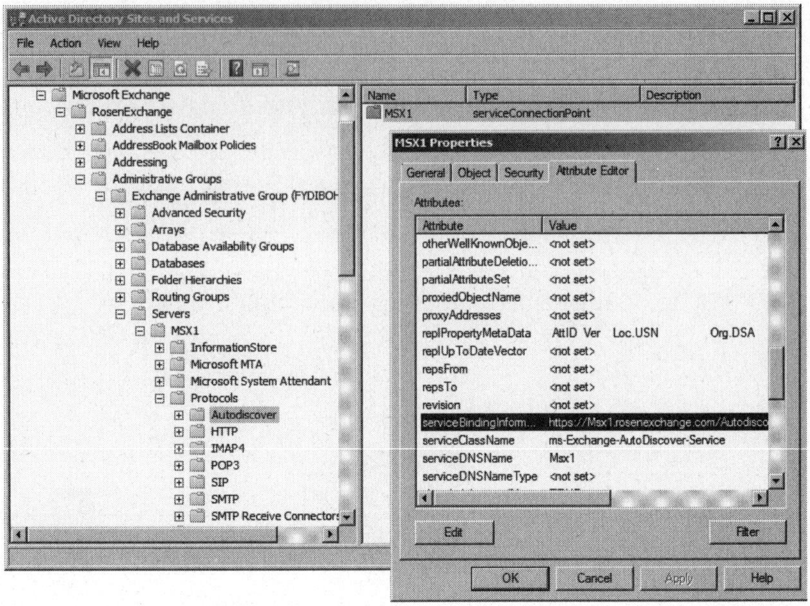

FIGURE 21.5
The location of
the SCP as seen
in Active Directory
Sites and Services

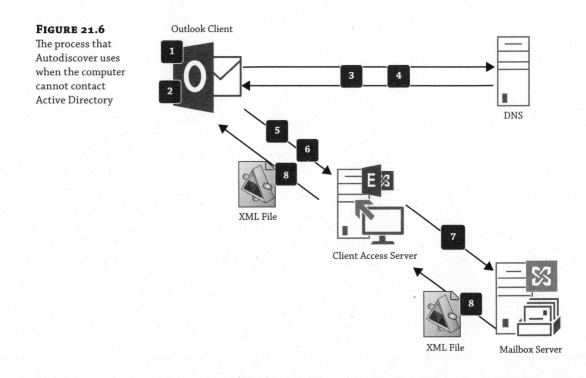

FIGURE 21.6
The process that
Autodiscover uses
when the computer
cannot contact
Active Directory

To find a Client Access server that can provide Autodiscover functions externally, the Outlook client will try to connect to one of these two URLs (where the domain is `rosenexchange.com`):

```
https://rosenexchange.com/Autodiscover/Autodiscover.xml
```

```
https://Autodiscover.rosenexchange.com/Autodiscover/Autodiscover.xml
```

For more information on this process, see the following URL:

```
http://msdn.microsoft.com/en-us/library/exchange/jj900169(v=exchg.150).aspx
```

The following steps take place when Outlook uses Autodiscover to configure the Outlook profile outside the LAN:

1. Outlook prompts the user to enter their name, password, and email address.

2. Outlook extracts the FQDN from the email address.

3. Outlook performs a DNS query for the namespace.

4. Outlook 2007 clients without a Service Pack will attempt to connect to `https://domain.com/Autodiscover/Autodiscover.xml`. If this fails, an attempt is made to connect to `https://Autodiscover.domain.com/Autodiscover/Autodiscover.xml`.

5. If the previous two attempts fail, Outlook attempts to connect using an HTTP redirect. Therefore, for the Autodiscover process to work correctly in Outlook with no Service Pack, one of the URLs must be resolvable in DNS.

6. If using Outlook 2007 SP1 or later, an additional DNS query will be performed, looking for a service locator (SRV) record that advertises Autodiscover. If this record is found, the client uses the hostname in the record to make another connection attempt to the Autodiscover service.

7. Once the connection has been made, the process continues in the same way as for internal connections, with the CAS locating a mailbox server to process the request. Exchange creates a specific XML file containing the relevant details for the user based on the credentials entered in step 1.

8. Outlook downloads the Autodiscover XML file and uses it to build the profile.

THE AUTODISCOVER XML

Now that we've discussed how Autodiscover works, let's take a look at how we can tune it. First, here's an example of the XML that is passed to the client. You can see how the XML is made up of nodes that describe the various services and their configurations:

```
<?xml version="1.0" encoding="utf-8"?>
<Autodiscover xmlns="http://schemas.microsoft.com/exchange/Autodiscover/
    responseschema/2006">
<Response xmlns="http://schemas.microsoft.com/exchange/Autodiscover/outlook/
responseschema/2006a">
```

```
  <User>
    <DisplayName>Isabel Rosen</DisplayName>
    <LegacyDN>/o=OEXCH015/ou=Exchange Administrative Group (FYDIBOHF23SPDLT)
/cn=Recipients/cn=Isabel Rosen</LegacyDN>
    <DeploymentId>996755d4-d79d-4cf9-94ba-fb91ec8877f8</DeploymentId>
  </User>
  <Account>
    <AccountType>email</AccountType>
    <Action>settings</Action>
    <Protocol>
      <Type>EXCH</Type>
      <Server>msx1.rosenexchange.com</Server>
      <ServerDN>/o=OEXCH015/ou=Exchange Administrative Group
(FYDIBOHF23SPDLT)
/cn=Configuration/cn=Servers/cn=msx1</ServerDN>
      <ServerVersion>720082AD</ServerVersion>
      <MdbDN>/o=OEXCH015/ou=Exchange Administrative Group (FYDIBOHF23SPDLT)
/cn=Configuration/cn=Servers/cn=msx1/cn=Microsoft Private MDB</MdbDN>
<ASUrl>https://mail.rosenexchange.com/EWS/Exchange.asmx</ASUrl>
<OOFUrl>https://mail.rosenexchange.com/EWS/Exchange.asmx</OOFUrl>
  <UMUrl>https://mail.rosenexchange.com/UnifiedMessaging/
Service.asmx</UMUrl>
      <OABUrl>Public Folder</OABUrl>
    </Protocol>
    <Protocol>
      <Type>EXPR</Type>
      <Server>mail.rosenexchange.com</Server>
      <SSL>On</SSL>
      <AuthPackage>Basic</AuthPackage>
      <OABUrl>Public Folder</OABUrl>
    </Protocol>
    <Protocol>
      <Type>WEB</Type>
      <External>
        <OWAUrl AuthenticationMethod="Fba">https://mail.rosenexchange.com/owa
</OWAUrl>
      <Internal>
        <OWAUrl AuthenticationMethod="Basic, Fba">
https://mail.rosenexchange.com/owa</OWAUrl>
        <Protocol>
          <Type>EXCH</Type>
<ASUrl>https://mail.rosenexchange.com/EWS/Exchange.asmx</ASUrl>
        </Protocol>
      </Internal>
    </External>
    </Protocol>
  </Account>
</Response></Autodiscover>
```

As you can see, a fair amount of information is included, in particular the URLs for the main services. So where does this information come from and how is it set?

When the CAS is installed, a virtual directory called Autodiscover is created in the IIS default website. It is from here that the configuration file is downloaded by the Outlook client. To determine which URLs to include in the XML file, Autodiscover uses the `InternalURL` and `ExternalURL` parameters from the various virtual directories. These two parameters are discussed in greater detail later in this chapter.

Outlook/Outlook Anywhere

One of the big changes with Exchange Server 2013 is the deprecation of MAPI/RPC connectivity to the Client Access server for clients, such as Microsoft Outlook. All client connectivity, both internal and external, now takes place using RPC over HTTP, also known as Outlook Anywhere. Outlook Anywhere has been updated to allow for two hostname settings, one for internal access and one for external access.

Clients use Autodiscover either through DNS or through Active Directory to get the URLs used for the various services. Autodiscover works by locating the user's mailbox and constructing an XML response containing the URLs of the various services. Outlook Anywhere's configuration is located in the EXHTTP nodes. In the sample environment in the following code, there is both an internal hostname (`msx1.rosenexchange.com`) and an external hostname (`mail.rosenexchange.com`):

```
<Protocol>
 <Type>EXHTTP</Type>
  <Server>msx1.rosenexchange.com</Server>
  <SSL>Off</SSL>
  <AuthPackage>Ntlm</AuthPackage>
  <ASUrl>https://msx1.rosenexchange.com/EWS/Exchange.asmx</ASUrl>
  <EwsUrl>https://msx1.rosenexchange.com/EWS/Exchange.asmx</EwsUrl>
  <EmwsUrl>https://msx1.rosenexchange.com/EWS/Exchange.asmx</EmwsUrl>
  <EcpUrl>https://msx1.rosenexchange.com/ecp/</EcpUrl>
  <EcpUrl-um>?rfr=olk&amp;p=customize/voicemail.aspx&amp;exsvurl=1&amp;realm=rose
nexchange.com</EcpUrl-um>
  <EcpUrl-aggr>?rfr=olk&amp;p=personalsettings/EmailSubscriptions.slab&amp;exsvur
l=1&amp;realm=rosenexchange.com</EcpUrl-aggr>
  <EcpUrl-mt>PersonalSettings/DeliveryReport.aspx?rfr=olk&amp;exsvurl=1&amp;IsOWA
=&lt;IsOWA&gt;&amp;MsgID=&lt;
      MsgID&gt;&amp;Mbx=&lt;Mbx&gt;&amp;realm=rosenexchange.com</EcpUrl-mt>
  <EcpUrl-ret>?rfr=olk&amp;p=organize/retentionpolicytags.slab&amp;exsvurl=1&amp;
realm=rosenexchange.com</EcpUrl-ret>
  <EcpUrl-sms>?rfr=olk&amp;p=sms/textmessaging.slab&amp;exsvurl=1&amp;realm=rosen
exchange.com</EcpUrl-sms>
  <EcpUrl-publish>customize/calendarpublishing.slab?rfr=olk&amp;exsvurl=1&amp;Fld
ID=&lt;FldID&gt;&amp;realm=rosenexchange.com</EcpUrl-publish>
  <EcpUrl-photo>PersonalSettings/EditAccount.aspx?rfr=olk&amp;chgPhoto=1&amp;exsv
url=1&amp;realm=rosenexchange.com</EcpUrl-photo>
  <EcpUrl-extinstall>Extension/InstalledExtensions.slab?rfr=olk&amp;exsvurl=1&amp
;realm=rosenexchange.com</EcpUrl-extinstall>
```

```
    <OOFUrl>https://msx1.rosenexchange.com/EWS/Exchange.asmx</OOFUrl>
    <UMUrl>https://msx1.rosenexchange.com/EWS/UM2007Legacy.asmx</UMUrl>
    <OABUrl>https://msx1.rosenexchange.com/OAB/36188335-bb9f-4efe-a5c1-
d4694f09b1ca/</OABUrl>
    <ServerExclusiveConnect>On</ServerExclusiveConnect>
    <CertPrincipalName>None</CertPrincipalName>
</Protocol>
<Protocol>
    <Type>EXHTTP</Type>
    <Server>mail.rosenexchange.com</Server>
    <SSL>On</SSL>
    <AuthPackage>Basic</AuthPackage>
    <ServerExclusiveConnect>On</ServerExclusiveConnect>
</Protocol>
```

If the internal hostname is not available, after a short time-out period the client will automatically roll to the second EXHTTP entry, which is the external hostname.

The Outlook Anywhere settings can be configured from EAC (Figure 21.7) or through PowerShell. In EAC, the settings are located on the Servers object; select a server and click the Edit (pencil) icon.

FIGURE 21.7
Enabling Outlook
Anywhere from
the EAC

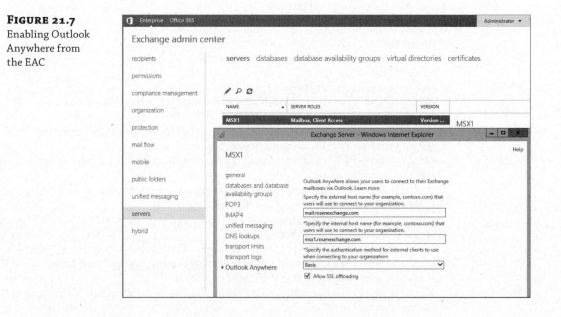

The same properties can be configured through PowerShell with the `Set-OutlookAnywhere` cmdlet. For example, to set the same configuration on all mailbox servers with properties configured as shown in the EAC example, you would use this code:

```
Get-OutlookAnywhere | Set-OutlookAnywhere -ExternalHostname "mail.rosenexchange
.com" -ExternalClientsRequireSSL $true -ExternalClientAuthenticationMethod basic
```

From within the Outlook 2013 client, these settings are shown in File ➢ Account settings ➢ Microsoft Exchange Connected Account ➢ More Settings ➢ Connection tab ➢ Exchange Proxy Settings. Other versions of Outlook may differ in the settings location.

IMAP4/POP3

IMAP4 and POP3 are largely unchanged in Exchange Server 2013. Both protocols continue to be disabled and can be enabled with Microsoft Management Console (MMC) or PowerShell. The PowerShell commands are as follows:

```
Set-service msExchangeIMAP4 -startuptype automatic
Start-service msExchangeIMAP4
Set-service msExchangePOP3 -startuptype automatic
Start-service msExchangePOP3
```

To enable this with the Services MMC, take the following steps:

1. Launch the Services snap-in. In the console tree, click Services (Local).

2. In the result pane, right-click Microsoft Exchange IMAP4, and then click Properties.

3. On the General tab under Startup Type, choose Automatic and then click Apply.

4. Under Service Status, click Start, and then click OK.

5. In the result pane, right-click Microsoft Exchange POP3, and then click Properties.

6. On the General tab under Startup Type, choose Automatic and then click Apply.

7. Under Service Status, click Start, and then click OK.

You must also enable the services on the Mailbox server role:

1. Launch the Services snap-in. In the console tree, click Services (Local).

2. In the result pane, right-click Microsoft Exchange IMAP4 Backend, and then click Properties.

3. On the General tab under Startup Type, choose Automatic and then click Apply.

4. Under Service Status, click Start, and then click OK.

5. In the result pane, right-click Microsoft Exchange POP3 Backend, and then click Properties.

6. On the General tab under Startup Type, choose Automatic and then click Apply.

7. Under Service Status, click Start, and then click OK.

There are a few changes to be aware of in Exchange Server 2013. First, for security reasons it is not possible to use anonymous or guest accounts. Also, administrator accounts are intentionally restricted. Organizations should look to leverage Exchange Web Services (EWS)–based clients as a possible replacement for IMAP4 and POP3. EWS provides for more functionality over IMAP4 and POP3, such as client throttling to prevent applications from consuming too many Exchange Server resources. Also, EWS is where Microsoft is making future investments in product innovation.

The Availability Service

The Availability service is installed by default as part of the Client Access server role in the Exchange Web Services interface. The primary job of the Availability service is to retrieve free/busy information about other users. Back in Exchange Server 2003, free/busy information was published in a public folder. Now that legacy or traditional public folders have been removed from Exchange Server 2013, all clients rely on the Availability service. When users use Outlook 2007 or later, or Outlook Web App, and access free/busy information for mailboxes on Outlook 2007 or later, then the Availability service retrieves that information straight from the user's mailbox. CAS 2013 is just the client connection point, and the work is really performed by the Mailbox server.

Here's how the Availability service works:

1. The Outlook client locates the Availability service URL using Autodiscover. The client then connects to the URL (on the Client Access server) given by Autodiscover.

2. CAS 2013 locates the Mailbox server where the requestor's active database is currently running. For example, in a database availability group, there may be more than one copy of the user's database. It uses this Mailbox server to proxy the EWS request to.

3. If the target users are located on this Mailbox server, the request will be handled locally. If the target users reside on another Mailbox server, the request will be proxied directly to the Mailbox server of each target user by using the EWS protocol.

    This process may vary if different Exchange Server versions are involved. For example, if the requesting mailbox is on Exchange Server 2013 and the target mailbox is on Exchange Server 2010, then the Exchange Server CAS 2013 will talk to the Exchange Server CAS 2010 and retrieve the free/busy information. This happens even if the servers are in the same site.

The Availability service enables some other great functionality. When coupled with the Outlook's scheduling assistant, it provides suggested meeting times, and Exchange Server suggests the time when all users and resources are available. It also allows users to share their calendar information in more granular ways. For each target person or group, users can choose one of four levels of sharing on the Properties page for their calendar.

On the Permissions tab of the Calendar Properties dialog, users can control the following settings:

◆ Whether items can be deleted or modified

◆ Item and detail visibility, such as the subject of a meeting, location, and meeting time

◆ How free/busy information is published

Positioning the Client Access Server Role

After you complete your design for the hardware on which the Client Access server role will run, the next step to consider is the positioning of the Client Access server role in your LAN. As a bare minimum, every Active Directory site hosting a Mailbox server also requires a CAS.

As with Exchange Server 2007, you want to avoid placing your Exchange Server 2013 Client Access servers in your perimeter network. This is important because the CAS uses RPCs to connect to the Mailbox server role. Because of this, the number of ports you must open to provide access for your CAS leaves a rather large hole for potential attack. You can either publish a CAS directly to Internet clients or you can use a reverse proxy to provide an additional layer of protection. We strongly urge you to put your Client Access servers on your internal network and use a reverse proxy to publish the servers to the Internet. In fact, placing your Client Access servers in the perimeter network is not a scenario supported by Microsoft. There is a great blog post about this (which still applies to Exchange Server 2013) on the Exchange Team Blog:

```
http://msexchangeteam.com/archive/2009/10/21/452929.aspx
```

So what are you expected to do? Our recommendation is to place the Client Access server role on your internal LAN and then proxy connections to it using a web-publishing server like Forefront Unified Access Gateway (UAG). Both Microsoft UAG and the previous product, Microsoft Threat Management Gateway (TMG), will receive updates for compatibility with Exchange Server 2013. TMG is no longer available for purchase, but if you already own it, it may also be used. These types of products give you many benefits, not the least of which is that the only thing being exposed directly to Internet traffic is the proxy/firewall—which is designed specifically for that exposure. When using UAG, you also get the benefit of preauthentication, which ensures that only authenticated traffic gets through to your internal LAN. On top of this, all inbound connection requests are inspected to ensure they are valid. Another possibility is to leverage a hardware load balancer. Today's hardware load balancers also perform much of this functionality. This makes things even more secure by closely checking all traffic to your Client Access servers for potential HTML exploits and nonstandard HTML requests before passing it through to your LAN.

Network Placement

One of the decisions to make is where to place the Client Access server role. First off, every Active Directory (AD) site that has a Mailbox server role must also contain a Client Access server role.

Figure 21.8 illustrates why this is the case. In this example, there are two AD sites—one with both CAS and Mailbox server roles, and the other with just a Mailbox server. Users in AD Site 2 cannot connect directly to the Mailbox server in the local AD site, since all client connectivity is provided by the CAS role. In this case the users are directed to the CAS server in AD Site 1, which provides access to the mailbox across AD sites. While it technically does work, the WAN becomes a single point of failure. If there are any issues with the WAN, users in AD Site 2 will not be able to access the Mailbox server in the same AD site. For this reason, it is required to have the both roles present.

FIGURE 21.8
Each AD site
requires a
CAS role.

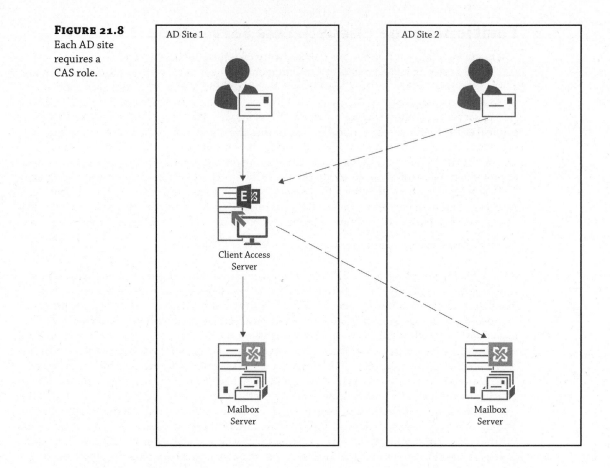

Multirole Servers

Now that you understand when you are required to have the CAS role, another design
question arises: Should it be collocated with the Mailbox server role? Exchange Server 2007
first introduced the ability to collocate the server roles, resulting in a *multirole server*. The idea
behind this is that administrators like to fully utilize resources on a server. In many customers'
environments, where each role was deployed on a separate server, they would appear to barely
consume any resources, except the Mailbox server role. The Client Access role used a lot of
memory but was fairly moderate on storage and CPU resources. The Hub Transport role, on
the other hand, didn't require significant memory resources and was slightly lower on CPU
but had higher storage requirements. Combining these two roles resulted in a more efficient
use of server resources. As more powerful servers became available, and hypervisors support
larger numbers of virtual CPUs (vCPUs), it became even more efficient to combine the CAS,
Hub Transport, and Mailbox server roles. The Unified Messaging (UM) role has high CPU
requirements and thus didn't combine well with the Mailbox role. The other bonus with this
architecture is that generally most implementations needed more Mailbox servers than the other
roles, but using multirole servers gave additional CAS and Hub Transport capacity and resulted
in overall lower total server counts.

Exchange Server 2013 follows the same principle. The Exchange CAS 2013 is very lightweight and has very little overhead when placed on the same server as the Mailbox role. CAS has no storage requirement and does not do any rendering or business logic. Because we get the same benefit of the overall additional capacity, and do not have the same concerns about versioning during patching, multirole Exchange Server 2013 servers are highly recommended.

You may be tempted to think *now that the CAS is just a stateless proxy for clients and transport, would it make sense to place it in a perimeter network?* Unfortunately, like in previous versions of Exchange, it is unsupported to put any Exchange server role, with the exception of the Edge Transport server, in a perimeter network.

Namespace Planning

Customers like to make it easier for their users to have access to their mailbox data. To achieve this goal, many customers want to use a single namespace—such as mail.rosenexchange.com for all client access, regardless of which protocol is being used. Exchange Server 2013 finally makes this option a reality. I can hear some administrators reading this section thinking, *wait a minute…we do this today on our legacy Exchange Server.* If, for example, you use a global traffic manager (GTM) with Exchange Server 2010 in order to use a single namespace, you are in effect going against what the product was designed to do. The communication in 2010 between the CAS and mailbox is RPC, while from the client to CAS it is HTTP. Therefore, you are better off making a client connection to the CAS closest to your Mailbox server since RPC connectivity requires low latency as compared to the client's connection to the CAS via HTTP, which works well on higher-latency links. The GTM, in this case, will try to get you to the closest CAS to where the client is located. This means a user who is traveling may get a CAS close to them, and that CAS is doing a cross-site connection back to the mailbox across the WAN over RPC. The user would have a better experience had they made a connection to the CAS local to the mailbox and used HTTP across the WAN. Now that you have the background, you can see that because CAS 2013 talks to the mailbox via HTTP, you can connect to any CAS and expect a good user experience. The next two sections further the discussion on namespace planning, by looking at two methods for getting users access to their mailboxes when there are multiple sites with Exchange Server.

CLIENT ACCESS SERVER PROXYING

Let's take a more detailed look at how remote access works and, more specifically, how your placement of Client Access servers and Internet connections affects what happens.

First, you need to understand how Client Access servers talk to Mailbox servers when users try to access their mailboxes. If you have a single Active Directory site (Baltimore) with Exchange servers in it, then you have a fairly simple scenario, as shown in Figure 21.9. You would provide remote access via a reverse proxy or some other type of firewall. In this scenario, the user talks to the CAS (either directly or through the firewall) and the CAS talks to the Mailbox server.

So what about when you introduce another Active Directory site (Honolulu) with Mailbox and Client Access servers? It depends. Let's look at a situation where a user, Nora, has her mailbox on a Mailbox server in Honolulu. If Nora were to use Outlook Web App to access the CAS in Baltimore (CAS-1), the server would look up Nora's mailbox location in Active Directory and find that her mailbox is actually hosted on a Mailbox server in Honolulu (MB-2).

FIGURE 21.9
A simple single-site
Exchange Server
setup

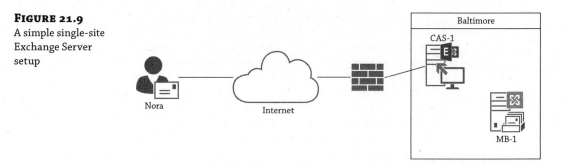

FIGURE 21.9
A simple single-site
Exchange Server
setup

At this point, the CAS in Baltimore (CAS-1) will determine if an external URL is configured for the CAS in Honolulu (CAS-2). If not, CAS-1 will contact CAS-2 and then proxy Nora's request to it. CAS-2 gets the info from Nora's Mailbox server and passes it back to CAS-1. From there the information is returned to Nora. So proxying is nothing more than one CAS telling another CAS to access the user's mailbox because it can't contact the Mailbox server itself. As shown in Figure 21.10, the cross-site traffic between Client Access servers uses HTTPS and not RPC. HTTPS is better to use than RPC for long-distance connections that are unreliable and susceptible to network latency.

When designing your Exchange Server topology to include Client Access servers, keep in mind that proxying only works in a point-to-point fashion between the requesting CAS and a CAS in the same site as the Mailbox server. If firewalls are in place that prevent this traffic, the CAS will not negotiate a hop-to-hop route via another site where there is connectivity.

FIGURE 21.10
A simple CAS
proxy scenario

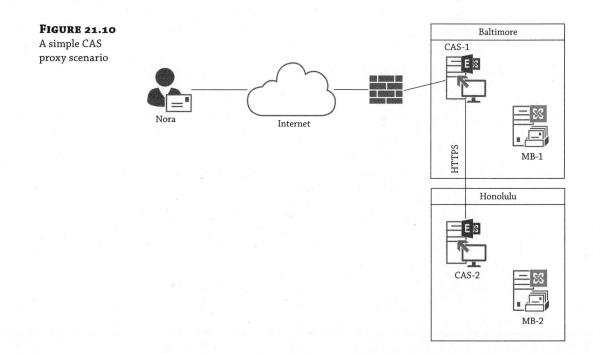

In addition to the web-based protocols, Exchange Server 2013 provides support for IMAP and POP3 proxying. Client Access servers are configured for proxying IMAP and POP3 by default.

To provide a better understanding of proxying, we want to introduce you to two important parameters. The `InternalURL` and `ExternalURL` parameters can be specified on web-accessible virtual directories, such as Outlook Web App, the Exchange Admin Center, Exchange ActiveSync, and the Offline Address Book virtual directories. These parameters define how the CAS performs proxying and redirection. In many cases, Client Access servers that are Internet-facing should have their public, Internet-accessible URL in the `ExternalURL` parameter for the web services that are accessible over the Internet, such as Outlook Web App or Exchange ActiveSync. For example, this URL could be `https://mail.rosenexchange.com/owa`. If you don't specify an `ExternalURL` for your Internet-facing servers, those servers won't be used for client redirection. If you are using a single-site configuration, you don't need the `ExternalURL` specified for OWA. However, if you want to take advantage of using Autodiscover for external client configuration, you will still need to configure `ExternalURL` for Exchange ActiveSync, Offline Address Book distribution, and Exchange Web Services. One change with Exchange Server 2013 is that if the `ExternalURL` parameter is configured with the same name, Exchange Server will proxy the connection rather than doing redirection.

In the `InternalURL` parameter, the CAS should have the URL that users inside the network will use to access it. This is important, because when a Client Access server (CAS-1) realizes that the mailbox it's looking for isn't in its site, it looks in Active Directory to find another Client Access server (CAS-2) that is in the same site as the mailbox that it wants to access. When CAS-1 uses CAS-2 as a proxy, CAS-1 uses the `InternalURL` parameter for CAS-2 to figure out how to connect to it. If your `InternalURL` is wrong or missing, that server can't be used for proxying.

Similar to Exchange Server 2010, the Exchange Server 2013 setup process allows administrators to configure the external URL during installation, and the appropriate virtual directories are configured for you.

The `InternalURL` is the server's fully qualified domain name (FQDN), which is also what the default self-signed certificate (see the section, "Certificates" later in this chapter) uses for its subject name. This could be the name that the clients inside your network will use to access the service on your CAS. If you are configuring a CAS only for internal access (either for use by internal clients or for other Client Access servers that proxy requests to it), you should set the `ExternalURL` parameter to `$Null` for the virtual directories listed here:

- Exchange ActiveSync
- Exchange Control Panel
- Exchange Web Services
- Offline Address Book
- Outlook Web App
- Unified Messaging

Table 21.1 summarizes the recommended `InternalURL` and `ExternalURL` configurations. There are some important things that you should note about this information. First, a split-brain DNS architecture is assumed. This means that the namespace used on your internal DNS servers is also the namespace used on your external DNS servers. Technically, both zones are authoritative, but the server used will depend on whether the client is coming from inside or outside your network. Second, this information assumes that you are using load-balanced Client Access servers, which we recommend as a standard practice in Exchange Server 2013. And finally, you should configure the AutoDiscoverServiceInternalUri property to be the FQDN of the load balancer on the CAS and the EWS property called InternalNLBBypassURL should be set to the Client Access server FQDN.

TABLE 21.1:   Recommended InternalURL and ExternalURL configurations

VIRTUAL DIRECTORY	InternalURL	ExternalURL (INTERNET-FACING SERVERS)	ExternalURL (NON-INTERNET-FACING SERVERS)
Exchange ActiveSync	Load-Balancer FQDN	Load-Balancer FQDN	$null
Exchange Control Panel	Load-Balancer FQDN	Load-Balancer FQDN	$null
Exchange Web Services	Load-Balancer FQDN	Load-Balancer FQDN	$null
Offline Address Book	Load-Balancer FQDN	Load-Balancer FQDN	$null
Outlook Web App	Load-Balancer FQDN	Load-Balancer FQDN	$null
Unified Messaging	Load-Balancer FQDN	Load-Balancer FQDN	$null

If you don't specify an external URL for your Client Access servers during Exchange Server setup, the ExternalURL parameter will already be empty. You only need to go back and clear the parameter if you've specified an external URL for your CAS but don't want every web service available externally. For example, you could disable the ExternalURL parameter for the Outlook Web App service but keep it enabled for the OAB distribution service. You can only clear the ExternalURL parameter on some of the virtual directories using the Exchange Management Console. For the rest, you will need to use the Exchange Management Shell. The following are the EMS cmdlets that you can use to clear the ExternalURL parameter on different virtual directories:

Exchange ActiveSync Set-ActiveSyncVirtualDirectory

Exchange Control Panel Set-EcpVirtualDirectory

Exchange Web Services Set-WebServicesVirtualDirectory

Offline Address Book Set-OabVirtualDirectory

Outlook Web App Set-OwaVirtualDirectory

PowerShell Set-PowerShellVirtualDirectory

The following example demonstrates the usage of the `Set-OwaVirtualDirectory` cmdlet in the EMS to set the default OWA virtual directory `ExternalURL` parameter to a null value:

```
Set-OwaVirtualDirectory "CAS-1\owa (Default Web Site)" -ExternalURL $Null
```

🌐 Real World Scenario

OUTLOOK WEB APP AND THE EXCHANGE ADMIN CENTER

Outlook Web App and the Exchange Admin Center are closely tied together. Users will be logging into OWA to read their mail and then using the EAC to access their options. If you set an `ExternalURL` for OWA but not for EAC, users may not be able to use the Options button in OWA. When setting the `ExternalURL` parameter on the OWA virtual directory, make sure that you set the `ExternalURL` parameter on the EAC virtual directory as well.

To demonstrate how the `InternalURL` and `ExternalURL` affect proxying, let's take another look at what happens when Nora tries to get to her mail from that Baltimore CAS. Here's what happens when Nora tries to open Outlook Web App:

1. The CAS in Baltimore (CAS-1) locates a CAS in the same Active Directory site as Nora's Mailbox server (Honolulu).

2. The Baltimore CAS determines if the Honolulu CAS has the `ExternalURL` property configured. If it does, Nora's web session is manually redirected to the Honolulu CAS (more on redirection in the next section of this chapter).

3. If the Honolulu CAS does not have the `ExternalURL` set, then the Baltimore CAS checks for an `InternalURL` on the Honolulu CAS.

4. If the `InternalURL` is configured and the web service is configured to use Integrated Windows authentication, the connection is proxied to the location specified in the `InternalURL` property.

CLIENT REDIRECTION

Redirection occurs when you set up multiple Internet-facing Client Access servers in different Active Directory sites. If a user connects to a CAS that is not in the same site as their mailbox, and if there is an Internet-facing CAS that is in the same site as the user's mailbox, the user will be redirected to the Internet-facing CAS in the site that their mailbox is in. Redirection is useful because it's generally a good idea to avoid proxying when possible. There's nothing inherently wrong with proxying, but the user will get the best experience when connecting to a CAS in the same site as their Mailbox server. Also, redirection puts less of a toll on WAN utilization.

For Outlook Web App, this redirection comes in the form of a web page redirection, where the user is warned to, "Use the following link to open this mailbox with the best performance." This is simply a web page that tells the user that they would be better off using the CAS closest to their site. This does not happen automatically; the user has to physically click the link to the site that they are being redirected to and reauthenticate.

For this process to work, the CAS that the user connects to needs to be able to determine whether the CAS near the user's mailbox is Internet-facing. To make this determination, the server uses the ExternalURL parameter. If the ExternalURL is filled out, the server is considered Internet-facing. Our recommendation is to configure your Internet-facing Client Access server web services with different URLs. Since Active Directory sites typically align to physical regions, many organizations use a geographic URL, such as ne-owa.domain.com or mail .europe.domain.com.

Load Balancing

One of the features you undoubtedly have seen advertised about Exchange Server 2013 is removing the need for layer 7 load balancing; it works with a layer 4 load balancer. This will simplify deployments and allow for less-costly infrastructure needed to support Exchange Server. Let's begin with a quick primer on load balancing and see what problem we are trying to solve by using a hardware load balancer. Also, this background is important because even though it is true that layer 4 is all that is required, layer 7 is still not appropriate for many designs.

Load balancers seek to solve multiple problems, one being how you can leverage multiple resources to act as one. For example, you have the need for multiple Client Access servers to provide higher availability. You may need to take a server offline for maintenance but not want to interrupt service. Or, because of scale limitations, you may need multiple servers to handle the load. Load balancers solve this by taking in the client connections and managing the traffic to downstream servers. This way a client knows it can connect to one location (namespace), and it does not need to know that physically there are many resources actually handing the processing. But this architecture may cause a new issue, one of persistence and affinity. A client connection now goes to a particular server, and subsequent conversations need to be directed to the same server to preserve things like authentication. In order to maintain this server affinity (sometimes referred to as *stickiness*), the load balancer must be able to map the client connection to the backend server somehow. In comes the Open Systems Interconnection (OSI) model. The OSI model describes a layered system used for communications in a network. Layer 7 refers to the Application layer in the OSI model. A layer 7 load balancer for our purposes is one that can look at the data from the application—in this case Exchange—and use it to make load-balancing decisions. One example of this is how the load balancer sees the target virtual directory (vDir), like /OWA or /Autodiscover.

In contrast, layer 4 is the Transport layer. For our purposes, we can think of layer 4 as where TCP and UDP (Transport Control Protocol and User Datagram Protocol) live. So, at layer 4, the load balancer has no idea what the target URL is; it simply knows the source and target IP addresses and ports and can only use this information for load balancing.

The reason this layer discussion is important comes back to the point about affinity. At layer 4, the load balancer is limited to using information like source IP to maintain affinity, whereas layer 7 has many options such as HTTP cookies or SSL Session ID. Source IP may not be adequate in some environments where many clients share the same source IP, typically when Network Address Translation (NAT) is used.

Due to changes in the 2013 architecture, all of the user's session state information is maintained on the Mailbox server role. This means the CAS truly acts as only a proxy, and there is no need to have requests maintain affinity. This sounds great because it's a much simpler design and may scale better since the load balancer has to do less work. Now for the trade-offs with using a layer 4 load balancer.

When the load balancer needs to send a connection to a CAS, how does it determine which one to choose? You would probably like the load balancer to base a decision on the health of the target, since it would not make sense to send a client to a CAS where the required service is unavailable. Remember, at layer 4 you do not have the information about the target protocol (vDir). Most load balancers provide some health-check functionality, such as a port ping to see if the server is healthy. Without knowledge at the individual protocol level, the best you can do is pick one of the vDirs as a representative for the whole server. An administrator may choose to pick /OWA, which is as good as any other protocol. What if the incoming request is for Outlook Anywhere (/RPC) but /OWA is unavailable? The load balancer in this case would mark the server as unhealthy, when really only OWA is affected, and the user is trying to make an Outlook Anywhere connection. This can be summarized by saying layer 4 with a single namespace (e.g., mail.rosenexchange.com for all protocols) results in health measured per server. With a layer 7 hardware load balancer, the hardware load balancer can terminate the SSL session, see that the request is destined for /RPC, determine that the vDir is healthy, and send the client traffic to the CAS despite /OWA being unavailable. In summary, layer 7 with a single namespace for all protocols results in the health being measured by protocol. So what? Well, the layer 4 model may result in a server not being used, even though it is really mostly healthy.

Finally, a common question for load balancing Exchange Server is *do I need to use a hardware load balancer; what about DNS round robin or Windows Network Load Balancer (WNLB)?* Both DNS and WNLB are able to load-balance Exchange Server traffic, but neither solution is recommended over a hardware load balancer. WNLB has a few major drawbacks:

◆ No ability to perform virtual directory or server health checks

◆ Scalability issues such as port flooding and limit of eight nodes

◆ Lack of good management tools

◆ Incompatible with Windows Failover Clustering, and the preferred deployment architecture is a multirole server

For these reasons, WNLB is not a very good choice for load-balancing Exchange Server 2013. DNS round robin (DNS RR) has many of the same issues as WNLB. DNS RR, however, may be appropriate if used in front of hardware load balancers. For example, where you may have deployed a global traffic manager (GTM), it is possible to simplify and just use DNS RR to replace it. Also, DNS RR works well for lab environments, removing the need to have costly hardware that is underutilized.

Coexistence with Previous Versions of Exchange Server

There is a good chance you are coming from a previous version of Exchange Server. This section should help administrators get an understanding of how Exchange Server 2013 Client Access can coexist with previous versions of Exchange Server. It is important to understand how client requests are routed between versions and what the end-user experience may be. Before we get into the details, let's look at the following high-level summary of supported environments.

Exchange Server 2003 or Earlier Unsupported

Exchange Server 2007 Requires update rollup 10 for Service Pack 3 on all servers in the org; requires Exchange Server 2013 CU1 on all servers in the org

Exchange Server 2010 Requires Service Pack 3 on all servers in the org; requires Exchange Server 2013 CU1 on all servers in the org

Office 365 with Exchange Server 2013–based Hybrid Tenant Supported; requires Exchange Server 2013 CU1 on all servers in the org

Coexistence with Exchange Server 2010

The good news is that Exchange Server 2013's coexistence with Exchange Server 2010 is very straightforward and provides a good user experience. The general coexistence steps are as follows:

1. Prepare the Exchange Server 2010 infrastructure by deploying Service Pack 3 or later across the org.

2. Install the Exchange Server 2013 servers.

3. Obtain and deploy certificates.

4. Move namespaces to CAS 2013.

5. Move mailboxes to Exchange Server 2013.

Before we take a look at the individual protocols and see how they work in coexistence with 2013, you should understand how CAS 2013 picks a target CAS 2010 server. At startup, a CAS 2013 server reads information from Active Directory to create its own view of the Exchange Server organization. Once per minute, the CAS 2013 sends a small HTTP HEAD request for each protocol to every target CAS 2010 server that it knows about from the Active Directory discovery. Based on the response, if the response is an HTTP 300 or 400, CAS 2013 knows the target server is healthy. If it receives a 503 error or time-out, it will retry to make sure the fault wasn't due to a transient error. If the retry produces the same result, CAS 2013 will mark it unavailable in its own view and will not use the CAS 2010 as the target endpoint. After the next minute, the process repeats and if the server is now healthy, the CAS 2013 server will resume using it as a target. Keep in mind that every CAS 2013 server does this independently and will try to communicate with every CAS 2010 server for every protocol. In some environments this results in a lot of additional network traffic—even though the HTTP HEAD request is quite small, your network administrators may notice an increase in traffic and want to understand what is going in. Currently, there is no ability to tune this process other than marking the CAS 2010 as unavailable with the following PowerShell cmdlet:

```
Set-ClientAccessServer -IsOutOfService
```

Now that the CAS 2013 has its own view of healthy target CAS 2010 servers, how does it pick one as a target? There is no special logic; CAS 2013 will pick any healthy CAS 2010 in the target AD site. CAS 2013 constructs its own URL, regardless of the internalURL settings. This allows you to configure the internalURL to a load-balanced name, and it will not affect CAS 2013's ability to proxy the connection. It also means that CAS 2013 ignores any certificate information (e.g., name mismatch) for that connection.

OWA

The first scenario to understand is OWA access when Exchange Server is configured for proxy (Figure 21.11). Remember, one of the first steps in coexistence is to redirect the namespaces to Exchange Server 2013. Once this is established, users' requests for `mail.rosenexchange.com` will go through the hardware load balancer to the Exchange Server CAS 2013. From there, CAS 2013 will proxy the request via HTTP to a CAS 2010, regardless of whether the mailbox is in the same site or needs to cross site boundaries. In this example, Site 2 could be a non-Internet-facing site.

FIGURE 21.11
OWA 2013
coexistence with
Exchange Server 2010
configured for proxy

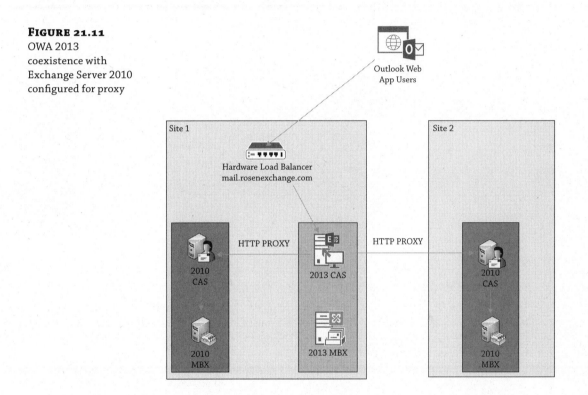

In Figure 21.12, the environment is configured for redirection. This scenario behaves just like previous versions. The user connects to the Exchange Server CAS 2013, which determines that the user's mailbox is in the other AD site. Since the CAS in Site 2 is configured with an `externalURL`, the user is redirected directly to Site 2 for mailbox access. Note that this is a silent redirection, meaning the user will automatically be redirected and not presented a link; however, this does not provide a single sign-on experience. Users will get forms-based authentication from the CAS 2010 in Site 2 and will be required to provide their credentials. To avoid this double authentication, users should use the `mail2.rosenexchange.com` URL to avoid the redirection.

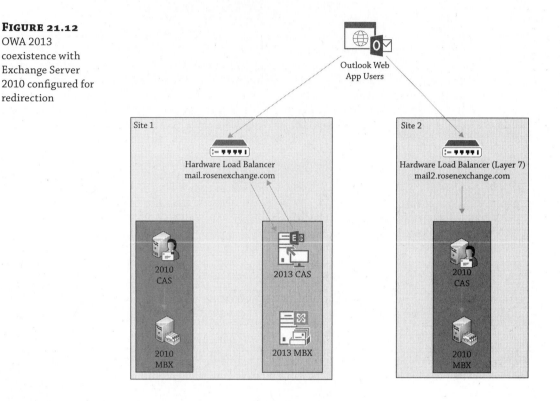

FIGURE 21.12
OWA 2013 coexistence with Exchange Server 2010 configured for redirection

EXCHANGE ACTIVESYNC

EAS is a similar experience to OWA. In Figure 21.13, a user's mailbox is on Exchange Server 2010 in the same site (Site 1) as the Exchange Server CAS 2013. The client will use Autodiscover to find the correct endpoint. In this case the client will connect to the CAS 2013, which will proxy the connection to the CAS 2010 in Site 1.

Extending this example further, Site 2 is a non-Internet-facing site. Again, the user will connect to Exchange Server 2013 in Site 1, which will proxy the connection to the CAS 2010 in Site 2.

If Site 2 is an Internet-facing site with its own namespace, the client will use Autodiscover to find the correct endpoint. This will send the client directly to the CAS 2010 in Site 2, and as Figure 21.14 shows, it does not go through the 2013 infrastructure.

EXCHANGE WEB SERVICES

At this point you are probably seeing a pattern emerging. Exchange Server 2013 coexistence with Exchange Server 2010 works pretty well out of the box. Like with the other protocols, a user will connect to the CAS 2013, which in turn will proxy the connection to the CAS 2010 in Site 1. Similarly, if Site 2 is a non-Internet-facing site, the CAS 2013 will proxy the connection to the CAS 2010 in Site 2; see Figure 21.15.

FIGURE 21.13
EAS 2013 coexistence
with Exchange Server
2010 configured
for proxy

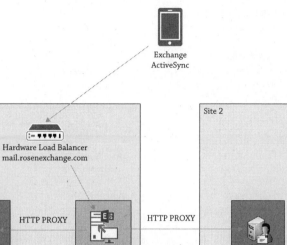

FIGURE 21.13
EAS 2013 coexistence
with Exchange Server
2010 configured
for proxy

Exchange
ActiveSync

Site 1

Hardware Load Balancer
mail.rosenexchange.com

HTTP PROXY   HTTP PROXY

2010 CAS   2013 CAS   2010 CAS

2010 MBX   2013 MBX   2010 MBX

Site 2

FIGURE 21.14
EAS 2013 coexistence
with Exchange Server
2010 configured for
redirection

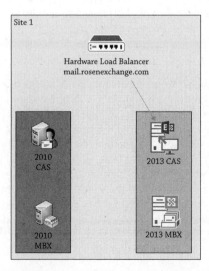

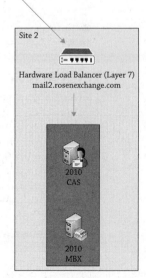

Exchange
ActiveSync

Site 1

Hardware Load Balancer
mail.rosenexchange.com

2010 CAS   2013 CAS

2010 MBX   2013 MBX

Site 2

Hardware Load Balancer (Layer 7)
mail2.rosenexchange.com

2010 CAS

2010 MBX

FIGURE 21.15
EWS 2013
coexistence
with Exchange
Server 2010
configured
for proxy

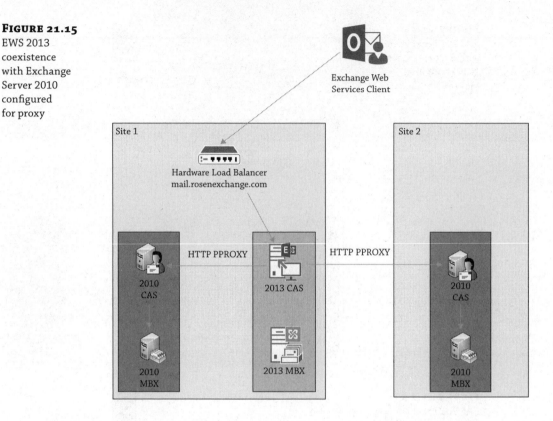

In Figure 21.16, where Site 2 has its own namespace, Autodiscover will return the correct URLs for the client's connection. EWS itself does not do any redirection. The user will perform an Autodiscover request and connect to Mail2 directly.

AUTODISCOVER

Since EWS and some of the other protocols rely on Autodiscover to work correctly, let's take a look at how it functions with Exchange Server 2010 coexistence. Remember, the first step is to move the Autodiscover namespace to CAS 2013. CAS 2013 will authenticate and perform mailbox discovery on the user (determine if the user's mailbox is on an Exchange Server 2010 or 2013 server). Since this example has the user on a 2010 Mailbox server, the CAS 2013 proxies the request to a CAS 2010 in the same AD site, or in the case where Site 2 is non-Internet-facing, to a CAS 2010 in the remote site. CAS 2010 is actually responding to the request and CAS 2013 is acting as the proxy. The client will do the initial discovery through either DNS or Active Directory. This depends on whether the client is domain-joined and on the corporate network, or non-domain-joined or externally connected. Figure 21.17 shows this concept.

FIGURE 21.16
EWS 2013 coexistence with Exchange Server 2010 configured for redirection

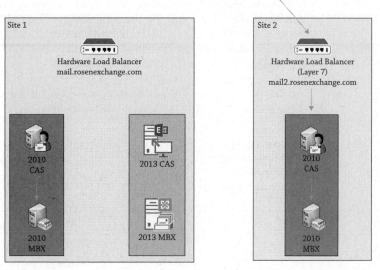

FIGURE 21.17
Autodiscover process with Exchange Server 2013 coexistence and Exchange Server 2010

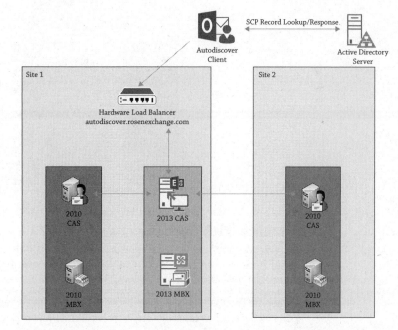

OUTLOOK ANYWHERE

CAS 2013 will happily proxy Outlook Anywhere connections for Exchange Server 2010 mailboxes. Outlook clients will connect to the Outlook Anywhere endpoint, which resolves to the CAS 2013 servers. CAS 2013 acts as an HTTP proxy to the Exchange Server CAS 2010. In order to proxy, every CAS 2010 must have Outlook Anywhere enabled.

There is one thing to be aware of in order for this to allow connections. In Exchange Server 2010 it was typical to configure the authentication mechanism to basic for both client and server authentication. If so, this will break authentication and a change to Exchange Server 2010 is required. It is possible to set client and system authentication differently. The client authentication method should be set to match the client authentication type of CAS 2013. The IIS authentication needs to be set to NTLM using the Set-OutlookAnywhere cmdlet. If you had previously configured Exchange Server 2010 for NTLM, you do not need to alter the configuration. Figure 21.18 illustrates this architecture.

FIGURE 21.18
Exchange Server 2013
Outlook Anywhere
coexistence with Exchange
Server 2010

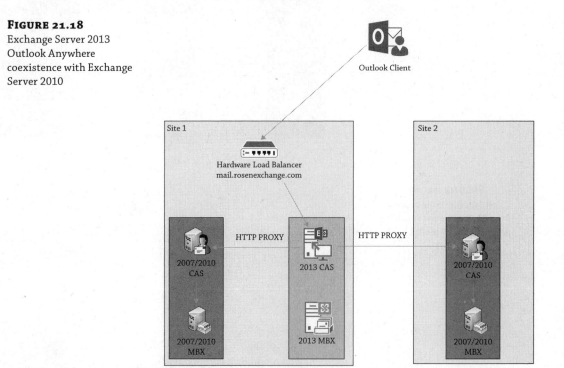

Coexistence with Exchange Server 2007

Exchange Server 2007 coexistence works a bit differently than 2010 coexistence. It requires additional steps to leverage a legacy namespace that is required for 2007 coexistence. The general coexistence steps are as follows:

1. Prepare the Exchange Server 2007 infrastructure by deploying Update Rollup 10 for Service Pack 3 or later.

2. Install the Exchange Server 2013 servers.

3. Create the Legacy namespace.

4. Obtain and deploy certificates.

5. Move namespaces to CAS 2013.

6. Move mailboxes to Exchange Server 2013.

Let's take a look at the individual protocols and see how they work in coexistence with 2013.

OWA

The first scenario to understand is OWA access when Exchange Server is configured for proxy. Remember, one of the first steps in coexistence is to redirect the namespaces to Exchange Server 2013. Once the namespace has been moved, users' requests for mail.rosenexchange.com will go through the hardware load balancer to the Exchange Server CAS 2013. This is where things are different than coexistence with Exchange Server 2010. Exchange Server 2007 requires a separate legacy namespace for redirection; there is no way for Exchange Server 2013 to proxy for Exchange Server 2007. In the scenario in Figure 21.19, a user in Site 1 on Exchange Server 2007 will reach the CAS 2013. The CAS 2013 will discover the user's mailbox is on Exchange Server 2007 and redirect the request to the legacy URL. If there is a non-Internet-facing site, such as Site 2 in this example, the CAS 2013 will redirect to the legacy URL, and the in-site CAS 2007 will then proxy the connection to the CAS 2007 in Site 2. The redirection is silent, meaning the user will not need to click a link, but it does not support single sign-on and the user will have to authenticate after the initial redirection.

In a scenario like Figure 21.20, in which Site 2 is in fact an Internet-facing site with its own namespace, the request will go to the CAS 2013 and simply be redirected to the CAS 2007 in Site 2 using its externalURL.

FIGURE 21.19
OWA 2013 coexistence
with Exchange Server
2007 configured for proxy

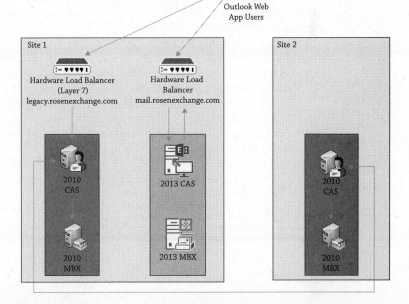

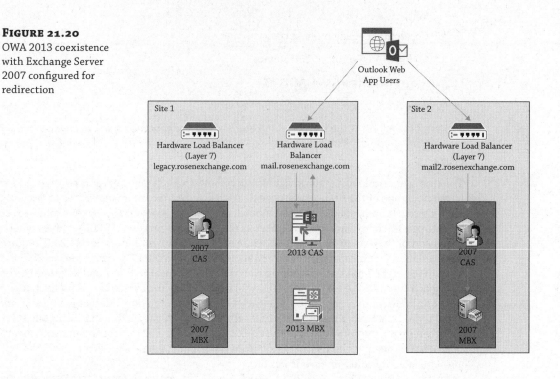

EXCHANGE ACTIVESYNC

EAS's coexistence model is a bit different than that of the other protocols. In Figure 21.21, a user's mailbox is on Exchange Server 2007 in the same site (Site 1) as the Exchange Server CAS 2013. The client will use Autodiscover to find the correct endpoint. In this case the client will connect to the CAS 2013, which connects to the 2013 Mailbox server role. The 2013 Mailbox server role then connects to the CAS 2007, which in turn connects to the user's 2007 Mailbox server role.

Extending this example further, Site 2 is a non-Internet-facing site. Again, the user will connect to Exchange Server CAS 2013 in Site 1, which will follow a similar path. The CAS 2013 connects to the 2013 Mailbox server role, which in turn connects to the CAS 2007 in Site2. Finally the CAS 2007 in Site 2 connects to the user's 2007 Mailbox server role.

EAS coexistence with Exchange Server 2013 and Exchange Server 2007 seems quite straightforward. The client, using Autodiscover, will connect directly to the CAS 2007 in Site 2, which connects to the user's mailbox on the 2007 Mailbox server role, as shown in Figure 21.22. One consequence of this design is that if a user in Site 2 is moved to Site 1, their ActiveSync device will stop syncing. This issue is because the CAS 2007 cannot understand the Exchange Server 2013 EAS virtual directory configuration, so the redirection fails. Also, EAS devices do not ever attempt to re-Autodiscover once their profile is successfully configured. In this case, a user must re-create their EAS profile after they have been moved. If Site 2 eventually will have Exchange Server 2013 installed into the site, this scenario will allow users to continue to work since it will follow the normal 2013 EAS proxy functionality.

FIGURE 21.21
EAS 2013 coexistence with Exchange Server 2007 configured for proxy

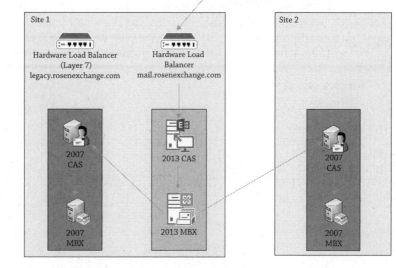

FIGURE 21.22
EAS 2013 coexistence with Exchange Server 2007 configured for redirection

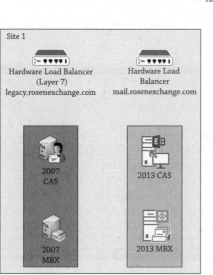
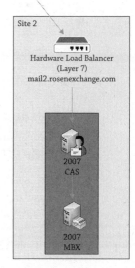

EXCHANGE WEB SERVICES

Exchange Web Services coexistence with Exchange Server 2007 is similar to that of the other protocols. Remember, the legacy namespace is required for Exchange Server 2007 coexistence. Even though the client gets their Autodiscover response from Exchange Server CAS 2013, it will return the legacy URL. The client will then connect to EWS directly from the legacy URL. In the case where Site 2 is not Internet-facing, the client will also talk to the CAS 2013 for Autodiscover, which will return the legacy URL of the CAS 2007 in Site 1. The CAS 2007 in Site 1 will then proxy the connection to the CAS 2007 in Site 2, as illustrated in Figure 21.23.

FIGURE 21.23
EWS 2013 coexistence with Exchange Server 2007 configured for proxy

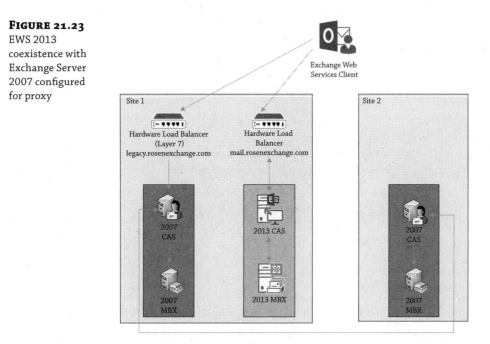

Now assume Site 2 is an Internet-facing site with its own namespace, as in Figure 21.24. The Autodiscover request will simply return mail2.rosenexchange.com and the client will connect to the CAS 2007 in Site 2.

AUTODISCOVER

Autodiscover in coexistence with Exchange Server 2007 is somewhat unique across the protocols in the way it handles requests. Let's examine the external, or non-domain-joined, client Autodiscover process (Figure 21.25). First, the Autodiscover namespace is moved to point to a CAS 2013 server. CAS 2013 authenticates the user and determines the user's mailbox version. In this case, the user's mailbox is located on a 2007 Mailbox server. CAS 2013 will not proxy or hand off the request to 2007, since 2007 would not understand the request. In this case, CAS 2013 sends the request to the nearest Mailbox 2013 server. The Mailbox 2013 server recognizes that the user is located on Exchange Server 2007 and will generate a well-formed Autodiscover XML response. If Site 2 is non-Internet-facing, the same process takes place. Autodiscover points to CAS 2013, which sends the request to MBX 2013 for it to generate the appropriate XML response.

FIGURE 21.24
EWS 2013 coexistence with Exchange Server 2007 configured for redirection

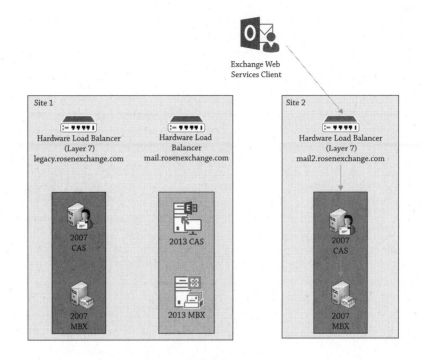

FIGURE 21.25
Autodiscover coexistence with Exchange 2007 with an external client

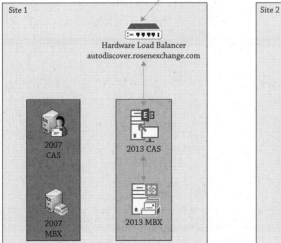

For internal clients, the process is slightly different (Figure 21.26). For internal clients that are domain-joined the mail client performs an Active Directory query for a service connection point (SCP) record that contains the URL of the server the client should use for Autodiscover. From there the process is the same as for the external clients discussed previously, where the Autodiscover is found via DNS. Keep in mind that the URLs returned by Autodiscover will be for Exchange Server 2007 services; what we are determining in this process is the server that can generate those correct URLs.

FIGURE 21.26
Autodiscover coexistence with Exchange Server 2007 with an internal client

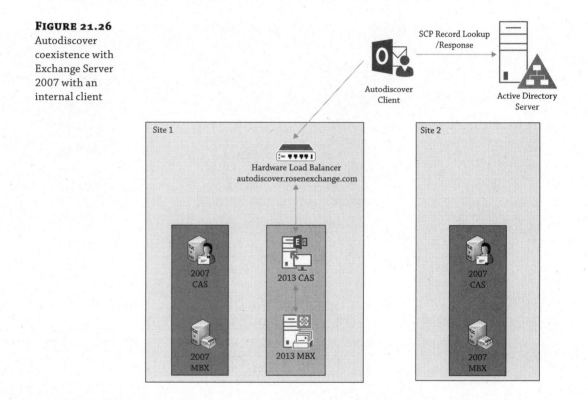

OUTLOOK ANYWHERE

CAS 2013 will happily proxy Outlook Anywhere connections for Exchange 2007 mailboxes. Outlook clients will connect to the Outlook Anywhere endpoint, which resolves to the CAS 2013 servers. CAS 2013 acts as an HTTP proxy to the Exchange Server CAS 2007. In order to proxy, every CAS 2007 must have Outlook Anywhere enabled.

There is one thing to be aware of in order for this to successfully allow connections. In Exchange Server 2007 it was typical to configure the authentication mechanism to Basic for both client and server authentication. Doing that will break authentication, and a change to 2007 is required. It is possible to set client and system authentication differently. The client authentication method should be set to match the client authentication type of CAS 2013. The IIS authentication needs to be set to NTLM using the Set-OutlookAnywhere cmdlet. If you had previously configured Exchange Server 2007 for NTLM, you do not need to alter the configuration.

After you have configured the namespaces, it is a good idea to validate the configuration with the Remote Connectivity Analyzer (`http://www.testexchangeconnectivity.com`). In summary, the coexistence for the protocols are shown in Table 21.2.

TABLE 21.2: Summary of protocols and coexistence with Exchange Server 2007 and 2010

PROTOCOL	COEXIST WITH EXCHANGE SERVER 2007	COEXIST WITH EXCHANGE SERVER 2010
Autodiscover	Proxy to Exchange Server 2013 Mailbox	◆ Proxy
EAS	Proxy	◆ Proxy
ECP	Does not apply	◆ Proxy ◆ Redirect if externalURL is configured
EWS	Autodiscover used to retrieve the EWS 2007 URL	◆ Proxy
Outlook Anywhere	Proxy	◆ Proxy
OWA	Redirect to legacy namespace	◆ Proxy ◆ Redirect if externalURL is configured

Certificates

In versions of Exchange Server prior to Exchange Server 2007, the use of certificates was simple. By default there were none installed, so if you wanted to use one, you requested a certificate with the principal name of your external access URL and installed it on the default website. This gave you secure access to OWA and RPC over HTTP. This process changed starting in Exchange Server 2007. In an effort to ensure that an out-of-the-box Exchange server secures traffic, a self-signed certificate is created by default, which is used for SMTP, POP3, IMAP4, and IIS.

Default Certificate Usage

When Exchange Server is installed, a self-signed certificate is created by default to offer some semblance of secure communications out of the box. In Exchange Server 2007, the expiration for this certificate was one year. In Exchange Server 2013, the default expiration period for self-signed certificates increased to five years.

You might be wondering what a self-signed certificate is. It's a certificate that is issued by the computer itself. This basically allows the server to vouch for itself. This is akin to you creating your own driver's license to prove who you are. If someone knows you already, like your parents, they don't need to verify your homemade driver's license with a third party. But when you present your state-issued driver's license when making a purchase in a store, they do care, and because they trust the state that issued the ID, then they can assume it is valid. In other words, if a service doesn't trust the server that issued the self-signed certificate, the certificate is considered invalid and most services will not accept it. This is important, for example, if your client, maybe your web browser, tries to access an Exchange server that is secured with a self-signed certificate. In this case, your client does not trust the server since it does not trust the signer (again, in this case it's the Exchange server itself). The web browser may warn the user and allow the user the choice to continue, or it will close the browser window. You either need to trust the certificate or issue a certificate to the server by a mutually trusted third party. In the case of your homemade driver's license, you would need to get a state-issued license in order for other people to accept it as valid.

Generally speaking, self-signed certificates don't scale well. They aren't trusted by your clients by default, so your users get annoying warnings. Some services, such as Outlook Anywhere, won't even work with self-signed certificates.

To illustrate, take a look at the default certificate, and you will notice some important details. Figure 21.27 shows the certification path details. In this case, the certificate is self-signed, so the certification terminates at the Exchange server that issued itself the certificate.

FIGURE 21.27
The Certificate window showing the certification path

Using Subject Alternative Name Certificates

As you've learned by now, Client Access servers can operate under the guise of many namespaces. A few of the ways that you can refer to a CAS are by the hostname, fully qualified internal domain name, fully qualified external domain name, Autodiscover name, and any aliases that you might use. This can be a tricky situation with certificates because certificates require that the subject name in the certificate be the same name that you use to access the server. For example, if you issued your certificate to your CAS with the Subject Name of cas-1.contoso.com, then if you were to browse to https://cas-1.contoso.com/owa, everything would check out fine. However, if you were to browse to https://mail.contoso.com/owa, the certificate would fail validation because the URL has a different name than the one shown in the Subject Name field in the certificate. The way to solve this problem in Exchange Server is to use a certificate that allows you to use multiple names. Two types of certificates allow you to do this:

- Wildcard certificates

- Subject Alternative Name (SAN) certificates

Wildcard certificates allow you to specify a wildcard character in the name. For example, a wildcard certificate for *.contoso.com will allow you to use mail.contoso.com, cas-1 .contoso.com, mail.europe.contoso.com, and so forth. Wildcard certificates tend to be a more expensive option, so many organizations choose the second option, SAN certificates, and may have compatibility issues with some clients.

SAN certificates have an additional field in the certificate called Subject Alternative Names. You input several other names in this field that you want the server to be accessed with. Certificates that support Subject Alternate Names are also referred to as Unified Communications Certificates. To find certificate authorities that will issue this type of certificate, search the Internet for "Subject Alternate Name" or "Unified Communications Certificates." Microsoft has also maintains a list of certificate authorities that it has partnered with to provide Exchange Server–specific websites for issuing the right certificates: http://support .microsoft.com/kb/929395.

When specifying the common name for a SAN certificate, you should use the name that will most frequently be used from the Internet, such as mail.contoso.com. Figure 21.28 shows a SAN certificate with a couple of entries in the Subject Alternative Names field. Keep in mind that you need to include only names in the certificate that will be used to access the server over SSL. If your users won't be using the NetBIOS name (contoso-ex01) or the server's FQDN (contoso-ex01.contoso.com), those names don't need to be included in the certificate.

You can get one of these SAN certificates either from yourself (self-signed) or from a third-party certificate authority like Comodo, DigiCert, and Entrust. One thing to bear in mind is that these certificates can be expensive and sometimes a little hard to obtain; not all third-party certificate authorities will issue you one. Check with the certificate authority you are planning to use.

Using the Exchange Certificate Wizards

The new web-based administration tool Exchange Admin Center helps you more easily configure your certificates. The wizards walk you through the process of generating certificate requests and importing existing certificates.

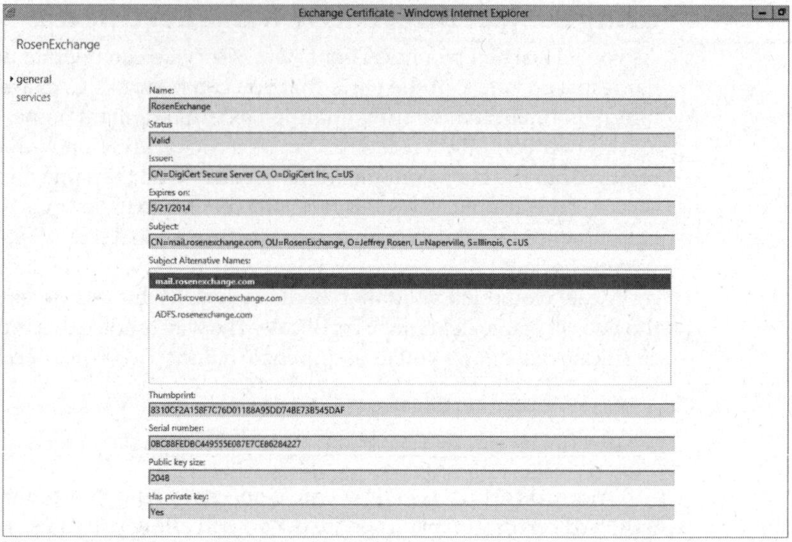

FIGURE 21.28
The Subject
Alternative Names
field of the certificate

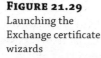

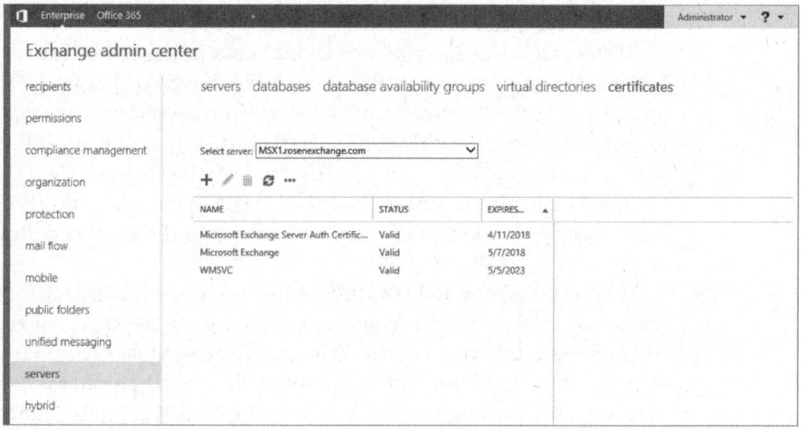

Exchange Certificate - Windows Internet Explorer

RosenExchange

▸ general
services

Name:
RosenExchange

Status:
Valid

Issuer:
CN=DigiCert Secure Server CA, O=DigiCert Inc, C=US

Expires on:
5/21/2014

Subject:
CN=mail.rosenexchange.com, OU=RosenExchange, O=Jeffrey Rosen, L=Naperville, S=Illinois, C=US

Subject Alternative Names:
mail.rosenexchange.com
AutoDiscover.rosenexchange.com
ADFS.rosenexchange.com

Thumbprint:
8310CF2A158F7C76D01188A9SDD74BE73B545DAF

Serial number:
0BCB8FEDBC449555E087E7CE86284227

Public key size:
2048

Has private key:
Yes

FIGURE 21.29
Launching the
Exchange certificate
wizards

Enterprise   Office 365   Administrator ▾ ? ▾

Exchange admin center

recipients

permissions

compliance management

organization

protection

mail flow

mobile

public folders

unified messaging

servers

hybrid

servers databases database availability groups virtual directories **certificates**

Select server: MSX1.rosenexchange.com ▾

+ ✎ 🗑 ⟳ •••

NAME	STATUS	EXPIRES... ▲
Microsoft Exchange Server Auth Certific...	Valid	4/11/2018
Microsoft Exchange	Valid	5/7/2018
WMSVC	Valid	5/5/2023

You will find these wizards in the Servers node of the EAC. Select the server that you want to acquire a certificate for and then choose the appropriate action, as shown in Figure 21.29. The + icon is to create a new certificate, and the ellipsis (…) allows for import/export of existing certificates.

To acquire a new certificate, you first need to use the New Exchange Certificate wizard to walk you through the process of generating your certificate request. The wizard does a nice job of presenting you with relevant certificate options, including the option to generate a request for a wildcard certificate. Exchange Server 2013 also includes the ability to create a new self-signed certificate. The Exchange Certificate configuration screen in the wizard presents the entire list of Exchange Server services that you might like to use the certificate for. You can go through each service and supply the appropriate options, as well as customize the names in the certificate. Figure 21.30 demonstrates this functionality in the wizard.

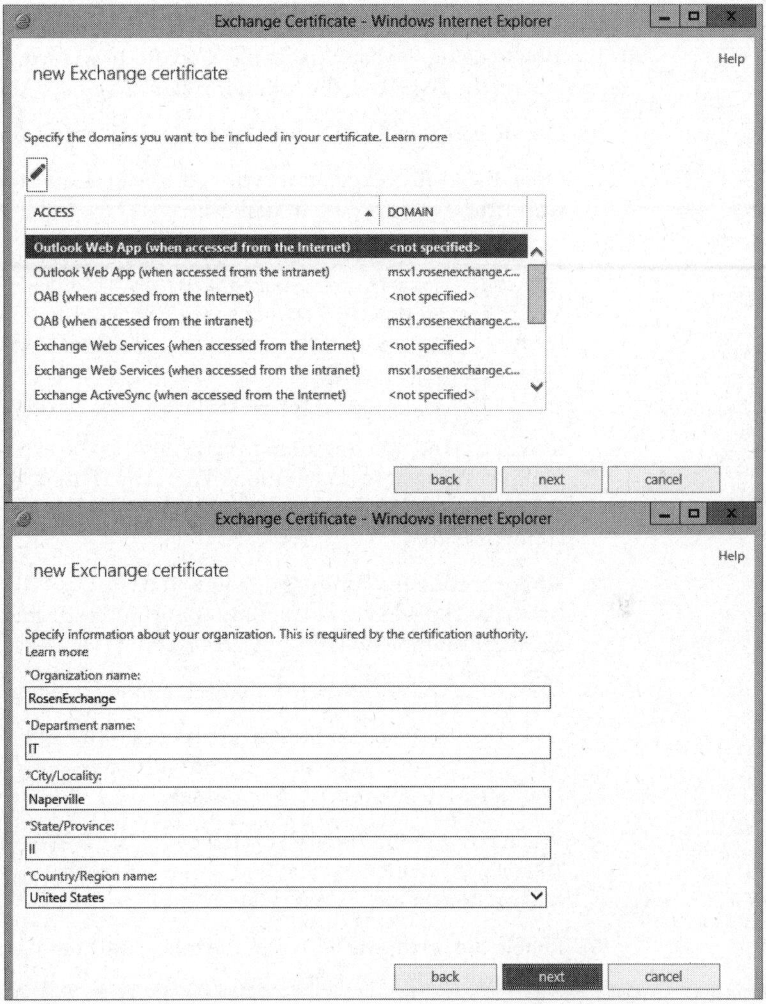

FIGURE 21.30
Configuring the
names for use in
the certificate using the
New Exchange
Certificate wizard

After you finish going through the wizard, a certificate request file is generated. You will need to give this certificate request to your certificate authority. They will use this request to issue you the certificate. When they issue the certificate, they will return it to you in the form of another file. This is the file that you will use to complete the certificate request.

After you have your certificate in hand, you can go back into the Server Configuration node in the EAC and complete the certificate installation. Select the server that certificate request is for, and the list of outstanding requests is displayed in the bottom pane. Select the request that you previously generated, and choose the Complete Pending Request task from the Actions pane. Follow the Complete Pending Request wizard to import your certificate.

Generating a Certificate Request in the EMS

In addition to using the New Exchange Certificate wizard, you can generate the certificate request using the EMS. Use the following steps to get a SAN certificate using the EMS:

1. Decide on the external name for your email access (in this case, email.domain.com).

2. Open the EMS and generate your certificate request using a command like the following (substituting your domain names):

   ```
   $Data = New-ExchangeCertificate -GenerateRequest -SubjectName "c=ES,o=domain,
   Cn=email.domain.com" -DomainName email.domain.com,
   Autodiscover.domain.com,hostname,internaldomain.com,
   hostname.internaldomain.com -FriendlyName "Exchange SAN cert"
   -PrivateKeyExportable:$true
   Set-Content -path "C:\MyCertRequest.req" -Value $Data
   ```

   Make sure that the first domain you enter is the external one that you will use for Outlook Anywhere and Outlook Web App. This domain goes into the Subject Name field of the certificate and is required by Outlook Anywhere in the Outlook client's configuration.

3. After running the command, you will have a text file in the path specified (in this case, C:\MyCertRequest.req). Submit it to your certificate authority (your internal one or a certificate authority like DigiCert or VeriSign).

4. Once you receive the certificate back, import it using the following command:

   ```
   Import-ExchangeCertificate -FileData ([Byte[]]$(Get-Content
   -Path c:\certificate.pfx -Encoding byte -ReadCount 0))
   -Password:(Get-Credential).password
   ```

5. When you run the `Import-ExchangeCertificate` command, the output will contain a `ThumbPrint`, which is what you will use to refer to the certificate in future commands. Make a note of it.

6. Enable the certificate by using the following command, which will enable use for all Exchange Server services:

   ```
   Enable-ExchangeCertificate -ThumbPrint [Value] -Services "IIS,SMTP,IMAP,POP"
   ```

When you check the Subject Alternative Names field after you configure your new certificate, you will see all the entries you specified.

The Front End Transport Service

The Front End Transport (FET) service is a stateless SMTP service that is part of the Client Access server role. FET has the following benefits:

- Provides a centralized, load-balanced ingress/egress point for SMTP traffic.
- Mailbox locator provides efficient routing by avoiding unnecessary hops.

◆ Provides a unified namespace for both authenticated and unauthenticated mail traffic.

◆ Scales based on numbers of connections.

The Front End Transport service's role is mainly to improve routing decisions and help provide high availability. It will route messages to the closest Mailbox server that can deliver a message to the recipients. In Exchange Server 2013, each Mailbox server delivers a message to the mailbox database that is active on that server. FET removes hops, which speeds up mail delivery to the destination mailbox by making these routing decisions. So, all inbound mail delivery must route through a CAS, but outbound mail can be routed through CAS or delivered directly by a Mailbox server.

Although FET does provide some similar functionality of the legacy Edge Transport server role, it is not a direct replacement. For one thing, as discussed earlier in this chapter, the CAS must not be placed in the perimeter network. This section will explore the FET architecture in more detail.

The Front End Transport Service Architecture

The FET architecture is simple, compared to the other transport components that are part of the Mailbox server role, to enable it to deliver the essential functionality needed. There are two main components: SMTP receive and SMTP send. Figure 21.31 shows the general architecture for FET. Note that FET does not inspect message content, bifurcate the message, or perform message queuing, and therefore it has a very streamlined transport pipeline. Figure 21.31 illustrates this architecture and associated ports.

FIGURE 21.31
Front End Transport architecture and ports

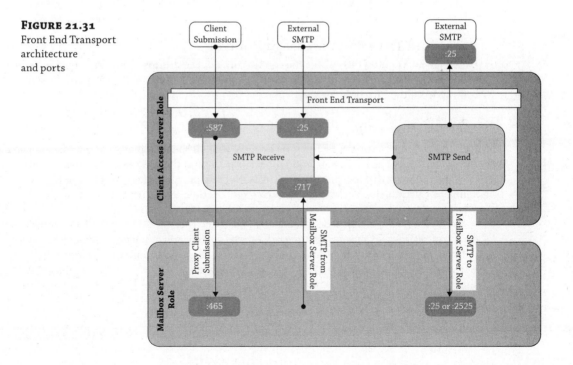

Let's take a deeper look at the mail flow and how FET provides its connectivity.

◆ Port 25 is the default SMTP port used for server-to-server communication. A default receive connector is created named Default Frontend <servername> during installation.

◆ Port 587 is the default SMTP port use for client mail submission. RFC 2476 specifies that it is preferred for clients, such as POP3 or IMAP4 to have a separate port for introducing new messages for routing. This allows for separate security policies and other features outlined in the RFC. A default receive connector named Client Frontend <server> is created during installation.

◆ Port 717 is the default port used for outbound mail proxy from the Mailbox Transport service to FET. A default receive connector named Outbound Proxy Frontend <server> is created during installation.

Figure 21.32 is a screenshot taken after running the PowerShell cmdlet `Get-Receive Connector` to show the default connectors. Note that it shows output from a multirole server. Since FET already uses port 25, transport defaults to port 2525.

FIGURE 21.32
Output from
`Get-ReceiveConnector`
for a multirole Exchange
Server 2013 server

Front End Transport Message Routing

Exchange Server 2013 introduces the concept of delivery groups. A *delivery group* is a collection of servers at the same version as the mailbox. The focus in this chapter is on understanding routing from the FET point of view.

INBOUND ROUTING

On inbound messages, the FET begins by resolving all the recipients of the message. The FET then determines the DAG, hub, and fallback hub to send the message. The next step is where front end routing differs from how the mailbox transport handles routing. The FET will not split, or bifurcate, the message for each recipient. Rather, it will try to find the target that provides the best destination for all users on the message.

Because FET is just a proxy, it needs to make these routing decisions quickly; otherwise it could interrupt mail service. For this reason, the CAS needs to have low-latency, good-quality network connectivity to the Mailbox servers. The FET prefers Mailbox servers in the same Active Directory site. If none of the recipients have delivery groups partially present in the local site, any local mailbox can be used. If more appropriate, FET can also proxy inbound messages to Exchange Server 2007 or 2010.

OUTBOUND PROXY

The transport on the Mailbox server role is capable of directly sending mail to external SMTP hosts. There is a new option in Exchange Server 2013 to force outbound mail traffic through the CAS. This is enabled with the following PowerShell cmdlet. Note this takes effect only if the send connector is also configured for IP or DNS routing.

```
set-sendConnector <name> -FrontEndProxyEnabled $true
```

This option can also be enabled in EAC, in the Mail Flow ➤ Send Connectors tab. There, select the send connector and click the Edit icon. Under the Connector Status options, check the option Proxy Through Client Access Server.

You may be wondering why you should enable this option. There are a few benefits—for one, the names of the internal servers are replaced with the CAS name. From a security standpoint, it is preferable to not expose internal server names.

When this option is configured, after mailbox transport determines it needs to send to an external host, it connects to a CAS in its Active Directory site with a special SMTP verb, XPROXYTO, after transport has authenticated itself. The CAS then connects to the external host using its DNS configuration, performs any authentication and session initiation, and then lets transport know it's ready for message transmission. From there the CAS relays the message information to the external host.

Unified Messaging

The final component of CAS is the Unified Messaging (UM) call router. Like transport, UM has components on both the CAS and Mailbox server roles. The former UM services from Exchange Server 2007 and 2010 are now integrated into the Mailbox server role, and new for 2013 is the client connection endpoint, also called the UM call router. Similar to the other CAS functions, the UM call router does not actually provide the UM services. Its role is to accept the incoming connection from IP Private Branch Exchange (PBX) gateways or Lync Server and determine where to redirect the connection to.

UM Front End Architecture

The CAS implements a new service called the Microsoft Exchange Unified Messaging Call Router service (`Microsoft.Exchange.UM.CallRouter.exe`). This listens on port 5060 (unsecured) or 5061 (secured) by default, but it can be configured with the `Set-UMCallRouterSettings` PowerShell cmdlet. Once it determines which Mailbox server should handle the call, it issues a `SIP 302 REDIRECT` message. From there the call is handed off to the Mailbox UM services, as depicted in Figure 21.33.

All of the configuration settings that applied to the Unified Messaging role in previous versions are still available; however, they are split between the CAS and Mailbox server roles. Very few configuration options are available for the UM Call Router service on CAS. The Client Access server is configured using the `Set-UMCallRouterSettings` cmdlet. The following parameters are available for this cmdlet on the CAS:

FIGURE 21.33
Exchange Server 2013
Unified Messaging
architecture and ports

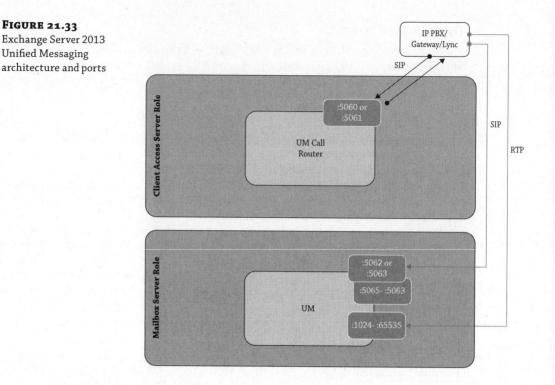

DialPlans Multivalued property used to specify the dial plan used by the CAS if integrating with Microsoft Office Communications Server 2007 R2 or Lync Server 2010 or 2013. It can be set to $null to remove existing values.

SipTCPListeningPort Specifies the TCP port the UM Call Router service is listening on for nonsecured connections; default is port 5060.

SipTLSListeningPort Specifies the TCP port the UM Call Router service is listening on for secured connections; default is port 5061.

UMStartupMode Specifies whether the CAS is running in TCP, TLS, or Dual mode.

The Bottom Line

Understand architecture changes in the CAS role. Now that clients connect to Client Access servers for all client connectivity, it's even more important that your Client Access servers be highly available. By placing your Client Access servers in load-balanced arrays, you can increase the redundancy and availability of your environment.

 Master It To increase the resiliency of the Client Access servers in your company's main datacenter, you have decided to place them behind a hardware load-balancer array. You want to ensure that your users can use Outlook while inside the network to access their email. What ports do you need to ensure are load-balanced in the array?

P 547

Design a CAS proxy and redirection solution.   For users to access their mailboxes, they need to go through a Client Access server that is in the same Active Directory site as their Mailbox server. Client Access servers need to communicate to the Mailbox server through HTTP. If the Client Access servers in the same site as a user's mailbox aren't exposed to the Internet, then Internet-based users will need to access their email from Client Access servers in another site. The Internet-facing Client Access servers will proxy the connection to the non-Internet-facing Client Access servers.

Master It   You have a Client Access server in two primary datacenters, one in Baltimore (cas-bal.contoso.com) and another in Honolulu (cas-hon.contoso.com). You also have a Client Access server in your branch offices in Seattle (cas-sea.contoso.com), Atlanta (cas-atl.contoso.com), and Amarillo (cas-ama.contoso.com). You want to ensure that only the Baltimore and Honolulu Client Access servers can be used over the Internet. You want users in Baltimore, Atlanta, and Amarillo to use mail-east.contoso.com and users in Honolulu and Seattle to use mail-west.contoso.com when accessing their email from outside the network. How should you configure your internal and external URLs for each of these Client Access servers to support your desired outcome?

Consider Client Access servers and coexistence with previous versions of Exchange Server.   When replacing your legacy Client Access servers, you will want to start from the edge of your network and work your way in. Therefore, you want to transition Internet-facing Client Access servers first. When transitioning from Exchange Server 2007, you will want to use a new legacy namespace for your Exchange Server 2007 URL and move the old namespace to the Exchange Server 2013 Client Access servers. When transitioning from Exchange Server 2010, you can use the same namespace on your Exchange Server 2013 Client Access servers.

Master It   Your current environment is composed of both Exchange Server 2007 and Exchange Server 2010 servers. You decide to install your Exchange Server 2010 Client Access servers in an Internet-facing site using the same namespace as your existing Exchange Server 2010 Client Access servers. You notice that users with mailboxes on Exchange Server 2007 can no longer access their email through OWA. However, users with Exchange Server 2010 mailboxes can use OWA just fine. What should you do to fix this problem?

Generate valid Subject Alternative Name certificates.   Each Client Access server has multiple names that clients use to access it. To secure access to the server using all of the names used, you need to issue Subject Alternative Name certificates to your Client Access servers. SAN certificates allow you to specify multiple names for your server in a single certificate.

Master It   Your company, Contoso Pharmaceuticals, implements a split-brain DNS architecture. Your main campus in Baltimore has an array of six Client Access servers called outlook.contoso.com. Each server in the array is named accordingly, starting at CONTOSO-CAS1 and ending at CONTOSO-CAS6. This same array of Client Access servers also serves Outlook Web App clients and Exchange ActiveSync clients under the name of mail.contoso.com. You need to make sure that your Client Access servers have the right certificates to operate correctly when accessed from both inside and outside the organization. What Subject Alternative Names need to be used in the certificate, and which name should be used for the Subject Name field?

Understand Front End Transport architecture changes. Transport has undergone significant changes in Exchange Server 2013. The Front End Transport service is a new feature on the Client Access server role and provides a stateless proxy to the backend Mailbox role.

Master It Your company, Contoso Pharmaceuticals, implements Exchange Server 2013 Client Access server with a default configuration. Your administrators use the Remote Connectivity Analyzer to view an email's message header information. The name of the Mailbox server is listed in the server conversation. The company security policy requires that the Mailbox server names not be exposed externally. How can the administrator hide the Mailbox server name on outbound mail?

Understand Unified Messaging CAS architecture changes. Unified Messaging no longer is a separate role in Exchange Server 2013. The UM Call Router service on the CAS handles the initial client connection and hands off media stream directly to the UM services on the Mailbox server role.

Master It After the Exchange Server 2013 deployment, your administrator needs to enable connectivity to her Lync server 2013 infrastructure. In order to provide the Lync administrators the correct information, should she use the CAS or Mailbox server IP address?

Chapter 22

Managing Connectivity with Transport Services

Exchange Server's primary purpose is to send, receive, and store messages. In previous versions of Exchange Server, message delivery was handled by an Exchange server running the Hub Transport role. A message would be generated on a Mailbox server, the Mailbox server would notify a Hub Transport server that a new message was ready, and the Hub Transport server would pick up the new message for processing.

Since there is no Hub Transport role in Exchange Server 2013, the responsibility for moving messages from one mailbox to another has been moved to the Mailbox and Client Access roles.

In this chapter, you will learn to:

◆ Understand the improvements in Exchange Server 2013 mail routing

◆ Create and manage Send connectors and Receive connectors

◆ Configure anti-spam and anti-malware technologies

Understanding the Transport Improvements in Exchange Server 2013

Before we delve into how internal email routing works, it's worth noting a few of the many improvements Exchange Server 2013 delivers in comparison to earlier versions of Exchange Server.

Prior to Exchange Server 2013, all messages were processed by a dedicated server role named Hub Transport. This approach worked well for many years, but having a separate server just for mail routing wasn't always practical. In fact, many companies would consolidate the Hub Transport and Client Access roles or the Hub Transport, Client Access, and Mailbox roles onto the same server. Due to many changes in Exchange Server 2013 (described in this and other chapters), Microsoft removed the Hub Transport server role from Exchange Server 2013 and moved most of the core email routing functionality to the Mailbox role. The Client Access role in Exchange Server 2013 also plays an important part in email routing; in fact, it usually acts as the first server in the Exchange Server organization to receive email messages.

In Exchange Server 2007 and Exchange Server 2010 mail routing was based on AD sites. If the source server and the target server of an email message were located in different AD sites, the AD site of the target server was used as the next hop for the email messages. As part of the new transport improvements, Exchange Server 2013 has introduced the concept of *delivery groups*.

The delivery group is the primary unit used to define a routing topology. AD sites are defined as a type of delivery group. Furthermore, if multiple Mailbox servers are members of the same DAG, those servers are considered to be in their own delivery group. This remains true even if a DAG spans multiple AD sites.

When routing an email message, a Mailbox server does not take into consideration the cost of AD site links when sending to another Mailbox server that is a member of the same DAG, even if that Mailbox server is in a different AD site. This change in routing architecture means that routing topologies in Exchange Server 2013 are significantly different than in previous versions of Exchange Server, especially for those that have a considerable amount of intra-organization email exchanges.

Another notable change is the introduction of the Safety Net feature. In Exchange Server 2007 and Exchange Server 2010, the transport dumpster was used as a fail safe mechanism to capture email messages that might have been otherwise lost during a lossy failover. Exchange Server 2013 has taken this technology one step further with removing the transport dumpster and introducing Safety Net. When Safety Net is enabled, which it is by default, messages are stored in a separate database called the queue database on each Mailbox server. The queue database will hold messages based on the Safety Net value, by default for two days. A Mailbox server will query the queue database of the Safety Net feature to restore any email messages that are missing from a mailbox database after a lossy failover.

Message Routing in the Organization

Again, the most significant change in transport in Exchange Server is the removal of the Hub Transport role. The Transport service that ran on the Hub Transport role has been moved to the Mailbox server role. As well, two additional transport services have been added to the Mailbox server: the Mailbox Transport Delivery service and the Mailbox Transport Submission service. Another notable service is the Front End Transport service that has been added to Exchange Server 2013 Client Access server role.

Not only are we now introduced to new services in Exchange Server 2013, but Microsoft has completely re-architected mail routing for both internal and external message deliveries. The overall design change of mail routing is based on the introduction of delivery groups (discussed in depth in this chapter).

In this chapter, we'll dig into the nuts and bolts of the email flow process, email delivery, and email queuing. Before we do, you should understand a few important points about the basics of Exchange Server 2013 message routing:

- All email messages are processed by the Transport service, Mailbox Transport Delivery service, and the Mailbox Transport Submission service. All services reside on the Mailbox servers.

- Inbound and outbound email messages exchanged with the Internet are *passed* through the Front End Transport service that runs on the Client Access server.

- All Active Directory sites that contain Mailbox servers must also contain at least one Client Access server.

The Mailbox server role is at the center of the message-routing architecture for messages being delivered internally, as well as messages leaving the organization. Though messages enter your organization through the Client Access servers, all messages are processed by the Mailbox server role regardless of whether they are being delivered locally or remotely. Figure 22.1 shows the components of the Mailbox server that handle message delivery.

FIGURE 22.1
The Mailbox server is at the center of all message delivery.

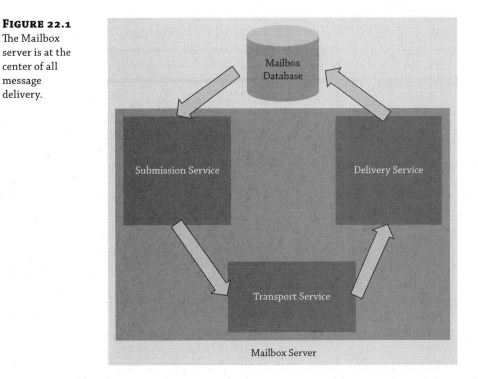

The Mailbox server role handles categorization, rule processing, transport-level journaling, and delivery for email messages that are intended for delivery to a local mailbox. Essentially, any email message sent by any recipient to any other internal or external recipient is always handled by the transport services that reside on the Mailbox servers.

The Exchange Server 2013 Mailbox server handles message categorization as well. Categorization is handled by a component of the Transport service, called the message categorizer. The message categorizer component figures out where an email message needs to go next when it is received by a Mailbox server, otherwise known as the next delivery hop. Here are some of the steps involved in message categorization:

◆ Expand distribution lists by querying the global catalog.

◆ Resolve recipient addresses to determine which recipients are local to that server, remote on another server, or outside the organization.

◆ Examine the message sender, recipients, message header, body, and attachments and apply message transport rules that apply to that message.

◆ Convert the message to the appropriate message format (Summary-TNEF, MIME, or UUencode) depending on the destination of the message.

◆ Determine the next hop for the message.

◆ Place the message into an appropriate queue.

When a message is transmitted from one Mailbox server to another inside the same Exchange Server organization, the Mailbox servers transport the message by using SMTP, the servers authenticate each other by using Kerberos, and the message data stream is encrypted by using Transport Layer Security (TLS). When messages are transmitted from a Mailbox server to an Exchange Server 2010 Edge Transport server, SMTP is used for message transfer, the servers authenticate each other by using mutual authentication using certificates, and the message data stream is encrypted by using TLS. Optionally, an organization that is sending messages to another Exchange Server organization that also contains Edge Transport servers can configure authenticated connections and TLS encryption. By default, messages delivered to other organizations are not encrypted, similarly to any email messages delivered between servers on the Internet.

Before we dig deep into routing, let's continue with a base understanding of the new services on the Mailbox and Client Access servers. During the installation of the Client Access server, the following transport service is installed:

Front End Transport Service   Proxies inbound email messages from the Internet to a Mailbox server and can be configured to relay outbound email messages from a Mailbox server to the Internet.

During the installation of the Mailbox server the following transport services are installed:

Transport Service   The Transport service is responsible for such tasks as mail queuing, categorization, protocol agents, and routing agents. Any message that is passed through the Exchange Server organization must go through the Transport service.

Mailbox Transport Submission Service   Using RPC, the Submission service connects to mailbox databases to retrieve outgoing email messages. The Mailbox Transport Submission service retrieves the message and sends the email message to the Transport service over SMTP.

Mailbox Transport Delivery Service   The Mailbox Transport Delivery service accepts email messages from the Transport service over SMTP and converts the email message to RPC for delivery to the mailbox database.

An essential part of message routing is determining the next hop in a delivery path. The identification of a next hop is driven by the delivery groups. The following delivery groups have been introduced in Exchange Server 2013:

Routable DAG Delivery Group   A collection of Mailbox servers that are a member of the same DAG.

Version Routing Delivery Group   A collection of Exchange servers that are determined by their version of Exchange Server.

AD Site Delivery Group   A collection of Exchange servers that are not members of the same DAG and that are not a member of any DAG. An AD Site delivery group normally occurs when there is a hub site along the least-cost route.

Connector Source Server Delivery Group   A collection of Exchange Server 2013 Mailbox servers or Exchange Server 2007 or Exchange Server 2010 Hub Transport servers that are scoped as source servers for a Send connector.

Distribution Group Expansion Server Delivery Group   An Exchange Server 2013 Mailbox server or Exchange Server 2007 or Exchange Server 2010 Hub Transport server that is set as the expansion server for a distribution group.

Exchange Server 2013 prefers certain delivery groups over other delivery groups. Figure 22.2 shows four Mailbox servers. The servers are located in two different sites, yet the preferred delivery group for servers EX2 and EX3 is the DAG boundary.

FIGURE 22.2
Mail flow between DAG members

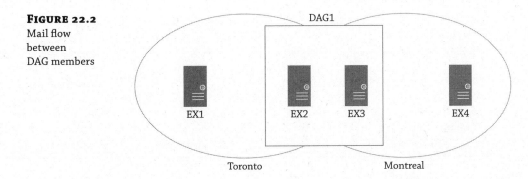

The Mailbox Transport Delivery service accepts email messages over SMTP from other Exchange servers and delivers them to an appropriate mailbox database in the same delivery group by using RPC. Figure 22.3 shows the two servers demonstrated in the previous figure. Here, an email message is received by EX2 for final delivery to a mailbox database active on EX3.

FIGURE 22.3
Mail routing between Exchange Servers in the same delivery group

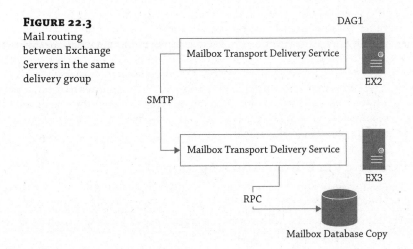

The reverse process would happen when an email message is sent from the Mailbox server. Sending an email message is the responsibility of the Mailbox Transport Submission service. The service retrieves the email from the mailbox database by using RPC and then sends the email to the Transport service on the appropriate Mailbox server. The Mailbox Transport Submission service directly communicates with the Transport service on any Exchange Server 2013 server inside or outside its own delivery group.

🌐 Real World Scenario

CUSTOMIZING ROUTING

In Exchange Server 2013, hub sites are no longer evaluated when message delivery occurs between DAG members. There is a good reason for this: a hub site must always be within a *least-cost route* for message delivery to be considered in the delivery path. However, with Exchange Server 2013, Mailbox servers that are members of the same DAG all share the same routing cost. Therefore, a hub site can never have a differing cost for any mailbox server in the DAG and therefore will never have a least-cost route. Although the hub site least-cost-path functionality is not new to Exchange Server 2013, the evaluation of delivery groups is new, and the DAG Member Delivery group definitely introduces a new design consideration for administrators involved in implementing message routing in an organization where hub sites are used.

Sending and Receiving Email

Mail routing to and from the Internet has changed in Exchange Server 2013. In Exchange Server 2007 and Exchange Server 2010, the Edge Transport role was an available option to accept email messages from the Internet. Even though Exchange Server 2013 Client Access servers and Mailbox servers can still be used to accept email messages from a previous version of Edge Transport, at the time of writing, Exchange Server 2013 no longer ships with the Edge Transport role. Will it return in a later release? It seems unlikely.

Unlike in previous versions of Exchange Server, the Client Access role can be used to proxy email messages from the Internet to a Mailbox server. In addition to accepting email messages from the Internet, the Client Access server can be used to proxy outbound email messages to the Internet. You may be asking yourself, "Why would I proxy SMTP messages through a Client Access server?" There are a few reasons for this proposed (*default*) implementation. For example, many organizations may not want the server hosting the mailboxes to communicate directly to a server on the Internet, or the organization may want to assign the role of sending email messages to the Internet to a single server. This last example is particularly relevant in implementing simplified troubleshooting scenarios.

Important Information When Receiving Email

When you are configuring Exchange Server to receive email from the Internet, what do you need to know? This might not seem like such a hard question, but there are a number of variables that you should consider so that you reliably receive email:

- You must determine the public- or Internet-facing IP address of all hosts that will accept mail for your organization. In small- and medium-sized businesses, this may be only one or two IP addresses at the same location. For large businesses, this may be multiple IPs spread across several physical locations.

- If you are using a managed provider or other external service to handle inbound mail, contact the provider to determine what you need to know.

- If you want to implement high availability for SMTP traffic, use a hardware load balancer to balance SMTP traffic between multiple Client Access servers, or ser.

- You must determine if inbound mail will pass directly through your firewall to your Exchange servers or if inbound mail will be routed to a third-party message-hygiene system.

- For each host that will accept inbound email for your organization, ensure that your Internet-facing DNS has a public host (A) record registered. For example, if your organization (netlogon.com) has two Client Access servers that will accept email, create two public host records for those servers. The actual host record names do not need to correspond to the actual server names. Here is an example for two Client Access servers:

```
mail1.netlogon.com      IN      A       192.168.244.10
mail2.netlogon.com      IN      A       192.168.244.11
```

- Ensure that the public DNS zone for your company's domain contains mail exchanger (MX) records for the host records. MX records should point to A records, not CNAME records. For the example of netlogon.com, the MX records would look something like this:

```
netlogon.com       MX      10      mail1.netlogon.com
netlogon.com       MX      10      mail2.netlogon.com
```

One of the practices mentioned earlier suggests that for each Client Access server that will receive email for your organization, you should create a separate host record and then create an MX record that points to the associated host record. This works best when you are trying to set multiple levels of priority so that certain hosts will accept mail only if servers with a lower preference value are not available. However, this does not necessarily work well if you are trying to load-balance multiple servers that should all have equal value. In the previous example, the domain netlogon.com has two MX records that have equal preferences values. Many SMTP servers will not properly load-balance or "round robin" between these two different servers (mail1.netlogon.com and mail2.netlogon.com.) Thus, one of these two servers will always be much busier than the other.

If you are trying to allow for round-robin load balancing across multiple inbound mail servers, there is a simple solution that most DNS servers will support. The solution requires that you configure the DNS servers to perform round-robin name resolution. First, create a single MX record like this:

```
netlogon.com       MX      10      mail1.netlogon.com
```

Then, create a single host record that has two IP addresses; to match the preceding example, the record would contain both 192.168.244.10 and 192.168.244.11 as valid IP addresses.

The MX record resolves to the host `mail1.netlogon.com`. When the TCP/IP address of the host `mail1.netlogon.com` is resolved, the DNS name server rotates the IP address values that are returned. By using this solution, DNS ensures that `mail1.netlogon.com` hosts are round-robin'ed and used equally for inbound mail. Also, this solution provides better control of your email infrastructure by ensuring that a single server is not overused by hosts on the Internet that *insist* on always connecting to the same server.

PRACTICE GOOD DNS RECORD MANAGEMENT FOR INBOUND MAIL

Poor DNS management contributes to many of the inbound mail problems organizations experience. Sometimes these things are a matter of simple oversight, and sometimes they are a result of sloppy management. Your Internet-facing DNS servers should be configured to provide all the necessary information for someone who needs to send you email, but they should be maintained so that stale information is removed:

◆ All Internet-facing mail servers should have an A record.

◆ MX records should point to your mail server's A records.

◆ Not all SMTP servers will use the MX record's weighting value. You may think that by setting your mail servers to an equal value you are load-balancing the inbound mail flow. Creating a single A record with multiple IP addresses (one for each of your inbound mail servers) will provide better inbound mail load balancing.

◆ Keep your MX records up to date and remove records that are no longer active.

◆ Don't confuse your external and internal DNS records. For most organizations, internal MX records are not necessary.

Receive Connectors

The Receive connector is the point where inbound SMTP mail is received on a Client Access server and a Mailbox server. Each Client Access server has three Receive connectors created by default:

Client Frontend   Accepts email messages from authenticated client using TLS over TCP port 587.

Default Frontend   Accepts anonymous email messages from external SMTP client over TCP port 25.

Outbound Proxy Frontend   Accepts email messages from Mailbox servers over TCP port 717 for outbound delivery.

The Mailbox server also has two Receive connectors that are created during the installation:

Client Proxy   Accepts email messages from authenticated clients that are proxied through the Client Access server over TCP port 465.

Default   Accepts email messages from Client Access servers over TCP port 25 or 2525 for inbound delivery. If the two roles are collocated on the same server, the Transport service hosted by the Mailbox server role will listen on TCP port 2525 instead of TCP 25, since TCP 25 will already be hosted by the Receive connector of the Client Access server. (Remember, two services cannot listen to the same port on the same IP, on the same server.)

The interaction between the Mailbox Receive connectors and the Client Access server Receive connectors is important to understand. Figure 22.4 illustrates the relationship between the connectors that run on both servers:

FIGURE 22.4
Mail flow between the Mailbox server and the Client Access server

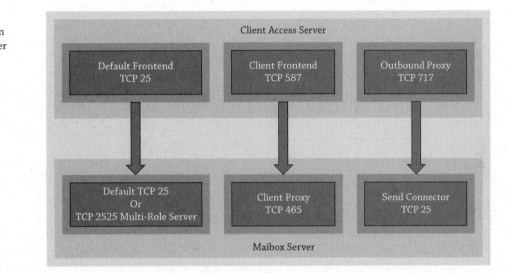

The Client Frontend Receive connector listens on TCP port number 587, not TCP port 25. TCP port 587 is the alternate port for POP3/IMAP4 clients to access SMTP, as per RFC 2476. The Client Frontend Receive connector is intended for receiving email from non-RPC over HTTPS clients, such as POP3 and IMAP4 clients. You would have to change the client's outbound SMTP port to use this connector for older clients, though most new POP3/IMAP4 client applications now default to TCP port 587. The Client Frontend Receive connector passes the client traffic over TCP port 465 to the Client Proxy Receive connector that runs on Mailbox servers.

The Default Frontend Receive connector is used to receive inbound SMTP mail from SMTP servers outside the organization. In Exchange Server 2007 and Exchange Server 2010, a Receive connector had to be manually created to accept email messages from anonymous senders. This is no longer the case in Exchange Server 2013; similarly to Exchange Server 2003, receiving email messages from the Internet happens "out of the box." In Figure 22.5 the Permission Groups properties of the Default Frontend Receive connector are shown. These permissions are the required set of permissions for receiving email messages anonymously from the Internet.

The Frontend Transport service, which is the service that is associated with the Default Frontend Receive connector, performs several actions on incoming email messages before starting an SMTP session to a Mailbox server. The Client Access server must perform these actions quickly because the Client Access server does *not* queue any email messages. Queuing occurs only on the Mailbox server.

One of the tasks that is performed on the Client Access servers is looking up the recipients of the email messages in Active Directory. Once the recipient is successfully looked up, the message is accepted by the Default Frontend Receive connector, and it is passed along to the Default Receive connector running on a Mailbox server. The Client Access server chooses the *best* Mailbox server to relay the email message. The *best* Mailbox server will vary. If the recipient of the email message is a distribution group, the Client Access server will pass the message to a Mailbox server in the same AD site. If the recipient's mailbox is located on a previous version of Exchange Server, the Client Access server passes the email message to an Exchange Server 2013 Mailbox server. The Client Access server never communicates directly to an Exchange Server 2007 or an Exchange Server 2010 server.

You can view the properties of a Receive connector by using the Get-ReceiveConnector cmdlet. Here is an example that displays all the properties of the Default Frontend Receive connector:

```
Get-ReceiveConnector "CAS-1\Default Frontend CAS-1" | fl
```

```
RunspaceId                          : c8f636cc-caa8-4031-b72d-a952b2771c67
```

```
AuthMechanism                              : Tls, Integrated, BasicAuth,
BasicAuthRequireTLS, ExchangeServer
Banner                                     :
BinaryMimeEnabled                          : True
Bindings                                   : {[::]:25, 0.0.0.0:25}
ChunkingEnabled                            : True
DefaultDomain                              :
DeliveryStatusNotificationEnabled          : True
EightBitMimeEnabled                        : True
BareLinefeedRejectionEnabled               : False
DomainSecureEnabled                        : True
EnhancedStatusCodesEnabled                 : True
LongAddressesEnabled                       : False
OrarEnabled                                : False
SuppressXAnonymousTls                      : False
ProxyEnabled                               : False
AdvertiseClientSettings                    : False
Fqdn                                       : CAS-1.netlogon.com
ServiceDiscoveryFqdn                       :
TlsCertificateName                         :
Comment                                    :
Enabled                                    : True
ConnectionTimeout                          : 00:10:00
ConnectionInactivityTimeout                : 00:05:00
MessageRateLimit                           : Unlimited
MessageRateSource                          : IPAddress
MaxInboundConnection                       : 5000
MaxInboundConnectionPerSource              : 20
MaxInboundConnectionPercentagePerSource    : 2
MaxHeaderSize                              : 128 KB (131,072 bytes)
MaxHopCount                                : 60
MaxLocalHopCount                           : 8
MaxLogonFailures                           : 3
MaxMessageSize                             : 36 MB (37,748,736 bytes)
MaxProtocolErrors                          : 5
MaxRecipientsPerMessage                    : 200
PermissionGroups                           : AnonymousUsers, ExchangeServers,
ExchangeLegacyServers
PipeliningEnabled                          : True
ProtocolLoggingLevel                       : Verbose
RemoteIPRanges                             : {::-ffff:ffff:ffff:ffff:ffff:ffff:ffff:
ffff, 0.0.0.0-255.255.255.255}
RequireEHLODomain                          : False
RequireTLS                                 : False
EnableAuthGSSAPI                           : False
ExtendedProtectionPolicy                   : None
LiveCredentialEnabled                      : False
```

```
TlsDomainCapabilities            : {}
Server                           : CAS-1
TransportRole                    : FrontendTransport
SizeEnabled                      : Enabled
TarpitInterval                   : 00:00:05
MaxAcknowledgementDelay          : 00:00:30
AdminDisplayName                 :
ExchangeVersion                  : 0.1 (8.0.535.0)
Name                             : Default Frontend CAS-1
DistinguishedName                : CN=Default Frontend CAS-1,CN=SMTP
Receive
                                   Connectors,CN=Protocols,CN=CAS-
1,CN=Servers,CN=Exchange Administrative Group
                                   (FYDIBOHF23SPDLT),CN=Administrative
Groups,CN=First
                                   Organization,CN=Microsoft
Exchange,CN=Services,CN=Configuration,DC=netlogon,DC=com
Identity                         : CAS-1\Default Frontend CAS-1
Guid                             : 775e96c4-469b-4d51-bc9d-b4c462236380
ObjectCategory                   : netlogon.com/Configuration/Schema/ms-
Exch-Smtp-Receive-Connector
ObjectClass                      : {top, msExchSmtpReceiveConnector}
WhenChanged                      : 4/8/2013 10:45:13 PM
WhenCreated                      : 4/8/2013 9:18:03 PM
WhenChangedUTC                   : 4/9/2013 2:45:13 AM
WhenCreatedUTC                   : 4/9/2013 1:18:03 AM
OrganizationId                   :
OriginatingServer                : DC1.netlogon.com
IsValid                          : True
ObjectState                      : Unchanged
```

The properties of the Default Receive connector are as follows:

```
Get-ReceiveConnector mbx1\"Default MBX1" | fl
```

```
RunspaceId                       : c8f636cc-caa8-4031-b72d-a952b2771c67
AuthMechanism                    : Tls, Integrated, BasicAuth,
BasicAuthRequireTLS, ExchangeServer
Banner                           :
BinaryMimeEnabled                : True
Bindings                         : {[::]:25, 0.0.0.0:25}
ChunkingEnabled                  : True
DefaultDomain                    :
DeliveryStatusNotificationEnabled : True
EightBitMimeEnabled              : True
```

```
BareLinefeedRejectionEnabled                : False
DomainSecureEnabled                         : False
EnhancedStatusCodesEnabled                  : True
LongAddressesEnabled                        : False
OrarEnabled                                 : False
SuppressXAnonymousTls                       : False
ProxyEnabled                                : False
AdvertiseClientSettings                     : False
Fqdn                                        : MBX1.netlogon.com
ServiceDiscoveryFqdn                        :
TlsCertificateName                          :
Comment                                     :
Enabled                                     : True
ConnectionTimeout                           : 00:10:00
ConnectionInactivityTimeout                 : 00:05:00
MessageRateLimit                            : Unlimited
MessageRateSource                           : IPAddress
MaxInboundConnection                        : 5000
MaxInboundConnectionPerSource               : Unlimited
MaxInboundConnectionPercentagePerSource     : 100
MaxHeaderSize                               : 128 KB (131,072 bytes)
MaxHopCount                                 : 60
MaxLocalHopCount                            : 8
MaxLogonFailures                            : 3
MaxMessageSize                              : 35 MB (36,700,160 bytes)
MaxProtocolErrors                           : 5
MaxRecipientsPerMessage                     : 5000
PermissionGroups                            : ExchangeUsers, ExchangeServers,
ExchangeLegacyServers
PipeliningEnabled                           : True
ProtocolLoggingLevel                        : Verbose
RemoteIPRanges                              : {::-ffff:ffff:ffff:ffff:ffff:ffff:ffff:
ffff, 0.0.0.0-255.255.255.255}
RequireEHLODomain                           : False
RequireTLS                                  : False
EnableAuthGSSAPI                            : False
ExtendedProtectionPolicy                    : None
LiveCredentialEnabled                       : False
TlsDomainCapabilities                       : {}
Server                                      : MBX1
TransportRole                               : HubTransport
SizeEnabled                                 : EnabledWithoutValue
TarpitInterval                              : 00:00:05
MaxAcknowledgementDelay                     : 00:00:30
AdminDisplayName                            :
ExchangeVersion                             : 0.1 (8.0.535.0)
```

```
Name                                    : Default MBX1
DistinguishedName                       : CN=Default MBX1,CN=SMTP Receive
Connectors,CN=Protocols,CN=MBX1,CN=Servers,CN=Exchange Administrative Group
                                          (FYDIBOHF23SPDLT),CN=Administrative
Groups,CN=First
Organization,CN=Microsoft Exchange,CN=Services,CN=Configuration,DC=netlogon,DC=com
Identity                                : MBX1\Default MBX1
Guid                                    : 410eca52-bd30-46a6-897b-ca72dc934b32
ObjectCategory                          : netlogon.com/Configuration/Schema/
ms-Exch-Smtp-Receive-Connector
ObjectClass                             : {top, msExchSmtpReceiveConnector}
WhenChanged                             : 4/23/2013 10:55:00 AM
WhenCreated                             : 4/8/2013 9:40:47 PM
WhenChangedUTC                          : 4/23/2013 2:55:00 PM
WhenCreatedUTC                          : 4/9/2013 1:40:47 AM
OrganizationId                          :
OriginatingServer                       : DC1.netlogon.com
IsValid                                 : True
ObjectState                             : Unchanged
```

CREATING A RECEIVE CONNECTOR

With few exceptions, you will usually not need to create additional Receive connectors, nor will you need to make many changes to the existing Receive connectors. The most common situation that should involve creating new Receive connectors is when you need to accommodate the needs of a custom application or server that needs to route email through your Exchange servers. For example, you may have a monitoring server that needs to send email internally to your server administrators. In this case, you could use the default Receive connectors but would then have to customize them for that need. To avoid messing around with the default Receive connectors, most organizations choose to create a new Receive connector that has a custom IP address range (which would allow only the monitoring server to communicate) and custom permissions (which would allow the monitoring server to relay email through the Receive connector). This solution minimizes the risk of inadvertently preventing an organization from receiving email because of misconfigurations on the default Receive connectors.

Creating a Receive connector in Exchange Server is not a simple as you might think. A multi-role server will have all of the default Receive connectors created for both the Mailbox and Client Access roles. On top of the default Receive connectors that are created, all the transport services for the Client Access and Mailbox servers will be running on the same server. This could cause a problem since the new Receive connector will listen on port 25 and will use the Transport service. If you recall from earlier in the chapter, the Transport service on a multi-role server normally listens to port 2525 and the Frontend Transport service listens to port 25. To create a new Receive connector that listens on port 25 and uses the Frontend Transport service, you can run the following:

```
New-ReceiveConnector -Name "Anonymous Relay" -Usage Custom -AuthMechanism
ExternalAuthoritative -PermissionGroups ExchangeServers -Bindings 192.168.1.20:25
-RemoteIpRanges 192.168.5.77 -TransportRole FrontendTransport
```

If you think creating a new Receive connector on a multi-role server is strange, wait until you see what you have to do to create a new Receive connector on a stand-alone Client Access server. As you know by now, when opening EMS on a Client Access server, the EMS session is running against a Mailbox server. So running the cmdlets to create a new Receive connector on a Client Access server from the EMS will actually create a new Receive connector on a Mailbox server. To create a new Receive connector on a Client Access server, you must force PowerShell to connect to a Client Access server by using the following steps on the client access server:

1. Open Windows PowerShell as an administrator.

2. Run add-pssnapin `Microsoft.Exchange.Management.PowerShell.SnapIn`.

3. Create your new Receive connector by using the `New-ReceiveConnector` cmdlet.

Important Information When Sending Email

Making sure that users on the Internet can send you email is fairly simple, but making sure they can receive email you send is a bit more challenging. Many of these challenges are because there are so many different types of anti-spam and anti-spoofing systems on the Internet. Unfortunately, these message-hygiene systems don't all follow the same set of rules. Why might a remote email server reject a connection from your public-facing server?

◆ The public IP address of your sending server may be on a real-time block list (RBL). This could be because that IP address had been a source of spam at one time, it could have been an open SMTP relay, or the IP address could be listed as part of a DHCP or dial-up IP address range.

◆ The public IP address of your sending server may not have a pointer (PTR) record registered in DNS. Some mail servers will not accept a connection from you unless your public IP has a PTR record.

◆ Your email domain may be missing or have an invalid sender policy framework (SPF) DNS record. You must take care during infrastructure changes and when your outbound IP addresses change; you must remember to keep your SPF record up to date, as well. While outright rejects because of this are not common yet, more organizations are using SPF as a way to protect against spoofing.

◆ The name that your sending server uses to introduce itself in the SMTP `HELO` or `EHLO` command may be an invalid domain name or may not match an existing DNS record.

To ensure that remote servers will accept connections from your email servers, there are a number of things you should do for your connections and in your public-facing DNS servers:

◆ Use a tool such as the Microsoft Remote Connectivity Analyzer (`www.testexchange connectivity.com`) or the DNSBL spam database lookup tool (`www.dnsbl.info`). If you find that your public-facing IP is on one of spam database lists, the list will usually have information on how to remove your IP. If the reason your IP is on the list is because they consider your IP part of a dial-up or DHCP range (common with cable service providers), you will need to work with your ISP to ensure you are removed from the list.

◆ Ensure that each public-facing IP address has a PTR record associated with it. Try to use the same name that the server uses for EHLO or HELO commands, such as `mail1` `.netlogon.com`. The owner of the IP address range will need to register the PTR records for you; this is usually the ISP.

◆ Create an SPF record in DNS that identifies the SMTP hosts that are authorized to send email for your domain. For small organizations this will be a simple matter of determining the public-facing IP addresses of your email servers. You can use the Sender ID Framework SPF Record Wizard to help you create this record; this wizard can be found at `www.microsoft.com/mscorp/safety/content/technologies/senderid/wizard/`. If you use a managed provider to deliver all of your outbound mail, you will need to contact the provider to get the information necessary to create SPF records for you. In the previous example for the mail servers for `netlogon.com`, the following SPF record indicates that only the listed host is authorized to send mail for `netlogon.com`:

```
netlogon.com    text =  "v=spf1 mx ip4:192.168.244.10 ip4:192.168.244.11 -all"
```

🌐 Real World Scenario

INCONSISTENT EMAIL DELIVERY FAILURES

A company that one of the contributors to this book worked with had been reliably sending email to the Internet for a number of years. The users rarely reported nondelivery reports (NDRs) or other outbound email problems.

During an upgrade of the speed of their Internet connection, the company changed their public IP addresses. The mail server and DNS manager dutifully changed the address and MX records on their public-facing DNS server. After the DNS changes took effect, they tested email to and from various domains. All their tests succeeded.

Since the IP address switch-over was so successful, it was quickly forgotten. Therefore, their administrators and their help desk were not quick to make a connection between the IP address change and occasional mail-delivery problems that the users were experiencing. Most of the NDR messages that the users were receiving were not very helpful and usually very cryptic.

Only after looking at the SMTP logs on their outbound smart host did the company determine that a few of the remote systems that were rejecting mail were doing so because there were no PTR records for the IP addresses.

The mail administrator contacted their ISP and asked the ISP to create the necessary PTR records for the IP subnet. This resolved the problem.

AOL is particularly strict on requiring IP addresses to have PTR records, but most organizations will accept mail from you regardless. Since only a small fraction of your outbound email is being rejected, it can make troubleshooting this problem more difficult.

Send Connectors

Whereas Receive connectors are configured for each server, Send connectors are organizational connectors that you can assign to a number of different Mailbox servers. This is an important distinction from some of the previous versions of Exchange Server. Send connectors in Exchange Server 2010 and Exchange Server 2013 are configured at the organization level and do not inherit settings from any specific server or site.

The Lowdown on Implicit Send Connectors

Each Mailbox server in an Exchange Server 2013 organization has an implicit Send connector, but that connector is used only for transferring email messages to other Mailbox servers. The implicit Send connector is not visible in the Exchange Admin Center or in the Exchange Management Shell. There are no properties that can be set for the implicit Send connector, and it cannot be used to deliver messages to the Internet or to an external host directly. This connector is actually *implicitly* created on demand whenever email messages need to be delivered to another mailbox server and then removed from the organization. You cannot configure this connector, so now that I've discussed it, and you know it, you can forget about it!

Send connectors accept only Mailbox servers as source servers, though proxying can be enabled on Send connectors. Proxying will mean that outbound email messages will be passed through a Client Access server before leaving the Exchange Server organization. In that case, the Mailbox server establishes an SMTP session with the Client Access server to deliver the email message. Once a proxy is enabled on a Send connector, the source Mailbox server will look for Client Access servers only in the same AD site as proxy servers for outbound SMTP connections.

Send connectors are managed in the EAC under the Send Connector tab when Mail Flow is selected from the Feature pane. Figure 22.6 shows the Source Server properties for a connector called Internet.

FIGURE 22.6
Managing send connectors

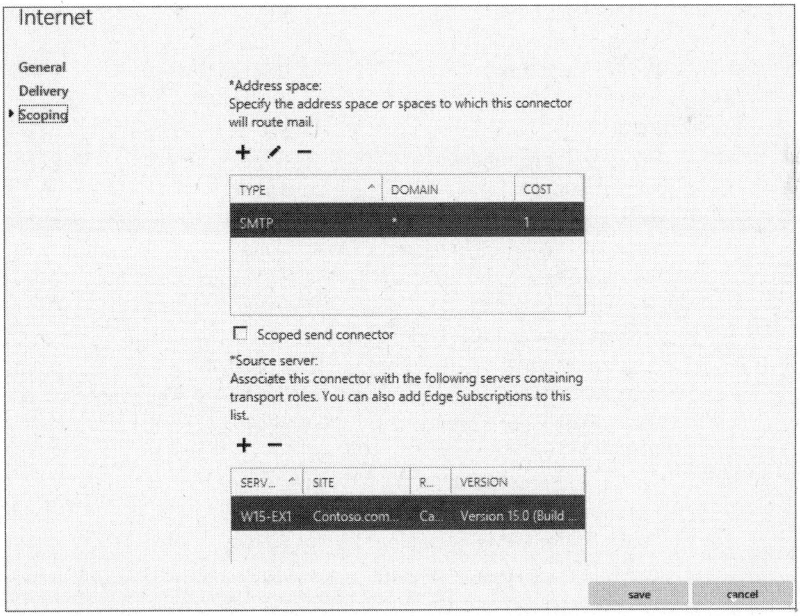

The Source Server properties page is where you designate which Mailbox server will deliver messages for a Send connector. When you assign more than one Mailbox server as a source server, the outbound messaging load will be balanced among the source servers.

You can also view the properties of a Send connector using the EMS cmdlet Get-SendConnector; here is an example:

```
Get-SendConnector "Internet" | FL
[PS] C:\Windows\system32>Get-SendConnector "Internet" | FL


AddressSpaces                 : {SMTP:*;1}
AuthenticationCredential      :
CloudServicesMailEnabled      : False
Comment                       :
ConnectedDomains              : {}
ConnectionInactivityTimeOut   : 00:10:00
DNSRoutingEnabled             : False
DomainSecureEnabled           : False
Enabled                       : True
ErrorPolicies                 : Default
ForceHELO                     : False
Fqdn                          :
FrontendProxyEnabled          : False
HomeMTA                       : Microsoft MTA
HomeMtaServerId               : MBX1
Identity                      : Internet
IgnoreSTARTTLS                : False
IsScopedConnector             : False
IsSmtpConnector               : True
MaxMessageSize                : Unlimited
Name                          : Internet
Port                          : 25
ProtocolLoggingLevel          : None
RequireOorg                   : False
RequireTLS                    : False
SmartHostAuthMechanism        : None
SmartHosts                    : {[192.168.1.171], [192.168.1.172]}
SmartHostsString              : [192.168.1.171],[192.168.1.172]
SmtpMaxMessagesPerConnection  : 20
SourceIPAddress               : 0.0.0.0
SourceRoutingGroup            : Exchange Routing Group (DWBGZMFD01QNBJR)
SourceTransportServers        : {MBX1}
TlsAuthLevel                  :
TlsCertificateName            :
TlsDomain                     :
UseExternalDNSServersEnabled  : False
```

Because Exchange Server 2013 does not have a default SMTP connector for outbound mail, you will need to create at least one Send connector. Most organizations will need to create only a single Send connector; this connector will be used to send email directly to the Internet, to an Edge Transport server, or to an SMTP smart host.

CREATING A SEND CONNECTOR

This section goes through an example of creating a Send connector that will be responsible for sending email to the Internet. To start, select Mail Flow from the Feature pane. Choose the Send Connector tab and click the + button. This launches the New Send Connector window shown in Figure 22.7. On the Introduction page, you must provide the name of the connector and its type (that is, its intended use).

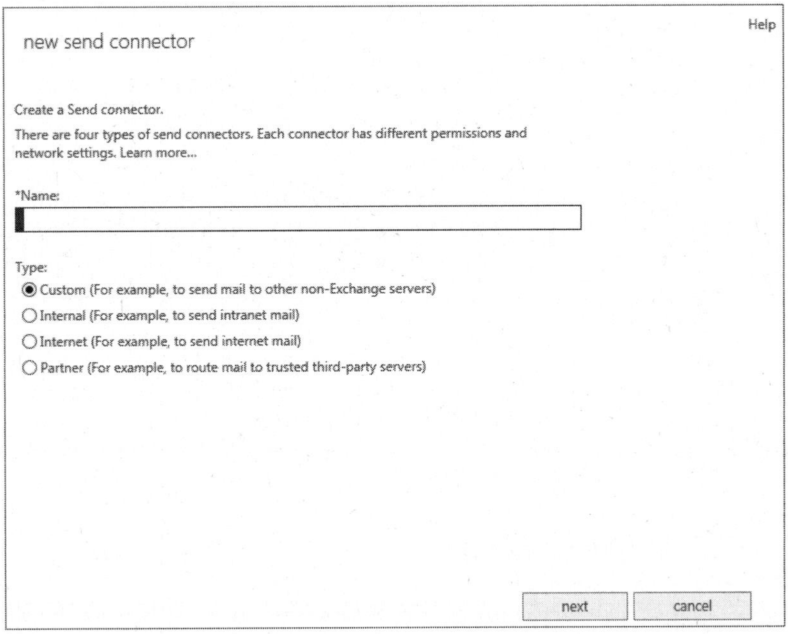

FIGURE 22.7
Introduction page of the New Send Connector window

The New Send Connector window will allow you to create four types of Send connectors. You should note that these types of connectors are nothing more than predefined configuration settings that can be changed at any point after the creation of the connector. Think of these connector types as templates, nothing more. The four types of Send connectors are listed here:

Custom Allows you to manually configure all the configuration settings, and has no preconfigured settings.

Internal Allows you to configure a connector that connects to Edge Transport servers in your organization or servers in another organization. Because all internal mail routing is automatic, you will usually not need to create an internal Send connector to another server in your organization.

Internet   Used to send mail to the Internet by using DNS MX records.

Partner   Used to send mail to specific Internet domains and to use certificate authentication and TLS encryption.

On the Network Settings properties page, you can configure a smart host for external delivery. Or, you can select the Use Domain Name System (DNS) "MX" Records To Route Mail Automatically setting to configure the Send connector to use name resolution to locate external hosts.

You must also specify the specific SMTP domains to which a Send connector will deliver email messages, in a setting called the *address space*. The address space with a value of * represents all SMTP domains that are not explicitly defined on another connector. (If a more precise address space is specified on another connector, such as konopizza.ca, that connector will be used instead of the connector that has the more general address space.)

The Source Server page allows you to specify the Mailbox servers that will deliver mail for this Send connector. If you have more than one Mailbox server, you should use additional servers for redundancy and load balancing.

Once you click the Finish button on the New Send Connector page, the EAC will execute the command necessary to create the new Send connector:

```
New-SendConnector -Name 'Internet Connector' -Usage 'Internet'
-AddressSpaces 'smtp:*;1' -DNSRoutingEnabled $true
-UseExternalDNSServersEnabled $false -SourceTransportServers 'EX1'
```

Once you have created the connector, you should set one additional configuration option. On the scoping tab of the Send connector, enter the public name of the FQDN for this server, such as MAIL.NETLOGON.COM.

This is the name that the Send connector uses to *announce* itself in the EHLO or HELO command when it connects to a remote SMTP system. If you don't specify an FQDN for the connector to use, the connector will use the default FQDN for the server. Often this is an internal name that is not recognized on the Internet. Some Internet hosts will reject a connection if the name cannot be resolved to a host record in your company's DNS zone.

Securing Mail Flow

One of the most common concerns with Exchange Server is how email messages are secured in transit. Out-of-the-box mail flow between Exchange servers inside an organization, is secured by using TLS. If a sniffer is placed in between source and destination servers, the traffic will be encrypted and unreadable. Not only is server-to-server communication secured by default, but so is all SMTP communication between transport services and SMTP clients, which is authenticated by default.

So if internal communication is secured by default, where does that leave us for communication to hosts on the Internet or third-party SMTP servers? Well, in short, it depends. There are several options available to secure email messages that are coming into or leaving your Exchange Server organization. Several of the most common options are covered in this section.

OPPORTUNISTIC TLS

The Frontend Default Receive connector is set to accept TLS connections from any source SMTP server. If a sending server accepts the SMTP verbs used to announce supportability for TLS, a TLS connection is established between target and source servers. Opportunistic TLS is effective because the servers are not validating the certificate being used to secure the SMTP session. Exchange Server *cares* only that a TLS session is established and that the traffic between source and target servers is encrypted.

DOMAIN SECURE TLS

Unlike opportunistic TLS when a certificate is not validated, domain secure TLS requires source and target servers to have valid certificates installed. When domain secure is enabled, sending and receiving servers exchange certificates. The subject name or subject alternate name of a certificate must match the FQDN set on the Send connector of the source organization. In the target organization, the subject name or subject alternate name of the certificate must match the FQDN set on the Receive connector. If the FQDN of the connector does *not* match any of the names on the certificate or if the certificate is not valid, email messages will not be exchanged between the organizations.

TRANSPORT RULE

Another method of enforcing TLS is through a new transport rule action that has been added to Exchange Server 2013 to require TLS to be established before transmitting any SMTP data. The new transport rule action is called Require TLS Encryption. As Figure 22.8 illustrates, the new action can be added to a transport rule.

FIGURE 22.8
Adding the Require TLS Encryption action to a transport rule

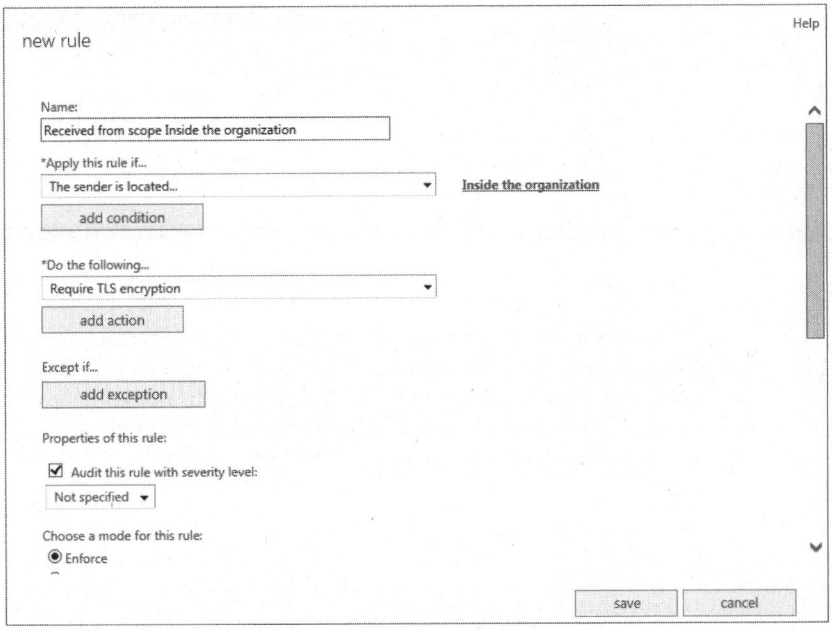

Accepted Domains

An accepted domain is an SMTP domain name (aka SMTP namespace) for which your Exchange Server 2013 organization will accept email messages. The servers in your organization will either deliver an email message to an accepted domain to an internal Exchange Server mailbox or relay it to an SMTP server. During a migration from a legacy version of Exchange Server, the accepted domains list will include the SMTP domains for your legacy version of Exchange Server. Accepted domains must be defined for all email addresses that will be routed into your organization or by your Exchange Server 2013 servers. Most small- and medium-sized organizations have only a single accepted domain.

SETTING UP AN ACCEPTED DOMAIN USING THE EAC

Accepted domains are found by choosing the Mail Flow tab in the Feature pane and selecting the Accepted Domains tab in the Results pane; you will see a list of the accepted domains that have been defined for your organization, such as those shown in Figure 22.9.

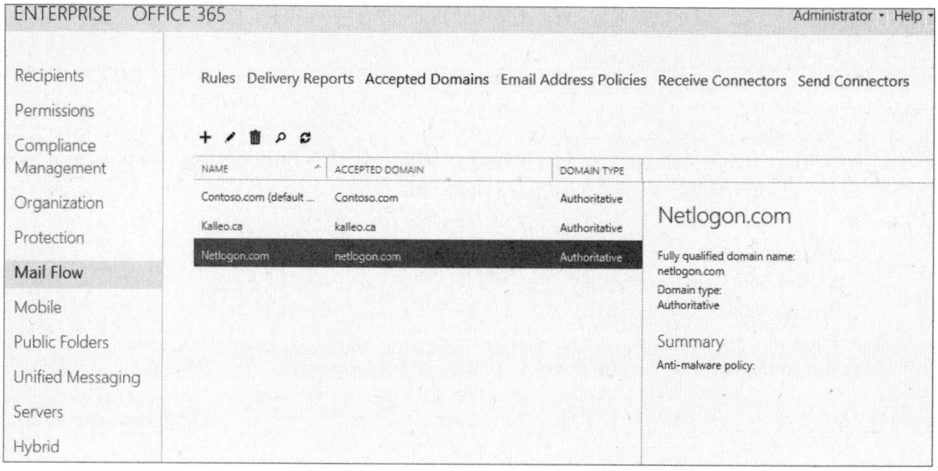

FIGURE 22.9
List of accepted domains

Accepted domains are simple to create and require little input. To create a new accepted domain using the EAC, click the + sign and you will see the New Accepted Domain window (shown in Figure 22.10). You then need to provide a descriptive name for the accepted domain, the SMTP domain name, and the domain type (how messages for this domain should be treated when messages are accepted by Exchange Server 2013).

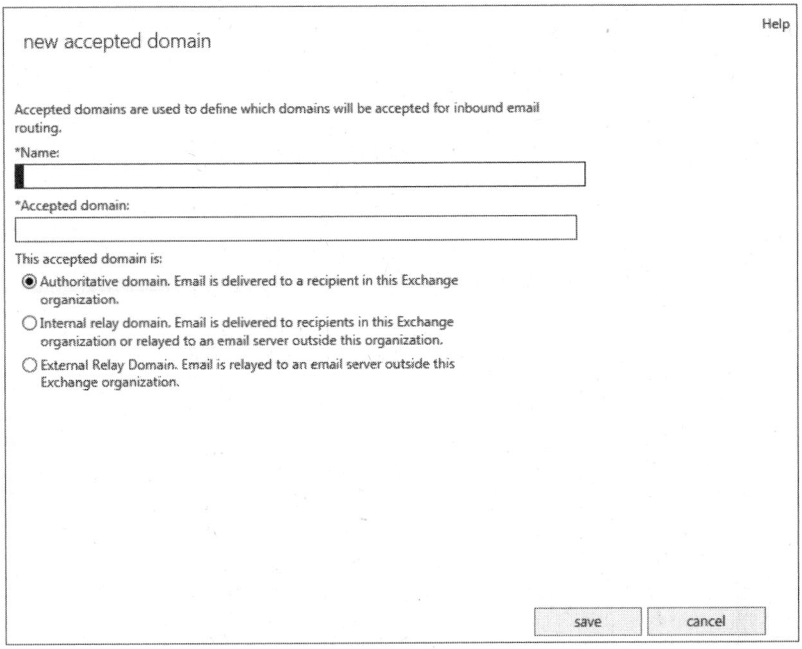

FIGURE 22.10
Creating a new
accepted domain

Keep in mind that you cannot modify the domain name of an accepted domain once it is created. (You can change the domain type, however.)

SETTING UP AN ACCEPTED DOMAIN USING THE EMS

You can also manage accepted domains by using the following EMS cmdlets:

- `New-AcceptedDomain`
- `Set-AcceptedDomain`
- `Get-AcceptedDomain`
- `Remove-AcceptedDomain`

For example, to create a new accepted domain, use the following EMS command:

```
new-AcceptedDomain -Name 'netlogon.com' -DomainName ↵
'netlogon.com' -DomainType 'Authoritative'
```

ABOUT DOMAIN TYPES

One tricky thing about defining an accepted domain is that you must define how Exchange Server is to treat a message addressed to that domain. You can choose from three types of domains when creating an accepted domain:

Authoritative Domain   These are SMTP domains for which you accept the inbound message and deliver it to an internal mailbox within your Exchange Server organization.

Internal Relay Domain   These are SMTP domains for which your Exchange server will accept inbound SMTP mail. The Exchange server must have mail-enabled contacts that specify forwarding addresses for users in those domains. The Exchange server then relays the message to another internal mail system. Internal relay domains are used when two Exchange organizations are using federation.

External Relay Domain   These are SMTP domains for which your Exchange Server organization will accept inbound SMTP mail and then relay that mail to an external SMTP mail server, usually one that is outside the organization's boundaries. If Edge Transport servers are used, the Edge Transport servers handle the external relay domains.

Remote Domains

When sending mail outside your organization, Exchange Server will make certain assumptions about message formatting and out-of-office replies. These types of settings can be controlled by creating remote domains. For a fresh installation of Exchange Server 2013, a single remote domain configuration is used for all outbound mail. To review the remote domains in your organization you just need to run Get-RemoteDomain.

Creating a new remote domain provides an organization with the ability to define the content that is shared with the remote domain and how email messages from the remote domain are processed by Exchange Server 2013 servers. Here are some of the common configurations the organization may use when creating remote domains:

AllowForwardEnabled   Allows auto forwards of email messages.

CurrentType   Specifies the message content type and format that are accepted by the remote domain.

IsInternal   Recipients in the remote domain are considered internal recipients. This setting will alter how transport rules and transport agents are applied to these recipients.

You can also create the remote domain from an EMS prompt by typing the following command:

```
New-RemoteDomain -Name "KALLEO Industries" -DomainName "kalleo.ca"
```

When an Exchange Server 2013 organization and Office365 are in a hybrid configuration, a new remote domain is created in the Exchange Server 2013 organization for the Office365 domain. Using the Get-RemoteDomain cmdlet, you can view the remote domain settings of an Office365 remote domain:

```
Get-RemoteDomain hy* | fl

RunspaceId                           : c8f636cc-caa8-4031-b72d-a952b2771c67
DomainName                           : elfassy.mail.onmicrosoft.com
```

```
IsInternal                           : False
TargetDeliveryDomain                 : True
ByteEncoderTypeFor7BitCharsets       : Undefined
CharacterSet                         :
NonMimeCharacterSet                  :
AllowedOOFType                       : External
AutoReplyEnabled                     : True
AutoForwardEnabled                   : True
DeliveryReportEnabled                : True
NDREnabled                           : True
MeetingForwardNotificationEnabled    : False
ContentType                          : MimeHtmlText
DisplaySenderName                    : True
PreferredInternetCodePageForShiftJis : Undefined
RequiredCharsetCoverage              :
TNEFEnabled                          :
LineWrapSize                         : Unlimited
TrustedMailOutboundEnabled           : False
TrustedMailInboundEnabled            : False
UseSimpleDisplayName                 : False
NDRDiagnosticInfoEnabled             : True
MessageCountThreshold                : 2147483647
AdminDisplayName                     :
ExchangeVersion                      : 0.1 (8.0.535.0)
Name                                 : Hybrid Domain - elfassy.mail.onmicrosoft.com
DistinguishedName                    : CN=Hybrid Domain - elfassy.mail.
onmicrosoft.com,CN=Internet Message
                                       Formats,CN=Global Settings,CN=First
Organization,CN=Microsoft
Exchange,CN=Services,CN=Configuration,DC=netlogon,DC=com
Identity                             : Hybrid Domain - elfassy.mail.onmicrosoft.com
Guid                                 : 019edd86-1861-43d8-ad96-0cfebea78cad
ObjectCategory                       : netlogon.com/Configuration/Schema/ms-Exch-
Domain-Content-Config
ObjectClass                          : {top, msExchDomainContentConfig}
WhenChanged                          : 4/19/2013 2:55:37 AM
WhenCreated                          : 4/19/2013 2:55:21 AM
WhenChangedUTC                       : 4/19/2013 6:55:37 AM
WhenCreatedUTC                       : 4/19/2013 6:55:21 AM
OrganizationId                       :
OriginatingServer                    : DC1.netlogon.com
IsValid                              : True
ObjectState                          : Unchanged
```

Messages in Flight

How does Exchange Server 2013 ensure that messages in flight are not lost during a server failure? Microsoft has taken lessons learned from Exchange Server 2007 and 2010 and expanded on their high-availability solutions for messages in flight. In this section we will cover the concepts of Shadow Redundancy and Safety Net. Even if you are familiar with Exchange Server 2010 shadow redundancy, please don't skip over this section, because Microsoft has made some changes to shadow redundancy in Exchange Server 2013.

Understanding Shadow Redundancy

Shadow redundancy protects organizations in the event of a Mailbox server or queue database loss. The main principle behind shadow redundancy is maintaining a copy of a message on the previous delivery hop until the server verifies that the email message has successfully delivered. Think about it as a fail-safe mechanism that waits for the recipient server to *confirm* that a message has been received instead of the sender server *assuming* that the message was successfully delivered. Inside the Exchange Server organization, before an email message is accepted by a receiving Mailbox server, a shadow copy of the email message is created, preferably on a server in a remote site. The shadow message is stored in a shadow queue.

An important thing to note here is that shadow redundancy is not unique to Exchange Server. This functionality is actually common among other third-party messaging systems.

Before diving into Shadow Redundancy, let's talk about some of the terminology that will be used in this section:

Primary message   An original email message

Shadow message   A copy of an original email message

Primary server   Mailbox server holding a primary email message

Shadow server   Mailbox server holding a shadow email message

Once a message has been accepted by a Mailbox server, the Mailbox server processes the message and delivers the email message to the appropriate mailbox database. After the message has been successfully delivered, the primary mailbox server notifies the Mailbox server holding the shadow copy to discard the message from the shadow queue.

The transport boundary for shadow redundancy is *Mailbox servers within the same delivery groups*. If an organization has two DAGs, shadow redundancy would occur within each delivery group.

A shadow message is not identical to a primary message. Since the receiving Mailbox server creates a shadow message before the message is accepted, the shadow message is an unprocessed message. This means that the email message has not yet gone through the transport pipeline. If the shadow message is ever called upon, the email message would have to go through the transport pipeline before being delivered.

Shadow redundancy is configured using `Set-TransportConfig`. It is enabled by default and should not be disabled unless you are troubleshooting specific email delivery issues. You can also view all the shadow redundancy settings by using the Get-TransportConfig cmdlet, the default settings of shadow redundancy are shown here:

```
Get-TransportConfig | fl *shadow*

ShadowRedundancyEnabled              : True
ShadowHeartbeatTimeoutInterval       : 00:15:00
ShadowHeartbeatRetryCount            : 12
ShadowHeartbeatFrequency             : 00:02:00
ShadowResubmitTimeSpan               : 03:00:00
ShadowMessageAutoDiscardInterval     : 2.00:00:00
RejectMessageOnShadowFailure         : False
ShadowMessagePreferenceSetting       : PreferRemote
MaxRetriesForLocalSiteShadow         : 2
MaxRetriesForRemoteSiteShadow        : 4
```

An important issue to note is that Exchange Server 2010 performed shadow redundancy by issuing the XSHADOW SMTP verb. Exchange Server 2013 servers do not issue an XSHADOW verb, therefore Exchange Server 2010 does not perform shadow redundancy when sending mail to Exchange Server 2013. However, when an Exchange Server 2013 server submits a message to an Exchange Server 2010 Hub Transport server in the same site, it will create a shadow copy of the message until it receives a notification of successful delivery.

For a detail architecture of shadow redundancy and all of the configuration parameters, review this TechNet article at http://technet.microsoft.com/en-us/library/dd351027(v=exchg.150).aspx.

Understanding Safety Net

In Exchange Server 2007 Microsoft introduced a new concept of holding email messages that haven't been delivered to their final destination in the queue database. The queue database is an Extensible Storage Engine (ESE) database, the same database type as a mailbox database, created on Hub Transport servers. As well as keeping copies of messages, the queue database took part in the transport dumpster. Hub Transport servers stored email messages in the queue database based on the transport dumpster settings and database replication. The transport dumpster was a big step forward for transport high availability, something that had long been criticized as being the Achilles' heel of high availability in Exchange Server. The transport dumpster, though, still had big gaps in its functionality.

In Exchange Server 2013, Microsoft has moved away from the transport dumpster and Safety Net has now taken its place. The queue database is no longer stored on Hub Transport servers; it's now stored on Mailbox servers, the only place where email messages can be queued.

Much like the transport dumpster, Safety Net utilizes the queue database to store email messages that have been successfully delivered. Unlike in legacy versions of Exchange Server, Safety Net defines how long email messages are retained in the queue database, by default for two days. So all messages that pass through the transport pipeline are stored in the queue database for two days after having been successfully delivered.

Another improvement that Safety Net offers over the transport dumpster is that each message now has two copies, each copy stored in a different queue database. To modify the amount of time that a message is retained in the queue database for Safety Net, change the value of the SafetyNetHoldTime parameter by using the Set-TranportConfig cmdlet.

It's nice that these messages are stored in the queue database, but how are those copies of email messages actually *used*? Well, for that to happen, Safety Net has to be invoked. When a database is mounted after a lossy failover, Active Manager generates a resubmit request to all Mailbox servers in its delivery group. The requesting server will always prefer the server that has the primary email message. If the Mailbox server holding the primary message is unavailable for 12 hours, Active Manager will make a request to the Mailbox server that holds the secondary or shadow copy of the original email message. The shadow copy of the message has not yet gone through the transport pipeline, so if there is a large quantity of email messages in the queue, you may notice a spike in transport service usage.

After 24 hours, a resubmit request will expire. To review the resubmit requests in your organization, you can use the Get-Resubmit cmdlet.

It's best if the Windows Server 2012 drive that contains the Safety Net database is configured as RAID 1 storage. As well, you should note that if you implement a lagged database copy in the organization, Microsoft recommends setting the SafetyNetHoldTime parameter and the ReplayLagTime parameter to the same value.

Using Exchange Server 2013 Anti-Spam/Anti-Malware Tools

Microsoft has continued to improve the anti-spam capabilities of Exchange Server over the past few years. On top of the anti-spam agents that can be enabled on an Exchange Server 2013 server, Microsoft has introduced an anti-malware solution that is built into Exchange Server 2013. Unlike many third-party solutions, the downside of the built-in anti-malware solution is that it contains only one scanning engine.

During the installation of Exchange Server 2013, you can choose to disable or enable anti-malware measures, as shown in Figure 22.11. Anti-spam functionalities, on the other hand, must be enabled after the installation of Exchange Server 2013.

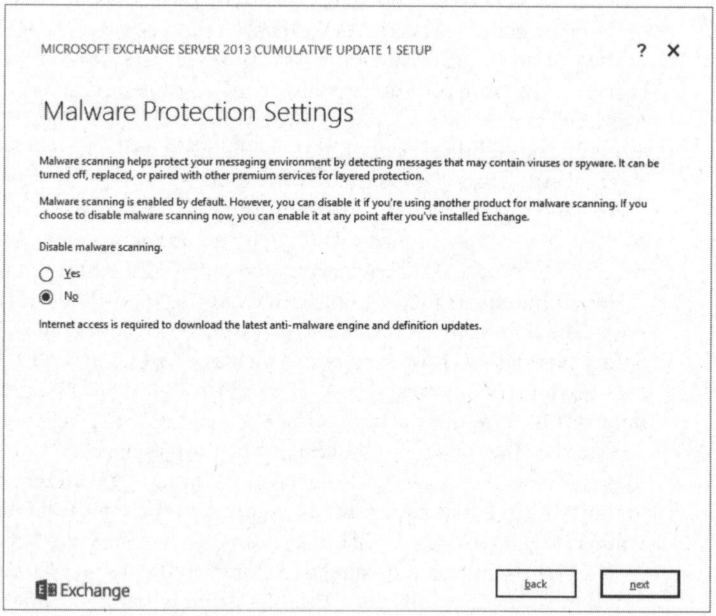

FIGURE 22.11
Enabling anti-malware during installation of Exchange Server 2013

Microsoft also recommends the use of Exchange Online Protection, which provides anti-spam protection before the message reaches your Exchange Server organization. There are plenty of third-party vendors that also supply on-premises or cloud solutions to assist with anti-spam and anti-malware. Every organization, no matter the size, should consider placing an anti-spam and anti-malware solution in front of Exchange servers. It's simply irresponsible to allow spam into your organization and malware onto your network.

Updating Anti-Malware Engines

After the installation of Exchange Server 2013, anti-malware engines and definitions can be updated by using the EMS. The following example uses the `Update-MalwareFilteringServer.ps1` script to download the latest updates:

```
& $env:ExchangeInstallPath\Scripts\Update-MalwareFilteringServer.ps1 -Identity all-1
```

Once the PowerShell script completes, you can confirm that the latest updates have been download by looking for event 6033 in the Application logs. If no new updates were found, you will see event 6023, as shown here, in the Application log.

```
Log Name:       Application
Source:         Microsoft-Filtering-FIPFS
Date:           6/20/2013 1:06:23 AM
Event ID:       6023
Task Category: None
Level:          Information
Keywords:
User:           NETWORK SERVICE
Computer:       Ex1.netlogon.com
Description:
MS Filtering Engine Update process has not detected any new scan engine updates.
 Scan Engine: Microsoft
 Update Path: http://forefrontdl.microsoft.com/server/scanengineupdate
```

Administrators sometimes forget this. You should update the anti-malware engines and definitions before placing production mailboxes on a Mailbox server.

Anti-Malware Policy

An anti-malware policy is a collection of settings that are used to define how an email message with malware is handled within your organization. Unlike the anti-spam features in Exchange Server 2013, anti-malware policy can be *managed* through EAC. However, from the EAC you cannot *create* a new anti-malware policy. To create a new policy, you must use the `New-MalwareFilterPolicy` command.

The core settings of the anti-malware policy are listed under the Settings tab, as shown in Figure 22.12.

FIGURE 22.12
Default anti-malware
settings

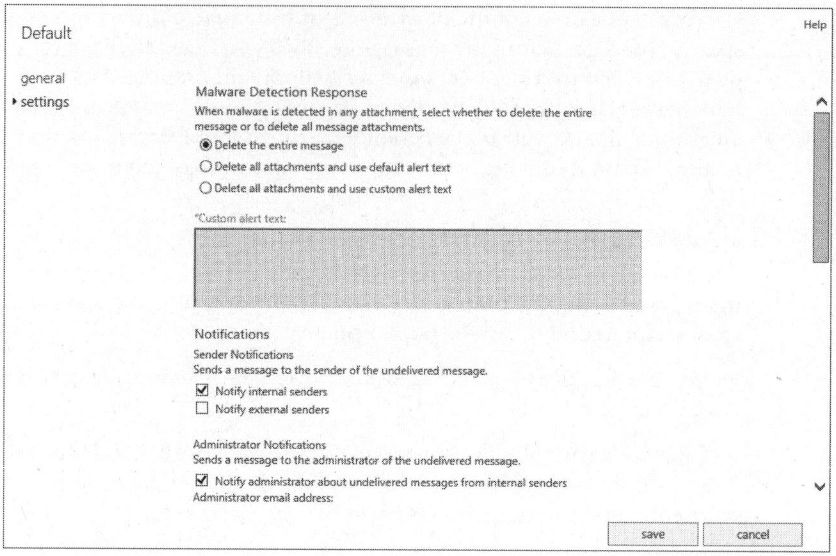

There are three possible settings that the Malware Detection Response can be set to:

Delete The Entire Message   Deletes the email message, thus preventing the message from being delivered. This is the default setting.

Delete All Attachments And Use Default Alert Text   Removes all attachments from the email message. Adds a text file as an attachment that informs the recipients that all attachments have been removed from the email message because malware was detected.

Delete All Attachments And Use Custom Alert Text   Removes all attachments from the email message. Adds a text file that contains the custom text created in the anti-malware policy.

The Notifications section defines the sender types that will be notified if malware is detected. There are two notification options:

Notify Internal Senders   Send notifications that malware was detected when the sender of the email message is within the organization.

Notify External Senders   Send notifications that malware was detected when the sender of the email message is outside the organization.

The Administrator Notifications section is used to send email messages to an SMTP recipient, most likely a distribution group containing your Exchange Server administrators, for undelivered messages. You can use a semicolon to separate multiple recipients.

The last option in the anti-malware policy is to create custom notifications. The custom notification is sent to the sender or administrator when a message is not delivered. This notification is used only when the entire email message has been deleted from the database.

To test the malware settings and the malware agent, you can download the EICAR (www.eicar.org) anti-malware test file, which masks itself as malware. Send the downloaded EICAR as an attachment to an internal recipient. Once the message is sent, you can use the message-tracking logs to review the actions taken by the malware agent, such as removing the email message from the transport pipeline. In the output shown here, notice that the malware agent detected the presence of malware and removed the infected email message:

```
Get-TransportService | Get-MessageTrackingLog -MessageSubject "Virus2" -event
fail | fl
```

```
RunspaceId              : c52ed2d3-e433-40e1-8038-9428479cb5d1
Timestamp               : 4/23/2013 12:44:57 PM
ClientIp                :
ClientHostname          : Ex1
ServerIp                :
ServerHostname          :
SourceContext           : Malware Agent
ConnectorId             :
Source                  : AGENT
EventId                 : FAIL>
Recipients              : {zoe@netlogon.com}
RecipientStatus         : {550 4.3.2 QUEUE.TransportAgent; message deleted by
transport agent}
```

Managing Anti-Malware Protection

For many organizations, the use of a third-party anti-malware application is preferred over the built-in Exchange Server solution. In these cases, anti-malware protection should be disabled on the Mailbox server. To disable anti-malware scanning, run the following command on each Mailbox server:

```
& $env:ExchangeInstallPath\Scripts\Disable-Antimalwarescanning.ps1
```

The following command will enable anti-malware scanning:

```
& $env:ExchangeInstallPath\Scripts\Enable-Antimalwarescanning.ps1
```

Once you enable or disable anti-malware scanning, the Transport service must be restated on the Mailbox server for the change to take effect.

When email messages are lost due to false positives that occur in anti-malware scanning, you can temporarily bypass filtering. Bypassing anti-malware filtering should be done with caution because the Mailbox server will no longer scan an email messages for malware. Enabling and disabling bypassing of malware filtering can take up to 10 minutes to take effect. To enable bypassing of anti-malware scanning use this command:

```
Set-MalwareFilteringServer -BypassFiltering $true
```

Using the Set-MalwareFiltering cmdlet, you can specify how malware filtering is configured within your organization. We already talked about bypassing malware filtering; you can also change settings, such as the update frequency of the malware engine. You can use the Get-MalwareFilteringServer cmdlet to see the settings that can be modified:

```
Get-MalwareFilteringServer | fl
ForceRescan                   : False
BypassFiltering               : False
PrimaryUpdatePath             : http://forefrontdl.microsoft.com/server/
scanengineupdate
SecondaryUpdatePath           :
DeferWaitTime                 : 5
DeferAttempts                 : 3
UpdateFrequency               : 60
UpdateTimeout                 : 150
ScanTimeout                   : 300
ScanErrorAction               : Block
MinimumSuccessfulEngineScans  : 1
```

Enabling Anti-Spam Agents

Out of the box, the Exchange Server 2013 anti-spam transport features are not enabled. Microsoft has included PowerShell scripts to enable anti-spam features in the Exchange Server script directory. Specifically, you will find two PowerShell scripts (Install-AntispamAgents .ps1 and Uninstall-AntispamAgents.ps1) in the folder C:\Program Files\Microsoft\ Exchange Server\v15\scripts.

On each of your Mailbox servers earmarked to use the anti-spam agents, you must run the Install-AntispamAgents.ps1 script. This script needs to be run only on the Mailbox servers that will receive inbound email from outside your organization.

To run the installation script, open the EMS, and change to the scripts folder (again, C:\ Program Files\Microsoft\Exchange Server\v15\scripts) by typing CD $exscripts, and then type this command: .\Install-AntispamAgents.ps1. After you run this command, you will need to restart the Microsoft Exchange Transport service for the change to take effect.

If you are familiar with managing anti-spam in Exchange Server 2010, you will quickly notice that in Exchange Server 2013 you can no longer manage anti-spam settings from a GUI management interface. All management of anti-spam settings is done through the EMS. The IP Allow lists' and IP Block lists' agents are not available in Exchange Server 2013. To use the IP Allow lists and IP Block lists, you must use an Exchange Server 2007 or Exchange Server 2010 transport server.

The most relevant anti-spam agents are discussed in the next sections.

Content Filtering

Content filtering is a feature in Exchange Server 2013 that was formerly known as the Intelligent Message Filter in Exchange Server 2003. Arguably it is the most useful of the anti-spam features. The content filter examines a message's content based on keyword analysis, message size, and other factors and then assigns the message a spam confidence level (SCL) ranking, a score essentially. This ranking is from 0 to 9. A message with a SCL ranking of 0 is not very likely to be spam, and a message with an SCL ranking of 9 is very likely to be spam. Based on the SCL value of a message, the Exchange server takes one of three possible actions:

Delete messages that meet or exceed a specific SCL threshold. This is the most drastic of actions. The sender is not notified that this has occurred, and you can't later evaluate whether the message really was spam.

Reject messages that meet or exceed a specific SCL threshold. The Mailbox server accepts the message, analyzes it, and kicks it back to the sender with text indicating that the message was rejected because it looks like spam.

Quarantine messages that meet or exceed a specific SCL threshold. Any messages with the specified SCL value or higher will be sent to an SMTP address where you can then analyze them to determine whether they are truly spam.

NEGATIVE SCL VALUES?

Is it possible to have an SCL value of –1? Yes, actually it is. For any message that is sent to your server via an authenticated connection, or if the sender's email address is on your safe senders list, the SCL value of the message is set to –1. So if one of your trusted senders is sending you a short message about low-interest-rate mortgages or buying cheap Viagra, you will still get the message.

If you are interested in seeing the SCL value that is assigned to any given message in your mailbox, you can use the column-filtering features of Outlook. Simply add the column named SCL to your view. The new column will display the score of each email message in the view.

You can activate none, one, two, or all three of the actions, but the SCL values must progress downward in accordance with the severity of the action. For example, you could set a reject value of 8 or higher and a quarantine value of 7 or higher. In that case, any messages with an SCL value of 8 or 9 will be rejected; messages with an SCL value of 7 will be sent to the quarantine email address. However, you cannot set a quarantine value of 9 but then delete everything with an SCL value greater than or equal to 7.

In Exchange Server 2013, a global value named the SCL Junk Threshold is set to 8 by default. This value determines that the information store must place any messages with a spam confidence level of 8 or higher into a user's Junk Email folder. Users can then review the contents of the Junk Email folder to determine whether a message was correctly identified as spam. However, if you set the quarantine value on the Mailbox server to 3, then only messages with an SCL value of 4 or higher will reach the Junk Email folder.

For most organizations, a global SCL Junk Threshold of 8 is sufficient, but depending on your business model and the types of email messages you receive, you might want to lower it. You can lower the SCL value to 5 or 6. To lower the Junk Email threshold for all users, type the following command:

```
Set-OrganizationConfig -SCLJunkThreshold 6
```

You can view the organization configuration using the Get-OrganizationConfig cmdlet. Here is an example:

```
Get-OrganizationConfig | FL SCLJunk*

SCLJunkThreshold : 8
```

In some cases, a specific user may need a different set of SCL values than the Mailbox server provides. The values the Mailbox server provides can be customized on a user-by-user basis. In the following command, we have disabled the Quarantine and Reject parameters for a particular user, and we have specified that this user's Junk Email threshold is 4:

```
Set-Mailbox "Zoe Elfassy" -SCLRejectEnabled $False -SCLQuarantineEnabled ~CR
$False  -SCLJunkThreshold 4 -SCLJunkEnabled $True
```

You can view the resulting configuration for the mailbox with the Get-Mailbox cmdlet. Here is an example:

```
Get-Mailbox "Zoe Elfassy" | FL Name,*scl*

Name                     : Zoe Elfassy
SCLDeleteThreshold       :
SCLDeleteEnabled         :
SCLRejectThreshold       : 7
SCLRejectEnabled         : False
SCLQuarantineThreshold   : 9
SCLQuarantineEnabled     : False
SCLJunkThreshold         : 4
SCLJunkEnabled           : True
```

🌐 Real World Scenario

WAY TOO MANY VALID EMAILS BEING FLAGGED AS SPAM

A company can set up filters to allow specific messages past anti-spam filters. Take, for example, a real estate services company. Much of their communication with customers and prospective customers is via email. They found when they started using the content filter that many of their customers' emails were being flagged as spam because of keywords in the message body.

They decided to use the content filter's custom-words feature to specify some words or phrases that the content filter would not block. These included words and phrases such as *mortgage*, *interest rates*, *real estate*, and *assessment*. The thought behind this was that it was better to possibly receive a few extra spam messages that use these words than it was to reject a message from a real customer.

You can enable two types of word lists. If the message contains words in the first list, even if the message appears to be spam, the message is accepted. If the words in the second list are contained in a message, the message is blocked unless it contains words from the first list. Using Add-ContentFilterPhrase, you can create a good or bad word list as shown here:

```
Add-ContentFilterPhrase -Influence BadWord -Phrase "Really bad"
```

The list with words and phrases that are always accepted can be particularly useful if legitimate messages to your company will frequently contain a particular word or phrase that might otherwise be filtered (see the, "Way Too Many Valid Emails Being Flagged as Spam" sidebar).

Recipient Filtering

When recipient filtering is enabled, the Mailbox server is configured to reject email messages intended for any SMTP address that is not found in the Active Directory or to reject email messages intended for specific SMTP addresses. This reduces the number of *garbage* messages that your Exchange Server organizations accepts, for which it has to issue nondelivery reports. The cmdlet Get-RecipientFilterConfig can be used to get the recipient filtering settings:

```
Get-RecipientFilterConfig
BlockedRecipients         : {}
RecipientValidationEnabled : False
BlockListEnabled          : False
Enabled                   : True
ExternalMailEnabled       : True
InternalMailEnabled       : False
```

If you are performing recipient filtering, newly created mailboxes may have their mail rejected by the Mailbox server until the new mailbox has been replicated throughout the organization.

Tarpitting

An Exchange Server can use tarpit to combat dictionary-spamming and directory-harvest attacks. The tarpit feature tells the SMTP server to wait a specified number of seconds (five seconds by default) before responding to a request to send a message to an invalid recipient. For example, if the recipient Celine@netlogon.com is an invalid recipient in your organization, but someone's mail server sends a message to that address, your server will wait five seconds and then respond with this error:

```
550 5.1.1 User unknown
```

Now, you may wonder why this feature is even worth mentioning. Spammers often hijack people's home (or work) computers with agents that send mail on their behalf. These "bots" can offer the spammer an almost unlimited supply of SMTP clients, all sending email. They can locate your domain and then go through a dictionary of common names and try to send mail to each one for example, sending to Zachary@netlogon.com, then Zoe@netlogon.com, then Savannah@netlogon.com, and so on. An Exchange server without a tarpit could send back dozens of 550 error messages each second. This makes dictionary spamming more practical. Another evil part of the dictionary-spamming attack is that the spammer can note which addresses are valid and use them in the future. This is called directory harvesting.

A five-second tarpit slows the spammer down by a factor of maybe 500 (depending on your server's speed and your Internet connection speed) by rejecting all the invalid delivery attempts. Most spammers' software programs can't handle the rejects, and they disconnect after some period of time.

You can view your Receive connector's tarpit interval by using the `Get-ReceiveConnector` cmdlet. For example, if you want to change the Ex1 Default Receive connector's tarpit interval to 30 seconds, you would type this command:

```
Set-ReceiveConnector "Ex1 Default" -TarpitInterval 00:00:30
```

We recommend that you do not set this value to more than about 30 seconds on any of your Exchange servers since it could start to impact delivery times of email messages to your organization.

Sender Filtering

Sender filtering is one of the oldest anti-spam features in Exchange Server; it is probably also the least effective. The premise is that you provide a list of SMTP addresses or domains that must be prevented from sending email messages to recipients in your organization. The problem is that most spammers rarely use the same email address twice, so this type of filtering is becoming less relevant to the needs of the users. To get the configuration of the sender filtering agent, you can run the `Get-SenderFilterConfig` cmdlet:

```
Get-SenderFilterConfig
BlockedSenders                : {}
BlockedDomains                : {}
BlockedDomainsAndSubdomains   : {}
Action                        : Reject
BlankSenderBlockingEnabled    : False
RecipientBlockedSenderAction  : Reject
Enabled                       : True
ExternalMailEnabled           : True
InternalMailEnabled           : False
```

A more interesting sender filtering anti-spam technique blocks a few pieces of mail by enabling the `BlankSenderBlockingEnabled` parameter. If a message does not have a sender (and it should), this feature will reject the message.

You can either reject the message entirely or stamp the message as having a blocked sender and allow it through by changing the `Action` value. If you stamp a message as being from a blocked sender, the content filter will rank the message as spam.

> **SENDER ID FILTERING—ANTI-SPOOFING, NOT ANTI-SPAM, BUT STILL IMPORTANT**
>
> Earlier in this chapter, we talked a bit about sender policy framework (SPF) records and DNS and how to make sure that yours are registered properly. Contrary to popular misconception, Sender ID is not an anti-spam technology but rather an anti-spoofing technology. Quite simply, to implement Sender ID, each organization on the Internet that sends email should register a sender policy framework record in their public DNS server. This SPF record contains a list of the servers authorized to send mail on behalf of their domain.

When an SMTP server receives a message from a particular domain, it analyzes the message to determine the actual sender and determines which server sent it. If the message originated from an authorized server, it is probably not being spoofed. If it is accepted from a server that is not in the DNS SPF record, the message might be from a spoofed sender.

Using the `Get-SenderIDConfig` cmdlet, you can export the settings of Sender IP using EMS:

```
Get-SenderIdConfig

SpoofedDomainAction   : StampStatus
TempErrorAction       : StampStatus
BypassedRecipients    : {}
BypassedSenderDomains : {}
Name                  : SenderIdConfig
Enabled               : True
ExternalMailEnabled   : True
InternalMailEnabled   : False
```

Sender Reputation

Sender reputation is the most promising feature of Exchange Server 2013 when it comes to reducing the amount of spam you receive. Why? First, let's outline the problem. Much of the spam that is received today is sent by bot or zombie networks. Spammers have joined forces with virus writers; the virus writers have written malware that infects hundreds of thousands of users' computers. Periodically, these computers check in with the spammer and download a new batch of spam. Blocking a single IP address becomes impractical because the spammers have so many of these computers all over the Internet. However, these zombie networks are usually not using correct SMTP commands and are not RFC compliant. A lot of spammers also use SMTP proxies by sending email messages through a proxy on the Internet.

Sender reputation allows Exchange servers to analyze the connections that are coming in to a Mailbox server and look for things, such as the number of protocol errors, invalid delivery attempts, and the number of messages from the same sender. These can be used to determine if a specific IP address is sending spam, which would give that IP address a bad reputation! Sender reputation can be managed using the `Get-SenderReputationConfig` cmdlet:

```
Get-SenderReputationConfig

MinMessagesPerDatabaseTransaction : 20
SrlBlockThreshold                 : 7
MinMessagesPerTimeSlice           : 100
TimeSliceInterval                 : 48
OpenProxyDetectionEnabled         : True
SenderBlockingEnabled             : True
OpenProxyRescanInterval           : 10
MinReverseDnsQueryPeriod          : 1
SenderBlockingPeriod              : 24
MaxWorkQueueSize                  : 1000
```

```
MaxIdleTime                  : 10
Socks4Ports                  : {1081, 1080}
Socks5Ports                  : {1081, 1080}
WingatePorts                 : {23}
HttpConnectPorts             : {6588, 3128, 80}
HttpPostPorts                : {6588, 3128, 80}
TelnetPorts                  : {23}
CiscoPorts                   : {23}
TablePurgeInterval           : 24
MaxPendingOperations         : 100
ProxyServerName              :
ProxyServerPort              : 0
ProxyServerType              : None
Name                         : Sender Reputation
MinDownloadInterval          : 10
MaxDownloadInterval          : 100
SrlSettingsDatabaseFileName  :
ReputationServiceUrl         :
Enabled                      : True
ExternalMailEnabled          : True
InternalMailEnabled          : False
```

The default value for the Sender Reputation Level (SRL) block threshold is 7; we recommend keeping it at this slightly moderate value and then monitoring to see if the value can be changed to a more aggressive number. If so, you can increase it slightly, but keep in mind that as you get more aggressive with this value, the possibility of valid connections getting rejected becomes higher, also known as *false positives*.

From the properties of the Sender Reputation settings, the Threshold Action section provides the ability to specify how long a sender is retained on an IP block list once the sender has been determined to be suspicious. The default is 24 hours, and I recommend that you keep that value.

Also as part of Sender Reputation checks, Exchange Server can test for open proxies and determine if the source of a connection is an open proxy. If a connecting SMTP host is identified as an open proxy, it will be added to the IP block list for the time specified. Run the following command to test for an open proxy:

```
Set-SenderReputationConfig - ProxyServerName All-1 -ProxyServerPort 80
-ProxyServerType HttpConnect
```

Troubleshooting Email Routing

Every Exchange Server administrator is involved in regular troubleshooting tasks. When troubleshooting transport, you often have to behave like an investigator trying to trace the path of a message and understanding what went wrong. Sooner or later, that process will lead you to transport logs. There are many transport-related logs, and the protocol-logging feature will increase the amount of information collected in those logs. Protocol logging can be enabled on the Mailbox server, Client Access server, Send connector, and Receive connector.

You can enable protocol logging using the following commands:

```
Get-TransportService | Set-TransportService-
IntraOrgConnectorProtocolLoggingLevel verbose

Get-FrontendTransportService | Set-FrontendTransportService-
IntraOrgConnectorProtocolLoggingLevel verbose

Get-ReceiveConnector | Set-ReceiveConnector -ProtocolLoggingLevel verbose

Get-SendConnector | Set-SendConnector -ProtocolLoggingLevel verbose
```

You will find the log files in the following locations:

◆ The `Set-TransportService` command creates protocol logs under this path:

```
C:\Program Files\Microsoft\Exchange Server\V15\TransportRoles\Logs\Mailbox\
ProtocolLog
```

◆ The `Set-FrontEndTransportService` command creates protocol logs under this path:

```
C:\Program Files\Microsoft\Exchange Server\V15\TransportRoles\Logs\FrontEnd\
ProtocolLog
```

◆ The `Set-ReceiveConnector` command creates protocol logs under this path:

```
C:\Program Files\Microsoft\Exchange Server\V15\TransportRoles\Logs\Hub\
ProtocolLog
```

◆ The `Set-SendConnector` command creates protocol logs under this path:

```
C:\Program Files\Microsoft\ExchangeServer\V15\TransportRoles\Logs\Hub\
ProtocolLog
```

The Bottom Line

Understand the improvements in Exchange Server 2013 mail routing.   Once you start sending messages between more than one Exchange server, you must understand how Exchange Server 2013 uses your existing Active Directory infrastructure to route messages between Mailbox servers. When you begin to discuss server placement and the message routing path with the networking team at your company, you need to understand exactly how messages will flow within your organization.

Master It   You have an Exchange Server organization that contains multiple sites, separated by WAN links. Another administrator handles all Active Directory configurations for your organization.

This kind of scenario means that you may want to alter the route that messages take within an Exchange Server organization. Although Exchange servers always attempt a direct connection to a final destination server, in some cases a connection is not established directly. This may be a good reason for modifying the site link costs used by Exchange servers when determining the least-cost path. What are your options in modifying these options?

Create and manage Send connectors and Receive connectors. All messages delivered by an Exchange server are routed through Exchange connectors. The source servers of Send connectors are always Mailbox servers. The Client Access servers can be used as proxy servers to send outbound email messages.

Master It You've been called in to deploy Exchange Server 2013 in a "greenfield" deployment, where no messaging system is present. Installing Exchange Server is pretty easy, even for the least experienced IT consultants.

But … surprise! After your successful installation, you notice that emails cannot be sent to the Internet. You need to connect this new organization to the Internet. What configuration will allow your customer to book his golf games by email?

Master It You need to plan for the deployment of an Exchange Server 2013 organization. You quickly notice that the organization is concerned with reducing the number of physical servers. Of course, virtualized installation of Exchange Server is always possible, but this customer has very little expertise in virtualization technologies.

They ask you a very important question: do they really need an Edge Transport server on their network?

Configure anti-spam and anti-malware technologies. Anti-spam and anti-malware management is a day-to-day reality of all email administrators. Finding the balance between keeping spam and malware out while maintaining free flow of all legitimate email messages is becoming increasingly difficult.

Master It You have deployed an Exchange Server 2013 organization that contains several servers that run the Exchange Server 2010 Edge Transport role.

Users report that they are increasingly receiving spam in their mailboxes. From the Exchange Admin Center, you modify the content-filtering settings, but you are not seeing any improvement in the number of spam email messages received. What should you do to ensure that spam is kept out of your organization?

Chapter 23

Managing Transport, Data Loss Prevention, and Journaling Rules

As you may have noticed by now, in spite of the extra features it offers, Exchange Server provides messaging as its core functionality. Messaging systems have been part of the business environment for years—long enough for the novelty of electronic messaging to wear off and for it to become a staple of the office. Email is now ubiquitous; right or wrong, your users think of it in the same class as utilities, such as electricity or telephone service. Because of this perception, the majority of messaging administrators must now deal with issues, such as regulatory compliance, that once were the province of only a few types of businesses.

Legacy versions of Exchange Server were not equipped with the tools and technology to allow administrators to affectively deal with these sorts of issues out of the box. Electronic discovery, regulatory compliance, preventing leakage of sensitive data, long-term message data archives, and effective retention policies—the basic Exchange Server architecture was designed without these needs in mind. But in today's business world, they are very real problems that some administrators may face. The solution has traditionally been the implementation of expensive, complicated, third-party software suites.

When setting the design goals for Exchange Server 2013, Microsoft wanted to ensure that it was better adapted for modern needs and problems. To combat the ever-growing needs for compliance, protection of sensitive data, archiving, and retention, Exchange Server 2013 has introduced new features that will allow administrators to design compliance solutions for the enterprise.

This chapter covers all the elements that work with a transport environment and allow you to control your messages as they flow through your environment. Whether it is to retain message information or to delete messages automatically, Exchange Server 2013 provides many options to administrators.

In this chapter you will learn to:

◆ Create and manage message classifications to control message flow

◆ Control message flow and manipulate messages by using transport rules

◆ Protect sensitive information by creating data loss prevention policies

Introducing the New Exchange 2013 Transport Architecture

In the two previous versions of Exchange, Exchange Server 2007 and 2010, most of the transport functionality had been moved to two distinct roles, Hub Transport and Edge Transport. Messages sent to any mailbox, no matter if the recipient was on the same mailbox database as the sender, were processed by a server with the Hub Transport role first and then delivered to the server with the Mailbox role holding the mounted copy of the mailbox database. This ensured that all messages would be processed by the Microsoft Exchange Transport service.

In contrast, the Mailbox role in Exchange Server 2013 is now responsible for the majority of the transport functionality. As you can guess, the Hub Transport role is no longer a valid role in Exchange Server 2013. So how does mail flow work now that the Hub role has been deprecated? Let's take a look:

1. When a message is submitted for delivery, the Mailbox Transport Submission service on the Mailbox server connects to a local database over RPC and captures the pending email message for delivery.

2. The Mailbox Transport Submission service submits the email message over SMTP to the Transport service on the local server or a remote Mailbox server.

3. After the message has been processed by the Transport service, the Mailbox Transport Delivery service on the Mailbox server receives the SMTP messages from the Transport service and delivers the messages using RPC to the local database.

All Messages Pass Through the Mailbox Server

Yes, you read that correctly. The Hub Transport role has been deprecated in Exchange Server 2013, and every single message you send in Exchange Server 2013 passes through the Microsoft Exchange Transport service, which is now a service on the Mailbox role. Although this might seem inefficient at first glance, the reality is that the resulting benefits make this a great design change. Mainly, and more importantly, it ensures that every single message can be captured by Exchange Server's transport components, which can then act upon that message. See Chapter 22, "Managing Connectivity with Transport Services," for more information about this design change and the underlying benefit.

This chapter covers four principal transport capabilities in Exchange Server 2013 in detail:

Message Classifications These are annotations to an email message that mark it as belonging to a designated category of information that Exchange Server and Outlook may need to treat in a special fashion. These annotations are exposed as properties of the message, allowing clients to display them visually for the users as well as permitting them to be exposed to the rules engine for automated processing. As an example, all messages with certain keywords can be classified as being confidential.

Transport Rules These are server-side rules that allow you to create and apply messaging policies throughout the entire Exchange Server 2013 organization. Much like Outlook rules, transport rules contain conditions, actions, and exceptions. Every message that passes through the transport pipeline is processed by your organization's transport rules.

Data Loss Prevention   Data loss prevention (DLP) entails identifying, monitoring, and protecting your organization from accidentally exposing sensitive information. A DLP policy combines transport rules, policy tips, and reporting. Each component of a DLP policy can be configured to meet regulatory or business requirements by protecting sensitive information sent through the transport pipeline and by notifying the sender before submitting an email message that contains sensitive information.

Message Journaling   This is the process of capturing complete copies and histories of specified messages within your organization. Journaled message reports are generated and sent to specified recipients, which can be within the Exchange Server organization or some external entity. Journaling may not be exciting or useful by itself, but it's one of the main ways to get messaging data into an external archival system. Note that Exchange Server 2013 also offers archival of content through the personal archive functionality, retention tags, retention policies, and many other technologies designed around the compliance needs of an organization. These features are discussed in the chapters that focus on Mailbox server and data storage technologies.

Setting Up Message Classifications

At their heart, message classifications are simply labels that are set on certain messages. These labels in turn allow other software, such as Outlook and Outlook Web App (OWA), to display a visual warning for the user and, optionally, take special action when processing the message with rules.

Message classifications have four principal properties:

◆ The *display name* determines how the classification is displayed in the client user interface and is scanned by the mailbox rules engine.

◆ The *sender description* allows the client interface to tell the sender the purpose of this classification if it isn't clear from the display name alone.

◆ The *recipient description* allows the client interface to tell the recipient the purpose of this classification.

◆ The locale is a code that defines the localized version of a classification.

Figure 23.1 illustrates how Outlook 2013 displays a message classification on a message by means of the additional field directly above the To line.

Out of the box, Exchange Server 2013 comes with three message classifications: Attachment Removed, Originator Requested, and Partner Mail. By default, these classifications are informational only; no associated rules enforce them, and their purpose is simply to display text to recipients. The default message classifications are not published to OWA or Outlook by default. Additional configuration is needed on the Outlook client and the Exchange servers for the clients to see the default message classifications.

You can modify these default classifications, and create new ones, to suit your business needs (see the message classifications shown in Figure 23.2). No GUI exists for creating and managing classifications; you must use the Exchange Management Shell (EMS). However, once the classifications are created, you can use the EAC (covered later in this chapter in the section, "Setting Up Transport Rules,") to apply them using transport rules.

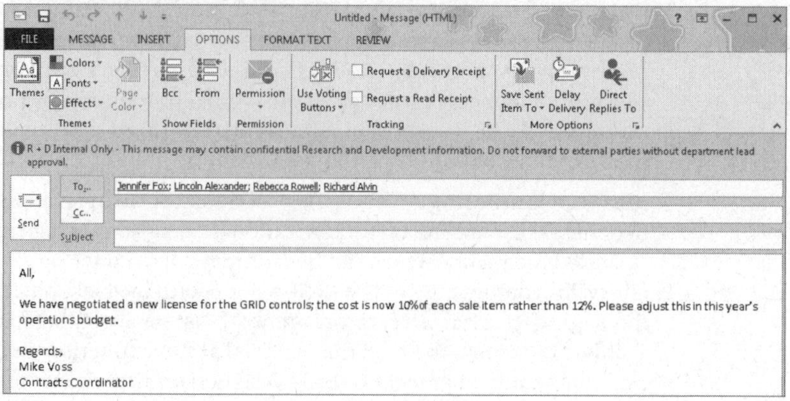

FIGURE 23.1
A message classification displayed in Outlook 2013: "R + D Internal Only—This message may contain confidential Research and Development information. Do not forward to external parties without department lead approval."

FIGURE 23.2
A sample list of message classifications.

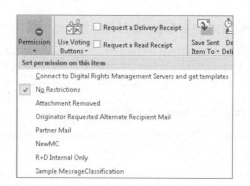

In addition to the basic classification properties, you can set some other properties:

◆ You can specify the precedence, which determines the order in which a given classification is applied to a message if multiple classifications are set. You have nine values (Highest, Higher, High, MediumHigh, Medium, MediumLow, Low, Lower, and Lowest) from which to choose.

◆ You can specify whether a given classification should be retained on the message if it is forwarded or replied to; some classifications, such as Attachment Removed, would make little sense when applied to a forwarded copy of a message or to its replies.

◆ You can create localized versions of message classifications if you are working in a multi-lingual organization. When working with localizations, Outlook 2013 and OWA will display the accurate classification based on the localization settings configured on the client.

By default, OWA supports the display and manual selection of message classifications. To use them in Outlook 2013, you must manually deploy them, which is covered in, "Deploying Message Classifications," later in this chapter.

> ### ADVANCED USERS AND MESSAGE CLASSIFICATION
>
> Advanced users (those with admin permissions) can control permissions on message classifications and thus restrict the use of some classifications to a subset of users. See the Exchange Server 2010 help topic, "Understanding Message Classifications," for instructions if you need this capability.

Modifying and Creating Message Classifications

To customize the properties of existing classifications or create new classifications, you must use the `Get-MessageClassification`, `Set-MessageClassification`, and `New-MessageClassification` cmdlets in the Exchange Management Shell.

Get-MessageClassification   This cmdlet shows you the existing message classifications in your organization:

```
Get-MessageClassification
```

Set-MessageClassification   This cmdlet modifies the properties of an existing classification. The following example takes an existing classification named NewMC, sets its precedence to High, and sets the `RetainClassificationEnabled` property so that the classification will be retained across forwards and replies:

```
Set-MessageClassification -Identity NewMC -DisplayPrecedence High ↵
-RetainClassificationEnabled $True
```

New-MessageClassification   This cmdlet creates a new message classification in your organization, configuring it on your Exchange Server 2013 servers and registering it in Active Directory:

```
New-MessageClassification -Name "RandDInternal" -DisplayName "R+D ↵
 Internal Only" -RecipientDescription "This message may contain ↵
 confidential and/or proprietary information. If you have received ↵
 this message in error, please delete it."  -SenderDescription "This ↵
 message may contain confidential Research and Development information. ↵
Do not forward to external parties without department lead approval. "
```

Deploying Message Classifications

When you create or modify classifications, they are automatically visible to OWA users. In what is a particularly painful oversight, the same is not true for Outlook 2013 users. If you want your Outlook 2013 users to benefit from message classifications, you have two tasks to complete:

1. Export the message classifications from Exchange Server 2013 to an XML file.

2. Configure Outlook 2013 to use the XML file that contains the classification information.

These steps must be performed every time you add new classifications or modify display properties of existing classifications. Just to make it even more annoying, these tasks are completely manual.

The following sections cover these steps in greater detail.

EXPORTING CLASSIFICATIONS FROM EXCHANGE

If you're looking for an EMS cmdlet to export all your classifications, stop. You have to use EMS, but no built-in cmdlet exists to perform this task. Here's how to do it:

1. Navigate to the Scripts subdirectory of the folder that you installed Exchange Server 2013 to (by default, this folder is located at `C:\Program Files\Microsoft\Exchange Server\V15\Scripts`) or just type **cd $ExScripts**.

Microsoft has provided several useful and complex EMS scripts in this folder; the one you want is named `Export-OutlookClassification.ps1`. Though you can use the `Export-OutlookClassification.ps1` script to export a single classification, you will probably want to export all classifications and configure Outlook to use them.

2. To export all of the classifications to a file called `c:\Classifications.XML`, type the following command:

```
.\Export-OutlookClassification.ps1 > c:\Classifications.xml
```

OUT-OF-SYNC CLASSIFICATIONS

If the XML file that Outlook uses is out of sync with the actual classifications specified on the Exchange server, Outlook will not display the classifications that are missing from the file. It will, however, retain them if they can be retained, and they will still be on the messages (and can be viewed in OWA). Once the file is updated, they will become visible to the user.

IMPORTING CLASSIFICATIONS IN OUTLOOK

This task has two parts: creating the necessary registry entries and copying over the XML file from the Exchange server on which you ran the `Export-OutlookClassification.ps1` script. Once you've created the registry settings on a given client, you don't need to keep setting them when you update the classifications XML file.

Copying the XML file to the desired location on all local workstations running a support version of Outlook is simple; you can do it manually, via a batch script, or through your existing desktop-management solution. If you are going to change the classifications on a regular basis, you might want to configure some sort of automated deployment system to minimize the need for manual involvement. For example, you might consider the use of a logon script to ensure that the latest copy of the classifications XML file is pushed out to your clients. If you've deployed Microsoft System Center Configuration Manager (or some third-party equivalent) in your environment, you can also use that mechanism.

PUBLISHING MESSAGE CLASSIFICATION TO VARIOUS VERSIONS OF OUTLOOK

Outlook reads the file in when it starts, so if the file is updated while Outlook is open, it will not use the updated information until it is next restarted.

The following registry key and values must be created on all Outlook computers whose users have mailboxes on Exchange Server 2013 servers and who are going to be sending message classifications. Until these registry entries are created, classifications will not be displayed in Outlook, even though they exist on messages.

For Outlook 2013, in the HKCU\Software\Microsoft\Office\15.0\Common key, create a new key named Policy.

For Outlook 2010, in the HKCU\Software\Microsoft\Office\14.0\Common key, create a new key named Policy.

For Outlook 2007, in the HKCU\Software\Microsoft\Office\12.0\Common key, create a new key named Policy.

Within this new key, create the following values:

```
"AdminClassificationPath"="C:\\ Path\\To\\Filename.xml"
"EnableClassifications"=dword:00000001
"TrustClassifications"=dword:00000001
```

You should set the values of these keys accordingly:

AdminClassificationPath   Specifies the full path and filename of the XML file you copied from the export process. Though this path can be on a network share, it might cause problems for laptop users or other users who lose network connectivity. The file is small, so there's no harm in copying it to the local hard drive.

EnableClassifications   Allows you to toggle whether message classifications are read and honored in Outlook on a per-user basis. The value 1 enables classifications, and the value 0 disables them.

TrustClassifications   Allows you to toggle whether Outlook actually trusts classifications on messages that are sent to users on legacy Exchange Server Mailbox servers. The value 1 enables trust; 0 disables it.

Keep in mind that there are other options as well. The Office Customization Tool allows you to specify additional registry keys that will be installed when Office is installed on a machine. If you want to ensure that message classification is universally deployed and supported in your organization, you might want to include these registry settings in your configuration when creating your installation scripts.

Setting Up Transport Rules

The transport rules in Exchange Server 2013 give you the ability to define and automatically enforce messaging policies within your organization. In Exchange Server 2013, the Transport Rule agent is triggered while the message is passing through the Transport service on the Mailbox role. The transport rules are enforced on the OnResolvedMessage transport event. You can use transport rules to append disclaimers to messages, search messages for certain types of content, require messages to be transmitted using Transport Layer Security (TLS), append classifications, insert text into a message, apply Rights Management Service templates, and more.

You can create and manage transport rules in both the Exchange Administration Center and the Exchange Management Shell. In the EAC, select Mail Flow from the Feature pane and then select the Rules tab, as shown in Figure 23.3.

Transport rules are similar to Outlook rules, but they are created using Exchange Server 2013 management tools. Like Outlook rules, transport rules have three parts:

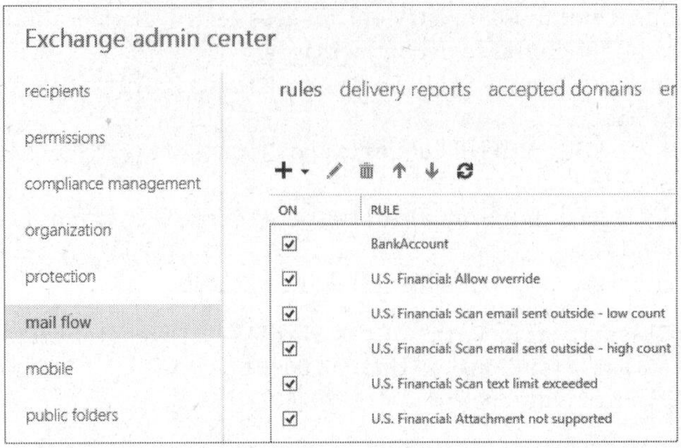

FIGURE 23.3
Locating the
transport
rules in the
Exchange
Administra-
tion Center

FIGURE 23.3
Locating the transport rules in the Exchange Administration Center

◆ Conditions identify the message properties that trigger the application of the rule to a given message. If you define no conditions, the rule will apply to all messages.

◆ Exceptions identify message properties that exempt a given message from being processed by the rule even if it matches the defined conditions. Exceptions, like conditions, are optional.

◆ Actions modify the properties or delivery of messages that match the conditions without matching the exceptions defined by the rule. In a given rule, there must be at least one action, and you can have multiple actions.

Transport rules are defined and stored in Active Directory; each server with the Mailbox role in the organization sees the entire set of defined rules and attempts to match them against all messages. This allows you to define a single, consistent set of message policies throughout your organization. Technically, you can define an unlimited number of transport rules. However, you should balance the number of transport rules against the server resources and latency of message delivery.

TRANSPORT EXPANDED GROUP CACHE IN EXCHANGE SERVER 2013

The Transport service on each Mailbox server maintains a list of mail objects of each distribution group in memory; this is referred to as the expanded group cache. The Transport agent and Journaling agent use the expanded group cache to apply transport rules and journaling rules. The cache is maintained to minimize further queries to Active Directory. By default, the expanded group cache is refreshed every four hours. This information can be particularly useful when troubleshooting transport rules that are not applied consistently in your organization.

The expanded group cache settings can be updated. To change the expanded group cache interval you need to modify the AppSettings section of the `EdgeTransport.Exe.Config` file on each Mailbox server. Modify the value for the `Transport_IsMemberOfResolver_ExpandedGroupsCache_ExpirationInterval` property. You must restart the Microsoft Exchange Server Transport service on all Exchange Server 2013 servers with the Mailbox role installed after making this change.

Transport Rules Coexistence

Transport rules can be a bit of a headache to manage and support during coexistence with legacy versions of Exchange Server. In this section we will cover how Exchange Server 2007 and 2010 transport rules interact with Exchange Server 2013.

Exchange Server 2007 transport rules created using the Exchange Server 2007 Management Console or Management Shell are stored in Active Directory under the Transport container, which is represented under the Configuration name context as `CN=Transport, CN=Rules, CN=Transport Settings, CN=<org name>, CN=Microsoft Exchange, CN=Services`. Transport Rule agents running on Exchange Server 2007 Hub Transport servers retrieve their rules from this Transport container.

To prevent the Exchange Server 2007 Transport Rule agents from loading rules created in Exchange Server 2013, a separate Active Directory container is created to separate the transport rules based on the version of Exchange Server used to create them.

Provisioning a separate Active Directory container for the new Exchange Server 2013 transport rules prevents legacy Exchange Server 2007 servers from loading rules that they are unable to read. In the case that an Exchange Server 2007 organization already has existing transport rules that they need to function in the new Exchange Server 2013 environment, Exchange Server 2013 provides two methods to migrate existing legacy transport rules to Exchange Server 2013: automatic and manual migration.

Automatic migration is performed during Exchange Server 2013 setup. If the setup program detects the existence of legacy rules, those rules are copied to Exchange Server 2013. Manual migration is performed by exporting and importing transport rules between the two messaging platforms or manually re-creating the rules using the Exchange Server 2013 management tools. Automatic migration of transport rules is only performed during the initial installation of an Exchange Server 2013 server, so new transport rules created after the setup process has run will not be read by Exchange Server 2013 servers.

To overcome this limitation, Exchange Server administrators can manually migrate a transport rule collection from Exchange Server 2013 to Exchange Server 2007 or from Exchange Server 2007 to Exchange Server 2013 by using the `Import-TransportRuleCollection` and `Export-TransportRuleCollection` cmdlets.

Coexistence between Exchange Server 2010 and Exchange Server 2013 at the time of writing this book is not well documented, but we will cover our experience. Just like with Exchange Server 2013, when creating transport rules using the Exchange Server 2010 Exchange Management Console or the Exchange Management Shell, the transport rules are stored in the TransportVersioned container, which is represented under the Configuration name context as: `CN=TransportVersioned, CN=Transport, CN=Rules, CN=Transport Settings, CN=<org name>, CN=Microsoft Exchange, CN=Services`.

During the coexistence with Exchange Server 2010, Exchange Server 2013 will apply the transport rules created in the Exchange Server 2010 management tools. So unlike with Exchange Server 2007, exporting and importing transport rules are not necessary. However, Exchange Server 2010 can't always apply transport rules created using Exchange Server 2013 management tools. Certain transport rules, especially those created for DLP, cannot be applied by an Exchange Server 2010 server. Each transport rule has a version associated with the transport rule, the version defines which version of Exchange can be used to manage the transport rule. The transport rule version is stored in the `msExchTransportRuleXml` property and can be viewed in the EAC, as shown in Figure 23.4. The number 15.x always refers to a version of Exchange Server 2013.

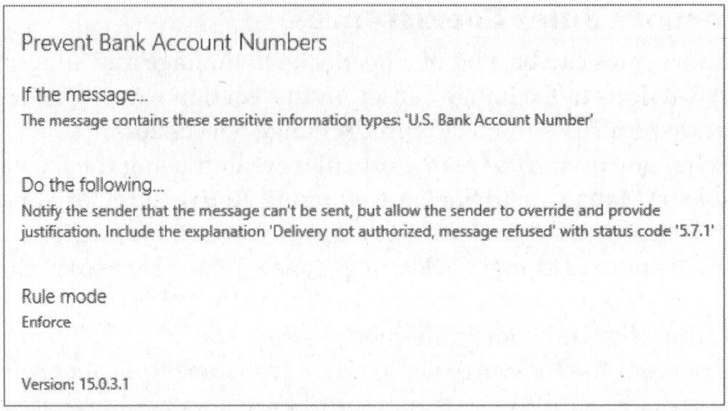

FIGURE 23.4
Transport rule version in the EAC

Prevent Bank Account Numbers

If the message...
The message contains these sensitive information types: 'U.S. Bank Account Number'

Do the following...
Notify the sender that the message can't be sent, but allow the sender to override and provide justification. Include the explanation 'Delivery not authorized, message refused' with status code '5.7.1'

Rule mode
Enforce

Version: 15.0.3.1

Similarly, transport rules created using the Exchange Server 2010 management tools can be managed using the EAC or the Exchange Server 2013 EMS, but some transport rules created using the Exchange Server 2013 management tools cannot be managed by Exchange Server 2010 management tools. This again is dependent on the version of the transport rule.

In hybrid deployments, transport rules are not replicated between Office 365 and your on-premises Exchange Server 2013 organization. The only way to ensure that the same transport rules are applied to all email messages is to create a matching pair of transport rules in your Office 365 organization and your on-premises organization. At the time of this writing, Office 365 has a limit of 100 transport rules and 100 recipients added to a message by all transport rules.

Transport Rules and Server Design Decisions

A number of factors come into play when you are sizing the server hardware. Exchange Server will run on top of and making server design decisions for your Exchange Server 2013 organization. One of the things to take into account is the number of transport rules you plan to implement. For example, an organization that sends 2,000 messages per hour and has 10 transport rules will need far less computing power than an organization that sends 10,000 messages per hour and has a few hundred transport rules.

Because rules are stored in Active Directory, modifications to your transport rules are subject to your normal AD replication. Depending on your site topology, it may take some time before your current changes replicate fully throughout your organization.

Another design decision point for Exchange Server 2013 transport rules is one of those features that requires previous implementation of non–Exchange Server components. Specifically, a Windows Server 2008 server with the Active Directory Rights Management Service role needs to be available to provide enhanced security through message encryption and authorization. Exchange Server is now Active Directory Rights Management Server (RMS or AD RMS) aware, ensuring that an administrator can create transport rules that can leverage built-in or custom RMS templates.

Selecting Conditions and Exceptions

Because conditions and exceptions are both involved in identifying whether a given message should be processed by the rule, it should be no surprise that they give you the same set of options.

TRANSPORT CONDITIONS AND EXCEPTIONS

The conditions of the rule define the circumstances under which the rule will apply. Conditions and exceptions are stored as parameters of a transport rule. To get a list of the conditions and exceptions of a transport rule use the Get-TransportRule cmdlet. Figure 23.5 shows some of the conditions that are available when creating a transport rule. A condition is represented as parameters within a transport rule.

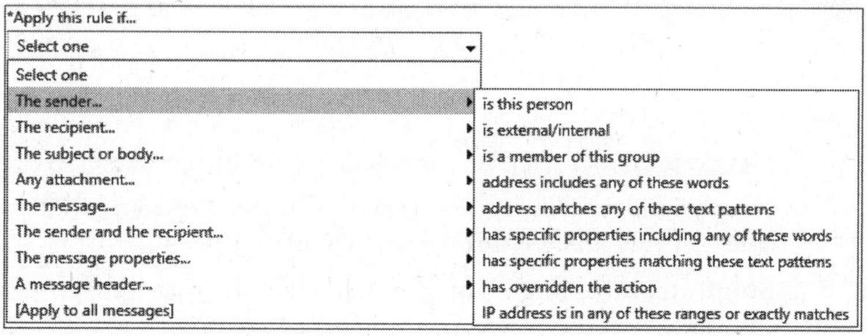

FIGURE 23.5
Transport rule conditions

The parameters in the following list are new in Exchange Server 2013. Most of the new parameters were introduced to support the implementation of Data Loss Prevention (DLP), which will be covered later in this chapter.

AttachmentExtensionMatchesWords   Use if you want to search for attachments with certain extensions, such as .JPG or .PNG.

AttachmentHasExecutableContent   Use to find an attachment that contains executable content.

HasSenderOverride   Use to determine if the sender overrode a DLP policy through a Policy Tip. (See the section, "Understanding DLP Policies," later in this chapter.)

MessageContainsDataClassifications   Used to find sensitive information types within an email message.

MessageSizeOver   Applies to all messages that exceed a certain size.

SenderIPRanges   Condition is met when the IP of the sender matches the value of this condition.

As with conditions and exceptions, your choice of possible actions is vast enough to meet most business needs. The Exchange 2013 Server helps files contain detailed descriptions of each condition and exception.

TRANSPORT ACTIONS

The actions of the transport rule specify what the rule will do to the message (or what it will do *about* the message). Figure 23.6 shows some of the actions available for transport rules.

The following actions are new to Exchange Server 2013:

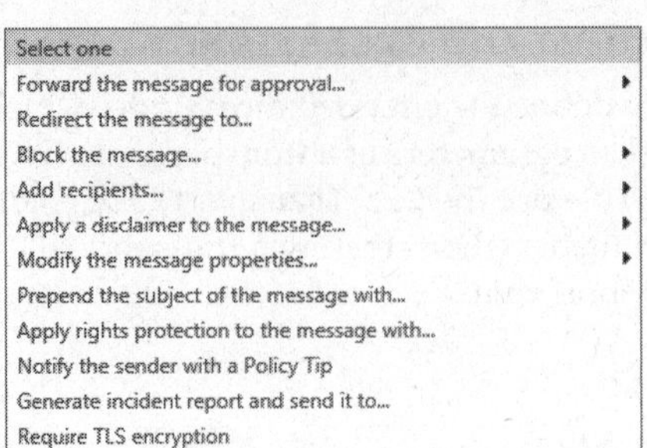

FIGURE 23.6
Viewing the actions from the EAC

Select one
Forward the message for approval... ▶
Redirect the message to...
Block the message... ▶
Add recipients... ▶
Apply a disclaimer to the message... ▶
Modify the message properties... ▶
Prepend the subject of the message with...
Apply rights protection to the message with...
Notify the sender with a Policy Tip
Generate incident report and send it to...
Require TLS encryption
Put message in the quarantine mailbox

GenerateIncidentReport Incident reports are generated when a DLP policy is triggered.

NotifySender This action is used to inform the sender that their email message contains sensitive information through a DLP Policy Tip.

StopRuleProcessing This action prevents further transport rules from processing this email message.

ReportSeverityLevel This action sets the severity level in the incident report.

RouteMessageOutboundRequireTLS Any message that meets the requirements of this transport rule must be delivered from a TLS SMTP session.

HTML DISCLAIMERS IN EXCHANGE SERVER 2013

In Exchange Server 2013, an administrator can create HTML disclaimers as a transport rule action. When using HTML disclaimers, a Mailbox server inserts disclaimers into email messages using the same message format as the original message. For example, if a message is created in HTML, the disclaimer is added in HTML. If the message is created as plain text, HTML tags are stripped from the HTML disclaimer text and the resulting disclaimer text is added to the plaintext message. The following images illustrate the output of an HTML disclaimer transport rule and an email message with the HTML disclaimer applied.

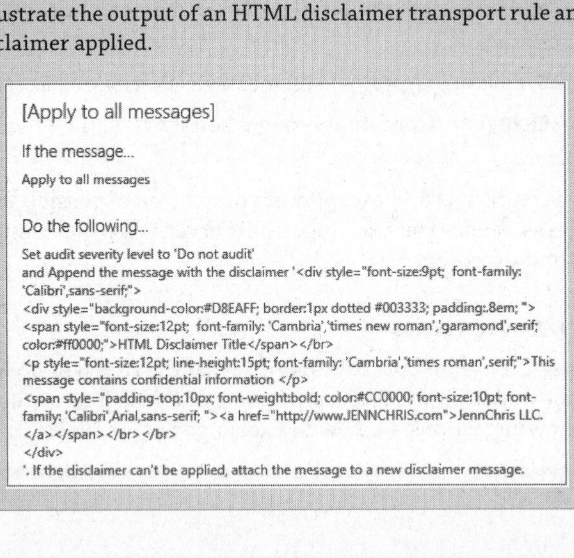

[Apply to all messages]

If the message...

Apply to all messages

Do the following...

Set audit severity level to 'Do not audit'
and Append the message with the disclaimer '<div style="font-size:9pt; font-family: 'Calibri',sans-serif;">
<div style="background-color:#D8EAFF; border:1px dotted #003333; padding:.8em; ">
<span style="font-size:12pt; font-family: 'Cambria','times new roman','garamond',serif; color:#ff0000;">HTML Disclaimer Title</span></br>
<p style="font-size:12pt; line-height:15pt; font-family: 'Cambria','times roman',serif;">This message contains confidential information </p>
<span style="padding-top:10px; font-weight:bold; color:#CC0000; font-size:10pt; font-family: 'Calibri',Arial,sans-serif; "><a href="http://www.JENNCHRIS.com">JennChris LLC.
</a></span></br></br>
</div>
'. If the disclaimer can't be applied, attach the message to a new disclaimer message.

```
From: Richard Alvin
Sent: Thursday, August 1, 2013 9:09 PM
To: Jenn Fox
Subject: Hi



HTML Disclaimer Title

This message contains confidential information
JennChris LLC.
```

Exchange Server 2013 HTML disclaimer text can include HTML tags. This allows you to create messages with rich functionality available in HTML code. For example, HTML tags can include inline Cascading Style Sheets. Messages sent in the HTML format can then display rich disclaimer messages.

More importantly, in Exchange Server 2013 you can add images to an HTML disclaimer by using IMG tags. You cannot actually drag and drop image files directly into the transport rule; you have to place the image files on a publicly accessible web server. Once you have verified that the image is available by using a URL, you can add the path to the disclaimer action in the transport rule, as in this example:

```
<IMG src="http://PublicServer.Netlogon.com/images/logo.gif"
```

Creating New Rules with the Exchange Administration Center

Creating a transport rule in the EAC is similar to creating a transport rule in the Exchange Management Console in Exchange Server 2007 and 2010. One of the striking differences is now all the transport rule options are listed on a single screen instead of going through a wizard. To create a transport rule you can use the following steps in the EAC:

1. On your client computer, open Internet Explorer and browse to the ECP URL. This URL should be the name of your Client Access server with /ECP appended to the end. If you don't know the URL for EAC, you can use the Outlook Web App URL and specify **/ECP** instead of **/owa** at the end of the URL. For example, for Contoso, the EAC URL might be https://mail.contoso.com/ECP.

2. When prompted with the authentication page, type in your name and password and log in.

3. In the Feature pane, on the left column of the EAC, select Mail Flow.

4. Tabs are listed across the top of the EAC; select the Rules tab. The transport rules should be listed below.

5. Click the Add (+) button to create a new transport rule. If you select the arrow next to the + button, a list of the most common transport rules will be displayed, as shown in Figure 23.7. These options provide you with the groundwork to build a transport rule.

6. In the New Rule window, select More Options to see the version in Figure 23.8, which contains all the options needed to create a new transport rule.

FIGURE 23.7
Templates to create new transport rules

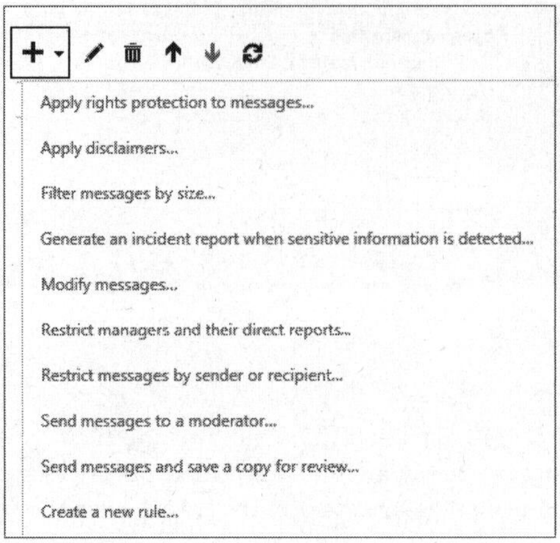

```
+ ▾   ✎   🗑   ↑   ↓   ↻

        Apply rights protection to messages...

        Apply disclaimers...

        Filter messages by size...

        Generate an incident report when sensitive information is detected...

        Modify messages...

        Restrict managers and their direct reports...

        Restrict messages by sender or recipient...

        Send messages to a moderator...

        Send messages and save a copy for review...

        Create a new rule...
```

FIGURE 23.8
New Rule window for EAC

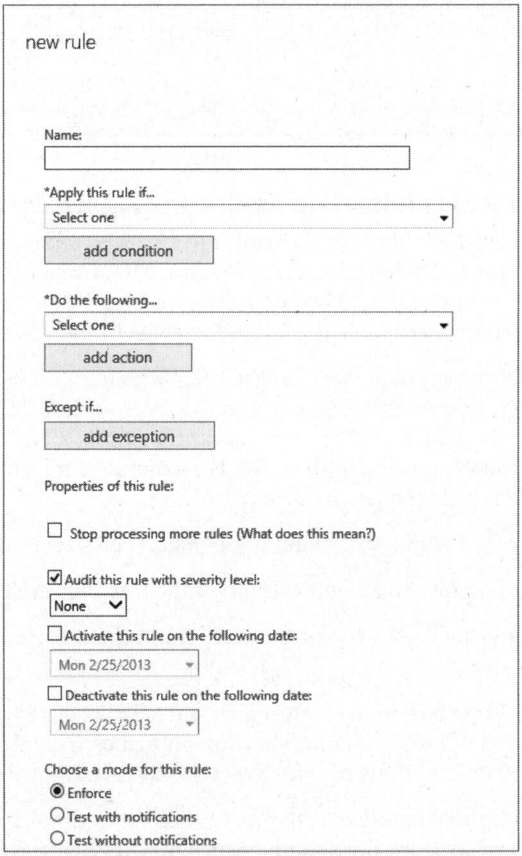

new rule

Name:

*Apply this rule if...
[Select one ▾]
[add condition]

*Do the following...
[Select one ▾]
[add action]

Except if...
[add exception]

Properties of this rule:

☐ Stop processing more rules (What does this mean?)

☑ Audit this rule with severity level:
[None ▾]
☐ Activate this rule on the following date:
[Mon 2/25/2013 ▾]
☐ Deactivate this rule on the following date:
[Mon 2/25/2013 ▾]

Choose a mode for this rule:
◉ Enforce
◯ Test with notifications
◯ Test without notifications

7. Provide a name for the new transport rule in the Name field.

8. To add a condition, select the drop-down box underneath Apply This Rule If, and choose the condition you want to apply to the transport rule.

9. To add an action, select the drop-down box underneath Do The Following.

10. To exclude the transport rule from applying to certain email messages, click Add Exception and select the drop-down box underneath Except If.

Up to this point, creating a new transport rule in Exchange Server 2013 is very similar to creating one in Exchange Server 2007 and Exchange Server 2010. Now it's time to look at the new bells and whistles that Microsoft has added to Exchange Server 2013. A brand-new set of options is presented for creating transport rules:

Audit This Rule With Severity Level   This topic will be covered more in the "Introducing Data Loss Prevention" section. This option defines the audit severity level of the transport rule.

Choose A Mode For This Rule   This topic will be covered more in the "Introducing Data Loss Prevention" section. This setting allows you to test a transport rule without enforcing the rule on email messages.

Stop Processing More Rules   A priority is associated with each transport rule. The Transport Rule agent analyzes messages against the transport rule with the lowest priority first and moves on to the transport rule with the next-lowest priority until the message has been analyzed by all the transport rules. If you enable this option, no subsequent transport rule will be processed against this email message.

Activate This Rule On The Following Date   This property is used to specify when the transport will begin processing email messages.

Deactivate This Rule On The Following Date   This property is used to specify when the transport will stop processing email messages.

TRANSPORT RULES: MORE FAMILIAR THAN YOU MIGHT REALIZE

Transport rules are always fun to describe to customers, since they have a familiar point of reference. We simply tell them that they are similar in experience to what they create with the Outlook Rules Wizard, except that these rules have many more available settings and run completely server-side.

One of the things that we often run into when we start diving a bit deeper is the ability to get *creative* around transport rules. Specifically, we had a customer who needed to define a disclaimer based on the user's department. This customer created a disclaimer transport rule in an Exchange Server 2007 organization and had not yet upgraded to Exchange Server 2013. So for users in the legal department, the outbound disclaimer had to state the legal requirements regarding client communication, while the sales department disclaimer had to state the company's warranty information.

Our first reaction was, "Sure, basic stuff!" So we fired up the New Transport Rules Wizard and found out quickly that creating a transport rule that applies based on the Department property in Active Directory cannot be done using Exchange Server 2007 management tools. Ouch!

Exchange Server 2013 now includes pretty much every Exchange Server recipient attribute as an available transport rule condition. So today, in Exchange Server 2013, we can create a new rule for this customer simply by selecting the Department attribute.

Creating New Rules with the Exchange Management Shell

The following Exchange Management Shell commands let you add, change, remove, enable, or disable transport rules that are used by the Transport Rule agent:

Get-TransportRule   This cmdlet shows you the existing transport rules in your organization:

```
Get-TransportRule
```

Enable-TransportRule   This cmdlet sets an existing transport rule as enabled, which means it will be applied to messages:

```
Enable-TransportRule -Identity MyTransportRule
```

Disable-TransportRule   This cmdlet sets an existing transport rule as disabled, which means that it will still be present in the configuration but will not be applied to messages:

```
Disable-TransportRule -Identity MyTransportRule
```

The Disable-TransportRule cmdlet is useful for troubleshooting problems with transport rules. You can also disable all transport rules with this command:

```
Get-TransportRule | Disable-TransportRule
```

Remove-TransportRule   This cmdlet allows you to delete an existing transport rule:

```
Remove-TransportRule -Identity MyTransportRule
```

Set-TransportRule   This cmdlet allows you to modify the parameters of an existing transport rule:

```
Set-TransportRule Project-X -Priority 3
```

New-TransportRule   This cmdlet allows you to create a new transport rule. Creating a new rule from the EMS is beyond the scope of this book, but it follows the same principles as the Set-TransportRule example. From the EMS, issue the following command for a full description of the cmdlet, including examples:

```
Help New-TransportRule -full
```

You can retrieve a list of the actions by using the Get-TransportRuleAction cmdlet and a list of the conditions using the Get-TransportRulePredicate cmdlet. Each transport rule has parameters defining the conditions, exceptions, and actions. Parameters are created based on the properties of a predicate. When using the Get-TransportRulePredicate and Get-TransportRule cmdlets, you can see the correlation between the transport rule parameter SentTo and the properties of the predicate SentTo.

```
Get-TransportRulePredicate SentTo

RunspaceId      : 6fc02408-b4c0-4e3d-9891-ee220f30dae4
Addresses       :
RuleSubTypes    : {None, Dlp}
Name            : SentTo
Rank            : 0
```

```
LinkedDisplayText : sent to <a id="SentTo">people</a>
Identity          :
IsValid           : False
ObjectState       : New
```

The property `LinkedDisplayText` holds two functions. First, it provides a description of the predicate, and second, the required properties are placed between `<a>` and `</a>`. Using the `SentTo` example, `people` represents any mail-enabled recipient.

Introducing Data Loss Prevention

A glaring flaw in Exchange Server 2007 and 2010 is the inability of the product to deeply analyze the content of an email message using a content engine to determine if the message contains sensitive information. To prevent sensitive information from being mishandled in Exchange Server 2007 and 2010, you could create a transport rule with a regular expression. A regular expression searches for a specific pattern within the email message. For example, you could create a regular expression that searches for the format of Social Security numbers. If a pattern in the email message matches the regular expression, the action within the transport rule will execute against the email message. A regular expression can be useful in certain circumstances, but in many cases it isn't flexible or advanced enough to meet business needs.

Microsoft has answered this problem with the introduction of Data Loss Prevention. DLP is designed to analyze, monitor, report, and prevent sensitive information from being exposed to unwanted parties. The classification of sensitive information varies for each company and region. For example, the United States uses Social Security Number as an identifier, but Canada uses Social Insurance Number as an identifier. DLP has been designed with the understanding that sensitive information is unique to each organization.

Understanding DLP Policies

The functionality of DLP is stored within a DLP policy. The DLP components are bound together in a DLP policy. The settings of the DLP policy and the components within the DLP policy define: the sensitive information to scan within an email message and attachments; the actions performed against an email message; level of reporting within the policy; if the DLP policy is enforced; and how to notify the end user that an email message they are composing falls in line with a DLP policy.

Armed with a sensitive information-detection engine that runs under the new Transport agent, DLP provides in-depth content analysis of an email message and certain types of attachments. The results of the content analysis are compared against sensitive information defined in a DLP rule. If sensitive content is found within the email message or attachment, the action specified in the transport rule is performed against the email message. Actions of a DLP rule can range from redirecting the email message to a compliance office to notifying the sender that the message contains sensitive information before the sender hits the Send button.

The file types that DLP can scan are shown in Table 23.1. Microsoft OneNote and Publisher are not supported file types unless the IFilters Filter Pack is registered on all the Mailbox servers. Attachments that are password-protected cannot be scanned by DLP.

TABLE 23.1:   Exchange Server 2013 DLP-scannable file types

CATEGORY	FILE EXTENSION
Office 2013, 2010, and 2007	DOCM, DOCX, PPTM, PPTX, PUB, ONE, XLSB, XLSM, XLSX
Office 2003	DOC, PPT, XLS
Additional Office files	RTF, VDW, VSD, VSS, VST
Adobe PDF	PDF
HTML	HTML
XML/OpenDocument	XML, ODP, ODS, ODT
Text	TXT, ASM, BAT, C, CMD, CPP, CXX, DEF, DIC, H, HPP, HXX, IBQ, IDL, INC, INF, INI, INX, JS, LOG, M3U, PL, RC, REG, TXT, VBS, WTX
AutoCAD drawing	DXF Note: AutoCAD 2013 files are not supported.
Image	JPG, TIFF Note: GIF and PNG are unsupported file types but the AttachmentIsUnsupported action will not execute against GIF and PNG files. The workaround to this problem is to create a transport rule explicitly looking for these file types.
Archive	ZIP, CAB, GZIP, RAR, TAR, UU Encode, TNEF, MSG

The Mode setting within a DLP policy defines how a DLP policy is applied to email messages within the organization and if end users are notified of the DLP policy using Policy Tips. Since every message is subject to DLP policies, a misconfiguration can cause havoc in an organization. Using the Test DLP modes allows you to test a new DLP policy before enforcing the DLP policy against all email messages. The three modes available are described here:

Enforce   If an email message meets the conditions of a DLP policy, the actions of the DLP policy are enforced. Content is added to the message-tracking log and Policy Tips are displayed to the sender.

Test DLP Policy With Policy Tips   If an email message meets the conditions of a DLP policy, the actions of the DLP policy are *not* enforced. Content is added to the message-tracking log and Policy Tips are displayed to the sender.

Test DLP Policy Without Policy Tips   If an email message meets the conditions of a DLP policy, the actions of the DLP policy are *not* enforced. Content is added to the message-tracking log and Policy Tips are *not* displayed to the sender.

The first part of preventing a leak of sensitive data is informing the sender through a Policy Tip that the email message they are composing contains sensitive data and violates a DLP policy. Policy Tips are similar to MailTips, in that a notification is provided to the sender before the sender submits the email message for delivery. A DLP policy can also be overridden through a Policy Tip. Within a DLP rule, you can specify if the rule can be overridden by the sender. You can also impose that a justification be provided when the sender overrides a DLP rule. The justification is registered and can be sent in an incident report.

The only clients that support Policy Tips are Outlook 2013 and Outlook Web App. Using EWS, the Outlook 2013 client downloads policies and classifications from servers with the CAS role. Policy definitions are downloaded on the local workstation running Outlook 2013 policy definition files (`PolicyNudgeClassficationDefinitions<GUID>.XML` and `PolicyNudgeRules<GUID>.XML`) and stores the files under `Users\<User>\Appdata\Local\Microsoft\Outlook`. Figure 23.9 shows an example of a Policy Tip in Outlook 2013. The Policy Tip notifies the end user that the content of the email message hit a DLP policy and the policy will prevent the delivery of the email message unless an override is specified.

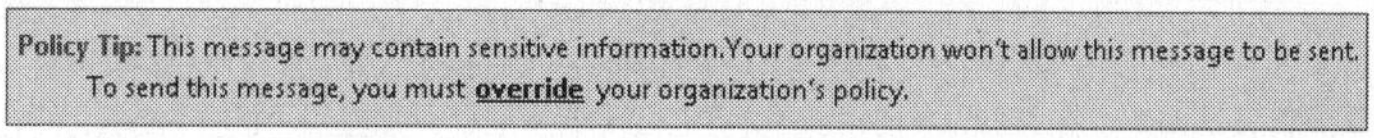

FIGURE 23.9
Policy Tip in Outlook 2013

Policy Tip: This message may contain sensitive information. Your organization won't allow this message to be sent. To send this message, you must **override** your organization's policy.

To take some of the complexity out of creating DLP policies, Microsoft has provided out-of-the-box DLP templates. A DLP template packages together transport rules and Policy Tips to identify, alert, and monitor sensitive information. Each built-in template is designed to cover a certain area of sensitive information. For example, let's say you create a new DLP policy from the U.S. Personally Identifiable Information (PII) Data template. The DLP policy will be composed of rules that will search email content for anything that matches U.S. taxpayer identification numbers, U.S. Social Security numbers, and U.S./U.K. passport numbers. The Exchange Server 2013 help file provides a list and description of each template.

Most DLP templates consist of similar rules. Continuing with the example, let's look at the rules created when using the DLP template U.S. Personally Identifiable Information (PII) Data. Figure 23.10 shows the rules created and the list following describes each rule:

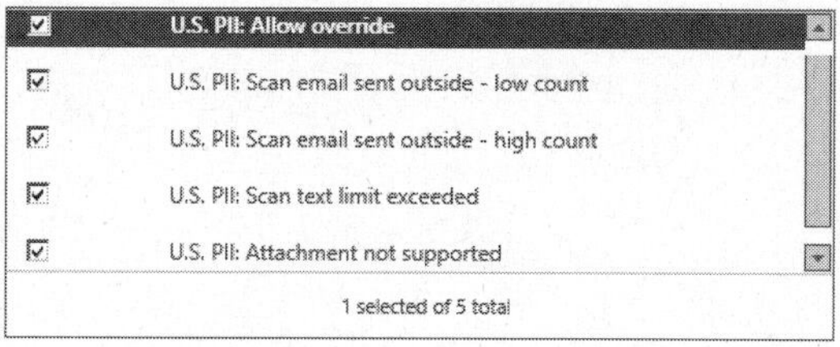

FIGURE 23.10
Rules created from DLP template U.S. Personally Identifiable Information (PII) Data

☑	**U.S. PII: Allow override**
☑	U.S. PII: Scan email sent outside - low count
☑	U.S. PII: Scan email sent outside - high count
☑	U.S. PII: Scan text limit exceeded
☑	U.S. PII: Attachment not supported

1 selected of 5 total

Allow Override   If the word *override* is in the subject of the email message, the DLP rules will be exempt from applying to the email message.

Scan Email Sent Outside – Low Count   During the evaluation of an email message, a record is kept each time sensitive information is found. If the total count of sensitive information is between 1 and 9, the user is notified via a Policy Tip that the message contains sensitive data but is allowed to send the email message.

Scan Email Sent Outside - High Count   The High Count rule is configured the same way as the Low Count rule except if the message exceeds 9 sensitive items, the message will be blocked unless a business justification is provided by the sender.

Scan Text Limit Exceeded   If the DLP engines and Transport agent don't complete scanning the email message, the email message will be audited.

Attachment Not Supported   If the email message contains an attachment that cannot be scanned, the email message will be audited.

We have covered the option of creating DLP policies from the Microsoft-provided templates. You can also create a DLP policy by importing your own template or a template provided by a third-party vendor. Using the New-ClassificationRuleCollection cmdlet, you can import an XML file that you created or was given to you by a third-party vendor, as shown here:

```
New-ClassificationRuleCollection -FileData ([Byte[]]$
    (Get-Content -Path "C:\rulepack.xml" -Encoding Byte -ReadCount 0))
```

The other way to create a new DLP policy is by creating a custom DLP policy. A custom DLP policy does not contain any default DLP rules; it is a blank canvas that you can use to create your own DLP policy based on the available DLP rules.

A custom DLP policy is a good option when none of the default templates meet your business requirements. For example, you may want to create a DLP policy that blocks U.S., German, and Japanese passport numbers. After selecting the sensitive information type, like Passport Number (U.S./U.K.), you can configure the options of the sensitive information. Figure 23.11 displays the options for sensitive information type Passport Number (U.S. / U.K.), and the following list describes each option.

FIGURE 23.11
Options for sensitive information type Passport Number (U.S. / U.K.)

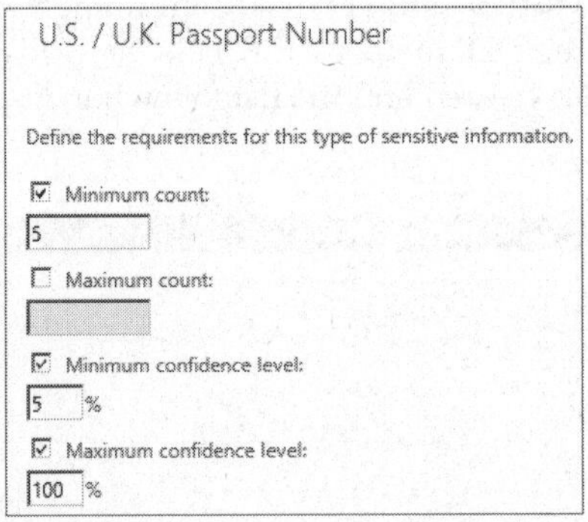

Minimum Count   The minimum number of times that data within the email message matches a message classification, such as Social Security numbers.

Maximum Count   The maximum number of times that data within the email message matches a message classification, such as Social Security numbers.

Minimum Confidence Level The lowest acceptable percentage used to count syntax as sensitive information.

Maximum Confidence Level The highest acceptable percentage used to count syntax as sensitive information.

Another part of the prevention process is being informed when an email message containing sensitive data was sent. A new transport rule action, GenerateIncidentReport, can be used to generate an incident report to a specific recipient. An incident report contains information regarding why the email message was flagged for containing sensitive information. Figure 23.12 shows an example DLP incident report and the list following describes each field with the report.

FIGURE 23.12
DLP incident report

```
Message Id: <eaaa93f15c9749c39b169178cbaeb241@All-1.jennchris.com>
Sender: Tad Thomas, tthomas@jennchris.com
Subject: SSN
To: 'David Scott', dscott@cbfive.com
To: 'tthomas@jennchris.com, tthomas@jennchris.com
Severity: Low
Override: No
False Positive: No
Data Classification: U.S. Social Security Number (SSN), Count: 1, Confidence: 85, Recommended Minimum Confidence: 75 Rule Hit: U.S. PII:
Scan email sent outside - low count, DLP Policy: 0ebf8e62-c10c-478a-ad4a-a205fd33cfeb, Action: AuditSeverityLevel, SenderNotify,
GenerateIncidentReport ID Match: U.S. Social Security Number (SSN), Value: 123-45-6789,
Context: SSN    Microsoft Word 15 (filtered medium)

Clients Name:  Jared Adam

Client Identifier or SSN:  123-45-6789

Address:  1234 Fake Street Baltimore, MD 21234
```

Message ID Shows the Message ID of the message sent.

Sender Shows the sender of the email message.

Subject Shows the subject of the email message.

To Lists the recipients of the email message.

Severity Shows the highest severity of any of the DLP policies that this email message triggered.

Override The sender can override the DLP policy by providing a justification for sending an email message containing sensitive information. The justification will be shown in the Override field.

False Positive Shows if the information worker reports the message as a false positive.

Data Classification Indicates the type of data that was found within the email message.

Count Gives the number of times that data within the email message matches a message classification, such as Social Security numbers.

Confidence Indicates the confidence level that the sensitive information found in the email message met the data classification in the DLP rule.

Recommended Minimum Confidence Indicates the minimum confidence level that will enforce the DLP rule.

Rule Hit   Shows the name of the DLP rule that was applied to the email message.

Action   Shows the action that was performed against the email message.

ID Match   Shows the type of message classification that was found in the email message.

Value   Shows the syntax that was found that matched a message classification.

DLP incidents are recorded in the message-tracking logs. As we talked about earlier in this chapter, when setting the mode of the DLP policy to test, the rules of the DLP policy are not applied to the email message. Instead, you can review the message-tracking logs to see if the DLP policy was applied to an email message. Using the `Get-MessageTrackingLog` cmdlet, you can export the transport rules that applied to an email message and the actions that were performed on the email message:

```
Get-TransportServer | Get-MessageTrackingLog -MessageSubject SSN | ↵
    where {$_.source -eq 'agent'}

Source    : AGENT
EventData : {[TRA, DC|dcid=a44669fe-0d48-453d-a9b1-2cc83f2cba77|count=1|conf=85],
[TRA,
ETRP|ruleId=5f4d29e2-4e12-411b-907c-a38ccb807ee5|ExecW=335|ExecC=15], [TRA,
ETR|ruleId=f31d282e-59e1-4505-aa6f-8b845dc2fcc2|st=3/1/2013 9:30:25
PM|action=ApplyHtmlDisclaimer|sev=1|mode=Enforce], [TRA,
ETR|ruleId=9ffe0714-b4de-4da0-8fc5-3e0d2c159a3f|st=3/3/2013 2:17:25 AM|action=
SetAuditSeverity|action=NotifySender|action=GenerateIncidentReport|sev=2|mode=E
nforce|dlpId=0ebf8e62-c10c-478a-ad4a-a205fd33cfeb|dcId=a44669fe-0d48-453d-a9b1-
2cc83f2cba77], [TRA, ETR|ruleId=67c4a4bf-46ff-4bc8-98f77bede9a907b4|st=3/1/2013
9:30:26PM|action=GenerateIncidentReport|sev=1|mode=AuditAndNotify|dlpId=1d4bb7
4b-1001-4919-b8e0-cc6ee4cb0eea|dcId=a44669fe-0d48-453d-a9b1-2cc83f2cba77]}
```

The output contains a lot of useful information. TRA in the output stands for Transport Rule agent. The `ruleId` is the GUID of the transport rule, which can be found using the `Get-TransportRule` cmdlet. The actions performed against this email message are registered under `action`. More information about message tracking can be found in Chapter 22.

Creating DLP Policies

DLP policies can be created, managed, and removed using the Exchange Server 2013 management tools.

Managing DLP Settings in the Exchange Administration Center

In the EAC you can create a new DLP policy from a template, import a DLP policy, and create a custom DLP policy. To create a DLP policy from a template in the EAC, use the following steps:

1. On your client computer, open Internet Explorer and browse to the ECP URL. This URL should be the name of your Client Access server with /ECP appended to the end. If you don't know the URL for EAC, you can use the Outlook Web App URL and specify **/ECP** instead of **/owa** at the end of the URL. For example, for Contoso, the EAC URL might be https://mail.contoso.com/ECP.

2. When prompted with the authentication page, type in your name and password and log in.

3. In the Feature pane, on the left column of the EAC, select Compliance Management.

4. In the toolbar across the top of the EAC, select the Data Loss Prevention tab. The DLP policies should be listed below.

5. Click the + button to create a new DLP policy from a template. To import a DLP policy or create a custom DLP policy, select the arrow next to the + button; a drop-down will display those options.

6. In the DLP Policy From Template window, which contains all the built-in templates for DLP, select U.S. Financial Data (Figure 23.13).

7. In the Name text box, type **U.S. Financial Data.**

8. At the bottom of the DLP Policy From Template window, select More Options.

9. Under Choose A Mode For The Requirements In This DLP Policy, select the Enforce radio button.

10. Click Save to create the new DLP policy.

FIGURE 23.13
DLP Policy
From Template
window from
EAC

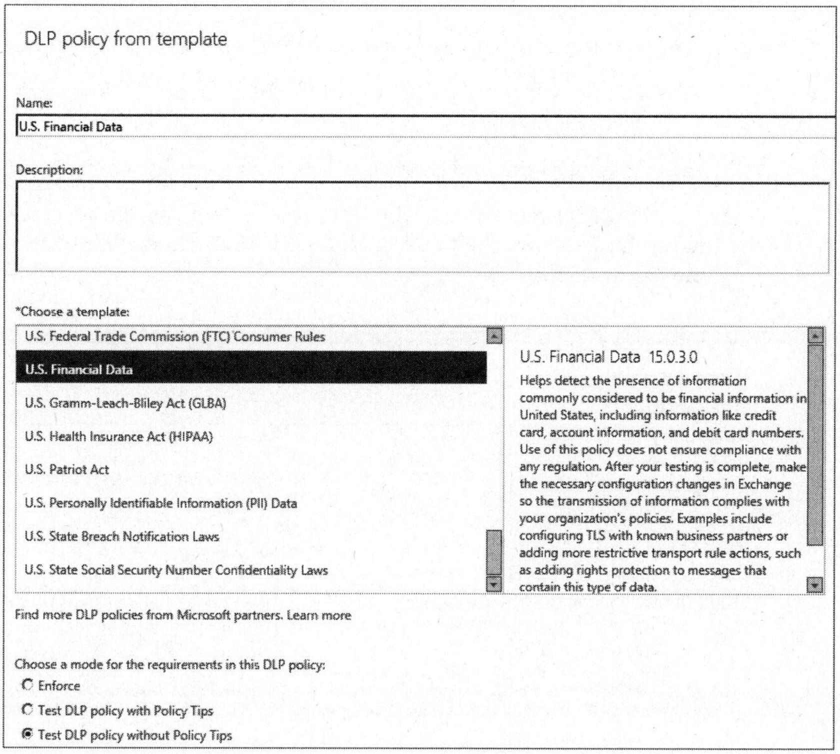

DLP policy from template

Name:

U.S. Financial Data

Description:

*Choose a template:

- U.S. Federal Trade Commission (FTC) Consumer Rules
- **U.S. Financial Data**
- U.S. Gramm-Leach-Bliley Act (GLBA)
- U.S. Health Insurance Act (HIPAA)
- U.S. Patriot Act
- U.S. Personally Identifiable Information (PII) Data
- U.S. State Breach Notification Laws
- U.S. State Social Security Number Confidentiality Laws

U.S. Financial Data 15.0.3.0

Helps detect the presence of information commonly considered to be financial information in United States, including information like credit card, account information, and debit card numbers. Use of this policy does not ensure compliance with any regulation. After your testing is complete, make the necessary configuration changes in Exchange so the transmission of information complies with your organization's policies. Examples include configuring TLS with known business partners or adding more restrictive transport rule actions, such as adding rights protection to messages that contain this type of data.

Find more DLP policies from Microsoft partners. Learn more

Choose a mode for the requirements in this DLP policy:
- ○ Enforce
- ○ Test DLP policy with Policy Tips
- ● Test DLP policy without Policy Tips

11. Highlight the U.S. Financial Data policy and select the Policy Tip Settings icon (the check box with the gear in the foreground).

12. In the Policy Tips window click the + button.

13. In the drop-down box under Action choose Allow The Sender To Override.

14. Select English from the drop-down underneath Locale.

15. Type **To override this policy add the word Override to the subject.** in the Text box.

The Policy Tip for the DLP policy U.S. Financial Data should look like the one in Figure 23.14.

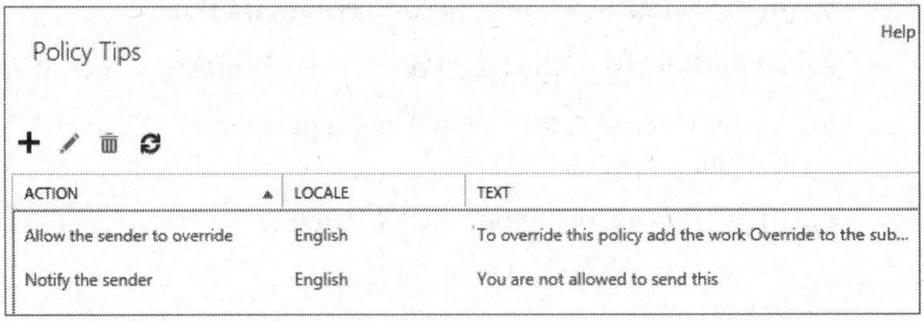

FIGURE 23.14
Policy Tip for DPL policy U.S. Financial Data

16. In the Feature pane, in the left column of the EAC, select Mail Flow.

17. In the toolbar across the top of the EAC, select the Rules tab. The transport rules should be listed below.

18. Highlight the transport rule, U.S. Financial: Scan Email Sent Outside - High Count.

In the display pane on the right side of the EAC, the sensitive information types this rule is searching for are: Credit Card Number, U.S. Bank Account Number, or ABA Routing Number (see Figure 23.15).

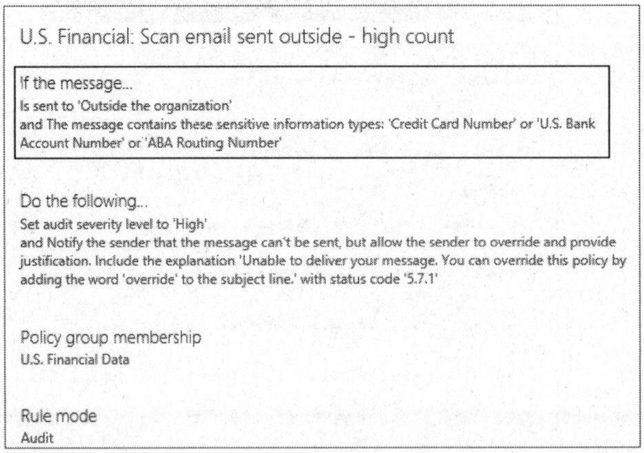

FIGURE 23.15
The sensitive information types covered by the transport rule U.S. Financial: Scan Email Sent Outside - High Count

Managing DLP Settings in the Exchange Management Shell

The following Exchange Management Shell commands let you add, change, remove, enable, or disable transport rules that are used by the Transport Rule agent on a Hub Transport server or an Edge Transport server:

`Get-DLPPolicy` Shows you the existing DLP policies in your organization:

```
Get-DLPPolicy
```

`Get-DLPPolicyTemplate` Shows the DLP policy templates that can be used when creating a DLP policy from a template:

```
Get-DLPPolicyTemplate
```

`New-DlpPolicy` Used to create new DLP policy within your organization:

```
New-DlpPolicy -Name "Patriot Act" -Template "U.S. Patriot Act"
```

`Set-DlpPolicy` Used to change the configuration of an existing DLP in your organization:

```
Set-DlpPolicy "Patriot Act" -Mode Enforce
```

`Remove-DlpPolicy` Removes a DLP policy from the organization:

```
Remove-DlpPolicy "Patriot Act"
```

`Export-DlpPolicyCollection` Used to export the DLP policy collection from your organization into an XML file. You can use this cmdlet to back up your DLP policies or to export the configuration in a lab environment and import it into a production environment. The `$ExportDLPpolicies` is a variable used in the following example to capture the `Export-DlpPolicyCollection` cmdlet:

```
$ExportDLPpolicies = Export-DlpPolicyCollection
Set-Content -Path C:\DLP\DLPpolicies.xml -Value ⮐
$ExportDLPpolicies.FileData -Encoding Byte
```

The contents of the XML file created by running the `Export-DlpPolicyCollection` will look similar to the output shown in Figure 23.16.

`Import-DlpPolicyCollection` Allows you to import a DLP policy collection from an XML file into an organization. Using this cmdlet will create the DLP policies and transport rules from an XML file:

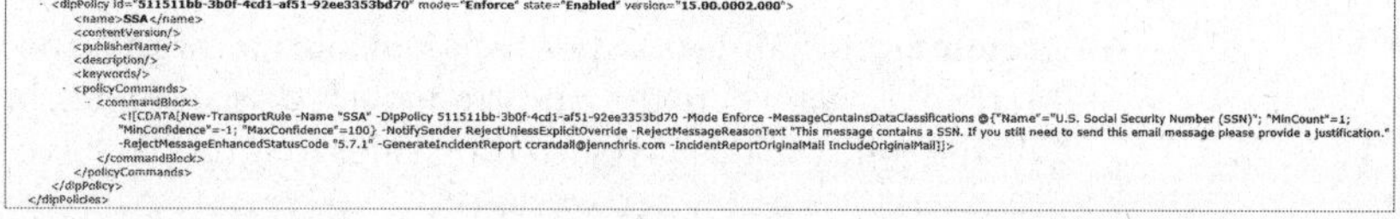

```
<?xml version="1.0" encoding="UTF-8" standalone="true"?>
- <dlpPolicies>
  - <dlpPolicy id="511511bb-3b0f-4cd1-af51-92ee3353bd70" mode="Enforce" state="Enabled" version="15.00.0002.000">
      <name>SSA</name>
      <contentVersion/>
      <publisherName/>
      <description/>
      <keywords/>
    - <policyCommands>
      - <commandBlock>
          <![CDATA[New-TransportRule -Name "SSA" -DlpPolicy 511511bb-3b0f-4cd1-af51-92ee3353bd70 -Mode Enforce -MessageContainsDataClassifications @{"Name"="U.S. Social Security Number (SSN)"; "MinCount"=1;
          "MinConfidence"=-1; "MaxConfidence"=100} -NotifySender RejectUnlessExplicitOverride -RejectMessageReasonText "This message contains a SSN. If you still need to send this email message please provide a justification."
          -RejectMessageEnhancedStatusCode "5.7.1" -GenerateIncidentReport ccrandall@jennchris.com -IncidentReportOriginalMail IncludeOriginalMail]]>
        </commandBlock>
      </policyCommands>
  </dlpPolicy>
</dlpPolicies>
```


Figure 23.16
Contents of the XML after running `Export-DlpPolicyCollection`

```
Import-DlpPolicyCollection -FileData ([Byte[]]$(Get-Content -Path ↵
C:\DLP\ DLPpolicies.xml -Encoding Byte -ReadCount 0))
```

Import-DlpPolicyTemplate Used to add a DLP template into an organization. Most of the time the imported templates will be provided by third-party applications:

```
Import-DlpPolicyTemplate -FileData ([Byte[]]$(Get-Content -Path ↵
"C:\DLP\DLPTemplate.xml" -Encoding Byte -ReadCount 0))
```

New-TransportRule Used to create rules within a DLP policy. If the specified DLP policy doesn't exist, a new DLP policy will be created:

```
New-TransportRule -Name "Prevent Bank Account Numbers" ↵
-MessageContainsDataClassifications @{Name="U.S. Bank ↵
Account Number"} -NotifySender RejectUnlessExplicitOverride –Mode ↵
 Enforce -GenerateIncidentReport HR@jennchris.com
```

Introducing Journaling

A lot of people confuse *journaling*, which is the process of capturing a set of communications for future use, with *archiving*, which is the practice of removing infrequently accessed or old message data from the message store in favor of a secondary storage location.

Archiving is all about getting stuff—usually old and bulky messages and attachments—out of your mailboxes, so you can reduce the performance hit on your comparatively expensive Mailbox server storage systems and reduce your backup windows. Archival solutions are discussed in Chapter 19, "Creating and Managing Mailbox Databases."

Journaling is record keeping; you're defining a set of users whose traffic you must keep track of, and Exchange Server dutifully captures faithful copies of every message they send or receive. As stated before, journaling is one of the main strategies that compliance and archival vendors use to get messaging data into their solutions.

Although you may not have any explicit applicable regulatory language that forces you to implement journaling, journaling can still be one of the easiest ways to meet the requirements you do have. As compliance becomes more of an issue, the ability to quickly and easily put your hands on complete and accurate records of messaging communications will become critical.

Exchange Server 2007 and 2010 journaling capabilities are essentially identical to those in Exchange Server 2013. The base journaling mechanism used by Exchange Server 2013 is envelope journaling, which captures all recipient information (even Bcc: headers and forwards). However, you have two options for journaling:

◆ Standard journaling (aka per-mailbox database journaling) uses the Journaling agent on a Mailbox server where the Hub Transport service resides, to journal all messages sent to and from recipients and senders whose mailboxes are homed on specified mailbox databases.

◆ Premium journaling (aka per-recipient journaling) also uses the Journaling agent on a Mailbox server where the Hub Transport service resides, but it's more granular. It offers you the ability to design journaling rules for groups or even specific users if need be.

You must have an Exchange Enterprise Client Access License (CAL) to use premium journaling.

Implementing Journaling

The Journaling agent, which is executed on the OnSubmittedMessage and OnRoutedMessage events, is responsible for detecting whether a given message falls under your journaling rules. Since the Transport service has been moved to the Mailbox role, all journaling is performed by servers with the Mailbox role installed. When you use standard journaling, you enable it for an entire mailbox database. Any messages sent to or by recipients whose mailboxes are located on a journal-enabled database will be detected by the Journaling agent and copies will be sent to a designated *journal recipient*. This journal recipient can be another recipient in the Exchange Server organization—if it is an Exchange Server mailbox, it must be dedicated to the purpose— or an SMTP address on another messaging system.

Journaling to an external recipient may seem like a crazy idea at first blush. However, this allows Exchange Server 2013 to be used with compliance and archival solutions that are not part of the Exchange Server organization or even with hosted solution providers.

If you use an external journal recipient, you should ensure that your SMTP transport connections to the external system are fully secure and authenticated. Exchange Server 2013 supports the use of the Transport Layer Security (TLS) protocol; see Chapter 22 for details on how to configure TLS connections to specific domains and how to enable SMTP authentication.

When you use premium journaling, you create journal rules that define a subset of the recipients in your organization. Premium and standard journaling rules are stored in Active Directory and retrieved by all servers with the Mailbox role, depending on the normal AD replication mechanism. The Journaling agent detects that the rule matches a given message and sends a copy of the message to the journaling recipient. Premium journaling rules are found under the Journal Rule tab of the compliance-management feature in the EAC.

Journaling rules can have three scopes, which helps the Journaling agent decide whether it needs to examine a given message:

◆ The Internal scope matches messages where all senders and recipients are members of the Exchange Server organization.

◆ The External scope matches messages where at least one sender or recipient is an external entity.

◆ The Global scope matches all messages, even those that may have already been matched by the other scopes.

To create a new journaling rule, run the New Journal Rule Wizard found on the Actions pane.

This same operation can be performed by using the Exchange Management Shell. The following command creates a new journal rule that will capture all messages for the members of the VIP distribution groups and send the journaled message to the Journal1 mailbox:

```
New-JournalRule -Name 'Journal VIP mail' –JournalEmailAddress ↵
'Journal1' -Scope 'Global' -Enabled $True -Recipient 'VIPs@somorita.com'
```

Managing Journaling Traffic and Security

If you are using an internal mailbox as your journaling recipient, you should be aware that it may collect a large amount of traffic. Though you can use the same mailbox for all journal reports generated in your organization, you may need to create multiple mailboxes to control mailbox size and ensure that your backup windows can be maintained. If you are using the Unified Messaging role in your organization, you may not want to journal UM-generated messages, such as voicemail, because of the large amount of storage space it requires. (On the other hand, you may be required to preserve these types of messages as well as your regular email.)

Journal mailboxes should be kept very secure and safe from everyday access because they may one day be material evidence in the event that your business is sued or must prove compliance to auditors.

To guard against the loss of journaling reports in the event of trouble within your Exchange Server organization, you can designate an *alternate journal mailbox*. This mailbox will receive any nondelivery reports that are issued if your journaling recipient cannot be delivered to.

Unfortunately, you can configure only a single alternate mailbox for your entire organization. Not only can this cause performance and mailbox size issues, but your local regulations may prevent you from mixing multiple types of journal information in one mailbox.

Using the `Set-TransportConfig` cmdlet, you can set the `JournalReportNdrTo` and the `VoicemailJournalingEnabled` parameters. Out of the box an alternate journal mailbox (`JournalingReportNdrTo`) is not set and voicemail messages (`VoicemailJournalingEnabled`) are journaled, as shown in the following example:

```
Get-TransportConfig | fl *journal*


JournalingReportNdrTo       : <>
VoicemailJournalingEnabled  :  True
```

Email messages that have an AD RMS template applied to them are protected using certificates from the AD RMS server. This could pose a problem when journaling is enabled in your organization. Luckily for us, Exchange Server 2013 can decrypt and journal an unencrypted version of a message. The decryption of journal reports is configurable using the `Set-IRMConfiguration` cmdlet. Using the `Get-IRMConfiguration` cmdlet, as shown here, will report the current value of the `JournalReportDecryptionEnabled` parameter:

```
Get-IRMConfiguration | fl *journal*


JournalReportDecryptionEnabled : True
```

INTEROPERABILITY WITH OFFICE 365

As mentioned earlier, journaling takes place when the message is passed through the transport pipeline. When your organization is in a hybrid configuration, some emails will not pass through the transport pipeline of your on-premises servers. For example, if an Office 365 user sent an email message to a recipient with a mailbox in Office 365, the message wouldn't pass through the transport pipeline of the on-premises servers; thus journaling wouldn't apply to that message. To combat this problem, create a mirror copy of the journaling rules in Office 365.

Another consideration to take into account is the placement of the journal mailbox while your organization is in a hybrid configuration. An Office 365 mailbox cannot be designated as a journal mailbox for an on-premises journaling rule. However, you can designate an on-premises mailbox as a journal mailbox in Office 365.

Reading Journal Reports

The journaling process creates a special Exchange Server message known as the *journal report*. This message is essentially a wrapper that contains a summary of the original message properties. It also contains a pristine copy of the original message that generated the report, neatly attached to the journal report.

The journal reports are designed to be human and machine readable, allowing you to automate processing of journal reports via a third-party application as well as perform manual checks on the data.

The following are the fields that Exchange Server 2013 places in the journal report:

To The SMTP address of a recipient in the To header or the SMTP envelope recipient. If the message was sent through a distribution list, this field contains the Expanded field. If the message was forwarded, this field contains the Forwarded field.

Cc The SMTP address of a recipient in the Cc header or the SMTP envelope recipient. If the message was sent through a distribution list, this field contains the Expanded field. If the message was forwarded, this field contains the Forwarded field.

Bcc The SMTP address of a recipient in the Bcc header or the SMTP envelope recipient. If the message was sent through a distribution list, this field contains the Expanded field. If the message was forwarded, this field contains the Forwarded field.

Recipient The SMTP address of a recipient who is not a member of the Exchange Server 2013 organization, such as Internet recipients or recipients on legacy Exchange servers.

Sender The sender's SMTP address, found in either the From or Sender header of the message.

On Behalf Of The relevant SMTP address if the Send On Behalf Of feature was used.

Subject The Subject header.

Message-ID The internal Exchange Message-ID.

The Bottom Line

Create and manage message classifications to control message flow. Message classifications provide a way to visibly tag selected messages and show that they require specific treatment. On their own, they're merely advisory, but combined with transport rules and mailbox rules, they can become powerful selection criteria for managing messages and ensuring policy compliance.

Master It You need to use message classifications to manipulate messages by using Outlook. You verify that custom message classifications are available from Outlook Web App. From Outlook, you look around but cannot find any options that relate to the custom message classifications. What do you need to do first?

Control message flow and manipulate messages by using transport rules. Transport rules give you a powerful, centralized method for creating automated policy enforcement in your environment.

Master It   You need to add a logo to an email disclaimer; you notice that you cannot include an image in the New Transport Rules Wizard. The availability of adding logos to a disclaimer was a major decision point of your Exchange Server 2013 implementation. What do you need to do to make the logo visible in the disclaimer?

Protect sensitive information by creating data loss prevention policies.   Using DLP policies you can enforce that all messages are subject to DLP rules, or you can allow users to bypass DLP rules by providing a business justification.

Master It   Your company's compliance officer requires that email messages containing U.S. bank routing numbers be redirected to the senders' manager for approval and that an incident report be generated and sent to the employees of the legal department. What do you need to do to make sure you meet the requirements of the compliance officer?

Part 5

Troubleshooting and Operating

Chapter 24

Troubleshooting Exchange Server 2013

Despite our care and attention, despite our best efforts to design the perfect Exchange server environment, something will inevitably go wrong at some point. Whether it's an unintended configuration setting, faulty hardware, a change to a dependency, or—*gasp*—a bug in the product, something invariably happens to cause problems for end users and ultimately for us, the administrators.

So what do you do when the lights go out on the Exchange server, figuratively speaking? The goal of this chapter is to outline tried-and-true strategies for recovering an Exchange server as quickly as possible.

In this chapter, you will learn to:

- ◆ Narrow the scope of an Exchange server problem

- ◆ Use basic Exchange Server troubleshooting tools

- ◆ Troubleshoot Mailbox server problems

- ◆ Troubleshoot mail transport problems

Basic Troubleshooting Principles

We can't overemphasize this key point: to troubleshoot Exchange Server, you have to understand the architecture. Understanding which functions of Exchange Server are controlled by which server roles is absolutely critical, or else you could spend a lot of time troubleshooting the wrong server.

Troubleshooting Exchange Server 2013 often involves collecting and reviewing information from a series of servers, rather than focusing on one. For example, a user complains that he isn't receiving new email. There are a number of possible causes for this:

- ◆ The user's client isn't receiving notifications of new email.

- ◆ The user's client can't connect to the Client Access server to retrieve new email.

- ◆ All copies of the relevant mailbox database are offline.

- ◆ The user's mailbox is full.

- ◆ Transport agents preclude delivery of email to this end user.

A closer look at this list shows an interesting breakdown. The first two issues could loosely be categorized as client-access issues, the next two as database issues, and the last as a transport issue. Unfortunately, this no longer corresponds nicely to the Exchange server roles since all those functions have now been rolled into only two roles. We'll cover troubleshooting in this chapter first by covering the general troubleshooting tools and then by troubleshooting client access, database storage, and then mail flow issues. However, before we dive right into the tools, let's take a moment to consider what troubleshooting involves.

When faced with a technical problem, your immediate impulse is often to jump right into the system and start clicking. While this can be successful, particularly when you're resolving a problem you've seen hundreds of times and know like the back of your own hand, it's not necessarily a reproducible strategy. What happens when you encounter a problem you haven't seen before? What do you do when you truly have no idea what the root cause could be?

The first step in troubleshooting a problem, any problem, is to define *what the problem is*. In many cases, this requires asking for more information. When an end user says that she can't send email, does she mean that she can't open Outlook? That she can't generate a new email? That she clicks Send but the email never leaves the Drafts or Outbox folder? Or that she's sent messages that were never received? The end result is the same—the user can't send email—but the root causes are very different.

Once the problem has been defined, the next step is to determine the scope of the problem. This often helps clarify the direction of further troubleshooting. By determining how many users are affected—and more importantly, determining what those users have in common—you can rule out some possibilities and focus on things with a greater impact. For example, if one user can't send email, the root cause could be many things unique to that user, from Outlook configuration to network connectivity to a disabled user account.

However, if a second user has a similar issue, it's more likely to be something they have in common. Are they in the same network segment, perhaps? If 10 users on different floors all report Outlook problems, there may possibly be a problem on an Exchange server. Are all 10 users in the same database, for example, or in the same Active Directory site?

There are a number of clarifying questions that are extremely useful in determining the scope of a particular problem:

◆ How many users are affected by the outage?

◆ Do all the affected users access Exchange Server through the same method, such as Outlook, Outlook Web App, or ActiveSync?

◆ What exactly are the users trying to do when they encounter the problem?

◆ Are other users able to perform the same task without problems?

◆ Are all of the users in the same database?

◆ Are all of the users in the same site?

◆ Does the problem occur all the time, only some of the time, or rarely?

The answers to these will often rule out possibilities right from the start. If one user can't log into Outlook successfully, but another in the same database can, you know immediately that the relevant database must be mounted and accessible, and you can then concentrate on other things.

Speaking of concentrating on other things, one of the most difficult things in troubleshooting is ignoring the unimportant distractions and focusing on what's causing the issue. It's often difficult to differentiate between what's important and what's not unless you know where to start (which is why defining the problem is so important).

Here's an example: an end user reports that he can't send email to a specific user, and during investigation you also discover that he can't access a particular public folder. Is the public folder problem directly related to the email problem? It might be—if the recipient's mailbox is on a server that also houses the only instance of that public folder, and that server is inaccessible, that would explain both problems. But in many cases it might not—the mailbox database that contains the public folder store might be dismounted or the user might not have permissions. Although there's at least one explanation that covers both problems, many more exist that are unique to the secondary problem. The steps to troubleshoot internal mail flow are different from those required to troubleshoot public folder access, so if you're trying to resolve a problem with internal email, concentrate on that and leave the public folder issue for later. Essentially, isolate the issue and start investigating it. Divide and conquer.

General Server Troubleshooting Tools

During troubleshooting, some steps should be the same no matter what the symptoms are. Yes, you need to define the problem, as discussed earlier, and you also need to understand the scope of the issue. But once you've determined that the problem is indeed server-based rather than specific to a group of clients, what next? This section will focus on the key tools you should use first.

Event Viewer (Diagnostic Logging)

Troubleshooting a server involves data collection and analysis, and the best ways to collect that data are the same regardless of server role. The Event Viewer includes detailed information about recent system and application errors, and this should always be an administrator's first move in the event of crisis.

Windows Server 2012 servers have two categories of event logs: Windows logs and Applications and Services logs. The Windows logs contain the event logs available in previous versions of Windows: Application, Security, and System event logs, as well as two new logs available only since Windows Server 2012: the Setup log and the ForwardedEvents log.

Windows logs store events from legacy applications and events that apply to the entire system. Applications and Services logs store events from a single application, such as Exchange Server, or components, such as a specific service, rather than events that might have system-wide impact.

Once you've determined the scope of a problem, and you've positively identified the root cause as server related, your next step should be to check the event logs on the relevant system. Because Exchange Server has so many moving parts, so to speak, you'll often find a large number of events clustered together at the time of the reported issue. The default logging level for the majority of services and categories is Lowest, which means that only critical, error, and warnings of logging level 0 will be written to the event log.

If the events generated during the problem aren't quite enough, you might need to increase the logging level for a specific service and category—for example, MSExchange Transport\ Mail Submission—to Low, Medium, or High. There is another logging level, Expert, but this generates so many events that it should be used only for short periods, typically when working directly with Microsoft support.

As with nearly everything in Exchange Server 2013, you can configure diagnostic logging through either the Exchange Admin Center (EAC) or the Exchange Management Shell (EMS).

ENABLING DIAGNOSTIC LOGGING

In the initial release of Exchange Server 2007, diagnostic logging was removed from the EMC, and the only way you could increase logging for a particular service was by using the Set-EventLogLevel cmdlet. Since PowerShell was still new at the time (Exchange Server 2007 was many administrators' first exposure to it), the change wasn't well received, and so Microsoft reintroduced diagnostic logging control to the console in Service Pack 2, and diagnostic logging control is still an administrator favorite in Exchange Server 2013.

If you run through the installation process of Exchange Server 2013, you will soon realize that logging is a major consideration from the outset. There have been many architectural and operational changes in Exchange Server 2013, but one that receives little fanfare is the minimum space requirement change for the installation partition of your Exchange servers. At minimum, you must have 30 GB of available space on the drive where you install Exchange Server, and I would recommend much more than that. The majority of this space will be filled by log files—not the database transaction log files that you have learned to love and respect but the diagnostic and performance log files you dread to dig through.

Figure 24.1 displays the default directory where all log files are found. Logging is enabled by default on all Exchange servers and cannot be disabled, at least in any way that I have found. Microsoft recommends that you open a call to product support should your entire installation drive become full and cause issues with your Exchange server.

The way to configure diagnostic logging in Exchange Server 2013 is through the Set-EventLogLevel cmdlet. This cmdlet does *not* take a server parameter. In other words, you have to run the command from the shell on the target server to configure logging. The syntax is relatively straightforward:

```
Set-EventLogLevel -Identity "MSExchange Transport\Mail Submission" ↵
-Level Medium
```

It's always a good idea to reset the logging back to Lowest when you're finished troubleshooting. Increased logging can add significantly to event log growth, and depending on your settings it might fill up your event log quickly or overwrite events.

Once you've identified the target server and configured logging, you might not see relevant events right away. You may need to reproduce the issue (for example, by having the user send another email or attempt to force a connection for a mail queue) before Exchange Server logs anything of value. Exchange Server events themselves will always appear in the Application event log and in the logging directories shown in Figure 24.1.

FIGURE 24.1
The logging
directory on
the Exchange
server

FIGURE 24.1
The logging
directory on
the Exchange
server

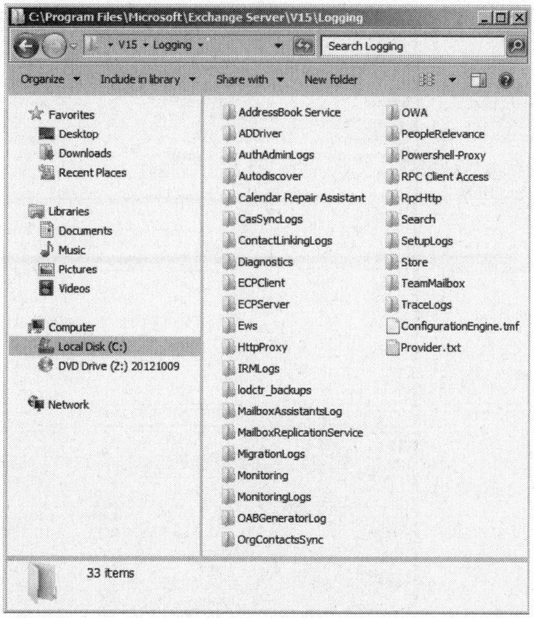

Diagnostic events include a wealth of information, but the most important pieces are the following:

Description   Although the field is unnamed in Windows Server 2012, it's the equivalent of the legacy Description field from previous versions of Windows. This includes the text of the event and will in many cases include additional error codes or critical information. For example, the well-known and widely feared-1018 error isn't an event—it's a JET error code that appears within the description text of other ESE events, like ESE error 474. The description may also include a link to further information on the Microsoft support site.

Source   This tells you which component logged the event. Note that this will typically be the underlying service name rather than the "friendly" name.

Event ID   This is the specific event number. Along with the Source, this is the most important information for the event.

Level   This reflects the severity of the event and can range from Informational to Error.

Logged   This displays the date and time of the event *in local time*. This information is stored in the event in UTC, and the Event Viewer displays the equivalent local time—if you're looking at a remote server, make sure you take this into account!

Task Category   This is the subcomponent of the service that logged the event. Not all services provide this additional information, but the majority of Exchange Server services do. This corresponds to the categories visible in the Manage Diagnostic Logging Properties Wizard or via `Set-EventLogLevel`.

Depending on the error, you should see information similar to the event shown in Figure 24.2.

FIGURE 24.2
Viewing an
event from the
Exchange
Application logs

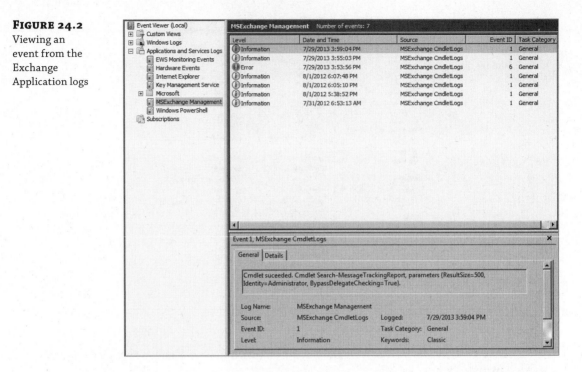

Many Exchange Server events include detailed diagnostic steps in the Description field, which is extremely convenient in times of trouble. Even if the event doesn't provide much information, you might be able to find more on the TechNet Events and Errors Message Center at www.microsoft.com/technet/support/ee/ee_advanced.aspx. Unfortunately, at the time of this writing this site hasn't been updated for Exchange Server 2013; thankfully, we still find relevant information regarding event IDs that have not changed since previous versions of Exchange Server. Simply select the appropriate product (Exchange Server, obviously); select the appropriate version (15.0 for Exchange Server 2013); enter the event ID, source, or both; and then click Go. Assuming the event appears in the TechNet database, you should see a link for additional information, which then provides a detailed explanation of the issue, as well as troubleshooting steps and recommendations. If you can't find information on the specific event here, there's always the Microsoft Knowledge Base (http://support.microsoft.com/search/?adv=1) or your favorite search engine.

The Test-* Cmdlets

PowerShell cmdlets control so much functionality in Exchange Server 2013 that it's not a surprise to see troubleshooting cmdlets as well. The Test-* cmdlets in Exchange Server are solid tools in the back pockets of Exchange Server administrators. My recommendation is to use them frequently since they use few resources on the servers and provide a wealth of useful information. For a complete list of all Test-* cmdlets, and a brief description of each cmdlet, just type the following command in an Exchange Management Shell window:

```
Help Test-*
```

TEST-SYSTEMHEALTH

One of the most basic troubleshooting cmdlets is `Test-SystemHealth`, a handy little tool that quickly collects data about the local server and analyzes it according to Microsoft-recommended practices. The standard syntax is mercifully simple: type **Test-SystemHealth**, press Enter, and then wait for the output. Unlike many cmdlets, `Test-SystemHealth` generates a progress bar at the top of the EMS window. This is a useful visual indicator—it's high contrast so you can see it from several feet away

When the cmdlet finishes, it displays the results in a simple list format (which you could format with the Format-List cmdlet if you wanted to). The tool displays warnings in yellow (shown here) and alerts in red (Figure 24.3).

FIGURE 24.3
Using the Test-System Health cmdlet

The resulting data is a mini-health check for your server. The `Test-SystemHealth` cmdlet will alert you to many common misconfigurations as well as recommended settings.

TEST-SERVICEHEALTH

Another extremely useful cmdlet is `Test-ServiceHealth`, which does what its name suggests: it checks the health of all required Exchange Server services on the server. Since the cmdlet recognizes roles as well, it doesn't check for every service; it only looks for the services the installed roles use. For example, if you're running the test on a Client Access server, it will not check for the MSExchangeMailSubmission service, which is available only on a Mailbox server.

This cmdlet also uses a very simple syntax; just type **Test-ServiceHealth**, press Enter, and peruse the results. The output from this cmdlet is preformatted into a table and simply reports on the status of the required services; an example of the output is shown in Figure 24.4.

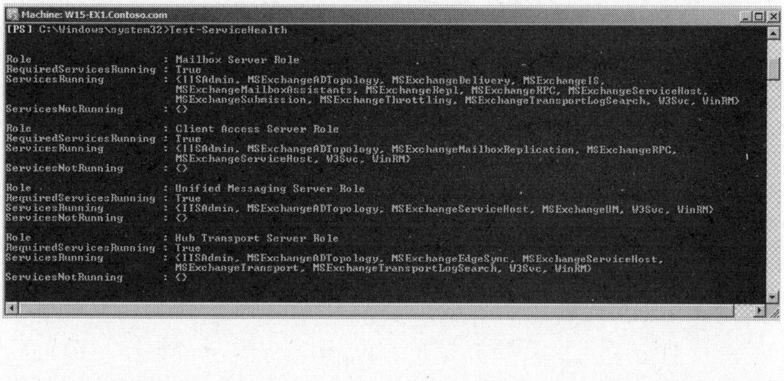

FIGURE 24.4
Using the Test-Service Health cmdlet

If you want to quickly check the status of a single server, the two preceding cmdlets can save a lot of time and effort. However, neither cmdlet runs against multiple servers at once. To check the configuration of a group of servers, or even every server in the organization, you need to script the cmdlets to run at a higher level.

New Cmdlets

Each version of Exchange Server since Exchange Server 2007 brings along a new stable of cmdlets. There are three new Test-* cmdlets in Exchange Server 2013, bringing the total to 32: Test-OAuthConnectivity tests application authentication, Test-SiteMailbox tests connectivity to a SharePoint 2013 site mailbox, and Test-MigrationServerAvailability tests connectivity to a migration server during a move of mailboxes to Office 365.

Replacing the Exchange Best Practice Analyzer

If you've been using Exchange Server for the last few years, you're probably familiar with the Exchange Best Practice Analyzer (generally known as ExBPA). You'll be sad to hear, as I was, that the ExBPA has been retired for this release of Exchange Server. I'm not sure what to make of the retirement of this tool, because it had become one of my best friends in troubleshooting deployments that I encountered infrequently. Being called in to a client site and running the ExBPA was a standard task to identify any major flaws quickly.

So one of the common questions that I get is, "How do you replace the functionalities provided by the ExBPA?" and the answer is not always a great one. First, in order to replace the ExBPA, you really need to be familiar with the Exchange Management Shell and its "troubleshooting" cmdlets. In fact, if you are new to managing Windows Server 2012 servers, you'll find that the PowerShell and Test-* cmdlets are prevalent there as well.

In a recent attempt to solve several configuration problems at a client site, I was able to identify the root cause of connectivity and certificate errors by running only two cmdlets: Test-MapiConnectivity and Test-ActiveSyncConnectivity. (See the section "Using Test-MapiConnectivity" later in this chapter.) Sure, both of these cmdlets require a bit of experience with their syntax, but at the end of the day they helped me resolve major configuration issues that would have required a full ExBPA test. This was in fact quicker and more efficient, though not as pretty and graphics-oriented.

Troubleshooting Mailbox Servers

With the shift of mailbox access over to the Client Access server in Exchange Server 2010 and the recent demise of the Hub Transport server role, the Mailbox server's role in Exchange Server 2013 essentially encompasses data storage, mail transport, and Unified Messaging functionalities. The primary focus of troubleshooting Mailbox servers rests on three things: database replication health, server performance, and email delivery. These aren't the only things Mailbox servers do, of course, but they're probably the most common troubleshooting topics. But before we get into those, let's recap some of the standard troubleshooting techniques you should apply to a Mailbox server.

General Mailbox Server Health

Although a Mailbox server is essentially useless without Client Access servers (as a good friend recently said, what good is a database if you can't access it?) to provide access and deliver mail, it's still the most important role in an Exchange Server environment. This is, of course, because the data is stored on the server—in the databases on the associated storage, to be precise. So when dealing with Mailbox server issues, you'll want to perform these basic checks:

- ♦ Are all required Exchange Server services able to start as necessary?

- ♦ Do you see any errors in the event log relating to MSExchangeDatabase, MSExchangeDatabase ➤ Instances, or MSExchangeSubmission Mailbox?

- ♦ Are there any Active Directory issues that might have a negative impact on Exchange Server?

Obviously, the Test-SystemHealth and Test-ServiceHealth cmdlets would be useful in detecting basic problems, like a dismounted database or a stopped service. They should always be the first two cmdlets you execute when troubleshooting a Mailbox server, simply because they group together so many common checks.

Using Test-MapiConnectivity

Like its close cousin, Test-OutlookConnectivity (which is no longer available), Test-MapiConnectivity will help you determine problems accessing a specific mailbox. It logs into a target mailbox (which you can specify with the -Identity parameter), the system mailbox in a specific database (which you can specify with -Database), or the system mailbox in every active database on a server (through -Server). The output for all three variants looks like the following:

```
Test-MAPIConnectivity -Server Server1

MailboxServer     Database         Result    Error
-------------     --------         ------    -----
Server1           MailboxDatabase... Success
Server1           MailBoxDatabase... Success


Test-MAPIConnectivity GTaylor

MailboxServer     Database         Result    Error
-------------     --------         ------    -----
Server1           MailBoxDatabase... Success


Test-MAPIConnectivity -Database MailboxDatabase-001

MailboxServer     Database         Result    Error
-------------     --------         ------    -----
Server1           MailBoxDatabase... Success
```

This is a useful (and quick) cmdlet for narrowing the possible scope of a problem; `Test-MapiConnectivity` essentially tests not only the Exchange Server information store but also ADAccess and RPCoverHTTP access, so a successful test against any mailbox on a server proves that those three components are at least functioning. If you can log into the system mailbox for a database but not into a user mailbox in that same database, the problem is clearly something unique to that user.

What is also very interesting about this cmdlet is that though it tests access to the mailbox database and essentially is a Mailbox server testing tool, it does *not* indirectly test the availability of Client Access servers. Client Access servers are the entry point of client requests to mailboxes, so if your `Test-MapiConnectivity` cmdlet retrieves a successful connection, that successful connection will be to the entry point on the Mailbox servers, not necessarily the one that users/Outlook/OWA and others will take to access the mailbox. I actually find that to be a positive aspect of this cmdlet, since it allows you to segment your troubleshooting results to pinpoint the source of a problem.

Checking Poison Mailboxes

One new feature that might lead to confusion for users (and more than a few administrators!) is poison mailbox detection. By default, Mailbox servers will tag any mailbox that causes a thread in the `store.exe` service to crash or that is connected to five or more "hung" threads. If a mailbox is tagged three times in two hours, Exchange Server 2013 will block access to that mailbox for up to six hours or until the administrator unblocks it, whichever comes first. If a user reports that she cannot connect to a mailbox, but other users have no difficulty, check to see if there are any quarantined mailboxes on the server. You can do this either through Performance Monitor (through the MSExchangeIS Mailbox\Quarantined Mailbox Count performance counter) or through the `Get-MailboxStatistics` cmdlet. For example, to find out if mailbox GillianK is quarantined, simply use this command:

```
Get-MailboxStatistics GillianK | Format-List DisplayName, IsQuarantined
```

Exchange Server 2013 will also write an event to the Application log when it quarantines a mailbox.

Do not confuse this feature with a poison message queue that is also stored on the Exchange Server Mailbox server. This queue contains messages that Exchange Server deems harmful to the environment while they are being transported in and out of an Exchange Server organization. These messages are not lost, since they will continue to exist in the poison message queue until an administrator deletes them manually.

Checking Database Replication Health

The introduction of continuous replication in Exchange Server 2007 dramatically changed the face of disaster recovery, because administrators could deploy two separate copies of a single database, each on a physically separate server. There were a few limitations, of course; end users still connected to the *server*, not just the database, so problems with the underlying cluster would render both database copies inaccessible. Standby continuous replication (introduced in Exchange Server 2007 Service Pack 1) provided another disaster-recovery option, but this had its limits as well—it was purely manual and, depending on the configuration, would require at least a setup "trick" (`setup /recovercms`) or even wholesale "rehoming" of users. A successful activation of a standby copy was also heavily dependent on replication of both DNS and Active Directory information, so users might still be unable to connect even after the issue was resolved.

Database availability groups (DAGs) in Exchange Server 2013 provide multiple copies of a single database on different servers, even in different datacenters, so a single server failure should have a significantly smaller impact on an Exchange Server deployment. Other architectural changes—namely Client Access namespaces—affectively hide the server object from the end user, so the actual location of the active database is immaterial from the end user's perspective.

Database replication health is, loosely speaking, how successful Exchange Server is at keeping database copies in sync. This depends on server configuration, network health, and a few other things (most of which Exchange Server checks automatically as part of the `Test-SystemHealth` and `Test-ServiceHealth` cmdlets). However, you can check the health of the replication infrastructure quite easily with two cmdlets. The first cmdlet, `Test-ReplicationHealth`, checks the health of the replication services and alerts you to any errors it finds. The output is extremely easy to read, as shown here:

```
Test-ReplicationHealth

Server          Check                      Result        Error
------          -----                      ------        -----
EX1        ReplayService                   Passed
EX1        ActiveManager                   Passed
EX1        TasksRpcListener                Passed
EX1        DatabaseRedundancyCheck         Passed
EX1        DatabaseAvailabilityCheck       Passed
```

Once you've validated the replication services, you can check the replication status for the databases themselves with `Get-MailboxDatabaseCopyStatus`. You can focus on a particular database by using the `-Identity` parameter or check the status for all mailbox database copies on a specific server by using `-MailboxServer`. You could even check the status of one specific database on one specific server by including both parameters. Here is an example of using the `Get-MailboxDatabaseCopyStatus` cmdlet where the results are filtered to show only a subset of the data being reported:

```
Get-MailboxDatabaseCopyStatus | Format-List ↵
Name,Status,LastInspectedLogTime,ContentIndexState

Name            Status     LastInspectedLogTime      ContentIndex
                                                        State
----            ------     --------------------      -----------
MDB001\EX1      Mounted    1/13/2013 8:44:03 AM      Healthy
MDB002\EX1      Mounted    1/15/2013 8:03:24 PM      Healthy
MDB003\EX1      Mounted    1/15/2013 8:12:56 PM      Healthy
```

There are many possible causes for replication errors, including the following:

◆ Transient network-connectivity issues

◆ Permissions issues

◆ Insufficient disk space on the target server

The general troubleshooting steps we covered in the beginning of this chapter will help you determine the exact cause of a replication problem.

With the reduction in functionality, Mailbox servers have become significantly easier to troubleshoot than in the past. There are a number of useful cmdlets for validating mailbox database availability and mailbox access, among them `Test-SystemHealth`, `Get-MailboxStatistics`, and `Test-MapiConnectivity`. Two additional cmdlets, `Test-ReplicationHealth` and `Get-MailboxDatabaseCopyStatus`, provide insight into the replication of those databases across member servers in the organization.

Troubleshooting Mail Flow

Message delivery is arguably the most important piece of Exchange Server 2013, and it's only fitting that Microsoft has provided a formidable arsenal of troubleshooting weapons to deal with pesky delivery failures. You'll have your pick of tools, from self-serve choices, such as message tracking in the Exchange Control Panel, to several forms of tracing, to the inevitable cmdlets.

However, just because you have an array of choices doesn't mean you have to use them right away. Again, it's important to approach a message-delivery problem with clear eyes and ask probing questions about what you're facing. Remember the example earlier in the chapter, with the end user who couldn't send email? There were a number of plausible explanations for this, some of which didn't involve message delivery at all! So it's still important to gather the essential information:

◆ Can the user send any emails at all? Is nondelivery restricted to a subset of users?

◆ Does the user receive a delivery status notification? If so, what is the delivery code?

◆ Is the recipient in the same Exchange Server organization or in a different organization (presumably on the Internet)?

◆ How close do messages get to their destination?

◆ What is the messaging path between the end user and the recipient?

These questions, though relatively simple, conceal a bewildering list of possible root causes. Consider the impact on message delivery on the following:

DNS Failure   Mailbox servers can't locate A records and therefore can't reach next-hop servers.

Site Link Failure   No site link exists between sender and recipient.

Transport Failure   Transport services on all of the Mailbox servers in the user's site are inaccessible.

Transport Agent   A transport rule prevents this email from reaching the recipient (because of sender restrictions, content restrictions, or recipient issues).

Mailbox Limits   The recipient's mailbox is full, but nondelivery reports do not reach the sender for whatever reason.

Messages Stuck in Queue A transient failure has temporarily stopped messages at a back-off location.

Back Pressure Transport services are temporarily throttling message delivery due to resource constraints.

This isn't even an exhaustive list, but it includes a wealth of possibilities. Now, there are few listed here that you would probably detect by performing the basic troubleshooting steps we covered earlier in this chapter (like DNS failure or transport failure). We'll begin with a simple cmdlet to check basic mail flow, which is typically the first step in locating undelivered messages, and then move on to message tracking and agent logging.

Using Test-Mailflow

Assuming you've done some of the basic checking (is the user's client connected to a database, are transport services available, and so on), you'll probably want to test that mail is flowing in the organization. There's an aptly named cmdlet for just this job: `Test-Mailflow`.

The cmdlet's basic function is simply to send and receive email from the system mailbox of the target server, but it can do so much more. The syntax is extremely simple: `Test-Mailflow` followed by the source server, then `-TargetMailboxServer`, `-TargetDatabase`, or `-TargetEmailAddress`. The different options mean that you can start with a Mailbox server, and if that test succeeds, focus on the user's database and then the user's email address. If you've deployed multiple databases in a DAG, you should skip the first step and start with `-TargetDatabase`.

```
Test-Mailflow EX1 -TargetEmailAddress zachary@netlogon.com


RunspaceId         : 0848e0b8-4228-4195-b1ee-c4c967ac9a41
TestMailflowResult : Success
MessageLatencyTime : 00:00:02.5631250
IsRemoteTest       : True
Identity           :
IsValid            : True
```

The output from `Test-Mailflow` doesn't need much interpretation. The most important piece is the `TestMailflowResult` property. If it reads `Success`, you know that you can reach that server, database, or email address, and you know that email is flowing, at least for some combination of user and database. The next property, `MessageLatencyTime`, lets you know the time it took for the message to reach the destination server. The `IsRemoteTest` property simply indicates whether the message left the server (this will also be `True` if you use the `-TargetEmailAddress` parameter).

However, if your test fails, the `TestMailflowResult` property reads `*FAILURE*`, and that's unfortunately the only indicator you receive—no messages about where the failure might have occurred or other useful information. That's when you need to start figuring out where the messages are stopped, and for that we need to move into different tools. We'll start with the Queue Viewer and then look into message tracking.

Utilizing the Queue Viewer

So, if you've been following along with this book, now in its 24th chapter, you've read plenty about the Exchange Admin Center (EAC) and how it is the primary graphical interface for managing Exchange Server 2013 servers. And that's true; I'm not backing down from this one. However, rarely you'll use the trusted Microsoft Management Console (MMC) to manage certain aspects of Exchange Server. The Queue Viewer is one of those rare examples.

The Queue Viewer is a tool that is available through an MMC snap-in named Exchange Toolbox. The Exchange Toolbox provides a virtual toolbox in the MMC that contains the Queue Viewer, alongside a number of other useful tools (some of which we'll cover later in this section). A big believer in truth in advertising, the Queue Viewer allows you to, yes, view the contents of the various delivery queues. Obviously, you need to connect to a Mailbox server to use this tool, but you can open the Queue Viewer from anywhere and then connect to the appropriate Mailbox server. The interface for the Queue Viewer is shown in Figure 24.5.

FIGURE 24.5
Using the
Queue Viewer
interface

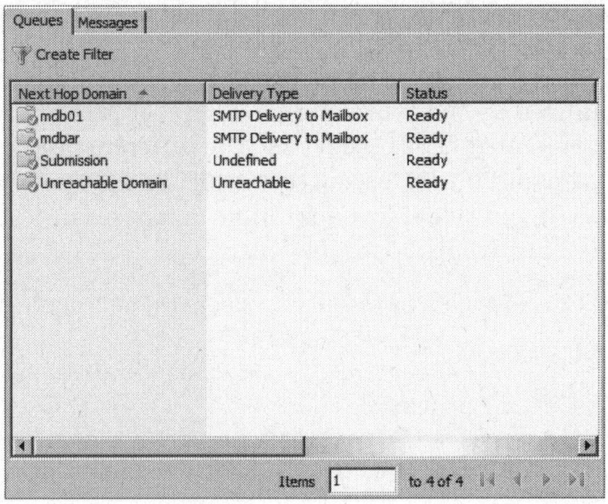

It's largely unchanged from Exchange Server 2007, but it didn't need any enhancements; it tells you the status of the queues, how many messages are pending delivery, and where the mail is heading, among other things. The list of queues is a bit thinner than in previous versions of Exchange Server (particularly when compared to the positively garrulous Exchange Server 2003), but if there's a problem with a particular queue, it'll be listed here.

Most of the columns in the Queues tab are relatively self-explanatory, but here's a brief rundown of what you'll see on this page:

Next-hop Domain   This is where the mail is heading next, whether a server in a different site, a server in the same site, or an Internet host.

Delivery Type   This indicates where the messages are heading next in their journey to the recipient.

Status   This simply indicates whether the queue state is Active (sending messages at the moment), Suspended (stopped through administrative action), Ready (able to send messages should any arrive), or Retry (unable to send messages). Queues in a Retry state are the most obvious candidates for additional review and analysis, but remember that queues can fail because of the sending server as well as the recipient.

Message Count   This lets you know how many messages are stuck in this queue.

Next Retry Time   This is applicable only to queues in a Retry state and lets you know the next time Exchange Server will attempt to "wake up" the queue for delivery.

You can perform a small number of tasks on the queues, including temporarily stopping them (Suspend), forcing them to connect if they've failed (Retry), or deleting all the messages (Remove messages with or without a non-delivery report). This can be useful for restarting mail flow after you've resolved a problem somewhere else in the environment or for deleting a quantity of undesired email. The Actions pane at the right of the MMC will display only valid actions for the queue you've selected.

The Messages tab has similar information to the Queues tab, and it's generally most useful when you've clicked a queue and then selected View Messages. You can click the Messages tab right away, but it'll show you every message queued on the server, which might take a little while for a busy system. The columns for the Messages tab are similar to those on the Queues tab:

From Address   This is the address of the sender, taken directly from the SMTP envelope.

Status   This indicates the message status, which is generally the same as the parent queue but is also influenced by administrator action (for example, if the administrator has tried to delete the message while it was being delivered, the message will appear as Pending Remove).

Size (KB)   This is the size of the message, displayed in kilobytes.

SCL   This is the spam confidence level (SCL) rating; the values range from –1 through 9, with –1 representing authenticated email and 9 representing email that is almost certainly unsolicited commercial email (UCE, or spam).

Queue ID   This value indicates the queue in which the message appears. If you chose a specific queue and then selected View Messages, this should be the same for all messages and should reflect the queue you chose on the Queues tab.

Message Source Name   This indicates the Exchange Server component that delivered the message to this particular queue. Depending on your architecture, this could be a Hub Transport server in another site, a Mailbox server in the same site, or possibly even an application or client submitting a message directly to the Hub Transport server via SMTP.

Subject   This is the subject of the email, taken from the SMTP envelope.

Last Error   This indicates the last error experienced when attempting delivery of this message. This typically appears only if the message is in a Suspended, Retry, or Pending state.

The Queue Viewer is useful for locating a message that hasn't been delivered, but the message-tracking feature is also useful for this in larger environments, and depending on the Last Error field for the queue or message in question, you may be able to figure out what your next move should be. However, the one drawback to the Queue Viewer is that unless you have a simple topology, you might not necessarily know exactly *how* a message reached that particular server. For that type of analysis, you need something a little more detailed (like message tracking, also known as Delivery Reports in Exchange Server 2013, which we'll cover next).

Using Message Tracking

With end-user message tracking in the Exchange Control Panel, Exchange Server 2010 introduced a new wrinkle into what used to be a purely administrative task. In a reversal, we now see the tool that was designed for end users make an appearance in the administrative management console, the Exchange Control Panel (for administrators, of course.) The conscientious administrator now has three choices for tracking messages:

◆ Allow the end user to search for messages via the Exchange Control Panel

◆ Track messages via the Exchange Control Panel

◆ Track messages via the Exchange Management Shell

These options are listed in order of power and usability, so we'll start with the simplest first: end-user message tracking.

SELF-SERVICE MESSAGE TRACKING IN THE EXCHANGE CONTROL PANEL

Before Exchange Server 2010, the only way an end user could determine the delivery status of a message was by requesting delivery receipts, but there were two drawbacks: many companies would block delivery (and read) receipts from leaving the Exchange Server organization, and many users elected to never send them at all. This left a functionality gap that the Exchange Control Panel helps fill. This option, available in Outlook Web App (OWA), allows end users to gather information about their own messages (or other people's messages if they have the permissions). This can be incredibly useful for environments with lots of tech-savvy users but would require a little investment in training, documentation, and, above all, communication. The security conscious among us need not fear: the message-tracking function in the ECP adheres to the same role-based access control regime as all the other Exchange Server components, so users couldn't use this interface to just browse their way through random users' message history.

To access the self-service message-tracking component, simply log into OWA as you normally would, and then select Options. Select Settings and then select Delivery Reports in the center pane. This displays the message-tracking screen shown in Figure 24.6.

FIGURE 24.6
Viewing message tracking in Outlook Web App

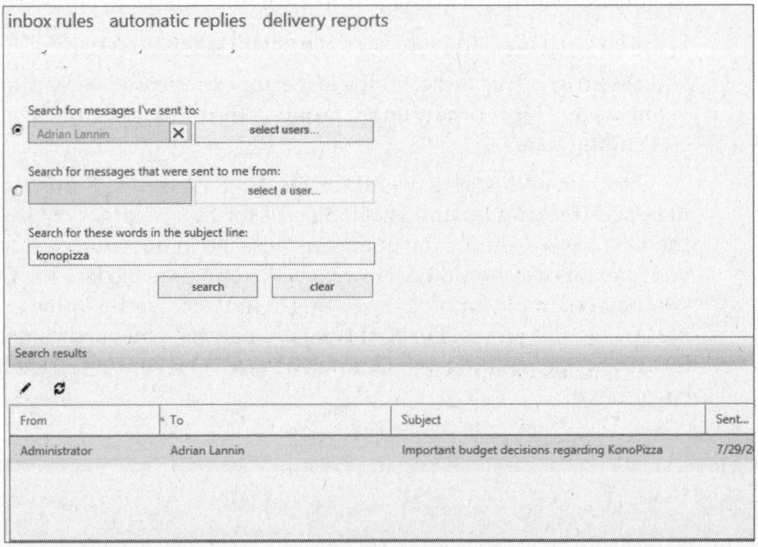

Although the title of the message-tracking pane seems to indicate that it's processing delivery reports, don't worry: Exchange Server hasn't been secretly appending delivery reports to every email your users have been sending! It's simply processing delivery information taken from the message-tracking logs (remember, message tracking is enabled by default in Exchange Server 2013).

Assuming the logs are still available, users should be able to determine information about their own messages, although as in medicine sometimes a little knowledge is a dangerous thing! Users might become so enamored of self-service message tracking that they check the status of all their messages, so any small delay could turn into *more* help desk calls, not fewer. You'll need to balance the needs of the community with the realistic expectations of delivery performance.

MESSAGE TRACKING VIA THE EXCHANGE ADMIN CENTER

The message-tracking tool, also listed as Delivery Reports in Exchange Server 2013, is very different than the one you encountered in previous versions of Exchange Server. Administrators can search for messages from any sender, to any recipient, with any subject line, using wildcards and filters as necessary to focus on the critical data. However, they are using the same interface used by Exchange Server users that is accessed from the Exchange Control Panel (From Outlook Web App).

To launch message tracking from within the Exchange Control Panel, select Mail Flow in the navigation pane at the left and then choose Delivery Reports in the display panel. This launches the web-based message-tracking tool, which is the same tool an end user would use but with a few additional options. The big difference is that as an administrator you will be able to track everyone's messages and not just your own, as shown in Figure 24.7.

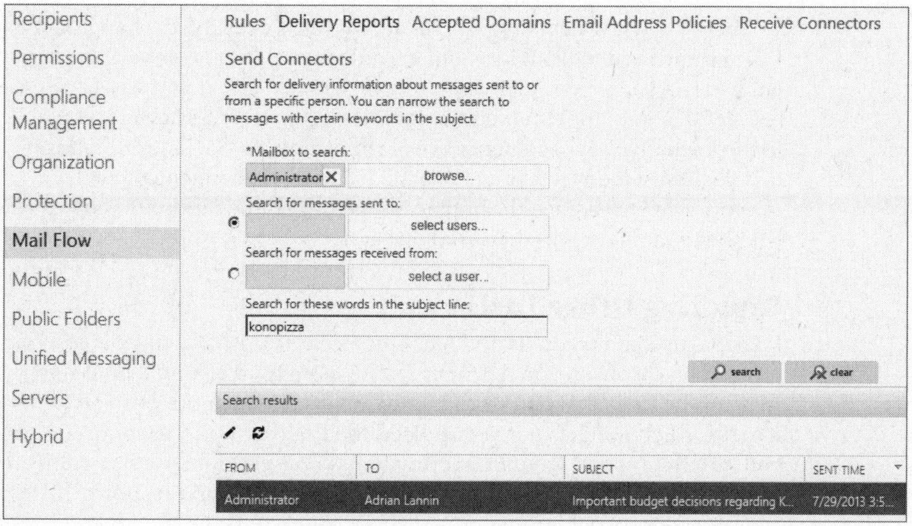

FIGURE 24.7
Tracking messages from the Exchange Admin Center

Once you've launched the tool, you'll be presented with what might be a bewildering array of possibilities. You can track on any of a number of fields, including the mailbox to search, the sender, and keywords that appear in the subject line.

Once you've entered all the relevant criteria, click Search to begin searching for messages. Depending on your search criteria, this process could take a significant amount of time.

The Message Tracking Results page is a little confusing when you first encounter it, but it makes sense after you've visited it a few times. Because messages pass through different stages during the mail-transfer process, you should (hopefully) see multiple entries for every message. At a bare minimum, a message should be listed three times, for the original notification to a Hub Transport server in the local site (SUBMIT), the delivery to the database on the receiving Mailbox server (DELIVER), and the ultimate delivery to the recipient (RECEIVE). If the recipient is in a different site, you'll see the delivery (SEND) of the message from one Hub Transport to another, and if there are multiple recipients, you'll probably see TRANSFER, which indicates that a message was bifurcated en route.

The message-tracking tool in the console can be useful, but it's a lot slower than building your own queries with PowerShell. After you've tracked messages a few times with the Exchange Control Panel, you'll probably be comfortable enough to forgo the GUI and just use the shell.

MESSAGE TRACKING USING THE EXCHANGE MANAGEMENT SHELL

Since the message-tracking tool in the Exchange Control Panel portion of Outlook Web App uses the `Get-MessageTrackingLog` cmdlet, there's little to do here but show the actual output of the cmdlet, with no input:

```
Get-MessageTrackingLog | Format-table EventID,Source,Sender, ↵
MessageSubject
```

There are a few advantages to using the shell over the Exchange Control Panel. Essentially, you get much more flexibility and granularity in your searches. You can initiate searches based on EventID, source event, or even source server. Now, if you were around before Exchange Server 2013, you might remember that these search criteria were available in previous versions in the Exchange Management Console (our previous GUI administrative console), but to have this flexibility today, you must use the Exchange Management Shell.

Now that we've gone through message tracking, you should be well equipped to determine whether a message was delivered and if not, where it stalled.

Exploring Other Tools

If you've used all the tools and techniques we've outlined to troubleshoot a mail issue and your problem isn't solved, you might be facing more than a simple mail-flow issue. If you long for some of the tools that you used in previous versions, force yourself to hone your shell technique. It's true: Microsoft has not yet updated the Routing Log Viewer or the Mail Flow Troubleshooter, both great transport troubleshooting tools from previous versions of Exchange Server; but you can still get by with the Exchange Management Shell and its powerful scripting ability.

If you've deployed transport agents in your environment, you may need to enable pipeline tracing, which essentially records every message to disk for later review. However, pipeline tracing is rather complex and is typically used only in conjunction with a Microsoft support case, so we won't cover it here—not to mention that it would deserve its own chapter! If you're curious about what pipeline tracing entails, what it offers, and (if you're brave enough) how to enable it, have a look at this page:

```
http://technet.microsoft.com/en-us/library/bb125018(v=exchg.150).aspx
```

TROUBLESHOOTING WHEN IPv6 IS INVOLVED

Many of you may have noticed by now that Windows Server 2008 R2 and Windows Server 2012 servers have IPv6 enabled for their network interfaces by default. In most cases, this is not of much concern to Exchange Server 2013 servers, except for some particular scenarios. The most common that I've come across recently is the lack of IPv6 DNS records. I've noticed that some ISPs now allow IPv6 traffic on their networks, yet most network administrators may not be ready for the trouble this might cause.

Here are the specifics. Some large cloud-based email companies, such as Google and Yahoo, in an effort to minimize the flood of SPAM received by their users, reject email messages sent by servers that do not have DNS records in the Reverse Lookup zones. Most organizations have created such DNS records for the IPv4 addresses, but failed to do so for the IPv6 address. Most will not feel any symptoms, until the day the Exchange Server starts to deliver email messages to @gmail.com addresses by using IPv6, and those emails are rejected.

To avoid the flood of users complaining about bounced email messages, do yourself a favor and create reverse DNS records for both IPv4 and IPv6 addresses used to deliver email messages to the Internet.

Troubleshooting Client Connectivity

Many of us subconsciously assume that "client" means Outlook (my favorite request to this day from an overzealous business owner was "David, can you please fix our Outlook server!"), but it's not the only client software (or device) capable of accessing Exchange Server 2013. Outlook is the most popular, but there's also Outlook Web App and ActiveSync-enabled devices like Windows Phone, Windows RT, Google's Android, and Apple's iPhone. Despite the obvious differences between these devices, they all rely on the same basic mechanisms to connect— locating the Client Access server and connecting to the appropriate interface. There have been many architectural changes introduced to the Client Access server role in this release of Exchange Server, but the basic premise still applies; identify your server's name, try to resolve its IP address, and attempt a connection to its required TCP/UDP ports.

Before troubleshooting the server components, it's a good idea to test the following:

♦ Verify that the client can successfully ping the Client Access server by both IP and fully qualified domain name. If the forest includes multiple domains, ping the Client Access server by short (NetBIOS) name as well so that you can verify that NetBIOS names are being resolved correctly.

♦ For a mobile device, verify that the device can access Internet-based content by browsing to a known website.

♦ Verify the username-and-password combination for the mailbox you're attempting to access.

If these tests fail, the problem may not be unique to Exchange Server, or if it is, it may not be unique to the Client Access role.

Troubleshooting Autodiscover

The Autodiscover service is the most important initial consideration for Outlook client connectivity. As described in Chapter 6, "Understanding the Exchange Autodiscover Process," the Autodiscover service generates an XML file with all the appropriate user settings and sends it to Outlook, which then uses that information to connect the user to their mailbox. But how does Outlook even know where to find Autodiscover in the first place? Depending on the client's location (on the corporate network or the Internet), the client will either check Active Directory for an appropriate record or look for a specific URL. There are a few different ways to check this, all of them very useful.

INTERNAL CLIENTS

Internal clients connect to Active Directory and check for the service connection point records, which are automatically published as part of the setup process. One easy way to validate Autodiscover for internal clients is with the Outlook Test E-mail AutoConfiguration tool. This useful little feature was introduced in Outlook 2007 and simply goes through the steps for Autodiscover without making changes to the current configuration. To access this wizard, start Outlook, Ctrl+right-click the Outlook icon in the notification area (system tray), and then select Test E-mail AutoConfiguration from the context menu. You can see a sample of the Test E-mail AutoConfiguration tool in Figure 24.8.

FIGURE 24.8
Using the Test Email Auto Configuration tool

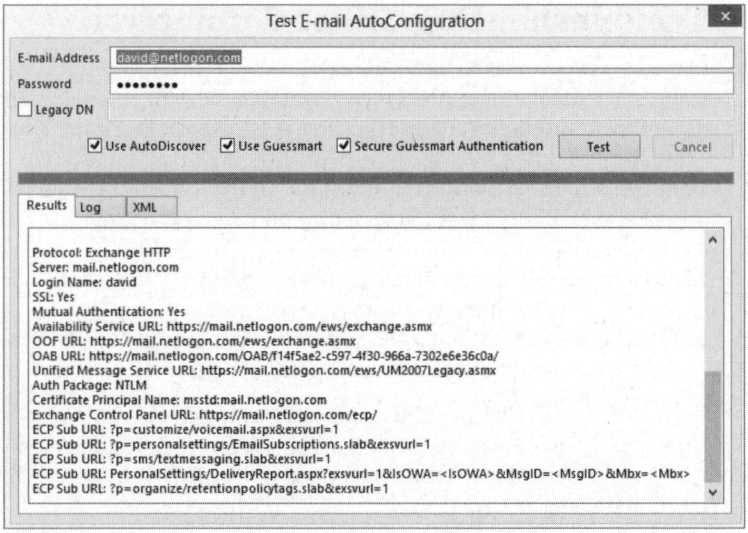

After providing appropriate user credentials and ensuring that only the check box for Use Autodiscover is selected, click Test to begin the configuration check. The AutoConfiguration test checks for much more than just Autodiscover: it also locates Availability Service, OOF, Offline

Address Book, Unified Messaging, Outlook Web App, and Exchange Control Panel URLs, making this one of the most useful client-based configuration tools.

If the AutoConfiguration test fails, the tool will display an error message. The four most common error codes, along with the most common root causes, are listed here:

0x80072EE7 – ERROR_INTERNET_NAME_NOT_RESOLVED A missing host record for the Autodiscover service in the domain naming service

0X80072F17 – ERROR_INTERNET_SEC_CERT_ERRORS An incorrect certificate configuration on the Exchange Server computer that has the Client Access server role installed

0X80072EFD – ERROR_INTERNET_CANNOT_CONNECT Issues that are related to the domain naming service

0X800C820A – E_AC_NO_SUPPORTED_SCHEMES Incorrect security settings in Outlook

Since Exchange Server 2013 requires Outlook Anywhere connectivity for both internal and external clients, the AutoConfiguration test checks the client configuration for Outlook Anywhere. When a client connectivity failure occurs, it's important to ensure that the names used to connect to Client Access services can be resolved both internally and externally.

EXTERNAL CLIENTS

If external clients can't connect to Exchange Server, you may need to ensure that you've configured your environment properly for remote access to the Exchange Server organization. Here are some of the configurations you would apply into an existing organization to configure access to Outlook with the name outlook.konopizza.ca. (In each case you'll obviously need to substitute your own domain name space.)

◆ To configure the external Autodiscover name for Outlook Anywhere, the appropriate command is as follows:

```
Enable-OutlookAnywhere -Server CAS01 -ExternalHostname "OUTLOOK.KONOPIZZA
.CA" -ExternalAuthenticationMethod "Basic" -SSLOffloading:$False
```

◆ The equivalent command for Web Service clients is as follows:

```
Set-WebServicesVirtualDirectory -identity "CAS01\EWS (Default Web
Site) " -externalurl https://OUTLOOK.KONOPIZZA.CA/EWS/Exchange.asmx
-BasicAuthentication:$True
```

◆ Here's the equivalent command for ActiveSync clients:

```
Set-ActiveSyncVirtualDirectory -identity "CAS01\Microsoft-Server-ActiveSync
(Default Web Site) " -externalurl https://OUTLOOK.KONOPIZZA.CA/Microsoft-
Server-ActiveSync
```

◆ And here's the equivalent command for the Offline Address Book:

```
Set-OABVirtualDirectory -identity "CAS01\OAB (Default Web Site) " -OUTLOOK.
KONOPIZZA.CA/oab
```

If you are in the process of configuring your organization for remote access, there is a great solution for troubleshooting your configurations in Exchange Server 2013: the Microsoft Remote Connectivity Analyzer (RCA). In 2008 Microsoft quietly released the beta of this extremely useful tool, then called the Exchange Server Remote Connectivity Analyzer. It simulates a number of connectivity scenarios, including Autodiscover, Exchange ActiveSync, Outlook Anywhere, and incoming Internet SMTP email. To use the RCA, simply browse to www.testexchangeconnectivity.com and select the appropriate option (see Figure 24.9).

Today this tool provides assistance to administrators who have hybrid environments with Office 365 and even coexistence with other technologies such as Lync Server 2013.

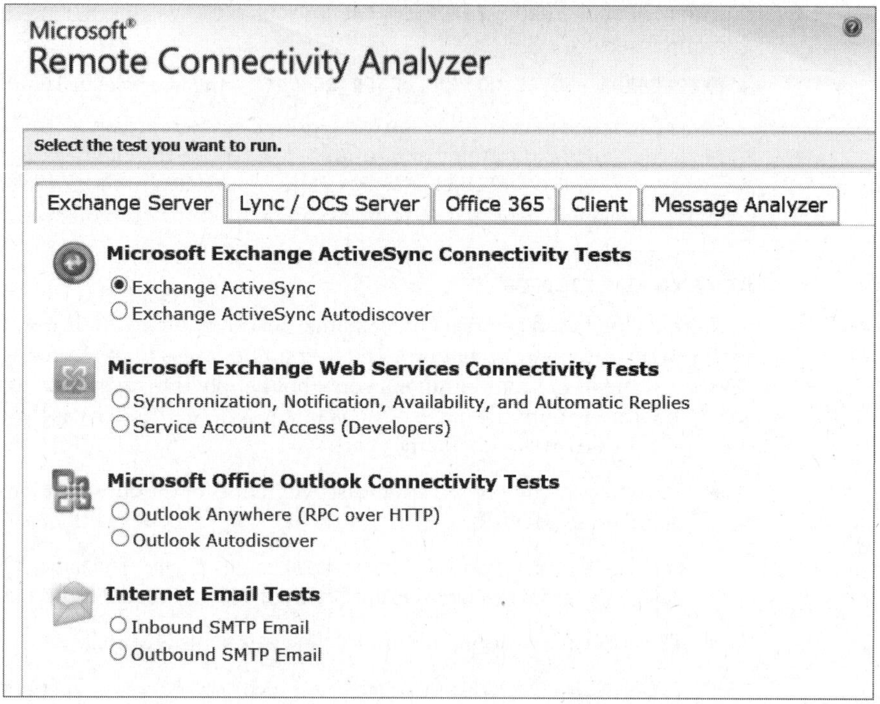

FIGURE 24.9
The main page
of the Remote
Connectivity
Analyzer
web page

Using the Test-* Connectivity Cmdlets

Microsoft has long recommended that to ensure full redundancy you deploy at least two Client Access servers in every site that houses a Mailbox server. This recommendation assumes that your site definitions correctly include all appropriate subnets, that your servers' IP addresses are correctly configured, and that all DNS records are properly registered in the appropriate zones. However, Exchange Server 2013's changes in role management have meant that Microsoft now recommends that each Exchange server have both roles installed. Based on this new math, you can expect that a one-to-one mapping of Mailbox servers and Client Access servers will be sufficient.

If your client can access Autodiscover, you know that you can connect to at least one Client Access server, but it's possible to access one service on a Client Access system but not others. How can you tell if other necessary components on the Client Access server are functioning properly? Earlier we talked about two very useful cmdlets—`Test-SystemHealth` and `Test-ServiceHealth`—that can help diagnose general issues on a server. However, sometimes you can take a more surgical approach and focus on one protocol. For this, we'll use a series of cmdlets called `Test-*Connectivity` (where * is the protocol or client you're testing).

TROUBLESHOOTING USING CMDLETS

You've probably noticed that troubleshooting Exchange Server 2013 involves a lot of cmdlets, and you're right! The Exchange Server product group worked hard to ensure that administrators had easy-to-use, robust, focused troubleshooting tools right at their fingertips, and the resulting family of cmdlets serves as a testament to those efforts.

Depending on the client you're testing, you'll want to use one of the following cmdlets:

- `Test-ActiveSyncConnectivity`
- `Test-ImapConnectivity`
- `Test-OwaConnectivity`
- `Test-PopConnectivity`
- `Test-WebServicesConnectivity`

These cmdlets are all pretty self-explanatory; they correspond to the most popular connectivity models (although it's important to note that the cmdlets to test POP3 and IMAP4 connectivity don't include the version numbers for the protocols—it's just POP and IMAP).

The suite of cmdlets listed here provides comprehensive coverage for connectivity issues. If you can run these successfully but still can't connect your client, there's a good chance that the problem isn't with Exchange Server at all.

The Bottom Line

Narrow the scope of an Exchange Server problem. One of the most important troubleshooting skills that an Exchange Server administrator must possess is the ability to quickly and effectively narrow the scope of problem. Determining the commonalities in a problem can help you quickly locate and solve a problem.

Master It Seven of your 400 users are reporting an error in Outlook that indicates that they cannot connect to the Exchange server. What are some things you would determine to narrow the scope of the problem?

Use basic Exchange Server troubleshooting tools. A number of tools are available that will help you in troubleshooting Exchange Server problems as well as possibly determining future issues. These include the Event Viewer, the Remote Connectivity Analyzer, Exchange Server diagnostics logging, and the `Test-SystemHealth` and `Test-ServiceHealth` cmdlets.

Master It After installing a recent Cumulative Update, you have started noticing intermittent issues with your Exchange server. What tool or tools could you run to help you identify potential issues?

Troubleshoot Mailbox server problems. The Mailbox server is at the core of your Exchange Server organization; all Exchange Server data is located and serviced via this Exchange server role. When the Exchange Mailbox server role is not functioning correctly, this will cause a fast-moving ripple effect through your organization that will affect more and more users. Tools such as the `Test-MapiConnectivity` cmdlet can help you determine whether a mailbox can be reached.

The Exchange Server 2013 database availability group high-availability feature is becoming increasingly prevalent in even small businesses as companies look to find ways to keep their Exchange Server infrastructure up and running as much as possible. The `Test-Replication Health` and `Get-MailboxCopyStatus` cmdlets can help in testing the health of the DAG replication.

Master It A user named Zoe is reporting that she cannot use Outlook to access her mailbox, yet she can access it via Outlook Web App. What tool could you use to determine whether the mailbox is accessible via Outlook?

Troubleshoot mail transport problems. The Exchange Server 2013 Mailbox role plays the all-important part of delivering all messages that are processed via the Exchange Server 2013 infrastructure. This is true even if a message is sent from one user to another on the same mailbox database, and the transport services are invoked to act in delivering the message.

A number of useful tools are available to help you and your users determine where a problem may exist. These include the Exchange Server 2013 Queue Viewer, the `Test-MailFlow` cmdlet, and message tracking.

Master It A user is reporting that they are sending email but that the recipient is never getting the message. The user is convinced your server is not delivering the message. You would like the user to determine whether the message is leaving your organization. What would you advise the user to do?

Chapter 25

Backing Up and Restoring Exchange Server

Exchange Server 2013 expands on the framework introduced in the previous version for protecting and recovering server data. Refinements to the product's architecture in the areas of message transport, client access, and database availability groups continue to drive Exchange Server's resiliency to new levels. However, there are still situations where a hardware failure, human error, or even a natural disaster can require manual intervention to restore data and return the system to normal service conditions. Fortunately, Exchange Server 2013 offers the ability to back up and restore data directly from Windows Server Backup in Windows Server 2012.

In this chapter, you will learn to:

◆ Back up Exchange Server

◆ Prepare to recover the Exchange server

◆ Use Windows Server Backup to back up the server

◆ Use Windows Server Backup to recover the data

◆ Recover Exchange Server data using alternate methods

◆ Recover an entire Exchange server

Backing Up Exchange Server

Exchange Server gives your organization the ability to store very large amounts of data. In most cases this data is considered mission-critical. Your users potentially send and receive hundreds of emails per day. Over time, this amount of email adds up. In some cases the only copy of an email or company data will be in the end user's mailbox.

Before you can successfully perform any backups, you must define your backup strategy. Your organization's requirements will drive the strategy that you need to deploy. Deploying a backup strategy without taking in the recovery scenarios or the backup requirements sets you up for failure. Knowing the backup requirements also helps you define the correct tool for the job.

You must understand why you are backing up the data. Once you know this, you will be able to define your goals and requirements. By establishing your goals and requirements, you will also have gathered the necessary information for the backup schedule.

With Exchange Server 2013, Volume Shadow Copy Service (VSS) backups are the only option for performing backups. VSS is a technology that allows you to take manual or automatic backup copies or snapshots of data, even if it has a lock, on a specific volume at a specific point in time over regular intervals. Make sure that your backup solution is capable of performing VSS backups.

Performing the backup is the easy part; restoring the data is tougher. Various VSS backup solutions are available for Exchange Server—including hardware-based VSS providers on a storage area network (SAN) and software-based VSS provider solutions. This chapter will focus on the solutions that Exchange Server provides out of the box.

IMPORTANT VSS-BACKUP TERMINOLOGY

The following are some VSS backup–related terms you'll see in this chapter:

Requestor The application that requests the creation of a shadow copy. This is typically the backup application itself. Windows Server Backup, Microsoft System Center Data Protection Manager, and many third-party backup applications have built-in VSS requestors.

Provider The interface that provides the functionality to make the shadow copy. Windows Server includes a VSS provider.

Writer Application-specific software that acts to ensure that application data is ready for shadow copy creation and is consistent upon backup completion.

Having functional backups is an extremely important part of the IT administrator's job. The first reason to keep a functional backup is for data recovery; the second (and sometimes forgotten) reason for backups is to provide transaction-log truncation. Exchange Server has always protected itself in case the system was not able to be backed up. As you know, when the transaction log location fills up, the mailbox database dismounts. So if you were not able to back up your server for several days, you risked having the server taken offline and thus answering to the end users.

Windows Server 2012 has kept up with the ever-changing backup technology by providing a plug-in that gives you the ability to make VSS backups of the Exchange Server data. VSS has enabled servers to be backed up in a fraction of the time of traditional tapes. What used to take hours now takes minutes.

When Windows 2012 backs up Exchange Server data, it also performs checks against that data. These checks make sure the files that have been backed up are in good shape and prepared for the recovery efforts. Once the snapshot has been taken of the Exchange Server data, verification is run against the data. If there are any issues with the snapshot, you will receive errors and be able to work on the data to figure out where the problem is. Once the issue has been located, you can make adjustments.

Determining Your Strategy

In the past there were several reasons why you needed to back up your databases. Some of the popular reasons were as follows:

◆ Single-message recovery

◆ Database recovery

◆ Entire-server recovery

Just as there are times when you will want to perform backups, there also will be times when you may choose not to restore an entire server. For example, if you are utilizing database availability groups (DAGs) you may not want or need to restore the entire server from your backup. Instead, you may choose to install another mailbox server, join it to the DAG, and then enable a database copy on the new mailbox server.

PRACTICING DATA RECOVERY

You are probably familiar with many scenarios in which you need to recover Exchange Server data. When such a scenario arises, you must know how to handle it. Some will be simple to handle, such as a deleted mailbox or deleted messages, while others will be more in depth and time-consuming, such as server or site recovery.

Regardless of the scenario, you need to have a well-documented recovery plan. Practicing recovery is just as important as having the recovery plan. We know that practicing is about as much fun as having your teeth pulled. But the wrong time to figure out how to do the recovery is when the recovery becomes necessary. When you are in the middle of a disaster, you don't have time to stumble through figuring it out.

Think of the practice as insurance. You put a lot of money in your insurance in the hope that you will not need it. But when you need it, you are glad you have it. Don't get caught without insurance in your organization.

ESTABLISHING YOUR RECOVERABILITY GOALS

Once you understand why you want to perform backups, you can determine the goals for data recovery. Think about how you are maintaining your backups, how long you are keeping the backups, and how quickly you need to restore the data. These scenarios will help you determine what your backup architecture should look like. One example is to keep your backups onsite (instead of storing them offsite) to meet your recovery-time objective (RTO).

Each scenario could have different recovery objectives. Table 25.1 shows how recoverability goals can differ based on the scenario.

TABLE 25.1: Sample scenarios with recovery goals

SCENARIO	DATA RETENTION GOAL	DATA RESTORATION GOAL
Corrupted database	Restored database must not be older than 1 day.	Must have empty mailboxes with basic send and receive capabilities up within 1 hour, and the database must be restored within 8 hours.
Mailbox deletion	Restored data must be less than 30 days old.	Mailbox must be restored within 1 hour.
Recover a message that was deleted more than 30 days ago	Must be able to restore messages for up to 60 days.	Message must be restored within 1 business day.

The key is to determine the minimum and maximum lengths of time that backed-up data must be kept and to select a backup methodology that allows you to restore the data within your target restoration goal.

SETTING A BACKUP SCHEDULE

Knowing what you are backing up is just as important as the other factors. To determine your backup schedule, you must know how much data you are going to back up and what the backup rate is for your specific environment. Look at the databases you are backing up, where you will place the data once it is backed up, and how the data will get there. All of these concerns factor into the design of your backup window. Once you put numbers to this information, you can do the simple math to figure out your backup window. Not only will you be able to determine your window, but you will also understand what your backup schedule will look like.

Your backup schedule will take into account the backup strategy you have identified, the recoverability goals, and the organizational requirements for the backups. You may also hear terms like recovery point object (RPO) and recovery time objective (RTO).

The RPO is the maximum acceptable amount of data loss after an unscheduled outage, defined as a measurement of time. This is generally the point in time before the event at which the data could be successfully recovered. The RPO varies from organization to organization. Some businesses might only need a backup since the most recent close of business, while other businesses may require a backup from the point of failure.

The RTO is the maximum acceptable length of time that Exchange Server can be down after a failure or disaster. It is a function of the extent to which the interruption disrupts normal operations. The RTO is measured in seconds, minutes, hours, or days and is an important consideration in disaster-recovery planning. Next, you need to determine a schedule that will map to your requirements.

If you have to back up 2.5 TB of Exchange Server data and you can back up and restore 500 GB per hour, then you are looking at 5 hours for the process to complete. (These numbers are completely random and are just used as examples.) If you need to restore your data in 4 hours, you are not going to make it. In this case, you would have to decrease the amount of Exchange Server data. You can do that by adjusting the settings for deleted-item retention or adding another Exchange server to the environment. By adding an additional server, you will be able to move some of the mailboxes, level out the amount of data per server, and fit your backup into your backup window.

Let's look at the example from Table 25.1. You see that the restored databases must be less than one day old, which tells you that the Exchange Server databases must be backed up daily. You also will note that you should be able to recover messages for a maximum of 60 days, which tells you that you must keep the database backups for 60 days. That means that no matter what solution you decide to implement, you must have enough tapes or disk space to hold the 60 backups that you will be keeping.

Alternatively, you could enable a feature that we will discuss more in this chapter—single-item recovery. However, enabling this for all mailboxes has the potential to increase the amount of disk space consumed by each mailbox, so that needs to be factored in as well. There may be more than one way to achieve an objective, and each solution may offer different advantages and disadvantages. It is important to explore all of your options to determine which solution is right for your organization.

Keep in mind that database backups should not be the primary recovery mechanism. The recommended solution would be to implement database copies. Having multiple copies online is much quicker to implement. You also don't have to worry about corruption during a restore of the database(s).

Backup Alternatives with Exchange Server

So far we have talked about the need for a successful backup of your data. Now let's look at another possibility. With Exchange Server 2010, Microsoft introduced an alternative to the standard backup methodology. Think about an environment in which you don't perform backups and you don't have to store backups. Microsoft chose this solution, known as native data protection (NDP), for their own internal deployment of Exchange Server 2010 and continues to use it within the Exchange Server 2013–based Office 365 Exchange Online service. NDP works by relying on log shipping and data replication to ensure that multiple copies of every database exist to provide redundancy within the datacenter and between datacenters. If ever there is a failure, causing an active database copy to become unavailable, another copy is activated automatically. By doing this, Microsoft has been able to minimize backup and maintenance costs.

This may be a lifestyle change for most IT shops. Imagine the conversation you will have with the CIO when you tell him that you are not going to be backing up his Exchange Server mailbox. Naturally, this will not be the most welcoming topic to begin with. We have all run across situations that we wanted to change but can't because things have always been done a certain way. Backups are just the next topic in that conversation. Even after you have had the discussion, you still may not be the most popular person in the room. The proof is in the pudding. As you know, Exchange Server 2013 brings about new technical capabilities that will help fill in the gap. Here are some of the most common issues and their solutions:

Individual Message Recovery   No more need for a third-party solution. Exchange Server gives you the ability to recover an individual item—just enable and configure. This is known as *single-item recovery*.

Corrupted Mailbox Database   If you know when the corruption occurred, you can use the transaction log replay lag on the DAG to recover the database minus the log that caused the corruption in the original database. This is known as using a *lagged mailbox database copy*.

Mailbox Recovery   By default, Exchange Server is set to keep deleted mailboxes for 30 days. This *deleted-mailbox retention policy* is an adjustable setting that can be specified based on the organization requirements.

Hard-Drive Failure   Multiple copies of the database placed in the DAG help protect against drive failures.

Complete Server Failure   Because no single server can host more than one copy of a given database, distributing the database copies across multiple servers in a DAG replicates data and provides redundancy for the server.

Site Failure   Stretch the DAG across to a remote datacenter instead of performing offsite backups.

Microsoft recommends that you have a minimum of three non-lagged copies in your DAG before you implement this backup alternative. How many times have you been told not to use circular logging unless you are performing a migration or are in a situation where recovery is not a high priority? Well, here is one of those situations. Since you are not performing a standard backup, you will not allow Exchange Server to truncate the logs. Because of this, circular logging is a must. If you don't enable circular logging, you will most certainly fill up the transaction logs and bring down the databases.

Native data protection uses a kind of circular logging. Unlike traditional circular logging on stand-alone databases, which is controlled by the Microsoft Exchange Information Store service, circular logging on mailbox database copies is controlled by the Microsoft Exchange Replication service. The two services communicate and work together to ensure that a given log file has been successfully replicated and replayed into all copies of the database, and is no longer needed, before it is discarded and reused. This form of circular logging is referred to as continuous replication circular logging.

Preparing to Recover the Exchange Server

Preparing the server and the environment is the first step to making sure that you are able to recover the server in case the worst happens. It is also one of the easiest things that you will do. Making sure that you have protected your servers and have a documented recovery plan will help you when the need arises for a recovery. It is not a matter of *if* you will need it but *when* you will need it.

Before you can perform a supported backup of your Exchange servers, you must prepare the operating system. Windows Server 2012 comes with the features to back up Exchange Server, filesystems, and other applications. These features are not installed during the normal setup of the server; you must manually install them. You can perform the installation from within Windows PowerShell or from Server Manager. The easiest way to do this is to open Windows PowerShell and type the following two commands:

```
Import-Module ServerManager

Add-WindowsFeature Windows-Server-Backup
```

You should receive the following when the command has completed:

```
Success Restart Needed Exit Code Feature Result
------- -------------- --------- --------------
True    No             Success   {Windows Server Backup}
```

Your server is now configured to allow you to back up your Exchange Server data.

If you are running Windows 2008 R2, there is an option to additionally install the Windows Server backup command-line tools. You should not install these tools. Those tools require an older version of PowerShell. This older version is not compatible with Exchange Server 2013. A command-line tool, WBAdmin.exe, is installed when you install the Windows Server backup features. This tool can be run against Exchange Server 2013 from the command prompt, cmd.exe.

Using Windows Server Backup to Back Up the Server

To back up the Exchange Server from within Windows, you don't just hit a few buttons and walk away. You need to select the correct settings for the backup to work, so that it can be restored and so that it's supported by Microsoft.

Since you have chosen to use the Windows 2012 server to perform the backups for your Exchange Server environment, we need to look at what the requirements are and what will make your backups and restores successful. Before you start configuring your backups, let's see what is required before and during the backup process.

All backups must be performed on the Windows 2008 R2 or Windows 2012 servers locally. You are not able to back up a remote server. For example, you are not able to install the backup features on a Windows 2012 domain controller named DC01 and then back up the Exchange Server mailbox server named EX-MBX01. In this scenario, the backup must be run from the server EX-MBX01.

Your account must also be delegated rights to either the local Backup Operators group or the local Administrator group. You cannot pick and choose the information that you want to back up. Your only option is to back up an entire volume. All of the Exchange Server data must be on the same dataset so you can restore the Exchange Server data.

You can either run a onetime backup or use the Task Scheduler to perform a recurring backup. Your backup strategy will help you determine which is best for your environment. Either way, the same basic information is needed. Remember, to truncate the transaction logs you must perform a full backup.

Most of the Exchange servers in your organization will have multiple databases. One thing to keep in mind is that you cannot restore a single database by using the Windows Server 2012 backups. All databases in the backup set will be restored. Keep this in mind because you will need enough space to perform the restores, and you don't want to be fooled into believing that you can piece a restore together.

Exchange Server provides the option to back up a passive copy of the database(s). However, this option is not available to you if you are using the Windows Server 2012 backup features. Since the Windows Server Backup VSS requestor is communicating with the Exchange Server 2013 VSS writer, the system knows if the database is not the active copy. You are only able to perform backups on the active copy of the database.

Backup copies of the Exchange Server database can be stored either locally on the server or on a separate storage device. You can use drive letters or a UNC path as the destination for the backup. You will have the opportunity to specify the location as you move through the backup wizard.

Performing the Backup

So, you know that you can perform a onetime backup or schedule the backups. We are going to look at everything involved with both options and then perform the backups.

VERIFYING THAT THE BACKUP FEATURES ARE INSTALLED

Make sure that you have installed the backup features on the server. You can run a command from within Windows PowerShell to verify. The following command will give you the information. (Just because you see the application icon for Windows Server Backup does not mean that you have installed the feature.)

```
Get-WindowsFeature
```

After this command runs, you will see a long list of features and roles for the server. The items with an empty set of brackets [ ] beside them have not been installed; the items with [X] beside them have been installed. Look for the line that pertains to Windows Server Backup, and confirm that it has the [X], indicating that the feature is installed.

If you are not a fan of PowerShell, you can follow these steps:

1. Click Start.

2. Choose Administrative Tools.

3. Select Windows Server Backup.

4. If you have already installed the Windows Server Backup feature, you will see the window shown in Figure 25.1, and you are all set to continue. If you have not installed the Windows Server Backup feature, you'll receive the message "Windows Server Backup is not installed on this computer," and you'll need to install it before you move on.

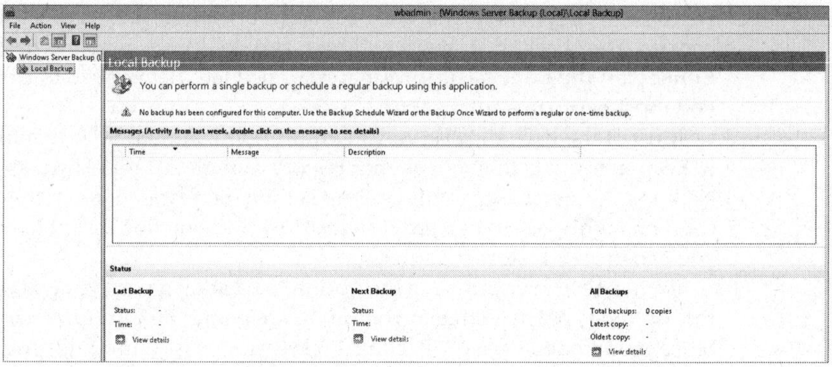

FIGURE 25.1
Windows Server Backup has been installed.

ONETIME BACKUP

With Windows Server Backup installed, it is time to perform the onetime backup of the data volume.

1. Click Start ➢ Administrative Tools ➢ Windows Server Backup.

2. In the Actions pane, click Backup Once. The Backup Once wizard appears.

3. On the Backup Options screen, select Different Options and click Next.

4. On the Select Backup Configuration screen, select Custom (so that you can select only the volumes that contain the Exchange Server data) and click Next.

5. On the Select Backup Items screen, click Add Items.

   This screen lets you decide which volumes to back up. Make sure you have selected the correct volumes for the location of the Exchange Server data, and click OK.

6. Click Advanced Settings. On the VSS Settings tab, select the VSS Full Backup radio button and click OK. Remember, only a full backup will truncate the logs if you are backing up a stand-alone database without circular logging enabled. Click Next.

7. On the Specify Destination Type screen, select the proper location for your backup. For this scenario, we are backing up to a local drive. Click Next.

8. On the Select Backup Destination screen, select the correct location from the Backup Destination drop-down list and click Next.

9. At the Confirmation screen, select Backup.

AUTOMATED BACKUPS

If you are going to be using the Windows Server 2012 backup mechanism, you can automate the process. Follow these steps:

1. Click Start ➤ Administrative Tools ➤ Windows Server Backup.

2. In the Actions pane, click Backup Schedule. The Backup Schedule Wizard appears. Click Next.

3. On the Select Backup Configuration screen, select Custom (so that you can select only the volumes that contain the Exchange Server data) and click Next.

4. On the Select Items For Backup screen, click Add Items and select the volumes containing the Exchange Server databases that you want to back up. Click OK.

5. Click Advanced Settings ➤ VSS Settings, and select VSS Full Backup. Click OK, and then click Next.

6. On the Specify Backup Time screen, select Once A Day, specify the time that you want to perform the backup, and click Next.

Make sure you are not selecting a backup time that will occur during online maintenance.

7. On the Select Backup Destination Type screen, select the appropriate radio button to choose where you want to store your backups. It is recommended to use a hard disk that is dedicated to only storing backups. Click Next.

8. On the Select Destination Disk screen, click Show All Available Disks.

9. Place a check mark in the box beside the drive you are backing up to, and then click OK (see Figure 25.2).

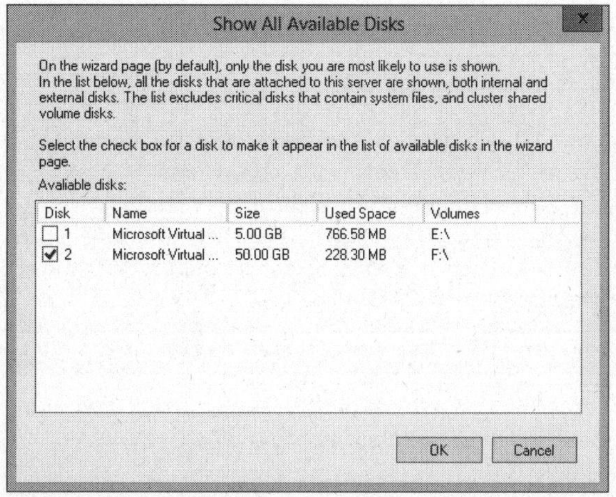

FIGURE 25.2
Selecting the backup location

10. You are now back to the Select Destination Disk screen. Notice that the Next button is unavailable; that's because you must place a check mark in the box beside the volume that you will be using, just as you did in the previous step.

Place a check mark in the box, and click Next.

11. You will see a warning dialog reminding you that Windows Server Backup will be formatting the disk. Click Yes after verifying there is no data on the volume you will be using.

12. Click Finish on the Confirmation screen.

13. Once the processing has completed, the Summary screen appears; click Close.

Your server is now backing up your Exchange Server data. At this point you are able to use the onetime method or the recurring method. Windows Server Backup will allow you to write to internal or external disks. You can also have a mixture of disks. You may choose to have your daily backups sent to an external storage device, while the onetime backups are backed up to a local disk for quick and easy recovery. Just make sure you have enough space on the destination drive, no matter where you write the backup.

The length of time the backup will take depends on several factors, such as the size of the Exchange Server databases and transaction logs that are being backed up. Another factor is the location of the data being copied and the location to which it is being written. If you choose to back up to a remote location, you need to think about the network bandwidth and latency from the server and the storage. Different types of storage make a difference as well. If you are using a SAN, your server may have a 4 GB connection to the storage. If you are using an iSCSI device, you may have only a 1 GB connection to the network and then to the storage. No matter what storage you are writing to, consider the type and speed of the drives that are writing the data. As you know, there is a big difference in performance between 15-K RPM drives in a SAN compared to 7,200 RPM SATA drives.

Using Windows Server Backup to Recover the Data

Now that you have backed up your Exchange Server data, let's perform a restore of that data. There are several ways to recover the data for the users and the organization.

USERS CAN RECOVER EMAIL

Although the ability has been around for several generations of Exchange Server, many users don't realize they can recover their own email. The easiest way for users to recover deleted email is to use the Recover Deleted Items option in Outlook or Outlook Web Access. We know this seems simple, but don't let that fool you. Education of the help desk and in turn the end users will go a long way. Once you train the users to recover their own messages within the allotted time, you will hopefully decrease the number of calls that you get.

Recovering the Database

Just because you backed up the entire volume during the backup sequence does not mean you need to restore the entire volume to recover your Exchange Server data. You are able to recover only the Exchange Server application data. At this point, you also have the opportunity to decide where you want the data restored. Do you want it restored to its original location or to an alternate location?

One of the key things to remember is that you cannot pick and choose the database(s) you want to recover. When you use Windows Server Backup to restore the database, all the databases in the backup set will be restored. Think about this before you give the command to restore the backup and overwrite all your data when you only needed a portion of the data.

RECOVERING TO THE ORIGINAL LOCATION

By restoring the data to the same location, you are recovering the data and overwriting the current Exchange Server data. You need to do this in case of database corruption. Only restore the data to the original location if you truly don't need the existing data. If you overwrite the data, you will not be able to recover it. When you are restoring to the original location, you can leave the database in a dirty shutdown. The recovery will perform the proper steps to get the database healthy. There are occasions where the database cannot be cleaned up without help. You can either perform more in-depth troubleshooting and maintenance with the `eseutil.exe` command, or you can pick a different backup to restore. You can make that call as you move through your restore.

To restore from a specific volume, follow these steps:

1. Open Windows Server Backup.

2. In the Actions pane on the right, select Recover.

3. On the Getting Started screen, select This Server (*ServerName*), and then click Next.

4. On the Select Backup Date screen, select the date from which you want to restore data. If there are multiple backups for that date, select the time of the backup that you want to use. Click Next when you have selected the backup date and time that you want.

5. On the Select Recovery Type screen, select Applications, and then click Next.

6. On the Select Application screen, make sure Exchange is highlighted and click Next (see Figure 25.3).

   By default, if you are recovering the last backup, Exchange Server will replay the log files for the backup. You must tell the backup application if you do not want to perform the log replay; select the "Do not perform a roll-forward recovery of the application databases" check box.

7. On the Specify Recovery Options screen, the option Recover To Original Location should be selected; if it's not, select it and click Next.

8. The Confirmation screen gives you a recap of the recovery you are getting ready to perform. Click Recover.

9. Once the recovery is complete, click Close.

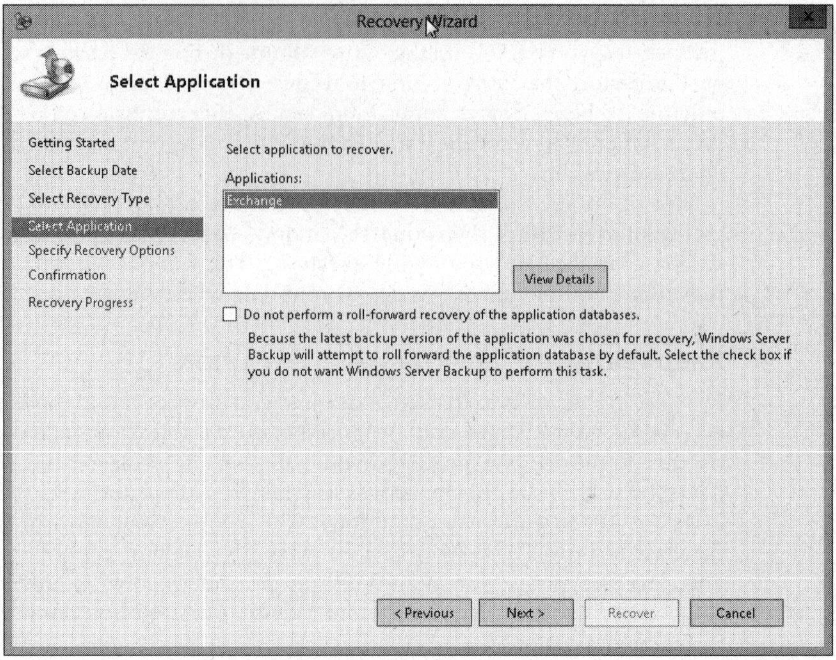

FIGURE 25.3
Selecting the
application to
recover

The recovery application will now start performing the recovery. You will be able to see the status throughout the recovery. If you told the backup application you did not want to perform the log replay, you can test the recovery by sending an email to an account on the system. Once you do, perform a backup and then make a change to the data in the account. When you have restored the Exchange Server database and logs, log into the account and look at the contents. You should see the information that was there before the backup. If there is any discrepancy, check the event log for any errors and then run the complete test again. If you kept the default settings and let the recovery play the transaction logs, your Exchange Server will be restored and up to date.

RECOVERING TO AN ALTERNATE LOCATION

When you recover to an alternate location, you can extract data from the restored data. Before you can perform any work on the restored database, you need to put it in a clean state. You will use the eseutil.exe command to accomplish this task.

1. Perform steps 1 through 6 from the procedure in the "Recovering to the Original Location" section.

2. On the Specify Recovery Options screen, select the option Recover To Another Location. Click Browse and browse to the location where you want to place the recovered files; click Next.

3. The Confirmation screen gives you a recap of the recovery you are about to perform. Click Recover.

4. Once the recovery is complete, click Close.

5. Open a command prompt and change to the location of the restore.

6. Run the `eseutil.exe` command against the database with the base name of the database.

   The base name is the first three characters of the log files for the restored database. If your log file is named `E0500000004.log`, your base name will be E05. Your command will look like this:

   ```
   Eseutil /r BaseName /L<path to logs>.
   ```

   You may receive the following error message:

   ```
   Operation terminated with error -1216 (JET_errAttachedDatabaseMismatch. ↵
   An outstanding database attachment has been detected at the start or end ↵
   of recovery, but database is missing or does not match attachment info) ↵
   after xx seconds.
   ```

   If you receive this message, run the command with the `/i` switch so that it will ignore any inconsistencies in the database:

   ```
   Eseutil.exe /r E05 /i
   ```

7. Now your database should be in a consistent state. You can redirect the original database and use the restored database. Run the `Move-DatabasePath` cmdlet from the Exchange Management Shell. You will also need to use the `ConfigurationOnly` parameter. Your command should look like this:

   ```
   Move-DatabasePath -Identity DB05 -EdbFilePath
   C:\RestoredExchange\DB05.edb ↵
   -LogFolderPath C:\RestoredExchange -ConfigurationOnly
   ```

   Your Exchange Server database is not ready yet because you must mount the database. You can mount the database via EMS or EAC, but before you do, be sure to designate the database as eligible for being overwritten by a restore. Otherwise, you will receive an error when you attempt to mount the database.

8. To designate the database as eligible to be overwritten by a restore, run the following command:

   ```
   Set-MailboxDatabase -Identity DB05 -AllowFileRestore $true
   ```

9. After you have successfully mounted the database, be sure to revert this setting by running the following:

   ```
   Set-MailboxDatabase -Identity DB05 -AllowFileRestore $false
   ```

USING BACKUPS FOR TESTING

You can test your backup by performing a recovery of the data to an alternate location. You use real Exchange Server data for testing. You may be testing mailbox recovery or single-item recovery scenarios.

Restoring to an alternate location gives you a perfect situation to test the recovery to verify that all the data is accessible. A successful backup does not mean that the successful recovery will give you good, usable data. By restoring the database(s) to an alternate location, you can run through a number of recovery options to verify that the data is there and that your staff is well equipped to handle restores when the pressure is on. By running through the recovery process when times are good, you and your staff will become familiar with the recovery steps and options needed to restore any of the server roles, configuration, and data. This will help you notice something that may be out of the ordinary if you are performing the emergency restoration.

Recover Exchange Server Data Using Alternate Methods

An Exchange Server administrator could find himself in a recovery situation where the restoration of a production database may not be desirable. Perhaps a user or administrator error has led to a situation that only impacts a single user. Or, as the Exchange Server product evolves and we start to see solutions designed with much larger databases and the use of NDP, administrators may need to rely on other methods besides database restoration for their data recovery needs.

Working with Disconnected Mailboxes

A mailbox becomes disconnected when it is no longer associated with an account in Active Directory. By default, all of the disconnected mailboxes are kept for 30 days before they are purged from the system. During this time the disconnected mailbox can be reconnected to a valid Active Directory account by using the `Connect-Mailbox` cmdlet or the Connect Mailbox Wizard from the EAC. This allows you to clean up from an accidental user deletion. Since the disconnected mailbox is not associated with any Active Directory account, you must have a way to identify the mailbox. There are three ways to do so:

◆ Display name of the mailbox

◆ Legacy distinguished name (LegacyDN)

◆ Globally unique identifier (GUID)

The following command shows you the list of disconnected mailboxes. You can see that we have also included a date command. This should help narrow your search for the specific mailbox.

```
Get-MailboxStatistics -Server CONTOSO-EX01 | where ↵
{$_.DisconnectDate -ne $null} | fl DisplayName, MailboxGUID, LegacyDN, ↵
DisconnectDate
```

🌐 Real World Scenario

MISSING DISCONNECTED MAILBOXES

Exchange Server administrators are sometimes surprised when a mailbox that was recently disabled in Active Directory is not immediately reflected as disconnected within the Exchange Information Store. This could occur for a number of reasons, such as a delay in Active Directory replication, or possibly the database where the mailbox was homed was dismounted at the time the user was disabled. That was the case for an organization that recently had an urgent need to reconnect a high-profile mailbox that had been mistakenly disabled. However, the disconnected mailbox was not showing up in the EAC or when running the `Get-MailboxStatistics` command discussed previously. The company's Exchange Server administrator tried to run the `Clean-MailboxDatabase` cmdlet but discovered it is no longer available in Exchange Server 2013. A quick explanation of the new `Update-StoreMailboxState` cmdlet, and how it can be used in Exchange Server 2013 to synchronize the mailbox state between Active Directory and the Exchange Information Store, soon put the customer back on track, and they were then able to see the disconnected mailbox and reconnect it.

Once you have the mailbox identifier, you can reconnect the mailbox to an account with the following command:

```
Connect-Mailbox MailboxID -Database DatabaseName -User UserToConnectTo ↵
 -Alias MailboxAlias
```

At any time, you have the ability to permanently delete the disconnected mailbox. The `Remove-Mailbox` cmdlet from the EMS will delete the mailbox. You must set the `Permanent` parameter to `$True` when you use this command.

By using the `StoreMailboxIdentity` parameter with the `Remove-Mailbox` cmdlet, you can permanently delete the data within the mailbox database of a disconnected mailbox. Use the `Get-MailboxStatistics` cmdlet with the `StoreMailboxIdentity` parameter to determine the values you need to supply for this cmdlet.

You can also adjust the number of days that you must keep the mailboxes. This setting will affect all the mailboxes in the database. However, it will affect only the database that is specified in the cmdlet. To change the retention time to 60 days, you would run this command:

```
Set-MailboxDatabase DB05 -MailboxRetention 60.00:00:00
```

You can also configure this setting using the EAC:

1. Select Servers from the Feature pane.

2. Click the Databases tab.

3. Select the database you want to adjust, and click the pencil icon from the toolbar to modify the database's properties.

4. In the Database Properties dialog, select Limits.

5. In the Keep Deleted Mailboxes For (Days) field, enter the number of days that you want to keep deleted mailboxes.

6. Click Save to save the changes and close the Properties dialog.

Using a Recovery Database

You may already be familiar with what was the Recovery Storage Group feature in earlier versions of Exchange Server, which became known as the recovery database in Exchange Server 2010. The basic concept is the same in Exchange Server 2013 in that you can mount a database and extract data from it. The recovery database allows you to mount a restored database and extract mailbox data from it via the New-MailboxRestoreRequest cmdlet. After the data has been removed, it can be exported or merged into an existing mailbox.

You are able to restore an existing database to a recovery database in one of two ways. If you already have a recovery database, Exchange Server can dismount the active database, restore it on the recovery database and log files, and then mount the database. You can also restore the database to an alternate location. Once Exchange Server has brought the database up to date, you can configure the recovery database to point to the recovered database.

Either method allows you to mount the database and perform a recovery and extraction of the target data. You can use databases only from Exchange Server 2013, not from previous versions of Exchange Server. If you need to extract data from previous versions of Exchange Server, you will have to use the Recovery Storage Group function on an Exchange Server 2007 server or a recovery database on an Exchange Server 2010 server. The target mailbox you will be using must be located in the same Active Directory forest as the database that will be mounted in the recovery database.

When you use the recovery database, there is no preservation of the folder access control lists. Due to the nature of the recovery database, there is no need to preserve any access control list information.

MAILBOX AND RECOVERY DATABASE DIFFERENCES

The recovery database is not the same as the standard mailbox database; here are the differences:

- ◆ Recovery databases are created in the EMS.

- ◆ Mail cannot be sent or received from a mailbox in the recovery database.

- ◆ The recovery database cannot be used to insert information into the Exchange Server environment.

- ◆ No client access is available to the recovery database through any protocols.

- ◆ No system or mailbox policy settings are applied.

- ◆ A single recovery database can be mounted at a time and does not count against the 100-database limit.

- ◆ You cannot use the recovery database to recover public folder data.

- ◆ You cannot perform a backup against the recovery database.

- ◆ Any mailboxes that are in the recovery database are not connected to the original mailboxes in any way.

There are several situations where a recovery database would be the proper selection for the restore:

- Dial-tone recovery (same server)

- Dial-tone recovery (alternate server)

- Mailbox recovery

- Individual item recovery

There are instances when a recovery database should not be used. You already know that you cannot use the recovery database to recover the public folder database. If you have to rebuild your Active Directory topology, thus restoring multiple Exchange Server databases, or you need to restore the entire server, you would not choose to use a recovery database.

WHAT IS A DIAL TONE RECOVERY?

A dial tone recovery refers to providing users with basic send and receive capabilities from their mailbox soon after an outage has occurred. Depending on the specifics of the environment and the outage, performing a full restore of the mailbox database(s) from tape can be a very time-consuming process, lasting hours or even days. This is especially true if the database size(s) is hundreds of gigabytes or even terabytes. Rather than having users completely non-operational for that period of time, an alternative is to create brand-new empty mailbox database and "move" the users to it by using the Set-Mailbox cmdlet with the -Database parameter.

Although the users will not have access to any historical data from prior to the outage, they can at least send and receive new messages. Once the original database is restored, it can be swapped with the dial tone database, and any changes made to the mailbox during the outage can be exported from the dial tone database and imported back into the restored database.

Recovering Single Messages

In the past, Exchange Server did not do a good job handling the recovery of a single message once the user had deleted it. Third-party companies have developed software to help organizations with this problem. Thanks to Dumpster 2.0, Exchange Server 2013 provides this ability out of the box. There is no need to purchase a third-party application to perform this task.

First introduced in Exchange Server 2010, Dumpster 2.0 changes the way messages are handled throughout the various phases of the deletion process. When a user removes an email item using the Recover Deleted Items tool, it is moved to a Purges folder that lives in the dumpster. This new feature is available only if single-item recovery has been enabled. Neither the Purges folder nor the messages within the folder can be seen by the end user. Any administrators who have been delegated the right to perform discovery searches can search the Purges folder and perform a recovery of the email item for the end user. By doing this, your standard administration staff can help the end user without needing the permission to restore and mount the user's database. Since the database does not need to be restored, the process is much easier.

The only individuals who can perform the discovery searches are those who have been granted the Discovery Management RBAC role.

Here is a breakdown of what happens to an email message (see Figure 25.4):

1. The email is delivered to the user's Inbox, where it remains unless it is moved to another folder by the user or a mailbox rule.

2. The user deletes the email.

3. The email is moved from the Deleted Items folder to the Deletions folder in Dumpster 2.0 automatically.

4. The email is purged by the user and moved to the Purges folder in Dumpster 2.0, where the user can no longer access it, but it is still accessible to the administrator.

5. The Versions folder is used to preserve items that are modified prior to their expiration by performing a copy-on-write.

6. If no action is taken to recover the email within the defined deleted-item retention windows (14 days by default), then it is permanently removed from the Exchange Server database.

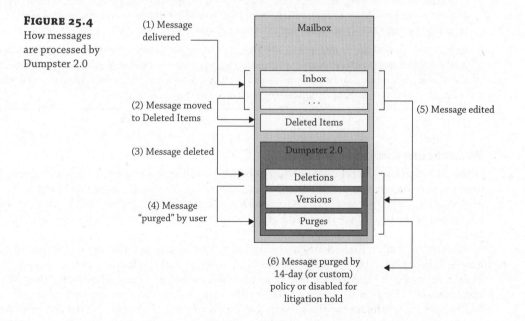

FIGURE 25.4
How messages are processed by Dumpster 2.0

As you can see, things have changed from earlier versions of Exchange Server. By moving the email messages to Dumpster 2.0, you now have an added safety feature to help your organization and users. In previous versions of Exchange Server, once a user removed the message from the Deleted Items Recovery utility or the age of the message surpassed the Deleted Items limit, it was gone forever.

All items in the Recoverable Items folder will be indexed and can be searched by using the discovery cmdlets. The Recoverable Items folder is located in the NON_IPM_Subtree of the user's mailbox, which means that if the mailbox is moved, the dumpster moves with it. Prior to Dumpster 2.0, a mailbox move meant that the user would lose access to items that had been deleted from the mailbox. There are three subfolders in the Recoverable Items folder:

Deletions   All soft-deleted items from the Deleted Items folder within the mailbox end up here. The user can see these items when they access the Recover Deleted Items feature in Outlook or OWA.

Versions   The original item and any modifications of the item are placed here, when either a litigation hold (covered in Chapter 18, "Getting Started with Email Archiving") or single-item recovery is enabled. This folder is not visible to the end user.

Purges   All hard-deleted items end up here, when either legal hold or single-item recovery is enabled. This folder is not visible to the end user.

Recoverable items are not counted against the user's quota. These messages are instead counted against the recoverable items size limits. There is a 20 GB soft limit for the recoverable items. At the 20 GB point, administrators are notified of the size by an event in the event log and by an Operations Manager alert if Operations Manager is in the environment. The alert fires as soon as the 20 GB limit is reached and once a day until it has been addressed. There is a hard limit of 30 GB on the recoverable items. You can run two EMS commands to set the warning level and the quota sizes:

```
Set-Mailbox -Identity MailboxName -RecoverableItemsWarningQuota 12GB

Set-Mailbox -Identity MailboxName -RecoverableItemsQuota 15GB
```

Earlier, we said email is removed from Exchange Server at the 14-day mark. This is the default setting for Exchange Server. If you have installed Exchange Server 2013 and have not made any changes, then your system is set up for the 14 days. You can change the amount of time that the messages will stay in the dumpster before they are removed. There are good and bad points to making this change. If you make the change to keep the messages for 30 days, you can recover a user's mail for the extra 16 days time; that is the good part. The not-so-good part is that now you have increased your storage requirements. Depending on the size of your organization and the amount of email that is sent and received, this may not be a huge problem. But if you have a large organization and your users send and receive a lot of email, this may end up being a large problem. Each organization is different—just be sure that before you make a change to the default settings you fully understand the impact on the environment.

Another thing to consider is the number of times that you have to perform these single-item restores of messages that are older than the default settings. If you find your organization is not performing this type of restore often or that the data is within the 14 days, then there is no reason to change the defaults. This information will help you decide if changing the defaults is the right way to go. If you are performing the restores past the 14 days but only a few times a year, what is the impact? Changing the defaults would fix the problem, but at what cost? Would it have been just as easy to perform a restore of the database for those few cases? That is something you will need to research. Table 25.2 shows the breakout for the single-item recovery features. It will help you see what the settings will provide you in the end.

TABLE 25.2:   Single-item recovery features

FEATURE STATE	SOFT-DELETED ITEMS KEPT IN DUMPSTER	MODIFIED AND HARD-DELETED ITEMS KEPT IN DUMPSTER	USER CAN PURGE ITEMS FROM DUMPSTER	MRM AUTOMATICALLY PURGES ITEMS FROM DUMPSTER
Item recovery disabled	Yes	No	Yes	Yes, 14 days by default and 120 days for calendar items
Single-item recovery enabled	Yes	Yes	No	Yes, 14 days by default and 120 days for calendar items
Litigation hold enabled	Yes	Yes	No	No

CONFIGURING FOR SINGLE-ITEM RECOVERY

Since you know you can change the default number of days from 14 to a new number, let's look at how to do it. For this example, we will change the limit to 30 days. A simple command from the EMS enables single-item recovery for a specific mailbox.

ENABLING SINGLE-ITEM RECOVERY

The following command will enable single-item recovery on a specific user's mailbox:

```
Set-Mailbox MailboxName -SingleItemRecoveryEnabled $True
```

Once you have enabled single-item recovery, you must specify the amount of time for which the items will be recoverable:

```
Set-Mailbox MailboxName -RetainDeletedItemsFor NumberofDays
```

You can combine these commands into a single one. To enable all the mailboxes on the same database and set the number of days to 30, type the following command:

```
Get-Mailbox -Database DatabaseName | Set-Mailbox ↵
-SingleItemRecoveryEnabled $True -RetainDeletedItemsFor 30
```

You can also set all mailboxes on a single server by changing the -Database switch to the -Server switch, as in the following command: (You must enable single-item recovery first.)

```
Get-Mailbox -Server ServerName | Set-Mailbox ↵
-SingleItemRecoveryEnabled $True -RetainDeletedItemsFor 30
```

You have enabled the mailboxes for single-item recovery; now perform the recovery. There are two ways to search mailboxes for deleted items: by using the Search-Mailbox cmdlet in

EMS, also known as Discovery Search, and by conducting an In-Place eDiscovery search in the EAC. However, only the `Search-Mailbox` cmdlet will allow you to search exclusively for items that have been purged. An In-Place eDiscovery search will search through the mailbox for deleted and non-deleted items, and present both in the results.

Next, you will use the EAC and an In-Place eDiscovery Search tool to locate the message that needs to be recovered. Once you have located the message, you will export it from the Discovery Search Mailbox into the user's mailbox.

You must know what item you are looking for in the Discovery Search Mailbox. You can use date ranges, keywords, sender or recipient address, or message type. First, you need to create the Discovery Search.

1. Open a web browser and navigate to the EAC URL on one of your Client Access servers (for example, `https://mail.jumprock.net/ecp`).

2. If you get a certificate error, you may be using a non-trusted self-signed certificate. Click the option Continue To This Website.

3. Log into the web interface with an account that has access to create and execute Discovery Searches. Any member of the Discovery Management Exchange security group will have the necessary permissions.

4. Select Compliance Management from the Feature pane. If you don't see Compliance Management in the Feature pane, you don't have permissions to perform Discovery Searches.

5. Select In-Place eDiscovery & Hold.

6. Click the plus (+) sign to create a new search. The New In-Place Discovery & Hold dialog will open.

7. Type a name for the search, and enter a description, if desired. It may be a good idea to put information, such as a help desk case number or details about the items being recovered, here. Other individuals with search permissions will be able to view your search, so make sure that you use a descriptive name (see Figure 25.5). Click Next.

8. Select the option Specify Mailboxes To Search, and click the plus (+) sign to select the mailbox that you want to recover items from.

9. Select the correct mailbox, click Add, and then click OK. Click Next.

10. On the Search Query page, you can specify characteristics about the message that you are trying to recover that will help filter it from other messages. The more details you can get from the end user about the message you are trying to recover, the more targeted the results of your search will be. Enter the information to build the search query, and click Next (see Figure 25.6).

11. On the In-Place Hold Settings page, just click Finish.

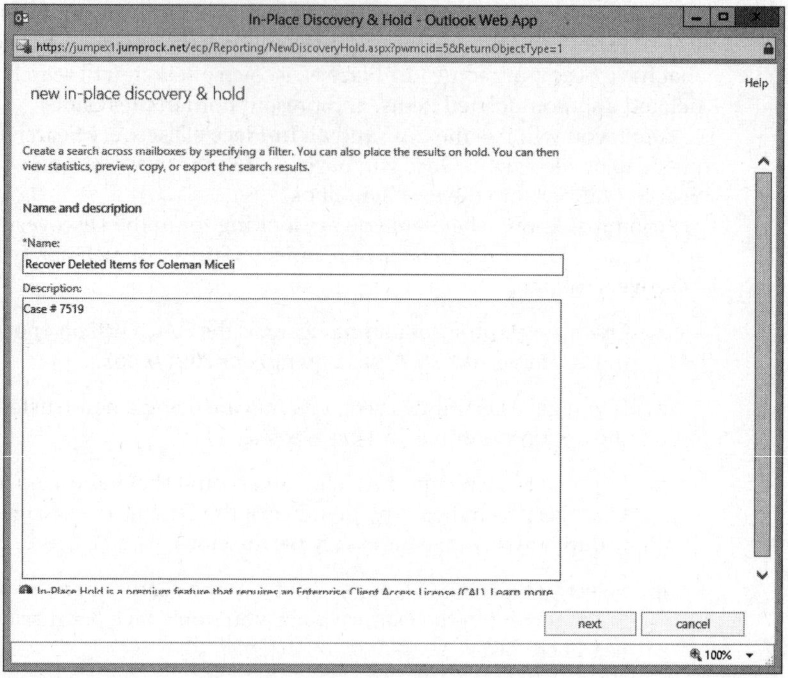

FIGURE 25.5
Search name and
description

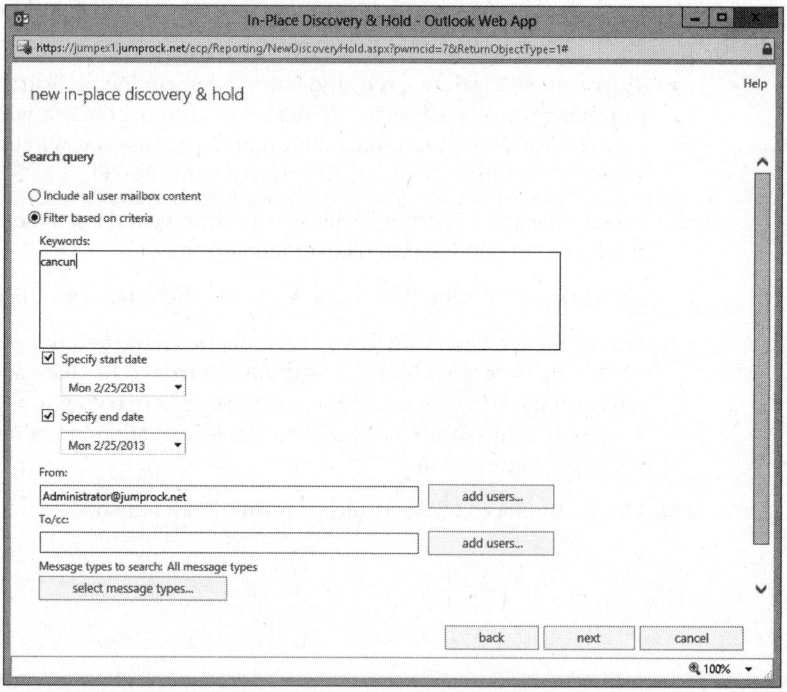

FIGURE 25.6
The Search
Query page

THE NEW IN-PLACE DISCOVERY & HOLD WIZARD

As its name suggests, the New In-Place Discovery & Hold Wizard can be used for multiple purposes. In addition to recovering deleted items for a single user, it can be used to search across multiple mailboxes simultaneously and consolidate results into one report or place the results on hold so that they are protected from permanent deletion. Be aware that using the tool for this purpose requires that each mailbox being searched be licensed with an Enterprise Client Access License (CAL).

At this point you should see your Discovery Search in the EAC, along with any other Discovery Searches that exist. By clicking on the Discovery Search that you created, you can see the current status in the Details pane, which will include the number of items found and the total size of the results. Next, you can preview the search results or export them to a Discovery Search Mailbox. To export the items, follow these steps:

1. On the In-Place eDiscovery & Hold tab in EAC, select the drop-down menu next to the magnifying glass in the toolbar, and select Copy Search Results.

2. Select any additional options you desire by checking the respective check box, and then click Browse to select the Discovery Search Mailbox that the results should be copied to.

3. Click Copy.

Now you can open the Discovery Search Mailbox and view the results for the search (see Figure 25.7). Once you have located the message(s), you can create a directory in which to place these items. All you need to do is drag the messages from the Recoverable Items folder to the folder you just created.

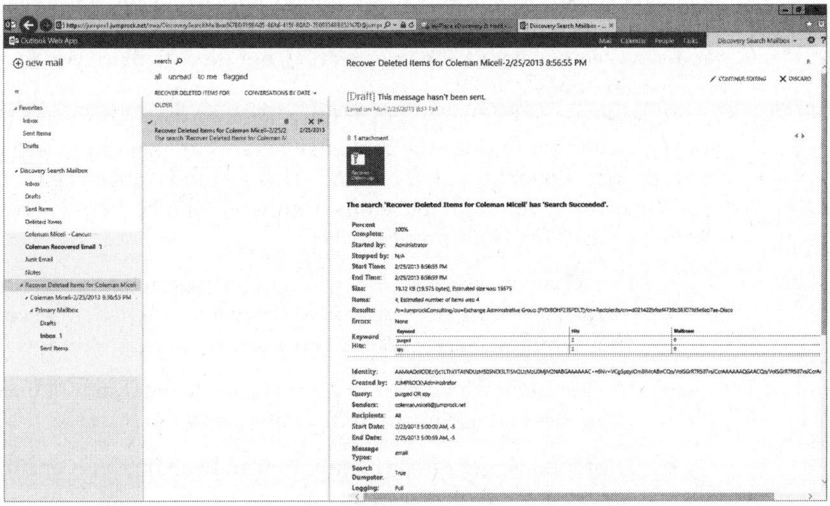

FIGURE 25.7
Search results in the Discovery Search Mailbox

The Discovery Search Mailbox is a resource mailbox. As such, it does not have an owner. You will only be able to view the Discovery Search Mailbox if you have permission to do so. When you ran the Discovery Search, all the email that fit the criteria was copied to this mailbox. To view the results of the search, click the Open link in the properties pane on the right. The Discovery Search Mailbox will open via OWA and you will see the results. The results will be under a folder with the same name as the search you created. If you searched multiple mailboxes, you will see separate folders for each mailbox containing messages that meet the criteria. You will notice the Primary Mailbox folder and the Recoverable Items folder. The Primary Mailbox folder contains the undeleted mail items. The Recoverable Items folder contains the mail items that the user had deleted and that are still within the retention window.

Now that the data has been recovered to the Discovery Search Mailbox, there are two options to get it back to the user. Both options involve EMS, and neither can be completed from the EAC. You can either use the `Search-Mailbox` cmdlet to simultaneously restore the data to the user's mailbox and delete it from the Discovery Search Mailbox, or you can use the `New-MailboxExportRequest` cmdlet to export the data to a `.pst` file. Regardless of the method used, the user running the command should be assigned the Discovery Management RBAC role. The following example command will export the mail items from the Discovery Search Mailbox to the Recovered Mail folder inside Coleman's mailbox:

```
Search-Mailbox "Discovery Search Mailbox" -SearchQuery "Cancun" ↵
-TargetMailbox coleman -TargetFolder "Recovered Mail"
```

Coleman's mail items have been recovered to the Recovered Mail folder in his active Exchange Server mailbox. At this point he is able to do anything that he needs to do with these mail items.

Recovering the Entire Exchange Server

Sometimes (hopefully not many times!) you will need to restore an entire server. We say not many because you should have engineered a good Exchange Server solution that includes proactive monitoring, good supporting resources for the services (people), and a well-thought-out and -tested disaster-recovery plan. These pieces will not ensure that you will never need to recover any of your Exchange Servers, but they do place you in a better position to deal with such a situation.

Recovering an Exchange Server is a relatively straightforward task. Since almost all the configuration settings for the Exchange Servers are kept in Active Directory, you will use the `setup /m:recoverServer` command. This method can be used for both Exchange Server 2013 roles. However, you cannot use this command for a Mailbox server that was part of a DAG without satisfying some prerequisites:

◆ The server on which recovery is being performed must be running the same operating system as the lost server. You cannot recover an Exchange Server 2013 computer that was running Windows Server 2008 R2 on a server running Windows Server 2012, or vice versa.

◆ The server on which recovery is being performed should have the same performance characteristics and hardware configuration as the lost server.

◆ The recovery steps must be run from an Exchange Server 2013 computer that has the Client Access or Mailbox role installed.

Client Access Server Role

It is likely that you have deployed multiple Client Access servers in your organization. So losing one of the servers should not result in a service outage to the user community. Because of the multiple Client Access servers, combined with the proper load balancing you have in place, all of your users will still be able to access their email using any method they choose: OWA, ActiveSync, or Outlook Anywhere. You will also be able to send and receive email since the Hub Transport server component now resides within the Client Access and Mailbox server roles and offers resiliency through its Shadow Redundancy and Safety Net functionality. In most cases, it is quicker and less error-prone to reinstall the OS and use the setup /m:RecoverServer command for these roles than it is to try to restore from a tape backup. Don't forget that your servers need to be at the same code level for the OS before you run this command. You must have the correct service pack and hotfixes or updates that were in use on the server before proceeding. After Exchange Server has been installed via the setup /m:RecoverServer command, update Exchange Server to the latest service pack to include any hotfixes or updates that have been approved by your organization.

Since you have the ability to configure OWA pages on your Client Access servers, be sure to back up any customizations. When you perform a restore with the /m:RecoverServer switch, the server will have only the configuration pieces that are stored in Active Directory. Make sure that you have a method for backing up your certificates and any other IIS customizations that you have performed.

Before you can begin to recover the Exchange Server, make sure that you have the correct permissions. To successfully perform the restore, you will need the Server Management permission. Here are the steps for performing the recovery:

1. Reset the computer account for the lost server through Active Directory Users and Computers.

2. Reinstall the operating system. The operating system and NetBIOS name must be the same as for the server you are replacing. If the name is not the same, the recovery will fail.

3. Join the server to the same domain as the lost server.

4. Install the necessary prerequisites and operating-system component.

5. Log on to the server being recovered and open a command prompt.

6. Navigate to the Exchange Server 2013 installation files and run the following command:

   ```
   setup /m:RecoverServer /IAcceptExchangeServerLicenseTerms
   ```

The /m:RecoverServer parameter operates under the same assumptions as in previous versions of Exchange Server, which is that the replacement server will be running the same OS and should have the same performance characteristics as the server you are recovering. The NetBIOS name and the IP address must be the same as well.

When you run a setup function with the /m:RecoverServer parameter, the Setup program will ask Active Directory for the relevant configuration information. This information will be pulled from Active Directory and used during the reinstallation of the server.

You can also use the Export-TransportRuleCollection cmdlet to export the transport rules from the Mailbox server. This data can be used to help document your environment in case you need to rebuild this information from scratch in a green-field scenario.

Database Availability Group Members

Mailbox servers that are members of a DAG require special consideration before a lost server can be recovered using the /m:RecoverServer switch:

1. If any of the database copies on the server are lagged copies, document what the replay lag and truncation lag settings are by running the following command:

```
Get-MailboxDatabase DB05 | FL *lag*
```

2. Remove all database copies that exist on the server by running the following command one time for each mailbox database copy:

```
Remove-MailboxDatabaseCopy DB05\EX-MBX01
```

3. Remove the failed server from the DAG's configuration in Active Directory by using the following command. Note that if the server is offline and not reachable via network communications, then the -ConfigurationOnly parameter must be included.

```
Remove-DatabaseAvailabilityGroupServer -Identity DAG01 ↵
-MailboxServer EX-MBX01 -ConfigurationOnly
```

4. Reset the Mailbox server's computer account in Active Directory.

5. Run Setup /m:RecoverServer /IAcceptExchangeServerLicenseTerms.

6. Once Setup is complete and all required post-installation patches have been installed, add the recovered Mailbox server back to the DAG by executing the following:

```
Add-DatabaseAvailabilityGroupServer -Identity DAG01 -MailboxServer EX-MBX01
```

7. After the Mailbox server has been added back to the DAG, reconfigure the mailbox database copies by running the following command one time for each database:

```
Add-MailboxDatabaseCopy -Identity DB05 -MailboxServer EX-MBX01
```

If the mailbox database copy being added back was a lagged copy, this can be compensated for using the information gathered in step 1, in combination with the command you just ran. For example, if the ReplayLagTime and TruncationLagTime for the database copy were 14 days, then this could be configured using the following:

```
Add-MailboxDatabaseCopy -Identity DB05 -MailboxServer EX-MBX01 ↵
-ReplayLagTime 14.00:00:00 -TruncationLagTime 14.00:00:00
```

The Bottom Line

Back up Exchange Server. Performing backups is the somewhat easy part of the equation. The more difficult part is defining the requirements for the backup.

Master It Document the goals for your backup solution.

Prepare to recover the Exchange server. Before you are able to perform any backups from Windows Server 2012, you must install the backup features.

Master It What do you need to do to install the backup features on Windows 2012?

Use Windows Server Backup to back up the server. There is always a need to back up your server(s). Since you have the requirements, you need to perform the backup.

Master It Perform a recurring backup utilizing the Windows Server 2012 backup features.

Use Windows Server Backup to recover the data. You may need to perform a restore of your Exchange Server data for several reasons. One of the reasons is that you need to give a user email that had been deleted but that is still recoverable.

Master It Perform a single-item restore for a user.

Recover Exchange Server data using alternate methods. If your organization is leveraging Exchange Server native data protection, performing a single-item restore for a user will be a different process that doesn't rely on Windows Server Backup.

Master It A user reports needing to obtain a message that was deleted from their dumpster. Their mailbox is enabled for single-item recovery. What action should you take to recover the message?

Recover an entire Exchange server. There may be occasions when you need to reinstall the entire Exchange Server. You have the ability to perform a reinstallation to either of the roles.

Master It How do you recover the Client Access server?

Appendix

The Bottom Line

Each of The Bottom Line sections in the chapters suggest exercises to deepen skills and understanding. Sometimes there is only one possible solution, but often you are encouraged to use your skills and creativity to create something that builds on what you know and lets you explore one of many possible solutions.

Chapter 1: Putting Exchange Server 2013 in Context

Understand email fundamentals. To gain the best advantage from Exchange Server 2013, you should have a good grounding in general email applications and principles.

Master It What two application models have email programs traditionally used? Which one does Exchange Server use? Can you name an example of the other model?

Solution The two models are *shared files*, in which a central shared filesystem is used to store messages and each client has access to those files, and *client/server*, where the central email server and clients communicate using a distinct protocol. The client/server model allows the system to provide stronger safeguards and permissions, better performance, and greater integrity for the data. Exchange Server has always used a client/server model. Its predecessor, Microsoft Mail, was a shared filesystem.

Identify email-administration duties. Installing an Exchange Server system is just the first part of the job. Once it's in place, it needs to be maintained. Be familiar with the various duties and concerns that will be involved with the care and feeding of Exchange Server.

Master It What are the various types of duties that a typical Exchange Server administrator will expect to perform?

Solution Recipient management tasks, basic monitoring tasks, daily troubleshooting tasks, security-related tasks, client administration tasks, and application integration tasks are typical duties of an Exchange Server administrator.

Chapter 2: Introducing the Changes in Exchange Server 2013

Understand the changes in the Exchange Server roles. Significant changes were made to the Exchange Server 2013 architecture to improve the scalability, security, and stability. Requiring an x64-based operating system and hardware dramatically provides scalability and performance of Exchange Server 2013. The database schema changes in this latest release have greatly reduced the performance toll that database writes and reads put on the server. This greatly improves the Exchange Server 2013 disk I/O profile over previous versions. The x64 architecture also means that Exchange Server 2013 can now access more than 3 GB of physical memory. Microsoft has tested server configurations with several hundreds of GB of physical memory. The additional physical memory means that data can be cached and written to disk more efficiently.

Master It You are planning your Exchange Server 2013 infrastructure to provide basic messaging functionality (email, shared calendars, and Windows phones). Which Exchange Server roles will you need to deploy?

Solution As of Exchange Server 2013, all Exchange Server deployments require the Mailbox and Client Access roles. The Hub Transport and Unified Messaging roles no longer exist.

Understand the changes in Exchange Server architecture. Microsoft introduced not only role consolidation in Exchange Server 2013, but also a new mechanism from client connectivity. RPC connectivity has not only been replaced by an "all-in" move to Outlook Anywhere, but Client Access is also now your entry point for email messages coming from the Internet. In Exchange Server 2010, Outlook Anywhere was the *recommended* mechanism for connectivity from Outlook clients. In Exchange Server 2013, Outlook Anywhere is the *only* mechanism for connectivity from Outlook clients. In Exchange Server 2010, the Hub Transport and Edge Transport roles were the *only* server roles that handled SMTP connectivity. In Exchange Server 2013, *neither* of those two roles exist, and all SMTP connectivity is handled by *both* the Client Access and Mailbox server roles.

Master It You are planning a training session for your junior administrators to prepare them in their SMTP connectivity troubleshooting tasks. Which server role should you recommend they inspect when attempting to troubleshoot email delivery problems?

Solution As of Exchange Server 2013, the entry for email from the Internet is the Client Access server. However, the Mailbox server also plays a role in handling email delivery. All inbound email messages from the Internet are proxied to a Mailbox server from a Client Access server. Administrators need to review the SMTP components on all server roles in Exchange Server 2013 when troubleshooting email delivery issues.

Chapter 3: Understanding Availability, Recovery, and Compliance

Distinguish between availability, backup and recovery, and disaster recovery. When it comes to keeping your Exchange Server 2013 deployment healthy, you have a lot of options provided out of the box. Knowing which problems they solve is critical to deploying them correctly.

Master It You have been asked to select a backup type that will back up all data once per week but on a daily basis will ensure that the server does not run out of transaction log disk space.

Solution Create a backup schedule that performs a full backup once per week and an incremental backup once per week.

Determine the best option for disaster recovery. When creating your disaster-recovery plans for Exchange Server 2013, you have a variety of options to choose from. Exchange Server

2013 includes an improved ability to integrate with external systems that will widen your recovery possibilities.

Master It What are the different types of disaster recovery?

Solution The two main types of disaster recovery are on-premises and off-premises. On-premises solutions include the use of out-of-the-box functionalities such as database availability groups, appliances, remote managed services, or some combination of these. Off-premises solutions are supplied by hosted service providers, who can offer other types of services.

Distinguish between the different types of availability meant by the term *high availability*. The term *high availability* means different things to different people. When you design and deploy your Exchange Server 2013 solution, you need to be confident that everyone is designing for the same goals.

Master It What four types of availability are there?

Solution Service availability is the overall availability of the Exchange Server service as a whole, rather than focusing on specific pieces of the Exchange Server organization. This includes needing to consider the availability of services that Exchange Server depends on but may be outside the control of your Exchange Server team.

Network availability is the ability to ensure that incoming client or server connections can still be processed even if an Exchange server or component is down.

Data availability is ensuring that multiple copies of Exchange Server mailbox data can be accessed, automatically if possible, by the Exchange Server system.

Storage availability concerns the design of the storage system to protect against individual disk failures and other single points of failure.

Implement the four pillars of compliance and governance activities. Ensuring that your Exchange Server 2013 organization meets your regular operational needs means thinking about the topics of compliance and governance within your organization.

Master It What are the four pillars of compliance and governance as applied to a messaging system?

Solution Discovery is the ability to quickly and efficiently search your messaging system for specific message data. This is often critical for auditing or legal reasons.

Compliance is the ability to define, manage, and monitor how the policies and regulations that govern your organization are applied to your messaging system.

Archival is the protection of key data that has entered the messaging system, often for a period of several years. Archival is useful for several purposes.

Retention is the ability to define and distinguish between messaging data that is critical to keep and messaging data that can be safely removed from the system.

Chapter 4: Virtualizing Exchange Server 2013

Evaluate the possible virtualization impacts. Knowing the impacts that virtualization can have will help you make the virtualization a success. Conversely, failure to realize how virtualization will impact your environment can end up making virtualization a poor choice.

Master It What kind of impact would virtualizing Exchange have in your environment?

Solution Gather performance information from your current email servers. After you have gathered the information, use the return-on-investment calculation tools and a tool such as Microsoft Hyper-Green to get an idea of where your organization will be once you have finished virtualizing Exchange.

Evaluate the existing Exchange environment. Before you can determine the feasibility of a virtualized Exchange environment, you must know how your current systems are performing.

Master It Are your Exchange servers good candidates for virtualization?

Solution Run the numbers. Verify that your servers are currently underutilized and can be virtualized successfully. Once you have verified that virtualizing is a positive solution, make sure the requirements will be upheld. Verify that you will be able to meet your SLAs, recovery-point objectives, and recovery-time objectives. Set the expectations for all stakeholders around the possibilities of the virtualization solution.

Determine which roles to virtualize. There will be times when virtualization of one or more roles is successful and times when it is not.

Master It Which roles will you virtualize?

Solution Define the virtual guests and how they will map to the virtual hosts. During this mapping, include disk space, RAM, virtual processors, and network information. Validate that you have enough physical resources for the virtual guests. Verify that the performance of the virtualized roles will meet the requirements of the organization.

Chapter 5: Introduction to PowerShell and the Exchange Management Shell

Use PowerShell command syntax. The PowerShell is an easy-to-use, command-line interface that allows you to manipulate many aspects of the Windows operating system, registry, and filesystem. The Exchange Management Shell extensions allow you to manage all aspects of an Exchange Server organization and many Active Directory objects.

PowerShell cmdlets consist of a verb (such as Get, Set, New, or Mount) that indicates what is being done and a noun (such as Mailbox, Group, ExchangeServer) that indicates on which object the cmdlet is acting. Cmdlet options such as -Debug, -Whatif, and -ValidateOnly are common to most cmdlets and can be used to test or debug problems with a cmdlet.

Master It You need to use the Exchange Management Shell cmdlet Set-User to change the telephone number (the phone property) to (808) 555-1234 for user Matt.Cook, but you want to first confirm that that the command will do what you want to do without actually making the change. What command should you use?

Solution `Set-User Matt.Cook -Phone "(808) 555-1234" -WhatIf`

Understand object-oriented use of PowerShell. Output of a cmdlet is not simple text but rather objects. These objects have properties that can be examined and manipulated.

Master It You are using the Set-User cmdlet to set properties of a user's Active Directory account. You need to determine the properties that are available to use with the Set-User cmdlet. What can you do to view the available properties?

Solution Use the following PowerShell command:

```
Set-User | Get-Member -MemberType Property
```

Employ tips and tricks to get more out of PowerShell.   PowerShell (as well as extensions for PowerShell, such as the Exchange Management Shell) is a rich, powerful environment. Many daily administrative tasks, as well as tasks that previously may have been difficult to automate, can be performed via PowerShell.

One of the most powerful features of PowerShell is the ability to pipe the output of one cmdlet to another cmdlet to use as input. While this is not universally true, cmdlets within the same family can usually be used, such as cmdlets that manipulate or output mailbox information.

Master It   You need to set the custom attribute 2 to have the text "Marketing" for all members of the marketing department. There is a distribution group called Marketing that contains all of these users. How could you accomplish this using a single command (a one-liner)?

Solution   Use the following PowerShell command:

```
Get-DistributionGroupMember "Marketing" | Set-Mailbox -CustomAttribute2
"Marketing"
```

Get help with using PowerShell.   Many options are available when you are trying to figure out how to use a PowerShell cmdlet, including online help and the Exchange Server documentation. PowerShell and the EMS make it easy to "discover" the cmdlets that you need to do your job.

Master It   How would you locate all the cmdlets available to manipulate a mailbox? You are trying to figure out how to use the Set-User cmdlet and would like to see an example. How can you view examples for this cmdlet?

Solution   Use one of the following two PowerShell commands:

```
Get-ExCommand *mailbox*
```
```
Get-Help Set-User -Examples
```

Chapter 6: Understanding the Exchange Autodiscover Process

Work with Autodiscover.   Autodiscover is a key service in Exchange Server 2013, both for ensuring hassle-free client configuration as well as keeping the Exchange servers in your organization working together smoothly. Autodiscover can be used by Outlook 2007, Outlook 2010, Outlook 2013, Entourage, Outlook for Mac 2011, Windows Mobile/Windows Phone 6.1 and later, and other mobile devices like Android, iOS, and even Windows RT devices.

Master It   You are configuring Outlook 2013 to connect to Exchange Server and you want to diagnose a problem that you are having when connecting. What tool can you use?

Solution   Use the Outlook 2013 Test E-mail AutoConfiguration tool.

Domain-joined Windows clients will make use of the service connection points in Active Directory. All other clients, and domain-joined Windows clients outside the firewall, will use DNS A and CNAME records.

Some clients can also use DNS SRV records.

Troubleshoot Autodiscover. In a large organization with multiple Active Directory sites or multiple namespaces, it is essential to track the Autodiscover traffic and understand where client queries will be directed.

Master It If you have multiple Active Directory sites, what should you do to control the client flow of requests for Autodiscover information?

Solution Use the `Get-ClientAccessServer` and `Set-ClientAccessServer` cmdlets in EMS to view and configure the SCP objects. Or, you can also edit them directly with Active Directory editing utilities such as the ADSI Edit MMC snap-in or `LDP.EXE`. Once you're finished configuring all Autodiscover settings, use the Microsoft Remote Connectivity Analyzer to test the Autodiscover settings.

Manage Exchange Server certificates. Exchange Server 2013 servers rely on functional X.509v3 digital certificates to ensure proper SSL and TLS security.

Master It Which tools will you need to create and manage Exchange Server certificates?

Solution Typically, you will use one or more of the following EMS cmdlets: `New-ExchangeCertificate`, `Get-ExchangeCertificate`, `Import-ExchangeCertificate`, and `Enable-ExchangeCertificate`. You can also use the EAC.

Chapter 7: Exchange Server 2013 Quick Start Guide

Quickly size a typical server. Having a properly equipped server for testing can yield a much more positive experience. Taking the time to get the right hardware will avoid problems later.

Master It What parameters must be kept in mind when sizing a lab/test server?

Solution CPU, memory, and storage are all critical. Storage must be allocated for binaries, mailboxes, transaction logs, and tracking logs.

Install the necessary Windows Server 2012 or Windows Server 2008 R2 prerequisites. Certain configuration settings must be performed before installing Exchange Server 2013.

Master It What is involved in installing and configuring the prerequisites?

Solution Verify that domain and forest functional levels are correct using Active Directory Domains and Trusts.

Install the filter pack, and use PowerShell and the `ServerManagerCmd.exe` program to quickly import the configuration settings via XML files and configure the newly installed services.

Install a multifunction Exchange Server 2013 server. You should provide a basic, bare-bones server for testing and evaluation.

Master It What installation methods are available for installing Exchange Server 2013?

Solution Use the `setup.exe` GUI to walk through the wizard and install Exchange Server 2013.

Use the `setup.com` command-line option to specify all parameters on a single line for a quick unattended installation.

Configure Exchange to send and receive email.   Your new Exchange server should be inter-acting with other email systems.

Master It   What are the configuration requirements for sending and receiving email?

Solution   Create Send and Receive connectors to configure mail flow for both internal and external (Internet-based) messages.

Configure recipients, contacts, and distribution groups.   Add mailbox-enabled users, mail-enabled contacts, and distribution groups to Exchange.

Master It   How are recipients created, and what's the difference between them?

Solution   Mailboxes are for mailbox-enabled users; distribution groups are for lists of people who can be addressed as one; resource accounts are for conference rooms, projectors, and so forth; and mail contacts are for external recipients you'd like to appear in your global address list.

Use `New-Mailbox`, `New-DistributionGroup`, and `New-MailContact` in the Exchange Management Shell to create these recipients, or use the Exchange Management Console to do the same.

Chapter 8: Understanding Server Roles and Configurations

Understand the importance of server roles.   For medium-size and large organizations, server roles allow more flexibility and scalability by providing you with the ability to isolate specific Exchange Server 2013 functions on different Windows servers. By installing only the necessary Exchange Server roles on a Windows server, there is less likelihood that one set of functions will consume all the server's resources and interfere with the operation of the other functions. The flip side of segregating roles onto different host Windows servers is that this normally increases the number of servers that are deployed within the organization. Increasing the number of servers in the organization will result in higher cost of support, man-agement, and licensing.

Consolidation and segregation of roles per host should be considered during the planning phase of an Exchange Server 2013 project. The path that you choose will directly impact the implementation of Exchange Server 2013 within your organization.

Master It   You are the administrator for an Exchange Server organization with 1,700 mailboxes. Your design calls for a dedicated Mailbox server based on hardware limita-tions. Your boss has asked you to explain some of the reasons why you need to segment the Mailbox role to a dedicated server.

Solution   The following are reasons you might need to segment the Mailbox role to a dedicated server:

◆ Reduce the complexity of the Windows server by installing only the necessary func-tions to perform the task at hand.

◆ The loss of a single server will impact only services running on the Mailbox server.

◆ Reduce the overall load on the Exchange Server Mailbox server by removing other components that might interfere with the Mailbox server functions.

Understand the Exchange Server 2013 server roles. Exchange Server 2013 supports two unique server roles. The features of the roles in Exchange Server 2007 and Exchange Server 2010 have been moved to the Client Access and Mailbox server roles in Exchange Server 2013. Also, some of the services that were performed by the Client Access role in Exchange Server 2010 have been moved to the Mailbox role in Exchange Server 2013.

The Mailbox server handles much more in Exchange Server 2013 than just the Exchange Server database engine. The Mailbox role now handles Unified Messaging, Client Access, and Transport services.

The Client Access server in many cases is a stateless server. A server running just the Client Access role can be quickly added or removed from an Exchange Server organization with little to no impact within the environment. With that said, a server running the Client Access role holds a lot of key responsibilities. It is still the end point for most of the protocols in the organization, such as SMTP, HTTP, and RTP. The main functions of the Client Access server are to authenticate an incoming request, locate the next hop for the request, and proxy or redirect the request to the next hop.

Master It Which Exchange Server role provides access to the mailbox database for Outlook Web App and Outlook clients?

Solution The Client Access server role.

Explore possible server role configurations. Server roles can be mixed and matched to meet most configuration requirements and organizational requirements.

For small organizations, a combined-function server that hosts the Mailbox and Client Access roles will suffice provided it has sufficient hardware even if it needs to support 500 or more mailboxes.

We do not recommend installing Exchange Server 2013 on a domain controller.

All server roles can be virtualized. Depending on the client load, Mailbox servers may also be virtualized as long as you remain within Microsoft's support boundaries. It is important to size out your Exchange Server 2013 deployment before committing to a virtual or physical server deployment.

Master It Your company has approximately 400 mailboxes. Your users require only basic email services (email, shared calendars, Outlook, and Outlook Web App). You already have two servers that function as domain controllers/global catalog servers. What would you recommend to support the 400 mailboxes?

Solution Install an additional Windows Server 2012 server that supports the Exchange Server 2013 Mailbox and Client Access servers.

Do not install Exchange Server 2013 on a domain controller/global catalog server.

Chapter 9: Exchange Server 2013 Requirements

Use the right hardware for your organization. There are several tools provided online to help you properly size the amount of RAM, as well as the hard disk configuration for your deployment. One other resource that you should not overlook is your hardware vendor. Very often vendors have created custom tools to aid in the proper sizing of your environment relative to your organizational needs.

If you want to get a fair idea as to what you should plan, use the tables in this chapter, based on both mailbox size and message volume. Remember, you should try both sizing methods and select the option that projects the most RAM and the largest storage volume. You can never have enough RAM or storage space.

Ensure that the processor core ratio for Client Access servers to Mailbox servers is adequate to keep up with the load clients will place on these servers. For Client Access servers, use a ratio of one processor core for every four Mailbox server processor cores.

Explore the possibilities with the Exchange Server 2013 Server Role Requirements Calculator, and try different combinations of options. It can serve as a solid guideline for deployments, from small- to medium-size companies, as well as large multinational organizations.

If you are missing a component, you will receive feedback from Exchange Server 2013 when you attempt to install the application. The components are going to differ from server operating system to server operating system and from role combination to role combination.

If you find it necessary to integrate Exchange Server 2013 with either Exchange Server 2007 or Exchange Server 2010, you will want to ensure that you have installed the latest Service Packs and updates for the host operating systems and the server applications.

Master It   What is the primary tool you can use to ascertain the appropriate configuration of an Exchange Server 2013 deployment based on the number of users and message volume?

Solution   You can use the Exchange Server 2013 Server Role Requirements Calculator; download it from:

```
http://gallery.technet.microsoft.com/Exchange-2010-Mailbox-Server-Role-
```

Configure Windows Server 2008 R2 and Windows Server 2012 to support Exchange Server 2013.   Make sure you have all of the prerequisite features and modules. Using PowerShell is the most efficient method for quickly and completely installing all of the necessary components.

Master It   You need to verify that all of prerequisites are met. How can you accomplish this from PowerShell?

Solution   You can open a PowerShell session, and from the prompt type in `Get-Module` to get a list of installed modules, and use the `Get-Module -ListAvailable` cmdlet to get a list of modules that are available to load into the operating system. The results from both of these cmdlets will vary from server to server.

Confirm that Active Directory is ready.   Make sure that you have set your Active Directory domain and forest functional levels to Windows Server 2003 at a minimum. You should not encounter any problems if you set your domain and forest functional levels to Windows Server 2008, 2008 R2, or Windows Server 2012.

Avoid frustration during installation or potential problems in the future that may result from domain controllers or global catalog servers running older versions of the software.

Master It   You must verify that your Active Directory meets the minimum requirements to support Exchange Server 2013. What should you check?

Solution   The Active Directory forest must be at Windows Server 2003 forest functional level at minimum.

All domain controllers should be running a minimum of Windows Server 2003 SP2.

Verify that previous versions of Exchange Server can interoperate with Exchange Server 2013.   Exchange Server 2013 will interoperate only with specific previous versions of Exchange Server.

Master It   You must verify that the existing legacy Exchange servers in your organization are running the minimum versions of Exchange Server required to interoperate with Exchange Server 2013. What should you check?

Solution   You should check the following:

◆ You can open `Control Panel\Programs\Programs and Features\Installed Updates`. From here you can take a look at all of the updates that have been installed on the system.

◆ Exchange Server 2007 servers should be at a minimum of Exchange Server 2007 Service Pack 3 with Update Rollup 10.

◆ Exchange Server 2010 servers should be at a minimum of Exchange Server 2010 Service Pack 3.

Chapter 10: Installing Exchange Server 2013

Implement important steps before installing Exchange Server 2013.   One of the things that slows down an Exchange Server installation is finding out you are missing some specific Windows component, feature, or role. Reviewing the necessary software and configuration components will keep your installation moving along smoothly.

Server hardware should match the minimum requirements, including at least 30 GB of free space and 4 GB of RAM for the Client Access role or 8 GB of RAM for the Mailbox server role. Ensure that you are using Windows Server 2008 R2 or Windows Server 2012 with the most recent updates. Install the Windows Server roles and features necessary for the Exchange Server's role requirements.

Master It   You are working with your Active Directory team to ensure that the Active Directory is ready to support Exchange Server 2013. What are the minimum prerequisites that your Active Directory must meet in order to support Exchange Server 2013?

Solution   All domain controllers must be running Windows Server 2003 Service Pack 1 or later.

The Active Directory forest must be at Windows Server 2003 Forest Functional level or higher.

Prepare the Active Directory forest for Exchange Server 2013 without actually installing Exchange Server.   In some organizations, the Exchange administrator or installer may not have the necessary Active Directory rights to prepare the Active Directory schema, the forest, or a child domain. Here is a breakdown of the steps involved and the associated group membership requirements to complete each:

◆ Running the Exchange Server 2013 `setup.exe` program from the command line with the `/PrepareSchema` option allows the schema to be prepared without installing Exchange. A user account that is a member of the Schema Admins group is necessary to extend the Active Directory schema.

◆ Running the Exchange Server 2013 `setup.exe` program from the command line with the `/PrepareAD` option allows the forest root domain and the Active Directory configuration partition to be prepared without installing Exchange. A user account that is a member of the Enterprise Admins group is necessary to make all the changes and updates necessary in the forest root. When preparing a child domain, a member of the Enterprise Admins group or the child domain's Domain Admins group may be used.

Master It   You have provided the Exchange 2013 installation binaries to your Active Directory team so that the forest administrator can extend the Active Directory schema. She wants to know what she must do in order to extend only the schema to support Exchange Server 2013. What must she do?

Solution   From the command line and in the same folder as the Exchange Server 2013 `setup.exe` program, run this command:

```
Setup.com /PrepareSchema /IAcceptExchangeServerLicenseTerms
```

Employ the graphical user interface to install Exchange Server 2013.   The graphical user interface can be used for most Exchange Server installations that do not require specialized pre-staging or nonstandard options. The GUI will provide all the necessary configuration steps, including Active Directory preparation.

The GUI allows you to install the Mailbox and Client Access roles on a server.

Master It   You are using the GUI for the Exchange Server 2013 installation program to install the Mailbox and Client Access roles onto the same Windows Server 2012 system. You must install both of these roles. Which setup option must you choose?

Solution   During setup, on the Server Role Selection page, select the Mailbox and Client Access roles.

Determine the command-line options available when installing Exchange.   The Exchange 2013 command-line installation program has a robust set of features that allow all installation options to be chosen from the command line exactly as if you were installing Exchange Server 2013 using the graphical user interface.

Master It   You are attempting to use the command line to install an Exchange Server 2013 Mailbox server role. What is the proper command-line syntax to install this role?

Solution   The command line looks like this:

```
setup.exe /mode:install /role:mailbox /IAcceptExchangeServerLicenseTerms
```

Chapter 11: Upgrades and Migrations to Exchange Server 2013 or Office 365

Choose between an upgrade and a migration. The migration path that you take will depend on a number of factors, including the amount of disruption that you can put your users through and the current version of your messaging system.

Master It   Your company is currently running Exchange Server 2010 and is supporting 3,000 users. You have a single Active Directory forest. You have purchased new hardware to support Exchange Server 2013. Management has asked that the migration path you choose have minimal disruption on your user community. Which type of migration should you use? What high-level events should occur?

Solution   You should pick a normal upgrade to Exchange Server 2013. The following high-level events should occur:

1. Evaluate and meet the prerequisites.

2. Install the Exchange Server 2013 servers.

3. Move email transport, messaging, and client access services to the new servers.

4. Remove the old servers from service.

Choose between on-premises deployment and Office 365.   A common choice today is deciding whether to move your mailbox data into the cloud. Office 365 is Microsoft's cloud solution, of which Exchange Online is a part.

Master It   You work at a university using Exchange Server 2007 on-premises for 10,000 students. You want to offer the functionality present in Exchange Server 2013 to your students, but you have budgetary constraints and cannot replace all of the required servers. What is your best course of action?

Solution   Microsoft offers Office 365 for Education, a basic-level subscription, at no cost to colleges and universities. Very little local hardware is required to have a fully hybrid solution that synchronizes the onsite Active Directory to Office 365.

Note that Office 365 may not be an ideal solution for non-educational environments or for companies that require a great deal of security. Each company should evaluate that choice carefully.

Determine the factors you need to consider before upgrading.   Organizations frequently are delayed in their expected deployments due to things that they overlook when preparing for their upgrade.

Master It   You are planning your Exchange Server 2013 upgrade from an earlier version. What are some key factors that you must consider when planning the upgrade?

Solution   You must consider the following factors:

◆ Confirm that all domain controllers are running Windows Server 2003 SP2 or later.

◆ Ensure that there are Exchange Server 2003, or older, servers.

◆ Review all third-party products currently in use and that interoperate with your messaging system. Confirm that you have versions that will work with Exchange Server 2013.

◆ Examine your current backup procedures, backup storage, and processes; determine if these need to change and, if so, what you will need to purchase.

Understand coexistence with legacy Exchange servers.   Coexistence with earlier versions of Exchange Server is a necessary evil unless you are able to move all your Exchange Server data and functionality at one time. Coexistence means that you must keep your old Exchange servers running for one of a number of functions, including message transfer, email storage, public folder storage, or mailbox access. One of the primary goals of any upgrade should be to move your messaging services (and mailboxes) over to new servers as soon as possible.

Master It   You are performing a normal upgrade from Exchange Server 2010 to Exchange Server 2013. Your desktop clients are a mix of Outlook 2003 and Outlook 2007. You quickly moved all your mailbox data to Exchange Server 2013. Why should you leave your Exchange Server 2010 mailbox servers online for a few weeks after the mailbox moves have completed?

Solution   Outlook 2003 clients cannot connect to Exchange Server 2013. Exchange Server 2013 has no support for the system public folders that Outlook 2003 requires, and Outlook 2003 has no support for Autodiscover. The Exchange Server 2010 Mailbox servers should be left online long enough for Outlook 2003 users to be upgraded to Outlook 2010 or Outlook 2013.

Perform an interorganization migration.   Interorganization migrations are by far the most difficult and disruptive migrations. These migrations move mailboxes as well as other messaging functions between two separate mail systems. User accounts and mailboxes usually have to be created for the new organization; user attributes such as email addresses, phone numbers, and so forth must be transferred to the new organization. Metadata such as "reply-ability" of existing messages as well as folder rules and mailbox permissions must also be transferred.

Although simple tools are provided to move mailboxes from one Exchange Server organization to another, large or complex migrations may require third-party migration tools.

Master It   You have a business subsidiary that has an Exchange Server 2007 organization with approximately 2,000 mailboxes; this Exchange Server organization is not part of the corporate Active Directory forest. The users all use Outlook 2010. You must move these mailboxes to Exchange Server 2013 in the corporate Active Directory forest. What four options are available to you to move email to the new organization?

Solution

◆ Use third-party migration tools.

◆ Issue the Exchange Server 2013 `New-MoveRequest` cmdlet.

◆ Issue the Exchange Server 2013 `New-MigrationBatch` cmdlet.

◆ Export the mailbox in the source organization to a PST file and then import it using `New-MailboxImportRequest`.

Chapter 12: Management Permissions and Role-based Access Control

Determine what built-in roles and role groups provide you with the permissions you need. Exchange Server 2013 includes a vast number of built-in management roles out of the box. Many of these roles are already assigned to role groups that are ready for you to use. To use these built-in roles, figure out which roles contain the permissions that you need. Ideally, determine which role groups you can use to gain access to these roles.

Master It As part of your recent email compliance and retention initiative, your company hired a consultant to advise you on what you can do to make your Exchange implementation more compliant. The consultant claims that he needs escalated privileges to your existing journal rules so he can examine them. Since you tightly control who can make changes to your Exchange organization, you don't want to give the consultant the ability to modify your journal rules, though you don't mind if he is able to view the configuration details of Exchange. What EMS command can you run to find out what role the consultant can be assigned to view your journal rules but not have permissions to modify them or create new ones? What role do you want to assign to the consultant?

Solution To determine which role has permissions to run the Get-JournalRule cmdlet, run the following command:

```
Get-ManagementRoleEntry "*\Get-JournalRule"
```

The two roles discovered with this command are the Journaling role and the View-Only Configuration role. To satisfy the consultant's requirements and satisfy your desire to not give him any more permissions than necessary, you can assign the View-Only Configuration role to the consultant.

Assign permissions to administrators using roles and role groups. When assigning permissions to administrators, the preferred method is to assign management roles to role groups and then add the administrators account to the appropriate role group. However, Exchange allows you to assign management roles directly to the administrator's account if you want.

Master It Earlier in the day, you determined that you need to assign a certain role to your email compliance consultant. You've created a role group called Email Compliance Evaluation and you need to add your consultant to this role group. What command would you use in the EMS to add your consultant, Sam, to this role group?

Solution To add Sam to the role group, you would run the following command:

```
Add-RoleGroupMember "Email Compliance Evaluation" -Member "Sam"
```

Grant permissions to end users for updating their address list information. RBAC doesn't apply only to Exchange administrators. You can also use RBAC to assign roles to end-user accounts so users can have permissions to update their personal information, Exchange settings, and their distribution groups.

Master It You've decided that you want to give your users the ability to modify their contact information in the global address list. You want to make this change as quickly as possible and have it apply to all existing users and new users coming into your Exchange organization immediately. You determine that using the EAC would be the easiest way to make this change. What would you modify in the EAC to make this change?

Solution In the EAC, you select the Permissions task, choose the User Role tab, and modify the Default role assignment policy. Check the option to assign the My Profile Information role to the policy. This is the default policy for the organization, so making the change on this policy would update all the existing mailboxes and ensure that new mailboxes also get that role.

Create custom administration roles and assign them to administrators. If you can't find an existing role that meets your needs, don't worry! You can create a custom role in Exchange Server 2013 and assign the permissions you need to the custom role.

Master It Your company has asked you to allow administrators in the Baltimore office to manage mailbox settings for all users in the Baltimore OU. Your company does not want the administrators in the Baltimore office to be able to change the mailbox storage limits for individual mailboxes. What would you implement to ensure administrators in the Baltimore office can only manage mailboxes in the Baltimore OU and are not able to change the mailbox storage limits?

Solution To create a custom role and assign the role to a role group, perform these steps:

1. Determine what parent role you should use for your custom role.

2. Create the custom role with the appropriate parent.

3. Remove the necessary management role entries to give the role the permissions that you want it to have.

4. If desired, create a custom role group that the custom role will have a role assignment for.

5. Create a role assignment to assign the custom role and scope to a role group.

6. Add your administrators in the Baltimore office to the role group that has the custom role assigned to it.

Audit RBAC changes using the Exchange Management Shell and built-in reports in the Exchange Administration Center. Assigning RBAC permissions is the easy part, determining who has been assigned what permissions can be a bit tricky. Luckily EMS can be used to determine the roles assigned to users.

Master It Your company has purchased a partner company, which has an administrator named Dave. You have been tasked with providing Dave with the same level of RBAC permissions in your Exchange Server 2013 organization that he has in his Exchange Server 2013 organization. What command would you run in your partner's organization to determine the roles assigned to Dave?

Solution The `Get-ManagementRoleAssignment` cmdlet with the `GetEffectiveUsers` parameter will display the roles that Dave has access to. In the following example, Dave has access to roles Legal Hold and Mailbox Search because he is a member of the Discovery Management role group:

```
Get-ManagementRoleAssignment -GetEffectiveUsers | ↵
?{$_.EffectiveUserName -eq "Dave"} | ft Name, Role, RoleAssigneeName

Name                                    Role        RoleAssigneeName
----                                    ----        ----------------
Legal Hold-Discovery Management         Legal Hol…  Discovery Management
Mailbox Search-Discovery Management     Mailbox S…  Discovery Management
```

Chapter 13: Basics of Recipient Management

Identify the various types of recipients.   Most recipient types in Exchange Server 2013 have been around since the early days of Exchange. Each serves a specific purpose and has objects that reside in Active Directory.

Master It   Your company has multiple Active Directory domains that exist in a single forest. You must make sure that the following needs for your company are met:

◆ Group managers cannot, by mistake, assign permissions to a user by adding someone to a group.

◆ Temporary consultants for your company must not be able to access any internal resource.

Solution   Create only distribution groups in your company. Ensure that security groups are never mail-enabled.

Create mail-enabled contacts for each of the temporary consultants. Do not create any mail-enabled users for the temporary consultants.

Use the Exchange Administration Center to manage recipients.   Historically, Exchange administrators mainly used a combination of Active Directory tools and Exchange-native tools to manage Exchange servers and objects. That has all changed with Exchange Server 2013, mainly with the advent of the remote PowerShell implementation of the Exchange Management Shell, but also with the browser-based version of the Exchange Administration Center.

Master It   You are responsible for managing multiple Exchange organizations and you need to apply identical configurations to servers in all organizations. If you are just starting out with Exchange Server 2013 and you are not yet familiar with Remote PowerShell and Exchange Management Shell, you need some guidance regarding the commands that must be used. What should you do?

Solution   One of our favorite features of the Exchange Admin Center is the *summary* page. The final page that appears once a task has been run, the summary page contains the PowerShell command that executed. A simple Ctrl+C will put that command in your clipboard, and away you go with some simple Notepad editing. Though that is a great way to get insight on some of the most advanced Exchange-related PowerShell commands, most administrators will find that the online Help files available with Exchange are simply invaluable as well.

Configure accepted domains and define email address policies.   Accepted domains and email address policies, once a single concept, have been broken up since Exchange Server 2007, and that it is still the case in Exchange Server 2013. It gives you more flexibility in managing email address suffixes and SMTP domains that will be accepted by your Exchange servers.

Master It You plan to accept mail for multiple companies inside your organization. Once accepted, the mail will be rerouted to the SMTP servers responsible for each of those companies. What do you need to create in your organization?

Solution Create an external relay domain for each of the SMTP domains. Ensure that all transport configurations and permissions have been set to be able to deliver mail to those SMTP servers.

Chapter 14: Managing Mailboxes and Mailbox Content

Create and delete user mailboxes. Exchange Server 2013 supports the same types of mail-enabled users as previous versions of Exchange Server. These are mailbox-enabled users who have a mailbox on your Exchange server and the mail-enabled user account. The mail-enabled user account is a security principal within your organization (and would appear in your global address list), but its email is delivered to an external email system.

There are four different types of mailbox-enabled user accounts: a User mailbox, a Room Resource mailbox, an Equipment Resource mailbox, and a Linked mailbox. You can perform mailbox management tasks via either the Exchange Administration Center or the Exchange Management Shell.

Master It Your Active Directory forest has a trust relationship to another Active Directory forest that is part of your corporate IT infrastructure. The administrator in the other forest wants you to host their email. What type of mailboxes should you create for the users in this other forest?

Solution You would create linked mailboxes. Linked mailboxes create a disabled user account in the forest with the Exchange server and assign external account permissions for a user account in the trusted forest.

Master It You must modify user Nikki.Char's office name to say Honolulu. You want to do this using the Exchange Management Shell. What command would perform this task?

Solution You would use the following command:

```
Set-User Nikki.Char -Office "Honolulu"
```

Master It You need to change the maximum number of safe senders allowed for user Jeff.Bloom's mailbox to 4,096. You want to make this change using the Exchange Management Shell. What command would you use?

Solution You would use the following command:

```
Set-Mailbox Jeff.Bloom -MaxSafeSenders:4096
```

Manage mailbox permissions A newly created mailbox allows only the owner of the mailbox to access the folders within that mailbox. An end user can assign someone else permissions to access individual folders within their mailbox or to send mail on their behalf using the Outlook client. The administrator can assign permissions to the entire mailbox for other users. Further, the administrator can assign a user the Send As permission to a mailbox.

Master It All executives within your organization share a single administrative assistant whose username is Chris.Rentch; all of the executives belong to a mail distribution group called #Executives. All of the executives want user Chris.Rentch to be able to access all of the folders within their mailboxes. Name two ways you can accomplish this.

Solution   Any of these solutions will accomplish your goal:

- Use the Exchange Administration Center's Manage Full Access Permissions Wizard to assign user Chris.Rentch permission to each mailbox one at a time.

- Use the `Add-MailboxPermission` cmdlet to assign the `FullAccess` permissions one executive user at a time.

- Use the `Get-DistributionGroupMember` cmdlet to retrieve the membership of the #Executives group and pipe the output of that to the `Add-MailboxPermission` cmdlet, as shown here:

```
Get-DistributionGroupMember #Executives | Add-MailboxPermission -User ↵
Chris.Rentch -AccessRights FullAccess
```

Move mailboxes to another database.   Exchange Server 2013 implements an entirely new way to move mailbox content from one mailbox database to another. The administrative tools (the Exchange Administration Center and the `New-MoveRequest` cmdlet) are no longer responsible for moving mailbox data. The Microsoft Exchange Server Mailbox Replication service that runs on each Client Access server role handles mailbox moves.

Master It   You want to use the Exchange Management Shell to move mailbox Brian .Desmond from mailbox database MBX-001 to MBX-002. The move should ignore up to three bad messages before it fails. What command should you use?

Solution   You would use the following command:

```
New-MoveRequest Brian.Desmond -TargetDatabase MBX-002 -BadItemLimit:3
```

Master It   You have submitted a move request for user Brian.Desmond. You want to check the status and statistics of the move request to see if it has completed; you want to use the Exchange Management Shell to do this. What command would you type?

Solution   You would use the following command:

```
Get-MoveRequestStatistics Brian.Desmond
```

Perform bulk manipulation of mailbox properties.   By taking advantage of piping and the EMS, you can perform bulk manipulation of users and mailboxes in a single command that previously might have taken hundreds of lines of scripting code.

Master It   You want to move all of your executives to a single mailbox database called MBX-004. All of your executives belong to a mail distribution group called #Executives. How could you accomplish this task with a single command?

Solution   You would use the following command:

```
Get-DistributionGroupMember #Executives | New-MoveRequest ↵
-TargetDatabase:MBX-004 -Confirm:$False
```

Use Messaging Records Management to manage mailbox content.   Messaging Records Management provides you with control over the content of a user's mailbox. Basic MRM features allow you to automatically purge old content, such as deleted items or junk email. You can create new managed folders within the user's mailbox as well as move content to these folders.

Master It You are managing an Exchange Server organization that was transitioned from Exchange Server 2010. You have found that many of your users are not emptying the contents of their Deleted Items and Junk E-mail folders. You want to automatically purge any content in these folders after 14 days. What are the steps you should take to do this?

Solution Follow these steps to automatically purge content:

1. Notify your users of the new policy and the date/time on which it will go in to effect.

2. Create a new retention tag on the Deleted Items folder that automatically purges items 14 days after they are moved to this folder.

3. Create a new retention tag on the Junk E-mail folder that automatically purges items 14 days after they are moved to this folder.

4. Create a new retention policy that includes the Deleted Items and Junk E-mail folders.

5. Assign the newly created retention policy to each user account.

Chapter 15: Managing Mail-enabled Groups, Mail-enabled Users, and Mail-enabled Contacts

Create and mail-enable contact objects. In some cases, you should *not* create mail-enabled users and instead choose the less-well-known mail-enabled contacts. Mail-enabled contacts can be used to provide easy access to external email contacts by using your internal address lists. Mail-enabled users can be used to provide convenient access to internal resources for workers who require an externally hosted email account.

Master It You periodically update the email addresses for your Active Directory contacts. However, some users report that they are not seeing the updated contact address and that they receive non-delivery reports (NDR) when sending mail to some contacts. What should you do?

a) **Solution** A problem could arise if a user has added the recipient to a local address book; the result is that the local object is not updated and can therefore result in NDRs. In that case, the user must delete and then copy again the recipient to the local address book.

Manage mail-enabled contacts and mail-enabled users in a messaging environment. All Exchange Server–related attributes for mail-enabled users and contacts are not available from Active Directory Users and Computers. To manage all Exchange Server–related attributes, you must use the Exchange Admin Center or EMS tools.

Master It Whether you want to manage users in bulk, need to create multiple users in your domain or multiple mail-enabled contacts in your organization, or simply want to change the delivery restrictions for 5,000 recipients, what tool should you use?

b) **Solution** Administrators who have experience with Exchange Server 2003 may be familiar with bulk-management tools such as `LDIFDE.exe` and Visual Basic Scripting. However, in Exchange Server 2013, you can achieve identical results by first using the `Get-object_type` command and then piping the results to a `Set-object type` command. Those are PowerShell commands available in the Exchange Management Shell. You *must* get comfortable with PowerShell if you plan to manage an Exchange Server messaging environment.

Choose the appropriate type and scope of mail-enabled groups. Although you can modify your group scope or group type at any time after the group has been created, it's always a best practice to create all groups as universal groups in an environment that contains Exchange servers.

Master It Your company needs to ensure that if an administrator adds a user to a distribution list, that user will not get any unnecessary access to resources on the network. How should you ensure that this type of administrative mistake does not impact the security of your networking environment?

Solution Ensure that security groups are not mail-enabled, and use only mail-enabled distribution groups. This separation prevents an unfortunate addition to a distribution list when a user who is added to a group inherits access rights. The information to which they may be given access could be sensitive.

Create and manage mail-enabled groups. Creating and managing distribution groups can mostly be done from the Exchange Admin Center, with only limited options that require the Exchange Management Shell.

Master It You want to simplify the management of groups in your organization. You recently reviewed the functionalities of dynamic distribution groups and decided that this technology can provide the desired results. You need to identify the tools that should be used to manage dynamic distribution groups. What tools should you identify?

Solution Dynamic distribution groups provide the ability to update membership automatically based on the Active Directory attributes defined on member recipients. Because this is a solution that is specific to Exchange Server, you can only create dynamic distribution groups by using the Exchange Server management tools. Active Directory Users and Computers cannot be used.

Explore the moderation features of Exchange Server 2013. Moderation and moderated groups are one of the features of Exchange Server 2013 that were only recently introduced. As part of the self-service focus of Exchange Server 2013, moderation allows a user to review messages sent to an email address on your server.

Master It If you want to use moderated groups in a mixed organization that contains both Exchange Server 2013 servers and Exchange Server 2007 Hub Transport servers, what group feature should you configure?

Solution In an organization that contains older versions of Exchange Server, you must specify an Exchange Server 2013 server as the expansion server for moderated groups. If a message that is sent to a moderated distribution group or dynamic distribution group is expanded on an Exchange Server 2007 Hub Transport server, it will be delivered to all members of that distribution group, bypassing the moderation process. By specifying an Exchange Server 2013 server as the expansion server, you ensure that all messages are moderated.

Chapter 16: Managing Resource Mailboxes

Understand how resource mailboxes differ from regular mailboxes. Resource mailboxes serve a different purpose in Exchange Server 2013 than standard user mailboxes and thus have different features and capabilities. Understanding how resource mailboxes are different, including what added features are provided, can help improve the end-user experience and increase adoption rate.

Master It   You are planning to create resource mailboxes to support conference room and other resource scheduling. Identify how the resource mailboxes are different from regular user mailboxes.

Solution   Resource mailboxes, such as conference room mailboxes, show up in the All Rooms address list. Room and equipment mailboxes have a different icon in address lists.

Resource mailboxes can have additional properties defined, such as the seating capacity of the room and details of a particular piece of equipment.

Create resource mailboxes.   Creating resource mailboxes is easy using various tools in Exchange Server. Users need resource mailboxes for conference rooms and equipment to allow for easier, more informative scheduling.

Master It   What tools are available to create resource mailboxes and to define additional schema properties for resource mailboxes?

Solution   Using the EAC, select the New Room Mailbox Wizard, and specify room or equipment when creating the mailbox. Using the EMS, use New-Mailbox with the -room or -equipment parameter to create a resource mailbox. Use Set-ResourceConfig in the EMS to define additional schema properties, and use the EAC or EMS to define capacity and features for each resource mailbox.

Configure resource mailbox booking and scheduling policies.   Properly configured resource mailboxes help users find the correct resource and determine whether it is available when needed. When the resource mailbox is properly configured, users can quickly and easily find conference rooms that have the proper capacity and features needed to hold a meeting.

Master It   You need to configure a resource mailbox to handle automatic scheduling. What tools can you use?

Solution   Use the Resource tabs in the EAC, the Resource settings in Outlook Web App, or the Set-ResourceConfig, Set-CalendarProcessing, and Set-MailboxCalendarConfiguration cmdlets in the EMS to configure resource accounts correctly.

Migrate resource mailboxes.   Moving resource mailboxes from legacy versions of Exchange Server requires proper planning and execution to ensure that Exchange Server 2013 features and capabilities for resource mailboxes are available. Resource mailboxes in Exchange Server versions prior to 2007 were standard user accounts, and they need to be migrated and converted to resource mailboxes in Exchange Server 2013.

Master It   You have moved a resource mailbox from an Exchange Server 2003 Mailbox server to an Exchange Server 2013 Mailbox server. You need to convert this resource to an Exchange Server 2013 resource mailbox. What steps should you take?

Solution   Follow these steps to convert the mailbox:

1. Disable any automated processing or scripts that were enabled in Exchange Server 2003.

2. Use the EMS Set-Mailbox cmdlet with the -Room option to convert the mailbox type.

3. Use Outlook Web App, the EAC, or the EMS to define the resource rules and to enable the automatic processing of schedule requests.

Chapter 17: Managing Modern Public Folders

Understand the architectural changes made to public folders. If you're coming new to Exchange Server 2013 or don't have a lot of investment in public folders in your current Exchange Server organization, you probably haven't been too worried about the rumors of the demise of public folders. These rumors are fortunately not true; public folders are still supported in Exchange Server 2013.

Master It You are the administrator of a distributed messaging environment that runs Exchange Server 2013. You plan to deploy a collaboration solution, and you are currently evaluating public folders as well as site mailboxes and shared mailboxes. You need to identify the limitations of each solution and present recommendations to your company's executives. What information should you present?

Solution Advantages of public folders:

◆ Public folders now use DAG to provide high availability.

◆ As the multi-master replication model has been deprecated, users will not have convergence issues that created problems in previous iterations of Exchange Server.

The following are disadvantages of public folders:

◆ The implementation of DAGs might have an effect on geographically dispersed implementations.

◆ Public folders cannot be accessed by POP3 and IMAP4 clients.

◆ Storing large files is not an efficient use of public folders.

Manage public folders. You are managing a large distributed Exchange Server infrastructure, and you want to create a hierarchy of public folders to reflect the organizational structure of your enterprise environment. How you can do it in Exchange Server 2013?

Master It Start with the Public Folder Mailbox, then define the various Departments within your folder structure. You can add various nested folders underneath the Departments parent folder, and manage the folder structure underneath, and make modifications to the permission structure to reflect the needs of the organization.

Solution All of this can be managed through the EAC, but very often you can get more feedback from the Exchange Management Shell.

```
New-Mailbox -PublicFolder
```

```
New-PublicFolder
```

```
Set-PublicFolderClientPermission
```

```
Get-PublicFolderStatistics
```

Explore all of the cmdlets to manage public folders, and you'll be able to more efficiently manage your public folder environment.

Chapter 18: Managing Archiving and Compliance

Understand the basic principles of email archiving. An archiving solution not only provides a way to ease the pain of storage problems on Exchange Server whether they are with the databases or with PST files but also assists in helping organizations become compliant and make discovery of email easier.

Master It How can government organizations actively comply with regulations on open records laws to taxpayers?

Solution The Freedom of Information Act allows for the full or partial disclosure of previously unreleased information and documents controlled by the U.S. government.

Ensure your company complies with regulations. It is extremely important that your messaging system be configured in such a way that email data is managed according to laws and regulations.

Master It Which laws and regulations are in effect in your business, and what does it mean for your organization?

Solution Work with your legal and HR departments to determine which laws and regulations you need to comply with. Once you have these policies, use Exchange Server 2013 retention-management policies to configure email retention and manage content as defined by the regulations.

Enable Exchange Server 2013 in-place archiving. Exchange Server 2013 allows for more efficient management of the user's primary mailbox by enabling the mailbox for archiving and using policies to move the content between the mailbox and the archive.

Master It How does archiving allow for moving older email content automatically from the primary mailbox to the In-Place Archive?

Solution You can archive-enable the mailbox by using the following PowerShell example:

```
Enable-Mailbox "John Doe" -archive
```

Use Exchange Server 2013 retention policies. Retention policies define how long data must be retained before it is automatically removed when the time setting has been met.

Master It You can create as many policies as you need; however, in many organizations retention policies will be created per department (for instance, finance).

Solution You can assign a retention policy to the mailbox by using the following PowerShell example:

```
Set-Mailbox "John Doe" -RetentionPolicy "Finance"
```

Use Exchange Server 2013 In-Place eDiscovery and Hold. In certain situations you may need to prevent deletion of email for a period of time while an end user is away and unable to attend to their mailbox.

Master It Without retention hold, and depending on the policies that may be active and applied to the user, messages may have been moved from the primary mailbox to the archive or even deleted. What is the cmdlet to put a mailbox on retention hold?

Solution   You have the option to temporarily suspend the retention policies from processing the mailbox for a set amount of time by placing the mailbox on a retention hold. You can place a mailbox on retention hold by using the following PowerShell example:

```
Set-Mailbox "John Doe" -RetentionHoldEnabled $true
```

Chapter 19: Creating and Managing Mailbox Databases

Identify the core components of Exchange Server database storage.   The ability to identify the components of your Exchange servers that provide storage functionality will allow you to properly plan and troubleshoot storage.

Master It   You plan to have redundancy for Mailbox servers. You need to establish how redundancy for databases has changed since Exchange Server 2003. What major change should you identify?

Solution   Placing your database and transaction log files on separate disks has been, and continues to be, the method of choice for administrators to ensure a complete data restore when mailbox database replication is not used. By using Exchange Server 2013 mailbox resiliency, complete data redundancy is achieved through replication and no longer requires separate spindles for transaction logs. Note also that transaction log files are automatically purged on Mailbox servers that are members of a DAG after replication has completed successfully, the truncation lag time has expired, circular logging is enabled, or a full database backup has been performed.

Plan for disk storage requirements for Exchange Server databases.   A major paradigm shift has occurred in the Exchange Server messaging world. Up to now, administrators have been focused on their IOPS and the capacity of their disks to handle the client requests. Today, administrators have to rethink the way they plan for server storage, though they still need to think about IOPS and capacity, new storage capabilities, and limits. Calculate your IOPS requirements based on the number and profiles of your users. By using Microsoft's user profile guidelines, you can reliably predict your IOPS requirements.

Master It   When planning for storage requirements for Exchange, you must take many factors into consideration. Many of them have to do with storage type, capacity, load, and redundancy. However, many administrators don't always plan for the number of databases that need be created and opt for a reactionary approach to mailbox database creation.

Solution   As more mailboxes are supported on a single Exchange Server Mailbox server, scaling the server upward to support more storage is important. Creating more mailbox databases will help you support larger mailboxes and more data while preventing any single database from growing too large. Smaller mailbox databases are faster to back up and manage.

Configure Exchange Server Mailbox servers with the appropriate storage solution.   Storage groups no longer exist in Exchange Server 2013 and Exchange Server 2010. All storage group configuration options have been moved to the mailbox database objects.

Master It   You need to prepare your junior administrator to manage the properties of your mailbox databases. Though most administrators have experience managing

Exchange Server, most of their experience was attained in previous versions of Exchange Server. What are some of the issues you want to be aware of when managing mailbox databases?

Solution To minimize loss of email and the necessity for restore operations, modify the Deleted Item retention settings. A high setting will have limited impact on your organization and can be advantageous.

Maximum mailbox size limit can be set at the mailbox database level but also at the individual mailbox level. When set at both levels, the mailbox-level configuration is the effective configuration.

When moving mailbox database files, always ensure that a recent backup of the mailbox database is available.

Chapter 20: Creating and Managing Database Availability Groups

Understand database replication. Mailbox databases can be replicated between Mailbox servers in different AD sites. Replicating databases between AD sites ensures mailbox services could be online and available if the Mailbox server in the primary site were to fail.

Master It Your company has a DAG that is stretched across two datacenters. All databases should be mounted in the primary datacenter where the end users are located. Last week, a server had a hardware failure, causing all the databases on that Mailbox server to fail over. After the failover you noticed that some of the databases were mounted on Mailbox servers in the secondary datacenter. What solution should be put in place to prevent mailbox databases from being activated in the secondary datacenter?

Solution On all the Mailbox servers in the secondary datacenter, run the `Set-MailboxServer` cmdlet while setting the `DatabaseCopyAutoActivationPolicy` parameter to Blocked. By making this change, databases cannot be automatically activated on the Mailbox servers in the secondary datacenter.

Manage a database availability group. Lagged database copies maintain an older database state by suppressing when transaction logs are written to the mailbox database. A lagged database can be used to restore mailbox content that has been removed or manipulated.

Master It A user has reported that email messages are missing from her Inbox. After checking the client and the dumpster, the messages are still missing. The user's mailbox is on a mailbox database that has a passive lagged copy. What steps should you perform to restore the lagged database copy?

Solution Here are the steps you should perform:

1. To preserve the state of lagged copy, suspend replication.

2. Copy the database and transaction logs to a different directory. You may also want to take a snapshot of the database and logs.

3. Once the copy and snapshot process have completed, resume replication to the lagged database copy.

4. From the copy of the lagged database, remove the check point file.

5. Once the mailbox database is in a clean state, create a recovery database.

6. Point the database file path of the Recovery Database (RDB) to the filename of the copied lagged database and mount the RDB.

7. Export the mail content of the user's mailbox from the RDB to a PST file.

Additionally, you can use eseutil (not covered in this chapter) between steps 4 and 5 to determine the state of the mailbox database and the log files needed to bring the database to a clean state.

Understand Active Manager. Behind the scenes you have a primary active manager (PAM) that is responsible for ensuring best copy and server selection in the event of a failure that causes a failover of the active database.

Master It You have a four-member DAG split evenly across two sites. You have configured your activation preferences for failover of active databases for your database; however, when you test the process by manually bringing down the server handling the active database, the failover never goes toward your preferred server. Why are your selections being ignored?

Solution The Active Manager has 10 different criteria sets for determining which passive copy of the database to mount. The activation preference only comes into play if all options are equal for the Active Manager to choose from. You can have a little more control over the process by using the AutoDatabaseMountDial parameter and adjusting the values to lossless, good availability, or best availability depending on your failover plan.

Understand site resiliency for Exchange Server 2013. When designing a DAG, Service Level Agreement (SLA), Recovery Time Objective (RTO), Recovery Point Objective (RPO), business requirements, and technical requirements should be used to model how the DAG is implemented.

Master It Your company has three datacenters spread across the continental United States. Each datacenter has a low-latency, high-throughput WAN connection to the other datacenters. Users are located in two of the three datacenters. Management requires that mailbox services must be online if the power fails in one of the datacenters. Due to budget restrictions, the solution must use the minimum number of servers. How would you design a DAG solution to meet management's requirements?

Solution Create a DAG that has an even number of Mailbox servers in the two datacenters that have end users. Place the file share witness in the third datacenter. If a power outage were to occur at any of the datacenters, Exchange Server services would still be online.

Chapter 21: Understanding the Client Access Server

Understand architecture changes in the CAS role. Now that clients connect to Client Access servers for all client connectivity, it's even more important that your Client Access servers be highly available. By placing your Client Access servers in load-balanced arrays, you can increase the redundancy and availability of your environment.

a) **Master It**   To increase the resiliency of the Client Access servers in your company's main datacenter, you have decided to place them behind a hardware load-balancer array. You want to ensure that your users can use Outlook while inside the network to access their email. What ports do you need to ensure are load-balanced in the array?

Solution   Internal Outlook users will use RPC over HTTP to access their mailboxes through Client Access servers. You will need to ensure that the HTTPS protocol on TCP port 443 is included in the load-balanced array.

Design a CAS proxy and redirection solution.   For users to access their mailboxes, they need to go through a Client Access server that is in the same Active Directory site as their Mailbox server. Client Access servers need to communicate to the Mailbox server through HTTP. If the Client Access servers in the same site as a user's mailbox aren't exposed to the Internet, then Internet-based users will need to access their email from Client Access servers in another site. The Internet-facing Client Access servers will proxy the connection to the non-Internet-facing Client Access servers.

b) **Master It**   You have a Client Access server in two primary datacenters, one in Baltimore (cas-bal.contoso.com) and another in Honolulu (cas-hon.contoso.com). You also have a Client Access server in your branch offices in Seattle (cas-sea.contoso.com), Atlanta (cas-atl.contoso.com), and Amarillo (cas-ama.contoso.com). You want to ensure that only the Baltimore and Honolulu Client Access servers can be used over the Internet. You want users in Baltimore, Atlanta, and Amarillo to use mail-east.contoso.com and users in Honolulu and Seattle to use mail-west.contoso.com when accessing their email from outside the network. How should you configure your internal and external URLs for each of these Client Access servers to support your desired outcome?

Solution   The InternalURL and ExternalURL values for each of the virtual directories on the Client Access servers should be configured as follows:

- Baltimore InternalURL: cas-bal.contoso.com

- Baltimore ExternalURL: mail-east.contoso.com

- Honolulu InternalURL: cas-hon.contoso.com

- Honolulu ExternalURL: mail-west.contoso.com

- Atlanta InternalURL: cas-atl.contoso.com

- Atlanta ExternalURL: empty

- Amarillo InternalURL: cas-ama.contoso.com

- Amarillo ExternalURL: empty

- Seattle InternalURL: cas-sea.contoso.com

- Seattle ExternalURL: empty

Consider Client Access servers and coexistence with previous versions of Exchange Server.   When replacing your legacy Client Access servers, you will want to start from the edge of your network and work your way in. Therefore, you want to transition Internet-facing Client Access servers first. When transitioning from Exchange Server 2007, you will want to use a new legacy namespace for your Exchange Server 2007 URL and move the old namespace to the Exchange Server 2013 Client Access servers. When transitioning from Exchange Server 2010, you can use the same namespace on your Exchange Server 2013 Client Access servers.

Master It   Your current environment is composed of both Exchange Server 2007 and Exchange Server 2010 servers. You decide to install your Exchange Server 2010 Client Access servers in an Internet-facing site using the same namespace as your existing Exchange Server 2010 Client Access servers. You notice that users with mailboxes on Exchange Server 2007 can no longer access their email through OWA. However, users with Exchange Server 2010 mailboxes can use OWA just fine. What should you do to fix this problem?

Solution   This problem is occurring because you are trying to use the same namespace as your existing Exchange Server 2007 servers. Both the Exchange Server 2007 Client Access servers and the Exchange Server 2010 Client Access servers are using the same external URL. When an Exchange Server 2007 user accesses Outlook Web App on Exchange Server 2013, they are redirected to the external URL specified on the Exchange Server 2007 Client Access server.

To fix this problem, you need to configure a new namespace for your existing Exchange Server 2007 Client Access servers and configure the external URLs on those servers to use the new namespace.

Generate valid Subject Alternative Name certificates.   Each Client Access server has multiple names that clients use to access it. To secure access to the server using all of the names used, you need to issue Subject Alternative Name certificates to your Client Access servers. SAN certificates allow you to specify multiple names for your server in a single certificate.

Master It   Your company, Contoso Pharmaceuticals, implements a split-brain DNS architecture. Your main campus in Baltimore has an array of six Client Access servers called `outlook.contoso.com`. Each server in the array is named accordingly, starting at CONTOSO-CAS1 and ending at CONTOSO-CAS6. This same array of Client Access servers also serves Outlook Web App clients and Exchange ActiveSync clients under the name of `mail.contoso.com`. You need to make sure that your Client Access servers have the right certificates to operate correctly when accessed from both inside and outside the organization. What Subject Alternative Names need to be used in the certificate, and which name should be used for the Subject Name field?

Solution   SAN certificates need to include each name that a Client Access server can be contacted with. Since certificates validate the name of the server, the validation will fail if the name that the server is accessed by is different than the name on the certificate. Outlook Anywhere clients require that the Subject Name in the certificate match the name in the Outlook configuration. Therefore, the Subject Name of the certificate should be `mail.contoso.com`. Here are the Subject Alternative Names:

◆   `outlook.contoso.com`

◆   `Autodiscover.contoso.com`

Understand Front End Transport architecture changes.   Transport has undergone significant changes in Exchange Server 2013. The Front End Transport service is a new feature on the Client Access server role and provides a stateless proxy to the backend Mailbox role.

Master It Your company, Contoso Pharmaceuticals, implements Exchange Server 2013 Client Access server with a default configuration. Your administrators use the Remote Connectivity Analyzer to view an email's message header information. The name of the Mailbox server is listed in the server conversation. The company security policy requires that the Mailbox server names not be exposed externally. How can the administrator hide the Mailbox server name on outbound mail?

Solution By default, outbound mail will bypass the CAS role and be delivered from the mailbox to a smart host or through DNS lookup. To enable outbound routing to use the CAS role with EAC, access the Mail Flow tab and select the appropriate send connector. In the send connector details, enable the Proxy Through Client Access Server option in the Connector Status section. Alternatively, in PowerShell use the Set-SendConnector cmdlet with the FrontEndProxyEnabled option set to $true.

Understand Unified Messaging CAS architecture changes. Unified Messaging no longer is a separate role in Exchange Server 2013. The UM Call Router service on the CAS handles the initial client connection and hands off media stream directly to the UM services on the Mailbox server role.

Master It After the Exchange Server 2013 deployment, your administrator needs to enable connectivity to her Lync server 2013 infrastructure. In order to provide the Lync administrators the correct information, should she use the CAS or Mailbox server IP address?

Solution Even though the media from the call is handled by the Mailbox server UM services, the initial call must be originated from the CAS. The Exchange Server administrator must ensure the Lync administrators establish the connection to CAS and not directly to the Mailbox server.

Chapter 22: Managing Connectivity with Transport Services

Understand the improvements in Exchange Server 2013 mail routing. Once you start sending messages between more than one Exchange server, you must understand how Exchange Server 2013 uses your existing Active Directory infrastructure to route messages between Mailbox servers. When you begin to discuss server placement and the message routing path with the networking team at your company, you need to understand exactly how messages will flow within your organization.

Master It You have an Exchange Server organization that contains multiple sites, separated by WAN links. Another administrator handles all Active Directory configurations for your organization.

This kind of scenario means that you may want to alter the route that messages take within an Exchange Server organization. Although Exchange servers always attempt a direct connection to a final destination server, in some cases a connection is not established directly. This may be a good reason for modifying the site link costs used by Exchange servers when determining the least-cost path. What are your options in modifying these options?

Solution Site link costs can be used to control the flow of email messages within an Exchange organization. Stay away from the Exchange-specific site link costs and the hub sites, unless you absolutely need to configure them to meet requirements. In fact, the more complexity that you incorporate into your Exchange design, the more complicated it will become to troubleshoot any kind of problem. Of course, if you opt against Exchange-specific site link costs, there is always the possibility of modifying the costs of the Active Directory site links directly. This may, however, have an impact on normal Active Directory replication.

The moral of the story? Unless you have some truly mitigating reasons for changing AD or Exchange link costs, don't. If you do have those reasons, then keep it as simple as possible, and document your changes adequately. And don't forget that if you add all the Mailbox servers to the same DAG, the AD site links and hub sites will not come into play because mail delivery occurs from source to destination within the same delivery group.

Create and manage Send connectors and Receive connectors. All messages delivered by an Exchange server are routed through Exchange connectors. The source servers of Send connectors are always Mailbox servers. The Client Access servers can be used as proxy servers to send outbound email messages.

Master It You've been called in to deploy Exchange Server 2013 in a "greenfield" deployment, where no messaging system is present. Installing Exchange Server is pretty easy, even for the least experienced IT consultants.

But… surprise! After your successful installation, you notice that emails cannot be sent to the Internet. You need to connect this new organization to the Internet. What configuration will allow your customer to book his golf games by email?

Solution By default, there are no Send connectors. When you install a new Exchange Server organization, you will not be able to send mail to the Internet until you create your first Send connector.

Administrators can manage and modify the Send connectors by using the Set-Send Connector cmdlet on any Mailbox server. If you need to enable outbound SMTP logging, this is where you will want to do it. Treat your Send connectors with respect; they deliver!

Master It You need to plan for the deployment of an Exchange Server 2013 organization. You quickly notice that the organization is concerned with reducing the number of physical servers. Of course, virtualized installation of Exchange Server is always possible, but this customer has very little expertise in virtualization technologies.

They ask you a very important question: do they really need an Edge Transport server on their network?

Solution For small organizations, a single server running the Mailbox and Client Access roles is truly all you need. The Receive connector is flexible enough and has practically all available filtering agents and tools necessary for most companies. There are downsides to having only a single multi-role server, such as the lack of redundancy for transport services and the possibility of overloading your server. However, for organizations that are trying to limit software and hardware costs, you can definitely get away with a single multi-role server.

When you are looking for more flexibility in configuring inbound mail flow, look at the options available for the Receive connectors—especially the remote IP address ranges configuration, which allows you to have multiple SMTP listeners with a single IP address and a single listening port.

Configure anti-spam and anti-malware technologies.   Anti-spam and anti-malware management is a day-to-day reality of all email administrators. Finding the balance between keeping spam and malware out while maintaining free flow of all legitimate email messages is becoming increasingly difficult.

Master It   You have deployed an Exchange Server 2013 organization that contains several servers that run the Exchange Server 2010 Edge Transport role.

Users report that they are increasingly receiving spam in their mailboxes. From the Exchange Admin Center, you modify the content-filtering settings, but you are not seeing any improvement in the number of spam email messages received. What should you do to ensure that spam is kept out of your organization?

Solution   Deploy an Edge Transport server that runs Exchange Server 2010. By default, the settings that you configure on your Exchange Server 2013 servers will not be replicated to the Edge Transport servers. If you have an Edge subscription, however, that will be replicated. Also, consider using Exchange Online Protection as a hosted anti-spam solution if spam starts to become unmanageable.

Chapter 23: Managing Transport, Data Loss Prevention, and Journaling Rules

Create and manage message classifications to control message flow.   Message classifications provide a way to visibly tag selected messages and show that they require specific treatment. On their own, they're merely advisory, but combined with transport rules and mailbox rules, they can become powerful selection criteria for managing messages and ensuring policy compliance.

Master It   You need to use message classifications to manipulate messages by using Outlook. You verify that custom message classifications are available from Outlook Web App. From Outlook, you look around but cannot find any options that relate to the custom message classifications. What do you need to do first?

Solution   The catch is that although message classifications work out of the box with OWA, using them with Outlook requires you to get your hands dirty copying files and adding registry entries.

Control message flow and manipulate messages by using transport rules.   Transport rules give you a powerful, centralized method for creating automated policy enforcement in your environment.

Master It   You need to add a logo to an email disclaimer; you notice that you cannot include an image in the New Transport Rules Wizard. The availability of adding logos to a disclaimer was a major decision point of your Exchange Server 2013 implementation. What do you need to do to make the logo visible in the disclaimer?

Solution   You can include HTML code that points to an image file that is stored on a web server on the Internet. The key here is that the image file is publicly available on a server on the Internet.

Protect sensitive information by creating data loss prevention policies.   Using DLP policies you can enforce that all messages are subject to DLP rules, or you can allow users to bypass DLP rules by providing a business justification.

Master It   Your company's compliance officer requires that email messages containing U.S. bank routing numbers be redirected to the senders' manager for approval and that an incident report be generated and sent to the employees of the legal department. What do you need to do to make sure you meet the requirements of the compliance officer?

Solution   Create a new custom DLP policy and set the mode to Enforce. Create a new rule within the DLP policy with the condition of The Message Contains Sensitive Information. Select the sensitive information type of U.S. Bank Account Number. Set the actions to redirect to the senders' manager and generate an incident report and send it to the legal department distribution group.

Chapter 24: Troubleshooting Exchange Server 2013

Narrow the scope of an Exchange Server problem.   One of the most important troubleshooting skills that an Exchange Server administrator must possess is the ability to quickly and effectively narrow the scope of problem. Determining the commonalities in a problem can help you quickly locate and solve a problem.

Master It   Seven of your 400 users are reporting an error in Outlook that indicates that they cannot connect to the Exchange server. What are some things you would determine to narrow the scope of the problem?

Solution   Ask yourself these questions:

- Are the users on the same database?
- Do they use the same Outlook client version?
- Are they on the same network or switch?

Use basic Exchange Server troubleshooting tools.   A number of tools are available that will help you in troubleshooting Exchange Server problems as well as possibly determining future issues. These include the Event Viewer, the Remote Connectivity Analyzer, Exchange Server diagnostics logging, and the `Test-SystemHealth` and `Test-ServiceHealth` cmdlets.

Master It   After installing a recent Cumulative Update, you have started noticing intermittent issues with your Exchange server. What tool or tools could you run to help you identify potential issues?

Solution   You could use the `Test-ServiceHealth` cmdlet or any of the several other `Test-*` cmdlets available in Exchange Server 2013.

Troubleshoot Mailbox server problems.   The Mailbox server is at the core of your Exchange Server organization; all Exchange Server data is located and serviced via this Exchange server role. When the Exchange Mailbox server role is not functioning correctly, this will cause a fast-moving ripple effect through your organization that will affect more and more users. Tools such as the Test-MapiConnectivity cmdlet can help you determine whether a mailbox can be reached.

The Exchange Server 2013 database availability group high-availability feature is becoming increasingly prevalent in even small businesses as companies look to find ways to keep their Exchange Server infrastructure up and running as much as possible. The Test-ReplicationHealth and Get-MailboxCopyStatus cmdlets can help in testing the health of the DAG replication.

> **Master It**   A user named Zoe is reporting that she cannot use Outlook to access her mailbox, yet she can access it via Outlook Web App. What tool could you use to determine whether the mailbox is accessible via Outlook?

> **Solution**   You can issue the following command:

> Test-MAPIConnectivity Zoe

Troubleshoot mail transport problems.   The Exchange Server 2013 Mailbox role plays the all-important part of delivering all messages that are processed via the Exchange Server 2013 infrastructure. This is true even if a message is sent from one user to another on the same mailbox database, and the transport services are invoked to act in delivering the message.

A number of useful tools are available to help you and your users determine where a problem may exist. These include the Exchange Server 2013 Queue Viewer, the Test-MailFlow cmdlet, and message tracking.

> **Master It**   A user is reporting that they are sending email but that the recipient is never getting the message. The user is convinced your server is not delivering the message. You would like the user to determine whether the message is leaving your organization. What would you advise the user to do?

> **Solution**   The user can use the Delivery Reports feature of Outlook Web App to track the message and determine if it was delivered to the Internet.

Chapter 25: Backing Up and Restoring Exchange Server

Back up Exchange Server.   Performing backups is the somewhat easy part of the equation. The more difficult part is defining the requirements for the backup.

> **Master It**   Document the goals for your backup solution.

> **Solution**   Interview the key stakeholders for the organization and determine what the requirements are for the organization. Define the RTO and RPO for the backup solution. Document the amount of Exchange Server data that will be backed up. Understand the various scenarios that you will be supporting.

Prepare to recover the Exchange server.   Before you are able to perform any backups from Windows Server 2012, you must install the backup features.

> **Master It**   What do you need to do to install the backup features on Windows 2012?

> **Solution**   Installing the Windows Server Backup feature is a simple process. Open PowerShell and issue the following two commands:

```
Import-Module ServerManager
Add-WindowsFeature Windows-Server-Backup
```

You can also install the features using Server Manager.

Use Windows Server Backup to back up the server.   There is always a need to back up your server(s). Since you have the requirements, you need to perform the backup.

Master It   Perform a recurring backup utilizing the Windows Server 2012 backup features.

Solution   Set up the Windows backup to perform a daily full backup of the Exchange Server data. Configure the backup to run every day at 10 p.m. Monitor the amount of time the backup takes to verify that you are not performing the backup during scheduled online maintenance. Also, make sure you are performing a VSS full backup, so that any necessary log files will be truncated. By default, Windows Server Backup performs a VSS copy backup, which will not truncate log files.

Use Windows Server Backup to recover the data.   You may need to perform a restore of your Exchange Server data for several reasons. One of the reasons is that you need to give a user email that had been deleted but that is still recoverable.

Master It   Perform a single-item restore for a user.

Solution   Pick a user in the organization who does not have single-item recovery enabled, and restore the volume that contains their Exchange Server data. Once you have restored the data, run through the steps to recover some of the email that they have deleted. Export this email to their email account and verify that they can perform operations with the restored email messages.

Recover Exchange Server data using alternate methods.   If your organization is leveraging Exchange Server native data protection, performing a single-item restore for a user will be a different process that doesn't rely on Windows Server Backup.

Master It   A user reports needing to obtain a message that was deleted from their dumpster. Their mailbox is enabled for single-item recovery. What action should you take to recover the message?

Solution   Use the In-Place eDiscovery Search tool in the EAC to locate the message that needs to be recovered. Once you have located the message, export it from the Discovery Search Mailbox into the user's mailbox using the Search-Mailbox cmdlet.

Recover an entire Exchange server.   There may be occasions when you need to reinstall the entire Exchange Server. You have the ability to perform a reinstallation to either of the roles.

Master It   How do you recover the Client Access server?

Solution   Since Active Directory holds information about the Client Access server, recovering this role is not difficult. You will need to perform the recovery by using the following command:

```
setup.exe /RecoverServer /IAcceptExchangeServerLicenseTerms
```

Before running the command, ensure the server has the same NetBIOS name, IP address, operating system, and hardware configuration as the original server. Once Setup has finished, apply all necessary patches and updates to the system. If any specific configurations have to be changed, make those changes.

Index

Note to the Reader: Throughout this index **boldfaced** page numbers indicate primary discussions of a topic. *Italicized* page numbers indicate illustrations.

property sets, 286
providers in VSS, 696
proxies
  Client Access server,
    567–571, *568*
  FET, **595**
PSS (Product Support Services),
  22–23
PST Capture tool, **464**
PST files
  characteristics, **13–14**
  and email archiving, **458,
    462–464**
  importing from, **279–280**
PTR records, 613
Public Folder Mailbox Wizard,
  433, *434*
public folders, **15–16**
  attributes, **444–445**
  databases
    administrators, **442**
    default servers, **442**
    EMS for, **445**
  EMS for, **442–447**
  hierarchy, **449**
  high availability, **450–451**
  limitations, **430–431**
  mail-enabled, **328**
  mailbox management,
    433–435, *434*
  Mailbox servers, **204**
  vs. mailboxes, **452–453**
  managing, **435–442**, *436–441*
  moving, **431–433**, *431–432*
  Outlook, **447–449**, *447–448*
  OWA, 552
  permissions, **446, 451–452**,
    452
  properties, **436–441**, *436–441*
  scripts, **446–447**
  support, **429–431**
Public Key property, 166
public keys
  Autodiscover, 164
  X.509 certificates, 166
PublicFolderToMailboxMap
  Generator.ps1 script, 446
Purges folder, 711–713
purging mailboxes, **373–374**

Purpose of the Policy/Policy
  Statement, 457

Q

Quarantine messages that meet
  or exceed a specific SCL
  threshold option, 631
Quest Software, 25
Queue ID setting, 685
Queue Viewer, **684–685**, *684*
Queues page, 684–685
quick start guide, **177**
  installation. *See* installation
  recipients, **197–199**
  server sizing, **177–181**, *178*
  Windows configuration,
    183–186, *184*
quorums in DAG, **511–512**
quotas
  email archiving, **474**
  mailbox databases, 499, *500*,
    504
quotes (' ") in cmdlets, 107

R

RAID (Redundant Array of
  Inexpensive Disks), **72–75**
RAM. *See* memory
raw disk mapping (RDM), 85
RBAC. *See* role-based access
  control (RBAC)
RBAC Manager, **293–294**, *293*
RBL (real-time block list)
  providers, 613
RCA. *See* Remote Connectivity
  Analyzer tool (RCA)
RDB (Recovery Database),
  710–711
RDM (raw disk mapping), 85
Readiness Checks, 190–191, *191*
reading journal reports, **667**
real-time block list (RBL)
  providers, 613
Receive connectors, 196
  creating, **612–613**
  overview, **606–612**, *607–608*
ReceiveConnector noun, 106

receiving email, **604–606**
recipient filtering, **633**
recipient scope for roles, 303–304
Recipient Update Service (RUS),
  329
RecipientRoot parameter, 307
recipients, **325**
  contacts
    EAC for, **407–409**, *408*
    EMS for, **409–410**
  email addresses. *See* email
    addresses
  journal, 665
  mail-enabled contacts,
    326–327
  mail-enabled groups,
    327–328
  mail-enabled public folders,
    328
  mail-enabled users, **326–327**
  mailbox-enabled users,
    325–326
  mailbox migration, 363
  management tasks, **17**
  in message classifications,
    641
  postmaster addresses, **199**
Recipients page, 363
RecipientType property, 415–416
RecipientTypeDetails property,
  415–416
reconnecting deleted mailboxes,
  374–375, *374*
records management.
  See messaging records
  management (MRM)
Recover Deleted Items tool, 501,
  704, 711
Recover To Original Location
  option, 705
Recoverable Items folder, 713,
  718
recovery, 56, **58–59**. *See also*
  backups
  vs. business continuity,
    59–60
  command-line options,
    255–256
  dial tone, **711**